The Oxford Encyclopedia of Islam and Politics

THE OXFORD ENCYCLOPEDIA OF ISLAM AND POLITICS

Emad El-Din Shahin

EDITOR IN CHIEF

Volume 1

Aal al-Bayt Institute–Kuttāb

OXFORD UNIVERSITY PRESS

OXFORD
UNIVERSITY PRESS

Oxford University Press is a department of the University of Oxford.
It furthers the University's objective of excellence in research,
scholarship, and education by publishing worldwide.

Oxford New York
Auckland Cape Town Dar es Salaam Hong Kong Karachi
Kuala Lumpur Madrid Melbourne Mexico City Nairobi
New Delhi Shanghai Taipei Toronto

With offices in
Argentina Austria Brazil Chile Czech Republic France Greece
Guatemala Hungary Italy Japan Poland Portugal Singapore
South Korea Switzerland Thailand Turkey Ukraine Vietnam

Published by Oxford University Press, Inc.
198 Madison Avenue, New York, NY 10016
www.oup.com

Library of Congress Cataloging-in-Publication Data
The Oxford encyclopedia of Islam and politics / Emad El-Din Shahin, editor in Chief.
volumes cm
Includes bibliographical references and index.
To be complete in 2 volumes—ECIP data.
ISBN 978-0-19-973935-6 (set : alk. paper)—ISBN 978-0-19-999805-0 (v.1 : alk. paper)—
ISBN 978-0-19-999806-7 (v.2 : alk. paper)
1. Islam and politics—Encyclopedias. I. Shahin, Emad Eldin, 1957-
BP173.7.O94 2013
297.2'72—dc23 2013016398

Printed in the United States of America
on acid-free paper

EDITORIAL AND PRODUCTION STAFF

Acquiring Editor
Damon Zucca

Development Editor
Anne Whittaker

Editorial Assistant
Lauren Konopko

Production Editor
Richard Johnson

Copyeditors
Dorothy Bauhoff
Michele Bowman
Mary Flower
Alan Hartley
Benjamin Saddock

Proofreaders
Heather Dubnick
Mary Flower
Carol Holmes
Diane Lange

Indexer
Katharyn Dunham

Compositor
SPi Global

Manufacturing Controller
Genieve Shaw

Cover Design
Brady McNamara

Managing Editor
Mary Araneo

Production Manager
David Ford

Executive Editor, Development
Alixandra Gould

Publisher
Damon Zucca

Contents

The Oxford Encyclopedia of Islam and Politics

List of Entries

Introduction to the Series

The **Oxford Islamic World Encyclopedia Series** is a series of four authoritative reference works, two volumes each, within a major subfield of Islamic studies: *Islam and Women*; *Islam and Politics*; *Islam and Law*; and *Philosophy, Science, and Technology in Islam*. Each multivolume set has its own editor in chief and editorial board.

Although *The Oxford Encyclopedia of the Islamic World* offers a comprehensive foundation of information, the four two-volume sets form an eight-volume series that provides far more detailed study of many aspects of the Islamic world. The Islamic World Encyclopedia Series has been designed to be a primary reference not only for scholars and students of religion, history, and the social sciences but also for government, media and corporate analysts, as well as interfaith organizations, which will find a reliable source of information for many topics and issues not covered by existing reference works and coverage in emerging areas.

Each multivolume set includes general overview articles from *The Oxford Encyclopedia of the Islamic World* as a foundation, drawing on its extensive coverage of Islam and Muslim societies and communities going back to the beginnings of Islam. However, the majority of articles are newly commissioned in-depth entries written by leading experts. Upon completion, the four sets will form an eight-volume series that taken together will provide an in-depth, comprehensive, and detailed study of key aspects of the Islamic world.

Each encyclopedia is offered in print and e-book format. Customers interested in a complete reference library in Islamic studies will be able to purchase the series. Because of the interdisciplinary nature of the research, we are also offering each set individually. All of the newly commissioned material will be included in the *Oxford Islamic Studies Online* website (http://www.oxfordislamicstudies.com), where it can be accessed in one place.

The Oxford Encyclopedia of Islam and Women
Editor in Chief
Natana J. DeLong-Bas
Boston College

Scholarship on Islam and women has expanded exponentially over the past twenty years, with increasing specialization within the field as well as cross-pollination between other fields and disciplines. Recent scholarship has tended to focus on expanding both historical and contemporary case studies relative to countries and regions through both archival and theoretical studies, as well as mapping out transnational trends and the reinterpretation of ideas and disciplines by Muslim women throughout the world.

With this surge in interest, a genuine need has developed for a systematic reference work to provide balanced comprehensive coverage of the field. An up-to-date, carefully organized reference source is urgently needed to help scholars assess the progress that has been made and to chart the path for future research. *The Oxford Encyclopedia of Islam and Women* is designed to meet this need by providing clear, current, comprehensive information on the major topics of scholarly interest within the study of women and Islam.

The Oxford Encyclopedia of Islam and Politics
Editor in Chief
Emad El-Din Shahin
The American University in Cairo

The Oxford Encyclopedia of Islam and Politics provides in-depth coverage of the political dimensions of Islam and the Muslim world. At no time has the understanding of the nature, political dimensions, and implications of these developments been more needed. Developments in Muslim societies in the nineteenth and twentieth centuries have highlighted the need for a major reference work focusing primarily on the political dimensions of Islam.

The recognition of internal decay and relentless quest for reform; the collapse of the Islamic caliphate; the fall of most parts of the Muslim world under Western colonialism; the emergence of nation-states; the dominance of secular ideologies; the rise of Islamic revivalist movements and faith-based political, economic, and social alternatives; and the confrontation between Islamic movements and secular-inspired regimes have constituted major turning points in the contemporary history of Muslim societies. *The Oxford Encyclopedia of Islam and Politics* seeks to target specialized users, scholars, students, experts, policy makers, and media specialists and offer them accurate and balanced scholarship on Islam and politics.

The Oxford Encyclopedia of Islam and Law
Editor in Chief
Jonathan AC Brown
Georgetown University

Recent years have witnessed an increase in scholarly publications on the subject of Islamic law, and the topic has received growing attention in the popular press. *The Oxford Encyclopedia of Islam and Law* is intended to be the primary reference source for questions of Islamic law. It is conceived to help scholars assess the progress that has been made and chart the path for future developments in this flourishing area of research.

The *Oxford Encyclopedia of Islam and Law* is designed to meet this need by providing clear, current, comprehensive information on the major topics of scholarly interest within the study of Islam and the law. It is intended to be the main reference source for questions of Islamic law among engaged readers in the West and academics in general and legal researchers in particular.

This encyclopedia contains conceptual entries that help readers from a Western legal background understand Islamic law and offers an extensive listing of Islamic legal technical terms, with an emphasis on discussing how Islamic law influences or exists in modern nation-states.

The Oxford Encyclopedia of Philosophy, Science, and Technology in Islam
Editor in Chief
Ibrahim Kalin
Georgetown University

Philosophy and science in the Islamic tradition have not yet been covered systematically in a single, authoritative reference work. *The Oxford Encyclopedia of Philosophy, Science, and Technology in Islam* builds on the subjects of philosophy, science, and technology presented in *The Oxford Encyclopedia of the Islamic World,* expanding them to provide comprehensive and in-depth coverage of the achievements of classical Islam as well as a detailed survey of the main features of philosophy, science, medicine, and technology in the Muslim world.

Like other major religious traditions before the modern period, the Islamic tradition treated philosophy, science, and technology as part of a single quest to understand the reality of things. Nature was studied and researched as a subject matter for both philosophy and science. The methodology and subject matter of the classical sciences allowed philosophy and the natural sciences to interact with one another in complementary ways. Technology, a field in which the Muslim world produced an immense body of work, from astrolabes to watermills, developed as an extension of both philosophy and science. Advanced techniques and technological devices quickly became a feature of urban life in the vast Muslim world stretching over the middle belt of the globe. Royal patronage was an important catalyst for the development of scientific institutions, including hospitals, libraries, and observatories.

This encyclopedia also covers the modern period during which interaction with modern (Western) philosophy and science as well as the transfer of modern technology into Muslim countries has led to the rise of new schools of thought and generated heated debates about Islam, tradition, and modernity up to the present time.

John L. Esposito
Georgetown University

Preface

The main idea behind *The Oxford Encyclopedia of Islam and Politics* is to provide in-depth coverage of the political dimensions of Islam and the Muslim world. It serves as a specialized supplement to *The Oxford Encyclopedia of the Islamic World* and treats Islam and politics through detailed and profound study. Over the past century and a half major turning points have taken place in the contemporary history of Muslim societies: the realization of internal decay, stagnation, and lack of innovation; the relentless quest for reform and vitality to fend off the western onslaught; the eventual collapse of the Islamic caliphate; the fall of most parts of the Muslim world under western colonialism and foreign domination; the emergence of nationalist movements raising Islamic values and symbols for resistance and reassertion of identity; the formation of nation-states; the dominance of secular ideologies; the rise of Islamic activist movements and faith-based political, economic, and social alternatives; the confrontation between Islamist movements and secular-inspired regimes; the collapse of some autocratic regimes following the Arab Spring; and the rise of Islamic parties to power. Most recently, the Muslim world has experienced major events that reasserted the role of Islam in politics as a main catalyst for change, resistance, liberation, and reassertion of identity and governance. These were manifested in the Islamic Revolution in Iran in 1979, the Gulf Wars, the Palestinian Intifadas, the September 11 attacks, and the popular uprisings that longed for dignity, freedom and social justice. The entries within the encyclopedia have been written by an outstanding group of scholars and experts whose knowledge and insights provide authoritative perspectives on the topics they deal with. Though the encyclopedia seeks to target specialized users, the authors have written the entries in a way that makes them accessible to the non-nuanced reader. We hope that readers find in *The Oxford Encyclopedia of Islam and Politics* a reliable and informative source on past and present interactions between Islam and Politics.

With a specific focus and an in-depth elaboration, the *The Oxford Encyclopedia of Islam and Politics* brings together some previously published entries from *The Oxford Encyclopedia of the Islamic World*, revised and rewritten as necessary, with a range of newly commissioned entries to create a single, specialized reference source on this important topic. Comprising 412 entries, more than 200 are entirely new and the rest are either heavily or lightly revised to reflect the political focus of the encyclopedia and expand its scope significantly. The editors realize that no encyclopedia can ever be completely comprehensive. We are certain that we may have overlooked entries. We also selected not to go in-depth with entries that the other encyclopedias in the series deal with from a specialized and extensive perspective. Instead, we included them within synthetic or principal articles such as Islam and Economics, Women and Politics, or Fiqh. However, we are hoping that the in-print and online series volumes will complement each other.

In designing the approach and thematic outline of this encyclopedia, the editors sought to blend theoretical dimensions of Islam and politics with practical and institutional aspects. As Muslim civilization spans centuries of intellectual and cultural contributions, we preferred not to restrict the focus of the encyclopedia to a limited time period, for example, focusing only on the contemporary period. We covered classical and modern developments, schools of thought, institutions, movements, and personalities. The encyclopedia follows the standard classification of modern political science references: concepts, values, thought, ideologies, structures, institutions, systems, as well as what is particular to an encyclopedia on Islam and Politics, such as basic religious beliefs, Muslim political history, Islam in specific geographic regions, thinkers and reformers, movements, society, economy, and international relations. The synthetic and principal articles provide an overview of Islam and its basic doctrines, the Sharīʿah law and Fiqh; Muslim Schools of Thought; Muslim History; Colonialism and Post-colonialism; Modernity and Modernization, Islamic Reform, and Education. We have assigned an entire section on regions in the Muslim World and dedicated a number of entries to the interaction of Islam and politics in these areas. This demonstrates our recognition of the universal and global reach of Islam; awareness that the majority of Muslims live outside the Middle Eastern region, whose population comprises only 20 percent of Muslims worldwide; and the need to focus on the increasing role of Islam in the politics of these regions. Another section focuses on Muslim institutions and structures: religious, social, economic, and political ones, past and present. The entries devoted to movements, organizations, and political parties address an extensive list of actors in Muslim societies that shape social, cultural, and political dynamics. We also emphasize Muslim political theories, thought and philosophy, combining classical and modern concepts that run the gamut from theories on the caliphate, rebellion, and obedience to contemporary Muslim perspectives on sovereignty, constitutionalism, and elections. We provide extensive coverage of major political thinkers and theorists, focusing on the main tenets of their intellectual frameworks and their contributions to Muslim political thought and practices. We selected main figures from the classical, premodern, and modern periods.

Acknowledgments

Like any major work, this encyclopedia is the product of the contributions of many able and supportive friends and colleagues who weathered many odds and difficulties to bring this project to fruition. As many endured to the end, some due to unforeseen circumstances had to leave at some point and move on to fulfill other commitments. John L. Esposito, a great friend and the Series Editor has been a source of inspiration behind this project. His continued support and encouragement were indispensable to the completion of the encyclopedia. He was always there with his stimulating optimism and indispensable guidance. Our initial editorial board—Peri Bearman, James Piscatori, and Robert Hefner—was helpful in conceptualizing and designing the preliminary outline of the encyclopedia. They brought their superb knowledge and expertise to bear, and together we managed to design a thematic blueprint and an elaborate headword list that despite later modifications still maintained their outstanding input and contributions. Peri Bearman was there from beginning to end, reminding me at moments of doubt and fatigue that this project would see the light and would come to an end. I am personally grateful to her for many things: her unabated support, positive attitude, and for sharing her brilliant scholarly and editorial expertise. James Piscatori, a great scholar of Islam and an invaluable mentor, improved the structure of the encyclopedia with his insightful comments and suggestions. It was unfortunate that Robert Hefner had to leave us to attend to other academic commitments, but we benefited greatly from his input on the early outline of the encyclopedia. Khaled M. G. Keshk spent long hours revising and improving the headword list and helping me with his insightful comments. His remarkable grace and reassuring confidence in the project made the process bearable. We appreciate Sohail H. Hashmi's efficiency and astute editorial skills. We are grateful to Joseph A. Kéchichian for joining the editorial board at a late stage. His revision of countless entries and contribution to the editorial process were key to the project.

Thanks are also due to the external reviewers and editors who contributed to the editorial process: Jennifer Bussell, Lyndon B. Johnson School of Public Affairs; Timothy P. Daniels, Hofstra University; Julie Chernov Hwang, Goucher College; Eric McGlinchey, George Mason University; Peter Mandaville, George Mason University; Jørgen S. Nielsen, University of Copenhagen; and Anita Weiss, University of Oregon.

We are deeply grateful to the authors who contributed to this encyclopedia. Prominent and long-established scholars from different fields—Islamic Studies, Arab/Middle Eastern Studies, Political Science, Sociology, History, and Anthropology—have enriched the quality of the entries with their knowledge and scholarship. We also welcomed young and promising scholars, giving them the opportunity to rise.

The managing and editorial team at Oxford University Press was instrumental in the production and completion of this work. We express deep appreciation to Damon Zucca, Acquiring Editor and Publisher, who initiated the project in 2009 and supervised it with valuable feedback on its overall structure and guidelines. We are grateful to Mary Funchion, Development Editor, who guided the project with great compassion and experience and helped us narrow down the list of entries and maintain focus. We were disappointed by her departure to pursue other professional tasks in May 2012. However, her interim replacement, Lauren Konopko, Editorial Assistant, proved to be as capable and managed the project until the new Development Editor, Anne Whittaker, took over and steered the encyclopedia with enthusiasm and commitment to the end. Thanks to Anne's persistence, we were able to keep on schedule.

I am thankful to my research assistants, Karin Brown, Mina Rizq, Christina Buchhold, and Khadiga Omar for helping me throughout the process, keeping track of the entries and following up with the contributors.

Emad El-Din Shahin
The American University in Cairo

Common Abbreviations Used in This Work

AD	*anno Domini*, in the year of the Lord
AH	*Anno Hijra*, in the year of migration from Meccato to Medina
b.	born
BCE	before the common era (= BC)
c.	*circa*, about, approximately
CE	common era (= AD)
cf.	*confer*, compare
d.	died
diss.	dissertation
ed.	editor (pl., eds), edition
f.	and following (pl., ff.)
fl.	*floruit*, flourished
l.	line (pl., ll.)
n.	Note
n.d.	no date
no.	Number
n.p.	no place
n.s.	new series
p.	page (pl., pp.)
pt.	Part
rev.	Revised
ser.	Series
supp.	Supplement
vol.	volume (pl., vols.)

The Oxford Encyclopedia of Islam and Politics

Aal al-Bayt Institute for Islamic Thought, The Royal. The Royal Aal al-Bayt Institute for Islamic Thought is an independent non-governmental institute headquartered in Amman, Jordan, whose ultimate purpose is to serve Islam and humanity at large.

Established in 1980 under the name of "The Royal Academy for Islamic Civilization Research (Aal al-Bayt Institute)" by the late Hussein bin Talal in the aftermath of the 1979 Islamic Revolution in Iran and the Soviet occupation of Afghanistan, the objectives of the institute are to serve Jordan, Arabs, Muslims, and mankind in general.

Well attuned to Western intellectual currents, the Jordanian monarch concluded that Muslim scholars needed to respond to exceedingly negative images of Muslims, especially as the American hostage crisis in Iran filled the airwaves. At the time, King Hussein and his advisors believed that Muslims ought to promote awareness of Islam and Islamic thought, to correct misconceptions about the faith, and, equally important, to highlight the many Islamic intellectual contributions to human civilization. Over the years, and because of the impact of the Iranian Revolution, the institute supported various activities that deepened dialogue between the various schools of Islamic jurisprudence. Members hoped that such cooperation would enhance moderation and tolerance, foster the encounter of Muslim scholars, strengthen intellectual links, and produce relevant academic products to promote peace and harmony among world civilizations.

These efforts gained additional urgency after the collapse of the Soviet Union in the early 1990s, when Francis Fukuyama penned his 1992 *The End of History and the Last Man* study, which was followed a year later by an equally problematic book by political scientist Samuel P. Huntington, who advanced a *Clash of Civilizations* theory that concluded with the startling notion that cultural and religious identities would henceforth be the primary sources of conflict in the post-Cold War world.

King Hussein's successor, Abdullah bin Hussein, maintained the Hashemite monarchy's support of the organization although the individual who carried the burden of work associated with the institute was the former Heir Apparent Prince Hassan bin Talal. Prince Ghazi bin Muhammad presided over the academy since 2000 as the Chairman of the Board of Trustees of the Royal Aal al-Bayt in his capacity as the Jordanian monarch's Personal Envoy and Special Advisor. He was assisted by a Vice-Chairman, the Jordanian Minister of Waqf and Islamic Affairs, Abdul Fattah Salah. Other members of the board included the Jordanian Minister of Education, Ibrahim Badran, the Jordanian Chief Sharīʿah Justice, Ahmad Hlayyil, the Grand Mufti of the Hashemite Kingdom of Jordan, Shaykh Abdul Kareem al-Khasawneh, the President of Aal al-Bayt University, Nabil Shawaqfeh, and the Grand Mufti of the Jordanian Armed Forces, Brigadier General Yahya Al-Btoush. Financially supported by Jordan, the institute conducted its activities under Law no. 32 (2007), known as the "Law of the Royal Aal al-Bayt Institute for Islamic Thought."

Admittedly, the institute gained valuable exposure after 138 Muslim scholars from around the world delivered an answer to Pope Benedict XVI in the aftermath of the Roman Catholic Pontiff's 13 September 2006 Regensburg address titled "Faith, Reason and the University—Memories and Reflections." In his lecture, delivered in his native German, the pope quoted an unfavorable remark about Islam made in the fourteenth century by Manuel II Palaiologos, a Byzantine emperor. The remarks sparked international reactions and controversy, reflecting a poor understanding of Islam and, more importantly, of significant ties that united Islam and Christianity. In the spirit of open intellectual exchanges and mutual understandings, Muslim scholars spoke with one voice about the true teachings of Islam, focusing on "Love in the Qurʾān." A similar effort husbanded by institute scholars was the November 2004 "Amman Message," which sought to declare what Islam is and what it is not, what actions represent it and what actions do not. Abdullah II wished to encourage Muslims to recognize the validity of all eight legal schools of Sunni, Shiah, and Ibadi Islam; of traditional Islamic theology (Asharism); of Islamic Mysticism (Sufism), and of true Salafi thought. The effort focused on how to forbid *takfir* (declarations of apostasy) between Muslims, and what preconditions needed to be fulfilled to issue *fatwas*, precisely to prevent ignorant and illegitimate edicts in the name of Islam. Ultimately, the institute hoped to "clarify to the modern world the true nature of Islam and the nature of true Islam."

BIBLIOGRAPHY

"A Common Word Dossier." *Islamica Magazine*, Issue 21, February 2009. Provides a complete discussion of Aal al-Bayt-sponsored dialogue between Christian and Muslim religious scholars, available at http://acommonword.com/en/a-common-word/11-new-fruits-of-a-common-word/251-a-common-word-dossier.html.

The Royal Aal al-Bayt Institute for Islamic Thought maintains a multilingual web page on its activities, including recent publications, at http://www.aalalbayt.org/en/news.html.

JOSEPH A. KÉCHICHIAN

ABANGAN. The term *Abangan* is applied to Javanese who identify as Muslims but do not strictly follow the prescribed Islamic practices. They are also called "statistical Muslims." Clifford Geertz in *The Religion of Java* (1960) discerned three subtraditions: Priyayi, Santri, and Abangan. The Priyayi descend from the precolonial Javanese nobility and are associated with a "refined" (*alus*) tradition that includes many Hindu-Buddhist elements. Some also practice what is called "Javanese mysticism" (*kebatinan* or *kejawen*). The Santri (or Putihan) are Muslims who follow Islamic prescriptions more strictly. They have tended to be traders or wealthier peasants. The Abangan are generally the mass of peasants and urban workers and servants. Their religious practice focuses on the local spirits and/or magical and curing rituals related to them.

Many scholars would drop the Priyayi category when discussing religion since Priyayi is a matter of social status. In fact some Priyayi do practice Islam strictly and so may be considered Santri, while the others may be considered a form of Abangan.

The word *abangan* means "red" or "brown," and its use in the present sense is first attested in the 1850s as a pejorative term applied by Santris, who considered themselves "white" or "pure" (*putihan*). According to Ricklefs the Priyayi-Santri-Abangan division developed in the later nineteenth century and become hardened and politicized in the twentieth. The Dutch used the Priyayi as administrators and encouraged them to get a Western-style education, thus distancing them to some extent from Islamic culture. Islamic reform efforts sharpened the difference between practicing and nonpracticing people and sometimes provoked anti-Islamic reactions.

The basic Abangan ritual, according to Geertz, is the *slametan*, a communal feast for neighbors and spirits held on a wide range of occasions. In its simplest form, food is prepared by the women of the house, neighbors (male) are invited and take their place in the room, the host gives a short speech in high Javanese, passages from the Qurʾān and prayers (*duʿāʾ*) are recited, and the guests eat the food fairly quickly and then leave, taking some with them. The general purpose is to encourage communal solidarity, placate the spirits, and induce a state of *slamet* (equanimity, emotional balance).

Abangan and Priyayi practices are commonly seen as syncretistic, combining Islamic and pre-Islamic elements, but many scholars rather see them as Javanese forms of Islam. The *slametan*, for example, not only includes Islamic elements but is done on occasions connected with Islam, such as circumcisions and the Prophet's birthday. In fact, the word *slamet* is derived from the Arabic *salāma(t)*, meaning "soundness, well-being, safety." The spirit beliefs and practices can be paralleled elsewhere in the Islamic world, and much that seems Hindu-Buddhist can be seen as derived from Sufism. It also appears that many Abangan increase their Islamic practice as they become older.

The movement for independence from the Dutch was under mainly secular, that is, Priyayi-Abangan, leadership. Sukarno, who led the struggle and became the first president of Indonesia (1950–1967), was of Priyayi background and named his ideology after a peasant, Marhaen, presumably Abangan, whom he had supposedly met. He described his father's religion as a mixture of Islam and Javanese mysticism and his own belief as "pantheistic." During his presidency the Communist Party (PKI), especially representing Abangans but including some Priyayis, was quite active. A political sect known as Permai combined Marxism with an effort to purify "original" Javanese beliefs and practices of Islamic accretions. Geertz states that "its opposition to Islam is extremely virulent and well worked out" (1960, 114). Santri political parties were active, though one was banned in 1960. In the 1955 national elections Sukarno's Indonesian Nationalist Party received 22.3 percent of the vote, the PKI received 16.4 percent, and three Santri parties received 42.5 percent among them. Violent clashes took place between Santris and Abangans during this period and culminated in the major slaughter of PKI supporters in 1965–1966.

Sukarno's successor, Suharto (1967–1998), was of Abangan background and said to be interested in Javanese mysticism, and the leading figures in his regime were either Abangan or non-Muslim. He suppressed dissent and sidelined the Santris politically for some time. Political parties were controlled and limited to three, one Santri and two Abangan/Priyayi, including Suharto's party,

Golkar. The resurgence of Islam from the 1970s, however, meant an increase in the numbers and influence of the Santris. In the 1990s Suharto took a more publicly Islamic stance and drew more Santris into his administration. Of his successors, Habibie and Abdurrahman Wahid were Santris, while Megawati and Yudhoyono are of Priyayi background, but their place on the Abangan-Santri spectrum is not so clear. Of the parties that won seats in the 2009 legislative elections, five, including the top three, Democratic Party (PD), Golkar, and Indonesian Democratic Party-Struggle (PDI-P), are Abangan oriented and received over half of the votes, while four, Prosperous Justice Party (PKS), National Mandate Party (PAN), United Development Party (PPP), and National Awakening Party (PKB), are Santri oriented and received almost a quarter of the votes.

It appears that the Priyayi-Santri-Abangan division has become less marked in recent years, probably because of increased social mobility and education along with Islamic resurgence.

BIBLIOGRAPHY

Geertz, Clifford. *The Religion of Java*. Glencoe, Ill.: Free Press, 1960.

Muhaimin, Abdul Ghoffur. "The Islamic Traditions of Cirebon: Ibadat and Adat among Javanese Muslims." Ph.D. diss., Australian National University, 1995. http://epress.anu.edu.au/islamic/itc/mobile_devices/index.html.

Ricklefs, M. C. *Polarizing Javanese Society: Islamic and Other Visions (c. 1830–1930)*. Singapore: NUS Press, 2007.

William E. Shepard

ʿAbbāsid Caliphate. The rise of the ʿAbbāsid caliphate was the first fissure in Islamic culture; it would eventually result in the Shīʿī and Sunnī sects that exist today. The ʿAbbāsid caliphate arose from the chaos resulting from the weak successors of the Umayyad caliph Ḥishām ibn ʿAbd al-Malik, which resulted in four caliphs in seven years, with scandal tainting two of them. Another proximate cause of the shift from the Umayyad dynasty was the changing demographics of the period; Ḥishām's efforts to consolidate the territory resulted in mass conversions of Persians, Turks, and Kurds; as Muslims they paid lower taxes, resulting in fiscal instability. In addition, several of the Ummayad caliphs had gained reputations for being more concerned with the pleasures of the flesh than piety or duty.

The formal proclamation of the first ʿAbbāsid caliph, Abū al-ʿAbbās al-Saffāḥ, in 750 CE forced the last Umayyad caliph to flee to al-Andalus, where the caliphate remained independent until the Frankish invasions and Spanish reconquista. The ʿAbbāsid dynasty ruled the caliphate until 1258 CE.

Origins of the Dynasty. The ʿAbbāsids claimed membership in the family of Prophet Muḥammad. They thus attracted support during the reign of the Umayyad Marwān II. Abū al-ʿAbbās became leader of a rebellion that began with isolated incidents and coalesced into a military uprising in Khorāsān in 747 CE, led by the Persian Abū Muslim. After taking Khorāsān, they advanced on Baghdad, which they occupied in 749, and proclaimed Abū al-ʿAbbās caliph (r. 750–754).

The early ʿAbbāsids faced opposition from supporters of the Umayyads, notably in Syria. Additional friction over rulership came from supporters of the house of ʿAlī, who felt the ʿAbbāsids had usurped their rights as descendants of the Prophet. The ʿAlid faction, most numerous in Iraq, staged uprisings, the most successful of which was led by Muḥammad al-Nafs al-Zakīyah ("the Pure Soul") in Medina and his brother Ibrāhīm in Basra in 762. Communication issues and rebellions close to court caused the ʿAbbāsid dynasty to abandon rulership of al-Andalus (modern Spain) and the Maghrib (modern Libya and Algeria).

Consolidation. ʿAbbāsid power was consolidated throughout the Middle East by al-Manṣūr (r. 754–775), who used the army, and their family members, to build his first government. These positions, prominently filled with Khorāsānī, and a bureaucracy, led by the Barmakid family, continued the Sassanian traditions of financial administration. The state was based in Iraq; in 762 al-Manṣūr founded a new capital at Baghdad. Most notably, al-Manṣūr focused on building a system of amirs and viziers, delegating authority and decentralizing much of the power he had accumulated. Much of this was done to appease the Persian supporters who dominated the bureaucracy.

Al-Manṣūr's immediate successor, al-Mahdī, continued his father's peaceful programs, and it was during his reign that Baghdad developed from a palace complex to a vibrant city and hub of trade across the Middle East; it became the largest city of its era outside of China. Al-Mahdī's successes included reorganizing the army (although the reasons for this included the prevention of a coup) and appointing secular judges. Technologically, al-Mahdī is notable for the introduction of paper to the Middle East. He was succeeded by his oldest son, al-Hādī, who was perceived as weak; this perception was coupled with uprisings both in the east and west and an invasion by the Byzantines.

Islamic Golden Age. Al-Hādī's successor was Hārūn al-Rashīd, who reigned during the apogee of the ʿAbbāsid dynasty over the next three decades. It was during the reign of Hārūn that the first actions against the increasingly powerful Barmakid family were taken and that the palace was moved from Baghdad to a more centralized location, in al-Raqqah, where lines of communication were better. His principal external rival was the Byzantine Empire, which paid tribute in all but four years of his reign as caliph.

In striking parallel to the succession of the sons of Charlemagne, Hārūn al-Rashīd was forced to divide his realm between his sons, al-Amīn (r. 809–813) in Iraq and the West and al-Maʾmūn (r. 813–833) in Iran. The agreement broke down immediately after his death in 809; a decade of destructive civil war ensued before al-Maʾmūn was able to establish himself as sole caliph in Baghdad. His reign was a period of great intellectual activity, and the caliph himself played an important part in the translation of Greek texts into Arabic; while al-Maʾmūn was a scholar and linguist and focused on the intellectual, the government proved less effective, with several provinces becoming independent in all but name, and getting away with acts that would have merited reprisals from his father.

The Rise of Turkish Influence. Al-Maʾmūn's successor, his brother al-Muʿtaṣim (r. 833–842), began his reign by dismantling his brother's military base at Tyana and sending his forces against the Khurramīyah revolt; the suppression was successful, and most of the rebels sought refuge with the Byzantines. Shortly after this rebellion was crushed, Muḥammad ibn al-Qāsim brought Khorāsān into rebellion; the fighting lasted a year and a half before al-Qāsim was captured. (He escaped from prison and was never heard from again.) The principal army of the rebellion, the Zult, were captured and presented to the caliph, who granted them clemency and sent them to fight the Byzantines. The final resolution of the Khorāsān rebellion involved bringing Babak Khorramdin to Sāmarrāʾ in 838; Khorramdin arrived at the palace on his own elephant and submitted to the rule of the caliph, resulting in him being beheaded by his own executioner.

Not without justification, Muʿtaṣim was concerned about internal rebellions and coup attempts; after repelling an invasion by the Byzantines, he acted on intelligence about a coup and killed a number of his senior military commanders. In an attempt to secure armed forces loyal only to himself, al-Muʿtaṣim instituted the *ghilman* system of slave-soldiers, in which the captured children from conquered regions were taken from their homes and trained as soldiers beholden only to the caliph. An unintended consequence of this, the creation of a corps of Turkish cavalry, was a growing discontent with the caliph by the Arab elements of his armed forces. After rioting in Baghdad, the capital was moved to Sāmarrāʾ, where it would remain for over fifty years.

While the capital was relocated to Sāmarrāʾ, the Ṭāhirid family was allowed a free hand in eastern Iran, including freedom from several intensely disliked taxes. Combined with the general dislike of the Arab populace for the mostly Turkish army, the isolation of the caliphate in Sāmarrāʾ persisted into the reign of al-Wathiq and was exacerbated in the reign of his successor, his brother, al-Mutawakkil.

The Rise of Intolerance and Impending Decline. Al-Mutawakkil was mistreated by his brother's vizier, Muḥammad ibn ʿAbd al-Malik; within a month of becoming caliph, al-Mutawakkil had him arrested and put to death and his property confiscated. Over the next two years, al-Mutawakkil began to deal systematically with those who had mistreated him during his brother's reign. This furthered the split between the Arab forces in the caliphate's army and the Turks who ran it. As most of the caliphs of this time did, al-Mutawakkil depleted his treasury and resources suppressing rebellions, notably in Albania and in Egypt, and fighting off incursions by the Byzantines. Although lacking the scholarly bent of his father and brother, he may have been the last effective ʿAbbāsid caliph.

Al-Mutawakkil involved himself in public works projects and in the religious sphere, where his proclamations resulted in a reopening of the rift between the Shīʿī and the caliph, and eventual repression of the Shīʿī, including the destruction of the shrine of Ḥusayn ibn ʿAlī. While he opened diplomatic avenues between Sāmarrāʾ and Constantinople, his treatment of the Christians and Jews in his own lands resulted in the proclamations that they must wear certain clothes, that every tenth Christian or Jewish home be torn down and replaced with a mosque, and that no Muslim should be ruled over by a Christian or Jew, effectively driving them from the government. The net effect of these proclamations was to make non-Muslims ready scapegoats when an unpopular decision had to be enforced.

The next three caliphs were virtual puppets of the Turkish army and various factions. Al-Mustaʿin, al-Muʿtazz, and al-Muhtadī put many of their heirs, rivals, and coconspirators to death and, in focusing on such issues, allowed the western part of the caliphate to slowly unravel and the Ṭāhirids to become an all-but-independent dynasty in northeastern Iran. The last of these three, al-Muhtadī, attempted a reformation—but was killed by the Turks four months after his ascension.

Relocation of the Capital to Baghdad and the Resurgence of the Caliphate. When ʿAbbāsid authority was restored by the second al-Muʿtaḍid (r. 892–902), the political influence of the caliphs was confined to Iraq, although Egypt was temporarily regained in 905. Many reforms were carried out, including reduction of some of the burdens on Christians and Jews imposed by al-Mutawakkil. Rapprochement with the Shīʿah was initiated, though the remaining Umayyads were removed from the mosques and the courts, and al-Muʿtaḍid's secret police and public executions made him feared rather than loved by his subjects. His son, al-Muktafī, won great popularity by ending some of his father's excesses, but his reign was marked by attacks by external forces.

While al-Muktafī desired to bring the caliphate back to its full expanse, circumstances did not allow it.

Al-Muqtadir and the Resumption of the Decline. The resurgence of the ʿAbbāsids was short lived; al-Muqtadir succeeded his father, with the assistance of his father's vizier, who wanted a weak caliph so that he could be the power behind the throne. Muqtadir is portrayed as caroming from one hedonistic pleasure to another, while thirteen viziers were nominated, assassinated, or brought up on charges and removed. His successor, al-Qāhir Billāh, was even worse; displaying an outward veneer of piety, he tortured those close to his predecessor for their wealth. He walled up his presumptive heir alive; eventually he was set upon by palace officials, blinded, and cast into prison. He died a beggar. His successor, al-Rādī, while not as maliciously cruel or paranoid, was functionally a puppet, as was the next caliph, al-Muttaqī.

In 945 CE, the caliphate came under the functional rule of the Būyids, who took Baghdad by force and sent the reigning caliph into hiding. After the caliph's capture and blinding, a civil war broke out between the Būyids and the Turkish elements of the army; the remaining caliphs served at the pleasure of the Būyids, and were ruled by their viziers.

In the early eleventh century, Būyid control crumbled, and the ʿAbbāsids returned to the life of the Muslim community. In opposition to the Shīʿī Būyids and their supporters, al-Qādir (r. 991–1031) put himself at the head of the emerging Sunnī movement, publishing the Risālat al-Qādirīyah, which established the bases of Sunnī doctrine. This influence grew after 1055 when Baghdad was taken by the Seljuk Turks, professed Sunnīs who accepted the religious leadership of the family. However, it was not until Seljuk power in turn began to collapse after the death of Sanjar in 1157 that this prestige could be translated into political power. Caliph al-Nāṣir (r. 1180–1225) reestablished ʿAbbāsid control over most of Iraq with the support of popular *futūwah* movements. His successors failed to maintain this momentum. When the ʿAbbāsids were faced by the still-pagan Mongols, who had no respect for their religious status, they were unable to put up an effective resistance. Baghdad fell to the invaders in 1258, and the last caliph, al-Mustaʿṣim (r. 1242–1258) was put to death.

The ʿAbbāsid caliphate enjoyed a certain afterlife in Cairo, where members of the family continued as titular caliphs, although they were in effect members of the Mamlūk court, kept to confer legitimacy on the sultanate but without any independent power. With the Ottoman conquest of Egypt in 1517, even this small survival of their ancient glory was swept away.

[*See also* Umayyad Caliphate.]

BIBLIOGRAPHY

Bowen, Harold. *The Life and Times of ʿAlí ibn ʿÍsa', 'the Good Vizier.'* Cambridge, U.K.: Cambridge University Press, 1928.

Glubb, John Bagot. *The Empire of the Arabs.* London: Hodder & Stoughton, 1963.

Kennedy, Hugh. *The Prophet and the Age of the Caliphate: The Islamic Near East from the Sixth to the Eleventh Century.* London and New York: Longman, 1986.

Le Strange, Guy. *Baghdad during the Abbasid Caliphate.* Oxford: Clarendon, 1900.

Muir, William. *The Caliphate, Its Rise, Decline, and Fall: From Original Sources.* Whitefish, Mont.: Kessinger, 2004.

Shaban, M. A. *Islamic History: A New Interpretation.* Vol. 2: *AD 600–750 (AH 132).* Cambridge, U.K.: Cambridge University Press, 1976.

Sharon, Moshe. *Black Banners from the East.* Vol. 1: *The Establishment of the ʿAbbasid State: Incubation of a Revolt.* Leiden, Netherlands: E. J. Brill, 1983.

Sourdel, Dominique. *Le vizirat ʿAbbāside de 749 à 936 (132 à 324 de l'hégire).* 2 vols. Damascus: Institut Français de Damas, 1959–1960.

al-Ṭabarī. *The History of al-Tabari*. Vols. 27–38. Edited by Ehsan Yarshater. Albany, N.Y.: State University of New York Press, 1984–1999.

Hugh Kennedy
Updated by Ken Burnside

ʿAbd al-Rāziq, ʿAlī. ʿAlī ʿAbd al-Rāziq, (1888–1966), was a Azharī scholar, Egyptian *qāḍī*, and government minister. ʿAbd al-Rāziq's contribution to Islamic political thought is his most enduring, as well as ambiguous, legacy. In 1925, his book *al-Islām wa uṣūl al-ḥukm: Baḥth fī al-khilāfah wa al-ḥukumah fī al-Islām* (Islam and the Foundations of Governance: A Study on the Caliphate and Government in Islam) was published. The main thesis of the book was responded to with indignation by major figures of the religious establishment, while it contributed to controversies over the caliphate, political authority, and the relationship of Islam to politics at the time.

An analysis of *al-Islām wa uṣūl al-ḥukm* and its historical context sheds light on political discourses in early twentieth-century Egypt, as well as controversies over the caliphate. The text is a touchstone for historians interested in the evolution of civic or political concepts in the Arab world. In addition, *al-Islām wa uṣūl al-ḥukm* informs our study of the historical events surrounding King Fuʾād's possible ambitions for the caliphate, subsequent to Mustafa Kemal Atatürk's abolition of the institution in 1924.

The central thesis of *al-Islām wa uṣūl al-ḥukm* is that authority is a natural concomitant to prophecy. Thus the Prophet Muḥammad possessed social authority, but he did not establish a political entity with the founding of Islam; therefore, religious authority is not synonymous with political authority. The Prophet Muḥammad issued orders, he was obeyed, he mitigated disputes, and he commanded in war; the author argues, however, that this authority was unique. As ʿAbd al-Rāziq insists: "The prophetic mission itself demands that the Prophet have some sort of primacy in his nation, a form of authority over his people. But this has nothing in common with the primacy of temporal sovereigns, nor with their authority over their subjects. Therefore, we should not confuse prophetic primacy with that of temporal sovereignty" (Donohue and Esposito, 2007, 24–31).

To understand *al-Islām wa uṣūl al-ḥukm's* theoretical import, we must acknowledge the political context of the time. At the turn of the twentieth century, Egyptians were contending with British domination. In order to challenge the British, some Egyptians sought greater solidarity with the Ottoman Empire; this alliance was predicated on notions of Islamic political sovereignty. Yet other Egyptians sought to instill in Egyptian society an acute sense of Egyptian identity. Both dispositions were important in rallying the common Egyptian against European domination. ʿAlī ʿAbd al-Rāziq had close ties to the Liberal Constitutionalists Party, Egyptian nationalists who gravitated toward the latter position. Although ʿAbd al-Rāziq's book was published after the collapse of the Ottoman Empire, notions of Islamic solidarity still loomed large on the Egyptian political horizon and Egyptian nationalists felt compelled to articulate more territorially based political concepts.

ʿAbd al-Rāziq's argument implies several things. First, it is being suggested that the Muslim community, or *ummah*, is not a political entity but a spiritual fraternity. In this case, no political institution, which the caliphate should be understood to be, has jurisdiction over spiritual affairs. Conversely, no spiritual institution should have jurisdiction over political affairs. This is perhaps the more important point that ʿAbd al-Rāziq wishes to make. His argument helps facilitate an autonomous space for the development of an

Egyptian national identity whose political sovereignty is articulated through an Egyptian state, rather than an Islamic polity. In *al-Islām wa uṣūl al-ḥukm* we thus have a contribution to debates over issues like "secularism," "nationalism," and civic identity. Lastly, ʿAbd al-Rāziq denies outright the spiritual necessity of the caliphate, long held to be the case. This latter point bring us to the case of King Fuʾād and his possible ambitions to the caliphate.

Throughout the 1920s King Fuʾād quietly but persistently pursued the caliphate through his contacts with the British. The British had interests in the caliphate question, as they now ruled over dozens of Muslim lands, particularly India. A caliph subservient to British interests could, perhaps, lend greater validity to British policy in Muslim lands, of which India was the most important. When ʿAbd al-Rāziq argued that the caliphate was unnecessary and incidental, he undermined Fuʾād's bid for that role; he subsequently faced a tremendous amount of political pressure both on the basis of his ideas and, most likely, because of his negative impact on Fuʾād's goals. An authoritative council of *ʿulamāʾ* removed him from his position as an Islamic judge. The book's themes remain highly relevant, however.

[*See also* Caliphate, Theories of the; Egypt; Governance; Nationalism; Ottoman Empire; Secularism; *and* Ummah.]

BIBLIOGRAPHY

ʿAbd al-Raziq, ʿAlī. "The Caliphate and the Basis of Power." In *Islam in Transition: Muslim Perspectives*, edited by John J. Donohue and John L. Esposito, pp. 24–31. New York: Oxford University Press, 2007.

ʿAbd al-Rāziq, ʿAlī. *al-Islām wa uṣūl al-ḥukm*. Cairo: Maṭbaʿat Miṣr, 1925.

Binder, Leonard. *Islamic Liberalism: A Critique of Development Ideologies*. Chicago: University of Chicago Press, 1988.

Hourani, Albert. *Arabic Thought in the Liberal Age, 1798–1939*. London: Oxford University Press, 1962.

Laith Saud

ʿAbduh, Muḥammad. Muḥammad ʿAbduh, (1849–1905), was an Egyptian reformer whose opinions and convictions were firmly based in the possibility of synthesizing Islam and modernity.

The historical, intellectual, and political importance of this figure in the succession of Muslim leaders formulating and seeking to implement social change in the modern era was that of a theorist of social and cultural transformation, rather than that of a revolutionary activist or charismatic political visionary. Scholarly observers' reception of Muḥammad ʿAbduh is divided. However, his importance as a representative of modernism and liberalism justified (if not conceived) in the medium of Islamic principles and precedents is accepted by scholars, however they may appraise him.

In the popular imaginary in Egypt ʿAbduh remains in some measure a figure of ambivalence, but at the same time his ideas comprise a landmark of liberal thought that emphasizes freedom and political development—one whose religiously inflected ideals are readily counterpoised by the essentially secular Egyptian and Arab nationalist intellectuals. ʿAbduh's references to Enlightenment ideals, which he appropriated with adaptations from Europe, ensure that his writings do not sit entirely comfortably with the realities of autocratic regimes of the past, nor with the values and commitments of the Muslim Brothers (*Ikhwān al-Muslimūn*) or the other Islamist or other extreme elements of Egyptian political history that emerged after his death.

Religious Training and Experience. Nothing in the formation of ʿAbduh's mind and the knowledge instilled in him as a student would presage his activist turn, nor his ascent to high office and social prominence. He was born in Ṭanṭa, in Egypt's Nile Delta; by an early age his exposure to and knowledge of the Qurʾān was extensive, as would be expected in a traditional Islamic education. As a youth, he gained an understanding of and dedication to Sufism, allying himself with mystics identifying themselves as the Shādhilī; he practiced *dhikr* (the ritual repetition of God's name) and *taʿwīdh* (incantation).

At the age of seventeen, ʿAbduh journeyed to Cairo to undertake further study and certification as an *ʿālim* at al-Azhar—the premier institution of Islamic learning in the Islamic world. There he gained competence in the familiar scholastic patterns of *tafsīr* (Qurʾānic exegesis and commentary) and *fiqh* (jurisprudence). Notwithstanding the authority al-Azhar had accumulated since its establishment in the tenth century and the resulting importance of the credentials he could secure there, ʿAbduh expressed dissatisfaction with its offerings; he identified aspects of the institution and the curriculum that he would later seek to alter.

Political Experimentation and Maturation. Like any person seeking to change the society in which he or she lives, Muḥammad ʿAbduh faced a choice of tactics: radical or revolutionary change effected in direct confrontation with the status quo, or incremental change and compromise pursued from within the corridors of power relying upon established authorities and institutions. Muḥammad ʿAbduh experimented with the former strategy before accommodating himself to the latter.

In 1880 he assumed a government post as editor of the government's official gazette *al-Waqāʾif al-miṣrīyah* (Egyptian Affairs). He also joined the anticolonial resistance, involving himself in the ʿUrābī revolt (1881–1882). As a consequence of his association with this forcibly suppressed uprising against the administrative tutelage of the British and their proxy local authorities, ʿAbduh was exiled from Egypt, for six years; sent to Beirut, he engaged himself in charitable activities and the foundation of an Islamic school.

ʿAbduh's stay at al-Azhar had overlapped with that of a man who would become his chief mentor: Jamāl al-Dīn al-Afghānī (1839–1897). During ʿAbduh's banishment from Egypt, he reconnoitered with Jamāl al-Dīn in Paris. The pair collaborated on the foundation and editing of a new (but short-lived) journal, *al-ʿUrwah al-wuthqā* (The Firmest Bond). Their aim was the liberation of Egypt from British occupation. The means to achieving that aim was the shaping of public opinion, mainly but not exclusively in Egypt. *Al-ʿUrwah al-wuthqā* propagated the thesis that Islam suffered corruption and atrophy through the ignorance of its adherents, necessitating their reform. Furthermore, there was no redemption in the leaders of Muslim countries who, motivated by greed and grandiosity, gave foreign powers access to Muslim lands. The colonial powers in turn maximized their advantage and profit by playing Muslims off one another, seeking to maintain the *ummah*'s divided, weakened, condition. ʿAbduh and Afghānī sought the realization of the pan-Islamic ideals of Muslim unity and collective cooperation to combat Western imperialism.

Al-ʿUrwah al-wuthqā inspired a subsequent generation of Muslim journalists, some of whom continued the pan-Islamic political project of Jamāl al-Dīn and the Islamic liberal revivalism of Muḥammad ʿAbduh; for example, Rashīd Riḍā, who sought to reconstitute an Islamic caliphate as the last bulwark against Western colonialism (when the Ottoman sultanate was no longer fit for this purpose). Riḍā founded the more persistent and also influential periodical *al-Manār* (The Beacon) in 1898, republishing in it selections and extrapolations from ʿAbduh's written works, lectures, and ideas; for instance, Riḍā posthumously published lectures by ʿAbduh on the Qurʾān and the Prophet Muḥammad. Riḍā also wrote a biography of his teacher Muḥammad ʿAbduh (*Tārīkh al-ustādh al-imām*).

Social and Political Thought. Unlike Jamāl al-Dīn al-Afghānī, who rejected the slower methods of popular organizing and mass education in favor of top-down revolution and elite pacts, Muḥammad ʿAbduh deemed the people of all classes essential to the Egyptian national cause—even as he recognized not all were or would be readily receptive to his ideas about how Muslims should change. ʿAbduh acquired a comparative, critical perspective on Egyptian society during his travels in Europe. He found the limitations and wasted potential of his country unacceptable, especially in the face of the already real, and intensifying, threat that Europeans posed Egyptian sovereignty.

In response, he called for human development: educational and spiritual liberation. He sought to reverse inertia born of religious and cultural habits. After his experiment with revolutionary foment from afar, Muḥammad ʿAbduh remained in Egypt for the rest of a career in which he made Egyptian people and institutions the object of his ministrations. He tended them through teaching, writing, jurisprudence, and administrative and curricular reform. In 1899 he ascended to Egypt's highest position in the Islamic clerical hierarchy, grand mufti, a position he occupied almost until the end of his life.

Science. The concept of science in ʿAbduh's thought transcends the positivistic or experimental methods associated with science today. For him science bundled together intellectual inquiry, moral development, progress, and freedom. ʿAbduh followed Ibn Khaldūn (1332–1406) in considering a just political order the sine qua non of intellectual effort. ʿAbduh's immediate predecessor in the Islamic defense of science in Egypt was Rifāʿah Rāfiʿ al-Ṭahṭāwī (1801–1873). In comparison with ʿAbduh, Ṭahṭāwī's admiration for France was effusive; Islamic references occupied a more prominent position in ʿAbduh's writings on science, research, and education than in Ṭahṭāwī's praise of French culture. The opposite of freedom of mind and the open exchange of information were what ʿAbduh found in Egypt—a blinkered mindset characterized by the unthinking emulation of the past, followed by the inevitable result: the stagnation and wastage of individual and collective capacity.

Some might dismiss as disingenuous ʿAbduh's efforts to find agreement between scientific theories and the Qurʾān; for example likening *jinn* to microbes, or asserting the compatibility of scientific evolution and the genesis narratives of the Qurʾān. More charitably, these efforts might be seen as pedagogical tools ʿAbduh deployed to reach out to a population that was not highly educated and clung to unexamined tradition. Further, he did not spare popular sensibilities regarding contemporary miracles and saints, manifestations of continuing prophecy, or what he regarded as superstition.

State and Economy. ʿAbduh's career as an educator and opponent of political repression demonstrate his principled commitment to the cultivation and encouragement of individual minds and agency. Although ʿAbduh's corpus is far from comprehensive concerning the economy of Egypt, it is apparent that his orientation was largely statist. Although an advocate of free enterprise, and to that extent capitalism, he considered the intervention of the state necessary to resolve disputes (for example those involving labor and management), to own and manage public land, to allocate scarce resources, to prevent exploitation, and to protect the disadvantaged. He noted the importance of savings accounts as an instrument for popular education in prudent financial planning. He sought to maintain fidelity to Islamic prohibitions on usury (*ribā*), while advocating investment.

Muḥammad ʿAbduh's writings on political theory are also suggestive rather than comprehensive and systematic. He took greater interest than his mentor Jamāl al-Dīn in democracy—broadly construed to include the painstaking development of a culture capable of self-governance and electoral contestation; he encouraged local participatory government at the village, regional, and national levels.

ʿAbduh followed both Islamic and European tradition in regarding the relationship of the people and their ruler as contractual, with each party bearing both rights and obligations. The ruler or government must attend to the public interest, including providing security and a national medical system; the clergy have a special obligation to minister to the moral and spiritual health of the people. The populace in turn must restrain the ruler, who they retain the authority to dismiss—although ʿAbduh did not counsel that they should do so with violence. ʿAbduh maintained that the Qurʾān was the source of state and governmental legitimacy, even as he acknowledged as inevitable and salubrious the resort to human ingenuity and (relatively) freewheeling interpretations of Islamic law (*Sharīʿah*).

Ethics, Law, and Theology. More than any constitution or any other human artifact, the binding element of the Egyptian nation (*waṭan*), according to ʿAbduh, was its continuity as a religious community circumscribed by *Sharīʿah*. Notwithstanding the pre-Islamic past, he saw Egyptian civilization as one in which religion was the primary force controlling public and, equally, private life. Schooled in jurisprudence, and a seasoned judge (*qāḍī*), ʿAbduh selectively emphasized precedents from Islamic law for his program of national integration and progress. He saw the legal system and its fit with present circumstances as essential to prosperity. As a jurist he sought to give scope to the values of equity and fairness by application of *istiḥsān* (the court's discretionary authority) and to take account of the broader interests of popular welfare with reference to *istiṣlāḥ* (the community's best interest).

As grand mufti he issued opinions (*fatāwā*, sing. *fatwā*) on family and tribal matters, ethics and social morality, labor relations, and commercial and business activities. He aimed to diminish divisions in Islamic law by synthesizing judgments from the four Sunnī legal schools (*madhāhib*). As grand mufti he sought to reform the religious courts, and the administration of religious trusts, or endowments (*awqāf*, sing. *waqf*). He sought to transform al-Azhar and to model it along the lines of a university. Ultimately he successfully added geometry, geography, arithmetic, and algebra to the curriculum.

As a theologian, ʿAbduh's most notable and systematic contribution was his *Risālat al-tawḥīd* (Treatise on the Oneness of God). In it he endeavored to reconcile the demands of reason and revelation, offering a defense of free will in order to uphold individual responsibility and morality. He recognized the value of informed speculation and independent thought while also drawing boundaries around it; there were things that were impossible to understand, where curiosity could lead only to "confusion of belief."

Strategic Cooperation or Collaboration?

Scholars differ in their retrospective assessment of Muḥammad ʿAbduh. The main axes of scholarly dispute are twofold. They concern his relationship with the agents of Western colonialism in Egypt and the subordinate if not subservient position from which ʿAbduh appropriated European ideas—particularly those broadly characterized as liberal.

First, the administrative system in which ʿAbduh participated—and to that extent abetted—was a foreign and a colonial order. Critics observe that he owed his status and specifically his promotion to grand mufti, to his cordiality with the British, and particularly to Evelyn Baring

(Lord Cromer), the British consul general and effective ruler of Egypt from 1883 to 1907. ʿAbduh's limited cooperation with the British may be seen as collaboration with an illegitimate imperialist power; alternatively, it might be seen as a strategic collaboration in the course of which Muḥammad ʿAbduh kept the overriding objectives of social reform and eventual national self-sufficiency ever in view.

Second, ʿAbduh's fidelity to Islam has been questioned by critics who discount the religious inflection of *Risālat al-tawḥīd* and his other works as a rhetorical veneer concealing an essentially secular worldview that lacked the piety it avowed. ʿAbduh's loyalty to Western values may be seen to eclipse his loyalty to Islam. In response it could be said that the attack on ʿAbduh's personal faith strains credulity, and that in any event ʿAbduh's personal convictions are of marginal importance when it comes to judging the validity of his interpretative construction of Islam. In any case, both of these criticisms may be directed at other Muslim thinkers reasonably categorized as Islamic modernists, including ʿAbduh's mentor Jamāl al-Dīn al-Afghānī and his student Rashīd Riḍā and others such as Qāsim Amīn (1863–1908).

An Islamic Modernity. Although he was of humble origins and far from revolutionary in his temperament, Muḥammad ʿAbduh's career—as author and editor, theologian and teacher, jurist and religious functionary—is remarkable both for the impact he had on his compatriots and on the trajectory of his country during his life and for the distillation of ideas and opinions that (irrespective of their European origins) were original within the context in which he applied them. As with other pan-Islamists and Islamic modernists, his agenda began with a narrative of the decline of Muslim societies. In the face of the Ottoman Empire's disintegration he began defending the integrity and Muslim character of the greater Middle East and North Africa, later narrowing his attention to Egypt alone. His overall aim throughout his career was the reversal of the decline he perceived not in Islam but in Muslim peoples.

Muḥammad ʿAbduh searched for an alternative modernity to that exhibited by the West. In his construction of a specifically Islamic modernism, Europe was at once a means and obstacle—a means because Egypt could learn from and even advance and perfect Western achievements, and an obstacle because it was European machinations in the Middle East that kept Egypt subordinate in geopolitics and the global economy. ʿAbduh's early and deep exposure to Islamic scriptural and pedagogical traditions, and his continuing commitment to Islamic faith and its propagation, ensured that he advanced his program of social reform and national development in a religious register that privileged morality and Islamic ethics. Despite his estimable successes within the channels of establishment and official Islam in which he operated, ʿAbduh never witnessed the fulfillment of the capabilities that he believed remained latent in Muslims and in Egyptian society.

Bibliography

ʿAbduh, Muḥammad. *The Theology of Unity*. Translated by Ishaq Masa'ad and Kenneth Cragg. London: Allen & Unwin, 1966.

Amin, Osman. *Muhammad ʿAbduh*. Translated by Charles Wendell. Washington, D.C.: American Council of Learned Societies, 1953.

Busool, Assad Nimer. "Shaykh Muḥammad Rashīd Riḍā's Relations with Jamāl al-Dīn al-Afghānī and Muḥammad ʿAbduh." *Muslim World* 66, no. 4 (October 1976): 272–286.

Kedourie, Elie. *Afghani and ʿAbduh: An Essay on Religious Unbelief and Political Activism in Modern Islam*. 2d ed. Portland, Ore. Frank Cass, 1997.

Kerr, Malcolm H. *Islamic Reform: The Political and Legal Theories of Muḥammad ʿAbduh and Rashīd Riḍā*. Berkeley: University of California Press, 1966.

Khoury, Nabeel A., and Abdo I. Baaklini. "Muḥammad ʿAbduh: An Ideology of Development." *Muslim World* 69, no. 1 (January 1979): 42–52.

Kurzman, Charles, ed. *Modernist Islam, 1840–1940: A Sourcebook*. Oxford: Oxford University Press, 2002.

Livingston, John W. "Muḥammad ʿAbduh on Science." *Muslim World* 85, no. 3 (July-October 1995): 215–234.

Sedgwick, Mark. *Muhammad Abduh*. Oxford: Oneworld, 2009.

Seferta, Yusuf H. R. "The Doctrine of Prophethood in the Writings of Muḥammad ʿAbduh and Rashīd Riḍā." *Islamic Studies* 24, no. 2 (Summer 1985): 139–165.

Scott Morrison

ABDÜLHAMID II. Abdülhamid II, (1842–1918), was the thirty-fourth Ottoman sultan (r. 1876–1909). A profound political and economic crisis brought Abdülhamid II to the throne. Since 1839 the open-door policy of the government, the commercial and legal privileges granted to European powers, and westernizing reform attempts—known as the Tanzimat—had ruptured the Ottoman social fabric. Trade and budget deficits soared. Heavy government borrowing abroad and at home delayed the inevitable financial crisis, but in 1875 the treasury declared insolvency. European creditors protested. Unrest mounted, fanning nationalist revolts among Christians in the Balkans and anti-Tanzimat movements among Muslims.

The government in Istanbul lost control of events. Since the death of the last powerful Tanzimat minister, Mehmed Emin ʿAli Pasha, in 1871, senior statesmen had been engaged in a struggle to control the government. In 1876 a group of ministers led by Midhat Pasha provoked the armed forces to effect a coup d'état and deposed the reigning sultan, Abdülaziz. His successor, Murad V, suffered a mental collapse and was deposed within three months. On 31 August 1876, Abdülhamid II succeeded him on the throne.

Meanwhile, nationalist uprisings in the Balkans turned into bloody ethnic and religious confrontations. The European powers put pressure on the Ottoman government to grant autonomy to the Christian population. Midhat responded by promulgating a constitution (23 December 1876) that ensured basic civil liberties, including the equality of all subjects before law, and provided for a parliament.

Forestalling foreign intervention was one objective of the constitution, and in this it failed. A disastrous war with Russia nearly brought the end of the Ottoman state in 1877. In a series of difficult negotiations that lasted until 1882, the Ottomans surrendered large tracts of territory not only to the Balkan states and Russia but also to other major powers.

The constitution was also intended as a solution to the crisis of authority afflicting the Ottoman state. As such, it reflected a consensus among the Ottoman political elite. The constitution set certain limits on executive authority but left the sultan with great powers vis-à-vis both the cabinet and the parliament. Indeed, Abdülhamid dismissed and exiled Midhat in February 1877 and suspended the parliament in February 1878 on the basis of his constitutional prerogatives. He did not meet any opposition, for the most influential Ottoman elite viewed him as a sensible sovereign capable of providing the leadership necessary to deal with the grave problems facing the government. In 1878 he began to establish an authoritarian regime that eventually breached the spirit of the constitution and brought his downfall.

In the meantime, however, his reign saw respectable accomplishments in the construction of highways, waterways, railroads, the telegraph, and other types of public infrastructure. Judicial and public security services improved and expanded significantly. Institutions were formed to supply credit and technical advice to agricultural producers. Public education and literacy improved. Many specialized schools were established, and old ones expanded with the specific purpose of training a corps of technical government personnel and better public administrators and jurists.

Abdülhamid made an effort to concentrate government investments and reforms in the predominantly Muslim parts of the empire. He emphasized Islam as a basis of internal social and political solidarity. Pan-Islamists such as Jamāl al-Dīn al-Afghānī viewed him as the symbol or focus of Islamic solidarity. Recent territorial losses and the immigration of large numbers of Muslims from the Balkans and Russia had rendered the Ottoman population overwhelmingly Muslim and had raised religious sentiments. Abdülhamid responded to this situation. He did not breach the principle of legal equality, because he believed in it, and he did not want to create pretexts for foreign intervention. He staunchly resisted, however, any attempt or pressure to obtain additional concessions and autonomy for the Christian population. He maintained that European protection had already put the Christians in an unduly advantageous position over the Muslims, who were in his mind the truly loyal subjects of the Ottoman state.

Abdülhamid's resistance to intervention in favor of Christians, particularly in eastern Anatolia and Macedonia, remained a sensitive issue in the government's relations with European powers. In this and other international problems, Abdülhamid tried to hold his ground by taking advantage of the rivalries among the powers and by resorting to delaying tactics. He hoped to gain time until the Ottoman government attained a stronger position to defend its interests, relying on a better-educated and unified population and a more prosperous economy.

His hopes were in vain. The state of Ottoman finances was a major problem: around 30 percent of the government revenue went directly into the coffers of the foreign-controlled Public Debt Administration, and an additional 40 percent was devoured by military expenditures. Given the consequent dearth of funds, the government awarded many of the planned projects and important mines to European concerns as monopolistic concessions. To a certain extent, Abdülhamid was able to use European vested interests to perpetuate his own policies, but the commercial and legal capitulations enjoyed by the European powers, backed by threats of force, left him with little room to maneuver.

The Ottoman regime looked increasingly helpless in defending local interests at a time when limited but real achievements aroused expectations, and nationalistic sentiments therefore gained momentum even among Muslims, undermining Abdülhamid's appeal to Islamic solidarity. There also developed a Muslim religious opposition to the sultan, not least because of his emphasis on modern secular schools at the expense of traditional religious ones. Ironically, it was among the graduates of the modern schools that the most formidable opposition to Abdülhamid's regime took form. Demanding a more institutionalized and participatory regime, a large group of Ottoman officials, officers, and intellectuals organized the Committee of Union and Progress (CUP), the indigenous organization of the Young Turks.

In 1908 sporadic mutinies broke out among the army corps in Rumelia and Macedonia, which rapidly evolved into a popular movement that forced Abdülhamid to call for elections and agree to serve as a parliamentary-constitutionalist monarch. Supporters of the CUP won the majority in the parliament. But as the parliament and the cabinet became bogged down in a struggle over their respective rights, and as the separatist movements in the Balkans intensified, the political situation remained tense. On 13 April 1909, a popular revolt broke out in Istanbul, led by certain religious groups and army units alienated by the CUP. An army of loyal units and volunteers rushed to Istanbul to crush the rebellion. Abdülhamid was falsely accused of having instigated the rebellion and was dethroned on April 27. He spent the rest of his life under house arrest until his death on 10 February 1918.

[*See also* Afghānī, Jamāl al-Dīn al-; Ottoman Empire; Pan-Islam; *and* Tanzimat.]

BIBLIOGRAPHY

Ahmad, Feroz. "Ottoman Perceptions of the Capitulations 1800–1914." *Journal of Islamic Studies* 11 (2000): 1–20.

Buzpinar, Ş. Tufan. "Opposition to the Ottoman Caliphate in the Early Years of Abdülhamid II: 1877–1882." *Welt des Islams* 36 (1996): 59–89.

Deringil, Selim. "Legitimacy Structures in the Ottoman State: The Reign of Abdülhamid II (1876–1909)." *International Journal of Middle East Studies* 23 (1991): 345–359.

Karpat, Kemal H., ed. *Ottoman Past and Today's Turkey*. Leiden: E. J. Brill, 2000.

Zhantiev, Dimitry R. "Islamic Factor in the Consolidation of the Ottoman Rule in the Arab Provinces during the Reign of Sultan Abdulhamid II (1876–1908)." In *Authority, Privacy, and Public Order in Islam: Proceedings of the 22nd Congress of L'Union Européenne des Arabisants et Islamisants*, edited by B. Michalak-Pikulska and A. Pikulski, pp. 453–458. Dudley, Mass.: Peeters, 2006.

ENGIN DENIZ AKARLI

ABIM. *See* Islamic Youth Movement of Malaysia.

ABŪ BAKR. The first caliph (*khalīfah*), or successor to the Prophet Muḥammad, ruled for only two years (632–634), but his tenure as caliph was decisive for the community. Insurrection had broken out in parts of Arabia, led in some cases by pseudoprophets, such as Musaylimah from the tribe of Banū Ḥanīfah and Tulayhah from the tribe of Banū Assad. These tribes refused to pay allegiance to the new government in Medina, assuming that their fealty to it, conceived in political rather than religious terms, had lapsed with the death of the Prophet. Consequently, they withheld the payment of *zakāt*, the obligatory alms giving that is one of the five "pillars," or duties binding upon Muslims. In response to the refusal of the rebellious tribes to pay their *zakāt* to Medina, Abū Bakr stated, according to tradition, that even if only the hobble of a young camel were withheld in payment of *zakāt*, he would fight those dissenters. Within a year of the Prophet's death, the rebellious tribes were defeated under the leadership of Khālid ibn al-Walīd, a famous military commander during and after the Prophet's time, in a series of battles known in Islamic history as the Riddah wars (political rebellion).

As the first of the Rightly Guided Caliphs (al-Rāshidūn), Abū Bakr is much lauded for his simple and abstemious lifestyle, his legendary generosity, and unwavering devotion to Muḥammad, whose father-in-law he became when ʿĀʾishah, his daughter, married the Prophet. At first Abū Bakr lived in a modest house in Sunh, a suburb of Medina, but then moved into the town for the sake of convenience. Under Abū Bakr the collection of the Qurʾānic verses is said to have begun, prompted by ʿUmar, who was alarmed by the death of a large number of Qurʾān reciters during the Riddah wars.

Abū Bakr's official title was Khalīfat Rasūl Allāh (the Successor to the Messenger of God), signifying his status as the only direct successor to the Prophet. In his often quoted accession speech, Abū Bakr laid out the foundational principles of consensual, restricted, and participatory government. Recognizing the people as the source of authority, he highlighted the importance of the rule of law, accountability of rulers, popular sovereignty, conditional obedience, public participation in policy making, and protection of the rights of the weak.

Among the honorifics conferred upon him were *al-Siddīq*, "the Truthful," and *al-ʿAtīq*, "the Freedman," the former because he had readily believed Muḥammad's account of his nocturnal journey to the heavens, and the latter because he had been, as Muḥammad himself said, freed from hellfire. Before his conversion, Abū Bakr had been a very wealthy merchant. On becoming Muslim, he is said to have given away most of his wealth, valued at forty thousand dirhams, in charity before the *hijrah* (emigration) to Medina in 622 CE.

During his last illness leading to his death in 634, he was nursed by his daughter ʿĀʾishah. As requested by Abū Bakr himself, he was laid to rest in ʿĀʾishah's apartment close to where the Prophet lay buried.

BIBLIOGRAPHY

Ibn Saʿd, Muḥammad. *Al-Tabaqāt al-kubrā*. Edited by Muḥammad ʿAbd al-Qādir ʿAtā. Beirut, 1997.

Shaban, M. A. *Islamic History: A New Interpretation*. Cambridge, U.K.: Cambridge University Press, 1971.

Asma Afsaruddin

Abū Ḥanīfah. *See* Sunni Schools of Jurisprudence.

Abū Yūsuf, Yaʿqūb ibn Ibrāhīm al-Anṣārī. (c. 731–798) Yaʿqūb b. Ibrāhīm b. Ḥabīb b. Khunays al-Anṣārī, (c. 731–798), known as Abū Yūsuf *al-qāḍī*, was a preeminent Ḥanafī jurist and judge who lived in Iraq in the early ʿAbbāsid era. His Qurayshī descent and close relationships in the circle of Kufan Sunnī traditionists and jurists propelled his career as a teacher and judge. His scholarship in prophetic traditions, *ḥadīth*, was considered trustworthy. Although a rationalist jurist, that is, one who employed personal opinion (*raʾy*), he earned the appreciation of Sunnī traditionist authorities such as Aḥmad ibn Ḥanbal (d. 855) and Yaḥyā Ibn Maʿīn (d. 848). Above all, he studied with Abū Ḥanīfah (d. 767), the eponym of the Ḥanafī school, and became his most prominent disciple. Ḥanafī biographers consider Abū Yūsuf to be the second founder of the school and accord him the title *ṣāḥib Abī Ḥanīfah* (Abū Ḥanīfah's companion). He is also praised for being the first to write on Ḥanafī principles of jurisprudence and to spread the school of Abū Ḥanīfah beyond Iraq.

He largely expanded Ḥanafī jurisprudence thanks to his status as chief judge, *qāḍī al-quḍāt*, appointed to this position by the fifth ʿAbbāsid caliph, Hārūn al-Rashīd (r. 786–809). Previously he had served as judge under al-Mahdī (r. 775–785) and al-Hādī (r. 785–786). Unlike Abū Ḥanīfah and other major jurists of early Islam, Abū Yūsuf was not reluctant to become an official. His involvement in state affairs provided his scholarship with practical insight, which can be seen in his most important work, *al-Kharāj*.

Abū Yūsuf's *al-Kharāj* is one of the earliest accounts of public finance in Islamic law. It displays the structure and the features of a responsum where Abū Yūsuf answers the alleged questions of Hārūn al-Rashīd on public finance, criminal punishment, and commercial and religious regulations. In particular, *al-Kharāj* covers topics of state income. Thus, Abū Yūsuf specifies the legal norms that should be respected in the collection and distribution of land tax, *kharāj*, and war booty. The centrality of land income might be considered an indicator of stability in the Hārūn al-Rashīd era and a prosperous time for agriculture. *Al-Kharāj* also testifies to the close relationship between the legal schools, the judicial system, and the early ʿAbbāsid caliphate, as Ḥanafī jurisprudence became involved in judicial decisions and state policies.

For this reason *al-Kharāj* is a significant milestone in the history of public law in Islam. It influenced later treatises on the subject of public law, in both their technical vocabulary and their legal reasoning. Abū Yūsuf emphasizes the distinction between land taxes paid by Muslims (*ʿushr*) and non-Muslims (*kharāj*). He also provides detailed regulations concerning the granting of fiefs, planting and sowing, reviving dead land, enclosing land, building and planting without permission, public water and its use, taxes on land irrigated by rain and artificial irrigation, the time for collecting taxes and giving alms, evasion, almsgiving, and the maximum taxable quantity. These minutiae show Abū Yūsuf's concern with real cases of public finance in the complex ʿAbbāsid society.

In addition to financial matters, Abū Yūsuf treats other issues of public law, such as apostasy, the status of belligerents who enter the territory of Islam, spies, and war against polytheists and rebels. A few questions of *dhimmī* law are also answered, such as the status of churches, synagogues, and crosses, as well as their clothing. He requests the caliph to treat the *dhimmī* with kindness and care, protecting him from injustice and harm.

Abū Yūsuf even responded to questions of commercial law, such as rental lands and issues of criminal punishment. Although the focus of his book is public finance, specialization in law was not yet a factor in early juristic literature. Furthermore, Abū Yūsuf was more of a responder to Hārūn al-Rashīd's queries than an author of a work on public finance, hence the thematic variety in *al-Kharāj*. Nevertheless, he answered Hārūn al-Rashīd's questions in a clear and direct way, which assures an easy readability of his text. To bolster his arguments he supports them with several traditions, accompanied by their chains of transmission (sing. *isnād*). Often the space occupied by the traditions exceeds that of his opinion.

Abū Yūsuf represents a Ḥanafī jurist who was keen to keep a balance between *sunnah* (including the caliphate practice), juristic opinion, and the ʿAbbāsid administration. In this regard *al-Kharāj* is an early example of a Sunnī reconciliation between the ideal caliphate and kingship. The book's preamble contains several motifs borrowed from the literature of mirrors for princes. For instance, Abū Yūsuf depicts the relationship between the ruler and his subjects as that of a shepherd and his flock. He also advises the ruler on the virtues of justice, moderation, and control. He masters an exalted literary style that indicates his integration within the elite group of scribes of Baghdad. In his preamble he uses rhymed prose in contrast with the dry and technical prose of the jurists or narrative style of the traditionists.

Although he addresses the caliph respectfully, Abū Yūsuf does not hesitate to display his religious authority. At one point he admonishes the caliph not to "go astray, otherwise the flock would go astray." His rhetoric sounds powerful and shows a self-confident jurist in service to a young ruler. He even orders him to study his book thoroughly, to reflect on it, and to repeat it until he has memorized it. Abū Yūsuf's main request to the ruler is to maintain justice with regard to both Muslim and non-Muslim landowners. He clearly states that the obedience and righteousness of the subjects is the result of the respect of laws, the removal of injustice, and the establishment of an effective judicial system.

Thus, Abū Yūsuf's significance lay in his ability to represent both the interests of the jurists and those of the state. On the one hand, he promoted the Ḥanafī school, firmly grounded in the legalist tradition of early Islam with a preference for rationalist methods but without neglecting traditions. On the other, he was sufficiently pragmatic to take on official positions within the ʿAbbāsid state as a chief judge and a political theorist.

[*See also* Taxation.]

BIBLIOGRAPHY

Ben Shemesh, Aharon. *Taxation in Islam*. Vol. 3, *Abū Yūsuf's* Kitāb al-Kharāj. Leiden, Netherlands: E. J. Brill, 1969.

Calder, Norman. *Studies in Early Muslim Jurisprudence*. Oxford: Clarendon, 1993.

Qurashī, ʿAbd al-Qādir b. Muḥammad b. Abī al-Wafāʾ al-. *Al-Jawāhir al-muḍīyah fī ṭabaqāt al-Ḥanafīyah*. Edited by ʿAbd al-Fattāḥ Muḥammad al-Ḥulw. Cairo: Dār Iḥyāʾ al-Kutub al-ʿArabīyah, 1978.

Schacht, Joseph. *The Origins of Muhammadan Jurisprudence*. Oxford: Clarendon, 1950.

Streusand, Douglas E. "Sir Hamilton A. R. Gibb, Abū Yūsuf, and the Concept of Islamic Civilization." In *History and Historiography of Post-Mongol Central Asia and the Middle East: Studies in Honor of John E. Woods*, edited by Judith Pfeiffer and Sholeh A. Quinn, pp. 542–554. Wiesbaden, Germany: Otto Harrassowitz, 2006.

ABDESSAMAD BELHAJ

ABŪ ZAHRAH, MUḤAMMAD. Muḥammad Abū Zahrah (1898–1974) was a scholar of Islamic law, an Egyptian public intellectual, and writer of conservative inclinations. He was born in El-Mahalla El-Kubra and attended elementary school at the Ahmadi School. He later studied at the Madrasat al-Qaḍāʾ al-Sharʿī for eight years, graduating in 1924, and at Dār al-ʿUlūm for an additional year. Following the completion of his studies, Abū Zahrah assumed professorships at the Azhar University's Faculty of Uṣūl al-Dīn and Cairo University's Faculty of Law, teaching classes on the history of religions and the Sharʿīah and producing scholarship on Islamic law. In 1962, Abū Zahrah was also chosen to serve at the Azhar University's Academy of Islamic Research. In the course of his career, he wrote more than forty works spanning a broad range of religious subjects, most notably a series of intellectual biographies on the "four imams" and notable classical Islamic scholars such as Zayd ibn ʿAlī, Jaʿfar al-Ṣādiq, Ibn Ḥazm, and Ibn Taymīyah. He also wrote on the subjects of religious trusts (*awqāf*), personal status and criminal law, and property in Islamic law.

Abū Zahrah had an interest in Egyptian politics that spanned his career. He is known for criticizing from the lectern deeds of Egyptian political figures that he viewed as hypocritical. In one famous story, he demanded that the president's daughter dismiss her bodyguards when attending his lectures. Abū Zahrah's public views earned him a number of political enemies, and in his mid-sixties, he was banned from teaching. Years later, President Sadat formed an assembly of Muslim *ʿulamāʾ* to which he invited Abū Zahrah. The latter presented a speech to the assembly in which he addressed Sadat by his first name. In those years, President Sadat displayed a certain reluctance to adopt Abū Zahrah's recommendations fully; many of Abū Zahrah's contemporaries traced this hesitance to Sadat's perception of a lack of respect on the part of the senior scholar. Abū Zahrah's political views and statements were well known to the Egyptian public thanks in part to the fame of his books and in greater part to his regular appearances on the weekly religious television show *Nūr ʿalā nūr* (Night after Night), in which he provided religious guidance to his audience.

Abū Zahrah's written works span a broad range of religious subjects. He authored general textbooks on the principles of jurisprudence and hermeneutics. Chief among these books are *ʿIlm uṣūl al-fiqh* (The Science of Juridical Principles) and *Zahrat al-tafāsīr* (The Flower of Interpretations.) He also lectured and wrote a number of comparative works on Christianity and other religions.

Among these, *Muqāranāt al-adyān* (The Comparison of Religions) is still taught and used as a reference at Azhar University. In addition, *Muḥādarāt fī al-naṣrānīyah* (Lectures on Christianity) chronicles the lectures on comparative religion that Abū Zahrah delivered over a number of years at Azhar University. The related volumes *al-ʿUqūbah fī al-fiqh al-islāmī* (Punishment in Islamic Jurisprudence) and *al-Jarīmah fī al-fiqh al-islāmī* (Crime in Islamic Jurisprudence) traced criminal law and mandatory sanctions (*ḥudūd*) across the four Sunnī schools.

Abū Zahrah's most famous books, however, were his biographical works tracing the output and historical implications of their subjects. Many of these remain influential and are still taught in Islamic studies departments in universities both within and beyond the Arab world. This series of works was not strictly biographical in nature; Abū Zahrah is best known for tracing the development of the intellectual contributions of his subjects and the formation of schools of thought around them in the context of the social and political conditions of their times. His biographical books also typically contained detailed discussions of the ways in which their followers developed and appropriated their work. Of these works, Abū Zahrah's detailed volumes recounting the intellectual lives of the four imams remain the most widely read. Each of these sought to trace the life, times, and jurisprudential views of the men who from whom the four classical Sunnī schools of interpretation take their names in a way that is sympathetic to the legacy of their thought but that gently suggests that modern scholars may sometimes build upon it to suit their times. In contrast, Abū Zahrah's book on the life of Ibn Taymīyah, *Ibn Taymīyah: Ḥayātuhu wa ʿaṣruhu; ʿĀraʾuhu al-fiqhīyah* (Ibn Taymīyah: His Life and Age; His Jurisprudential Views), is frequently critical of its subject's intellectual legacy, arguing for the deviance of a number of positions adopted by Abū Zahrah's Wahhābī contemporaries. By the author's own admission, Abū Zahrah's writing and lectures influenced some of Egypt's most important Islamic intellectuals in the twentieth century, a number of whom were his students. Muḥammad al-Ghazālī, for instance, cited Abū Zahrah as an influential figure in his life and expressed his view that the author of these biographies on the four imams was himself worthy of the title imam.

BIBLIOGRAPHY

Abu Zahra, Muhammad. *The Four Imams: Their Lives, Works and Their Schools of Thought*. Translated by Aisha Bewley. London: Dar al-Taqwa, 2001.

Ghaffār, ʿAbd al-Rasūl. *Bayna al-Kulaynī wa-khuṣūmih: Mawqif Muḥammad Abū Zahrah min al-Kulaynī*. Beirut: Dār al-Muḥajjah al-Bayḍāʾ, 1995.

Kelly Al-Dakkak

Acquisition. *See* Religious Beliefs.

Adalet ve Kalkinma Partisi. The Adalet ve Kalkınma Partisi (Justice and Development Party; AKP) is a Turkish political party that was formed in 2001 and came to power in 2002. By the beginning of the twenty-first century, it had become evident that all the political parties that had governed Turkey since the republic's founding had failed to secure a stable constituency. Their political bankruptcy was demonstrated by their failure in the elections of November 2002 to secure the 10 percent threshold necessary to enter parliament. The only significant winner in those elections was the AKP. AKP won 34 percent of the national vote, and ultimately controlled 60 percent of parliamentary seats—a majority unsurpassed since the 1950s. This was the first time in almost two decades that a single party won enough votes to be able to form a government on its own. AKP's ascendency continued for a decade, with a 47 percent win in the 2007 elections, and a landslide victory of over 50 percent in the 2012 elections—an unprecedented performance since the advent of multiparty politics six decades earlier. Equally significant was the election of a party member to the presidency, despite the fierce resistance of secular parties and the misgivings of the top generals. This was the first time since the 1940s that the president and prime minister belonged to the same party.

The origins of the AKP may be dated to the 1970s, when a series of Islamist parties began to challenge the politically dominant understandings of Turkish secularism. The most successful was the Refah Partisi (Welfare Party), which formed a coalition government in the summer of 1996, only to be ousted from power by the military in February 1997 and dissolved by a court order the following year. Its Islamist successor, the Fazilet Partisi (Virtue Party), was remarkably similar and seemed destined to suffer the same fate; it was in fact dissolved in 2001. Young party cadres believed that Turkish voters (and the military) were weary of ideological politics and yearned for a pragmatic and conservative party instead. When they failed to impress this point on their colleagues in the party's 2001 congress, they broke away to found their own party, the AKP. The new party's motto in its successful 2002 campaign was "We have changed."

In contrast to the ailing leaders of most Turkish parties, the founders of AKP were young, dynamic, media savvy, and particularly attentive to business interests. Recep Tayyip Erdoğan, AKP's leader and Turkey's prime minister since 2003, came from Istanbul's violent and underprivileged Kasımpaşa neighborhood. He studied economics at Marmara University, played soccer semiprofessionally, and became involved in grassroots organizing with various Islamist parties in the 1980s. At the age of forty he became mayor of Istanbul (1994–1998) and was credited with revamping the city's administration. His popularity soared when, after his remarkable achievements as mayor, he was banned from politics for five years and sentenced to prison for ten months for reciting what were perceived as inflammatory verses in a public address in December 1997.

Abdullah Gül, the party's second in command, who would become foreign minister and later president of the republic, came from the central Anatolian city of Kayseri, whose business community was made up of archetypical AKP supporters: export-oriented businessmen. He studied economics in Istanbul and England, and after receiving his doctoral degree he was employed at the Saudi-based Islamic Development Bank until 1991, before devoting himself fully to politics. Thus, his social, educational, and professional background was particularly reassuring to Turkey's bourgeoisie.

AKP's pragmatism was manifest in its substitution of Islamism as an ideology with what its leaders proclaimed was "conservative democracy"—a catchall label meant to help the party garner as many votes as possible through posing as a perfect (and admittedly odd) synthesis between everything that Turks cherished: Islamism and nationalism on the one hand and free market liberalism and state welfare on the other. The party's core supporters were the Anatolian-based small- and medium-sized manufacturer-exporters, the so-called Anatolian tigers. They preferred AKP to other Islamist parties because of its distinctive position toward the economy. While Islamists generally upheld the sanctity of private property, they also emphasized social justice, full employment, and providing a decent livelihood for all, and frowned upon consumerism and the accumulation of excessive wealth. By contrast, AKP believed in the virtues of the open market and free trade, where middle-class entrepreneurs, protected from state intervention, would bring prosperity and leadership to their communities. This was exactly the story the Anatolian tigers were promoting, and it is therefore not surprising that they and the rest of Turkey's bourgeoisie provided unyielding support to AKP. What was surprising was AKP's popularity among the lower classes despite its faithful adoption of "a neo-liberal regimen with the fervour of a convert" (Anderson, 2009, p. 449). This popularity was partly explained by Erdoğan's humble origins, militant roots, common-man piety, traditional Turkish machismo, and plain-talking populism, which all combined to garner the support of the masses on an unprecedented scale. Moreover, AKP provided "neo-liberalism with a human face"; it combined respect for market forces with systematic efforts to alleviate poverty and improve public services (Öniş, 2009, p. 24).

Finally, AKP radically altered Turkey's foreign policy. In 2002, AKP declared its intention to make Turkey a global power by 2023, the one hundredth anniversary of the establishment of the republic. This was a paradigmatic shift from Turkey's conventionally isolationist and defensive foreign policy to what is now referred to as "neo-Ottomanism" (*Osmanlicaler*), an active and assertive foreign policy geared to establishing Turkey as a global power in its own right. The intellectual underpinnings of AKP's foreign policy shift were articulated almost singlehandedly by the party's foreign minister, Ahmet Davutoğlu, whose "strategic depth" (*stratejik derinlik*) doctrine, published in 2000, held that strategic depth is predicated on geographical and historical depth, and that Turkey is uniquely positioned to benefit from both. This doctrine found particular resonance with Erdoğan (Murinson, 2006, pp. 946–948). As a result, Turkey became very active in Middle East politics and threw its weight unhesitatingly behind the Arab revolts starting in 2011. More important, AKP dramatically improved Turkey's chances of joining the EU by curbing the political influence of the armed forces and adopting democratic reforms. In return, the EU and the United States came to see in AKP a good model for Muslims worldwide: the party's ideological moderation, respect for democracy, and probusiness attitude helped transform Turkey—from a Western viewpoint—into a "beacon of democracy in the Muslim world" (Keyder, 2004, p. 84).

BIBLIOGRAPHY

Anderson, Perry. *The New Old World.* London: Verso, 2009.

Keyder, Çağlar. "The Turkish Bell Jar." *New Left Review* 28 (2004): 65–84.

Murinson, Alexander. "The Strategic Depth Doctrine of Turkish Foreign Policy." *Middle East Studies* 42, no. 6 (2006): 945–964.

Öniş, Ziya. "Conservative Globalism at the Crossroads: The Justice and Development Party and the Thorny Path to Democratic Consolidation in Turkey." *Mediterranean Politics* 14, no. 1 (2009): 21–40.

Tuğal, Cihan. "Islamism in Turkey: Beyond Instrument and Meaning." *Economy and Society* 31, no. 1 (2002): 85–111.

Tuğal, Cihan. "NATO's Islamists: Hegemony and Americanization in Turkey." *New Left Review* 44 (2007): 5–34.

HAZEM KANDIL

ADMINISTRATION. Despite its diversity in different times and places, premodern Islamic governance was based on a number of distinctive administrative institutions and practices. Under the governing logic of Islam, these institutions were largely adopted and adapted from the pre-Islamic Arab tribal and monarchical traditions and the Sassanian and the Byzantine empires.

Early Caliphate: The Conquest Period (632–749). The first recognizable administrative institution has been traced to the practice of the second caliph, ʿUmar (r. 634–644), who reportedly established the public treasury (*bayt al-māl*), understood as public wealth as opposed to private ownership, by two measures: setting aside conquered lands as property of all Muslims rather than just the participants in the conquest, and establishing a register or bureau (*dīwān*) after the Sassanian model, in order to deal with the collection of taxes and recording stipends (*ʿaṭāʾ*) of Muslims. The register increasingly included expanding functions pertaining to the governing and taxing of the conquered sedentary peoples. The Muslim policy of conquest comprised two principles: preventing damage at the hands of the conquering armies—especially the ones fighting the Sassanians, as they consisted of chiefly nomadic tribes not used to relations with city dwellers—to the established Iranian cities and their agricultural system, thus disturbing the conquered populations as little as possible religiously, socially, or administratively, and seeking the cooperation of the previous elite in governance. The first principle was underpinned by the Qurʾānic injunction of "no compulsion in religion" (2:255) allowing religious autonomy to the "people of the book," a general pattern actualized by the Prophet himself in his pact with the Jewish and pagan tribes of Medina, to leave each tribe to live by its own religion and tradition and form an alliance of mutual defense with authority of final arbitration resting in the Prophet (for questions around the authenticity of this document, see ʿUmarī, 1991, vol. 2, p. 102). The overall effect was that, rather than settle as agriculturalists, Muslims in this era were to engage in governance and carry on further conquests. To prevent the Bedouins from raiding indiscriminately or destroying the productive agricultural lands and to segregate the Muslim Arabs from the conquered non-Muslims, the Bedouins were settled in garrison cities called *amṣār* (sing. *miṣr*), the three earliest ones being Basra and Kufa in Iraq and Fusṭāṭ in Egypt; a little later, others such as Qayrawān in Tunisia and Marv in Khorāsān were established. The old elites and the administrative machinery of the Byzantine and Sassanian empires were incorporated into the new regime. Non-Muslim scribes retained their jobs and served the new rulers. The old landowners, chiefs, and headmen kept their authority in the villages and assisted in collecting taxes. The Umayyads maintained a *dīwān al-kharāj* where revenue was brought in from the provinces and recorded before being deposited in the *bayt al-māl* (treasury).

Apart from these basic principles and practices, the relationship between the caliphate and the conquered peoples varied, due in part to the treaties and deals that were made with the chiefs or rulers during conquest. The old city-state status that had been the unit of political organization in Mesopotamia, Syria, and Egypt since antiquity was replaced by a central administration that appointed governors. The governor oversaw the collection of tributes and taxes, supervised the distribution of stipends, led the Muslims in prayer and war, and disseminated religious knowledge among Muslims. In the more remote areas or where the strong resistance of the old rulers had earned them favorable arrangements, only annual tribute was collected, at least for a time. In Iran, Muslims established garrisons in or near established cities such as Hamadān, Isfahan, Qazvīn, Rey, Nishapur, and Marv. In Iraq, the Sassanian chancery (*dīwān*), the old system of collecting taxes and distributing stipends, was adopted, and the taxes included both a land tax (*kharāj*) and a poll tax for non-Muslims (*jizyah*).

Non-Arab converts to Islam were absorbed organically into the old clan structure as clients (*mawālī*, sing. *mawlā*) into a multigenerational, symbiotic relationship, in which loyalty and protection were exchanged, along with social capital such as knowledge (many of the chief scholars of Islam had been clients of Arab scholars), marriages, and economic benefits, but the superior status of the old Arab clan was retained. The Marwānid-Umayyads, with important exceptions, attempted to fashion the Caliphate as an Arab phenomenon against the threat to their interests posed by non-Arab conversions to Islam, and were ultimately toppled.

The High ʿAbbāsid Period (749–945). The ʿAbbāsids, although rejecting the Umayyads' Arab-centered conception of rule and restoring a universalist Islamic basis for legitimacy, inherited the personnel and traditions of the Umayyads and the early caliphs, who had in turn adopted and adapted the Byzantine and Sassanian practices in granting tax revenues for military service. The ʿAbbāsids' was a loose, tolerant empire, rather than homogeneous or monolithic one; it governed a vast territory composed of communities that were quite varied, including large cities that were divided into many communities, in addition to peasants, semi-sedentarized villagers, nomads, and mountain peoples. For obvious reasons, the level of bureaucratic control varied; the farther a city was from the ʿAbbāsid capital in Baghdad, and the farther a region from a city, the less control the empire wielded. In Islamic political and legal tradition, the caliph was vested with the authority to rule on behalf of the Muslim community, and from him all other offices drew their authority; in practice, challenges to the authority of the caliph were constant. The directly controlled provinces were Iraq, Egypt, Syria, western Iran, and Khūzestān. The term *wazīr* first applied to the high secretaries close to the caliph, but by the middle of the ninth century, the office of the *wazīr* headed all administration and drew from established families that often succeeded in passing it on hereditarily. The Sassanian registers, or bureaus (*dīwān*), were further developed into the *dīwān al-rasāʾil* (chancery), *dīwān al-kharāj* (tax collection), and *dīwān al-jaysh* (payment of salaries); later, there also developed from these bureaus the *dīwān al-ʿazīmmah* (internal auditors or controller's office), *dīwān al-tawqīʿ* (countersignature), and *barīd* (the official messenger and information service). A different kind of elite, the *ʿulamāʾ*, in particular the Ḥanafīs, served as judges (*quḍāt*, sing. *qāḍī*).

To ensure provincial loyalty to the center, several means of check and balance were employed in times and places where centralization could be achieved, such as frequent rotation of governors (*wulāt*, sing. *wālī*), a practice established early on by ʿUmar, and division of functions, such that the governor served as the military commander, a representative of the central treasury (*ʿāmil*) oversaw financial affairs, and the judge drawn from the *ʿulamāʾ* class performed a range of functions besides dispensing justice, all being subject to the oversight of the *barīd*. Local government was minimal, limited to taxation, hierarchically divided into *rustāq* (also called *dīh* or *qaryah*; subdistrict, consisting of a market and an administrative town, surrounded by villages); larger units were called *kūra* and *tassūj*.

In addition, of the cultivated lands that were privately owned and taxed, there were two other kinds, the crown lands that belonged to the caliphate and those ceded to individuals on a revocable basis, called *iqṭāʿ*. One kind was *iqṭāʿ tamlīk*, usually created out of wastelands for the sake of stimulating agricultural investment with a three-year grace period and other incentives; such lands ended up becoming private property. Another kind, *iqṭāʿ istighlāl*, was akin to tax farming in which an insolvent caliph received a sum of money equivalent to the tithe (*ʿushr*) for the period in question, in return for the right to tax the peasantry at a higher rate. The sum thus received was used to finance administration, pay off political debts, and offset budget deficits or pet projects. Tax collection was enormously demanding on a bureaucracy suited for communication and record keeping; it required visiting the villages with a team of specialists including those who could survey, estimate, adjudicate disputes (*qāḍīs*), register deeds, provide intelligence, and extract, violently if necessary, the revenues. This would be impossible without the cooperation of the middlemen, called *aʿwān* (helpers), who were the local headmen (*raʾīs* and *dihqān* in Iran, *shaykh al-balad* in Egypt), who were prone to pocketing commissions from either side. Family ties, extended by patronage, were crucial to this system.

The Period of Patronage States. After the fall of ʿAbbāsid power, the caliphate became a symbolic office, and the Seljuks, who came in as converts to and saviors of Sunnī Islam, ruled through a mix of Persianate bureaucracy and central Asian tribal ruling custom. As horse-warriors, not able to maintain a central empire, they molded the *iqṭāʿ* system of the late ʿAbbāsid times into a system of financial administration that, under various names, was later adapted by the Mongol, Timurid, Ottoman, Ṣafavid, Uzbek, and Mughal empires. The *iqṭāʿ*, *timār*, *tuyūl*, and *jāgīr* (all names for grants of tax revenues) all represent a similar principle of decentralized financial compensation to the military elite. Other examples of administrative uniformities among Muslims states are taxation on a *kharāj-jizyah* or land- and poll-tax basis, and the endowment of *waqf*s for religious purposes. In many cases, as in central Asia and North Africa, these uniformities were due to the direct transfer of Middle Eastern institutions, but in many others, they were due to the inheritance of similar institutions from earlier non-Muslim regimes, and to the adoption of a common Muslim terminology for separate precedents.

The Empires of the Early Modern Period: Ottomans, Ṣafavids, Mughals. Nearly the entire Muslim world in the early modern period was divided between three great empires: the Ottoman, Ṣafavid, and Mughal. While on the intellectual plane, even in administrative practices, there is little that was drastically new, each of the empires erected strong centralized bureaucratic institutions unprecedented in their coherence since classical ʿAbbāsid times, and the general populace achieved a considerable level of prosperity. Of the three, the Mughals of India were the grandest and most populous, but also the shortest lived. Central supervision reached its peak in the Ottoman Empire. The rulers of all three empires shared central Asian stock; the Ottomans were Oghuz Turks whose ancestors had immigrated to Anatolia after their Seljuk cousins had settled in the old Islamic lands; the ancestors of the Ṣafavids hailed from Azerbaijan, near the Caspian coast, and the Mughals traced their ancestry to Tamerlane (Timur Lang), who was proud of his mixed Turkish and Mongol lineage. Among central Asian tribes, the rule of succession was that there was no rule, and the tradition continued even as they ruled mainly sedentary empires. The Ottomans even employed fratricide to eliminate the threat of competition, a practice common between the fifteenth and seventeenth centuries. Ṣafavid succession relied on a more peaceful contest in an assembly of the chief courtiers to choose which son would succeed after the monarch's death. In any case, unlike earlier military patronage states, centralized power was highly valued and none of the empires were allowed to be parceled between the male heirs of a monarch as had been the case among the Seljuks. The leadership of the Sunnī world, contested briefly by the Mughals, fell to the Ottomans when they vanquished the Mamlūk rulers of the central Arab regions of Syria and Egypt. The caliph residing in Cairo was decommissioned and the title of caliphate claimed by the Ottoman sultan for himself.

In administration, the Ṣafavids build on preexisting Turko-Persian patterns, whereas the Ottomans created distinct military and civilian offices out of the diverse populations they ruled over in Anatolia and eastern Europe; Turkish was established as one of the official languages in the Ottoman court and literature alongside the rich and ancient Persian. Eventually, Turkish largely replaced Persian in bureaucracy and literature and Arabic in religious discourse. But this did not mean privileging Turkic ethnicity, and ethnic Turks were limited in their political and military roles, opting often to advance through *madrasah* education to become *ʿulamāʾ* or scribes. For the military-administrative elite, the Ottomans created a new "Roman" race, a new blend, Turkish-speaking and Muslim, but from non-Muslim, non-Turkish origins. Ottoman writers took pride in how the Ottomans took the best qualities of many nations and blended them into a new, superior race. The Ottoman state was the rule and reign of the sultans, but in an important sense it was the conglomeration of all the households, the sultans' as well as those of this "Ottoman Roman" elite. In contrast, the Ṣafavid empire was centered on a charismatic shah, who was seen as divinely anointed and even divine by some of his early followers; this conception abated with the death of Shah Ismāʿīl in 1524.

The Ottoman-Ṣafavid military rivalry lasted from 1578 until 1639, when a treaty was concluded. In both empires the emperor needed to bolster revenues for military ends; military service was rewarded through temporary revenue grants (*timārs*, Turkish equivalent of *iqṭāʿ*)—a system that had been in place since ʿAbbāsid times. The rulers' own revenues mostly came from customs duties on international trade and commercial taxes, and so increase in foreign trade enhanced the ruler's revenues, hence the age-old tradition of building caravansaries, bridges, and roads to facilitate trade, and providing security at mountain passes and river crossings. Both empires learned from each other; the Ṣafavids discovered that ideology alone will not guarantee success; the Ottomans realized that administration was not sufficient, and over the course of sixteenth century various ideological bases were posited. While the Ottoman rulers had claimed to be "commanders of the faithful" earlier on, the conquest of Egypt in 1517 and confrontation with the Ṣafavid "heretics" led them to emphasize the sultan as the caliph, the leader of the Sunnī world. Süleyman I Kanuni (the "Lawgiver"; d. 1566) wanted to ensure that his sultanistic edicts were fully in accord with the *Sharīʿah*, and by the end of the century, the sultan was presented routinely as the champion of Sunnī Islam.

Prior to 1600, the "classic" Ottoman rule was based on the principle of an egalitarian agrarian society. The peasants were allocated plots of equal productivity sufficient for a family. In the Ottoman realm there were about fifty thousand cavalrymen and several hundred provincial officers who lived close to their revenue sources alongside peasants and townsmen. The holders of larger revenue grants were distant in proportion to the size of the grant in both empires. The Ṣafavids allowed their Turkoman commanders to hold large land grants in the provinces. After 1600, the more efficient and superior Ottoman system that had relied on large number of small-scale holdings came to resemble the Ṣafavids' as the need for revenue and military expenses against the Ṣafavids and Habsburgs put pressure on the Ottomans to make larger grants. The power and protection of the Ottoman state, which reached individual subjects directly before this time now devolved upon civic, religious, or ethnic communities.

A crucial difference between the two empires—with the Mughal one resembling the Ottomans in this respect—was the position of the *ʿulamāʾ*. The Shīʿī *ʿulamāʾ* were empowered by the religious ideology of the Ṣafavid realm, and after the founding dynasty lost its sway, the *ʿulamāʾ*'s power, based in secure economic grants, only increased, whereas the Ottoman *ʿulamāʾ*, by contrast, had become state functionaries. An Ottoman *qāḍī* administered not only *Sharīʿah* to Muslims but also the sultan's *qānūn* law to all subjects. To be considered for the judiciary, the *ʿulamāʾ* had to not only follow the Ḥanafī school that the Ottomans preferred but also learn Turkish and join provincial rotation. This put an end to the Arab *ʿulamāʾ*'s traditional role of socioreligious leadership that had long acted as check against political abuse.

The Poll Tax on Non-Muslims (*Jizye,* or *Jizye-isherʿī*) in the Ottoman Empire. Sanctioned by scriptural text (*naṣṣ*) and juristic convention, as asserted in the *firmān*, *jizyah* was for the Ottomans a religious tax whose collection and spending had to be done with special care. It was collected as a rule directly for the state treasury. As a *sharʿī* tax belonging to the *bayt māl al-muslimīn* its administration was put under the supervision of the *qāḍīs* and not infrequently its actual collection was made by them. The *jizyah* revenues were usually spent for military purposes. Exemption from *jizyah* was usually made in return for military services. In accordance with the *Sharīʿah* the Ottoman government always exempted from *jizyah* children, women, disabled and blind men, and the unemployed poor. Earlier, monks (*ruhbān*) and clerics were exempted from *jizyah*, but in the reform of 1691 all able clerics were subjected to *jizyah*. In 1692 the *ruhbān* sent a petition to the sultan stating a *sharʿī* opinion about the necessity of the exemption of those *ruhbān* who were in retirement and not earning their own living, but it was rejected on the basis of the differing opinion of Imām Abū Yūsuf.

Like the first Muslim conquerors of Egypt and Syria, the Ottomans used varied administrative modes of collecting *jizyah*, in some cases identifying previous taxes as *jizyah* (as in Hungary). When a conquered land was to be organized as an Ottoman province, a census of people subject to *jizyah* was made by the *qāḍī* appointed there, and a book called *defter-i jizya-i gabrān* was drawn up and two copies made, one for the central treasury and the other for the provincial administration. The census was not always punctually renewed.

Islamic jurisprudence distinguished two kinds of *jizyah*, that fixed by *ṣulḥ*, agreement, the amount of which could not be altered (called by Ottomans the fixed *jizyah*, or *maqṭūʿ*) and that was levied from individuals, *al-jizyah ʿala ʾl-ruʾūs* (poll tax). Considering the basic *sharʿī* character of the poll tax, the government often insisted on its payment individually. On the other hand, the *maqṭūʿ* might become too onerous when the population of such a group for one reason or another decreased. In such cases a new census was often asked for, to reduce the amount or to return to the payment by individuals. The *maqṭūʿ* system in *jizyah*, however, came to be more and more extensively applied in the period of decline during which the central government had increasingly lost control of tax collection in the provinces. It was the sultan's responsibility to declare every new year the rates of *jizyah* to be collected on the basis of a *fatwa* given by the *shaykh al-Islām*, who determined it according to the *sharʿī* scale. The wealthy, middle-income, and poor paid 48, 24, and 12 dirhams, respectively; payment could be made in silver and gold coins in circulation. If a non-Muslim visitor (*mustāʾmin*, one given *amān*) prolonged his stay in the Ottoman dominions longer than one year he was treated as a *dhimmī*, subjected to *jizyah*. Later on under the capitulations, the Ottoman government became more and more tolerant in this matter.

Corruption appeared in the form of bribery; collectors could allow the wealthy a lower rate and force the poor to pay higher, or burden the people for their expenses, or be unduly harsh.

The Tanzimat decree of 1839 brought a new concept of citizenship to the society of the Ottoman state: the idea that both the Muslims and the

Christians living in the empire were to be treated as equal before the law. This involved the question of taxation, including the *kharāj*, which there was pressure to abolish from Western diplomats in Istanbul. A decision on this was made only after the 1856 reforms, when both *kharāj* and *jizyah* were abolished, and instead non-Muslim subjects were taxed in lieu of military service (*bedel-e asker*).

India. A recognizably Islamicate administration that more or less replicated the *dīwān* system developed under the ʿAbbāsids was introduced into India during the rule of the Ghaznavids, whose seat of administration was at Lahore, and the administration was organized under it into as many as ten different departments. This system of government seems to have been fully developed during the sultanate period, as we find quite a number of departments in existence.

The question of the levy of *jizyah* in India is contested, and there is evidence that it was not normally levied under the Dihlī Sultanate [*q.v.*] in the sense of a discriminatory religious tax. Under the Dihlī Sultanate, political conditions do not appear to have been apt for the imposition of a novel discriminatory tax by a minority upon a majority; authors employ *jizyah* to mean tribute from Hindu kings. Efforts were made by Fīrūz Shāh Tughluq (but the context suggests it was not distinguished from land revenue). In the Sayyid and Lodhi periods nothing is heard of the levy of *jizyah*. There is mention of Akbar's abolition of it, but it is dubious and appears to be panegyrical. Following a number of orthodox measures discriminating against non-Muslims, Awrangzīb (d. 1707) imposed an unpopular *jizyah* in 1679 on the urging of the *ʿulamāʾ*; in this, government servants were exempted. and there were three rates of tax—owners of property worth 2,500 rupees were assessed at 16 rupees, those worth 250 rupees at 6 rupees 8 annas, and those worth 52 rupees were assessed at 3 rupees 4 annas, the blind, the paralyzed, and the indigent being exempt. Awrangzīb's successors largely abolished it; Muḥammad Shāh made a futile attempt in 1725 to restore it.

REFERENCES

Cahen, Cl.. "Bayt al-Māl." *Encyclopaedia of Islam*. 2d ed. Brill Online, 2013.

Duri, A.A. "Dīwān." *Encyclopaedia of Islam*. 2d ed. Brill Online, 2013.

Halm, H., "Rawk." *Encyclopaedia of Islam*. 2d ed. Brill Online, 2013.

İnalcik, Halil, and P. Hardy. "Djizya." *Encyclopaedia of Islam*. 2d ed. Brill Online, 2013.

Johns, Jeremy. *Arabic Administration in Norman Sicily: The Royal* Dīwān. Cambridge, U.K.: Cambridge University Press, 2002.

Kunt, Metin. "Ottomans and Safavids: States, Statecraft, and Societies." In *A Companion to the History of the Middle East*, edited by Youssef Choueiri, pp. 192–206. Blackwell, 2005.

Lapidus, Ira M. *A History of Islamic Societies*. 2d ed. Cambridge, U.K.: Cambridge University Press, 2002.

Tyan, Émile. *Institutions du droit public musulman*. 2 vols. Paris: Recueil Sirey, 1954–1957.

ʿUmarī, Akram Ḍiyāʾ al-. *Madinan Society at the Time of the Prophet*. Translated by Hudā Khaṭṭāb. 2 vols. Herndon, Va.: International Institution of Islamic Thought, 1991.

OVAMIR ANJUM

AFGHĀNĪ, JAMĀL AL-DĪN AL-. Jamāl al-Dīn al-Afghānī, (1838/1839–1897), was a writer, orator, reformer, and Pan-Islamist political activist. Controversial during his lifetime, al-Afghānī has become since his death one of the most influential figures in the Muslim world.

Life and Activities. Despite his claim to Afghan origin—whence his name—overwhelming evidence shows that al-Afghānī was born and raised in Iran of a Shīʿī family. Among this evidence are several documents in the papers he left in Tehran when he was expelled from Iran in 1891, of which a catalog was published in 1963. No such early documentation is found for Afghanistan, where the first published reference to him dates from World War I and consists of a paraphrase of an Egyptian biography. His passport also identified him as Iranian.

Sunnī Muslims are often reluctant to admit that al-Afghānī was raised in Shīʿī Iran. Al-Afghānī apparently feared the repercussions of an Iranian identification. Moreover, he knew he would have less influence in the Sunnī world if he were thought to be from Shīʿī Iran.

Documents indicate that after his education in his hometown of Asadābād in northwest Iran and in Qazvīn and Tehran, he went for higher education in the 1850s to the Shīʿī shrine cities in Ottoman Iraq. The earliest treatises found among al-Afghānī's papers and dated from this period are Shaykhī treatises; he annotated them in a way that makes it clear that he followed, at least for a time, this innovative and philosophically oriented school of thought. Al-Afghānī's books and papers also confirm the influence of the rationalist Islamic philosophers, especially such Iranian thinkers as Avicenna (Ibn Sīnā) and Nāṣir al-Dīn al-Ṭūsī.

In his late teens al-Afghānī traveled to India and was almost surely there at or near the time of the Indian Mutiny of 1857. It is likely that his lifelong hatred of the British, and especially of their power in colonized countries, dates from his contact with them in India. It is also possible, as one later account says, that he was in Būshehr, Iran, at the time of the British–Persian War of 1856–1857.

Al-Afghānī seems then to have embarked on a journey that probably included Mecca, and certainly a trip across Iran into Afghanistan in the early 1860s. According to an Indian journalist in Afghanistan at this time, al-Afghānī came to Afghanistan with secret papers (which the journalist thought were from the Russians) that gained him rapid access to the *amīr*. He was reported as speaking Persian like an Iranian, and also Turkish (widely spoken in northwest Iran), and he was believed to be from Anatolia (and therefore called Rūmī). His conversations of this period, the earliest ones documented, already have the fiercely anti-British ring that was to characterize the rest of his life. A change in *amīrs* brought a pro-British ruler to the throne, and al-Afghānī's attempts to keep his position failed; he was expelled in late 1868.

In 1869 he went briefly to Cairo and then to the Ottoman capital, Istanbul. He was involved in the council of education and the new university, where he gave one of a series of public lectures. A speech gave conservative *ʿulamāʾ* an excuse to attack the new university, which they disliked, and the head of the university was compelled to resign, while al-Afghānī was expelled from the country.

From 1871 to 1879 al-Afghānī lived in Cairo, where he spent most of this time teaching. As Egypt entered a political and financial crisis in the late 1870s, al-Afghānī encouraged his disciples to publish political newspapers; he himself gave speeches and carried out political activities as head of a secret society. His followers included several young men who later became the leaders of Egyptian political and intellectual life, notably his closest disciple, the young Muḥammad ʿAbduh, as well as ʿAbd Allāh Nadīm, Saʿd Zaghlūl, and Yaʿqūb Ṣannūʿ. Al-Afghānī blamed Egypt's plight on both the British and Khedive Ismāʿīl. When Ismāʿīl was replaced by Tawfīq in 1879, however, it was the work of the British and French, and Tawfīq responded to al-Afghānī's continued fiery anti-British speeches by expelling him from Egypt.

Al-Afghānī returned to India, going to the Muslim state of Hyderabad. Here he did much of his important writing, including his most famous treatise, known in English as *The Refutation of the Materialists* (1881). It was intended to refute the work of the pro-British (though liberal) Sayyid Aḥmad Khān. The writings from this and the Egyptian period include a great deal on nationalism, and nothing of the Pan-Islamism with which his name is now associated.

At the time of the ʿUrābī revolt in Egypt (1881–1882), al-Afghānī left India. Muḥammad ʿAbduh joined him in Paris, where they edited an Arabic newspaper, *al-ʿUrwah al-wuthqā* (The Strongest Bond, i.e., the Qurʾān). The paper lasted only eight months (from March to October 1884) but was influential; its main themes were Pan-Islamist and anti-British, and it also included theoretical articles.

In 1884 al-Afghānī went to Britain, where he became involved in an abortive plan to accompany Sir Henry Drummond Wolff to Istanbul with the aim of inducing Britain to end its occupation of Egypt. Ironically, Blunt's writings on these events persuaded some Muslims to consider al-Afghānī a British spy.

In 1886 al-Afghānī went to Iran, where he gathered liberal disciples, and thence to Russia, where he tried but failed to arouse Russian leaders to wage war against Britain. Returning to Iran in 1890–1891, he encouraged growing activity against the shah's economic concessions to foreigners. A pamphlet against these concessions probably inspired by al-Afghānī led to his expulsion to Iraq in early 1891. From Iraq al-Afghānī went to Britain, where he joined another reformer, Malkom Khān, in written and spoken attacks on the Iranian government.

Abdülhamid II invited al-Afghānī to Istanbul but became increasingly suspicious of him; he was kept in comfort but prevented from publishing or giving speeches. He might have encouraged an Iranian disciple, Mīrzā Riẓā, to kill Nāṣir al-Dīn Shāh. In 1897 al-Afghānī died of cancer of the jaw. No evidence supports the story that he was poisoned by the sultan. In 1944, his remains were transferred to Kabul, Afghanistan, and a mausoleum was erected there.

Contributions to Modern Islam. Al-Afghānī did not do extensive writing or conceive of a complex theoretical system. He was rather an intellectual who picked up, combined, and developed a number of existing themes to create a novel whole.

His background in Muslim philosophy allowed al-Afghānī to give his modernizing teaching an Islamic base. He spoke vehemently against blind faith and argued that Islam is compatible with modern science. But he seems to have favored preaching orthodox religion to the masses and a kind of rationalist, natural-law deism to the elite. He also called for giving women greater rights on the grounds that men are first educated by their mothers.

His political thought was impelled by hostility to British rule, especially in Muslim lands. Although al-Afghānī expressed himself in friendlier terms toward the French and Russians, his anti-British speeches and writings could be, and were, extended to a more general anti-imperialism, one that has increased in the Muslim world since his time.

Al-Afghānī is associated with two movements that he did not originate but that he propagated. One is nationalism, supported in Egypt with references to the glories of ancient Egypt and in India with praise of the ancient Hindus. The other is Pan-Islamism, which started with the nineteenth-century Ottoman sultans and was then voiced in more progressive, anti-imperialist forms by the Young Ottomans, especially Namık Kemal. As al-Afghānī's works on this subject were written in Arabic, he had more influence internationally than the Young Ottomans did. Nationalism and Pan-Islamism were seen as different but not necessarily contradictory strategies for communal unity and anti-imperialism.

Al-Afghānī stressed pragmatic aspects of internal reform and self-improvement and was a staunch supporter of technical and scientific education. He frequently worked with autocratic rulers, and only near the end of his life spoke of the need to awaken the people.

Al-Afghānī's reputation has continued to grow since his death. His chief disciple, Muḥammad ʿAbduh, even though he renounced al-Afghānī's political activism, carried on one aspect of al-Afghānī's work when he tried to elaborate modern and pragmatic interpretations of Islam. ʿAbduh's pupil Muḥammad Rashīd Riḍā specifically stressed al-Afghānī's influence.

Pan-Islam, in the sense of either a political or a more general unity of Muslim countries as a barrier to further European conquest of Muslim territory, became especially strong after the British conquest of Egypt in 1882, the establishment of the French protectorate of Tunisia in 1881, and the European taking of Muslim territories in the Russo-Turkish war and the Congress of Berlin in 1877–1878. In the more general sense of Muslim solidarity against the Christian and imperial West, Pan-Islam has continued to be popular to the present. This, combined with his anti-British activities, is one reason al-Afghānī has remained popular in the Muslim world.

[*See also* ʿAbduh, Muḥammad; Aḥmad Khān, Sayyid; Arab Nationalism; Modernity; Pan-Islam; *and* Rashīd Riḍā, Muḥammad.]

BIBLIOGRAPHY

ʿAbduh, Muḥammad. *The Theology of Unity*. Translated by Ishaq Masaʿad and Kenneth Cragg. London: Allen & Unwin, 1966.

Afghānī, Jamāl al-Dīn al-. *Réfutation des matérialistes*. Translated by Amélie-Marie Goichon. Paris: P. Geuthner, 1942.

Afshār, Īraj, and Aṣghar Mahdavī, eds. *Documents inédits concernant Seyyed Jamal al-Din Afghani*. Tehran: University of Tehran, 1963.

Chaghatai, Mohammad Ikram, comp. and ed. *Jamal al-Din al-Afghani: An Apostle of Islamic Resurgence*. Lahore, Pakistan: Sang-e-Meel, 2005.

Cole, Juan R. I. *Colonialism and Revolution in the Middle East: Social and Cultural Origins of Egypt's ʿUrabi Movement*. Princeton, N.J.: Princeton University Press, 1993.

Hourani, Albert. *Arabic Thought in the Liberal Age, 1798–1939*. London: Oxford University Press, 1962.

Keddie, Nikki R. *An Islamic Response to Imperialism: Political and Religious Writings of Sayyid Jamāl al-Dīn "al-Afghānī."* Rev. ed. Berkeley: University of California Press, 1983.

Keddie, Nikki R. *Sayyid Jamāl al-Dīn "al-Afghānī": A Political Biography*. Berkeley: University of California Press, 1972.

Kedourie, Elie. *Afghani and ʿAbduh: An Essay on Religious Unbelief and Political Activism in Modern Islam*. London: Cass, 1966.

Kohn, Margaret. "Afghānī on Empire, Islam, and Civilization." *Political Theory* 37, no. 3 (2009): 398–422.

Moaddel, Mansoor. "Conditions for Ideological Production: The Origins of Islamic Modernism in India, Egypt, and Iran." *Theory and Society* 30, no. 5 (October 2001): 669–731.

Mohamed, Aishah. "A Critique of Jamal al-Din al-Afghani's Reformist Ideas and Its Importance in the Development of Islamic Thought in the Twentieth Century." *Islamic Quarterly* 45, no. 1 (2001): 49–66.

Montada, Josep Puig. "Al-Afghânî, a Case of Religious Unbelief?" *Studia Islamica* 100/101 (2005): 203–220.

NIKKI R. KEDDIE
Updated by NAEL SHAMA

AFGHANISTAN. *This entry contains two subentries:*

Overview *and*
Afghanistan, 2001 U.S. Invasion of.

OVERVIEW

In the nineteenth century Afghanistan emerged as a buffer state between the contending British Indian and tsarist Russian colonial empires. This overwhelmingly Muslim (more than 99 percent) landlocked nation covers an area of 251,825 square miles (652,225 square kilometers) consisting primarily of rugged mountains, deep valleys, deserts, and arid plateaus.

Muslim Arab armies penetrated the region at the turn of the eighth century CE. Muslim empires rose during the following centuries and expanded the frontiers of Islam into Central and South Asia. Modern Afghanistan is the remnant of one of the last such Muslim empires in the region, the Durrānī Empire founded by Aḥmad Shāh Durrānī (r. 1747–1772). The Durrānī Empire began to disintegrate at the turn of the nineteenth century because of bloody struggles over succession as well as growing external military and political pressures. The prolonged fratricidal wars (1800–1880) encouraged British and Russian colonial encroachments, resulting in two Anglo-Afghan Wars (1839–1842 and 1879–1880) and considerable territorial losses. These civil wars and colonial interventions left powerful legacies, notably the increasing economic, military, and technological dependence of Afghan governments on European colonial and postcolonial powers.

The effects of foreign assistance and interventions became apparent immediately after the Second Anglo-Afghan War (1879–1880), when Britain installed Amīr ʿAbd al-Raḥmān Khān (1880–1901), a member of the Muḥammadzai branch of the Durrānīs. With substantial annual British subsidies and technical assistance, Amīr ʿAbd al-Raḥmān Khān, the "Iron Amir," consolidated power over the territory carved out by British India and tsarist Russia as a buffer state under the official name the Kingdom of Afghanistan.

Amīr ʿAbd al-Raḥmān's policies were maintained unchanged during the reign of his son, Amīr Habīb Allāh (r. 1901–1919). Toward the end of Habīb Allāh's reign, as a result of the introduction of modern schools and the press, such new political ideals as constitutionalism, nationalism, liberal secularism, reformism, and Islamic modernism entered the political culture of Afghanistan, both complementing and competing with the traditional ideals of kingship, kinship, and Islam. These ideals found adherents among the nascent intelligentsia, members of the royal family, the court page boys, and some *ʿulamāʾ*. King Amānullāh (r. 1919–1929), a grandson of Amīr ʿAbd al-Raḥmān and a supporter of modernist-nationalist thought, introduced the first constitution of Afghanistan in 1923. He attempted to promote the idea of equality and develop a national ideology based on traits common to all citizens of Afghanistan, but he failed. His rule was challenged by popular armed rebellions supported by some conservative *ʿulamāʾ* and *ruḥānīs* (spiritual or Ṣūfī dignitaries), under the banner of a *jihād* against an "infidel king," and he was forced into exile in 1929.

Muḥammad Nādir Shāh (r. 1929–1933), who succeeded King Amānullāh after a nine-month interregnum, abandoned many of Amānullāh's Western-inspired reforms, and attempted to legitimize his own dynastic rule by constitutional means. He called a grand assembly (*loya jirga*) of the tribal elders, religious dignitaries, and local aristocrats to ratify a new constitution (1931). He established the Jamʿīyatul ʿUlamāʾ (Supervisory Council of Muslim Scholars). Reverting to Amīr ʿAbd al-Raḥmān's practices, both civil and criminal cases were brought within the domain of *Sharīʿah* courts, making them the most important vehicles of centralization. Southeastern frontier Pashtun tribes that had helped him in his bid for power were granted exemptions from taxes and conscription, and members of the influential Mujaddidī family of *ruḥānīs* were awarded cabinet posts for their support.

Response to Musahiban Rulers. During the crucial decades of the 1960s and 1970s, when economic development programs were failing and development-related corruption was rampant,

Afghan leaders became preoccupied with prolonging their rule by employing Western-style governance techniques to appease their foreign patrons, instead of extending social services and equitably meeting the needs of all citizens. After the promulgation of the "liberal" constitution of 1964 and the onset of New Democracy in Afghanistan, Marxist and Maoist parties formed. In response, Islamist movements emerged, not only to address the potential communist threat but also to challenge the legitimacy of the Musahiban monarchy. The rise of both communist and Islamist parties and movements—each with ideological ties and financial patrons (actual or potential) outside the country—was without precedent in the political history of Afghanistan. The government's dependence on foreign assistance for economic development programs and the maintenance of its large military and police forces had also reached new heights.

The Afghan state depended on Soviet patronage for survival. Hence, the government opposed Islamist movements, while the communist groups, especially the pro-Soviet Marxist parties, were given free rein. As a consequence, in July 1973 Prince Muḥammad Dāʾūd, a former prime minister (1953–1963) and paternal first cousin and brother-in-law of King Zahīr Shāh (r. 1933–1973)—also a longtime royal supporter of the pro-Soviet Marxists—staged a military coup, abolished the monarchy, and proclaimed himself president of the Republic of Afghanistan (1973–1978). Only five years later Dāʾūd himself fell victim to a coup led by the People's Democratic Party of Afghanistan (PDPA) that ended Durrānī dynastic rule by establishing a communist government (1978–1992). The Islamist movements, already seriously weakened by the monarchy and Dāʾūd's regime, suffered devastating new attacks from the Marxist government. Ironically, however, the usurpation of state power by the PDPA and the direct military intervention of the Soviet Union (1979–1989) offered the fledgling Islamist movements a new lease on life.

Following the PDPA coup, elements of Islamist groups living in exile in Pakistan and elsewhere joined with traditional tribal and religious leaders in rural areas to launch a nationwide popular armed struggle, a *jihād*, that eventually drove out the invading Soviet army (1989), defeated the Afghan communists, and declared Afghanistan an Islamic state (April 1992).

The military triumph gradually deteriorated into humiliating and bloody interethnic and sectarian warfare. The vastly popular Islamist armed struggle, despite its remarkable military success, did not produce a coherent Islamic ideology, political unity, or a functioning state. The manner in which the Islamist victory by Afghan Mujāhidīn turned into a spectacular political and ideological failure not only raised serious doubts, especially among the educated Muslim youth, about the future viability of militant Islamist political struggles but created the conditions for the rise of even more regressive and violent movements such as the Taliban.

The *jihād* struggle was spearheaded and sustained by two major factions of the original Islamist movement: the Jamʿīyat-i Islāmī (Islamic Society) headed by Burhanuddin Rabbani, an al-Azhar-educated former professor of Islamic studies; and the Ḥizb-i Islāmī (Islamic Party) led by Gulbuddin Hekmatyar, a former undergraduate engineering student at Kabul Polytechnic University.

The impact of these differences in Rabbani and Hekmatyar's political outlooks—combined with their distinct ethnic affiliations (Rabbani is Tajik and Hekmatyar Pashtun) and serious interpersonal tensions—became evident when the two leaders took refuge in Pakistan. In the economically and politically volatile environment of the Afghan exile community in Peshawar, animosities and factional conflicts flourished.

Two other developments also played a significant role in the creation and perpetuation of factional divisions within the *jihād* movements in Afghanistan. First, the Pakistan government created or officially recognized five additional, primarily Pashtun-dominated resistance organizations. These groups included two led by traditional *ʿulamāʾ* (Mawlawī Yūnus Khāliṣ and Mawlawī Muḥammad Nabī Muḥammadī), two led by *ruḥānī* families (Ṣibghat Allāh Mujaddidī and Sayyid Aḥmad Gīlānī) with strong ties to the defunct monarchy, and one led by another al-Azhar–educated former Kabul University professor, ʿAbd al-Rabb Rasūl Sayyāf. In addition, at least eight Shīʿī resistance groups were organized in Iran and one in Pakistan. The Iranian groups during the early 1990s formed an alliance called Ḥizb-i Waḥdat-i Islāmī (Islamic Unity Party), led by Muḥammad ʿAlī Mazārī, who was brutally murdered by the Taliban (1995). Scores of other nonofficial Mujāhidīn groups active in the resistance complemented these groups.

Second, nearly all these groups were headquartered in neighboring Pakistan and Iran and were completely dependent on outside sources, both Muslim and non-Muslim, for money and arms. Because of direct Soviet intervention, there were no shortages of foreign supporters (covert and overt) to help defeat and destroy the USSR, especially during the Reagan era. Mujāhidīn parties and organizations representing many diverse interest groups (ideological, sectarian, ethnolinguistic, tribal, regional, and local) competed with one another for the patronage of numerous international aid organizations.

When an arrangement between the forces of Aḥmad Shāh Masʿūd, a Tajik Mujāhidīn commander, and ʿAbd al-Rashīd Dūstam, a powerful Uzbek leader of a militia force in northern Afghanistan, brought about the collapse of Najibullah's Marxist government in Kabul, the Mujāhidīn had a chance to end the war and establish a credible Islamic government. They failed because of powerful feelings of mistrust, encouraged by their foreign patrons, among the factions.

On the fall of the communist regime, the forces of the Iranian-backed Islamic Unity Party of eight Shīʿī and other predominantly Hazāra groups had occupied significant areas of Kabul. Dūstam, forming and leading the Junbush-i Millī-i Islāmī-i Shimālī Afghānistān (National Islamic Movement of Northern Afghanistan), demanded a role in the new Islamic State of Afghanistan. Similarly, other armed and newly empowered ethnic and sectarian minorities, such as the traditionally oppressed Shīʿī Hazāras, asked for fair representation in the new government.

Pashtun groups, notably those led by Sayyāf and Hekmatyar, responded with armed attacks against Masʿūd, Dūstam, and the Shīʿī coalition forces in and around Kabul. Sayyāf, who enjoyed the support of powerful Saudi patrons and allegedly introduced controversial Wahhābī practices, began armed attacks against the pro-Iranian Shīʿī Islamic Unity Party. Hekmatyar, formerly willing to recruit Pashtun communist officers for his failed military coups against the communist regime, condemned Aḥmad Shāh Masʿūd's alliance with Dūstam's militia. He opposed the inclusion of members of Dūstam's militia in the government while welcoming numerous high-ranking communist Pashtun military officers into his own camp. Hekmatyar's devastating rocket attack against Kabul, which ruined much of the city, was apparently motivated by fear that non-Pashtun minorities might dominate the central government, and this was not acceptable to him.

Crisis of the 1990s. The availability of an ever-larger number of competing foreign sponsors (governmental and nongovernmental, Muslim and otherwise), with their divergent or conflicting strategic, ideological, political, and economic agendas, offer ideal conditions for the growth of extremist militia organizations such as the Taliban within the political culture of Afghanistan. Not surprisingly, the same conditions are also aiding the continuing bloody resurgence of Taliban and al-Qaʿida insurgency in Afghanistan into the early twenty-first century.

The hastily arranged UN-brokered Bonn Accord (December 2001) installed the Karzai regime to power and spelled out the so-called peace process in post-Taliban Afghanistan. The process consisted of holding a series of elections (for emergency and constitutional *loya jirgas*, for president, and for parliament), drafting and ratifying a new constitution, building a national army and police force, reforming the judiciary, repatriating the refugees, and undertaking the political, social, and economic reconstruction of the country. It has, so far, fallen far short of domestic expectations. The often chaotic and contradictory policies and practices of state building have, for the most part, recreated the dysfunctional sovereignty-based presidential system, which remains a person-centered, Kabul-centered, and kin- and crony-based system of rule.

[*See also* Ḥizb-i Islāmī Afghānistān; Jamāʿat-i Islāmī; Loya Jirga; Muslim Brotherhood; *and* Taliban.]

BIBLIOGRAPHY

Abd al-Raḥmān Khān. *The Life of Abdur Rahman, Amir of Afghanistan*. 2 vols. Edited by Sultan Mahomed Khan. Karachi: Oxford University Press, 1980.

Arnold, Anthony. *Afghanistan's Two-Party Communism: Parcham and Khalq*. Stanford, Calif.: Hoover Institution Press, Stanford University, 1983.

Gregorian, Vartan. *The Emergence of Modern Afghanistan: Politics of Reform and Modernization, 1880–1946*. Stanford, Calif.: Stanford University Press, 1969.

Kakar, M. Hasan. *Government and Society in Afghanistan: The Reign of Amir ʿAbd al-Rahman Khan*. Austin: University of Texas Press, 1979.

Poullada, Leon B. *Reform and Rebellion in Afghanistan, 1919–1929: King Amanullah's Failure to Modernize a Tribal Society*. Ithaca, N.Y.: Cornell University Press, 1973.

Roy, Olivier. *Afghanistan: From Holy War to Civil War*. Princeton, N.J.: Darwin, 1995.

Shahrani, M. Nazif. "War, Factionalism, and the State in Afghanistan." *American Anthropologist* 104, no. 3 (September 2002): 715–722.

Shahrani, M. Nazif, and Robert L. Canfield, eds. *Revolutions and Rebellions in Afghanistan: Anthropological Perspectives*. Berkeley: Institute of International Studies, University of California, 1984.

Tapper, Richard, ed. *The Conflict of Tribe and State in Iran and Afghanistan*. New York: St. Martin's, 1983.

M. Nazif Shahrani

Afghanistan, 2001 U.S. Invasion of

American support for the Mujāhidīn added to the burden of the brutal civil war (1992–1996) in which 1.5 million Afghans died, 7 million were displaced, and the country was devastated. With the collapse of the state, the aid community increasingly performed the role of a surrogate state, providing food, health care, and education. Opium production increased as a means of surviving the rural and urban destruction and poverty. Violence, especially against women, escalated to an unprecedented level.

American support for the Mujāhidīn also led to the emergence of Osama Bin Laden as the leader of al-Qaʿida, a jihādist organization that used violence to realize political objectives. Bin Laden, a wealthy Saudi businessman, was close to the Saudi royal family and may have received CIA financial support in 1980 to build a major arms storage depot, as well as training and medical centers for the Mujāhidīn. He and other Arab militants allied with the extremist Pashtun Mujāhidīn, alienating the non-Pashtuns and Shīʿah ethnic and religious groups. However, by 1990 he was disillusioned by factions fighting within the Mujāhidīn and left Afghanistan. Bin Laden objected to Riyadh's close relationship with Washington, as he committed himself to a *jihād* against the United States, allegedly because it was the greatest enemy of Islam. He sponsored terrorist attacks in Somalia, Egypt, Sudan, Yemen, Kenya, Tanzania, Saudi Arabia, and Afghanistan. According to American government sources, Bin Laden may have sponsored the 1993 attacks on the north tower of the World Trade Center, which killed six people and injured more than a thousand. In 1996, Bin Laden returned to Afghanistan under the protection of the Taliban. Washington was not involved with the country, its simmering civil war, or the Taliban until the events of 9/11.

Aftermath of 9/11. In October 2001 the United States and the United Kingdom, operating under a NATO mandate that was sanctioned by the Security Council of the United Nations, led a bombing campaign against the Taliban government and invaded Afghanistan. After eleven years of war, the death of thousands of Afghans and hundreds of foreign troops, as well as ongoing violent attacks on civilians, Western governments began negotiating with the Taliban, who cooperate and share funding with al-Qaʿida and who together control much of the country. This policy is designed to split the Taliban and al-Qaʿida to secure U.S. economic and political interests in the region.

As of 2013, the Afghanistan International Security Assistance Force and U.S. and NATO forces had no workable strategy to create a stable and peaceful Afghanistan and to combat widespread drug cultivation, growing insurgency, crime, and corruption. The processes of nation and state building from outside have exacerbated ethnic, religious, class, and gender conflicts. Afghanistan's economy relies on international aid and drug income, although investments in the agricultural sector could become a viable alternative if specific policies are implemented to encourage wealth creation.

After the fall of the Taliban, Afghanis were promised peace, security, development, democracy, and liberation, which never materialized. On the contrary, their world is full of anxiety, and the killing of Bin Laden by the CIA in 2011 hardly reduced their pain, as the social conditions that existed under the Taliban and al-Qaʿida were being reconstituted.

[*See also* Bin Laden, Osama; *and* Taliban.]

BIBLIOGRAPHY

Jalalzai, Zubeda, and David Jefferess, eds. *Globalizing Afghanistan: Terrorism, War, and the Rhetoric of Nation Building*. Durham, N.C.: Duke University Press, 2011.

Johnson, Chris, and Jolyon Leslie. *Afghanistan: The Mirage of Peace*. London: Zed, 2004.

Rostami-Povey, Elaheh. *Afghan Women, Identity, and Invasion*. London: Zed, 2007.

Rostami-Povey, Elaheh. *Iran's Influence: A Religious-Political State and Society in Its Region*. London: Zed, 2010.

ELAHEH ROSTAMI-POVEY

AFRICA MUSLIM PARTY. The Africa Muslim Party (AMP) of South Africa was founded in 1994, with Gulam Sabdia as its chairman and Imtiaz Suleman as its national leader. It competed rather unsuccessfully in the 1994 elections for the National Assembly and also for the Council of Provinces. While it did not contest the 1999 elections for the National Assembly, it did compete again, however, for the elections but exclusively in the Western Cape Province. Once again it failed to secure any seats. The 2004 national elections were contested by AMP, with the same abysmal results as before.

It was in the 2000 elections for the Cape Town metropolitan area that AMP finally managed to secure two seats in the city government. Similarly, it gained three seats in the 2006 Cape Town Metro Council elections. This limited electoral success was followed by AMP's tactical move to join the multiparty coalition headed by the Democratic Alliance (DA) with close ties to the mayoral government of Helen Zille of DA. This too did not last long as it was expelled in January 2007 when it was learned that AMP councilor Badih Chaaban had attempted to make a secret coalition deal with the African National Congress (ANC) that supposedly would have seen him become the mayor if he succeeded in dislodging the DA-led coalition. This unfortunate political misadventure by Chaaban, suspected of bribing local councilors in his bid to gain power at any cost, tarnished AMP's image further, especially among its detractors who saw it as a peripheral and parochial organization. While it calls itself the African Muslim Party, it has very little to do with Africans or African Muslims as its name suggests. It is a mainly Malay/Colored and even Indian Muslim party.

Why was AMP created in the first place? What interests did it serve, and what did it hope to gain by contesting the general elections as a Muslim party in a country where Muslims formed less than 2 percent of the total population? On its official website AMP admits rather frankly that it was not under any illusion that it could form the government of the country; rather, it hoped to be able to make an input in the democratic process of a country with a multiethnic, multireligious, and multilingual society. It claims that this diversity is borne out by the fact that there were nineteen parties registered for the National and Provincial Assembly elections in 1994. It believed in devolution of powers from the national government to the provinces and the communities (which is where AMP comes in). It also wanted to promote morality, support religious freedom, abolish poverty and hunger, fight racism, enhance adult education, and promote free and fair trading conditions, as well as supposedly fighting nepotism and corruption.

In the period preceding the 1994 multiparty general elections Muslim groups/organizations became active in voter education and public campaigns to convince Muslims to vote for the secular party/ANC (headed by Nelson Mandela) as the progressive Muslim organizations such as the Muslim Youth Movement and the Call of Islam did, or to boycott elections as the pro-Iran Qibla did, or to vote for newly established fringe Muslim parties such as AMP and the Islamic Party (IP) as their supporters did. Both Muslim parties came in for criticism (IP, for instance, stood for elections only in the Western Cape Province) as they were seen as "vote spoilers," whereas, in fact, Muslims voted for the mainstream parties, predominantly for Mandela's ANC, though some voted for the National Party. Even the Jamiatul Ulama Transvaal, which had endorsed the idea of a single Muslim party, found itself distancing itself from the AMP when it was established by pointing out that it was formed without consultation of the Muslim community.

Both Muslim parties (IP and AMP), as Inga Niehaus points out, "represented the predominantly conservative sectors of the community and demanded a return to the traditional values and norms of Islam and the criminalisation of abortion, gambling and prostitution" (Niehaus, 2006). This is partly suggested by what we have mentioned above, that is, AMP's ethical concerns about the direction the country would take under a secular party such as ANC. Clearly, therefore, AMP positioned itself differently from other Muslim organizations with regard to political power in the postapartheid era. It did not seek accommodation with the African National Congress (ANC) but hoped both to create a platform for its ethical message (opposed to societal secularization) and to gain some political leverage in whatever way was possible, though the political fiasco that Chaaban created in 2007 did not help the party's image as a fringe organization.

Bibliography

Anon. "Liberation Movements Have Strong Support among Muslims." *Muslim Today* 1, no. 3, April 1994.

Bangstad, Sindre, and Aslam Fataar. "Ambiguous Accommodation: Cape Muslims and Post-Apartheid Politics." *Journal of Southern African Studies* 36, no. 4 (2010): 817–831.

Call of Islam 11, no. 7, 1994.

Moosa, Ebrahim. "Muslim Conservatism in South Africa." *Journal of Theology for Southern Africa* 69 (1989): 73–81.

Niehaus, Inga. "South Africa's Muslims between Participation and Exclusion: The Political Role of a Religious Minority during the Transition to Democracy." Paper presented at the Islamic Civilisation in Southern Africa conference, University of Johannesburg, 31 August–3 September 2006. http://www.africamuslimparty.org/Index_files/.

Abdin Chande

Aḥbāsh, al-. Officially registered as the Association of Islamic Philanthropic Projects (Jamʿīyat al-Mashariʿ al-Khayrīyah al-Islāmīyah), al-Aḥbāsh was established in Beirut in 1983 and has grown to become one of Lebanon's leading Sunnī organizations, operating an educational network at all levels, a radio station, and a journal (*Manār al-hudā*, Guiding Beacon) and organizing a variety of social, cultural, and welfare activities. It has also opened branches in other Middle Eastern countries, western Europe, the United States, Australia, and Africa, and it claims a quarter of a million members. In recent years the Aḥbāsh has become a leading factor in the heated debate between moderates and radicals over the essence of Islam.

Though members of the association represent several ethnic backgrounds, they identify themselves as Ethiopians, "al-Aḥbāsh." This nickname reflects their admiration for their founder and spiritual leader, Shaykh ʿAbd Allāh ibn Muḥammad ibn Yūsuf al-Hararī, a native of Harer, the seat of Ethiopian Islam. Shaykh ʿAbd Allāh adopted the name "the Ethiopians" to stress his message of Islamic moderation in the spirit of Islamic-Christian coexistence.

Born in the mid-1910s, Shaykh ʿAbd Allāh grew up absorbing the blend of Ṣūfī spirituality and moderate orthodoxy that was followed by the local merchant class of Harer. This urban elite had come under Ethiopian imperial rule in 1887 and has since chosen to cooperate with the Christian state. However, as of the 1930s an emerging local middle class, influenced by the Saudis through the *ḥajj*, began opposing the elite, adopted a Wahhābī doctrine, and opted for secession from Ethiopia. Shaykh ʿAbd Allāh became the leader of the pro-Ethiopian wing, which clashed bitterly with the local Wahhābīs. In 1947, however, he had to leave Ethiopia and in 1950 settled in another Christian-Muslim state, Lebanon.

By 1983, when he established the association, Shaykh ʿAbd Allāh had gained a reputation as a leading scholarly interpreter of Sunnī moderation, by combining Sunnī and Ṣūfī influences. The Aḥbāsh have gained a substantial following through the establishment of schools and other institutions, and they participated in the Lebanese parliamentary elections of 1992, the first after the civil war, when their candidate, Adnan Trabulsi, was elected. The *shaykh* has published some twenty books, and his sermons are recorded and disseminated by his admirers. They all convey a dual message.

One aspect of the *shaykh*'s writings and preaching is Islamic tolerance and flexibility. He stands for the separation of religion and state, cooperation between Islamic scholars and modern nationalist—mainly Arab—leaders, and the coexistence of Muslims and Christians. He thus was able to establish constructive relations with Lebanon's Christians as well as political ties with the Syrian Baʿthist regime. Moreover, following the example of the "first *hijrah*" to Ethiopia and the Prophet's command that the *ṣaḥābah* (companions) seek asylum with the Christian king of Ethiopia, the *shaykh* and the Aḥbāsh accept the legitimacy of non-Islamic governments in the West and participate in the public lives of those countries. The moderation of the "Ethiopians" extends also to social matters such as women's rights, music, and clothing. Much of the *shaykh*'s scholarship in this spirit derives from early Islamic thought—like that of the Muʿtazilī and the Ashʿarī schools of theology—adapted and reinterpreted.

The other notable aspect of al-Aḥbāsh is an ideological offensive against people seen as radicals. Admittedly, the *shaykh* is inspired in part by his old rivalry with the Hararī Wahhābīs of the 1940s, whose leader, Shaykh Yūsuf ʿAbd al-Rahman al-Hararī, resides in Medina and with whom he still exchanges bitter polemics. One of Shaykh ʿAbd Allāh's main targets is the writings of the Wahhābīs' medieval inspiration, Ibn Taymīyah, and their doctrine of *tawḥīd*. He mocks the Wahhābīs' beliefs and calls them infidels. His followers are active in spreading these messages, especially in what has become almost a war on the Internet. The Aḥbāsh denounce the Wahhābīs as terrorists and destroyers of Islam and are in turn proclaimed infidels and traitors. In Lebanon, the Aḥbāsh play a concrete, visible role, but one that is complicated by their association with the Syrians (in April 2001, al-Aḥbāsh militants organized a series of public rallies to counter anti-Syrian demonstrations on the anniversary of the Lebanese civil war) and by the 1995 assassination of their president, Shaykh Nizār al-Ḥalabī. (Aḥmad ʿAbdul Karīm al Saʿīd, known as Abū Miḥjin, the head of the ʿUṣbat al-Anṣār [League of Partisans], was later charged and sentenced to death in absentia for masterminding the crime.) The Aḥbāsh also have a more abstract but important significance for the greater Islamic world as militant guardians of what might be termed universal or cross-sectarian flexibility.

In 2005, the Special Tribunal for Lebanon issued a report into the assassination of Lebanese prime minister Rafīq Ḥarīrī, which featured the names of three brothers: Aḥmad ʿAbd al-ʿAll, an active member of al-Aḥbāsh currently in Lebanese custody; Walīd, a member of the Presidential Guard; and Maḥmūd, also a member of al-Aḥbāsh, who, according to the United Nations investigation, telephoned Lebanese president Emile Lahoud moments before the bombing that targeted the former prime minister's convoy on 14 February 2005. It remains to be determined whether any of the three, or other al-Aḥbāsh members, were involved in the murder or acted on behalf of a foreign power.

[*See also* Lebanon.]

BIBLIOGRAPHY

Erlich, Haggai. *Saudi Arabia and Ethiopia: Islam, Christianity, and Politics Entwined.* Boulder, Colo.: Lynne Rienner, 2007.

Hamzeh, A. Nizar, and R. Hrair Dekmejian. "A Sufi Response to Political Islamism: Al-Ahbash of Lebanon." *International Journal of Middle East Studies* 28 (1996): 217–229.

Kabha, Mustafa, and Haggai Erlich. "Al-Ahbash and Wahhabiyya: Interpretations of Islam." *International Journal of Middle East Studies* 38 (2006): 519–538.

Mustafa Kabha
and Haggai Erlich
Updated by Joseph A. Kéchichian

Ahl al-Ḥall wa-al-ʿAqd. Those who are qualified to act on behalf of the Muslim community in electing a caliph are known as *ahl al-ḥall wa-al-ʿaqd* ("the people who loose and bind"; less frequently, *ahl al-ʿaqd wa-al-ḥall*).

In premodern political theory, their main function was contractual, namely, to offer the office of caliphate to the most qualified person and, upon his acceptance, to administer to him an oath of allegiance (*bayʿa*). They were also entrusted with deposing him should he not fulfill his duties. They must be Muslim, of age, just, free, and capable of exercising *ijtihād* (interpretation of religious sources). The implication of the last requirement is that *ahl al-ḥall wa-al-ʿaqd* are jurists of the highest caliber, whose consensus is binding.

In the absence of any revealed text stipulating the number of *ahl al-ḥall wa-al-ʿaqd*, scholars were in disagreement concerning this issue. Some argued that they must represent all regions of the Islamic empire. The prevailing opinion, however, seems to have been that one person suffices; this reflects the historical reality in which a caliph normally designated his successor. Since the caliph appointed by *ahl al-ḥall wa-al-ʿaqd* must enjoy the same qualifications required of the members of the appointing body, the caliph himself was deemed a most qualified member, who might alone designate a successor. This is perhaps why some Muslim political theorists, such as the eleventh-century Shāfiʿī jurist al-Māwardī, maintain that the *bayʿa* of *ahl al-ḥall wa-al-ʿaqd* is a subsidiary process, resorted to when the caliph fails to appoint an heir.

Theory diverged from practice in at least one respect. In later times, military commanders played the role of *ahl al-ḥall wa-al-ʿaqd*, although they did not fulfill the theoretical qualifications. Most notably, they were not deemed *mujtahid*s (interpreters of the law) and were thus not empowered to form a consensus on behalf of the Muslim community. Their assumption of this role was finally justified on the basis of public interest (*malaḥa*), mainly in terms of the doctrine that however objectionable the appointments of military commanders may be, they are preferable to a situation in which the community is left without leaders. The historical practice, however, has rarely been devoid of consultation, whereby appointing caliphs sought counsel among the leading jurists.

The title *ahl al-ḥall wa-al-ʿaqd* has gained particular significance in modern political thought. The title is now intimately connected with an expanded meaning of *shūrā*, a term that previously meant consultation among the oligarchs on political matters, including the appointment of a caliph. In nineteenth- and particularly twentieth-century political thought, the *ahl al-ḥall*, through the medium of *shūrā*, speak for the full community. Khayr al-Dīn al-Tūnisī (d. 1890), a Tunisian reformer, equates *ahl al-ḥall* with a European-style parliament, and Muḥammad Rashīd Riḍā (d. 1935) entrusts them with powers to elect and depose rulers by virtue of their influential status in the community and their mutual consultation. Their decisions, though they may be at variance with those of the ruler, are binding upon him because *ahl al-ḥall* are the deputies of the community and express its will. For Rashīd Riḍā the ruler thus becomes subservient to *ahl al-ḥall*, who express through their consultation the will of the community on matters of public law and policy. More recent political thinkers deem the ruler a servant of the people, elected by a process of consultation whose medium is *ahl al-ḥall*. No rule, they argue, can be legitimate unless it is based on this process.

[*See also* Caliphate, Theories of the; *and* Succession.]

BIBLIOGRAPHY

Crone, Patricia. *God's Rule: Government and Islam*. New York: Columbia University Press, 2004.

Faḍl Allāh, Mahdī. *Al-Shūrā: Ṭabīʿat al-ḥākimīya fī al-Islām* [The *Shūrā*: The nature of sovereignty in Islam]. Beirut: Dār al-Andalus, 1984.

Kerr, Malcolm H. *Islamic Reform: The Political and Legal Theories of Muḥammad ʿAbduh and Rashīd Riḍā*. Berkeley: University of California Press, 1966. Pp. 34–36, 159–165, 183.

Kurzman, Charles, ed. *Modernist Islam, 1840–1940: A Sourcebook*. Oxford: Oxford University Press, 2002.

Lambton, Ann K. S. *State and Government in Medieval Islam: An Introduction to the Study of Islamic Political Theory*. Oxford: Oxford University Press, 1981. Summarizes the theories of various medieval scholars on the subject. See pp. 18, 73, 89, 105, 111–114, 139, 141, 184, 311.

al-Māwardī, Abū al-Ḥasan ʿAlī ibn Muḥammad. *Al-Aḥkām al-sulṭānīya* [The laws of the caliphate]. Edited by M. Engri. Bonn, 1853. Translated by Wafaa H. Wahba as *The Ordinances of Government* (Reading, U.K.: Center for Muslim Contribution to Civilization; London: Garnet, 1996); translated by Léon Ostrorog as *Traité de droit public musulman* (Paris: Éditions Leroux, 1925). Well-known classical work on constitutional theory. See pp. 6–7, 21–22.

Meri, Josef W., ed. *Medieval Islamic Civilization: An Encyclopedia*. 2 vols. London: Routledge, 2006.

Shaltūt, Maḥmūd. *Min tawjīhāt al-Islām* [Concerning the guiding principles of Islam]. 7th ed. Cairo and Beirut: Dār al-Shurūq, 1983. Pp. 471ff.

WAEL B. HALLAQ

AHMAD, EQBAL. A critical thinker on world politics and the contemporary Arab-Islamic world, Eqbal Ahmad (1933–1999) wrote prolifically on the rise of anticolonial movements, the Vietnam War, the Palestinian-Israeli conflict, and the Cold War from the standpoint of its Third World victims. He focused upon the legacy of the anti-Soviet war in Afghanistan, religious fundamentalism of all stripes, terrorism, nuclear proliferation, and Middle Eastern and South Asian politics. He agitated against nuclear arms testing on the Indian subcontinent until his death in Islamabad on 11 May 1999.

Ahmad was born in Irki, Bihar, to an Indian Muslim landowning family. His father was murdered shortly after parceling out the estate to landless peasants. Upon the partition of India, the remaining family members immigrated to Pakistan on foot.

After obtaining an MA from the Punjab University in Lahore, Ahmad studied political science at Princeton University, where he received a Proctor Fellowship for excellence in graduate studies and he wrote a doctoral dissertation on the Tunisian labor movement. This work formed the basis of a lifelong interest in working-class politics, political mass movements, and revolutionary change. Along with Stuart Schaar, he wrote about North African trade union activists and progressive voices such as the Tunisian feminist and modernizing intellectual Ṭāhir al-Ḥaddād. In 1961, Ahmad accompanied the Algerian delegation as an observer to the ongoing peace talks in Évian, France that eventually ended the Algerian War and achieved national independence.

His pioneering works on Vietnam, Algeria, and the decolonizing world explored the rise of insurgencies and failures of counterinsurgencies. His analysis of revolutionary warfare is embedded in the film *The Battle of Algiers*, on which he consulted. Ironically the counterinsurgency doctrines that he critiqued decades earlier have regained a measure of respectability in the war on terror.

A staunch anticolonialist activist, he regarded as risible the idea that the West granted human rights to the decolonized world. He instead argued that the colonized struggled for those rights with great loss of life and that the fight for human rights was born in opposition and resistance to colonialism. Meanwhile, Ahmad condemned the furies of nationalism that soon convulsed the postcolonial world.

Ahmad received international notoriety in January 1971 when the U.S. government arrested him. He and seven Roman Catholic peace activists were accused of having plotted in August 1970 to kidnap National Security Advisor Henry Kissinger in order to charge the Nixon administration's foreign policy architects with war crimes. A jury could not reach a verdict, and the government dropped its case. Previously Ahmad had rallied support for the dissident Roman Catholic priests, Daniel and Philip Berrigan. Ahmad liked to recount how his octogenarian mother in Pakistan expressed exasperation about his ecumenical activism, "How did he get mixed up with the Catholics?"

After a decade as a senior fellow at the Institute for Policy Studies in Washington, D.C., Ahmad taught at Hampshire College in Amherst, Massachusetts, from 1982 to 1997. Upon his retirement, he moved back to Pakistan, where he remained until his death from cancer two years later.

In the 1990s, he attempted to establish Khaldunia University (named for the Arab scholar Ibn Khaldūn), a progressive, alternative educational institution and college in Islamabad, Pakistan, patterned on Hampshire College. The project never met Eqbal's lofty goals of developing independent thinkers at the college level in Pakistan, although the elementary school thrived.

Eqbal Ahmad insisted on the importance of democracy to developing societies, especially in the Muslim world. He wrote caustically of the dictators who rule the Muslim world, claiming that they serve the interests not of their people but of themselves and their benefactors. His writing on Pakistan explored the failure of democracy. He argued that a badly run democracy was still better than an efficient military dictatorship and that the rise of fundamentalism in Muslim settings was a result of the failure of the state and the absence of meaningful secular alternatives. He also wrote about the rise of sectarian *jihādī* forces in Pakistan. One of his concerns was the increasing "Talibanization" of Pakistan by *jihādī* organizations and their patrons. His writings thus anticipated the Arab Spring and the post-9/11 rise of the Taliban.

Eqbal Ahmad wrote for both mass circulation and scholarly publications including *Dawn* (Pakistan's oldest English-language newspaper), *Al-Ahram Weekly*, the *New York Times*, *The Nation*, *Race and Class*, and *Middle East Report*.

Unlike many secular Muslim intellectuals, Ahmad took the Islamic tradition seriously and was well-schooled in Islamic history and theology. He argued that any meaningful reform of Muslim societies required an understanding of Islamic tradition and change would have to be congruent with past traditions. He was scathingly critical of modern Islamic fundamentalist movements and believed them to be sectarian, ahistorical, and not rooted in the Islamic tradition. Instead they represented a clear rupture from Islam's heritage. He noted in particular the pathologies of the Taliban: "They are devoid of the ethics, aesthetics, humanism, and Sufi sensibilities of traditional Muslims, including Afghans of yesteryear. To call them 'mediaeval'...is to insult the age of Hafiz and Saadi, of Rabi'a Basri and Mansur al-Hallaj, of Amir Khusrau and Hazrat Nizamuddin. The Taliban are the expression of a modern disease, symptoms of a social cancer which shall destroy Muslim societies if its growth is not arrested and the disease is not eliminated" (Eqbal Ahmad, What after Strategic Depth, *Dawn*, 23 August 1998).

Eqbal Ahmad never published a single classic text but was an influential public intellectual whose speeches and lectures moved those who struggled against colonialism, intolerant nationalism, and injustice. Toward the end of his life, he narrated a BBC documentary titled *Stories My Country Told Me* (1996), in which he explored the partition of the Indian subcontinent and the rise of nationalist communal identities. He also had a lifelong fondness for the poetry and literature of the Indian subcontinent, in particular that of Faiz Ahmad Faiz and Rabindranath Tagore.

His insight and opinions were sought out by heads of national liberation movements, third world leaders, progressive activists, and journalists. His insightful criticisms of the decolonized state and third world elites particularly in South Asia and the Middle East remain enduring lessons for the present moment. A democrat, his writings were imbued with a concern for the poor, the downtrodden, and the powerless. His writings also reflected a repudiation of the coercive pathologies of violence, and he demonstrated how this could be non-violently resisted especially in his native Pakistan.

Edward Said, his long-time confidant and friend, noted his "almost instinctive attraction to liberation movements, movements of the oppressed and the persecuted, causes of people who were unfairly punished—whether they lived in the great metropolitan centres of Europe and America, or in the refugee camps, besieged cities, and bombed or disadvantaged villages of Bosnia, Chechnya, south Lebanon, Vietnam, Iraq, Iran, and, of course, the Indian subcontinent" (*The Guardian*, 14 May 1999).

[*See also* Democracy; *and* Pakistan.]

BIBLIOGRAPHY

Ahmad, Eqbal. *Confronting Empire: Interviews with David Barsamian*. Cambridge, Mass.: South End, 2000.

Ahmad, Eqbal. *Between Past and Future: Selected Essays on South Asia*. Edited by Dohra Ahmad, Iftikhar Ahmad, and Zia Mian. Karachi: Oxford University Press, 2004.

Ahmad, Eqbal. *The Selected Writings of Eqbal Ahmad*. Edited by Carollee Bengelsdorf, Margaret Cerullo, and Yogesh Chandrani. New York: Columbia University Press, 2006.

Ahmad, Eqbal, and Stuart Schaar. "M'hamed Ali: Tunisian Labor Organizer." In *Struggle and Survival in the Modern Middle East*, edited by Edmund Burke III. Berkeley: University of California Press, 1993, pp. 191–204.

Ahmad, Eqbal, and Stuart Schaar. "Tahar Haddad: A Tunisian Activist Intellectual." *Maghreb Review* 21, nos. 3–4 (1996), pp. 240–255.

Barsamian, David. "Tribute and Interview." *Massachusetts Review* 41, no. 4 (Winter 2000–2001): 449–464.

Chomsky, Noam. "Thoughts of a Secular Sufi." 2000. Onlineathttp://www.chomsky.info/articles/2000----.htm.

Kumar, Amitava. "A Civilizing Mission." *The Nation*, 27 November 2006, pp. 32–36.

Said, Edward. "Eqbal Ahmad: He Brought Wisdom and Integrity to the Cause of Oppressed Peoples." *Guardian*, 14 May 1999.

EMRAN QURESHI
and JOHN TRUMPBOUR

AHMAD, ISRAR. Israr Ahmad, (1932–2010), was the spiritual and political leader of the Pakistani Sunnī Islamist organization Tanzīm-i Islāmī (Islamic Organization). He advocated Islamic revival and the establishment of an Islamic state based on the *khilāfat* (caliphate) system.

Ahmad was born on 26 April 1932 in Hisar (a district of pre-partition Indian Punjab, now a part of the Indian state of Haryana). He graduated as a medical doctor from King Edward Medical College, Lahore, in 1954 and later received his master's degree in Islamic studies from the University of Karachi in 1965.

Ahmad came under the influence of Sayyid Abū al-Aʿlā Mawdūdī, the founder of Pakistan's oldest Islamist party, Jamāʿat-i Islāmī, as a young student. Following the creation of Pakistan in 1947, Ahmad worked for the Islāmī Jamʿīyat-i Tulabā (Jamāʿat-linked Islamic Students Organization) and then for the Jamāʿat-i Islāmī. However, he resigned from the Jamāʿat in April 1957 because of its involvement in Western-style electoral politics, which he believed was irreconcilable with the revolutionary Islamic methodology adopted by the Jamāʿat prior to Pakistan's creation. Despite parting ways with the Jamāʿat,

Ahmad persisted in his attempts to advance his views on Islam. He gave up his medical practice in 1971 in order to launch a full-fledged and vigorous movement for the revival of Islam. As a result of his efforts, the Markazi Anjuman-i Khuddāmulqurʾān, Lahore, was established in 1972; Tanzīm-i Islāmī was founded in 1975, and Tehrik-i Khilāfat (Movement for the Establishment of Khilāfat) was launched in 1991. His launching of the Tehrik-i Khilāfat was influenced by his discussions with the Pan-Islamic organization Hizb-ut-Tahrir, which also advocated the establishment of a system of *khilāfat* in the Islamic world.

Ahmad's interpretation of orthodox Sunnī Islam was eclectic. He had repeatedly acknowledged the deep influence of Shāh Walī Allāh al-Dihlawī, the eighteenth-century Sunnī Indian Islamic revivalist, who was at once a spiritual leader, a jurist, and a prolific scholar, on his perception of Islam. Paradoxically, Ahmad's thought and views had also been influenced by the modernist Islamic philosophy of Muhammad Iqbal (1877–1938). Ahmad claimed that his admiration of Iqbal was due to the latter's comprehensive knowledge of the Qurʾān as exhibited in his Islamic poetry. For Israr Ahmad, Iqbal's emphasis on a pan-Islamic revival and the need for Muslims to rediscover themselves (*khūdī*) and thereby revive the spirit of true Islam was of particular interest. Regarding Islam's relationship with politics, Ahmad also borrowed heavily from the thought of Sayyid Abū al-Aʿlā Mawdūdī and the Indian nationalist Muslim politician Abū al-Kalām Azād. Nonetheless, Ahmad's understanding of the *Sharīʿah* remained close to the orthodox Sunnī versions advocated by the Deoband school in India. In the context of Qurʾānic exegesis and understanding, he remained a traditionalist in the mold of Mawlānā Maḥmūdulḥasan and Shabbīr Aḥmad ʿUsmānī of the Deoband school, although he presented his Qurʾānic teachings in what he claimed to be a scientific and enlightened manner.

Like most Islamists of the time, Ahmad believed in what he called "Islamic revolutionary thought," the idea that Islam—the teachings of the Qurʾān and the *sunnah* (the customs of the Prophet Muḥammad) must be implemented in the social, cultural, legal, political, and economic spheres of life. Ahmad's revivalist movement differed substantially from its parent organization, the Jamāʿat-i Islāmī, in that it rejected democratic and electoral means to create an ideal Islamic society. Ahmad claimed that he had realized early on that establishing an Islamic political/social/economic system in a country was a revolutionary process and unlikely to occur through parliamentary politics based upon Western liberal-democratic traditions. Consequently, he rejected involvement in the political process and sought to change society by influencing its ideas and values through nonviolent means, although he remained vague on how his movement could gain power if it remained outside the democratic political process and also opposed violent revolutionary methods.

For the realization of his objectives, Israr Ahmad used the Markazi Anjuman-i Khuddāmulqurʾān as a largely educational organization focused on propagating Islamic education and an understanding of the Qurʾān, while the Tanzīm-i Islāmī was specifically created as a political grouping seeking revolutionary change via mass communication and propaganda. The goal was to emphasize that *īmān* (faith) must be revived within "a significant portion of the Muslim society" before there can be an Islamic revival. Ahmad emphasized that it was a religious obligation of all Muslims to struggle toward the establishment of an Islamic state in the form of a caliphate uniting the Muslim world.

Ahmad was a prolific writer and wrote over sixty books in Urdu related to Islam and Pakistan.

Within his own country, his often controversial and extremely conservative views on the role of women in Muslim society aroused resentment among a sizeable section of Pakistan's Westernized elite as well as the middle classes. He had also disapproved of some aspects of Shīʿī interpretation of Islam in his formative years. Ahmad's newspaper articles, written mainly in Urdu, aired his perceptions on the developments in the wider Islamic world. His criticism of Israel and his apocalyptic visions of a showdown between the Muslim world and what he perceived as a supposedly Jewish-dominated non-Muslim world raised considerable controversy. He also remained supportive of the Taliban movement in Afghanistan and its resistance to the U.S.-led occupation of that country from 2001. Ahmad was even reportedly contacted by emissaries from al-Qaʿida in 2003. However, he did not explicitly endorse al-Qaʿida's philosophy but remained silent about its violent methods.

Israr Ahmad remained actively engaged in his efforts to revive Islamic values with the ultimate objective of establishing a true Islamic state, or caliphate, until his death. Nonetheless, the overall impact of his thought and efforts to inspire an Islamic ethos within Pakistani society remained marginal at best.

Bibliography

Ahmad, Israr. *Iqbāl awr Hum* (Iqbal and Us). Lahore: Markazi Anjuman Khuddam-ul-Quran, 1989.

Ahmad, Israr. *Islamic Renaissance: The Real Task Ahead.* Translated by Absar Ahmad. Lahore: Markazi Anjuman Khuddam-ul-Quran, 1980.

Ahmad, Israr. *Khilafah in Pakistan: What, Why, and How?* Lahore: Markazi Anjuman Khuddam-ul-Quran, 2001.

Ahmad, Mumtaz, Dietrich Reetz, and Thomas H. Johnson. *Who Speaks for Islam? Muslim Grassroots Leaders and Popular Preachers in South Asia.* NBR Special Report 22. Seattle: National Bureau of Asian Research, 2010.

Ahmad, Shagufta. "Dr. Israr Ahmad's Political Thought and Activities." M.A. thesis, Institute of Islamic Studies, McGill University, 1993.

Shahzad, Syed Saleem. *Inside al-Qaeda and the Taliban: Beyond Bin Laden and 9/11.* London: Pluto, 2011.

Rizwan Hussain

Ahmadinejad, Mahmoud. Mahmoud Ahmadinejad (Ahmadi Nejad) was popularly elected as the sixth president of Iran on 24 June 2005 to serve a four-year term, becoming the first noncleric president of Iran in more than twenty years. He was reelected for a second term on 12 June 2009 in a disputed election.

Born on 28 October 1956 in Aradan, near Garmsar, Ahmadinejad moved to Tehran in 1957 with his family, where he completed his education. In 1975, he earned high marks on the university entrance exam and enrolled at the prestigious Science and Technology University (STU) to study civil engineering. He earned a master's degree in 1986, joined the Board of Civil Engineering Faculty in 1989, and obtained a doctorate in 1997 in transportation engineering and planning. At STU Ahmadinejad became engaged in political activities while studying, teaching, conducting scientific research, and supervising student theses. His interest in religious and political meetings peaked with the 1979 Islamic Revolution, when he became a founding member of the STU Islamic Student Association. Ahmadinejad joined the volunteer Basīj forces and served in the engineering division throughout the 1980–1988 Iran-Iraq War. In the early 1990s, he served in various political capacities, including governor of Maku and Khoy provinces, advisor to the governor general of Kordistan Province, advisor for cultural affairs to the minister of culture and higher education (1993), and governor general for Ardabil Province (1993–1997). He was elected mayor of Tehran in 2003 and served until his election as president in 2005.

While campaigning, the populist Ahmadinejad emphasized his own modest life, and promised to create an "exemplary government for the people of the world" in Iran. Ayatollah Muḥammed Taghi Mesbah Yazdī, a senior cleric from Qom, acted as his ideological mentor and spiritual guide.

Succeeding the very popular Muḥammad Khatami, Ahmadinejad became president with 62 percent of the vote in the run-off poll, nearly twice that of former president ʿAlī Akbar Hāshimī Rafsanjānī, and may well have been Supreme Leader Khameneʾi's preferred candidate to address many of the country's socioeconomic challenges. Within a year, however, his spending priorities were heavily criticized, as were his recommendations for family planning and petroleum imports. No matter how hard he tried, Iran's unemployment hovered around 25 percent, which necessitated heavy subsidies on a variety of items. Ahmadinejad proposed a US$1.3 billion fund, called "Reza's Compassion Fund"—named after Imām ʿAlī al-Riḍā—which was intended to help young people with job opportunities and affordable housing. Parliament rejected it, although Ahmadinejad allegedly brought much of the fund into being by ordering the administrative council to create it. His sudden 2006 announcement that nothing prevented women from watching men playing sports in stadiums angered many supporters, including Mesbah Yazdī and other clerics, which necessitated an intervention by Iran's supreme leader to confirm the ban.

Ahmadinejad's gravest controversy was his support for Iran's nuclear program, which pitted him against the international community. The government repeatedly argued that its nuclear program was for peaceful purposes, and Ahmadinejad as well as other leaders repeatedly denied any military intentions. Few believed him, especially since the president was not responsible for the country's nuclear policy. That responsibility fell to the National Security Council appointed by the supreme leader, consisting of key military officials and members of the executive, judicial, and legislative branches of government. Ahmadinejad's threatening declarations against the West in general and the United States in particular created controversy. He refused to end Iran's nuclear program, repeatedly called for Israel to be "wiped off the map," and described the Jewish Holocaust as a "myth." Despite expectations of a tight race in the 2009 presidential election, Ahmadinejad secured more than 60 percent of the vote in the first round. His chief rival, Mir-Hossein Mousavi, received only 34 percent. Blatant electoral irregularities triggered widespread popular protests, the largest since the Islamic revolution in 1979. Khameneʾi, however, endorsed the election results, and an inquiry by the Council of Guardians confirmed Ahmadinejad's victory. He was sworn in for a second term as Iran's president in August of that year.

During his second term, a power struggle with Khameneʾi curtailed much of Ahmadinejad's authority in the Iranian political system. In 2011, Khameneʾi revoked Ahmadinejad's decision to dismiss the minister of intelligence and blocked his attempt to name himself acting minister of oil. Ahmadinejad was also questioned by parliament in 2012 over mismanaging the economy and challenging the authority of the supreme leader.

A controversial figure both at home and overseas, Ahmadinejad continues to have widespread support among the poorer classes of Iran.

BIBLIOGRAPHY

Ansari, Ali M. *Iran under Ahmadinejad: The Politics of Confrontation*. Abingdon, U.K.: Routledge, 2007.

Ansari, Ali. "Iran under Ahmadinejad: Populism and its Malcontents." *International Affairs* 84, no. 4 (2008): 683–700.

Jafarzadeh, Alireza. *The Iran Threat: President Ahmadinejad and the Coming Nuclear Crisis*. New York: Palgrave, 2007.

Melman, Yossi, and Meir Javedanfar. *The Nuclear Sphinx of Tehran: Mahmoud Ahmadinejad and the State of Iran*. New York: Carroll & Graf, 2007.

Naji, Kasra. *Ahmadinejad: The Secret History of Iran's Radical Leader*. Berkeley: University of California Press, 2008.

JOSEPH A. KÉCHICHIAN
Updated by NAEL SHAMA

AḤMADĪYAH. A messianic movement in modern Islam, the Aḥmadīyah has been one of the most active and controversial movements since its inception in British India in 1889. It has sustained its activities for more than a century and has been unrivaled in its dedication to the propagation of the faith. Aḥmadī mosques and missionary centers have been established not only in the Indian subcontinent but also in numerous cities of the Western world, Africa, and Asia.

The core of Aḥmadī thought is prophetology, which draws its inspiration from the great medieval Muslim mystic Muḥyī al-Dīn ibn al-ʿArabī (1165–1240), who postulated an uninterrupted succession of nonlegislative prophets following Muḥammad. Claiming for its founder messianic and prophetic status, the Aḥmadī movement aroused the fierce opposition of Sunnī Muslims and was accused of rejecting Islamic dogma, according to which Muḥammad was the last prophet. While India was under British rule, the controversy remained a doctrinal dispute among private individuals or voluntary organizations, but in 1947, when the Aḥmadī headquarters moved to the professedly Islamic state of Pakistan, the issue became a constitutional problem of major importance. Religious scholars belonging to the Sunnī mainstream demanded the formal exclusion of the Aḥmadīs from the Islamic fold and achieved that objective in 1974. The history of the Aḥmadī movement thus affords a unique example of the intricate relationship between religion and state in Islam, an example in which secularly elected members of political institutions arrogated to themselves the authority to determine the religious affiliation of a group of citizens, and to draw constitutional conclusions from this determination.

History. Mīrzā Ghulām Aḥmad, the founder of the Aḥmadī movement in Islam, was born in the late 1830s in Qādiyān, a village in the Punjab. His claim to special spiritual standing was first announced in the early 1880s. The movement was established in March 1889, when Ghulām Aḥmad accepted a pledge of allegiance from a number of his followers in the Punjabi city of Ludhiana. He devoted the following years to prolific literary activity, to the organization and expansion of the new community, and to many polemical encounters with Sunnī ulema (*ʿulamaʾ*, religious scholars), Christian missionaries, and members of the Hindu revivalist movement of Ārya Samāj. A number of periodicals were launched in Qādiyān, including the monthly *Review of Religions*, the main English organ for the propagation of the Aḥmadī view of Islam.

Ghulām Aḥmad died on 26 May 1908. He was succeeded in the leadership of the community by Nūruddīn, one of his first supporters, who became the first "Successor of the Messiah" (*khalīfat al-masīḥ*). During his leadership, the unity of the movement was threatened by differences of opinion on issues such as the relationship with non-Aḥmadī Muslims and the nature of the community's leadership.

Nūruddīn died in 1914 and was succeeded by Ghulām Aḥmad's son Bashīruddīn Maḥmūd Aḥmad. The differences in the movement came to a head, and the Aḥmadīyah split into two factions, known as the Qādiyānīs and the Lāhōrīs. The Qādiyānī faction, which was larger and retained control of the movement's headquarters and main publications, was headed by Maḥmūd Aḥmad, now known as Khalīfat al-Masīḥ II; the prominent personalities among the Lāhōrīs were Muḥammad ʿAlī and Khvājah Kamāluddīn. In addition to personal friction among members of the two groups, the focal points of disagreement were the nature of Ghulām Aḥmad's religious claim, the extent of Maḥmūd Aḥmad's authority in community affairs, and the attitude to be adopted toward non-Aḥmadī Muslims. The Qādiyānīs stressed Ghulām Aḥmad's claim to prophethood, maintained that Maḥmūd Aḥmad's religious authority was not less than that of Ghulām Aḥmad, and left little doubt that they considered non-Aḥmadī Muslims infidels. The Lāhōrīs, on the other hand, held that Ghulām Aḥmad never claimed to be more than a "renewer" (*mujaddid*) of religion; they suggested that the community leadership be entrusted to a group such as the Supreme Council of the Aḥmadīyah (*Ṣadr Anjuman-i Aḥmadīyah*) rather than to one Successor of the Messiah; and they deemed infidels only those Muslims who regarded the Aḥmadīs in that way. This attitude toward non-Aḥmadīs was intended to minimize friction with other Muslims.

Following the split, the Aḥmadīs continued their missionary and literary activity. The two factions renounced any connection with each other. The Lāhōrī publications deal almost exclusively with familiar themes of Islamic modernism. They contain few references to ideas that distinguish the Aḥmadīyah from the Islamic mainstream. The Qādiyānī *Review of Religions*, however, continued to stress the crucial role of Ghulām Aḥmad in the spiritual history of mankind. Its pages provide translations from Ghulām Aḥmad's works and details of such Aḥmadī missionary activities as the establishment of mosques and centers and cases of conversion to Islam. Several new institutions were established in Qādiyān by order of Maḥmūd Aḥmad in order to coordinate the worldwide missionary and literary endeavors of the movement.

Following the partition of the Subcontinent in 1947, the headquarters of the movement moved to Pakistan, where a town called Rabwa (after Qurʾān 23:51) was built in order to serve as the new center of the Aḥmadīyah. In Pakistan the movement faced increasing difficulties. Various Islamic groups, led by the Jamāʿat-i Islāmī, insisted that the Aḥmadīs be declared a non-Muslim minority and excluded from public office. In the early 1950s, this agitation was directed primarily against Muhammad Zafrullah Khan, a prominent Aḥmadī who served at that time as Pakistan's foreign minister. The demand was accompanied by widespread anti-Aḥmadī riots in the Punjab, but the government stood its ground.

The Aḥmadī issue came to the fore again in 1974. Following a clash between Aḥmadī and non-Aḥmadī students in Rabwa, pressure to exclude the Aḥmadīs from the fold of Islam was renewed; it was accompanied by riots and threats of a general strike by the religious leadership. After some initial resistance, Prime Minister Zulfiqar Ali Bhutto's government gave way, and the National Assembly decided "to discuss the status in Islam of persons who do not believe in the finality of the prophethood of Muḥammad (peace be upon him)." After lengthy deliberations behind closed doors, the Assembly met in open session on 7 September 1974 and unanimously decided to amend the constitution of Pakistan by adding a clause asserting that

> A person who does not believe in the absolute and unqualified finality of the prophethood of Muḥammad (peace be upon him), the last of the Prophets, or claims to be a Prophet, in any sense of the word or of any description whatsoever, after Muḥammad (peace be upon him), or recognizes such a claimant as a Prophet or a

religious reformer, is not a Muslim for the purposes of the Constitution or Law.

In April 1984, in the context of intensifying the Islamic characteristics of public life in Pakistan, President Muhammad Zia ul-Haq promulgated an ordinance (known as Ordinance XX) making Aḥmadī religious observance a punishable offense. Among other things, the Aḥmadīs were forbidden to refer to their faith as Islam, to honor their leaders by traditional Muslim epithets, to preach or propagate their faith, or to call their places of worship mosques. Since the Constitutional Amendment of 1974 declared the Aḥmadīs non-Muslims, Aḥmadīs who engaged in those and similar activities were described as "posing as Muslims." All these offenses were made punishable by three years of imprisonment and a fine.

Starting in the late 1980s, the treatment of the Aḥmadī movement was influenced by the so-called "blasphemy laws" that were promulgated in Pakistan and imposed life imprisonment, fines, and even capital punishment for blasphemy. Aḥmadī views were considered blasphemous because the belief in the prophethood of Ghulām Aḥmad was seen as defiling the name of the prophet Muḥammad as the last prophet, according to an interpretation of Qurʾān 33:40. Responding to these attempts to exclude them from the Muslim fold, the Aḥmadīs made sustained efforts to assert their Muslim identity. Wearing a badge containing the Muslim declaration of faith (*shahāda*) or inscribing it on walls of Aḥmadī houses or mosques became the most common components of this endeavor.

An organization called the Council for the Preservation of the Finality of Prophethood" (*majlis-i taḥaffuẓ-i khatm-i nubuwwat*) was instrumental in the initiation of numerous legal proceedings against Aḥmadīs on the basis of the "blasphemy laws." The most celebrated case of this kind resulted from the prosecution of a few Aḥmadīs who wore a badge with the Muslim declaration of faith. They were prosecuted for posing as Muslims and sentenced to one year of imprisonment and fines. All defendants lost their appeals at the Lahore High Court but were granted leave to appeal before the Supreme Court of Pakistan. The Aḥmadīs argued that Ordinance XX violated their freedom of religion, guaranteed by Article 20 of the Constitution. The majority of the court, however, viewed the matter differently. On 3 July 1993 the court asserted that the Aḥmadīs had been declared non-Muslims; thus, behavior designed to demonstrate adherence to Islam was a dangerous fraud that might encourage people to join their fold rather than the fold of Islam. Since the exercise of religious freedom was "subject to law, public order and morality," the fraudulent behavior of the Aḥmadīs was not protected by Article 20 of the Constitution. The arguments of the court majority were strengthened by reference to those pronouncements of Ghulām Aḥmad in which non-Aḥmadī Muslims had been pronounced non-Muslims. The court drew from these pronouncements the conclusion that nobody can simultaneously be an Aḥmadī and a Muslim, dismissed the appeals, and ordered the appellants to serve their sentences.

In addition to legal proceedings of this nature, Aḥmadīs were subjected to various types of harassment. In the wake of Ordinance XX, Mīrzā Ṭāhir Aḥmad, the fourth successor of the founder, moved to London. The headquarters of the Qādiyānī branch of the Aḥmadī movement moved with him. As of August 2010, the movement was headed by Mirzā Masrūr Aḥmad, the fifth successor of the founder, who assumed office in 2003.

Religious Thought. The religious thought of the Aḥmadīyah until 1914, and of its Qādiyānī branch since then revolves around Ghulām Aḥmad's persistent claim to be a divinely inspired religious thinker and reformer. The many ways in which Ghulām Aḥmad expressed his convictions enabled both his supporters and his rivals to make diverse and often contradictory interpretations of his claim to spiritual eminence. As has often been the case with Muslim revivalist and messianic movements, the starting point of Ghulām Aḥmad's thought was the assertion that Muslim religion and society had deteriorated to the point that divinely inspired reforms were essential in order to arrest the process of decline and restore the pristine purity of Islam. It was against this background that Ghulām Aḥmad claimed to have been chosen by God for the task of revitalizing Islam.

Ghulām Aḥmad's mission is described in his writings in diverse terms. The definition of his spiritual claim that was most acceptable to the Sunnī point of view was his declaration that God appointed him to be the renewer (*mujaddid*) of Islam in the fourteenth century. More controversial was his claim to be the Mahdī and the Promised Messiah (*masīḥ-i maw'ūd*). He supported this claim by an elaborate Christology arguing that Jesus did not die on the cross but only swooned; that he was taken down and cured of his wounds; and that he went to India and died a natural death at the age of 120 in the city of Srinagar. The Christian belief in the resurrection of Jesus and his return in glory at the end of days is, according to Ghulām Aḥmad, groundless. It is incontrovertibly refuted in several verses in the Qur'ān (e.g., 3:55) and is a Christian invention designed to prove that the living Jesus is superior to the deceased Muḥammad and that Christianity is consequently superior to Islam. Whenever a Muslim tradition seems to suggest the second coming of Jesus, it should be taken to indicate not the coming of Jesus himself, but that of a person similar to him. This person is Ghulām Aḥmad, whose spiritual role bears complete affinity with that of Jesus, in that both Jesus and Ghulām Aḥmad appeared when their people were subjected to foreign rule; both were rejected by their religiously decadent communities; both repudiated *jihād*; and neither brought a new law but rather vowed to revive laws brought by Moses and Muḥammad, respectively.

Ghulām Aḥmad's repeated assertion that God made him a prophet was the most controversial formulation of his claim. Since it contradicted the Muslim dogma of Muḥammad as the last prophet, it brought upon Ghulām Aḥmad and his followers the most vociferous denunciations by the Sunnī ulema. However, Ghulām Aḥmad was able to maintain that his theology was compatible with the Muslim belief in the finality of Muḥammad's prophethood. Following in the footsteps of Ibn al-'Arabī, he divided prophets into two categories: legislative (*tashrī'ī*) prophets, who were entrusted with bringing a new book of revealed divine law and were usually founders of new communities; and nonlegislative (*ghayrtashrī'ī*) prophets, who did not receive a new book of divine law but were sent to an existing community to urge it to implement the divine law brought by an earlier, legislative prophet.

According to Ghulām Aḥmad, the belief in the finality of Muḥammad's prophethood applies only to the first, legislative category. This classification of prophets enabled Ghulām Aḥmad to attest that Muḥammad was, indeed, the seal of the prophets and to claim at the same time that God could not possibly leave Muslims without prophetic guidance after the death of Muḥammad, a condition that would make Muslims an accursed and abandoned community. Therefore, while it is true that no law-giving prophet can appear after Muḥammad, prophetic perfections are continuously bestowed upon his most accomplished followers, such as Ghulām Aḥmad, to whom God spoke and revealed his secrets. However, since Ghulām Aḥmad attained this position only by his faithful following of Muḥammad, his prophethood does not infringe upon Muḥammad's status as the seal of the prophets. Rather, the fact that the Prophet of Islam was capable of bestowing prophetic perfections on his accomplished followers proves Muḥammad's superiority over his predecessors in the prophetic office. Muslims are thus the only community privileged with divine communication and prophethood after the completion of Muḥammad's mission. Although this prophethood does not involve the revelation of new laws and is given only as a shadow of the prophethood of Muḥammad, its existence is a decisive indication of Islamic superiority over other religions.

Ghulām Aḥmad's claim to be the Mahdī is closely related to his view of *jihād*. The classical tradition according to which the Mahdī "will break the cross, kill the swine, and abolish war" is interpreted in a way that transforms the Mahdī into an entirely peaceful figure. The statement that the Mahdī will "abolish war" is understood literally, and great stress is laid on it; on the other hand, the killing of the swine and the breaking of the cross are understood metaphorically and are said to indicate the Mahdī's victory over Christianity by means of argument and spiritual power. *Jihād* with the sword has thus come to an end with the advent of the Mahdī. Even before that, however, *jihād* was far from all-out aggressive war; it was allowed only in response to persecution by infidels. This interpretation rejects the traditional view that the idea of *jihād* developed from a total prohibition in Mecca to a command of unrestricted validity in Medina. According to the Aḥmadīs, Islam has always been a religion dedicated to peace. Ghulām Aḥmad repeatedly denounced Muslims who preached violent *jihād*: they not only distorted an essential part of Islamic teaching, but also assisted Christian missionaries in misrepresenting Islam as a religion committed to expansion by violent means; the only *jihād* sanctioned by Islam is spreading the faith by preaching and persuasion.

Summary. The dispute between the Aḥmadīyah and mainstream Sunnī Islam stems from different approaches to the question of religious authority. As a messianic movement claiming a certain kind of prophethood for its founder and continuous divine inspiration for his successors, the Aḥmadīyah was bound to clash with the ulema, who felt that their authority as custodians of Islamic learning and interpreters of Islamic law was being undermined. The dispute was exacerbated by the fact that the ulema focused their opposition to the Aḥmadīyah on the emotional issue of Muḥammad's honor, which was said to have been tarnished by Ghulām Aḥmad's claim to have received divine revelation after the completion of Muḥammad's mission.

As far as the Aḥmadī struggle within Islam is concerned, the main point of contention is thus the religious claim of Ghulām Aḥmad, which is couched in terms derived from medieval Sufism. In its relationship with the non-Muslim world, however, the Aḥmadīyah is primarily engaged in defending Islam and depicting it as a liberal, humane, and progressive religion that has been systematically slandered by non-Muslims. This aspect of Aḥmadī teaching is well in line with that of modernist Muslim thinkers, though in other matters—for example, in their support for purdah and polygamy—the Aḥmadīs follow the traditional point of view. One of the essential differences between them and other contemporary Muslim movements is that the Aḥmadīs consider the peaceful propagation of their version of Islam among Muslims and non-Muslims alike to be an indispensable activity; in this they are persistent and unrelenting.

[*See also* Pluralism.]

BIBLIOGRAPHY

Aḥmad, Bashīruddīn Maḥmūd. *Invitation to Aḥmadiyyat*. Rabwah, Pakistan: Aḥmadīyya Muslim Foreign Missions Office, 1961. The most comprehensive description of Aḥmadī beliefs in English,

translated from the Urdu original of Ghulām Aḥmad's son and second successor.
Aḥmad, Ghulām. *Jesus in India: Being an Account of Jesus' Escape from Death on the Cross and of His Journey to India.* London: London Mosque, 1978.
Aḥmad, Ghulām. *Rūḥānī khazā'in.* 23 vols. Rabwah, Pakistan. The collected works of the founder in Urdu, Arabic, and Persian.
Binder, Leonard. *Religion and Politics in Pakistan.* Berkeley: University of California Press, 1961. The Aḥmadī controversy during the first years of Pakistan's existence.
Brush, Stanley E. "Aḥmadīyyat in Pakistan: Rabwa and the Aḥmadīs." *Muslim World* 45 (1955): 145–171.
Fisher, Humphrey J.*Aḥmadiyya: A Study of Contemporary Islam on the West African Coast.* London: Oxford University Press, 1963. Excellent study of the Aḥmadiyya in an African setting.
Friedmann, Yohanan. *Prophecy Continuous: Aspects of Aḥmadī Religious Thought and Its Medieval Background.* Berkeley: University of California Press, 1989. New ed., New York: Oxford University Press, 2003. The new edition includes a new preface, by Zafrira and the author, describing the developments since 1984). History of the Aḥmadiyya and its expansion. Includes analysis of the prophetology of both factions. The chapter on Aḥmadī *jihād* surveys relevant beliefs in medieval Muslim tradition. Extensive bibliography.
Gualtieri, Antonio R. *The Ahmadis: Community, Gender, and Politics in a Muslim Society.* Montreal: McGill-Queen's University Press, 2004. A detailed description of the Aḥmadīs in Rabwa.
Gualtieri, Antonio R. *Conscience and Coercion: Aḥmadī Muslims and Orthodoxy in Pakistan.* Montreal: Guernica, 1989. A passionate advocacy of the Aḥmadī cause.
Khan, Amjad Mahmood. "Persecution of the Ahmadiyya Community in Pakistan: An Analysis under International Law and International Relations." *Harvard Human Rights Journal* 16 (2003): 217–244.
Khan, Muhammad Zafrullah. *Aḥmadīyyat: The Renaissance of Islam.* London: Tabshir, 1978. History of the movement from the Aḥmadī point of view.
Khan, Muhammad Zafrullah, trans. *Tadhkirah: English Translation of the Dreams, Visions, and Verbal Revelations Vouchsafed to the Promised Messiah on Whom Be Peace.* London: Saffron Books, distributed by the London Mosque, 1976.
Mujib-ur-Rehman Dard v. Pakistan, C. A. 148/89.
Pakistan National Assembly. "Verdict on Finality of Prophethood of ḥaẓrat Muḥammad (peace be upon him)." Islamabad, 1974.
Smith, Wilfred Cantwell. "Aḥmadīyya." In *The Encyclopaedia of Islam*, new ed., edited by H. A. R. Gibb et al., vol. 1, pp. 301–303. Leiden: Brill, 1960.

YOHANAN FRIEDMANN

AḤMAD KHĀN, SAYYID. The family of Sir Sayyid Aḥmad Khān (1817–1898), an Indian Islamic modernist writer and political activist, claimed lineal descent from the prophet Muḥammad; his ancestors had settled in Herāt in Afghanistan and then migrated to Mughal India in the seventeenth century. Despite their residence in India for nearly two hundred years, Sir Sayyid's family retained a consciousness of their foreign origin. This extraterritorial consciousness determined their outlook, and that of other upper-class Muslims, in the Indian environment. They viewed the culture and political problems of Muslims from this perspective, generally detaching themselves from the indigenous Muslim masses but associating with them closely in periods of political crisis.

Sir Sayyid's formal education was strictly traditional and was never completed; he ceased formal schooling at eighteen. What traditional education he had acquired was neither comprehensive nor intensive, and this later exposed him to the ridicule of conservative critics, who considered him unqualified to undertake his bold modernization of Islam. Yet this weakness was his real strength: unfettered by the discipline of rigorous traditional education, through personal study and independent investigation he reached out to new horizons of intellectual creativity and laid the groundwork for a modern interpretation of Islam.

Sir Sayyid was loyal to the British colonial regime, which appointed him *sarishtahdār* (recorder) in the criminal department of a lower court. In 1839 he was appointed deputy reader in the office of the divisional commissioner in Uttar Pradesh province, eventually rising to the position of subjudge. In 1855 he was transferred to Bijnor, where he participated in the upheavals of1857. He emerged from this ordeal as both a loyal functionary of the British government and a staunch Muslim nationalist.

Immediately after 1857 Sir Sayyid undertook three projects: to initiate an ecumenical movement in order to create understanding between Muslims and Christians; to establish scientific organizations that would help Muslims understand the secret of the West's success; and to analyze objectively the causes of the 1857 revolt. He was the only Muslim scholar ever to have ventured a commentary on the Old and New Testaments, in his *Mohomedan Commentary on the Holy Bible* (1862).

Against the British view that the rebellion of 1857 was led by Muslims, he advanced the thesis that a large number of Muslims had remained loyal to the British government. Between 1860 and 1861 he published a series of articles, collected in *An Account of the Loyal Mahomedans of India*, attempting to show that the majority of influential Muslims remained loyal to the British government. At the same time Sir Sayyid continued to urge Muslim loyalty to the British in order to elicit British support for a fair Muslim share in the Indian political system. His mission also fostered respect and understanding between Muslims and Christians.

In May 1869 Sir Sayyid arrived in London and remained in Britain for fifteen months. There he internalized positive aspects of British culture, including the value system of modern scientific education and the capitalistic form of economy characterized by social and political laissez-faire.

In London he published twelve essays on the life of the prophet Muḥammad, *A Series of Essays on the Life of Mohammed* (1870). In order to study British educational institutions he visited the universities of Cambridge and Oxford, as well as private preparatory schools. These educational models enabled him to plan the Mohammedan Anglo-Oriental College, which he established in 1875 at Aligarh; in 1920 the college became Aligarh Muslim University.

Equipped with modern ideas and orientations, Sir Sayyid returned to India in 1870 and initiated his movement of religious and cultural modernism among Muslims. He resigned his position in the judicial service in 1876 and until his death in 1898 devoted his life to modernizing the life of Muslims on the Indian subcontinent.

Sir Sayyid devoted most of his energies to promoting modern education among Muslims, especially through the All-India Mohammedan Educational Conference, which existed from 1886 to 1937. From 1886 to 1898 the Educational Conference was pitted against the All-India National Congress, which espoused secular Indian nationalism. Sir Sayyid, on the contrary, promoted a form of Muslim nationalism that accentuated separatist Muslim politics in India; this gave rise to the All-India Muslim League, which in the 1930s and 1940s spearheaded the movement for the creation of Pakistan.

In the field of religion Sir Sayyid promoted an Islamic modernism that drew inspiration from the writings of Shāh Walī Allāh (1703–1762) and emphasized a rational approach to Islam and social reforms in Muslim culture. What made Sir Sayyid controversial was his emphasis on a religious modernism that rejected the traditional practices and orientations of the orthodox, and his advocacy of modern education, which lured young Muslims from orthodox religious seminaries into Western-style schools and colleges. In recognition of his accomplishments, the British government knighted him in 1888.

[*See also* All-India Muslim League.]

BIBLIOGRAPHY

Abdullah, S. M. *The Spirit and Substructure of Urdu Prose under the Influence of Sir Sayyid Ahmad Khan.* Lahore: Muhammad Ashraf, 1940.

Ahmad Khan, Sayyid. *Causes of the Indian Revolt: Three Essays.* Compiled and edited by Salim al-Din Quraishi. Lahore: Sang-e-Meel, 1997.

Ahmad Khan, Sayyid. *Selected Essays by Sir Sayyid Ahmad Khan.* Translated by John W. Wilder. Lahore: Sang-e Meel, 2006.

Ahmad Khan, Sayyid. *Sir Sayyid Ahmad Khan's History of the Bijnor Rebellion.* Translated by Hafeez Malik and Morris Dembo. Delhi: Delhi Idarah-i Adabiyat-i Delli, 1982.

Baljon, J. M. S. *The Reforms and Religious Ideas of Sir Sayyid Ahmad Khan.* Lahore: Orientalia, 1958.

Dar, Bashir Ahmad. *Religious Thought of Sayyid Ahmad Khan.* Lahore: Institute of Islamic Culture, 1957.

Donohue, John J., and John L. Esposito, eds. *Islam in Transition: Muslim Perspectives.* 2d ed. New York: Oxford University Press, 2007.

Graham, G. F. I. *The Life and Work of Sir Syed Ahmed Khan.* Rev. ed. London: Hodder & Stoughton, 1909.

Lelyveld, David. *Aligarh's First Generation: Muslim Solidarity in British India.* New Delhi: Oxford University Press, 2003.

Malik, Hafeez, ed. *Political Profile of Sir Sayyid Ahmad Khan: A Documentary Record.* Islamabad: Institute of Islamic History, Culture and Civilization, Islamic University, 1982.

Malik, Hafeez. *Sir Sayyid Ahmad Khan and Muslim Modernization in India and Pakistan.* New York: Columbia University Press, 1980.

Malik, Hafeez, ed. *Sir Sayyid Ahmad Khan's Educational Philosophy: A Documentary Record.* Islamabad: National Institute of Historical and Cultural Research, 1989.

Robinson, Francis. *Islam and Muslim History in South Asia.* New Delhi: Oxford University Press, 2000.

Troll, Christian W. *Sayyid Ahmad Khan: A Reinterpretation of Muslim Theology.* New Delhi: Vikas, 1978.

Hafeez Malik

Al-ʿAdl wa-al-Iḥsān. *See* Justice and Benevolence Party.

Al-Aḥkām al-Khamsa. *See* Sharīʿah.

Alevis. *This entry contains two subentries:*

Overview *and*
Turkey.

Overview

The Alevis are a group whose members stem from Anatolia and, to a lesser extent, the Balkans. They are characterized by their strong emphasis on the mystical side of Islam: the idea that a part of God lies within all human beings, and that appropriate ethical conduct is more important than any strict following of the orthodox rules of faith. This they sometimes encapsulate by drawing a contrast between the "five pillars" of Sunnī Islam in Turkey, and their "three conditions": "Be master of thy hands, thy tongue, and thy loins" (i.e., do not steal, do not tell falsehoods, and do not commit adultery). Known as *edep*, this prescription is known widely within Turkish mystical Islam. What is notable about the Alevis is the priority that *edep* is given within their religious culture: everyone—men and women—is part of this mystical tradition by virtue of being born into it.

Until recently, the Alevis have inhabited primarily rural, often mountainous locations, predominantly in the central and eastern regions of Anatolia, that is, the provinces of Tokat, Yozgat, Sivas, Amasya, Erzincan, Erzurum, Kahramanmaraş, and Tunceli, though they may be found also in the west, notably Balıkesir. There is no single overarching Alevi organization, but many Alevis, particularly those toward the central and western regions, are influenced by the Bektāshī brotherhood, whose tenets they may regard as following theirs very closely. Locally, leadership is usually conferred through hereditary patrilineages (known variously as *dede*, lit. grandfather, or *pir*) whose founder or later descendants are regarded as being sacred by virtue of being favored by God with a miraculous sign. The hierarchical relationship between *dede* and their followers is crucial to Alevi life: the *dede* has a duty to teach the tenets of the Alevis (*Alevilik*) to his followers, to advise them in times of difficulty, to lead collective religious ceremonies within the community, and to act as mediator in times of dispute.

The principal Alevi ceremony is the *cem*, which usually takes place during the winter months. Held at night, it is a complex and rich ritual whose central rite marks the passing of God's secrets to ʿAlī, from whom they are believed to have been passed to his martyred children Ḥasan and Ḥusayn, and their descendants down to the Alevi community. The congregation collects in a large room, men and women together, grouped around a central space that is known as ʿAlī's *meydan*. If there are disputants, they are called to this space, and until their problem is resolved, worship cannot take place. The *dede* leads the ceremony and is accompanied by a minstrel (*âsık*), who plays a prominent role, singing laments celebrating the Twelve Imams and otherwise accompanying the unfolding ritual. The culmination of the ceremony is the *sema*, or sacred dance of the forty. There are different versions of this *sema*, but it usually consists of two or three pairs of mature, married couples, dancing in a circle in unison. Traditionally, outsiders were not permitted at this ceremony, though among the migrant communities abroad, such a prescription is often lifted.

Though clearly influenced by Shiism, the Alevis themselves do not typically regard themselves as Shīʿī. The word *Alevi* itself appears to be of comparatively recent origin, dating perhaps to the end of the nineteenth century. It is best to conceive of them as a number of disparate groups, perhaps not clearly defined, that have gradually, as the Turkish republic has taken shape, come to see themselves as being part of a similar religious tradition. Though there is no one text that unites all Alevis, many refer to a work known as the *Buyruk*, or decree, said to be written by Imām Jaʿfar. This exists in different versions but is thought to have been compiled in the sixteenth century in the time of Shāh Ismāʿīl, perhaps as an attempt to create support against the Ottomans. Alevi traditions may draw upon older forms of Islam too: many may refer back to eastern schools, such as those of Aḥmad Yasavī at Khorāsān. There may also be an affinity with the Mevlevîs, or with Anatolian figures such as Yunus Emre.

The Alevis have never quite been accepted within the Turkish state, as their highly devolved organization and culture often creates an uneasy relationship with authority, particularly in the tribal east. Nevertheless, relations with the republic have often been good, and the Turkish Alevis, and at least some of the Kurdish Alevis, strongly supported Atatürk and his secular reforms. Indeed, the history of the left-wing republican parties in Turkey could hardly be written without including the role of the Alevis, who regarded them as a defense against the re-Islamification of the public sphere.

There is no accurate idea of the population of Alevis. Estimates range from as low as 10 percent to as high as 30 percent of Turkey's population. In recent decades there has been rapid migration from the countryside, whether to urban centers within the republic or further abroad, particularly Germany, Holland, and Austria. In these new milieus there is a strong intellectual movement toward the reformulation or codification of Alevi tradition, often led by young intellectuals who are not necessarily themselves of *dede* descent. In terms of modern ethnicity, Alevis may be both Turkish and Kurdish. In Germany at least, this ethnic distinction may become apparent in the form of Alevi religion that is regarded as most appropriate for the community to pursue, and can give rise to lively internal debate. The current situation is fluid, and as the republic itself moves away from secularism and toward the acceptance of a form of political life based on Sunnī Islam, it is potentially tense.

Bibliography

Mélikoff, Irène. *Hadji Bektach: Un mythe et ses avatars: Genèse et évolution du soufisme populaire en Turquie.* Leiden: Brill, 1998.

Shankland, David. *The Alevis in Turkey: The Emergence of a Secular Islamic Tradition.* London: Routledge-Curzon, 2003.

David Shankland

Turkey

Alevis are the second largest religious community in Turkey after the Sunnīs, with a population in Turkey that is estimated at between 15 and 20 million. A great majority of Alevis lived in rural areas until the mid-twentieth century, though today, most Alevis live in urban centers. There are approximately 1 million Alevi immigrants outside Turkey, the majority in Germany. Alevis are a multiethnic religious group whose members speak various languages including Turkish, Kurmanji, Dimili, Arabic, and Azeri, among others. Alevis do not proselytize and practiced strict endogamy until very recently.

The term *Alevi*, often used to refer to descendants of ʿAlī ibn Abī Ṭālib, has also come to denote, since the sixteenth century, a person who is a member of a sect that holds ʿAlī in high esteem. In the contemporary Turkish, Alevi is used as an umbrella concept to refer to a range of groups including Kızılbaş, Bektaşi, Tahtacı, Çepni, and Amucalı, among others. From the late nineteenth century on, the term Alevi became a popular euphemism to refer to these groups, particularly owing to the pejorative connotations of the term Kızılbaş in conservative Sunnī parlance. The Ottoman political and religious establishment propaganda (since the sixteenth century) claimed that the Kızılbaş, who were supporters of the Ṣafavid rivals of the Ottomans, practiced incestuous orgies during their religious ceremonies. Beginning with the Alevi revival of the 1990s, however, Alevis started to reappropriate the word *Kızılbaş* and use it in affirmative ways.

The Alevi faith is often puzzling to outsiders, because its adherents do not see themselves as either Sunnī or Shīʿī. Alevis never recognized the authority of the Sunnī caliphs. Instead, they pay allegiance to the Twelve Imams. Alevis are often characterized by their Sunnī rivals by reference to their failure to follow the Sunnī orthopraxy, particularly their refusal to perform the five daily prayers, the Ramadan fast, and the pilgrimage to Mecca. Alevis, however, present the teaching of four gates and forty stations (*dört kapı kırk makam*) as the central tenet of their spiritual path (*yol*). This mystical journey begins by following the formal religious rules (*şeriat*) and ends with the discovery of the divine within, and ultimately in union with the divine (*hakikat*). The goal of human beings in life is to attain the status of a perfect human being called *insan-ı kâmil.* Other distinguishing features of Alevi teachings involve the belief in reincarnation and metempsychosis as well as the mystical unity between the Prophet Muḥammad and ʿAlī ibn Abī Ṭālib. Although Alevi teachings are for the most part transmitted orally by religious guides and minstrels, there are also various important written documents. A collection of manuscripts attributed to Imām Jaʿfar al-Ṣādiq called *Buyruk* (the Command) is accepted as one of the most important sources of Alevi belief and practice.

The central ritual of Alevis is the *âyin-i cem*, a congregational ceremony of men and women that comprises various different practices called twelve services (*oniki hizmet*). The *cem* ceremony involves chanting, music, and ritual dance (*semah*). It is modeled after the archetype of the congregation of the forty saints (*kırklar cemi*), which is believed to have taken place on the prophet Muḥammad's return from his ascent to heaven. Two key Alevi practices that are based on *kırklar cemi* are spiritual brotherhood (*müsahiblik*) and people's courts (*görgü*). Becoming a *müsahib* involves the establishment of a lifelong relationship between two married couples whereby they are expected to stand in solidarity with each other in all aspects of life. This fictive kin relationship is as strong as a consanguinal relationship, and the intermarriage of children of *müsahibs* is considered incestuous. The practice of *görgü* in *cem* ceremonies involves the settling of disputes and reconciliation of differences in the presence of religious guides. In rare cases in which members of the community are guilty of serious offenses, people can be declared *düşkün* and ostracized from the community.

Alevi men and women carry out *cem* ceremonies in worship halls called *cemevi* and do not attend mosques. Alevis used to carry out *cem* ceremonies secretly, out of fear of persecution by the Ottoman Sunnī establishment. This secrecy continued until the late twentieth century. Although *cem* ceremonies have become public for the most part, the Turkish state still does not recognize *cemevi* as worship halls, although these halls are considered and tolerated as cultural centers.

Alevi communities are served by male religious guides called *dede* or *baba*, although there are few instances of women serving as well. Most of the religious guides are members of patrilineages, and they putatively demonstrate agnatic descent from the Twelve Imams. Religious guides are also assisted by *zakirs*, who play a stringed instrument called *bağlama* during the *cem* ceremony. Alevis refer to *bağlama* as *telli Kur'an*, the stringed Qur'ān. This is connected to the Alevi belief that human beings are *Kuran-ı natık*, the speaking Qur'ān. Spiritually mature people, Alevis believe, can speak out or sing the divine wisdom to the tunes of the *bağlama*.

There is no universally accepted central and hierarchical organization of Alevis. The town of Hacıbektaş, where the shrine of the patron saint Hacı Bektaş is located, is believed to be the spiritual center of the Alevi faith. The Ulusoy family residing in Hacıbektaş is recognized by some Alevis as the descendants of the saint Hacı Bektaş. Most Alevis in Turkey, however, are organized in Alevi associations and foundations, the number of which exceeds three hundred. These organizations are members of umbrella organizations, the most important one being the Alevi Bektaşi Federation (ABF). The Federation of Alevi Associations (ADF) and the Federation of Alevi Foundations (AVF) were also established recently as umbrella organizations alternative to the ABF. These two more recent federations, however, bring together fewer organizations. The European Confederation of Alevi Unions (AABK) based in Germany, which also includes ABF of Turkey as a member, is currently the most important transnational organization representing Alevis around the world. Alevis, once a closed and secretive community practicing dissimulation for fear of Sunnī persecution, have become public within the last two decades. Today there is a rich array of Alevi TV channels, radio stations, popular and academic journals, publishing houses, and websites.

BIBLIOGRAPHY

Birge, John Kingsley. *The Bektashi Order of Dervishes*. London: Luzac; Hartford, Conn.: Hartford Seminary Press, 1937.

Shankland, David. *The Alevis in Turkey: The Emergence of a Secular Islamic Tradition*. London: Routledge-Curzon, 2003.

Shindeldecker, John. *Turkish Alevis Today*. Istanbul: Şahkulu Sultan Külliyesi Vakfı, 1996.

Yaman, Ali, and Aykan Erdemir. *Alevism-Bektashism: A Brief Introduction*. London: England Alevi Cultural Centre & Cem Evi, 2006.

AYKAN ERDEMIR

ALGERIA. Islam provided the principal expression of social cohesion in Algeria's Arab and Berber societies from the seventh century to the modern period. The French conquest of Algeria from 1830, and subsequent colonization of the territory until independence in 1962, had a major impact on the social and political significance of Islam, making it a central rallying point for an Algerian national community. After independence, the single-party regime of the National Liberation Front (FLN) sought to monopolize the religious sphere as part of its state-building project. From the 1960s, dissidence expressed in Islamic terms, as well as a moralizing discourse promoted by the religious, cultural, and educational institutions of the state, provided alternative expressions of what by the late 1970s became an Islamist agenda for society and politics. The Islamist movement that became a populist focus of opposition to the incumbent regime in the late 1980s, however, disintegrated under the pressure of internal dissent and repression by the military and security services from 1992 onward. With parts of the more radical Islamist groups engaged in armed insurgency against the regime and, increasingly, against civilians, in a decade of civil violence that killed an unknown number of Algerians (estimates range between one and two hundred thousand), more moderate Islamist figures sought to reintegrate the political system and by the late 1990s operated within a regime-sanctioned multiparty arena. With widespread popular disaffection from the political process, widely perceived as corrupt and unrepresentative, and the exhaustion and delegitimization of *jihādist* violence, older, less overtly political forms of Islam returned to prominence in the early 2000s. Islamic public piety and personal morality remain important aspects of Algerian society, while the association of religion with politics is increasingly viewed with skepticism, as either dangerous extremism when in opposition to the system or as compromised by association with it.

Early History and Colonialism. From its emergence, Islam in Algeria took similar forms to those found elsewhere in the agrarian world of the medieval and early modern periods, and these forms have survived into the present. Local spiritual landscapes were marked by the passage of saintly men, "friends of God" (*walīs*), often called *mrabtīn*, "marabouts." Their tombs became centers of spiritual and social power, inherited by saintly families that often became affiliated with the Ṣūfī orders (*ṭarīqahs*), or "brotherhoods." The *ṭarīqahs* gained political significance through their wealth, transregional connections, spiritual legitimacy as arbiters of good and evil, and the local preeminence of their leaders. In the early nineteenth century, rural revolts against the Ottoman state were organized and led by the brotherhoods whose *zāwiyahs*, centers of learning and pilgrimage focused around founders' tombs, became strongholds of regional political influence. The Ottoman state had institutionalized Islamic law and learning in the country's urban centers, where judges from the Mālikī and Ḥanafī *madhhabs* (schools of jurisprudence) ruled on civil and commercial matters. While the overwhelming majority of the country's people were by this time Sunnī Muslims, a small and distinctive Ibāḍī community settled in the valley of the Mzab in the northern Sahara maintained its own variant of Islamic law and community self-regulation. The country's urban centers were also home to a small Jewish population that shared many aspects of language and culture with their Muslim neighbors.

The colonial conquest of Algeria and the incorporation, from 1848, of Algerian territory under the "internal" jurisdiction of metropolitan France created a completely new situation. With the creation of a large European settler society dominating landownership, urban space, and political institutions, Algerians were disenfranchised as noncitizen subjects. After the indigenous Jewish community was granted French citizenship by decree in 1870, adherence to Islam combined with a set of racial stereotypes defined Arab and Berber Muslim Algerians as a subordinate population in colonial law and administrative practice. Initially, the *zāwiyah*s and Ṣūfī brotherhoods served as centers and networks of resistance to the conquest. As the conquest was consolidated, the brotherhoods were ultimately obliged to reach accommodation with the French, who attempted, sometimes successfully, to coopt their leaders as intermediaries for colonial power in the countryside. The official system of Islamic law and learning was also subordinated to the colonial state. As a result, the current of religious reform and Arab-Islamic cultural revival that swept the Arab world in the late 1800s and early 1900s took on particular significance in Algeria, most of whose people were technically "French" nationals but were excluded by their religious (and "racial") identity from French citizenship. While not initially advocating political independence from France, the reformist movement led from the mid-1920s by Shaykh ʿAbd al-Ḥamīd Ibn Bādīs (1889–1940) spoke for an Islamic social, cultural, and moral authority independent of the state as well as for the "purification" of Islam from the popular, everyday religious practices and forms of authority and learning associated with the Ṣūfī brotherhoods and their saints' shrines and saintly lineages. It thus became implicitly political, and from the early 1940s onward played an increasingly important role in nationalist activity against the colonial status quo. Reformist religious leadership was not directly connected with the small group of nationalist radicals who launched the FLN's war of independence in November 1954, and the FLN's nationalist project was not primarily an "Islamic" one. But Muslim community solidarity and Islamic moral discipline, as well as *jihād* against the colonial occupier that was easily understood by the peasantry and mountain populations, contributed to forging the broad social base of the revolution. A cultural vision of national communal self-realization and "authenticity" based on the values of reformist Islam informed the outlook of some of the more religiously inclined leaders of the revolution. Although they were less central to the emerging structures of power in the wartime FLN than were the military leaders of the National Liberation Army or its internal security apparatus, they exercised considerable influence on the formulation of a "puritanical" nationalist cultural vision that was officialized after independence.

Independence. In independent Algeria, however, the religious and cultural fields, the jurisdiction of Islamic law, and the training of preachers and Islamic teachers were firmly subordinated to the ministerial bureaucracies of the authoritarian state. Opposition by religious conservatives could not prevent the enactment in 1971 of an "agrarian revolution" aimed at bettering the lot of poor peasants (and seen as an attack on private property) along with other measures of a government committed to a socialist, state-led economic and social development program. Opposition to the regime's perceived sidelining of religion began to appear in early 1964, with the appearance of a group of functionaries and educators who formed Jamʿīyat al-Qiyam al-Islāmīyah (The Islamic Values Society). Most prominent among them was the educationalist Malek Bennabi (1905–1973), who in a series of philosophical and sociological works attempted to construct a critique of the Muslim world's "colonizability" by the West and a vision of contemporary Islamic revival. Al-Qiyam was banned by the government in 1966, but many of its ideas, articulated around the need for "cultural decolonization" and a communal "authenticity," began to be propounded by the Ministry of Religious Affairs. As pressures on the regime grew toward the end of the 1970s and in the early 1980s, currents of Islamist critique outside the regime and toleration of Islamist-leaning currents within it were curbed; the official *al-Aṣālah* was closed in 1981, as a younger and more radical Islamist militancy began to appear on university campuses and around the country. In 1981–1984, a series of clashes between leftist and Islamist students and between security forces and Islamist militants indicated rising tensions around a social demand for a "remoralization" of society and a political system perceived as increasingly "inauthentic," corrupt, and out of touch with Islam, morality, and a "true" (Arab-Muslim) Algerian identity. The slow retreat from a socialist developmental agenda that had failed, by the late 1970s, to keep pace with demographic expansion, social change, and global economic trends, accentuated the alienation felt by many as the gap between the wealthy and poor grew rapidly. The regime now responded with a strategy of appeasement; in 1984, Islamist leaders arrested in 1982 were amnestied, and an intensely conservative family law was passed, severely restricting the legal autonomy of women. Arabization and "Algerianization" were pursued more vigorously against the remaining influence of the French.

Crisis and Civil War. These measures, however, failed to limit Islamist critiques of a political system increasingly unable to cope with the social and economic pressures facing it, and lacking any mechanism for channeling and responding to dissent. In 1985–1987, a group calling itself the Armed Islamic Movement, led by Mustapha Bouyali, a veteran of the war of independence, waged a minor guerrilla campaign in the mountains of Blida, south of Algiers. When discontent turned to rioting in the east of the country in November 1986 and, most notably, in Algiers in October 1988, the deaths of protestors in the army's crackdown precipitated a major political crisis on which the Islamist movement was able to capitalize. Leaders of different tendencies—"*jaza'iristes*" ("Algerianists") identifying with the Islamic component of a specifically Algerian nationalism—and Pan-Islamists came together to form FIS (Front Islamique du Salut; Islamic Salvation Front). Led by the independence war veteran and sociology teacher ʿAbbāsī Madanī, FIS won local and regional elections in June 1990, coming to power in municipalities across the country. In January 1991 it gained more popular visibility by leading protests against the U.S.-led coalition forces' campaign against Iraq. Seeking to avoid marginalization by FIS's growing populism and militancy, other Islamist leaders now organized rival parties: Mahfoud Nahnah's Ḥarakah li-al-Mujtamaʿ al-Islāmī (Movement for Islamic Society, known as "Ḥamās"; later renamed Ḥarakat Mujtamaʿ al-Silm, Movement for the Society of Peace) and ʿAbdallah Djaballah's Nahḍah (Renaissance) Party. Tensions rose as FIS, demanding a presidential election, called for a general strike—which was generally ignored—and organized protests in Algiers. In June 1991 the army moved against the protestors with overwhelming force, and the FIS leaders ʿAbbāsī Madanī and ʿAlī Bel Ḥajj were arrested. In the first round of legislative elections in December 1991, FIS candidates won 188 of the 232 contested seats and looked set for a landslide victory. Under pressure from the army, on 11 January 1992, President Chedli Benjedid (in office since 1979) resigned and was replaced by a High Council of State, which canceled the election and instituted a state of emergency. As Islamist militants began to launch attacks on state targets, FIS was banned, and its militants were rounded up and interned in detention camps in the Sahara, beginning a cycle of violence that was to escalate and last throughout the 1990s. In the course of the war, Islamist movements bifurcated between those increasingly engaged in more radical violence and rejection of political process—identified with the various Armed Islamic Groups (Jamaʿāt al-Islāmīyah al-Musallaḥah; GIA)—and those, often with a more doctrinally developed and less populist stance, accepting a position within the party-political arena reconstructed and tolerated by the regime since 1997. After the winding down of the violence, with the exhaustion of the insurgency by the early 2000s, the latter groups, notably the political parties Ḥamās and Nahḍah and their offshoots, regularly took part in elections and accepted positions in government coalitions. After 2001, however, the remnants of the more radical groups, especially the GSPC (Salafist Group for Preaching and Combat), an offshoot of the GIA, rebranded themselves as parts of a global *jihād* inspired by, and from 2007 notionally affiliated with, al-Qaʿida. Sporadic attacks against security forces continued; in April 2007 coordinated suicide bombings targeted major government offices and police headquarters in Algiers, and in December that year the United Nations Development Programme office in the capital was bombed.

Such attacks showed the continued existence and capability of radical splinter groups, but also underlined their marginality from the political sphere, which was firmly back under regime control, as well as the absence of any broader social movement to which they might appeal. Popular piety in everyday life was greater than it had ever been since independence, but increasingly divorced from the kind of directly oppositional political activism seen in the 1980s. Instead, popular religious devotions in new mosque buildings and Ṣūfī centers expressed a desire for peace, stability, and solace after the violence of the 1990s. At the same time, as a counterweight to Islamist ideas "imported" from Saudi Arabia and Egypt, the regime of President Abdelaziz Bouteflika (since 1999) promoted the revived *zāwiyahs* as expressions of an "Algerian Islam", and promised to build the world's largest mosque near the Algiers waterfront.

BIBLIOGRAPHY

Ahnaf, M. al-, Bernard Botiveau, and Franck Frégosi, eds. *L'Algérie par ses islamistes*. Paris: Karthala, 1991.

Clancy-Smith, Julia A. *Rebel and Saint: Muslim Notables, Populist Protest, Colonial Encounters: Algeria and Tunisia, 1800–1904*. Berkeley: University of California Press, 1994.

Colonna, Fanny. *Les versets de l'invincibilité: Permanence et changements religieux dans l'Algérie contemporaine*. Paris: Presses de la Fondation Nationale des Sciences Politiques, 1995.

McDougall, James. *History and the Culture of Nationalism in Algeria*. Cambridge, U.K.: Cambridge University Press, 2006.

McDougall, James. "Islam(s) and Politics: Post-Traumatic States in Algeria." *OpenDemocracy*, 10 July 2007, http://www.opendemocracy.net/democracy_power/africa_islam/algeria_politics.

Roberts, Hugh. *The Battlefield Algeria, 1988–2002: Studies in a Broken Polity*. London: Verso, 2003.

Rouadjia, Ahmed. "Discourse and Strategy of the Algerian Islamist Movement (1986–1992)." In *The Islamist Dilemma: The Political Role of Islamist Movements in the Contemporary Arab World*, edited by Laura Guazzone, pp. 69–104. Reading, U.K.: Ithaca, 1995.

Willis, Michael. *The Islamist Challenge in Algeria: A Political History*. Reading, U.K.: Ithaca, 1996.

JAMES MCDOUGALL

ʿALĪ IBN ABĪ ṬĀLIB. *See* Companions of the Prophet.

AL-KHOEI BENEVOLENT FOUNDATION. Established in 1989 with headquarters in London, the Imam al-Khoei Benevolent Foundation has centralized religious institutions acquired through pious donations managed by the late Ayatollah Abol-Qāsem al-Khoʾi (Abū al-Qāsim Khūʾī, d. 1992) in his position as *marjaʿ al-taqlīd* (supreme juridical authority) of the majority of Shīʿī Muslims. Practical considerations prompted the establishment of the foundation to supervise the religious endowments and other assets that had been managed by al-Khoʾi's *wukalāʾ* (personal representatives). Shīʿī religious law recognizes the *marjaʿ* as the superintendent of religious assets as long as he lives. In the absence of any established legal procedure for the succession of juridical authority, there is no provision to ascertain legal conveyance of these assets to the subsequent *marjaʿ* acknowledged by the Shīʿah. The convention is to treat these assets as pious endowments supervised by appointed trustees or by the ministries of *awqāf* (pious endowments; sing. *waqf*) in various Muslim countries.

Another concern that led to the creation of a multinational foundation in the name of al-Khoʾi—who was not the actual owner of the trust—was that foreign assets were registered in accordance with national laws that did not recognize Islamic law or the ayatollah's supervisory role. The mandate of the al-Khoei Foundation was expanded through registration as a nonprofit corporation, empowering it to solicit, accept, administer, and invest funds and other property. Unlike the traditional method of the *marjaʿ*—who does not publicize any accounts because of the great trust in which he is held by his followers—the foundation had to abide by the standards of accountability in the West, such as the UK Charity Commission's reporting requirements. According to its published reports, its activities have included the establishment of religious and educational institutions in the United Kingdom, France, the United States, Canada, Pakistan, India, Thailand, and, for a short period, Malaysia. The foundation has also provided emergency humanitarian aid to victims of war and natural disasters, and more recently engaged in human development projects to tap into international sources of funding.

Al-Khoʾi's death in August 1992 left a vacuum in Shīʿī religious leadership and tested the al-Khoei Foundation's capacity to continue its mission within the *marjiʿīyah*'s framework. The foundation's bylaws of 1989 had anticipated the need to hand over its supervision to the next religious leader after al-Khoʾi. One article stipulated that such a person had to be recognized and confirmed by three-quarters of the foundation's trustees. It took almost a year for the trustees to acknowledge Ayatollah Muḥammad Rizā Gulpāygānī of Iran as the foundation's new patron. After Gulpāygānī's death in December 1993, they requested at once the patronage of ʿAlī al-Sīstānī of Najaf, also receiving the permission to use 50 percent of the religious dues collected on his behalf for the foundation's projects. Thus, the trustees reserved the legally and traditionally recognized supervisory role for themselves while assigning the ceremonial role of patron to the *marjaʿ*. This empowerment of the trustees marked a clear departure from the traditional role of the supreme juridical authority as the trustee of the Hidden Imam, as conceived in Shīʿī jurisprudence. It also raises questions in the Shīʿī community regarding the limited authority invested in the *marjaʿ* by the *Sharīʿah* and the ever-expanding mandate claimed by the foundation in the name of the *marjaʿ*.

Moreover, the danger that the al-Khoei Foundation might turn into a family empire was foreseen, and it stems from the foundation's internal organization. Al-Khoʾi dictated that the position of general secretary should be entrusted to one of his sons or grandsons who is a cleric. The ayatollah's son, Muḥammad Taqī al-Khoʾi, assumed this position from Najaf until his death in 1994. He was replaced by his younger brother, ʿAbd al-Mājid al-Khoʾi, who was killed in April 2003 when he traveled to Najaf under American protection. During the 1990s and early 2000s, the foundation under ʿAbd al-Mājid's leadership had engaged in an advocacy movement to denounce human rights violations in Iraq, for which it established sustained political contacts with government circles. Since 2003, another al-Khoʾi brother, ʿAbd al-Sāhib, has acted as the foundation's general secretary.

In the twenty-first century the al-Khoei Foundation continues to fulfill its charitable mission through projects worldwide. Its successful application for general consultative status at the United Nations in 1998 was also a recognition of its role as representative of Shīʿī interests at large. However, the competition from other leading *marājiʿ* (plural of *marjaʿ*), some of whom have also established their own charitable foundations in London, has diluted the foundation's once exclusive claim to leadership.

[*See also* Khoʾi, Abol-Qāsem al-; *and* Waqf.]

BIBLIOGRAPHY

Corboz, Elvire. "The al-Khoei Foundation and the Transnational Institutionalisation of Ayatollah al-Khu'i's *Marjaʿiyya*." In *Shiʿi Islam and Identity: Religion, Politics and Change in the Global Muslim Community*, edited by Lloyd Ridgeon, pp. 93–112. London: I. B. Tauris, 2012.

Leichtman, Mara A. "A Day in the Life of the Khoei Foundation: A Transnational Shi'ite Institution in London." *The Middle East in London* 3, no. 5 (November 2006): 5–6.

Rahe, Jens-Uwe. *Irakische Schiiten im Londoner Exil: Eine Bestandsaufnahme ihrer Organisationen and Untersuchung ihrer Selbstdarstellung, 1991–1994*. Al-Rafidayn 4. Würzburg: Ergon, 1996.

Official websites of the al-Khoei Foundation: http://www.alkhoei.org/ (headquarters); https://www.al-khoei.org (New York branch); http://www.khoei.ca (Montreal branch).

Abdulaziz Sachedina
Updated by Elvire Corboz

Allāh. *See* Religious Beliefs.

All-India Muslim League. The origins of the All-India Muslim League lie in what is commonly called the Aligarh Movement. Sir Sayyid Aḥmad Khān in 1875 founded a college (later a university) in the town of Aligarh, with the intention of providing Western education to the upper strata of Indian Muslim society. Some of the college's early graduates saw their role as providing a political lead to the country's Muslims. The initial forum for this task was the Muhammadan Educational Conference. At its Dhaka meeting in December 1906, it transformed into the Muslim League. The political context was provided by the election in Britain of a Liberal government and subsequent moves toward limited representative institutions in India. In October 1906, with the help of the British principal of Aligarh, a delegation of Muslim notables called on the viceroy in Simla, Lord Minto, and presented a petition asking for various forms of special protection for the Muslim population, notably separate electoral rolls. These were in fact incorporated into the 1909 Indian Councils Act.

Founded initially as a loyalist organization, the Muslim League was taken over a few years after its creation by a new group of Aligarh graduates, most prominently Muḥammad ʿAlī and his brother Shaukat ʿAlī, who emphasized Pan-Islamic themes on the one hand and cooperation with the Indian National Congress on the other. In 1916 the League leaders, including Mohammad Ali Jinnah, who had joined in 1913, negotiated an agreement with the Congress that secured separate electorates in return for support for a common program of constitutional change. After the end of the war, however, the League as an institution was temporarily swept aside by the force of the Khilāfat movement, although several of its leaders played prominent parts in the latter. Muslim politics during the 1920s and early 1930s were dominated by provincial leaders and parties, such as Sir Fazli Husain in the Punjab. Jinnah himself had retired to London in 1931 following the failure of efforts to negotiate new agreements or understandings with the Congress, and Muslim interests at the national level were represented by conservative loyalists.

By the mid-1930s, the political environment had changed substantially following the civil disobedience campaign by the Congress, and the 1935 Government of India Act appeared to presage an elected government at the all-India level. The possibility that the government in India might represent the Congress's views and attitudes and emphasize either secular or Hindu values forced a rethinking of the Muslim position. Jinnah, seen as having the negotiating skills and contacts to represent the Muslim cause, was called back from London in 1935 and took on the presidency of the League. His first task was to contest the initial elections under the 1935 act, which were held in early 1937. An electoral organization had to be created from scratch, and the overall League performance was poor compared with that of both the Congress and regional parties such as the Unionists in the Punjab. A further setback came when the Congress refused to allow Muslim League representatives in the United Provinces, where the League had won a number of seats, to join the Congress government there. This confirmed Jinnah's view that the Congress was unwilling to allow the Muslim League political space in any future constitutional arrangements.

From the middle of 1937 Jinnah succeeded in projecting the League as the representative agent of the Muslims. In September 1937 he persuaded the premiers of the Muslim-majority provinces of the Punjab and Bengal to join the League while maintaining their provincial party structures. Simultaneously the League launched a sustained attack on the Congress, portraying it as fundamentally hostile to Muslim interests. In a meeting in Lahore in March 1940 the Muslim League passed what has become known as the Pakistan Resolution, calling for independent states in Muslim-majority areas. Jinnah's own speech at this meeting set out his view of the Muslims of India as a separate nation. Although the resolution apparently called for the partition of the subcontinent into separate states, there has been much controversy over whether this was in fact Jinnah's aim. Some writers have argued that it was primarily intended as a bargaining chip.

During World War II Jinnah and the Muslim League made progress on various fronts. The League moved from being mainly an agent of other groups to a principal actor. In the Punjab and elsewhere it began to attract the support of prominent landlords and of some sections of the *'ulamā'* and Ṣūfī *pīrs*. An unbroken string of by-election victories paved the way for landslide results in the 1945 and 1946 elections. With solid political support from the Muslim community, Jinnah then moved into the final stage of tripartite negotiations with the Congress and the outgoing British. Against a background of increasing violence, the only solution that could be found involved the partition of India and also of the provinces of Punjab and Bengal, which formed the bulk of the new state of Pakistan.

After independence and Jinnah's death in September 1948, the League had difficulty establishing a separate role for itself. Within a short time the army and bureaucracy came to dominate the political process, and the only role for the League was as a vehicle for rival groups of provincial politicians. Splits occurred from time to time along factional lines. It has, however, been a convenient label for politicians to adopt, and in elections in1988 the Pakistan Muslim League–Nawaz or PML–N under Nawaz Sharif formed the core of the successful Islāmī Jumhūrī Ittiḥād (Islamic Democratic Alliance), which ruled until 1993.

Subsequently, Nawaz Sharif and the PML–N led another coalition government from 1997 to 1999 and it was overthrown in a military coup led by General Pervez Musharraf. Musharraf himself chose another fraction of the League, the PML–Q, as a political front. In the May 2013 elections, Nawaz Sharif returned to power for a third time at the head of the PML–N.

[*See also* India; Jinnah, Mohammad Ali; Khilāfat Movement; *and* Pakistan.]

BIBLIOGRAPHY

Hardy, P. *The Muslims of British India*. Cambridge, U.K.: Cambridge University Press, 1972. Masterly synthesis.

Jalal, Ayesha. *The Sole Spokesman: Jinnah, the Muslim League, and the Demand for Pakistan*. Cambridge, U.K.: Cambridge University Press, 1985.

Pirzada, Sayyid A. S., ed. *Foundations of Pakistan: All-India Muslim League Documents, 1906–1947*. 2 vols. Karachi: National Publishing House, 1969–1970.

Pirzada, Sayyid A. S. "The Demand for Pakistan and the *ʿUlamāʾ* and *Mashāʾikh*." *Hamdard Islamicus* 18, no. 4 (1995): 83–102.

Qureshi, Ishtiaq Husain. *The Muslim Community of the Indo-Pakistan Subcontinent, 610–1947: A Brief Historical Analysis*. 2d ed. Karachi: Maʿaref, 1977. Standard Pakistani account of the history of the subcontinent.

Shaikh, Farzana. *Community and Consensus in Islam: Muslim Representation in Colonial India, 1860–1947*. Cambridge, U.K.: Cambridge University Press, 1989.

Talbot, Ian. "Planning for Pakistan: The Planning Committee of the All-India Muslim League, 1943–46." *Modern Asian Studies* 28, no. 4 (October 1994): 875–889.

Wells, Ian Bryant. *Jinnah: Ambassador of Hindu-Muslim Politics*. London: Seagull, 2006.

David Taylor

Al-Wefaq National Islamic Society. Al-Wefaq National Islamic Society, also known as the Islamic National Accord Association, is an Islamic political organization that represents a large segment of the disenfranchised Shiite majority in Bahrain. Under the leadership of Shaykh ʿAlī Salmān, it is the most influential political society and the largest Shiite bloc in the country. Perceived as a moderate group, it earned a wide appeal thanks to the provision of social services and mosque outreach programs before it engaged in the political process. It is the largest opposition movement against the Āl Khalīfah Sunnī regime, but it is not the sole representative of Bahraini Shiites. Another political movement, Al Haq (Movement of Freedom and Democracy), is outlawed because it is deemed radical in its demands, which call for a change of regime.

For decades Bahrain has enjoyed a vibrant civil society. The Al-Wefaq Society was established on 7 November 2001 as an umbrella group for different Shiite groups active in the opposition in the 1980s and 1990s. Its aims, as outlined in its charter, are the betterment of living standards of its constituency; halting discrimination in terms of housing, jobs, and political representation; and putting an end to the sectarian discrimination, fighting corruption and ultimately establishing a truly constitutional monarchy based on Islamic teachings and the rule of law, not kinship or sectarian affiliations.

In 1999, King Hamad of Bahrain initiated a top-to-bottom political reform process. Yet, even though Al-Wefaq supported this regime-controlled liberalization initially, it soon became apparent that the pace and direction of these reforms fell short of assuaging the Shiite majority, who called for a more fundamental political reorientation to end decades of political exclusion and economic marginalization.

After having boycotted the 2002 elections, Al-Wefaq partook in the 2006 parliamentary elections and won sixteen out of the forty seats in the Council of Representatives. It thus proved that it is the largest political society both in terms of its membership and its results at the polls. In the 2010 elections, Al-Wefaq increased its representation to eighteen seats, but still fell short of a majority. Coalition blocs of opposition Sunnī parties and independent members of parliament have often outvoted it. It has increasingly focused on the issue of "political naturalization," an unofficial Āl Khalīfah policy that grants citizenship to Sunnīs from other Arab countries to counterbalance the Shiite demographic majority.

Following the Arab Awakening, a Bahraini uprising started on 14 February 2011. It culminated in a political crisis that defied resolution for years, especially after the intervention of the Saudi-led Gulf Cooperation Council troops. This uprising demonstrated that reforms initiated by the regime fell short of Shīʿī goals. On 27 February 2011, following a crackdown by security services on the demonstrators in Pearl Roundabout, which left many dead, the eighteen Al-Wefaq members of parliament submitted letters of resignation to protest regime violence against proreform Bahraini protestors.

Following the conclusion of the "National Dialogue" aimed at resolving the political crisis, a special election was scheduled on 24 September 2011 to fill the eighteen vacated seats. Al-Wefaq boycotted the election on the grounds that the National Dialogue was not inclusive enough and its reform recommendations were not substantial. Sunnīs now overwhelmingly dominate the Council of Representatives with thirty-two seats as against eight for Shīʿīs.

BIBLIOGRAPHY

Bahry, Luayy. "The Socioeconomic Foundations of Shiite Opposition in Bahrain." *Mediterranean Quarterly* 11, no. 3 (2000) 129–143.

Davidson, Christopher M., ed. *Power and Politics in the Gulf Monarchies*. New York: Columbia University Press, 2011.

Younes Abouyoub

AMAL. A populist movement of Lebanese Shīʿī Muslims that emerged in 1974, Amal (*afwāj al-muqāwama al-lubnānīya,* Lebanese Resistance Detachments) became an important political force in Lebanon, although its influence is waning.

Political Mobilization of the Shīʿī. Well into the twentieth century, the Shīʿī were marginal players on the Lebanese political stage. Socialized into a religious tradition that extolled sacrifice and presumed temporal injustice, the Shīʿī found ready confirmation for their beliefs in their deprived sociopolitical status.

Lebanon's confessional (sectarian) political equation—in which privilege, office, and political rights are allocated according to sect size—operated to the disadvantage of the Shīʿīs, who, among the top governmental posts, are granted only the position of Speaker of the House. Moreover, despite the fact that their population grew disproportionately to the country's other two major sects—the Maronite Christians and Sunnīs—the number of seats in parliament to which they were entitled remained unchanged until 1990, when the imbalance was rectified. Adding to the frustration and bitterness of members of this predominantly agricultural community, its leading politicians, who were for the most part conservative scions of large landowning families, were quite content with the political and economic status quo.

The rapid modernization that had marked Lebanon since independence in 1943 transformed the Shīʿīs. Access to education produced a growing pool of individuals who were no longer content to confine their prospects to subsistence farming. Improved transportation and communications eroded the geographic isolation of the community, whose members were concentrated in the Bekáa Valley and the south. At the same time, changes in the agricultural sector, including an increasing emphasis on cash crops and farm mechanization, led to underemployment and joblessness. Many Shīʿīs were forced to move off the land in order to survive. Fleeing the poverty of the village and the drudgery of farm labor, many took work where they could find it in Beirut, usually as petty laborers or peddlers. Although some actually escaped from poverty, most remained dreadfully poor. Not surprisingly, these migrants from the country became a fertile pool for recruitment by leftist secular parties that claimed to have answers to their difficulties.

The dearth of economic opportunities within Lebanon also factored into the movement of many Shīʿī men overseas, where opportunities in the Gulf States and especially West Africa provided a way out of poverty. Though the Shīʿīs as a whole are still relatively impoverished, many have done well as merchants, building contractors, and professionals. The money earned by these Shīʿī migrants would later play a crucial role in financing the growth of Shīʿī political activism within Lebanon.

The 1960s and 1970s exposed the Lebanese Shīʿīs to the leadership of Sayyid Mūsā al-Ṣadr, a populist leader with an agenda of reform. Although born in Iran, Ṣadr traced his ancestry back to southern Lebanon and the village of Marakah. He moved to Lebanon in 1960 from Najaf, Iraq, where he had been studying Islamic *fiqh* (jurisprudence) under several of the most important *ayatollah*s of the day. It was under his direction and leadership that the Ḥarakat al-Maḥrūmīn (Movement of the Deprived)—the forerunner of the Amal movement—emerged in 1974.

While the Movement of the Deprived claimed to represent all of the politically dispossessed Lebanese, regardless of confession, it was transparently a party of the Shīʿīs. The charismatic Ṣadr skillfully exploited Shiism's potent symbolism to remind his followers that they were people with a heritage of resistance and sacrifice. He revitalized the epic martyrdom of Imam Ḥusayn (the grandson of the prophet Muḥammad) at Karbala in 680 and inspired his followers to emulate the imam's bravery, particularly southern Shīʿīs, who faced economic hardships and were increasingly subjected to cross-border clashes between the Israelis and the Palestine Liberation Organization (PLO).

Yet despite the leader's magnetic appeal for many Shīʿīs, Ṣadr's movement was only one in a field of organizations that successfully mobilized the community into political action. The Communist Party and the Syrian Social National Party were the prominent parties of the 1970s. As the civil war began in 1975 many Shīʿī youths were recruited by a number of militia organizations, including the Christian Lebanese Forces and the Palestinian Fidāʾīyān. Only later, and mainly as a result of tensions with the PLO and Israel's full-scale invasion of South Lebanon in 1978, did Ṣadr's movement assume center stage for the Shīʿīs.

Amal's Development. By the 1970s many politicized Shīʿīs deserted the political left and joined or supported Amal. The organization began to take shape as a loose grouping of village home guards, intent on circumscribing the influence of the PLO, thereby reducing the exposure of the Shīʿīs to Israeli attacks.

With the Iranian Revolution gathering momentum in 1978, many Lebanese Shīʿīs took inspiration from the actions of their Iranian coreligionists. If the Islamic Revolution was not a precise model for Lebanon, it was still an exemplar for action, and Amal, as an authentically Shīʿī movement, was the momentary beneficiary of this enthusiasm. Ṣadr was known to be a key supporter of Ayatollah Ruhollah Khomeini (1902–1989) and an adversary of the shah (although his opposition had been tempered by a good dose of realism). Moreover, several key Amal officials, including the Iranian Muṣṭafā Chamrān, took up key positions in the new regime.

Ironically, it was Ṣadr's disappearance on a trip to Libya with two companions in 1978 that helped to bolster the promise of his earlier mobilizing efforts. The symbol of a missing imam—reminiscent of the central dogma of Shiism—is a powerful one, and his disappearance mitigated some of the accusations of corruption brought against Ṣadr by his enemies. By 1982 when Israel launched its invasion, the reform movement Ṣadr founded had become the largest Shīʿī organization in Lebanon and a dynamic force in Lebanese politics despite the fact that all attempts at reform had proven unsuccessful.

Activities of Amal. With the disappearance of Ṣadr, Nabih Berri, the Sierra Leone–born son of a Shīʿī trader who had assumed leadership of the Movement of the Deprived's fighting wing of Amal, came to power. Under Berri's guidance and with arms supplied by Syria, Amal became a major combatant force in the fourteen-year struggle against the Lebanese government and the Israeli-backed Christian militias that supported it. At the same time Amal also found a military role in the Lebanese resistance movement that was created after the expulsion of PLO fighters in 1982 and the Israeli occupation of Lebanon.

The Lebanese resistance (*al-muqāwama al-lubnānīya*) emerged as a result of Syria's determination to undermine Israel's gains and America's ambitions in Lebanon. Damascus found a willing partner for this project in Ayatollah Khomeini, who wished to export the Islamic Revolution and, simultaneously, end his country's regional isolation. Aided by these two states, an increasingly potent Lebanese resistance emerged. Based initially on the parties of the left, major resistance activities were soon delegated to Ḥizbullāh (the Party of God), a Shīʿī organization whose Lebanese founders were originally part of Ṣadr's movement. Organized, armed, and trained in the Bekáa Valley by Iran's Revolutionary Guards and managed by Syria, the Party of God came into its own as a guerrilla force when Israel established a so-called Security Zone on Lebanese territory in 1985. Amal's resistance activities, like Ḥizbullāh's, began during the 1982 Israeli invasion. In later years Amal fighters were active along the fringes of the "Security Zone," where they carried out various operations against the Israelis and their Lebanese surrogates. Unlike Ḥizbullāh, Amal combatants fought on two fronts in the 1980s—in the south against Israel and its local allies, and in the civil war that raged in and around Beirut until it was contained in 1989.

The high point of Amal's organized military power was in the Beirut war theater in 1984, where its fighters confronted the central government. After heavy shelling of the densely populated southern suburbs by the army, Nabih Berri called successfully on Shīʿī soldiers to lay down their arms. It was clear, however, that Amal had become the dominant force of the moment in West Beirut.

Given the extant hatreds, Amal did not need much prodding to suppress surviving PLO positions in the Shīʿī environs of Beirut where its militiamen held sway. Clashes dubbed the "war of the camps" that were fueled by Syrian arms and assistance continued sporadically until 1988.

Amal's ascendancy, however, was promptly checked, when a tactical alliance with the Druze leader Walīd Jumblatt crumbled and fears of Shīʿī suzerainty among the Sunnī Muslims sparked a variety of organizational ripostes. Amal's moment of singular power was over.

Competition and Cooperation with Ḥizbullāh. Amal, an organization that had promised in the early 1980s to become the dominant organizational voice for the Shīʿīs, faced a serious erosion in its following in later years. Ineffective and even incompetent leadership, corruption, and more than a modicum of arrogance have undermined its support, especially in the environs of Beirut.

Ḥizbullāh, on the other hand, has emerged since 1982 as a competent, dedicated, and well-led challenger. Although young Shīʿī clerics dominate the leadership of Ḥizbullāh, Ḥizbullāh has been especially effective in recruiting among well-educated Shīʿīs from secular professions, many of whom have lost confidence in Amal. In the May 1988 fighting throughout the Beirut suburbs, which saw Ḥizbullāh triumph over the Amal militia, the Islamic organization's steady success in enlisting Shīʿīs, many of whom are ex-Amal members, was confirmed. Moreover, Amal's relegation to a relatively minor role in the resistance effort in comparison to its rival has also cut into Amal's popular support, as have the extensive public and social services delivered by Ḥizbullāh to residents in areas under its political influence. This negative turn of events for Amal has engendered tensions among its partisans that occasionally erupt into violent confrontations with Ḥizbullāh members. These incidents are nevertheless quickly contained by the leaders of the two organizations in the interest of maintaining the unity among resistance ranks.

For the same reason Amal agreed with Ḥizbullāh to avoid the divisiveness of electoral campaigns for seats in parliament within the resistance area. This has been done since 1992 by placing Amal and Ḥizbullāh candidates on the same electoral ticket for each southern district. In Beirut and the Bekáa-Hermel elections and in the municipal elections, however, political competition between Amal and Ḥizbullāh is unrestrained and elections are hotly contested. The results of the local elections from 1998 on indicate that Amal's fiefdom in the south has suffered some erosion as a result of Ḥizbullāh's rising popularity, while the Party of God dominates the Bekáa and Beirut's southern suburbs. The Shīʿī community, estimated to be at least one million, or 30–35 percent of the total Lebanese population, appears to be divided almost equally between these three areas. In the 2009 elections, Amal secured 13 of the 128 seats in the Lebanese parliament, while Ḥizbullāh garnered 12.

Despite the inroads into Amal's constituency made by Ḥizbullāh, there appear to be serious limits to the latter's capacity to overwhelm its opponent. Many Shīʿīs, for example, find the Party of God's Islamic ideology off-putting, and Amal's secular underpinnings more consistent with Lebanese social norms. In addition, Nabih Berri's ready wit, political astuteness, and well-oiled political machine with which he distributes government largesse to his constituents help him retain the allegiance of supporters and maintain the dynamics that have underpinned Amal's development as a political party and a resistance partner.

Amal in Parliament and on the Battlefield. Amal's transition from a freewheeling militia to a mainstream political organization with considerable strength was made clear in 1992 when its candidates triumphed in Lebanon's first postwar parliamentary elections and quickly formed themselves into a parliamentary bloc. Today, the Reform and Liberation Bloc comprises eight Shīʿī members of Amal and seven "allies" of varying faiths including two "independent" Shīʿīs; all are residents of the south. This bloc is one of the largest in the 128-member parliament.

Amal's emergence as a powerful political actor was further demonstrated in 1992 when Nabih Berri was elected Speaker of the House, a role he has since retained with reelections in 1996, 2000, 2005, and 2009. While these events signaled Amal's coming of political age, they also bore witness to the routinization of the energetic reform and protest movement begun by Mūsā Ṣadr in 1974.

In addition to the prestige of his position and its capacity to divert state funds for communal assistance and Amal's aggrandizement, Berri has used the speaker's podium to defend the resistance in the face of domestic and foreign criticism and threats by Israel and the United States. Since the election of a pro-Western cabinet in 2005 the Amal leader has applied his leadership skills and constitutional prerogatives to help deter any efforts on the part of the government, its 14 March supporters, and foreign backers to eliminate Syrian influence in Lebanon and to disarm Ḥizbullāh and Amal cadres.

Amal's rank-and-file members play their own part in this strategy by adding their considerable numbers to the opposition coalition formed in the fall of 2006 to challenge the government. Spearheaded by Ḥizbullāh, the coalition began a campaign of civil disobedience to pressure the government to provide equal representation in the cabinet for opposition members. If successful, this tactic would have enabled the latter to block any actions by the government deemed unfavorable to opposition objectives.

In 2007 and 2008, members of Amal's parliamentary bloc joined other opposition deputies to derail majority plans to elect a president favorable to its anti-Syrian agenda. Since the Lebanese constitution calls for the presence of two-thirds of the members of parliament to elect a president, Amal MPs and their colleagues simply boycotted the electoral sessions called by the speaker, thus nullifying them, while Berri shut down parliament for long stretches of time after 2005.

Amal continues to play an active role in the resistance, although major military operations against Israel have been denied its cadres since 1998. Amal partisans nonetheless play important supportive roles when called to do so during conflicts between Ḥizbullāh and Israel. During the 2006 Ḥizbullāh-Israel War, Amal fighters patrolled the beaches of the south and manned major intersections of coastal and inland roads. They performed emergency evacuations, helped move humanitarian aid to the battered residents of the south, and located housing for thousands of displaced families in the Bekáa and Beirut. Posted near major installations, these cadres also provided on-the-spot information to Ḥizbullāh field commanders during the heated thirty-three-day land, sea, and air battle. They also participated in the 7 May 2008 attempt to take over Beirut, which resulted in the death of ninety-four, including thirty-five civilians.

A strong supporter of Syria, Amal saw its reputation dwindle after the 2005 assassination of former prime minister Rafīq Ḥarīrī, which led to a Syrian withdrawal of its military troops. While Amal officials boast of their nationalist credentials, competition between Amal and Ḥizbullāh for the hearts and minds of the Shīʿī community remains intense. However, Amal's cooperation with its political rival on critical foreign policy and domestic issues has advanced its own political interests and further empowered Lebanon's Shīʿī community.

[*See also* Ḥizbullāh; Lebanon; *and* Ṣadr, Mūsā al-.]

BIBLIOGRAPHY

Agha, Hussein. "The Syrian-Iranian Axis in Lebanon." In *Lebanon on Hold: Implications for Middle East Peace*, edited by Rosemary Hollis and Nadim Shehadi, pp. 24–31. London: Royal Institute of International Affairs, 1996.

Ajami, Fouad. *The Vanished Imam: Musa al Sadr and the Shia of Lebanon*. Ithaca, N.Y.: Cornell University Press, 1986.

Brom, Shlomo. *Israel and South Lebanon in the Absence of a Peace Treaty with Syria*. Tel Aviv: Jafee Center for Strategic Studies, 1999.

Cobban, Helena. "The Growth of Shiʿa Protest in Lebanon and its Implications for the Future." In *Shiʿism and Social Protest*, edited by Juan R. I. Cole and Nikki R. Keddie, pp. 137–159. New Haven, Conn.: Yale University Press, 1986.

Faour, Ali. "Migration from South Lebanon with a Field Study of Forced Mass Migration." *Population Bulletin* of the *ESCWA* 21 (1981): 27–61.

Harik, Judith Palmer. "The Grass Roots Speak: The 1998 Municipal Elections." In *Hezbollah: The Changing Face of Terrorism*, pp. 94–110. London: I. B. Tauris, 2004.

Harik, Judith. *The Public and Social Services of the Lebanese Militias*. Papers on Lebanon 14. Oxford: Centre for Lebanese Studies, 1994.

Harik, Judith. "Syrian Foreign Policy and State/Resistance Dynamics in Lebanon." *Studies in Conflict and Terrorism* 20 (1997): 249–265.

Harik, Judith, and Hilal Khashan. "Lebanon's Divisive Democracy: The Parliamentary Elections of 1992." *Arab Studies Quarterly* 15, no. 1 (1993): 41–59.

Mallat, Chibli. *Shi'i Thought from the South of Lebanon*. Oxford: Centre for Lebanese Studies, 1988.

Nir, Omri. *Nabih Berri and Lebanese Politics*. New York: Palgrave Macmillan, 2011.

Norton, Augustus Richard. *Amal and the Shi'a: Struggle for the Soul of Lebanon*. Austin: University of Texas Press, 1987.

Picard, Elizabeth. "The Lebanese Shi'a and Political Violence in Lebanon." In *The Legitimization of Violence*, edited by David Apter, pp. 189–233. Basingstoke, U.K.: United Nations Research Institute for Social Development, 1997.

Picard, Elizabeth. "Political Identities and Communal Identities: Shifting Mobilization among the Lebanese Shi'a through Ten Years of War, 1975–1985." In *Ethnicity, Politics, and Development*, edited by Dennis L. Thompson and Dov Ronen, pp. 159–177. Boulder, Colo.: Lynne Riener, 1986.

Shanahan, Rodger. *The Shi'a of Lebanon: Clans, Parties and Clerics*. London: Tauris Academic Studies, 2005.

AUGUSTUS RICHARD NORTON
Updated by JUDITH HARIK
and JOSEPH A. KÉCHICHIAN

AMĀNAH. The word *amānah* (trusteeship) is derived from the Arabic root *a-m-n*. Derivatives of this root revolve around two basic senses, security and confidence. *Amānah* itself can be a verbal noun, meaning, among other senses, being secure from or confided in, and it can refer to something that is entrusted to someone. A notable mention of this term in the Qur'ān is 33:72, "Surely we offered the trust [*al-amānah*] to the heavens and the earth and the mountains, but they refused to undertake it and were afraid of it. But man has assumed it; he was indeed unjust and foolish." The meaning of *amānah* in this verse was interpreted variously by early Muslim authorities, but according to a famous interpretation, *amānah* here refers to a contract, whereby God offers eternal bliss in paradise in return for worshipping him alone and abiding by his rules. The heavens, the earth, and the mountains knew that they would not be able to fulfill their duties in this contract, so they shied away from accepting it. The primordial man, being unjust to himself and foolishly confident of his ability to carry out his duties, accepted it. Thus, *amānah* in this context refers to a primordial contract between God and mankind, whereby the latter is required to obey and worship God in return for divine reward.

Another use of this word is in 4:58, "Surely Allāh commands you to make over trusts [*amānāt*, pl. of *amānah*] to their owners, and when you judge between people you judge with justice; surely Allāh admonishes you with what is excellent." In the Sunnī Qur'ānic exegetical tradition, this verse is often interpreted to refer to the relationship between the Muslim ruler and his subjects. Many early Muslim authorities are reported to have determined Muslim rulers to be the intended addressees of this verse, which establishes a contract between these rulers and their subjects. For example, 'Alī ibn Abī Ṭālib, the Prophet Muḥammad's cousin and fourth successor, held that according to this verse, Muslim subjects only need to obey their rulers if they fulfill the duties mentioned in this verse. What rulers are required to return to their subjects could be any of their rights, such as their shares in the treasury of the state. In other words, the Muslim subjects entrust *their* rights to the ruler who is religiously required to protect them in return for obedience. A similar interpretation of *amānah* in this verse exists in the Imāmī Shī'ī exegesis, although there is a clear inclination to interpret it as referring particularly to the imamate (the political and religious leadership of the Muslim community), which every imam has the duty to hand over to his successor. Likewise, the Prophet Muḥammad is reported to have used the word *amānah* in the context of leadership, warning Muslim rulers of not fulfilling their duties as its trustees.

While 4:58 is not mentioned in all medieval Muslim works on the rights and duties of rulers and subjects in Islam, the famous Sunnī scholar Taqī al-Dīn Ibn Taymīyah (1328) considered it, along with 4:59 ("O you who believe! Obey Allāh and obey the Messenger [Muḥammad] and those of you who are in authority. And if you have a dispute in any matter, refer it to Allāh and the Messenger"), the basis of his long discussion of this subject. In this view, just as the subjects are required to obey their rulers so long as they do not ask them to commit a prohibited act or disobey God, the rulers have the duty to fulfill the terms of their *amānah* (trust) and rule with justice. The fulfillment of the *amānah* and just rule require, among other things (1) appointing the best candidates in leadership positions without consideration of kinship, race, freedom, legal affiliation, friendship, or even the personal feeling of the ruler towards the best fit to the position; (2) the efficient, honest, and fair administration of public monies by collecting them according to Islamic law and redistributing them to those entitled to them; and (3) the application of the Islamic law and punishment of offenders who terrorize people and rob them of their property. Ibn Taymīyah discusses the first of these points at great length, considering appointing anyone other than a person whom the ruler knows to be the most qualified for a particular position to be a betrayal of the *amānah* whose terms Muslim rulers are required to fulfill according to 4:58.

Surprisingly, this use of the Qurʾānic term *amānah* in modern Muslim "reformist" discourse is virtually absent, despite the fact that a central contention in this discourse is that the relationship between the ruler and the people in Islam is contractual. This idea is reminiscent of some aspects of social contract theory, where both rulers and people have rights and duties. The Qurʾān gives a religious sanction to this contract, commanding rulers in straightforward language to be just toward their subjects by fulfilling the terms of the *amānah*.

BIBLIOGRAPHY

Ibn Taymiyyah, Ahmad ibn ʿAbd al-Halim. *Al-Siyasah al-Sharʿiyyah fi Islah al-Raʿi wa al-Raʿiyyah*. Mecca: Dar ʿAlam al-Fawaʾid, n.d.

Lewis, Bernard. "Islam and Liberal Democracy: An Historical Overview." *Journal of Democracy* 7, no. 2 (1996): 52–63.

Tabari, Muḥammad ibn Jarir al-. *Jamiʿ al-Bayan fi Taʾwil Ay al-Qurʾan*. Cairo: Maktabat Mustafa al-Babi al-Halabi, 1954.

Tusi, Muḥammad ibn al-Hasan al-. *Al-Tibyan fi Tafsir al-Qurʾan*. Qom, Iran: al-Muʾassasah, 1992–.

AMR OSMAN

ANARCHISM. *See* Rebellion.

ANAVATAN PARTISI. Turkey was governed from 1983 to 1991 by the Anavatan Partisi (Motherland Party), better known by the Turkish acronym ANAP. It was formed in April 1983 after the military regime that had seized power on 12 September 1980 allowed the return of electoral politics. The junta, which had ruled as the National Security Council (NSC), had dissolved all parties and banned their leaders from political activity for periods of five to ten years. The generals thus hoped to introduce a "new politics" involving people who had little or no prior political experience. ANAP's founder, Turgut Özal (1927–1993), was such a figure; ANAP soon became identified with him as the vehicle for his ambitions.

ANAP Under Özal. Özal was born in Malatya in eastern Turkey into a humble provincial family, his father a minor bank official and his mother, Hafize Hanım, a primary-school teacher. His mother was the stronger influence. She emphasized the importance of education and may have initiated her sons into the Naqshbandī Ṣūfī order, with which he was affiliated. After completing his schooling Özal entered Istanbul Technical University, where he met future politicians like Süleyman Demirel, prime minister in the 1960s and 1970s, and Necmettin Erbakan, prime minister in 1996–1997. He graduated in 1950 and entered the bureaucracy as a technocrat. Özal rose through the ranks and in 1966 became Prime Minister Demirel's technical adviser. The following year he was appointed undersecretary at the State Planning Organization, where he assembled a team of like-minded conservatives, many of whom became prominent in ANAP. When Demirel was ousted by the coup of 12 March 1971, Özal also lost his position. He worked at the World Bank in Washington, D.C., from 1971 to 1973; there he became infatuated with American technology and know-how. Meanwhile his younger brother Korkut Özal joined the Islamist National Salvation Party (Millî Selamet Partisi; MSP), was elected to parliament in 1973, and became a minister in the 1974 coalition of the Republican People's Party (Cumhuriyet Halk Partisi) and the MSP. Turgut Özal ran for election on the MSP ticket in 1977 but lost; had he been elected, he too would have been disqualified from politics by the NSC. In November 1979 he was appointed Demirel's economic adviser, a post he continued to hold under the junta until July 1982, when the "Bankers' Scandal" forced him to resign.

ANAP, Özal claimed, had brought together all the ideological tendencies represented in the recently dissolved parties. The influence of the NSP and the neofascist Nationalist Action Party (Milliyetçi Hareket Partisi, MHP) was especially strong and was reflected in the attempt to reconcile ultranationalism and Islam with the so-called Turkish-Islamic synthesis. ANAP was a center-right party that appealed largely to provincial elements most comfortable with the traditional cultural values generally associated with Islam; for example, ANAP women tended to prefer modest attire, including the head scarf, over fashions imported from the West. Such people had had a peripheral political role in the old system; now they filled the vacuum created by the NSC's policies. Many of the new politicians were technocrats like Özal whose familiarity with the modern world did not go beyond their field of expertise, and they had little appreciation of Western mores or culture; such people formed the Islamist faction. There was also a secular faction to which Özal belonged, with his wife, Semra, an important role model for Turkish women. Özal mediated between these factions and manipulated them to safeguard his own hegemony in the party.

ANAP won the November 1983 elections largely because only parties approved by the NSC were allowed to run, and ANAP seemed to be the one least tied to the military. However, the policies the ANAP government pursued were virtually laid down by the NSC. In economic matters, Özal as prime minister continued to favor free-market and supply-side economics. Ever-rising prices and low wages curbed consumption, enabling Turkey to export its goods and improve its balance of payments. Inflation remained very high, hovering between 60 and 85 percent through the 1980s. In order to stay in power ANAP used patronage with great skill and manipulated the electoral laws to its advantage.

Islamists and Secularists. ANAP largely adopted the policies of the NSC in other areas as well. Despite its promise to restore Kemalism, and thus secularism, as the nation's ideology, the

NSC had promoted Islamic indoctrination in schools as the antidote to social democracy and socialism. It went further than any previous government in making religious lessons a statutory part of the curriculum, countering the previous stress upon critical thinking. The Higher Education Law of 1981 even legislated a dress code for students, forbidding beards for men and head scarves for women; this led to protests in the universities. The Saudi-financed organization Rabita ül-Alem ül-İslâmî (Ar., Rābiṭat al-ʿĀlam al-Islāmī, Muslim World League) was permitted to subsidize the activities of Turkey's Directorate of Religious Affairs in Europe so as to insulate Turkish workers from foreign ideologies. At home, Saudi influence is thought to have worked through the agency of the Intellectuals' Hearth (Aydınlar Ocağı). This body, founded in the mid-1970s, planned political strategies for Islamist parties and factions and attempted to reconcile nationalism and Islam by proposing a synthesis of the two.

The Islamist faction in ANAP, led by Vehbi Dinçerler and Mehmed Keçeciler, fought hard to further the NSC's policies in education. They challenged the theory of evolution, claiming that it served only materialism; like the creationists in America, they wanted "the errors of the theory of evolution exposed and what the Holy Books said about creation to be taught." The Istanbul daily *Cumhuriyet* (9 September 1985) noted that Islamization of education was causing confusion: "Religion speaks of creation, science of evolution: the students are confused as to what to believe."

For ANAP, state support for religious education was also part of its strategy of remaining in power. Qurʿānic schools run by orders like the Naqshbandīyah and the Qādirīyah were patronized in return for political support. State-run schools for chaplains and preachers (the İmam Hatip schools) also flourished under ANAP, so that in the 1980s religious education had overtaken secular education—especially in English—and the latter became the preserve of the upper classes.

This strategy failed to bring political rewards in an atmosphere of economic stagnation and high inflation. The voters refused to elect Islamist parties. Despite its generous use of patronage, ANAP's vote in the 1987 elections declined to 36 percent from 45 percent in 1983. The Welfare Party (Refah Partisi, the MSP reincarnated) failed to win even the 10 percent necessary to enter parliament. Thereafter ANAP's fortunes declined until its popularity had slipped below 20 percent. A struggle between the nationalist and Islamist factions followed Özal's election as Turkey's eighth president in October 1989. Mesut Yılmaz's election as ANAP's leader in June 1991 suggested that the modern wing had won, but the party's defeat in the October 1991 elections left its future in the balance. Throughout the 1990s, ANAP continued to play a secondary role in coalition politics. President Süleyman Demirel even appointed Mesut Yılmaz prime minister in June 1997 when Necmettin Erbakan was virtually forced to resign. Yılmaz was himself forced to resign under accusations of corruption. That marked the eclipse of ANAP as a political force, and it failed to enter parliament in the general election of November 2003. After the 2003 election members of the party were absorbed into center-right parties of Turkey, including the governing Adalet ve Kalkınma Partisi (AKP; Justice and Development Party).

Bibliography

Ahmad, Feroz. "Islamic Reassertion in Turkey." *Third World Quarterly* 10, no. 2 (April 1988): 750–769.

Ahmad, Feroz. *The Making of Modern Turkey*. London: Routledge, 1993.

Ahmad, Feroz. "The Transition to Democracy in Turkey." *Third World Quarterly* 7, no. 2 (April 1985): 211–226.

Ergüder, Üstün. "The Motherland Party, 1983–1989." In *Political Parties and Democracy in Turkey*, edited by Metin Heper and Jacob M. Landau, pp. 152–169. London: I. B. Tauris, 1991.

Kedourie, Sylvia, ed. *Turkey: Identity, Democracy, Politics*. London: Frank Cass, 1996.

Tapper, Richard, ed. *Islam in Modern Turkey: Religion, Politics, and Literature in a Secular State*. London: I. B. Tauris, 1991.

FEROZ AHMAD

ANDALUSIA. The name "Andalusia," for Muslim Spain, is derived from "al-Andalus," the name used in Arabic sources to indicate those parts of the Iberian peninsula under Muslim control between the initial invasion of 711 CE and the fall of Granada in 1492 CE. The extent of this territory varied considerably over nearly eight centuries of Muslim rule, ranging from an early hold on most of the peninsula to the small Nasrid kingdom of Granada during Muslim Spain's final two and a half centuries. Modern Spain's southernmost autonomous region, Andalucía, reflects the legacy of Islamic rule in southern Spain but should not be confused with historical Andalusia.

Political History. The Muslim invasion of Spain followed the conquest of North Africa, which was completed in the early 700s. Apparently without consulting the Umayyad caliph in Damascus, the North African governor Mūsā ibn Nuṣayr authorized Ṭāriq ibn Ziyād to lead a primarily Berber army into the Iberian peninsula in 711 and he defeated the Visigothic King Roderic that same year. Mūsā followed with a larger army, laying the foundations for a new province centered in Córdoba. Additional military expeditions by the early Andalusian governors reached across the Pyrenees before being repelled by the Frankish ruler Charles Martel in 732; thereafter, small Christian kingdoms retained control of most of the lands north of the Duero River.

Andalusia's distance from the caliphal center of power increased after the ʿAbbāsids defeated the Umayyads in 750 and established their capital in Baghdad. One member of the Umayyad dynasty, ʿAbd al-Raḥmān I (r. 756–788), fled west, where in 756 he established a new Umayyad emirate in Iberia, independent of the ʿAbbāsid caliphate. The region was torn by revolts and civil wars throughout the ninth century. The eighth Umayyad *amīr*, ʿAbd al-Raḥmān III (r. 912–961), eventually unified it and enjoyed a long reign characterized by economic prosperity and intellectual and artistic development. In 929 he proclaimed himself caliph, the legitimate ruler of all Sunnī Muslims, a move that symbolized the wealth and power of Córdoba and served as a countermeasure to the recently established Shīʿī Fāṭimid caliphate in North Africa.

Following the fruitful reigns of ʿAbd al-Raḥmān III and his son, the caliphate began to disintegrate as several contenders vied for control in the late tenth and early eleventh centuries, and in 1031, the last caliph was deposed. Centralized authority was replaced by petty principalities known as *ṭawāʾif*, or factions, ruled by rival "party kings" whose shifting alliances included strategic relationships with Christian kingdoms. In 1085, Alfonso VI captured Toledo, marking a significant advance in the ongoing Reconquest of Spain.

In response to Christian expansion, the *ṭawāʾif* kings appealed to the Almoravids, a North African Berber dynasty centered in Marrakech. Led by their ruler Yūsuf ibn Tāshufīn (r. 1061–1106), the Almoravid army crossed into Andalusia and won a major victory against Alfonso VI in 1086 at al-Zallaka. The Almoravids were unable to retake Toledo, but reunified Muslim Spain by assuming control of the *ṭawāʾif*. By the mid-twelfth century the Almoravids were replaced by the Almohads, a reformist movement originating in southern Morocco. Although the Almohads maintained Muslim control over much of the peninsula until the early thirteenth century, the Reconquest continued to gain ground, reaching a decisive point in 1212 with the defeat of the Almohads at the Battle of Las Navas de Tolosa. Muslim political unity again gave way to small states that were conquered by the Christian kingdoms over the next quarter century, including Córdoba (1236), Valencia (1238), and Seville (1248). After Ferdinand of Aragón and Isabel of Castile unified their kingdoms near the end of the fifteenth century, the Catholic monarchs completed the Reconquest with the surrender of Granada in 1492. Jews were expelled from Spain the same year, and forced conversion of Muslims followed in the first decade of the sixteenth century; by the early seventeenth century, these last crypto-Muslims, or Moriscos, were also expelled.

Muslims, Christians, and Jews. The population of Andalusia comprised a rich mixture of ethnic and religious groups. Berbers formed the majority of the initial conquering armies, and continued to migrate to Andalusia in later centuries. Originally, Arabs were a small minority, but their numbers rapidly increased as a result of intermarriage with the local Hispano-Roman population as well as through patron–client relationships. The number of Muslims in Andalusia also increased exponentially, through both reproduction and conversion. Although the local population was not forced to convert, they had ample political and socioeconomic incentives for doing so. Muslims are estimated to have become the majority in Andalusia by the mid-tenth century.

The local Iberian population under Visigothic rule had been primarily Christian, with a small Jewish minority. Muslim rule permitted these groups to retain their religious identities as *dhimmīs*, or protected peoples, provided they submitted to Muslim authority and paid a special tax. Andalusian Christians and Jews became increasingly Arabized over time, and by the twelfth century, Arabic had replaced Latin and the Romance languages as the dominant spoken language.

The term *convivencia*, or living together, is often used to describe the coexistence of these three religious communities in Islamic Spain. In Spanish historiography, this concept has tended to refer to mutual cultural influence alongside a competitive rivalry. More recently, *convivencia* has come to represent the romanticized vision of a uniquely tolerant and symbiotic pluralism, a version of Andalusian *convivencia* especially attractive to those striving to improve interreligious relations between the Islamic world and the West.

Supporters of a romanticized *convivencia* highlight the flowering of a Hebrew Golden Age among Jewish intellectuals and poets living under Muslim rule, the influential positions held by some Jews and Christians within Muslim administrations, and culturally hybrid forms of architecture and poetry. Critics of this romantic view of interreligious relations stress that conflict and violence were also an integral part of ethnic and religious coexistence in medieval Spain.

Islamic Thought. Islamic scholarship in Andalusia centered on the development of legal literature in general and the Mālikī school of law in particular. Immediately following the conquest, Andalusian judicial practice was based on that of the Syrian jurist al-Awzāʿī (d. 774). The doctrines of Medina's Mālik ibn Anas (d. 795) were introduced during the reign of al-Hishām I (r. 788–796), supplanting those of al-Awzāʿī and becoming the dominant legal school in Andalusia from the reign of al-Hishām's son al-Ḥakam I (r. 796–822) forward. By the tenth century, the Mālikī school had solidified its position as the official caliphal school and was followed by most Andalusian jurists. Thereafter, the Andalusian Mālikī school faced only two significant competitors: the strictly literalist and now-defunct Ẓāhirī school and the reformist creed of the Almohad dynasty. Both challenges were overcome, and Mālikī scholars from this region made important contributions to the elaboration of school doctrine throughout Andalusian history.

Sufism, theology, and philosophy were not seriously cultivated, especially by Andalusian scholars trained in the religious sciences, until the eleventh century. In the twelfth century, a number of prominent masters aided the spread of Sufism, but it was not embraced as widely as in North Africa.

Artistic and Scientific Heritage. Andalusia was a thriving cultural center, celebrated for the brilliant literary, artistic, and scientific accomplishments of its poets, scholars, and craftsmen. This was particularly true of tenth-century Córdoba, which was described by a contemporary poet as the "ornament of the world" and boasted a caliphal library with an estimated 400,000 volumes. Among these collected works were Arabic translations of Greek philosophical and scientific works and Persian and Indian astronomical and mathematical treatises. Córdoba's caliphs also collected original Arabic religious and scientific works drawn from both Andalusia and the greater Muslim world.

Much of this accumulated intellectual wealth was subsequently transferred to Christian Europe. Toledo's "school of translators," particularly active in the twelfth century, translated Arabic texts into Latin, Hebrew, and the Romance languages; many of the multilingual translators were Arabized Jews. One of the most influential works translated from Arabic into Latin in thirteenth-century Spain was an extensive set of commentaries on the works of Aristotle, composed by the Córdoban jurist and philosopher Ibn Rushd al-Ḥafīd (1126–1198), known in the West as Averroës.

The legacy of Andalusia also remains tangible in the form of unique architectural monuments. The Great Mosque of Córdoba incorporated local Roman and Visigothic elements while evoking the Great Mosque of Damascus and reinforcing the *amīr*'s Umayyad lineage. The mosque remains largely intact despite the insertion of a cathedral in the sixteenth century. Madīnat al-Zahrā', the legendary palace city begun by ʿAbd al-Raḥmān III in 939, was destroyed in the civil wars that brought down the caliphate but has been partially restored. Under the Almoravids and Almohads, the art and architecture of Andalusia both influenced and were influenced by that of North Africa. The most important remaining Almohad monument in Spain is La Giralda, the beautiful minaret of the former Great Mosque of Seville (begun in 1172), now converted into a cathedral belltower. Granada's Alhambra (Ar., al-Ḥamrā', "The Red"), dating primarily from the fourteenth and fifteenth centuries, remains one of the most celebrated architectural monuments in the Islamic world.

[*See also* ʿAbbāsid Caliphate; Expansion of Islam; Fāṭimid Dynasty; *and* Umayyad Caliphate.]

BIBLIOGRAPHY

Clarke, Nicola. *The Muslim Conquest of Iberia: Medieval Arabic Narratives*. London and New York: Routledge, 2011. A rich collection of local and regional texts offering a detailed and nuanced narrative of the Muslim conquest of the Iberian peninsula.

Harvey, L. P. *Islamic Spain, 1250 to 1500*. Chicago: University of Chicago Press, 1990. Provides particularly good coverage of the various Mudéjar communities and the kingdom of Granada.

Jayyusi, Salma Khadra, ed. *The Legacy of Muslim Spain*. 2d ed. 2 vols. Leiden: Brill, 1994. A comprehensive collection of essays on aspects of Islamic Spain including political history, economy, literature, music, art and architecture, religion, and science.

Mann, Vivian B., Thomas F. Glick, and Jerrilynn D. Dodds, eds. *Convivencia: Jews, Muslims, and Christians in Medieval Spain*. New York: George Braziller, 2007. A richly illustrated collection of essays covering literature, architecture, science, and the concept of *convivencia*.

Menocal, María Rosa, Raymond P. Scheindlin, and Michael Sells, eds. *The Literature of Al-Andalus*. New ed. Cambridge, U.K.: Cambridge University Press, 2006. A rich collection of essays covering Iberian Muslim, Christian, and Jewish literature, music, art, and architecture.

Reilly, Bernard F. *The Medieval Spains*. Cambridge, U.K.: Cambridge University Press, 2000. A good single-volume introduction to medieval Spanish history before, during, and after Muslim rule.

JOCELYN HENDRICKSON
Updated by RONALD BRUCE ST JOHN

APOSTASY. In classical Islamic law apostasy (*riddah*) is understood to be a reversion from the religion of Islam to unbelief. This may occur in a number of ways, including denying the existence of God or his attributes or refusing to accept any one of the fundamentals of religion, such as the five obligatory daily prayers or declaring something prohibited (*ḥarām*) that is clearly permissible (*ḥalāl*). Muslim jurists classified acts or behaviors that could take a person out of Islam into three categories: those that related to belief, action, or utterance.

The jurists also set down certain qualifications to define who could commit apostasy. Legally, *riddah* could only be committed out of free will by someone of adult age and of sound mind. Jurists agreed that both men and women could become apostates. The penalty for apostasy is death according to the almost unanimous agreement of the classical Muslim jurists.

Although the punishment of death has fallen into disuse in much of the Muslim world today, the civil penalties associated with apostasy are still commonly enforced. These can relate to property ownership, marriage, and inheritance. For the Mālikīs, as well as some Shāfiʿīs and Ḥanbalīs, an apostate's right to own property was suspended until his or her situation, in terms of Islam, became clear. For the majority of jurists apostates also lost the right to dispose of their property. Upon returning to Islam their rights were fully restored.

Under classical Islamic law, if either party to a marriage committed apostasy, the marriage contract was immediately nullified. The jurists disagreed, however, on whether a new marriage had to be conducted if the apostate returned to Islam. This was the view of the Mālikīs and Ḥanafīs, but the Shāfiʿī and Shīʿī schools held that an apostate's marriage was simply in a state of suspension: if the apostate repented during his wife's waiting period (*ʿiddah*) the marriage could be reinstated. Any children born prior to the apostasy of their parents were to be considered Muslim.

The jurists determined that an apostate may not inherit, even from those of another religion. In the event of a person dying while in a state of apostasy, most of the classical legal schools declared that the apostate's property would be appropriated by the state treasury. According to the Ḥanafī school of law, however, any property that had been acquired before the deceased committed apostasy could be passed on to the apostate's heirs, while any property accumulated afterwards would become the property of the state treasury; for a female apostate, her entire estate passed to her Muslim heirs.

Concerning the penalty for apostasy, there was general agreement among the jurists that apostasy required a sentence of death (*qatl*), and this must be applied. This consensus was often justified on the basis of prophetic traditions (*ḥadīth*). The first (and perhaps the most important) tradition cited in support of the death penalty was the *ḥadīth* "Whoever changes his religion, kill him." This *ḥadīth* is of the solitary type (*āḥād*), although it is considered authentic by Sunnī Muslims because of its inclusion in collections of *ḥadīth* by authoritative figures such as al-Bukhārī. Other similar traditions are also used to support the death penalty.

Although there was unanimous agreement among classical jurists on this punishment, a number of Muslim scholars today argue against the death penalty. They note that the Qurʾān never calls for punishing apostasy with death, despite the subject of apostasy occurring several times in the Qurʾān. Verses such as 2:217 and 3:86–91 clearly envisage a natural death for the apostate. Verse 16:106 refers to the punishment of the "wrath of God" awaiting the apostate. Verse 22:11 also makes no reference to temporal punishment. Moreover, 4:137 seems to provide a strong argument against the death penalty for apostasy because it refers to those who repeatedly believe and then disbelieve, yet a worldly punishment is not specified for these repeat offenders.

Critics of the death penalty have also reconsidered those traditions that appear to support the death penalty. For the critics of the death penalty the *ḥadīth* "Whoever changes his religion, kill him" is a general (*ʿāmm*) command that needs specification (*takhṣīṣ*). In its general form it may apply equally to cases that fall outside its intended scope, as, for example, to Christians who convert to Judaism or Islam. Given that this is an unlikely interpretation, classical jurists recognized a number of exceptions. Several Muslim scholars today have also followed this reasoning and argued for further exceptions.

To make this *ḥadīth* more specific, recourse is often made to others. According to one *ḥadīth*, it is the person "who repudiates his religion and separates himself from the [Muslim] community" (*al-tārik al-islām al-mufāriq li-l-jamāʿa*) who is to be executed. A number of versions of this *ḥadīth* exist, including one that says: "And a man who leaves Islam and engages in fighting against God and His Prophet shall be executed, crucified, or exiled." Critics argue that this version makes a clear connection between apostasy and fighting against the Muslim community. Such evidence suggests that the punishment of death is meant for those who not only repudiate Islam but join the enemy and aim to inflict harm upon the Muslim community and Islam. As such the issue of apostasy could be said to be largely a political issue, and less a religious one.

For those who criticize the death penalty, the Qurʾān emphasizes that no one should be forced to embrace Islam; all have the freedom to choose their belief system in this life (6:1–8). The Qurʾān rejects forced conversion, as in the well-known verse "There shall be no coercion in matters of faith" (2:256). Indeed, a strong theme of personal responsibility runs through the Qurʾān. According to 16:9, God's plan for humankind is not that everyone should follow the same path. Instead, all will be asked about their actions on the Day of Judgment, and individuals will ultimately bear the responsibility for that choice. This also applies to Muslims, and a number of Qurʾānic verses refer to the serious consequences of rejecting Islam.

Although the issue of apostasy is still of great concern in Muslim-majority states, there are changes taking place today regarding religious freedom, such as the move away from implementing the death penalty for apostasy. There have also been new initiatives to recognize, to some extent, the beliefs of other religious groups and to promote interfaith dialogue. Leading Muslim thinkers such as Mohammad Hashim Kamali and Taha Jabir al-Alwani argue that freedom of religion, including the freedom to change and renounce one's faith, is supported by the Qurʾānic position that there is no coercion in matters of faith. Despite these views and positions, among Muslims there is still strong opposition to rethinking the death penalty for apostasy.

[*See also* Religious Beliefs.]

BIBLIOGRAPHY

al-Jazīrī, ʿAbd al-Rahmān. *Min kitāb al-fiqh ʿalā l-madhāhib al-arbaʿa*. Vol. 5. Beirut: Dār al-Fikr, n.d.

Ibn Qudāma. *al-Mughnī*. Vol. 8. Riyadh: Maktabat al-Riyāḍ al-Ḥadītha, n.d.

Kamali, Mohammad Hashim. *Freedom of Expression in Islam*. Cambridge, U.K.: Islamic Text Society, 1994.

Peters, Rudolph, and Gert J. J. de Vries. "Apostasy in Islam." *Die Welt des Islams*, n.s., 17 (1976–1977): 1–25.

Saeed, Abdullah, and Hassan Saeed. *Freedom of Religion, Apostasy, and Islam*. Aldershot, U.K.: Ashgate, 2004.

Shawkānī, Muḥammad b. ʿAlī al-. *Nayl al-Awtār*. Vol. 7. Beirut: Dār al-Kutub al-ʿIlmiyya, n.d.

Subaşi, Turgut. "The Apostasy Question in the Context of Anglo-Ottoman Relations, 1843–44." *Middle Eastern Studies* 38 (2002): 1–34.

Zuhayli, Wahba al-. *al-Fiqh al-islāmi wa-adillatuhu*. Vol. 6. Damascus: Dār al-Fikr, 1997.

ABDULLAH SAEED

AQḤIṢĀRĪ, ḤASAN KĀFĪ AL-. Ḥasan ibn Ṭūrkhān ibn Dāwud ibn Yaʿqūb al-Aqḥisārī (1544–1615 or 1616) was a prominent Bosnian *qāḍī* (judge) and scholar from the village of Prusac (known in Ottoman times as Aqḥisār). The most important source for Ḥasan Kāfī's life is his own autobiography, still unedited but translated into English. According to this account, Ḥasan Kāfī spent his youth in his native village, then traveled to Istanbul for his education. After some time in the capital, he was appointed to the office of *qāḍī* in the district of Sirem (north of Belgrade). Subsequently, he was appointed to a permanent judgeship in Aqḥīsār and a pension contingent upon his teaching the students of the region. He is said to have founded a village named Banū Ābād close to Aqḥiṣār with a mosque, *madrasah*, Sufi lodge, library, bathhouse, and a caravansary for travelers. The famous Ottoman traveler Evliyaʾ Çelebi (d. 1683) visited Ḥasan Kāfī's grave after his death and describes his uncorrupted corpse as a place of local piety. The Ottoman poet and scholar Nevʿīzāde (d. 1634) also reported that he was engaged in the persecution of the Balcan disputed Sufi order of the Ḥamzawiyya, but al-Aqḥisārī does not mention this episode in his autobiography.

Ḥasan Kāfī participated in the Ottoman campaign of Eğri (Eger, Hungary) against the Austrians in 1596. During this expedition he presented to the highest representatives of the sultan his most famous work, *Uṣūl al-ḥikam fī niẓām al-ʿalam* (The Principles of Wisdom Regarding the Order of the World), a short treatise on good government that he had composed the year before. The book was originally written in Arabic, then translated into Ottoman Turkish by Ḥasan Kāfī himself, so that it could be read by the sultan and used by the court (*divan*) officials.

Uṣūl al-ḥikam fī niẓām al-ʿalam is a short work in which the author reacts to the social, economic, military, and political crisis of the Ottoman empire at the turn of the sixteenth century. Ḥasan Kāfī analyzes the causes for the crisis and proposes remedies to what was perceived within the Ottoman government as a calamitous period of decline. *Niẓām* ("order") is the conceptual pivot of this booklet. It is in the renewal and the corroboration of a (temporarily) lost social, military, and political order that resides the key to stability. On the contrary, confusion, turbulence, disorder, and depravation redundantly occur to represent the current state of affairs. Al-Aqḥiṣārī's advice is meant to restore this lost harmony.

The treatise is divided into an introduction and three chapters. The introduction (*muqaddimah*) focuses on the societal order that was established by God to keep society stable and harmonious. Men are divided into four classes: the rulers and the military, scholars and pious men, farmers, and artisans and traders, each class having its own duties. To prevent disorder, each person should accept the role assigned to him and fulfill his obligations to society.

In the first chapter following the introduction, Ḥasan Kāfī expands on the bases of public order, namely, justice and good governance (*ḥusn al-siyāsah*). These are achieved by delegating power to the most suitable people, by constant consultation of the rulers with religious scholars, and by generosity with the subjects. The second chapter develops further the importance of taking counsel from religious scholars and those who have experience in government. The third chapter focuses on military matters and recommends greater control of the armies by their commanders and adoption of the most advanced military technology. When a region is conquered, the local governors should be replaced to avoid future rebellions, as happened in Transylvania, Moldavia, and Walachia at that time (1596). What brings about victory is piety, rectitude, observance of religious duties, and enduring reliance upon God. The sultan should exhort and reward his soldiers but also punish them severely if they flee from battle. Soldiers should not fight for material reasons but to glorify God's word. What brings about defeat is disobedience and rebellion. Finally, in a somewhat surprising departure from the preceding discussion, Ḥasan Kāfī ends the book by writing that peaceful resolution of conflicts is to be preferred to the hardships of war.

Each chapter presents an explicit reference to the circumstances of the author's time: soldier rebellions, turmoil in the countryside and the subsequent migrations to cities, recruitment of farmers into the army, technological military superiority of the Austrians, economic crisis, corruption of the elite, and the growing isolation of the Sultan. These elements were highly prized by modern scholars when examining al-Aqḥiṣārī's work as an important source for the late sixteenth-century crisis.

A more promising approach considers *Uṣūl al-ḥikam*as an example of the sixteenth- and seventeenth-century Ottoman "literature of decline." In fact, *Uṣūl al-ḥikam* belongs to the long-standing genre of *naṣīḥat al-mulūk* (advice to kings), which was meant to offer rulers practical recommendations and moral guidance and was usually written by people familiar with state administration. *Uṣūl al-ḥikam* reflects the viewpoint of a provincial *qāḍī*on the concepts of Ottoman legitimacy and sovereignty but is also part of a specific intellectual climate which was voiced through the classical tropes and topoi of this literature (order, justice, piety) combined with the stress on military strength. Sayings of the Prophet Muḥammad, Alexander the Great, and Ardashīr, the founder of the Sassanid dynasty, are interspersed throughout the book. In this way, Ḥasan Kāfī blends his political advice with the literary history of the great empires of the past. But the treatise also reflects the author's particular class interests and, probably, his attempt to ascend into the circle of educated bureaucrats who usually composed the "mirrors for princes" literature. Some twentieth-century scholars detect in *Uṣūl al-ḥikam* a radical reformist attitude and thus see it as a forerunner of the Ottoman reformist movements that emerged in the late eighteenth century (Tlili, 1974).

Today, Ḥasan Kāfī al-Aqḥiṣārī represents a major reference point in the revival of the Bosniac Islamic legacy, in the spirit of which some of his theological works are now being edited. In spite of this, his theological views remain to be studied, and many of his works are still in manuscript form.

BIBLIOGRAPHY

Aqḥiṣārī, Ḥasan Kāfī al-. *Uṣūl al-ḥikam fī niẓām al-ʿalam*. Edited by Iḥsān Ṣidqī al-ʿAmd. Kuwait: Dhāt al-Salāsīl, 1987.

Babinger, Franz. *Die Geschichtsschreiber der Osmanen und ihre Werke*. Leipzig: Otto Harrassowitz, 1927. See esp. pp. 144–145.

Howard, Douglas A. "Ottoman Historiography and the Literature of 'Decline' of the Sixteenth and Seventeenth Centuries." *Journal of Asian History* 22, no. 1 (1988): 52–77.

Mehmed, Mustafa A. "La crise ottomane dans la vision de Hasan Kiafi Akhisari (1544–1616)." *Revue des Etudes Sud-Est Européenne* 13 (1975): 385–402. This article stresses the importance of *Uṣūl al-ḥikam* as a factual source of the history of the causes of the so-called Ottoman decline.

Petráček, Karel. "Die Chronologie der Werke von Ḥasan al-Kāfī al-Aqḥīṣārī." *Archiv Orientální* 27, no. 1 (1959): 407–412.

Tlili, Béchir. "Aux origines de la pensée réformiste ottomane moderne: Un important document du Sayh al-Aqhisari (XVII° s)." *Revue de l'Occident Musulman et de la Méditerranée* 18 (1974): 131–148.

CATERINA BORI

ARAB-ISRAELI CONFLICT.

Overview

The origins of the Arab-Israeli conflict can be traced back more than a century, when Jews, disillusioned with prospects for integration into European societies, began to migrate to Palestine in 1882. In 1897, the First Zionist Congress called for the creation of a Jewish homeland in Palestine, thus spawning the modern Jewish national movement, Zionism. The land, which the Jews considered theirs by virtue of God's will and historic rights, was, however, inhabited by another people, the Palestinians, who had lived there for centuries.

The first Jewish immigrants to Palestine did not encounter resistance from the local population. Only decades later was the Zionist movement perceived as a threat by the indigenous Palestinian population, as well as by other Arabs. In the Balfour Declaration of 1917, British foreign minister Lord Balfour promised a "national home for the Jewish People" in Palestine. This move by the British government resulted in an eruption of violence that continued, intermittently, into the twenty-first century. The Palestinians were further alienated by the massive Zionist immigration to Palestine, which had brought the number of Jews from 24,000 in 1881 (less than 5 percent of the total population) to 85,000 by 1914 (12 percent). Immigration intensified further following the Balfour Declaration and the rise of Nazism in Germany in 1933, swelling the number of Jewish immigrants to 368,845 by 1945. In Jerusalem (Arabic: al-Quds) alone, the most significant city in Palestine for both Jews and Arabs (Muslim and Christian alike), the number of Jews grew from 53,000 in 1931 to 70,000 in 1935.

In 1936 the Palestinians began a revolt against British policy in Palestine that lasted until 1939. One of the leaders of this revolt was al-Ḥājj Amīn al-Ḥusaynī, mufti of Jerusalem and president of the Supreme Muslim Council in Mandatory Palestine. When the revolt began, al-Ḥājj Amīn assumed the presidency of the Arab Higher Committee.

Britain's regional strategic considerations during the rise of German military power and its fear of losing credibility with the Arabs forced it in subsequent years to balance its policy in Palestine. This led to the White Paper of 17 May 1939, in which the British government seemed to accept the Palestinian demand for national independence with an Arab majority (within ten years), restricting Jewish immigration to Palestine and the sale of lands to the Jews. This angered the Jews, who were meanwhile building a formidable military force and a complex social infrastructure.

United Nations Resolution 181. Resolution 181 of the United Nations, issued on 29 November 1947, recommended the partition of Palestine into an Arab state and a Jewish state but failed to avert a conflict. David Ben-Gurion—one of the founders of the Jewish state and later the first prime minister of Israel—and the other Zionist leaders reluctantly accepted the UN resolution, because they understood that this was the best the Jewish community in Palestine could achieve under the given circumstances. The Arabs, however, elected to fight to reverse what they considered an injustice that would force them to relinquish parts of their homeland.

After approximately six months of fighting between Arab and Jewish forces (December 1947–May 1948), the Palestinian and Arab volunteer forces were defeated, and on 14 May 1948, Ben-Gurion announced the establishment of the Jewish state of Israel in parts of historic Palestine. As a result of the war, approximately three-quarters of the 10,400 square miles (27,000 square kilometers) of Palestinian land came under the control of the state of Israel; the remaining portions—the West Bank and the Gaza Strip—came under the control of Jordan and Egypt, respectively. More than one million Palestinians fled or were forced to leave by the Israeli forces. Many Palestinian cities, above all, the western part of Jerusalem, were largely abandoned by the Arab Palestinian population.

From Suez to the June 1967 War. Nine years after winning its first battle against Palestinian and Arab forces, Israel collaborated with France and Britain in defeating the Egyptian army in the Suez War of 1956, during which Israeli forces occupied the Sinai and the Gaza Strip. Upset by the fact that Israel, France, and Great Britain had secretly planned the campaign to evict Egypt from the Suez Canal, thus ignoring American interest in the Middle East Region, the United States joined the Soviet Union in a political campaign to force the invading forces to withdraw from the Sinai, the Suez Canal, and the Gaza Strip.

In May 1967, Soviet and Syrian intelligence reports indicated that Israel was massing troops on its border with Syria. Egypt rushed to mobilize troops and station them along the southern borders of Israel, acting on the principle that aggression against any Arab country was aggression against Egypt.

Three weeks of high military and political tension erupted into war on 5 June 1967, when Israel attacked and destroyed the air forces of Egypt, Syria, and Iraq. This defeat in the Six-Day War was a major turning point in the history of the Middle East. In those six days the Israelis occupied the remaining 22 percent of the Palestinian lands. They also reoccupied the Sinai Peninsula and the Golan Heights of Syria, considering it a vital security zone. Gamal Abdel Nasser took full responsibility for the defeat and submitted his resignation as president of Egypt. Because of enormous public pressure, however, he remained in power until his death in 1970.

Ascendance of Local Nationalism. After the Arab defeat in 1967, the Palestine Liberation Organization (PLO), which had been founded in 1964, gradually gained recognition among Palestinians, Arab nations, and their leaders. The PLO began to assert itself as an independent organization in the complex arena of Arab politics and became the champion of the Palestinian cause. The Palestinian issue, despite the efforts of Israel and its supporters, regained its status as the crux of the Arab-Israeli dispute.

Egypt, led by Anwar el-Sadat (r. 1970–1981), continued to see itself and to be seen by others as the heart of the Arab world. The war of October 1973 against the Israeli forces in the Sinai and Golan Heights was intended above all to put Egypt and Syria in a better position to negotiate a political settlement. Sadat's trip to Jerusalem in November 1977 and the subsequent Camp David Accords (signed in September 1978) brought about a "cold peace" between Israel and Egypt. Solving Egypt's economic problems was Sadat's main goal during his presidency, one for which he was willing to sign a peace treaty with Israel. Although it was not a high priority, Sadat also wanted to solve the Palestinian problem; he even negotiated an autonomy plan with the Israelis for the Palestinians, although his formula was not accepted by the Palestinians or by the rest of the Arab world, and dissatisfaction with it brought about Egypt's isolation by the rest of the Arab world for several years and eventually led to Sadat's assassination on 6 October 1981.

Widening of the Conflict. Since the 1967 War, Palestinians have established diplomatic relations with most countries worldwide and have launched guerrilla attacks from any Arab country that has allowed them to do so or could not prevent them, mainly Jordan and Lebanon. However, the PLO lost its bases in Jordan following the September 1970 civil war, which King Hussein (d. 1999) and forces loyal to him launched against the Palestinian organizations. Consequently, the focus of military activity moved to Lebanon, a militarily weaker northern neighbor of Israel. With three hundred thousand Palestinians living there in refugee camps, a weak central government, and sympathy for the Palestinian cause from several political and religious factions, the conditions in Lebanon were conducive to the establishment of a Palestinian military and even social infrastructure.

Responding to repeated Palestinian raids on Israel, most of which had no military value, Israel occasionally launched counterattacks (such as the Litani River Operation in March 1978) and other full-scale military operations. With the cooperation of a Christian military faction led by Saʿd Ḥaddād and his successor, Anṭūn Laḥd, the Israelis created a "security zone" in southern Lebanon to protect their northern settlements from shelling and raids by Palestinian forces and their supporters in Lebanon. The Israeli counterraids on Palestinian positions disrupted the life of the southern Lebanese. Consequently, support for the Palestinians in Lebanon eroded, and the last significant Palestinian military force was eradicated following the Israeli invasion of southern Lebanon (in Operation Peace for Galilee) in June 1982 and the eventual takeover of Beirut. Although PLO forces held out for eighty-two days against the strongest army in the Middle East, they were ultimately forced to leave Lebanon and move their headquarters to Tunis.

The move to Tunis marked the beginning of the end of Palestinian attempts to confront Israel militarily. Already in 1974, Palestinian intellectuals close to the PLO chairman Yasir Arafat wrote several articles hinting at a willingness of the Palestinian leadership to live side by side with a Jewish state. They first proposed a solution based on a secular democratic state in which all parties, Palestinians and Israelis, could live together. Israel reacted negatively to this proposal. The Israeli government felt no pressure to relinquish its claim to the entire Palestinian land. The Palestinians, although in many ways important actors in the Middle East conflict, had limited political and military options, or so it seemed until 9 December 1987, when Palestinians launched their uprising (*intifāḍah*). This sociopolitical endeavor is a major landmark of Palestinian history. The Palestinian people decided to take their fate into their own hands and not wait for salvation from the outside, not even from the PLO. They fought their occupiers with all means available, including stones, knives, boycotts, and strikes. The Israelis adopted even harsher measures than those they had been practicing against the Palestinians since the occupation began in 1967.

In November 1988, in the midst of the *intifāḍah*, the Palestinians, through the PLO, expressed their desire for a historic compromise with the state of Israel, one based on a two-state solution. Once again Israel felt no obligation to respond positively to the proposal. The Palestinian Declaration of Independence and the verbal declarations associated with it, which laid out the new attitude of the Palestinians and their desire to reach a compromise, were overshadowed by other political events.

In August 1990, after Iraqi forces invaded Kuwait, many Palestinians expressed sympathy with Iraq, and the PLO was perceived as doing so as well. The rich Arab Gulf states halted financial aid to the Palestinians, and most living in Kuwait were forced to leave.

From the Madrid Conference to the 1993 Oslo Accords. After the collapse of the Soviet Union and the cooperation between the West and the majority of the Arab world to expel Iraq from Kuwait, the United States and Russia jointly sponsored a peace conference dealing with the Middle East problem. The parties (Israel, Palestinians, Syria, Lebanon, and Jordan) held their first meeting in Madrid on 30 October 1991. The process led nowhere, however, and once again the Palestinians lost hope for a peaceful, let alone just, solution, while the PLO lost further credibility among its supporters.

Meanwhile, however, some Israelis and Palestinians met secretly in Oslo, Norway, and struck an agreement on certain principles for the first stage of Palestinian-Israeli conflict resolution. This agreement was signed by Israel's prime minister and the PLO chairman in Washington, D.C., on 13 September 1993, leading to a major breakthrough in Middle East politics.

The pragmatic Yitzhak Rabin and the visionary Shimon Peres led Israel toward a better future as an integral part of the Middle East, and Yasir Arafat, leader of the PLO and of the Palestinian Authority (PA), concluded that there was no alternative to peace and to a historic compromise with the Jewish national movement. King Hussein of Jordan, whose secret relations with various Israeli leaders were known to almost everyone in the Middle East, signed a peace agreement with Israel in 1994. Israeli leaders, after almost fifty years of boycott, were welcome in many Arab capitals.

Still, many Palestinians and Israelis thought that the Oslo agreement fell short of their vision for peace. Palestinians expressed their opposition through suicide bombings, and Israelis by launching an ugly campaign against Rabin, creating an atmosphere that led to his assassination by an Israeli religious youth in November 1995.

Six months later, with the election of Benjamin Netanyahu as the next prime minister of Israel, a new era of mistrust began in the Middle East. Netanyahu's narrow win brought to power a right-wing coalition. Some aspects of the Oslo agreement were implemented during the three years that this government was in power, but the momentum of the peace process had been lost. Netanyahu's failed policies brought back the Labor Party, headed by General Ehud Barak. Only six days after he was elected in May 1999 and eager to fulfill his campaign promise, Barak withdrew the Israeli army from the security zone in southern Lebanon, confirming the widespread belief that Ḥizbullāh's armed resistance against the Israeli occupation in southern Lebanon had liberated occupied land through armed struggle. This withdrawal convinced many that armed struggle rather than political negotiation was the way to liberate lands occupied by Israel. The Israelis became more reluctant to give up occupied land.

Camp David II. President Clinton, in the final months of his presidency, invited Israeli and Palestinian leaders to a Camp David summit to try to resolve the conflict. The leaders met for two weeks in July 2000 but achieved nothing other than creating conflict among the leaders involved. The Israelis accused the Palestinians of turning down what they considered a very generous offer of the return of 92–95 percent of occupied Palestinian land in exchange for peace. This attempt failed, primarily because of the leaders' inability to reach a final-status agreement on essential issues such as Palestinian refugees and Jerusalem.

Increasing the enormous tensions between the two parties that followed the failure to reach an agreement at Camp David II was the permit granted by Prime Minister Ehud Barak to Ariel Sharon, Israel's opposition leader, to visit the Temple Mount (Ḥaram al-Sharīf) on 28 September 2000. This led to Palestinian mass demonstrations which evolved into open warfare with the Israelis in what has been called the al-Aqṣā or Second Intifāḍah.

Twenty-First Century

Camp David 2000 and the Dissolution of the Peace Process to 2012. George W. Bush, who was elected president of the United States in 2000, admired Ariel Sharon, who shared Netanyahu's determination to expand settlements in the West Bank and the Golan Heights to guarantee their permanent retention by Israel. Sharon pursued these efforts, tolerated in part because of Washington's distraction after the 9/11 al-Qaʿida terrorist attacks on New York and Washington and the decisions to invade Afghanistan and Iraq.

In the midst of these developments, the Arab League in 2002 approved and announced a peace initiative sponsored by Saudi Arabia that would offer Israel full peace with all Arab states in return for Israel's withdrawal from the Golan Heights and from the West Bank, which would permit creation of a Palestinian state with East Jerusalem as its capital. Prime Minister Sharon ignored the offer, as have his successors, including Benjamin Netanyahu, who has headed the Israeli government since 2009.

The question of the Palestinian state became even more contentious with Barack Obama's accession to the U.S. presidency. He and his advisers proposed initiatives to halt Israeli settlement construction as a prelude to Israeli's withdrawal from the West Bank in exchange for a peace agreement with Palestinians. Netanyahu successfully stymied this initiative, at times rejecting it out of hand, and relied on the U.S. Congress to back him against the Obama administration. Domestic political pressures forced Obama to backtrack and to ultimately oppose a Palestinian bid for statehood recognition at the United Nations in 2011.

Nonstate Actors, Demography, and the Arab Spring. Various problems threaten the future of Palestinian-Israeli and Arab-Israeli relations. Ḥamās has controlled the Gaza Strip since Israel's withdrawal of its settlements there in 2005 in order to consolidate its hold on the West Bank. Israel has retained control of most points of entry into and exit from Gaza and has encircled it with barriers. Reports of political reconciliation between the Islamist Ḥamās and Fatah have proved false, in part because neither can agree on the specifics of power sharing arrangements.

In Israel, Netanyahu's Likud Party was reelected in 2013 and formed a government in coalition with parties further to its right who insist on full Israeli retention of the West Bank. Netanyahu has openly pushed settlement expansion in the West Bank proper and in expanded East Jerusalem to bar any possibility of a true two-state solution.

A series of uprisings known as the "Arab Spring" first erupted in Tunisia in December 2010. These popular protests quickly forced out existing regimes in Tunisia, Egypt, and then Libya. The impact of these developments on the Arab-Israeli conflict is as yet unclear. Egypt has pledged to maintain its peace treaty with Israel. Syria has long had a stable truce with Israel, but the Assad government now struggles to retain power as civil strife has intensified. A destabilized Syria could come to resemble Lebanon, where Ḥizbullāh, a Lebanese Shīʿī group initially formed by Iran to resist the Israeli invasion of Lebanon in 1982, has become a significant military force and part of the Lebanese political system. In Syria, however, the strongest militia appears to be a Sunni entity loyal to al-Qaʿida, but equally hostile to Israel.

The prospects of further destabilization of Arab governments on Israel's peripheries may well further threaten Israeli security at a time when the Palestinian Arab population of Gaza, Israel, and the West Bank now equals Israel's Jewish population and will soon exceed it. This combination of the Palestinian demographic threat to Israel's dominance in the occupied territories, coupled with external challenges from destabilized states on Israel's borders will create new challenges to regional stability in the near future.

[*See also* Arab Nationalism; Ḥamās; Ḥizbullāh; International Relations and Diplomacy; Israel; Jerusalem; Nasser, Gamal Abdel; Organization of Islamic Cooperation; Palestine; *and* Palestine Liberation Organization.]

BIBLIOGRAPHY

Anglo-American Committee of Inquiry. *A Survey of Palestine*, Vol. 1. Washington, D.C.: Institute for Palestine Studies, 1991. Reprint; originally published in 1946.

Barrett, Roby C. *The Greater Middle East and the Cold War: U.S. Foreign Policy under Eisenhower and Kennedy*. London and New York: I. B. Tauris, 2007.

Center for Policy Analysis on Palestine. *Facts and Figures about the Palestinians*. Washington, D.C.: Center for Policy Analysis on Palestine, 1992.

Flapan, Simha. *The Birth of Israel: Myths and Realities*. New York: Pantheon, 1987.

Kimmerling, Baruch, and Joel S. Migdal. *Palestinians: The Making of a People*. New York: Free Press, 1993.

Kurtzer, Daniel C., and Scott B. Lasensky, eds. *Negotiating Arab-Israeli Peace: American Leadership in the Middle East*. Washington, D.C.: United States Institute of Peace Press, 2008.

Lesch, David W., and Mark L. Haas, ed. *The Middle East and the United States: A Historical and Political Reassessment*. 5th ed. Boulder, Colo.: Westview, 2013.

Moinuddin, Hasan. *The Charter of the Islamic Conference and Legal Framework of Economic Co-operation among Its Member States*. New York: Oxford University Press, 1987.

Muslih, Muhammad Y. *The Origins of Palestinian Nationalism*. New York: Columbia University Press, 1988.

Roy, Sara. *Failing Peace: Gaza and the Palestinian-Israeli Conflict*. London: Pluto, 2007.

Shlaim, Avi. *The Iron Wall: Israel and the Arab World*. New York: W. W. Norton, 2000.

Smith, Charles D. *Palestine and the Arab-Israeli Conflict*. 8th ed. Boston: Bedford/St. Martin's, 2013.

Swisher, Clayton E. *The Truth about Camp David: The Untold Story about the Collapse of the Middle East Peace Process*. New York: Nation, 2004.

Tannous, Izzat. *The Palestinians: A Detailed Documented Eyewitness History of Palestine under British Mandate*. New York: IGT, 1988.

Overview by SHUKRI B. ABED
Twenty-First Century by CHARLES D. SMITH

ARAB LEAGUE. Ottoman, British, and French colonial authorities dominated political life throughout much of the Arab world in the nineteenth and twentieth centuries. The first opportunity to regain independence and unity came in the early twentieth century when the Hashemite sharīf, Ḥusayn ibn ʿAlī, ruler of the Hejaz (r. 1916–1924), launched the 1916 Arab revolt against the Ottoman Empire, then the ultimate source of power. Although Britain pledged Ḥusayn its support in his quest to establish a unified Arab state, the British had secretly signed the Sykes-Picot Agreement a month earlier with France, dividing the Arab East between them. London's quest was to strengthen land links to India even if the accord with Paris was duly endorsed by the League of Nations in 1922. Accordingly, Britain secured a mandate over Transjordan and Palestine, while France obtained similar authorization over Syria and present-day Lebanon.

Birth of the Arab League. Sharīf Ḥusayn's sons, particularly Fayṣal and Abdullah, joined several groups to induce London to accept Arab independence and unity. Anthony Eden, then foreign minister of Great Britain, responded to these pressures by declaring in May 1941 that Britain supported the Arab quest for unity through an institution that looked after their interests. Ironically, London simultaneously promised Jewish leaders its favorable view for the establishment of an independent Jewish State in Palestine. Abdullah and Fayṣal supported the idea of an Arab League that would include Syria, Lebanon, Palestine, Jordan, and Iraq, but Britain, wary of a rising Arab power, preferred to headquarter the group in Egypt, the center for British activities in the region, and excluded Palestine.

Throughout 1943 and 1944, Egyptian leaders discussed with officials and representatives from Iraq, Transjordan, Saudi Arabia, Syria, Lebanon, Yemen, and Palestine various proposals for some form of union. When these officials consented to an Egyptian proposal for the establishment of an Arab League, representatives of the seven states met in September 1944 in Alexandria, Egypt, and eventually agreed on a specific structure. Member-states retained their respective sovereignties with binding initiatives applied only when unanimously resolved. With these critical accords sealed, and under British tutelage, Arab representatives met in Cairo and signed the Pact of the League of Arab States on 22 March 1945. The founding members were Egypt, Iraq, Jordan (then Transjordan), Lebanon, Saudi Arabia, Syria, and Yemen. In addition to the original members, the following states have joined the League since: Libya (1953); Sudan (1956); Tunisia and Morocco (1958); Kuwait (1961); Algeria (1962); the People's Democratic Republic of Yemen (1967, united in 1990 with the Yemen Arab Republic); Bahrain, Qatar, Oman, and the United Arab Emirates (UAE; 1971); Mauritania (1973); Somalia and Palestine (1974); Djibouti (1977); and Comoros (1993). In January 2003, Eritrea acceded as an observer.

Six Egyptians and a Tunisian have led the League as Secretary-Generals since 1945: Abd al-Rahman Hassan Azzam (1945–1952), Abdul Khalek Hassouna (1952–1972), Mahmoud Riyad (1972–1979), Chedli Klibi (Tunisian, 1979–1990), Dr. Ahmad Esmat Abd El-Meguid (1991–2001), and Amr Moussa (2001–2011). Nabil Elaraby, Egypt's foreign minister, was elected unanimously in May 2011 to succeed Moussa.

The League after 1945. Little of the organization's structure has changed since 1945. The League comprises six major bodies: the Council, the supreme body of the organization, composed of the representatives of the member states; Permanent Commissions, which includes the important Political Committee; the General-Secretariat, comprising the Secretary-General, assistants, and other officials; the Common Defense Council; the Social and Economic Council; and the Specialized Arab Organizations. The goals of these bodies include encouraging close cooperation of the member states in political, security, economic, communications, cultural, social, and financial matters.

In the area of social and economic welfare, numerous joint ventures have been formed, such as the Arab Potash Company, the Arab Maritime Companies, the Arab Satellite Communications Organization, the Arab Monetary Fund, and the Arab Fund for Economic and Social Development. The last two institutions provide financial assistance for social and economic development in the Arab world, especially in the poorer states. Other specialized organizations present recommendations to assist member states in solving socio-economic problems. In the area of cultural cooperation, the Arab Organization for Science, Culture, and Education organizes educational conferences and publishes studies on science and education.

Dissent within the League. The Arab League pact prohibits the use of force for the settlement of disputes between member states, but various cross-border incursions doomed its otherwise remarkable record. Its efforts to mediate such disputes have been largely ineffective.

To counter Egypt's domination of the league, Saudi Arabia, supported by other Arab and Muslim states, founded the Muslim World League (1962), followed by the Islamic Pact (1965) and the Organization of the Islamic Conference (OIC). In March 1979, when Egypt signed a peace treaty with Israel, Arab leaders met in Baghdad, expelled Egypt from the League, moved its headquarters to Tunis, and appointed a Tunisian as the new secretary-general.

Yet, soon after the Baghdad summit, Iraq was at war with Iran (1980–1988), which exacerbated Arab divisions and further weakened the institution. Several Arab leaders, notably King Hussein of Jordan and King Hassan of Morocco, sought to reestablish Arab solidarity. Hussein was instrumental in the return of Egypt to the League during the 1987 Arab Summit in Amman although the August 1990 Iraqi invasion of Kuwait resulted in further divisions. Disgruntled by foreign interferences in Arab affairs, and emasculated of his authority, the Tunisian secretary-general resigned his post. An Egyptian official was appointed in his place at the August 1990 emergency summit, which condemned the Iraqi invasion of a fellow Arab country, even if eight states sided with Baghdad.

These schisms were further accentuated in 1994, when the League voiced strong opposition to the Gulf Cooperation Council's decision to end secondary and tertiary trade embargoes against Israel. The six conservative Arab Gulf monarchies rejected a League rule—that only the Council could make such a policy change—asserting, instead, their rights to act independently. Further divisions developed over the U.S. campaign against Iraq during the 1990s. Secretary-General Chedli Klibi condemned the use, or even the threat, of force against Iraq in 1998. League officials sided with Baghdad while aggressively pursuing peace initiatives and, equally important, adopted policies to combat terrorism. Arab interior and justice ministers signed an agreement to strengthen cooperation against terrorism, denouncing the attacks on American diplomatic missions in Kenya and Tanzania. Simultaneously, the League voiced strong reservations against the Clinton administration's missile strikes against Afghanistan and Sudan.

The most important recent initiatives of the League include the 2002Beirut Summit meeting when King ʿAbdallah bin ʿAbd al-Azīz Āl Saʿūd of Saudi Arabia proposed that all League members normalize relations with Israel in exchange for Israeli withdrawal to the 1967 borders, as well as the right of those Palestinian refugees or their descendants who wished to return to do so. Also significant is the 2003 vote (21–1, Kuwait casting the lone dissent) calling on the unconditional removal of all foreign forces from occupied Iraq. The Beirut Peace Plan was again endorsed at the July 2007 Riyadh Summit, when the League dispatched an official mission—the Jordanian and Egyptian foreign ministers—to Israel to promote the initiative. Israel showed little interest.

In the aftermath of the 2008–2009 Israel–Gaza conflict, League Secretary-General Amr Moussa visited the Gaza Strip to pressure Israel to lift its economic blockade against the territory. The 13 June 2010 visit was the first by a League official since Hamas came to power in 2007, and while Moussa pledged to ask UN Security Council assistance, the blockade was not lifted. In April 2011, Moussa declared that the League would ask the Security Council to impose a no-fly zone over Gaza, which Israel has pounded with air strikes periodically since 2008 in response to rocket fire from the territory.

League rifts continued in earnest at the March 2009 Cairo Summit, when Muʿammar al-Qadhdhāfī of Libya denounced King ʿAbdallah as a "British product and American ally." According to various news reports, Shaykh Ḥamad bin Khalīfah Āl Thānī of Qatar attempted to defuse tensions, which only heightened the Colonel's ire:

"I am an international leader," interjected Qadhdhāfī, "the dean of the Arab rulers, the king of kings of Africa and the imam of Muslims, and my international status does not allow me to descend to a lower level" (Otterman).

Such diplomatic fireworks aside, League summiteers were deeply divided over which Palestinian faction to support—Fatah or Ḥamās—and what to do about Iran's rising influence in the Arab world. They rallied around 'Umar Ḥasan Aḥmad al-Bashīr, the president of Sudan, who was indicted by the International Criminal Court for war crimes and crimes against humanity in Darfur, as they rejected the arrest warrant issued against him.

This was the sole unifying position reached by the League before the Winter 2010–Spring 2011 uprisings that started in Tunisia and rocked regimes in Egypt, Yemen, Oman, Bahrain, and Syria. An anti-Qadhdhāfī alliance emerged in Libya, which mobilized the U.N. Security Council and NATO forces to impose a no-fly-zone over the North African country. On 12 March 2011, the Arab League approved the no-fly zone to prevent Colonel Qadhdhāfī's air force from attacking civilians. According to Egyptian officials, only Syria and Algeria opposed the decision, although that was before serious uprising against the Assad and Bouteflika regimes started. Qatar and the UAE dispatched air units to join NATO forces. Secretary-General Moussa, who planned to run for president in Egypt in late 2011, deplored the broad scope of the U.S.-European bombing campaign in Libya and said that he would call a League meeting to reconsider Arab approval of the Western military intervention although that did not occur. The Libyan leader stood firm and, allegedly, hired foreign mercenaries to defeat the rebellion against his regime. He chastised the Arab League after Moussa announced on 22 February 2011 that Libya's membership in the League had been suspended. In one of his more colorful statements, Qadhdhāfī proclaimed that the League was illegitimate, shouting: "The Arab League is finished. There is no such thing as the Arab League" (Reuters, 16 March 2011).

[*See also* Organization of Islamic Cooperation.]

BIBLIOGRAPHY

Anderson, Krister. "Going Major: Reforming the League of Arab States." *Harvard International Review* 25, no. 4 (2004): 7.

Barnett, Michael N. *Dialogues in Arab Politics*. New York: Columbia University Press, 1998.

Gomaa, Ahmed M. *The Foundation of the League of Arab States*. London and New York: Longman, 1977.

Hasou, Tawfiq Y. *The Struggle for the Arab World: Egypt's Nasser and the Arab League*. Boston and London: KPI, 1985.

Hassouna, Hussein A. *The League of Arab States and Regional Disputes*. Dobbs Ferry, N.Y.: Oceana Publications, 1975.

Hätinger, Benjamin. *The League of Arab States*. Norderstedt, Germany: Druck und Bindung: Books on Demand GmbH, 2006.

MacDonald, Robert W. *The League of Arab States: A Study in the Dynamics of Regional Organization*. Princeton, N.J.: Princeton University Press, 1965.

Maddy-Weitzman, Bruce. *The Crystallization of the Arab State System, 1945–1954*. Syracuse, N.Y.: Syracuse University Press, 1993.

Muḥāfaẓah, 'Alī, et al. *Jāmi'at al-Duwal al-'Arabīyah: Al-wāqi' wa-al-tumūh* [The League of Arab States: The reality and the aspiration]. 2d ed. Beirut, Lebanon: Markaz Dirāsāt al-Wahdah al-'Arabīyah, 1983.

Otterman, Sharon. "Arab League," *New York Times*, http://topics.nytimes.com/topics/reference/timestopics/organizations/a/arab_league/index.html.

Reuters. "Qaddafi: Arab League Is Finished," *Arab News*, 16 Mar 2011 at http://arabnews.com/middleeast/article318542.ece?comments=all.

Riyād, Mahmūd. *The Struggle for Peace in the Middle East*. London and New York: Quartet Books, 1981.

Salamé, Ghassan, ed. *The Foundations of the Arab State*. London: Routledge, 2006.

Tawfiq Y. Hasou
Updated by Joseph A. Kéchichian

ARAB NATIONALISM. Like other strands of third-world nationalism, *qawmīyah ʿarabīyah* (Arab nationalism) is best understood within an anticolonial ethos, as is its glorification of the Arab origins and history in the face of Western dominance. Arab nationalism must be assessed as a political movement essentially confined to the twentieth century. Its bases and components originated with the presence of the Arabic language itself or with aspects of Arab social, intellectual, and political culture. At present there is consensus around the view of Sāṭiʿ al-Ḥusrī (1882–1968) that Arabs are identified by their language, having Arabic as their mother tongue and consciously identifying with it. Indeed, al-Ḥusrī defined nationalism as love of the nation and organic identification with it, and the bases of such a national collectivity are language and common history. To these bases must be added common traditions and interests as well as a common culture shaped by the same environment. In its most modern form (with Nasser, the Baʿth party, or Muʿammar al-Qadhdhāfī), Arab nationalism aimed at the political reunification of all Arabic-speaking states from the Persian Gulf to the Atlantic Ocean, and their transformation from a *Kulturnation* into a *Staatsnation*.

This interplay between the doctrine's cultural and political phases attracts attention to the sequences in its evolution, for the movement reached its zenith only gradually. Its vicissitudes are a function of various factors: intervention of external powers in the region; defining events or political upheavals that shook the area; the type of leadership at the head of the movement; and its competition with two other loci of people's loyalty—the territorial state and Pan-Islamism. Consequently, the movement's evolution may be divided into four phases, along with a fifth that highlights its decline.

Nineteenth Century to World War I. Under Ottoman rule, Islamic solidarity was challenged by modernizing forces at the empire's center, especially after unruly provinces demanded their autonomy. Though interest in Western science and technology united the Young Turks and many Arabs, the drive of the revolutionary Committee of Union and Progress in Constantinople for Turkification alienated Arabs and accelerated their demand for autonomy. Cultural clubs—organized mostly by Lebanese Christians in collaboration with American missionaries—proliferated (prominent leaders of such clubs include Nāṣīf al-Yāzijī, 1800–1871, and Aḥmad Fāris al-Shidyāq, 1805–1887). When the Syrian Buṭrus al-Bustānī (1819–1883) pleaded for girls' education, or when the Egyptian Rifāʿah Rāfiʿ al-Ṭahṭāwī (1801–1873) emphasized *waṭan* (fatherland), they presented secularist challenges to the Islamic establishment of the Turkish caliph. ʿAbd al-Raḥman al-Kawākibī (1848–1902) tried to find a compromise and called in his *Umm al-qurā*for the return of the caliphate to its originators, the Arabs. It was not long before the first Arab nationalist conference, limited to Asian Arabs, was held in Paris in 1913. World War I thus marked the beginning of an explicitly political phase, with the Hashemite Sharīf Ḥusayn, in collaboration with Britain and France and with the active help of T. E. Lawrence, revolting against the empire to seek the establishment of a single Arab kingdom in its Arab provinces.

Interwar Period to the Establishment of Israel. Rather than forming a unified Arab kingdom, however, the Arab provinces were divided between France and Britain according to the secret 1916 Sykes-Picot Agreement, and in November 1917, Lord Balfour pledged to establish a national home for Jews in Palestine. Directed against European domination (rather than against Muslim authority as before), the basic us/them dichotomy of nationalism facilitated the movement's politicization. Given the predominantly hereditary leadership at the time and the increasing imposition of European-type administrative divisions, Arab nationalism was locally rather than regionally oriented. Pan-Arab writings such as al-Ḥusrī's, with their secularist orientation and objective of a unified Arab state, compensated for this localism.

In addition to al-Ḥusrī, critical Arab nationalist voices emerged in the interwar period, including those of Amīn al-Riḥānī (1876–1940), Constantine Zurayk (1909–2000), Zakī al-Arsūzī (1899–1968), and Michel ʿAflaq (1910–1989). Although these erudite theorists favored largely secularist views, various ideologies competed for attention. Local nationalist tendencies emerged in Lebanon, promoted by predominantly Christian thinkers and politicians, favoring the establishment of a Greater Syria. Elsewhere, but especially in Iraq and Syria, communism gained adherents even if it was generally hostile to specific pan-Arab political projects.

Revisionist and Mass-Oriented Movements, 1945–1967. Increasingly dominated by a new middle class (military or otherwise), this period was dense with major political events, including the establishment of the League of Arab States in 1945, which, with its exclusive Arab membership, institutionalized the Arab/non-Arab distinction in the region. In addition, the disastrous end of the 1948 Arab-Israeli war made Palestine a core issue in inter-Arab politics and in the Arabs' relations with outside powers. Moreover, disillusioned young officers soon toppled corrupt civilian regimes—there were three coups in Syria alone in 1949—and came to be the region's new leaders, such as Gamal Abdel Nasser after the 1952 Egyptian coup. Nasserism, whether or not in alliance with the Baʿth, aimed at the establishment of a unified, nonaligned Arab state, with its own development model of Arab socialism. This "third road" policy represented a consensus among different nationalist forces, from revolutionary Algeria to opposition forces in the Gulf.

Another, more activist conceptualization, distinct from that of Michel ʿAflaq and the Baʿth establishment, was also in the making. Its reading of experiences of unification in history resulted in the distinction between secondary and primary determinants. Secondary determinants such as language and history were necessary but not sufficient for unification, whereas primary determinants were both necessary and sufficient. The latter included a base region or pole of attraction (e.g., Egypt), a transnational charismatic leadership (e.g., Nasser), and an external threat (e.g., Israel and Western encroachment). Unity between Egypt and Syria, which produced the United Arab Republic between 1958 and 1961, seemed to confirm this theory. Yet its dissolution and the failure of unity negotiations in 1963, which also included Baʿthist Iraq, cast doubt on the theory's immediate applicability and long-term viability. A protracted civil war in Yemen following Imām Muḥammad Badr's ouster in 1962, with Egypt and Saudi Arabia championing opposite camps, further deepened Arab divisions. Regionally, opposition intensified between radical Arab nationalism and a conservative Pan-Islamic strategy promoted by Saudi Arabia, Jordan, and Morocco that emphasized the convening of Islamic conferences. In this context, the region was shaken to its roots in 1967 by the third Arab-Israeli war. The magnitude of Arab defeat restructured regional leadership, culminating in the decline of revisionist forces and the rise of the oil-producing powers, especially Saudi Arabia under King Fayṣal. The August 1967 Arab Summit in Khartoum sealed the withdrawal of Egyptian forces from Yemen and resulted in Egyptian dependency on oil-state subsidies.

Arab Territorial State and Militant Pan-Islam, 1968–1992. Influential leadership bases shifted from *thawrah* (revolution) to *tharwah* (wealth), from ideologists and officers to rich royalty and "wealthy merchants who flitted between East and West, between royal palaces and the offices of oil companies (examples are Kamal Adham, Mahdi al-Tajir, and Adnan Khashoggi)." The public was more drawn to the riches of the oil fields than by the hardships of the battlefields.

Neither the 1969 coup by the young and fiery al-Qadhdhāfī in Libya nor the revolutionary but stateless Palestinians could stop the decline of the radical pole. Quantitative indicators confirm this. By 1979, 55 percent of the capital of inter-Arab joint economic ventures was contributed by oil-rich Saudi Arabia, Kuwait, the United Arab Emirates, Qatar, and Libya. Oil states gradually became the locale of an increasing number of new Arab organizations. In 1970 Cairo hosted twenty-nine, or 65 percent, of these organizations, whereas Iraq hosted none and Saudi Arabia only one. Eight years later, Baghdad had become the locale for twelve organizations, thereby occupying the second place, after Egypt. Saudi Arabia was in third place with eight organizations. In addition, fewer Arab League meetings were held in Egypt and more in the oil states. The proportion of meetings held in Cairo decreased from 70.5 percent in 1977 to 42.2 percent in 1978. Egypt's share in the Arab League budget also dropped; it was above 40 percent until the late 1950s but declined until 1978—the year the Arab League moved to Tunis—when it was only 13.7 percent, equivalent to that of Kuwait.

It might be supposed that the movement of migrant labor from densely populated Egypt or the West Bank to the Gulf, and the transfer of capital in the form of remittances and investments in the opposite direction, would promote Arab integration. Nasser's death in 1970, amid the ashes of the Jordanian-Palestinian civil war, concretized this change by eliminating one of the postulated primary determinants of political unification—charismatic leadership. Egyptian rapprochement with Israel, culminating in the 1978 Camp David Accords, seemed to take away the second primary determinant, the existence of a threat. Indeed, the rise of independent diplomacy concerning one of the most sacred causes of the Pan-Arab ideal confirmed—if it needed to be confirmed—the primacy of *raison d'état* over *raison de la nation*. Moreover, hindsight tells us, it presaged the integration of Israel into the regional system. Naturally, such a possibility diluted Arab regional exclusiveness and promoted an enlarged Middle East. Ironically, the radical pole was engaged from quite a different direction in an equally diluting process when, in the Iran-Iraq war (1980–1988), Syria, Libya, and Algeria sided with non-Arab revolutionary Islamic Iran against Arab Iraq. Harassed on two fronts by territorial *raison d'état* and revolutionary Islamism, Arab nationalism was wounded but not dead. Its troubles reflected both its own weakness as a political program and the disappearance of the simple world of heroic politics and categorical formulas.

Pan-Islamism and the End of Arab Nationalism, 1993–Present. To take control over a complex situation, Arabs tried to form subregional groupings: the Gulf Cooperation Council (GCC, including Bahrain, Kuwait, Oman, Qatar, Saudi Arabia, and the United Arab Emirates) in 1981, the Union du Maghreb Arabe (Algeria, Libya, Mauritania, Morocco, and Tunisia) in 1989, and the Arab Cooperation Council (Egypt, Iraq, Jordan, and Yemen), also in 1989. Inasmuch as these moves were a way to escape the double bind of nation versus state and replace it with a sequential logic, a step-by-step strategy (with the exception of the GCC) did not survive the political upheaval of the 1991 Gulf War following Iraq's invasion of the sheikhdom. In its discourse Iraq appealed to the opposition of many Arabs to artificial colonial frontiers and the division of the Arab nation, and to their demand for a fairer redistribution of Arab wealth between haves and have-nots. Though tempted, many Arabs mistrusted

Saddam Hussein's cynical exploitation of Pan-Arabism and Pan-Islamism. Arabs both at the state level and in transnational civil society were seriously divided and traumatized, with the Arab League (now back in Cairo) paralyzed, and foreign troops stationed near the holy sites in Saudi Arabia, poised to decide the issue for them.

After Saddam Hussein invaded Kuwait in August 1990, the twentieth-century quest for Arab unity ended. Baghdad sought Kuwaiti oil wealth to fill its empty treasury, and, remarkably, while Hussein maintained that the sheikhdom was its nineteenth province, it could not justify the invasion as an act of Arab nationalist unification. Still, imbued by *qawmīyah*, some Arab nationalists elevated the Baʿthi to Nasserite levels, faithful to chimerical visions of past recklessness on the banks of the Nile. Many welcomed lackluster Iraqi claims that whatever military might the country possessed would serve all Arabs, even if most preferred to ignore its appalling losses in the eight-year war with Iran.

Dejected Arab nationalists, who had suffered so much humiliation, saw raw power as a panacea, and Saddam Hussein fit the bill. Yet, when most Arab states joined the international coalition against Iraq, Arab nationalism was replaced with the tenets of a state system, especially since few Arabs perceived the Iraqi leader as a genuine Pan-Arab figure. Most concluded correctly that the dictator was primarily advancing Iraqi national interests. Ironically, with the March 1991 liberation of Kuwait, millions of Arabs in Kuwait and elsewhere claimed victory, even if triumphant Arab "states" failed to translate that feat into tangible political gains.

For many Arab intellectuals, Arab nationalism became anachronistic, because it espoused ideology at a time when the rest of the world experienced the first pangs of postideology. Arab nationalists lost their champion outside support—the Soviet Union—and, equally importantly, faced a growing internal rejection of economic stagnation. New voices called instead to shift priorities to domestic concerns, including economic growth, to better equip young Arabs not to swell unemployment ranks. Regional organizations like the GCC promoted financial development and collective security but soon were mired in a massive arms race. In the aftermath of the post-1967 military defeats, and faced with limited capabilities to introduce effective socioeconomic changes, an "end of Arab nationalism" was identified as a new reality.

At the dawn of the twenty-first century, few Arabs championed nationalism, even if many hoped that the eventual rejection of Islamism might rekindle hopes for unity. Yet the slow rejection of a single nation was increasingly evident, as liberal philosophies gained momentum in one of the birthplaces of Arab nationalism: Beirut.

After a thirty-year Syrian occupation, Lebanon rejected the classic *waṭanīyah* espoused by Damascus, insisting that authoritarianism be replaced with genuine democracy. If Arab nationalism was not a natural ally of democracy or of Islam, the 2005 Cedar Revolution featured young Lebanese Arabs insisting on the creation of political parties and similar institutions. Even among large numbers of Lebanese Muslims, a yearning for authenticity was evident, as respect and tolerance for religious diversity grew. Few Lebanese, or Egyptians, or Syrians awaited another Nasser to save the Arabs from themselves and unite them, aware that political solace may best be found among nascent institutions that ensured liberty for the masses. Even fewer were willing to be stirred into a frenzy to satisfy chimerical windmills.

When Saddam Hussein was ousted from power in 2003, an avowedly secular Arab Socialist Baʿth Party that ruled against Western imperialism briefly in 1963 and again between 1968 and 2003 came to an end. Michel ʿAflaq and Ṣalāḥ Bīṭār, who established the organization in 1947, believed in their motto: "Unity, Liberty, Socialism" (*Waḥdah, ḥurrīyah, ishtirākīyah*), even if this never materialized. Instead, in the words of Kanan Makiya, it gave rise to the "republic of fear." By the end of 2010, and especially in the spring of 2011, young Arabs took to the streets of Tunisia, Egypt, Yemen, Syria, and elsewhere, as they rejected the lies of the past century. Few looked to Salafīs or any combination of Islamists as answers to intrinsic challenges, especially as they assessed the consequences of the 1979 Islamic Revolution in Iran. Still, many Arab men and women were inspired by the 2009 "Twitter Revolution" in Iran, where the notorious paramilitary Basīj forces beat protesters with impunity. Arab potentates imitated Tehran, but neither Arab nationalism nor the idealized Islamic State appealed to members of the young generation that shed their cloak of fear. From Cairo to Dara, and from Misrātah to Sanaa, Arabs no longer fancied *waḥdah* and *ishtirākīyah*. They simply longed for *ḥurrīyah* from dictators generous with vague ideological promises.

[*See also* Arab League; Congresses; Nasser, Gamal Abdel; *and* Pan-Islam.]

BIBLIOGRAPHY

Sources in Arabic

Bibliyūghrāfiyāh al-waḥdah al-ʿArabīyah, 1908–1980 (Bibliography of Arab Unity, 1908–1980). 3 vols. Beirut: al-Markaz, 1983–1986.

Al-Ḥiwār al-qawmī-al-dīnī (The Nationalist-Religious Dialogue). Beirut: al-Markaz, 1989.

Al-Qawmīyah al-ʿArabīyah fī al-fikr wa-al-mumārasah (Arab Nationalism: Thought and Practice). Beirut: al-Markaz, 1980.

Al-Qawmīyah al-ʿArabīyah wa-al-Islām (Arab Nationalism and Islam). Beirut: al-Markaz, 1981.

Yawmīyāt wa-wathāʾiq al-waḥdah al-ʿArabīyah (Chronology of Arab Unity). Annual.

Western-Language Sources

Al-Barghouti, Tamim. *The Umma and the Dawla: The Nation-State and the Arab Middle East.* London: Pluto, 2008.

Choueiri, Youssef M. *Arab Nationalism—A History: Nation and State in the Arab World.* Oxford: Blackwell, 2000.

Citino, Nathan J. *From Arab Nationalism to OPEC: Eisenhower, King Saʿūd, and the Making of U.S.-Saudi Relations.* Bloomington: Indiana University Press, 2002.

Cleveland, William L. *The Making of an Arab Nationalist: Ottomanism and Arabism in the Life and Thought of Satiʿ al-Husri.* Princeton, N.J.: Princeton University Press, 1971.

Dawisha, Adeed. *Arab Nationalism in the Twentieth Century: From Triumph to Despair.* Princeton, N.J.: Princeton University Press, 2003.

Hopwood, Derek, ed. *Arab Nation, Arab Nationalism.* Basingstoke, U.K.: Palgrave Macmillan, 2000.

Khoury, Philip S.*Urban Notables and Arab Nationalism: The Politics of Damascus 1860–1920.* Cambridge, U.K.: Cambridge University Press, 1983.

Korany, Bahgat, and Ali E. Hillal Dessouki, eds. *The Foreign Policies of Arab States: The Challenge of Globalization.* Rev. ed. Cairo: American University in Cairo Press, 2008.

Louis, William Roger. *The British Empire in the Middle East, 1945–1951: Arab Nationalism, the United States, and Postwar Imperialism.* Oxford: Clarendon, 1985.

Tibi, Bassam. *Arab Nationalism: Between Islam and the Nation-State.* 3d ed. New York: St. Martin's, 1997.

Wien, Peter. *Iraqi Arab Nationalism: Authoritarian, Totalitarian, and Pro-Fascist Inclinations, 1932–1941.* London: Routledge, 2006.

Yaqub, Salim. *Containing Arab Nationalism: The Eisenhower Doctrine and the Middle East.* Chapel Hill: University of North Carolina Press, 2004.

BAHGAT KORANY
Updated by JOSEPH A. KÉCHICHIAN

ARAB SOCIALISM. The notion of Arab socialism was never articulated precisely, but it can be taken as representing the economic and social aspirations of Nasserism and Bathism, the state ideologies, respectively, of Egypt in the late 1950s and 1960s and Iraq and Syria from the 1960s until 2003 (although officially until the present time in Syria). During the years following World War II, a widespread consensus developed among the educated middle classes and the largely unofficial opposition in each of these states to the effect that the country's most urgent needs were national independence and economic development, and that the state was the natural vehicle to carry out the necessary transformations. After the revolutions of the 1950s and 1960s, this notion became an important part of the political discourse of the various successor regimes.

In practice, the word "socialism" is something of a misnomer in that neither a socialist revolution nor exclusive state ownership of the means of production was envisaged. The postrevolutionary economies of Egypt, Iraq, and Syria might have had some superficial similarities with the command economies of their contemporary Eastern European states, but it was no accident that all three countries continued to maintain substantial and indeed often buoyant private sectors. Thus the "socialism" in Arab socialism is best understood as state-sponsored economic development with specific legitimizing political attributes.

Apart from the various land reforms of the 1950s (1952 in Egypt, 1958 in Iraq and Syria) and the nationalization of the Suez Canal in 1956, it was not until the early 1960s that the nationalization of large private and foreign-owned companies took place, and the governments of all three states began to act more determinedly to bring the various sectors of the economy under state control. More stringent land reforms were introduced, and banking, insurance, foreign trade, and large industrial enterprises were all nationalized. This took place in Iraq under ʿAbd al-Salām ʿĀrif in 1964. In spite of its socialist rhetoric, the Baʿth's only further step in this direction after 1968—admittedly a crucial one—was the nationalization of the Iraq Petroleum Company and its various subsidiaries in 1972. In fact, the considerable enhancement of Iraqi state power that the nationalization of oil facilitated was only the most extreme example of what would turn out to be one of the salient features of Arab socialism, namely, that the concentration of economic power in the hands of a largely unaccountable political authority facilitated the emergence of increasingly repressive and dictatorial state structures.

Alongside this economic dirigisme came a considerable expansion in social, welfare, health, and educational services. Naturally, the quality of provision varied considerably both between and within states and was generally much better and more comprehensive in the larger cities than in the countryside. But, at least in theory, free education, for example, was available from primary school through university for every child. At the same time, most basic foodstuffs were subsidized and/or made available in exchange for coupons from special government establishments, and government stores sold such items as clothing, footwear, and furniture at subsidized prices.

Insofar as it had ideological underpinnings, the notion of Arab socialism was probably most clearly articulated in some of the writings of Michel ʿAflaq, one of the founders and principal ideologues of Bathism. It is important to stress, however, that ʿAflaq formulated his ideas in the 1950s and did not significantly modify them when Baʿth parties came to power in Syria and Iraq in the 1960s. It is also important to note that, although socialism is the third member of the Bathist trinity—*waḥdah, ḥurrīyah, ishtirakīyah* (unity, freedom, socialism)—it was far less important to ʿAflaq, and the object of much less of his attention, than either (Arab) unity or (Arab) nationalism. Article 26 of the party constitution says: "The Party of the Arab Baʿth is a socialist party. It believes that the economic wealth of the fatherland belongs to the nation." Article 34 reads: "Property and inheritance are two natural rights. They are protected within the limits of national interest." The only other reference to socialism in the Baʿth Party constitution is the expression of the belief that "socialism is a necessity which emanates from the depth of Arab nationalism itself," and that it "constitutes the ideal social order which will allow the Arab people to realize its possibilities." There is no exposition of the meaning of these assertions, although it is clear from ʿAflaq's other writings, and also from the Nasserist version of Arab nationalism, that socialism is essentially non-Marxist, and in fact anti-Marxist, in that it stresses the primacy of ethnic and national identity and rejects the notion of antagonistic social classes. Once the Arabs are liberated and united, it is asserted, class conflict will somehow melt away.

In general, some of the vogue enjoyed by Arab socialism and Islamic socialism probably reflected a need to incorporate several of the more unexceptionable aspects of socialist ideology (the extension of state power as an expression of the transfer of power to the people; the introduction of comprehensive social reform and welfare measures) into the nationalist and Islamic religious discourse of the time. Naturally, such a synthesis produces its own contradictions, such as the coexistence of the notion of the sanctity of private property with the notion of equality and equality of opportunity.

It is clear, however, from the writings and speeches of Arab nationalists and Muslim Brothers in the 1950s that invocations of socialism were necessary for both groups to assert their progressive credentials and intentions; the aspiration for social justice, together with the sense that the state was the appropriate instrument to spearhead social and economic development, was almost universally shared at the time. It was also the case that Arab communists had their own much more precise and elaborate version of socialism. Arab socialism and Islamic socialism, because of their allegedly "homegrown" nature, could thus be useful weapons in blunting or deflecting the appeal of communism at the time of its greatest popularity in the Middle East, which coincided with the height of the Cold War.

With the fall of the Baʿth regime in Baghdad in 2003, Arab socialism suffered a major defeat, even if the Republic of Iraq is far from a free society today. Instead of fulfilling a socialist agenda that served citizens, Saddam Hussein's dictatorial rule gave rise to a "republic of fear" (Makiya, 1989) where there was no *ḥurrīyah*. Likewise, Damascus confronted a genuine uprising that was multi-pronged, but mainly dominated by a quest for political and economic reforms that would end the Baʿth Party's rampant corruption. In all Arab socialist states, unsuitable policies ensured little or no economic prosperity, which disappointed many. Even Colonel Muʿammar al-Qadhdhāfī in Libya could only deliver a Jamāhīrīyah that advocated socialism without any of its benefits. Instead, the self-appointed "King of Kings of Africa" wasted billions while Libyans were left to fend for themselves. In 2011, Arab socialism was on the wane, as many Arabs rejected failed post–World War II ideologies. They demanded *ḥurrīyah*, including in the economic arena, to better protect and serve their intrinsic interests.

[*See also* Arab Nationalism; *and* Baʿth Parties.]

BIBLIOGRAPHY

Aksikas, Jaafar. *Arab Modernities: Islamism, Nationalism, and Liberalism in the Post-Colonial Arab World.* New York: Peter Lang, 2009.

Baker, Raymond William. *Egypt's Uncertain Revolution under Nasser and Sadat.* Cambridge, Mass.: Harvard University Press, 1978. Interesting analysis of the balance of continuity and change in Egypt between 1952 and the mid-1970s.

Batatu, Hanna. *The Old Social Classes and the Revolutionary Movements of Iraq: A Study of Iraq's Old Landed and Commercial Classes and of Its Communists, Baʿthists, and Free Officers*. Princeton, N.J.: Princeton University Press, 1978.

Beinin, Joel. "Labour, Capital, and the State in Nasserist Egypt, 1952–1961." *International Journal of Middle East Studies* 21, no. 1 (February 1989): 71–90.

Choueiri, Youssef M. *Arab Nationalism—A History: Nation and State in the Arab World*. Oxford: Blackwell, 2000.

Farouk-Sluglett, Marion. "Socialist Iraq, 1963–1978: Towards a Reappraisal." *Orient* 23, no. 2 (1982): 206–219.

Farouk-Sluglett, Marion, and Peter Sluglett. "The Iraqi Baʿth Party." In *Political Parties in the Third World*, edited by Vicky Randall, pp. 57–74. London: Sage, 1988.

Hinnebusch, Raymond A. "Syria under the Baʿth: State Formation in a Fragmented Society." *Arab Studies Quarterly* 4, no. 3 (Summer 1982): 177–199.

Makiya, Kanan. *The Republic of Fear: The Politics of Modern Iraq*. Berkeley: University of California Press, 1989.

Moaddel, Mansoor. *Islamic Modernism, Nationalism, and Fundamentalism: Episode and Discourse*. Chicago: University of Chicago Press, 2005.

PETER SLUGLETT
Updated by JOSEPH A. KÉCHICHIAN

ARAB SPRING. "Arab Spring" refers to the popular mass uprisings throughout the Middle East and North Africa (MENA) that have been going on since 2010. The 17 December 2010 self-immolation of Muhammad Bouazizi, a twenty-six-year-old unemployed computer science graduate in the town of Sidi Bouzid, Tunisia, not only launched the "Jasmine Revolution" in Tunisia but is widely credited for sparking revolutions in Egypt, Libya, and elsewhere in MENA. The people of the MENA do not describe their revolt against the political order as "Arab Spring." They prefer to describe their uprising as *thawrah* (revolution), *thawrāt* (revolutions), *intifāḍah* (uprising), *ṣaḥwah* (awakening), or *nahḍah* (resistance).

The Arab Spring has two major aims: to remove from power long-serving despotic rulers and to replace the old autocratic political systems with democratic and economic orders based on the rule of law and social justice. The first of these objectives have been achieved in Tunisia, Egypt, Libya, and Yemen. President Zine El-Abidine Ben Ali of Tunisia, President Hosni Mubarak of Egypt, Colonel Muʿammar al-Qadhdhāfī of Libya, and President ʿAlī ʿAbd Allāh Ṣāliḥ of Yemen were forced to give up power in the face of mass uprisings. The rulers of Syria, Bahrain, Oman, Saudi Arabia, and the United Arab Emirates (UAE) faced demonstrations demanding reforms but managed to cling to power. The second objective of Arab Spring—to build new democratic political orders guaranteeing freedom of the people, the rule of law, and transparency in the system—proved challenging in the MENA. Khair El-Din Haseeb provided four factors accounting for the success and failure of achieving the objectives of Arab Spring: breaking the barrier of fear; the nonviolent nature of the uprisings; the presence of sufficient social cohesion and national unity in opposing the regimes; and the stance of the military towards the mass uprisings (Haseeb, 2012, pp. 185–186).

The rapid onset and spread of the Arab Spring took political observers by surprise. People of the MENA states were accustomed to long-standing autocratic rule: President Hosni Mubarak ruled Egypt from 1981 to 2011; in Libya, Qadhdhāfī led the country from 1969 until he was overthrown and killed during the uprising in Libya in 2011. President Zine El Abidine Ben Ali of Tunisia held power from 1987 until he fled to Saudi Arabia in 2010. Yemen's President ʿAlī ʿAbd Allāh Ṣāliḥ remained in power from 1978 until mass demonstrations forced him to step down in 2012 and transfer power to his deputy, Abd Rabbuh Mansur Al-Hadi.

The revolt of the Arab masses was directed against social deprivation and injustices blamed on long periods of dictatorial and family rule. *The Arab Human Development Report 2009* quoted data from the Arab Labor Organization pointing out that, in 2005, the average unemployment rate in the Arab countries was 14.4 percent of the labor force compared to 6.3 percent for the rest of the world (p. 10). Rising food prices have also been cited as one catalyst—with social networks as an accelerator—of the Arab Spring. High levels of corruption and long-entrenched autocratic regimes meant that the region's young, educated populations not only wanted more jobs and better economic prospects; they also yearned for greater democracy (*Strategic Survey*, 2011, vol. 2). Concentration of wealth in too few hands was a contributing factor to the Arab Spring as well. It can also be argued that the gradual and painful process of democratization in Iraq may have encouraged the Arab masses in the region to seek greater freedom.

Leadership and Organizational Structure. Revolutions in MENA were not plotted and launched by any ideologically driven leadership, but in the countries where armed resistance against the rulers broke out, such as Libya and Syria, an identifiable group of leaders ultimately took over the direction of the struggle. In countries such as Tunisia and Egypt, where mass collective peaceful demonstrations managed to drive the rulers from power, there were no recognizable groups of leaders guiding the revolutions. Tunisian youth, imbued with the idea of seeking justice and a better life and throwing out a corrupt government, were mobilized by the use of social media sites. On 25 January 2011, Egyptians began their revolution by going out to the streets demanding the resignation of eighty-two-year-old President Hosni Mubarak and the end to his three-decade-long regime. Wael Ghonim, a Google marketing executive, is credited with organizing thousands of Egyptians using Facebook. Mubarak was arrested, tortured by security forces, and then released. Wael was treated as a hero of the opposition to Mubarak's rule. Mohamed ElBaradei, the former chief of the International Atomic Energy Agency (IAEA) was perhaps the most visible face of the Egyptian revolution. He returned to Cairo from Vienna to take part in the revolution. The Muslim Brotherhood, the largest of the Islamist groups, played a low-profile role in the revolution, initially refusing to take part in it or participate in elections, but it changed its position, and its presidential candidate Mohamed Morsi was elected president of Egypt in June 2012.

The revolutions in Tunisia and Egypt were not driven by young educated members of an expanding middle class, although a handful of lawyers and university professors took part in the uprising in Benghazi. In Libya, soon after the uprising on 15 February 2011, the residents of eastern Libya formed an interim rebel administration named the National Transitional Council (NTC). The primary aim of the NTC was to provide military and political leadership for the rebels. Other aims included organizing basic local services and representing Libyans abroad. By May 2011, the NTC emerged as the interim government with thirty-one members from different parts of Libya under the prime ministership of Mahmoud Jibril el-Warfally. The NTC was composed of various factions: the east and the west; Tripoli and Benghazi; the mountains and the cities; the religious and the secular; the Arabs and the Berbers. Each faction demanded a greater share in power in postrevolution Libya.

Syrian society is divided along many religious and ethnic lines: Sunni Muslims, ʿAlawīs, Kurds, Christians, Druze, and others. Therefore, it is not surprising that organizing an effective national opposition leadership to the regime of President Bashar al-Assad proved difficult. The opposition is divided into two main factions: the Syrian National Council (SNC) and the National

Coordination Committee for the forces of Democratic Change. Once demonstrations against the Bashar regime began, local coordination committees sprung up throughout the country. To galvanize this opposition, after much effort, on 23 August 2011, the SNC was created in Istanbul. It consists of exiled members of the Syrian Muslim Brotherhood, Kurdish dissidents, and many other dissident groups. It is aimed at organizing political support for bringing about democratic revolution in Syria and developing a roadmap for democratic change in Syria. The forces opposing the Assad regime in Syria have employed both political negotiations and armed resistance to achieve their objectives. The SNC runs the Free Syrian Army. The SNC has been criticized for its shortcomings. Burhan Ghalioun, a Paris-based Syrian academic, was named chair of the council in September 2011. Because of the criticism of his leadership style, he was forced to resign, and on 10 June 2012, Sweden-based Abdulbaset Sida, a Kurdish leader, took over as the chair of the SNC.

Evolution and Major Transformations. In Tunisia large-scale demonstrations broke out on 24 December 2010, a week after the self-immolation of Muhammad Bouazizi, and spread to other towns. About one thousand protestors staged demonstrations in Tunis on December 27. They organized these gatherings through the use of social media sites. President Ben Ali warned the demonstrators of consequences. However, his warnings and the crackdown by his security forces failed to stop the spread of antigovernment demonstrations throughout the country. People from all walks of life joined in the uprising to oust Ben Ali's government. By January 2011, the antigovernment demonstrations gained ground in Tunis and other major towns as the number of demonstrators killed by government security forces and snipers increased to sixty-six. In a major televised speech on January 13, President Ben Ali promised to carry our major reforms and vowed not to contest the 2014 elections. He also vowed to try those responsible for killing protestors. However, as part of a major crackdown the very next day, a state of emergency was imposed throughout Tunisia. President Ben Ali fired his government, promising fresh parliamentary elections within six months to quell the demonstrations. But this announcement failed to stop violent clashes between protestors and security forces. It now appears that this was a last ditch attempt by the former president to try to stop the mass uprising against his rule; it did not work. The next day, 15 January 2011, reports started circulating in Tunis that the military had taken control of key government installations including the airport. Reports also began to appear that Tunisian airspace had been closed. The Saudi government admitted that Ben Ali had resigned as the president of Tunisia and he and an unspecified number of his family members were being hosted by Riyadh.

Within ten days of the escape of Ben Ali and his family to Saudi Arabia, on 25 January 2011, thousands of Egyptians began to pour into Tahrir Square in Cairo. Their appearance was in response to a call on Facebook and Twitter to observe a Day of Rage. Surrounded by heavily armed riot police, and shot at with rubber bullets and tear gas, the demonstrators nevertheless remained peaceful. However, they shouted slogans calling for the removal of the Mubarak government. Thus a movement calling for limited reforms was swiftly transformed into a revolutionary movement (Lesch, 2011). Tahrir Square would remain the center of the anti-Mubarak movement until the announcement of his resignation on 11 February 2011. The Egyptian people paid a heavy price for the success of their revolution as they became the targets not only of the state security apparatus but the supporters of the Mubarak regime in the city of Suez, Alexandria, and other cities.

The Libyan revolution began on 15 February 2011 with demonstrations in Benghazi against the arrest of the human rights activist Fethi Tarbel. Within four weeks of the start of these demonstrations, the Libyan uprising had transformed from a spontaneous uprising into a full blown uprising. On February 24, the coastal city of Misrata was taken over by militias opposed to Qadhdhāfī forces. A Transitional National Council (TNC) was formed in Benghazi and on March 5 declared itself the sole representative of the opposition forces. The pro-Qadhdhāfī forces regrouped and launched counterattacks on Benghazi, Misrata, and a number of other Libyan cities. In a significant move on March 17 the UN Security Council declared a no-fly zone over Libya to protect civilians from pro-Qadhdhāfī forces. NATO air strikes on Qadhdhāfī's forces stopped their advance toward Benghazi and saved the population from massacre. As NATO airstrikes systematically began to target and destroy Qadhdhāfī's air defenses, the forces opposed to Qadhdhāfī began to gain ground, and on August 21, they entered Tripoli. Qadhdhāfī was finally captured and killed on 20 October 2011, in his birthplace, E.

In Syria, in July 2000, a young Bashar al-Assad had taken over power in Damascus amid increased optimism. It was hoped that a Western-educated president would transform Syria into a modern state in the Arab world. The anti-Bashar uprising in Syria began in March 2011 in the province of Derra with the arrest of fifteen school children who had written antigovernment slogans on their school's wall. On March 18, demonstrations broke out in five Syrian cities including Damascus with protestors demanding the release of arrested children in Derra and reforms in the political system. However, the brutalities of the Syrian security forces in suppressing the Syrian popular uprisings led to the demands for the removal of President Bashar al-Assad and caused the deaths of several thousand civilians. Province after province rose up against the government rule. Assad dug in, unleashing tanks, artillery, and other heavy weapons against civilian targets, causing the deaths and injuries of thousands of civilians. In particular, massacres of civilians have been committed by government forces in places such as Homs, Houla, Hama, Jisr al-Shugour, Qubair, Taftanaz, and Jabal al-Zawiya. The failure of the UN Security Council to speak with one voice to deal with the Syrian situation ultimately led to the announcement of Kofi Annan's Six Point Plan on 16 March 2012. This called for a military pullback, temporary cease-fire, and political dialogue. Both the Assad government and the opposition accepted this plan, but the violence continued. Three hundred UN peacekeepers were deployed to Syria following an April 21 UN Security Council decision to do so. However, because of continued violence, their activities were halted. In Geneva on 30 June 2012, at a UN-sponsored conference, a communique was adopted that called for the formation of a transitional government of national unity, to consist of all parties involved in the Syrian conflict. There are sharp differences between Russia and the Western powers over the interpretations of this communique. The United States and the United Kingdom maintain that President Assad must give up power and cannot be part of an interim government. Russia, on the other hand, maintains that only the Syrian people have the right to choose their president.

Impact on Political Dynamics and Future Prospects. The political upheavals of 2010–2011 in the MENA have changed the region forever. However, as Katerina Delacoura has pointed out, it is clear that comparisons of the Arab Spring to the end of communism in Eastern Europe in 1989 were premature (Delacoura, 2012). While it is a fact that countries like Tunisia and Egypt have thrown out their despotic regimes, these societies still have a long way to go in establishing democratic order. Egypt elected a new parliament and a new president—Mohamed Morsi of Muslim Brotherhood. Before he could take his oath of office, the Military Council dissolved the newly elected parliament and assumed the legislative powers. The newly elected president took his oath of office on 30 June 2012, before the Supreme Constitutional Court instead of the Egyptian parliament.

In Tunisia, the first ever democratic elections for parliament were held in October 2011. These were won by the moderate Islamist Ennahda Party, which got 41 percent of the vote, winning ninety seats in the 217-member Constituent Assembly. Tunisia's constitution is being debated although it had been proposed to be ready by 23 October 2012. Parliamentary elections are to be held by December 2013. The Ennahda has vowed to respect the secular nature of the Tunisian state. The July elections in Libya saw liberals as the main winners. The Arab Spring has left its mark on the domestic reform agenda in the MENA region. Bahrain, which faced sustained and often violent demonstrations against the ruling family, had to commission an independent judiciary body to examine the charges of torture. This judiciary body's recommendations were implemented by the government of Bahrain. Jordan and Morocco also carried out limited reforms in their political systems.

Syria remains arguably the most problematic state in the MENA. The downing of a Turkish Air Force jet by Syria in June 2012 shows that the situation there may dissolve into regional conflict. Turkey refrained from invoking the NATO security clause that might have described the Syrian downing of Turkish jet as an attack on the entirety of NATO. The June 30 meeting at Geneva once again showed the existence of fundamental differences between Russia and China on the one hand and the United States, the United Kingdom, and France on the other. The Annan plan does not indicate any confidence about the prospect for peace in a troubled Syria.

Bibliography

Ammar, Tawnia Sanford. "Where Are the Leaders of Tunisia's Jasmine Revolution?" *The Mark*, 27 January 2011, http://www.themarknews.com/articles/3866-where-are-the-leaders-of-tunisias-jasmine-revolution#.T-pv5cWgSHQ.

Delacoura, Katerina. "The 2011 Uprisings in the Arab Middle East: Political Change and Geopolitical Implications." *International Affairs* 88, no. 1 (January 2012): 63–79.

Haseeb, Khair El-Din. "The Arab Spring Revisited." *Contemporary Arab Affairs* 5, no. 2 (April 2012): 185–197.

Lacher, Wolfram. "Families, Tribes, and Cities in the Libyan Revolution." *Middle East Policy* 18, no. 4 (Winter 2011): 140–154.

Lesch, Ann M. "Egypt's Spring: Causes of the Revolution." *Middle East Policy* 18, no. 3 (Fall 2011): 35–48.

Ramadan, Tariq. *The Arab Awakening: Islam and the New Middle East.* London: Allen Lane, 2012.

"Strategic Geography 2011." *Strategic Survey* 111, no. 1 (2011): i–xx.

Ishtiaq Hossain

Arslān, Shakīb. Shakīb Arslān, (1869–1946), was a Druze leader, a nobleman known as the "Prince of Eloquence" (*Amīr al-Bayān*), a prolific and influential writer, poet, and historian, as well as an astute Lebanese politician. Though supportive of the Ottoman Empire, Arslān was largely influenced by the epochal ideas of the great Egyptian thinker, Muḥammad ʿAbduh. Long before he settled in Switzerland, where he created a powerful mouthpiece, the journal *La Nation Arabe*, Arslān traveled extensively, believed in the Pan-Islamism espoused by Sultan Abdülhamid in Constantinople, supported the survival of a dying Ottoman Empire as the last guarantee against the division of the *ummah*, and vociferously opposed Western colonialism. Notwithstanding inherent incompatibilities between an empire's political aspirations and devotion to a deity, Arslān articulated a vision that saw commonality between Ottomanism and Islam. He assumed that intrinsic religious reforms would naturally lead to the revival of the Ottoman Empire which was a victim of secular nationalism and gradually succumbed to the rise of the nation-state system throughout the Muslim world.

Born into a powerful Druze clan, Shakīb Arslān was destined for a position of leadership, and benefited from an exposure to Mount Lebanon's Christian communities. For seven years at the Hikmah School, Shakīb worked to master the Arabic language, delving into classical literature with Shaykh ʿAbd Allāh al-Bustānī, who authored the key and still widely used dictionary *al-Bustān*. In 1866, Arslān moved to the Sultaniyyah School in Beirut, where Arslān met Egyptian reformer Shaykh Muḥammad ʿAbduh, with whom he formed a long-lasting relationship.

Shakīb was appointed governor of Choueifat and served his followers in the Chouf Mountains starting in 1887. Two years later, the young governor went to Constantinople, where he embarked on a writing career. A firm believer that only the Sublime Porte could successfully face Europe, Arslān overlooked the Ottoman Empire's inherent weaknesses, which would lead to its fatal demise.

Arslān's visceral hatred of French and British imperialism caused him a lot more trouble than many predicted as he was exiled from Lebanon by French Mandate authorities. Whether his putative sympathies toward Germany were colored by this revulsion remains to be determined, although it is widely known that Arslān went to Berlin in the summer of 1917. In the German capital, he met with several high-ranking officials and drew attention by blaming allied powers for the famine then spreading throughout Syria. Importantly, he could not find the courage to simultaneously denounce Ottoman officials, whose policies were largely responsible for the starvation.

Arslān moved to Switzerland at the beginning of 1920, from where he observed the collapse of the Ottoman Empire and the rise of a secular Turkey. Among very few Lebanese who rendered such a level of service to Ottoman officials, Arslān's choice led to his permanent exile, as he witnessed "his military idols smashed, [and] his homeland occupied by a foreign power" (Kramer, 2008, p. 104). Still, he never gave up on Arab unity, spending most of the interwar years in Geneva as the unofficial representative of Syria and Palestine at the League of Nations. It was in Switzerland that his prolific pen was unleashed with gusto.

The periodical became an influential mouthpiece, even if critics insisted that Arslān "never made the full passage to Arabism," concentrating instead on "an all-embracing Islamic nationalism, which included but transcended the Arab cause" (Kéchichian, 2011). In 1937, Arslān submitted twenty-eight volumes of his writings on behalf of Arab nationalism to the Syrian ministry of foreign affairs, though Damascus never latched on to his ideas.

Arslān argued that lack of justice led to the current malaise, as leaders protected their own lives instead of addressing national concerns. In his magnum opus, *Our Decline: Its Causes and Remedies*, which was a response to a letter written by Shaykh Muhammad Basyuni ʿImran of Borneo, Arslān compared Muslims with Europeans and the Japanese, and identified faith as the source of the latter two groups' power and wealth. He thus recommended adopting similar tactics.

Shakīb Arslān married Salimah al-Khass, a Circassian woman, who gave him a son, Ghalib, and two daughters, Nazimah and Mayy. In turn, Mayy married into another Druze family, becoming the wife of Kamal Jumblatt; Walīd Jumblatt, the current scion of the family, was the product of that union. Arslān died in 1946, a few months after returning to his native Lebanon.

BIBLIOGRAPHY

Arslān, Shakīb. *Our Decline: Its Causes and Remedies.* Kuala Lumpur, Malaysia: Islamic Book Trust, 2004.

Cleveland, William L. *Islam against the West: Shakib Arslan and the Campaign for Islamic Nationalism.* Austin: University of Texas Press, 1985.

Kéchichian, Joseph A. "The Prince of Eloquence." *Gulf News*, 20 May 2011. Available online: http://gulf-news.com/life-style/people/the-prince-of-eloquence-1.809019.

Kramer, Martin Seth. *Arab Awakening and Islamic Revival: The Politics of Ideas in the Middle East.* Piscataway, N.J.: Transaction, 2008.

Joseph A. Kéchichian

Ashʿarīs. Ashʿarīs (Ashʿarites) are followers of the mainstream Sunnī theological school founded by Abū al-Ḥasan al-Ashʿarī (d. 935) who crafted a *kalām* synthesis of Ḥanbalī theological doctrines and Muʿtazilī dialectical methodology. However, since his method displays Muʿtazilī influences, Ḥanbalīs and traditionalists attacked Ashʿarites for their use of rational arguments in matters of divine unity and theodicy. Al-Ashʿarī's combination creates several contradictions on divine attributes and acts. For example, the best known contribution of al-Ashʿarī to Sunnī theology, his theory of acquisition, *kasb*, is highly criticized by his opponents for its incoherence. Al-Ashʿarī argues that God is the only creator of acts (giving credit to Ḥanbalīs), but human agents acquire them by an ad hoc capacity created by God (failing to please Muʿtazilīs but losing Ḥanbalī support, as his position implies determinism, *jabr*).

Early Ashʿarīs, known as *mutaqaddimūn al-ashāʿirah*, such as Abū Bakr al-Bāqillānī (d. 1013) and Abū Bakr Ibn Fūrak (d. 1015), maintained al-Ashʿarī's line; while endorsing a rational argument, they were faithful to the positions of Sunnī orthodoxy. The impact of traditionalism can be clearly perceived in their writings. However, later Ashʿarites, known as *muta'akhkhirūn al-ashāʿirah*, such as Abū Ḥāmid al-Ghazālī (d. 1111) and Fakhr al-Dīn al-Rāzī (d. 1209), considerably changed Ashʿarī theology. It was influenced by Sufism, Islamic philosophy, and Muʿtazilism, which countered the traditionalist component. After the twelfth century, Ashʿarīs became the dominant school throughout the Muslim world. Its close ties with Sunnī dynasties, Ṣūfī brotherhoods, and the Mālikī and Shāfiʿī schools secured its supremacy over its adversaries. With regard to the problem of divine attributes, looseness is one specific aspect of Ashʿarism, which allows its followers either to interpret divine attributes (*ta'wīl*) as later Ashʿarīs did or to defer their meaning as early Ashʿarīs did (*tafwīḍ*). This laxity of the Ashʿarīs appears above all in their political ideas.

Political Doctrines. With reference to the issue of the imamate, al-Ashʿarī's position reflected the Sunnī orthodoxy's acknowledgment of the historical reality. Simultaneously, he justifies the obligation of the imamate by *sharʿī* arguments and reasons on its functioning by interest. The starting point of his political thought is the necessity of a ruler to manage the legal, economic, and political affairs of the community. For al-Ashʿarī, there are two sets of qualities needed in such a ruler: There is a maximalist one in which the *imām* is required to be Qurashī and a *mujtahid*—he has to be able to issue legal opinions independently and have numerous moral and physical qualities. No one can be called an *imām* unless he possesses all these qualities. But if there is nobody with these qualities, al-Ashʿarī turns minimalist. He approves even an unjust ruler (*sulṭān jā'ir*) or king (*malik*) as long as he applies Islamic law and preserves the community's unity. Al-Ashʿarī's approach appears in the mode of the designation of the *imām*. He states that the normal mode of appointing an *imām* is by contract (*ʿaqd*), where a qualified group of Muslims (*ahl al-ḥall wa-al-ʿaqd*) agree to choose a candidate as *imām*. However, al-Ashʿarī is willing to recognize other modes of choice, as in the case of the designation of ʿUmar ibn al-Khaṭṭāb (d. 644) as an heir by Abū Bakr al-Ṣiddīq (d. 634). Finally, if a rebellion contests the leadership of a ruler, al-Ashʿarī supports the legal *imām*, but he also justifies the position of his adversaries. For him, they act by interpretation, or *ijtihād*, and therefore they are erroneous but not sinners or unbelievers.

Ashʿarīs' relationship to the state is best illustrated by al-Ghazālī. As with many of his predecessors and successors, he took on the function of providing advice, *naṣīḥah*, for the Seljuk political authorities with the conviction that *sharīʿah* should govern public order, according to the religious duty of commanding right and forbidding wrong. However, the latter is the task of the ruler and not that of the jurist. For him, the jurist's role is to maintain the centrality of Muslim legal-ethical principles in any political system adopted by Muslims, by way of preaching. Al-Ghazālī does not embrace the submissive role of a mirror for princes seeking effective governance, but recalls the principles of Islam in governance according to the legacy of Muḥammad and the early Islamic caliphate. In his political ideas, al-Ghazālī is a conservative, defending social and political stability. Although he aspires to a legitimate political-religious order (the imamate), he accepts the sultanate as a necessary way to maintain order.

Ashʿarīs endorse the duty of commanding right and forbidding wrong as a communitarian responsibility, but delegate it to the state's authority. Although they agree with traditionalist on the obligation of commanding right, they reject its excessive application by some zealous Ḥanbalīs. On the other side, they discard the Muʿtazilī view that considers commanding right as a principle of belief incumbent on all believers. The apprehension of civil war, hardship, and disintegration of the community is a major axis of the Ashʿarī political thought. Therefore, Ashʿarīs always warn against the threat of chaos, *fitnah*, which could become real if commanding right is not regulated. Accordingly, commanding right should not threaten the public order and hence should be carried out by the state or with its approbation. They establish several conditions that make fulfilling the duty almost unfeasible. In al-Ghazālī's view, the performer of the duty should meet the following five conditions: legal competence, belief, probity, official permission, and power. As for the performance of the duty, one must go through eight levels, which start with seeking information and end with military violence. In fact, there are no available accounts of Ashʿarīs taking part in any violent cases of commanding right. Rather, they were negative-quietist, recognizing fully the authority of the state in this matter. With these various conditions, Ashʿarīs reduce the duty to its minimalist sense, seeking mainly cooperation rather than confrontation.

Since the tenth century, Ḥanbalīs became the main adversaries of Ashʿarīs. Their rivalry began as a theological debate, but was stimulated and intensified by political factors. This controversy became public and even violent in Baghdad and Damascus, where a competition between the two Sunnī schools of thought took place. After the arrival of the Seljuks in Baghdad, the opposition became sharp owing to the fact that they created the Niẓāmīyah schools and adopted Ashʿarism as an official dogma. Ḥanbalīs, allies of the ʿAbbāsid caliphs, opposed Ashʿarīs violently and led a terrorizing campaign under the leadership of al-Sharīf Abū Jaʿfar (d. 1077). In Mamlūk Damascus, the Ḥanbalī minority had to face Ashʿarī persecution. For example, Ibn Taymīyah (d. 1328) criticized later Ashʿarīs for following Muslim philosophers and Muʿtazilīs and spent several years in jail. With the gradual isolation of Ḥanbalīs in Nejd and the eastern Arabian coast, the conflict between Ḥanbalīs and Ashʿarīs in medieval Islam almost came to an end. However, the movement of Muḥammad b. ʿAbd al-Wahhāb (d. 1792) in Nejd revived the controversy and spread it across the Muslim world.

Modern Ashʿarīs. Modern Ashʿarīs pursue mainly the later Ashʿarī doctrine, with Ṣūfī leanings and Salafī reformist influences (especially of Muḥammad ʿAbduh [d. 1905]). Modern official religious adherence to Ashʿarī belief can be seen in Morocco (the Ministry of Endowments and Islamic Affairs and al-Qarawīyīn make it a pillar of Moroccan identity) and in Egypt (the *shaykh al-Azhar* and the mufti of Egypt are overtly Ashʿarī). In addition, the majority of Muslim religious learning centers teach the Ashʿarī creed (northern, western, and eastern Africa; Syria-Jordan-Lebanon; and Southeast Asia). In most modern Islamic colleges, there is a conflict between teachers of Ḥanbalī and Ashʿarī doctrines. Today's most outstanding Ashʿarī theologian is Muḥammad Saʿīd Ramaḍān al-Būṭī of Syria. In Jordan, Saʿīd Fūda, who wrote a brief refutation of Ibn Taymīyah, actively claims and disseminates Ashʿarism. Nonetheless, in Jordan it is Ḥasan al-Saqqāf who is considered the voice of scholarly Ashʿarism. In Syria and Jordan, Ashʿarism has the asset of state-supported Islamic colleges. As for Lebanon, Ashʿarism is diffused by the al-Aḥbāsh movement, a strong Ṣūfī and charitable association founded by ʿAbd Allāh al-Hararī (d. 2008). Ḥabib ʿAlī al-Jifrī (Yemen), another influential Ashʿarī, combines Ashʿarism, Sufism, and popular televised preaching. Most modern Ashʿarīs support established regimes in Muslim countries, harshly criticize Ḥanbalī Salafīyah, and discredit radical Islamism violence.

BIBLIOGRAPHY

Allard, Michel. "En quoi consiste l'opposition faite à al-Ashʿarī par ses contemporains Ḥanbalites?" *Revue des Études Islamiques* 28 (1960): 93–105.

Cook, Michael. *Commanding Right and Forbidding Wrong in Islamic Thought*. Cambridge, U.K.: Cambridge University Press, 2000.

Frank, Richard M. "Moral Obligation in Classical Muslim Theology." *Journal of Religious Ethics* 11 (1983): 204–223.

Gimaret, Daniel. *La doctrine d'al-Ashʿarī*. Paris: Cerf, 1990.

Hillenbrand, Carole. "Islamic Orthodoxy or Realpolitik? Al-Ghazālī's Views on Government." *Iran* 26 (1988): 81–94.

Kabha, Mustafa, and Haggai Erlich. "Al-Ahbash and Wahhabiyya: Interpretations of Islam." *International Journal of Middle East Studies* 38 (2006): 519–538.

Makdisi, George. "Ashʿarī and the Ashʿarites in Islamic Religious History." *Studia Islamica* 17 (1962): 37–80.

ABDESSAMAD BELHAJ

ATATÜRK, MUSTAFA KEMAL. Mustafa Kemal Atatürk (1881–1938) was the founding father of the Turkish Republic. Born of modest parentage to Zübeyde Hanım and Ali Rıza Efendi in the cosmopolitan Ottoman port of Selânik (Thessaloniki) into a markedly Muslim environment, Atatürk opted for a military education against his parents' wishes, graduating from the Military Staff College in Constantinople as an infantry staff captain in 1905. Various sources question Mustafa's Turkish origins, with *Time* magazine asserting that his father was Albanian and his mother Macedonian (*Time*, 12 October 1953, "Turkey: The Land a Dictator Turned Into a Democracy." http://www.time.com/time/magazine/article/0,9171,860057-2,00.html). According to the *Encyclopaedia Judaica*, Kemal Atatürk was of Dönmeh—crypto-Jewish—origins, an assertion denied by the Turkish government even if his father was believed to be of Albanian stock. Atatürk was a participant in the Young Turk movement; his early military career ran concurrently with his secret, illegal political activities against the despotism of Sultan Abdülhamid II—itself a misconstrued attempt to inoculate the empire against a slow throttling by the Great Powers.

Early Military Career. Atatürk saw no contradiction between his military profession and his founding, joining, and propagating of various revolutionary societies. He was active in quelling uprisings in the capital (1909) and Albania (1910), as well as in the defense of Ottoman Libya against Italy (1911–1912). It was the disastrous Balkan Wars of 1912–1913, however, that really accelerated his conversion to Turkish nationalism.

Atatürk emerged from World War I a brigadier general, and when Mehmed VI became the new sultan of the Ottoman Empire in July 1918, he appointed Mustafa Kemal as commander of the Seventh Army, in Palestine. By November 1918, Kemal was forced to organize the return of the battle-hardened Yıldırım Army Group, which was then officially dissolved, as Kemal confronted an occupied Constantinople. Yet with the finality of their defeat, the Turks faced the problem of preserving their existence in the face of the victorious Allies' attempts to dismember what remained of the empire. Atatürk shared the officers' belief in the efficacy of the regular military to resist such pressures, and assumed decisive military and political leadership. In May 1919, he joined the nascent Turkish national movement to fight in what became the Turkish War of Independence. His supervision and centralization of spontaneous and widespread local resistance by establishing an alternative national assembly to represent the resistant Turkey grew out of his conviction that a nation's claim to full independence must be fought for, not granted—a postulate central to the National Struggle of 1919–1922 demanded the absolute loyalty of the professional soldiers to it.

The Republic. With the foundation of the Republic of Turkey in 1923, Atatürk concentrated on advancing his nationalist revolution. Through a series of predominantly political reforms, he endeavored to establish an inherently capitalist nation-state based on the principle of popular sovereignty; the state's moral substance would be a conscious synthesis of indigenous and universal elements. The new social order he envisaged assumed a modern state inclining toward democracy, in which ideas that had taken root in Enlightenment Europe would be grafted onto a liberated Turkey. He aimed to teach individuals to take control of their own affairs, to stimulate a nationalist economy free from foreign dominance, and, significantly, to secularize the polity.

Atatürk and Islam. The depth of Atatürk's religious conviction is still unclear, though Zübeyde Hanım allegedly encouraged Mustafa to attend a religious school, something he did reluctantly and only briefly; what is certain is that his drive toward secularism (called *lâiklik*, a Turkish adaptation of the French word *laïcisme*) in Turkey was not conceived as an attack on Islam, which he considered the most rational, natural, and therefore final religion. In 1926, he introduced laws that separated *Sharīʿah* law from secular regulations, which seriously restricted the autonomy enjoyed by religious authorities.

Assessment. Atatürk lived his life seeking to impose the possible but not attempting to impose the not-yet-possible. Atatürk's attempted reform of Turkish religious life comprises, with his other social reforms, a consistent political philosophy. His ultimate objective, in a generally applicable formula, was the achievement of a genuine and modernizing nation, responsible for and answerable to its citizens individually and collectively, which would survive, conscious and assured, in the contemporary world.

BIBLIOGRAPHY

Hanioğlu, M. Şükrü. *Atatürk: An Intellectual Biography*. Princeton, N.J.: Princeton University Press, 2011.

Iğdemir, Uluğ, et al. *Atatürk: Biography*. Translated by Andrew J. Mango. Ankara: Turkish National Commission for UNESCO, 1981. This is a complete translation of the entry "Atatürk, Gazi Mustafa Kemal" in *İslâm Ansiklopedisi*, vol. 1, fasc. 10, pp. 719–807. Istanbul: Milli Eğitim Basımevi, 1950.

M. Naim Turfan
Updated by Joseph A. Kéchichian

Australia and Oceania. Muslim communities in Australia and Oceania form a very small proportion of the populations of their countries of residence as well as of the global Muslim population. However, their presence has had a disproportionate political impact, largely due to the international security environment in the years since 11 September 2001.

History. Small numbers of Afghan, Malay, and Turkish Muslim migrants began to arrive in Australia as hawkers, cameleers, and pearl divers during the nineteenth century. However, their wives and families were not permitted entry. Elsewhere in Oceania, Muslim indentured laborers were brought to Fiji from the Indian subcontinent by the British colonizers to work in the sugarcane fields in the late nineteenth century, while the leaders of an 1871 Muslim insurgency against the French colonization of Algeria were deported to New Caledonia.

Muslim migration to Australia and New Zealand was limited throughout much of the twentieth century by policies excluding nonwhite applicants. This policy eased in Australia in 1967 with the signing of an agreement to facilitate migration from Turkey. In the decades that followed, conflicts in Lebanon, Afghanistan, Iraq, and Somalia generated substantial numbers of Muslim refugees to Australia, while others took up residence as international students or as skilled and business migrants. New Zealand has seen a dramatic rise in the number of Muslim migrants (like Australia, highly ethnically diverse) since the 1980s. The recent emergence of Muslim communities in Vanuatu, the Solomon Islands, and Papua New Guinea is mainly due to conversion rather than migration (Flower, 2008).

Communities, Institutions, and Leadership. Islamic organizations and institutions in Australia and New Zealand were established within particular ethnic communities and have retained strong ethnic and sectarian identities. Given the high degree of diversity among such communities, the issue of who may legitimately claim to represent Muslims has proved both complex and contentious. The Australian Federation of Islamic Councils (AFIC) was established as an umbrella organization of Muslim community organizations in 1964. AFIC's main role has been the building of mosques and schools, the certification of *ḥalāl* meat (an important source of revenue for the organization during its early years), and as a national advocacy organization (Saeed, 2003). The Federation of Islamic Associations of New Zealand (FIANZ) was formed in 1979 and has taken a similar role, with a strong emphasis on an education (Federation of Islamic Associations of New Zealand, 2011).

In 1988, AFIC created the position of mufti of Australia, mostly in order to boost the residency application of the position's first incumbent, Shaykh Taj al-Din al-Hilali. Hilali, who was facing deportation proceedings at the time, is imam of a major mosque in Lakemba, a Sydney suburb with a large Lebanese population. Given the diversity of the Australian Muslim community, the creation of the position of a national mufti was disputed by many analysts. Mohamad Abdalla writes that since multiethnic communities encompass a diversity of religious understanding and practice, "clearly the legitimacy and authority of one Mufti for all Australian Muslims will not be recognised" (Abdalla, 2011, p. 223). This dispute has been compounded by a series of public controversies over Hilali's reported sermons on issues such as "the Jews," sexual violence, and Australian identity. These controversies eventually led to Hilali being passed over in favor of the Melbourne-based Shaykh Fehmi Naji el-Imam.

Muslims in Fiji initially sought representation as members of the Indian community rather than as Muslims. However, rising Hindu-Muslim tensions during the 1920s led to the deepening of religious identity and the formation of the Fiji Muslim League in 1926. Sectarian divisions have hampered unified political organization (Ali, 2004).

Muslims in Australia and New Zealand attracted intermittent political attention during the 1990s, mostly in the wake of international stories such as the first Gulf War, the "Rushdie affair" after the publication of *The Satanic Verses*, and the conflicts in Bosnia and Kosovo. However, initial participation by Muslims in Australian public life was primarily defined according to ethnic rather than religious identity.

Like Muslims living in other Western societies, Muslims living in Australia and New Zealand have come under an intense and often hostile scrutiny in the years since 11 September 2001, largely due to their perceived status as a security hazard, but also due to the cultural threat that they are supposed to pose to "mainstream values." This has led to a shift from ethnic to religious identity in terms of both public perception and self-identification.

Australian Muslims David Hicks and Mamdouh Habib were imprisoned in Guantanamo Bay after being detained in Pakistan and Afghanistan in the weeks following September 11. The detention of Hick and Habib was a high-profile political controversy until their eventual repatriation to Australia and release (Habib in 2005, Hicks in 2007).

The 2002 bombings in Bali, in which eighty-eight Australians and three New Zealanders were killed, were widely perceived as an attack on Australia and its lifestyle because of Bali's proximity and its long-standing popularity with Australian tourists. The 2005 London bombings, in which an Australian and a New Zealander were killed, focused attention on the possible hazard posed by "homegrown terrorists" within Australian Muslim communities. This led to measures such as the introduction of counterterrorism legislation and the referral of eight "extremist" Islamic books to the Literature Classification Board by the Commonwealth attorney general. Two books by Abdullah Azzam were eventually banned.

The alleged incompatibility of Islamic gender norms with "mainstream" values has played a prominent role in political discourse in Australia and New Zealand. Although neither country has introduced regulations regarding the wearing of hijab or burqa in public space, Muslim women's dress codes have been the subject of extensive public debate, and women wearing hijab are vulnerable to abuse and harassment, as well discrimination in employment. The entitlement of Muslim women to leave their faces covered when giving evidence in court has also been contested. In the New Zealand case, it was decided that the women should unveil behind a screen, hidden from the public and most of the court staff. In the case in Western Australia, the woman was ordered to uncover her face in court.

A religious vilification case brought by the Islamic Council of Victoria (ICV) against the Christian organization "Catch the Fire" received international media coverage, partly because religious legislation was then under consideration in the United Kingdom. The ICV's case was initially upheld but dismissed on appeal.

A series of sexual assaults by Muslim men upon non-Muslim women (referred to in media coverage as "the Sydney gang rapes") were reported as having been motivated by the offenders' religious identity and contempt for non-Muslim women. Anger over the alleged assault of lifeguards and the harassment of Australian women by young Muslim men was cited as a trigger for the 2005 "Cronulla riots" in Sydney (Ho, 2007). The perception of Islam as mandating sexual violence against non-Muslim women was reinforced by the reporting of a sermon by then-mufti Shaykh Hilali, in which he likened immodestly dressed women to "uncovered meat" left out for cats to devour (Mattar, 2006).

The unregulated arrival of asylum seekers from Muslim-majority countries such as Afghanistan, Iraq, and Iran by boat from Southeast Asia has been a high-profile political issue in Australia. The government led by Prime Minister John Howard introduced the so-called "Pacific Solution" in response to rescue of 438 asylum seekers by the Norwegian freighter MV *Tampa* in August 2000. Until the policy was declared unconstitutional by the high court in 2007, asylum seekers entering Australia by boat were transported to Nauru and to Manus Island in Papua New Guinea rather than having their applications processed on the Australian mainland.

The building of community facilities such as mosques and schools has generated flashpoints for anti-Muslim sentiment in Australia. In particular, the application to build an Islamic school in Camden, a regional town on the outskirts of Sydney, met with widespread opposition from locals and was ultimately rejected by the local council in 2008.

The recent appearance of small Muslim communities in Papua New Guinea, the Solomon Islands, and Vanuatu has sparked hostility from Christian organizations, as well as security concerns. However, substantial evidence supporting such fears is yet to be documented (Flower, 2008).

BIBLIOGRAPHY

Abdalla, Mohamad. "Do Australian Muslims Need a Mufti? Analyzing the Institution of *Ifta* in the Australian Context." *Law and Religion in Public Life: The Contemporary Debate*, edited by Nadirsyah Hosen and Richard Mohr, pp. 214–228. New York: Routledge, 2011.

Ali, Jan. "Islam and Muslims in Fiji." *Journal of Muslim Minority Affairs* 24, no. 1 (2004): 141–154.

Evans, Martin. "Culture and Empire, 1830–1962: An Overview." *Empire and Culture: The French Experience, 1830–1940*, edited by Martin Evans, pp. 1–26. New York: Palgrave Macmillan, 2004.

Flower, Scott. "Muslims in Melanesia: Putting Security Issues in Perspective." *Australian Journal of International Affairs* 62, no. 3 (2008): 408–429.

Ho, C. (2007) "Muslim Women's New Defenders: Women's Rights, Nationalism, and Islamophobia in Contemporary Australia." *Women's Studies International Forum* 30, no. 4 (2007): 290–298.

Kolig, Erich, and Nahid Kabir. "Not Friend, Not Foe: The Rocky Road of Enfranchisement of Muslims into Multicultural Nationhood in Australia and New Zealand." *Immigrants and Minorities* 26, no. 3 (2008): 266–300.

Mattar, Delia, trans. "What Sheik Hilali Said." *Australian*, 22 October 2006.

Pennell, Richard, Pam Pryde, and Emmett Stinson. *Banning Islamic Books in Australia*. Melbourne: Melbourne University Press, 2011.

Saeed, Abdullah. *Islam in Australia*. Sydney: Allen & Unwin, 2003.

SHAKIRA HUSSEIN

AUTHORITY AND LEGITIMATION.

The reality of inner-Islamic diversity is reflected in the multifaceted ways in which Muslims of today view authority and legitimation. The twenty-first century heralds three competing directions within Islam, each in disagreement with the others, on how to determine authority and legitimation. These directions refer first to the use of Islam by rulers to legitimate their authority, second the opposite, namely to use religion to legitimate the political opposition by Islamist movements. The third direction of civil Islam revives the buried tradition of Islamic humanism and is critical of the first and second directives. At issue is the question of who is entitled to the authority and legitimation. Among the concerns is who has the authority to declare *jihād* on non-Muslims and on those Muslims in power whose legitimacy is contested. In the recent past, some secular leaders (such as Saddam Hussein prior to the Iraq War of 2003) and Islamist oppositionists (such as Osama Bin Laden) claimed they had authority to declare *jihād*, but were delegitimated by the establishment of the al-Azhar *ʿulamāʾ*. Since the Arab Spring Islamist movements have been driven by the intention to seize power and combine this agenda with a claim to authority and legitimacy in contemporary Islam. They are opposed by a minority of Muslims who are at pains to revive a buried tradition in Islamic civilization, one that can be identified as rationalism and humanism. It elevates reason to a major source of legitimation of political authority (al-Jabri, 1999). This tradition can be understood as a form of Islamic enlightenment once pursued by philosophers such as al-Farabi, Avicenna, Averroës, and Ibn Khaldun. The work of the late Moroccan philosopher Mohammed al-Jabri documents an effort to revive this classical rationalism in contemporary Islam (al-Jabri, 1991; Tibi, 2009, ch. 8).

The old Islamic tradition of determining the authority of the ruler as the imam of the Islamic *ummah* still exists. In this tradition, a distinction is made between the rightful imam (*al-imam al-salih*, or "true imam" [Tibi, 1996]) and the unjust imam (*al-imam al-jaʾir*). A rudimentary form of this tradition is seen today only in two Sunnī countries, Morocco and Saudi Arabia, in which the king claims a religious title associated with his political authority (Tibi, 1985). The title of the Moroccan king is *amīr al-muʾminīn* (commander of the faithful), and the Saudi king is *khādim al-ḥaramayn al-sharīfayn* (custodian of the holy shrines [of Mecca and Medina]). In Saudi Arabia the Qurʾān is considered the constitution, while Morocco has a modern constitution.

In 1992 the late Moroccan king Hassan II showed a willingness to amend the constitution to enhance the power of his prime minister, who is constitutionally subordinate to royal authority. The amendment also refers to human rights mentioned in the constitution. When the constitutional change was submitted to a referendum, the king responded to opposition criticism by emphasizing the authority of an Islamic ruler. He said, "Islam does not permit a constitutional monarchy like the one that exists in western Europe. As a Muslim ruler, I am entitled to temporarily delegate some of my authority to others, but I have no right to give up my own power privileges." This raises the question of whether the king's view represents an authentic perspective on authority and legitimacy in Islam. The al-Azhar University scholar ʿAlī ʿAbd al-Rāziq, in *Islam and the Principles of Government* (1925), held that Islam does not entail a system of government. ʿAbd al-Rāziq argued further that Islam historically has been abused in order to legitimize unjust rule. This position of depoliticizing Islam to prevent its abuse as a device for the legitimation of a political authority is continued in contemporary Islamic thought (al-Najjar, 1977) in the Islamic rejection of the Islamist idea of a *sharīʿah* state (Ashmawi, 1983).

Tawḥīd and Political Authority. In contrast to the enlightened view of a truly liberal Islam, both the religious establishment and Islamist opposition groups believe that Islam is characterized by a holistic view of the world in which politics, law, and all other spheres of life are merged into one (Tibi, 2005, ch. 2). The governing principle of this thinking is the application of *tawḥīd* (the oneness of God, the supreme authority) to politics. God rules not only the world, but also the lives of Muslims and their political order. It follows that Muslims in principle are not allowed to separate political and religious authority, and that political authority has to be religiously grounded; that is, its legitimation has to be related to *tawḥīd*. According to this view, no Muslim ruler can therefore claim to have sovereign authority, because that is God's alone. The rulers legitimate their authority as an execution of the divine will of God as fixed in Islamic revelation. It is this provision to which the Moroccan king's statement refers. However, the Islamist opposition, that shares the same view, denies that a king may legitimate his authority on Islamic principles and legitimates herewith their opposition.

The medieval Islamic theologian Ibn Taymīyah (d. 1328) coined the term *taʿṭīl* for claims by humans to govern the world. His work is a major source for contemporary Islamism. Another source is the authoritative pamphlet *Maʿālim fī al-ṭarīq* (Milestones) by the spiritual father of Islamic fundamentalism, Sayyid Quṭb (1906–66). He reactivated this precept in his challenge to democratic legitimacy and the idea of popular sovereignty. In contrast, contemporary liberal Islam draws on al-Farabi and on the rationalism of Ibn Rushd (Averroës).

Although the outlined basic understanding of authority and legitimacy is shared by most Muslims, Islamic history reveals many competing sectarian patterns of authority and legitimacy. Historians of Islam have described this disagreement as a conflict over how to identify the true imam or authority for Muslims (Hartmann, 1944; Tibi, 1996). The wide range of political rulers who have been legitimized through Islam shows the extent that Muslims have disagreed about legitimacy. In classical Islam, Sunnī and Shīʿī rulers and their opponents have legitimized their authority on the basis of their specific understanding of Islam. The lack of a tradition of a generally accepted pluralism has contributed to the growth of religious controversies over authority and legitimacy (Watt, 1968). All Muslim rulers refer to the Qurʾānic commandment, "Oh ye who believe, obey Allāh, obey the Prophet and those in authority [*ulu al-amr*] among you" (4:59); whether "authority" here means "power" is a matter of interpretation. In contrast to this tradition, al-Farabi determines order as *al-madīnah al-fāḍilah* (perfect state), based on human reason and ruled by a philosopher as the "true imam" (Farabi, 1985).

In modern times, the disintegration of the Ottoman Empire and the subsequent abolition of the caliphate in 1924 smoothed the way for the introduction of the European nation-state based on the concept of popular sovereignty among Muslims (Enayat, 1982, pp. 111f.; Tibi, 1997). In Arab lands the notion of an Islamic *ummah* (community) has been superficially secularized to refer to an Arab *ummah* that unites Muslims and Christians as distinguished from other non-Arab Muslims. Islamism, the Islamic variety of the global phenomenon of religious fundamentalism, has challenged this new secular concept of the *ummah* (Choueiri, 1990, pp. 63ff.; Tibi, 2002) and has contested the assumption that the legitimacy of the modern state is secularly grounded.

In his monograph *The Legitimation of Power* (1991), David Beetham devotes a chapter to Islam, in which he points out that the politicization of Islam presents a challenge to Western notions of the exclusively secular basis of political legitimacy. At the core of this challenge is the idea of the Islamic state. Islamists argue that the Islamic *sharīʿah* state can only be based on a specific pattern of authority and legitimacy (Kurdi, 1984; Feldman, 2008). Given that Islamic fundamentalists are not traditionalists—they themselves are both a product of modernity and a reaction to the process of modernization (Tibi, 1993)—the question is whether the concept of an Islamic state is based on a new rather than a traditional type of legitimacy. The term "state" (*dawlah*) occurs neither in the Qur'an nor in the *ḥadīth* of the Prophet. The idea of an Islamic state is based on an Islamist invention of tradition (Tibi, 2012).

Divine Sanction of Political Authority. In a departure from the politicized principle of *tawḥīd* and thus from the belief that God governs the entire world, all spheres of life in the Islamic state are expected to be organized in accordance with Islamic revelation. According to this understanding, political authority in Islam must always be grounded in divine legitimacy. In classical Islam, the caliph's authority was supposed to be based on his submission to the *sharīʿah*. Although he, as the imam of the *ummah*, is the absolute political leader of the Islamic community, he has no right to legislate; his authority is restricted to administering *Sharīʿah*. In practice, however, Islamic rulers have deviated from this principle by introducing the autonomous realm of *siyāsah* (administration), in which the caliph retained some sovereignty. As Joseph Schacht writes in his introduction to Islamic law, "This *siyasah* is the expression of the full juridical power which the sovereign...can exercise whenever he thinks fit...a double administration of justice, one religious and exercised by the Kadi [*qāḍī*] on the basis of the *sharīʿa*, the other secular and exercised by the political authorities" (1964, p. 54). This system of separation of politics from *Sharīʿah* was practiced by the caliphs from the Umayyad period onward.

Contemporary Islamic rulers who base their political authority on Islamic legitimacy draw on a tradition in the political history of Sunnī Islam. The political systems of classical and contemporary Islamic societies are not very institutionalized. According to Samuel P. Huntington's *Political Order in Changing Societies* (1968), one of the consequences of this lack of highly institutionalized structures and processes is the personalization of political power. Thus the authority of the political ruler in Islam, classical and contemporary alike, has been highly personal, not institutional, and has been legitimized in an arbitrary manner by the *ʿulamāʾ* and jurists submissive to the ruler. This fact explains the lack of continuing institutional power in Islamic history. The focus in Islamic political thought on the quality of the ruling imam, not on the political institutions, is an indication of this flaw (Tibi, 1996).

Shīʿī and Sunnī. The sectarian division most pertinent to authority and legitimacy is that which differentiates the doctrines of the caliphate in Sunnī Islam from the imamate in Shīʿī Islam. For Sunnī Muslims the caliph is an imam both as the symbolic leader of congregational prayers and as the political leader, but for the Shīʿīs, the imam is not a political leader. Whereas Sunnīs believe that prophecy ended with the death of the Prophet, Shīʿīs believe in the continuation of prophecy through the imams; they conceive the imamate not as temporal leadership but as religious guidance "for preserving and explaining the Divine Law" (Momen, 1985, p. 147). Thus the legitimacy of the Shīʿī imam is not based only on the interpretation of divine law: "the Imam's knowledge is coextensive with that of the prophets.... Thus the Imam as a result of his knowledge is perfectly able to give judgement on all matters of religious law" (Momen, 1985, p. 156). Some Shīʿī scholars interpret the authority of the imam as political insofar as he is "a person who takes the lead in a community in a particular social movement or political ideology" (ṭabāṭabāʾī, 1975, p. 173).

Until the advent of Ayatollah Ruhollah Khomeini, however, this was not a common view among Shīʿīs. Khomeini's revisionist interpretation of *vilāyat-i faqīh* (mandate of the religious jurist; Persian variant of the Arabic *wilāyat al-faqīh*) "obliterates some of the most important differences between Sunnīs and Shīʿīs. He minimizes the extent of the rift by...his appeal to the Shīʿīs to...install an Islamic state [that] indicates his denunciation of... Shīʿī practices that have become staple themes of Sunnī polemics against Shīʿīsm" (Enayat, 1983, pp. 174–175). It is not surprising that current treatises by Sunnī fundamentalists resort to Khomeini's ideas of authority and legitimacy, which endorse harmony and reconciliation between Sunnīs and Shīʿīs. The Sunnī writer Muḥammad Salīm al-ʿAwwā, in his book *Fī al-niẓām al-siyāsī lil-dawlah al-Islāmīyah* (On the Political System of the Islamic State, 1983), presents such a case.

In the period between the abolition of the Ottoman Empire in the early 1920s and the rise of political Islam as a variety of religious fundamentalism in the early 1970s, the idea of the nation-state and its secular legitimacy seemed to have superseded the idea of an Islamic order. Islamism, like all other varieties of religious fundamentalism, envisions a "remaking of the world" (Tibi, 2002). Earlier, in the nineteenth century, ʿAbd al-Raḥmān al-Kawākibī (d. 1903) was the most important Muslim Arab author seeking to revive the caliphate under Arab rule against the Sunnī Turks, and Muḥammad Rashīd Riḍā's book *The Caliphate or the Supreme Imamate* (1922/1923) was the last significant Islamic work to defend the caliphate. The scholar Shaykh ʿAlī ʿAbd al-Rāziq (d. 1966) held that those who have legitimated political authority by recourse to Islam have abused Islam for their political ends. ʿAbd al-Rāziq's argument, which provoked his dismissal from al-Azhar, was that Islam is a religion and an ethical system, not a system for legitimizing political authority. Despite his dismissal, ʿAbd al-Rāziq's argument had already come to represent the spirit of the times. To be sure, the Islamist gear for an "Islamic state" is not the restoration of the caliphate; it is rather an invention of tradition.

The two Arab Muslim monarchies, Morocco and Saudi Arabia, are legitimized by Islam, and although they differ considerably from one another, both do in some measure reflect Islamic political culture. In his book on legitimacy in Arab politics, Michael Hudson writes:

> The ideal Arab monarchy, perfectly legitimized, entirely congruent with the values of the traditional political culture, would be an Islamic theocracy governed by the ablest leader of a tribe tracing its lineage to the prophet. The ruler would be guided by the substantive ethic of Islam and by the patriarchal consultative procedures of tribal decision-making. The ruler's authority would rest not only on his coercive power but in the respect of his people for a leader on the right path (the Sunna).... By this legitimate behavior alone, he would earn the deference of his people and thus acquire authority. (1977, p. 167)

Contemporary Islamists who deny the claims of Morocco and Saudi Arabia to be "Islamic states" based on the *Sharīʿah* envision a political order legitimized by a "sharīʿatization" of Islam (Tibi, 2009, ch. 3), not merely on the "substantive ethic of Islam" as Hudson argues.

Secularization. Morocco and Saudi Arabia, however, did not fit the dominant pattern of secularization during the period of early decolonization, up through 1967. Between the 1930s and the early 1970s, the secular nation-state was the most widely accepted form of legitimated government in the Arab world, even though the processes of secularization and structural differentiation needed as underpinnings for the nation-state had not taken place in the Islamic world (Tibi, 1997). In the world of Islam, secularization has been normative rather than structural in nature and has thus failed to take root, but also has been replaced in a contemporary process of de-secularization (Tibi, 2009, ch. 6).

The turning point in the resurgence of political Islam and its views on authority and legitimacy was the Arab defeat in the Six-Day War in 1967. The Arab countries were at the center of the contemporary politicization of Islam long before the Islamic revolution in Iran drew the attention of the West to this process that has sharpened the focus on authority and legitimacy in Islam. The crisis of the secular Muslim state has given rise to the claim for an Islamic state as a religious order in place of the existing secular ones. This is the new concept of the Islamic state. As exemplified in the case of ʿAlī ʿAbd al-Rāziq, debates on these issues have persisted in modern Islam, even when secular ideologies prevailed (Tibi, 1986). During the 1950s and 1960s, some important publications revived these debates and reopened the arguments against ʿAbd al-Rāziq's views; significant among them were the works of al-Rayyis (1953), Mūsā (1962), and Mutawallī (1966).

However, prior to 1967, these books could not compete in dissemination and popularity with prevailing secular positions, such as that laid out in Khālid Muḥammad Khālid's *Min hunā nabdaʾ* (From Here We Start). Khālid's book was reprinted ten times between 1950 and 1963 and distributed far beyond Egypt. Khālid's strong argument against what he called *kahānah Islāmīyah* (Islamic theocracy) culminates in a clear commitment against the use of Islam as a legitimation of political authority:

> We should keep in mind that religion ought to be as God wanted it to be: prophecy not kingdom, guidance not government, and preaching, not political rule. The best we can do to keep religion clean and pure is to separate it from politics and to place it above it. The separation between religion and the state contributes to keeping religion away from the shortcomings of the state and from its arbitrariness. (1963, p. 184)

The Islamic State. Such views have been superseded since the early 1970s. Even Khālid now supports the idea of the Islamic state (Khālid, 1988). The strongly articulated plea of Islamism for an "Islamic solution" (Qaradawi) began to replace the secular writings of the enlightened Arab Muslim authors. The roots of this Islamist thinking can be traced back to 1953, when Muḥammad Ḏiyaʾ al-Dīn al-Rayyis asserted that Islam provides a pattern of legal rule because political authority is bound to the legal framework of *Sharīʿah*. He blames those who disagree with him, in particular those whom he calls Orientalists, for viewing Islamic governments as despotic: "The Orientalists, in their allegation that the government of Islam is despotic, are mistaken. . . . The source of their mistake is that they look at the Caliphate that really existed in history. . . . Thus they confuse Islam as a legal idea with what really happened in the Muslim world" (1953, pp. 225–226). Al-Rayyis thus sees Islam as an ideal for a political order. A similar case is also made by ʿAbd al-Ḥāmid Mutawallī in his authoritative book *Mabādiʾ niẓām al-ḥukm fī al-Islām* (Principles of the System of Government in Islam, 1966), where he writes, "As far as the science of government is concerned, Islam provides general principles valid for every time and place." These principles, he says, guarantee the practice of the "Islamic constitutional norms," justice, freedom, participation (*shūrā*), and equality (p. 548). Contemporary Islamists translate this thinking into a political agenda.

Today, these issues of authority and legitimation are no longer relevant just to the world of Islam. The rapidly increasing Islamic diaspora in the West, particularly in Europe, is confronted with the question to what authority diasporic Muslims must submit. While liberal Muslims argue for a Euro-Islam, secular and moderate (Baran, 2010, 157–174), Islamists want to establish, in the name of freedom of faith, a "counter culture" (Berman, 2010, p. 150) with its own terms of authority and legitimation.

In the recent past, Islamism has been wrongly identified as Islamic revivalism. In fact, Islamism engages in an invention of tradition with regard to authority and legitimacy. This is no revival, but rather an indication of a crisis of legitimacy in contemporary Islamic civilization. The legitimacy of rulers is challenged by Islamism in the Islamic world where rulers have no popular legitimizing basis. The alleged return to Islam is presented in the guise of an Islamic state as a *hall Islami* (Islamic solution) for a perceived moral decline. Even though the proponents of the Islamic state derive the legitimacy of their model from the distant past, the pattern of authority and legitimacy they propose is an artifact of the modernity they rhetorically reject. The current crisis brings to light a predicament with modernity. The invention of tradition is no solution to this predicament (Allawi, 2009; Tibi, 2009).

The most sophisticated current treatments of authority and legitimacy are those of Muḥammad Salīm al-ʿAwwā (1983) and Muṣṭafā Abū Zayd Fahmī (1981). They emphasize the legal and participatory meanings of Islamic political norms and so provide an Islamic model of authority and legitimacy seemingly compatible with modernity. However, even these Islamists fail to tell us why Islam has never achieved the democratic, legal, and participatory Islamic values they present. From the early history of Islam (Mottahedeh, 1980) until the present, the personal political authority of imams and emirs (*khuri*) has been legitimated with a reference to Islam. However, it was a personal rule that used Islam to justify the ruler's status as an imam. The historical context of authority and legitimacy has changed, but the fact of personal rule has not. The invention of tradition in the guise of an Islamic *sharīʿah* state is not an Islamic revival that may help Muslims to come to terms with their predicament with modernity. A true revival would be more promising if it were based on a modern interpretation of the tradition of Islamic humanism and on al-Farabi's concept of a truly Islamic *madīnah fāḍilah*, a proper polity in which the authority of the rulers is legitimized by a combination of free elections and the political culture of democracy.

[*See also* ʿAbd al-Rāziq, ʿAlī; Caliphate, Theories of the; Dawlah; Ibn Taymīyah, Taqī al-Dīn Aḥmad; Imamate, Theories of the; Kawākibī, ʿAbd al-Raḥmān al-; Khālid, Khālid Muḥammad; Quṭb, Sayyid; Rashīd Riḍā, Muḥammad; Ummah; *and* Wilāyat al-Faqīh.]

BIBLIOGRAPHY

ʿAbd al-Rāziq, ʿAlī. *al-Islam wa usul al-hikm* [Islam and the Principles of Government] (1925; Repr. *al-Hayat* [Beirut, Lebanon], 1966).

Abou El Fadl, Khaled. *And God Knows the Soldiers: The Authoritative and Authoritarian in Islamic Discourses*. Lanham, Md.: University Press of America, 2001.

Ahmed, Ishtiaq. *The Concept of an Islamic State*. London: Frances Pinter, 1987.

Allawi, Ali A. *The Crisis of Islamic Civilization*. New Haven, Conn.: Yale University Press, 2009.

Ashmawi, Mohammed Said. *Uṣūl al-shariʿa* [The Origins of *Sharīʿah*]. Cairo: Madbuli, 1983.

ʿAwwā, Muḥammad Salīm al-. *Fī al-niẓām al-siyāsī lil-dawlah al-Islāmīyah* [On the Political System of the Islamic State]. Cairo: al-Maktab al-Miṣrī al-Ḥadīth, 1983.

Baran, Zeyno, ed. *The Other Muslims: Moderate and Secular*. New York: Palgrave, 2010.

Beetham, David. *The Legitimation of Power*. Basingstoke, U.K., and Atlantic Heights, N.J.: Humanities Press International, 1991.

Berman, Paul. *The Flight of the Intellectuals: The Controversy over Islamism and the Press*. New York: Melvillehouse, 2011.

Choueiri, Youssef M. *Islamic Fundamentalism*. Boston: Twayne Publishers, 1990.

Enayat, Hamid. "Iran: Khumayni's Concept of the 'Guardian of the Jurisconsult.'" In *Islam in the Political Process*, edited by James P. Piscatori, pp. 160–180. Cambridge, U.K.: Cambridge University Press, 1983.

Enayat, Hamid. *Modern Islamic Political Thought*. Austin: University of Texas Press, 1982.

Fahmī, Muṣṭafā Abū Zayd. *Fann al-ḥukm fī al-Islām* [The Art of Government in Islam]. Cairo: al-Maktab al-Miṣrī al-Ḥadīth, 1981.

al-Fārābī, Abū Nasr. *Al-Farabi on the Perfect State*, edited by Richard Walzer. Oxford: Oxford University Press, 1985.

Feldman, Noah. *The Fall and the Rise of the Islamic State*. Princeton, N.J.: Princeton University Press, 2008.

Hartmann, Richard. *Die Religion des Islam: Eine Einführung*. Darmstadt: Wissenschaftliche Buchgesellschaft, 1992. Reprint of the 1944 edition.

Hudson, Michael C. *Arab Politics: The Search for Legitimacy*. New Haven, Conn.: Yale University Press, 1977.

al-Jabri, Mohammed Abed. *Arab-Islamic Philosophy: A Contemporary Critique*. Austin, Texas: CMES, 1999.

al-Jabri, Mohammed Abed. *al-Turath wa al-hadatha* [The Cultural Legacy in the Context of Modernity]. Beirut: al-Markaz al-Thaqafi, 1991.

Khālid, Khālid Muḥammad. *al-Dawlah fī al-Islām* [The State in Islam]. Cairo, 1988. Originally published in 1981.

Khālid, Khālid Muḥammad. *Min hunā nabda'*. 6th ed. Cairo: Mu'assasat al-Khanjī, 1963. Translated from the third edition by Ismā'īl R. al-Fārūqī as *From Here We Start* (Washington, D.C.: American Council of Learned Societies, 1953). The original edition was published in 1950.

Khūrī, Fu'ād Isḥāq. *Imams and Emirs: State, Religion, and Sects in Islam*. London: Saqi Books, 1990.

Kurdi, Abdulrahman A. *The Islamic State*. London: Mansell, 1984.

Madelung, Wilferd. *The Succession to Muhammad: A Study of the Early Caliphate*. New York: Cambridge University Press, 1998.

Madigan, Daniel. *The Qur'ân's Self-Image: Writing and Authority in Islam's Scripture*. Princeton, N.J.: Princeton University Press, 2001.

Momen, Moojan. *An Introduction to Shi'i Islam*. New Haven, Conn.: Yale University Press, 1985.

Mottahedeh, Roy P. *Loyalty and Leadership in an Early Islamic Society*. Princeton, N.J.: Princeton University Press, 1980.

Mūsā, Muḥammad Yūsuf. *Niẓām al-ḥukm fī al-Islām* [The System of Government in Islam]. Cairo: Jami'ā t al-Duwal al-'Arabīyah, 1962.

Mutawallī, 'Abd al-Ḥamīd. *Mabādi' niẓām al-ḥukm fī al-Islām* [Principles of Government in Islam]. Alexandria: Dār al-Ma'ārif, 1966.

al-Najjar, H. Fawzi. *al-Islam wa al-siyasah* [Islam and Politics]. Cairo: Daral-Sha'b, 1977.

al-Qaradawi, Yusuf. *Hatmiyat al-hall al-Islami* [The Islamic Solution is Determined]. 3 vols. al-Rissala: numerous editions.

Rayyis, Muḥammad Ḍiyā' al-Dīn al-. *al-Naẓarīyah al-siyāsīyah al-Islāmīyah* [The Political Theory of Islam]. Cairo: Maktabat al-Anjalū al-Misrīyah, 1953.

Schacht, Joseph. *An Introduction to Islamic Law*. Oxford: Clarendon Press, 1964.

ṭabāṭabā'ī, Muḥammad Ḥusayn. *Shi'ite Islam*. London, 1975.

Tamadonfar, Mehran. *The Islamic Polity and Political Leadership*. Boulder, Colo.: Westview Press, 1989.

Tibi, Bassam. *Arab Nationalism: Between Islam and the Nation-State*. 3d ed. New York: St. Martin's Press, 1997.

Tibi, Bassam. 1998. *The Challenge of Fundamentalism: Political Islam and the New World Disorder*. Updated Edition. Berkeley: University of California Press, 2002.

Tibi, Bassam. *The Crisis of Modern Islam*. Translated by Judith von Sivers. Salt Lake City: University of Utah Press, 1988.

Tibi, Bassam. "Islam and Modern European Ideologies." *International Journal of Middle East Studies* 18, no. 1 (1986): 15–29.

Tibi, Bassam. "Islam and Secularization: Religion and the Functional Differentiation of the Social System." *Archives for Philosophy of Law and Social Philosophy* 66, no. 2 (1980): 207–222.

Tibi, Bassam. *Islam and the Cultural Accommodation of Social Change*. Translated by Clare Krojzi. Boulder, Colo.: Westview Press, 1990.

Tibi, Bassam. *Islam between Culture and Politics*. 2d ed. New York: Palgrave Macmillan, 2005.

Tibi, Bassam. *Islamism and Islam*. New Haven, Conn.: Yale University Press, 2012.

Tibi, Bassam. *Islam's Predicament with Modernity: Religious Reform and Cultural Change*. New York: Routledge, 2009.

Tibi, Bassam. *Political Islam, World Politics and Europe: Democratic Peace and Euro-Islam versus Global Jihad*. New York: Routledge, 2008.

Tibi, Bassam. "A Typology of Arab Political Systems (with Special Reference to Islam and Government as Exemplified in Arab Monarchies Legitimized by Islam: Morocco and Saudi Arabia)." In *Arab Society: Continuity and Change*, edited by Samih Farsoun, pp. 48–64. London: Croom Helm, 1985.

Tibi, Bassam. *Der wahre Imam*. Munich: Piper, 1996.

Tibi, Bassam. "The World View of Sunni Arab Fundamentalists." In *Fundamentalisms and Society*, edited by Martin E. Marty and R. Scott Appleby, pp. 73–102. Chicago: University of Chicago Press, 1993.

Watt, W. Montgomery. *Islamic Political Thought: The Basic Concepts*. Edinburgh: Edinburgh University Press, 1968.

Bassam Tibi

Āzād, Abū al-Kalām. Abū al-Kalām Āzād (1888–1958) was an Urdu journalist, Islamic thinker, and religious universalist who symbolized the Muslim option of composite Indian nationalism. Mawlānā Āzād was born in Mecca, where his father Khairuddīn Dihlawī (1831–1908) had migrated in 1858 and later married the daughter of a mufti of Medina. The ancestors of Āzād had intellectual and spiritual links with Shaykh Aḥmad Sirhindī (d. 1624), Shah Walī Allāh Dihlawī (d. 1762), and Shah ʿAbd al-ʿAzīz (d. 1824). Khairuddīn was an influential *ʿālim-pīr* (learned Ṣūfī authority) with outspoken anti-Wahhābī leanings. The family moved to Calcutta around 1898.

Āzād was taught at home under the strict supervision of his father and completed, at the age of fifteen, the *dars-i niẓāmī* course of higher Islamic studies. His phenomenal memory, as well as his public preaching, prose, and verse, made him famous as a child prodigy. Very early, however, he became critical of his father's bitter opposition to the scripturalist Wahhābīs and of his practices of *taqlīd* (reliance on tradition) and the *pīr-murīdī* relationship (between spiritual guide and disciple). For some time Āzād fell under the spell of the reformist ideas and rationalistic theology of Sayyid Aḥmad Khān (1817–1898). This was followed by a period of doubts, unbelief, and sensuous living. A deep experience of mystic love induced by earthly love led him back to faith in God by the end of 1909.

Āzād's journalistic career started in 1903, when he launched the short-lived reformist journal *Lisān al-Ṣidq*. Thereafter he worked for short periods with *al-Nadwah*, the organ of the Nadvat al-ʿUlamāʿ academy in Lucknow, under the guidance of Muḥammad Shiblī Nuʿmānī (d. 1914), and with the renowned newspaper *Vakīl* in Amritsar. He was familiar with the contemporary writing of the Arab world in the vein of Jamāl al-Dīn al-Afghānī and those associated with the influential journal *al-Manār* with its roots in neo-Ḥanbalī theology. In 1908–1909 on a visit to western Asia he met Iranian nationalists in Iraq and Arab nationalists and Turkish revolutionaries in Cairo, followers of Mustafa Kemal Atatürk (d. 1938). He synthesized their ideas with his own experience of contact with the Bengal Hindu revolutionaries in the wake of the 1905 partition of Bengal.

In 1912 Āzād, through his widely influential weekly journal *al-Hilāl* (The Crescent), set out first to revive among the Muslims of India the true spirit of Qurʾānic Islam as the only solution to the nation's problems, and second to move them to political revolt through participation in the struggle of the Indian Congress Party for self-government. The fight for independence was a religious duty for Muslims, but they first had to be freed of their "pathological fear of the Hindus." Āzād emerged as a forerunner of Mohandas Gandhi, who was to launch his anti-British noncooperation agitation in 1919. However, nonviolence for Āzād was a matter of policy, not of principle.

When the government forced *al-Hilāl* to close down, upon the outbreak of war between Turkey and Britain, Āzād started another journal, *al-Balāgh*. He was soon exiled from Bengal and spent three and a half years interned near Ranchi. Immediately upon his release in January 1920, he joined the nationwide struggle for political freedom led by Gandhi. The address that Āzād delivered in February 1920, as president of the Bengal

Provincial Khilafat Conference, served as a strong inspiration and theoretical basis for the Khilāfat movement. Referring to the covenant concluded in 622 between Muḥammad and the people of Medina, including Jews and pagans, Āzād described Muslim together with non-Muslim parties as a single community (*ummah wāḥidah*).

Āzād was again arrested toward the end of 1921 and formally put on trial. His defense, later published under the title *Qawl-i fayṣal*, occupies a prominent place in both the political history of India and the history of Urdu literature. In 1929 Āzād, in cooperation with thirty other nationalist Muslim leaders, convened the Nationalist Muslim Conference, but his real field of political activity was within the Congress. During the 1930s and 1940s he was imprisoned four times; he eventually spent one-seventh of his life interned or in jail. In 1940 Āzād was elected president of the All-India National Congress and held this position until 1946. He failed to prevent the partition of India, which was for him a lasting tragedy overshadowing the achievement of independence. In 1947 he joined the interim government of India as Minister of Education. This post, as well as that of deputy leader of Congress, he held until his death.

Āzād's overall religious perspective is marked by his unique temperament; he combined aesthetic experience and religious consciousness. The charming letters to his friend from the British prison at Ahmadnagar (*Ghubār-i khāʿir*, edited by Malik Ram, New Delhi, 1967; rev. ed. 1983) provide insight into his multifaceted Islamic sensitivity. Earlier, in his fragmentary autobiography *Tazkirah* (edited by Fazluddin Ahmad, Calcutta, 1919; rev. ed. Malik Ram, New Delhi, 1968), Āzād had offered a passionate discussion of such moral and religious issues as the eternal validity of the word of God, the affinity between earthly and sacred love, and the appreciation of beauty in its varied forms, including music, which he held to be compatible with the Qurʾān. All of Āzād's writings had a deeply religious tenor and were marked by his artistic, highly personalized diction, appealing to intuition rather than discursive reason.

Āzād's mind accommodated conflicting elements without any attempt to reconcile them in a conceptual whole. His countless writings and speeches all refer to a few fundamental attitudes and options sponsored by his interpretation or *tafsīr* of the Qurʾān. However, in *Tarjumān al-Qurʾān*, Āzād's annotated Urdu rendering of chapters 1 to 23, and especially in his commentary on the opening verses of the Qurʾān, his main concern is to let the Qurʾān speak for itself. The Qurʾān is a spiritual text concerning God and humanity, enjoining good and prohibiting evil. Pseudoscientific attributions of medieval or modern provenance must not distort its divine beauty and simplicity.

In their essence, all faiths are one (*dīn*); their distinctiveness, expressed in different laws, is neither original nor inherent. Islam as the religion of the Qurʾān does not have to be politically and nationally separatist to be viable and effective in history. Moreover, God's attributes are readable in their qualities of nurture, harmony, and guidance as imprinted on the created universe. The Qurʾān indicates the middle path between transcendentalism and anthropomorphism. Praise, gratitude, and universal brotherhood are the obvious human responses. Although Āzād believed that human obduracy generates destructive "groupism," he preferred not to probe the depths of sinful perversion in individuals or societies.

A basic lacuna in Āzād's religious scholarship is the absence of an updated hermeneutics of the fundamental sources of Islam—the Qurʾān and *ḥadīth*—and, based on that, a reformulation of the principles of legal construction. However, although he did not initiate a school of thought, his vision of Islam as Qurʾān-based universal humanism continues to inspire Muslim sensitivity, especially in the Urdu-speaking world.

BIBLIOGRAPHY

Āzād, Abū al-Kalām. *India Wins Freedom*. Bombay: Orient Longman, 2005. Reprint containing thirty pages originally withheld from publication.

Āzād, Abū al-Kalām. *Khuṭubāt-i Āzād*. New Delhi, 1981. The chief public speeches of Āzād, 1914–1948, in the Urdu original.

Āzād, Abū al-Kalām. *Speeches of Maulana Azad, 1947–1955*. New Delhi: Government of India, 1956.

Āzād, Abū al-Kalām. *Tarjumān al-Qur'ān*. 2 vols.Delhi, 1931–1936. Critical edition by Malik Ram. 4 vols. New Delhi, 1964–1976. Translated and edited by S. A. Latif, The Tarjumān al-Qur'ān. 3 vols. Bombay, 1962–1967.

Douglas, Ian Henderson. *Abul Kalam Azad: An Intellectual and Religious Biography*. Edited by Gail Minault and Christian W. Troll. New York: Oxford University Press, 1988. The most penetrating study of Āzād's life and works. Comprehensive bibliography.

Faruqi, I. H. Azad. *The Tarjuman al-Qur'an: A Critical Analysis of Maulana Abū al-Kalām Azad's Approach to the Understanding of the Qur'an*. New Delhi: Vikas, 1982. Elucidates the links of Tarjumān with earlier Qur'ān exegesis and brings out its distinguishing features.

Hameed, Syeda Saiyidain. *Islamic Seal on India's Independence: Abul Kalam Azad—A Fresh Look*. New York: Oxford, 1998.

Hasan, Mushirul, ed. *Islam and Indian Nationalism: Reflections on Abul Kalam Azad*. New Delhi, 1992. Delineates Āzād's political trajectory in the context of nationalist struggles in West Asia and India.

Kabir, Humayun, ed. *Maulana Abul Kalam Azad: A Memorial Volume*. Bombay: Asia Publishing House, 1959. Remains the most important collection of views and analyses of Āzād's personality and work by contemporaries.

Sarkar, Ichhamuddin. "Mawlana Abul Kalam as Azad: A Study of His Religious Views." *Hamdard Islamicus* 21, no. 4 (1998): 33–39.

CHRISTIAN W. TROLL

AZERBAIJAN. Situated on the Caspian Sea, between Russia, Georgia, Armenia, and Iran, Azerbaijan gained independence with the collapse of the USSR in 1991. Its population, estimated at just over 8 million in 2012, identifies itself almost entirely as Muslim, roughly 75 percent of them Shīʿah. Polls of 2011–2012 show that only 15–20 percent of those who consider themselves Muslims have more than a superficial familiarity with Islam, so the majority must be considered "cultural Muslims." Azerbaijan is a secular republic, but religious leaders have occasionally had a high profile in the country's post-Soviet history. The government, fearful of radicalism, has repressed religious groups, including during 2011 in response to the Arab Spring. The head of the state-affiliated ecclesiastical board, Shaykh al-Islām Allashukur Pashazade, came to prominence in 1990 for speaking out against Russian repression of the nationalist movement. He subsequently played a smaller political role, though he cultivated relations with Iran and Saudi Arabia. He participated in the presidential inaugurations of Azerbaijan Popular Front leader Abulfez Elchibey in June 1992 and, when Elchibey was overthrown in a coup a year later, of Heydar Aliyev, former Communist Party first secretary. Because of his consistent support of Aliyev and his son Ilham, who succeeded him in October 2003, Pashazade lost much of the credibility he had gained during his oppositional activism.

Religious parties were tiny and few and religion had played no role in political mobilization in the first years after the Soviet collapse. Post-Soviet rulers have maintained the secular tradition of Azerbaijan codified during independence in 1918–1920 and the Soviet period. Yet independence opened the doors to knowledge of Islam and to foreign Muslim missionaries and organizations. It also led Azerbaijan to rebuild its religious infrastructure. The appeal of Islam appears to stem from popular disillusionment with the lack of morality in Soviet and now post-Soviet society, its materialism, corruption, and the danger of drugs and crime. It is unclear whether Islam's popularity is because of individuals' search for morality or its utility as a political instrument, nor is it clear whether, when it is used for political ends, these ends are reformist or radical as the government normally charges.

Foreign Influence. Iran and Turkey, using both official structures and independent religious groups, helped to build mosques and schools in Azerbaijan in the 1990s. Observers inside Azerbaijan report that more than a hundred small mosques were built with Iranian money and staffed with Iranian mullahs in villages throughout the countryside. Many such mosques, schools, and other institutions were closed down after the 11 September 2001 attacks, but Iranian influence is still apparent in the southern areas, in several villages near Baku such as Nardaran and Mashtaga, and in a few political organizations. Some pious Shīʿīs are seeking to identify a spiritual guide, or *marjaʿ al-taqlīd*, a concept that was suppressed with modernization in the nineteenth and twentieth centuries and has been rediscovered. Political analysts in Azerbaijan and abroad remain concerned about the Iranian-Israeli antagonism that flared in 2012. The rhetoric and some isolated incidents have raised fears that both powers are using Azerbaijan as an arena for their struggle, including assassinations and cyber attacks. Iran claims Azerbaijan is pro-Zionist and thus anti-Islamic, thereby appealing to the population over the heads of the secular rulers.

Investment by the Turkish government has been mainly secular and shaped by the ethnic bond between Turkey and Azerbaijan. The Turkish government's Diyanet (Ministry for Religious Affairs) funded several secular schools in Baku and one small but ornate mosque near the Shahid Khiyabani (Martyrs' Lane) for those killed in the Karabakh conflict with Armenia. The Turkish Nurcu movement of Fethullah Gülen has also founded schools and one university in the Baku area. Its blend of moderate religion, emphasis on education, and Kemalism has been appealing to the urban elites as well as moderate Muslims who seek a climate of morality for their children. Though a Sunni movement, its appeal is transsectarian.

Islamic Activism. There has been some evidence of the rise of political Islam, beginning with demonstrations around the village of Nardaran, just outside the capital, Baku, in the summer of 2002. The village was known for its conservative Shīʿī character, but religion had not been used politically before this incident. Villagers demanded fulfillment of promises made by the government in 2000 to supply gas and electricity to their village. When Baku police came to suppress the demonstrations, the villagers used Islamic symbols and rhetoric to denounce the regime. Aliyev's regime was unyielding and linked the unrest to international Islamic groups and "Islamic fundamentalism." Local commentators raised the specter of a population, frustrated by lack of services despite the country's petroleum wealth, turning to Islamic movements as a source of inspiration, if not outright support.

A second case around this time involved Baku's Juma mosque in the Old City, which had been turned into a carpet museum by Soviet authorities in the 1920s. Haji Ilgar Ibrahimoğlu fought for its restoration as a mosque and became its imam in 2002, at about age thirty. His background as a journalist and human-rights activist was stressed by the Western press, but he studied at the University of Tehran before working in Poland on human rights. His use of legal arguments and international human-rights norms distinguishes him and his generation from the older cohort that matured in the Soviet Union. He was prosecuted for his political activism, and the Juma mosque was closed down for alleged extremism in 2004.

Ibrahimoğlu defends freedom of religion as a basic human right. He is the founder and director of the Religious Faith and Freedom of Conscience Defense Center (Dini Etiqad və Vicdan Azadlıqlarını Müdafiə Mərkəzinə, DEVAMM). It has a website (http://www.deyerler.org) and a journal *Dəyərlər/Tsennosti* (Values) that is written half in Azerbaijani and half in Russian. In the July 2005 issue (its second), İbrahimoğlu stressed the benign character of his congregation: "The majority has a higher education. . . . There was no hatred. There was a respectful approach to those who think differently. Social projects were being carried out." Moreover, the preaching from the pulpit, he said, invited people to civility, decency, love of humanity, and the ideals and values of God. At the same time, the message of *Dəyərlər/Tsennosti* is socially conservative, idealizing traditional roles for women and the wearing of the *hijāb* (headscarf). İbrahimoğlu and men in the congregation will not shake hands with female visitors. With later electoral losses by the Popular Front and the other major secular opposition party, the Yeni Müsavat, the relative size of Haji Ilgar's group—some three thousand members by his count—could put it ahead of the secular democratic parties. Ibrahimoğlu's Web presence was hurt by state repressions, especially in 2011, as indicated by the complete lack of posts on Ibrahimoğlu's blog for that year, compared to 196 for 2010.

Growth of Radicalism. There have been hints of radical political Islam. In the spring of 2007, two Baku journalists were put on trial for "insulting Islam" because of an article they wrote arguing that Christianity had coped more successfully with historical challenges than Islam had. A group of Islamist demonstrators was reported to have shouted "*Allāh akbar*" (God is great) in court, for which they received stiff sentences. Local analysts note frequent repressions against men with beards (forcibly shaving them while in police custody) or distinctive "Muslim" dress and discrimination in jobs against women in the *hijāb*.

The Aliyev regime may have encouraged political Islam, if inadvertently, by its consistent repression of the weak and fragmented democratic opposition. Since the overthrow of President Elchibey in the summer of 1993, no election in Azerbaijan has been deemed "free and fair" by international monitors. Under Ilham Aliyev, ever greater repression of opposition parties, newspapers, and journalists has resulted in worsening ratings from human rights and democratization groups such as Amnesty International, Freedom House, and Transparency International. In the parliamentary election of fall 2010, the democratic opposition parties were completely excluded and no longer have any representative in the National Assembly. Without any viable secular opposition, the government targeted the small but active religious groups, which, in turn, are more attractive with the apparent failure of secular parties to win demands.

Just after parliamentary elections, in December 2010, the Ministry of Education banned the *hijāb* for school girls. In January 2011, Movsum Samadov of the Islamic Party of Azerbaijan was arrested after his YouTube sermon denouncing the Aliyev government and calling for its overthrow. Samadov, along with two assistants and two close relatives, was arrested, tried in October of that year, and sentenced to over ten years in prison. Repressions continued throughout 2011 in fear of the Arab Spring, with the government targeting youth and social media. Continued Western support for Azerbaijan's leaders contributes to public disillusionment with democratic politics, which seem to bring no gains, even though the export of oil creates pockets of conspicuous wealth in Baku. Growing gaps between rich and poor and between urban and rural may create more fertile ground for appeals to action for social justice, which is associated with Islam.

BIBLIOGRAPHY

Altstadt, Audrey L. *Azerbaijani Turks: Power and Identity Under Russian Rule*. Stanford, Calif.: Hoover Institution Press, Stanford University, 1992.

Altstadt, Audrey L. "The Forgotten Factor: The Shīʿī Mullahs of Pre-Revolutionary Baku." In *Passé turco-tatar, présent soviétique:Études offertes à Alexandre Bennigsen / Turco-Tatar Past, Soviet Present: Studies Presented to Alexandre Bennigsen*, edited by Ch. Lemercier-Quelquejay, G. Veinstein, and S. E. Wimbush, pp. 345–365. Louvain, Belgium: Editions Peeters, 1986.

Balci, Bayram. "Between Sunnism and Shiism: Islam in Post-Soviet Azerbaijan." *Central Asian Survey* 23 (2004): 205–217.

Bennigsen, Alexandre, and Chantal Lemercier-Quelquejay. *Islam in the Soviet Union*. Translated by Geoffrey E. Wheeler and Hubert Evans. London: Pall Mall, 1967.

Bennigsen, Alexandre, and S. Enders Wimbush. *Mystics and Commissars: Sufism in the Soviet Union*. London: Hurst, 1985.

Hacibeyli, Ceyhun. *Antiislamistskaia propaganda i ee metody v Azerbaidzhane*. Munich, 1957.

Kotecha, Hema. *Islamic and Ethnic Identities in Azerbaijan: Emerging Trends and Tensions*. OSCE discussion paper, July 2006, http://www.osce.org/baku/23809.

Malashenko, Alexey, Bayram Balci, and Thomas de Waal. "Political Islam in the Caucasus." Panel at the Carnegie Endowment for International Peace Conference, 22 February 2012, Washington, D.C., http://carnegieendowment.org/2012/02/22/political-islam-in-caucasus/9cwd.

AUDREY L. ALTSTADT

AZHAR, AL-. Situated in the heart of the medieval Cairo neighborhood, al-Azhar is one of greatest mosque-universities in the world today, if not the greatest.

After al-Jawhar al-Ṣiqillī began constructing al-Azhar in 970 as Cairo's official mosque, al-Azhar introduced organized instruction in 978, which makes it one of the oldest teaching universities in the world.

Ṣalāḥ al-Dīn and his Ayyūbid heirs downgraded the status of al-Azhar when they restored Egypt to Sunnī Islam in 1171. Successive sultans and *amīrs* of the Mamlūk dynasty (1250–1517) patronized and restored the now Sunnī mosque, but it was as yet only one among many seats of Islamic learning in Cairo.

The Ottoman conquest of 1517 diverted power and patronage to Istanbul, but al-Azhar emerged as the preeminent seat of Arabic-Islamic learning. During the French occupation (1798–1801) al-Azhar became a rallying point for revolt against the French, who bombarded, occupied, and desecrated the mosque. In 1805, the Azharī *ʿulamāʾ* sanctioned the ouster of Egypt's Istanbul-appointed governor by Muḥammad ʿAlī and his Albanian troops, but the commander of the Ottoman Army, who became governor and self-declared khedive (viceroy) of Egypt and Sudan, soon felt strong enough to begin the long campaign to subordinate al-Azhar to the "state." He ignored the ruler's obligation to consult the *ʿulamāʾ*, chose the *shaykhs al-Azhar* himself, played Ṣufī leaders against the Shaykh al-Azhar, and confiscated many religious endowments.

As was usual in premodern Islamic schools, al-Azhar had no formal educational practices. Professors lectured from a favorite pillar of the mosque, the students gathering at their feet. Memorization and commentary, often on epitomes and commentaries rather than on the original classics, were the means of instruction. Qurʾānic exegesis, *ḥadīth*, and jurisprudence were taught in the morning; grammar, rhetoric, and other "auxiliary sciences" after the noon prayers; and various nonessential subjects after the sunset prayers. Many Azharīs were active Ṣūfīs as well as *ʿulamāʾ*.

The departure of progressive Azharīs like Rifāʿah Rāfiʿ al-Ṭahṭāwī, Muḥammad ʿAbduh, and Saʿd Zaghlūl to work for the state reinforced al-Azhar's conservatism. Beginning in 1872, state reformers tried to overhaul al-Azhar, despite resistance from conservative elements of society. Eventually, competition with state-school graduates for government jobs fostered a reformist minority within al-Azhar.

Khedive Ismāʿīl had opened a School of Law (originally Administration and Languages) and the Dār al-ʿUlūm teachers' college to bypass al-Azhar. The opening of the School for Qāḍīs (1907) and the state-run Egyptian University (1925) dealt a further blow to job prospects for the unspecialized Azharī graduates. In fact, the two elderly Mālikī *shaykhs al-Azhar* between 1909 and 1927 responded not with reforms but with pressure on the state to hire Azharīs. King Fuʾād agreed to do so, for he needed Azharī endorsement of his caliphal ambitions and a counterweight to the following of Saʿd Zaghlūl and the Wafd Party among secondary and university students in Egypt.

The Wafdist–Liberal Constitutionalist cabinets of 1926–1928 canceled the state's commitment to hire Azharīs, seized the prerogative of naming the Shaykh al-Azhar, and brushed aside the king's candidate, Muḥammad al-Aḥmadī al-Zawāhirī, in favor of Muḥammad Muṣṭafā al-Marāghī. Still, King Fuʾād soon turned the tables on al-Marāghī, a Ḥanafī and an admirer of ʿAbduh, when he suspended the constitution, reclaimed the prerogative of appointing the Shaykh al-Azhar, and reappointed Zawāhirī to his post.

Disappointed in the conservatism of Shaykh al-Azhar ʿAbd al-Raḥmān Tāj (1954–1958) despite his Sorbonne education, a hurried President Gamal Abdel Nasser looked for a replacement and found the reformist *shaykh* he wanted in Maḥmūd Shaltūt (1958–1963). When in June 1961 Nasser had Speaker Anwar el-Sadat ram a bill—Law No. 103—for radical reform of al-Azhar through a surprised parliament in a single night, Shaltūt was disillusioned. A withering press attack on the *ʿulamāʾ* followed that also upset him.

The Azhar law of 1961 provided for a supreme council under the Shaykh al-Azhar, an Islamic Research Academy, a Department of Cultural and Islamic Mission at al-Azhar University, and the precollegiate institutes. The existing Colleges of Theology, *Sharīʿah*, and the Arabic Language (renamed Arabic Studies) were further reformed. The College of Arabic Studies drifted farthest from its old moorings; in 1974, 93 percent of its credit hours were in "secular" subjects. The College of *Sharīʿah* added Qānūn (secular law) to its name and curriculum, and even the College of Theology now requires social sciences and a Western language. The opening of the College of Islamic Women (literally "Girls") was a radical step, as was the addition of Colleges of Engineering, Medicine, Commerce, Science, Agriculture, and Education.

Over the years, al-Azhar's Preaching and Guidance department sent preachers and lecturers throughout Egypt, acquired its own press, and published the *Majallat al-Azhar* (Journal of al-Azhar, originally *Nūr al-Islām*, Light of Islam), which was established in 1930. Its *Voice of al-Azhar* radio program began broadcasting in 1959, as Azharī preachers increasingly saturated Egyptian radio and television airwaves, before diving into the Internet toward the end of the twentieth century.

Outside Egypt, al-Azhar is prized as a champion of Sunnī Islam and the Arabic language. Students returning from studies at al-Azhar and Azharī professors and preachers on mission abroad are in demand throughout the Islamic world.

Al-Azhar is conservative. It held Islamist activists at arm's length, from Jamāl al-Dīn al-Afghānī, Muḥammad ʿAbduh, and Muḥammad Rashīd Riḍā to Muslim Brotherhood leaders Ḥasan al-Bannā and Sayyid Quṭb. It is significant that al-Bannā and Quṭb were products of Dār al-ʿUlūm, not al-Azhar, and that in Egypt most leaders of today's "Islamic groups" are not Azharīs. Azharī *shaykhs* sometimes dismiss radical Islamists as extremists who, they insist, are only superficially familiar with Islam, and many Islamists disparage Azharīs as "official *ʿulamāʾ*," cravenly subservient to the state that pays them.

Islamists generally approve, however, of the condemnation of controversial books by al-Azhar's Islamic Research Academy, which sees itself as the guardian of true Islam. In the 1920s, al-Azhar stripped ʿAlī ʿAbd al-Rāziq of his degree and drove him from his judgeship for reinterpreting the Caliphate in secular terms, and it hounded Ṭāhā Ḥusayn for his provocative book *On Pre-Islamic Poetry*. Certain books by Nobel Prize–winner Naguib Mahfouz and literary critic Louis Awad were banned in Egypt until 2011, and al-Azhar has condemned Salman Rushdie's *Satanic Verses* and works by the outspoken secularist Saʿīd ʿAshmāwī. Not a few Azharīs privately agree with Shaykh ʿAbd al-Ḥamīd Kishk, the blind Azharī graduate whose radical, populist sermons drew an enthusiastic Islamist following in the 1970s and 1980s. Kishk chided his alma mater for accepting Western-educated *shaykh*s al-Azhar, demanded elections to fill that office, and called for the elimination of the colleges added since 1961.

Al-Azhar walks a fine line between provoking another state assault and discrediting itself in the eyes of the people through subservience to the state. Azharī authorities issued *fatwas* endorsing family planning, the Egyptian-Israeli peace treaty, and Egypt's participation in the Gulf War of 1990–1991. Jād al-Ḥaqq condemned terrorism by Ayatollah Ruhollah Khomeini's Iranian partisans, yet he refused to sanction the payment of interest on funds invested for national development, as the government wanted. In 2010, President Mubarak appointed Shaykh Muḥammad Ṭanṭāwī as the new Shaykh al-Azhar, who noted that among his priorities were efforts that would allow Muslims "to master all knowledge of the world and the hereafter, not least the technology of modern weapons to strengthen and defend the community and faith." Ṭanṭāwī added that "mastery over modern weaponry is important to prepare for any eventuality or prejudices of the others, although Islam is a religion of peace." The controversial Ṭanṭāwī reasserted that his is the best faith to follow (not an uncommon tenet among men of the cloth) and that Muslims were duty bound to propagate *daʿwah*. Although he issued several declarations about Muslims interacting with non-Muslims, including the oft-neglected statement that Egyptian Copts are not a threat to Muslims, his efforts were not always successful. In one confused claim, the Shaykh al-Azhar declared that "Muslims are allowed to undertake exchanges of interests with these non-Muslims . . . so long as these ties do not tarnish the image of the faith." Clashes between Muslim extremists and Christian Copts received mild Azhar commentaries, though Cairo funded the rebuilding of burned churches.

In October 2007, Muḥammad Ṭanṭāwī, then the grand imam of al-Azhar and a strong Mubarak supporter, called for limitations on freedom of speech, ostensibly to prevent false rumors circulating about the sick president's health and imminent death. This was not the last time he criticized the Egyptian press, although he conspicuously kept a low profile after the March 2011 uprisings that toppled the Mubarak regime, perhaps to preserve al-Azhar's reputation.

[*See also* Education, Muslim; Egypt; Nasser, Gamal Abdel; Shaltūt, Maḥmūd; *and* Universities.]

BIBLIOGRAPHY

Badrawi, Malak. *Al-Azhar and the Arab World: Moulding the Political and Ideological Consciousness*. London: RoutledgeCurzon, 2008.

Dodge, Bayard. *Al-Azhar: A Millennium of Muslim Learning*. Memorial edition. Washington, D.C.: Middle East Institute, 1974.

Eccel, A. Chris. *Egypt, Islam, and Social Change: Al-Azhar in Conflict and Accommodation*. Berlin: K. Schwarz, 1984.

Gesink, Indira Falk. *Islamic Reform and Conservatism: Al-Azhar and the Evolution of Modern Sunni Islam*. London: Tauris Academic Studies, 2009.

Hefner, Robert W., and Muhammad Qasim Zaman. *Schooling Islam: The Culture and Politics of Modern Muslim Education*. Princeton, N.J.: Princeton University Press, 2006.

Heyworth-Dunne, James. *An Introduction to the History of Education in Modern Egypt*. London: Luzac, 1939.

Reid, Donald Malcolm. *Cairo University and the Making of Modern Egypt*. Cambridge, U.K.: Cambridge University Press, 1990.

Zaman, Muhammad Qasim. *The Ulama in Contemporary Islam: Custodians of Change*. Princeton, N.J.: Princeton University Press, 2002.

DONALD MALCOLM REID
Updated by JOSEPH A. KÉCHICHIAN

AZZAM, ABDULLAH YUSUF AL-.

Shaykh Abdullah Yusuf al-Azzam (1941–1989) was a Palestinian-born Islamic cleric and a leading theorist of Islamic radicalism. He rose to prominence during the Afghan war against the Soviets (the Afghan Jihād, 1979–1989). Al-Azzam was not only the main architect of the political-religious dimensions of the Afghan jihād, but also one of its most tireless supporters, traveling the world to recruit fighters and financial assistance for the *mujāhidīn*. Through such efforts his ideas took on heightened visibility and widespread acceptance among radical communities. Moreover, despite a later ideological split, his ideas were formative for the nascent jihādi community that was emerging in Afghanistan, Pakistan, and Sudan in the late 1980s. In this way, al-Azzam's work and thinking left a deep ideological mark on figures such as Osama Bin Laden, Ayman al-Zawahiri, and Abu Musʿab al-Suri, and remain a theoretical cornerstone of militant, radical thinking in contemporary Islam.

Al-Azzam was born in the northern Palestinian village of Selat al-Harithia in 1941. After the 1967 Arab-Israeli War, al-Azzam fled to Jordan, where he was actively involved in Palestinian activism and militancy against the state of Israel. In 1966 he obtained a degree in *Sharʿīah* studies from Damascus University in Syria and in 1973 a master's degree and a Ph.D. in Islamic jurisprudence from al-Azhar University in Cairo. Al-Azzam then took a position at the University of Jordan, where he taught Islamic law. This was followed by a move to Saudi Arabia, where he took a position at King Abdul Aziz University in Jiddah.

It was during his time in Saudi Arabia that al-Azzam met several Afghan *mujāhidīn* and was quickly won over to their cause. While he continued to advocate for the liberation of Palestine, Afghanistan quickly came to occupy the majority of his time and thinking. To assist the *mujāhidīn*, al-Azzam moved to Pakistan and became intensely involved in recruitment efforts. In 1984, with the help of Osama Bin Laden, he started Maktab al-Khidamat, the "Services Bureau" in Peshawar—an organization that sought to recruit non-Afghan *mujāhidīn* to fight alongside the Afghans.

However, al-Azzam's framing of the Afghan jihād as a Muslim struggle (as opposed to a specifically Afghan struggle) was his most important contribution. For al-Azzam, the Afghan jihād marked a pivotal moment in Islamic history. The struggle of the *mujāhidīn*, he argued, was a symbolic battle for the soul of Muslims, as well as a very real battle for the survival of the *ummah*. According to al-Azzam, the Afghan jihād reflected the current religious and political conditions of the broader Muslim world, as lack of piety and adherence to God's law had weakened the *ummah*, leaving Muslims unable to resist encroachment and subjugation by foreign (non-Muslim) powers. The only way for Muslims to restore their former power and glory was to take up arms and to ignite a revolution—spanning the breadth of the Muslim world—that would expel all foreign powers from Muslim territory. This revolution, he argued, began at the front door of the Afghans. Winning the war against the Soviets, al-Azzam insisted, would transform Afghanistan into a spiritual and geographical base from which this global Muslim revolution could be waged.

Moreover, he argued, this revolution required an unceasing and unyielding armed struggle that, in light of the current state of the Muslim world, was the religious duty of every able-bodied Muslim. Referencing evidence from the Qurʾān, the *ḥadīth*, and the work of prominent Islamic jurisprudents, al-Azzam argued that it was the individual religious duty—*farḍ ayn*—of every able-bodied Muslim to expel foreign invaders from Muslim lands. Therefore, taking up arms in defense of Afghanistan was an obligation for every Muslim, and would continue to be the obligation of every Muslim until all lands formerly under Muslim rule—including Palestine, Lebanon, Somalia, the Philippines and southern Spain—were "liberated."

At the end of the Afghan-Soviet war, al-Azzam and Bin Laden had significant disagreements regarding the future direction of the jihād. While the evidence remains inconclusive on this point, the most widespread accounts tell of an ideological split between al-Azzam on one side and al-Zawahiri and Bin Laden on the other. Bin Laden and al-Zawahiri were advocating for the liberation of Muslims through the violent overthrow of regimes across the Muslim world. Al-Azzam, however, was adamantly opposed to this idea, arguing that it would lead to political upheaval as well as inter-Muslim strife and fracturing. This rupture came to a head in November 1989, when a roadside bomb in Peshawar killed al-Azzam and his two sons—ultimately opening the way for the most radical elements within al-Qaʿida to impose their vision of jihād.

BIBLIOGRAPHY

Azzam, Abdullah Yusuf. *Defence of the Muslim Lands: The First Obligation after Imam*. Circa 1979. http://www.religioscope.com/info/doc/jihad/azzam_defence_1_table.htm.

Azzam, Abdullah Yusuf. *Join the Caravan*. Circa 1987. http://www.hoor-al-ayn.com/Books/Join%20the%20Caravan.pdf.

Wright, Lawrence. *The Looming Tower: Al-Qaeda and the Road to 9/11*. New York: Vintage Books, 2006.

NAHED ARTOUL ZEHR

B

Bābism. *See* Bahāʾī.

Bahāʾ Allāh. *See* Bahāʾī.

Bahāʾī. It is debatable whether an article on "Bahāʾī" should appear in an encyclopedia on Islam, since the members of the Bahāʾī Faith, and increasingly scholars of religion, regard it as a separate religion. Insofar as the religion was founded in the Islamic world and has historically interacted with that world, it can, however, be considered as having roots in that cultural realm, even though it has developed Islamic terms and concepts well beyond their evolution within the Islamic civilization.

The origins of the Bahāʾī Faith lie in the Bābī movement in Iran, founded by Sayyid ʿAlī Muḥammad Shīrāzī, the Bāb (1819–1850). The Shīʿī clerical class of Iran perceived this movement as a direct threat to their interests. They initiated, and then dragged the state into, a campaign of persecution that saw three major upheavals in different parts of Iran in 1848–1850, where government troops were pitted against the Bābīs for months. A small group of Bābīs then attempted to assassinate the shah in 1852.

The intense persecution that followed the attempted assassination drove the movement underground, but it was to reemerge less than two decades later transformed into the Bahāʾī Faith, founded by Bahāʾ Allāh (Mīrzā Ḥusayn ʿAlī Nūrī, 1817–1892). Bahāʾ Allāh had been exiled as a leading Bābī to Baghdad by the Iranian government in 1853 and, at the insistence of the Iranian government, was subsequently exiled by the Ottoman government further away from the Iranian border to Istanbul (1863), Edirne (1863), and ʿAkkā (1868). He advanced his claim to be the founder of a new religion, at first to a small number of followers in 1863, and then more openly in 1866. A very small group of Bābīs (probably about 5 percent of surviving Bābīs) rejected Bahāʾ Allāh's claim and followed the leadership of his half-brother Mīrzā Yaḥyā Azal. The Azalī Bābīs played an important role in the Iranian Constitutional Revolution of 1906–1911 but were never a structured religious community.

From the 1870s onwards, Bahāʾ Allāh and his son and successor, ʿAbd-al-Bahāʾ (ʿAbbās Effendi, 1844–1921), began to issue books and treatises on the social reforms needed in both the Middle East and the world as a whole. The topics covered in these writings include democratic government with the establishment of parliaments, constitutional monarchy, the importance of education in transforming individuals and society, the elimination of clerics from the business of government, the need for international treaties to define borders and mutually guarantee peace, and the eventual establishment of international institutions for justice, governance, and the management of the world's resources. The proposals in the Bahā'ī texts differed from those of contemporary Middle Eastern advocates of reform in that they were much wider in their scope and emphasized that these social reforms could not occur without a spiritual and moral dimension. This latter dimension includes the abolition of the concept of "ritual impurity" (*najāsa*) and "holy war" (*qitāl, jihād*); the need for all individuals to tackle their prejudices and regard all humanity as members of one family; the advancement of the social role of women; probity and justice among government officials; the belief that individuals should move away from self-centeredness and toward an ethos of service; and the need for all to move from parochial concerns toward a global consciousness ('Abdu'l-Bahá, 1970; Bahá'u'lláh, 1978; Lerche, 2004).

During the last part of the nineteenth century, the Bahā'ī leaders were in contact with many of the Iranian social reformers such as Malkom Khān and Jamāl al-Dīn al-Afghānī, as well as many of the leading lights of the Young Ottoman and Young Turk movements, such as Midhat Pasha, Ebüzziya Tevfik, Nuri Bey, Bereketzade İsmail Hakkı Bey, and Abdullah Cevdet. During the course of the Constitutional Revolution in Iran, 'Abd-al-Bahā' met with such leading figures among the Constitutionalists as Ḥājī Shaykh al-Ra'īs, Muḥammad Valī Khān Naṣr-us-Salṭaneh, and Sardar As'ad Bakhtiyārī; Bahā'īs were owners of several key reformist newspapers, while in a number of towns, such as Sari and Barfurush in Mazandaran, Bahā'īs were among the leading supporters of the Constitutionalist cause. Around February 1907, however, 'Abd-al-Bahā' instructed his followers to desist from all political activity. Although this may have been due to particular factors operating at that time, this instruction was continued by Shoghi Effendi (1897–1957), 'Abd-al-Bahā''s successor as leader of the Bahā'ī Faith, and by the Universal House of Justice (established 1963), the elected body that is the present head of the religion.

'Abd-al-Bahā' corresponded and, during his journeys to the West, met with many Western leaders of thought including the British suffragette leader Emmeline Pankhurst; the treasurer of the United States, Lee McClung; the philosophers Henri Bergson, John Dewey, and Auguste Forel; and the writers Leo Tolstoy and Khalil Gibran. In the Middle East, he met with such figures as the khedive of Egypt, 'Abbās II Ḥilmī; Shaykh Muḥammad Bakhīt, the *mufti* of Egypt; Lord Kitchener; and Amīr (later King) Abdullah of Jordan. After World War I, 'Abd-al-Bahā' was among those informally consulted by the British Mandate authorities about such matters as reconciling Arabs and Jews in Palestine.

Throughout the twentieth century, most figures who tried to introduce reform in Iran were accused by their enemies of being Bahā'īs. During the late Pahlavi era and especially since the Islamic Revolution of 1979, the Bahā'īs of Iran have also appeared in the public discourse of Iran as scapegoats for political failure, as an "enemy within" and as the focus of far-fetched conspiracy theories. The clerical and secular enemies of the Bahā'īs in Iran have falsely accused a number of prominent political figures from the Pahlavi era, such as Prime Minister Amīr 'Abbās Hoveydā, of having been Bahā'īs.

Although Bahā'īs do not engage with the divisive and competitive nature of party politics, judging this to be antithetical to the unity and cooperative ethos that they wish to build in society, Bahāʾīs do engage in the discourse on political governance in ways that involve consensus building and are nonpartisan and devoid of power struggles. For several decades, for example, the Bahāʾī International Community has been one of the most active of nongovernmental organizations at the United Nations, supporting proposals for social development that are in accord with its teachings, while national Bahāʾī communities have supported such causes as interracial harmony in the United States and human rights in Iran.

Bahāʾīs administer their communities through elected councils at the local, national, and international level. The distinctive features of this administration include a noncompetitive electoral system, consultative decision making, and the absence of a clerical class or of individuals in positions of power. Bahāʾīs consider this a model for future society. The main social action of Bahāʾī communities around the world at present is engagement in a collaborative learning process designed to empower people to become active participants in their own social, material, intellectual, and spiritual development and to assist them in developing projects for the betterment of their communities. The present world leadership of the Bahāʾī community, the Universal House of Justice, considers that this pathway of action when pursued on a global scale will contribute more to the building of a better world civilization than engagement in partisan politics.

BIBLIOGRAPHY

ʿAbdu'l-Bahá. *The Secret of Divine Civilization*. Translated by Marzieh Gail. Wilmette, Ill.: Bahá'í Publishing Trust, 1970. Written on Bahāʾ Allāh's instructions in 1875, this book engaged with the discourse on reform in Iran following the attempts at reform initiated by Ḥusayn Khān Moshīr-ud-Dawleh.

Alkan, Necati. *Dissent and Heterodoxy in the Late Ottoman Empire: Reformers, Babis and Baha'is*. Istanbul: Isis, 2008. Describes the contacts between the Bahāʾī leaders and the Ottoman reformers.

Amanat, Abbas. *Resurrection and Renewal: The Making of the Babi Movement in Iran, 1844–1850*. Ithaca, N.Y.: Cornell University Press, 1989. The standard academic account of the Bāb and his religion.

Bahá'í Reference Library. http://reference.bahai.org/en/. Contains most published Bahāʾī scripture and other authoritative texts in original languages and English translation.

Bahá'u'lláh. *Tablets of Bahá'u'lláh Revealed after the Kitáb-i-Aqdas*. Translated by Habib Taherzadeh et al. Haifa, Israel: Bahá'í World Centre, 1978. The writings of Bahāʾ Allāh that contain his social teachings.

Cole, Juan R. I. *Modernity and Millennium: The Genesis of the Baha'i Faith in the Nineteenth-Century Middle East*. New York: Columbia University Press, 1998. An attempt to place Bahāʾ Allāh's thought in the context of the nineteenth-century Middle East.

Lerche, Charles O., ed. *Healing the Body Politic: Bahá'í Perspectives on Peace and Conflict Resolution*. Oxford: George Ronald, 2004. A collection of essays covering such subjects as peace, governance, conflict resolution, human rights, collective security, and globalization from a Bahāʾī perspective.

Momen, Moojan. "The Constitutional Movement and the Baha'is of Iran: The Creation of an 'Enemy Within.'" *British Journal of Middle Eastern Studies* 39, no. 3 (December 2012): 328–345. The role of Iranian Bahāʾīs in the Constitutional Revolution and ʿAbd-al-Bahāʾ's instructions about this.

Smith, Peter. *The Babi and Baha'i Religions: From Messianic Shiʿism to a World Religion*. Cambridge, U.K.: Cambridge University Press, 1987. The best academic survey of Bābī and Bahāʾī history and teachings.

MOOJAN MOMEN

BALKAN STATES. "Balkans" is the name used since the early eighteenth century to refer to the region consisting of the present-day states of Bulgaria, Romania, Greece, Albania, Serbia, Macedonia, Montenegro, Bosnia and Herzegovina, Croatia, Slovenia, and the European part of the Republic of Turkey. In modern European geopolitical discourse, the Balkans consist of

Serbia (including the former Ottoman administrative unit of the Sancak (Sandžak) of Novi Pazar), Kosovo, Montenegro, Bosnia and Herzegovina, Croatia, Albania, Bulgaria, and occasionally Slovenia.

Islam was present in the Balkans even before the Ottoman period, by means of trading contacts or via Slav mercenaries and slaves in the courts of Muslim Spain and Sicily. However, Islam became one of the Balkan region's principal religions as a result of the Ottoman conquest.

Following the end of Ottoman rule and the withdrawal of its military garrisons from Inner Serbia in 1867, and the 1878 Berlin Congress, when the European powers agreed that Austria-Hungary should occupy Bosnia and Herzegovina, the Muslims of the Balkans experienced a civilizational shock. For centuries they had lived in the Ottoman Empire, where Islam was the state religion, but now they had to define their religious status within nation-states with a Christian majority. Muslims were neither a minority nor a major national group in Bosnia and Herzegovina in 1878. This need became particularly acute after the 1912–1913 Balkan wars, when the Ottoman Empire lost most of its territories in the Balkans.

After 1878, European powers called upon the newly formed Christian states in the Balkans to recognize Islam as a religion and to grant the Muslims legal status. This included the right to profess the teachings of Islam, to manifest it in worship and practice, and to assemble with other believers in a religious community.

Serbia. In 1868 Mihailo Obrenović issued a decree permitting Muslims to use the Bajrakli mosque in Belgrade. State funds were allocated for the maintenance of the mosque. Not long after this, Serbia enlarged its territory to the south by means of war, particularly in clashes with the Ottoman Empire in 1876–1878, when Serbian forces seized many areas with a large indigenous Muslim population. In 1878 an interim law was promulgated in Niš, granting protection to "the Serbian citizen of the [Orthodox] Christian faith and the Serbian citizen of the Muslim faith." The Serbian authorities enacted an almost identical law in Belgrade in 1913, following the conquest by Serbian forces of the Sandžak of Novi Pazar, Kosovo, and Metohija.

Montenegro. In Montenegro, the recognition of Islam became relevant following the 1876–1878 wars, when five Turkish *kadılıks*—regions under the jurisdiction of a *qāḍī* [*kadı, kazi*] or judge—became part of the state of Montenegro. At first there was no legislation in Montenegro governing the rights and freedoms of Muslims to profess Islam, apart from the statements and documents issued by Prince Nikola, which amounted to the recognition in public law of Islam in the state. A few years after 1878, Prince Nikola appointed a mufti of Montenegro as the "religious elder of the Muslims of Montenegro," granting him the authority to judge the Muslims under *Sharīʿah* law "in the same way as in the Turkish period." The 1888 General Property Code for the Principality of Montenegro recognized mosques as the common property of the Muslims.

In 1905, speaking at the Montenegrin Assembly held on Nikoljdan, the Montenegrin leader noted that the Muslims were equal in rights and freedoms with their baptized brothers in the state, and were not prevented from maintaining spiritual relations with the caliph in the imperial city of Istanbul. The Judicial Procedure Law, enacted in Montenegro in 1905, extended the powers of the *Sharīʿah* courts, and the 1905 Constitution of Montenegro confirmed all previous legislative provisions pertaining to the Muslims.

The Kingdom of Yugoslavia (1918–1941). The 1921 Constitution of the Kingdom of Serbs, Croats, and Slovenes, known as the Vidovdan (St. Vitus's Day) Constitution, proclaimed the principle of equality of religious confession. In the Kingdom of Yugoslavia, too, between 1918 and

1941, *Sharīʿah* law was recognized in regard to Muslim family and inheritance law and in matters of Islamic pious endowments (*vakf*, from the Arabic *waqf*).

The Kingdom of Yugoslavia also sought to locate the headquarters of the supreme Islamic leader or Reisu-l-Ulema in Belgrade, and for a time he was based there.

Bosnia and Herzegovina. Several important laws dealing with Islam and the Muslims were enacted during the Austro-Hungarian period in Bosnia and Herzegovina (1878–1918). The Convention Governing the Occupation of Bosnia-Herzegovina, adopted in 1879, set out the obligation to respect the Islamic faith. By Imperial Decree of 1882, the Islamic religious hierarchy was established, headed by the Reisu-l-Ulema. This decree, issued in Vienna, introduced the Ulema Medžlis (Council of Scholars) in Sarajevo, appointing the Reisu-l-Ulema and another four members to the council, following the model of the Synod of the Orthodox Church. In 1910 Austria-Hungary promulgated a Provincial Constitution for Bosnia and Herzegovina, which proclaimed a "system of recognized religious communities."

In 1902 the Austro-Hungarian authorities enacted a law that required the word "Muslims" to be used to denote the followers of Islam and "the Islamic faith" to denote Islam itself.

In 1916, Austria-Hungary enacted a Law on the Recognition of the Islamic Faith, guaranteeing freedom of religion and state protection for the Muslims of Bosnia and Herzogovina. This had been already enacted in Austria in 1912 and elsewhere at earlier dates. Under the terms of this law, polygamy was not permitted in the Dual Monarchy but was allowed in Bosnia and Herzegovina.

Croatia. Islam was recognized by the Croatian Parliament in 1916, a few weeks after its recognition by the Austro-Hungarian monarchy. In 1919 an Imam's Office was established in Zagreb, and in 1922 a Mufti's Office was established there but was abolished in 1923 by the Kingdom of Yugoslavia, on the grounds that there were no more than two thousand Muslims in Croatia.

Islam and Muslims in the Balkans, 1945–1992. In socialist Yugoslavia (1945–1992), religion and religious communities were marginalized, particularly in the early decades. After 1945, the socialist states not only of Yugoslavia, but also of Albania, Bulgaria, and Romania, systematically introduced an atheistic system in their schools and universities, as well as in the workplace.

Between 1945 and 1955 many imams, *hojjas*, priests, and friars were imprisoned. The practice of incarcerating religious figures, as well as other ideological enemies of socialism and communism, continued even after this.

There was no specific law governing the status of Islam and the Muslims or that of *vakufs* in the early years of socialist Yugoslavia. There were, however, two instances of laws in which the Bosnian Muslims and those of Albania were singled out. The first was the 1946 Law on the Abolition of *Sharīʿah* Courts in the People's Republic of Bosnia and Herzegovina, and the second was the 1950 Law Prohibiting the Wearing of the Veil, both specifically targeting Islamic believers.

In the early decades of socialist Yugoslavia, the Islamic community was known as the Islamic Religious Community, headed by the Reisu-l-Ulema, who chaired a body known as the Supreme Islamic Leadership. At the time it was a centralized institution, interpreting Islam in the manner then regarded as socially acceptable: Islam interpreted progressively, Islam backing the workers and peasants, Islam for the honest intelligentsia, and so forth. There were only two active madrasahs in socialist Yugoslavia, the Gazi Husrev-bey madrasah in Sarajevo and the Alauddin madrasah in Priština (Kosovo).

A special police campaign was conducted in Serbia, Macedonia, and Bulgaria in the late 1960s and during the 1970s to have the Muslims settle in Turkey. In Bulgaria, Muslim names were changed by law into Bulgarian ones. In Yugoslavia, Tito's authorities put a stop to the campaign, and Tito dismissed Aleksandar Rankovič, the Minister of Police. During this period, Kosovo gained a large measure of autonomy, effectively giving it equal status with the six Yugoslav republics.

Recent History. Bosnian Muslims were granted the status of Muslims as a nationality in 1971. In the later years of Yugoslav socialism, there was a marked renaissance among the Muslims and their institutions in the Balkans, particularly in the western Balkan countries. Numerous mosques were built in Bosnia and Herzegovina, the former Novi Pazar Sandžak, Kosovo, and Macedonia. During the 1970s and 1980s the Gazi Husrev-bey madrasah, founded in 1537, flourished, and in 1977 the Faculty of Islamic Theology was established (renamed the Faculty of Islamic Studies in 1992). The Faculty of Islamic Studies in Sarajevo is between six hundred and seven hundred students.

After the dissolution of socialist Yugoslavia, which began in 1990, war broke out, first in Slovenia, then in Croatia and, in 1992, in Bosnia and Herzegovina. All three republics were recognized as independent, sovereign states, first by the European Union and the United States and then, in 1992, by the United Nations. Serbian politics in Bosnia and Herzegovina and official Belgrade were opposed to this, and wars ensued, particularly in Bosnia and Herzegovina (1992–1995) and Kosovo (1999). More than 70 percent of the victims in the wars of 1992–1995 and 1999 were Bosnian Muslims and Albanians. More than a thousand mosques, *tekke*s (Ṣūfī lodges), and *maktab*s (Islamic schools) were destroyed, along with about two hundred churches.

The war ended in Bosnia in 1995 by NATO strikes, and at the end of the year the Dayton Peace Agreement was signed. Bosnia was divided administratively into the Federation of Bosnia and Herzegovina and Republika Srpska, with a weak central government in Sarajevo. In Kosovo, NATO strikes in 1999 put a stop to the persecution and the forced expulsion of the Albanian population by the Serbian army and police.

Since 1992, five madrasahs (Islamic high schools) have been opened, along with another two faculties of Islamic studies. Under the auspices of the Islamic Community of Bosnia, madrasahs have also been opened in Novi Pazar (Serbia) and Zagreb (Croatia).

The Islamic community in Bosnia and Herzegovina has several muftis' offices (Sarajevo, Bihać, Mostar, Banja Luka, Tuzla, Travnik, Zenica, Goražde), headed by the Reisu-l-Ulema as Grand Mufti, headquartered in Sarajevo. There is also a Bosnian mufti in Zagreb and Dubrovnik (Croatia), Ljubljana (Slovenia), Novi Pazar, and Belgrade. The Reisu-l-Ulema heads the executive body of the Islamic community of Bosnia and Herzegovina, known as the Rijaset. The supreme governing body of the Islamic community in Bosnia and Herzegovina is the Sabor (Assembly), which issues decrees and regulations binding only by virtue of the moral will and conscience of the Muslims, because in Bosnia and Herzegovina, as indeed throughout the Balkans, *Sharīʿah* law is no longer applied. In Kosovo, a Faculty of Islamic Studies has recently been opened, and the Islamic community there is headed by amufti. In Montenegro, the Islamic community is headed by a Reis in Podgorica.

The headquarters of the Islamic community in Macedonia is in Skopje, also headed by a Reisu-l-Ulema. In Albania, the headquarters of the Islamic community is in Tiranë, under amufti.

Most Muslims or Islamic communities in the Balkan states, from Bulgaria to Croatia and Slovenia, are keen for their countries to join the European Union, in which they see their security. In these Balkan Muslim communities, Islam is seen as a religion and a moral system.

Since 2008 the countries of the western Balkans have been making an effort to improve their mutual relations. The Republic of Serbia, under the leadership of its president, Boris Tadić, has been pursuing a largely moderate policy towards her neighbors. Serbia under his presidency has been doing the best it can on the sensitive issue of Kosovo's recognition: the Serbian government does not declare approval of the recognition of Kosovo, but it does accept negotiations with Priština. With its softer stand on Kosovo, Serbia is trying to take advantage of EU funds. Serbia's rhetoric in recent years has been mainly pro-European. There is an attempt to pacify or neutralize the appetites of the Serb population in Kosovo. The EU is well aware of the old diplomatic issue that, if Serbia were to remain in the East, it would mean remaining under the influence of the Russian Federation. It suits the EU and pro-European forces in Serbia to integrate Serbia into the EU as quickly as possible to stabilize the Balkans.

Muslim politicians in Bosnia support the integration of Croatia and Serbia into the EU. Croatia has signed the accession treaty with the EU and became the EU's twenty-eighth member state on 1 July 2013, while Serbia is also a few steps ahead of Bosnia. Bosnia, especially her Muslim politicians, hopes that the EU umbrella over the western Balkans will bring stability to the region. Muslim religious and political leaders in Montenegro and Macedonia share this hope. There is a pronounced positive Muslim view and discourse about the EU and its future role in the western Balkans.

[*See also* Bosnia and Herzegovina; Ottoman Empire; *and* Turkey.]

BIBLIOGRAPHY

Agović, Bajro. *Islamska zajednica u Crnoj Gori* (Islamic Community in Montenegro). Podgorica: Mešihat Islamske zajednice, 2007.

Aslan, Ednan, ed. *Islamic Education in Europe*. Vienna: Böhlau, 2009.

Bougarel, Xavier, Elissa Helms, and Gerlachus Duijzings, eds. *The New Bosnian Mosaic: Identities, Memories and Moral Claims in a Post-War Society*. Aldershot, U.K.: Ashgate, 2007.

Disolucija Jugoslavije (Procesi, uzroci i pozicija Bosne i Hercegovine kroz prizmu djelovanja političkog vodstva na čelu sa Alijom Izetbegovićem). Zbornik sa Međunarodnog naučnog simpozija. Sarajevo: Muzej Alija Izetbegović, 2010.

Donia, Robert J. *Sarajevo: A Biography*. Ann Arbor: University of Michigan Press, 2006.

Ghodsee, Kristin. *Muslim Lives in Eastern Europe: Gender, Ethnicity, and the Transformation of Islam in Postsocialist Bulgaria*. Princeton, N.J.: Princeton University Press, 2010.

Gradeva, Rossitsa, ed. *Istoriya na myusyulmanskata kultura po balgarskite zemi* (History of Muslim Culture in Bulgarian Lands). Sofia: IMIR, 2007.

Halit Eren, ed. *The Ottoman Legacy and the Balkan Muslim Communities Today*. 2nd ed. Istanbul: Balkanlar Medeniyet Merkezi, 2011.

İnalcik, Halil. *The Ottoman Empire: The Classical Age, 1300–1600*. London: Phoenix, 2001.

Jezernik, Božidar. *Wild Europe: The Balkans in the Gaze of Western Travellers*. London: Saqi in association with the Bosnian Institute, 2004.

Karčić, Fikret. *The Bosniaks and the Challenges of Modernity*. Sarajevo: El-Kalem, 1999.

Malcolm, Noel. *Bosnia: A Short History*. London: Macmillan, 1996.

Malcolm, Noel. *Kosovo: A Short History*. New York: New York University Press, 1998.

Nielsen Jorgen S., et al., eds. *Yearbook of Muslims in Europe*, vol. 2. Leiden, Brill, 2010.

Nielsen, Jorgen S., et al., eds. *TheYearbook of Muslims in Europe*, vol. 3. Leiden, Brill, 2011.

Poulton, Hugh, and Suha Taji-Farouki, eds. *Muslim Identity and the Balkan State*. London: Hurst, 1997.

Quataert, Donald. *The Ottoman Empire, 1700–1922*. New York: Cambridge University Press, 2005.

Zirojević, Olga. *Srbija pod turskom vlašću 1459–1804* (Serbia under Turkish Rule 1459–1804). Belgrade: Srpski genealoški centar, 2007.

Alexandre Popovic
Translated from the French by Harry M. Matthews Jr.
Updated by Enes Karić

BANNĀ, ḤASAN AL-. Ḥasan al-Bannā (1906–1949) was the founder of the Muslim Brotherhood, which became one of the largest and most influential religious movements in the Islamic world. Al-Bannā was born in Maḥmudīyah, near Alexandria in Egypt, to the family of the local religious notable Shaykh Aḥmad ʿAbd al-Raḥmān al-Bannā (1881–1958). From his youth onward, he took part in the Ḥaṣāfīyah Ṣūfī Welfare Society, which was a predecessor of the Muslim Brotherhood. After attending the Damanhūr teachers' training college, from 1923 to 1927 he studied at the Dār al-ʿUlūm in Cairo, founded by Muḥammad ʿAbduh (d. 1905) and made famous by Muḥammad Rashīd Riḍā, who taught there until his death in 1935. In September 1927, al-Bannā began teaching primary school in Ismailia, Egypt. There he was known to be skeptical toward official Islam and started an unconventional preaching campaign in coffee shops. In March 1928, six followers urged him to found a "religious association devoted to the promotion of good and the rooting-out of evil." Al-Bannā agreed to be their leader and named it the Society of the Muslim Brothers (Jamʿīyat al-Ikhwān al-Muslimūn). Al-Bannā was the acknowledged leader of the Brotherhood as it expanded into other parts of Egypt. During the 1930s and 1940s, he started a publishing house, which put out the newspaper *al-Ikhwān al-Muslimūn* from 1933 to 1938 and 1942 to 1948, as well as the weekly magazine *al-Taʿāruf* (The Instructions) from 1940 to 1942. Additionally, it published *al-Manār* (The Lighthouse), inherited from Rashīd Riḍā, from 1939 to 1941.

By the mid-1930s, the Muslim Brotherhood had begun to take on a more political character, defining Islam as a comprehensive system that included political affairs. Additionally, it started to move toward a more charismatic organization centered on the figure of al-Bannā himself, a magnetic personality and stirring orator. The *Qānūn al-Ikhwān al-Muslimīn al-ʿAmm* (General Law of the Society of the Muslim Brothers), drafted by al-Bannā in 1934, allotted extensive powers to the executive body, whose members were chosen directly by al-Bannā himself. Decisions made by the executive committee required unanimity, and al-Bannā alone had final decision-making power. He believed that the Muslim Brotherhood could never be successful unless it commanded its members' total confidence and obedience. In the unstable political environment of the time, he saw limited uses for consultation (*shūrā*), was skeptical of democratic elections within the organization, and eventually assumed the title of *al-Murshid al-ʿAmm* (General Guide).

Another shift in the organization occurred with the triumph of pan-Islamic ambitions over the local focus in Ismailia. The growth of the movement, which moved its headquarters to Cairo in 1933, was rapid: It numbered four branches in 1929, fifteen in 1932, one hundred–fifty in 1936, three hundred in 1938, and eventually two thousand in 1948, according to its own journals. Estimates of the total membership in July 1944 ranged from a hundred thousand to half a million, many of whom were students. Al-Bannā attached a fundamental importance to student cadres in the Islamic mission. The Muslim Brotherhood was able to expand its organization from Ismailia to all parts of Egypt and to recruit a mass following. Additionally, the Muslim Brothers established branches in Palestine, Sudan, Iraq, and Syria. These appear to have been established mainly by foreign students who had been influenced by the Muslim Brothers' teachings in Cairo.

Parallel to the political organization was a military wing, the Special Apparatus. There was strong internal pressure for more military activism from more radical members prior to the Fifth Congress in 1939. The formation of the Special Apparatus offered a temporary solution to resolve this internal friction, as it offered opportunities for those who wished to prepare for armed struggle against the British. Moreover, the rumors surrounding the military wing also gave the society a touch of mystique and secrecy. The armed units of the Special Apparatus demonstrated their ability and their stock of weaponry when they took part in the Arab revolt in Palestine in 1936 and later in the Arab-Israeli war of 1948–1949.

By late 1939 some of the society's radical cadres had seceded and formed the rival society Shabāb Muḥammad (Muḥammadan Youth). The dissidents voiced their grievance against al-Bannā's autocratic leadership and his willingness to enter into political compromise.

The formal independence of Egypt, declared in 1922, and the 1923 constitution were both attributable to the Wafd Party, a popular movement born in 1919 during nationalist demonstrations and riots. Both were eroded by the 1936 Anglo-Egyptian treaty that confirmed Egyptian dependence. From that time onward, the Wafd Party increasingly lost its credibility and popularity. The enthronement of the young King Farouk in 1937 gave al-Bannā the opportunity to acclaim him enthusiastically, in hopes of being able to enhance the standing of the Muslim Brotherhood, which was highly critical of the Wafd Party and preparing itself for a larger role in the Egyptian political arena. In an internal document from 1939 (later published in the Sixth Congress in 1941) it was declared that the Muslim Brotherhood intended to present candidates for the next parliamentary election. During these years of alignments with the palace, al-Bannā stressed the right to criticize the palace if the Muslim Brothers deemed it necessary.

World War II presented immediate obstacles for the realization of the Muslim Brotherhood's political ambitions. In 1942, Great Britain demanded general support for the Wafdist government it had installed in February of that year. Al-Bannā, alongside all the members of the Egyptian nationalist movement, expressed hopes that an Axis victory would undermine British colonialism, but al-Bannā condemned the racism underpinning their ideologies. At the beginning of the war, he relied on the support of King Farouk and his prime minister, ʿAlī Māhir Pasha. When the king was forced to submit to British authority in 1941–1942, al-Bannā found himself harassed and even incarcerated briefly in Cairo in 1941 and again in 1945. Muslim Brothers were subjected to government harassment and restrictions because of their anti-British propaganda. This did not, however, prevent al-Bannā from maintaining close contact with the government during these years.

In his letter to the Fifth Congress of the Muslim Brotherhood in 1939, al-Bannā was already advising the king to dissolve the parties and to form a "People's Union" that would "work for the good of the nation in conformity with the principles of Islam." His criticism was directed toward the corrupt Egyptian party system, and he did not reject a multiparty system, as such, in an Islamic state. Al-Bannā successfully formed the Muslim Brotherhood's program independent of names, families, and parties, which was pivotal for strengthening the organization's support base, which consisted of the educated lower middle class.

The Muslim Brotherhood weakened in the 1940s. Al-Bannā withdrew from the 1943 elections in favor of the Wafd party. He suffered outright defeat in the 1945 elections, which were widely assumed to have been fraudulent. Al-Bannā again advocated forming a "People's Union" and refused to join the Wafd, as his friend Aḥmad al-Sukkarī had suggested. Sukkarī left the Muslim Brotherhood in 1947. Al-Bannā reassured the king and the British that there was no threat of military action by the Muslim Brotherhood against the government.

The volunteer units of the Muslim Brotherhood in the Arab-Israeli war of 1948–1949 were compelled to become part of the Egyptian army and to observe the ceasefire. Although al-Bannā submitted, not all of the fighting members of the Muslim Brotherhood followed him. Some kept their weapons, and, under the leadership of Shaykh Farāghlī, they withdrew to the Suez Canal until 1952, with the intention of armed struggle against the British. Faced with the Wafd party and the Socialist (formerly Young Egypt) party in 1948, al-Bannā even allied himself with the communist groups in participating in demonstrations and writing tracts against the British and the government, but not the king.

The assassination on 22 March 1948 of a judge by a young Muslim Brother seems to have occurred completely independently of al-Bannā's authority. In November 1948, a large student demonstration of Muslim Brothers ended in the deaths of two British officers, and a jeep loaded with explosives and weapons was intercepted in Cairo, on its way to Brotherhood members. A military decree dissolved the Muslim Brotherhood on 6 December 1948. On 28 December, Prime Minister Maḥmūd Fahmī al-Nuqrāshī, who had issued the decree, was assassinated by a student affiliated with the Brotherhood. Al-Bannā denied responsibility for any of these actions in three papers that were printed only after his death. The secret police assassinated al-Bannā on 12 February 1949. The funeral ceremonies took place under heavy military escort and without a procession. The founder of the Muslim Brotherhood was regarded as a martyr, and a 1951 trial found him innocent of the criminal actions of 1948. After 1954, Nasser and his associates, who were at first respectful of al-Bannā and his memory, wrongfully imputed the 1945 assassination of Prime Minister Aḥmad Māhir to him. The beliefs about al-Bannā and his movement held by Nasser and his circle were often echoed in general works on contemporary Egypt.

Replacing al-Bannā was to prove difficult for the Muslim Brotherhood. In 1951, as an underground movement, it was moving in two different directions. One school of thought, that of the al-Bannā family, was moderate and loyal to the reformist policy of the majority of al-Bannā's writings. The new guide of the Muslim Brothers, Ḥasan al-Huḍaybī, who was appointed in 1951 after the relegalization of the movement, also represented a moderate tendency. At the beginning of the twenty-first century, al-Bannā's moderate stance is the guiding principle of the Muslim Brothers in Egypt.

A more radical school of thought was led by Ṣāliḥ ʿAshmāwī, who was al-Bannā's successor in the underground movement. He started the publication *al-Daʿwā* (The Call) in 1951. Sayyid Quṭb, who officially joined the Muslim Brotherhood in 1951, was to inspire radical groups from the 1970s to the 1990s. The ideologue of the Organization of the Islamic Jihād, Muḥammad ʿAbd al-Salām Faraj, in his 1981 tract *al-Farīḍah al-ghaybah* (The Missing Precept), deemed al-Bannā and the Muslim Brotherhood to have compromised with "the pagan power" and become enemies of the "minority of activist believers." However, the Muslim Brotherhood's traditional adversaries mistakenly believed that violent extremism was contained in letters written by al-Bannā himself, in particular the *Letter of the Jihād* and the *Letter of Teachings*.

Al-Bannā's writings marked a watershed in modern Islamic discourse by making the successful transition of Islam into an ideology. Al-Bannā regarded Islam as "an all-embracing concept that regulates every aspect of life, adjudicating on every one of its concerns and prescribing for it a solid and rigorous order," and he called for the Islamization of the state, the economy, and society. He shared with earlier Muslim reformers such as Jamāl al-Dīn al-ʿAfghānī and Muḥammad ʿAbduh the belief that Muslim weakness in the face of European domination stemmed from Muslims' deviation from "true" Islam. The solution to Egypt's political, economic, and social problems lay in a return to Islam as a comprehensive system and in making "the Qur'ān our constitution." However, the ideology of the Muslim Brotherhood does not represent a stern anti-Westernism. For example, in one of al-Bannā's theological treatises, *al-ʿAqāʾid* (Dogmas), he quotes extensively from Réné Descartes, Isaac Newton, and Herbert Spencer to underpin his arguments about the existence of God. Although the ideology called for anti-imperialism, his thinking was marked by an openness to ideas from the West. His pamphlet from 1929, *Mudhakkirah fī al-taʿlīm al-dīnī* (A Memorandum on Religious Education), does not quote the Qur'ān or the sunnah. It refers exclusively to Western sources and Western examples.

An important element in the ideology was pan-Islamic nationalism with a strong emphasis on Islamic unity. Al-Bannā considered all Muslims to exist in a sole *ummah* (nation). For him, "Islam knows no geographical frontiers, nor racial or civic differentiations." However, he recognized the pivotal role of the state in the making of an Islamic system in modern times. His message was tailored to a specific Egyptian audience with a strong focus on the liberation of Egypt from the British colonial powers through jihād. According to al-Bannā, it was necessary to "free the Islamic homeland from all foreign authority, for this is a natural right belonging to every human being which only the unjust oppressor will deny."

"Jihād of the spirit" became a keyword denoting self-initiated productive work or activities aimed at bettering the conditions of the Islamic community. Al-Bannā stipulated that "God ordained jihād for the Muslims not as a tool of oppression but rather as a defense for the mission, a guarantee of peace." Furthermore, "the greatest struggle to utter a word of truth in the presence of a tyrannical ruler" became one of the guiding principles of the Muslim Brothers and continued to serve as such into the twenty-first century. It was in this spirit that they began from the mid-1930s to submit their reform proposals and letters of protest to the government. Al-Bannā did not call for the overthrow of Egypt's political order; rather, he sought to reform it from within. He considered Egypt's Constitution of 1923 as valid because it stated that all legislation had to conform to Islamic principles. For al-Bannā, the fundamental flaw in Egypt's political order was that its laws did not strictly forbid things prohibited in Islam, such as alcohol, prostitution, gambling, and usury (*ribā*).

Al-Bannā also rejected the adoption of foreign law codes for commerce and banking, because Islam possessed regulations for all matters. He therefore condemned bonds at a fixed interest rate, but not stock dividends. Al-Bannā envisioned an Islamic economic reform in Egypt. In the Muslim Brotherhood's political program of 1943 he pointed to the failure of the Egyptian state to provide welfare for its citizens by stating, "Remember, brothers, that more than 60 percent of Egyptians live in conditions worse than those in which animals live; they can only get their food by breaking their backs. Egypt is threatened with deadly famine, exposed to economic problems which have no solutions except through God." Al-Bannā constructed a rigorous fiscal system under which "Islam consecrates the alms (*zakāt*) entirely to social expenses," which would strive to reduce the inequalities between rich and poor.

Al-Bannā also emphasized a social and educational reform of society where the Islamic state should guarantee public morality. The state should also exercise the power to censor songs, lectures, films, plays, and books. According to al-Bannā, no society can run its affairs in an Islamic manner without an Islamic state. In general the state should encourage Egyptians to abandon Western customs, for instance in dress, and return to Islamic ones in their homes and in public. Women were regarded as the guardians of Islamic morality, and al-Bannā spoke of "the problem of woman," which was described as "one of the most important social problems" of the day. Furthermore, religious instruction (such as memorization of the Qurʾān), Arabic grammar, and Islamic history should be part of the education from primary school to university.

BIBLIOGRAPHY

Carré, Olivier, and Gérard Michaud. *Les Frères musulmans: Egypte et Syrie, 1928–1982*. Paris: Galimard, 1983.

Commins, David. "Hasan al-Banna (1906–1949)." In *Pioneers of Islamic Revival*, new ed., edited by Ali Rahnema, pp. 125–153. New York: Zed, 2005.

Husaynī, Isḥāq Mūsā al-. *The Moslem Brethren: The Greatest of Modern Islamic Movements*. Beirut: Khyat's College Book Cooperative, 1956.

Imām, 'Abd Allāh. *'Abd al-Nāṣir wa-al-Ikhwān*. Cairo, 1981.

Jansen, Johannes J. G. "Ḥasan Al-Bannā's Earliest Pamphlet." *Die Welt des Islams*, New Ser., 32, no. 2 (1992): 254–258.

Kotob, Sana Abed. "The Accommodationists Speak: Goals and Strategies of the Muslim Brotherhood of Egypt." *International Journal of Middle East Studies* 27, no. 3 (1995): 321–339.

Lia, Brynjar. *The Society of the Muslim Brothers in Egypt: The Rise of an Islamic Mass Movement, 1928–1942*. Reading, U.K.: Ithaca, 1998.

Kraemer, Gudrun. *Hasan al-Banna*. Oxford, U.K.: Oneworld, 2009.

Moussalli, Aḥmad. "Ḥasan Al-Bannā's Islamist Discourse on Constitutional Rule and Islamic State." *Journal of Islamic Studies* 4, no. 2 (1993): 161–174.

Wendell, Charles, trans. *Five Tracts of Ḥasan al-Bannā (1906–1949): A Selection from the Majmū'at al-rasā'il al-Imām al-Shahīd Ḥasan al-Bannā*. Berkeley: University of Calififornia Press, 1978.

Olivier Carré
Translated from the French by Elizabeth Keller
Updated by Liv Tønnessen
and Abdullah A. Al-Arian

Bāqillānī, Abū Bakr Muḥammad ibn al-Ṭayyib al-. Abū Bakr Muḥammad ibn al-Ṭayyib al-Bāqillānī (950–1013), was an Ashʿarī theologian and Mālikī jurist credited with playing a significant role in systemizing and popularizing Ashʿarī doctrine and developing the earliest known political theory of the caliphate.

Born in Basra, al-Bāqillānī spent most of his life in Baghdad, where he gained acclaim for his writing, lecturing, and skill at debating. Not much is known about his early life, and very little is mentioned about his early studies, though a few accounts mention that he studied *uṣūl al-dīn* (fundamentals of faith) under a number of disciples of Abū al-Ḥasan al-Ashʿarī (d. 935), the eponymous founder of the Ashʿarī school of theology. He also studied *fiqh* (jurisprudence) under the leading Mālikī of Baghdad, Abū Bakr al-Abharī (d. 985). His lectures, such as those at al-Manṣūr Mosque in Baghdad, on a variety of Islamic subjects, including *usūl al-dīn* (teaching al-Ashʿarī's *Kitāb al-lumaʿ*, or Book of Illumination) and *fiqh*, are said to have attracted large audiences. Bāqillānī is buried near the grave of Aḥmad ibn Ḥanbal in the Baghdad cemetery of Bāb Ḥarb.

Al-Bāqillānī was among the foremost Mālikī jurists of his period and held the office of chief *qāḍī* (judge) for some time. He had an influence on the legal thought of, among others, al-Baghdādī (d. 1037/1038), al-Māwardī (d. 1058), and Abū Yaʿlā (d. 1067). It was, however, his adeptness in the science of *kalām* (dogmatic theology) that won him great notoriety among his contemporaries and prominent Muslim figures in generations that followed. Al-Bāqillānī employed al-Ashʿarī's methods to refute followers of various sects including the Shīʿah, Khawārij, Muʿtazilah, Rawāfiḍ, Ḥashwīyah, Jahmīyah, Mushabbihah, and Karrāmīyah. The caliph ʿAḍūd al-Dawlah (d. 983), recognizing al-Bāqillānī's outstanding debating skills, dispatched him on a diplomatic mission to the Byzantine court in Constantinople, where al-Bāqillānī debated with Christian scholars in the presence of their emperor.

Al-Bāqillānī authored some fifty-two works, several them on tenets of Islamic belief. Six of his works are known to be extant. His *Tamhīd* (Preface) is regarded as the most complete manual of the Ashʿarī doctrine (similar in content to al-Ashʿarī's *Kitāb al-lumaʿ*) and the earliest extant example of a manual on theological polemic. It also includes a substantial section on his political theory. His *Kitāb manāqib al-aʾimmah* (The Good Deeds of the Imams) defends the Sunnī position regarding the caliphate. His *Kitāb al-inṣāf fī asbāb al-khilāf* (Justice in Disputation) expounds the Sunnī creed and offers a relatively thorough discussion on common theological issues including *qadar* (destiny), seeing God, *shafāʿah* (intercession), and the question of whether the Qurʾān is created or eternal. His *al-Intiṣār fī al-Qurʾān* (Victory through the Qurʾān) is a refutation of those who reject the Qurʾān, and his *Iʿjāz al-Qurʾān* (The Miracle of the Qurʾān) is a popular treatise that deals with the wonders of the Qurʾān and its stylistic perfection.

Al-Bāqillānī's political theory, expounded in his *Tamhīd*, is regarded as the earliest analytical rendering of the Sunnī theory of the caliphate and the most thorough attempt to justify the *ijmāʿ* (consensus) of the Muslim community. Al-Bāqillānī's theory aimed to uphold the legitimacy of the caliphate and to establish it upon the principles of the *Sharīʿah*. For Bāqillānī, the Muslim community could only be governed according to the *Sharīʿah*, and the *Sharīʿah* could only be implemented by means of the caliphate. Al-Bāqillānī therefore maintained that the establishment of the caliphate was necessary and that the caliph's ultimate responsibility was to obey the *Sharīʿah*. He deemed it obligatory upon the community, in return, to obey the caliph. As to how the caliphate was to be established, Bāqillānī argued that it should be through a process of *ikhtiyār* (election), and he refuted the Shīʿī claim that it should be by *naṣṣ* (designation). He further held that the *Sharīʿah* had not imposed a limit on the number of electors needed to validate the contract of the caliphate, and that an unlimited number of Muslims should be present to witness this contract and the *bayʿah* (oath of allegiance), making it publicly known. Bāqillānī also maintained that there could only be one caliph serving at a time, regardless of the distance between Muslim lands.

As for the requirements necessary to be caliph, Bāqillānī mentions several, including being a descendant of the Quraysh (refuting the Shīʿī position that the caliph must be from *ahl al-bayt*, or "people of the house of the Prophet"), possessing knowledge of religious and legal matters minimally equivalent to that required for a *qāḍī*, and being adept in state, military, and administrative affairs. He also believed, contrary to the Shīʿah, that the caliph did not need to be *maʿṣūm* (sinless).

According to al-Bāqillānī, the community could not depose the caliph without just cause from the principles of the *Sharīʿah*. He gives the reasons justifying the deposition of the caliph to be the following: committing heresy (e.g., openly declaring disbelief in a fundamental tenet of Islam), committing an act of evil, being unjust, having a physical or mental infirmity that would inhibit the carrying out of those duties and responsibilities associated with the office (i.e., insanity, deafness, or old age), and being taken into captivity by the enemy. Al-Bāqillānī, however, offers no rules of procedure for deposing the caliph. Though he deplored rebellion against an unjust caliph (fearing anarchy), he reserved the right of Muslims to disobey acts contrary to the principles of the *Sharīʿah*.

[*See also* Fiqh.]

BIBLIOGRAPHY

Al-Bāqillānī, Muḥammad ibn al-Ṭayyib. *Kitāb al-tamhīd*. Edited by R. J. McCarthy. Beirut: al-Maktabah al-Sharqīyah, 1957. Arabic text with English introduction. Al-Bāqillānī's *Tamhīd* is regarded as the most complete manual of the Ashʿarī doctrine, and it includes a substantial section on his political theory.

Grunebaum, Gustave E. von. *A Tenth-Century Document of Arabic Literary Theory and Criticism*. Chicago: University of Chicago Press, 1950. Includes an annotated English translation of the sections of al-Bāqillānī's *Iʿjāz* that deal with poetry.

Ibish, Yusuf. *The Political Doctrine of al-Baqillani*. Beirut: American University of Beirut, Faculty of Arts and Sciences, 1966. The only known published work in English on al-Bāqillānī's political thought, based on the respective section in his *Tamhīd*. Also contains a brief but informative section on his life and works.

Tritton, A. S. *Muslim Theology*. London: Luzac, 1947. See especially pp. 177–182.

MOHAMMAD A. ABDERRAZZAQ

BARANĪ, ḌHIYAʾ AL-DĪN AL-. (1285–1357)

Baranī ranks among the most preeminent political theorists and historians of the Delhi Sultanate (1206–1526) of India. He served as courtier for seventeen years under Muḥammad Ibn Tughluq (r. 1325–1351) but fell into disgrace under that sultan's successor, Firūz Tughluq, spending his final years impoverished and in jail, where he wrote Persian-language treatises on governance and history, drawing from memory. Prominent among his numerous writings was his history of the Delhi Sultanate, *Tārikh-i Firūz-Shāhī*, which covers the period from Ghiyās al-Dīn Balban (r. 1266–1286) to Firuz Tughluq (r. 1351–1388) and was intended, in part, to serve as an instructive guide for Delhi's rulers. As a rhetorical device for his works, Baranī puts his own words into the mouths of Muslim rulers such as Balban, ʿAlāʾ al-Dīn Khaljī, and especially Maḥmūd of Ghazna, who is held up by Baranī as the ideal Muslim king. Although Baranī's narrative of events is not always reliable, his history of the sultanate nevertheless upholds the principle of generating historical knowledge based on observable social and political phenomena, in order to discern underlying religious truths and to exalt the achievements of Sunnī Islam.

Baranī's interest in history informed his major effort to reformulate, for conditions in India at the time, the Islamic political tradition in which religion and the state were conceived of as being inextricably bound together. In his *Fatāwā-i Jahāndārī*, Baranī therefore attempts to define the obligations of the sultan to the state as well as to Islam, while simultaneously grappling with one of the most pressing challenges faced by the rulers of Delhi, namely, how Muslim sovereigns were to govern in a society where the majority of subjects were non-Muslims. Baranī makes it clear that he views the imperatives of effective imperial governance—reliance on military force, support of monarchical hierarchy and royal splendor, an unending concern with replenishing the treasury—as unavoidable hindrances to living the life of a pious Muslim in the mold of the first four caliphs, since whose time empires have spread wherein "the appearance and character of Islam have greatly changed." This conclusion leads Baranī to draw a sharp distinction between the religious injunctions of the *Sharīʿah* on the one hand and the requirements of state or "secular" law (*ḍawābiṭ*) on the other. State law, the province of kings, defers to political expediency but is nevertheless designed ultimately to protect the religious realm in which *Sharīʿah* holds sway and thereby spread the glory of Islam. In this schema,

God-fearing Muslims are to adhere strictly to the holy law, while sovereigns and their officials forgo religious poverty in the ineluctably sinful service of the state.

Baranī provides a description of how the sultan should fulfill his duty as he conducts matters of state, so that he might prevent tyranny, promote political and economic stability, enforce justice, and eliminate wickedness and unbelief. Here Baranī draws upon the legacy of the pre-Islamic Persian Sassanid kings, who represented a model of effective governance, if not religious virtue. In Baranī's texts we encounter detailed advice for the proper manner by which the sovereign should select wise counsel, criteria to develop an efficient and righteous cadre of administrators and military officers, strategies to promote the well-being of the peasantry, and considerations for a tempered system of punishment and reward in the administration of justice (*ʿadl*). In his prescriptions, Baranī repeatedly emphasizes that only elite, high-born Muslims merit the support of the state, as the promotion of low-born men to office by the sultan leads invariably to social chaos and political decline, while the appointment of well-born and hence loyal, bold, and wise men would ensure the kingdom's success.

In stressing the king's responsibility to suppress heresy and unbelief, Baranī denounced Muslim philosophers and rationalists and proved to be zealously anti-Hindu. His writing is marked by frequent incitement of the king to humiliate as well as kill Hindus, particularly their Brahman leaders, to demolish idols, and to generally extirpate Hinduism from the public realm. For Baranī, the exaction of discriminatory taxes including the *jizyah* was not enough; Hindus should be given the choice of Islam or death, and he considers it praise to say that, had Maḥmūd of Ghazna had further opportunity, he would have wiped out Hinduism altogether. While Baranī at times suggests his prescriptions in this regard be confined to the environs of the imperial capital of Delhi, even there they were in fact by and large blithely ignored by Muslim rulers. Indeed, most of the sultans whom he sought to influence were inclined from their contacts with the powerful Ṣūfī mystic orders to develop an approach of general accommodation and tolerance toward non-Muslims. Although Baranī attempted to bolster his authority by highlighting his association with the great Ṣūfī *shaykhs* of his time, his worldview was generally bereft of the same accommodation and tolerance.

BIBLIOGRAPHY

Alam, Muzaffar. *The Languages of Political Islam: India, 1200–1800*. Chicago: University of Chicago Press, 2004.

Habib, Muhammad, and Afsar Umar Salim Khan. *The Political Theory of the Delhi Sultanate (Including a Translation of Ziauddin Barani's Fatāwā-i Jahāndārī, circa, 1358–9* AD). Allahabad, India: Kitab Mahal, [1961].

Haq, S. Moinul. *Baranī's History of the Tughluqs (Being a Critical Study of the Relevant Chapters of Tārikh-i Firūz-Shāhī)*. Karachi, Pakistan: Pakistan Historical Society, 1959.

Hardy, P. "Unity and Variety in Indo-Islamic and Perso-Islamic Civilization: Some Ethical and Political Ideas of Ḍiyā' al-Dīn Baranī of Delhi, of al-Ghazālī and of Naṣīr al-Dīn Tūsī compared." *Iran* 16 (1978): 127–135.

BRENDAN LAROCQUE

BARELWĪS. The Barelwī movement emerged during the 1880s from the north Indian town of Bareilly. The movement is so called because of its close association with the writings of Maulānā Aḥmad Riẓā Khān Barelwī (1856–1921). The followers of Maulānā Aḥmad Riẓā, however, also identified themselves as the Ahl al-Sunnat wa-al-Jamāʿat, or "people of the (prophetic) way and the majority (community)." The significance of this nomenclature is their relation with the earliest

Muslim community, the Companions and followers of the prophet Muḥammad.

The significance of the Barelwī movement should be viewed against the background of the failure of the Indian revolt of 1857, followed by the formal colonization of India by the British. These events, traumatic from the Indian Muslim point of view, led to a period of lively religious debate among the scholars of Islamic law (*ʿulamāʾ*). They could all agree that Indian Muslims had lost political power because of internal weakness and decay, but they differed widely in their understanding of how renewal (*tajdīd*) and reform (*iṣlāḥ*) should proceed. The Barelwī movement emerged in this context of identity and action deemed necessary to reverse a politically unfavorable situation. The main trait of this movement, however, lies in its staunch favoring of indigenous characteristics of South Asian Islamic tradition. Because of its more Sufist inclination, it contains many differences from the religious beliefs present in Arab Islamic societies.

In scholarly terms, Aḥmad Riẓā had a strong orientation toward the "rational" (*maʿqūlāt*) sciences and jurisprudence. His voluminous writings, estimated at one thousand texts, consist for the most part of *fatwas* (religious rulings). The rapid growth of telecommunications and railway networks in late nineteenth-century British India facilitated the wide dissemination of Aḥmad Riẓā's views.

Aḥmad Riẓā and his followers were also Ṣūfī *shaykhs* (masters of select circles of disciples), owing particular though not exclusive allegiance to the Qādirī order. In this capacity, Aḥmad Riẓā enjoyed close relations with a number of prominent Qādirī Ṣūfī families in the region, which affected his practices twofold: by a strong emphasis that a "good" Muslim should accord primacy to the *Sharīʿah* (Islamic law) over *Ṭarīqah* (the Ṣūfī path), and an insistence that being a "good" Muslim was contingent on personal devotion to the prophet Muḥammad as a loving guide and intercessor between Allāh and the individual through a chain of *pīrs*, to whom each individual was bound by an oath of loyalty (*bayʿah*). Barelwī ritual practices centered on Sufism and on Ṣūfī shrines, particularly the periodic observance of their death anniversaries (*ʿurs*). Another prominent Barelwī belief is that individual believers needed the Prophet's intercession (*waseela*) with Allāh if they hoped for Allāh's closeness and forgiveness. On the other hand, according to Barelwi beliefs, the intervention of notable saints (Ṣūfīs) of Islam is also helpful in gaining closeness to Allah. Those who denied the importance of intercession on the grounds of the equality of all believers before Allāh were deemed by Aḥmad Riẓā to be guilty of arrogance. The more extremist views of the Deobandī School were regarded as apostasy.

What brought the Barelwīs into conflict with other Sunnī Muslim reform movements, particularly with the *ʿulamāʾ* associated with the Dār al-ʿUlūm Deoband, was primarily the Barelwī vision of the prophet Muḥammad's attributes. These attributes included his ability to see into the future, to have knowledge of the unseen (*ʿilm al-ghayb*). Aḥmad Riẓā argued on the basis of certain verses of the Qurʾān, as well as *ḥadīth* and *fiqh* scholarship, that the prophet Muḥammad had been invested with these qualities by God, with whom his relationship was that of a beloved. Denial of these prophetic attributes was interpreted by Aḥmad Riẓā as denial of some of the "fundamentals of the faith" (*ḍarūrīyat al-dīn*). These fundamentals, which fall under the rubric of *ʿaqāʿid* (articles of faith), broadly interpreted, were indivisible. Denial of these prophetic qualities, in Aḥmad Riẓā's view, was implicit in the position taken by those he designated as "Wahhābīs," a term he applied variously to prominent Deobandī *ʿulamāʾ*s. By "Wahhābīs," he meant the similarities in views of Deobandī *ʿulamāʾ*s with that of Muḥammad ibn ʿAbd al-Wahhāb, who founded Salafism in the Arabian peninsula.

During Aḥmad Riẓā's lifetime, the Barelwī movement centered on a small core of followers, personally loyal to him. But afterwards his followers, returning to their own towns after receiving *khilāfat* (the right to accept students of their own), carried his vision beyond the confines of learned *ʿulamāʾ* circles into a wider arena. Since Aḥmad Riẓā's death in 1921, "Barelwī" leaders—among them Maulānā Naʿīmuddīn Murādābādī (d. 1948), Shāh Aulād-i Rasāl Marharvī (d. 1952), Ẓafaruddīn Bihārī (d. 1950s), Aḥmad Riẓā's son Muṣṭafā Riẓā Khān Barelwī (d. 1981), and Burhānulḥaqq Jabalpūrī (d. 1984)—have led the movement in varying directions in terms of the leading political issues of twentieth-century British India, most importantly that of partition in 1947. A significant feature of the Barelwīs' political views was their staunch support of Jinnah and the Muslim League for the creation of a separate Muslim homeland, Pakistan, in a milieu where the majority of Deobandī *ʿulamā*'s were opposing this idea. Although the Barelwī movement has been viewed as largely rural in terms of its following, it is currently in the throes of a resurgence among urban, educated Pakistanis and Indians, as thousands of religious *madrasahs* identifying themselves as "Ahl al-Sunnat wa-al-Jamāʿat" or Barelwīs are to be found in big and small cities of South Asia.

[*See also* Deobandīs; India; Pakistan; *and* Sufism.]

BIBLIOGRAPHY

Khan, Aḥmad Riẓā. *Al-ʿAṭāyā lil-nabawīyah fī al-fatāwá al-Riḍawīyah*. Vols. 1–7, 10–11. Bareilly: Saudagaran, 1981–1987.

Khan, Aḥmad Riẓā. *Malfūẓāt-i Aʿlā Ḥazrat*. 4 vols. Gujarat, Pakistan, n.d.

Metcalf, Barbara D. *Islamic Revival in British India: Deoband, 1860–1900*. Princeton, N.J.: Princeton University Press, 1982.

Qādrī Rizvī, Shāh Muḥammad Ẓafaruddīn. *Ḥayāt-i Aʿlā Ḥazrat*. Vol. 1. Karachi, 1938.

Sanyal, Usha. *Devotional Islam and Politics in British India: Aḥmad Riẓā Khān Barelwī and His Movement, 1870–1920*. New York: Oxford University Press, 1999.

Sanyal, Usha. "In the Path of the Prophet: Maulānā Aḥmad Riẓā Khān Barelwī and the Ahl-e Sunnat wa Jamaʿat Movement in British India, c. 1870–1921." Ph.D. diss., Columbia University, 1990.

USHA SANYAL
Updated by MUḤAMMAD ATIF KHAN

BAʿTH PARTIES. The Arab Socialist Baʿth Party was founded in Syria in the early 1940s by a group led by two Damascene teachers, Michel ʿAflaq (Greek Orthodox by origin) and Ṣalāḥ al-Dīn al-Bīṭār (a Sunni Muslim), together with followers of the philosopher Zakī al-Arsūzī.

The party took as its rallying cry the revitalization, reunification, and liberation of "one Arab nation with an eternal mission," an expression inspired by Johann Gottlieb Fichte. Its original ideology rested on the concept of an Arab nation defined not by race but by cultural reality. From the outset, Baʿthist ideologues viewed the role of Islam (and/or any other religious heritage of the Arab nation) as contributing to the totality of the Arab peoples' experience. The party's basically secularist identity was reinforced in successive stages of its existence.

Three elements underlay the notion of a common Arab identity. These included a common history and unity of opposition to enemies, and the Arabic language—the natural language of humanity, according to philosopher al-Arsūzī. Finally there was Islam, which is seen not as a religion, but as a culture and spiritual experience for all Arabs.

A serious political miscalculation came only fifteen years after Syrian independence, when Baʿthist leader al-Bīṭār tried to save the party from a downward political spiral by tying its destiny to the ill-fated United Arab Republic under Nasser (1958–1961). In the aftermath of several coups d'état in Syria and Iraq in the early 1960s, opportunities for long-term Baʿthist "eras" emerged in both countries, even if the ideology proved more successful in the Levant.

The Baʿth party came to power in Iraq in February 1963, but only secured power for a period of nine months, though cadres returned in stages after gaining support among the military. In Syria, the party took over in March 1963 and maintained almost continuous hegemony for over forty years, before it faced serious challenges in 2011.

Bolstered by the political upheavals of the 1960s, Baʿth leaders hosted in Damascus their Sixth National Pan-Arab Congress, which in October 1963 adopted a report entitled *Baʿḍ al-munṭalaqāt al-naẓarīyah* (*Some Theoretical Points of View*). The report recommended the immediate adoption of socialism in the form of agrarian reforms and widespread nationalizations when and where the party could assume control. Still guided by the leadership of Michel ʿAflaq (and not yet faced by the divisions that would set the Damascus regional branch of the party against the Iraqi regional branch), a program of "democratic centralism" was adopted in April 1965. This plan provided for a "national command" framework: a single apparatus to link both the leadership and rank and file party members from "regional commands" in different Arab countries.

The year 1963 marked a problematic high point of Pan-Arabism for the party as several Syrian leaders intervened in an internal struggle among Iraqi Baʿthists. An open rupture between Syrian and Iraqi militants came after February 1966 (and before the start of a strong Baʿthist "recovery" in Iraq) with the triumph of the neo-Baʿthist leftists of Ṣalāḥ Jadīd in Damascus. From July 1968, when the party returned to power in Baghdad, the National Command was clearly divided into two rival camps, one under the radical leftist neo-Baʿthists in Syria (whose ascendancy was broken by Hafeẓ al-Assad in the early 1970s) and the other Iraqi-influenced.

Over time, the apparent organizational conflict became a conflict of competing ambitions between two determined leaders, Hafez al-Assad and Saddam Hussein. Generally speaking, the Baʿth parties in Syria and Iraq sought to rule without sharing power with any of their putative allies. After eliminating rivals and reducing the number of likely candidates for leadership, each party allied itself with small leftist groups to form what they called a Progressive National Front (Syria in 1972; Iraq in 1973). Formerly avant-gardist parties, the Baʿth in Syria and Iraq gradually transformed themselves into the supposed parties of the masses, by taking control of trade unions and popular organizations. As an apparatus of recruitment and mobilization, each party became a privileged channel of social advancement and the redistribution of the advantages associated with positions of power, a process that became typical of Saddam Hussein's methods of control after the 1970s.

Indeed, despite its broadly based social agenda, the Baʿth progressively changed into a coterie of minority solidarity, often involving particular regional ethnic identities. The non-Sunni Arab minorities in Syria, especially the ʿAlawīyah, came to be overrepresented in the party with the advent of the neo-Baʿth in the mid-1960s. Following Hafez al-Assad's seizure of power early in the 1970s, this trend may have been tempered, but Assad (himself ʿAlawī) still permitted leaders of the ʿAlawī community to dominate in the name of party ideals.

In Iraq, the Sunnis of the Tikrīt region (the homeland of Saddam Hussein) progressively dominated the party. They controlled the executive at the expense of the Kurds and especially the Arab Shiite majority. This situation received its first near-catastrophic shock in the wake of the 1991 Gulf War that, as a sequel to Saddam Hussein's involvement in the Iran-Iraq war (1980–1988), presaged an inevitable drift toward the collapse of the Baʿth regime in Iraq.

As in Syria, Baʿthists in Iraq incorporated references to Sunni Islam into the rhetoric of their popular propaganda. Yet by imposing official control over mosques and the *ʿulamāʾ* the Baʿth consistently reaffirmed the domination of politics over religion, which illustrated how Baghdad drifted from Baʿthism.

Although the Baʿthist party was obviously the major actor in Syrian and Iraqi politics at least until the last years of the twentieth century, proponents of its ideology (if not of the symbol of repressive rule associated with the persons of Assad and Hussein) attempted over the years to play a role in other political systems, most notably in Jordan and Lebanon. Specific characteristics governing the politics of other Arab countries, however, reduced this to a minor role when compared to the course of events in Syria and Iraq.

Analysts generally agreed that, during the tenure of Saddam Hussein, the Iraqi Baʿth party lost the last vestiges of actual political autonomy. Access to any position of influence in government required not only party membership, but "clearance" to assure proper loyalty to the ruling executive under Saddam Hussein. In Syria what appeared to be an evolutionary succession of Bashar al-Assad in 2000 (following his father's iron-handed leadership of the party since the 1970s) left many observers uncertain as to the future of the Baʿth party in Syria.

The overthrow of the Saddam Hussein regime in 2003 ushered in a new era. The military invasion of Iraq by a U.S.-led force and the subsequent outlawing of the Iraqi Baʿth party contributed to changes in the possible status of the party at home as well as in other regions of the Middle East. A notable if unexpected example seemed to surface in the Republic of Yemen, although the military regime of ʿAli ʿAbdallah Saleh tolerated little ideological independence from his own cult-based tribal loyalties. A wide spectrum of announcements emanating from Baʿthist party spokesmen there gave the impression of unprecedented international activities beyond the Middle East by Yemeni Baʿthists but this was a mirage.

In June 2003, the Iraq Coalition Provisional Authority (CPA) formally banned the Baʿth party in its imperial Order 1, which deleted the Baʿth party influence with the stroke of a pen. The purpose was ostensibly to purge the nascent republic of its ossified political system, but it created a significant sociopolitical vacuum, given that most experienced people could no longer participate in civil society. Physicians, university professors, school teachers, bureaucrats, and others were simply removed from their posts even if their Baʿth affiliation was pro forma. The hastily devised and hurriedly applied de-Baʿthification was finally rescinded in June 2004 when a putative transfer of sovereignty reverted to the Iraqi Interim Government. Still, a new constitution, which was approved by a referendum on October 15, 2005, reaffirmed the Baʿth party ban, even if Iraqi society was not "cleansed" of Baʿthist influence, as deteriorating security conditions were partly attributed to former Baʿthist officers organized against Baghdad.

A major question began to emerge in Iraq after nearly five years of U.S.-led military and political efforts to "reconstruct" the country in the post–Saddam Hussein era: could the recurrent violence sparked by inter-sectarian and/or apparent external terrorist infiltration be reduced by loosening the total exclusion of former Baʿthists from the reconstruction process? Baghdad tackled this challenge in January 2008, when the Iraqi parliament voted to reorganize the "official" De-Baʿthification Committee under the highly controversial "Accountability and Justice Act" that was supposed to ease the policy but was, in fact, geared to accomplish two specific tasks: see competent individuals who happened to be Baʿthists return to the folds of government, and provide incentives for Sunni Arabs to abandon insurgency elements. This controversial move opened the possibility of allowing, under carefully defined conditions, many lower-level party members to return to government jobs, including posts in the critical Ministry of Interior. The law allowed an estimated 35,000 Baʿthists to be eligible for public-sector employment and limited pension payments for services rendered to the state over the past few decades. De-Baʿthification continued to threaten Sunni Arabs whose participation in the 2010 parliamentary elections was "regulated" by the Justice and Accountability Council that denied candidates believed to harbor pro-Baʿth sentiments the right to run for office. Baʿth leaders Saleh al-Mutlaq and Dhafir al-Ani were barred from running because their party was illegal.

The Baʿth Party in Syria held 134 of the 250 seats in the Syrian Parliament in 2011, though this was an inaccurate depiction since the figure was dictated by election regulations rather than by voting patterns. According to the Syrian Constitution, the Baʿth Party was "the leading party of society and state," which was a technical definition of a legally enforced monopoly on real political power. Starting on January 26, 2011, protests against the Assad regime engulfed Syria, as demonstrators called for political reforms and the reinstatement of civil rights. Because demands included an end to the state of emergency that was introduced by the Baʿth in 1963, the public rage was clearly targeted against party officials, as well as against Bashar al-Assad. Protesters in several Syrian cities took to the streets after Friday prayers, regularly chanting "God, Syria, freedom, that is enough," which challenged the Baʿth slogan "God, Syria, Bashar, that is enough." Although the 1963 Emergency Law was rescinded on April 21, 2011, violent crackdowns continued unabated, which raised existential problems for a party leadership that gradually lost its legitimacy.

[*See also* Arab Nationalism; Arab Socialism; *and* Iraq.]

BIBLIOGRAPHY

ʿAflaq, Michel. *Choice of Texts from the Baʿth Party Founder's Thought*. Rome, 1977. Available online at: http://ia600302.us.archive.org/3/items/ChoiceOfTextsFromTheBathPartyFoundersThought/Baath.pdf

ʿAflaq, Michel. *Fī sabīl al Baʿth* (On the Baʿth Path). Beirut: Dār al-Ṭalīʿah, 1963.

Baram, Amatzia. *Culture, History and Ideology in the Formation of Baʿthist Iraq, 1968–1989*. New York: Palgrave Macmillan, 1991.

Batatu, Hanna. *The Old Social Classes and the Revolutionary Movements of Iraq: A Study of Iraq's Old Landed and Commercial Classes and of Its Communists, Baʿthists, and Free Officers*. Princeton, N.J.: Princeton University Press, 1978.

Hinnebusch, Raymond A. "Syria under the Baʿth: Social Ideology, Policy, and Practice." In *Social Legislation in the Contemporary Middle East*, edited by Laurence O. Michalak and Jeswald W. Salacuse, pp. 61–109. Berkeley: University of California Press, 1986.

Khalil, Samir. *Republic of Fear: The Politics of Modern Iraq*. Berkeley and Los Angeles: University of California Press, 1989.

Lesch, David W. *The New Lion of Damascus: Bashar al-Asad and Modern Syria*. New Haven, Conn.: Yale University Press, 2005.

Nūnū, Muṭīʿ. *Dawlat al-Baʿth wa Islām ʿAflaq* (The Baʿth State and ʿAflaq's Islam). Cairo: M. al-Nūnū, 1994.

Omar, Saleh. "Philosophical Origins of the Arab Baʿth Party: The Work of Zaki Al-Arsuzi." *Arab Studies Quarterly* 18, no. 2 (March 1996): 23–38.

Rangwala, G., and Colin Rowat. *Iraq and the West: The Politics of Confrontation*. Cheltenham, England: Understanding Global Issues, 2002.

BYRON D. CANNON
Revised by JOSEPH A. KÉCHICHIAN

BAYʿAH. *See* Succession.

BAYT AL-ḤIKMAH. (House of Wisdom) Commonly refers to the public library of the early ʿAbbāsid caliphs al-Rashīd (r. 170–193 / 786–809) and al-Maʾmūn (r. 198–218 / 813–833). This library was also referred to as *khizānat al-ḥikmah* (storehouse of wisdom), although the latter phrase may refer to any collection of books, such as the *khizānat ḥikmah* of al-Fatḥ ibn Khāqān (al-Nadīm, p. 143; Yāqūt, p. 2008).

Primary sources offer scant information on the holdings, associates, and activities of Bayt al-Ḥikmah. In the *Fihrist*, al-Nadīm records that among the holdings of *khizānat al-Maʾmūn* (the storehouse of al-Maʾmūn) were a piece of hide (*jild*) with the handwriting of ʿwi al-Muṭṭalib (p. 5), a text in the Ḥimyarī script (p. 5), and an example of Ḥimyarī-style Abyssinian letters (p. 19). His comment that a book on revealed scriptures written in "old-fashioned script" (*qadīm al-naskh*) "appears (*yushbihu*) to be from the storehouse of al-Maʾmūn" (p. 21) suggests that *khizānat al-Maʾmūn* was known for its collection of works in old-fashioned scripts. He mentions that the directors (sing. *ṣāḥib*) of the library were Sahl ibn Hārūn (pp. 10, 120, 125, 305) and Salm (pp. 120, 243, 268, 305); and that associates of the library were Saʿīd ibn Hārūn al-Kātib (pp. 120, 125; Yāqūt, p. 1379), the bookbinder Ibn Abī al-Ḥarīsh (p. 10), the copyist ʿAllān al-Shuʿūbī (p. 105; Yāqūt, p. 1631), and the astronomers Abū Sahl al-Faḍl ibn Nawbakht (p. 274) and Muḥammad ibn Mūsā al-Khwārazmī, who was "attached" (*munqaṭiʿ*) to the library (p. 274). Ibn al-Qifṭī adds that Hārūn al-Rashīd charged al-Faḍl ibn Nawbakht with maintaining the storehouse (*wallāhu al-qiyām bi-khizānat kutub al-ḥikmah*) (*Taʾrīkh*, p. 255), and that al-Maʾmūn "registered" the Banū Mūsā (*athbatahum*) at Bayt al-Ḥikmah (p. 441).

Since many associates were Persian translators, it is likely that a portion of the caliphal library's collection was devoted to Persian political theory and didactic literature for kings, and thus that the library served as an important venue for preserving and propagating Sāsānian kingship ideology for the ʿAbbāsid caliphs. However, such was clearly not the only area of interest, as shown by the collection of old-fashioned scripts and the association of astronomers and mathematicians. In light of the broad application of the term *ḥikmah* in classical Islamic epistemological discourses (Nasr, pp. 21–2), it is conceivable that Bayt al-Ḥikmah reflected a diverse array of intellectual interests.

The predominant picture of Bayt al-Ḥikmah in modern scholarship has been that of a research and translation institute specializing in Greek sciences. O'Leary (1922) was the first to assert that al-Maʾmūn founded Bayt al-Ḥikmah in 217/832 as a school of science modeled on preexisting Nestorian or Zoroastrian schools (p. 112), but he does not cite any supporting evidence. Meyerhof (1926) expanded on this claim, proposing, also without substantiation, that Bayt al-Ḥikmah imitated the medical school of Alexandria and functioned as the focal point of the Greek translation movement (pp. 702, 722). More recent reassessments of the primary evidence offer a more convincing interpretation. Dimitri Gutas (1998) explains that Bayt al-Ḥikmah was a palace library in the Sāsānian tradition and a state bureau for preserving the Persian literary heritage (pp. 55–57). While the existence of Bayt al-Ḥikmah suggests the ʿAbbāsids' general interest in non-Arab culture and support of translators, there is no solid evidence to prove that the

Greek translation movement of the early ʿAbbāsid period was carried out in any substantial way at Bayt al-Ḥikmah.

Since Bayt al-Ḥikmah is mentioned almost exclusively in connection with al-Rashīd and more often al-Maʾmūn, it seems that the library ceased to exist in its original form after al-Maʾmūn's reign. Yet al-Nadīm's reports of personally accessing material from al-Maʾmūn's storehouse indicates that titles once copied or stored there remained identifiable as such even if they were no longer held in the original collection.

BIBLIOGRAPHY

Gutas, Dimitri. *Greek Thought, Arabic Culture: The Graeco-Arabic Translation Movement in Baghdad and Early ʿAbbāsid Society (2nd–4th/8th–10th Centuries).* New York: Routledge, 1998. Pp. 53–60. A critical assessment of the Greek translation theory in light of primary evidence, and a convincing proposal of a primarily Persian character to Bayt al-Ḥikmah.

Ibn al-Qifṭī. *Taʾrīkh al-ḥukamāʾ*. Edited by Julius Lippert. Leipzig: Dieterich'sche Verlagsbuchhandlung, 1903. Much of his information on Bayt al-Ḥikmah is copied from al-Nadīm's *Fihrist*.

Makdisi, George. *The Rise of Humanism in Classical Islam and the Christian West, with Special Reference to Scholasticism*. Edinburgh: Edinburgh University Press, 1990. Pp. 54–59. A concise typology of independent public libraries like Bayt al-Ḥikmah, as well as libraries associated with other *waqf* (endowment) institutions, like *madrasah*s and *ribāṭ*s.

Meyerhof, Max. "New Light on Ḥunain ibn Isḥāq and His Period." *Isis* 8 (1926): 685–724. Reprinted in *Studies in Medieval Arabic Medicine: Theory and Practice*, edited by Penelope Johnstone. London: Variorum Reprints, 1984. Claims that Bayt al-Ḥikmah was a major research academy largely responsible for the translation of Greek medical works, but fails to support this claim with evidence from primary sources.

Nadīm, Muḥammad ibn Isḥāq al-. *Fihrist*. Edited by Gustav Flügel. Leipzig: Vogel, 1871. Reprint, Beirut: Maktabat Khayyāṭ, [1966]. Translated by Bayard Dodge as *The Fihrist*. New York: Columbia University Press, 1970. Page references are to the 1966 Arabic printing. A fourth/tenth-century source on books and writers, with references to Bayt al-Ḥikmah being the most numerous.

Nasr, Seyyed Hossein. "The Meaning and Concept of Philosophy in Islam." In *History of Islamic Philosophy*, edited by Seyyed Hossein Nasr and Oliver Leaman. New York: Routledge, 1996. A brief exposition of the concept of *ḥikmah* among Islamic philosophers until the time of Mullā Ṣadrā.

O'Leary, De Lacy. *Arabic Thought and Its Place in History*. London: K. Paul, Trench, Trubner, and Co., 1922. Rev. ed. New York: E. P. Dutton, 1939. Page references are to the 1939 edition. The earliest assertion that al-Maʾmūn founded Bayt al-Ḥikmah as a center for medical studies, but lacking any evidence to support this claim.

Yāqūt al-Ḥamawī. *Muʿjam al-udabāʾ*. Edited by Iḥsān ʿAbbās. 7 vols. Beirut: Dār al-Gharb al-Islāmī, 1993. A seventh/thirteenth-century biographical dictionary of literary personalities that includes many references to private libraries (*khazāʾin*).

VANESSA DE GIFIS

BAYT AL-MĀL. In the classical Islamic period, *bayt al-māl* (lit. "the house of [public] property, wealth") denoted the state treasury. Since the earliest caliphs, the term was used interchangeably with *bayt māl al-muslimīn* ("the house of Muslim property"), *bayt māl Allāh* ("the house of God's property"), and *bayt māl al-islām* ("the house of the property of Islam"). The idea of ascribing the treasury to Muslims or God rather than to the state or the ruler represents the essence of public finances in Islam.

According to early Muslim historians, the second caliph ʿUmar (r. 634–644) borrowed the concept of *bayt al-māl* from the Sasanids along with other administrative institutions and procedures. However, a similar concept—*bayt māl al-āliha*, "house of the property of the gods"—existed already in late antiquity in southern Arabia (ʿAlī 1968). The Umayyads (r. 661–750) later took over the administration of *bayt al-māl* from the Byzantines and put into practice an arabized system of taxes and procedures. Thus, the religious notion that wealth belongs to God (or to the Muslim community) commingled with the Sasanid and Byzantine sophisticated administration of finances.

In spite of its being a bureaucratic institution, the state treasury still maintained its religio-communitarian sense during the ʿAbbāsid era (750–1258). This can be seen in the Shāfiʿī jurist al-Māwardī's (d. 1058) treatise *al-Aḥkām al-sulṭāniyya*, where al-Māwardī defines the wealth that belonged to the treasury as any property entitled to the Muslim community and not owned by any specific person.

Among the legal schools, the religio-communitarian significance of *bayt al-māl* was best formulated by the Shāfiʿīs (followed by the Mālikīs), who described the state treasury as income that was not designated for another purpose by *Sharīʿah* law and belonged to the Muslim community as a whole. It was to be managed by the legitimate ruler on behalf of the Muslim community and any property that could be a source of revenue to the state belonged to the treasury. The Ḥanafīs were more bureaucratic; for them the public treasury could only appropriate state income as determined by Islamic law.

Under the ʿAbbāsids the treasury was one of the four institutions of the *dīwān* administration (together with the army, provincial administration, and the appointment of governors). The treasury's function was to manage state income and expenditures. It was entitled to three types of income: *fay'* (spoils of war acquired without force), *ghanīma* (spoils of war acquired by force, as in battle), and *ṣadaqāt* (taxes). Of *fay'*, a share (one-third of the fifth) went to the family of the Prophet (and their descendants); one-fifth of *ghanīma* went to the treasury and the warriors took the rest; and the treasury was entitled to taxes on crops, fruits, and animals.

As regards expenditures, the community had the right to claim funding from the treasury in two cases. The first was that the treasury paid all military salaries and war costs, whether there was enough money or not. This was a binding liability, as in principle the treasury was indebted to the army. Accordingly, payment was to be made immediately. It could be delayed if the treasury was unable to pay, but it remained a financial obligation. The second case was the requirement that the treasury pay for facilities in the public interest, such as damaged city walls, an inadequate water supply, etc., but only if it had sufficient funds.

Muslim jurists allowed the treasury to be indebted if it could not meet its financial obligations, but only for non-essential expenditures. Thus, if the ruler believed that the army would be harmed without financial support, he could charge the treasury, incurring any necessary debts. Once the treasury had recouped funds, the ruler or his successor was obliged to fulfill the debt. The funding of facilities in the public interest on the other hand—which for the jurists would not lead to chaos and corruption if unmet, as cutting military funds would—was not considered to be a necessary expenditure for which the treasury could be burdened with debt.

In the event of income exceeding expenditures, the Ḥanafīs—more inclined to saving than spending—maintained that money should be set apart for inexorable contingencies. Because of their pragmatism, the Ḥanafīs were favored by the ʿAbbāsid state. In contrast, the Shāfiʿī school, which was more prone to support public spending than saving, held that the extra moneys should not be stored. Rather, they should be used for those ventures that were of common interest to the community. Shāfiʿīs argued that the state imposed taxes on people when it needed the money, so it should distribute the wealth when it had enough.

The treasury excluded *dhimmīs*—non-Muslim individuals under Muslim rule—or their institutions from receiving funds. An exception was a *dhimmī* starving from hunger. In such a case it was incumbent upon the *imām* to urge the state treasury to provide for the *dhimmī*. According to the *dhimma* contract, the *imām* must protect the life and property of his *dhimmī* subjects.

In contemporary Islam, *bayt al-māl* is still the term for a treasury or a fund. The most notable example is the Treasury of Jerusalem, *Bayt Māl al-Quds al-Sharīf*, an Islamic agency, established in 1995, whose headquarters is located in Casablanca. The agency is one of the institutions of the Organization of the Islamic Conference (OIC), and its primary objective consists in financially assisting Jerusalem in order to maintain its Islamic character. The appellation *bayt al-māl* gives an Islamic touch to the financial character of the agency. For its revenues, the agency disposes of its own assets and properties. In addition, it benefits from voluntary contributions of the OIC member states as well as from gifts and donations of individuals and organizations.

Bibliography

Aghnides, Nicolas P. *Mohammedan Theories of Finance, with an Introduction to Mohammedan Law and a Bibliography*. New York: AMS, 1969.

ʿAlī, Jawād. *al-Mufaṣṣal fī taʾrīkh al-ʿArab qabla l-Islām*. Beirut: Dār al-ʿIlm li-l-Malāyīn, 1968.

Imamuddin, S. M. "*Bayt al-Māl* and Banks in the Medieval Muslim World." In *Islamic Culture* 34 (1960): 22–30.

al-Māwardī, ʿAlī b. Muḥammad. *al-Aḥkām al-sulṭāniyya wa-l-wilāyāt al-dīniyya*, tr. Wafaa Hassan Wahba, as *The Ordinances of Government*. Reading, U.K.: Garnet, 2000.

Bayt Māl al-Quds, http://www.bmaq.org

Abdessamad Belhaj

Bearing Witness. *See* Religious Beliefs.

Bedouin. *See* Tribes.

Bennabi, Malek. Malek Bennabi (Mālik bn Nabī) (1905–1973) was a renowned but inadequately studied Algerian intellectual. He was a prolific writer, and his books, articles, and speeches naturally link him with Islamic revivalism (*tajdīd*) and reformism (*iṣlāḥ*). He is identified with the ideals of Islamic modernism's *nahḍah* (renaissance, revival) as promulgated by the Association des Oulémas Musulmans Algériens (Association of Algerian Muslim Ulama; AUMA). Bennabi's Islamism pursued a fundamental objective—to renew, reform, and restore Islam as the principal idea and moral force in Muslim society. Nevertheless, he possessed an independent, critical spirit and intellect, which inhibits any kind of simplistic "Islamist" labeling. For example, Bennabi enthusiastically embraced the intellectual and cultural heritage of European as well as Islamic civilization and viewed it, despite its colonial legacy, as vital and instructive. Although deeply engrossed in the colonial and postcolonial condition of Algeria and the rise and decline of Muslim civilization, he was especially concerned with the Muslim personality. Bennabi aimed to raise or reinstill within the individual an authentic historical and social consciousness linked to Islamic spirituality, fundamentally an existential project, in order to reanimate a creative Muslim community (*ummah*) and civilization (*ḥaḍārah*).

Born in 1905 in Constantine, Algeria, Bennabi spent his childhood there and in Tébessa, a city approximately 62 miles (100 km) to the southeast. His father earned a living as a minor bureaucrat in the colonial administration, and he and his mother insisted that Bennabi acquire an education. He attended Qurʾānic classes and a French school for "indigènes," as the locals were called. Given his lackluster performance in Qurʾānic studies, his parents decided that he should only attend the French school, and he eventually received a scholarship to continue secondary studies in Constantine, where he took Qur'ānic (theological and juridical) courses along with French courses. Graduates were expected to serve the colonial administration.

During his years of secondary study in Constantine, Bennabi's acquisitive mind devoured French literature, including Orientalists Pierre Loti, Claude Farrère, Isabelle Eberhardt, and Alphonse de Lamartine. He discovered Rabindranath Tagore's poetry, proving that the subaltern did have a voice—a profound one. He also admired John Dewey's philosophical pragmatism. As his Arabic improved, he read classical poets and modern exponents such as Kahlil Gibran (Jibrān Khalīl Jibrān). Constantine was also the epicenter of Algeria's *iṣlāḥ* movement. Bennabi studied the writings of Islamic reformers Jamāl al-Dīn al-Afghānī and Muḥammad ʿAbduh.

After completing his secondary studies, he traveled to France in 1925 and suffered the consequences of under- and unemployment before returning to Algeria. This exhausting experience made him sensitive to the desperate plight of Algerian emigrant workers. He eventually received a position as a legal assistant in the Muslim court of Aflou in western Algeria. There he discovered an Algeria that seemed relatively unaffected by colonialism, which buoyed his spirits. With his parents' blessings, he returned to France, anticipating entering the prestigious École des Langues Orientales (School for Oriental Languages). To his astonishment, he was informed that he failed the admissions exam. Bennabi believed that this decision was politically influenced. Nevertheless, he evinced remarkable resilience after this bitter disappointment and enrolled in the École Spéciale de Mécanique et d'Électricité (ESME), to become an electrical engineer. By this time, Bennabi had discovered a Christian youth organization, the Union Chrétienne de Jeunes Gens de Paris (Young People's Christian Union of Paris; UCJG), which encouraged his membership. He engaged in ecumenical discussions, which made him think about his own devotion to Islam. He also married a French woman (Paulette Philippon), who converted to Islam and took the name Khadījah.

Bennabi became involved in the Association des Étudiants Musulmans Nord-Africains (Association of North African Students; AEMNA). His activism earned a police visit and then an invitation by the eminent Orientalist Louis Massignon. Bennabi brusquely refused Massignon's invitation, because he associated the renowned scholar with his well-known role as a consultant for the French government on Muslim affairs.

As he took his classes at ESME, Bennabi's intellectual exploration intensified in a vibrant Paris, where his circle of friends discussed *iṣlāḥ*, Wahhābīyah, and Maghrib unity. He delved into the Pan-Arabism of Shakīb Arslān. His closest friend was Hamouda Ben Saï (Ḥammūdah bn Issāʿi), a Massignon student, who introduced him to Friedrich Nietzsche's ideas; they also discussed Baruch Spinoza. Bennabi studied Charles Darwin, Arnold Toynbee, Oswald Spengler, Jacques Maritain, and Henri Massis. He met Maghribī nationalists, including ʿAllāl al-Fāsī of Morocco, Habīb Bourguiba of Tunisia, and Algeria's Messali Hadj (Aḥmad Maṣṣālī al-Ḥajj), and considered Messali to be more concerned with his status as a nationalist leader than with mobilizing an authentic nationalist movement. He opposed Shaykh Ibn Bādīs's affiliating his Association des Oulémas Musulmans Algériens with nationalist political parties. Although Bennabi did not belong to a political party, he identified with the cultural positions of the AUMA, and opposed Farhāt ʿAbbās's identification with France, even if he found him more ideologically compatible during the postwar period and wrote articles for his newspaper. Although Bennabi performed admirably in his coursework and passed examinations, he was informed that he would receive a document certifying his coursework but not an official diploma from the state, which he correctly attributed to his political activism. His efforts to find work were ineffective or, he believed, purposely blocked. In 1938, he engaged in a volunteer literacy project for emigrant workers in Marseille.

When World War II broke out, he stayed in Dreux, France, and took on odd jobs. Searching for steady employment, Bennabi journeyed to Paris, where he heard of an employment opportunity in the planned "Arab section" of the Parti Populaire Français (French Popular Party) led by Jacques Doriot. He left Paris and labored in Germany before returning to France, then being liberated, though his and his wife's apparent collaborations with Germans landed them jail sentences. They were released after months of imprisonment, for lack of proof.

The Bennabis then spent several years in Algeria before returning to France, and it was in his native land that wrote some of his most important works. After the Algerian War of Independence broke out in 1954 and with Khadījah suffering from rheumatoid arthritis, Bennabi settled alone in Egypt. Wishing to serve the revolutionary cause, his relations with "external" leaders of the Front de Libération Nationale (FLN) were distant and distrustful, even if he cultivated close connections with members of the Egyptian government, who sponsored and promoted more of his publications. He also traveled to Syria, Lebanon, and Libya, where he married a second wife and eventually fathered several daughters.

Bennabi returned to Algeria in 1963 and assumed the post of director of higher studies at the University of Algiers a year later. He participated also in the Qiyām (Values) Society, an Islamist discussion group, which the government disbanded in 1966. Disenchanted, he left his university position in 1967, but continued to publish, travel, and teach. He organized conferences and held seminars in his home until his death in October 1973.

Selected Works and Assessment. In the early twenty-first century, particularly because of the contributions of Nour-Eddine Boukrouh (Boukrouh, 2006; Bennabi, 2006, *Mémoires d'un témoin du siècle*), a former presidential candidate (1995), minister in the Algerian government, and attendee of Bennabi's seminars, scholars and students have increasingly recognized Bennabi's importance as an insightful and innovative thinker. His extensive interdisciplinary interests distinguished his work and enhanced his significance, which was why he became known as the greatest Maghribī intellectual since Ibn Khaldūn (1335–1406).

Bennabi's two-volume autobiography describes his life until the late 1930s. In the first volume, titled *Mémoires d'un témoin du siècle: Enfant*, the reader discovers an inquisitive and acquisitive mind who describes his childhood in Algeria. He completed the second volume (*Mudhakkirāt shāhid al-qarn: Al-ṭālib* [Memories (Memoirs) of a Witness of the Century: The Student]) after he returned to Algeria. Composed in Arabic, it recounts his life in Paris during the 1930s, an invaluable period in his intellectual development. There are other important, if unfinished, autobiographical narratives (e.g., Boukrouh, 2006; Bennabi, 2007, *Pourritures* [Rottennes]).

His first original work, *Le Phénomène coranique: Essai d'une théorie sur le Coran*, published in 1946, illustrated Bennabi's epistemological apprehension regarding the effects of European Orientalists' influence and interpretation on young Muslim scholars. He offers an exceptional exegesis of the Qur'ān and Islam, reconciling reason and science with revelation. The book posits an ecumenical goal to raise Muslim consciousness and to educate non-Muslims, while underscoring Islam's natural place in the heritage of monotheism. It includes an exceptional psychological study of the Prophet Muḥammad, reaffirming his humanity. In 1948, *Lebbeik: Pèlerinage de pauvres* appeared, a novel of Islamic redemption set during a *ḥajj*. (Bennabi also composed poetry, but it is not extant.) In *Discours sur les conditions de la renaissance algérienne* (1949), the thinker gauges the potential of Algerian society and Muslim civilization to achieve spiritual and secular renewal, by overcoming centuries of decadence or "colonizability," which he equated with the loss of identity. Reiterating this idea in successive works, Bennabi perceives the history of Muslim civilization as cyclical, proceeding through spiritual, rational, and primitive instinctual "psycho-temporal" stages founded on the changing, transformative synergy of man (*insān*), soil (*turāb*), and time (*zamān*). Like Ibn Khaldūn, Bennabi was interested in historical evolution, although regarding the rise and fall not so much of states as of civilizations. He considered religion as foundational to any civilization. The spiritual stage served as the principal liberating, disciplining, and civilizing force from natural, primitive instincts. In Islamic civilization, this marked the beginning of Muḥammad's revelation to the battle of Ṣiffīn (657). In the rational stage reason plays a complementary social role along with religion as the civilization flourishes until primitive instinct eventually erodes the civilization through decadence, corruption, and superstition. In his next book, *Vocation de l'Islam* (1954), he elaborates the idea that the decline of Muslim civilization (the primitive instinctual stage) coincided with the moral and intellectual indolence (the loss of a "civilizing élan") of the individual, a "post-Almohad man," who emerged in the fourteenth century after the end of the Almohad (Muwaḥḥidūn) state. Despite this centuries-old condition, Bennabi contended that Muslim civilization was reawakening, as signaled by Islamic modernism (the *nahḍah*).

While living in Egypt during the Algerian War of Independence, he perceived the importance of the emerging third world, as illustrated by the Bandung Conference of 1955. In *L'Afro-asiatisme: Conclusions sur le Conférence de Bandœng* (1956), Bennabi describes the postwar appearance of two geopolitical axes, that of the superpowers (Washington-Moscow) and that of the third world (Jakarta-Tangier). He considered the Afro-Asiatic phenomenon a new civilization. Bennabi perceived the dangers, however, of "co-colonialism," which he identified as a strategic neocolonialism that qualified independence and exploited the ex-colonized still afflicted with "colonizability."

In postwar articles dealing with politics, culture, economics, and foreign affairs, which are collected in the posthumous *Pour changer l'Algérie* (1989) and in a second important work dealing with state formation, *Perspectives algériennes: De la civilisation, de la culture, de l'idéologie* (1964), Bennabi refined his seminal ideas and especially his call for the articulation of an authentic national identity. *Naissance d'une société: Le faisceau des relations sociales* (1962) and *Le problème des idées dans la société musulmane* (1971) examine the role of ideas in the generation and degeneration of societies.

Bennabi often referred to one of his favorite *āyāt* (verses) from the Qur'ān: "Verily, God changes not what is in a people until they change what is in themselves (their souls)" (13:11). If one is receptive, the power of an idea could transform a person and a society as Islam (and Christianity) historically had done. For Bennabi, influenced undoubtedly by Nietzsche, will empowered (*vouloir/pouvoir*). To be transformative, however, an idea must have moral force. Bennabi castigated insincere politicians and self-righteous intellectuals. He dismissed the idea that Frantz Fanon was the "theoretician of the Algerian Revolution," because Fanon's "atheism" was not compatible with core Algerian convictions, even if he admired Fanon's fervent engagement in the Algerian Revolution and welcomed his ideas regarding African liberation (Bennabi, 1976, *Les grands thèmes*, pp. 77–78). Nevertheless, Bennabi's concept of "colonizability" resembles the idea of a "psycho-existential" complex that Fanon diagnosed among the colonized in Martinique (as described in *Black Skin, White Masks*). Each shared convictions regarding the potential of the third world and the emergence of a new, moral humanity. Bennabi genuinely believed in the possibility of mutual reconciliation of civilizations despite different spiritual beliefs and historical traditions. He embodied the "ecumenical man" as described in *L'afro-asiatisme*. His erudition served an Islamic humanism (Christelow, 1991), a vivid imagination of civilization, nation, and the catalyzing potential of an idea upon self and society.

BIBLIOGRAPHY

Primary Works

Bennabi, Malek. *Les grands thèmes: De la civilization, de la culture, de l'idéologie, de la démocratie en Islam, de l'orientalisme*. Algiers: Omar Benaissa, 1976.

Bennabi, Malek. *Mémoires d'un témoin du siècle: L'enfant, l'étudiant, l'écrivain, les carnets*. Algiers: Samar, 2006.

Bennabi, Malek. *Pourritures: Mémoires*. Algiers: Dar El Oumma, 2007.

Secondary Works

Bariun, Fawzia. "Malik Bennabi and the Intellectual Problems of the Muslim Ummah." *American Journal of Islamic Social Sciences* 9, no. 3 (Fall 1992): 325–337.

Benaïssa, Omar. *Malek Bennabi: Dans l'histoire de l'intellect Islamique, dans le future de la société Islamique*. Damascus: Dar al-Fikr, 2008.

Boukrouh, Nour-Eddine. *L'Islam sans l'Islamisme: Vie et pensée de Malek Bennabi*. Algiers: Samar, 2006.

Christelow, Alan. "An Islamist Humanist in the 20th Century: Malik Bennabi." *Maghreb Review* 17, nos. 1–2 (1991): 69–83.

El-Mesawi, Mohamed El-Tahir. "Religion, Society, and Culture in Malik Bennabi's Thought." In *The Blackwell Companion to Contemporary Islamic Thought*, edited by Ibrahim M. Abu-Rabiʿ, pp. 213–256. Malden, Mass.: Blackwell, 2006.

Naylor, Phillip C. "The Formative Influence of French Colonialism on the Life and Thought of Malek Bennabi (Malik bn Nabi)." *French Colonial History* 7 (2006): 129–142.

Walsh, Sebastian J. "Killing Post-Almohad Man: Malek Bennabi, Algerian Islamism and the Search for a Liberal Governance." *Journal of North African Studies* 12, no. 2 (June 2007): 235–254.

Phillip C. Naylor

Bin Laden, Osama. Global jihādist, Saudi militant, and founder of al-Qaʿida, Osama Bin Laden (1957–2011) remains an icon for Islamic extremism and violent opposition to both the United States and its allies and domestic authoritarian regimes in the Muslim world.

Osama Bin Laden was born in Riyadh, Saudi Arabia. His father, Muḥammad bin ʿAwaḍ bin Lādin, was the founder of the multi-billion dollar commercial construction company, the Saudi Binladin Group, which provided Bin Laden with business and construction experience, access to heavy equipment, contacts with the Saudi royal family and business communities, and financial assets. Although Bin Laden was only ten years old when his father was killed in a plane crash, he credits his father with inspiring him to religious service, particularly through *jihād* (struggle), hard work, and concern for the Palestinians.

Bin Laden began studying economics at King Abdulaziz University in Jiddah in 1976 but did not complete his degree. Although he received no formal religious training at the university, he is known to have studied the ideas of the Egyptian scholar-activist Sayyid Quṭb, who developed a framework for *jihād* against *jāhilī* (ignorant, pre-Islamic) societies, particularly the West, and a vision of Islam as an alternative to capitalism and Marxism.

In 1979, Bin Laden left the university to join the *jihād* against the Soviet Union in Afghanistan. There he met Abdullah Yusuf Azzam, a

Palestinian religious scholar and ideologue of militant *jihād* against non-Muslims living in historically Muslim lands, who became Bin Laden's mentor, and Ayman al-Ẓawāhirī, an Egyptian medical doctor and militant activist who also encouraged him to expand his vision of *jihād* beyond Afghanistan to include fighting against authoritarian, "un-Islamic" regimes in the Middle East.

During these early years, Bin Laden supported the Afghan *mujāhidīn* by providing financial and logistical support, including the transfer of equipment and engineers from his construction company, which he used to build roads, arms depots, training facilities, a medical center, and a complex of tunnels that are believed to have facilitated his escape in 2001. Bin Laden's willingness to live a simple and austere life in the trenches, his personal piety, and his generous support of the *jihād* earned him folk-hero status in Afghanistan.

Initially, Bin Laden recruited Muslims from other countries via the cofounding of the Services Office in 1984 with Azzam. In 1987, he sought to expand his own military role in the Afghan *jihād* through the foundation of his own exclusively Arab Afghan military base, al-Masada (The Lion's Den), to demonstrate Arab dedication to self-sacrifice and martyrdom in the conflict with the Soviets. His desire for military activity is attributed to his growing contact with Egyptian militants by 1986, most notably al-Zawāhirī, Mohammed Atef (Abu Hafs al-Misri), and Abu Ubaidah al-Banshiri, all of whom became key members of al-Qaʿida when it was founded in 1988/89.

The 1989 defeat of the Soviet Union was interpreted as the ideological victory of Islam over atheistic communism, marking an important psychological victory for the *mujāhidīn* and inspiring *jihād* against other "infidel" regimes. Unable to reach a consensus about where to begin this global *jihād*, the Arab Afghans returned to their home countries, where many began to oppose their domestic regimes. Bin Laden returned to Saudi Arabia in 1990. When Saddam Hussein invaded Kuwait shortly afterward, Bin Laden offered the services of his Arab Afghans to protect Saudi Arabia. King Fahd's refusal in favor of American troops resulted in Bin Laden declaring that the king and the religious establishment had abandoned their faith. Bin Laden went into exile in the Sudan in 1991–1992, where he established the Advice and Reform Committee (ARC) to call for Saudi domestic political and religious reform. Stripped of his Saudi citizenship in 1994 and having survived several assassination attempts, Bin Laden called for the overthrow of the monarchy in 1997.

During his exile in Sudan, Bin Laden founded several profitable construction and agricultural business ventures that are believed to have generated income and provided cover for his vision of *jihād*, which expanded to include Palestine, Iraq, and American foreign policy in the Middle East. International pressure on Sudan resulted in Bin Laden's departure for Afghanistan in 1995/96.

Bin Laden declared *jihād* against the United States on 23 August, 1996, with the goal of removing American troops from Saudi Arabia. In 1998, he joined with other jihādist groups to form the World Islamic Front for Jihād Against Crusaders and Jews, declaring attacks on American financial and military targets to be the most important duty for Muslims after belief in God. Since then, attacks have occurred against both the "near enemy" of domestic authoritarian regimes and the "far enemy" in the West, including attacks on the U.S. embassies in Tanzania and Kenya in 1998, the USS *Cole* off the coast of Yemen in 2000, Washington, D.C., and New York City in September 2001 (9/11), nightclubs in Bali in 2002, a train in Madrid in 2004, the London transit system in 2005, and both government facilities and

Westerners in Saudi Arabia between 2003 and 2005. Although Bin Laden consistently denied personal responsibility for planning the 9/11 attacks in particular, he nevertheless did claim responsibility for setting the political objectives and goals for terrorist attacks against the United States and its allies, as well as providing financial and logistical support.

Bin Laden's whereabouts were unknown following his escape from Afghanistan in October 2001, although he was believed to be hiding somewhere along the border between Pakistan and Afghanistan. From 2001 through 2011, periodic intelligence reports announced his death. Despite the reports, video appearances attributed to him continued to be released, allowing him to maintain figurative and symbolic status as the head of al-Qaʿida, although he was not necessarily directly involved in the logistical aspects of what has increasingly become an amorphous entity. Bin Laden was killed during a covert operation by U.S. Navy SEALs on 2 May 2011, in Abbottabad, Pakistan, and was reportedly buried at sea. Although some conspiracy theorists continue to maintain that he is alive, al-Qaʿida officially confirmed his death on 6 May 2011.

Bin Laden's jihādist ideology has been rejected as a heretical violation of Islamic values and beliefs by the overwhelming majority of the global Muslim population, including Muslim scholars who point to the major differences between mainstream interpretations of *jihād* as defensive, geographically limited in scope, and seeking to end discord, and Bin Laden's call for uncompromising, unending, and unrestricted global *jihād* that does not respect classical Islamic prohibitions of attacks against civilians and Qurʾānic provisions for cooperative, peaceful relations between Muslims, Christians, and Jews. Despite these challenges to his religious legitimacy, he has remained an influential figure with some populations because of the broad resonance of the political causes he engaged—the suffering of the Palestinians, Iraqis, Chechens, and Kashmiris under occupation, and opposition to both U.S. foreign policy and domestic authoritarian regimes in the Muslim world.

[*See also* Azzam, Abdullah Yusuf al-; Jihād; Qaʿida, al-; *and* Ẓawāhirī, Ayman al-.]

BIBLIOGRAPHY

Bergen, Peter L. *Holy War, Inc.: Inside the Secret World of Osama Bin Laden*. New York: Free Press, 2001.

Bergen, Peter L. *The Osama Bin Laden I Know: An Oral History of al Qaeda's Leader*. New York: Free Press, 2006.

DeLong-Bas, Natana J. *Wahhabi Islam: From Revival and Reform to Global Jihad*. New York: Oxford University Press, 2004.

Fandy, Mamoun. *Saudi Arabia and the Politics of Dissent*. London: Palgrave, 1999.

Kepel, Gilles, ed. *Al-Qaʿida dans le texte: Écrits d'Oussama ben Laden, Abdallah Azzam, Ayman al-Zawahiri et Abou Moussab al-Zarqawi*. Paris: Presses Universitaires de France, 2005.

Lawrence, Bruce, ed. *Messages to the World: The Statements of Osama Bin Laden*. London: Verso, 2005.

Lo, Mbaye. *Understanding Muslim Discourse: Language, Tradition, and the Message of Bin Laden*. Lanham, Md.: University Press of America, 2009.

Scheuer, Michael. *Through Our Enemies' Eyes: Osama Bin Laden, Radical Islam, and the Future of America*. Revised ed. Washington, D.C.: Potomac Books, 2006.

NATANA J. DELONG-BAS

BISHRĪ, ṬĀRIQ AL-. Ṭāriq al-Bishrī (1933–) is a prolific, incisive, and influential Egyptian public intellectual whose primary career has been as a judge in the country's highest administrative court. He is best known for two major monographs on modern Egyptian history and essays on a variety of historical and political themes. The author of several important legal opinions, he was chosen to chair the committee that drafted amendments to the 1971 constitution in the wake of the 2011 uprising, which overthrew the government of Hosni Mubarak. In his writings, Bishrī has explored themes of national identity, the conflicts between hierarchical administration and democracy, the relationship between Islamic and positive law, and the possibility of massive nonviolent protest in Egyptian society.

Bishrī was born on 1 November 1933 and spent his childhood in his grandfather's house in Hilmīyah Zaytūn, which was then still a rural suburb of Cairo. His grandfather, Salīm al-Bishrī, twice served as Shaykh al-Azhar (1900–1904 and 1909–1916). True to his legacy, he has written that in this environment he gained an appreciation for the worlds of both the turban and the tarboosh, by which he meant the traditional religious world of al-Azhar and the world of secular legal practice in which his father, ʿAbd al-Fattaḥ al-Bishrī, worked as the president of the Egyptian Court of Appeals until his death in 1951. The Appeals Court (Cour de Cassation, or Majlis al-Naqd) was then, with the State Council still in formation and in the absence of a supreme court, the country's most important judicial body.

Bishrī began his legal studies at Fouad al-Awwal University (today Cairo University) in 1949. Bishrī's professor in *fiqh*, Azharī *shaykh* ʿAbd al-Wahhāb Khallāf, profoundly affected him. Khallāf wrote extensively on the role of Islamic law in the contemporary world. His 1931 book *al-Siyāsah al-sharʿīyah* addressed the need for a new legal system in the wake of the collapse of the Ottoman caliphate. Later work emphasized the importance of separation of powers, including the independence of the judiciary. On graduation Bishrī entered the then recently created Majlis al-Dawlah, or State Council. The State Council had been created in 1946 to enhance the rule of law by resolving disputes involving any state administrative body, including those of individual citizens. In 1998 Bishrī retired as first deputy of the council where he had spent his entire legal career.

Bishrī is sometimes referred to in the West as an ex-Marxist and is more frequently described as one of several Islamist moderates in the so-called Wasaṭīyah group including such other prominent legal figures as Salīm al-ʿAwwā and Kamāl Abū al-Majd, as well as the journalist Fahmī Huwaydī. Bishrī's work suggests a stronger intellectual affiliation with Max Weber than with Karl Marx and a greater concern with the role of bureaucratic institutions and the social structures and attitudes that promote local democracy than with Islamic law or political organizations.

Bishrī, early in his career, associated with the Egyptian left and saw himself as a secularist, by which he meant that religion was an individual relationship with God rather than a source of social cohesion. The unexpected and complete Egyptian defeat in the 1967 war with Israel shocked many Egyptians. As Bishri has noted in print, it provided him with the emotional impetus to profoundly reconsider his world view, and it appears to be the moment when he, along with many others, ceased to see his role as part of a Westernizing elite and came to view himself as part of the local elite that dedicated itself to renewal.

Bishrī's first monograph, *al-Ḥarakah al-siyāsīyah fī Miṣr, 1945–1952* ("The Political Movement in Egypt, 1945–1952"; [Cairo]: al-Hayʾah al-Miṣrīyah al-ʿĀmmah lil-Kitāb, 1972), is a history of the background to the 1952 Free Officer's coup that established the Egyptian republic, eliminated parliamentary democracy, and undertook some important social reforms. He explored the development of various trends within the parameters of Egyptian nationalism and argued that the Muslim Brothers, despite their size, were less influential than the more highly organized communist and socialist organizations. In 1980 the book was reissued with a lengthy new introduction in which Bishrī argued that, in fact, the

Muslim Brothers rather than the left were the true bearers of democracy in Egypt. The core of his argument was that democracy in Egypt (and perhaps the Arab world more generally) necessarily required the implementation of widely held values by popular movement such as the Muslim Brothers.

One of Bishrī's early essays, *al-Dīmūqrātīyah wa-al-Nāṣirīyah* ("Nasserism and Democracy"; Cairo: Dār al-Thaqāfah al-Jadīdah, 1975), sets out themes that recur in his later work. Among the most important of these is the conflict between the hierarchical nature of state institutions and the possibility for the participation in governance that forms the core of Bishrī's understanding of democracy. Another is the negative influence that the personalization of rule plays in a political system.

Bishrī's second major monograph, *al-Muslimūn wa-al-Aqbāt fī iṭār al-jamāʿah al-waṭanīyah* ("Muslims and Christians in the Framework of National Community"; Cairo: al-Hayʾah al-Miṣrīyah al-ʿĀmmah lil-Kitāb, 1980), is a history of Egypt in the nineteenth and twentieth centuries. In it, the author argues that Muslims and Christians in Egypt share a common cultural history that seals their membership in a national community. He views joint participation in the 1919 revolution as an indication of national community but also in some sense constitutive of it in the twentieth century. In writing the book, Bishrī seemed to argue that Islamic law was as much a shared cultural artifact of Egyptian life as a system of religious commitment. He also strongly asserted the necessity in a national and democratic government of the Islamic movements accepting in principle that Christians could serve in all offices (including the presidency).

Bishrī has published studies composed of collected essays on diverse topics. These included democracy and the regime established by the Free Officers as well as the relationship between Egyptian codification and Islamic law. He has argued that the Egyptian legal system in its present form was largely consonant with *Sharīʿah*. This was not uncontroversial, but it may have had widespread support in the legal community. It allowed Bishri and many attorneys and judges to argue in favor of *Sharīʿah* as a source of legitimacy while not requiring a radical transformation of the existing statutes and institutions.

Bishrī authored two important legal decisions. In December 1992 he issued the decision of the administrative court that the practice of trying civilians in military courts was invalid. In response, the Egyptian government simply changed the law sufficiently to ensure that the Supreme Constitutional Court would find that, given a wave of terrorist violence, even the broad use of such courts would be valid. In 1994, he wrote the opinion of the State Council asserting the right of al-Azhar to censor films, music, and video cassettes in regard to their religious content, thereby expanding the institution's role from overseeing books and magazines. From the viewpoint of classical liberal thought there was an obvious contradiction between these two opinions, but from within the framework of administrative (rather than constitutional) law each opinion was primarily grounded in existing enactments rather than in an argument about underlying principles.

In the years since his retirement from the State Council, Bishrī has become more directly involved in politics. He has acted as an advisor, rather than as a leader, of some of the protest movements in the first decade of the twenty-first century, such as Kifāyah. For the most part, however, he increased his role as a public intellectual. During the same period there were several high-profile cases of Christian women who were said to have converted to Islam. Bishrī published several articles that were extremely critical of the hierarchy of the Coptic Church and its relationship to the Mubarak government. While his argument was couched in terms of equal treatment, he seemed to no longer take seriously claims about systematic discrimination against Christians in Egypt.

He publicly called for massive nonviolent protests against the Mubarak government, notably in a booklet titled *Miṣr bayna al-ʿiṣyān wa-al-tafakkuk* ("Egypt between Disobedience and Disaster"; Cairo: Dār al-Shurūq, 2006). There, he reiterated his earlier critique of the Nasserist government from which the Mubarak administration had sprung, but in far more severe terms. He indicted the politics of personalized rule and corruption and called for civil disobedience as a tool for democratization.

In February 2011, after the collapse of the Mubarak government in the wake of sustained and massive but unexpected demonstrations, the Supreme Council of the Armed Forces (SCAF) called on Bishrī to chair a committee to amend the 1971 constitution. After several weeks of intense discussion the committee provided a limited set of amendments for a referendum, though Bishrī was chagrined that the SCAF suddenly put his committee's proposals up for a vote, not as amendments but within the framework of a newly rewritten constitutional document. Since then, Bishrī has continued to publish occasional articles in the press and supported the constitutional referendum but has, like most of the so-called Wasatīyah group, become a vocal critic of the government now dominated by the Muslim Brothers.

Bishrī has played an important role in Egyptian intellectual life since the 1970s. His illumination of the strengths and weaknesses of the Egyptian bureaucracy and of the possible paths to devolution of power from the highly centralized state remains of the utmost importance as Egypt moves into a new political future.

BIBLIOGRAPHY

Binder, Leonard. *Islamic Liberalism: A Critique of Development Ideologies*. Chicago: University of Chicago Press, 1988.

Bishrī, Ṭāriq. *Al-Dīmūqrāṭīyah wa-niẓām 23 Yūliyū, 1952–1970*. Cairo: Dār al-Hilāl, 1991.

Bishrī, Ṭāriq. *Al-Ḥiwār al-Islāmī al-ʿalmānī*. Cairo: Dār al-Shurūq, 1996.

Ellis, Goldberg. "Ṭāriq al-Bishri and Constitutional Revolution," *nisralnasr* (blog), 15 February 2011. http://nisralnasr.blogspot.com/2011/02/tariq-al-bishri-and-constitutional.html.

Kirkpatrick, David D., and Kareem Fahim. "In Egypt, a Panel of Jurists Is Given the Task of Revising the Country's Constitution." *New York Times*, 15 February 2011. http://www.nytimes.com/2011/02/16/world/middleeast/16egypt.html?pagewanted=all&_r=0.

Meijer, Roel. *History, Authenticity, and Politics: Ṭāriq al-Bishri's Interpretation of Modern Egyptian History*. Amsterdam: Middle East Research Associates, 1989.

Rutherford, Bruce K. *Egypt after Mubarak: Liberalism, Islam, and Democracy in the Arab World*. Princeton, N.J.: Princeton University Press, 2008.

Ellis Goldberg

Bosnia and Herzegovina.

Usually referred to as Bosnia or Bosnia-Herzegovina and located in the midst of the western Balkans, between the Sava River to the north, the Una River to the northwest, the Dalmatian region to the south, and the Drina River to the east. Bosnia covers an area of just over 51,000 square kilometers. No census has been taken in Bosnia since 1991, when over 44 percent of the country's population were Muslims. Many Bosnians now live in Western Europe and the United States, having emigrated primarily because of the effects of war. Muslims in Bosnia today, as in the past, are Sunnī and follow the Ḥanafī legal school.

Early History. The earliest mention of "the land of Bosnia" was in 958 CE in a treatise written by the Byzantine emperor Constantine Porphyrogenitus, referring to the area between the towns of Sarajevo and Zenica in central Bosnia. This area constitutes the historical nucleus of Bosnia as a country and a state.

The medieval Bosnian state began its territorial expansion from this historical nucleus, especially during the reigns of Kulin (r. 1180–1204), Stjepan Kotromanić (r. 1322–1353), and Tvrtko I (r. 1353–1391). After Tvrtko I, local feudal lords began fighting for power, and by the time of Stjepan Tomaš (r. 1443–1461) and Stjepan Tomašević (r. 1461–1463), medieval Bosnia had lost its independence. In 1463, Bosnia was conquered by the Ottoman sultan Mehmed II, known as Fatih (the Conqueror).

Despite conquest, Bosnia largely retained its territorial integrity and, as a province within the Ottoman Empire, expanded. Beginning in 1453, it had the status of a frontier *sanjak* (a first-level subdivision of Ottoman administration, with military personnel under the leadership of a *sanjak-beg*, appointed by the sultan). In the early sixteenth century, Bosnia-Herzegovina became an *eyalet* (an intermediate administrative level) that included present-day Bosnia-Herzegovina, Croatia, Serbia, and Montenegro. After 1580, Bosnia became a *paşalık* (a sanjak ruled by a pasha appointed by the sultan).

The Spread of Islam under the Ottomans. Islam spread slowly in Bosnia from the mid-fifteenth to the early seventeenth centuries. Many historians, led by Noel Malcolm and Mustafa Imamović, take the view that the spread of Islam was neither rapid nor forcible, and that Ottoman authorities did not use administrative powers to enforce conversion. The mass acceptance of Islam can instead be explained in terms of specific local factors and internal historical developments in Bosnia. Before the Ottoman conquest, the Roman Catholic, the Greek Orthodox, and the no longer extant Bosnian Church competed for adherents. Islam spread among adherents of all of these traditions. The common denominator for the converted population was that it was Slavic and Bosnian.

Under the Ottoman Empire, Bosnia developed dynamically. The Ottomans developed and improved many towns and cities, such as Sarajevo, Mostar, Travnik, Višegrad, Foča, and Banja Luka. It provided roads and bridges, the most magnificent of which include the Mehmed Pasha Sokolović bridge in Višegrad, the Mostar Bridge, and the Goat's Bridge near Sarajevo, all built in the sixteenth century. Numerous schools and Ṣūfī centers were built in Sarajevo, Mostar, Travnik, Foča, Banja Luka, Tuzla, and elsewhere. The most famous of them is the Gazi Husrevbegova *madrasah* in Sarajevo which still exists and has about five hundred students. Throughout the Ottoman and Austro-Hungarian periods, the skylines of Bosnian towns and cities were graced with mosques and churches. During this period Bosnia's towns developed strong commercial centers (*bedestans*) and trade links with other parts of the Empire and beyond. This development may have attracted converts to Islam. In addition, the Ṣūfī orders preached actively in Bosnia-Herzegovina, and the Mevlevi, Naqshbandi, Qadiri, and Halveti orders retain a presence in the country today.

The Modern Era. During the Austro-Hungarian period (1878–1918), Bosnia's territorial integrity was recognized and was treated as a special area (*corpus separatum*). Bosnia largely kept its integrity also under the Kingdom of Yugoslavia (1918–1941). Within the Socialist Federal Republic of Yugoslavia (1945–1990), Bosnia was one of the six republics with equal federal status. In the modern era, as under Austro-Hungarian rule, Bosnian Muslims played a prominent role in the political and legal struggle for preserving Bosnia's territorial integrity.

Since 1992, Bosnia has been a sovereign state and a member of the United Nations. Following its declaration of independence in 1992, a war broke out in which the remnant Yugoslavia, comprising Serbia and Montenegro and dominated by Serbs, attacked Bosnia with the support of rebel Bosnian Serbs. On several occasions the international community accused Serbia of aggression against Bosnia. In 1995 NATO intervened and brought the conflict to an end. The bloody and horrific war ended with the signing of the U.S.-sponsored Dayton Peace Accord, as a result of which Bosnia remained a sovereign country comprising two entities, the Bosnia-Herzegovina Federation and the Serb Republic.

During the war, ethnic cleansing was carried out mainly against Bosnian Muslims (Bosniaks), although a significant number of Croats and Serbs were also victims. The number of war casualties is still being investigated: the figure ranges between 120,000 and 200,000 killed and missing. Because 70 percent of the victims were Bosnian Muslims, however, the government of Bosnia charged Serbia with complicity in genocide in Bosnia and Herzogovina. In February 2007 the International Court of Justice ruled that neither the army nor the police of Serbia had perpetrated genocide or conspired to do so in Bosnia-Herzegovina, but it found that Serbia had failed to prevent genocide in Srebrenica in 1995, which was its obligation under the Genocide Convention.

The effects of war in Bosnia are still visible, even though destroyed mosques, schools, and Ṣūfī centers are being rebuilt and Islamic learning is undergoing a revival. Politically, Bosnia has been experiencing a crisis of Dayton arrangement since 2006. When the so-called April package of constitutional changes did not receive the backing of the Bosnian Parliamentary Assembly in 2006, representatives of the international community in Bosnia decided to let the domestic politicians produce a "solution" option. Hardline politicans from Republika Srpska, especially Milorad Dodik (formerly the Republic prime minister, now president), openly declared their secessionist views. This provoked protests by Bosnian Muslim politicians. In relation to Bosnian-Croat politicians, the Croat Democratic Party (HDZ) is putting its stakes on the creation of the so-called third entity. However, the support for the establishment of the third entity is not supported by many Bosnian Croat intellectuals, Bosnian Franciscans, and the Catholic Church. International community representatives in Bosnia oppose the creation of the third entity, because they are aware that it would cause tensions between Bosnian Croats and Bosnian Muslims.

Since 2006, Bosnia has taken steps toward closer relations with the EU. There is, however, continued filibustering by the Republika Srpska with respect to adopting the necessary legislature of the so-called European laws. Some progress has been made, making Bosnia's closer relations with NATO possible and opening the way to the EU's pre-accession funds. The position of Croatia and Serbia toward EU to a great extent determines the views of many in Bosnia towards the country's integration into the EU. However, central government or state institutions in Bosnia are being blocked. As already mentioned, this blocking comes above all from the Republika Srpska. Such a policy elicits angry reactions from Bosnian Muslim politicians. The EU encourages reaching a common agreement but also encourages Bosnia's integration into the EU. By taking decisive action, the OHR, the OSCE, and the EU have stopped some destructive moves by the Republika Srpska, such as the attempt by the Republika Srpska Assembly to adopt the Referendum Law.

There has been substantial progress in Bosnia following the war of 1992–1995. There is a visible regeneration of educational and cultural institutions and rebuilding of infrastructure. The ideology that moderate policies bring results has been adopted by Bakir Izetbegović, the current Bosniac member of state presidency.

Bosnian Muslim intellectuals and the majority of religious intellectuals inside the Islamic community support Bosnia's path to Europe, and there are European trends in the interpretation of Islam and Muslim tradition. With its centuries-long blend of cultures, Bosnia is considered a forerunner of present-day European multilateralism.

[*See also* Balkan States.]

BIBLIOGRAPHY

Agović, Bajro. *Islamska zajednica u Crnoj Gori* (Islamic Community in Montenegro). Podgorica: Mešihat Islamske zajednice, 2007.

Aslan, Ednan, ed. *Islamic Education in Europe*. Vienna: Böhlau, 2009.

Bougarel, Xavier, Elissa Helms, and Ger Duijzings, eds. *The New Bosnian Mosaic: Identities, Memories and Moral Claims in a Post-War Society*. Aldershot, U.K.: Ashgate, 2007.

Disolucija Jugoslavije (Procesi, uzroci i pozicija Bosne i Hercegovine kroz prizmu djelovanja političkog vodstva na čelu sa Alijom Izetbegovićem), zbornik sa Međunarodnog naučnog simpozija. Sarajevo: Muzej Alija Izetbegović, 2010.

Donia, Robert J. *Sarajevo: A Biography*. Ann Arbor: University of Michigan Press, 2006.

Filipović, Nedim. *Islamizacija u Bosni i Hercegovini* (Islamization in Bosnia and Herzegovina). Tešanj, 2005.

Ghodsee, Kristin. *Muslim Lives in Eastern Europe: Gender, Ethnicity, and the Transformation of Islam in Postsocialist Bulgaria*. Princeton, N.J.: Princeton University Press, 2010.

Gradeva, Rossitsa, ed. *Istoriya na myusyulmanskata kultura po balgarskite* zemi (History of Muslim Culture in Bulgarian Lands). Sofia: IMIR, 2007.

Halit Eren, ed. *The Ottoman Legacy and the Balkan Muslim Communities Today*, 2nd ed. Istanbul: Balkanlar Medeniyet Merkezi, 2011.

Izetbegović, Alija. *Inescapable Questions: Autobiographical Notes*. Leicester: Islamic Foundation, 2003.

Jezernik, Božidar. *Wild Europe: The Balkans in the Gaze of Western Travellers*. London: Saqi in association with the Bosnian Institute,2004.

Karčić, Fikret. *The Bosniaks and the Challenges of Modernity*. Sarajevo: El-Kalem, 1999.

Nielsen, Jørgen. S., et al., eds. *Yearbook of Muslims in Europe*, vol. 2. Leiden: Brill, 2010.

Nielsen, Jørgen. S. et al., eds. *TheYearbook of Muslims in Europe*, vol. 3. Leiden, Brill, 2011.

Pinson, Mark, ed. *The Muslims of Bosnia-Herzegovina: Their Historic Development from the Middle Ages to the Dissolution of Yugoslavia*. Cambridge, Mass.: Harvard University Press, 1993.

Zirojević, Olga. *Srbija pod turskom vlašću 1459–1804* (Serbia under Turkish Rule 1459–1804), Belgrade: Čigoja, 2007.

ENES KARIĆ

BRETHREN OF PURITY. The Ikhwān al-Ṣafāʾ (Brethren of Purity) were the anonymous affiliates of a tenth-century learned esoteric fraternity based in the Iraqi city of Basra with an operative branch in Baghdad. This secretive urban brotherhood occupied a prominent place in Islamic intellectual history due to the wide dissemination and adaptive assimilation of its monumental encyclopedic compendium the *Rasāʾil Ikhwān al-Ṣafāʾ* (Epistles of the Brethren of Purity). The exact identity of the lettered adepts of this clandestine coterie, their doctrinal and sectarian affiliation (*madhhab*), the dating of their textual corpus, and the chronology of its compilation and composition are all vexing questions that are still shrouded in mystery and debated amongst historiographers and medievalists in Islamic studies. Coining a nom de plume for this underground organization may have been necessitated by the politically tumultuous conditions in Iraq under Būyid confederate governance and the challenged suzerainty of the Abbasid caliphs in Baghdad. Their true identity concealed, the Ikhwān operated in dissimulation. Whilst it is conventionally proclaimed that they might have flourished around the 960s to 980s CE, or perhaps at the eve of the Fatimid conquest of Egypt (c. 969 CE), other historiography accounts situate them in much earlier epochs.

The *Rasāʾil Ikhwān al-Ṣafāʾ* contained fifty-two treatises that offered synoptic explications of the classical philosophical and scientific traditions of the age. Divided into four classificatory parts, the *Rasāʾil* compendium treated themes such as arithmetic, geometry, astronomy, music, logic, natural philosophy cum physics, psychology, metaphysics, and theology, in addition to containing moral tales, didactic odes, and ecological fables. The compilation of philosophical and scientific theories in the *Epistles* constituted one of the paradigmatic legacies in the canonization of philosophy and the sciences in medieval Islamic civilization, which also led to the popularization of rational knowledge in urban locales. This encyclopedic corpus, with its elegant architectonic unity, allowed for the convergence of its constituent elements in a remarkable *oeuvre des belles lettres* within the high Arabic literature of Islam.

The Ikhwān al-Ṣafāʾ occasionally referred to themselves as the "righteous friends of God" (*Awliyāʾ Allāh*), in affirmation of their continual obedience of divine decrees, and in expression of their declared aim to found a utopian mystical polis, which they named *Dawlat al-khayr* (Reign of Goodness), and constituted their vision of a spiritual polity that represented their own version of a "virtuous city" (*madīna fāḍila*), as inspired by Plato's *Republic*.

Even if the Brethren of Purity were not directly affiliated with the Ismāʿīlī communities of the Fertile Crescent, the ʿAbbāsids would have been ideologically hostile to their critical doctrines, which may have been perceived as being subversive in diluting the centrality of the teachings of Islam by way of drawing excessively upon other sources of guidance from within other traditions of monotheism, or from pre-Islamic pagan legacies. This would have forced the Brethren to veil the identity of their own revolutionizing members. Although one can detect Ismāʿīlī conceptual leitmotifs in the *Epistles*, which also stress the Shiite character of this compendium, it is nonetheless the case that the Brethren drew inspiration from various sources in Abrahamic monotheism and from the ancient wisdoms of polytheistic cultures. It is therefore unclear how a precise determination of the Brethren's creed can be established without controversy. It is perhaps closest to the spirit of their teachings to describe them as classical free thinkers, even if they displayed clear signs of Shiite leanings or of Ismāʿīlī proclivities besides their broader interests in gnosis and esotericism. In philosophical terms, they can be described as neo-Pythagorean and Neoplatonists, while also being influenced by the Aristotelian corpus.

Marked by a perceptible openness to otherness, and eschewing fanaticism, the Brethren's epistles seemed to embody a form of heterodoxy and syncretism in Islam, which accommodated miscellaneous ancient and monotheistic traditions. The Brethren found "veracity in every religion" and grasped knowledge as "a pure nourishment for the soul." They also associated the attainment of happiness with the development of rational pursuits and intellectual quests. They also promoted an ethical "friendship of virtue" amongst their companions, and asserted the eschatological aspiration to found a spiritual ecclesiastic and ecumenist sanctuary that would assist their coreligionists in overcoming the sectarian discord plaguing their age. They avowedly affirmed that their companions came from all stations and classes in society, bringing together aristocrats and commoners, sons of "kings, emirs, viziers, secretaries, tradesmen, and workmen." Ultimately, they pictured the ideal human being as a noble who is graciously "Persian in breed, Arab in faith, *ḥanīf* in jurisprudence, Iraqi in culture, Hebrew in tradition, Christian in comportment, Syrian in piety, Greek in knowledge, Indian in contemplation, Ṣūfī in intimation and lifestyle."

BIBLIOGRAPHY

Brethren of Purity. *The Case of the Animals Versus Man Before the King of the Jinn: An Arabic Critical Edition and English Translation of Epistle 22*. Translated by Lenn E. Goodman and Richard McGregor. Oxford: Oxford University Press, 2009.

Callataÿ, Godefroid de. *Ikhwan al-Safa': A Brotherhood of Idealists on the Fringe of Orthodox Islam*. Oxford: Oneworld, 2005.

El-Bizri, Nader, ed. *The Ikhwān al-Ṣafā' and Their Rasā'il: An Introduction*. Oxford: Oxford University Press, 2008.

Netton, Ian Richard. *Muslim Neoplatonists: An Introduction to the Thought of the Brethren of Purity (Ikhwān al-Ṣafā')*. London: Routledge Curzon, 2002.

Nader El-Bizri

Bughāt. *See* Rebellion.

Būyids. The Būyids, or Buwayhids, were a series of kingdoms in the Daylamite region (south of the Caspian Sea) that ruled western Iran and later part of Iraq from 935 to 1055. The dynasty were first believed to have been Zaydis but converted to Twelver Shiism for political expediency after the Greater Occultation of the twelfth Imam. This allowed them to keep the ʿAbbasid caliphate while resisting the Fāṭimids. The dynasty consisted of the three sons of a local leader named Būyeh, who joined Mardāvīj, a fellow Daylami, a founder of the Ziyārids, and a leader who brought the Būyid brothers south. He was murdered in 935, and the eldest Būyid brother, ʿAlī, started his career as a general in the service of Nasr bin Aḥmad, the Samanid ruler. After several other stints in the service of others, ʿAlī conquered the city of Arrajan for himself and then established himself in Isfahan and Fars. The second brother, Ḥasan, consolidated power in Rayy and Hamadan, and the third brother, Aḥmad, occupied Kerman, but later moved to Khuzestan.

In 934 ʿAlī was invested with a standard and robes of honor by the ʿAbbasid caliph al-Radi. We know this because of a coin dating to that period that was struck in Shīrāz. But it was not until the ʿAbbasid caliph al-Mustakfi, and Aḥmad's conquest of the city of Baghdad in 945 that honorific titles were bestowed on the family. Aḥmad became known as Muʿizz al-Dawlah (one who honors or dignifies the state), ʿAlī became known as ʿImād al-Dawlah (pillar of the state), and Ḥasan became Rukn al-Dawlah (support of the state). These honorific titles, the most accurate way of determining the pecking order of the family, were struck on their coins. One finds the name of the Būyid who struck the coins on the obverse side, and on the reverse side the name of the ʿAbbasid caliph, with the head of the family underneath. Thus the Sunnī caliph became a client of the Shīʿī Būyids. Ḥasan installed his son Fana Khusraw, also known as ʿAdūd al-Dawlah (strength of the state), in Shīrāz, and on Ḥasan's death in 976, ʿAdūd al-Dawlah united all the Būyid domains, entering Baghdad in 977. By 980 he ruled most of Iraq and the Iranian plateau except Khurasan. Upon his death in 983, the Būyids fell into disputes and each acquired his own principality. The first loss of territory was to Maḥmud of Ghaznah, who took Rayy in 1029, but the final end of Būyid authority was the taking of Baghdad by the Seljuk sultan Tugrul Beg.

Though the Būyids were Twelver Shīʿī, they supported the Sunnī caliphs and were tolerant of the majority Sunnīs in their realm. But they were hostile toward the Fāṭimids, who were Ismāʿīlīs. The highpoint of Būyid rule was the reign of ʿAdūd al-Dawlah, who is remembered as an enlightened monarch and the builder of such works as the dam of the Amir near Shīrāz, as well as mosques in various cities of Iran, such as those in Nāʿīn and Neyrīz.

Under Būyid rule, relative peace and security prevailed and trade flourished, but the system of fiefs (*iqṭāʿ*) granted to soldiers weakened the agricultural base of the economy. Scholarship flourished, sometimes under state support. For example, ʿAdūd al-Dawlah was the patron of the Arab poet al-Mutanabbi.

The Būyids brought into prominence the commemoration of the death of Ḥusayn ibn ʿAlī, ʿĀshūrāʿ, on the tenth day of the month of Muḥarram. In addition to mosques, they built many *turbahs*, saints' tombs or places of pilgrimage, especially in Sāmarrāʿ, in Iraq, where the Twelver Shīʿī believe the Twelfth Imām vanished and will reappear in the fullness of time. They left the caliphs, beginning with al-Muṭīʿ, as titular rulers and permitted them to appoint Sunnī religious officials. Throughout all of this, the Būyid right to govern was based on recognition of the caliph.

Whereas the Sāmānids, who reigned in Central Asia in the ninth and tenth centuries and share credit for reasserting Persian dominance in the region, ruled over a predominantly Sunnī Muslim society, the Būyids in western Iran had a large Zoroastrian and Christian population. For this reason, the written record includes Pahlavi, Syriac, and Arabic, and several Būyid rulers composed poetry in Arabic. Thus, although the Būyids made little contribution to Persian literature, Arabic literature flourished under such literati as Badīʿ al-Zamān of Hamadan (d. 1008), who wrote only in Arabic.

[*See also* ʿAbbāsid Caliphate; *and* Dawlah.]

BIBLIOGRAPHY

Busse, Heribert. *Chalif und Grosskönig: Die Būyiden in Iraq (945–1055)*. Wiesbaden: F. Steiner, 1969. A standard account of the Būyids in Iraq. Discusses the relation of the Būyid rulers to the caliphs, as well as the bureaucracy in Baghdad. Also discussed are cultural and Muslim scholarship.

Kraemer, Joel L. *Humanism in the Renaissance of Islam: The Cultural Revival during the Būyid Age*. Leiden, Netherlands: E. J. Brill, 1992. Connects the brilliant development of Arabic literature and Muslim scholarship under the Būyids with former and later times. Cultural matters are also treated.

Mottahedeh, Roy P. *Loyalty and Leadership in an Early Islamic Society*. London: I. B. Tauris, 2001. The author explains the rules for and values behind Būyid political and social actions with reference to ethical, political, and religious issues.

Richard N. Frye
Revised by Khaled M. G. Keshk

C

Caliphate, Theories of the. The term "caliphate" (Ar. *khilāfah*) refers to the office of the caliph (Ar. *khalīfah*), the "successor, vicegerent, or deputy" in charge of the affairs of the Muslims. Sunnī Muslims consider the Caliphate to be the ideal and divinely sanctioned form of Islamic government, instituted upon the death of the Prophet Muḥammad in the year 632 CE. From the outset of the institution, Muslim political theorists, theologians, and legists have been occupied with two main fields of concern: (1) What is the nature and scope of caliphal authority, and (2) what are the criteria for eligibility and accession to the position? The Caliphate continued in various forms and locations until its official abolition in March 1924. Since then, discussions of the Caliphate typically revolve around the question of its revival as an ideal or practical reality.

Nomenclature. The endeavor to define the nature and scope of the caliph's power is epitomized in the debates over nomenclature. The earliest extant documentary sources that provide a title for the caliph are silver coins (*darāhim*) dating from the caliphate of Muʿāwiyah (r. 661–680) bearing the title *amīr al-mu'minīn* (commander of the faithful). The term *khalīfah* first appears in documentary sources dating from the late seventh century CE, notably on coins struck by the Umayyad caliph ʿAbd al-Malik ibn Marwān (r. 685–705), which read *amīr al-mu'minīn khalīfat Allāh*, with *khalīfat Allāh* meaning "deputy of God," or, as Aram Shahin (2009, p. 623) suggests, "successor by [the agency of] God." A variant on this phrase that appears in literature from the early ʿAbbāsid period is *khalīfat rasūl Allāh* (deputy of the messenger of God, or successor by [the agency of] the messenger of God), although literary sources from the Umayyad and ʿAbbāsid caliphates suggest that both *khalīfat Allāh* and *khalīfat rasūl Allāh* were in use from the time of Abū Bakr (r. 632–634) or ʿUmar (r. 634–644). According to Crone and Hinds (1986), the title *khalīfat Allāh* was used less frequently than *amīr al-mu'minīn*, yet *khalīfat Allāh* was the most essential designation, getting to the heart of the nature and function of the office as divine deputyship. They argue that the notion of *khalīfah* was almost always understood in the sense of *khalīfat Allāh* rather than *khalīfat rasūl Allāh*, meaning that the caliph was considered the deputy of God and not of the Prophet, and that the traditionist scholars in the later Umayyad period devised the phrase *khalīfat rasūl Allāh* in an effort to subordinate the caliph to the Prophetic *sunnah*. While

Crone and Hinds claim that the Umayyad caliphs saw their own power independently from that of the Prophet, Uri Rubin (2003) insists that they embraced their role as the Prophet's legatees. Looking at the same Umayyad evidence as Crone and Hinds (namely the epistolography of al-Walīd II and the poetry of Farazdaq), Rubin shows how the Umayyad caliphs considered their legacy to stem from the Prophet as the indispensable hereditary link between them and the universal divine legacy of which they are defenders. Hakim (2005) basically agrees, proposing that the presence or absence of the word *rasūl* in the title is less significant than Crone and Hinds suppose, that the phrases *khalīfat Allāh* and *khalīfat rasūl Allāh* were interchangeable, and that the older usage in no way nullified the importance of the Prophet as a source of divine sanction for caliphal authority.

Qurʾānic References. The claim to divine sanction has led medieval and modern scholars alike to look for a Qurʾānic basis for the political concept of the *khalīfah*. While neither *khalīfat Allāh* nor *khalīfat rasūl Allāh* appears in the Qurʾān, the term *khalīfah* appears twice, both times referring to a vicegerent whom God places on earth. In Qurʾan 2:30, *khalīfah* appears in connection with Adam, the first man:

> Behold, thy Lord said to the angels: "I will create a vicegerent [*khalīfah*] on earth." They said: "Wilt Thou place therein one who will make mischief therein and shed blood?—Whilst we do celebrate Thy praises and glorify Thy holy [name]?" He said: "I know what ye know not." (Trans. A. Yusuf Ali)

In Qurʾān 38:26, *khalīfah* appears in connection with the prophet-king David:

> O David! We did indeed make thee a vicegerent [*khalīfah*] on earth: so judge thou between men in truth [and justice]: Nor follow thou the lusts [of thy heart], for they will mislead thee from the Path of Allāh: for those who wander astray from the Path of Allāh, is a Penalty Grievous, for that they forget the Day of Account. (Trans. A. Yusuf Ali)

In Muslim exegesis (*tafsīr*), it seems that from al-Ṭabarī (d. 923) onward the dominant interpretation is that Qurʾān 38:26 refers to political rule and the meting out of justice. However, there is some question as to whether this interpretation reflects the earliest understandings of the verse or of the political office from its inception. Al-Qāḍī (1988) shows that there is little evidence in the earliest exegeses to connect these verses with the political institution of the Caliphate, and that the early exegetes did not use the phrase *khalīfat Allāh* in their exegeses, suggesting either that the political concept of *khalīfat Allāh* was not yet established or, contrarily, that it was already so well established as to not require any explanation.

Umayyad and ʿAbbāsid Periods. The most influential early theorizer on the Caliphate is ʿAbd al-Ḥamīd al-Kātib (d. 750), a secretary (*kātib*) for the Umayyad caliphs Hishām (r. 724–743) and Marwān II (r. 744–749/750). When the ʿAbbāsid revolution threatened to topple the Umayyad Caliphate, ʿAbd al-Ḥamīd was head of the chancellery and wrote passionately enjoining obedience (*ṭāʿah*) and warning against civil discord (*fitnah*). Although his epistles do not contain a systematic theory of the Caliphate, they introduce seminal ideas about the nature and scope of caliphal authority. Obedience to "God's caliphs" (also called "God's friends") is equivalent to obedience to God and therefore is the backbone of the religion. To disobey the caliph is to support "the Devil's friends," which is not merely an earthly rebellion but a sin against God and his Prophet and a deliberate rejection of Islam, leading not only to worldly perdition but eternal damnation (al-Qāḍī, 2005, p. 8). Thus the *khilāfah* is essential to Islam and obedience to the Caliph is a fundamental religious obligation.

Another epistolographer on the Caliphate was Ibn al-Muqaffaʿ (d. c. 756), famed for his translations of Sassanian literature from Middle Persian into Arabic, and whose advice to the ʿAbbāsid caliph al-Manṣūr (r. 754–775) in his *Risālah fī al-ṣaḥābah* (Epistle Concerning Courtiers) gives us a glimpse of how Perso-Sassanian absolutist ideology dovetailed with the developing theory of the Caliphate. Keenly aware that the rapidly growing Islamic empire required an unambiguous institutional basis, Ibn al-Muqaffaʿ proposes a number of reforms to centralize the religious, judicial, civil, and military branches of government under the caliph's control. As the title of the letter suggests, an important aspect of this is the careful delegation of duties to reliable administrators. Ibn al-Muqaffaʿ advises the caliph to support the possessors of good judgment (*dhū al-raʾy*) who can offer trustworthy suggestions and defend him from corrupt governors, but ultimately the caliph is the final authority in secular and religious matters of state. At a time of many differing legal opinions, Ibn al-Muqaffaʿ insists that it is the caliph's prerogative—indeed duty—to apply his sound and binding judgment to the codification of the *Sharīʿah*, so that justice and equality may be fulfilled throughout Islamdom. He admits the possibility, at least theoretically, that the caliph may err, and while the caliph should not be obeyed in disobedience to God, at the same time, and perhaps more importantly, error on the part of the caliph cannot be used as an inducement for rebellion. Similar themes appear in *Kitāb al-kharāj* (The Book of Taxation) of the famous ʿAbbāsid chief judge and Ḥanafī jurist Abū Yūsuf (d. 798 CE), who emphasizes the role of the caliph as the shepherd of God's flock, the upholder of the divine law, and the dispenser of justice and wisdom to his subjects. Although with Ibn al-Muqaffaʿ and Abū Yūsuf we do not yet find a systematic theory of the Caliphate, nonetheless their writings offer valuable insights into the conception and functions of the office under the ʿAbbāsids.

Further insight may be gleaned from the classical Muslim sectarian discourses of the early ʿAbbāsid era, which dealt in earnest with evaluating the criteria for legitimate accession to the Caliphate. These discourses were typically cast in the light of the initial contest for the Caliphate among the Companions of the Prophet, a pivotal era for defining the institution. From these formative events Muslims highlighted several criteria (precedence in conversion and service to Islam, proximity to the Prophet through companionship or kinship, inherited and earned merits, and piety) and modes of accession to the Caliphate (popular consent, testamentary designation, election, and seizure). Proto-Sunnī and proto-Shīʿī positions on these matters are recorded in the treatises on the Imamate (meaning Caliphate) by the prolific theologian and litterateur al-Jāḥiẓ (d. 869). He not only relates the views of the various emerging sects but proposes (albeit implicitly) his own theory of the Caliphate, which culminates in a comprehensive definition of virtue (*faḍl*) as the qualitatively best combination of proximity to the Prophet, piety, service, and strategic acuity, and in his proposition that this definition of virtue applies in toto to deserving the Caliphate. In accordance with his theory of virtuous leadership, al-Jāḥiẓ defends each of the first four caliphs as the most virtuous (*afḍal*) candidate at the time of his accession. This affirmation of the "rightly guided" caliphs is foundational to the orthodox Sunnī understanding of the Caliphate from the tenth century onward.

The gradual waning of ʿAbbāsid autocracy in the tenth century led to increasing flexibility in Sunnī theories of the Caliphate. In 945, the Shīʿī Būyids took control of the ʿAbbāsid Caliphate, reducing the caliph to a figurehead with little direct power. Not long after, in 969, the Shīʿī Fāṭimids extended their reach from Tunisia to Egypt and directly challenged the ʿAbbāsid claim to the Caliphate. The task of justifying the continued relevance of the ʿAbbāsid caliphate in such a context was taken up by al-Māwardī (d. 1058), who, in his *al-Aḥkām al-sulṭānīyah* (Eng. trans., *Ordinances of Government*: Māwardī, 2000), is less concerned with having the caliph retain real power than with having his symbolic power continually acknowledged. He affirms the already clearly established requirements that the caliph must be of Qurayshī descent and of sound mind and body, but beyond these minimal criteria, al-Māwardī takes a flexible approach, especially with respect to the mode of accession (election or designation). Perhaps most significantly he recognizes the legitimacy of governorship by usurpation, suggesting that the caliph quickly recognize those who set themselves up and possess authority so as to transmute their independence into subordination. Thus he accommodates the decentralization of practical political power while requiring the Caliphate as a legitimizing institution, and entrusting the cohesion of the Muslim *ummah* to a continued common commitment to the ideal of *Sharīʿah*-minded rule that the Caliphate represents.

Mamlūk and Ottoman Periods. The coming of the Mongols in 1258 brought an end to ʿAbbāsid rule in Baghdad and ushered in a new era of increased marginalization of the Caliphate. Although the Mamlūk sultan Baybars (r. 1260–77) installed an ʿAbbāsid caliph in Cairo (al-Mustanṣir II, r. 1261), the caliph's purpose was apparently only to validate the sultan and delegate to him all powers previously assigned to the caliph, including religious as well as political prerogatives. The caliph wrote, "I entrust to you the interests of all the Muslims and I invest you with all which I am invested in the matters of religion" (quoted in Black, 2001, p. 143). The sultanate's effective absorption of the Caliphate finds legitimation in the political theory of the Shāfiʿī chief judge in Cairo, Ibn Jamāʿah (d. 1333), who goes beyond al-Māwardī in justifying usurpation not merely through being delegated a portion of caliphal authority but in fact through totally co-opting the Caliphate itself. The contemporaneous Ḥanbalī jurist Ibn Taymīyah (d. 1328) and the historian Ibn Khaldūn (d. 1406) similarly accommodate such realpolitik into their political theories, emphasizing the effective enforcement of laws and norms as the most essential characteristic of legitimate Islamic rule. Modern scholars differ in interpreting the significance of such co-optation for the relevance of the Caliphate by this time. On the one hand, its continued function as a tool for legitimation suggests its continued relevance, while, on the other, the caliph's divestment of any real personal power suggests its ultimate irrelevance. It seems that in the case of the Mamlūks the caliph is theoretically relevant but practically ineffectual.

With the demise of the Mamlūks in 1517, the Ottomans formally absorbed the Caliphate into their own sultanate-Caliphate. The Ottoman sultan-caliphs, as God's deputies and guarantors of justice, assumed authority over both political and religious affairs, the latter being achieved in part through a thorough incorporation of the religious scholars (*ʿulamāʾ*) into the state bureaucracy as a distinct class of ruling elite. In his *Naṣīḥatu s-selāṭīn* (Eng. trans., *Counsel for Sultans*: ʿAlī, 1979–1982), the Ottoman bureaucrat Muṣṭafā ʿAlī (d. 1600) echoes many of the most salient themes found in the classical works on the Caliphate in the early ʿAbbāsid period, notably the role of the sultan-caliph as a shepherd of the flock, the delegation of trustworthy administrators, the dispensing of justice, and the enforcement of the *Sharīʿah*.

The Caliphate in Modern Times. In 1924 the Grand National Assembly of Turkey officially abolished the Caliphate. Since the Caliphate was, by this time, more ideal than real, its abolition had more of a psychological impact than a practical one. Those who lamented its passing mounted an intellectual defense of its existence and called for its necessary revival, while many more took little notice of the Caliphate's extinction and directed their efforts to adopting new forms of Islamic governance.

One of the more influential treatises calling for the revival of the Caliphate was written shortly before its official abolition. Muḥammad Rashīd Riḍā (d. 1935) was a major early leader of the still-active Salafī movement, which advocates a return to the golden age of the pious ancestors (*al-salaf al-ṣāliḥ*), that is, the first generation of Muslims. In his treatise titled *al-Khilāfah*, Riḍā argues that the *sunnah* of the Prophet demands the existence of the Caliphate to assure that society is properly governed according to the *Sharīʿah*. His main concern is the enforcement of Islamic law, which he believed requires strong central leadership, hence the need for a caliph. Thus the restoration of the Caliphate is part of a larger program of Islamic legal reform. In this program the caliph is not to be an absolute ruler, but rather a moderator presiding over a consultative assembly of *ʿulamāʾ* and serving as the supreme *mujtahid* in matters of public welfare. In this respect his theory of the Caliphate somewhat resembles a representative government along the lines of the modern European parliamentary models of the time.

In contrast, the prominent secularist ʿAlī ʿAbd al-Rāziq (d. 1966) claims in his *al-Islām wa-usūl al-ḥukm* (Islam and the Bases of Government) that neither the Qurʾān nor the sunnah require the institution of the Caliphate. The Prophet never designated a successor, and never mentioned anything about the formation of government after him. Moreover, the Prophet's authority was wholly religious, inimitable, and nontransferable, so it is impossible that the caliph, in the sense of the Prophet's appointed political successor, can ever really exist. Consequently, Muslims are at liberty to abandon the institution of the Caliphate and devise new political systems that are more realistic and viable in their current circumstances.

For many modern Islamists the Caliphate remains an ideal symbol for pan-Islamic unity, while militant movements like Hizb ut-Tahrir and al-Qaʿida use the restoration of the Caliphate as a rallying banner for global *jihād*. The founder of Hizb ut-Tahrir, Taqī al-Dīn al-Nabhānī (d. 1977 CE), saw the Caliphate as a necessary institution for the liberation of Muslims from un-Islamic tyranny and the restoration of the *Sharīʿah*. Conceived as a grassroots movement, Hizb ut-Tahrir has an agenda consisting of three phases: (1) ideological attack on un-Islamic intellectual and political systems, (2) large-scale recruitment and consolidation, and (3) erection of the Caliphate. In similar fashion, the well-known al-Qaʿida ideologue Āyman al-Ẓawāhirī (b. 1951) describes the phased objectives of al-Qaʿida in his *Knights under the Prophet's Banner* (2001):

> The jihād movement must follow a plan aimed at establishing an Islamic state it can defend on a territory in the Muslim world; from there, it will lead the struggle to restore the rightly guided caliphate after the Prophet's model. (Quoted in Keppel and Milelli, 2008, pp. 198–199)

For both groups, the establishment of the Caliphate is a distant and ill-defined goal. Neither of them offers any substantive details on precisely how or where the Caliphate is to be restored, nor do they address the most critical questions about who would be qualified to hold the position, how he would accede, the specific functions he would perform, or the procedures by which such functions would be fulfilled. Meanwhile, in the twenty-first century, the question of reviving the Caliphate is situated within larger postmodern discourses on the role of religion in public life and the challenges of globalization and plurality. If the history of the theory as outlined above is any indication, contemporary theories of the Caliphate will have to grapple with the exigencies of Muslims living in a dynamic world.

BIBLIOGRAPHY

Primary Sources

ʿAbd al-Rāziq, ʿAlī. "The Problem of Caliphate." Excerpt from *al-Islām wa-usūl al-ḥukm*; translated by Kamran Talattof. In *Contemporary Debates in Islam: An Anthology of Modernist and Fundamentalist Thought*, edited by Mansoor Moaddel and Kamran Talattof, pp. 95–100. New York: St. Martin's, 2000.

ʿĀlī, Muṣṭafā. *Mustafā Ali's Counsel for Sultans of 1581.* Edited and translated by Andreas Tietze. 2 vols. Vienna: Verlag der Österreichischen Akademie der Wissenschaften, 1979–1982.

Ibn Khaldūn, ʿAbd al-Raḥmān. *The Muqaddimah: An Introduction to History.* Translated by Franz Rosenthal. Abridged ed. edited by N. J. Dawood. Princeton, N.J.: Princeton University Press, 1969.

Ibn al-Muqaffaʿ. "Al-Risālah fī al-ṣaḥābah." In *Rasāʾil al-bulaghāʾ*. Edited by Muḥammad Kurd ʿAlī. Cairo: Lajnat al-Taʾlīf wa-al-Tarjamah wa-al-Nashr, 1946.

Kepel, Gilles, and Jean-Pierre Milelli. *Al Qaeda in Its Own Words.* Translated by Pascale Ghazaleh. Cambridge, Mass.: Belknap Press of Harvard University Press, 2008.

Māwardī, al-. *The Ordinances of Government: Al-Aḥkām al-sulṭāniyya wʾal-wilāyāt al-dīniyya.* Translated by Wafaa H. Wahba. Reading, U.K.: Garnet, 1996.

Secondary Sources

Black, Antony. *The History of Islamic Political Thought: From the Prophet to the Present.* New York: Routledge, 2001.

Crone, Patricia, and Martin Hinds. *God's Caliph: Religious Authority in the First Centuries of Islam.* Cambridge, U.K.: Cambridge University Press, 1986.

De Gifis, Adrian. "The Theory of Virtuous Leadership in the Works of al-Jāḥiẓ: An Analysis of the Depictions of ʿAlī ibn Abī Ṭālib." Ph.D. diss., University of Chicago, 2010.

Enayat, Hamid. *Modern Islamic Political Thought.* London: I. B. Tauris, 2005.

Hakim, Avraham. "ʿUmar b. al-Khaṭṭāb and the Title *Khalīfat Allāh*: A Textual Analysis." *Jerusalem Studies in Arabic and Islam* 30 (2005): 207–230.

Qāḍī, Wadād al-. "ʿAbd al-Hamid al-Katib (c. 689–750)." In *Arabic Literary Culture, 500–925*, edited by Michael Cooperson and Shawkat M. Toorawa, 3–11. Dictionary of Literary Biography 311. Detroit: Thomson Gale, 2005.

Qāḍī, Wadād al-. "The Term 'Khalīfa' in Early Exegetical Literature." *Die Welt des Islams* 28 (1988): 392–411.

Rubin, Uri. "Prophets and Caliphs: The Biblical Foundations of the Umayyad Authority." In *Method and Theory in the Study of Islamic Origins*, edited by Herbert Berg, 73–99. Leiden, Netherlands: Brill, 2003.

Shahin, Aram. "Struggling for Communitas: Arabian Political Thought in the Great Century of Change (c. 500–c. 600 AD)." 5 vols. Ph.D. diss., University of Chicago, 2009.

Taji-Farouki, Suha. *A Fundamental Quest: Hizb al-Tahrir and the Search for the Islamic Caliphate.* London: Grey Seal, 1996.

Taji-Farouki, Suha. "Islamists and the Threat of *Jihad*: Hizb al-Tahrir and al-Muhajiroun on Israel and the Jews." *Middle Eastern Studies* 36 (2000): 21–46.

Wegner, Mark. "Islamic Government: The Medieval Sunni Islamic Theory of the Caliphate and the Debate over the Revival of the Caliphate in Egypt, 1924–1926." Ph.D. diss., University of Chicago, 2001.

ADRIAN DE GIFIS

CAPITULATIONS. A system of commercial and legal privileges granted by the Ottoman ruler (or one of his provincial governors) to European citizens, supplemented and renewed by each new ruler in Constantinople. Though the Sublime Porte issued the Capitulations in the form of unilateral edicts, they were treated as irrevocable treaties by the European powers that benefited from them. Yet the fact that they were decreed rather than agreed upon meant that they were rarely reciprocal.

The Ottomans did not freely negotiate the first of these pledges; when they conquered Egypt in 1517, the caliph agreed to uphold the Treaty of

Capitulations already signed between the Mamlūks and the French over fifteen years earlier. Soon, however, the Ottomans were entering into similar conventions. In 1535, Caliph Süleyman the Magnificent permitted the subjects of King Francis I of France to trade throughout the Caliphate without incurring extra dues in addition to those paid by Muslim subjects. The legal privileges bestowed gave the Franks rights of residence, travel, and work; accepted the extraterritorial jurisdiction of French consular courts in cases involving French citizens; and obliged Ottoman authorities to enforce their rulings; in addition, France was allowed to act as guardian over Christian holy sites, in effect turning these into French protectorates, as well as allowing Catholic missionaries to journey across Muslim lands. The goal of this first installment of Capitulations was to furnish an Franco-Ottoman alliance to undermine European efforts to encircle the capital of the Caliphate on the Mediterranean. The extent of the concessions, however, created the precedent that Muslim rulers were ready to compromise their sovereignty for protection. In 1583 similar privileges were extended to Elizabeth I, and between 1609 and 1612 to the Dutch Republic, then to Austria in 1615, before being offered to the majority of European subjects in 1740. The Ottomans then offered the Russians in 1774 navigation rights and tax exemptions, as well as recognition of the self-avowed role of Catherine the Great as protector of Orthodox subjects.

In the realm of justice, the Ottomans established in 1847 what became known as mixed courts, comprising an equal number of Islamic and European judges, to try civil or criminal cases where at least one of the plaintiffs or defendants was European. The court procedures, however, were entirely based on European positive law rather than the *Sharīʿah*. A new commercial code was promulgated in 1850, followed by a criminal one the following year, introducing European laws into the main canons of Ottoman justice, and setting the first historical precedent of Muslims accepting governance by legal systems other than their own. This was later adopted in 1875 by the khedive Ismāʿīl of Egypt, and in less than a decade became so prominent that the British extended the application of positive laws to Muslim subjects themselves through so-called Native Courts, established in 1883, a year after its occupation of Egypt. These legal concessions were officially justified by the wide differences in Islamic and Western laws and customs, though in reality they reflected increased dominance of European powers in the political and economic life of the Ottoman Empire.

As corruption plagued the Sublime Porte, capitulations were granted by courtiers who wanted to enrich themselves and enhance their status in the eyes of the ruler. Adding to the divisiveness and chaos, privileged foreigners, especially the French and British, carried on their rivalries within the Caliphate securing native allies, lobbying for contradictory legislations, and undercutting each other. By the time of the Tanzimat (1839–1876), foreign consuls, interpreting the Capitulations in the broadest possible terms, became power centers in their own right, intervening in political organization, overruling laws, and making demands in the name of Christian minorities.

In that sense, the Capitulations can be said to have opened the door to foreign domination of the Ottoman state, and eventually its overthrow. Although Constantinople strove to retract many of these concessions after the Paris Congress of 1856, the Capitulations survived until the final days of Ottoman rule. When the Treaty of Lausanne abolished them in 1923, the new Turkish Republic was on its way to adopting a Western-style secular constitution that did not impart these rights to Europeans. The last remaining Capitulations in the Muslim world were abolished in Egypt as late as 1949, though the decision to revoke them was stipulated in the Anglo-Egyptian Treaty of 1936 and the 1937 Montreux Convention Regarding the Abolition of Capitulations in Egypt. Egypt's new National Courts did not return to ruling in accordance with the *Sharīʿah* but rather in light of the positive laws first introduced for trying foreigners.

BIBLIOGRAPHY

Ahmad, Feroz. "Ottoman Perceptions of the Capitulations, 1800–1914." *Journal of Islamic Studies* 11, no. 1 (2000): 1–20.

Angell, James B. "The Turkish Capitulations." *American Historical Review* 6, no. 2 (1901): 254–259.

Finkel, Caroline. *Osman's Dream: The History of the Ottoman Empire, 1300–1923*. New York: Basic Books, 2006.

Kinross, Patrick Balfour. *The Ottoman Centuries: The Rise and Fall of the Turkish Empire*. New York: William Morrow, 1977.

Ravndal, G. Bie. *The Origin of the Capitulations and of the Consular Institution*. Washington, D.C.: Government Printing Office, 1921.

Scott, James Harry. *The Law Affecting Foreigners in Egypt*. Rev. ed. Edinburgh: William Green and Sons, 1908.

HAZEM KANDIL

ÇELEBI, KÂTIP. Kâtip Çelebi (1609–1657) was a prominent Ottoman intellectual of the seventeenth century, the author of important works on history, geography, and bibliography. He was also known as Ḥājjī Khalīfah (Hacı Kalfa) to the rulers and officials because of his posts in the Ottoman bureaucracy.

Born Muṣṭafā ibn ʿAbd Allāh in 1609 in Istanbul, Çelebi received private lessons from a number of teachers during his early years. He then served in clerical positions in the army as his father's apprentice and in later years participated in several campaigns. At the same time, he developed his scientific training by studying with the leading Ottoman scholars of his time, such as Kadızâde Meḥmed, who was one of the most controversial figures of Ottoman history and had a great influence on him, and Aʾrec Muṣṭafā Efendī, whom he mentioned with great admiration and respect. After having participated in the Revan campaign in 1634–1635, he devoted himself only to scientific studies and writing, spending the greater part of two inheritances purchasing books. He died suddenly in 1657 in Istanbul, at age forty-eight, in the midst of the most productive period of his life.

Kâtip Çelebi was such a prolific writer that he has been described as the "Ottoman Suyūṭī," a reference to the equally prolific fifteenth-century Egyptian writer Jalāl al-Dīn al-Suyūṭī. Some of Çelebi's writings remained either unfinished or in draft. The language he preferred for his works is Arabic, in line with the academic tradition of his time, but he also wrote in Turkish to be accessible to ordinary people. He wrote more than twenty books on a wide variety of subjects in the fields of history, geography, biography, bibliography, politics, and others. In addition, he made several translations of European—primarily Latin—works with the help of a French convert, Meḥmed Ihlâsî. These translations served mainly as sources for his major studies. Among Ottoman scholars, Çelebi was one of the first to draw from Western scientific sources. In turn, some of his works have been wholly or partially translated into European languages.

The works that made him well known in both Muslim and Western circles are *Kashf al-ẓunūn*, *Cihânnümâ*, and *Mīzān al-ḥaqq*. *Kashf al-ẓunūn* is a bibliographical dictionary in Arabic, listing some 14,500 book titles, and is an essential reference in classical Islamic literature. The *Cihânnümâ* is a book on geography written in Turkish in two versions. The first version followed the classical Islamic texts on geography and cosmology and remained incomplete because, at the time, Çelebi lacked sufficient information about Europe and the Western Hemisphere. When he learned about these places from Western sources, he wrote a second version with different content and format. Unfortunately, this version also remained unfinished at the time of his death. *Mīzān al-ḥaqq* is Çelebi's last and most widely read work. Written in Turkish, it deals with the religious controversies between the Kadızâde movement and the dervishes of Khalwatī (Halveti) order. Çelebi tries in the *Mizan* to find a middle way and to prevent serious conflicts between the two sides.

Kâtip Çelebi lived in an era when the Ottoman Empire had reached its maximum growth and was beginning its slow decline. As a bureaucrat, Çelebi could not remain indifferent to the problems of his time. His scholarship has a clearly pragmatic and instrumental, rather than purely academic, character. For instance, he studied history because he viewed it as a means to learn from the mistakes of the past. Çelebi was deeply influenced by Ibn Khaldūn's cyclical theory of history and viewed the Ottoman Empire as having reached Ibn Khaldūn's stage of decline. But Çelebi thought the decline could be reversed or slowed by proper ameliorative measures by the state, most importantly the reform of the education system.

BIBLIOGRAPHY

Çelebi, Kâtip. *The Balance of the Truth*. Translated by G. L. Lewis. London: Allen & Unwin, 1957. English translation of Çelebi's *Mīzān al-ḥaqq*.

Gökyay, Orhan Şaik. "Kātib Čelebi." In *Encyclopaedia of Islam*, edited by H. A. R. Gibb, vol. 4, pp. 760–762. 2d ed. Leiden, Netherlands: E. J. Brill, 1978.

Gökyay, Orhan Şaik. "Kâtib Çelebi." In *Türkiye Diyanet Vakfı İslâm Ansiklopedisi*, vol. 25, pp. 36–40. Ankara: Türkiye Diyanet Vakfı, 2002.

KADIR GÖMBEYAZ

CHARITY. Every civilization esteems the principle of altruism. The essence of charity may be thought of as a bodily act, such as reaching out with a hand to a traveler in distress, or, in the Islamic tradition, even smiling at a neighbor. Yet, just as these minimal gestures may be ambiguous, so all acts of charity imply an inequality between benefactor and recipient. This opens the way to political activity as soon as actions coalesce into institutions.

All ulama and Islamic intellectuals agree on the vital importance of charity. The Christian concept of charitable action bears connotations of spiritual love that are absent in the Qurʾānic terms *zakāt* and *ṣadaqa*. *Zakāt* bears lexical connotations of both purity and growth. The meaning is taken to be that, by giving up part of one's wealth, one purifies that which remains, and also oneself—through a restraint on one's selfishness and indifference to others' privations. The recipient, too, is purified—from being jealous of those who are well off. *Ṣadaqa* bears connotations of justice, but is so closely associated with *zakāt* that the key verse in the Qurʾān that defines the purposes of *ṣadaqa* (Q 9:60) is treated as referring also to *zakāt*. *Zakāt* is closely linked in Islamic teaching with prayer, held to be ineffective if the *zakāt* obligation is not met, and with sacrificial offerings.

Whereas *ṣadaqa* refers to optional almsgiving, *zakāt* is a religious obligation—the third of the five pillars (*arkān*) of Islam. Muslims are enjoined to donate about one-fortieth of their assets, after deducting the value of their home and working necessities, to a list of eight categories of people. These are (to borrow the most usual descriptions): the poor; the destitute; those employed to administer the *zakāt*; those who might be converted to Islam, or assist in the cause; slaves; debtors; those committed to the "way of God"; and travelers in need. Theologians have debated the interpretation of this list. For instance, "slaves" may include prisoners of war, or the subjects of oppressive regimes and military occupations. The "way of God" is taken to mean the same as *jihād*, hence as either a spiritual engagement or a more aggressive type of campaign.

The Qur'ān urges Muslims not only to be generous themselves, but to encourage others to be generous. In common with Judaism and Christianity, Islam teaches that all wealth belongs to God. Giving is specially enjoined, and earns special merit, during the holy month of Ramadan, at the end of which a small additional payment to the needy is required (*zakāt al-fiṭr*, "*zakāt* of the breaking of the fast"), which is probably more widely observed in practice today than the annual levy. Alms given discreetly are better than those that are publicized. Those whose wealth is below a fixed threshold are exempt from almsgiving. Despite the importance ascribed in the Qur'ān to *zakāt*, no sanctions to enforce the obligation are specified. *Zakāt* has inspired a body of texts detailing how the original prescriptions should be interpreted in response to economic realities. For instance, mineral rights are subjected to a low rate, and treasure trove to a high rate since it incurs no labor.

Shiite Muslims are required to pay, in addition to *zakāt*, a religious tithe called *khums*, one fifth of residual income, to a *marja'*, or spiritual authority, of their choice, for him to spend as he sees fit. The *khums* is a major source of wealth and power for Shiite leaders.

Zakāt: A Flexible Principle. At various junctures in Islamic history, *zakāt* became a mere vehicle for extracting taxes. We find this in medieval Cairo, before the Mamlūk dynasty decided to make it a private matter for individuals; in the nineteenth-century Ibāḍite imamate of Oman, when it was the only tax levied by government; and in Malaysia in the 1970s, when the state's attempt to monopolize *zakāt* collection was obstructed by peasants. The Taliban in Afghanistan have been reported as levying a *zakāt* tax on the value of truckloads of opium.

These practices are at odds with a long tradition of extolling the importance of *zakāt* as a form of "financial worship." Al-Ghazālī, the great medieval Persian philosopher, wrote a chapter on *zakāt* in his magnum opus *Iḥyā' 'ulūm al-dīn* (Revival of the Religious Sciences), which integrated legal doctrines with a Sufi concern for the spiritual obligations of both donors and recipients. In the very different idiom of the latter part of the twentieth century, the Egyptian Islamist Sayyid Quṭb maintained that *zakāt*, "the outstanding social pillar of Islam," had nothing to do with Western ideas of charity. He reiterated a fundamental tenet of Islam, that whenever an individual is destitute, blame should fall on the community as a whole. *Zakāt* is often presented as the opposite of *ribā*, that is, usurious lending. One of the sources of support for Islamic charities today is the "halalization" by Islamic financial institutions of funds deriving from bank interest into *zakāt* contributions. *Zakāt* is a major support in the standard Islamic case against both capitalism and communism.

Amy Singer (2008) has shown that throughout its history, *zakāt* has always been a malleable principle. Today, no state in the world has it organized as Islamic teaching prescribes. In Saudi Arabia, at one extreme, a Department of Zakat and Income Tax in the Ministry of Finance distributes to quasi-governmental charities such as the Al-Birr Foundation for orphan programs, which are an almost universal feature of Islamic charities. In Oman, at the other extreme, *zakāt* is not institutionalized at all, but left for individuals to elect to pay through informal channels to people they know of. Among Muslim countries, Jordan has found an intermediate solution. A directorate of *zakāt* was established under the Ministry of Religious Affairs, but local committees are also allowed to raise and distribute funds.

However, frequent appeals by Prince Hassan of Jordan and others for the foundation of an international *zakāt* fund, for relief and development within the Muslim world, have not been taken up by Jordan's richer neighbors.

In many conservative mosques throughout the world, alms are still collected locally for the benefit of local Muslims in need. Classical interpretations insisted for the most part that they had to be paid to Muslims only. However, a more liberal interpretation has gained ground: that the first category of "the poor" (*al-fuqarāʾ*) means all the poor. In an industrial country such as the United Kingdom, the dominant view among Muslim donors is that true poverty is not to be found in a country with welfare safety nets, and they accept that all, or most of, their charitable contributions should be disbursed overseas.

A further evolution has been toward the professionalization of Islamic charities and their adaptation to the international aid system. Traditionally, Arab societies were based on networks of kinship and clientelism. The obligation of *nafaqa*, or maintenance—the provision of food, clothing, and shelter to one's dependents—shaded into acts of charity. According to one *ḥadīth*, interceding on behalf of an inferior is "*ṣadaqa* of the tongue," so that whoever makes such an intercession becomes a donor. The Arabic word *wasṭa* ("clout") has equivalents in every language, and the importance of the endowed trust, *waqf*, in Muslim history demonstrates the strength in Islam of the principle of the common good. However, patron-client relations are still particularly strong in conservative Arab societies. A movement in charitable institutions to neutralize them by means of impersonal bureaucratic procedures has been led from Europe and from Europe-influenced jurisdictions such as Jordan.

Politics of the Modern Islamic Charity Sector. Some major Islamic voluntary associations such as the Muhammadiyah in Indonesia and the Jamʿiyya Sharʿiyya in Egypt date back to the early twentieth century. Islamic charities working at an international level began to be founded in the 1970s. They represent a confluence of two historical movements: the general rise and diversification of NGOs and the Islamic resurgence. One of the difficulties holding back most of the Muslim world today is that, for understandable reasons, it is preoccupied by politics. Humanitarian politics is an arena of its own, even without the admixture of disputes concerning some of the world's most troubled regions of conflict. Hence the Islamic charity sector today is steeped in controversy. In Saudi Arabia, for instance, overseas aid charities that were once mighty have been obliged by the authorities to scale down.

Such controversy may be traced back at least as far as the foundation in 1928 of the Muslim Brotherhood, since it has always combined welfare with religious and political goals. One type of Islamic charity today is associated with opposition movements. Whereas Hezbollah in Lebanon controls an important network of Shiite welfare organizations quite openly, the *zakāt* committees in the Palestinian Territories established legal independence for themselves in the 1990s. Though these committees have been criminalized by the governments of Israel and the United States as fronts for Hamas, other analysts contend that they were authentic community-based charities administered by "social coalitions" and responding to needs without discrimination. Unlike many Fatah-based institutions they were not accused of personal malpractice. In 2007, however, soon after the takeover by Hamas of Gaza, the Palestinian Authority and Hamas took control of the *zakāt* committees in the West Bank and Gaza, respectively.

Charges that Islamic charities were acting as conduits for terrorist finance date back to the 1990s. Yet in the 1980s the United States government used its then permissive charity regime to bring support of all kinds to the Afghan mujahideen in the campaign to defeat the Soviet Union. Some Islamic charities continued to support Afghan and Bosnian militants after the United States had reidentified them as terrorists. After the attacks of 9/11, the U.S. government intensified its effort to purge the Islamic charity sector of abuse, publishing an extensive blacklist of "Specially Designated Terrorist Groups," closing down charities in the United States, and punishing their organizers under wide-ranging legislation that treats any kind of "material support" for terrorism as equivalent to terrorism itself. The doctrine that money is "fungible," that is, transferable, means that if a donation is sent to a hospital deemed to be affiliated to a designated organization, this releases funds for that organization to buy bombs—even if it can be shown that the hospital is providing its services according to accepted humanitarian and medical ethics.

The result of these measures, followed by numerous other governments, has been to depress the growth of international Islamic charities. In the United States only a few small ones have survived the purge. In the period following September 2001, the mainstream (non-Muslim) charities in the United States did not react immediately, but by the end of the decade many were coming to the view that draconian counter-terrorist measures might actually have the reverse effect to that intended—preventing aid from reaching beneficiaries, aggravating resentment in the Muslim world, and leaving a vacuum in humanitarian aid for extremist groups to penetrate. Thus in Pakistan, after the Kashmir earthquake in 2005 and the floods in 2010, welfare groups closely associated with the extremist group Lashkar-i-Tayyiba were conspicuous in bringing relief aid, and an audio interview attributed to Osama Bin Laden in 2010 called on Arab governments to do more for flood relief and economic development.

Positive Trends. That this decline of a sector was not inevitable is indicated by the healthy record of Islamic Relief Worldwide, founded in 1984 in Birmingham, England. The supportive policies of the British government and its Charity Commission were helpful, as was the precedent of agencies such as Christian Aid, which had opted thirty years earlier to eschew proselytism and concentrate on relief and development. Islamic Relief decided to embrace the principle of non-discrimination, which opened the door to government funding and cooperation with non-Muslim NGOs such as the Catholic Fund for Overseas Development. Islamic Relief gradually developed the traditions of *zakāt*, *qurbān* (the annual festive sacrifice; Persian *qorbānī*), and Ramadan as fundraising opportunities. In 2005 it was elected a member of the Disasters Emergency Committee, the elite of British overseas aid agencies, which coordinates joint fundraising through the media.

Islamic Relief, like the Aga Khan Foundation, founded in 1967, has set a standard for Islamic charities to engage with current debates about aid and development. But the wider Islamic charity sector has remained conservative and paternalistic, still disconnected from wider trends. The potential of *zakāt* as a vehicle for modern development aid may be retarded by the role that conservative Islamic teaching allocates to the poor as necessary for the spiritual wellbeing of the wealthy. But current interest in the role of faith-based organizations in general, with their access to huge civil society networks, is likely to stimulate innovation.

[*See also* Waqf.]

BIBLIOGRAPHY

Alterman, Jon B., and Karin von Hippel, eds. *Understanding Islamic Charities*. Washington, D.C.: Center for Strategic and International Studies, 2007.

Collection of articles, with an emphasis on the tradeoff between security and humanitarian concerns.

Benthall, Jonathan, and Jérôme Bellion-Jourdan. *The Charitable Crescent: Politics of Aid in the Muslim World.* London: I. B. Tauris, 2003; paper ed., 2009. A general overview.

Islamic Charities Project. http://graduateinstitute.ch/ccdp/religion-politics-islamic-charities.html

Montagu, Caroline. "Civil society and the Voluntary Sector in Saudi-Arabia." *Middle East Journal*, 64 (Winter 2010): 67–83.

al-Qaraḍāwī, Yūsuf. *iqh al-Zakah: A Comparative Study of Zakah, Regulations and Philosophy in the Light of Qur'an and Sunnah.* Eng. trans. Monzer Kahf. Jeddah: Scientific Publishing Centre, King Abdulaziz University, n.d. Exhaustive study by one of the most prominent, though controversial, Sunni religious authorities. Freely downloadable.

Schaeublin, Emanuel. *Role and Governance of Islamic Charitable Institutions: The West Bank Zakat Committees (1977–2009) in the Local Context.* Geneva: Graduate Institute of International and Development Studies, 2009; also available in Arabic trans. Fieldwork-based enquiry into differing interpretations of the status of the *zakāt* committees. Freely downloadable.

Singer, Amy. *Charity in Islamic Societies.* Cambridge, U.K.: Cambridge University Press, 2008. Valuable historical overview.

Zysow, Aron. "Zakāt," in *Encyclopaedia of Islam*, vol. 11. Leiden: Brill, 1960–2004. Foundational article on the classical law of *zakāt*.

JONATHAN BENTHALL

CHECHNYA. The mountainous northern Caucasus zone is the historic homeland for numerous ethnic groups. For centuries potentially dominant neighbors, be they Christian or Muslim, have viewed the northern Caucasus region as an environment inviting divide-and-rule policies. For most of the twentieth century until the early 1990s, two ethnic groups, the Chechens and the Ingush, whose homelands are bordered to the east by Daghestan and to the west by Ossetia, had special status as Autonomous Soviet Socialist Republics (ASSRs). Both have since attempted to declare full independence from post-Soviet Russian control.

Although the Caucasus became a theater for Russian expansion in the early years of the Romanov Dynasty, the area had been a target even earlier for the Ottoman Turks after their conquest of the Kingdom of Trabzon in 1461. The Ottomans, however, never ruled directly in any part of the Caucasus. Russian pressure on the Caucasus became serious when Peter the Great took Derbent in Daghestan and Baku in the 1720s. His contacts with Georgia to the west probably contributed to a significant increase in religious conversion in some mountainous areas of the interior. Mainly Muslim areas, especially Chechnya, thus felt challenged to defend their political and cultural identity.

The first resistance against the Russians in the late eighteenth century, although led by an ethnic Chechen, aimed at uniting peoples of the entire north Caucasus. Although anti-Russian goals were essential to the movement organized by the Naqshbandī Shaykh Manṣūr, his followers were urged to use Islam to forge bonds of equality and justice that could transcend local ethnic identity. Manṣūr's defeat in 1791 made him a martyred champion of Caucasus resistance movements for the next two centuries. One result of this period of turbulence was the Russian decision to intimidate locals by building a fortress at Grozny in 1818.

A second revered Naqshbandī leader, Shaykh Shāmil, was an ethnic Avar from Daghestan. His initial goal was to oppose the Avar ruling elite, but, in the turbulent period of the Crimean War, hopes ran high that he could unite Muslim ethnic groups to oppose the tsar. After Shāmil was defeated in 1859, fear of reprisals led to major Muslim emigration from Chechnya and its neighbors to Ottoman territory.

Several factors spawned sporadic resistance movements up to the end of the tsarist era.

Some drew from the underlying cultural fabric of Chechen identity and the inspiration of Islam—particularly the added influence of the Qādirīyah order "imported" by another Daghestani, Kunta Haji Kishiev. Until his death in prison in 1867 Kishiev took over veterans from Shaykh Shāmil's time and tried to establish more centralized structures in comparison to earlier Naqshbandī methods.

The discovery of oil in areas near Grozny and Baku just before World War I clearly increased tensions just prior to the fall of the tsar. Early in the Russian Revolution the Bolsheviks professed sympathy for a nucleus of Naqshbandī *shaykhs* who had sought a religious monarchy uniting Daghestan and Chechnya. Since the aims of the two movements were obviously incompatible, the Bolsheviks tried, but failed, to co-opt apparently more compromising Qādirīyah elements.

By 1920 an Autonomous Mountain Soviet Socialist Republic, joining seven north Caucasian ethnic groupings, was established. By 1922 the Chechens—followed in 1924 by the Ingush and Ossetes—were given separate *oblast* (autonomous district) status. In 1934 Ingush and Chechens were joined in a single *oblast*. Two years later this administrative creation changed again: three ASSRs, including the Chechen-Ingush ASSR, were declared. Hard reality was, however, reflected in two ways. First, actual control of all the ASSRs was held by a Russian-dominated Executive Committee of the Northern Caucasus. Second, an influx of mainly Russian oil field workers and administrators occurred. Thus, on the eve of World War II, Chechnya faced what amounted to Russian colonization. This was reflected not only economically but culturally; use of the Chechen language declined as a medium of the press and in educational institutions, and Islamic groups were forced underground.

When Soviet forces retreated from the Caucasus in 1942, there was a brief feeling of relief from Russian control. By 1944 and the Soviets' return, however, Chechens suspected of having aided the Nazis—in fact, the population as a whole—paid a high price for having "abandoned" the Russians. Wholesale deportation affected half a million people, and many Islamic sites were destroyed. A policy of denial of the very existence of a Chechen people only began to change under Nikita Khrushchev in the mid-1950s. Early returnees essentially lived as refugees until a decree in 1956 established a four-year schedule for orderly rehabilitation. Even after a financial aid program and restoration of the Chechen-Ingush ASSR in 1957, violence broke out in 1957 over contradictory property claims, then tensions rose over the preponderance of Russians in industrial managerial and educational posts. Moscow's proclamation of a "New Soviet Man" program for Chechnya had mixed results in the 1960s and 1970s. Demands for independence were bound to resurface.

By the time Mikhail Gorbachev led the USSR in the direction of *glasnost* (openness) and *perestroika* (restructuring), underground currents of political and religious activism in Chechnya led to a call for an All-National Congress of the Chechen People in Grozny in 1990. Forty-seven-year-old Dzhokhar Musaevich Dudaev, who had spent over a decade of his youth in exile in Kazakhstan (later rising to a high rank in the Soviet air force), chaired an executive committee charged with redefining Chechnya's status. Dudaev's task was seriously hampered as different tendencies arose in the Ingush-Ossete region, and a separate Ingush Republic was declared. Then, following Gorbachev's removal in 1991, more divisions surfaced between subgroupings in Chechnya. Some aligned with the emergent Islamic Path Party; others were suspected of wanting to keep the local Communist Party in control.

When Boris Yeltsin took control he faced a fait accompli: parliamentary and presidential elections had been held, and Dudaev had been named head of a self-declared Chechen-Ingush Republic. In November 1991 Yeltsin failed to obtain support for a military move to squash the breakaway republic, and—surprisingly—he announced a planned withdrawal of Russian forces. By January 1992 Dudaev became embroiled in, but then removed himself from, contradictory relations with other Caucasus political movements, especially rising levels of violence and confusion in Georgia. Failure of short-lived plans for a joint Chechen-Ingush Republic in June 1992 was only one sign that Dudaev could not build a broader basis for Caucasus regional autonomy. Until 1994, when Yeltsin launched a costly and disastrous invasion of Chechnya, he kept trying to balance the declaration of a Chechen constitution (which avoided any references to ethnic or religious subgroupings) with a competing call from beyond Chechnya for a (pan-Caucasus) Confederation of the Peoples of the Caucasus.

Russia's military intervention between 1994 and 1996 crumbled when they were driven out of Grozny and then harassed by guerrilla forces operating in both the valleys and the mountains. The Russians became desperate and resorted to massive bombardment of Grozny, causing very heavy civilian casualties. Their successful use of a guided missile to kill President Dudaev was followed by a temporary cease-fire in May 1996. This phase of the brutal struggle ended with the Khasavyurt Accord of August 1996. The agreement, essentially recognizing the failure of Russia's military tactics, provided for withdrawal by December. It stipulated that a formal definition of relations should be concluded within five years' time. However, matters appeared to advance more rapidly. After a series of long-demanded internal reforms were concluded—at least on paper—a peace treaty was signed with the Chechen Republic of Ichkeria in May 1997.

Despite attempts by Dudaev's successors to normalize relations, conditions again deteriorated seriously, leading to a second massive military confrontation in August 1999. The breakdown was sparked by cumulative tensions over bombings in Moscow (assumed to have been the work of Chechen terrorists) and an abortive "invasion" of Daghestan by Chechen splinter groups. Early in 2000 Russian forces reversed their failure of 1996, capturing Grozny in May. Direct rule reminiscent of the Soviet period was reimposed. The spread of Russian control of all formal governmental and security agencies during the next five years did not succeed in stamping out resistance groups, who began attacking civilian targets beyond Chechnya's borders. International concern for obvious human rights issues focused on several terrorist initiatives and Russian reactions involving Chechen hostage takers. Heavy losses of innocent lives occurred in a Moscow theater in 2002 and following violent assault tactics used by the Russians in 2004 to free hundreds of hostages held by Chechen terrorists in a school in Beisan (in the Autonomous Republic of North Ossetia-Alania).

In the same year of the Beisan tragedy (in May 2004), the detonation of a large bomb during a celebration at Grozny Dynamo Stadium of Nazi Germany's defeat killed Chechen president Akhmad Kadyrov who—after resisting Russian forces in his capacity as chief mufti during the first Russo-Chechen conflict—had shifted his loyalty and supported Moscow during the Second Chechen War. Before his violent death, Kadyrov had fostered initiatives to reduce the influence of radical Islam. Kadyrov was replaced by another Russian protégé, Chechen interior minister Alu Alkhanov, who assumed the presidency following very controversial elections. Soon the stage was set for Kadyrov's son Ramzan to challenge, from his position as prime minister, Alkhanov's tenuous leadership. Ramzan Kadyrov's ambitions were aided by his close relations with Russian president Vladimir Putin. Putin's support led to the thirty-one-year-old's ascendancy to the presidency in February 2007.

Ramzan Kadyrov's mode of leadership during the next several years combined continuation of his father's campaign against extremist Islam with strong-arm tactics of repression. Use of private militia forces (dubbed the "Kadyrovtsky") earned President Ramzan Kadyrov the controversial title of "Warrior King of Chechnya."

[*See also* Islam and Politics in Central Asia and the Caucasus; *and* Terrorism.]

BIBLIOGRAPHY

Chechnya Society and Culture Complete Report. Petaluma, Calif.: World Trade, 2010.

Dunlop, John B. *Russia Confronts Chechnya: Roots of a Separatist Conflict*. Cambridge, U.K.: Cambridge University Press, 1998.

Gammer, Moshe. *The Lone Wolf and the Bear: Three Centuries of Chechen Defiance of Russian Rule*. London: Hurst, 2006.

Gilligan, Emma. *Terror in Chechnya: Russia and the Tragedy of Civilians in War*. Princeton, N.J.: Princeton University Press, 2010.

Jaimoukha, Amjad. *The Chechens: A Handbook*. New York: RoutledgeCurzon, 2005.

BYRON D. CANNON

CHINA. Islam in China has been propagated since the seventh century primarily among the people now known as "Hui," but many of the issues confronting them are also relevant to the Turkic- and Indo-European–speaking Muslims on China's Inner Asian frontier. "Hui teaching" (*Hui jiao*) was the term once used in Chinese for Islam in general; it probably derives from an early Chinese rendering of the name for the modern Uighur people. According to the 2000 census of China, the total Muslim population is 20.3 million, including: Hui (9,816,805); Uighur (8,399,393); Kazakh (1,250,458); Dongxiang (513,805); Kirghiz (160,823); Salar (104,503); Tajik (41,028); Uzbek (14,502); Bonan (16,505); and Tatar (4,890). The Hui speak mainly Sino-Tibetan languages; Turkic-language speakers include the Uighur, Kazakh, Kirghiz, Uzbek, Salar, and Tatar; combined Turkic-Mongolian speakers include the Dongxiang and Bonan, concentrated in Gansu's mountainous Hexi Corridor; and the Tajik speak an Iranian language. The Chinese census registered people by nationality, not by religious affiliation, so the actual number of Muslims is still unknown, and the interpretation and use of all population figures are clearly influenced by politics. Nevertheless, there are few Han converts to Islam and perhaps even fewer members of the ten nationalities listed above who would choose to disavow Islam. Muslim identity in China can best be described as ethno-religious, because history, ethnicity, and state nationality policy have left an indelible mark on contemporary Muslim identity; it is almost impossible to discuss Islam without reference to ethnic and national identity.

The Pre-Communist Era. As the result of a succession of Islamic reform movements that have swept across China since the fifteenth century, one finds among the Muslims in China today a wide spectrum of Islamic belief. Archaeological discoveries of Islamic artifacts and epigraphy on the southeast coast suggest that the earliest Muslim communities in China were descended from Arab, Persian, Central Asian, and Mongolian Muslim merchants, soldiers, and officials who settled first along that coast in the seventh to tenth centuries; there followed larger migrations to the north from Central Asia under the Mongol Yuan dynasty in the thirteenth and fourteenth centuries, followed by intermarriage with the local Chinese populations and the raising of their children as Muslims. Practicing Ḥanafī Sunnī Islam and residing in independent small communities clustered around a central mosque, these relatively isolated Islamic village and urban communities interacted via trading networks and their recognition of membership in the wider Islamic *ummah*. Each was headed by an *ahong* (from Persian *ākhūnd*) or *imām* who was invited to teach on a more or less temporary basis.

Sufism began to make a substantial impact in China proper in the late seventeenth century, arriving mainly along the Central Asian trade routes with saintly *shaykh*s, both Chinese and foreign, who brought new teachings from the pilgrimage cities. These charismatic teachers and tradesmen established widespread networks and brotherhood associations, most prominently the Naqshbandīyah, Qādirīyah, and Kubrawīyah. The hierarchical organization of these Ṣūfī networks helped to mobilize large numbers of Hui during economic and political crises in the seventeenth to nineteenth centuries, assisting widespread Muslim-led rebellions and resistance movements against late Ming and Qing imperial rule in Yunnan, Shanxi, Gansu, and Xinjiang. The 1912 Nationalist revolution allowed further autonomy in regions of Muslim concentration in the northwest, and wide areas came under virtual control by Muslim warlords, leading to frequent intra-Muslim and Muslim-Han conflicts until the eventual Communist victory led to the reassertion of central control. In the late nineteenth and early twentieth centuries, Wahhābī-inspired reform movements known as the Yihewani (from Arabic *ikhwān*, "brothers"), and later the Salafīyah, rose to popularity under Nationalist and warlord sponsorship; they were noted for their criticism of traditionalist Islam as too acculturated to Chinese practices and of Sufism as too attached to the veneration of saints and their tombs.

The Communist Era. Many Muslims supported the early communist call for equity, autonomy, freedom of religion, and recognized nationality status and were active in the early establishment of the People's Republic, but they became disenchanted by growing criticism of their religious practice during several radical periods in the People's Republic of China beginning in 1957. During the Cultural Revolution (1966–1976), Muslims became the focus of antireligious and antiethnic nationalist criticism, leading to widespread persecutions, mosque closings, and at least one massacre of a thousand Hui following a 1975 uprising in Yunnan province. Since Deng Xiaoping's post-1978 reforms, Muslims have sought to take advantage of liberalized economic and religious policies while keeping a watchful eye on the swinging pendulum of Chinese radical politics. In the post–11 September 2001 environment, Muslims in China have become more engaged in international affairs and connected with global Islamic movements. There are now more mosques open in China than there were before 1949, including a large number of exclusively women's mosques led by women *ahong* in north China, and Muslims travel frequently on the *ḥajj* to Mecca and engage in cross-border trade with coreligionists in Central Asia, the Middle East, and Southeast Asia.

Increasing Muslim political activism on a national scale and the rapid response of the state indicate the growing importance Beijing places on issues related to Muslims. In 1986 Uighurs in Xinjiang marched through the streets of Ürümqi protesting a wide range of issues, including the environmental degradation of the Zungharian plain, nuclear testing in the Taklimakan, increased Han immigration to Xinjiang, and ethnic insults at Xinjiang University. Muslims throughout China protested the publication of the Chinese book *Sexual Customs* in May 1989 and of a children's book in October 1993 that portrayed Muslims—particularly their proscription of pork, which Mao once called "China's greatest national treasure"—in derogatory fashion. In each case the government responded promptly, meeting many of the Muslim demands, condemning the publications, arresting the authors, and closing down the printing houses. Uighur Muslim activism in China peaked in the late 1990s; there has been little organized resistance domestically since 2001, but there has been increased activism internationally among Uighur expatriate communities.

Cross-border trade between Xinjiang and Central Asia has grown greatly since the independence of the Central Asian states, especially with the reopening in 1991 of the Eurasian Railroad linking Ürümqi and Alma-Ata with markets in China and eastern Europe. Overland travel between Xinjiang and Pakistan, Tajikistan, Kyrgyzstan, and Kazakhstan has also increased dramatically with the relaxation of travel restrictions based on Hu Jintao's prioritization of trade over security interests in the area. The government's policy of seeking to buy support through stimulating the local economy seemed to be working as of 2007, as income levels in Xinjiang are often far higher than those across the border, but increased Han migration to participate in the region's lucrative oil and mining industries continues to exacerbate ethnic tensions. Muslim areas in northern and central China continue to be left behind, as China's rapid economic growth expands unevenly, enriching the southern coastal areas far more than the interior.

While further restricting Islamic freedoms in the border regions, the state has become more keenly aware of the importance foreign Muslim governments place on China's treatment of its Muslim minorities as a factor in China's lucrative trade and military agreements. The establishment of full diplomatic ties with Saudi Arabia in 1991 and increasing military and technical trade with Middle Eastern Muslim states enhances the economic and political salience of China's treatment of its Muslim minority. The increased transnationalism of China's Muslims will be an important factor in their ethnic expression and in their accommodation to Chinese culture and state authority.

BIBLIOGRAPHY

Bai Shouyi, ed. *Huimin qiyi*. 4 vols. Shanghai: Shenzhouguo Guangshe, 1953.

Ben-Dor Benite, Zvi. *The Dao of Muhammad: A Cultural History of Muslims in Late Imperial China*. Harvard East Asian Monographs 248. Cambridge, Mass.: Harvard University Asia Center, 2005.

Broomhall, Marshall. *Islam in China: A Neglected Problem*. Philadelphia: China Inland Mission, 1910.

Chen Dasheng, ed. *Islamic Inscriptions in Quanzhou*. Translated by Chen Enming. Yinchuan, China: Ningxia Renmin Chubanshe, 1984.

Forbes, Andrew D. W. *Warlords and Muslims in Chinese Central Asia: A Political History of Republican Sinkiang, 1911–1949*. Cambridge, U.K.: Cambridge University Press, 1986.

Gillette, Maris Boyd. *Between Mecca and Beijing: Modernization and Consumption among Urban Chinese Muslims*. Stanford, Calif.: Stanford University Press, 2002.

Gladney, Dru C. *Dislocating China: Reflections on Muslims, Minorities, and Other Subaltern Subjects*. Chicago: University of Chicago Press, 2004.

Gladney, Dru C. *Muslim Chinese: Ethnic Nationalism in the People's Republic*. Cambridge, Mass.: Council on East Asian Studies, Harvard University, 1991.

Israeli, Raphael, and Lyn Gorman. *Islam in China: A Critical Bibliography*. Westport, Conn.: Greenwood, 1994.

Jaschok, Maria, and Shui Jingjun. *The History of Women's Mosques in Chinese Islam: A Mosque of Their Own*. London: Curzon, 2001.

Leslie, Donald Daniel. *Islam in Traditional China: A Short History to 1800*. Canberra, Australia: Canberra College of Advanced Education, 1986.

Lipman, Jonathan N. *Familiar Strangers: A History of Muslims in Northwest China*. Seattle: University of Washington Press, 1997.

Ma Tong. *Zhongguo yisilan jiaopai yu menhuan zhidu shilue*. Yinchuan, China: Ningxia Renmin Chubanshe, 1983.

Millward, James A. *Eurasian Crossroads: A History of Xinjiang*. New York: Columbia University Press, 2007.

Perdue, Peter C. *China Marches West: The Qing Conquest of Central Eurasia*. Cambridge, Mass.: Belknap Press of Harvard University Press, 2005.

Pillsbury, Barbara. "Cohesion and Cleavage in a Chinese Muslim Minority." Ph.D. diss., Columbia University, 1973.

DRU C. GLADNEY

CHIRĀGH ʿALĪ. Chirāgh ʿAlī (1844–1895) was an Indian modernist author who came to prominence as a supporter of Sir Sayyid Aḥmad Khān and the Aligarh movement. He came from a Kashmiri family settled in the United Provinces and served the British administration in North India in various judicial and revenue positions. In 1877, thanks to the recommendation of Sir Sayyid, he entered the service of the *niẓām* of Hyderabad. There he rose to the position of revenue and political secretary and was known by the title Nawāb ʿĀzam Yār Jang.

Chirāgh ʿAlī agreed with Sir Sayyid that there could be no conflict between the word of God as contained in the Qurʾān and the work of God as expounded in modern science. His writings are modernist apologetics designed to refute missionary and orientalist criticisms of Islam as incapable of reform. Among his works are *The Proposed Political, Constitutional and Legal Reforms in the Ottoman Empire and Other Mohammedan States* (1883) and *A Critical Exposition of the Popular Jihad* (1885). He also wrote frequently in Sir Sayyid's journal of Muslim social reform, *Tahdhīb al-Akhlāq* (The Muslim Reformer), published in Aligarh.

Chirāgh ʿAlī maintained that Islam inculcated no set political or social system and that the schools of Islamic law, as human institutions, were subject to revision. Muslim governments were in no way theocratic, nor did *jihād* imply a forcible expansion of the faith. On the contrary, all the Prophet's wars were defensive in nature. Chirāgh ʿAlī, as a modernist, based his ideas on the teachings of the Qurʾān; all other sources of law, including *ḥadīth*, were subject to interpretation. He was particularly dismissive of the founders of the classical schools of Islamic law, whose writings, he felt, reflected the needs of their times but had little applicability to the modern age.

Chirāgh ʿAlī's writings were influential among Western-educated Muslims of the Aligarh school in the late nineteenth and early twentieth centuries. He championed education for women and was critical of polygamy and divorce. He also argued that slavery was incompatible with the true spirit of Islam. His favorable discussion of political reforms in the Ottoman Empire was a factor, albeit a minor one, in the Indian Muslims' growing sympathy for Turkey in the period before World War I.

[*See also* Aḥmad Khān, Sayyid.]

BIBLIOGRAPHY

Kurzman, Charles, ed. *Modernist Islam, 1840–1940: A Sourcebook.* New York: Oxford University Press, 2002.

Moaddel, Mansoor, and Kamran Talattof. *Contemporary Debates in Islam: An Anthology of Modernist and Fundamentalist Thought.* New York: St. Martin's, 2000.

GAIL MINAULT

CITIZENSHIP. The concept and form of citizenship evolved gradually from the time of the Greek city-state to the formation of nation-states in the nineteenth century. The modern concept of citizenship within democratic principles allows the citizen to participate in public decisions and imposes various duties, most commonly paying taxes and serving in the military. In modern democracies, sovereignty belongs to the citizens of a nation as defined by its laws.

Early Islam. In early Islamic history the caliph/sultan ruled over the Islamic community in accordance with *Sharīʿah* (Islamic law) based on the

Qurʾān and the sunnah (the traditions of the Prophet Muḥammad).

In principle, the members of the Islamic community, the *ummah*, were equal, without deference to race, color, or ethnic background. Also, membership in the *ummah* had no geographical boundaries. In practice, however, during the rule of the Umayyad dynasty (661–750 CE), for instance, more than one class emerged. The *mawālī* (sing. *mawlā*), or Muslims who were non-Arabs or not full members by descent of an Arab tribe, did not receive equal economic and social benefits and were not fully accepted by the Umayyad aristocracy. Non-Muslims living in *dār al-Islām* (territories under Islamic rule) had protected but unequal status based on the concept of the *dhimmī*, by which *ahl al-kitāb* (people of the book: Jews and Christians) were permitted freedom of religious worship, security of property and person, and protection against external threats in exchange for recognition of the dominion of Islamic rule and payment of a poll tax (*jizyah*).

During the rule of the ʿAbbāsid caliphs (750–1258), the practical social order of the Muslim *ummah* was central to the philosophy of the state. Nevertheless, Muslim philosophers and jurists, such as al-Fārābī (d. 950) and al-Māwardī (d. 1058), raised fundamental questions regarding the relations between the ruler and the ruled and their mutual duties. In his *Al-madīnah al-fāḍilah* (The Virtuous City), al-Fārābī set the standards by which states should be judged. For al-Fārābī, the duty of the state is to put aside funds for education, taking a portion from the alms tax (*zakāt*) and land tax (*kharāj*), as well as other state resources. Later, during the Mamlūk period, Ibn Taymīyah (1263–1328) listed the criteria for "just" rulers and the political and social obligations of the community: respectability, intelligence, judgment, and courage. The position of the ruler and the subjects were placed in an Islamic framework as interpreted by the *ʿulamāʾ*. Ibn Taymīyah stated that the imam must be obeyed at all costs since he held political power, whether he was just or unjust, a ruling that was supported by the *ʿulamāʾ*.

The Ottoman Empire. In the Ottoman Empire, from the mid-fifteenth century on, the population was organized into *millets*, legally recognized religious-communal organizations. The four *millets*, Greek Orthodox, Armenian, Jewish, and Muslim, were differentiated according to their religious affiliations and not according to their ethnic and linguistic differences. With privileges granted by the ruler, the *millets* assumed several social and economic responsibilities. The leaders of the *millets* also had extensive civil authority over the membership, including matters related to internal organization, education, and personal status.

The *millet* system continued long into the nineteenth century (throughout the Tanzimat era). With two major reform edicts in 1839 and 1856, the Ottoman government reaffirmed equality among its subjects and their right to security of life, honor, and property, preconditions to the modern concept of citizenship. Ottoman subjects at this time, however, still identified themselves as members of the *millet*.

Ideas dealing with equality of Muslim and non-Muslim subjects and the protection of rights in return for specific obligations to the state were expressed by some Muslim intellectuals, such as Rifāʿah Rāfiʿ al-Ṭahṭāwī (d. 1873) and Mehmed Sadık Rifat Pasha (d. 1858). Al-Ṭahṭāwī, in *Manāhij al-albāb al-miṣrīyah fī mabāhij al-ādāb al-ʿaṣrīyah* (Methods for Egyptian Minds on the Joys of Modern Manners), outlined the citizens' duties toward their country (Egypt) as well as their rights. The chief duty was patriotism. As a result, citizens had a right to political education, since they were required to love their country and obey its laws. Al-Ṭahṭāwī assigned an active role to the members of the political community.

Sadık Rifat Pasha, in his monumental book *Müntehabat-ı âsar* (Selections of Works), made frequent use of the term *halk* (the people) and discussed the rights of subjects to liberty.

During the nineteenth century, various nationalist tendencies emerged in the Ottoman territories. In 1869, the Ottoman government, in its efforts to provide a viable ideology for the unity of the empire and to curb the interference of European powers and Russia in its domestic affairs, issued the law of nationality and naturalization. Article 1 of the law stated that all people born to an Ottoman father are Ottoman subjects. Article 2 provided that all people born in Ottoman territories to parents of foreign nationality can, at the age of maturity, claim Ottoman nationality.

This was a landmark in the development of the concept and form of citizenship among Muslims, as the law provided an updated legal concept regarding the status of Ottoman subjects. The latter were no longer merely members of a *millet* but Ottoman nationals. A person's relation to the state was now more direct, and his or her obligations toward it went beyond those to a *millet*. The central government, however, did assume certain social and economic responsibilities that previously had fallen under the purview of the *millet* administrations. Moreover, by recognizing the right of individuals born in the empire—even to foreign parents—to become Ottoman subjects, the Sublime Porte came closer to establishing a modern concept of citizenship based on the territorial boundaries of nation-states.

During the remainder of the nineteenth century, Ottoman intellectuals, notably Namık Kemal (1840–1888), discussed the nature of the political system and the individual's role within it. They recognized certain natural rights for citizens and argued for their preservation, even if few voiced their disapproval of the genocide perpetrated against Ottoman citizens, both Armenians and Greeks, living within the empire. Within the Western liberal political tradition, these writers emphasized the "people's will" and the people's rights to exercise sovereignty. At the beginning of the twentieth century, similar arguments were heard among Egyptian intellectuals, the nationalist Young Tunisians, and members of the Young Algeria movement.

The Modern Muslim State. From the early decades of the twentieth century, as modern nation-states emerged among Muslim populations, governments defined the rights and duties of their citizens. In Turkey, the National Assembly, established in 1920 during the war of independence by the nationalist government under Mustafa Kemal (later Atatürk), declared that "sovereignty unconditionally belongs to the people," thus establishing de facto a republic before its official declaration in 1923. The removal of the last Ottoman sultan in 1922 and the abolition of the caliphate in 1924 eliminated any legal basis for a challenge to a people's exercise of political will. The extension of full franchise to women in 1934, permitting them to vote and stand for election and giving them full political rights and duties, meant that now all Turkish citizens could become active participants in the political process.

With the 1936 Anglo-Egyptian Treaty, which recognized Egypt's independence, fresh interpretations of citizenship emerged. As other Muslim countries gained their independence—for instance, Indonesia (1945), Transjordan (1946), Libya (1951), Tunisia and Morocco (1956), and Algeria (1962)—each country established its own criteria for citizenship, based on its own political ideology, historical experience, and social customs. Although some countries provided their citizens, men and women, Muslim and non-Muslim, with extensive political and social rights (e.g., Egypt, Iraq, and Indonesia), others (e.g., Kuwait and Saudi Arabia) limited the privileges of citizenship. In Kuwait, two classes of citizenship are still in effect: first-class citizens, whose forebears lived in

Kuwait before 1922; and second-class citizens, who belong to families that came to Kuwait between 1922 and 1945. Those who arrived after 1945 are not considered citizens, while an entire community, the Bedouin, are simply "stateless" even though most were born in the shaykhdom. In Saudi Arabia, women, who are considered citizens, remain disenfranchised, although new laws are gradually granting previously denied privileges, including education. Saudi female attorneys, for example, earned the right to appear in court for the first time in 2010, though society remains segregated. Women's full exercise of citizenship in many countries is further constrained by unequal access to resources, restrictions on travel without the permission of *maḥrams* (fathers, husbands, or male relatives), and patriarchal legal statutes that regulate marriage, divorce, child custody, and inheritance.

While legal citizenship in Muslim countries is now defined with reference to national boundaries rather than membership in the *ummah*, the rise of political Islam in the latter part of the twentieth century and accompanying calls for application of Islamic law has renewed discussion of the status of non-Muslims in Islamic societies. Many Islamists have attempted to articulate modern conceptions of citizenship based on Islamic values. Some thinkers associated with the *wasaṭīyah* (moderate) trend have argued that the historical institution of *dhimmī* is no longer a suitable basis for citizenship and that non-Muslims should enjoy all the rights and duties of Muslims in contemporary society. In the words of the Egyptian Islamist Fahmī Huwaydī, non-Muslim members of Islamic societies should be considered *muwāṭinūn lā dhimmīyūn* (citizens, not *dhimmī*s). Other moderate Islamists, such as Muḥammad Salīm al-ʿAwwā and Ṭāriq al-Bishrī, maintain that non-Muslims can hold any office in society—except those that are specifically religious—including the office of president. At the same time, the boldness of these positions is tempered by the authors' stated assumption that non-Muslims will not be elected head of state in Muslim-majority countries and by their ambiguity regarding the status of some non-Muslim groups, such as Bahāʾīs, as well as of apostates.

BIBLIOGRAPHY

Baker, Raymond William. *Islam without Fear: Egypt and the New Islamists*. Cambridge, Mass.: Harvard University Press, 2003.

Botman, Selma. *Engendering Citizenship in Egypt*. New York: Columbia University Press, 1999.

Butenschøn, Nils A., Uri Davis, and Manuel Hassassian, eds. *Citizenship and the State in the Middle East: Approaches and Applications*. Syracuse, N.Y.: Syracuse University Press, 2000.

Davison, Roderic. *Reform in the Ottoman Empire, 1856–1876*. Princeton, N.J.: Princeton University Press, 1963.

Esposito, John L., and John O. Voll. *Islam and Democracy*. New York: Oxford University Press, 1996.

Ghannouchi, Rashid al-. *The Right to Nationality Status of Non-Muslim Citizens in a Muslim Nation*. Translated by M. A. El Erian. Springfield, Va.: Islamic Foundation of America, 1990.

Hourani, Albert. *Arabic Thought in the Liberal Age, 1798–1939*. London: Oxford University Press, 1962.

Joseph, Suad, ed. *Gender and Citizenship in the Middle East*. Syracuse, N.Y.: Syracuse University Press, 2000.

Lapidus, Ira. *A History of Islamic Societies*. Cambridge, U.K.: Cambridge University Press, 1988.

March, Andrew F. *Islam and Liberal Citizenship: The Search for an Overlapping Consensus*. New York: Oxford University Press, 2009.

Mardin, Şerif. *The Genesis of Young Ottoman Thought: A Study in the Modernization of Turkish Political Ideas*. Princeton, N.J.: Princeton University Press, 1962.

Qaradawi, Yusuf al-. *Non-Muslims in the Islamic Society*. Translated by Khalil Muhammad Hamad and Sayed Mahboob Ali Shah. Indianapolis, Ind.: American Trust, 2005.

Stephanous, Andrea Zaki. *Political Islam, Citizenship, and Minorities: The Future of Arab Christians in the*

Islamic Middle East. Lanham, Md.: University Press of America, 2010.

A. ÜNER TURGAY
Updated by MICHAELLE BROWERS
and JOSEPH A. KÉCHICHIAN

CIVILIZATION. The genius of Islamic civilization is twofold. First, it was founded on a literary and religious tradition grounded in the Arabic language. At the same time, it expanded through the confident tolerance and integration of far-flung, diverse cultures. The confident tolerance of Islam, enshrined in religious law, allowed for strategic acceptance of difference and the integration of new and variable political systems and ideas while maintaining core tenets rooted in Arabic. In this way Islam was able to expand outward, integrating different influences and enjoying the benefits of other cultures even as it remained rooted to a solid, inward core. As much as it was grounded in Arabic letters and in the immutable notion of the Qurʾān as an Arabic text at the center of faith, Islamic civilization was, for the first centuries, defined as much by the contributions of nonnative Arabic speakers as by Arabs. In Islam the toleration of non-Muslim Christians, Jews, and Zoroastrians—the *Ahl al Kitaab*, "People of the Book"—was part of its founding creed. This toleration allowed the gradual inclusion of different cultures during and after the Arabic conquests. Even later, as the Arab caliphs lost authority, the ease of conversion to Islam and its flexible ideals of equality for all believers, ideals unsuccessfully challenged by an Arab elite, allowed the integration of militarily powerful peoples such as the Turks and Mongols. This same religious tolerance also allowed for the flowering of sciences, art, and architecture even as the common language of Arabic facilitated the sharing of ideas across the Islamic world. At the same time Arabic maintained roots in the Arabic pre-Islamic times. There was a prohibition on translating the Qurʾān, which was only fully revealed in Arabic; the Arabic language formed the basis of civilizational revival and interchange in lands touched by conquest and conversion.

It would be inaccurate to claim that Islamic civilization was based on temporary, elite political arrangements or even that Islamic civilization could be encapsulated by one particular form of governance in one particular era. Rather, Islamic civilization was a durable and integrated social and political system that persisted over time and often in spite of serious political fragmentation. In this way, Islamic culture can be considered an example of a "civilization" in that it has persisted over a grand scale of time despite various changes in power structures. Although the impetus of *jihād*, was strong, Islamic civilization did not merely "conquer." It united beliefs and cultures, peoples, languages, and rich civilizations across the Middle East, Europe, and Central and South Asia: a union of world-historical importance. Islam made much of Eurasia and North Africa part of an interlocking cultural and civilizational system.

Conversely, even when political systems were weakened by internal divisions, Islamic civilization itself was not easily conquered or overthrown. Its integrative power remained resilient. Over time, most non-Muslim dynasties of predominantly Muslim regions, having first been converted to the civilization, with its attendant benefits in trade and the relative equality of believers under Islamic law, would later convert to the faith. A good example of this was the Ilkhans, the medieval Mongol rulers of Central Asia who, though far superior in military technology, quickly abandoned their traditional religion and converted to Islam. Even in those rare instances when Islam and Islamic social politics was replaced by another faith, as in the Christian conquest of Muslim Spain, some of the cultural and civilizational aspects of Islam persisted for centuries. Arabic vocabulary, for example, still forms a major part of Spanish language and cultural heritage more than five centuries after the conquest of the last Muslim rulers of Granada in 1492.

Origins. Some converted, conquered peoples resisted the influence of Arabic. In a movement called *shuʿubiyya*, prominent Persian speakers claimed that Persia, not Arabia, was the main source of Islamic civilization. Calling for the enforcement of Islamic ideals of equality for all believers, they resisted the privileged status of Arabs in the *ummah*, or community of believers. Despite these important exceptions, Muslims throughout history have looked to Arabia and the region of the Hejaz containing the two holy cities of Mecca and Medina not only as a place of pilgrimage, the yearly *ḥajj*, but as the central well-spring of Islamic cultural heritage.

While the revelation of the Qurʾān to Muḥammad in the seventh century was the most important point in Islamic civilization, Arabic language and culture predates it. In the centuries before Islam, pre-Islamic poets of the so-called *jāhilīyah*, or "age of ignorance" before the revelation of the Qurʾān are revered and memorialized for their profound and evocative use of the language. Even so, the Qurʾān remained the primary reference for Islamic civilization.

Influence of the Qurʾān. Praised as an ideal standard of Arabic writing, the Qurʾān itself insisted on being separate from the work of the poets. For Muslims, their holy book was a unique form of writing revealed by God. As such, it had an impact on civilization and politics even greater than the writings of the famed pre-Islamic poets. Its stories became the basis of literature. Generations of Muslims, both scholars and nonscholars, memorized its beautiful passages. Mere recitation of the words of the Qurʾān was even used to cure illnesses and bring about "*barakah*," or blessing. Its proclamations were elaborated and interpreted for cultural contexts far different from the seventh-century Arabia in which it was revealed. Yet the Qurʾān always maintained a prominence that, by default, elevated Arabic culture and language everywhere Islam spread.

The Qurʾān was compiled and canonized from oral memory and written fragments under the third "rightly guided" caliph, or successor to Muḥammad, ʿUthmān ibn ʿAffān (d. 656). This standardizing of the holy book corresponded with a burst of cultural and civilizational expansion for the caliphate. ʿUthmān's predecessor, ʿUmar (d. 644), not only expanded the Islamic world through the conquest of important cities such as Jerusalem, he enshrined the so-called pact of ʿUmar, outlining the specific limitations and privileges of conquered "People of the Book," who were allowed to continue to worship even as they paid a special poll tax. Many Jews and Copts were treated far better under Muslim than under Byzantine orthodoxy. As Islam solidified its hold over the Middle East and North Africa, many converted for economic and political reasons as much as spiritual ones. Arabic came to slowly replace Greek, Syriac, and, in North Africa and Spain, Berber or Latin as the primary language of speech and government. Arabic also became a language of science, medicine, and high culture as different rival courts around the Islamic world attracted religious scholars, astrologers, poets, and others. Philosophy also flourished as works translated from Greek and Persian later inspired the work of scholars such as al-Fārābī, Ibn Sīnā, and Ibn Rushd—scholars whose work was read widely in medieval Europe. Even in medical texts the Qurʾān and the *ḥadīth*, the saying of the Prophet, inspires scholarship: "Pursue knowledge as far as China." The Qurʾān explicitly encourages interpretation by "men of understanding." It is full of evocative descriptions of the natural world and even a scientific portrayal of human conception. The Qurʾān could be used to encourage, or at least justify, learning and science.

The Golden Age. The Muslim Caliphate was at its strongest politically and economically under the ʿAbbāsid caliphs. The arts and sciences flourished. Architecture, including entire caliphal cities such as Sāmarrāʾ, achieved a new state of grandeur as Islamic architects integrated both classical and Persian influences to create an original, distinctive, decorative style of building. Names such as Hārūn al-Rashīd and al-Maʾmūn still resonate throughout the Muslim world, evoking a time when Islamic civilization seemed to be at the peak of influence and power. Indeed, Baghdad, like the former Umayyad capital, Damascus, became a thriving center of civilizational vitality as Greek, Persian, and other texts were translated at the "House of Wisdom." Translations at the house of wisdom inspired generations of scholars who integrated a newly confident Islamic theology with the questions of Greek philosophy. In the sciences medicine and chemistry, from the Arabic *al-kīmiyāʾ*, was encouraged by rulers. Chemical terms and mathematical vocabulary such as "algebra" and "algorithm," the latter named after the Persian mathematician al-Khwārizmī (d. 850 CE), reflect the development of the sciences under Islam.

Under the caliph Maʾmūn, however, there was an attempt to standardize religious law and interpretation under the caliph—vesting the caliph with a power similar to the popes of Europe. This attempt to centralize spiritual power, however, failed. Instead, scholars such as Ibn Ḥanbal and other experts in the *ḥadīth*, or sayings of the prophet, extracted laws that outlasted the power of the caliphs. Although attacked by Mongol and Turkish invaders who ultimately destroyed the ideal caliphate, Islamic civilization survived and continued to prosper as scholars such as al-Ghazālī developed a legal code that ensured the survival of Muslim thought, law, and practice regardless of political change. In the medieval period, after the fall of the caliphate, Muslim arts and letters continued to prosper as different princes and rulers vied to renew the power and splendor of the ʿAbbāsid golden age. Indeed, the dream of restoring the golden age of Islam remains to this day. Restoring the unity and prosperity of the caliphate is a political and religious dream of Muslims the world over. This yearning for an idealized past, according to scholars such as Ali A. Allawi, has created a modern crisis of Islamic civilization.

BIBLIOGRAPHY

Allawi, Ali A. *The Crisis of Islamic Civilization*. New Haven, Conn.: Yale University Press, 2009.

Grunebaum, Gustave E. von, ed. *Unity and Variety in Muslim Civilization*. Chicago: University of Chicago Press, 1955.

Hodgson, Marshall G. S. *The Venture of Islam*. 3 vols. Chicago: University of Chicago Press, 1974.

Humphreys, R. Stephen. *Islamic History: A Framework for Inquiry*. Rev. ed. Princeton, N.J.: Princeton University Press, 1991.

Kennedy, Hugh. *When Baghdad Ruled the Muslim World: The Rise and Fall of Islam's Greatest Dynasty*. Cambridge, Mass.: Da Capo, 2005.

Lapidus, Ira M. *A History of Islamic Societies*. 2d ed. Cambridge, U.K.: Cambridge University Press, 2002.

ALLEN FROMHERZ

CLASH OF CIVILIZATIONS. In a 1993 article in *Foreign Affairs* and in a 1996 book entitled *The Clash of Civilizations and the Remaking of World Order*, the Harvard-based political scientist Samuel Huntington argued that the post–Cold War world order would be characterized by competition and divisions across civilizations, with cultural differences replacing the ideological fault lines of the Cold War era. Although states would remain the central actors in world politics, alliances would be dictated largely by civilization politics. The most important dividing line separates

Western societies from the other six civilizations Huntington identifies, an idea referred to by Huntington's critics as "the West and the Rest." Huntington and like-minded scholars emphasize in particular the value differences between the West and the Islamic world.

According to Huntington, Western cultural invasion and political domination has prompted resentment and heightened attachment to non-Western cultures in other parts of the world. At the same time, the declining relative economic and demographic power of the West has brought growing political challenges to Western hegemony on the part of rising states representing rival civilizations. In response to these circumstances, the West should strengthen and unify its own civilization against possible internal or external challenges to its fundamental values and interests. Instead of further Western intervention, which can only exacerbate resentments or challenges, efforts should be directed toward the maintenance of a stable balance of power across civilizations.

The civilizations identified by Huntington are the West (Europe, North America, Australia, and New Zealand); Latin America; the Slavic-Orthodox world of Russia, the Ukraine, and portions of the Balkans; the Sinic or Confucian world (China, Japan, Korea); the Islamic world; Hindu civilization; and sub-Saharan Africa.

Interestingly, Huntington distinguishes modernization and Westernization; non-Western cultures can modernize in ways distinct from Europe and North America, he argues. But in contrast to classic modernization theorists or contemporary world culture theorists, Huntington argues that modernization does not lead to convergence and cooperation but rather to divergence and competition—hence the "clash of civilizations." Another claim is that the power of the West has peaked and is being challenged by other civilizations. The Islamic world in particular is growing in strength due to its demographic surge. However, unlike the architects of the Project for the New American Century in and around the administration of U.S. president George W. Bush, Huntington counsels not foreign adventures and interventions—and even less so the coercive export of electoral democracy—but rather unity within Western civilization toward the strengthening of its own cultural values and political institutions.

Huntington's essentially culturalist view of international relations has inspired many scholars, especially those curious about cultural and political developments in the Islamic world. Some have identified the major fault line between Western and Islamic civilizations as concerning democracy, while others note that surveys show Muslim societies to be largely in favor of a democratic polity. Survey-based research has pointed to a democratic deficit in the Middle East as compared with other parts of the Muslim world. The true clash of civilizations between Muslims and Westerners, the political scientists Robert Inglehart and Pippa Norris argue, lies in attitudes toward sex and gender. Results from the World Values Survey may show that Muslims want democracy, but Muslims and Westerners are a world apart when it comes to attitudes toward divorce, abortion, gender equality, and gay rights—which may not bode well for democracy's future, especially in the Middle East, they assert.

Critics have questioned the validity of Huntington's definition of civilizations as well as his emphasis on essential cultural values. For example, Latin America was colonized and settled by Europeans and shares many of the values of the West. It is unclear why Japan and China are placed in the same civilization. The grouping of the highly differentiated sub-Saharan Africa into one civilization appears arbitrary. Huntington seems oblivious to cultural cross-fertilizations; he also attaches excessive weight to cultural differences rather than to inequalities of economic and political power in a hierarchical world-system. Scholars of Muslim societies have criticized the clash of civilizations thesis for erroneously constructing a unitary and homogeneous Islamic world; as Vartan Gregorian has argued, the world of Islam should be regarded as a mosaic and not a monolith. John Voll, John Esposito, and Ray Takeyh, among other scholars; Nobel Peace Prize–laureate Shirin Ebadi of Iran; and former Iranian president Mohamed Khatami have contested Huntington's claim that Islam is incompatible with democratic values. They note efforts in the Muslim world to develop and legitimize democratic concepts through reinterpretation of Islamic texts and traditions, and to engage in parliamentary government. Others have stressed the emergence of dynamic women's movements in the Muslim world; some of these movements take as their cultural and political point of departure the global women's rights agenda as defined by the United Nations, while others engage in a woman-centered reinterpretation of Islamic texts and early history to legitimize gender equality.

[*See also* Democracy; Khatami, Mohamed; *and* Modernity.]

BIBLIOGRAPHY

Gregorian, Vartan. *Islam: A Mosaic, Not a Monolith.* Washington, D.C.: Brookings Institution Press, 2003.

Hunter, Shireen T., and Huma Malik, eds. *Modernization, Democracy, and Islam.* Westport, Conn.: Praeger, 2005.

Inglehart, Ronald, and Pippa Norris. "The True Clash of Civilizations." *Foreign Policy* 135 (March/April 2003): 63–70.

Moghadam, Valentine M. "Islamic Feminism and Its Discontents: Towards a Resolution of the Debate." *Signs* 27, no. 4 (Summer 2002): 1135–1171.

Saliba, Therese, Carolyn Allen, and Judith A. Howard, eds. *Gender, Politics, and Islam.* Chicago: University of Chicago Press, 2002.

Skidmore, David. "Huntington's Clash Revisited." *Journal of World-Systems Research* 4, no. 2 (Fall 1998): 180–188.

VALENTINE M. MOGHADAM

COLONIALISM AND THE MUSLIM WORLD. Colonialism has been present since the dawn of civilization. Greeks, Romans, and Phoenicians had colonies, as did many other states throughout history. Colonizing and being colonized has been in no way specific to the Muslim world. All of the Americas were at one time colonies, as was virtually all of Africa, both the Muslim-majority and non-Muslim-majority countries. In the broadest definition of colonialism—the domination by imperial political centers of peripheries—it can be said that virtually all peoples have been either colonized or colonizers, and often both, at one time or another (e.g., Britain under Roman rule roughly two millennia ago and a British Empire on which "the sun never set" during the reign of Queen Victoria).

For present purposes, coverage of colonialism is limited spatially to the Muslim world, not the entire formerly colonized world, and temporally from roughly the latter half of the eighteenth century until the end of formal Western colonial rule, achieved in most cases by the 1960s but for Russian/Soviet colonial possessions with the breakup of the Soviet Union in 1991. A suggested beginning point for this periodization might be the 1757 British East India Company's victory in India at the Battle of Plassey, setting in motion the long British domination of the Indian subcontinent. From that time the different Western powers (including Russia) established, in fits and starts, colonial rule over most of the Muslim world.

Although the title "Colonialism and the Muslim World" suggests a certain unity of subject, at least at an abstract level (Western colonialism vis-à-vis the colonized Muslim world) it is important to set out the diversity revealed in the history of colonialism during these roughly two centuries. That diversity includes six different imperial colonizers (British, Dutch, French, Italian, Russian, and Spanish) of sharply different importance as colonizers. These six imperial powers established several times their number of discrete "colonies" (Tables 1–3).

Nor can all of these diverse imperial holdings be properly labeled "colonies." Many were indeed colonies, but others were protectorates, mandates, or even in one case (Algeria) juridically an integral part of the home country (France). Also, Muslim Central Asia and the Caucasus, slowly "colonized" by Russia beginning in the latter part of the eighteenth century, became during the Soviet period organized into separate Soviet Republics of the USSR. While scholars can properly write of the Soviet Empire and Soviet "colonies,"

Table 1: Muslim Majority States Once British Colonial Possessions

	Duration	Present population 000	% Muslim	Area sq mi 000
Aden/South Yemen	1839–1967[1]	n/a	98	n/a
Bahrain	late 19th c.–1971	1,215	81	(472)
Bangladesh	See India	158,571	90	89
Brunei	1888–1984	402	67	3
Egypt		82,080	90	621
Occupation	1882–1914			
Protectorate	1914–1922			
Formal Indep.	1911–1936			
Formal Indep.	1936–1956[2]			
Gambia	late 18th c.–1965	1,798	90	6
India		1,189,172	13	2042
East India Co.	c. 1757–1858			
Imperial Raj	1858–1947[3]			
Iraq	1920–1932	30,400	97	272
Jordan[4]	1922–1946	6,508	92	8955
Kuwait	1899 –1961	2,596	85	11
Malaysia		28,729		205
Straits Settlement since 18th Century			60	
Colony and Protectorate	1948–1957[5]			
Maldives	1887–1965	395	98	(185)
Nigeria		155,216	50	574
Royal Niger Company	1885–1900			
Colony & Protectorate	1901–1960			
Pakistan	See India	187,343	95	494
Palestine Mandate	1920–1948[6]	3,760	97	3
Qatar	1878–1971	848	78	7
Sierra Leone		5,364	60	44
Sierra Leone Co.	1792–1808			
Colony & Protectorate	1808–1961			

TABLE 1: CONTINUED

Somalia	1880s–1960	9,926	99	1
Sudan	1898–1956[7]	45,048	99[8]	1,156
United Arab Emirates	early 19th c.–1971	149	96	52

[1] From 1967 to 1990. The People's Democratic Republic of South Yemen, and later united with North Yemen in that year. A secessionist movement to restore South Yemen has gained strength since 2008.
[2] Accepted into the League of Nations 1936, but British troops remained in Egypt until 1956.
[3] 1947 partition created separate states of India and Pakistan. Bangladesh split off from Pakistan in 1971.
[4] Transjordan until 1946, thereafter Jordan.
[5] Malaya united with Sabah, Sarawak, and Singapore in 1963 creating Malaysia. Singapore separated from Malaysia in 1965.
[6] Creation Israel 1948. Remainder Palestine mandate taken by Jordan and Egypt until 1967 war when these territories (West Bank & Gaza) taken by Israel. Israel later withdrew from Gaza but maintains blockade. Population and Muslim percentage is for those now living in these occupied territories.
[7] Technically Anglo-Egyptian Condominium.
[8] Excludes South Sudan created in 2011.

TABLE 2: MUSLIM STATES ONCE FRENCH COLONIAL POSSESSIONS

	Duration	Present Population 000	% Muslim	Area sq mi 000
Algeria	1830–1962	34,995	99	1,480
Burkino Faso	1896–1960	16,751	61	170
Chad	c. 1920–1960	10,759	53	782
Djibouti[1]	1894–1977	757	94	14
Guinea	1890s–1958	10,601	85	152
Lebanon	1920–1943	4,143	60[2]	6
Mali	c. 1905–1960	14,160	90	770
Mauritania	Late 19th c.–1960	3,282	99	640
Morocco	1912–1956	31,968	99	277
Niger	Late 19th c.–1960	16,469	80	787
Senegal	Mid 19th c.–1960	12,644	94	122
Syria	1920–1946	22,518	90[3]	114
Tunisia	1881–1956	10,629	98	101

[1] As French Somaliland.
[2] Highly disputed and only a best guess in the absence of census. One source suggests 59.7% Muslim of which 27% Shīʿa, 27% Sunni, 5.7% other Muslim (such as Nusayris & Druze) and 39% Christian.
[3] Estimated 74% Sunni, 16% Shīʿa.

the leadership of the USSR, true to its Marxist-Leninist ideology, insisted that no such thing existed in the Soviet Union; imperialism and colonialism reigned only in the capitalist West.

Moreover, colonized entities were differently classified over time. India, for example, was at first governed by the East India Company and only later absorbed into the British Empire. Likewise, the Dutch East India Company exercised control over limited parts of what is now Indonesia until it went bankrupt in the last years of the eighteenth century. It was then replaced in 1800 by the Dutch

TABLE 3: FORMER DUTCH, ITALIAN, SPANISH, AND RUSSIAN/SOVIET MUSLIM COLONIAL POSSESSIONS

	Duration	Present Population 000	% Muslim	Area sq mi 000
Indonesia		245,614	86	1,183
Dutch East India Company	1602–1800			
Dutch East Indies	1800–1948			
Libya[1]	1911–1951	6,598	87	1,093
Somalia[2]	1880s–1960	9,926	99	396
Spanish Protectorate Morocco	1912–1956	See Morocco under French Colonial Possessions		See Morocco under French Colonial Possessions
Spanish Sahara [3]	1884–1975	507	99	165
Azerbaijan	1812–1918/ 1920–1991	8,372	93	54
Chechnya	late 18th c.–[4]	1,269	94	10
Dagestan	late 18th c.–[5]	2,910	91	31
Kazakhstan	mid-19th c.–1991	15,522	47[6]	1,693
Kyrgyzstan	late-19th c.–1991	5,587	75	124
Tajikistan	c.1860–1991	7,627	85	88
Turkmenistan	c.1865–1991	4,998	89	303
Uzbekistan	late-19th c.–1991	28,129	88	277

[1] Eritrea, controlled by Italy from 1890 until the Italians were ousted by the British in 1941, has a slight Christian majority and is thus not included.
[2] Union of Italian Somaliland and British Somaliland.
[3] Now the "Western Sahara" it remains contested by Morocco and the Saharan Polisario.
[4] Briefly independent after 1991, but restored to the Russian Federation during the Second Chechnyan War.
[5] Still a part of the Russian Federation.
[6] According to the CIA World Fact Book Kazakhstan has a slightly greater number of Muslims than Christians.

government. Egypt was at first simply "occupied" by Britain and only later became a protectorate and thereafter nominally independent.

Colonial rule began for some colonies (using that term to embrace all of the many forms of imperial domination) as long ago as the latter half of the eighteenth century, with roots even further back in time. Others were colonized as recently as after World War I. The duration of colonial rule was equally diverse, ranging from almost two centuries (British India) to only a few years (the British mandates for Transjordan and Iraq).

Most colonies were literally overseas possessions, separated by oceans from the imperial base, although the Russian (later Soviet) colonial experience was a matter of pushing out territorially from the existing home country. It is thus appropriate that the nineteenth-century "great game" of confrontation between the British and Russian Empires could be depicted as a contest between the Leviathan and the Behemoth.

Another major distinction in the era of the colonization of Muslim countries by the West was whether colonial rule brought with it an influx of settlers from the home country (or from other European countries). Such was the case for the French possessions in Morocco, Algeria, and Tunisia and the Italians in Libya. Significant numbers of non-Muslims also settled into some of the Russian possessions in Central Asia during both the pre-Soviet and Soviet period. At the other end of the settler spectrum, British subjects (and other Europeans) were barred from establishing permanent residence in the Anglo-Egyptian Sudan.

There was equal diversity distinguishing the many different countries colonized. Some, such as Egypt, Tunisia, and Morocco, had been for centuries (millennia in the case of Egypt) urban-based organized polities with relatively unchanged borders. Other countries subject to colonization such as Chad, Mali, and large parts of the Caucasus and Central Asia were uncentered, hinterland polities characterized by mountainous or semi-nomadic regions. The small states of the Persian Gulf can be best described as tiny city-states, whereas India by contrast was a subcontinent. Indonesia is a constellation of over seventeen thousand islands; Mali is landlocked.

Should this long list of diverse Muslim states colonized by Western colonizers include even a few more entries? Why not Iran? It was twice divided into spheres of influence between Britain and Russia, first according to the terms of the 1907 Anglo-Russian Convention, and again in 1941 during World War II. If measured by the intensity of outside domination, including the overthrow of Iran's ruler (Reza Shah Pahlavi) and military occupation, Iran, it could be argued, was much more "colonized" than the small states of the Persian Gulf during the period of Britain's control. This would be to embrace the notion of "informal empire," extending the use of "empire" to include states under the sway of an outside power without the accoutrements of formal colonial control.

Or what about including Afghanistan, a very different case, among the colonized? It was recognized in that same 1907 Anglo-Russian Convention as a British protectorate, but the actual British presence in Afghanistan was limited by both British choice and Afghan resistance.

The list of those Muslim states colonized employed by this entry stops short of including those "colonized" de jure but not de facto (such as Afghanistan) or those controlled by means of "informal empire" such as prevailed in the British Empire during roughly the first half of the nineteenth century. Even so, this idea of "informal empire" does reflect an important dual reality: (1) the actual impact of Western control short of colonization over many peoples and polities was greater than that of several in the list of colonized countries presented here; and (2) the era of Western colonialism in the Muslim world witnessed a concurrent creation of diverse Western empires and a sundering of existing Muslim states, including empires and states such as those of the Ottomans and the Moghuls in the Indian subcontinent. Indeed, a study of the Western impact on those states experiencing "informal empire" (e.g., Turkey or Iran) compared to states undergoing explicit colonial rule (e.g., Algeria or Malaysia) would be useful.

Here, however, a more focused set of questions is under consideration: What was the "Islamic factor" in this two-century-old confrontation between Western colonizers and Muslims confronting colonization? To what extent did Muslims respond qua Muslims? What changes in Muslim institutions and ideologies emerged from this confrontation?

One may begin to answer these questions by noting that the "Muslim world" experiencing Western colonialism in one form or another is defined here as those states with a majority Muslim population. It was in most cases an overwhelming majority. Twelve of the twenty former British colonies, eight of the thirteen former French colonies, and five of the twelve former Dutch, Italian, Spanish, and Russian colonies today have Muslim majorities of 90 percent or more. With only two exceptions, that proportion of Muslims was essentially the same throughout the colonial era. Those exceptions are India under the British Raj, where until the 1947 partition into India and Pakistan the Muslims were a minority, no more than 30 percent, and Lebanon, which until the creation of "greater Lebanon" following World War I had a Christian majority.

Moreover, most of the forty-five counties listed had been Muslim for centuries, and in the case of the Arab core for over a millennium. The combination of these historical, geographical, and demographic factors underscores the appropriateness of the usage "Muslim world."

The Mediterranean portion (the Middle East and North Africa) of this Muslim world had been in contentious contact with Europe since the rise of Islam. A quick overview reveals the early and rapid Muslim conquest of all of Northern Africa from Egypt to Morocco, followed by Spain only to be stopped deep in France at the Battle of Tours in 732. Then there were the Crusades beginning during the last years of the eleventh century and sputtering on for several centuries thereafter. Roughly the same era witnessed the fascinating territorial exchange of the western and eastern ends of the Mediterranean as Muslim Spain gave way to the Christian Reconquista and Byzantine Christian Anatolia fell to Islam. There was also the Ottoman penetration into Southeastern Europe, stopped only at the outskirts of Vienna (in 1529 and 1683).

The larger Muslim world beyond the Middle East did not have the same history of contentious contact with the West over the centuries, but it, too, was accustomed to prevailing against its non-Muslim enemies until a few decades before the advent of Western colonialism. This historically shaped outlook would make the virtually unbroken chain of military defeats that the Muslim world experienced after the 1757 Battle of Plassey even more acutely felt.

Western colonial rule also presented a shock to Muslim thinking about politics and international relations. The Muslim view presupposed a world divided into *dār al-islām* (abode of Islam) and the non-Muslim *dār al-ḥarb* (abode of war). The underlying assumption was that while a temporary truce (*hudnah*) might be acceptable, the long term assumption and mission entailed the expansion of *dār al-islām*, certainly not its contraction. The Muslim ruler should abide by the *Sharīʿah*. The individual Muslim could not opt out of the Muslim *ummah* (Muslim community), and the status of non-Muslims in the *ummah* was as a protected minority (*dhimmī*) absorbed into full membership in the *ummah* only by conversion. Admittedly, these categorical statements do violence to the many complexities of classical Muslim political thought with its rich nuances that can only be ferreted out by an in-depth reconstruction of the many *fatwas* and treatises penned over the centuries, but it may be said to stand generally as the received wisdom understood by the political elite and the people.

Put differently, classical Muslim political thought was a coherent, self-contained worldview, comparable to other coherent, self-contained worldviews such as that of the European Holy Roman Empire during the Middle Ages. That worldview, at the advent of Western colonialism, was to be challenged by the infidel invader, not from within, as was the case with the Holy Roman Empire.

Thus, Western colonialism was a major shock to the Muslim world, and the response was understandably expressed in Islamic terms. How then did the Muslim world respond? One might begin by placing the question within a general interpretative schema: peoples and polities confronting invasion may be seen as choosing to respond by fight, flight, or accommodation. The options to fight may range from outright war, to guerrilla warfare, to such activities as strikes and boycotts, down to the least violent choice of passive resistance. Flight may involve actual physical emigration, or it may take the form of what might be called psychic emigration leading to political quietism. Accommodation can range from temporizing to embracing, in varying degrees, the institutions and ideas brought by the invader. The response(s) chosen may vary over time, and more than one of the three patterns—fight, flight, or accommodation—may often coexist—in fact will usually coexist—at a given time.

In adapting this schema to the Muslim world confronting Western colonialism, we can even, without undue semantic violation, convert the triad—fight, flight, and accommodation—to Islamic terms—*jihād*, *hijrah*, and *iṣlāḥ*. The interaction of the three categories over two centuries and across multiple countries, colonizers and colonized, reveals the following pattern:

Most early resistance to Western colonialism took the form of *jihād*. Such *jihāds* were eventually defeated or neutralized, some quickly, others in a matter of one or more decades. Examples from when this early period ended include the French defeat of Algeria's ʿAbd al-Qādir in 1847, the British suppression of the 1857 mutiny in India, and the 1898 Battle of Omdurman ending the Sudanese Mahdīyah. Yet what might be dubbed the *jihād* syndrome was more nearly dormant than dead. Later militant resistance movements include the several different Mahdist movements, the struggle of Ṣūfī brotherhoods such as the Naqshbandīyah and Sānusīyah, and violent decolonization as in Algeria from 1954 to 1962 or the final phase of the decolonization of the Dutch East Indies to create Indonesia from 1945 to 1949.

Examples of *hijrah* include Sayyid Aḥmad Barelwī in India calling for a withdrawal in 1826 in order to be better positioned for his *jihād* against the British and the Sikhs. Another *hijrah*, which reenacted the Prophet Muhammad's move from Mecca to Medina, was the Sudanese al-Mahdī's move from Khartoum to the Nuba Mountains. *Hijrahs* confined to emigration without hope or intent of returning to resistance took place in Algeria's most traditional city, Tlemcen, in 1911 and in India during the 1920s. The Tlemcen exodus resulted in a few hundred emigrants but was emblematic of a broader malaise throughout the country. Psychic *hijrah* or opting out of politics can be seen in such originally apolitical organizations as the Deobandī movement and the Tablīghī Jamāʿat.

Accommodation is the most varied and the most important response in tracking the history of this colonizer/colonized era. The earliest instances occurred as Muslim states or protostates, bested by invading outsiders, sought to come to terms with the invading outsider by submitting to the outsider in the hope of maintaining some autonomy within the outsider's power network. This pattern was especially prominent in India, and the system of autonomous princely states may be seen from the "colonized" perspective as having resulted from efforts to "get along by going along" with the British Raj. An example of such an accommodation missed was the French decision in 1830 to send the Algerian leaders into exile and disband their army even though those defeated were probably prepared to work with the victorious French. It would have been comparable to the way the Egyptian Mamlūk, defeated by the Ottomans in 1517, were then integrated into the Ottoman system.

Such accommodation, or, to use that much more pejorative word, "collaboration," takes place in the colonial context not only in responses to defeat but in efforts to line up a useful outside patron. This can be seen, for example, in the much disputed diplomacy during World War I that led to two members of the Arab Hashemite family ruling the British mandate states of Transjordan and Iraq.

This pattern of accommodating the colonizer, of coming to terms with the infidel outsider, clearly has little that is "Islamic" about it. Thus, it is not surprising to find that many of the *jihāds* and *hijrahs*, both early and late in the colonial era were in no small measure an outraged reaction to just such accommodationist or collaborationist actions that indigenous political actors undertook.

More truly "Islamic" and more deserving of the rubric *iṣlāḥ* was a different accommodation that emerged later in the colonial era and was in large measure a response to the many ideas and institutions that colonialism brought to the colonized. This phenomenon must be carefully explained, lest this article appear as an uncritical paean of praise for Western colonialism (with echoes of "white man's burden," *mission civilisatrice*, and the "ethical policy" in the later years of the Dutch East Indies). Instead, what is intended is a value-free appraisal starting with the proposition that the confrontation between Western colonialism and the Muslim world, like any colonizing enterprise, was always a matter of institutionalizing an unequal power relationship between ruler and ruled imposed by violence, potential or actual. Moreover, it can be assumed that the ruler seeks to maintain that unequal power relationship and the ruled to change it.

Even so, in all colonizer/colonized situations some ideas and institutions brought by the invader are accepted and adapted. They are "indigenized." These would include in the case of the colonized Muslim world secular education and legal changes that greatly reduced the role of the *ʿulamāʾ* and created a new elite speaking the colonizer's language and adopting, at least in part, the colonizer's worldview. This new elite included those natives recruited into colonial administration who, although often crudely abused and "othered" by the colonial system, were adopting new values even while competing with their overlords. So, too, were all classes of the colonized wrestling with the changes wrought, be it in economics, urbanism, gender roles, or even such seemingly banal matters as clothing.

The *iṣlāḥ* aspect of all this is associated with Islamic reformism or modernism, including the Salafīyah of Egypt's Muḥammad ʿAbduh, Sayyid Ahmad Khan and his Aligarh movement in India, and Ismail Gasprinskii (1851–1914) and his Jadīd (*uṣūl al-jadīd*) movement in Russian Central Asia. Generally speaking, Islamic reformism sought to demonstrate that Islam, properly understood, was a rational, moderate religion in accord with what might be dubbed the ethical and practical precepts of modernity as set by the West. An indication of this orientation is the way Islamic reformists, challenging the Western image of Islam as a religion of the sword, began to reinterpret *jihāds* as being primarily a matter of individual moral improvement ("the greater *jihād*," according to a *ḥadīth* of the Prophet Muḥammad) and also restricted *jihād* to defensive war against invaders.

ʿAbduh's movement, the Salafīyah, is, confusingly, also the name proudly claimed by today's most fundamentalist Muslims, and an ideological connection between today's Salafīs and ʿAbduh's Salafīyah of well over a century ago is not lacking. In its time, however, ʿAbduh's Salafīyah and the other reformist movements noted above, by presenting Islam as a peaceful and reasonable religion and by implicitly softening the distinction between *dār al-islām* and *dār al-ḥarb* paved the way for the emergence of a new, also Western-imported, worldview. This was nationalism, according to which loyalty and identity would shift from the *ummah* to the *waṭan* (fatherland) or the *qawm* (nation) (and often a mix of both *waṭan* and *qawm*), and the basis of individual membership in the political community would be citizenship rather than status as a Muslim or *dhimmī*. This, in turn, by downgrading the public role of religion and of religious leadership (without, interestingly, the anticlericalism that prevailed at times in the West) facilitated a de facto separation of religion and state.

This notion of the proper tie between Islam and politics was tested in what may be described as the last contest between the options of *jihād* and *hijrah* vis-à-vis *iṣlāḥ* during the era of Western colonialism. This was when the ideology of Pan-Islamism emerged in the later decades of the nineteenth century. Associated with the mercurial Jamāl al-Dīn al-Afghānī and adopted as a policy by the Ottoman sultan Abdülhamid II, Pan-Islamism preached the political unity of all Muslims under the caliph. When in November 1914 the Ottoman Empire entered World War I on the side of the Central Powers, a *fatwa* was issued calling on all Muslims, not just Ottoman subjects, to join in the struggle against the enemies of Islam. Yet the impact of the *fatwa* on Muslims was limited. The many Muslim colonials serving in the armed forces of the British and French during that war continued to fight for the enemy as designated by the *fatwa*. Even within the Ottoman Empire the celebrated "Arab Revolt" was in no way deterred by this call for the unity of Muslim ranks.

Accordingly, the strictly Islamic aspect of this complex two-century-long confrontation between Western colonizer and Muslim colonized would lead to a ratcheting down of the Islamic influence in terms of both ideology and institutions. Certainly, the period of decolonization left the Muslim world with new, essentially secular nation-states ruled by such nationalists as Egypt's Abdel Nasser, Bourguiba in Tunisia, Indonesia's Sukarno, and even Pakistan's founder, Jinnah (who was clearly more dedicated to creating a state for Muslims than a Muslim state). Moreover, at the time of decolonization the significant transnational movements were Pan-Arabist and Pan-Turkist, not Pan-Islamist.

Yet there are many countervailing tendencies to challenge this broad appraisal. Among the discrete items that challenge such a metanarrative are the following:

1. The appeal to an overall Islamic political unity did not die out following the 1914 Ottoman *fatwa*. Witness the later Khilāfat movement in pre-Partition India and the many ultimately futile efforts to agree upon a new line of caliphs and a new caliphal capital (Yemen? Mosul?) in response to the abolition of the caliphate (1924) by Atatürk's Turkey.
2. A careful look at the "Arab Revolt" during World War I reveals a much more "Islamic" mind-set (especially on the part of its leader, Sharif Husayn) than popular Western historiography presents.
3. ʿAbduh's Salafīyah never won over the majority of the *ʿulamāʾ*, and one of his followers, ʿAlī ʿAbd al-Rāziq, published in 1925 *Islām wa uṣūl al-ḥukm* [Islam and the Foundations of Political Power]. He argued that Islam was based on the separation of religion and state, and was "defrocked" by the *ʿulamāʾ* for his effort.
4. Jihadist movements did not die out later in the colonial period, as is shown by the Sānusīyah resisting Italian colonization in Libya or the long (c. 1900–1920) Somali movement against the British and Italians led by Muḥammad ʿAbd Allāh Ḥasan, dubbed the "mad mullah" by the British.
5. The continued importance of a Muslim political identity is shown in the great stimulus given to Moroccan decolonizing nationalism by the French imposition of the "Berber Dhahir" in 1930, which provided for the replacement of *Sharīʿah* law by Berber customary law even though Berber customary law had been in use all along.
6. Ḥasan al-Bannāʾs Muslim Brotherhood, created in 1928, grew thereafter not just in Egypt but throughout much of the Muslim world.
7. The limits of accommodation to the Western polity is highlighted in the celebrated public debate in Algeria in 1936 between Ferhat Abbas and the ʿAbd al-Ḥamīd Ibn Bādīs, founder of the reformist Algerian

Association of Ulama. Abbas, working for Algerian equality within a French framework proclaimed: "If I had discovered an Algerian nation, I would be a nationalist.... [but] such a homeland does not exist.... We must tie forever our future to that of the work of France in this land." Ibn Bādīs retorted that he, too, had searched history and had "found the Algerian Muslim nation;.... this Algerian and Muslim nation is not France."

8. Abū al-Aʿlā Mawdūdī (1903–1979) wrote a book in the 1920s restoring to prominence a hard-line interpretation of *jihād*. He also militated against Muslim separatism in India, insisting that nationalism had no place in Islam. Then after partition in 1947 he moved to Pakistan. This, of course, highlights the unique case of pre-Partition India, in which Muslims were a minority (unlike the other forty-plus countries listed). Even so, Mawdūdī was probably the most influential Sunnī scholar and public intellectual of his age.

While the *jihād-hijrah-iṣlāḥ* triad can be of use in organizing the study of Western colonialism and the Muslim world, it is perhaps more accurate to see the "Islamic factor" not in linear fashion as leading toward either greater secularization or its opposite, increased Islamization. The confrontation is best seen as a dialectical process still continuing. Accordingly, as we look at that era with today's eyes, shaped by the "return of Islam" beginning so soon after most decolonization was achieved, we are inclined to conclude that one can understand Western colonial rule over the Muslim world only with a good knowledge of Islamic ideology and institutions, but one cannot adequately decipher developments of that period by the "Islamic factor" alone.

BIBLIOGRAPHY

Anderson, Lisa. *The State and Social Transformation in Tunisia and Libya, 1830–1980* (1986) Fine comparative appraisal of these neighboring states under different (French and Italian) colonial rule, and much more.

Brown, L. Carl. "The Many Faces of Colonial Rule in French North Africa." *Revue de l'Occident Musulman et de la Mediterranee* (1973) pp. 171–191. Highlights the difference settler colonization makes.

Brown, L. Carl. "The Sudanese Mahdiya." In *Protest and Power and Protest in Black Africa*, edited by Robert I. Rothberg and Ali A. Mazrui, pp. 145–168. New York: Oxford University Press, 1970.

Burke, Edmund, III. "A Comparative View of French Native Policies in Morocco and Syria, 1912–1925." *Middle Eastern Studies* 9 (1973) pp. 175–186.

Etemad, Bouda. *Possessing the World: Taking the Measurements of Colonisation from the 18th to the 20th Century*. Translated by Andrine Everson. New York: Berghahn, 2000. A treasure trove of quantitative data on Western colonialism in all its aspects.

Lapidus, Ira M. *A History of Islamic Societies*. Cambridge, U.K.: Cambridge University Press 1988. Roughly one-half of this huge tome (1,002 pages) treats all parts of the Muslim world, region by region, during the nineteenth and twentieth centuries.

Lewis, Bernard. *The Political Language of Islam*. Chicago: University of Chicago Press, 1988. The best single book on political thought in Islam, including the doctrine and practice on such matters as non-Muslim rule over Muslims, jihad and more.

Lieven, Dominic. *Empire: The Russian Empire and Its Rivals*. New Haven, Conn.: Yale University Press, 2002. Treatment of empire in its global context, chapters on the British, Ottoman and Habsburg empires and then in-depth treatment of the Russian/Soviet colonial experience.

Osterhammel, Jurgen. *Colonialism: A Theoretical Overview*. Translated from the German by Shelley L. Frisch. 2d ed. Princeton, N.J.: Markus Wiener, 2005.

Pervillé, Guy. *De l'empire francais français aà la decolonisation decolonization*. Paris: Hachette, 1991. Good overview with useful bibliography.

Peters, Rudolph. *Islam and Colonialism: The Doctrine of Jihad in Modern History*. The Hague: Mouton, 1979. This book by Peters provides splendid coverage of the classical doctrine, modern adaptations, and several examples of jihadi movements in modem times with translations of *fatwās*.

Peters, Rudolph. *Jihad in Classical and Modern Islam: A Reader*. Princeton, N.J.: Markus Wiener, 1996.

Roberts, Stephen H. *The History of French Colonial Policy, 1870–1925*. London: Frank Cass, 1929, reprinted 1963. First published 1929. Interesting early study showing the great attention in that era to the nuts and bolts of colonial administration. The conclusion (pp. 634–679), which compares French and British colonial rule will strike many of today's readers as quaint, demonstrating that each age must rewrite its history.

Robinson, Francis. "The British Empire and the Muslim World," In *The Oxford History of the British Empire*, edited by Wm. Roger Louis. Vol. 4, *The Twentieth Century*, edited by Judith M. Brown and Wm. Roger Louis, pp. 398–420. Oxford: Oxford University Press, 1999.

Wesseling, H. L. *Imperialism and Colonialism: Essays on the History of European Expansion*. Westport, Conn.: Greenwood, 1997. Includes a number of articles on Dutch colonialism as well as colonialism in general.

L. CARL BROWN

COMBAT. The Qurʾān and *sīra* (life of the Prophet) narratives present an evolving conception of combat that transformed significantly in the course of the Prophet Muḥammad's life. It is reported that during the early, Meccan phase of Muḥammad's mission, his followers were frequently persecuted by the Quraysh, the Prophet's tribe. Yet Muḥammad prohibited his followers from defending themselves with force, calling for them to "be steadfast, for I have not been commanded to fight." Around the time of his migration to Medina in 622, new Qurʾānic verses that gave Muḥammad permission to fight were revealed:

> Permission is given to those who fight because they have been wronged. God is well able to help them—those who have been driven out of their houses without right only because they said God is our Lord. Had not God used some men to keep back others, cloisters and churches and oratories and mosques wherein the name of God is constantly mentioned would have been destroyed. Assuredly God will help those who help Him. (Qurʾān 22:39–41)

These verses suggest that warfare was necessary and permissible for the survival of Abrahamic communities, as long as it was fought in their defense.

Muḥammad's first act as a military leader was to propose the Constitution of Medina, a defensive pact between his followers and the Jewish tribes of Medina. Both groups, the constitution stipulated, were forbidden from offering protection to the Quraysh and their allies. Muḥammad was also willing to make alliances with polytheist tribes that agreed to aid his campaigns against the Quraysh. Indeed, his numerous alliances with polytheist tribes eventually enabled him to conquer Mecca with a force of 10,000 men. After the conquest of Mecca, however, a new verse of the Qurʾān declared, "God and His Messenger dissolve [treaty] obligations with the polytheists." Muḥammad's followers were to refrain from fighting polytheist tribes for a grace period of a few months, the verse maintained, "but when the forbidden months are past, then fight and slay the polytheists wherever you find them, and seize them, beleaguer them, and lie in wait for them in every stratagem [of war]; but if they repent, and establish regular prayers and practice regular charity, then open the way for them: for God is Oft-forgiving, Most Merciful" (Qurʾān 9:5).

This verse illustrates a shifting conception of the meaning and nature of combat. All polytheists are potential combatants, the sura goes on to explain, because "they obstruct [others] from His [God's] Way.... In a believer they respect not the ties either of kinship or of the covenant" (Qurʾān 9:9–10). That is, polytheists must be fought because they prevent their clansmen from living in submission to God's will. Whereas the Quraysh posed an immediate threat to the survival of the Muslim community, the remaining polytheists hindered the expansion of Islam. Combat is permissible not just for the sake of ensuring the Muslim community's survival but also as part of a civilizing mission to destroy oppressive regimes that prevent others from embracing Islam. In Muḥammad's final years, polities led by peoples of the Book (non-Muslim believers) were counted among such regimes. Muḥammad's followers were commanded to fight them "until they pay the *jizya* [the tax on non-Muslim believers] with willing submission and feel themselves subdued" (Qurʾān 9:29). At the time of his death in 632, Muḥammad was in the midst of organizing military raids against the Byzantine territory of al-Jurf.

By the mid-eighth century, military combat constituted a central theme of Muslim historiography. Narratives of the Prophet's campaigns (*maghāzī*) and the early Islamic conquests (*futūḥ*) presented these military victories as the providential expansion of the territory of Islam. With this interpretation of history, the earliest jurists opined that Muslim rulers should continue the Prophet's civilizing mission to extend the boundaries of the territory of Islam and the influence of Islamic values. Early works of *fiqh* (Muslim jurisprudence) express a concern to ensure that combat is conducted rightly, so that Muslims "fight in the name of God and in the path of God." Hence, Mālik ibn Anas's *Muwaṭṭaʾ* and Muḥammad al-Shaybānī's *Siyar*, to give two prominent examples, addressed the proper procedures for declaring war, pledging protection, dividing the spoils of war, and other practical matters that confronted Muslim rulers and commanders upon invading enemy territory. To illustrate, al-Shaybānī (d. 805) drew from the example of Muḥammad's military campaigns to establish procedures for declaring war. Muḥammad reportedly told his commanders that before invading an enemy territory, they must invite its ruler to accept Islam. If he refuses, then he should be asked to pay the *jizya*. If he refuses that, then the enemy's territory can rightfully be attacked. Scholars generally agreed that after such nonmilitary means had been attempted, combat was a legitimate means of extending the territory of Islam.

The weakening of the ʿAbbāsid central government radically altered Islamic conceptions of the nature and meaning of combat. In the absence of a strong, centralized government capable of providing the resources and organization necessary to wage expansive wars, scholars had to look to other sponsors. In his treatise *Al-Aḥkām al-sulṭāniyya*, al-Māwardī (d. 1058) argued that it was permissible for local governors to wage *jihād* on the caliph's behalf. With the advent of the Crusades, however, decentralized political authority became an especially pressing problem as isolated local provinces fell to European armies. In *Kitāb al-Jihād*, Ali ibn Tahir al-Sulamī (d. 500/1106) addressed the subject of fighting "imposed," or defensive, wars. Such wars, he argued, impress new duties upon believers. All Muslims were responsible for waging wars of defense. Fighting in defensive wars was an individual duty that could not be satisfied by the performance of others. In contrast, the caliph was responsible for waging wars of expansion. Fighting wars of expansion was considered a communal duty not incumbent upon each member of the community, as long as a sufficient number performed the task. Most likely, al-Sulamī's work was intended to encourage Muslim sultans from distant principalities to join in the defense against invaders.

Writing after the fall of Baghdad in 1250, Taqī al-Dīn Aḥmad Ibn Taymīyah (d. 1328) also acknowledged that all Muslims have an individual duty to participate in defensive wars. He emphasized, however, the duty to wage combat against apostate Muslims who refuse to abide by prescriptions of the *Sharīʿah*, or religious law. Departing from the general trend of Sunnī *fiqh*, Ibn Taymīyah extended this duty even to combatting Muslim rulers. Most likely this innovation was motivated by Ibn Taymīyah's refusal to acknowledge the legitimacy of recently converted Mongol sultans. Despite their profession of Islam, Mongol rulers continued to practice pre-Islamic tribal customs and enforce dynastic laws that contradicted the *Sharīʿah*.

By Ibn Taymīyah's standards, such departures from the *Sharīʿah*, constituted apostasy, making Mongol sultans legitimate targets of attack.

Like scholars writing after the decline of the ʿAbbāsid caliphate, contemporary Islamist militants view the Muslim world as under attack. As they see it, the territory of Islam has been usurped by apostate regimes supported by Western imperialist powers. These circumstances call for defensive combat. Like their medieval predecessors, contemporary militants have stressed each Muslim's individual duty to fight defensive wars. But whereas al-Sulamī's and Ibn Taymīyah's insistence on individual duty was intended to encourage local rulers to come to the aid of distant, beleaguered provinces, contemporary militants have appealed to this individual duty to encourage the formation of radically decentralized, popular resistance groups. In his tract *al-Farīḍah al-ghāʾiban*, Muḥammad ʿAbd al-Salām al-Faraj (d. 1982), for example, classified Anwar al-Sadat as an apostate on account of his creation of a "mixed regime" that implemented European-inspired laws. He encouraged Egyptians to fight Sadat's regime by reminding them of a Muslim's individual duty to combat the apostates living in their midst. Al-Qaʿida, in contrast, has emphasized the individual duty of every Muslim to fight the "far enemy"—at present, the United States and its allies. Since apostate regimes of the Muslim world are supported by Western imperialist powers, the defense of Muslim lands requires that these distant powers be attacked.

The military operations of terrorist groups like al-Qaʿida have raised new questions concerning the conduct of Islamic warfare. Many Muslims, including the legal scholars Muḥammad Sayyid Ṭanṭāwī (d. 2010) and Yūsuf al-Qaraḍāwī, have judged al-Qaʿida's policy of attacking civilians as a departure from the *Sharīʿah's* prohibition of targeting noncombatants. Numerous reports (*ḥadīth*) assert that Muḥammad forbade attacking women, children, and other civilian groups. According to one report, he reprimanded soldiers for killing a woman because "she was not one who would have fought." In light of this precedent, scholars of *fiqh* from the earliest generations have generally prohibited the killing of women and children. Some scholars, including Ibn Taymīya, extended this prohibition to include other groups incapable of fighting, such as the elderly, the blind, monks, and slaves. Representatives of al-Qaʿida have attempted to justify their actions with appeals to reciprocal justice, in retaliation for attacks on Muslim lands. Other al-Qaʿida sympathizers have argued that U.S. citizens, as voters, bear responsibility for their country's military policies. As new generations attempt to adjust norms of combat in ways that best fit contemporary circumstances, such debate illustrates the discursive character of *Sharīʿah* reasoning concerning combat.

[*See also* Faraj, Muḥammad ʿAbd al-Salām; Jihād; *and* Māwardī, Abū al-Ḥasan al-.]

BIBLIOGRAPHY

Bonner, Michael. *Jihad in Islamic History: Doctrines and Practice*. Princeton, N.J.: Princeton University Press, 2006.

Kelsay, John. *Arguing the Just War in Islam*. Cambridge, Mass.: Harvard University Press, 2007.

Peters, Rudolph. *Jihad in Classical and Modern Islam: A Reader*. Princeton, N.J.: Markus Wiener, 1996.

Shaybānī, Muḥammad al-. *The Islamic Law of Nations: Shaybānī's Siyar*. Translated by Majid Khadduri. Baltimore, Md.: Johns Hopkins University Press, 2001.

JAMES BROUCEK

COMMANDING RIGHT AND FORBIDDING WRONG. The phrase "commanding right and forbidding wrong" (*al-amr bi-l-maʿrūf wa-l-nahy ʿan al-munkar*) refers to a duty that is generally believed to be incumbent upon Muslims, namely, to command that which is considered obligatory and to forbid that which is considered prohibited. The language comes from the Qurʾān, where it appears eight times, as in 3:104: "Let there be one community of you, calling to good, and commanding right and forbidding wrong; those are the prosperers."

The verses that contain this language appear to be directed at the Muslim community generally, although they do not provide answers to the many questions that arise as soon as the actualization of such a duty is contemplated. A vast body of scholastic literature, both Sunnī and Shīʿī, developed to elucidate the details of the duty (see Cook, 2003, for an extensive and thorough examination of this literature). While some general contours are generally agreed upon, many variations depend on sect, school of law (*madhhab*), individual scholar, and time and place.

One issue is the meaning of the terms "right" (*maʿrūf*) and "wrong" (*munkar*). A basic question is whether they match any of the five legal classifications for acts developed by the jurists. *Maʿrūf* was largely understood to refer to the same acts covered by the term *wājib* ("required"), but the definition of *munkar* is more complicated. According to al-Ghazālī (d. 1111), for example, *munkar* contains two categories: forbidden (*ḥarām*) and disapproved of or repugnant (*makrūh*). In his view, preventing a wrong that is merely *makrūh* is commendable but not obligatory.

As a related question, who determines that an act is right or wrong such that a Muslim is obliged—or permitted—to command or forbid it? In general, jurists required a particular act to be agreed upon as right or wrong before an individual could command or forbid it. Matters that were subject to disagreement were excluded, such as when the schools held differing views, and, further, a view reached by *ijtihād*, individual reasoning, could not be enforced under this duty. This position meant that, for example, an act permissible in one school of law but forbidden in another should not be forbidden by a Muslim acting under the banner of this duty, even if both the actor and the individual being reproached are themselves adherents of the school that forbids the act.

Jurists further limited the duty to acts that were publicly manifest, meaning that the commission of a wrongful act must be done in public or the omission of an obligatory act must be publically visible. An example of the latter might be when a Muslim man is present in public at the time of the Friday noon prayers but not participating in them. Thus, an individual may not spy to carry out this duty, except in limited circumstances when reliable evidence indicates that an irremediable wrong is imminent, such as a murder or a rape. Another point of disagreement was how a Muslim was supposed to carry out the duty; *sunnah* (and juridical literature) refer to a hierarchy of approaches to be used when acting—first using the hand, then the tongue, and then the heart. Some jurists cautioned against exercising the duty when it was likely to lead to harm to the actor or to a greater wrong than the failure to act would cause. A further issue is the role of non-Muslims, who might be the target of the duty if their public behavior violated agreed-upon rights or wrongs.

While there is extensive literature about the concept of commanding right and forbidding wrong, the extent to which individual Muslims carried out this duty remains an important historical question that calls for further research. Some reports about practitioners are well known, such as the story of the goldsmith of Marv, who reportedly confronted and reproached the leader of the ʿAbbāsid revolution. The goldsmith, who apparently believed that he was carrying out this duty, was executed as a result. Entries in biographical dictionaries occasionally mention that an individual was devoted to commanding and forbidding, but it is not possible at this stage of research to draw general conclusions about the extent to which daily life at any particular place and time was affected by the duty as carried out by individuals.

While the concept theoretically applies to all Muslims, as a separate matter, rulers of Muslim societies historically typically appointed particular individuals (sg. *muḥtasib*) to carry out the duty to command right and forbid wrong as an official and public matter. The term *ḥisbah* describes the jurisdiction of this official. Technically, the concept of *ḥisbah* is narrower than the concept of "commanding right and forbidding wrong," referring only to the *muḥtasib*'s function and not to Muslims who undertake the duty as individuals. According to al-Māwardī (and generally), while the *muḥtasib* is personally obligated by nature of the appointment, for individual Muslims, *ḥisbah* is a collective duty (*farḍ kifāyah*), satisfied for all when carried out by someone within the society.

[*See also* Ḥisbah; Māwardī, Abū al-Ḥasan al-; *and* Religious Beliefs.]

BIBLIOGRAPHY

Cook, Michael. *Commanding Right and Forbidding Wrong in Islamic Thought*. Cambridge, U.K.: Cambridge University Press, 2000.

Cook, Michael. *Forbidding Wrong in Islam: An Introduction*. Cambridge, U.K.: Cambridge University Press, 2003.

Ghazālī, Abū Ḥāmid Muḥammad b. Muḥammad al-. *Iḥyā' 'ulūm al-dīn*. Edited by Muḥammad al-Dālī Balṭa. 5 vols. Sidon, Lebanon: al-Maktaba al-ʿAṣriyya, 1992.

Ibn Taymiyya, Taqī al-Dīn. *Al-Ḥisba fī l-islām*. Edited by Sayyid b. Muḥammad Ibn Abī Saʿda. Kuwait: Maktabat Dār al-Arqam, 1983. Translated by Muhtar Holland as *Public Duties in Islam: The Institution of the Ḥisba*. Leicester, U.K.: Islamic Foundation, 1982.

Madelung, W. "Amr Be Maʿrūf." *Encyclopaedia Iranica*, http://www.iranicaonline.org/articles/amr-be-maruf-arabic-al-amr-bel-maruf-wal-nahy-an-al-monkar-enjoining-what-is-proper-or-good-and-forbidding-what-is-reprehensible-or-evil-one-of-the-principle-religious-duties-in-islam.

Māwardī, Abū al-Ḥasan al-. *Al-Aḥkām al-sulṭāniyya wa-l-wilāyāt al-dīniyya*. Beirut: Dar al-Kutub al-ʿIlmiyya, 1985.

KRISTEN A. STILT

COMPANIONS OF THE PROPHET. Known in Arabic as al-Ṣaḥābah or al-Aṣḥāb, the Companions of the Prophet are credited by tradition with having played a seminal role in shaping the early Muslim community and laying the bases of religious, legal, and political thought. The Companions collectively were eulogized by the early biographer Ibn Saʿd (d. 845):

> All the Companions of the Messenger of God, peace and blessings be upon him, were models to be emulated, whose actions are remembered, whose opinions were consulted, and who voiced their opinions. Those who were the most prominent among the Companions of the Messenger of God, peace and blessings be upon him, listened to *ḥadīths* and transmitted them.

As this statement points out, of particular significance is the role of the best-known Companions in the preservation of the memory of the Prophet, his actions, and particularly his speech—that is to say, their role in the formation of the sunnah, the second most important source of law after the Qur'ān. The primary component of the sunnah is Muḥammad's recorded speech, known as *ḥadīth* (literally, "statement" or "speech").

Because of the importance of *ḥadīth* transmission in the development of the religious sciences after the Qur'ān and the indispensable role of the Companions in this activity, interest in recording the details of their lives emerged early. Biographical works written specifically to assess the reliability of the *ḥadīth* transmitters known as *rijāl* (literally, "men," although entries on women transmitters are included as well), as well as works on the *ḥadīth* sciences, contain valuable information about the Ṣaḥābah and are often remarkably candid in documenting both the positive and negative traits of individual Companions. Thus the scholar Ibn Qutaybah (d. 889) relates in regard to the prominent Companion Abū Hurayrah, for example, that ʿUmar, ʿUthmān, ʿĀʾishah, and ʿAlī rejected *ḥadīths* related by him as unreliable.

The candid portrayals of Companions found in early authoritative sources did not impede, however, the development of an image of the Companions as near-perfect individuals who exemplified the highest Islamic ideals in both their private and public conduct. One of the main impetuses for this evolution was the growing dialectical exchanges between the Sunnīs and the Shīʿīs. The Shīʿīs would progress from an earlier neutral stance toward the Ṣaḥābah to outright denunciation of the majority of the Companions for having withheld from ʿAlī what was assumed to be his preordained right to become the caliph or imam after the Prophet's death. The Sunnīs, in turn, formulated the collective moral excellence of the Companions, who were defined as those who had interacted with the Prophet on a regular basis as well as those who had met him only once. The chronological excellence imputed to the generation of the Companions followed by the next two generations of Muslims finds full expression in a statement attributed to the Prophet, in which he remarks: "The best of people are from my generation, then from the second [generation], then from the third. Then will come a group of people in whom there will be no good."

BIBLIOGRAPHY

Afsaruddin, Asma. *The First Muslims: History and Memory*. Oxford: Oneworld, 2008.

Ibn Saʿd, Muḥammad. *Al-ṭabaqāt al-kubrā*. Edited by Muḥammad ʿAbd al-Qādir ʿAtā. 9 vols. Beirut, Lebanon, 1990–1991.

ASMA AFSARUDDIN

CONGRESSES. Although the sentiment of international Muslim solidarity is intrinsic to the faith of Islam, it took no organized form until modern times. In the course of the twentieth century, modernized communications made it possible to translate vague principles of solidarity into periodic congresses of Muslims from different lands. Some of these congresses have evolved into international Islamic organizations that promote political, economic, and cultural interaction among Muslim peoples and states.

First Initiatives. Muslim reformists were the first to suggest the holding of Islamic congresses, in writings dating from the late nineteenth century. These reformists sought a forum to promote and sanction the internal reform of Islam, and they believed that an assembly of influential Muslims would strengthen Islam's ability to resist Western imperialism. The advent of easy and regular steamer transport made it possible to imagine regular gatherings of Muslim thinkers, activists, and notables. As an observer wrote in 1896, such a congress would "clear Islam of many unjust accusations, and establish its place in the concert of modern civilizations."

A number of émigré intellectuals in Cairo first popularized the idea in the Muslim world. In 1900 one of them, ʿAbd al-Raḥmān al-Kawākibī of Aleppo, published an influential tract titled *Umm al-qurā*, which purported to be the secret protocol of an Islamic congress convened in Mecca during the pilgrimage of 1899. The imaginary congress culminated in a call for a restored Arab Caliphate, an idea then in vogue in reformist circles. Support for such a congress also became a staple of the reformist journal *al-Manār*, published in Cairo by Muḥammad Rashīd Riḍā of Syrian Tripoli. Kawākibī and Rashīd Riḍā both believed that Mecca during the pilgrimage offered the most appropriate stage for such a congress, but other reformists favored Istanbul or Cairo. The Crimean Tatar reformist Ismail

Gasprali̇ (Gasprinskii) launched the first concrete initiative in Cairo, where he unsuccessfully attempted to convene a "general" Islamic congress in 1907–1908.

Kawākibī's book, Rashīd Riḍā's appeals, and Gasprali̇'s initiative all aroused the suspicion of Ottoman authorities, who believed that a well-attended Islamic congress would fatally undermine the religious authority claimed by the Ottoman sultan-caliph. They feared the possible transformation of any such congress into an electoral college for choosing an Arab caliph who would champion the separation of the Arabic-speaking provinces from the Ottoman Empire. Steadfast Ottoman opposition thwarted all the early initiatives of the reformists and associated the congress idea with political dissidence. In 1911 Rashīd Riḍā wrote that "the Muslims are not yet ready to convene a general Islamic congress for discussion of their interests and how to improve their lot. Intellectuals have repeatedly advocated this step, but no one heard them, noticed them, or showed them any sympathy."

Early Congresses. The final dismemberment of the Ottoman Empire after World War I removed the Ottoman obstacle and created a void, which a number of Muslim leaders and activists rushed to fill by convening Islamic congresses. In each instance they sought to mark their causes or their ambitions with the stamp of Islamic consensus. Some conveners sought wider Muslim support against non-Muslim enemies; others coveted the title of caliph, which they hoped to secure through the acclaim of a Muslim assembly.

In 1919, Mustafa Kemal Atatürk convened an Islamic congress in Anatolia to mobilize foreign Muslim support for his military campaigns. After his victory, however, Kemal took no further initiatives, and he ultimately severed Turkey from wider Islam by abolishing the caliphate in 1924. During the pilgrimage season of 1924, King Ḥusayn ibn ʿAlī of the Hejaz summoned a "pilgrimage congress" in Mecca to support his own short-lived claim to the caliphate, but he was driven into exile by ʿAbd al-ʿAzīz ibn Saʿūd, who occupied Mecca and convened his own "world" congress during the pilgrimage season of 1926. This congress, which ʿAbd al-ʿAzīz hoped would confer Islamic sanction to his administration of the holy cities, instead drew many criticisms, and he did not reconvene it.

Also in 1926, the leading clerics of al-Azhar University in Cairo summoned a "caliphate congress" to consider the effects of the Turkish abolition of the caliphate. The congress enjoyed the support of Egypt's King Fuʾād, who reputedly coveted the title of caliph, but no decision issued from the gathering. In 1931, Amīn al-Ḥusaynī, *mufti* of Jerusalem, convened a "general" congress of Muslims in Jerusalem to secure foreign Muslim support for the Arab struggle against the British Mandate and Zionism. In 1935, the Pan-Islamic activist Shakīb Arslān convened a congress of Europe's Muslims in Geneva to carry the protest against imperialism to the heart of Europe. And in 1938, Abdürräshid Ibragimov, the Volga Tatar Pan-Islamist, convened a "world" congress in Tokyo in a bid to link Japan and Islam in a common struggle against European imperialism.

Each of these early congresses resolved to create a permanent organization and convene additional congresses, but all such efforts were foiled by internal rivalries or by the intervention of the European powers. Each of the early congresses also revolved around political rather than doctrinal matters. Following this precedent, subsequent congresses remained far more concerned with the defense of Islam than with its reform.

The painful partitions of India and Palestine, as well as improvements in air travel, encouraged new initiatives in the 1940s and 1950s. In 1949 Pakistan sponsored the creation of the Karachi-based World Islamic Congress, presided over by the exiled Palestinian leader Amīn al-Ḥusaynī.

The organization aimed to promote solidarity between Pakistani and Arab Muslims against India and Israel. Beginning in 1953, many of the leading figures in Islamic activism attended the meetings in Jerusalem of the General Islamic Conference for Jerusalem, which operated under the auspices of the Muslim Brotherhood. It served to organize international Islamic support against Israel and enjoyed the active support of Jordan. These congresses briefly succeeded in creating secretariats and even reconvened at wide intervals before they too became practically defunct.

Obstacle of Arabism. With the progress of decolonization, several Muslim leaders floated new plans for the creation of a permanent organization of independent Muslim states. Pakistan, anxious to secure wider Muslim support against India, took a number of initiatives, especially during a failed 1952 campaign for a conference of Muslim prime ministers. During the Meccan pilgrimage of 1954, an "Islamic congress" assembled the heads of state of Pakistan, Saudi Arabia, and Egypt in Mecca and created a standing organization headquartered in Cairo. The initiative for an organization of Muslims states ran aground, however, as Egypt moved increasingly toward a revolutionary Pan-Arabism under its leader Gamal Abdel Nasser. By the mid-1950s Egypt's secular Pan-Arabism had become the dominant ideology in the Arab world. In the name of this ideology Egypt suppressed the Muslim Brotherhood at home and launched a cold war against Saudi Arabia, culminating in Egyptian military intervention in Yemen.

Saudi Arabia, under siege by Pan-Arab Egypt, responded by developing a rival Pan-Islam, around which it rallied other besieged regimes and the Muslim Brotherhood. For this purpose the Saudi government sponsored the establishment in 1962 of the Mecca-based Muslim World League, which built a worldwide network of Muslim clients. The league not only operated among pilgrims but also assembled many congresses of Muslim activists and *ʿulamāʾ* (religious scholars) from abroad, especially from among the Muslim Brotherhood. Beginning in 1964, Egypt responded by organizing congresses of Egyptian and foreign *ʿulamāʾ* under the auspices of al-Azhar's Academy of Islamic Research. These rival bodies then convened a succession of dueling congresses in Mecca and Cairo, each claiming the sole prerogative of defining Islam in such a way as to legitimate Saudi or Egyptian policy. In 1965–1966 Saudi Arabia's King Fayṣal launched a campaign for an Islamic summit conference that would have countered the Arab summits dominated by Egypt; however, Nasser had sufficient influence to thwart the initiative, which he denounced as a foreign-inspired "Islamic pact" designed to defend the interests of Western imperialism.

Organization of the Islamic Conference. Israel's 1967 defeat of the combined Arab armies and annexation of East Jerusalem eroded faith in the brand of Pan-Arabism championed by Egypt. These events damaged Nasser's standing and inspired a return to Islam, setting the scene for a renewed Saudi initiative. In September 1969, following an arson attack on the al-Aqṣā mosque in Jerusalem, Muslim heads of state set aside their differences and met in Rabat, Morocco, in the first Islamic summit conference. King Fayṣal took this opportunity to press for the creation of a permanent organization of Muslim states. This time the effort succeeded, and in May 1971 the participating states established the Organization of the Islamic Conference (OIC). The new organization, headquartered in Jiddah (pending the restoration of Jerusalem to Islam), adopted its charter in March 1972.

The OIC eventually achieved minor prominence in regional diplomacy, principally through the organization of triennial Islamic summit conferences and annual conferences of the foreign ministers of member states. The OIC's activities fell into three broad categories. First, it extended moral support to Muslim states and movements engaged in conflicts with non-Muslims. Most of these efforts were devoted to the causes of Palestine and Jerusalem, although the OIC supported many other Muslim resistance movements, from Afghanistan to the Philippines. Its conferences passed hundreds of resolutions on these issues, although its support for embattled Muslims remained strictly declaratory. Second, the organization offered mediation in disputes and wars between its own members. However, the deep divisions among member states limited the moral force of the OIC's calls for peace, and in any case it lacked armed force for truce supervision or peacekeeping. In practice, the United Nations played a far greater role than the OIC in mediating conflicts between Muslim states. Finally, the OIC sponsored an array of subsidiary and affiliated institutions to promote political, economic, and cultural cooperation among its members. The most influential of these institutions was the Islamic Development Bank, established in December 1973 and formally opened in October 1975. The bank, funded by the wealthier OIC states, financed development projects that promoted cooperation and trade among member states. Yet despite these economic efforts, the amount of trade among member states, as a percentage of their overall trade, continued to decline throughout the 1980s.

The OIC represented the culmination of government efforts to organize Muslim states, but it remained a weak organization, supported largely by Saudi funds and biased in favor of Saudi policies. For this reason, the existence of the OIC did not prevent several of its members from independently organizing international Islamic congresses and organizations. They did so to garner Muslim support for their own policies, often in defiance of Saudi Arabia and the OIC.

Impact of Libya and Iran. In September 1969, shortly before the first Islamic summit, Muʿammar al-Qadhdhāfī carried out a coup in Libya and instituted a revolutionary regime based upon his own interpretation of Islam. Qadhdhāfī made it clear that he intended to promote his own leadership of Islam, and the following year he convened a conference that laid the foundations of the Tripoli-based Islamic Call Society (later the World Islamic Call Society). This organization convened frequent conferences in later years and through its far-flung branches did much to disseminate Qadhdhāfī's eclectic vision of Islam beyond Libya's borders.

Iran played an even more important role in stimulating the rapid increase in the variety of Islamic conferences in the 1980s. After the revolution in 1979, and especially after the outbreak of war with Iraq in 1980, Iran conducted a vigorous campaign against Saudi Arabia's claim to organize the consensus of Islam. For a decade Iran virtually ignored the OIC and convened frequent conferences of its own clients and supporters from abroad. Secretariats based in Tehran supported a succession of organizations, including the World Congress of Friday Imams and Prayer Leaders (from 1982), the Conference on Islamic Thought (from 1983), and the International Conference to Support the Islamic Revolution of the People of Palestine (from 1991). Despite their different names, these congress initiatives reassembled many of the same foreign participants, who placed an Islamic stamp of approval on Iran's policies. Iran also convened many extraordinary conferences after the killing of several hundred Iranians in Mecca during the pilgrimage season of 1987, and after Ayatollah Ruhollah Khomeini's edict against the novelist Salman Rushdie in 1989.

Saudi Arabia, Egypt, and Iraq were aligned in opposition to Iran throughout the 1980s and cooperated in convening congresses of those

Muslim figures that were prepared to sanction their own policies in the name of Islam. Existing organizations such as Saudi Arabia's Muslim World League and Egypt's Academy of Islamic Research expanded their cooperation. Saudi Arabia and Egypt also combined with Iraq in 1983 to establish the Baghdad-based Popular Islamic Conference, which mobilized Muslim support for Iraq's war against Iran. (When the Iraqi invasion of Kuwait in 1990 turned Iraq and Saudi Arabia from allies into enemies, each side simultaneously convened the Popular Islamic Conference in Baghdad and Mecca, respectively, where each passed resolutions condemning the other.)

Islamist Congresses. In the 1990s a growing number of semiclandestine Islamist movements came into the open as governments adopted policies of political liberalization. These movements had strengthened their ties during the 1980s in little-publicized conferences, often held in Europe. As they began to acquire legitimacy and even power, they launched their own congress initiatives. In 1990 ʿAbd al-Raḥmān Khalīfah, leader of the Jordanian Muslim Brotherhood, convened a World Islamic Popular Gathering in Amman that was attended by the leading figures of the Muslim Brotherhood worldwide. In 1991 Ḥasan al-Turābī, the Islamist guide of the Sudanese regime, convened a Popular Arab Islamic Conference in Khartoum attended by many of the most notable Islamists. The conference created a permanent secretariat, and Turābī presented the new organization as the populist alternative to the OIC.

The plethora of organizations that summoned Islamic congresses and conferences reflected the intensified competition for authority in contemporary Islam. This competition had long pitted states against one another. But as Islam became the common language of protest, congresses increasingly brought together Islamist movements of opposition seeking to help one another in the pursuit of power. Less than a century after Kawākibī's dream, a crowded calendar of congresses binds the world of Islam together as never before. It remains uncertain, however, whether these often competing institutions bridge the differences between Muslims or serve to widen them.

[*See also* Atatürk, Mustafa Kemal; Daʿwah; Ḥusayn ibn ʿAlī; Kawākibī, ʿAbd al-Raḥmān al-; Nasser, Gamal Abdel; Organization of Islamic Cooperation; *and* Turābī, Ḥasan al-.]

BIBLIOGRAPHY

Brown, L. Carl, ed. *Diplomacy in the Middle East: The International Relations of Regional and Outside Powers*. Rev. ed. New York: I. B. Tauris, 2004.

Brown, L. Carl. *Religion and State: The Muslim Approach to Politics*. New York: Columbia University Press, 2000.

Dawisha, Adeed, ed. *Islam in Foreign Policy*. Cambridge, U.K.: Cambridge University Press, 1983. Ten country studies on the general role of Islam in the formulation of foreign policy.

Esposito, John L., and François Burgat, eds. *Modernising Islam: Religion in the Public Sphere in the Middle East and Europe*. London: C. Hurst, 2003.

Khan, Saad S. *Reasserting International Islam: A Focus on the Organization of the Islamic Conference and Other Islamic Institutions*. Karachi: Oxford University Press, 2001.

Kramer, Martin. *Islam Assembled: The Advent of the Muslim Congresses*. New York: Columbia University Press, 1986. Event-by-event account of the development of Islamic congresses, from the first initiatives through World War II, with extensive bibliography.

Landau, Jacob M. *The Politics of Pan-Islam: Ideology and Organization*. Oxford: Clarendon, 1990. Detailed survey of the political role of Pan-Islam beginning from the late Ottoman period, with extensive bibliography.

Moinuddin, Hasan. *The Charter of the Islamic Conference and Legal Framework of Economic Co-operation among Its Member States: A Study of the Charter, the General Agreement for Economic, Technical, and Commercial Co-operation and the Agreement for Promotion, Protection, and Guarantee of Investments among Member States of the OIC*. Oxford: Clarendon, 1987. Examines the constitutional foundation of the OIC.

Sheikh, Naveed S. *The New Politics of Islam: Pan-Islamic Foreign Policy in a World of States*. London: Routledge Curzon, 2003.

Martin Kramer

Constitutional Movement.

The reinstatement of the Ottoman constitution (*kanun-ı esasî*) on 24 July 1908 followed a carefully orchestrated mutiny by military officers and soldiers in Macedonia. Its immediate origins went back to 1907, when the Committee of Progress and Union (CPU), an underground political organization that opposed the autocratic rule of Sultan Abdülhamid II (r. 1876–1909), merged with the Salonika-based Ottoman Freedom Society, a secret group of military officers. Having lost control of the army, the sultan declared that the constitution—suspended in 1878—was in force once again, that elections were to be held soon, and that a new parliament, or chamber of deputies (*meclis-i mebusan*), was to be formed. In a moment of unity, Ottomans across the multiethnic and multireligious empire celebrated the news of the constitution and the apparent arrival of representative government. The group that staged the revolution, now renamed the Ottoman Committee of Union and Progress (CUP, *Osmanlı İttihad ve Terakki Cemiyeti*), and its leaders—Enver, Resneli Niyazi, Talat—became canonized on postcards and placards in mass gatherings as the "heroes of freedom." Elections were held in late 1908, with all taxpaying men over the age of twenty-five eligible to vote. While bans on political activity and restrictions on the press were lifted, the high hopes for representative government remained unfulfilled as the empire was buffeted by crisis after crisis, including Austria-Hungary's annexation of Bosnia-Herzegovina (1908), an armed movement against the CUP (1909), massacres of Christians in Adana (1909), the Italian attack on Ottoman Libya and its occupation of the Dodecanese Islands (1911–1912), the two Balkan Wars (1912 and 1913), and the CUP's own tendencies toward authoritarianism. The CUP's constitutionalism, it turned out, had been born not out of liberal conviction but out of the desire to sideline the sultan, to grab the reins of state for itself, and to save the empire from what it considered a dual threat—external invasion and occupation and growing internal divisions within the empire. The so-called Young Turk Revolution of 1908 built on an older constitutional movement that reached back into the nineteenth century (and an Ottoman-Islamic tradition of limited government, based on the principles of the "circle of justice" and the Islamic concept of "consultation," which go back much further). In the 1860s, a group highly critical of the state's foreign and domestic policies and known as the Young Ottomans, led by Namık Kemal, Ali Suavi, and Ziya Bey, began demanding representative government and a constitution through their publications, especially their newspaper *Hürriyet* (Liberty). In 1876, the liberal reformer and grand *vezir*, Midhat Pasha, succeeded in persuading the sultan to grant a constitution, at a time of violent unrest in the Balkans and the threat of invasion. The First Constitutional Period came to an abrupt end, however. In the Arab provinces, Buṭrus al-Bustānī became an ardent supporter of constitutionalism in the Ottoman Empire in the 1860s. The empire's Armenians adopted their own constitution in 1863 and formed an Armenian national assembly, with the primary objective of limiting the powers of the Armenian patriarch in Istanbul.

Bibliography

Çiçek, Nazan. *The Young Ottomans: Turkish Critics of the Eastern Question in the Late Nineteenth Century*. New York: I. B. Tauris, 2010.

Hanioğlu, M. Şükrü. *Preparation for a Revolution: The Young Turks, 1902–1908*. Studies in Middle Eastern History. New York: Oxford University Press, 2001.

MUSTAFA AKSAKAL

CONSTITUTIONAL REVOLUTION. The Iranian Constitutional Revolution (1905–1911) was one of two major revolutions in modern Iran that, together with several rebellions, made Iran the most revolutionary Middle Eastern country of the modern era. Iran owed its revolutionary character largely to the country's semicolonial status (much like revolutionary China); the alliance among merchants, *ʿulamāʾ* (religious scholars), and modern intellectuals; and the central role in revolutions of many cities. The particular causes of the 1905–1911 movement included dissatisfaction with the growth of Western power and with economic stagnation, as well as the influence of modern ideas and of the Russo-Japanese war of 1904–1905 and the Russian revolution of 1905.

The immediate cause of the revolution was, as is often the case, trivial. In December 1905, the governor of Tehran beat the feet of a sugar merchant accused of raising prices, after which many *mullahs* and merchants took *bast* (sanctuary) in Tehran's royal mosque. After their dispersal, many *ʿulamāʾ* took *bast* in a shrine and presented demands to the shah, the crucial one being for an undefined "house of justice." The shah dismissed the governor and in principle acceded to the demand for the house of justice in January 1906 but did nothing further. There followed preaching by radical preachers and the killing of a *sayyid* by an officer; as a result, many *mullahs* and others took *bast* in Qom in July 1906. Thousands of merchants and tradespeople took *bast* in the British legation in Tehran and began to demand a parliament. In August, Muẓaffar al-Dīn Shāh (d. 1907) accepted this demand, and the first parliament, or *majlis*, was elected under a six-class system, which gave more power to the popular-class guilds than they were to enjoy in subsequent parliaments, elected under a nonclass system.

The first majlis opened in October 1906, and a committee wrote a Fundamental Law, which the shah signed only when he was mortally ill, in December 1906. A longer Supplementary Fundamental Law was signed by the new shah, Muḥammad ʿAlī, in October 1907. Together, these made up the Iranian constitution that remained in effect, with minor amendments, until the 1979 revolution. It was based largely on the Belgian constitution of 1830, but, on the insistence of the *ʿulamāʾ*, it included references to Islam and a provision that a committee of five *mujtahids* (authorities on the interpretation of Islamic law) would pass on the constitutionality of parliamentary laws. This remained a dead letter. The intent of the parliamentarians was to set up a Western-style constitutional monarchy with power held by parliament and its chosen ministers, but this rarely was the case.

There was a flowering of liberal and radical newspapers and societies during the revolutionary period. The new shah brought back a conservative prime minister, called the Atābak (Atabeg), and the majlis majority did not insist on making this choice itself. Several groups opposed autocracy: merchants and tradespeople; the *ʿulamāʾ* opposition, led by the liberal *sayyid* Muḥammad Ḥusayn Ṭabāṭabāʾī and the opportunistic *sayyid* ʿAbd Allāh Bihbahānī; and liberals and radicals, such as the then-socialist deputy (from Tabrīz) Sayyid Ḥasan Taqīzādah. The far left and the shah were both involved in the killing of the Atābak on 31 August 1907, by coincidence the same date as the signing of the Anglo-Russian Treaty dividing Iran into spheres of influence. The introduction of Russo-British cooperation in Iran helped doom the revolution.

The shah, with the aid of the Russian-led Cossack Brigade, staged a successful coup against the majlis and the opposition in June 1908. Only Tabrīz, led by two guerrilla leaders from the popular classes, held out. When Russian troops moved in, in 1909, the guerrillas moved to Gilan, where the constitutionalist movement was also strong. In the south, the Bakhtiārī tribe had its reasons to oppose the shah, and in July 1909, the Bakhtiārīs and the northern revolutionaries converged on Tehran. They deposed the shah and installed his minor son, Aḥmad Shāh, under a regency. Although leftists, including those influenced by Russian social democrats, were strong in the opposition and in the Democrat Party, most power went to a conservative, Bakhtiārī-led cabinet.

Severe financial problems led the government to seek a foreign adviser not tied to Britain and Russia, and they brought in an American expert, Morgan Shuster, to reform Iranian finances. Shuster wanted to appoint a British subject to head a tax gendarmerie, but the Russians said this violated the Anglo-Russian Treaty, and Britain acquiesced. In November 1911, the Russians issued an ultimatum and sent in troops, and for several years Russia and Britain controlled the government, marking the real end of the revolution, although the constitution and the experience of political participation remained as its legacy.

[*See also* Iran, Islamic Republic of; *and* Majlis.]

BIBLIOGRAPHY

Afary, Janet. *The Iranian Constitutional Revolution, 1906–1911: Grassroots Democracy, Social Democracy, and the Origins of Feminism*. New York: Columbia University Press, 1996.

Bayat, Mangol. *Iran's First Revolution: Shiʿism and the Constitutional Revolution of 1905–1909*. New York: Oxford University Press, 1991. Questions the importance usually given the *ʿulamāʾ* and incorporates Russian material, especially on the role of the left.

Berberian, Houri. *Armenians and the Iranian Constitutional Revolution of 1905–1911: The Love for Freedom Has No Fatherland*. Boulder, Colo.: Westview, 2001.

Bonakdarian, Mansour. *Britain and the Iranian Constitutional Revolution of 1906–1911: Foreign Policy, Imperialism, and Dissent*. Syracuse, N.Y.: Syracuse University Press, 2006.

Browne, Edward G. *The Persian Revolution of 1905–1909*. Cambridge, U.K.: Cambridge University Press, 1910. The classic work, a partisan pro-revolution book written during the revolution; still useful for its translated and summarized primary sources and as a primary source from one perspective.

Kasravi, Ahmad. *History of the Iranian Constitutional Revolution*. Translated by Evan Siegel. Costa Mesa, Calif.: Mazda, 2006.

Keddie, Nikki R. *Iran: Religion, Politics, and Society: Collected Essays*. London: Frank Cass, 1980. Collection of articles, including "Religion and Irreligion in Early Iranian Nationalism" (pp. 13–52) and others discussing the constitutional revolution.

Keddie, Nikki R. *Modern Iran: Roots and Results of Revolution*. New Haven, Conn.: Yale University Press, 2003.

Lambton, Ann K. S., ed. *Qājār Persia: Eleven Studies*. Austin: University of Texas Press, 1988.

Martin, Vanessa. *Islam and Modernism: The Iranian Revolution of 1906*. London: Tauris, 1989. The first of three recent comprehensive books on the revolution, readable and strong in its discussion of Shiism and the role of the *ʿulamāʾ*.

NIKKI R. KEDDIE

CONSTITUTIONS AND CONSTITUTIONALISM. Accompanying the rise of Islam in Arabia, Islamic constitutional principles began to emerge consistently along with the revelation of the Qurʾān and the foundation of *sunnah*. The first Qurʾānic word revealed was the command "Read" (96:1). This command, with other Qurʾānic verses (20:114, 39:9), laid the foundation for a fundamental right, namely, the equal right to education for both men and women, because the command for gaining knowledge is gender-neutral. Throughout the twenty-three years of its revelation, the message of Islam's remaining constitutional principles had to be solidified and tested in various situations through the use of the Qur'ān and *sunnah*. The Qur'ān emphasizes numerous constitutional principles, including those related to preservation of human dignity (17:70), maintenance of the sanctity and security of private life (24:27, 49:12), and ensuring the right to life and personal security (17:33, 2:193). The Prophet Muḥammad's actions and sayings, his *sunnah*, also introduced a large number of constitutional principles. In a notable incident that is entrenched in the rule of law of the developing Islamic state, the clan of a noble woman who had committed theft sent a close companion of the Prophet Muḥammad to dissuade him from inflicting the punishment for theft upon the woman. The Prophet summarily rejected the request, noting that the selective application of punishment based on the offender's social status had been the cause of the destruction of earlier nations (Ṣaḥīḥ al-Bukhārī). The Prophet Muḥammad, in his farewell speech, emphasized the sanctity of life and human dignity, especially that of women, and the right to acquire private property.

After the death of the Prophet Muḥammad, Islamic constitutional principles were applied in full. This is especially true during the golden era of the Islamic State, that of the Rāshidūn (the Rightly Guided Caliphs). Even rights that were uncommon in old civilizations were matured and implemented in Islam. For example, social-welfare rights were fully elucidated in the Qur'ān (2:177, 51:19, 70:24–5, 4:36, 9:60). The religion, race, or cultural background of a citizen of the Islamic State was never a factor in determining the applicability of these rights. In a notable incident, the second caliph, ʿUmar ibn al-Khaṭṭāb, had endorsed social-welfare payments to a destitute Jewish citizen of the Islamic State and criticized the officials who failed to recognize the deprived status of that citizen. In the reign of the first caliph, Abū Bakr, the Muslim army commander Khālid ibn al-Walīd made a treaty with the Christians of Hira, a city in Iraq, and affirmed their right to social welfare, equivalent to that of Muslims, and guaranteed tax exemptions for the poor and the disabled.

In the Prophet Muḥammad's lifetime, the first Islamic constitutional document was produced, commonly known as the Charter of Medina or the Constitution of Medina. This agreement was made between Muslims and the people of Medina, including its Jewish community. Numerous Islamic constitutional principles are manifest in the document, including the right to social welfare, citizenship, and the free exercise of religion. This document was followed by a number of constitutional documents that were produced when a need arose. For example, the Najrān treaty between the Muslims and the Christians of Najrān bound Muslims to its terms from the moment of its inception until the Day of Judgment. The second caliph, ʿUmar ibn al-Khaṭṭāb, concluded a peace treaty with the people of Jerusalem that reemphasized a number of constitutional principles, including the free exercise of religion, the freedom of movement, and the equal protection of the law. Modern Muslim states have incorporated Islamic constitutional principles in their constitution either singularly or collectively, as in the Cairo Declaration on Human Rights in Islam (1990).

While most of the constitutional principles are clear, several conditional principles are subject to misrepresentation or misapplication by the Muslim States. Equality has always been subject to misrepresentation. The general principle of equality has been stated several times in the Qur'ān as follows:

> O mankind! We created you from a single (pair) of a male and a female, and made you into nations and tribes, that ye may know each other (not that ye may despise each other). Verily the most honored of you in the sight of Allah is (he who is) the most righteous of you.

And Allah has full Knowledge and is well-acquainted (with all things). (49:13)

This verse promulgated the concept of unity of origin and, if applied properly, would eliminate any basis for inequality because the basic premise of discrimination requires unlikeness in race, gender, religion, or otherwise. If all are of one origin, then all are alike, and any grounds for discrimination would be unsustainable. In this context, various rules in Islam that appear superficially discriminatory need to be interpreted within the framework of the concept of unity of origin. Examples of superficially discriminatory rules are *jizyah* and women's rights.

Jizyah is a financial obligation levied on non-Muslims who reside in the Islamic State. Because Muslims do not have to pay *jizyah*, non-Muslims may view paying *jizyah* as a discriminatory practice aimed to convert non-Muslims to Islam. The eminent Islamic scholar Yūsuf al-Qaraḍāwī explained that the *jizyah* ratio must be equal to *zakāh*, a mandatory charity imposed on Muslims. If the term *jizyah* is offensive to non-Muslims, it may be called mandatory charity or alms or some such, so long as it is paid. Christians of the Banū Taghlib tribe during the reign of the second caliph, ʿUmar ibn al-Khaṭṭāb, approved the principle of paying some financial obligation; however, they expressed their dissatisfaction with the term *jizyah*. Caliph ʿUmar granted their request and changed the term to *ṣadaqah* (alms). A Muslim government that violates these guidelines for collecting *jizyah*—either by collecting *jizyah* in a dishonorable manner or by collecting a higher rate of *jizyah* than of *zakāh*—to such a degree that it forces non-Muslims to convert to Islam not only violates the principle of equality and the proper application *jizyah* but also violates other constitutional principles such as freedom from compulsion in religion, as delineated in the Qurʾān (2:256). In this context, *jizyah* can be understood as an Islamic institution intended to make non-Muslims pay their fair share of financial obligations to the state as do Muslims in paying *zakāh*, and there thus is no discrimination.

Typically, women's right of inheritance is suggestive of discrimination. The Qurʾān (4:176) determines that women, as a general rule, should receive one-half of a man's share of an inheritance. The application of this rule in a vacuum, absent other rules that balance it out would plainly result in discrimination. However, as Professor Rashad Hassan Khalil, dean of the Faculty of *Sharīʿah* and Law at al-Azhar University, explains, Islamic law mandates that a woman have the right to be supported her entire life, either by a family member such as a father, husband, or uncle or by the state. Also, a woman is under no obligation to support anyone including, herself, her husband, or any other family members. On the other hand, men, fulfilling a social function as father, husband, son, or otherwise, bear the entire responsibility of supporting women. Consequently, whatever a woman earns from work or inherits shall serve only one purpose—as an additional joy in her life.

Misapplication of Islamic constitutional principles in Muslim states is more commonplace than misrepresentation. Political struggles are typical motives for misapplication of Islamic constitutional principles. For instance, the Islamic historian Aḥmad Amīn concluded that the Fāṭimid dynasty in general was marked by excellent treatment of non-Muslims to a degree that approaches preferential treatment over Sunnī Muslims. He suggested that the Fāṭimid caliphs were Shīʿah who were attempting to expand their territories and influence the public with Shīʿah ideologies; they thus took a very lenient approach to all religious groups in order to attain recognition. Accordingly, it was only the political environment in this era that had granted non-Muslims their rights. When the political environment changed, individuals became subject to non-Islamic ill treatment. Al-Ḥākim bī ʾAmr Allāh (1021), the sixth of the Fāṭimid caliphs, in advancing his religious ideology, persecuted Sunnī Muslims, Christian, and Jews alike. This example demonstrates that a basic Islamic constitutional right such as human dignity, as delineated in the Qurʾān (17:70), can be subject to the whims of a ruler.

Several constitutional principles have been subject to various political interpretations throughout Islamic history. Chief among them is the concept of *shūrā* (mutual consultation) that is delineated in the Qurʾān twice (3:159 and 42:36). The interpretation of this concept has shaped the Islamic State and has dramatically affected Muslim political life from the death of the Prophet Muḥammad to the twenty-first century. The concept of *shūrā* is critical in deciding two distinct matters, the succession process for the ruler of the Muslim State and the composition and rule of the Muslim State's parliament or *shūrā* council. The Prophet Muḥammad, the exemplary model for Muslims, had exercised *shūrā* by creating a *shūrā* council with up to seventy members. He consulted with them regarding the emerging Islamic State's affairs. He championed the idea that women could be included in the *shūrā* council. He solicited and then followed the advice of his wife Umm Salamah after the al-Ḥudaybīyah treaty, which made Muslims more accepting of the treaty terms. However, he never put forward a means of succession for the ruler of the Muslim State. After the death of the Prophet, al-Khulafāʾ al-Rāshidūn (the four Rightly Guided Caliphs) presented three models for the appointment of subsequent rulers. The first model was the imperfect election process of the first caliph, Abū Bakr. On this occasion, al-Anṣār (the Muslims of Medina) met in the Saqīfah banī Sāʿidat to elect one of them to be the new leader, but three of the Muhājirūn (the Muslims of Mecca) rushed to the meeting to join the election process, driven by the fear that al-Anṣār, who were only a portion of the population, might make a decision without the consultation of the rest of the Muslims. The meeting resulted in the election of the closest companion of the Prophet Muḥammad, Abū Bakr, as the new leader. This election process was far from perfect, because many Muslims neither voted nor were consulted in the election process. However, this imperfect procedure did not stir Muslims' disapproval for a number of reasons. The elite status of Abū Bakr, as the closest companion to the Prophet Muḥammad, was well appreciated by the populace. The fact that the Prophet Muḥammad asked Abū Bakr to lead the Muslims in prayers shortly before the Prophet's death may have indicated to many Muslims the Prophet's desire to appoint Abū Bakr as the first caliph. Before his death, Abū Bakr appointed ʿUmar ibn al-Khaṭṭāb as his successor. ʿUmar, before his death, used new procedures. He nominated six community leaders and gave Muslims the power to elect one of them through sophisticated procedures. This process resulted in the election of ʿUthmān ibn ʿAffān. ʿUthmān's assassination triggered a civil war in the Islamic State and eventually resulted in the creation of the Umayyad monarchy, which was followed by various monarchies including the ʿAbbāsid and Fāṭimid monarchies. It is difficult to find any trace of *shūrā* doctrine in the ruler-succession process of the Umayyad, ʿAbbāsid, and Fāṭimid monarchies.

This history is influential in modern succession practices in Muslim states such as Saudi Arabia, the Persian Gulf States, and various autocratic republics. Article 5 of the current constitution of Saudi Arabia declares monarchy to be the system of governance. Only children of the founding king, ʿAbd al-ʿAzīz ibn ʿAbd al-Raḥmān Āl Saʿūd, are eligible to rule. Article 7 emphasizes that this system of governance is based upon the Qurʾān and *sunnah*. Article 8 declares that the system of governance is based on the Islamic principles of equality, *shūrā*, and justice. These articles are difficult to reconcile. If equality is a constitutional doctrine, why then are only the children of the founding king eligible to rule? Why is it that only the royal family may exercise *shūrā* in the succession process, excluding the rest of the Muslim population?

Many other Muslim states' constitutions contain similar provisions. Article 20 of the Moroccan constitution declares Morocco a monarchy, in which only the children of King Ḥasān II are eligible to rule. Article 1 of the constitution of Bahrain declares that only Ḥamad bin ʿĪsā bin Salmān Āl Khalīfah's children are eligible to rule. Several Muslim "republics," especially in the Middle East, do not differ fundamentally from the overt monarchies. Article 83 of the Syrian constitution was hastily amended in the year 2000 to lower the required minimum age of the president from forty to thirty-four, which was, at the time, the age of Bashar al-Assad, son of President Hafez al-Assad, in order to make him eligible for the presidency. He won the election with more than 97 percent of the vote. The historic and current state of affairs of the transfer of power in many Muslim states might be the result of the failure to create and implement a succession mechanism consistent with the doctrine of mutual consultation, but several Muslim states, such as Malaysia and Turkey, have created a free election mechanism to elect parliament members and the head of the state, consistent with the concept of mutual consultation mandated by *shūrā* doctrine.

This raises a question: what are the similarities and/or differences between a democratic election and a *shūrā* election of a ruler? If democracy is defined as government by the people with officials elected and the majority ruling while respecting minority rights, then *shūrā* is democracy with only one stipulation, that the people's will cannot override Islamic law. Accordingly, what has been practiced in the three models presented by the four Rightly Guided Caliphs is both democratic and in accordance with *shūrā* doctrine. These caliphs were either expressly elected or their appointment was ratified by the people. The people were satisfied with the result and did not challenge the appointment of any of them. The monarchies and the dictatorial regimes that followed were not a product of the lack of principle; rather, they are a product of the lack of a mechanism to ensure proper application of the doctrine. This line of analysis has been consistently presented by Islamic legal scholars. The renowned scholar al-Māwardī concluded that a ruler can assume power only if he is elected by those who have the right to vote or by appointment by the previous ruler, providing that the people ratify the appointment. In essence, the relationship between the ruler and the people is governed by a *bayʿah*, or contract, upon whose terms two parties, the people and the ruler, agree. If there is no agreement, as in case of many contemporary Muslim monarchies, or one party to the contract, namely, the ruler, violates the conditions of the contract, there is no contractual relationship, and consequently the ruler does not have legitimate authority to rule.

Because the Qurʾān mandated *shūrā* among Muslims in their affairs and the Prophet Muḥammad exercised *shūrā* in his life, it became indispensable in modern Muslim states to establish a parliament or *shūrā* council. However, there was variation in the rule of the council and the membership eligibility requirements. A number of Islamic legal scholars have suggested that the *shūrā* council's task should be limited to offering nonbinding advice to the ruler. They have relied on Qurʾānic verses asserting that the majority opinion may not be correct. Accordingly, the government ought not to be bound to the majority opinion. The following is one of the Qurʾānic verses they relied upon to form this opinion: "And if you obey most of those on the earth, they will mislead you far away from Allah's Path. They follow nothing but conjectures, and they do nothing but lie" (6:116).

Obviously, this interpretation is problematic because it institutes a rule in the wrong context. The verse states only that obedience of the entire population of earth will mislead. The Muslim State is different; what applies to the Islamic State differs from what is applicable to the people of the earth, who are mainly non-Muslims. Moreover, numerous *ḥadīth* and study of the practice of the rightly guided caliphs suggest that the majority opinion should prevail, so long as it is consistent with basic sources of Islamic law, the Qur'ān and *sunnah*. The Prophet Muḥammad commanded Muslims to adhere to the opinion of the *jamā'ah* (main group of Muslims) and avoid divisiveness (al-Tirmidhī). The Rightly Guided Caliphs also followed in the footsteps of the Prophet. The election process that was developed by 'Umar ibn al-Khaṭṭāb, the second caliph, suggests that majority opinion should prevail. Furthermore, in the early days of the Islamic State, the Muhājirūn (Muslims who migrated with the Prophet from Mecca to Medina) played a positive role in representing the collective consciousness of Muslims and supervised the caliph's affairs.

Several Muslim states, such as Saudi Arabia, follow this narrow interpretation of *shūrā* doctrine. Saudi Arabia, for example, established a *shūrā* council of 150 members appointed by the king. The council has very limited powers and is closer to advisory in nature, because they cannot legislate without the consent of the king. In contrast, other Islamic states, such as Turkey, Malaysia, and post-2011 revolutionary Egypt, adopted the prophetic approach where the parliament discusses state affairs and the majority opinion prevails. In these states, the parliament legislates and supervises the executive branch of the government.

Representation by women in the parliament also varies varies among states. The majority of Muslim states allow women to be members of parliament. Until 2011, Saudi Arabia barred women from joining the *shūrā* council. King Abdullah of Saudi Arabia on 25 September 2011 approved the participation of women as members in the *shūrā* council in accordance with *Sharī'ah* guidelines. He granted women the right to nominate themselves or participate in the nomination of other candidates for membership in municipal councils. This wind of change is indeed significant in Saudi Arabia, a state that has been dominated by conservative scholars. This has opened the door to speculation about the cause of this historic move, given that the rules of *shūrā* have not changed since the time of the Prophet Muḥammad, in the seventh century. Accordingly, it is surprising that the right of women to become members of the *shūrā* council was recognized in Saudi political life only as recently as 2011.

Representation of non-Muslims in the parliament/*shūrā* council of Muslim states has been a controversial issue among Islamic legal scholars. Several scholars have suggested that non-Muslims ought not to be represented, because the Qur'ān prohibits Muslims from taking non-Muslims as *awliyā'* (supporters, helpers). This opinion often cites two supporting verses in the Qur'ān: "Let not the believers take the disbelievers as Auliya' instead of the believers, and whoever does that will never be helped by Allah in any way, except if you indeed fear a danger from them. And Allah warns you against Himself (His punishment), and to Allah is the final return" (3:28), and, "O you who believe! Take not for Auliya' disbelievers instead of believers. Do you wish to offer Allah a manifest proof against yourselves?" (4:144).

An opposing argument suggests that the older interpretation of these Qur'ānic verses involved unwarranted and overly broad generalizations of the role of non-Muslims in the Islamic state. The exclusion of non-Muslims as *awliyāʾ* is limited to forbidding Muslims from blindly following non-Muslims with respect to law, way of life, and culture and forsaking the Islamic way. This is true especially when the non-Muslim lifestyle clearly contradicts Islamic law. However, it does not follow that Islam bans all sorts of cooperation with non-Muslims. Indeed, Muslims throughout the centuries have lived harmoniously with non-Muslims, whether in Muslim or in non-Muslim states. They have shared common ethical standards, allied for the general good, and built together mighty civilizations. The Prophet Muḥammad spoke highly of the pre-Islamic Ḥilf al-Fuḍūl (Oath of Fuḍūl), which aimed to uphold justice and aid the oppressed, and expressed his wish to join such an alliance if it occurred after the revelation of the message of Islam. What the Qurʾānic verse 58:22 prohibits is taking non-Muslims as *awliyāʾ* if they express enmity to Muslims and Islam and are wrongdoers. This interpretation clearly is in harmony with the obvious meaning of verse 60:1. Ultimately the Qurʾānic verses 60:8–9 declare that Allah does not forbid Muslims from dealing justly and kindly with those who neither fought them on account of religion nor drove them out of their homes. On this basis, the vast majority of Muslim states have allowed non-Muslims to be represented in the parliament.

Problems appear, however, when non-Muslims attempt to define or modify Islam. Drafting of the post–2011-revolution Egyptian constitution is under way. The newly elected pope of the Coptic Orthodox Church of Egypt did not object to a proposed constitutional provision that maintains Islamic law as the source of legislation. Instead, he objected to another constitutional provision that defines Islamic law as resolutions decreed by Islam according to the Sunnī sect. Such an objection was distasteful to many Egyptian Muslims and raised the question of non-Muslims' role in defining Islamic law and the possibility of limiting non-Muslims' voting power in the parliament.

In sum, while Islamic constitutional principles are delineated in the basic sources of Islamic law—the Qurʾān and *sunnah*—its application, representation, and interpretation are subject to the political system that governs the Muslim state. A state may brand itself as Islamic, but it may not be the case that that state truly applies Islamic constitutional principles.

BIBLIOGRAPHY

Ahmed, Manzooruddin. *Islamic Political System in the Modern Age: Theory and Practice*. Karachi: Saad, 1983.

ʿImārah, Muḥammad. *Al-Islām wa-falsafat al-ḥukm*. Cairo, 2009.

ʿImārah, Muḥammad. *Al-Islām wa-al-ākhar: Man yaʿtarifu bi-man? Wa-man yunkiru man??* Cairo: Maktabat al-Shurūq, 2001.

Khalīl, Rashād Ḥasan. *Naẓarīyat al-musāwāh fī al-sharīʿah al-Islāmīyah*. Cairo: Dār al-Fārūq lil-Nashr wa-al-Tawzīʿ, 2007.

Khayyāṭ, ʿAbd al-ʿAzīz al-. *Al-Niẓām al-siyāsī fī al-Islām*. Cairo and Alexandria: Dār al-Salām lil-Ṭibāʿah wa-al-Nashr, 2004.

Maḥallī, Jalāl al-Dīn al-, and Jalāl al-Dīn al-Suyūṭī. *Tafsīr al-Jalālayn*. Riyadh, 2002.

Māwardī, ʿAlī ibn Muḥammad al-. *Al-Aḥkam al-sulṭānīyah*. Cairo: Muṣṭafā al-Bābī al-Ḥalabī, 1966.

Najjār, ʿAbd al-Wahhāb al-. *Al-Khulafāʾ al-rāshidūn*. Cairo, 2003.

Qaraḍāwī, Yūsuf al-. *Min fiqh al-dawlah fī al-Islām*. Cairo, 2009.

Ramadan, Hisham M., ed. *Understanding Islamic Law: From Classical to Contemporary*. Lanham, Md.: Rowman & Littlefield, 2006.

Rayyis, Muḥammad Ḍiyāʾ al-Dīn. *Al-Islām wa-al-khilāfah fī al-ʿaṣr al-ḥadīth: Naqd kitāb al-Islām wa-uṣūl al-ḥukm*. Cairo: Manshūrāt al-ʿAṣr al-Ḥadīth, 1972.

HISHAM M. RAMADAN

COUNCIL ON AMERICAN-ISLAMIC RELATIONS. The Council on American-Islamic Relations (CAIR) is a nonprofit civil-liberties and advocacy organization promoting civil rights, diversity, and freedom of religion.

CAIR was cofounded in 1994 by Omar Ahmad and Nihad Awad. Both cofounders were born in Jordan and hold degrees in engineering from American universities. Ahmad led the organization until 2005, followed by Awad as national executive director. Along with its headquarters in Washington, D.C., CAIR maintains around thirty-two autonomous chapters in twenty states, with a concentration on the East and West Coasts. While each chapter is organized and operated independently by local activists, a national board of directors oversees CAIR. CAIR is community supported and raises its funding mainly at annual banquets organized all over the country.

CAIR is a faith-based organization identifying with the "Islamic middle way" based on the Qurʾān and the life of Prophet Muhammad. The organization promotes (religious) pluralism, interfaith dialogue, public service, and civic engagement. It takes positions on international issues and educates the public about Islam, such as by means of its "Share the Quran" campaign. However, the lion's share of CAIR's activism is concerned with civil rights. CAIR claims to have processed over 9,500 civil-rights discrimination cases in the past decade. Its casework draws heavily on the Civil Rights Act of 1964, especially by reminding employers of Title VII's prohibition of discrimination against employees on the basis of race, color, religion, sex, and national origin.

As one of CAIR's main concerns is to ensure religious accommodation in the workplace, the first discrimination case treated by CAIR in 1995 was directed against an employer who refused to allow an employee to wear the hijab. From 1996 to 1999 CAIR gained public attention by bringing advocacy cases against prominent corporations, such as the publisher Simon & Schuster as well as against Nike. After 9/11 CAIR was asked for assistance by Muslim Americans and others perceived as Muslims that were targets of harassment and hate crimes.

By 2009, CAIR's training of the Muslim community concentrated on three primary areas: the fostering of individual awareness of rights, civic participation, and the building of media relations. This type of focus can be considered as key to CAIR's success: the organization takes action locally, on a grassroots level, by assisting Muslims in cases of discrimination, and raises awareness of its positions and deeds publically through media work. In line with this, CAIR has put effort into training its affiliates to deal effectively with the media, with its executive director, Nihad Awad, setting a good example for this. In 1997 he was a part of Vice President Al Gore's Civil Rights Advisory Panel to the White House Commission on Aviation Safety and Security. He has appeared on national and international media outlets, such as CNN, BBC World Service, PBS, C-SPAN, NPR, and published in the *New York Times*, the *Washington Post*, *Voice of America*, and Al Jazeera, and was listed as one of the five hundred most influential Muslims in the world in a 2009 publication produced by the Royal Islamic Strategic Studies Center and Georgetown University's Prince Alwaleed Bin Talal Center for Muslim-Christian Understanding.

CAIR has taken an active stand against terrorism, especially immediately after the terrorist attacks of 9/11. Along with over 120 other Muslim American individual and collective actors, CAIR has backed a *fatwa* against terrorism that was issued by the Fiqh Council of North America in 2005. In addition, the organization launched various initiatives condemning terrorism and its association with Islam. Nonetheless, CAIR has repeatedly been a target of defamation, mainly via online campaigns

CAIR has promoted the civic engagement of Muslim Americans in various nonpartisan campaigns. CAIR's encouragement of Muslim Americans to vote included voter registration, education about how to get involved in the electoral process, and meetings with candidates as well as running phone banks on Election Day to call on Muslims to go to the polls. CAIR also provides surveys of the attitudes of Muslim American voters.

As an outspoken public player, CAIR will continue to challenge the stereotyping of and discrimination against Muslim Americans and thereby take an important part in shaping Muslim collective identity and Islam in the United States.

BIBLIOGRAPHY

Council on American-Islamic Relations Web Site, http://www.cair.com/.

Nimer, Mohammed. "Muslims in the American Body Politic." In *Muslims' Place in the American Public Square: Hope, Fears, and Aspirations*, edited by Zahid H. Bukhari, Sulayman S. Nyang, Mumtaz Ahmad, and John L. Esposito, 145–164. Walnut Creek, Calif.: AltaMira, 2004.

Unus, Nada, and Emily Tucker. "Council on American-Islamic Relations." In *Encyclopedia of Islam in the United States*, edited by Jocelyne Cesari, vol. 1, 163–168. Westport, Conn.: Greenwood Press, 2007.

Sabina von Fischer

Council(s) of Senior ʿUlamāʾ. The practice of *iftāʾ* (the issuing of religious-legal opinions, *fatwas*) in the modern Muslim world is characterized by the emergence of the Council(s) of Senior *ʿUlama*ʾ, enabling more than one religious scholar to submit and sign the same *fatwa*. Councils of Senior *ʿUlamā*ʾ have existed since the start of the twentieth century; for instance, the Council of Senior *ʿUlamā*ʾ was founded in 1911 at al-Azhar University in Cairo, Egypt. This council consisted of thirty leading *ʿulama*ʾ, from among whom the Shaykh al-Azhar was selected. Other councils were established during the twentieth and early twenty-first centuries, both within the Islamic world and in the West, such as Nahdatul Ulama in East Java, Indonesia (1926); the Council of Islamic Ideology in Lahore, Pakistan (1962; now located in Islamabad); the World Muslim League in Mecca (1962); the Islamic Society of North America in Plainfield, Indiana (1963); the Council of Senior *ʿUlamā*ʾ in Riyadh, Saudi Arabia (1971); the International Islamic Fiqh Council in Jeddah, Saudi Arabia (1981); the European Council for Fatwa and Research in London (1997; now located in Dublin, Ireland); and finally the International Union of Muslim Scholars, also established in Dublin (2004).

These councils vary in their composition, function, and authority. Thus, some are state agencies, founded and funded by governments, while others are nongovernmental and/or global. For example, the Council of Senior *ʿUlamā*ʾ in Saudi Arabia is a governmental agency, designated "to issue legal opinions, based on the *Sharīʿah*, on matters submitted by the king [*walī al-amr*], and to act as an advisory body regarding Common Law issues, to facilitate the king's decisions." (Royal Decree A/137, 29 August 1971) Ordinarily, members of this council must be selected from among the Saudi senior *ʿulamā*ʾ. However, with certain provisos and the king's approval, non-Saudi *ʿulamā*ʾ may become members. Led by the grand mufti, this council is the apex of the religious pyramid, providing the ultimate decrees on *Sharīʿah* in Saudi Arabia today.

The International Union of Muslim Scholars (IUMS), on the other hand, best represents the independent and global councils of senior *ʿulamā*ʾ, cutting across the sociocultural and political differences among Arab and Islamic societies. It was founded in Europe by a group of scholars led by Shaykh Yūsuf al-Qaraḍāwī. In October 2010, the

IUMS headquarters was moved to Doha, Qatar, and two additional branches were established in Egypt and Tunisia. The structure and composition of the IUMS has been transformed since its creation. Today, the IUMS is considered the largest-ever Islamic religious body, with around sixty thousand members, representing thousands of religious councils and organizations from all over the Arab and Islamic worlds: Sunnīs, Shīʿīs, Ṣūfīs, and Ibāḍīs. This is reflected, among other things, by the makeup of the IUMS leadership: Shaykh Yūsuf al-Qaraḍāwī (president; Sunnī), Shaykh Aḥmad ibn Ḥamad al-Khalīlī (vice president; Ibāḍī); Shaykh ʿAbd Allāh Ibn Bīyah (vice president; Ṣūfī); Ayatollah Muḥammad Wāʿiẓ Zādah (vice president; Shīʿī).

One common major goal of these councils is the exercise of collective *ijtihād* (juristic reasoning) when facing the challenges of modernity. For many modern Muslim scholars in complex modern societies, individual *ijtihād* no longer makes sense. That is, an individual mufti is still entitled to give his opinion, but *ijtihād* on important questions, especially those related to public affairs, must be collective. Muslim scholars rely on the premise that an opinion formulated by a group of scholars is much better than that of an individual; the individuals in the group may consult one another, thus addressing neglected aspects of the problem under discussion. Therefore, collective decisions are considered to be much more solid, regardless of the intellectual prowess of any individual scholar.

The emergence of these councils may indicate a tendency toward restructuring religious authority in modern Islamic societies. Collective *iftāʾ*, by which a group of senior scholars sign the same *fatwa*, is supposed to earn respect and trust in the Muslim community, hence fostering the religious authority of these councils. Indeed, decisions made by state councils are generally respected by their governments. For example, in Saudi Arabia, the Council of Senior Ulema continues to have some sway over royal policies and decisions. This is manifested, for instance, whenever the Saudi government adopts the council's decisions and *fatwas*, rendering them state laws. Instances of Islamic involvement in the legislative process may be found, especially in cases of controversial issues, such as criminal procedure, ethical and moral issues, family law, and ritual prescriptions. Substantive legislation is often formulated with full interaction and cooperation between the religious and the political establishments.

Yet the emergence of these Muslim councils falls short of centralizing religious authority with the goal of establishing a global Islamic religious authority. Religious authority still evokes many controversies among modern Muslim scholars and in the councils of the senior *ʿulamāʾ*. There is an ongoing debate over the scope of these councils' authority and the extent to which the public complies with their decisions. It seems that some official, governmentally appointed councils suffer from public mistrust, more than the independent councils do. The fact that governments may influence these councils, to a greater or lesser extent, or that people may perceive this to be the case, increases the community's mistrust of the official councils.

BIBLIOGRAPHY

Atawneh, Muhammad al-. *Wahhābī Islam Facing the Challenges of Modernity: Dār al-Iftā in the Modern Saudi State*. Leiden, Netherlands: E. J. Brill, 2010. See esp. ch. 2.

Masud, Muhammad Khalid, Brinkley Messick, and David S. Powers, eds. *Islamic Legal Interpretation: Muftis and Their Fatwas*. Cambridge, Mass.: Harvard University Press, 1996. See esp. pp. 3–30.

Mudzhar, Muhammad. "Fatwas of the Council of Indonesian Ulama: A Study of Islamic Legal Thought in Indonesia, 1975–1988." Ph.D. diss., University of California, Los Angeles, 1990. See esp. pp. 6–7.

Skovgaard-Petersen, Jakob. *Defining Islam for the Egyptian State: Muftis and Fatwas of the Dār al-Iftā.* Leiden, Netherlands: E. J. Brill, 1997. See esp. pp. 284–285.

MUHAMMAD AL-ATAWNEH

COUP D'ÉTAT. *See* Rebellion.

COURTS. In Medina, the Prophet Muḥammad acted as an arbiter in the early community (*ummah*). His role was sanctioned by the Qurʾān, which prescribed that he judge according to the divine revelation (5:48–49). After his death in 632, the first caliphs took over his role and dispensed justice in Medina. When the first judge (*qāḍī*) was delegated is still the subject of controversy. Reports that the Prophet himself sent judges to Yemen are rejected by modern scholarship. According to Islamic sources, the second caliph, ʿUmar (r. 634–644), appointed *qāḍīs* in conquered territories soon after the beginning of the conquest. Although the status of these first judges and of their legal rulings is unclear, the first Muslim armies certainly needed men appointed by an authority to arbitrate the inevitable conflicts among the soldiers. However, because of the contradictory sources, some scholars dismiss these reports and defer the appearance of the first judiciary system until the reign of Muʿāwiyah (r. 661–680).

The *Sharīʿah* Court. One judge alone dispensed justice in every large Muslim city, except in a capital such as Baghdad, which was, from the late eighth century, divided into three districts and from the eleventh century on into four districts. After the conquest, only cities with Friday mosques had a *qāḍī*. As an increasing number of conquered peoples converted to Islam, especially from the ninth century on, jurisdictions were created in secondary towns, where the judge was usually a deputy (*nāʾib*) of the *qāḍī* of a larger city. Judgeships were held exclusively by adult Muslim males of unsullied reputation.

The main task of the *qāḍī* was to dispense justice between litigants. During the classical period, he sat in a public place, usually the mosque (some *qāḍīs* preferred holding court in their home), where a plaintiff could come and lodge a complaint against an adversary. If the defendant refused to appear, the judge could summon him and even have him forcibly brought. If the defendant did not confess his guilt, the burden was on the plaintiff to prove his claim by providing at least two honorable witnesses (a process known as *bayyinah*, or testimonial proof). Alternatively, Medinan doctrine would accept one witness if the plaintiff took an oath. If there were no witnesses (or if the witnesses were not reliable), the judge would ask the defendant to swear that he was innocent. Ḥanafīs regarded the defendant's refusal to take an oath as a proof of his culpability. However, according to Mālikīs and Shāfiʿīs, the defendant's decline to swear was no proof and in this situation the judge had to refer the oath to the plaintiff. Some circumstantial evidence could also be taken into consideration in favor of the defendant, on the word of an expert (Johansen, 2002, "Signs as Evidence," p. 174). On the basis of this legal evidence, the judge then issued a written and binding decision, which could only be repealed if there were a serious breach of law. The judge was assisted in his task by one or more clerks and by a body of professional witnesses—these first appeared in Egypt at the turn of the ninth century, and thereafter this custom seems to have spread to other provinces. With the help of other assistants, the *qāḍī* also performed "administrative" tasks, such as the supervision of endowed foundations (*waqf*s) and the control of the property of orphaned, disabled, or bankrupt people.

Relationships with the Rulers. From the very beginning of Islam, justice was the prerogative of the ruler. He delegated his judicial authority to *qāḍīs*, who were appointed for an indeterminate length of time. At any moment, the ruler could dismiss them and appoint other judges in their place. The *qāḍī* received a salary and was therefore considered a civil servant.

Under the Umayyads (661–750), who ruled from Syria, provincial governors were usually responsible for the appointment of their *qāḍīs*. Although some Umayyad caliphs, such as ʿUmar II (r. 717–720), Yazīd II (r. 720–724), and Hishām b. ʿAbd al-Malik (r. 724–743), attempted to overrule the authority of some governors by appointing provincial *qāḍīs* themselves, centralization of the judgeship under the authority of the caliph was only completed under the ʿAbbāsids. The second ʿAbbāsid caliph, al-Manṣūr (r. 754–775), began to appoint judges in the principal Iraqi cities, and later in the provinces. This reform was part of a larger political agenda that was meant to reinforce central power, the main symbolic expression of which was the foundation of the round city of Madīnat al-Salām (Baghdad) in 762. Provincial governors did not easily accept the undermining of their power, however, and attempts were made to regain control of the judiciary, especially when the central power was at its most vulnerable (as, e.g., during and after the civil war between the caliphs al-Amīn and his brother al-Maʾmūn, in 811–813). On the whole, ʿAbbāsid control of the *qāḍīs* became widely accepted except in territories where the caliph was not recognized, as in al-Andalus (Muslim Spain, where a dynasty of Umayyad governors came to power in 756). The clearest representation of the centralization of the judiciary was the creation of the office of chief judge (*qāḍī al-quḍāt*, literally, judge of judges) in Baghdad around 790, under the caliph Hārūn al-Rashīd (r. 786–809). Although the chief judge rarely appointed other *qāḍīs* himself, he was a close advisor of the caliph, and he had a decisive influence on the selection of judges. In al-Andalus, the judge of Córdoba, who had held the title of *qāḍī al-jamāʿah* (judge of the community) since the beginning of the Umayyad rule, tended to be regarded as the western counterpart of the *qāḍī al-quḍāt*.

From the late ninth century onward, when provinces began to claim political and financial autonomy from the ʿAbbāsid caliphate, asserting centralized authority over local judgeships became a major issue. With the political decline of the ʿAbbāsid caliphate in the early tenth century, the vizier (chief of the central administration) played an increasingly important role in the appointment of judges, but after 945, the Būyid *amīrs* soon extended their authority over the judiciary. They were replaced in 1055 by a Seljuk sultan who claimed the same prerogative over the judgeship, even though the vizier Niẓām al-Mulk (d. 1092) acknowledged that the *qāḍī* was still theoretically a deputy of the caliph.

The selection of *qāḍīs* according to their schools of law (sing. *madhhab*) was also a political issue. The ʿAbbāsids selected their first *qāḍīs* from among the Hijazī jurists, perhaps because promoting Medinan law (which relied on *ʿamal*, the uninterrupted practice of the Medinan community since the death of the Prophet) would reinforce their legitimacy. From the reign of the caliph al-Mahdī (r. 775–785) onward, the ʿAbbāsids gravitated toward the followers of the Iraqi scholar Abū Ḥanīfah (d. 767), the eponym of the Ḥanafī school of law, whom they appointed as *qāḍīs* in the principal regions of the empire. This policy met with resistance from urban communities who were still attached to their local legal traditions. During the ninth century, *qāḍīs* were increasingly selected for their theological beliefs, and the Ḥanafīs lost their hegemony after 871. Thereafter, rulers appointed judges mainly from the Ḥanafī, Mālikī, and Shāfiʿī legal schools (except for the Shīʿī Fāṭimids, r. 909–1171, who preferred Ismāʿīlī *qāḍīs*), with each dynasty favoring one or another of these schools for the chief judgeship. In 1265 the legal pluralism at play was formalized under the Mamlūks (1250–1517), when Sultan Baybars appointed four chief judges, one for each Sunnī school (Shāfiʿī, Ḥanafī, Mālikī, and Ḥanbalī), first in Cairo and then in Damascus. This reform, which was notable from a legal point of view, has also been interpreted as a political act undertaken to weaken the authority of a single chief judge who had been showing annoying signs of independence.

Tension and Judicial Independence. Tension between the ruler and the judiciary existed since the Umayyad period. The *qāḍī* was a mere deputy of the ruler and depended on him for the execution of some of his judgments. For example, judges had no authority over the prisons in which they incarcerated debtors, and local governors or chiefs of police could release prisoners without the judge's consent. Rulers could easily overrule or interfere with the judiciary, whereas the *qāḍīs*, who were hired from among the scholars who were the authors of the Islamic jurisprudence, considered themselves the main judicial authority. The centralization of legal appointments under the caliph al-Manṣūr allowed judges to be free of the authority of local governors, but they were beholden to the caliph, who also interfered in the judicial process.

Under the ʿAbbāsids, *qāḍīs* became a major political tool. The dynasty had seized power by denouncing the impiety and the injustice of the Umayyads. In order to maintain their legitimacy, at a time of intense legal development that led to the birth of the classical schools of law, the first ʿAbbāsid caliphs surrounded themselves with scholars and used *qāḍīs* to embellish the official facade of the state. *Qāḍīs* were used as advisors, witnesses, and emissaries. Caliphs also used them to conduct political trials, or to issue *fatwas* allowing the execution of political enemies. The political use of *qāḍīs* reached its peak during the *miḥnah* (examination), instituted at the end of the caliph al-Maʾmūn's reign and lasting until the beginning of that of al-Mutawakkil (c. 833–848). In an effort to restore his authority, which was being challenged by the traditionalist movement, the caliph sought to impose his control over the judicial system and through it impose his control over the whole Muslim community. He determined that only *qāḍīs* who adhered to the official theological dogma that the Qurʾān was a part of God's creation were to remain in office, and they had to check that all witnesses (who usually belonged to the social and religious elite) professed the same dogma.

Religious scholars in general and *qāḍīs* in particular argued increasingly against such manipulation of the judiciary. They disseminated prophetic reports (*ḥadīths*) insisting on the individual responsibility of the judge, who would be held responsible for his actions in the hereafter. They emphasized that the judge's decision relied on scriptural sources—including the consensus (*ijmāʿ*) of jurists—or on his own assessment (*ijtihād*), and that left no place for caliphal intervention. During the ninth century, Ḥanafī jurists began to question the link between the caliph and his *qāḍīs*. According to the jurist al-Khaṣṣāf (d. 874), the *qāḍī* could issue a judgment against the caliph, despite his being a deputy of the latter. A century later, al-Jaṣṣāṣ (d. 981) asserted that the caliph did not appoint a judge in his own name but that the judge acted as a deputy for the whole community. The *qāḍī* served Muslims (and not the caliph) on the basis of the law formulated by the legal scholars (*fuqahāʾ*). According to this theory, a *qāḍī* could be appointed by rebels (Khārijīs), and even by the community itself in the absence of a ruler. Al-Jaṣṣāṣ's theory was later adopted by other scholars, such as the Mālikī al-Bāqillānī (d. 1013). Although the caliphate recognized a greater independence of the *qāḍīs* after the end of the *miḥnah* and the victory of Sunnism under al-Mutawakkil (r. 847–861), Muslim rulers never ceased in their attempts to manipulate the judiciary.

Shīʿī Discourse on the Judiciary. Imāmī Shīʿīs, who believe that the only true rulers (imams, in Shīʿī discourse) were the fourth caliph, ʿAlī ibn Abī Ṭālib (r. 656–661), and eleven of his descendants, regarded the Umayyads and the ʿAbbāsids as illegitimate leaders. According to al-Kulaynī (d. 940), the imam Jaʿfar al-Ṣādiq (d. 765) forbade people to appeal to official *qāḍīs*. Instead, Shīʿī followers were advised to seek the judgment of a Shīʿī scholar, who would be considered a deputy of the true imam. The Imāmī doctrine evolved under the Būyid dynasty (945–1055), which was of Shīʿī persuasion. According to al-Ṭūsī (d. 1067), an Imāmī Shīʿī appointed *qāḍī* by an illegitimate ruler could dispense justice as long as he remained faithful to his own doctrine and regarded himself as a deputy of the true imam. It was the duty of an Imāmī jurist to accept his appointment, lest an unjust (Sunnī) scholar be appointed *qāḍī* in his place.

Parallel Judicial Institutions. The administration of law was exercised in forums other than the *Sharīʿah* court, which allowed rulers to assert their judicial authority. Himself a source of judicial power, the ruler could preside over the litigations and give binding decisions, or he could appoint deputies who unlike *qāḍīs* were not bound by the rules of the *Sharīʿah* (even if these deputies could be *Sharīʿah* court judges at the same time). Often called "secular" justice because it took place outside the *Sharīʿah* court, it manifested itself in different ways.

The Maẓālim Court. The *maẓālim* (literally, "wrongs") court symbolized the discretionary authority vested in the ruler. It had a broad jurisdiction—it received petitions against officials and abuse of power, and could occasionally serve as court of appeal against the *qāḍīs*' judgments. The judge—theoretically the ruler, but more often his deputy—was usually assisted by jurists and *qāḍīs*, who guaranteed the legitimacy of the decision, as well as by clerks and witnesses. Procedure was not restricted by legal doctrine, however. Whereas the *qāḍī* was bound by the accusatory procedures formulated by the religious law and could not violate the evidentiary rules, the *maẓālim* judge had procedural powers that went beyond those—he could use the inquisitorial method, order investigations, proceed without waiting for a case to be brought, and rely on noncanonical types of proof. The ruler could thus base his decision on principles of equity or follow the dictates of the state rather than *Sharīʿah* law as such.

Following the Sassanian model, *maẓālim* court sessions were probably organized on a regular basis during the early ʿAbbāsid period. Caliphs al-Mahdī and al-Hādī (r. 785–786) presided in person over a court. Later, the *maẓālim* were mostly supervised by the vizier, until the Shīʿī Būyids handed them to the Imāmī *naqīb al-ashrāf* (who ran the affairs of ʿAlī's descendants). From the eleventh century on, the *maẓālim* court was characterized by increasing bureaucratization and placed under the responsibility of different officials (sultans, governors, military officers). No specific locale was reserved for these public sessions until Nūr al-Dīn Zankī (r. 1146–1174) established a "house of justice" (*dār al-ʿadl*) in Damascus. A similar structure was built in Cairo under the Mamlūks.

From the early ʿAbbāsid period on, the *maẓālim* competed with the *qāḍīs*' jurisdiction, even though *qāḍīs* were occasionally appointed to head this court. ʿAbbāsid caliphs used the *maẓālim* forum to reinstate their authority when confronted with a *qāḍī*'s excessive autonomy or noncompliance with official ideology, as during the *miḥnah*. Through this institution, provincial governors seeking autonomy from the caliphate could also reinforce their power. In the late ninth century, when local dynasties first appeared in the east, provincial *qāḍīs* were still appointed by the caliph. Governors who sought autonomy had to regain control of the judiciary, but they could not easily dismiss a *qāḍī* dispensing justice in the name of the caliph. Rulers such as Ibn Ṭūlūn (r. 868–884), his son Khumārawayh (r. 884–896), and later the Ikhshīds (935–969) in Egypt therefore regularly used the *maẓālim* court to bypass the ordinary judicial system. Moreover, during the Mamlūk period, the *maẓālim* tended to encroach on matters regulated by the *Sharīʿah*, which fell under the jurisdiction of the *qāḍī*, such as cases involving pious foundations.

The proliferation of centers of power after the eleventh century increased the importance of justice dispensed by rulers. Other courts, such as the *yarghu* of the Īl-Khān Mongols (1256–1335), which dealt specifically with disputes among Mongols as well as state affairs, were assimilated into the *maẓālim* when the dynasty converted to Islam.

The Police. The *shurṭah* (also called *maʿūnah* from the ninth century onward), was an elite unit of the army that served as a security and police force. It was established under the first caliphs or the early Umayyads to protect cities and villages against riots and banditry and to ensure the night watch. Its chief, the *ṣāḥib al-shurṭah* (also called *shiḥnah* after the end of the ninth century), was appointed by the caliph or the governor, and he was often the head of the ruler's personal bodyguard. In early Islamic Egypt, the *ṣāḥib al-shurṭah* was the second highest official of the province after the governor, and he acted as his deputy when the latter was away. The *shurṭah* could be called upon to maintain order at the *qāḍī*'s court or to carry out his rulings.

The *shurṭah* was not only a military unit with control and security functions. The *ṣāḥib al-shurṭah* also presided over a court where he dispensed criminal justice. Like the *maẓālim*, his court was not bound by the rules of the *Sharīʿah*, and the *ṣāḥib al-shurṭah* operated much more freely than the *qāḍī*. He could conduct investigations and rule on the grounds of physical evidence. His discretionary powers allowed him to inflict punishments harsher than those prescribed by Islamic law. The *ṣāḥib al-shurṭah* probably judged criminals arrested and brought before him by his troops. He prosecuted on his own authority, without the necessity of a plaintiff.

Finally, the *ṣāḥib al-sūq* or *muḥtasib*, chief of the "market police," also heard complaints and dispensed justice. His principal task was the supervision of moral behavior in public. He intervened on his own accord and passed punitive judgment based on custom (*ʿurf*) against offenders.

Summary. In early Islam, the *qāḍī* was no more than a legal official under the ruler's supreme judicial power. Between the eighth and the tenth centuries, as Islamic law developed into a specific field governed by legal scholars, the *qāḍīs* were increasingly identified with a religious jurisdiction that necessarily had to escape from under the authority of the ruler. Therefore, two sets of judicial institutions developed, which came to complement and sometimes compete with each other. For a ruler who needed to govern according to the public interest, to ensure security beyond the prescriptions of the *Sharīʿah*, or simply to serve state interests, it was necessary to rely on institutions that were not bound by the strict prescriptions of Islamic law and could be monitored more easily. During the Mamlūk period, authors such as Ibn Taymīyah (d. 1328) and Ibn Qayyim al-Jawzīyah (d. 1350) attempted to repair the rupture between the two types of institutions by developing the concept of *siyāsah sharʿīyah* (governance in accordance with the sacred law). According to their theory, many practices of the extra-*Sharīʿah* institutions conformed to the spirit of Islamic law and could be justified on this ground; *Sharīʿah* legitimacy thus extended to actual states. Their theory would strongly influence the Ottoman legal system.

The question of the boundaries between the various courts is still unresolved. Most scholars today think the *qāḍī* had little jurisdiction in penal law, although the *Sharīʿah* holds that the *qāḍī* has authority in criminal cases. As Émile Tyan remarked (Tyan, 1938–1943, Vol. II, p. 411–412), procedural law limited the involvement of the *qāḍī* in criminal cases—both a claimant and a defendant were required, and the judge could neither act on his own nor conduct inquiries. Most penal law cases were probably heard by the security forces (especially the police). Only on rare occasions, such as when a crime was witnessed and an accusation could be leveled, did the judge's competence in criminal matters become a reality. As Christian Lange has argued (Lange, 2008, p. 48), the situation may be described as a network of overlapping jurisdictions, subject to variations according to era, place, and specific cases.

[*See also* Ḥisbah; Justice; *and* Sharīʿah.]

BIBLIOGRAPHY

Bligh-Abramski, Irit. "The Judiciary (*Qāḍīs*) as a Governmental-Administrative Tool in Early Islam." *Journal of the Economic and Social History of the Orient* 35 (1992): 40–71.

Hallaq, Wael B. *The Origins and Evolution of Islamic Law*. Cambridge, U.K.: Cambridge University Press, 2005.

Johansen, Baber. "Signs as Evidence: The Doctrine of Ibn Taymiyya (1263–1328) and Ibn Qayyim al-Jawziyya (d. 1351) on Proof." *Islamic Law and Society* 9 (2002): 168–193.

Johansen, Baber. "Wahrheit und Geltungsanspruch: Zur Begründung und Begrenzung der Autorität des Qadi-Urteils im islamischen Recht." In *La giustizia nell'alto medioevo (secoli IX–XI)*, edited by Ovidio Capitani, pp. 975–1074. Spoleto, Italy: Centro Italiano di Studi sull'alto Medioevo, 1997.

Lange, Christian. *Justice, Punishment, and the Medieval Muslim Imagination*. Cambridge, U.K.: Cambridge University Press, 2008.

Nielsen, Jørgen S. *Secular Justice in an Islamic State: Maẓālim under the Baḥrī Mamlūks, 662/1264–789/1387*. Leiden, Netherlands: Nederlands Historisch-Archaeologisch Instituut te Istanbul, 1985.

Nielsen, Jørgen S. "Sultan al-Ẓāhir Baybars and the Appointment of Four Chief *Qāḍīs*, 663/1265." *Studia Islamica* 60 (1984): 167–176.

Rapoport, Yossef. "Legal Diversity in the Age of *Taqlīd*: The Four Chief *Qāḍīs* under the Mamlūks." *Islamic Law and Society* 10 (2003): 210–228.

Tillier, Mathieu. *Les cadis d'Iraq et l'État abbasside (132/750–334/945)*. Damascus: Institut français du Proche-Orient, 2009.

Tillier, Mathieu. "*Qāḍīs* and the Political Use of the *Maẓālim* Jurisdiction under the ʿAbbāsids." In *Public Violence in Islamic Societies: Power, Discipline, and the Construction of the Public Sphere, 7th–19th Centuries CE*, edited by Christian Lange and Maribel Fierro, pp. 42–66. Edinburgh: Edinburgh University Press, 2009.

Tsafrir, Nurit. *The History of an Islamic School of Law: The Early Spread of Hanafism*. Cambridge, Mass.: The Islamic Legal Studies Program, Harvard Law School, 2004.

Tyan, Émile. *Histoire de l'organisation judiciaire en pays d'Islam*. 2d ed. Leiden, Netherlands: Brill, 1960.

MATHIEU TILLIER

CRUSADES. Ranging from the late eleventh to the thirteenth century and initially seeking to restore Christian control over Jerusalem and the Holy Sepulcher, the Crusades mobilized medieval European societies for religious warfare against the rise of Islam. Crusading also encompassed papal authorizations for campaigns designed to extirpate heresy and paganism in Europe from the eleventh to the sixteenth centuries, including at various times the Iberian Peninsula and the Baltic region, as well as southern France and Italy. Historians are, however, divided between "traditionalists," who designate as Crusades primarily the campaigns in the Holy Land and the East, and "pluralists," who place special stress on religious crusades throughout Europe. This article deals with Crusader campaigns primarily in the Holy Land and their later ramifications in political thought for centuries to come.

The term "Crusade" is derived from the Latin word *crux* (cross), a symbol prominently displayed on the military regalia of Crusaders. Many Muslim chroniclers of the medieval era preferred "Frankish invasions," a term that used the Arabic word *al-ifranj*, designating specifically the French but often applied generally to Westerners.

In 1095 at the Council of Clermont, Pope Urban II called for a combination of warrior commitment and pilgrim piety that would restore the Holy Land to Christian rule. The pope had five initial aims:

1. Curtailing the internal warfare that had racked parts of Europe by directing military activities outside Christian communities
2. Asserting papal supremacy over secular kings who had recently challenged papal authority over such matters as lay investiture
3. Ending the disruption of pilgrimages
4. Healing the East-West schism within Christendom, which had been made official in 1054, by assisting Constantinople in regaining control of cities such as Antioch and, perhaps ultimately, bringing Eastern Orthodoxy back into the Roman fold
5. Continuing to reverse the expansion of Islam, following Iberian Muslim defeat in Toledo in 1085, which secured northern and central Spain for Christians, and the Norman defeat of Muslims in Sicily in 1091.

In the late eleventh century, Christians fired volleys of accusations that the Seljuk Turks were unleashing marauding attacks on pilgrims en route to the Holy Land. While later historians such as Hans Eberhard Mayer have raised many doubts that the Seljuks were engineering assaults on Christian pilgrims, various brigands and bandits from Muslim backgrounds took part in robberies of and interference with European travelers. Graphic stories of Christian humiliation soon were mobilized to inspire concerted action against Muslim control over the Holy Land. The Fatimid caliph Al-Ḥakīm demolished the Church of the Holy Sepulcher in 1009, and the efforts to rebuild it in the mid-eleventh century had not restored its former splendor. Many Christians seemed unaware that the Seljuks were fierce opponents of the Fatimids.

The Seljuk Turks had delivered a stinging defeat to the Byzantine Empire at the Battle of Manzikert in 1071 through swift horsemanship, deft use of bow and arrow, and the eagerness of Turkish mercenaries to abandon their service to the Byzantine military. In the battle's aftermath, various Turkoman nomads soon flowed into Anatolia. Even though they did not always support the in-migration of these Turkish tribes, the Seljuks were on their way to achieving mastery over Asia Minor. The Byzantine emperor eventually requested papal assistance in reversing and repelling Muslim forces in the east.

The Early Crusades. Officially Christian leaders promoted the Crusades as being animated by chivalric warrior practices and the spirit of saintly pilgrimage. Very quickly, these high ideals broke down. Rogue bands of ill-equipped Crusaders, for example, sacked several cities of the German Rhineland and massacred thousands of Jews in 1096. Archbishop Ruthard of Mainz, Archbishop Hermann III in Cologne, and eventually the papacy denounced the Crusader orgy of terror in the Rhineland.

Jews and Muslims fought together, though unsuccessfully, to repel invading Crusaders at Jerusalem. As Crusader forces poured into the breached fortresses of Jerusalem in 1099, Muslim women and children were hacked to death, and Jews perished in a burning synagogue set on fire by exultant Christian warriors. Medieval Christians blamed Muslims for allowing Jews to become entrenched in Jerusalem against the Augustinian vision of the new Christian world order. In the dying days of the Roman Empire, Saint

Augustine had promulgated the theology of the Jews as a "witness" people who were rendered abject for all to see as earthly punishment for denying Christ's divinity. On a brighter, less punitive note, Augustine asserted that Jews should be afforded protection under Christendom following Psalm 59:11: "Slay them not, lest they should at last forget Thy law." But Augustine had also stressed that Jews were now a Diaspora people who faced perpetual banishment from the Holy City of Jerusalem.

By 1109, the Christians had established four Levantine Crusader states also known by their collective French name, Outremer (overseas): the Kingdom of Jerusalem, the County of Edessa, the Principality of Antioch, and the County of Tripoli.

The Muslim world had been racked by many internal conflicts, and it took several decades to mount an effective counterthrust to the new Crusader states. Edessa was the first place to have been seized from Muslim control by the Crusaders, and it was the first to fall. In 1144, Imād al-Dīn Zangī, the Seljuk Turkish ruler of Mosul and conqueror of Aleppo, met Christian talk of holy war with a new spirit of Islamic unity and *jihād*. Although murdered in 1146 by a disgruntled slave, Zangī had inspired a new tradition of counter-Crusaders led by his son Nūr al-Dīn and his Kurdish general, Ṣalāḥ al-Dīn, known in the West as Saladin. Saladin had unified Egypt and Syria, effectively surrounding the Crusader states. His forces took back Jerusalem in 1187, securing his legend as a hero and chivalric figure who honored treaties and treated his enemies fairly.

The early Crusades had been spearheaded by what medievalist Robert Bartlett calls a "knightly-clerical-mercantile consortium," and many spoke of how the fighting forces of the First Crusade operated "without lord, without prince" or "fought without king, without emperor" (Bartlett, 1993, p. 308). With Saladin's triumph, European monarchs soon jumped into the fray, as Richard the Lionheart of England, Philip II Augustus of France, and Frederick Barbarossa of the Holy Roman Empire joined forces in an attempt to take back Jerusalem. Their enterprise met with stiff resistance, though Saladin eventually allowed unarmed Christian pilgrims access to Jerusalem. Richard secured Crusader control over Cyprus, an island that could be used for projecting sea power and facilitating the delivery of provisions. Many Crusaders developed an ardor for spices and sugar, the latter a relatively rare delicacy in most of Europe. Learning to harvest sugar cane in Cyprus, they sometimes competed with Muslim producers in the Middle East.

Frustrated with Crusader failure to retake Jerusalem, Pope Innocent III, who represented the pinnacle of papal power in medieval Europe, promoted a new Crusade at the commencement of the thirteenth century. This enterprise was diverted to Constantinople when Venetian warriors sought to collect debts from the Byzantine emperor for his use of their ships and provisions. The sacking and pillaging of the city in 1204 led some inhabitants of Constantinople to express the heretical view that they would be better off under the Turkish sultan than being ruled by Christian Crusaders. Innocent III's outrage at Venice mounted when he later saw that some of its merchants had grown comfortable making cozy trade deals with Muslims.

Later Crusades. In the thirteenth century, Crusaders launched several more attempts to retake the Holy Land with invasions during 1217–1221, 1228–1229, and 1248–1254, and then the last abortive foray of Louis IX of France in 1270. Despite many devastating setbacks, the Crusaders on occasion won concessions. The Egyptian ruler al-Kāmil Muhammad al-Malik reached an agreement in 1229 with the invading Frederick II, King of Sicily and Holy Roman Emperor, allowing Christian rule over most of Jerusalem for the next ten years. Muslims opposed this concession to the invaders, and certain Crusaders railed against the provisions forbidding them from fortifying the city's walls. In 1244, Muslim forces took back control of Jerusalem.

In 1258, the Mongols rampaged through Baghdad, destroying a city that many regarded as the jewel of the Islamic world. The Mamlūk general Ẓāhir Baybars halted the march of these nomadic invaders at the Battle of Ain Jalut in 1260. Baybars and his successors then took a much harder line toward Frankish settlers, who in 1268 encountered a level of atrocities that shocked some Muslims accustomed to rulers seeking a measure of coexistence with Christians and Jews.

Papal preeminence from the twelfth century was giving way to more powerful monarchies in western Europe in the thirteenth century. But the kings squabbled among themselves and, despite exhibiting some devastating fighting techniques at home, were unable to assemble the kind of formidable military force that could take on the large Mamlūk armies. The Mamlūks benefitted from fresh infusions of experienced troops recruited from the defeated Mongols, who had previously ravaged the Muslim world and threatened Europe. Meanwhile, monarchs in the Iberian Peninsula from time to time asserted their preference for battling Muslims close to home, rather than in distant Jerusalem.

In 1290, newly arrived Crusader troops in Acre killed several Muslim merchants. When the Christians refused to turn over to the Mamlūk authorities the soldiers responsible for the murders, alleging that the merchants had provoked the attacks, the Egyptian sultan Qalāwūn assembled one of the Crusade era's largest armies to retake Acre. The military orders of Hospitalers, Templars, and Teutonic Knights made their last stand. Acre fell to the Mamlūk forces—as did the rest of Louis IX's carefully constructed fortifications throughout the region—and the age of the Crusaders in the Holy Land was over.

The Crusading impulse was not dead. Christopher Columbus repeatedly spoke of how the wealth of Cathay (China) would be delivered through his expeditions to the New World, and these fabulous riches could allow Europe to liberate Jerusalem with monumental force. In the sixteenth century, the Pope helped assemble the Holy League to stymie Ottoman imperial expansion, and Crusader themes could still be found in the ensuing propaganda onslaught.

Implications for Political Thought and Statecraft. Europeans produced a voluminous literature about the Crusades, by some measures the most studied event in Mediterranean history. However, by comparison, Islamic writing on the topic seems somewhat sparse until the age of modern imperialism in the nineteenth and twentieth centuries. Al-Ghazālī (1058–1111) is recognized as the greatest Islamic theologian and jurist at the time of the First Crusade, and it is striking that in his seventy extant works of philosophy and jurisprudence he seems to have little direct to say about non-Muslim invaders in the region. This seemingly aloof demeanor has provoked scathing rebuke from twenty-first-century Salafists and myriad proponents of puritanical Islam, who prefer the stern calls for resistance to foreign invaders from the anti-Mongol thinker Ibn Taymiyya (1263–1328) and in muscular anti-Crusader tracts such as *The Forty Hadiths for Inciting Jihad* by Ibn 'Asākir of Damascus (1105–1176).

And yet, al-Ghazālī remained focused on the dangers of civil war and division within Islam, and he was at pains to stress the primacy of the greater *jihād* (*jihād al-akbar*), the spiritual struggle from within, over the lesser *jihād* (*jihād al-aṣghar*) encompassing war on the infidel. When Muslims are divided and living in spiritually unsound ways, this opens the possibility for mayhem from external forces, in the view of adherents to al-Ghazālī's political philosophy. In his *Kitāb al-'aṣā* or *Book of the Staff*, Usāma bin

Munqidh (1095–1188), a nephew of the ruler of the small north Syrian principality of Shaizar and the author of vivid descriptions of the Franks, confessed his admiration for the spiritual devotion of Christian priests he witnessed at Nablus by the tomb of Saint John the Baptist: "I saw [there] a sight that moved my heart but also grieved me and made me lament that I had never seen exertions like theirs among the Muslims" (Cobb, 2005, p. 119). According to the thirteenth-century chronicler Abu Shama (d. 1258), Saladin pointed to the power of Christian piety: "We shall never cease to be amazed at how the Unbelievers…have shown trust, and it is the Muslims who have been lacking in zeal" (Gabrieli, 1969, p. 214).

After the death of Alp Arslan (r. 1063–1072), the second Seljuk sultan, profound divisions emerged among Muslims that allowed for Crusader attacks to succeed and possibly foment the earlier breakdown of law and order that antagonized Christian pilgrims. Ibn al- Athīr (d. 1233), author of the *Universal History*, summed up the reasons for Muslim defeat in the First Crusade: "The sultans disagreed, as we shall relate, and the Franks seized the lands."

Nevertheless, the Byzantine emperor failed to recognize that Sultan Alp Arslan had been open to cooperation with Christian powers, as he was much more preoccupied with the threat of his Shīʿah rivals, the Fatimids. The Seljuks came to be regarded as enforcers of Sunni orthodoxy, and they looked on Shīʿah dynasties with a wary eye. Christian rulers sometimes saw the Islamic world as a monolith and lacked the diplomatic finesse to benefit from these divisions. Just as much of the Muslim world had a tendency to call all Christians "Franks," the European Christians commonly saw Muslims as undifferentiated teeming masses whom they routinely referred to as "Turks," even when they were confronting Arabs, Persians, Berbers, or Kurds. And yet the Christian Crusader attacks on their Eastern Orthodox brethren in Constantinople tarnished the image of Latin Christians in the eyes of some Muslims, who could now behold the frightening disunity of the Christian world. Already many Christians dwelling in the Near and Middle East resented the Frankish settlers who, after all, had provoked Muslim dynasties to curtail more tolerant practices toward the indigenous Christian communities.

The comparative neglect of the Crusades among Muslim thinkers in the medieval and early modern period gave way to prolific and vociferous criticism with the rise of European imperialism and then the emergence of the United States as a global power. When France assumed its mandate rule over Syria in 1920, General Henri Gouraud marched to Saladin's tomb, allegedly gave it a swift kick, and then crowed triumphantly: "Saladin, we have returned. My presence here consecrates the victory of the Cross over the Crescent." Upon seizing Jerusalem from the dying Ottoman Empire in 1917, British general Edmund Allenby found himself frequently hailed as a conquering Crusader, even though he chafed at this later in life. Major Vivian Gilbert in *The Romance of the Last Crusade: With Allenby to Jerusalem* (1923) exclaimed, "At last Jerusalem was in our hands! In all ten crusades organized and equipped to free the Holy City, only two were really successful, the first led by Godfrey de Bouillon, and the last under Edmund Allenby" (p. 171). The *New York Times* (18 May 1925) in an editorial saluted Allenby as "the Deliverer of the Holy Land" and "worthy to be remembered… beyond the greatest of the Crusaders of the Middle Ages."

Writing in the 1960s, Muhammad Jalal Kishk, an Islamic author and journalist, produced a militant historical vision of the Crusades as having three phases: the First Crusade, launched in 1095; the Second Crusade, commencing with Napoleon's invasion of Egypt in 1798, and the Third Crusade, starting in 1967 in which the Zionist and U.S. war and cultural complex resumed

Napoleon's work, leading to the subordination and enervation of Muslim peoples. Taking note of pious Israeli soldiers praying at the Wailing Wall and semisecularized Arab warriors who now seem ashamed of open displays of religiosity, Kishk affirms that only a turn to authentic Islam can arrest the decay and deliver meaningful resistance.

In the aftermath of the 9/11 bombings, Osama bin Laden told Al Jazeera on 21 October 2001 that "the *ummah* is asked to unite itself under this Crusaders' campaign, the strongest, most powerful, and ferocious Crusaders' campaign to befall the Islamic nation since the dawn of Islamic history. There have been past Crusader wars, but there has never been a campaign like this before.... Either you are with the Crusades, or you are with Islam." During the early days of the response to the 9/11 atrocity, U.S. president George W. Bush steadfastly affirmed on the South Lawn of the White House that "this crusade, this war on terrorism, is going to take a while" (Waldman, p. A1). Then in a speech before the U.S. Congress, he added, "Either you are with us, or you are with the terrorists" ("World-Wide," *Wall Street Journal*, 21 September 2001, p. A1) In testimony before the National Commission on Terrorist Attacks upon the United States on 23 March 2004, U.S. secretary of state Colin Powell also referred to his demand to Pakistan's Pervez Musharraf to get behind "this crusade" ("Public Testimony Before 9/11 Panel," *New York Times* online, 23 March 2004, p. 23 at http://www.nytimes.com/2004/03/23/politics/23CND-PTEX.html?pagewanted=23). Though firmly repudiated by bin Laden loyalists as a reprobate enemy of true Islam, Iraqi dictator Saddam Hussein actively propagandized that he should be looked upon as the second coming of Saladin, doubly ironic given brutal Baʿthist repression of the medieval warrior's Kurdish descendants.

With the waning of the cold war, preeminent political scientists such as Samuel P. Huntington and the Middle East historian Bernard Lewis made regular appeal to the persistence of "the clash of civilizations," a construct that regards the storm and stress from the Crusades as a permanent feature of Islamic-Christian relations. Openly embraced by U.S. vice president Dick Cheney, Lewis's thought earned the Princeton professor the nation's highest honor for a humanist scholar, the National Medal for the Humanities, personally bestowed on 9 November 2006 by President Bush at the Oval Office. There have been many efforts at demolishing the clash of civilizations idea as a flawed and frozen construct, but the Crusades have remarkable tenacity in modern memory, retaining political potency even in the twenty-first century.

BIBLIOGRAPHY

Ali, Tariq. *The Clash of Fundamentalisms: Crusades, Jihads, and Modernity*. London: Verso, 2002.

Bartlett, Robert. *The Making of Europe: Conquest, Colonization and Cultural Change, 950–1350*. Princeton, N.J.: Princeton University Press, 1993.

Bhatia, Umej. *Forgetting Osama bin Munqidh, Remembering Osama bin Laden: The Crusades in Modern Muslim Memory*. RSIS Monograph 12. Singapore: S. Rajaratnam School of International Studies, 2008.

Cobb, Paul M. "Usāma Ibn Munqidh's *Book of the Staff*: Autobiographical and Historical Excerpts," *Al-Masāq*, vol. 17, no. 1, March 2005, 109–123.

Daniel, Norman. *Islam and the West: The Making of an Image*. Rev. ed. Oxford: Oneworld, 1993.

Gabrieli, Francesco. *Arab Historians of the Crusades*. Trans. by E. J. Costello. London: Routledge & Kegan Paul, 1969.

Gilbert, Vivian. *The Romance of the Last Crusade: With Allenby to Jerusalem*. New York: W. B. Feakins, 1923.

Halliday, Fred. *Islam and the Myth of Confrontation: Religion and Politics in the Middle East*. London: I. B. Tauris, 1996.

Hillenbrand, Carole. *The Crusades: Islamic Perspectives*. New York: Routledge, 2000.

Mourad, Suleiman A., and James E. Lindsay. *The Intensification and Reorientation of Sunni Jihad Ideology in the Crusader Period: Ibn ʿAsākir of Damascus*

(1105–1176) and His Age, with an Edition and Translation of Ibn ʿAsākir's *The Forty Hadiths for Inciting Jihad*. Leiden: Brill, 2013.

Riley-Smith, Jonathan. *The Crusades, Christianity, and Islam*. New York: Columbia University Press, 2008.

Tyerman, Christopher. *God's War: A New History of the Crusades*. Cambridge, Mass.: Belknap Press of Harvard University Press, 2006.

Waldman, Peter, and Hugh Pope. "Worlds Apart: Some Muslims Fear That a War on Terrorism is a War on Them," *Wall Street Journal*, 21 September 2001, p. A1.

JOHN TRUMPBOUR

CULTURAL INVASION. Western cultural hegemony provoked resistance in a variety of non-Western settings, not only in the Islamic world. During the nineteenth century, dynasties as diverse as Manchu China, Tokugawa Japan, and Romanov Russia, as well as the Ottoman caliphate felt threatened by the economic and military expansionism of Western Europe. To avert ruin at the hands of mightier powers, they all sought to learn from their adversaries, and, to their dismay, they all ended up borrowing more than they had originally intended.

In the Islamic world, the Ottoman caliphate's power centers proved more vulnerable to culture invasion than its periphery. By virtue of their leading position in the realm, Turkey and Egypt were more susceptible to Western incursion than others, and hence their need to respond was greatest. Mahmod II (r. 1808–1839) of Constantinople and Muḥammad ʿAlī (r. 1805–1849) of Cairo began to study how the West advanced in order to protect their rule and maintain their capacity to project regional power. They sent emissaries to Paris, Vienna, and other European capitals to master the secrets of industry and bureaucratic and military organization. They then promptly applied that knowledge at home, notably through the replacement of slave corps (the janissaries in Turkey and the Mamlūks in Egypt) with conscript armies along Western lines. Still, both leaders were defeated by an alliance of Western powers (Britain, France, Austria, and Russia): the Ottomans on the shores of Greece in 1827 and the Egyptians at the borders of Constantinople in 1840. Their heirs—substantially weakened and increasingly in awe of Western power—inaugurated the second phase of cultural borrowing. This time the careful, selective learning of the first reformers gave way to wholesale imitation.

As Ibn Khaldūn so adeptly described, the weak, driven by a blinding desire to emulate the strong, do not stop at simply adopting those elements of strength that they lack; instead, their internalized sense of inferiority encourages them to mimic the habits and lifestyle of their conquerors in the most irrational way. Hence, the era of the Tanzimat (1839–1876) in Turkey and the reign of Khedive Ismāʿīl of Egypt (r. 1863–1879) witnessed the total embrace of all things Western: language, art, music, and architecture, down to even clothing and cuisine. In the minds of many, as famously articulated by Malek Bennabi, this led to the weakening of the cultural character and religious bonds that held these societies together, thus increasing their "susceptibility to be colonized" (Bennabi, 1996) by the West. And duly so, before the nineteenth century came to a close, almost every single Muslim province fell prey to one form of Western domination or another. Ironically, it was anti-imperialist campaigns within the Muslim world that cemented cultural dependency on the West, giving rise to a plethora of Islamic forces intent on breaking away from this foreign orbit.

It was toward the end of World War I, with the breakup of the Ottoman Empire and the ending of the caliphate, that national independence movements sprang up throughout Muslim societies. Their struggle to secure political independence from the colonial powers of the West was cheered by their fellow countrymen, though only a few noticed that their demands were framed in distinctively Western vocabulary: constitutionalism, nationalism, and—curiously—secularism, which they believed to be the guardian of civil liberties, citizenship rights, and modernization. The leaders of nationalist movements in Turkey, Egypt, India, Algeria, and other parts of the Muslim world were avid students of Western philosophy, law, and literature. They upheld the ideals of humanism and the Enlightenment, accepting the claim that Western history represented the Muslim present, and that its present represents the only conceivable Muslim future. The tension resulting from their abandonment of Islamic traditions, which they replaced partly or wholly with Western institutions and laws, was resolved firstly by religious scholars, such as Muḥammad ʿAbduh (d. 1905) in Egypt and Aḥmad Khān (d. 1898) in India, who espoused Western-style reforms and reinterpreted Islam in a way that synthesizes tradition and progress. But the cultural agenda of these Westernized political elites was ultimately legitimatized by their success in achieving political independence from the West and their subsequent attempt to develop their societies mostly against the will of Western powers. The voice of Islamic resistance was stifled for a while.

But the obscurity of Islamic reform doctrines, combined with the meager results of secular modernization projects, paved the path for Islamic resurgence in the second half of the twentieth century. The premise upheld by moral reform movements (such as the Nurculuk movement in Turkey) as well as political organizations (such as the Muslim Brothers in Egypt) was that cultural independence was no less significant than political or economic independence, and that after two centuries of going astray a nation must first "return to itself" before it could hope to achieve power.

BIBLIOGRAPHY

Bennabi, Malek. *Shurūṭ al-nahḍah* (The Conditions for Renaissance). Damascus: Dar al-Fikr, 1996.

Bishrī, Ṭāriq. *al-Malāmiḥ al-ʿāmmah lil-fikr al-siyāsī al-Islāmī fī al-tārīkh al-muʿāṣir* (General Features of Islamic Political Thought in the Contemporary Age). Cairo: Dār al-Shurūq, 1996.

Ibn Khaldūn, ʿAbd al-Raḥmān. *al-Muqaddimah* (Prolegomena). Alexandria, Egypt: Dar Ibn Khaldūn, 2003.

Kishk, Muḥammad Jalāl. *al-Ghazw al-fikrī* (The Intellectual Invasion). Cairo: Dār al-Qawmiyyah, 1966.

Shariati, Ali. *al-ʿAwdah ilá al-dhāt* (The Return to Self). Cairo: Al-Zahra' lel-ʿIlam al-ʿArabi, 1986.

HAZEM KANDIL

CUMHURIYET HALK PARTISI. A major political organization in Turkey for ninety years, the Cumhuriyet Halk Partisi (Republican People's Party, or CHP) was founded on 9 September 1923. The CHP maintained authoritarian single-party rule until 1946 and continued in power under a multiparty system until 1950, when it lost in the free general elections. Following the military intervention of 1960, it led several coalition governments, three during 1961–1965, one in 1974, and one during 1978–1979.

The CHP was in many ways a continuation of the Union and Progress Party that ruled from the last decade of the Ottoman Empire until its defeat in World War I. It originally developed from Association for the Defense of the Rights of Anatolia and Rumelia created at the Sivas Congress in autumn 1919 in response to the Greek invasion. Its ideology was that of Ottoman patriotism and Islamism rather than Turkish nationalism. It aimed at preserving the offices of the caliphate and the sultanate, securing the integrity of the Ottoman motherland, and safeguarding national independence. In the absence of a widespread national consciousness, it rallied the people through religion.

The DRAAR was transformed into the Grand National Assembly of Turkey (GNAT) early in the war, and the "First Group" was formed in the assembly to secure party discipline. After the military victory, the leader of the nationalist struggle, Mustafa Kemal (Atatürk), was commander in chief, president of the GNAT, and the head of the First Group. He reorganized the latter into a political party, utilized the slogan "Popular Sovereignty," and called this the People's Party.

The CHP was initially only a parliamentary party, but it soon began to expand into the provinces, purging any potential opponents (yet it did not open branches in the Kurdish-majority eastern provinces until the 1940s). The party obeyed Atatürk's charismatic authority and assimilated his modernization program.

Republicanism, populism, nationalism, and laicism became the main principles of the CHP in 1927. Four years later two more principles, statism and reformism, were added. Various sociopolitical reforms were carried out under these principles, ranging from changes in headgear and dress to the adoption of Western laws and Latin alphabet—all moves in the direction of secularism.

The identification of the party with the state occurred in 1936–1937. The minister of internal affairs became the general secretary of the party, and the governors became the provincial heads of local CHP organizations. The monopolistic state apparatus could not tolerate the existence of a distinct party structure apart from itself.

Under İsmet İnönü, the second president of the republic and the CHP, the party went through important changes, particularly after three successive election defeats in the 1950s. It first became a "democratic" opposition party. Beginning in the mid-1960s it adopted a left-of-center course. The general secretary of the party, Bülent Ecevit, who strongly opposed the military coup of 12 March 1971, toppled İsmet İnönü and gained control of the party in an extraordinary convention in 1972, advocating a democratic leftist platform. The metamorphosis helped the party win two election victories, in 1973 and 1977. The CHP's previously strict laicism had already been softened. Indeed, in 1974 it even formed a coalition government with the fundamentalist National Salvation Party.

After the 1980 military coup, its activities were stopped by the junta, together with those of other political parties; it was formally dissolved on 16 October 1982 by decision of the National Security Council. Shortly thereafter, a number of center-leftist political parties were established and claimed the mantle of the dissolved CHP, including the Social Democratic People's Party (SHP) and the Democratic Leftist Party (DSP). Upon the granting of permission to reform previously banned political parties in 1992, a new CHP was established.

The new CHP was founded by Deniz Baykal, a former member of parliament of the party in the 1970s, with the same emblem and party principles. It joined coalition governments during 1993–1995 and 1995–1996, and it merged with the SHP in 1995. The party's "Anatolian leftist" course and strict laicism could not prevent it from being overshadowed by Ecevit's DSP. It failed to pass the threshold in the 1999 elections and remained outside the assembly.

Since 2002, the new CHP has emerged as the second party in all three general elections, with about one-fifth of the overall votes. In 2010, Baykal resigned as the president of the CHP, and Kemal Kılıçdaroğlu, the deputy speaker of the party's parliamentary group, took over. Seeking to revive the spirit of the 1970s, Kılıçdaroğlu has called for a social-democratic transformation. In the 2011 general elections, the party's vote share increased to 25.9 percent, the highest since 1977, bringing a 33.3 percent increase in the number of seats in the new parliament.

BIBLIOGRAPHY

Bilâ, Hikmet. *Sosyal Demokrat Süreç içinde CHP ve Sonrası*. 2d ed. Istanbul: Milliyet Yayınları, 1987.

Ciddi, Sinan. *Kemalism in Turkish Politics: The Republican People's Party, Secularism, and Nationalism*. London: Routledge, 2009.

Güneş-Ayata, Ayşe. "The Republican People's Party." In *Political Parties in Turkey*, edited by Barry Rubin and Metin Heper, pp. 102–122. Portland, Oreg.: Frank Cass, 2002.

Mete Tunçay
Updated by H. Ozan Ozavci

Customary Law. *See* Sharīʿah.

D

Dār al-Iftā'. A *fatwa*, a nonbinding response to a question of religion, law, or morality asked of an authoritative legal scholar (mufti), can, in modern times, be issued by an official mufti or institution as well as an independent mufti. The Arabic term for the issuing of a *fatwa* is *iftā'*, and, if state-run, the mufti's office is called *dār al-iftā'*. The best known of these institutions is the Egyptian Dār al-Iftā', but such legal institutions exist in other countries as well, notably Saudi Arabia.

The Egyptian Dār al-Iftā' was established around 1895 when Ismā'īl Pasha (1830–1895) appointed Ḥassūna al-Nawāwī (d. 1924), at that time Shaykh al-Azhar, as the first grand mufti of Egypt. The government appointment took over the function of the Ḥanafī chief mufti, who until then had been the person consulted by institutional bodies about religious or legal matters pertaining to the state, such as the time of the new moon for the beginning and end of Ramadan, or, as in 1952, the right of women to vote. Al-Nawāwī held the position for four years, until 1899, and his office issued a total of 687 *fatwas* (or sixteen per month); as of 1996, when the grand mufti Muḥammad Sayyid Ṭanṭāwī (d. 2010) stepped down, having held the position since 1986, the total of *fatwas* issued by the Dār al-Iftā' had reached approximately 4,500. It is estimated that the Egyptian Dār al-Iftā currently issues up to one thousand *fatwas* each year. Its only real competition is the *fatwa* committee (Lajnat al-Fatwa) of al-Azhar, the Egyptian religious university, which prides itself on not being an official organ of the state but is regarded by many nevertheless as being coopted.

The Saudi Arabian Dār al-Iftā' is the popular name for Lajnat al-Dā'imah lil-Buḥūth al-'Ilmīyah wa-al-Iftā' (Permanent Committee for Scientific Research and the Issuing of Fatwas), an arm of the Council of Senior *'Ulamā'*, whose members are appointed by the Saudi regime. The first grand mufti in Saudi Arabia, Muḥammad Ibrāhīm Āl al-Shaykh (d. 1969), a descendant of Ibn 'Abd al-Wahhāb, the founder of modern Saudi Arabia, was named in 1952, but he retained, for the most part, his independence from the state; upon his death his office was merged into the new Permanent Committee in 1971. An influential grand mufti was Bin Bāz (d. 1999), who wielded great authority in that position.

A large percentage of *fatwas* issued by these institutions, whether solicited by the state or by individuals, affects state policy, such as *fatwas* on medical ethics. Questions on organ transplants, sex change, euthanasia, and circumcision reverberate in society—a case in point is the *fatwa* issued in Egypt in 2006 by Grand Mufti ʿAlī Jumʿa (Ali Gomaa) decrying female circumcision as un-Islamic and forbidding it. One of the controversial *fatwas* issued during Ṭanṭāwī's tenure in 1989 was the legitimization of most banking operations, including the taking of interest (*ribā*) and the issuing of government bonds. Some of the *fatwas* that have been issued in the twentieth century by these and other *fatwa* institutions are staunchly political and have been used by regimes to legitimize their existence or their policies, for example, the Saudi *fatwa* authorizing the use of force to oust the insurgents occupying the Grand Mosque of Mecca in 1979 and the *fatwa* issued by the Egyptian Grand Mufti ʿAlī Jād al-Ḥaqq (d. 1996) endorsing the peace treaty between Egypt and Israel in 1979.

BIBLIOGRAPHY

ʿAbduh, Muḥammad, ed. *Al-Fatāwā l-islāmīyah min Dār al-Iftāʾ al-miṣrīyah* (Islamic Fatwas from the Egyptian Dar al-Ifta'). Cairo: Jumhūriyyat Miṣr al-ʿArabīyah, 1980–.

Al-Atawneh, Muhammad K. *Wahhābī Islam Facing the Challenges of Modernity: Dār al-Iftā in the Modern Saudi State*. Leiden, Netherlands: Brill, 2010.

Brown, Nathan J. "Egypt: Cacophony and Consensus in the Twenty-First Century." In *Shariʿa Politics: Islamic Law and Society in the Modern World*, edited by Robert W. Hefner, pp. 94–120. Bloomington: Indiana University Press, 2011.

Lajnat al-Dāʾimah lil-Buḥūth al-ʿIlmīyah wa-al-Iftāʾ. *Fatāwā al-Lajnah al-Dāʾimah lil-Buḥūth al-ʿIlmīyah wa-al-Iftāʾ* (*Fatwas* from the Permanent Committee for Scientific Research and the Issuing of *Fatwas*). Riyadh: al-Mamlakah al-ʿArabīyah al-Saʿūdīyah, 1992–.

Mallat, Chibli. "Tantawi on Banking Operations in Egypt." In *Islamic Legal Interpretation: Muftis and Their Fatwas*, edited by Muhammad Khalid Masud, Brinkley Messick, and David S. Powers, pp. 286–296. Cambridge, Mass.: Harvard University Press, 1996.

Peters, Rudolph. "Muḥammad al-ʿAbbāsī al-Mahdī (d. 1987), Grand Muftī of Egypt, and His Fatāwā al-Mahdiyya." *Islamic Law and Society* 1 (1994): 66–82.

Skovgaard-Petersen, Jakob. *Defining Islam for the Egyptian State: Muftis and Fatwas of the Dār al-Iftā*. Leiden, Netherlands: Brill, 1997.

PERI BEARMAN

DARUL ISLAM MOVEMENT. Darul Islam (House of Islam) had its roots in West Java in the early 1940s, but it was not until 1948 that a group of Islamic activists established its state structure upon Islamic principles. Its base was in traditional areas of West Java, particularly in the Preanger (Parahyangan) region, where it could develop within a strong Islamic community that was confronted by economic hardship and Dutch colonial rule. Separate Darul Islam movements developed later in South Kalimantan, South Sulawesi, and Aceh. On Java it led to the establishment of an autonomous government, the Islamic State of Indonesia (Negara Islam Indonesia), and a military force, the Indonesian Islamic Army (Tentera Islam Indonesia). Initially, the new state was based upon Islamic principles and law with leadership formally in the hands of *kiais* and teachers of Islam. Its head was Sukarmadji Kartosuwiryo, the founder of a religious school in Java. Darul Islam initially targeted the Dutch and their allies and proclaimed loyalty to the Indonesian Republic, although Kartosuwiryo and others in the organization were suspicious of secular aspects of the republic from its beginning. They were opposed to its religious pluralism and rejection of Islam as the basis of the state and were apprehensive about the power of secular nationalists and communists in the new nation. Even before the end of Dutch rule there was armed conflict between the armed forces of the republic and Darul Islam, which continued until the late 1960s.

From almost the beginning of the organization, the leadership had trouble controlling its members and maintaining its Islamic principles. From the early 1950s Darul Islam was under pressure from the military, which further eroded central control. Increasingly, its fragmented military adopted their own methods and sought more secular goals. Militant groups from within the organization and others who attached themselves to it turned from the movement's Islamic roots. Many engaged in banditry, extortion, and other criminal acts, forcefully extracting food and services from the peasantry. The economic hardships arising from the conflict, combined with the unregulated actions of its armed forces, led to diminishing support from the population.

Darul Islam's leader was captured in 1962 and executed, but fragmented parts of the organization continued to be active. Its legacy lies in the ideological foundations of militant Islamic groups that arose in Indonesia over the following decades. The original vision of Darul Islam has been proclaimed as a model for the return of an Islamic state, and present and former members have been active in some militant factions. For example, it is claimed that Darul Islam members were part of a violent Islamic group, Komando Jihad, in the 1970s and early 1980s. Abu Bakar Bashir, leader of Southeast Asia's most notorious Islamic militant group, Jemaah Islamiyah, was a member of Darul Islam in the 1970s. In the twenty-first century Darul Islam veterans and ideals were important in more militant Muslim organizations such as the anti-Christian Laskar Jihad and Majelis Mujahidin Indonesia (Council of Holy Warriors of Indonesia, MMI).

BIBLIOGRAPHY

Kahin, George McTurnan. *Nationalism and Revolution in Indonesia*. Ithaca, N.Y.: Cornell University Press, 1952.

van Dijk, C. *Rebellion under the Banner of Islam: The Darul Islam in Indonesia*. The Hague: Martinus Nijhof, 1981.

FRED R. VON DER MEHDEN

DAʿWAH. Literally meaning "claim, prayer, invocation," *daʿwah* is "a religious outreach or mission to exhort people to embrace Islam" (Denny, 1987, p. 244), although the concept acquired meanings other than "mission" and "conversion." In Islamic theology, the very purpose of *daʿwah* is to invite people, both Muslims and non-Muslims, to understand the worship of God. Because a believer is subject to potential conversion, *daʿwah* strengthens Islam, which in turn consolidates the power of the *ummah*. *Daʿwah* is indeed the means by which the Prophet Muḥammad spread the message of the Qurʾān to mankind as he commanded the faithful to continue in his footsteps. In contemporary Islamic thought, *daʿwah* is also described as the duty to "actively encourage fellow Muslims in the pursuance of greater piety in all aspects of their lives."

Qurʾānic Concepts. In the Qurʾān (2:186) a basic meaning for *daʿwah*—perhaps its cardinal meaning—is the single act of prayer: "When My servants ask thee about Me, I am indeed close by and answer the prayer [*daʿwah*] of everyone when they pray to Me." *Daʿwah*, therefore, can indicate a certain person's prayer or an entreaty addressed to God; such are the prayers of Moses and Aaron (*sūrah* 10:89) and of Abraham, Solomon, and Jonah (asserted in a *ḥadīth* reference to Qurʾānic passages). Prayer can also mean the call to formal prayer rituals, as in a *ḥadīth* that specifies *daʿwah* ("calling to prayer") as an office of the Ethiopian, but it is more commonly an individual's invocation of God for a special purpose, such as the granting of a favor. In fact, many Qurʾānic passages are warnings or admonitions against trying to call on a god other than the One True God, and a primary lesson in the Qur'ān is that to make a *da'wah* to other gods is in vain either in this life or in the next. Such a *da'wah* cannot and will not receive an answer; it yields no result, and to persist in it once apprised of its uselessness is a wickedness.

The Qur'ān is replete with examples of those who wrongly call on false gods and, naturally, of the correctness of directing a *da'wah* to the True God, who alone grants the appeal of his servants. Equally, each servant must recognize that God's own *da'wah*, his summons, requires their response. The ultimate *da'wah* is that of God himself. This double principle—that God both summons through *da'wah* and that God alone answers the *da'wah* of all servants—results in a sense of the true *da'wah*, the *da'wat al-ḥaqq* of *sūrah* 13:14: "To Him is the prayer of truth [*da'wat al-ḥaqq*], and all those they pray to, other than Him, answer them not at all, no more than if they stretched out their hands to reach for water, which reaches them not, for the prayer of the unbelievers is futile."

From such examples, the fundamental meaning of the Islamic *da'wah* emerges, which is the declaration that there is no god other than the True God (Allāh). The *da'wah* is Islam, and Islam is the *da'wah*.

The second duty of a Muslim is to answer the *da'wah* of God's *dā'ī*, the Prophet Muḥammad. Muḥammad, like prophets before him, issues his own call as he summons his people to the true faith; he thus fulfills God's *da'wah* by instituting his own. Although the opening *sūrah* of the Qur'ān is an invocation addressed to God, and as such the *sūrah* itself is called the *da'wah*, it also contains the message of the "straight path," which is true religion itself.

These extensions of the notion of each prophet's call lead to an extremely important concept—that of community in the sense of community of believers, no longer merely the people summoned by a single prophet. Although the faithful summoned by the prophet may not respond to his summons, those who do henceforth constitute the *ummah* of Muslims: "Oh you who believe, fear God as He should be, and die not except having become *muslim*" (*sūrah* 3:102). The idea of *da'wah* thus moves one step further, becoming an activity of the whole community; it is the command to promote good and fight injustice at large. *Sūrah* 3:104 begins to articulate a sense of *da'wah* as a synonym of *ummah* and of righteousness itself, and it is thus not far from this to the equation of *da'wah* and *Sharī'ah* (the divine law), which, like *da'wah*, is the "straight path."

Main Thinkers on *Da'wah*. *Da'wah* was used as a call to establish an alternative political order in the early history of Islam, for instance by the Khawārij and 'Abbāsids against the Umayyads and by the Ismā'īlīs against the 'Abbāsids, but it was gradually divested of this political orientation in later periods. Political theorists generally mentioned *da'wah* as one of the duties of a caliph, but this duty was rarely realized in practice until the nineteenth century, when the doctrine was revived in by the Ottoman sultan Abdülhamid II (r. 1876–1909). Instead of referring to preaching and *jihād*, this caliphal duty was now defined to extend the caliph's authority over Muslims in other countries, analogous to the Catholic pope. Although Abdülhamid II used the idea for his own political purposes, it was also readily accepted by the West, where it was argued that the Ottoman caliph should only be the spiritual head of all Muslims, while executive and administrative powers should be placed in the hands of local and regional rulers.

In this context *da'wah* immediately became a political instrument to propagate Islamic unity. The doctrine of *da'wah* as a caliphal function brought Muslims in different territories together under one spiritual head, an idea that was systematically developed by Jamāl al-Dīn al-

Afghānī (d. 1897), who founded the Jamʿīyat al-ʿUrwah al-Wuthqā (Society of the Reliable Bond), a *daʿwah* organization promoting Muslim solidarity.

Improved means of communication and news media in the twentieth century increased socio-political awareness among Muslim communities, which had remained largely isolated from one another until then. This awareness led to the growth of a sense of solidarity. The political context of democracy and nation-states heightened the importance of attracting large numbers of supporters. The vigorous Christian missionary work of this period was also viewed by Muslims as a political threat, because it was seen as an effort to increase the number of Christians in Muslim areas. *Daʿwah* organizations like al-Daʿwah wa-al-Irshād (*Daʿwah* and Guidance), founded by Muḥammad Rashīd Riḍā (d. 1935), were established in response to the perceived threat.

Evolution during Various Periods. Throughout the history of Islam, except during the Fāṭimid and Ismāʿīlī dynasties, *daʿwah* was largely an individual and noninstitutionalized activity. In modern times, however, it has become increasingly institutionalized in response to the global Christian missionary activities that began to reach the Muslim world in the sixteenth century. A formal institutionalized and organized *daʿwah* began after 1915, as clear parallels with Christian missionary organizations attested; for example, the World Council of Mosques and the Organization for the Distribution of the Qurʾān are comparable to the World Council of Churches and various Bible societies.

In a different manner, the Society for Teaching and Propagation (Jamāʿat al-Tablīgh wa-al-Daʿwah; more commonly referred to as the Tablīghī Jamāʿat) of the Indian Mawlānā Muḥammad Ilyās (1885–1944) had already stressed the necessity of a missionary duty of *daʿwah*. Of Ṣūfī background, the Tablīghī Jamāʿat focused on Muslim communities on the peripheries as well as on neighboring non-Muslims. The large mystical organizations were better able to cover the needs of proselytes in the peripheries than the political associations of the neo-Salafīyah. In West Africa, it was mainly the Sanūsīyah and the Tijānīyah that helped to spread Islam to previously non-Muslim territories. Likewise, such sects as the Aḥmadīyah and the Ismāʿīlīyah used the concept of *daʿwah* to proselytize chiefly in communities to which Muslims had migrated but in which they constituted a minority.

Missionary activities of the new Islamic organizations were still marginal and restricted to sporadic activities of several centers of Islamic learning. Thus, during the sessions of the General Islamic Congress of Jerusalem in 1931, Muḥammad Rashīd Riḍā (1865–1935) was able to revive his small Society of Call and Guidance (Jamʿīyat al-Daʿwah wa-al-Irshād), which he had founded in 1911 as a putative cornerstone of Ottoman Pan-Islamic activities. Only after the end of World War II did the political tendency to establish transnational Islamic bodies lead to the idea of propagating Islam outside the sphere of the *ummah* as well. The short-lived Islamic Conference, established by Saudi Arabia, Egypt, and Pakistan in 1954, demanded that the spread of Islam become a major task of "Islamic work." *Daʿwah* was now understood to be an integral part of the concept of *waḥdat* (unity): transnational organizations should simultaneously represent the will of the Muslim community to live in a single, at least culturally unified *ummah* and to work to spread the true teachings of Islam.

The justification for the centralization of *daʿwah* is sought in the doctrine of *al-amr bi-al-maʿrūf*, the Qurʾānic injunction to do good, defined as a distinct duty of the Muslim *ummah*. This duty is understood as applying to all humankind, but in its doctrinal details its scope is generally restricted to Muslims. Another justification is derived from the doctrine of *tartīb al-daʿwah* (the order of priority in the spread of *daʿwah*), an early Islamic doctrine. As explained by Ibn Amīr al-Ḥājj (d. 1474), a Ḥanafī jurist, in *Al-taqrīr wa-al-taḥbīr*, this doctrine has reference to the *daʿwah* of Muʿādh ibn Jabal (d. 639), which stressed a graded approach in communicating religious duties and doctrines to new converts. Since there were deficient Muslims who needed to be converted to true Islam, the conversion of non-Muslims became secondary in importance.

Significance of the Concept in Modern Times. Since the beginning of the twentieth century, modern Islamic *daʿwah* has become a major issue of newly established Islamic institutions and organizations. The Ottoman sultan Abdülhamid II had already included the concept of *daʿwah* in his "imperial ideology," supporting his claim to be the caliph of the Islamic *ummah*. ʿAbd al-Raḥmān al-Kawākibī embodied the call to the righteous of (Salafī) Islam into the duties of his fictitious Society for the Edification of the Unitarians (Jamʿīyat Taʿlīm al-Muwaḥḥidīn). But whereas the classical Salafīyah had stressed the concept of *tarbīyah* (educating the Muslim believers), independent non-scholarly organizations of the neo-*salafīyah* put *daʿwah* at the foreground of their political and cultural activities. During the 1930s in Egypt, two competing organizations, the Muslim Brotherhood (al-Ikhwān al-Muslimūn) and the Association of Young Muslims (Jamʿīyat al-Shubbān al-Muslimīn), not only called for a temporary withdrawal from society (*hijrah*) but also called on Muslim youth to join the new groups in accordance with the Qurʾān (3:104): "Let there arise out of you a band of people inviting to all that is good, enjoining what is right and forbidding what is wrong. These are the ones to attain felicity." By using this Qurʾānic verse, they tried to legitimate their claim to independent authority in a nation-state community. In a way, *daʿwah* still meant the call to become a member of the only righteous Islamic community within the Muslim *ummah*.

During the Arab Cold War (1957–1967), *daʿwah* work attained greater recognition in Saudi Arabia as Saudi leaders realized the possibility of broadening their political and cultural influence by promulgating the word of God, promoting the message of Islam, and bringing the Muslims back to the orbit of Islam. Saudi Arabia established the Islamic University in Medina in 1961 for the education and training of *daʿwah* workers. In 1962 the Muslim World League (Rābiṭat al-ʿĀlam al-Islāmī) was founded to organize various transnational *daʿwah* activities. While it succeeded early on in bringing together various reformist *daʿwah* groups in India, Pakistan, Morocco, and Saudi Arabia, results were mixed. In 1970, the institution extended its activities within the nascent Organization of the Islamic Conference, which proved to be an effective body on all five continents.

In the early 1970s, when Islamic politics was becoming a major focus of political and cultural struggle, the *daʿwah* of the transnational organizations gained greater attention from the Islamic public. In December 1972, the Wahhābī community in Saudi Arabia organized the International Youth Conference for Islamic Daʿwah, which became the cornerstone of the new Saudi-sponsored World Assembly of Muslim Youth (al-Nadwah al-ʿĀlamīyah li-al-Shabāb al-Islāmī). Regrettably, in May 1972, the Libyan government inaugurated a new transnational *daʿwah* organization, the Islamic Call Society (Jamʿīyat al-Daʿwah al-Islāmīyah), which, during the first ten years of its existence, exercised hardly any influence, because its raison d'être was to act as a competitor of the Saudi-based Muslim World League and a mouthpiece for Muʿammar al-Qadhdhāfī's Third International Theory.

The disappointing results of international *daʿwah*, the foundation of new state agencies, and the spontaneous emergence of new radical Islamic political groups highlighted the need for coordination and cooperation. In 1973, the Muslim World League accepted volunteers from the Azhar Academy of Islamic Research (Majmaʿ al-Buḥūth al-Islāmīyah), founded in 1961, in order to fulfill the duties of Islamic work in Africa and Southeast Asia. In September 1975, the Muslim World League held the Mosque Message Conference, an international *daʿwah* conference, in Mecca at which it proposed the total reorganization of *daʿwah* activities and the highlighting of mosques. Accordingly, the World Council of Mosques was established in 1975. Within ten years, the league succeeded in founding several regional branches of this council, which was clearly regarded as a counterweight to the World Council of Churches. After this reorganization of the institutional field of *daʿwah*, the major transnational Islamic organizations were confronted with new developments resulting from the revolutionary propaganda of the Islamic Republic of Iran. The Iranian leadership had set up the Organization for Islamic Propaganda (Munaẓẓamat-i Iʿlām-i Islāmī) as a state ministry whose purpose was to win non-Shīʿī Muslims over to the cause of the Islamic revolution. *Daʿwah* was again aimed more at attracting supporters for a specific political ideology than at recruiting proselytes. Depending on the direct support of the patron regime, political *daʿwah* also followed fluctuations in the government's domestic and foreign policy strategies: in 1982, the Iranian regime began to emphasize its Shīʿī background, thus forcing the propaganda organization to join in this spirit.

After 1982, the competition among the major transnational organizations created a new geographical distribution of *daʿwah* activities: the Iranian activists stressed the importance of working among Muslim communities in the Western world; the Muslim World League tried to consolidate its *daʿwah* activities in East Africa, Southeast Asia, Afghanistan, India, and Pakistan; the Libyan Islamic Call Society chiefly intervened in West Africa and in South America. The Cairo-based Higher Council of Islamic Affairs tried to steer clear of this competition and continued to recruit its activists from those parts of the Islamic world that maintained contacts with al-Azhar University.

BIBLIOGRAPHY

Abedin, Syed Z. "Dawa and Dialogue: Believers and Promotion of Mutual Trust." In *Beyond Frontiers: Islam and Contemporary Needs*, edited by Merryl Wyn Davies and Adnan Khalil Pasha, pp. 42–55. London: Mansell, 1989.

Āl Kāshif al-Ghiṭā, Muḥammad al-Ḥusayn. *Al-Dīn wa-al-Islām, aw al-Daʿwah al-Islāmīyah* (Religion and Islam, or The Islamic Call). Beirut: Dar al-Maʿrifah, 1960.

Canard, Marius. "Daʿwa." In *The Encyclopaedia of Islam*. Rev. ed. Edited by H. A. R. Gibb, Vol. 2, pp. 168–170. Leiden, Netherlands: E. J. Brill, 1965.

Denny, Frederick M. "Daʿwah." In *The Encyclopedia of Religion*, edited by Mircea Eliade, vol. 4, pp. 244–245. New York: Macmillan, 1987.

Engineer, Asghar Ali. "Daʿwah or Dialogue?" *Journal of Ecumenical Studies* 39:1–2 (January 2002): 26–32.

Fadl Allāh, Muḥammad Ḥusayn. *Uslūb al-daʿwah fī al-Qurʾān* [Style of the Call in the Qurʾān]. Beirut: Dar al-Malak, 1994.

Mendel, Miloš. "The Concept of 'ad-Daʿwa al-Islāmīya': Towards a Discussion of the Islamic Reformist Religio-Political Terminology." *Archiv Orientální* 63 (1995), pp. 286–304.

Poston, Larry. *Islamic Daʿwah in the West: Muslim Missionary Activity and the Dynamics of Conversion to Islam*. New York: Oxford University Press, 1992.

Racius, Egdunas. "The Multiple Nature of the Islamic *Daʿwa*." Ph.D. diss., University of Helsinki, 2004. http://ethesis.helsinki.fi/julkaisut/hum/aasia/vk/racius/.

PAUL E. WALKER, REINHARD SCHULZE, *and* MUḤAMMAD KHALID MASUD
Updated by JOSEPH A. KÉCHICHIAN

DAWLAH. An Arabic term from the root *d-w-l*, meaning to rotate, alternate, take turns, or occur periodically, *dawlah* in a modern context refers to the state. In modern Persian *dawlat* sometimes refers to the government, and is in that sense interchangeable with Persian *ḥukūmat* (Ar. *ḥukūmah*). In modern Turkish, *devlet* (also derived from the Arabic) refers only to the state, not government. As early as 1837 an official of the Ottoman Empire wrote a memorandum that distinguished between the two meanings in reference to European states and their governments. Hence, in the modern period, it appears that only in Persian is the word potentially ambiguous.

Development of the Concept of State. In the classical and medieval periods of Islam (622–1453), Muslims lacked a theoretical concept of a juridical, territorial, sovereign state as it is understood today. Still, it could be argued that a political organization consisting of "a set of governmental institutions which constitute the supreme political authority within a given territory"—such as the city of Medina—was known to the early Muslims (Crone, 1988, p. 4).

In the Qurʾān Allāh is said to "cause the days to alternate" (3:140). In a later chapter, the word is used in the sense of something that is given alternately from one hand to another (59:7). Apparently, evidence exists that *dawlah* was used in the Jāhilīyah (pre-Islamic era) by poets to mean "times of success." The first ʿAbbāsid caliph, al-Saffāḥ (r. 749–754), declared on his accession: "You have reached our time and Allāh has brought you our *dawlah*" (i.e., "turn/time of success"). His successor, al-Manṣūr (r. 754–775), praised "our *dawlah*." Here, the word apparently refers to the dynastic house of the ʿAbbāsid caliphs. It was also applied sometimes in the sense of "victory" in this period. Hence, the evidence for equating *dawlah* with dynasty or even more narrowly with the ʿAbbāsid house is inconclusive. Over time, *dawlah* came to connote a "turn of success." The word was also used by the philosopher al-Kindī (c. 801–866) as the equivalent of *mulk*, kingship. In the 900s *dawlah* came into use as a sobriquet bestowed on or appropriated by various princes, such as those of the Ḥamdānid (929–1003) and Būyid (932–1055) houses—hence such titles as *rukn al-dawlah* (pillar of the state) and *sayf al-dawlah* (sword of the state).

Ibn Khaldūn (d. 1406) preferred the terms *mulk* and *siyāsah ʿaqlīyah* (the latter meaning politics or government based on positive law and human reason), but his meaning was close to the modern understanding of *dawlah*.

The modern understanding of *dawlah* as a sovereign state with the attributes of statehood did not develop until the Ottoman Empire's confrontation with Christian Europe in the sixteenth and seventeenth centuries. During the Qājār (1796–1925) and Pahlavi periods in Iran (1925–1979), among the official titles of the shahs was "ruler of the *dawlat-i shāhī*" and, subsequently, the *dawlat-i shāh-in-shāhī* (the royal or imperial state). In short, as commercial and diplomatic intercourse quickened between the Middle East and Europe—and ambassadors were exchanged, treaties signed, and economic agreements consummated—the political vocabulary of the region crystallized. By the mid-nineteenth century, the word *dawlah* had taken on the meaning of Weber's celebrated definition of state as a political organization that, based on its juridical sovereignty, monopolizes the legitimate means of violence within a given territory.

Islam and the Secular State. Muslim writers had to deal with this increasing secularization of the political realm (i.e., the separation of religion and state), and the debate continues over the appropriate response. Typically, Islamists seeking total implementation of what they regard to be the *Sharīʿah* (the holy law) are uncomfortable with the term *dawlah*, preferring to refer to the Muslims as an *ummah* (community of believers) whose political institution is the *khilāfah* (caliphate) or *imāmah* (imamate). An exception to this is Saʿīd Ḥawwā (1935–1989), the former leader of the Syrian Muslim Brotherhood, who employed the word *dawlah* in his call for the establishment of *dawlat Allāh*. But in this case, the translation is the religiously accommodating "kingdom of Allāh," not the laicized "state of Allāh."

In international relations, the period since the Treaty of Westphalia of 1648 has been the era of the nation-state, and territoriality has become a decisive factor of life, with the *ummah* split into a variety of units, each with its own attributes of statement and government. Muslim reformers had to take these developments into account. Among the most celebrated attempts to do so is that of Shaykh ʿAlī ʿAbd al-Rāziq (d. 1966), a former rector of al-Azhar. In 1925, he published a book entitled *al-Islam wa-usūl al-ḥukm* (Islam and the Foundations of Rule). ʿAbd al-Rāziq scandalized religious scholars by rejecting the thesis that Islam was both religion and state. Indeed, he went as far as to say that an Islamic order does not require a caliph ruling on the basis of the *Sharīʿah*.

Modern Interpretations. Islamic liberals today, the heirs of ʿAbd al-Rāziq, maintain that the political sphere should be left entirely to the deliberations of Muslim people, in accordance with the saying of the Prophet, as attributed to him by three of the seven authoritative codices of *ḥadīth*—those of Ibn Ḥanbal (d. 855), Muslim ibn al-Ḥajjāj (d. 874/875), and Ibn Mājah (d. 886–887)—that "if it is a matter of religion, then have recourse to me, but if it is a matter of your world, you know better about it [than I do]." They do add, of course, that the state must not violate general religious principles and so must "command the right and forbid wrong" and "not allow what God has prohibited nor forbid what God has permitted."

However, the more radical Islamist tendency dissents over the issue, condemning the long-term trend of relegating the state to the secular sphere. They maintain that separation of religion and politics (i.e., religion and the state) was never intended by the Prophet or his successors. Accordingly, they aim to restore the integration of the two spheres, as symbolized by the slogan *al-islām dīn wa-dunyā [dawlah]* (Islam is religion and the world [state]). In the words of one Islamist, the Egyptian Khālid Muḥammad Khālid: "We find no religion…whose nature demands the establishment of a state as…does Islam." Islam may be a religion legislated by Allāh, but "in its human applications it represents a 'social contract' [sic] that includes the establishment of an authority that discharges the obligations of this contract and stands guard over its implementation" (Khālid, 1989, pp. 25, 29). In current Shīʿī theories, associated with Ayatollah Ruhollah Khomeini, the relationship between religion and state has gone beyond merger. In *fatwas* (authoritative religious opinions) that he issued in late 1987 and early 1988, Khomeini said that doctrine of the "mandate of the jurist" (Ar. *wilāyat al-faqīh*; Pers. *vilayāt-i faqīh*) empowered the leader of the Islamic Republic of Iran to suspend secondary ordinances of religious belief (such as the pilgrimage or prayer) if he believed it was necessary to prevent the state's interests from being undermined. The reasoning was that the Islamic Republic of Iran was a truly Islamic state, so it was an obligation to protect it at any cost.

The efforts of twenty-first-century Islamists are ironic, because the great founders of the schools of Islamic law, who lived in the eighth and ninth centuries, did not contest the separation of the spheres of religion and state by the ruling caliphs of those times. In modern times, Islamists interpret the expression *inna al-ḥukm illa li Allāh*

(Qur'ān 12:47, 60) to mean that rule is God's alone, whereas the legal exegetes did not take such a radical position. If those luminaries had had differences with caliphs, these differences were theological in nature, not political. For example, Ibn Ḥanbal quarreled with and was punished by the caliph al-Ma'mūn (r. 813–833) over whether or not the Qur'ān was created. But Ibn Ḥanbal did not suggest that the separation of religion and state that had been effected by al-Ma'mūn's predecessors and sustained by him was wrong or cause for pronouncing unbelief on the ruler. Today's Islamists, who recognize the contributions of the great founders of the schools of law as central to the identity of Islam, are implicitly criticizing these same jurists for accommodating themselves to the caliphs of their eras.

Radical Islamists today have regarded as apostates those rulers who have openly followed secular policies, such as Hafez al-Assad (d. 2000) of Syria and Saddam Hussein (d. 2006) of Iraq. Pro-Western rulers, such as those in Saudi Arabia, Jordan, or Egypt since 1970, are also seen as un-Islamic or even anti-Islamic by such radicals.

Yet the criteria for inclusion in or exclusion from the category of the genuine Islamic state are not unambiguous. Even in Iran, governmental institutions are based on the notion of a constitution, separation of powers, a parliament, and popular sovereignty (though the last is undermined by other provisions), which are all legacies of eighteenth-century Western history. It is also difficult to imagine a genuine Islamic state whose economic policies are shaped by arrangements that are immune to *Sharī'ah* provisions on contracts, loans, ownership, fiduciary responsibilities for joint investments, and international capital flows that are dependent on the exigencies of the capitalist world economy. An authentic Islamic state, as defined by radical Islamists, would be unable to assume membership in international organizations that operate on the basis of secular international law. Nor could a political system be called an exemplary Islamic state if its government's conduct violated a standard canon of the Islamic law of war and peace (such as the doctrine of *amān*, a guarantee of safe conduct for the emissaries of infidels in the lands of the Muslims).

Moderate Islamists, however, explain the apparent deviations from Islamic canons either by reference to established concepts in Islamic experience, such as the concept of *shūrā* (deliberative consultation) to justify reliance upon a parliament, or by reference to principles in Islamic law that allow Muslims to make adjustments to enhance their prospects, such as the doctrine of *istiṣlāḥ/maṣlaḥah murāsalah* (deeming something to be good, beneficial, fitting). The more radical Islamists, however, forthrightly repudiate as *bid'ah* (heretical innovation) or even *kufr* (unbelief) what they regard as un-Islamic influences on the thinking and conduct of political leaders in their societies.

The concept of state in Islam has evolved over time. Although in theory many Muslims believe that there should be no separation between religion and state, in practice the separation was achieved early in Islamic history. Since Islamists today live in a world of nation-states, a world in which secularization is a fact of life, they cannot escape its effects. Among moderate Islamists, it is an article of faith that Islam has anticipated developments in the modern world either through venerable concepts in the scripture or the actual practice of leaders in Islamic history. They are not alarmed by mechanisms such as constitutions and parliaments. But the radicals among them have condemned both their more moderate colleagues and virtually all national leaders in the Muslim world today for having either engineered or acquiesced to the deliberate separation of religion and state.

The Future of the Issue. Debates on the nature of the state and its relationship to religion will continue. Among the major questions relevant to this relationship is what happens if the ruler of the state violates religious principles. Religious scholars in the past generally frowned upon rebellion, either because they wrote in the service of rulers or because they believed that oppositional activity would lead to anarchy. In the modern era, radical Islamists have endorsed the overthrow of such rulers.

[*See also* ʿAbd al-Rāziq, ʿAlī; Ibn Taymīyah, Taqī al-Dīn Aḥmad; Khomeini, Ruhollah al-Musavi; Sharīʿah; *and* Taliban.]

BIBLIOGRAPHY

Ayubi, Nazih N. *Over-Stating the Arab State: Politics and Society in the Middle East*. London: I. B. Tauris, 1995.

Binder, Leonard. *Islamic Liberalism: A Critique of Development Ideologies*. Chicago: University of Chicago Press, 1988.

Crone, Patricia. *Medieval Islamic Political Thought*. Edinburgh: Edinburgh University Press, 2004.

Enayat, Hamid. *Modern Islamic Political Thought*. Austin: University of Texas Press, 1982.

Ghazālī, Muhammad al-. "Hadha dinuna" (This Is Our Religion). *Al-Shaʿb* (Cairo), 9 July 1992.

Ibn Khaldūn, ʿAbd al-Raḥmān. *The Muqaddimah: An Introduction to History*. Translated by Franz Rosenthal. 3 vols. New York: Pantheon, 1958.

Khālid, Khālid Muḥammad. *al-Dawlah fī al-Islām* (The State in Islam). 3d ed. Cairo: Dār Thābit, 1989.

Lewis, Bernard. *The Political Language of Islam*. Chicago: University of Chicago Press, 1988.

Piscatori, James P. *Islam in a World of Nation-States*. Cambridge, U.K.: Cambridge University Press, 1986.

Rosenthal, Erwin I. J. *Islam in the Modern National State*. Cambridge, U.K.: Cambridge University Press, 1965.

Rosenthal, Franz. "Dawla." In *The Encyclopaedia of Islam*. Rev ed., edited by H. A. R. Gibb, vol. 2, pp. 177–178. Leiden, Netherlands: Brill, 1960.

Zubaida, Sami. *Islam, the People, and the State: Political Ideas and Movements in the Middle East*. 2d ed. London: I. B. Tauris, 1993.

SHAHROUGH AKHAVI

DEMOCRACY. Around the middle of the nineteenth century, new ways of thought began to emerge in the Middle East, primarily as a result of contact with European industry, communications, and political ideas and institutions. While they were not breaking with the Islamic past, there was a modern element in the thought of some Muslim thinkers and officials—such as Rifāʿah Rāfiʿ al-Ṭahṭāwī (Egypt, 1801–1873), Ali Suavi (Turkey, 1839–1878), and Khayr al-Dīn al-Tūnisī (Tunisia, 1822–1890)—who argued that Muslims could increase their strength by selectively adopting Western institutions and practices that were compatible with *Sharīʿah* (Islamic law).

Some writers of this period maintained that the principles of social action are rational and that they change as society changes. The Egyptian reformer Muḥammad ʿAbduh (1848–1905) sought to strengthen the moral roots of Islamic society by returning to the past, recognizing and accepting the need for change and linking that change to the teachings of Islam. Disseminating his ideas through the periodical *al-Manār* (The Beacon), ʿAbduh asserted that Islam could form the moral basis of a modern, progressive society while moving in the direction of new ideas about social and political organization. Other modernist thinkers argued further that human society constitutes its own judge and master, and its own interest should reign supreme. Some reformists of the period, such as the Egyptian Qāsim Amīn (1863–1908), went so far as to affirm the benefit of the active participation of all citizens, including women, in matters of public concern.

From about 1900 until the early 1950s, two lines of thought regarding the proper bases of government coexisted in the Middle East. Supporters of the first advocated the principles of secularism and constitutional democracy, including representative government based on broad political participation. Following the dissolution of the Ottoman state, this principle was advanced by leaders of political groups and national liberation movements; it seemed to have reached its logical end with the establishment of quasi-constitutional systems in a number of Arab countries on the model of Western-style democracies. Experimentation with democracy was not, however, a happy experience. Rigged elections, puppet governments, arbitrary arrests, and rubber-stamp parliaments raised serious doubts about the ability of the Arabs to create and tolerate democratic institutions and practices.

Following a second line of thought were those who believed that Islamic law and institutions should be the basis of political and social organization. For most of this school, the ideal was to live in the inherited Islamic framework and to preserve the continuity of the Islamic tradition. This contrasts in many ways with the thinking of the advocates of democratic reform, most of whom accepted Islam as a body of principles but believed that secular norms of nationalism and liberal democracy were best suited to the reorganization and regulation of Arab society and politics.

Following the Arab-Israeli War of 1948 and especially with the advent of revolutionary regimes in key Arab states (Egypt, Syria, and Iraq), the balance of political thought tilted decisively in favor of the radicalism of the revolutionary state. The new ways of thought and action were embodied in a form of nationalism that expressed social reform in the idiom of Arab socialism and that expressed foreign policy in the language of anti-colonialism and positive neutrality. In the 1950s and 1960s, many secularists as well as Islamists were engaged in attempts to prove that Islam and socialism were compatible, and that the pursuit of Arab unity was more important than the pursuit of democracy and pluralism. In North Africa and in the Arab East, the principle of Arab unity held first place, on the grounds that socialism, freedom, and the liberation of Palestine could not be achieved without it. This was a position clearly articulated by the representatives of Arab nationalism—Egyptian president Gamal Abdel Nasser (1918–1970), and such Baʿthist activists and intellectuals as the Syrian Michel ʿAflaq (1910–1989), the Palestinian ʿAbd Allāh Muḥammad Rīmāwī, and the Jordanian Munīf al-Razzāz.

In the 1970s and 1980s, the unrest generated by war and civil strife in some Arab countries, the failure of Arab governments to stand up to Israel, the rising discontent with socioeconomic performance, and the unchecked growth of the power of the state brought about a change in the scale of political life: there was a broader agenda of grievances and a larger public for new ideas and rhetoric. The movement for the revival of Islam as the only valid basis for social and political life was perhaps the most significant aspect of this change.

With the rise of Islamic political movements in the 1970s and 1980s, writers and activists formulated diverse ideas about social and political organization. This article deals in a general way with three of them—the rejectionist, moderate, and liberal Islamic perspectives—because they are broadly representative of certain attitudes and positions with respect to the notion of democracy. However, we should neither impose a false unity on the ideas of a particular category nor view the categories as mutually exclusive, particularly because the works of many of the writers have evolved over several decades. The term "fundamentalist" is likewise too narrow to be applicable to any of the intellectual trends discussed here.

In fact, advocates of each of the views were influenced by the modernizing impulse and the call for *ijtihād* (independent reasoning) of Muḥammad ʿAbduh, who encouraged Muslims to establish their government by reasoning from Islamic principles in the interest of the Islamic community. What distinguishes the three perspectives is not only their assessment of democracy, but the scope permitted to, and the basis of, their *ijtihād*.

The Rejectionist Islamic View. ʿAbduh's student Muḥammad Rashīd Riḍā (Syria/Egypt 1865–1935) edited *al-Manār* from 1898 until his death. Like ʿAbduh, Rashīd Riḍā encouraged Muslims to emulate the scientific and technological achievements of the West but discouraged the imitation of foreign ideas and practices. He maintained that the backwardness in Muslim countries arose from the neglect of the true principles of Islam.

The Egyptian thinker Sayyid Quṭb (1906–1966), who was a leading member of the Muslim Brotherhood and whose writings became very popular after his execution by the Egyptian authorities, shared Rashīd Riḍā's concern with emulation of the foreign. Quṭb condemned the Arab nation-state systems as un-Islamic and as part of what he called the modern *jāhilīyah*, a term that originally denoted the period prior to the emergence of Islam in the seventh century but which, for Quṭb, corresponds to the prevailing aspects of modern life, including Western institutions and beliefs inconsistent with Islam. Quṭb believed that the comprehensiveness and universality of Islam made it good for all peoples, regardless of place and time. Quṭb asserts that the Islamic political order is an eternal system that rests on three fundamental bases: "justice on the part of rulers, obedience on the part of the ruled, and consultation between ruler and ruled" (Quṭb, pp. 119–120). For Quṭb, a just political and social order based on the Qurʾān and the *sunnah* (tradition) will lead to the implementation of the *Sharīʿah* and will thus achieve the main political goal of Islamists, which is the establishment of the Islamic state. The main value is not democracy but the implementation of the *Sharīʿah*, and the only political system of any type that can claim Islamic legitimacy is one that enforces the *Sharīʿah*.

An even sharper distinction between democracy and "consultation between ruler and ruled" is drawn by Abū al-Aʿlā Mawdūdī (India/Pakistan, 1903–1979), who believed that the notion of popular sovereignty that lies at the basis of democracy violates the principle of *ḥākimīyah* (the absolute sovereignty of God over the world) and is tantamount to *shirk billāh* (the sacrilegious attribution of partners to God). Mawdūdī terms the proper Islamic system of government a "theo-democracy," distinct from European theocracies because, rather than rule by a clerical class that enforces its decisions upon the people in the name of God, the entire Muslim population is to run the state in accordance with the *Sharīʿah*, which rules over all aspects of life.

While this perspective remained common throughout the 1970s and 1980s among various groups calling for the establishment of an Islamic state, the number of thinkers adopting an outright rejectionist stance toward democracy—generally the most radical Islamists—has diminished in recent years. Many Islamist groups, including most factions of the Muslim Brotherhood, have moderated their stance on democracy. Nonetheless, much contemporary scholarship has questioned whether Islamic thinkers who have claimed the mantle of democracy merely exploit the popularity of the term for political opportunity or cloak more radical stances in moderate language.

The Moderate Islamic View. Three concepts are central to the moderate Islamic understanding of democracy: *shūrā* (consultation), *maṣlaḥah* (public interest), and *ʿadl* (justice). There are disagreements among Muslim scholars with regard to *shūrā*, but in essence they all agree, on the basis of the Qurʿān, that God instructed the Prophet to consult with his advisers, even those whose advice had led to defeat in battle, and that good Muslims should consult with each other in conducting their affairs. While Quṭb, Mawdūdī, and others have rejected the equation of *shūrā* and democracy, others consider this principle of mutual consultation to be a basis for the election of representative leaders and government institutions, as in the case of Western democracies. *Fatwa* (legal opinions), it is further argued, have allowed and will continue to allow different systems of government to legitimize their authority in the name of Islam.

Maṣlaḥah means doing what is good for the people and avoiding what is injurious. Critical here is the extent to which the people can be involved in determining what is good and what is not good for them. Theoretically speaking, this can be resolved by means of mutual consultation through the representative organs of the state, but regardless of the extent of consultation, just rule is a sine qua non for the promotion of the public interest. Islamic political leaders are considered to be just insofar as they follow policies that are consistent with the public interest as defined through *shūrā* and insofar as they do not inflict unnecessary hardship on their people.

Representing this perspective is Ḥasan al-Turābī (b. 1932), a leading Islamic thinker and the primary ideologist of the Sudanese Islamic National Front, the main pillar of the Sudanese government. He argues that any political or social system must be based on *tawḥīd*, the unification of all Muslims as a fulfillment of the *rabbānīyah* (lordship) of God. Shūrā and *tawḥīd* should go hand in hand. *Shūrā* is needed to interpret *Sharīʿah* and to deal with constitutional, legal, social, and economic matters. Al-Turābī distinguishes between *shūrā* and Western-style democracy: *shūrā* represents the ultimate sovereignty of God as embodied in the Qurʿān, while democracy connotes the ultimate sovereignty of the people.

According to al-Turābī, liberal democratic systems have two flaws. First, they are based on factional interests and therefore cannot promote real political equality, unity, and freedom. Because wealth, and therefore power, are concentrated in the hands of a few, ultimate authority is vested in a small elite. Second, liberal democracies are based on human reason, and regardless of how people may try to perfect the political and social order, reason still suffers from the limitations that God has imposed on humans.

For al-Turābī, Islam thus has a unique advantage in postulating the divinely ordained connection between political *shūrā* and *tawḥīd*. This connection prevents tyranny because it resolves ideological conflicts and unifies Muslim actions. It also leads to an *ʿaqd al-bayʿah* (contract of allegiance) between the people and their ruler. The origin of this *ʿaqd* is *ijmāʿ* (consensus) through political *shūrā*. Al-Turābī believes that by following this course Muslims will be able to create a democratic system free from the flaws of liberal democracies. This system will be able to deliver the Islamic *ummah* from *jāhilīyah* and will provide through *shūrā* a means of participation and adaptation, as well as a mechanism for the realization of true political equality.

The Tunisian thinker Rāshid al-Ghannūshī (b. 1941) has considered how present-day Muslims might best pursue the political ideals of *shūrā*, *maṣlaḥah*, and *ʿadl*. Acknowledging that Islamic government exists only as an idea, unrealized in contemporary circumstances, al-Ghannūshī encourages Muslims to participate in existing non-Islamic governments as a nonviolent means of laying the foundation for a truly Islamic social order. He defends this strategy as necessitated by the exceptional circumstances of the present, where Muslims are unable to establish Islamic rule directly and where the choice is not between Islamic and non-Islamic rule, but between dictatorship and democracy. Further, this approach is rendered permissible by the Islamic principle of *maṣlaḥah*: Muslims must actively pursue the (even partial) implementation of Islamic laws and values in order to serve mankind. In those countries in which Muslims form the majority, Islamic movements will benefit from working with other groups to topple dictatorships that stand in the way of the realization of respect for human rights, security, and freedom of expression, essential bases for preparing the way for the longer-term goal of establishing an Islamic government. In those countries where Muslims are minorities, they should work to transform the values of their society in order to secure their freedom of worship and belief.

The development of a moderate Islamic discourse has influenced some of the most prominent Islamist thinkers. Shaykh Yūsuf al-Qaraḍāwī (Egypt/Qatar, b. 1926), who, in a 1977 work, placed democracy at the top of a list of "imported solutions" to be rejected, revealed a change in stance in a widely circulated 1990 work, in which he argued that the main objective of the Islamist movement is to oppose political despotism and the usurpation of the people's rights and to stand for political freedom and true democracy. Al-Qaraḍāwī argues that Islam and democracy are different things. The former is a comprehensive system of values, while the latter is a means. Democracy, in al-Qaraḍāwī's view, means that Muslims would be permitted to rule themselves according to their own beliefs in those countries in which they are majorities. Only in an atmosphere of freedom and democracy has Islam flourished. Al-Qaraḍāwī shares with Quṭb and Mawdūdī the belief that the Islamic community is charged with ensuring that rulers govern within the limits of Islamic law, to which everyone is held accountable. However, while Quṭb and Mawdūdī seem to assume a unified Islamic community and a narrow legislative space, al-Qaraḍāwī believes that Islam's binding texts are few, leaving a wide space capable of accommodating multiple permissible interpretations of Islam. Further, whereas Quṭb and Mawdūdī rely upon that which unites the Islamic community, al-Qaraḍāwī trusts the Muslim masses to assert Islamism through majority rule.

The Liberal Islamic View. Like the moderate Islamic view, that of Islamic liberals is influenced by ʿAbduh's emphasis on the role of reason in understanding religion and in dealing with the demands of modern life. According to the Islamic liberals, the challenge in coping with worldly matters is to enter social transactions and relations on a basis that allows for adaptation to changing conditions. The liberal Islamic view is, however, distinguished by its emphas is on the importance of a plurality of positions and the freedom of thought for the emergence and proper functioning of a democratic system. Liberal Islamic thinkers argue that the Qurʾān allows for political and religious diversity. The often-cited verse 2:256, *lā ikrāh fī al-dīn* (there is no compulsion in religion), is interpreted to mean the equality of Muslims and non-Muslims in civic rights and duties. There is inequality in matters of faith, but that is something that should be left to God. Human beings are not entitled to pass judgment on other people's religious beliefs.

Islamic thinkers such as Egyptians Fahmī Huwaydī (b. 1937) and Ṭāriq al-Bishrī (b. 1933) have constructed important justifications for the full citizenship of non-Muslims in an Islamic state. Based on Muḥammad's ruling in the Charter of Medina regarding *ahl al-kitāb* (people of the book), they assert that Christians, Jews, and Zoroastrians are *muwaṭinūn* (citizens), not *dhimmīyūn* (protected subjects), and thus share rights and duties equal to Muslims. Other thinkers, such as Mohammed Arkoun (Algeria/France, b. 1928) and Naṣr Ḥāmid Abū Zayd (Egypt/Netherlands, b. 1943), have attempted further to assert the value of plurality and freedom by extending the boundaries of acceptable interpretations of Islam through the incorporation of postmodern or literary modes of textual interpretation. These approaches are unified by a willingness to forego the literal interpretation of scriptures when it is believed to harm the interests of Muslims.

The Iranian thinker Abdolkarim Soroush (b. 1945) is exemplary in this regard. He argues that reason, freedom, and democracy are universal, primary values that cannot be constrained by religious or political dictates. Going further than moderate Islamic thinkers, Islamic liberals affirm not just the possibility of the coexistence of religion and democracy but the necessity of the constant examination of religious understanding, which can only be done in a democratic context. What Soroush calls "religious democracy" does not require that democracy be religious, but that religious thought be democratic, tolerant, and just. Religion needs freedom and tolerance to flourish. Soroush maintains that religious democracy is thus more demanding and substantive than secular democracy, because whereas the latter removes matters of faith and belief from the realm of politics, the former necessitates the constant engagement with and renewal of understandings of faith and belief.

One finds within these three Islamic trends distinct, though not necessarily conflicting, elements of modernity and tradition that echo the thoughts of nineteenth-century Islamic writers. They show the point at which certain ideas about political organization have entered contemporary Arab intellectual discourse. They also illustrate intellectual attempts to restructure Islamic society and politics, on the basis of an inherited Islamic past that is believed to contrast with Western political traditions, on the basis of the selective appropriation of modern democratic thought made to conform to Islamic values and law, or on the basis of a theory of liberal norms that becomes the basis for a reinterpretation of Islamic thought.

BIBLIOGRAPHY

Abou El Fadl, Khaled, et al. *Islam and the Challenge of Democracy*. Princeton, N.J.: Princeton University Press, 2004.

Bayat, Asef. *Making Islam Democratic: Social Movements and the Post-Islamist Turn*. Stanford, Calif.: Stanford University Press, 2007.

Browers, Michaelle. *Democracy and Civil Society in Arab Political Thought: Transcultural Possibilities*. Syracuse, N.Y.: Syracuse University Press, 2006.

Diamond, Larry, Marc F. Plattner, and Daniel Brumberg, eds. *Islam and Democracy in the Middle East*. Baltimore: Johns Hopkins University Press, 2003.

Esposito, John L., and John O. Voll. *Islam and Democracy*. Oxford: Oxford University Press, 1996.

Hashemi, Nader. *Islam, Secularism, and Liberal Democracy*. New York: Oxford University Press, 2009.

Hefner, Robert W. *Civil Islam: Muslims and Democratization in Indonesia*. Princeton, N.J.: Princeton University Press, 2000.

Hefner, Robert W., ed. *Remaking Muslim Politics: Pluralism, Contestation, Democratization*. Princeton, N.J.: Princeton University Press, 2005.

Jahanbakhsh, Forough. *Islam, Democracy, and Religious Modernism in Iran, 1953–2000: From Bāzargān to Soroush*. Leiden: E. J. Brill, 2001.

Kurzman, Charles, ed. *Modernist Islam, 1840–1940: A Sourcebook*. Oxford: Oxford University Press, 2002.

Lowrie, Arthur L., ed. *Islam, Democracy, the State, and the West: A Round Table with Dr. Hasan Turabi*. Tampa, Fla.: World & Islam Studies Enterprise, 1993.

Moussalli, Ahmad S. *The Islamic Quest for Democracy, Pluralism, and Human Rights*. Gainesville: University Press of Florida, 2001.

Qaradāwī, Yūsuf. *Priorities of the Islamic Movement in the Coming Phase*. Swansea, U.K.: 2000.

Quṭb, Sayyid. *Social Justice in Islam*. Translated from the Arabic by John B. Hardie and Hamid Algar. Oneonta, N.Y.: Islamic Publications International, 2000.

Soroush, Abdolkarim. *Reason, Freedom, and Democracy in Islam: Essential Writings of Abdolkarim Soroush.* Translated and edited by Mahmoud Sadri and Ahmad Sadri. New York: Oxford University Press, 2000.

Tamimi, Azzam S. *Rachid Ghannouchi: A Democrat Within Islamism.* Oxford: Oxford University Press, 2001.

MUHAMMAD MUSLIH
Updated by MICHAELLE BROWERS

DEMOKRAT PARTI. Turkey was ruled by the Demokrat Parti (DP) from 1950 until its overthrow by a military coup on 27 May 1960. Its founders, Celâ Bayar (1884–1986), Mehmet Fuat Köprülü (1890–1966), Refik Koraltan (1891–1974), and Adnan Menderes (1899–1961), were all ranking members of the governing Cumhuriyet Halk Partisi (Republican People's Party, CHP). Bayar, a banker in his early life, played a critical role during the Kemalist period in the liberal, anti-statist wing of the party and served as prime minister in 1937–1938. Köprülü, a historian and Turcologist, proposed a reformation that would Turkify Islam; his proposal was, however, not taken seriously. Koraltan was a bureaucrat and Menderes a large landowner from the prosperous Aegean region. Together they represented the liberal wing of the CHP; in forming the DP, they responded to the rising bourgeoisie's demand for political and economic liberalization and an end to the state's hegemony over civil society. The Turkish people had also come to hate the single-party regime, which had become increasingly repressive, especially during World War II. The imposition of militant secularism was especially resented by the population. The pressure for political change that came from a victorious America, which encouraged pluralism and a free-market economy, ought not be discounted either.

The introduction of multiparty politics and the lively competition for votes made Islam a burning issue and forced all parties to reevaluate their religious policy. Between 1945 and the 1950 elections, the CHP abandoned its militant secularism and made concessions to Islamic sentiment. When the Democrats won power in May 1950, they merely accelerated the process, realizing that the overwhelmingly Muslim population had been alienated by state interference in religious life.

The Democrats' first concession was quite dramatic: in June 1950, they lifted the ban on the call to prayer (*ezan*) being made in Arabic and permitted muezzins to issue the *ezan* in either Arabic or Turkish. Most chose Arabic, and the impact of this reform resounded throughout the country. On 5 July they permitted the broadcasting of religious programs over the radio, and the Qurʾān was heard over the airwaves. In October, religious lessons in schools (introduced by the CHP) became virtually obligatory when parents were asked to inform the authorities in writing if they did not want their children to attend such lessons. Few Muslim parents did so.

There was a bipartisan consensus on religious policy as long as the secular reforms of Atatürk were not threatened. In fact, both parties welcomed the director of religious affairs' pronouncement against communism. "Islam," declared Ahmed Hamdi Akseki, "rejects communism absolutely, its ideology in any form and all its practices. Faith and spirit are the most powerful weapons against communism. It is not possible for a genuine believer to reconcile himself to the ideas and practices of communism."

The more liberal atmosphere marked by an emphasis on populist politics also led to the reappearance of a variety of religious orders popular with the masses. Their leaders believed that Islamist political pressure would compel the DP government to reverse some of the major reforms of the republic, notably the Western code of law and the Latin script. In the DP's congress in Konya in 1951, there were demands for the restoration of the fez, the headwear banned in 1925, and the veiling of women. Politics also entered the mosque, and the Friday sermon was often used to denounce the opposition for being anti-Islam. Even Mustafa Kemal Atatürk's busts and statues, found in every village and town, were vandalized.

The CHP, founded by Atatürk and claiming his mantle, blamed the Democrats for failing to protect the Kemalism to which both parties were constitutionally committed. Prime Minister Menderes responded by taking stern measures against the reactionaries. In March 1951 orders were issued to protect Atatürk's statues, and men like Necip Fazıl Kısakürek, who led the Islamic resurgence, were prosecuted. Islamist publications were proscribed. In June 1951, members of the Tijānīyah order, who were agitating for the restoration of a theocratic monarchy (also a violation of the constitution), were arrested. Their *shaykh*, Kemal Pilavoĝlu, was sentenced to ten years at hard labor. The "Atatürk Bill" passed by the Assembly on 25 July gave the state greater powers to prosecute those who threatened the secular republic. Under this law, the Islamic Democrat Party was dissolved in March 1952, Kısakürek was sent to jail, and Bediüzzaman Said Nursî (Nurculuk), the leader of the Nurists, was put on trial. Finally, the Law to Protect the Freedom of Conscience was passed in July 1953 to prevent Islam from being used for political ends. Under this law, when the Nation Party, founded in July 1948 by a right-wing splinter group in the DP, made Islam a part of its political platform, it was dissolved by court order on 27 January 1954.

In the 1954 election, however, all parties exploited religion to attract votes, though with little success. The DP's victory was even more resounding than in 1950; its triumph was based on its economic policies, which initially brought the country prosperity as well as a great sense of dynamism and hope. Only in Kırşehir was Islam's role critical; there the Republican Nation Party, supported by the Bektaşi order, won all seats.

After 1955 the DP too began to exploit Islam more openly. There were two principal reasons for the change. First, the liberal Kemalist wing broke away and formed the Freedom Party, strengthening the right wing. Second, the economy began to stall, leading the Democrats to flaunt their religious image as a distraction. They cultivated the religious orders because they controlled local voting blocs. More money was spent on mosques, and the Democrats boasted that they had spent 37.5 million liras (over 13 million dollars) in seven years, while the CHP had spent only 6.5 million liras in their twenty-seven years.

The decline of the DP's vote from 56.6 percent in 1954 to 47.3 percent in 1957 suggests that its religious policy was not paying off. The economic crisis turned voters away, and religious appeal was a poor substitute. Religious activity flourished in 1958, a disastrous year for the economy with the lira devalued by almost 400 percent. Radio was now allowed to devote more airtime to religious programs, and the Nurists were free to spread their propaganda.

The Democrats had become identified with the resurgence of Islam. After Menderes survived an airplane crash in London in February 1959, that identification became more explicit; the hand of providence was seen in the escape, described as miraculous. The myth of Menderes's immortality emerged, and it has been suggested that the junta that overthrew Menderes executed him to destroy this myth.

The Demokrat Parti facilitated the Islamic resurgence, as any ruling party would have done to survive the challenge of competitive politics. In fact, the resurgence was more the consequence of the mass politics that replaced the politics of elites in 1945. The center of political gravity shifted to the provinces largely untouched by Kemalist reforms or modern secular culture. This was recognized after the fall of the Democrats, and any party that has won power since has had to cope with this element of political life.

There were two attempts to exploit the DP's name when a new center-right was formed. In December 1970 dissidents from the Justice Party formed the Demokratik Parti, but it was closed down by the military intervention of March 1971. Another attempt was made in May 2007, when the Demokrat Parti tried to merge with the Motherland Party (Anavatan Partisi). The merger failed, and the newly formed DP won only 6 percent of the vote in the 2007 general election and failed to have a presence in parliament. The DP and the Motherland Party finally merged in November 2009. The party is still functioning, hoping for a center-right revival when the fortunes of the governing Justice and Development Party may decline.

BIBLIOGRAPHY

Ahmad, Feroz. *The Turkish Experiment in Democracy, 1950–1975*. London and Boulder, Colo.: Westview Press, 1977.

Lewis, Bernard. *The Emergence of Modern Turkey*. 3d ed. London and New York: Oxford University Press, 2006.

Sarıbay, Ali Yaşar. "The Democratic Party, 1946–1960." In *Political Parties and Democracy in Turkey*, edited by Metin Heper and Jacob Landau, pp. 119–133. London and New York: Oxford University Press, 1991.

Sayari, Sabri, and Yilmaz Esmer. *Politics, Parties, and Elections in Turkey*. Boulder, Colo.: Westview Press, 2002.

VanderLippe, John M. *The Politics of Turkish Democracy: İsmet İnönü and the Formation of the Multi-Party System, 1938–1950*. Albany: State University Press of New York, 2005.

Feroz Ahmad

Deobandīs. The *ʿulamāʾ* associated with the Indo-Pakistani reformist movement centered in the Dār al-ʿUlūm of Deoband are known by the name Deobandīs. The school at Deoband, a country town some ninety miles northeast of Delhi, was founded in 1866. It was a pioneer effort to transmit the religious sciences, specifically the *dars-i niẓāmī* identified with the Lucknow-based *ʿulamāʾ* of Farangī Maḥall, by utilizing institutional forms derived from British schools. The goal of the school was to preserve Islamic teachings in a period of non-Muslim rule and considerable social change by holding Muslims to a standard of correct practice; central to that goal was the creation of a class of formally trained and popularly supported *ʿulamāʾ*. The school had classrooms, a bureaucratically organized faculty, formal examinations, and an annual convocation. The founders created a system of popular contributions utilizing mail and money orders; donors, many from the *ashrāf* classes involved in government service and trade, were listed in an annual report. Several men central to the foundation of the school were educated in Delhi in the 1840s and participated in two critically important institutions: the reformist milieu of *ʿulamāʾ* linked to the family of Shāh Walī Allāh al-Dihlawī and Sayyid Aḥmad Barelwī; and Delhi College, founded by the British to teach both European and "Oriental" subjects through the medium of Urdu rather than in the former court language of Persian.

In its six-year course the school emphasized *ḥadīth* and the Ḥanafī legal tradition, using both as a framework to scrutinize customary practices and to enjoin correct observance of ritual and life-cycle events. In the mid-nineteenth century, the British had replaced Persian with the vernacular language of Urdu across north India, and the Deobandīs also used Urdu as their medium of instruction and the language of much of their writing. Beyond formal learning, Deobandīs also typically sought the personal transformation of Sufism with the help of a spiritual guide; multiple initiation into various *silsilahs* (chains of transmission) was common, but the influence of

Chishtī-Ṣābirī and Naqshbandī Mujaddidī traditions was particularly strong. Hallmarks of Deobandī practice included opposition to some shrine-based customs, including the *urs* (annual death-anniversary celebrations), the so-called *fātiḥah* food offerings for the dead (distributed after reciting the Fātiḥah Sūrah of the Qurʾān), and to the elaborate ceremonies associated with birth, marriage, and death. By emphasizing individual responsibility for correct belief and practice, the Deobandīs provided an alternative to an intercessory religion focused on the Ṣūfī shrines and elaborate customary celebrations. The term "Deobandī" designates one of the main divisions (*maslak*) of *ʿulamāʾ* of the Subcontinent, distinguished from a range of other sectarian orientations including the Shīʿī, Aḥmadī, Jamāʿat-i Islāmī, Aligarh and other modernists, and rival Sunnī groups like the Barelwīs (Ahl-i Sunnat wa-al-Jamāʿat) and the Ahl-i Ḥadīth.

The Deobandīs from the beginning envisaged a network of schools; the multiple ties of education, Ṣūfī affiliation, and family linked many teachers among them. By the end of the nineteenth century, there were more than a dozen schools known as Deobandī from Peshawar to Chittagong to Madras. The number of Deobandī schools grew substantially both in South Asia and among Muslims of South Asian descent elsewhere, especially from the 1980s on, as did enrollment at the central seminary itself, where, in the early twenty-first century, annual enrollment surpassed 3,000. Among the most important early Deobandī schools was the Mazahirul ʿUlum, founded in nearby Saharanpur. Notable schools in Pakistan include the Darul Uloom and the Jamia Farooqia, both in Karachi, and the Jamia Ashrafia, Lahore.

Deobandīs have served as teachers, imams, guardians, and trustees of mosques and tombs, preachers, writers, debaters with opponents, and publishers of religious works. Many offer *fatwas* to provide spiritual counsel and guidance on legal matters apart from state institutions. Among the most celebrated early graduates of the school was the prolific writer and revered spiritual guide Mawlānā Ashrāf ʿAlī Thānvī (1864–1943). His manual for Muslim girls, the *Bihishtī zevar*, written at the turn of the century, has been widely circulated in Urdu and in translations into many regional languages. Today, many Deobandī institutions have a substantial presence on the Internet.

Originally quiescent politically, individual Deobandīs, if not the school itself, became politically active in the course of the nationalist movement. Maulānā ʿUbaidullāh Sindhī (1872–1944) was one of the first to forge links between the *ʿulamāʾ* and those educated at Aligarh. During World War I he went to Afghanistan to work with German and Turkish agents with the blessing of Mawlānā Maḥmūdulḥasan (1851–1920), a celebrated teacher at the school. Because of these sympathies, Maḥmūdūlḥasan, along with Maulānā Ḥusain Aḥmad Madanī (1879–1957) and three others linked to Deoband, were exiled to Malta during World War I. Honored as the "Shaykh al-Hind" upon his return in 1920, Maḥmūdulḥasan was one of many Deobandīs who participated in the Jamʿīyatul ʿUlamāʾ-i Hind, organized in 1919, which supported the short-lived postwar movement to preserve the Ottoman caliphate and consistently supported the Indian National Congress. The Jamʿīyatul ʿUlamāʾ-i Hind favored a religiously plural, democratic, and secular state and emphasized the importance of guaranteeing cultural autonomy through religious freedom and the continuance of separate, religiously defined systems of personal law. As independence approached, most Deobandīs opposed the partition of India and saw Pakistan as the creation of Westernized forces and an enforced confinement of Muslim influence. Foremost among the politically active was Maulānā

Ḥusain Aḥmad Madanī, who engaged in a public exchange with Muhammad Iqbal over the priority of territorial rather than religious identity for statehood.

A minority of Deobandīs, led by Maulānā Shabbīr Aḥmad ʿUṣmānī (1887–1949) and including Muftī Mian Muḥammad Shāfiʿ, Maulānā Ihtishāmul Ḥaqq Thānvī, and Mawlānā ʿAbdulḥamīd Badāʿunī (d. 1969), supported the Muslim League's demand for Pakistan; in 1945 in Calcutta they founded the Jamʿīyatul ʿUlamāʾ-i Islām, which continued as a political party in Pakistan.

Deobandīs have demonstrated pragmatic responses to the varying environments in which they find themselves. The Indian Deobandīs have sustained the apolitical strand within the school's teaching and participate only as individuals in India's vibrant democratic system.

The Pakistani Deobandīs are organized as a political party in the Jamʿīyatul ʿUlamāʾ-i Islām, which, in 2002 became part of a coalition of religious parties in control of the two provinces bordering Afghanistan. Many of the Pakistani Deobandīs have had close ties to the Afghan Taliban, many of the leadership of which were trained in Deobandī schools in Pakistan, and some Deobandī offshoots have been involved in sectarian violence as well as militancy in Afghanistan and Kashmir. The Taliban represent a third pattern of Deobandī political activity. They, like the others, took on the shape of their political environment—in their case, as an ethnic group seeking national domination in the 1990s, albeit with a distinctive pattern of enforcing an extreme version of Islamic rituals and social norms. They turned for support, however, to Arab extremists who shared their Islamic program but, unlike them, were driven by a vision of global *jihād*. Their support for al-Qaʿida led to their removal from power by U.S. coalition forces after the 11 September 2001 attack on the United States.

The historical pattern launched by the Deoband *ʿulamāʾ*, however, for the most part treated political life on a primarily secular basis, typically, de facto if not de jure, identifying religion with the private sphere, and in that sphere fostering Islamic norms and practice. This is seen most clearly in yet another orientation rooted in the Deoband movement, that of the apolitical, transnational movement of inner renewal known as Tablīghī Jamāʿat, which originated in India in the 1920s and today draws millions among millions of participants worldwide. The Tablīgh movement demonstrates that the goals and satisfactions that come from participation in Islamic movements may well have little to do with explicit opposition or resistance to non-Muslims or "the West." Tablīghī concerns focus on other Muslims—an internal, not an external "Other." What they offer participants is the hope of individual empowerment, transcendent meaning, and moral sociality that does not engage directly with national or global political life at all.

[*See also* India; Iqbal, Muhammad; Islam and Politics in South Asia; Pakistan; *and* Tablīghī Jamāʿat.]

BIBLIOGRAPHY

Faruqi, Ziya-ul-Hasan. *The Deoband School and the Demand for Pakistan*. New York: Asia Pub. House, 1963. Brief but useful treatment of the role of Deobandīs in support of the Congress movement.

Friedmann, Yohanan. "The Attitude of the Jamīʿyat ʿUlamāʾ-i Hind to the Indian National Movement and the Establishment of Pakistan." In *The ʿUlamāʾ in Modern History*, edited by Gabriel Baer, pp. 157–183. Jerusalem, 1971. Detailed treatment of the first major political organization of the *ʿulamāʾ*, primarily Deobandī, which opposed the Pakistan movement. Friedmann notes the parallel opposition of respected Jewish religious leaders to the Zionist movement.

Hardy, Peter. *The Muslims of British India*. London: Cambridge University Press, 1972. The best overall survey, providing a good context for specific educational and political movements.

Metcalf, Barbara D. *Islamic Revival in British India: Deoband, 1860–1900*. Princeton, N.J.: Princeton University Press, 1982. Study of Deoband in its early decades based on institutional records, government records, and writings of the Deobandīs themselves, including biographies, memoirs, diaries, tracts, letters, and *fatwas*. It also includes an overview of other movements of the period: that of the Ahl-i Ḥadīth, the Barelwīs, the Nadwah *'ulamā'*, and Aligarh.

Metcalf, Barbara D. "Traditionalist Islamic Activism: Deobandīs, Tablighīs, and Talibs." In *Understanding September 11*, edited by Craig Calhoun et al., pp. 53–66. New York: New Press, 2002. A survey of three fundamentally distinctive positions of Deobandīs in relation to different state structures.

Reetz, Dietrich. *Islam in the Public Sphere: Religious Groups in India, 1900–1947*. New Delhi: Oxford University Press. 2006. This work places the Deoband movement in the context of a wide range of reformist and revivalist Islamic traditions and includes material through the turn of the twenty-first century.

Thānvī, Ashraf 'Alī. *Perfecting Women: Maulana Ashraf 'Ali Thanawi's Bihishti Zewar*. Translated with commentary by Barbara D. Metcalf. Berkeley: University of California Press, 1990. Partial translation and study of one of the most influential Deobandī texts.

Zaman, Muhammad Qasim. *The 'Ulamā' in Contemporary Islam: Custodians of Change*. Princeton, N.J.: Princeton University Press, 2002. Included in this volume are case studies of Deobandīs, emphasizing the role of such traditionalist scholars in creative interpretation of the historic tradition.

BARBARA D. METCALF

DERWISH. *See* Sufism.

DEWAN DAKWAH ISLAMIYAH. Also known as the Indonesian Propagation Council or DDII, founded in 1967 by former Prime Minister Mohammad Natsir and others from the then-banned (1960) Islamic modernist Indonesia Masyumi Party (Majelis Sjuro Muslimin Indonesia or Council of Indonesian Muslim Associations). Key members of the DDII's early leadership had roots in the Masyumi, and the relationship between party members and the DDII lasted for several decades. The DDII purposely did not join other *dakwah* organizations. Unable to be active in politics and rejected in its efforts to implement the *Sharī'ah* in Indonesia, their aim was to concentrate on Islam as both a religious and a political struggle. The DDII initially reflected a more flexible Islamic character, although there were early attempts to stem what were perceived as Hindu and Christian inroads into the Muslim community. The organization grew more conservative in reaction to the efforts of the military-dominated New Order to weaken Islam and the impact of anti-pluralist ideas injected from outsde Indonesia.

The DDII came under the increasing influence of Wahhābī-Salafī interpretations of Islam. It was also one of the major conduits for introducing ideas of the Egyptian Muslim Brotherhood to Indonesia. The role of Saudi Arabia was vital to this development, as various Saudi organizations provided funds, publications, and the opportunity for DDII students to study in the Kingdom. Returning students, along with other Saudi-trained cadre, became spokesmen for Wahhābī-Salafī beliefs. In 1962 Saudi Arabia had formed the Rābiṭat al-'Ālam al-Islāmī (Muslim World League) to propagate Wahhābī interpretations, and the DDII later became its main partner in Indonesia, with Natsir as one of its vice presidents.

The DDII attempted to reach out through mosques, religious schools, university campuses, and its own preachers, but its more public face was the magazine *Media Dakwah*, which began as an irregular publication of DDII speeches and activities. During the New Order, the journal was unable to obtain a printing license from the government and thus could not be widely disseminated, although continued outreach efforts were made through flyers. Now a monthly news magazine, it reflects conservative views through opposition to the treatment of Muslims in Indonesia and the rest of the world and by fostering strong, uncompromising views on Islam. Its reporting does not manifest sympathy for religious or political pluralism.

In 1998 the DDII formed a charitable organization, KOMPAK (Komite Aksi Penanggulangan Akibat Krisis, Action Committee for Crisis Response), to aid Muslims perceived as persecuted in the Moluccas, Kalimantan, and Sulawesi. It was abetted by the Saudi Islamic Relief Organization, which foreign observers of militant Islam declared to be a financier of "terrorist" activities elsewhere in Southeast Asia. They also accused KOMPAK of being a conduit for domestic and international support for Islamic militancy in Indonesia. While some observers differentiate between the charitable activities of the organization and the more militant *mujāhidīn* KOMPAK, others do not make that distinction when accusing it of affiliating itself with violent groups such as Jemaah Islamiyah. KOMPAK officials deny accusations of "terrorism," although some members of its more militant wing have been arrested for sectarian violence.

BIBLIOGRAPHY

Abuza, Zachery. *Political Islam and Violence in Indonesia*. London: Routledge, 2007.

Feillard, Andree, and Mardinier, Remy. *The End of Innocence: Indonesian Islam and the Temptations of Radicalism*. Translated by Wong Wee. Leiden, Netherlands: KITLV Press, 2011.

Hefner, Robert. *Civil Islam: Muslims and Democratization in Indonesia*. Princeton, N.J.: Princeton University Press, 2000.

FRED R. VON DER MEHDEN

DIPLOMACY. *See* International Relations and Diplomacy.

DĪWĀN. A term used throughout Islamic history to cover a number of institutions and practices, *dīwān* can most inclusively be defined as a homogeneous collection of written materials, literary or documentary, or a state administrative office. It is in the latter sense that the term is salient to the political sphere.

Many early Muslim historians report that the caliph ʿUmar ibn al-Khaṭṭāb (r. 634–644) instituted the *dīwān* in conscious imitation of Sassanian practice; they often frame the institution as one of his signal achievements. The *dīwān* of ʿUmar is supposed to have kept records of the spoils of conquest, in particular the portions owed to combatants. These were allotted according to such criteria as precedence in conversion to the Prophet's cause and tribal affiliation. As the Islamic state gained in administrative sophistication, the term was applied more generally to other kinds of archival registers, and then to the bureaus that generated such registers. Folk etymologies associate its origins with the Persianate cultural ethos that permeated urban populations and especially scribal milieus since the early caliphate. One etymology of the term derives it from the Persian *dīv* (spirits of evil and of darkness), supposedly describing the fiendish ingenuity of bureaucrats. Another envisions bureaucrats muttering tax figures to themselves and applies to this behavior the Persian word *dēvāna* (insane, bewitched). It seems, in fact, that the term derives, by uncertain channels, from the Old Persian *dipi* (inscription, document).

The most common usage was eventually with respect to offices that administered important governmental functions. The central administration of different Islamic states was often called simply the *dīwān*. Various branches of the government were also called *dīwān*s, in combination with an appropriate modifier (e.g., *dīwān* of taxation, *dīwān* of oversight). As the central administration, a *dīwān* (also given such loftier titles as *dīvān-i aʿlā* or *divan-i hümayun*) would often be headed by the vizier or grand vizier. By a further leap of meaning, the term (usually with the spelling "dewan" in English) was also used to denote a vizier on the Indian subcontinent, after the time of the Mughal Empire. The East India Company, for instance, was appointed *dīwān* of the Province of Bengal.

There naturally existed much diversity among various kinds of *dīwān* over time and space. Ad hoc arrangements led to the creation or abolition of specific *dīwān*s even under a single government. Still, a remarkable continuity can be observed in certain structural features whereby a threefold division was quite characteristic of *dīwān*s from al-Andalus to Central Asia: a *dīwān* of the chancery (often known as *dīwān al-rasāʾil* or *dīwān al-inshāʾ*); a *dīwān* of finances (*amwāl*); and a *dīwān* of the military (*jaysh*). Separate *dīwān*s were commonly responsible for the administration of pious foundations, fiefs, various taxes, alms, confiscations, customs (hence the word for customs in some European languages: e.g., *douane*, *dogana*), and so forth. Provincial administrations might also have their own local *dīwān* and divisions into subsidiary *dīwān*s that might parallel those at the center. All these might be subject to inspection by *dīwān*s of control (*zimām*, *azimma*). Finally, various governments instituted *dīwān*s of *maẓālim*, which functioned like a court of appeals or complaints and dealt with allegations of abuse of authority and miscarriage of justice. In the sense of tribunal or bureau, *dīwān* survives in the usages of some modern states, such as the *dīwān al-khidmah al-madanīyah* (Civil Service Bureau) in Jordan or the *dīwān al-muḥāsabah* (State Audit Bureau) in Kuwait. It has however been largely eclipsed in these senses by the term *wizārah* (ministry).

The functioning of the Ottoman *divan-i hümayun* is well documented. The procedures and hierarchies that governed its functioning and related ceremonies were codified in writing under Mehmed II Fatih (r. 1444–1446, 1451–1481). Since the decisions of the *dīwān*, recorded and kept in *mühimme* registers, are extant from around the mid-sixteenth century, its order of business can be studied in particular detail after that point. The Ottoman *dīwān* met every day until sometime before the end of the sixteenth century, when meetings were reduced to four days a week. It would include, in addition to the viziers, heads of the chancery and treasury departments and the two top experts in *Sharīʿah* (the divine law). Since Mehmed II, the Ottoman sultans did not participate in the meetings of the *dīwān* but might follow the proceedings from behind a grilled window, just as the ʿAbbāsid caliphs followed from behind a curtain. In addition to functioning as some form of cabinet and state council, the Ottoman *dīwān* held hearings on all kinds of cases brought before it by any subject or foreigner with legitimate business. The complaint of a monkey-player whose monkey was killed by the grand vizier's men might be heard on the same day as preparations for war were discussed or Istanbul's firewood shortage considered.

[*See also* Administration; Governance; *and* Wizāra.]

BIBLIOGRAPHY

Balādhurī, Aḥmad ibn Yaḥyā al-. *Futūḥ al-buldān*. Edited by ʿAbd Allāh Anīs al-Ṭabbāʿ and ʿUmar Anīs al-Ṭabbāʿ. Beirut, 1958. Translated by Philip K. Hitti as *The Origins of the Islamic State*. 2 vols. New York: AMS Press, 1968–1969.

de Blois, François, and C. E. Bosworth. "Dīvān." In *Encyclopaedia Iranica*. Vol. 7, pp. 432-438. London: Routledge and Kegan Paul, 1982. In-depth discussions of the term's etymology and the institution's evolution in Iran and Central Asia.

Dūrī, ʿAbd al-ʿAzīz al-, et al. "Dīwān." In *Encyclopaedia of Islam*. New ed., vol. 2, pp. 323–337. Leiden: Brill, 1960–. An authoritative account of the premodern institution.

Ibn Khaldūn, ʿAbd al-Raḥmān. *Muqaddimat Ibn Khaldūn*. 2d rev. ed. by ʿAlī ʿAbd al-Wāḥid Wāfī. Cairo, 1965. Translated by Franz Rosenthal as *The Muqaddimah*. 3 vols. New York: Pantheon Books, 1958.

Jahshiyārī, Muḥammad ibn ʿAbdūs al-. *Kitāb al-wuzarāʾ wa-al-kuttāb*. Edited by Muṣṭafā al-Saqqā, Ibrāhīm al-Ibyārī, and ʿAbd al-Ḥafīẓ Shalabī. Cairo: Muṣṭafā al-Bābī al-Ḥalabī, 1938. Among the most concentrated sources of information on the early development of the institution.

Johns, Jeremy. *Arabic Administration in Norman Sicily: The Royal Dīwān*. New York: Cambridge University Press, 2002. Discusses the imitation of Fāṭimid administrative practices by the Christian Norman kings of Sicily.

Marcinkowski, Muhammad, trans. *Mirzā Rafīʿā's Dastūr al-Mulūk: A Manual of Later Ṣafavid Administration*. Kuala Lumpur: ISTAC, 2002. An administrative manual on which depended the well known but less richly detailed *Tadhkirat al-Mulūk: A Manual of Ṣafavid Administration (c. 1137/1725)*. Edited and translated by Vladimir Minorsky. London: Luzac, 1943.

Mumcu, Ahmet. *Divan-ı Hümayun*. Ankara: Sevinç Matbaası, 1976.

Qalqashandī, Aḥmad ibn ʿAlī al-. *Ṣubḥ al-aʿshā fī ṣināʿat al-inshāʾ*. 5 vols. Cairo: al-Maṭbaʿah al-Amīrīyah, 1987. The most extensive primary source for early and medieval administration in the central Islamic lands, especially in Egypt.

Cemal Kafadar
Revised by Luke Yarbrough

Dīwān al-Maẓālim. The Islamic legal system had a multi-court system. In addition to the *Sharīʿah* court, presided over by the *qāḍī*, there were courts for police and army jurisdictions, and, most importantly, a special tribunal presided over by the ruler—caliph or sultan—or his delegate that addressed grievances (*maẓālim*, from *ẓulm*, injustice, oppression) suffered by the population at large, as for instance in matters of unjust treatment by powerful persons. The contemporary function of the *maẓālim* institution will be described further.

The *maẓālim* tribunal continues in the present day in a form similar to what is better known in the West as arbitration or as an ombudsman institution. In Saudi Arabia, a Board of Grievances (*dīwān al-maẓālim*) was created in 1955, as a department within the Council of Ministers (*majlis al-wuzarāʾ*), to hear complaints brought against a government action or official. The board has considerable legal cachet since it is made up of judges trained in the religious law (*Sharīʿah*) and is legitimated by the authority of the Saudi king, to whom it reports. Its jurisdiction was further extended in 1982 when its judicial scope and prosecutorial capacity were enlarged to include the enforcement of foreign judgments and criminal trials of corruption, such as forgery and bribery. In 1987 its jurisdiction was again expanded to cover all disputes of commercial law. A new law of 2007 has restricted its competence in commercial disputes, transferring their settlement to courts of first instance; but the Board of Grievances remains the most important legal forum in Saudi Arabia for administrative disputes against government authorities and for arbitral awards, in addition to its competence in enforcing foreign judgments.

In Morocco the *dīwān al-maẓālim* was created by King Muḥammad VI on 1 December 2001 as a tribunal to hear complaints against government agencies. Its mandate is "to advance mediation between citizens as individuals or groups and the administration or any body having public authority, and to encourage the latter to respect the primacy of law and justice" (Royal Decree no. 1-01-298). It has forty-four members: fourteen named by human rights associations, nine by political parties, six representing various professional groups (such as doctors and judges), and fifteen appointed by the king, including the ombudsman or mediator, the *walī al-maẓālim*. According to some human-rights organizations, the Moroccan *dīwān al-maẓālim* is not completely free of abuse of the system or political influence.

[*See also* Courts; *and* Sharīʿah.]

BIBLIOGRAPHY

Cotran, Eugene, and Martin Lau, eds. *Yearbook of Islamic and Middle Eastern Law* 8 (2001–2002): 299. The Hague: Kluwer Law International, 2003.

Global Integrity Report. *Global Integrity Index: Morocco*. 2008. http://report.globalintegrity.org/Morocco/2008/scorecard/69.

Vogel, Frank E. *Islamic Law and Legal System: Studies of Saudi Arabia*. Leiden, Netherlands: Brill, 2000.

PERI BEARMAN

DĪWĀNĪYAH. The term *al-dīwānīyah* derives from *dīwān* (pl. *dawāwīn*), which is a registry or a logbook containing army personnel, scribes, and poets. It was also known as a collection of papers, as well as a reference to army records, monetary establishments, and other such places. Some claim it has Assyrian origin. In modern parlance, it refers to a secluded room that is part of the house but with its own entrance to the outside. The room is used for guests or as a place for gathering. All of these meanings and connotations revolve around a common concept: to meet, discuss, and exchange views. Despite their modernization and urbanization, societies in the Arabian Gulf States still retain a private *dīwānīyah* for each tribe or family. These *dīwānīyāh* were the headquarters of leaders and notable *shaykhs* in the past, but later evolved and became specialized with time into fundamental foundations in the lives of ordinary individuals. They are now a distinguishing cultural and political characteristic of Arabian Gulf society as they play an important role in spreading political awareness among citizens and fill a vacuum in some of those societies where there are no political parties and, hence, no real political participation.

In the Arabian Gulf States, the *dīwānīyāh* are currently considered the most important social phenomenon as they function as a place where men can periodically gather to discuss social, political, cultural, or economic affairs of their society. This is true particularly in Kuwait, where the *dīwānīyāh* played a very important and unique role in the politics of the country. Their role was especially significant in the crisis periods (1921–1938) and during the Iraqi invasion in 1990 when they immediately became active venues for political articulation. Moreover, during periods of parliamentary dissolution, the *dīwānīyāh* were used to pressure the government into resumption of parliamentary rule despite restrictions imposed on their political practices. The *dīwānīyāh* were apparently active on Mondays when political figures, parliamentarians, and opposition activists met to exert pressure on the government to resume parliament. Until the present day, *dīwānīyāh* in the Gulf region, and especially in Kuwait, have been the most effective institution in managing active political and social participation across a clear and mature framework relevant only to public welfare, while conforming to the heritage and traditions of each segment of society. They have been deservedly referred to as "informal parliaments."

[*See also* Gulf States.]

BIBLIOGRAPHY

Alhajeri, Abdullah Mohammad. "The Development of Political Interaction in Kuwait through the "Dīwānīyas" from Their Beginnings until the Year 1999." *Journal of Islamic Law and Culture* 12, no. 1 (2010): 24–44.

ʿAlī,āGāwād. *Al-Mufaṣṣal Fī Tārī Al-ʿArab Qabl Al-Islām*. Beirut: Dār al-ʿIlm li-'l-Malāyīn, 2001. See p. 273.

Ghabra, Shafeeq. "Voluntary Associations in Kuwait: The Foundation of a New System?" *Middle East Journal* 45, no. 2 (1991): 199–215.

Ibn al-Athīr, ʿIzz al-Dīn. *Al-Kāmil fī al-Tārīkh*. c. 1. See p. 428.

Ibn Manẓūr, Muḥammad ibn Mukarram. *Lisān al-ʿArab*. 1968. See part 15, p. 463.

Qalqashandī, Ahmad ibn ʿAlī al-. *Ṣubḥ Al-Aʿsha*. 23, 4, 90, la, xvii.

Tétreault, Mary Ann. "Kuwait's Democratic Reform Movement." *Middle East Executive Reports*, October 1990.

ABDULLAH M. ALHAJERI

DRUZE. The Druze are a monotheistic religious group of over one million adherents. They emerged in the eleventh century CE, from the Ismāʿīlī school of Shiism. Today they are located primarily in the eastern Mediterranean/Levant region.

Druze Beliefs. Several beliefs and characteristics set the Druze apart from other religions. Their faith is exclusive and secret, not universal. Their theology, while deriving from Ismāʿīlī theology, accepts the Christian Old and New Testaments as divine texts, reveres several figures (including Jesus Christ and the Prophet Muḥammad) as prophets, and includes aspects drawn from other religions and from secular philosophers. The Druze separate themselves from Islam irrevocably by declaring that the revelations of al-Ḥākim ibn ʿAmr Allāh, the sixth Fāṭimid caliph (r. 996–1021), not those of the Prophet Muḥammad, contain the ultimate truth. The Druze believe that God is beyond human comprehension or definition, and that God is a universal intellect resident in every aspect of existence. They adhere to seven principles, drawn from scripture: belief in the unity of God; truthfulness in their conduct; loyalty and aid to other Druze; renunciation of all other religions; submission to God's will; contentment with God's deeds; and the rejection of any behavior that distracts from their spiritual conduct and endeavors.

Because of their strict secrecy, a Druze is permitted outwardly to deny the faith as protection in times of mortal danger. The Druze believe in the transmigration of souls (*tanāsukh*), which is not a feature of the mainstream monotheistic religions. They believe that the number of souls was finalized at the closure of conversion, and that transmigration lets the soul have a breadth of experience and build a greater knowledge of God than would be possible in one lifetime and is thus seen as a generous, definitive act of divine justice. Male circumcision, universal among Muslims, is not ritually practiced among the Druze. Gender issues also set the Druze apart from some other religions: polygamy, concubinage, and temporary marriage (*mutʿah*) are forbidden to Druze. Divorce is not an easy process, and a Druze woman can initiate proceedings.

Although known to outsiders as Druze, the Druze refer to themselves as al-Muwaḥḥidūn (Unitarians), a sign of their emphasis on absolute monotheism. Many details about the religion have been held secret since the closing of the *daʿwah* and are shared only by a small number within the community. In each succeeding generation, a few are initiated into the ranks of the *al-ʿuqqāl* (the enlightened), which has, from the earliest days, included both men and women. *Al-ʿuqqāl* live ascetic lives focused on the pursuit of enlightenment and are initiated only after years of study and observation. Other Druze, the *juhhāl* (the ignorant, or the uninitiated), protect the secrecy and sanctity of the religion through group loyalty and solidarity.

The Theological and Political History of the Druze. The Druze faith grew from the Ismāʿīlī theology that prevailed in early Fāṭimid Cairo. It promised a radical political change within Islam that failed to materialize once the Ismāʿīlīyah gained political power in North Africa, especially in Egypt in 969 CE. People still looked for messianic rule, and many came to believe that the caliph al-Ḥākim would be that messiah.

The leading champion of al-Ḥākim and his divinity was Ḥamzah ibn ʿAlī ibn Aḥmad al-Zūzanī, a Persian Ismāʿīlī theologian. In 1017 CE, a year after Ḥamzah's arrival in Cairo, al-Ḥākim issued a proclamation in which he revealed himself to be the manifestation of the deity. Ḥamzah pursued the *daʿwah* (divine call) of the new faith throughout the empire and beyond to Damascus and Aleppo, aided in his missionary endeavors by two disciples in particular, Muḥammad al-Darāzī and al-Muqtanā Bahāʾ al-Dīn. Al-Darāzī generally is regarded as having given converts the name "Druze" by which they are now known to non-Druze.

The Druze were not so much a sect of Islam as a new religion—certainly they saw themselves as such—that aimed to establish a millennial world order. Within a year of al- Ḥākim's proclamation, however, a disagreement between Ḥamzah and al-Darāzī arose over issues of political power and the process of conversion. Ḥamzah publicly rebuked al-Darāzī, and in 1019 CE the latter was assassinated and then anathematized by the Druze faith as a heretic. Less than two years later al-Ḥākim disappeared suddenly under mysterious circumstances. His successor, ʿAlī al-Ẓāhir (r. 1021–1036 CE) denied his predecessor's divinity and worked for the destruction of those who believed in the Druze message. Despite the persecution, Bahāʾ al-Dīn continued pursuing the missionary *daʿwah*, gaining new converts and nurturing those who had survived the imperial reprisals, particularly in the remoter regions of Mount Lebanon. During this time he codified the religious teaching of the Druze into six books known as *al-Ḥikmah al-sharīfah* (The Noble Knowledge), which contain 111 texts composed by al-Ḥākim, Ḥamzah, and himself. In 1043 CE, the *daʿwah* was formally ended; since that time no new adherents have been admitted to the faith, though there remains some uncertainty as to whether the *daʿwah* was closed forever or merely suspended.

The closure of the *daʿwah*, along with geographic isolation, meant that the Druze evolved semi-independent communities within wider Sunnī empires. A local Druze dynasty, the Tanukhs, ruled Mount Lebanon from the twelfth century to the sixteenth, during which time the Druze developed most rapidly as a distinct religious and social community. They developed a reputation for martial capability around this time by repelling Crusaders in the thirteenth century, which also brought favor from the Mamlūk rulers of the Levant. After the decline of the Tanukhs, the Maʿn became the principle Druze clan after the Ottoman conquest of the Mamlūks, though the Maʿn fiercely resisted the Ottoman attempt to subjugate them. It is at this time that Druze political power and autonomy reached its peak. In the seventeenth century Fakhr al-Dīn I was permitted by the Ottomans to form his own military; he was followed by Fakhr al-Dīn II, who ruled Mount Lebanon and much of the coast effectively and with considerable autonomy.

After a century of political prominence under the Maʿn, the Druze split over the succession of the rival Shihāb clan, and many fled in the early eighteenth century to the region of southern Syria known thereafter as the Jabal al-Durūz. When the Shihāb converted to Maronite Christianity in the mid-eighteenth century, Druze leadership passed to the Jumblatt (Junblāṭ) family, who were relatively recent arrivals from Aleppo, reputedly of Kurdish origin. Rivalry between the Druze and Maronites saw fierce tensions, especially in 1842 when Lebanon was effectively partitioned, albeit briefly, into separate Christian and Druze districts. This partition did not reduce tensions, however, and fighting flared on several occasions in the nineteenth century. French support to the Maronites resulted in violence in 1860, leading to the creation of an autonomous Christian governorate that became the basis of an enlarged Lebanon, first under a French mandate in 1920, and then as an independent republic in 1943 in which the Druze counted for only 6.7 percent of the population. Kamal Jumblatt was the leading Druze leader (*za'īm*) from independence until his assassination in 1976 during the Lebanese Civil War. He was succeeded by his son Walīd, who still presides with unquestioned authority over the political interests of the Lebanese Druze. The political leadership of the Druze in Syria has traditionally been exercised by the al-Aṭrash family. Traditional Druze leadership in Israel has come from the Ṭarīf clan of Julis, in Galilee. Since independence, the Druze, alone among the Arabs of the former Palestine mandate, have served in the Israeli military and occasionally been given minor posts in the government and diplomatic service.

Druze Political Demography Today. Still largely a rural- and village-based community, the Druze are usually found today in small communities of under 10,000, and sometimes in small villages and other such units, the exceptions being al-Suwaydā' in Syria and Ba'qlin in Lebanon. In Lebanon the Druze number an estimated 300,000 to 350,000 out of a population of about 4.2 million, and in Syria between 450,000 and 500,000 out of a total population estimated at about 22 million. A smaller community of 60,000 to 70,000 lives in Israel proper, augmented since 1967 by another 15,000 in the occupied Golan Heights. In addition there are some 15,000 to 20,000 Druze in Jordan and perhaps as many as 100,000 living outside the Middle East, giving a total Druze population of about one million worldwide. The Druze of Lebanon are found primarily in small towns and villages in the Shūf district on the western slope of Mount Lebanon from the Beirut-Damascus highway south to the Jazzin escarpment. A second concentration is located in the southeast of the country, in the Wādī al-Taym district in the western foothills of Mount Hermon, around the towns of Hasbayya and Rashayya. A third center is Beirut, where a small number have permanent residence. In Syria, 80 percent of the Druze are found in the district of al-Suwaydā' (Jabal al-Durūz) in the south. A second concentration is located on the eastern slope of Mount Hermon in Damascus province and in the city itself. A third, historic center is the Jabal al-A'lā region west of Aleppo near the Turkish frontier, where some 30,000 to 40,000 Druze live in a dozen villages dotted with ruined Byzantine churches (e.g., Qalb Lawza). The Druze of Israel live primarily in sixteen towns and villages (nine of them exclusively Druze) in Galilee, and two major settlements on Mount Carmel southeast of Haifa.

[*See also* Lebanon.]

BIBLIOGRAPHY

Abu-Izzeddin, Nejla M. *The Druzes: A New Study of Their History, Faith, and Society*. Leiden, Netherlands: Brill, 1984.

Alamuddin, Najib. *The Druzes: Lebanon and the Arab-Israeli Conflict*. London: Quartet Books, 1993.

Atashi, Zeidan. *Druze & Jews in Israel. A Shared Destiny?* Brighton, U.K.: Sussex Academic Press; Portland, Oreg., 1997.

Betts, Robert B. *The Druze*. New Haven, Conn.: Yale University Press, 1988.

Firro, Kais M. *The Druzes in the Jewish State: A Brief History*. Leiden, Netherlands: and Boston: Brill, 1999.

Firro, Kais M. *A History of the Druzes*. Leiden, Netherlands: Brill, 1992.

Joumblatt, Kamal. *I Speak for Lebanon*. Translated from the French by Michael Pallis. London: Zed Press, 1982.

Najjār, 'Abd Allāh. *Madhhab al-Durūz wa-al-tawḥīd*. Cairo: Dār al-Ma'ārif, 1965. Translated by Fred Massey as *The Druze: Millennium Scrolls Revealed*. Atlanta: American Druze Society, Committee on Religious Affairs, 1973.

ROBERT BRENTON BETTS
Updated by MATTHEW GRAY

E

EDUCATION, MUSLIM. The guardianship and study of religious knowledge (*ʿilm*) have always been at the heart of Muslim culture and politics. The Qurʾān and *sunnah* abound with references to the importance of learning. The education or "culturing" (*tarbīyah*) of Muslims as to their obligations as believers has long been an imperative of religious life, and one to which rulers were enjoined to lend support.

In the absence of a centralized church hierarchy like that of Western Christianity, religious study also played a key role in creating the network and hierarchy of scholarly dignitaries who came to exercise religious authority in Muslim communities. From the early Muslim period to today, however, the identification of religious leaders has often been a point of contention. Equally contentious has been the task of determining the scope of these leaders' authority and their rights and obligations to the state. Rulers often had their own ideas as to the aims of education and the place of religious dignitaries in political affairs.

In the modern period, the tensions surrounding religious education became even more pervasive. Modern states have educational ambitions more varied than those of classical schooling. Modern societies are marked by a heightened circulation of people and ideas, as well as a plurality of actors and movements claiming authoritative knowledge of Islam. The modern period has also given rise to broad movements of educational reform, including many dedicated to the idea that modern science and learning are thoroughly compatible with Islam.

Early and Classical Education. Although the transmission of knowledge has long been at the heart of Muslim societies, the institutions through which this transmission takes place have changed over time. During the Muslim world's Middle Ages (1000–1500 CE), the religious college or *madrasah* emerged as the dominant institution for advanced religious learning. The *madrasah* was distinguished from institutions of more elementary religious study, such as the *kuttāb* or *maktab*. These taught youths to read and recite the Qurʾān, but did not delve into legal or exegetical matters. *Kuttāb*-like institutions emerged in the first century of the Islamic era, not long after scholars completed their recensions of the Qurʾān per the instruction of the caliphs ʿUmar (r. 634–644) and ʿUthmān (r. 644–656).

The first *madrasah* appeared a full three centuries later, in the province of Khorāsān in eastern

Iran. The institution spread quickly to other Muslim regions, reaching Spain and northern India in the first decades of the thirteenth century. Political patronage aided the institution's diffusion. In the second half of the eleventh century, the great Seljuk vizier Niẓām al-Mulk established eleven *madrasahs* in Iraq and Syria. In later centuries, the Turkic conquerors of Arab lands often sponsored *madrasahs* in an effort to win favor with the local populace.

For most of the Middle Ages, the *madrasah* was not the sole center for higher learning. Hospitals and libraries—the latter the largest in the medieval world—hosted study circles, too, some of which engaged the heritage of Greek philosophy and natural science. Ṣūfī lodges also served as major centers of esoteric learning, sometimes merging with *madrasahs*. Notwithstanding the plural educational environment, by the fourteenth century the *madrasah* had emerged as *the* core educational institution in the Muslim heartland. It trained not only youth aspiring to become religious scholars but children of the urban trading classes and political elite.

Prior to the *madrasah*'s emergence, advanced study in the religious sciences took place in informal study circles (*ḥalaqāt*, sg. *ḥalqah*) in mosques, homes, or merchant shops. Neither the content nor the method of education was systematized to the degree that it would be after the *madrasah*'s ascendance. The localization of advanced religious learning in *madrasahs* was related to a broader change in the economy of the Islamic sciences. By the eighth and ninth centuries, the growing complexity of religious knowledge, especially that associated with the study of *ḥadīth* and legal commentaries, meant that advanced learning required prolonged periods of study. Faced with this practical challenge, mosques specializing in advanced religious study at first built hostels for resident students. The tenth-century *madrasah* took this innovation one step further, providing classrooms, dormitories, and washrooms for students, all of whom were male. Although elite women often sponsored the establishment of *madrasahs*, their formal religious education was limited to tutorial instruction in the privacy of their homes.

School Curricula and Pedagogy. In their first centuries, some *madrasahs* provided instruction in subjects other than the religious sciences. From the eleventh to the fourteenth century, Middle Eastern scholarship in mathematics, astronomy, and medicine was the most advanced in the world, and some larger *madrasahs* excelled in these sciences, as well as in philosophy and poetry. However, in the late Middle Ages, *madrasahs* made jurisprudence (*fiqh*) and related disciplines the focus of study, eventually providing only ancillary instruction in nonreligious sciences. The curricular situation remained more complex in the arc of Muslim societies extending from Anatolia to northern India. In these regions, *madrasahs* provided instruction in basic mathematics and the nonrevealed sciences well into the eighteenth century.

Medieval *madrasahs* developed a core curriculum, portions of which are used still today in tradition-minded schools. They offered instruction in Qurʾān recitation (*qirāʾah*), Qurʾānic interpretation (*tafsīr*), jurisprudence (*fiqh*), the sources of the law (*uṣūl al-fiqh*), and didactic theology (*kalām*). Instruction was also provided in sciences complementary to the transmitted traditions, including Arabic grammar, lexicology, morphology, metrics, rhyme, prosody, and history.

As an educational institution, the *madrasah* was organized differently from the colleges that appeared in western European cities in the late Middle Ages. Recruitment and daily study were organized around each student's disciple-like relationship with his teacher, not around a corporate institution. Students were subject to examinations, which took place when a student had mastered a particular text in the Islamic sciences. The scholar who had provided instruction in the text then licensed its teaching by providing the student with a written certificate known as an *ijāzah*. Otherwise, however, *madrasahs* had no standardized curricula, institution-awarded degrees, or system of college governance. As with many other aspects of the Islamic tradition, the informal and networked quality of religious education was to undergo a great transformation in the modern period.

Educational Patronage and Politics. In the Middle Ages and at many traditionalist institutions today, students were not charged tuition, so funding for school operations depended in large part on religious endowments provided by local notables. The legal basis for these donations was the institution of the *waqf*. The *waqf* was a private endowment set aside in perpetuity for the purpose of providing funds for some public good or service, typically of a religious nature. In medieval times, those who established a *waqf* for *madrasahs* included rulers, military elites, and male and female members of prominent families.

The precise role of the state in *madrasah* funding varied by locale. The state everywhere had to provide the legal guarantees that allowed for *madrasahs* to operate. But the state's direct contribution to *madrasah* endowments varied. Where civil society was strong, as in northeastern Iran in the tenth and eleventh centuries, landed aristocrats and other nonstate notables led the way in establishing and maintaining *madrasahs*. Elsewhere, as in Iraq during the Seljuk Empire (1040) or Egypt and Syria under the Mamlūks, rulers provided the lion's share of *waqf* endowments. Court officials in the latter lands even appointed professors to endowed chairs. The Turkic rulers in these countries patronized *madrasahs* in an effort to bolster their legitimacy in the eyes of the local Arab population. In farther regions, as at the frontiers of Muslim expansion in Africa, the Balkans, and South and Southeast Asia, ruling elites patronized *madrasahs* to promote orthodoxy and political loyalty among Muslim converts still only nominally conversant with the details of their faith.

Centering and Canonizing Knowledge and Authority. The rise of the *madrasah* was part of a far-reaching reorganization of religious knowledge and authority in medieval Muslim societies. The main characteristic of this change was the recentering and standardization of scholarly learning in *madrasahs*. Jurisprudence (*fiqh*) became the centerpiece of advanced religious education, and although interpretive plurality still characterized the broader religious field, mastery of a written canon became imperative for those aspiring to advanced learning. This heightened dependency on a textual canon and study with a recognized master created clearer criteria for identifying who qualified as a religious authority. The development of a corpus of authoritative Islamic texts and agreed methods for their mastery also brought about a greater uniformity of knowledge in those circles where *madrasah*-educated scholars exercised influence.

Beyond these educated circles, however, nonstandard streams of religious knowledge and practiced thrived. Muslim societies in the Middle Ages were overwhelmingly rural, and some 98 to 99 percent of the population was illiterate. Even in educational centers such as twelfth-century Cairo, known as "a city of schools," there were popular traditions of healing, magic, and mysticism that appeared heterodox from the perspective of the *madrasah* canon. Unlettered religious masters with no background in *madrasahs* abounded. They based their claim to religious eminence on knowledge acquired from visions and dreams of the Prophet, not from books studied under an erudite master.

The plurality of religious knowledge and practice was all the greater in places such as West

Africa, the Balkans, Bengal, Kazakhstan, and Indonesia, all of which were brought into the Muslim fold well after the high medieval period. *Madrasahs* arrived late in these regions, and even after their establishment they typically had a nonhegemonic impact on popular Islam. Nonstandard traditions of Islamic learning survived and thrived there well into the modern era. Their practitioners maintained that their healing cults and saint venerations were Islamic, even when some among the religious establishment might insist otherwise.

***Madrasahs* and Political Modernity.** In the nineteenth and twentieth centuries, Muslim societies experienced new religious movements that aimed to recenter and standardize religious learning in new ways. Ultimately these movements effected the greatest changes in Muslim education since the rise of the *madrasah* in the Middle Ages. The changes in religious education were linked to three developments: the advance of Western colonialism into Muslim lands, the rise of Islamic reform movements, and, in the mid-twentieth century, the expansion of mass education.

Together these events created conditions in which received institutions of religious learning seemed inadequate to meet the political challenges of the day. With education no longer an elite affair, growing numbers of people were drawn to the study of Islam, often in movements outside the control of *madrasah* scholars. Large numbers of reformists also came to regard their faith as objective, systemic, and applicable to the whole of their lives. Processes of religious "authentication" also became socially pervasive. Growing numbers of believers concluded that all observant Muslims, not just religious scholars, must survey the cultural field so as to eliminate customs and practices antithetical to Islam.

The form and intensity of these educational changes, and their implications for Muslim politics, varied in a manner that reflected each society's political circumstances. In Muslim-majority societies that escaped direct colonial rule, such as Iran and the Ottoman Empire, Muslim rulers launched educational reforms of their own. Rulers sought to follow the example of their Western counterparts by creating a citizenry endowed with new educational tools and a common national culture.

In undertaking these reforms, Muslim governments grappled with the question of where Islamic education fit into the institution of the nation. Different rulers resolved the question in different ways. Some intervened directly in *madrasah* affairs. Others attempted an end run around the *madrasah* establishment and founded public schools of their own. Whichever option it pursued, the modern state ended the *ʿulamāʾ*'s monopoly on education. It created new knowledge elites and raised questions about education and the state that have remained at the heart of Muslim politics to this day.

The general trend in the early portion of the modern period, then, was a greater étatization of Islamic education, but the precise timing and scope of the change varied by country. In the most powerful Muslim realm of the modern era, the Ottoman Empire, state intervention in religious education had actually begun several centuries before the ascent of the European powers; educational modernity was not a postcolonial effect of Western rule. From the late fifteenth century on, Ottoman authorities launched reforms aimed at centralizing and controlling Islamic schooling. The Ottomans ranked *madrasahs* according to a strict hierarchy; they also established educational criteria whereby scholars passed from lower to higher ranks in the religious establishment. By the eighteenth century, this bureaucratic rationalization had created eleven levels in the *madrasah* hierarchy, each differentiated from the others by prestige, staffing, and salaries. By this late period, however, Ottoman power had also begun to wane relative to the empire's fast-rising European rivals. In seeking to understand the reasons for the European advantage, some Ottoman officials concluded that one key was the European emphasis on technical and nonreligious education.

In a pattern of defensive educational reform seen a few years later in Egypt and Iran, Ottoman officials responded to the European challenge with initiatives intended to narrow the gap with the West. In the late eighteenth century they established military academies, recruiting Europeans as instructors. In the early nineteenth century, they opened colleges for medicine, military training, civil administration, and law. All of these institutions adopted Western schools as their model. State officials had concluded that it was not politically expedient to draw *madrasahs* into these reforms, not least because in the early decades of the nineteenth century religious scholars had rebuffed proposals for reform made by the Ministry of Education.

The Ottoman defeat in World War I strengthened the political elite's resolve to reform the entire school system, including its Islamic branch. Mustafa Kemal, the Republic of Turkey's founder and first president, abolished all but eight of Turkey's *madrasahs*, replacing them with a School of Theology and thirty-three schools for training preachers and mosque officials. Over the next few years, his administration eliminated religious instruction entirely from public education. After Kemal's death in 1948, the state reintroduced religious education into its schools, and higher religious education under state supervision was also allowed.

No Muslim-majority country undertook reforms as comprehensively secularizing as those of Republican Turkey. In Qājār Iran, the state responded to the disasters of the Russo-Persian War of 1803–1815 by inviting French officers to Iran to train troops in European military arts. Fearing resistance from the *madrasah* elite, Qājār officials resolved not to interfere in the *madrasah* sector and deferred the implementation of programs of mass education.

Elsewhere, in colonized Muslim lands, European rule subordinated the development of general education to the interests of the colonial state. The precise pattern varied by country, in a manner that sometimes worked to the advantage of reform-minded Muslim educators. In the absence of a Muslim-led state, Muslims leaders in India concluded that the best way to defend Islam was by making religious education public, rather than concentrating school resources on the training of a small scholarly elite. Muslim educators remained divided, however, on the question of the curriculum most appropriate for the new religious schooling. Some called for the incorporation of mathematics, science, and history into the *madrasah* curriculum. Others insisted that, in the absence of Muslim rule, *madrasahs* should become the frontline of struggle against all manner of European influence, including nonreligious subjects of study.

The advance of European colonialism over Muslim lands, then, did not bring educational reforms where previously there were none. The Ottoman and Mughal empires had harnessed the institutions of Islamic education to state programs well before the Europeans arrived. In both empires, Muslim educators' ties to the state led to an emphasis on the rational as well as religious sciences. In the colonial period, the boldest attempts to reform Islamic education took place in countries like India, Indonesia, and Nigeria, where Muslim leaders concluded that the best way to defend and promote Islam was by taking religious learning to the masses. In the absence of a Muslim state, a pious people with a clear understanding of their faith seemed to offer the best prospect for upholding Islam. The late colonial period also witnessed the emergence of institutional hybrids blending instruction in the Islamic sciences with Western-influenced study of science, history, and mathematics. National independence would greatly accelerate these reformist trends.

The Politics of Postcolonial Education. For rulers in the newly independent Muslim lands, the first order of business was not the reform of Islamic education but the building of a modern nation and a shared national culture, not least through programs of general education. The nonreligious public schools established in the early independence era had a powerful effect on Islamic education. State schools challenged religious styles of learning, created a new class of Muslim intellectuals apart from religious scholars, and changed the ways ordinary Muslims thought about religion and identity.

In 1800 literacy rates across most of the Muslim world hovered around 1–2 percent of the population. By 1960, state-sponsored education had changed this entirely. The percentage of primary-age youths enrolled in school (for both sexes) had risen to 47 percent of the population in Bangladesh, 66 percent in Egypt, 71 percent in Indonesia, 65 percent in Iran, 30 percent in Pakistan, 12 percent in Saudi Arabia, and 75 percent in Turkey. By 1990, the proportion of the school-age population in elementary school had climbed further, to 70 percent or higher in all countries, with the notable exception of Pakistan (37 percent). In many countries, the education of young girls still lagged behind that of boys, but even here there was progress. In 1960 the percentage of girls enrolled in primary school was 26 percent in Bangladesh, 52 percent in Egypt, 58 percent in Indonesia, 27 percent in Iran, 13 percent in Pakistan, 2 percent in Saudi Arabia, and 58 percent in Turkey. By 1990, the rates of female participation in primary school education were 68 percent in Bangladesh, 90 percent in Egypt, near 100 percent in Indonesia, Iran, and Turkey, and 72 percent in Saudi Arabia. Pakistan was the outlier, with just 26 percent of its school-age girls enrolled in primary school.

In the eyes of some Western and nationalist observers, state-sponsored schooling held the promise of a far-reaching secularization of Muslim society. Enrollments in the private Islamic school sector did decline in many Muslim lands in the 1950s and 1960s, as parents concluded that state schools offered a better path to their children's employment and prosperity. However, the situation changed in the 1970s and 1980s in the aftermath of a powerful resurgence in Islamic observance. The resurgence affected religious education in three ways. First, governments in most Muslim-majority societies heightened their investment in religious education. Second, a growing number of Islamic schools incorporated instruction in general subjects (math, science, social studies) into their curricula. Third, even as the state increased its involvement in religious education, growing numbers of pious youth opted to pursue their religious learning in study circles and social movements apart from established educational institutions. The result was that religious learning and authority underwent a powerful but often destabilizing pluralization.

The combination of mass education and Islamic resurgence had broader political consequences as well. On the one hand, as piety movements gained momentum, governments in many countries reintroduced religious instruction into the state school curriculum. On the other hand, mass education and Islamic resurgence also contributed to a shift from the personalized and hierarchical discipleship of classical religious education to a more impersonal and varied educational regimen. Islamic knowledge came to be viewed not as an ineffable part of a way of life but as a systemic and rationalized knowledge whose study was incumbent on all believers. The removal of religious learning from established educational institutions also prompted some to conclude that they had the right to determine the tenets of their faith without official authorization. Inevitably they reached conclusions different from those of state officials and the religious establishment. Through these and other developments, and in contrast to what government officials had intended, mass religious education created a more pluralized, competitive, and, sometimes, politicized religious marketplace.

The political consequences of the new landscape of religious learning nonetheless remained varied. In most countries the great majority of people sought to use religious learning to be more pious, but not to effect radical political change. In a few settings, however, the resurgence inspired radical social movements. In Afghanistan, the collaboration of the Taliban with al-Qaʿida militants raised concerns that *madrasahs* might be the root cause of religious extremism. The Taliban leadership did emerge from *madrasahs* located along the Afghan-Pakistan border. However, their militancy owed less to South Asian educational traditions than to a twenty-year conflict that pulverized Afghan society, created millions of desperate refugees, and propelled religious students away from their traditional political quietism and out into the political sphere. Elsewhere, as in western Europe, small circles of disaffected militants used secretive study circles to promote an understanding of Islam at variance with most of the Muslim public, and in opposition to democratic governance.

Notwithstanding a few radical currents, the general trend in modern Muslim education has been the effort to revive the legacy of rational inquiry balanced with religious piety for which classical Islamic civilization had been renowned. New initiatives in Islamic education seek to overcome the lag some Muslim societies still experience in the fields of women's education, scientific achievement, and book publishing. In an age in which the intensive cultivation of knowledge has become essential for public well-being, the lag is serious. But the speed with which it is diminishing as a result of the Muslim world's educational transformation is one of the least remarked but important changes taking place in Muslim culture and politics today.

[*See also* Azhar, al-; *and* Universities.]

BIBLIOGRAPHY

Arjomand, Said Amir. "The Law, Agency, and Policy in Medieval Islamic Society: Development of the Institutions of Learning from the Tenth to the Fifteenth Century." *Comparative Studies in Society and History* 41 (April 1999): 263–293. A historical sociology of the rise of the *madrasah* set against its social and political context.

Berkey, Jonathan. *The Transmission of Knowledge in Medieval Cairo: A Social History of Islamic Education*. Princeton, N.J.: Princeton University Press, 1992. One of the richest historical studies of Islamic education in a medieval setting.

Chamberlain, Michael. *Knowledge and Social Practice in Medieval Damascus, 1190–1350*. Cambridge Studies in Islamic Civilization. Cambridge, U.K.: Cambridge University Press, 1994. A historical analysis of the political and economic context for classical Muslim education.

Eickelman, Dale F. "Mass Higher Education and the Religious Imagination in Contemporary Arab Societies." *American Ethnologist* 19 (1992): 643–665. A concise analysis of the impact of modern mass education on ideas of religion and religiosity in the Muslim Middle East.

Fortna, Benjamin C. *Imperial Classroom: Islam, the State, and Education in the Late Ottoman Empire*. Oxford: Oxford University Press, 2002. A history of educational reform in the late Ottoman period.

Hefner, Robert W., and Muhammad Qasim Zaman, eds. *Schooling Islam: The Culture and Politics of Modern Muslim Education*. Princeton, N.J.: Princeton University Press, 2007. Comparative studies of Islamic education in eight national settings today.

Makdisi, George. *The Rise of Colleges: Institutions of Learning in Islam and the West*. Edinburgh: Edinburgh

University Press, 1981. A historical study of the origins of the *madrasah* in comparison with the rise of colleges in the late medieval West.

Metcalf, Barbara Daly. *Islamic Revival in British India: Deoband, 1860–1900*. Princeton, N.J.: Princeton University Press, 1982. A history of the rise of modern India's most important educational reform movement.

Starrett, Gregory. *Putting Islam to Work: Education, Politics, and Religious Transformation in Egypt*. Berkeley: University of California Press, 1998. An anthropological analysis of the politics and uses of Islamic education in modern Egypt.

Zaman, Muhammad Qasim. *The Ulama in Contemporary Islam: Custodians of Change*. Princeton, N.J.: Princeton University Press, 2002. A study notable for its insights into religious debates raging in educational circles in contemporary Pakistan and India.

Zeghal, Malika. *Gardiens de l'Islam: Les oulémas d'Al Azhar dans l'Égypte contemporaine* (Guardians of Islam: The Ulemas of al-Azhar in Contemporary Egypt). Paris: Presses de la Fondation Nationale des Sciences Politiques, 1996. A political and historical study of the single most influential Islamic university in the world.

ROBERT W. HEFNER

EGYPT. With approximately 80 million Muslims (some 90 percent of the total population), Egypt is the most populous Arab country and among the top five most populous Muslim countries. Islam has played a central and complex role in the country's politics since the mid-seventh century and has assumed greater prominence since the uprising of January and February 2011 that overthrew the government of Hosni Mubarak.

From Islamic Conquest to Ottoman Rule. Prior to the Islamic conquest, Saint Mark the Evangelist had founded the Church of Alexandria in the first century, which established itself in 451 as the Coptic Orthodox Church. Muslim rule in Egypt dates back to 639, when, under the caliphate of ʿUmar ibn ʿAbd al-Khaṭṭāb, Arab armies led by ʿAmr ibn al-ʿĀṣ advanced into the territory and defeated Byzantine forces by 641. The new rulers founded al-Fusṭāṭ as Egypt's first Arab capital. In 706, during the Umayyad caliphate (661–750), Arabic was made the official language of administration in Egypt, but conversion to Islam of the native population would be a long and gradual process.

The Ismāʿīlī Shīʿī dynasty of the Fāṭimids established the city of Cairo in 969, and in 971, the mosque-university of al-Azhar was founded. Al-Azhar became a highly influential institution of Sunnī jurisprudence, transforming Egypt into a leading religious and cultural center. After several internal power struggles, Ṣalāḥ al-Dīn (Saladin) founded the Ayyūbid dynasty (1171–1250), restoring Sunnī political prominence in Egypt. The Mamlūks, Turco-Circassian slave soldiers, took power in Egypt in 1240 and continued to rule even after the Ottoman Empire (1300–1923) conquered Egypt in 1517, as the Ottomans turned to the Mamlūks to administer Egypt.

The early Islamic period crystallized multiple connections between Islam and political rule. First, religion came to dominate conceptions of identity, social status, and citizenship. Second, religion became the unifier and legitimizer of successive dynasties. The early Islamic period also inaugurated the theme of revivalism; already under the ʿAbbāsids, many were professing nostalgia for a golden age of Islam, a trope that continues to resonate powerfully today.

The Challenge of European Imperialism and Modernization. By the eighteenth century, the Ottoman Empire had begun to experience, and respond to, the military and economic encroachment of the Western European states. In Egypt, Napoleon's expedition (1798–1801) launched this process. Muḥammad ʿAlī (1805–1849), the "founder of modern Egypt," enshrined the Egyptian state's response to Europe's advances—defensive reforms along European lines. He introduced new technologies into military training; diminished *ʿulamāʾ* control in the fields of law, administration, and economy; and introduced new secular colleges of education in medicine and science. Khedive Ismāʿil (1863–1879) continued this process, at first consulting the *ʿulamāʾ* but then reverting to Muḥammad ʿAlī's top-down methods.

These policies disturbed the way in which Islam had determined identity and social status, as a dual education system created a majority with religious attachments and a minority with a secular worldview. Political ideology was now built upon effective command of Western technologies more than religious sanction. Both state institutions and the law were secularized, with *Sharīʿah* courts now confined to the realm of family law and the influence of the *ʿulamāʾ* reduced. In response, new impulses for revivalism were generated.

Nineteenth-Century Revivalism. By the mid-nineteenth century, the challenge from the West was intensifying. Muḥammad ʿAlī was forced to sign the Treaty of London in 1840, imposing restrictions on Egypt's army and industry. Khedive Ismāʿil plunged Egypt into debt until Anglo-French "dual control" was established over the economy in 1876.

New social actors now elaborated an Islamic modernist alternative. Between conservative rejectionism and the state's Westernization, they used tradition in the call for change. Jamāl al-Dīn al-Afghānī (1838–1897) and his Egyptian disciple Muḥammad ʿAbduh (1849–1905) stressed first the political and cultural ascendancy of Islam's past, fostering a shared identity and heritage in which Muslims could take pride and have faith. Second, they emphasized the dynamic character of Islam, able to draw on the sources of Europe's strength while preserving its own identity. Third, they affirmed the permissibility of such modernization, against conservatives who saw this as illicit innovation (*bidʿah*). Their aim was to restore solidarity among Muslim communities and effect a renaissance that would overthrow imperialism.

ʿAbduh and al-Afghānī were exiled for supporting Aḥmad ʿUrābī's revolt against the British (1879–1882). From Paris, they published the journal *al-ʿUrwah al-wuthqā*. Returning in 1888, ʿAbduh worked toward reforming al-Azhar's curriculum and the religious courts. In 1898 he began publishing the journal *al-Manār*, insisting that there was no conflict between Islam and science and that the basis for change already existed within Islam through the distinction between fixed duties to God and changeable duties in society. In 1899 he became mufti of Egypt, issuing progressive legal opinions, including a critique of polygamy that inspired generations of Egyptian feminists.

Resisting British Occupation. The British occupation of 1882 launched a period of direct colonialism that lasted until 1956. The enlightened revivalism of the nineteenth century infused subsequent trends, having encouraged both nationalist and pan-Islamic ideas. The setting was now the fall of the Ottoman Empire in 1918 and British declaration of a protectorate in Egypt. This spawned three connected movements, whose figures were all al-Afghānī's and ʿAbduh's associates: the secular Egyptian nationalism of Aḥmad Luṭfī al-Sayyid and Saʿd Zaghlūl, the conservative Islamism of the Salafīyah and Muslim Brotherhood, and secular pan-Arabism, in which Islam was both political symbol and identity-marker.

Salafīyah. One of ʿAbduh's students and *al-Manār* collaborator, Muḥammad Rashīd Riḍā (1865–1935), moved away from his teacher's ideas. Riḍā reacted conservatively to the abolition of the caliphate in 1924, the liberal party politics of the 1920s and 1930s, and the influence of the secular nationalism of European-educated elites. He drew closer to the conservative Ḥanbalī school of

Islamic law and to the premodern Islamic revivalism of Muḥammad ibn ʿAbd al-Wahhāb. He called for institutional innovations that would restore Islam's social role in the contemporary age.

The Muslim Brotherhood. In 1928, Ḥasan al-Bannā (1906–1949) founded the Muslim Brotherhood (Ikhwān al-Muslimīn) in Ismāʿīlīyah. He was influenced by Muḥammad Rashīd Riḍā's teachings, the 1919 anticolonial uprising, and his membership in Islamic associations. He emphasized the self-sufficiency of Islam as a "cure" to the decay brought on by colonialism and Westernization. By 1949, the Brotherhood had approximately two thousand branches, built around mosques, schools, and small businesses offering services. This network advanced the Brotherhood's "social Islam" project. Meanwhile, al-Bannā used modern dissemination strategies to establish his political organization and mobilize support. The Brotherhood remains a hierarchical organization, with a Supreme Guide, Guidance Bureau, a Shūrā Council that elects a Political Bureau, and a Brotherhood mufti.

The Brotherhood championed anticolonialism, tapping widespread popular sentiment in rejecting British rule and the Israeli colonization of Palestine, which continues to mobilize members today. In the late 1940s, the Brotherhood fostered ties beyond Egypt through its involvement in anti-British and anti-Zionist resistance. Westernized Egyptians who made up the colonial political class also became targets. In 1949, when a young Muslim Brother assassinated Prime Minister Maḥmūd Fahmī al-Nuqrashī, the ensuing government crackdown drove an estimated one million members underground, and al-Bannā himself was assassinated by secret police.

The Brotherhood's message was further radicalized by Sayyid Quṭb (1906–1966), a teacher and Education Ministry bureaucrat inspired by al-Bannā and Pakistan's Abū al-Aʿlā Mawdūdī. In such influential tracts as *Signposts on the Road*, Quṭb affirmed martyrdom in the revolutionary quest to establish an Islamic state, but also emphasized the spiritual and moral decay of contemporary Muslims, which left them prey to the materialist West, transforming them into legitimate targets. Quṭb was charged with plotting to overthrow the state and executed in 1966.

The Brotherhood formalized a new revivalism and new political identity and ideology, insisting on every Muslim's obligation to participate in modern-day *jihād* against the twin enemies of the corrupting West and corrupted Muslims. The Brotherhood did not elaborate its conception of the Islamic state's institutions, save for the rule of *Sharīʿah* law. In practice, it affirmed the right to private property, and the permissibility of income differences, as tempered by charity and social duty.

Independence and the July 1952 Revolution. Also emerging from the extra-parliamentary political ferment of the 1930s and 1940s were the young military men who formed the Free Officers Movement in 1949. They overthrew the monarchy on 23 July 1952, led by Gamal Abdel Nasser. In official discourse, Nasser stressed the equality of all faiths and used ad hoc policies to improve Christian citizens' standing in politics and society. He also used Islamic references, often in contexts of anticolonial resistance, such as his speech at al-Azhar during the Suez War of 1956.

In policy, Nasser pursued his vision of secularism through redistributive developmentalism as well as state religious institutions. During 1952–1953, Nasser instated land reforms that included religiously endowed property (*waqf*). After the failure of the 1954 Islamic Congress, Egypt created its own Supreme Council for Religious Affairs in 1960, which published the progressive journal *Minbar al-Islām*. In 1961 Egypt passed the law of al-Azhar, introducing state appointments and bureaucrats into its administration. Its curriculum was reformed, adding four non-religious faculties and a women's college. The government solicited the *'ulamā'*'s opinions to validate birth control, scientific research, and the doctrines of Arab socialism.

Meanwhile, Nasser fostered a symbiotic relationship with popular Islam in Egypt. Indeed, the al-Azhar establishment traditionally included members of Ṣūfī orders. Islamic mysticism, arising in the early Islamic period, remains deeply popular among Egyptians. Millions participate in heterodox rituals such as commemorating the saints' days, and gathering at Ṣūfī *shuyūkh* lodges (*shuyūkh* is the plural of *shaykh*), while millions more identify less consistently with its spiritual emphasis.

Nasser had exempted the Brotherhood from the dissolution of political parties, but in 1954, an assassination attempt by Brotherhood members led Nasser to ban the organization. The conflict emerged from considerations of power rather than ideology, though Nasser strongly disliked the Brotherhood's combination of religion and politics. Many Brothers were jailed, while others emigrated to Saudi Arabia, where they came into more direct contact with Wahhābī clerics and ideas. Many accumulated personal fortunes and contributed these to the budding Islamic finance sector in Egypt. This legitimized their ties, as a new transnational Islamist bourgeoisie, with Gulf business and shielded their wealth from the nationalizations of the state banking sector.

Regional and international politics have indeed been crucial. Saudi Arabia, with American backing, was a powerful rival to Nasser's Egypt. Its Wahhābī brand of political Islam and its support for Egypt's exiled radicals formed part of its soft power arsenal against Nasser's secular pan-Arabism. In 1962, members of the Saudi religious establishment, working with some of these Muslim Brothers, founded the Muslim World League in Mecca to proselytize Wahhābīyah. Saudi funding of the Egyptian Islamist movement have had a massively empowering effect on their growth.

1970–1981: Sadat and the Muslim Brotherhood. Israel's victory in the June 1967 War was a critical event in the growth of Egypt's and the broader Arab world's Islamist movements. After Egypt's defeat, Nasser's secular pan-Arabist project was left vulnerable to critique from Islamist quarters. Disparate groups began to speak in the name of Islam, blaming secularism for Egypt's moral and material weakness. They contended that the solution was the "return" to Islam.

But it was only after Nasser's death in 1970, when Anwar el-Sadat became president in 1971, that Egypt's Islamists received their political opportunity. After arresting several of the Nasserist political elite in 1971, Sadat promptly released many of the imprisoned Islamists and allowed many exiles to return. He strategically built up these groups and offered funds to Islamist student associations through the secret services in order to counter the leftist and Nasserist opposition to his policy shifts to the right. Sadat had begun forging an alliance with the United States and later introduced sweeping economic liberalization policies. In 1976, Sadat permitted the publication of the Brotherhood-affiliated *al-Da'wah* magazine edited by future supreme guide, 'Umar al-Tilimsānī. Sadat played a large role in enabling Egypt's Islamist currents to challenge and eclipse the religious establishment from outside.

At the same time, Sadat remodelled Egyptian state discourse in order to claim religious legitimacy and outbid the Islamists, referring to Egypt as "the state of knowledge and faith" and calling himself "the believer president." He cultivated his own pious image, making ostentatious visits to mosques and interspersing his speeches with Qur'ānic verses. He also increased Islamic television programming, poured funds into expanding al-Azhar and securing its supportive *fatāwā*, and invented new posts in the Ministry of Religious Endowments.

The Brotherhood took an accommodationist line, vowing to effect change from within the political system. With an enabling state policy environment, this period saw the development as well as differentiation of the Islamist trend. The number of private mosques doubled from twenty thousand to forty thousand, only six thousand of which were publicly owned. With financial support from Saudi networks, many of the Islamist intelligentsia who had graduated in the 1970s began to disseminate their political message. They focused on morality and behavioral norms rather than socioeconomic policy, in order to attract both the urban migrant poor and the pious middle class.

Here again, regional and international contexts were key. The Gulf oil boom following the 1973 Arab-Israeli war saw an increase in Egyptian immigration. There was also a shift in the balance of power toward Gulf states and their ideologies. The increased numbers of Egyptian migrants were all exposed to the spread of Wahhābī ideas through Saudi state and Muslim World League efforts. The Sadat regime made sure to woo members of this devout new middle class enabled by Saudi money, easing their access to the private sector.

Sadat and the Rise of Islamist Militancy. By the mid-1970s the first signs of the backfiring of Sadat's policies of outbidding with the Islamic movement had appeared: the regime came under pressure from Islamists inside and outside parliament calling for stricter interpretations of religious law in Egyptian politics. Furthermore, in the late 1970s, certain sectors of the Brotherhood splintered. The new groups' membership came often from the educated unemployed and often migrant youths who had been the losers in Sadat's economic liberalization.

The Jamāʿat al-Muslimīn group, popularly named Jamaʿat al-Takfir wa-al-Hijrah, took Quṭb's teaching to extremes. Its leader, Shukrī Muṣṭafā, defined everyone outside his own group as infidels, whose lives and property were licit to believers. Members had to swear allegiance to *amīr*s, who rallied their followers to a secluded existence, until they were strong enough to conquer society for Islam. When the group kidnapped and murdered an Azharī cleric, Muṣṭafā was arrested and executed in 1978.

In the late 1970s, the militant theorist Muḥammad ʿAbd al-Salām Faraj formed Tanẓīm al-Jihād, which attacked not only Sadat but also the pliant *ʿulamāʾ* and the Muslim Brotherhood as a loyal opposition. Al-Jihād was a continuation of Muḥammad's Youth (the Islamic Liberation Organization), which originated in the military engineering college and had attempted a coup against Sadat in 1974. Where al-Takfir wa-al-Hijrah claimed that all fellow citizens were infidels, Tanẓīm al-Jihād held only the rulers guilty.

Sadat exercised a policy that alternated between outbidding and repression to manipulate the Islamist groups. In 1977, they condemned his visit to Jerusalem, and in 1979, Sadat attacked them and banned his erstwhile protégés, the Islamic student organizations. Ultimately, Sadat had unleashed forces he could not control, and after he signed his peace treaty with Israel in 1979 and cracked down even harder on internal dissenters, he was assassinated by disgruntled youths from Tanẓīm al-Jihād in 1981.

1981–2011: Mubarak–Outbidding, Control, and Co-optation. Succeeding Sadat in 1981, Mubarak began by cracking down harshly on radical Islamists such as those in Tanẓīm al-Jihād but releasing Sadat's more moderate Islamist political prisoners. While the Brotherhood remained illegal, members could participate in politics by forming alliances with liberal parties such as al-Wafd. They strengthened themselves among the middle class through professional syndicates and among the working class through charity. These networks of patronage were crucial during elections. By 1992 the Brotherhood had won elections in the Egyptian lawyers', doctors', engineers', dentists', and pharmacists' syndicates. Meanwhile, private voluntary associations flourished, in tandem with the enrichment of a devout middle class, and the pro-business attitude of the leadership. This "social Islam" was a barometer of the state's public service failures. Social processes, such as the return of migrant labor, also swelled the Brotherhood's ranks. They infiltrated the religious establishment, with associates among the *'ulamā'*.

Mubarak preserved his predecessor's policy of reinforcing the state's own religious infrastructure through sponsorship of Islamic initiatives and devoting more airtime to television preachers such as Muḥammad Mutawallī al-Sha'rāwī and Muḥammad al-Ghazālī, who focused on morality censorship. Soon, however, the regime came under pressure in parliament and outside, as Sadat's had, to implement *Sharī'ah*.

Mubarak was unable to control violent extremism in the 1990s. In jail in the 1980s, Tanẓīm al-Jihād had split into two factions: Abbūd al-Zumar and Āyman al-Ẓawāhirī had helped to reform al-Jihād, aiming at an Islamic coup, while a second faction, al-Jamā'at al-Islāmīyah, followed Omar Abdel Rahman, who preached the creation of Islamist zones outside the state's control, legitimizing attacks on those outside them. Keeping low profiles since their releases, these groups had built power bases by 1992, in, for example, Asyūṭ and El Minya, where unemployed graduates were stirred up against the Coptic middle class. An ensuing wave of violence included the murder of the author Faraj Foudah in 1992, the attempted murder of Nobel laureate Najīb Maḥfūẓ in 1994, and the massacre of sixty people, mostly tourists, at Luxor in 1997.

From 1993 to 2011, regime relations with the Brotherhood became confrontational. It had to adopt a more complex strategy against the militants and the Brothers, who had penetrated the religious establishment to which the regime looked for help. In 1993, a mediation committee composed of al-Sha'rāwī, al-Ghazālī, and Kishk proposed the conciliation and unity of all Islamists. Instead, the regime opted for a crackdown, stopping the formation of a joint front.

In 1996, the Center (al-Wasat) Party was formed by Brotherhood defector Abu al-'Ila Madi and the self-declared New Islamists. Al-Wasat was geared toward the educated middle class, championing democracy and civil liberties. The ruling National Democratic Party (NDP), tightening its grip on power during Mubarak's last ten years, ensured that al-Wasat remained illegal and took to imprisoning Brotherhood leaders—many of them powerful businessmen—every time political hegemony or economic interests were threatened.

Since the 2011 Egyptian Revolution. By all accounts, the popular protests that toppled Mubarak in January and February 2011 were secular; their slogans focused on social justice and dignity; they emphasized Muslim-Christian unity; and organizations calling for *Sharī'ah* rule were notably absent. Revolutionary activists came from coalitions such as Kifaya, which had united leftists, Nasserists, al-Wasat, and individual Muslim Brothers in campaigning against Mubarak's rule since the 2000s. The Brotherhood leadership would not endorse the protests and the Salafīs forbade them, but youth members broke away from each movement to participate.

However, with Mubarak gone and the political field opened, Islamist leaders swiftly formed political parties. Meanwhile, Egypt's ruling military council revived Sadat's policy of empowering the Islamist trend against secular left and liberal alternatives. It immediately released several jailed Islamists and appointed an Islamist legal scholar to head the March 2011 constitutional committee.

When some Salafīs were involved in violence against Christians, the generals invited Salafī preachers to form reconciliation committees. In return, they have received near consistent support from the Islamist bloc—which includes the newly licensed al-Wasat—in their repression of dissent since. By contrast, Ṣūfī organizations have positioned themselves alongside the secular left-liberal parties; for example, the Ṣūfī Liberation Party joined the liberal Egyptian Bloc coalition in summer 2011.

The Freedom and Justice Party. The Brotherhood's Freedom and Justice Party (FJP) was licensed in May 2011. It endorsed positions echoing protesters' demands in January 2011 for a civilian-led state and social justice, with the framework of the *Sharīʿah* added. However, as the rift grew between revolutionary youth coalitions and the military council into 2012, the FJP supported the latter, demanding that elections be held before the constitution was written and expressing disapproval of labor strikes and protest. Though institutionally separate, the FJP and Brotherhood work closely together, and all Brothers are banned from joining other parties. Some left in 2011 to form the Egyptian Current Party. Having pledged not to contest more than 50 percent of parliamentary seats, the FJP, through the Democratic Alliance electoral coalition, ultimately contested 70 percent in the November 2011 first electoral round. The FJP was able to secure parliamentary representation that outweighed the Brotherhood's role in the 2011 protests, winning 77 of the 156 parliamentary seats contested in the first round. In 2012, the Supreme Constitutional Court dissolved this parliament, citing constitutional violations.

The presidential elections of May and June 2012, which brought Muhammad Mursi to power, were similarly controversial, as was his support for a constitution drafted by an Islamist-dominated constituent assembly and put successfully to referendum despite widespread protests in December 2012. Mursi's rule has been characterized by polarization, with mounting criticism during 2013 that he is reproducing Mubarak-era policies of neoliberal authoritarianism.

Salafism and Al-Nūr Party. Salafism began in Egypt in the early 1900s through the Jamāʿat Anṣār al-Sunna (Advocates of the Sunna) organization. Not to be confused with ʿAbduh's Salafīyah, this movement received financial support and ideas from counterparts in Saudi Arabia. It attracted a lower-middle class membership. Under Mubarak, in a tacit pact with the regime, Egyptian Salafīs described obedience to the ruler as a religious obligation. In a turnaround after the revolution, leading Salafīs now argued that in a secular state, Muslims were obliged to participate rather than abstain. The Salafīs demand the establishment of an Islamic state based on *Sharīʿah*. They call for the independence of religious institutions, including al-Azhar, from the Ministry of Religious Endowments. The al-Nūr party was formed by the Daʿwah (Call) movement and licensed in June 2011. The smaller al-Aṣālah and al-Faḍīlah parties also formed, as well as the al-Bināʾ wa-al-Tanmīya party of al-Jamāʿat al-Islāmīyah. After testing various coalitions with liberals and Muslim Brothers, Salafī parties formed their own Islamic Alliance in October 2011, agreeing to share parliamentary lists. Al-Nūr dominated, winning thirty-three seats.

Conclusion. Islam has informed identity and ideology consistently in modern Egypt, always allied with some form of Egyptian and Arab nationalism. The 1970s marked a qualitative change, however, with the state engaging in its own revivalism, encouraging the assertion of religious identity in political and public life, and demoting secular nationalist alternatives which had been prevalent since the turn of the century, and the rule of Gamal Abdel Nasser.

The same period saw heterogeneous groups, shaped by variously permissive and repressive state environments, advocating political Islam. In the 1970s, the Muslim Brotherhood embraced "change from within," precipitating the defection of extremist groups, who violently opposed the entire order, and later the New Islamists, who opposed the regime.

These groups' collective pressure on the state has been reflected in Egypt's constitutional documents. Egypt's 1923 and 1954 constitutions had included articles affirming *Sharīʿah* as one of the main sources of legislation. In 1962, the Charter for National Action held freedom of religious belief "sacred," making no reference to state religion. By 1964, after demands by religious figures, a clause was inserted into Egypt's constitution declaring Islam the state religion. Sadat formalized this in the 1971 constitution, and in 1980, upgraded *Sharīʿah* to the main source of law, beginning efforts to update existing law accordingly. The 2012 constitution has further substantiated *Sharīʿah* with technical terms from traditional Sunnī jurisprudence. Post-Mubarak Egypt marks a rupture in which Islamists, alongside their secular nationalist competitors, now confront challenges of rule rather than repression, which will see the influence of Islam in Egyptian politics mediated in new ways.

[*See also* ʿAbduh, Muḥammad; Afghānī, Jamāl al-Dīn al-; Muslim Brotherhood; Rashīd Riḍā, Muḥammad; Salafī Movements; *and* Sharīʿah.]

BIBLIOGRAPHY

Al-Anani, Khalil, and Maszlee Malik. "Pious Way to Politics: The Rise of Political Salafism in Post-Mubarak Egypt," *Digest of Middle East Studies* 22, no. 1 (2013): 57–73.

Baker, Raymond William. *Islam Without Fear: Egypt and the New Islamists.* Cambridge, Mass.: Harvard University Press, 2003.

Baker, Raymond William. *Sadat and After: Struggles for Egypt's Political Soul.* London: I. B. Tauris, 1990.

Beinin, Joel and Joe Stork, eds. *Political Islam: Essays from Middle East Report.* London and New York: I. B. Tauris, 1997.

Eickelman, Dale F., and James Piscatori. *Muslim Politics.* Princeton, N.J.: Princeton University Press, 2004.

El-Ghobashy, Mona. "The Metamorphosis of the Muslim Brotherhood." *International Journal of Middle Eastern Studies* 37, no. 3 (2005): 371–395.

El-Hamalawy, Hossam. "Comrades and Brothers." *Middle East Report* 242, 2007.

Esposito, John L. *Islam and Politics.* 4th ed. Syracuse, N.Y.: Syracuse University Press, 1998.

Hopkins, Nicholas, ed. *Political and Social Protest in Egypt.* Cairo Papers in Social Science 29, nos. 2 and 3. Cairo: American University in Cairo Press, 2009.

Ismail, Salwa. *Rethinking Islamist Politics: Culture, the State and Islamism.* London: I. B. Tauris, 2006.

Kepel, Gilles. *Jihad: The Trail of Political Islam.* London, I. B. Tauris, 2006.

Mitchell, Richard P. *The Society of the Muslim Brothers.* London: Oxford University Press, 1969.

Said, Edward. *Culture and Imperialism.* New York: Alfred A. Knopf, 1993.

Shehata, Samer, and Joshua Stacher. "The Brotherhood Goes to Parliament." *Middle East Report* 240, no. 36 (2006).

Shorbagy, Manar. "The Egyptian Movement for Change—Kefaya: Redefining Politics in Egypt Public Culture." *Arab Studies Quarterly* 19, no. 1 (2007): 175–196.

Singerman, Diane. *Avenues of Participation: Family, Politics, and Networks in Urban Quarters of Cairo.* Princeton, N.J.: Princeton University Press, 1996.

Sullivan, Denis J., and Sana Abed-Kotob. *Islam in Contemporary Egypt: Civil Society vs. the State.* Boulder, Colo., and London: Lynne Rienner, 1999.

Tadros, Mariz. *The Muslim Brotherhood in Contemporary Egypt: Democracy Redefined or Confined?* London: Routledge, 2012.

Waterbury, John. *The Egypt of Nasser and Sadat: The Political Economy of Two Regimes.* Princeton, N.J.: Princeton University Press, 1983.

Zubaida, Sami. *Islam, the People and the State: Political Ideas and Movements in the Middle East.* London and New York: I. B. Tauris, 2009.

REEM ABOU-EL-FADL

ELECTIONS. Long considered conspicuously absent or purely procedural, elections have taken center stage in the Islamic world since 2009 and may prove pivotal in its political future. Elections have occurred with regularity in, among other places, Turkey and Iran and, in the Arab world, Egypt, Jordan, Lebanon, Morocco, Kuwait, and Yemen. Beyond the Middle East, they have formed part of the political landscape of Pakistan, Bangladesh, Indonesia, Malaysia, Nigeria, and Senegal, and Muslim minorities have been actively engaged in the electoral politics of India, Europe, North America, and Australia. Islamists—Muslims who are committed to political action to implement what they regard as an Islamic agenda—have routinely participated in many of these elections. Yet some doubts remain about their intentions and whether the elections themselves substantially contribute to democratization or are merely cosmetic.

Elections as Principle. The idea of elections came into its own in the Ottoman Empire of the nineteenth-century Tanzimat period. The principle of representation was first recognized in a *firmān* (edict) of January 1840 whereby administrative councils were established in the major districts of the empire. The majority of members were chosen by a complex and indirect process of selection in which non-Muslims were allowed a place. The Hatt-ı Hümayun (Imperial Edict, 1856) created an assembly of indirectly elected delegates within each *millet* (religious community), while elections were first formally recognized in the *vilâyet* (district) laws of 1864 and 1867. But the constitution of 1876 had a broader reach, establishing a chamber of deputies whose members were to be elected. Power remained mainly in the hands of the sultan, the *ʿulamāʾ* were steadfast in their opposition, and the electoral process did not live up to its promise, instead following the *vilâyet* precedent of corporate representation. Yet, with these developments, the notion of popular sovereignty began to penetrate Islamic political consciousness.

The electoral principle became further entrenched in the Muslim world as a result of the Constitutional Revolution in Iran (1906–1911). The momentum for a consultative assembly of some kind was unstoppable, though disagreement ensued as to whether this should be an Islamic or national (*millî*) assembly. An imperial rescript in August 1906 announced "the establishment of a *majlis* of elected representatives" of various social classes, which would provide advice to the shah's ministers and would devise reforms to be "enforced in accordance with the *Sharīʿah*." The electoral law was based on the Belgian constitution but adapted to local circumstances. The few hundred electors in each social category had to be literate males, Persian nationals, over twenty-five, and substantial property owners or engaged in a recognized trade or business. No mention was made of religious affiliation, although heretics, as well as women, minors, bankrupts, and convicts, were specifically excluded.

With the Tanzimat and the Constitutional Revolution the electoral principle thus put down early and partially formed roots, but differing views emerged and have solidified among Muslim intellectuals. One school of thought accepts that elections are fully consistent with Islamic principles. Khayr al-Dīn al-Tūnīsī (d. 1889), prime minister of Tunisia from 1873 to 1877, likened a parliament to *ahl al-ḥall wa-al-ʿaqd*, "those who loose and bind," and the Islamic scholar Muḥammad Rashīd Riḍā (1865–1935) wrote approvingly of the Turkish Grand National Assembly.

The idea that government rests upon the consent and participation of the people came into its own, however, only from the mid-twentieth century. Muhammad Asad (1900–1992) argued, for example, that, although the real source of sovereignty is the will of God, the community is subject to the control of the people. The *majlis al-shūrā* (consultative assembly) must be both representative of the entire community, men and women, and the result of free and general election based on universal suffrage.

A second, contrasting line of argument rejects any notion of popular sovereignty. The influential Egyptian thinker Sayyid Quṭb (1906–1966), in commenting on the Qur'ānic verse that says, "were you to follow the majority (*aktharīyah*) of those on earth, they will lead you away from the path of God" (6:116), inferred that majoritarianism and popular opinion were suspect. In Algeria, one leader of the Jabhat al-Inqādh al-Islāmī (Islamic Salvation Front), ʿAlī Bel Ḥajj (b. 1954), has similarly argued that popular sovereignty leads to the rule of scoundrels, is the antithesis of God's authority, and undermines the Islamic way of life. This argument is associated most strongly with contemporary Salafī movements, which represent small but vociferous constituencies throughout the Muslim world.

Straddling these lines of thought is Abū al-Aʿlā al-Mawdūdī (1903–1979), founder of the Jamāʿat-i Islāmī in South Asia, who argued that elections are acceptable but must avoid the distortions of Western parliamentary systems. Although he felt that the number of votes could not be equated with what is true or right, he accepted majority voting in an advisory body as a practical necessity. But, because the source of legislative authority, *shūrā* (consultation), is itself based on *ijtihād* (independent judgment), it must be limited to a select few who are well-versed in the appropriate subjects.

Beyond the question of adopting or rejecting liberal democratic values through electoral processes, devout Muslims—and Islamist organizations in particular—often choose to participate in elections as a form of *daʿwah* (proselytizing) even, and some argue especially, when the elections are known to be fraudulent or unwinnable. Instead of fighting for electoral victory or influence over domestic policy, Islamist organizations set long-term goals to maximize programmatic appeal and expand constituencies by consistently contesting elections, thereby granting them space in otherwise controlled public spheres to disseminate their sociopolitical platforms and values.

The case of Egypt's Ikhwān al-Muslimūn (Muslim Brotherhood) under Hosni Mubarak's regime exemplifies this principle of political *daʿwah* and illustrates its benefits. In spite of known ballot stuffing, vote-buying, and regime intimidation against its supporters, the Brotherhood ran in both parliamentary elections during Mubarak's presidency (2005, 2010), knowing that each election represented an opportunity to spread its message, broaden its support base, and strengthen its political organization. Thus, after years of political *daʿwah*, the Brotherhood emerged from the 25 January 2011 uprising as the only organization in post-Mubarak Egypt with any serious electoral experience and capacity for mobilization, thereby enabling its offshoot political party, Ḥizb al-Ḥurriya Wa-al-ʿAdala (Freedom and Justice Party), to win 47 percent of the seats in the 2011–2012 parliamentary election.

Elections as Process. Though contested, the vocabulary of participation and representation has gradually become part of modern Muslim political discourse. There is less agreement, however, as to how to interpret the unfolding practice. For example, some once saw hopeful signs in the experience of Iran—eight parliamentary and nine presidential elections since the revolution of 1978–1979. However, the experience of the June 2009 presidential election, widely regarded as fraudulent both in and outside Iran, and the Green Movement uprising it inspired—with its slogan, "Where is My Vote?"—erased whatever tenuous claim the Islamic Republic had to electoral legitimacy. Some argue that examples from the Iranian experience and the many other elections throughout the Muslim world suggest that elections in the majority of Muslim states are nothing more than procedural, contrived, and, in the end, counterproductive.

One form of this argument concerns governments—monarchies and semi-authoritarian states in particular, but also fledgling post-authoritarian democracies. There is concern that external and some internal pressures may force governments to stage elections, while the hope of controlling the result compels them to manipulate electoral rules. In either case, elections may transform the political system only superficially and may reinforce authoritarianism. This has been argued of the limited elections in Gulf societies such as Saudi Arabia (2005), Bahrain (2006), and Qatar (2007), as well as Mubarak's Egypt (2005, 2010) and Musharraf's Pakistan (2008), among others.

Another form of this argument concerns Islamists, who are also regarded as calculating—"one person, one vote, one time"—intending through the ballot box to acquire the means by which to render democratic development impossible. Some see the electoral victories by Ḥamās in Gaza (2006), An-Nahda in Tunisia (2011), and the Muslim Brotherhood's Freedom and Justice Party in Egypt (2012) as worrisome cases in this regard; others, however, see great potential for democratization and institutional development in states now governed by majority or coalition Islamist parliaments.

Indeed, elections may prove transformative, routinizing democratic procedures and socializing participants into accepting democratic values, snaring in their logic even reluctant but tactical Islamists. Elections may formalize existing informal networks, in effect bringing new actors into the game, and acquaint them with the rules of intergroup bargaining. The majority rule, since 2001, of the Adalet ve Kalkınma Partisi (Justice and Development Party) in Turkey is perhaps the strongest example of this moderating and conciliating imperative, with Ḥizbullāh's two decades of electoral and parliamentary participation in Lebanon (since 1992) offering another.

Although it remains unclear whether elections will lead to the democratization of Muslim societies, they now appear firmly part of the political landscape in the twenty-first century. The political changes inaugurated by Iran's Green Movement and the so-called Arab Spring forced surviving semi-authoritarian and monarchical regimes to reevaluate their approaches to increased calls for democratization from among their publics: cosmetic changes and fraudulent, purely procedural elections have so far proven incapable of placating largely young and restive populations that monitor and share political information with all the tools afforded them by the digital age.

Democratic change—however Muslim societies choose to shape it—appears to be an inescapable fact, and popular elections are one of its increasingly prominent fixtures. To the extent that they will be seen as unavoidably or naturally so, elections are likely to become an increasingly useful political instrument for modern Islam.

[*See also* Arab Spring; Constitutional Revolution; Democracy; Ḥamās; Islamism; Majlis; Mawdūdī, Sayyid Abū al-Aʿlā; Muslim Brotherhood; Rashīd Riḍā, Muḥammad; Secularism; *and* Tanzimat.]

BIBLIOGRAPHY

Brown, Nathan J. *When Victory is Not an Option: Islamist Movements in Arab Politics*. Ithaca, N.Y.: Cornell University Press, 2012.

Brumberg, Daniel. "The Trap of Liberalized Autocracy." *Journal of Democracy* 13, no. 4 (October 2002): 56–68.

Hamdy, Iman A., ed. *Elections in the Middle East: What Do They Mean?* Cairo and New York: American University in Cairo Press, 2004.

Hashemi, Nader, and Danny Postel, eds. *The People Reloaded: The Green Movement and the Struggle for Iran's Future*. New York: Melville House, 2011.

Hefner, Robert W. *Civil Islam: Muslims and Democratization in Indonesia*. Princeton, N.J.: Princeton University Press, 2000.

Lewis, Bernard. "Islam and Liberal Democracy: A Historical Overview." *Journal of Democracy* 7, no. 2 (1996): 52–63.

Lust, Ellen. "Voting for Change: The Pitfalls and Possibilities of First Elections in Arab Transitions." *Brookings Doha Center-Stanford Project on Arab Transitions Paper Series* 2 (2012): 1–12.

Piscatori, James. *Islam, Islamists, and the Electoral Principle in the Middle East*. Leiden, Netherlands: Isim, 2000.

Sadiki, Larbi. *Rethinking Arab Democratization: Elections Without Democracy*. Oxford: Oxford University Press, 2009.

Shehata, Samer S. "Political *Daʿwa*: Understanding the Muslim Brotherhood's Participation in Semi-Authoritarian Elections." In *Islamist Politics in the Middle East: Movements and Change*, edited by Samer S. Shehata. New York: Routledge, 2012.

JAMES PISCATORI
Updated by DOUGLAS H. GARRISON

ELIJAH MUHAMMAD. *See* Nation of Islam.

EQUALITY. In one of his last speeches, the Prophet Muḥammad is reported to have said, "All of you are from Adam, and Adam is created from dust. An Arab is not superior to a non-Arab, nor a non-Arab to an Arab. A white person is not superior to a black person, nor a black person to a white person, except by piety and good deeds."

Equality (*musawah*, in modern Arabic) as a modern notion was not discussed as such in early and medieval Islamic literature, but the Prophet's statement was established as part of the Islamic Weltanschauung. However, despite the "modernist" Muslim interpretation of it, this statement, addressed to a predominantly Muslim audience, does not necessarily eliminate all forms of inequality among individuals as citizens of the Muslim state. The Qurʾān itself distinguishes clearly between people according to the purity of their creed, knowledge, and deeds (cf. 32:18, 39:9, and 57:10). In practice, social stratification based on birth, lineage, wealth, profession, religion, gender, and knowledge always existed in medieval (and modern) Muslim societies. This stratification, at times influenced by Hellenistic and Persian cultures, was not necessarily associated with a denial of the essentially equal human nature of all individuals as God's creatures and servants, but it had implications, not necessarily sanctioned by Islam itself, with regard to the duties, rights, and social status of individuals as members in the community and citizens of the Muslim state.

This variation in the textual evidence relevant to the issue of equality and the historical interpretations and practices of medieval Muslim societies points to the complexity of the issue of equality in Islam. Therefore, it is now one the most pressing and contentious issues in most Muslim societies. But perhaps because of the clear position of Islam against racial and ethnic discrimination, religious and gender (in)equality in modern Muslim societies receive more attention from Muslim scholars than other forms of inequality. When dealing with these issues, these scholars seek to disentangle the "genuine" teachings of Islam from the historical views and practices of Muslim societies.

Religious Equality. Islam recognizes other monotheistic religions, notably Judaism and Christianity. Early and medieval Muslim scholars agreed that Jews and Christians living in Muslim states are protected people, *dhimmīs*. As such, they are exempt from fighting in the Muslim armies, but are required to pay a certain tax to the Muslim state in return. Although these religious minorities enjoyed a great deal of tolerance in Muslim states, they were not typically regarded as equal to the Muslim populations. For example, in juridical discussions, Muslim jurists debated whether non-Muslim citizens of Muslim states were qualified to hold public offices or serve as witnesses in the courts of law. They also debated whether a Muslim should be killed in retaliation for murdering a non-Muslim.

Perhaps the only one of these issues that Muslim jurists agreed on was that non-Muslims cannot hold the position of caliph, a position that has a religious as well as a political nature and functions, and do not therefore participate in electing him. Other than that, some jurists held that non-Muslims qualified as witnesses, and that they must be protected by the Muslim state, such that a Muslim who kills a protected non-Muslim must be killed in retaliation (although they did not necessarily agree that this retaliation was due to the equality of the killer and the victim). Other scholars did not see non-Muslims qua non-Muslims as qualified to give testimony, and they rejected killing a Muslim for a non-Muslim. Others went as far as suggesting that non-Muslims should wear specific clothes that distinguished them, or that they were to be forbidden from displaying their religious symbols or celebrating their religious occasions in public. The extent to which these views were reflective of the reality when they were expressed is hard to tell. However, they may well indicate that the opportunities that were made available to non-Muslims simply stirred the ire and jealousy of the Muslim scholars and populations.

Gender Equality. The Qurʾān states that men and women are created from one soul (4:1), a statement that was invariably understood to indicate that men and women are equal in humanity. Muslim women are required to observe almost the same religious duties as men, and are generally subject to the same punishments. They share inheritance with men (although their shares are not always equal) and can have their own property and money. On the other hand, the Qurʾān grants authority to men over women, and in a certain context it considers the testimony of two women equal to that of one man. Relying on some statements attributed to the Prophet Muḥammad, medieval Muslim scholars agreed that women could not hold the position of caliph, serve as judges, or lead the congregational prayers in which men participate.

The historical practices of medieval Muslim societies were shaped by differing views inferred from these pieces of textual evidence, as well as by the status of women in their cultures. For example, some women, known for their piety and religious knowledge, taught men as well as women. While this does not necessarily prove that women in general were regarded as equal to men, it does indicate that women were able, both in theory and in practice, to be superior to men even in fields that men traditionally dominated, such as scholarship. At the same time, it is not uncommon to find reference to women as slaves to their male guardians. At any rate, there is hardly any evidence that gender equality was an issue that medieval scholars felt the need to discuss.

Modernist Muslim Discourse. Starting from the nineteenth century, the issue of equality has been the subject of extensive discussions among modernist Muslim scholars, Sunnī and Shīʿī alike. The trend has been to insist that Islam is essentially egalitarian, and that egalitarianism reflects the spirit of its teachings. To demonstrate this, these scholars employ many strategies.

One strategy is appealing to what they regard as the broad principles of Islam. For example, they maintain that discrimination against religious minorities or women is inconsistent with "justice," a central notion in Islam. To ensure the perpetuation of the original Islamic disposition to equality and justice, Islamic teachings must be regularly revised to take into consideration new social realities and understanding of justice.

Another strategy is contextualizing historical Muslim views and practices, some of which were instigated by specific historical circumstances. For example, discriminatory views and practices prejudicial against non-Muslims were often the product of times when Muslims were extraordinarily suspicious of non-Muslims for alleged collaboration with foreign aggressors. The Qurʾānic distinction between the weight of the testimony of men and women must be understood against the backdrop of the Arab culture at that time, where women did not have much expertise in the kinds of dealings that the Qurʾān addresses. Other restrictions on women's freedom were the product of medieval cultures and prevalent misogynistic reading of the foundational texts of Islam. A third strategy is to emphasize specific historical incidents (and, naturally, to deemphasize others). The first thing that the Prophet Muḥammad did when he established his "state" was to write a document (generally known now as the Constitution of Medina) in which he considered all Muslims and non-Muslims in Medina citizens of the new state who enjoyed equal rights and bore the same responsibilities. Other reports show women participating actively in public life in early Islam, suggesting that they were not regarded as unequal citizens of the state. It is this kind of historical practice, modernist Muslim scholars maintain, that reflects the true nature of Islam and its egalitarian ethos.

This discourse is regularly criticized by some "traditional' and "conservative" religious scholars, who feel that Islam is being reconfigured to match "alien" values. Further, the view that the teachings and practices of Islam must be historically contextualized remains unpopular among many of them. In their view, this approach requires a total break with how Muslims have traditionally regarded their scripture and believed in the immutability of its teachings, some of which may appear unfair to human understanding but serve purposes that God may not have revealed to believers.

Equality in Modern Muslim Countries. Modern Muslim states have predominantly adopted constitutions that grant full legal, political, social, and economic equality to all citizens regardless of their faith, gender, etc. However, the headship of these states remains an exception in many Muslim countries where the head of state must be Muslim. In 1990, the Organization of the Islamic Conference promulgated the Cairo Declaration of Human Rights in Islam, the first article of which declares, "All men are equal in terms of basic human dignity and basic obligations and responsibilities, without any discrimination on the grounds of race, color, language, sex, religious belief, political affiliation, social status or other considerations." This strong statement does not truly reflect the social and political reality in most Muslim countries, where the degree of gender equality, for example, varies depending on the local cultures, female literacy, the struggle between conservative and modernist readings of Islam and power relationships of their proponents, as well as foreign pressures on Muslim countries. Whereas women in some Muslim countries can rise to the highest ranks in all branches of the government, in other Muslim countries, such as Saudi Arabia, they hardly participate in political life. Discrimination against religious minorities—which can be Muslim religious minorities, such as the Sunnīs in Iran and the Shīʿīs in the Arab countries of the Persian Gulf—varies from one country to another and is motivated by religious as well as political considerations.

BIBLIOGRAPHY

Friedmann, Yohanan. *Tolerance and Coercion in Islam: Interfaith Relations in the Muslim Tradition*. Cambridge, U.K.: Cambridge University Press, 2003.

Hunter, Shireen T., and Vartan Gregorian. *Reformist Voices of Islam: Mediating Islam and Modernity*. Armonk, N.Y.: M. E. Sharpe, 2009.
Kamali, Mohammad Hashim. *Freedom, Equality and Justice in Islam*. Cambridge, U.K.: The Islamic Texts Society, 2002.
Kamrava, Mehran, ed. *The New Voices of Islam: Reforming Politics and Modernity, A Reader*. London: I. B. Tauris, 2009.
Marlow, Louise. *Hierarchy and Egalitarianism in Islamic Thought*. Cambridge, U.K.: Cambridge University Press, 1992.

AMR OSMAN

ERBAKAN, NECMETTIN. A Turkish political leader who briefly served as Turkey's first Islamist prime minister, Necmettin Erbakan (1926–2011) was a native of the Black Sea port of Sinop and was affectionately known as "Hodja" (teacher). Erbakan spent his childhood in provincial cities where his father, Mehmet Sabri Erbakan, came from the prestigious Kazanoğlu clan from Cilicia and served as one of the last Islamic judges of the Ottoman Empire, whose system of religious courts was replaced by a secular legal code after the founding of modern Turkey by Mustafa Kemal Atatürk in 1923. The future Hodja attended primary school in Trabzon and high school at the internationally renowned Istanbul Lisesi (Lycée Français), and completed his higher education at the Istanbul Technical University in 1948, where he remained for his doctoral studies, before moving to Germany. At the Rhenish-Westphalian Technical University of Aachen, Erbakan earned a doctorate, which allowed him to work in the motor industry for Humboldt Deutz, specializing in diesel engine design, as well as serving as chief engineer on the team that designed the German Leopard tanks for the Wehrmacht. His German was fluent and lyrical. Upon his return to Turkey, Erbakan embarked on an academic career at Istanbul Technical University, where he was promoted to full professor in 1965. While teaching, Erbakan played a key role in the early development of the Turkish motor industry at the Gümüş Motor Factory, which produced diesel engines; he served as the factory director between 1956 and 1963 and assumed a leadership position to mobilize workers. It was at this time that his political career gelled, especially after he was elected general secretary of the Union of Chambers.

In 1969, Erbakan left his academic career when he was elected to the Grand National Assembly as an independent candidate from Konya, as he planted the seeds of the country's Islamist movement. A year later Erbakan founded the Millî Nizam Partisi (MNP, National Order Party). The Millî Nizam was a neo-Islamist party that called for a spiritual reawakening as well as a return to religious values combined with technical development programs. This platform defied the secular consensus in the country and while the party survived several closures, it was banned from political activity by the Constitutional Court in 1972, allegedly for its violation of legislation forbidding the use of religion for political purposes. The party literally disappeared in the 1971 military coup before reemerging in 1973 as the Millî Selamet Partisi (MSP, National Salvation Party), with Erbakan as its leader. The National Salvation Party program, much like the Millî Nizam Partisi's, was critical of the republican course of development, which it saw as a failed effort to industrialize and a disastrous project that destroyed national values in the name of Westernization. The Millî Selamet ideology, called the Milli Görüş (National View), emphasized rapid industrialization accompanied by moral and spiritual reconstruction.

Under Erbakan's leadership the Millî Selamet participated in three coalition governments between 1973 and 1978, with Erbakan as deputy prime minister in all three, acting more like a kingmaker. In fact, with a significant electoral victory in 1973—winning forty-eight seats—Erbakan served in the coalition government led by the Republican People's Party of Prime Minister Bülent Ecevit. The party was outlawed after the 1980 coup d'état, along with all the other parties of the pre-1980 period. Erbakan and the leaders of the other parties were banned from political activity. With the return to civilian politics in 1983, the defunct Millî Selamet was replaced by the Refâh Partisi (RP, Welfare Party), with Erbakan as its de facto leader, a position that he kept as its rightful leader after the 1990 referendum that lifted the earlier ban.

The Refâh ideology developed into a criticism of capitalism as a Zionist plot and called for regional cooperation among Muslim countries. A fiercely anti-Western leader who decried the European Union as a "Zionist Christian" club, Erbakan railed against usury and the free market. In domestic politics, moreover, he argued for a change of the legal system along confessional lines, an argument that later furnished the major rationale for the closure of the party by the constitutional court even if Erbakan disavowed all forms of violence and, at least on this front distinguished his party from other Islamist groups like the Tarikat Ṣūfī Islamic fraternities. Refâh supported what it called the "Just Order" in economic policy, on the basis of which neighborhood committees would decide on the moral credibility of investors and manufacturers, and the state would become the sole buyer of products. Its educational policy rested on giving parents the right to educate their children according to their own beliefs and values rather than through the centralized secular system of education.

Thanks to its effective grassroots organization in poor neighborhoods—it was known for delivering services and goods to poor families—Refâh gained the support of the lower middle classes and the poor, especially in large cities. It had an economic network of what Erbakan called the "Anatolian tigers," pious businessmen in Anatolian cities who used this economic network to promote upward social mobility, even if his success among the downtrodden led one Turkish general to call him "a pimp." Despite such distasteful comments generously bestowed by some of Erbakan's opponents, Refâh policies carried the party to power, initially in municipal governments, and finally in a coalition government; Erbakan became prime minister in 1996 when the party received the highest percentage of votes (21.4) in the 1995 elections. However, increased polarization between the secularists and Islamists meant that the party could not hold its majority long, and Erbakan had to resign from his post in 1997 after the so-called "post-modern military coup." Clearly, his mistake was to challenge the secular, pro-Western foundations of modern Turkey and to invest heavily in ties with other Muslim countries. Westernized military officers concluded that Refâh's rural and religious styles were incompatible with Turkey, and the party was banned for violating the principle of secularism in the constitution. Prohibited by the military-dominated Constitutional Court in 1998, the epochal decision to shut down the Islamist party was endorsed by the European Court of Human Rights in 2001, as Erbakan himself was sentenced to one year in prison for violating Article 312 of the Criminal Code that forbade "provoking hatred among citizens based on religious or ethnic differences"; he was banned from political activity for five years.

Erbakan was an active figure behind Recai Kutan's Fazilet Partisi (FP, Virtue Party) that was established in 1997 as an alternative to the defunct Refâh. When Fazilet was also closed by the Constitutional Court in 2001, the Milli Görüş movement split, with the so-called reformers under the leadership of Recep Tayyip Erdoğan (the influential ex-mayor of Istanbul from Refâh), establishing the Adalet ve Kalkınma Partisi (AKP, Justice and Development Party). Erdoğan entered the 2002 elections on a platform of liberal democratic reforms and commitment to European Union membership and emerged with 34.2 percent of the votes as he offered a milder, less anti-Western brand of Islamic politics. This carried Erdoğan to power as the prime minister of a single-party government. The old Erbakan line was organized under Saadet Partisi (SP, Felicity Party) but was effectively marginalized by Erdoğan. Saadet elected Recai Kutan as party leader although Erbakan continued to have great influence as spiritual guide and adviser, still sporting a suit and tie (usually Versace). Saadet received a meager 2.4 percent of the votes in the 2002 elections and while Erbakan was an independent candidate from Konya in 2002, he was prevented from entering the elections by the electoral commission because of his earlier sentence under Article 312. In 2007, he was tried on embezzlement charges in what came to be known as the Missing Trillion case in which cash reserves ordered to be seized after Refâh was closed down went missing. Sentenced to two years and four months, Erbakan was found guilty of "forgery of personal documents," a form of "corruption" that necessitated his imprisonment, although the sentence was commuted to house arrest due to his age. President Abdullah Gül, one of his early protégés and a long-time Erbakan foreign-policy adviser, pardoned him on health grounds. He became a candidate for Saadet in the July 2007 elections, but was once more turned down by the Electoral Commission because of his criminal record. Necmettin Erbakan died in Ankara on 27 February 2011. Ironically, and despite the military's established loathing of his ideas and political positions, the top brass were among thousands of Turks at his funeral on 1 March 2011, poignantly, a day after the coup's fourteenth anniversary. The chief of the general staff hailed Erbakan's "great services to [Turkey] as a valued man of science and politics."

Necmettin Erbakan contributed much to the legitimation of Islamist politics in a secular state and the formulation of Islamist political programs within the limits of parliamentary democracy. He was the major influence in the formulation of the Milli Görüş ideology in Turkey and published books and pamphlets to explain the party's views on development, cultural issues, the educational system, foreign policy, and social welfare. Erbakan's Milli Görüş movement gained supporters among Turkish workers in Europe as the National View organizations in various European countries became influential in promoting political Islamism among diaspora Turks. Prime Minister Recep Tayyip Erdoğan, Erbakan's former pupil who became prime minister, declared that his master "was a scientist who devoted his life to learning [and who would be] remembered with gratitude," as the father of political Islamism in contemporary Turkey.

[*See also* Adalet ve Kalkinma Partisi; *and* Refâh Partisi.]

BIBLIOGRAPHY

Alkan, Türker. "The National Salvation Party in Turkey." In *Islam and Politics in the Modern Middle East*, edited by Metin Heper and Raphael Israeli, pp. 79–102. London and Sydney: Croom Helm, 1984.

Cizre, Ümit, ed. *Secular and Islamic Politics in Turkey: The Making of the Justice and Development Party*. London: Routledge, 2007.

Gülalp, Haldun. "Globalization and Political Islam: The Social Bases of Turkey's Welfare Party." *International Journal of Middle East Studies* 33 (2001): 433–448.

Gülalp, Haldun. "Political Islam in Turkey: The Rise and Fall of the Refah Party." *The Muslim World* (January 1999): 22–41.

Gülalp, Haldun. "The Poverty of Democracy in Turkey: The Refah Party Episode." *New Perspectives on Turkey* 21 (Fall 1999): 35–59.

Hale, William, and Ergun Ozbudun. *Islamism, Democracy and Liberalism in Turkey: The Case of the AKP.* London: Routledge, 2009.

Kaylan, Muammer. *The Kemalists: Islamic Revival and the Fate of Secular Turkey.* Amherst, N.Y.: Prometheus Books, 2005.

Öniş, Ziya. "The Political Economy of Islamic Resurgence in Turkey: The Rise of the Welfare Party in Perspective." *Third World Quarterly* 18, no. 4 (1997): 743–766.

Sarıbay, Ali Yaşar. *Türkiye'de modernleşme, din ve parti politikası: MSP Örnek Olayı.* Istanbul: Alan Yayıncılık, 1985.

Toprak, Binnaz. "Politicization of Islam in a Secular State: the National Salvation Party in Turkey." In *From Nationalism to Revolutionary Islam*, edited by Said Arjomand, pp. 119–133. London: MacMillan, 1984.

White, Jenny B. *Islamist Mobilization in Turkey: A Study in Vernacular Politics.* Seattle and London: University of Washington Press, 2002.

Yavuz, M. Hakan. *Islamic Political Identity in Turkey.* New York: Oxford University Press, 2005.

Yavuz, M. Hakan, ed. *The Emergence of a New Turkey: Democracy and the AK Parti.* Salt Lake City: University of Utah Press, 2006.

BINNAZ TOPRAK
Updated by JOSEPH A. KÉCHICHIAN

ESCHATOLOGY. *See* Religious Beliefs.

ETHIOPIA. Since antiquity, the region of the Horn of Africa, stretching south of Egypt and east of the Nile Valley, has been known as Ethiopia or Abyssinia. The name "Ethiopia" was derived from the Greek term for the biblical "land of Cush." Abyssinia (al-Ḥabashah in Arabic) was named for the Ḥabashah, one of the peoples that migrated to Africa from Arabia, bringing with them Semitic languages and urban culture. The local state that consequently developed, with the town of Aksum as its capital, was one of the first political entities to adopt Christianity in 333–334 C.E. It persisted officially as a Christian kingdom until Emperor Haile Selassie was deposed by military revolutionaries in 1974. With the rise of Islam in the seventh century, the country was perceived as a "Christian island," an image that began to fade only in the 1990s. From an Islamic historical point of view, Ethiopia was relevant both as a Christian neighbor and as the home of substantial Islamic communities.

Formative Concepts. The Christian empire of Ethiopia was Islam's first foreign-relations case. The "first *hijrah*" to Aksumite Ethiopia was a formative episode that left enduring and significant legacies for later Muslims. It had two parts. First, in 615–616 C.E., the Prophet told the tiny Islamic community of the Ṣaḥābah (companions), then still persecuted in Mecca, to seek asylum with the righteous Christian ruler of Ethiopia, the *najāshi* (*negus*) Ashama (*negus* is the Ethiopian word for "king"). By all Islamic accounts (there was no mention of the episode in Ethiopian sources), nearly all members of the community fled to Christian Ethiopia and were given refuge by its king. The *najāshi* himself then corresponded with the Prophet and helped him in various ways. Gratitude to the benevolent neighbor was eternalized in the *ḥadīth*, "Leave the Ethiopians alone as long as they leave you alone." For many, this meant that Christian Ethiopia should be tolerated and exempted from *jihād*, and that Muslims could live under a righteous non-Islamic government. Thus, the concept of Ethiopia remained relevant in internal Islamic debates on interpretations of Islam and politics.

The second part of the same episode gave rise to a different approach. In 628 CE, the Prophet, already established in Medina, initiated his international diplomacy, calling on rulers he knew to accept his Islamic mission. The only positive response came from his friend the *najāshi*, but the king's generals and priests revolted against him, and he died in isolation two years later. Thus, in the eyes of many, Ethiopia had joined the land of

Islam, and her defiant existence as a Christian state was tantamount to *irtad* (apostasy). For them, the Ethiopian case represented the first defeat of Islam—the "first Spain"—and their interpretation of the initial story was expressed in the slogan *Islām al-najāshi* (Islam of the *negus*), meaning that a Muslim king should be reinstalled over Ethiopia. Whenever Ethiopia appeared on the agenda of Muslims, their debates revolved around the dichotomous meanings of this formative chapter. This polarization in the concepts of the Ethiopian Christian "other" was reinforced by various contradictory traditions, from praise for the purity, kindness, tolerance, and bravery of the Ethiopians, to their ultimate demonization as enemies destined to destroy the Kaʿbah at the end of time.

After the Prophet. Relations between Ethiopia and the major Islamic empires and countries were influenced primarily by the fact that the Christian state managed to retain its independence. No Middle Eastern power successfully invaded Ethiopia, and Egypt in particular was also restrained by the fact that Ethiopia was the source of most of the Nile's waters. Moreover, independent Ethiopia remained influential at crucial junctures of Islamic and Middle Eastern history: the above-mentioned rise of the Prophet, the rise of Egyptian nationalism in the last quarter of the nineteenth century (also stimulated by the Egyptian defeat by the Ethiopians in 1876), and the emergence of modern pan-Arabism in the 1930s (also indirectly energized by the crisis stemming from Mussolini's conquest of Ethiopia in 1935–1936).

More direct and continuous were relations between Ethiopia's Christian ruling establishments and the various Islamic communities in Ethiopia and the Horn of Africa. The local Muslims—to whom the Arabic terms *ḥabasha* or *aḥbāsh* or *ḥubshān* have also been applied by Muslims of the Middle East—were never linguistically or politically united. Where the empire was Christian, Islam was adopted mainly by those who tried to maintain a peripheral, centrifugal identity. Islam began to spread in Ethiopia in the days of the *ṣaḥāba* but remained only remotely connected to the major Islamic empires or to Arabic language and culture. As of the ninth century, Islam in the Horn, Sunnī Orthodox, yet practiced mainly in popular forms, helped to build local emirates in the coastal zones and the southern plateau, among Somali, Afar, Sidama, Oromo, Gurage, and other ethnic groups. Among the highlanders of central and northern Ethiopia, Islam was adopted mostly by traders and immigrants. Muslim speakers of Amharic or Tigrinya—the languages of the mostly Christian center and north—were called *Jabartīs* (there are various traditions about the initial source of this term). Traders and slavers from Arabia who settled on the coast also helped to spread Islam, and in the interior, the town of Harar emerged as the most important Islamic urban center, beginning in the twelfth century.

Until the sixteenth century, Christian Ethiopia, flourishing under the Solomonian dynasty (1270–1529), enjoyed superiority, and taxed and raided the various Islamic entities. However, inspired and aided by the rising Ottomans and by Arabian scholars, the local Harari *amīr*, Aḥmad ibn Ibrāhīm al-Ghāzī, nicknamed Gragn (in Amharic *grañň*, left-handed), unified the various Islamic peoples and conquered Ethiopia, occupying the country between 1529 and 1543. Ethiopian sources report that nine out of ten Ethiopian Christians were forced to adopt Islam and nearly all churches and monasteries were destroyed. Portuguese military reinforcements helped the Ethiopians regaining independence, but the traumatic memory of the episode remained alive among Christians. Some of the Oromo tribes took advantage of the chaos in the sixteenth century: they penetrated the core

Christian highlands and, in the seventeenth century, adopted Islam to further solidify their local independence.

The Modern Era. Modern Ethiopian rulers worked to revive and centralize the political system by extending Christian superiority. Emperor Tewodros II (r. 1855–1868) viewed Muslims in Ethiopia and abroad as enemies, and Emperor Yohannes IV (r. 1872–1889) was said to have forced nearly half a million Oromo Muslims to adopt Christianity. Emperor Menelik II (r. 1889–1913) conquered southern Ethiopia and imposed his Christian government on Oromo Muslims and other Islamic peoples, including the city of Harar (occupied in 1887). The late-nineteenth-century annexation of what became Ethiopia's southern regions eroded the traditional Christian majority and significantly enlarged the Islamic populations. Menelik was succeeded by his grandson, Lij Iyasu (r. 1913–1916), son of a Muslim Oromo chief, who gambled on Ottoman victory during World War I, flirted with Islam, was accused of converting to it, and was therefore deposed in 1916 by a group of Christian warlords led by future emperor Haile Selassie (r. 1930–1974).

At a time when Ethiopia's Islamic communities were thus expanding, various Islamic influences were radiating from the greater Arab world through immigrating scholars and traders. In general, there were three movements of Islamic revival which presented their influence in Ethiopia at that time. Two were movements of militant, political Islam: Wahhābīyah, from Saudi Arabia, and Mahdīyah, from the Sudan. Their messages, however, with minor exceptions, were mostly rejected. Far more influential were the messages of various Ṣūfī movements, with their rather apolitical culture and more flexible acceptance of local traditions and customs. The pragmatic nature of Ethiopia's Islam enabled coexistence with the political nature of Ethiopian Christianity.

Following the demise of Lij Iyasu and the rise of Haile Selassie, Ethiopian Christian supremacy was revived. Discrimination against Muslims reached its peak with the abolishment in 1934 of the last Islamic autonomous entity in the emirate of Jimma. The hegemony of Christians was however interrupted during Italian occupation between 1936 and 1941, when Mussolini, presenting himself in the Middle East as "the champion of Islam" reenacted autonomy for Muslim regions, authorized the building of mosques (hitherto forbidden in urban centers), and encouraged the study of Arabic. Following the return of Haile Selassie's government in 1941, Islamic communities were again marginalized. The official end to Christian hegemony came with the military regime of Mangistu Haile Mariam (1974–1991), when Islam was proclaimed one of the state religions. And even though, under his communist-oriented government, all religions were in practice marginalized, Muslims, as traders, suffered more than others from the communist economy. They were further persecuted as the pro-Soviet Mangistu pursued hostilities with Somalia, Egypt, Saudi Arabia, and Sudan. At the same time, an Eritrean separatist movement, which in the 1960s had been led by pan-Arab Muslims, came under the domination of Christian Eritreans who would win independence for Eritrea following the collapse of Mangistu's regime in 1991.

The new Ethiopia that emerged in 1991, when local Tigreans took over the government from the Amhara, was decentralized. A federation of nine "ethnic" states, a relatively free economy, elements of cultural openness, and renewed relations with most Middle Eastern countries created new horizons for local Islam. Muslims, said to account for about half of the total population (though an official census in 1994, believed to be distorted, put their share at 32.8 percent), took advantage of the new market economy, the somewhat more open political competition, and the growing religious permissiveness. Thousands of mosques and Islamic schools have been built; Islamic literature is published locally or imported from abroad. Most significantly, the Arabic language is being adopted rapidly by the young and is creating a new sense of supra-ethnic unity among the various Islamic communities. All other institutions and legacies of orthodox Islam, of the various judicial schools and ideological trends, are quickly blending into local popular Islamic traditions. The reawakening of Islam in Ethiopia is already presenting local Muslims with the ancient dilemma: whether to accept an Ethiopia led by Christian elites (but now in a more "righteous" way) and help to create a bridge between Ethiopia and the greater world; or to work with Islamic radicals from abroad for the fulfillment of *Islām al-najāshi*, and try to gain control over Ethiopia rather than participating in its new pluralism.

BIBLIOGRAPHY

Ahmed, Hussein. "The Historiography of Islam in Ethiopia." *Journal of Islamic Studies* 3, no. 1 (1992): 15–46.

Ahmed, Hussein. *Islam in Nineteenth Century Wallo.* Leiden: Brill, 2001.

Cerulli, Enrico. "Ethiopia's Relations with the Muslim World." In *General History of Africa*, edited by M. Elfasi, pp. 575–585. Berkeley: University of California Press, 1988.

Cerulli, Enrico. *L'Islam di Ieri e di Oggi* (The Islam of Yesterday and Today). Rome: Istituto per l'Oriente, 1971.

Couq, J. *L'Islam en Éthiopie, des Origines au XVI Siècle* (Islam in Ethiopia, from Its Origins to the Sixteenth Century). Paris: Nouvelles Editions Latines, 1981.

Erlich, Haggai. *The Cross and the River: Ethiopia, Egypt, and the Nile.* Boulder, Colo.: Lynne Rienner, 2002.

Erlich, Haggai. *Ethiopia and the Middle East.* Boulder, Colo.: Lynne Rienner, 1994.

Erlich, Haggai. *Islam and Christianity in the Horn of Africa: Somalia, Ethiopia, Sudan*, Boulder, Colo.: Lynne Rienner, 2010.

Erlich, Haggai. *Saudi Arabia and Ethiopia: Islam, Christianity, and Politics Entwined.* Boulder, Colo.: Lynne Rienner, 2007.

Trimingham, J. Spencer. *Islam in Ethiopia.* 2d ed. London: Frank Cass, 1965.

ʿUlayyān, Muḥammad ʿAbd al-Fattāḥ. *Al-Hijrah ilā al-Habashah wa-munaqashat qadiyat Islām al-naj101zshi* (The Hegira to Ethiopia and the Arguments over the Issue of Islam al-Najashi). Cairo: Dār al-Turāth, 1987.

HAGGAI ERLICH

ETHNICITY. The Qurʾān states in several verses that individuals, not groups, are responsible for what they do, stressing the unity of the Islamic *ummah* (community) and emphasizing the primacy of bonds created through Islam over those based on shared identities of kinship, descent, region, and language—bonds which the philosopher Ibn Khaldūn (d. 1406) collectively called *ʿaṣabīyah* (group cohesiveness). Other verses reiterate the theme that humankind has been made into nations and tribes to "know one another" (49:13) and to "compete in goodness" (5:48).

The Ties that Bind: Ethnicity and Descent. Muslims say that commitment to Islam supplants ties of ethnicity, the ways in which individuals and groups characterize themselves on the basis of shared language, culture, descent, place of origin, and history. Yet from the first Muslim conquests in seventh-century Arabia, as Muslim armies spread forth from the Arabian Peninsula to peoples who neither spoke Arabic nor could claim Arab descent, such concerns frequently surfaced in practice. Under the Umayyad dynasty (661–750), those claiming Arab descent obtained economic and political benefits. Muslims claiming descent from the Prophet Muḥammad, called *sharīf*s or *sayyid*s, often enjoy religious prestige and legal entitlements.

Ethnicity is an observer's term, although those who assert ethnic ties often regard them as fixed and "natural." Ethnicity is often thought to be a matter of birth, but the exceptions are as frequent as the rule: the social and political significance of ethnic and religious identities differs significantly according to historical and social contexts. For example, take the term *qawm* (people) in Afghanistan. Depending on the context it can mean a tribe or a subdivision of one, a people sharing a common origin or region of residence, or more generally a shared religious and linguistic identity. Moreover, since the latter half of the twentieth century, the experience of large-scale migration in search of wage labor—Pakistanis to Saudi Arabia, Turks and Kurds to western Germany, and North Africans to France—or as refugees—Afghans to Iran and Western Europe, and Bosnian Muslims to Austria and Germany—has had a major impact on changing the significance and political implications of ethnic identity.

In the Arabian Peninsula, claims to ethnic or tribal identity—the two notions are almost indistinguishable in countries such as Saudi Arabia, Oman, Yemen, and the Gulf States—are usually framed in genealogical terms as descending from one of two eponymous ancestors. "Northern" Arabs claim descent from ʿAdnān; "southern" Arabs, including those who speak Semitic languages other than Arabic, claim Qaḥṭān as their ancestor. The possibility for some groups claiming either ʿAdnān or Qaḥṭān as eponymous ancestors allows for flexibility in making descent claims, although genealogies are considered fixed. Ex-slaves (Ar., *khuddām*) attached to tribes and ruling families throughout the Arabian Peninsula, and other groups lacking tribal descent, have traditionally had an inferior social status, as shown by occupation and the lack of intermarriage with other groups. Modern economic conditions have eroded some of these distinctions.

Ethnic and Linguistic Identities: North Africa. It is crucial to consider how social distinctions such as ethnicity and religion figure in the overall context of social and personal identity and not stop at a mosaiclike enumeration of ethnic group, sect, family origin, locality, and occupation. In North Africa, for example, the first Arab invaders arrived with the advent of Islam in the seventh century from the Arabian Peninsula, followed by a second, larger wave of migrations in the eleventh and twelfth centuries. Nonetheless, the peoples of the region claim both Berber (Amazigh) and Arab descent, and these claims to ethnic identity are based on language and cultural characteristics. Arabic is the dominant language of the region, and Arab civilization is pervasive, but there are still groups in the mountainous regions and in certain oases, particularly in Morocco and southern Algeria, who retain Berber languages and traditions.

In Morocco, for example, nearly half the population speaks one of the several Berber languages, although most Moroccan Amazighs, especially men, speak Arabic as a second language. The most important language (and ethnic) clusters are Tashilḥīt, spoken in Morocco and Mauritania; Shāwiyah and Kabyle in Algeria; Tamāshek, spoken by the Tuareg of the central Sahara and south of the Niger; and Zanāga, in Senegal. Since the mid-1990s in Morocco, television news has been given in the major Amazigh dialects, as well as in Arabic and French, and since 2005 a unified Berber language based on Tamazight has been used in schools in Berber-speaking regions and on state television. Tamazight, banned from schools and most public places in Morocco until the mid-1990s, subsequently was encouraged as a means of diminishing the political appeal of separatism, as was occurring in neighboring Algeria.

In Morocco, the categorizations Arab and Berber are often situational. People stress different aspects of their identity depending on context.

Identity as Arab and/or Berber is best thought of as a continuum rather than as a sharp, mutually exclusive distinction. Diverse patterns of occupation, residence, marriage, urban and rural origin, and other factors show that the ethnic distinctions of Arab and Berber in North Africa lack the all-pervasive typification that ethnicity takes in contexts elsewhere, including being Kurdish in northern Iraq or Muslim in Bosnia.

Ethnic and Religious Identities in South Asia. Assertion of an ethnic identity is often a political claim. In Afghanistan, opposition to the Soviet-dominated state which took power in 1978 and to the 1979 Soviet invasion came largely from tribally organized ethnic groups, for whom attachment to Islam served as a common denominator. In Pakistan, especially after the secession of Bangladesh in 1971, the country's ruling Punjabi elite viewed other ethnic groups with suspicion, including Sindhis, Pashtuns, Muhājirs (Muslim refugees who migrated after 1947 from what is now India), and Baluch. The Pakistani state emphasizes Islam as an identity more important than the common ethnic ties of its minority groups, including the Baluch, who from 1973 to 1977 fought for regional autonomy. The insurgency was unsuccessful, but it contributed to a heightened Baluch national consciousness that cut across tribal divisions.

Ethnic stereotyping involves shared notions concerning the motivations and attributes of the members of other ethnic groups and what can be expected of them, as well as those of one's own ethnic group. Ethnic identities, like those of language, sect, nation, and family, can be comprehended only in the context of more general assumptions made in a given society concerning the nature of the social relationships and obligations. Such understandings can be benign, as in most Arab-Berber relations in North Africa, or they can menace the destruction of civil society, as with Muslims in Bosnia or the Kurds in northern Iraq under Saddam Hussein.

Changing Representations of Identity: The Kurds of Turkey and Iraq. Modern notions of ethnicity emphasize how such distinctions are generated, produced, and maintained in society. Ethnic identities are constantly adjusted to changing requirements, even if some advocates of ethnic nationalism maintain that ethnic identities are irreducible and self-evident.

The Kurds are a case in point. How Kurds construct their ethnic and religious identity, or have the label "Kurd" applied to them by others, indicates the difficulties involved in treating ethnic identities as primordial givens or as locally held aggregations of collective interests.

Kurdistan is a region that crosses several international boundaries. Most Kurds live in Turkey (15 million, about 18 percent of the country's population), although several million live in neighboring Iran and northern Iraq, with smaller numbers in Syria and elsewhere, including western Germany. The number of Kurds is itself a significant issue, with Kurdish spokespersons offering higher figures than those wishing to diminish the political importance of Kurds. For many years, Kurds in Turkey were officially designated as "mountain Turks," possessing an incomplete command of Turkish. Although other minorities in Turkey had their non-Turkish mother tongues recorded in official censuses, the Kurdish languages were not, and only in recent years has speaking and writing them become legal. Many Kurds in Turkey are also Alevi (Ar., ʿAlawī) Muslims, a sectarian group looked on with disdain by many Sunnī Turks. Kurds differ from other Turks not only in terms of language but also in religious doctrine and practice. Until recently, their largely rural origin has placed them at a disadvantage because some Muslims have considered Alevi doctrines and practices to deviate from "acceptable" Islamic practices. The repressive treatment of Kurdish speakers in eastern Anatolia, combined with the region's poverty, has led to their high level of emigration from Turkey, where they form around 20 percent of the Turkish immigrant community of some 3.5 to 4 million in Germany.

Identity as Alevi Kurds in Turkey is continually negotiated. From an early age, Alevi children are socialized into seeing themselves as a subordinated people whose religious identity is suppressed by a Sunnī majority, who view them as religiously deviant and backward. The memory of shared injustices and suppression is carried from generation to generation. In contrast, Kurdish-speaking Alevis in western Germany find themselves freer than in Turkey to express themselves as Kurds and as Alevis. Moreover, second-generation migrants in Germany often rework their identity as Turks or Kurds in terms learned from European nationalist and ethnic discourse. Sunnī and Alevi Turks in Germany critically rethink their differences since they interact with one another more intensely than they do in Turkey. This has had an impact on improving the situation of Kurds in Turkey.

Central Asia and the Caucasus. Contemporary ethnic and religious identities in the new states of Central Asia and the Caucasus merit special consideration. During the Soviet era, Stalin created ethnic identities—"national" identities in the political language of the former Soviet Union—to weaken the possibility of resistance to Soviet domination. Beginning in the nineteenth century, Russian imperial expansion led to the forced migration of the Muslim populations of the region, creating hostility against Russians. Subsequently, those speaking Turkic languages, including the Turkmen, Kazakh, and Kyrgyz (whose traditional lifestyles involved pastoralism), and the Uzbeks, primarily agricultural and urban, were considered separate for administrative purposes, as were the Persian-speaking Tajiks. The frequent displacement of populations, heavy Russian immigration to the major towns and to certain regions (such as northern Kazakhstan), and frequent shifts of language policy, including changes of alphabet and the substitution of Russian for the Turkic languages and Persian in schools, served to fragment ethnic identities. The newly independent republics are rapidly reversing this situation. In Azerbaijan, for example, schools shifted in the early 1990s from the Cyrillic to the Latin alphabet and to Azeri Turkish as the language of instruction instead of Russian. Uzbekistan and Kazakhstan have made similar moves. In all cases, the demise of the Soviet Union has led to a growth in ethnic consciousness and ethnic conflicts linked to competing claims over land, water, and other national resources. Because the various ethnic populations often live side-by-side—many Tajiks, for example, live in Uzbekistan, and many Uzbeks live in the neighboring republics (including Kyrgyzstan, for example)—the possibilities of conflict are enormous.

China and Southeast Asia. The same situation exists in China, where ethnic and religious boundaries can be seen to be cultural and political constructions rather than territorial ones. The attribution of an ethnic, or even a religious, identity to a group or an individual depends on the speaker, the audience, and the context. Such identities are constructed in competition between local communities and the state, classes, and leaders and followers. Not infrequently one answer is given when governments make inquiries, and another when scholars do. Of the 55 national minorities listed in China's 2000 census, ten are Muslim by tradition, including the Hui, Uighur, Kazakh, and others, for a total of over 21 million, which is probably an underrepresentation. Some groups claim Turkic descent, while others, such as the Hui, consider themselves a mixture of Han, Mongol, and Arab.

The decision under post-1949 communist rule to classify the Hui as a national identity rather than a religious one suggests that the authorities regarded ethnic identity as more amenable to control than a religious one. (In a similar manner, Tito's Yugoslavia treated the country's Muslims as a national rather than as a religious identity.) Since the 1980s, China's Muslims were given limited autonomy. Mosques were opened and ties restored with Muslim communities elsewhere, so that China's Muslims have become increasingly aware of their collective identity and are stressing it more than their complementary identities. Even if such a shift did not result in demands for greater autonomy, it has obliged the central government to take claims for resources and just treatment seriously.

There is a subtle interplay between ethnic and religious identities throughout the Muslim world, an interplay not unique to it. The intercommunal tensions between Hindus and Muslims in India, a formally secular state, parallel in many respects the interplay of religion and ethnicity between Hindu Tamils and Buddhist Sinhalese in neighboring Sri Lanka. In Malaysia, claims to ethnic identity are inextricably linked to religion and, since the Islamization movement of the late 1970s, have led to economic, educational, and legal preferences and entitlements. In neighboring Indonesia, in contrast, the official ideology, the *pancasila*, encompasses general principles from several world religions, including Islam—although at least 90 percent of Indonesians consider themselves Muslim—and the government frequently limits the participation of religious organizations in politics. Nonetheless, international corporations and organizations often impute leadership skills to personnel based on ethnic origin. Batak and Ambonese, for example, are sometimes favored over Javanese because of their reputation for being good administrators and for not favoring their relatives.

Ethnicity and Transnationalism. Ethnic identity is now transregional and transnational. The Yemeni grocer in Brooklyn, New York, might serve as a link for others from his tribe and village in Yemen, and the Turkish factory worker in Germany might facilitate the adjustment for others from his home region or country in adjusting to life in a foreign land. Yet ethnicity and sectarianism are products of global economic and political circumstances that encourage the formation of such identities, which are then used for obtaining political and economic advantage. Understanding claims to ethnic identity entails attention both to constructed collective meanings and to the economic and political contexts in which such identities are created and sustained. Ethnic distinctions, like those of region, sect, gender, language, and even tribe, are not being erased by modern conditions but instead provide the base from which newer social distinctions are created and sustained.

Some governments and political leaders, like their religious counterparts, often seek to ease possible tensions that arise from making such group definitions by officially denying their existence, but it would appear more reasonable to recognize them for what they are and constructively to seek to harness them. Shared notions of community by ethnic group or region often can provide the basis of trust and solidarity necessary for the effective functioning of and participation in modern society. Unfortunately, they can also be used to intimidate and to destroy.

BIBLIOGRAPHY

Barfield, Thomas. *Afghanistan: A Cultural and Political* History. Princeton, N.J.: Princeton University Press 2010.

Eickelman, Dale F. *The Middle East and Central Asia: An Anthropological Approach*, 4th ed. Englewood Cliffs, N.J.: Prentice Hall, 2002.

Fuller, Graham E. *Central Asia: The New Geopolitics*. Santa Monica, Calif.: Rand, 1992.

Garthwaite, Gene R., "Reimagined Internal Frontiers: Tribes and Nationalism—Bakhtiyari and Kurds." In *Russia's Muslim Frontiers: New Directions in Cross-Cultural Analysis*, edited by Dale F. Eickelman, pp. 130–45. Bloomington: Indiana University Press, 1993.

Gladney, Dru C. *Dislocating China: Muslims, Minorities, and Other Subaltern Subjects*. Chicago: University of Chicago Press, 2003.

Kaiser, Robert J. *The Geography of Nationalism in Russia and the USSR*. Princeton, N.J.: Princeton University Press, 1994.

Liu, Morgan Y. *Under Solomon's Throne: Uzbek Visions of Renewal in Osh*. Pittsburgh, Pa.: University of Pittsburgh Press, 2012.

Maddy-Weitzman, Bruce. *The Berber Identity Movement and the Challenge to North African States*. Austin: University of Texas Press, 2011.

Mutalib, Hussin. *Islam and Ethnicity in Malay Politics*. New York and Singapore: Oxford University Press, 1990.

Stewart, Pamela J., and Andrew Strathern, eds. *Contesting Rituals: Islam and Practices of Identity-Making*. Durham, N.C.: Duke University Press, 2005.

Tapper, Richard. "Ethnicity, Order, and Meaning in the Anthropology of Iran and Afghanistan." In *Le fait ethnique en Iran et en Afghanistan*, edited by Jean-Pierre Digard, pp. 21–31. Paris: Éditions du CNRS, 1988.

Dale F. Eickelman

Executive. In liberal-democratic regimes today, the executive branch is one of three separate branches of government (the others being legislative and judicial). Executive systems in the Islamic world vary according to the economic, social, and political contexts and historical experiences of different Muslim societies. There is no single model of executive system shared by all Muslim states. Executive systems depend on local social, economic, political, and cultural variables rather than universal Islamic rules.

During the first Islamic empires of the Umayyads and ʿAbbāsids, the respective caliphs served at the head of the state executive organs as absolute dynastic monarchs. In theory, they did not have legislative and judicial authority. This did not, however, lead to a separation among executive, judicial, and legislative powers. Caliphs-sultans attempted to make the laws, affect legislation and judicial authority, and exercise absolute authority over their subjects.

Except for some Islamic religious duties, *Sharīʿah* law generally played the role of a flexible constitution, which was open to wide interpretation and manipulation by rulers. The *ʿulamāʾ* (Islamic scholars) were, in theory, at times an autonomous group. In practice, however, they mostly became salaried administrators of executive authority, especially the ʿAbbāsids, who centralized political authority and placed it in the hands of an absolute monarch who served as both secular king and spiritual head of the Islamic community. The Ottoman Empire's political system was an absolute monarchy. Ottoman sultan-caliphs and their administrators who acted as executive authorities wielded almost unlimited power in practice.

With the modernization attempts of the nineteenth and twentieth centuries and the codification, modernization, and secularization of laws, legislative processes, and state bureaucracy transferred the *ʿulamāʾ*'s theoretical authority over the content and implementation of law to the state, mostly to the executive authorities and to an elected legislature. These legislative bodies have, however, been mostly dominated or monopolized by authoritarian parties, charismatic leaders, ethnoreligious oligarchs, or tribal leaders.

In the contemporary Muslim world, the executive branch exerts a powerful influence over other branches of government. Dynastic and constitutional monarchies are still widespread, albeit not prevailing, forms of government. These regimes are based on independent and strong executive elements, such as king, sultan, or emir. In some constitutional regimes without dynastic succession, presidents regularly expand their executive authority over legislative and judicial bodies and extend their mandated term of office, unlike in liberal democratic constitutional monarchies or presidential systems where executive authority is exercised by elected governments led by prime ministers or presidents according to the laws made by autonomous legislative bodies.

Today, a few Muslim states based on Islamic law continue to follow traditional systems of government. Current Islamic monarchies have two governmental branches: the head of the state or main executive organ titled sultan, emir, or president; and the bureaucracy or state administration. Even in some neo-Islamist regimes, such as Iran, which were established by the organized *ʿulamāʾ* which replaced the secularist monarch, executive organs and the highest *ʿulamāʾ* are interrelated. In the Islamic world, executive organs are generally not restricted effectively. In a few hybrid regimes they are partly restricted by the legislative and judicial elements that balance the government. Nevertheless, sultanates and one-party governments, as executive organs, monopolize or have great power over law-making councils and judicial functionaries. The main reasons for this are not only Islamic principles, but also imperial legacy, strong tribal ties, oil-rich ruling strata free from tax revenues, poverty, Arab-Israeli conflict that promotes authoritarian ideologies, and the world political system partly favoring some of the authoritarian regimes.

BIBLIOGRAPHY

Black, Antony. *The History of Islamic Political Thought: From the Prophet to the Present*. Edinburgh: Edinburgh University Press, 2012.

Gelvin, James L. *The Arab Uprising: What Everyone Needs to Know*. Oxford: Oxford University Press, 2012.

Hallaq, Wael B. *An Introduction to Islamic Law*. Cambridge, U.K.: Cambridge University Press, 2009.

MURAT METINSOY

EXPANSION OF ISLAM. This article understands the "expansion of Islam" to mean primarily the geographical expansion of the Muslim *ummah* and its correlate, Dār al-Islām. According to the Qurʾān and Muslim tradition there were many prophets and *ummahs* thoughout history, but these *ummahs* either did not survive or survived with essential corruptions, as in the case of Jews and Christians.

The Beginnings. The continuing Muslim *ummah* began when the Prophet Muḥammad (c. 570–632) about the year 610 received the first of a series of revelations that continued until his death and gathered a small group of followers, including his wife, Khadījah; his cousin ʿAlī; and a close friend, Abū Bakr. He soon encountered opposition from the leaders of the dominant tribe in Mecca, where he lived, since his revelations called for a strict monotheism that impugned the gods they worshipped and challenged various injustices of their society. Persecution led him to send some of his followers to Ethiopia, where they were favorably received. Soon after this Muḥammad's clan was boycotted for two years.

Muḥammad then began to seek support outside of Mecca. After some failures he was approached by representatives from Yathrib, a farming oasis some 230 miles (370 kilometers) to the north of Mecca, to come as a mediator in tribal conflicts there. In 622 he and most of his followers moved to Yathrib, which became known as Madīnat al-Nabī (city of the prophet), or Medina for short. This significant event is known as the *hijrah* (emigration), and it marks the beginning of the *ummah* as a polity. From being a mediator Muḥammad gradually became the effective ruler, though facing internal opposition from three Jewish tribes, eventually eliminated, and less than fully loyal Muslims referred to as "hypocrites."

External opposition came primarily from the Meccans, who saw in the nascent *ummah* a threat to their position. There were a number of skirmishes and battles, of which the three most important were Badr (624), where the Muslims defeated a larger Meccan force; Uḥud (625), where the Meccans defeated the Muslims but failed to follow up; and the Trench (627), where new technology staved off the Meccans. In 628 a truce was made between the Muslims and the Meccans, and in the following two years Muḥammad was able to gain the allegiance of a number of the surrounding tribes and strengthen his position so that the Meccans capitulated in 630, on generous terms, and accepted Islam. There followed expeditions against opposing tribes and a couple of expeditions in the direction of Syria, while deputations came from many tribes to affirm their allegiance. The *ummah* was now established as a new kind of community, transcending tribal allegiances in the name of God, and raids for booty and tribal honor were superseded by *jihād*, which involved booty but was done in the name of God and his rule.

First Wave of Expansion. When Muḥammad died in 632 many but not all of the Arabian tribes had accepted Islam. Under Abū Bakr, Muḥammad's successor as ruler, or caliph, the remaining tribes were brought into the fold and some "copycat" prophetic movements were defeated. In the *Riddah* (Apostasy) wars some tribes were compelled to pay the *zakāt* tax after they had refused to pay on the grounds that their allegiance had been only to Muḥammad, a position that threatened the unity of the *ummah*.

Under the second caliph, ʿUmar, Muslim armies began to conquer, or "open" (*fatḥ*, the Arabic word for these conquests), lands beyond Arabia. Syria and Palestine fell after decisive battles in 634–636 over the Byzantines, with the caliph himself negotiating the surrender of Jerusalem in 638. Egypt was taken from the Byzantines between 639 and 646 and Tripoli about 647. The battle of Qādisīyah in 637 opened Sassanian Iraq to the Muslims and after the battle of Nihawand in 641 or 642 they advanced through Iran, reaching Khorāsān by 654. During this period key precedents were set for settling and taxing these lands, including the establishment of *amṣār* (garrison towns, sing. *miṣr*), garrison towns where the Arab troops were expected to live.

Conquests continued under the Umayyads (661–750). To the west, Qayrawān (Tunisia) was founded in 670, and in 711 Muslim Arabs and Berbers (converted early) entered the Iberian Peninsula (to be known as al-Andalus). They conquered most of it and advanced into France until they were stopped at Poitiers in 732. Between 827 and 896 Sicily was occupied. To the east the Muslims reached Sind (now in Pakistan) in 712 and to the northeast they captured the main cities of Central Asia in 712 and 713 and fought a Chinese army in 751. To the north, three expeditions against Constantinople, in 660, 668, and 717, failed, and the border with the Byzantines remained more or less stable for several centuries.

Consolidation. A large empire having been conquered, the next step was to incorporate its population into the *ummah*. Initially all Muslims were Arabs, and these constituted a thin ruling layer (with Berbers in the Maghreb) over the much larger *dhimmī* population. There seems initially to have been little expectation that they would convert to Islam. As *dhimmīs*, they had to pay special taxes and recognize Muslim preeminence in other ways, provisions not unlike what previous empires had imposed on minorities, but otherwise they were self-governing in their own affairs, and life went on much as before. Conquest had involved little material destruction, and government administration continued largely in the hands of the same people as before and in the same languages. Coins even retained the Byzantine and Sassanian designs.

This changed under the Umayyad caliph ʿAbd al-Malik (685–705), who undertook major administrative reforms, such as making Arabic the language of administration and introducing distinctively Islamic coins. He also built the Dome of the Rock, signaling the self-view of Islam as a distinctive and permanent order replacing the previous empires.

At about this time *dhimmīs* began to convert to Islam in significant numbers. Reasons included an attraction to its doctrines, a feeling that God did indeed favor the Muslims, and greater opportunities for social and political advancement. Under the Umayyads the sense that Muslim meant Arab was still strong, and converts had to become *mawālī* (clients) of an Arab tribe in order to become Muslim, and they still suffered social disadvantages. By 750 the *mawālī* had become sufficiently numerous that their disaffection was a major factor in the overthrow of the Umayyad dynasty and its replacement by the ʿAbbāsids. Since then Islam has been the multiethnic religion that it is today. Conversions continued, and in the lands of the first wave of conquests it took about two centuries for the majority of the population to become Muslim and a few more centuries to reach the much larger proportions that have remained more or less stable since. Pre-Islamic symbols and practices were sometimes incorporated into the growing religion of Islam and were sometimes criticized and/or eliminated by reformers.

Some Reverses. While the premodern history of Islam is mainly a story of expansion, there were a few significant reverses. In 1099 the western European Crusaders captured Jerusalem and established themselves along the Mediterranean coast of Syria. They held Jerusalem until they were forced out by Ṣalāḥ al-Dīn (Saladin) in 1187, regained it briefly from 1229 to 1244, and were finally driven out of the area in 1291. While the Crusades were significant events for Europeans, they were little more than ephemeral "barbarian" incursions from the overall Muslim point of view.

Much more serious was the challenge of the Mongols, who entered the Muslim world in the thirteenth century, extending their sway over central Asia, Iran, and Iraq and sacking Baghdad in 1258, terminating the caliphate there. Their devastation set back the conquered lands economically and culturally for some time. Their advance was stopped by the Mamlūks at Ain Jalut in Syria in 1260, but they ruled as non-Muslims over Muslim peoples until their leader converted to Islam in 1295, and his followers followed suit over the next decade. Later Mongol rulers patronized Islamic culture and contributed to its blossoming.

An important permanent loss took place with the Christian *reconquista* of al-Andalus, beginning with the capture of Toledo in 1085 and ending with the termination of the Kingdom of Granada in 1492. Practice of Islam was forbidden by 1526, and even Muslim converts to Christianity were expelled by 1611. Sicily was retaken by the Normans between 1061 and 1092, though a Muslim population remained for a time, among them the great geographer al-Idrīsī.

Second Wave of Expansion. The long stalemate between the Muslims and the Byzantines ended in 1071 when the Seljuk Turks defeated the Byzantines at the battle of Manzikert and added much of Anatolia to their realm. The struggle against the Byzantines was taken up by the Ottomans after 1281. They conquered northwestern Anatolia and moved into the Balkans in a number of campaigns; finally, in 1453 they took Constantinople and brought an end to the Byzantine Empire. *Dhimmīs* often prospered under their *millet* system, and the Balkan population remained predominantly Christian. Anatolia become predominantly Muslim, thanks particularly to the efforts of Ṣūfīs, but had a significant Christian population in parts until the twentieth century.

Muslim expansion into India had begun with the conquest of Sind in 712–713. The Ghaznavids (961–1186), initially based in Afghanistan, took Lahore in 1030 and controlled much of northwest India. Their successors, the Ghūrīds, extended their control as far as Delhi, and in 1209 one of their generals founded what became known as the Sultanate of Delhi, which extended Muslim rule to cover almost all of India. The existing social system was left largely intact and Hindus were treated as *dhimmīs*, their chiefs often cooperating with the Muslim rulers, who functioned as a ruling caste in a society organized by caste. Ṣūfī *ṭarīqahs* played a major role in converting about 25 percent of population of the subcontinent as a whole, a majority in much of the north. This was probably facilitated by at least apparent similarities between Sufism and the Bhakti devotional movement. The greatest of the Muslim dynasties in India, both politically and culturally, was the Mughal dynasty, beginning in 1526. Its greatest ruler, Akbar (r. 1556–1605), was both a warrior and a reformer and was known for his tolerance in religious matters. He abolished the *jizyah* tax for non-Muslims and sponsored debates among scholars of different religions. The empire remained strong for about a century but lost strength quickly after the death of Akbar's third successor, Awrangzīb, in 1707. The eighteenth century saw a significant revival of Hindu and Sikh power, as well as the beginning of British intervention.

Islam penetrated China through merchants and Ṣūfīs via Central Asia, where a confederation of Uzbeks ruled from the sixteenth to the nineteenth century, and through merchants in Chinese seaports. The descendants of the latter group along with others are called the Hui and are Chinese in language and culture. The Uighurs and other Muslims of Xinjiang were brought under Chinese rule in the eighteenth century but have maintained their ethnic identities and have been less happy to accept Chinese rule.

Islam appears to have been brought to Southeast Asia by traders and Ṣūfīs from both India and the Arabian Peninsula sometime before 1300. It spread south along the coasts of Sumatra and the Malay Peninsula, and thence to Java, where the last Hindu kingdom was replaced by a Muslim state by 1550 and at least superficial conversion was nearly complete two and a half centuries later. Meanwhile, the Europeans were beginning to make their presence felt. The Portuguese took Malacca in 1511 and were replaced about a century later by the Dutch, who began to extend their control. This stimulated the spread of Islam as a form of cultural and political resistance. *Jihād* became a form of anti-imperialist struggle, as would happen elsewhere. Islam spread as far as the southern Philippines in the fourteenth and fifteenth centuries.

Traders brought Islam to the East African coast and Somalia beginning in the ninth century, while between the twelfth and early sixteenth centuries Muslims pushed south from Egypt and north from the Blue Nile region to conquer Christian kingdoms in what is now the Sudan. Ethiopia resisted and remains a Christian state today, though much of its population is Muslim. Elsewhere in sub-Saharan Africa Islam was usually brought first by merchants and Ṣūfīs and later accepted by the rulers. In the central and western parts the elites of several kingdoms, including Ghana, Mali, Songhay, and Kano, became Muslim between the eleventh and the sixteenth centuries. From the sixteenth to the nineteenth centuries *jihād* movements sought to reform pagan practices and spread the faith and practice of Islam.

The Impact of the West. Modernity, coming on the back of Western imperialism, has been a major challenge to the *ummah*. Beginning in the eighteenth century but with full force in the nineteenth century, the descendants of the "barbaric" Franks of earlier times spread their power over Muslim lands until, by 1920, almost all of the *ummah* was under their direct or indirect control. After 1920 this control began to loosen, and by 1970, or in 1991 for those under Soviet rule, most of the *ummah* had gained formal independence. Even though the Western armies had left, however, they were prepared to return if they felt it necessary, as they did in Iraq in 1991 and 2003 and Afghanistan in 2001.

No less important is the form in which independence came, the nation-state. Invented in the West and for Western conditions, the nation-state probably divides the *ummah* more deeply than any previous political system has. Moreover, it demands a level of loyalty that many Muslims believe should be given only to God, that is, nationalism is seen by these Muslims as a form of *shirk* (polytheism).

Western influence goes much deeper than politics, moreover. In the nineteenth century the *ummah* was incorporated into the worldwide capitalist system, also made in the West, usually to its disadvantage, although in the twentieth century oil has permitted some Muslim states to play the capitalist game successfully. Western technology of various sorts has usually been welcomed, as has Western education, though with greater reservation. The same is true of much Western pop culture. The so-called resurgence of Islam since about 1970 and the political Islamism connected with it has modified this but not reversed it.

Postcolonial Advance. Western imperialism has affected the nature and quality of Muslim life, but has not meant a major geographical retreat of the *ummah*. Ottoman control over Greece and the Balkans was lost between 1830 and 1918, and the loss of Palestine since 1948 has been deeply felt. There have also been two major population exchanges, both connected with the creation of nation states, between Turkey and Greece in 1923 and between Pakistan and India in 1947.

Apart from these the *ummah* still occupies most of the territories that it did in 1800, and its people still identify as Muslims and perform the pillars of Islam probably at least as faithfully as in 1800. Although at least one nineteenth-century leader asserted that Muslims lands under non-Muslim rule were no longer Dār al-Islām, most rejected this assertion on the grounds that Muslims were still free to practice their religious rites, most of their customs, and much of their law. Moreover, the *ummah* has continued to spread geographically in the last two centuries in sub-Saharan Africa, although at present it confronts vigorous Christian churches originally planted by Western missionaries.

Another form of advance of the *ummah* is a product of imperialism and modernity. Under the British Empire, for example, South Asian Muslims emigrated to places such as South Africa and Fiji and formed permanent communities there. Since the 1950s considerable numbers of Muslims have emigrated to Western countries, primarily for economic reasons. Others have gone as students, some remaining and some returning to their home countries. In many cases they have moved to the lands of their former rulers, such as South Asians to the United Kingdom and Maghribīs to France. Most European countries have Muslim communities of some significance. There is also a considerable population of Muslims in the United States, Canada, Australia, New Zealand, and other countries. (We should also note the existence of a homegrown American Muslim movement deriving from the Nation of Islam movement of Elijah Muhammad.) While many of the first generation of immigrants expected to return to their home countries, most, along with their descendants, have remained and form permanent diaspora communities and are often citizens of their host countries.

These communities raise a number of issues for themselves, for their host communities, and for the *ummah* as a whole. For themselves there is the issue of identity. Can they be Muslims and Europeans (etc.) at the same time, and if so on what terms? How should they deal with prejudice and discrimination from the host country? Can/should there be a distinctive European or American (etc.) Islam?

For the host country questions include: To what extent can distinctively Muslim practices, for example, in clothing, be tolerated (or encouraged)? Can there be a place for the *Sharīʿah*? What should be done about the popular fear of Muslims generally labeled Islamophobia? For the *ummah* as a whole, does their intimate connection with the West make them traitors or enable them to make distinctive contributions? Does the freedom of expression generally provided in the West allow them to present innovative ideas and practices that will benefit the whole *ummah*? Are they part of Dār al-Islām? An interesting suggestion is that they are *dār al-daʿwah or dār al-shahādah*, the abode of witness, a new category for a new situation.

Thus, while the general geographic configuration of Dār al-Islām, if understood as Muslim-majority areas, has not changed much since the eighteenth century, the situation and character of the *ummah* has changed considerably and will undoubtedly continue to do so.

Bibliography

Balādhurī, Ahmad ibn Jabir. *The Origins of the Islamic State*. Translated by Philip Khûri Hitti. Beirut: Khayats, 1966. Translation of one of the early Arabic sources for the conquests; reprint of the 1916 edition.

Bonner, Michael. *Jihad in Islamic History: Doctrines and Practice*. Princeton, N.J.: Princeton University Press, 2006. A good study of the topic.

Donner, Fred McGraw. *The Early Islamic Conquests*. Princeton, N.J.: Princeton University Press, 1981. Detailed study of the earliest conquests, including Syria and Iraq; stresses social, political, and ideological factors.

Gervers, Michael, and Ramzi Jibran Bikhazi, eds. *Conversion and Continuity: Indigenous Christian Communities in Islamic Lands, Eighth to Eighteenth Centuries*. Toronto: Pontifical Institute of Mediaeval Studies, 1990. Good collection of articles.

Haddad, Yvonne Yazbeck, and Jane I. Smith, eds. *Muslim Minorities in the West: Visible and Invisible*. Walnut Creek, Calif.: AltaMira, 2002. Articles on a number of countries and situations, with particular attention to America.

Hodgson, Marshall G. S. *The Venture of Islam: Conscience and History in a World Civilization*. 3 vols. Chicago: University of Chicago Press, 1974. Detailed and innovative study that has more than stood the test of time.

Ikram, S. M. *Muslim Civilization in India*. Edited by Ainslie T. Embree. New York: Columbia University Press, 1964. Detailed account of the Muslim period from 712 to 1857.

Kennedy, Hugh. *The Great Arab Conquests: How the Spread of Islam Changed the World We Live In*. Philadelphia: Da Capo, 2007. Detailed but accessible and attractively written account of the conquests to 750 CE with attention to the sources. Forward has a good discussion of the historical value of the sources.

Lapidus, Ira M. *A History of Islamic Societies*. 2d ed. Cambridge, U.K.: Cambridge University Press, 2002. The most recent detailed and authoritative study of Muslim history.

Lewis, Bernard. *The Arabs in History*. Rev. ed. New York: Harper & Row, 1958. Older work; still useful; very readable.

Ramadan, Tariq. *To Be a European Muslim: A Study of Islamic Sources in the European Context*. Leicester, U.K.: Islamic Foundation, 1999. By a leading participant in the debate about Islam in Europe.

Robinson, Francis, ed. *The Cambridge Illustrated History of the Islamic World*. Cambridge, U.K.: Cambridge University Press, 1996.

William E. Shepard

F

FAḌLALLĀH, MUḤAMMAD ḤUSAYN. The spiritual leader of Ḥizbullāh (Party of God), Sayyid Faḍlallāh (1935–2010) was born in Najaf, Iraq, into a Lebanese family from ʿAynata, a village close to Bint Jubayl. Faḍlallāh's father was an *ʿalim* (religious scholar) in the Iraqi shrine and university city, where his son excelled in religious studies. One of his principal teachers was Abol-Qāsem al-Khoʾi (Abū al-Qāsīm al-Khūʾī), whose doctrine and practice rejected direct political participation by the *ʿulamāʾ* (community of religious scholars). Faḍlallāh cited the influence of his other teacher, Muḥsin al-Ḥakīm, and of his fellow student Muḥammad Bāqir al-Ṣadr. Al-Ṣadr was politically active in the 1960s, turning the Shīʿī university at Najaf into a center of political and religious opposition to the Iraqi regime. The regime had at first been favorably inclined toward the Communists, but was soon dominated by Arab nationalists within the Iraqi Baʿth party.

As early as 1964, at the age of 29, Faḍlallāh defined the function of a Muslim intellectual: "to bridge the deep divide that exists between youth and religion." At 31, he was appointed cleric to the eastern suburb of Beirut, in Nabʿah, an impoverished area. There, Faḍlallāh established cultural youth clubs as well as free clinics and community centers, harbingers of future Ḥizbullāh activities. The success of these clubs encouraged him, by 1972, to spread his message in his native region.

The late 1960s and early 1970s witnessed significant encroachments by Israel against Palestinians in south Lebanon, causing a Shīʿī exodus toward Beirut. Faḍlallāh completed a major treatise, *al-Islām wa-manṭiq al-quwah* (Islam and the Logic of Power), in March 1976 at the height of these confrontations. In the course of the Lebanese civil war, Nabʿah was destroyed, emptied of its inhabitants by extremist Christian militias, and Faḍlallāh was taken prisoner. He recounted that he began his book on the contemporary requirements of Islam while the bombs were still falling. In a 1977 postscript, he emphasized how he placed himself "squarely in the experience of the have-nots," which further defined his philosophy.

Released, Faḍlallāh was immersed in the country's Shīʿī refugee crisis. He was mobilized by the 1978 disappearance of Mūsā al-Ṣadr, the charismatic head of the Harakat al-Maḥrūmīn (Movement of the Disadvantaged), abducted and perhaps executed by Libyans. Within one year, Iran ushered in Ayatollah Ruhollah Khomeini, who received Faḍlallāh in 1984 and named him *marja' al-taqlīd* (source of imitation) in 1986. From that point forward, the balance of political and spiritual obligations became his main focus.

Political Life in Lebanon. In the civil war configuration of Lebanese politics, Amal—the successor to Harakat al-Maḥrūmīn—was pro-Syrian, anti-Palestinian, increasingly Lebanese, and disposed to compromise with the Katā'ib (the Phalanges, a Maronite party) and Israel. When a splinter Shī'ī group emerged in 1982, Faḍlallāh called them *al-islāmiyūn* (roughly, "Islamists"). These groups were united within the Organization of the Islamic Jihād. By 1983, the group was ready to conduct its "first operations of the popular Islamic resistance against Israeli occupation," which was openly acknowledged in 1985.

Throughout the early 1980s, Faḍlallāh delivered sermons and lectures. His firm and radical pronouncements gained popularity, both at home and overseas. On 8 March 1985, he was the target of an attempted assassination—one of several over a period of years—by car bomb. Allegedly, the attack was organized by Western intelligence. Faḍlallāh claimed that the then-director of the CIA, William J. Casey, had told an Arab ambassador that he "had become annoying to U.S. policy and should be removed." American intelligence was persuaded that Faḍlallāh blessed the devastating 1983 attacks in Beirut that killed 241 U.S. Marines and 58 French paratroopers, which Faḍlallāh denied. After 1985, Faḍlallāh became the president of the Lebanese council of Ḥizbullāh.

The Palestinian Conflict. In the spring of 1985, Faḍlallāh defended Beirut's Palestinian camps, which were besieged by Amal acting on Syrian orders. This effort complicated matters as Iran and Syria, which were nonetheless allied powers, clashed in Lebanon. By early 1986, Ḥizbullāh and its pro-Iranian allies rejected the inter-Lebanese agreement that had been drawn up at Damascus in December 1985. In this rejection, Ḥizbullāh followed the example of the Maronite Lebanese Forces and opposed Amal.

In the second "war of the (Palestinian) camps," waged after September 1986, Ḥizbullāh was neutral and clashed only with Syrian troops, which were eventually deployed in West Beirut. Damascus yielded to the Islamist enclave. Faḍlallāh attended two formal scholarly meetings in Tehran and Lausanne, which produced a draft of the Lebanese Islamic Constitution. Although Faḍlallāh harbored doubts about the Islamic state and the risks of absolute personal power, he nevertheless contemplated such a blueprint for multi-confessional Lebanon.

Further Political Developments in Lebanon. Faḍlallāh's political commitment engendered and nourished his theological reflections, especially since he was no longer an active participant in military affairs. Remarkably, it was Sayyid Ḥasan Naṣrallāh—not Faḍlallāh—who succeeded 'Abbās al-Mūsawī as general secretary of Ḥizbullāh, after he was assassinated by Israel in 1992. A tenuous situation emerged after Ḥizbullāh opposed the October 1989 Ṭā'if Accord, which introduced constitutional readjustments for Lebanon, followed by low-intensity clashes in the Israeli-declared "security zone" in the south. Without denouncing resistance, Faḍlallāh nevertheless favored political participation, supporting the August 1992 Lebanese legislative plebiscite, ostensibly because the new system of confessional secularism somewhat favored the Shī'ī community.

Although Ḥizbullāh originally aimed to transform Lebanon into an Islamic republic, this goal was abandoned, according to Faḍlallāh. In 1998 Faḍlallāh spoke at a conference on women's rights at the American University of Beirut, making visible additional concessions to modernizing influences. Faḍlallāh recommended that, within the framework of a trial, stoning for "crimes of honor" should not result in death. In effect, the *ḥudūd* (Qurʾānic penalties) were considered the concern of the judicial powers and not the victims, further illustrating the influences of a multiconfessional system.

Views on Terrorism. Faḍlallāh continued to be an outspoken leader for the Shīʿī community in Lebanon, supporting Ḥizbullāh despite repeatedly condemning various terrorist attacks against civilians. He and Naṣrallāh condemned the 11 September 2001 assaults on New York and Washington, DC. Nevertheless, Faḍlallāh issued a fatwa forbidding any Muslim from assisting the United States in its occupation of any Muslim country.

In 2004, he made clear that he feared that U.S. foreign policy increased terrorism. Faḍlallāh insisted that the roots of terrorism stemmed from U.S. foreign policy, which "[led] to a psychological state that oppose[d] the U.S. administration." He cited Washington's support of Arab elites as a central cause for generating terrorism. Moreover, the occupation of Iraq "increased acts of terrorism against the U.S. and everyone going along with it, including the Iraqis themselves." Faḍlallāh reiterated a widely held belief, especially among Shīʿī Lebanese, that the war for Iraq as well as the United States' absolute commitment to Israel served the Israeli interests—or so many believed—rather than Arabs or Muslims.

United Nations Involvement. In the aftermath of the Cedar Revolution that mobilized Lebanon after former prime minister Rafiq Ḥarīrī was assassinated on 14 February 2005, Faḍlallāh and other Ḥizbullāh leaders backed Syria. He rejected the Syria Accountability Act, which called for a withdrawal of Syrian troops from Lebanon, believing that the country would not be affected by whatever sanctions were imposed on Damascus. In fact, Lebanon was mired in internal conflict from then on, especially following the devastating August 2006 war between Ḥizbullāh and Israel. Faḍlallāh insisted that the expanded United Nations force in Lebanon was deployed to protect Israel, which naturally engendered disapproval. Faḍlallāh urged the Lebanese to treat the United Nations Interim Force in Lebanon (UNIFIL) with caution, saying that the international forces were doing little to stop Israel's violations of UN Resolution 1701, which imposed a cease-fire on 14 August 2006 to end the month-long conflict.

Resolution 1701 called for the disarmament of Ḥizbullāh, the withdrawal of Israeli troops from southern Lebanon, and the deployment of 15,000 Lebanese soldiers to be backed by an equal number of UN peacekeepers in mainly Shīʿī south Lebanon. The 34-day Israeli offensive in Lebanon claimed the lives of more than 1,200 Lebanese civilians and wounded at least 4,000 others. Faḍlallāh and others noted with contempt that the deadly Israeli assault left much of southern Lebanon in ruins and displaced nearly a million civilians from their homes.

In early 2007, Faḍlallāh spoke to the vast, mostly Arab Sunnī audience of Al Jazeera (estimated at over 45 million) on Sunnī-Shīʿī clashes in Lebanon and Iraq. He denounced bloodshed of any kind and called for an end to intra-Muslim killings. Yet he complained about *takfīrīs* (excommunicators) who allegedly tolerated the killing of Shīʿī Muslims.

Sayyid Faḍlallāh died on 4 July 2010 at the age of 74. Several of his followers "launched a school of beliefs and thoughts, a school that would always be committed to the main causes of Islam, from Jihād to Resistance, and face all foreign threats against the region" (Hussein Assi, "Ayatollah Sayyed Fadlullah's Last Wish: Israel's Vanishing," *Al-Manar*, 6 July 2010) that further committed Ḥizbullāh to the central Arab cause, Palestine, as well as persisting with its abhorrence of American policies. Although Faḍlallāh was known for his relatively liberal views on women, his political perceptions were controversial. Still, Faḍlallāh was respected by all sides in his ancestral country, as the Lebanese bade farewell to their last great Shīʿī *marjaʿ al-taqlīd.*

Political Thought. Although the Lebanese Islamic Constitution, which Faḍlallāh helped to develop in the 1980s, provided for a *lajnah* (commission) of *wilāyat al-faqīh* (rule of the jurisconsult) to exist alongside the president of the republic, the Shīʿī leader quickly realized its pitfalls ashe developed a unique political perspective. Faḍlallāh's democratic views and his misgivings about the totalitarian *wilāyat al-faqīh,* excluding the *marjaʿ al-taqlīd,* were no longer apparent in this key document. The ultimate source of legitimacy of this Lebanese *lajnah* was to be Ayatolloh Khomeini, anticipated as the sole *faqīh qāʾid* of all Muslims. The Lebanese president of this local *lajnah* would be presented simply as Khomeini's representative, designated by him. In this regard, Faḍlallāh finally acknowledged a unique supreme authority (*wilāyah*), as well as delegated, dependent local authorities. The theory of the pluralist *marjaʿīyah* thus collapsed. Faḍlallāh had at this same time pondered the question, which he termed "agonizing," of the choice between a sole *wilāyah* for the world or multiple authorities in Muslim countries; the choice was thus between an imperial Muslim state under one single authority, or a confederation of autonomous Islamic states that would meet periodically in a central assembly led by Khomeini. The Lebanese Islamic Constitution adopted the former solution, which proved to be a non-starter, and which colored his political viewpoints.

Faḍlallāh faced the delicate issue of how to handle non-Muslims in a professed Islamic state. For him, secular individual freedom did not exist. Going against the great Muslim tradition that had existed in practice as well as in theory since the eleventh century, he rejected the fundamental distinction between political and religious powers. He opposed those who did not wish to become involved in political activity, in particular his own mentor in Najaf, al-Khoʾi. Moreover, he praised the involvement of Muḥammad Bāqir al-Ṣadr in the Daʿwah party in Iraq, and explained al-Ṣadr's eventual withdrawal, and even his refusal to let his disciples be politically active, as only a tactical decision of superior wisdom (*taqīyah*) in the face of the all-powerful police strength of Saddam Hussein. Faḍlallāh himself emphasized the necessity of a disciplined political party to serve Islam.

It might have been expected that Faḍlallāh's experience in Lebanon, his commendation of coexistence with Christians, his desire for a substantive dialogue, and his desire for an open and humanized *fiqh* (jurisprudence) would have brought him to discover new solutions. This was not the case, as he maintained that Christians must renounce political sectarianism yet did not expect Muslims to do likewise. Consequently, the desired Muslim state was not founded on the legal equality of all people, regardless of their religious and family ties, even though these ties might be taken into account, as in the present-day Lebanese constitution.

The Nature of Authority. As to politics in general and war in particular, Faḍlallāh, like Khomeini, adhered to the Uṣūlī (fundamentalist) tradition of modern Shīʿism that was established at the end of the eighteenth century as an alternative to the great tradition then called *akhbārī* (textual). To be Uṣūlī was to valorize *ijtihād* (effort) in modern circumstances, to give authoritative opinions, advice, and decisions to individuals facing new problems. In the fundamentalist tradition, these opinions and authorities were numerous and varied, and each great leader (*marjaʿ*) had his particular tradition (*taqlīd*). Faḍlallāh saw *taqīyah* (dissimulation) as a rule governing concrete daily conduct without the supervision of a *marja' al-taqlīd*. He accused the Akhbārīs of confirming and even sanctifying the gap between the immutable and ideal norms (*Sharī'ah*) of the golden age of the imams and daily life, which had no link with those norms and was guided only by the light of mysticism.

Rebellion and Revolution. According to Faḍlallāh, the possibility of a violent revolution at an appropriate juncture was not excluded, because of the breach between the intangible ideal of *Sharī'ah* and traditional customs and new conditions. In addition, Faḍlallāh sought to emulate the revolutionary examples of 'Alī and Ḥusayn more than the quietist examples of the subsequent imams. He even claimed to draw inspiration from the rebellion movements that were crushed by the Shī'ī powers, backed by the *'ulamā'* in the name of *taqīyah*. He made such claims as early as the first year of the civil war in Lebanon, in 1976. At the same time, he accused the Islamic extremists of indulging in impulsive and disorganized actions—"without *taqīyah*." The time of *taqīyah* was the time of education, preparation, and organization in a party that was disciplined and adhered to a firm doctrine.

Islamic Government. Nothing that Faḍlallāh suggested concerning the modernization of *fiqh* has gone beyond the level of generalities, which appeared to his youthful listeners, but lacked concrete revolutionary application. Following the model of al-Ṣadr, and not Khomeini, he emphasized the entire scope of *fiqh*, especially its social and political aspects. Thus he intended that the role of *faqīh* (especially that of the *marja' al-taqlīd*) should go beyond simple director of individual consciences. He affirmed the existence of an Islamic economy, an elaborate social structure, and various political views, according to certain general principles that, however, did not establish a specific type of political regime.

More specifically, in the applications of the supposedly modernized *fiqh* Faḍlallāh ruled out the restoration of the caliphate and was wary of Khomeini's own theory of *wilāyat al-faqīh al-qā'id* (governance of the jurisprudent). It was true that he clearly stated his allegiance to Khomeini, but this allegiance was to his jihadist (struggle) movement rather than to the man himself. Thus, Faḍlallāh excluded the notion that Khomeini was the representative or the forerunner of the imam Mahdī, a position that differed from the one held by his successor. Rather, Khomeini's legitimacy lay in the reality of his Islamic government that, Faḍlallāh said, was truly the first to be established after long centuries of expectation. He implicitly denied the Islamic character of all other existing regimes in the Muslim world that did not sit well with most *'ulamā'*s.

For Faḍlallāh, the very nature of authority was thus subjected to concrete political visions that recognized justified rebellion without engaging in perpetual revolutions. He supported the establishment of an Islamic government that did not impose rule by fiat. His political thought, in short, was distinctive. It was tolerant of his adoptive country's multiculturalism that necessitated compromises.

[*See also* Ḥizbullāh; Lebanon; Ṣadr, Muḥammad Bāqir al-; *and* Wilāyat al-Faqīh.]

BIBLIOGRAPHY

Works by Muḥammad Ḥusayn Faḍlallāh

Al-Ḥaraka al-islāmīyah: Humūm waqaḍāyā. 4th ed. Beirut: Dār al-Malāk, 2001.

Al-Islām wa-manṭiq al-qūwah (Islam and the Logic of Power). 2d ed. Beirut: Al-Mu'assasah al-Jami'iyyah, 1981.

Al-Marja'īyah wa-harakat al-waqi'. Beirut: Dār al-Malāk, 1994.

Al-muqawamah al-Islamiyyah. Beirut: Dār al-Malāk, 1985.

"'Alā' ṭariq ḥarakat al-qūwah fī al-dawlah al-islāmīyah." *Al-Tawḥīd* (March 1986): 85–102.

"Fī ḥiwār al-dīn wa-al-mar'a wa-al-siyāsah wa-al-mufawaḍāt." *Al-Majalla* (June 17, 1995): 23–26.

Fiqh al-Sharīʿah. Vol. 1. 5th ed. Beirut: Dar al-Malak, 2001.

Irādat al-qūwah: Jihād al-muqāwamah fī khiṭāb al-Sayyid Faḍlallāh. Beirut: Dār al-Malāk, 2000.

Khatawat ʿala ṭariq al-Islām. 3d ed. Beirut: Dār al-Malāk, 1982.

Secondary Sources

Carré, Olivier. *L'Utopie islamique dans l'Orient arabe*. Paris: Presses de la Fondation nationale des sciences politiques, 1991. See chapter 9, "Khomeinisme libanais: Orgueilleux et déshérités chez Faḍlallāh," and chapter 10, "La Révolution islamique selon Fadlallah."

Kramer, Martin. "Muhammad Husayn Faḍlallāh." *Orient* 2 (1985): 147–149.

Kramer, Martin. "The Oracle of Ḥizbullāh: Sayyid Muhammad Husayn Faḍlallāh." In *Spokesmen for the Despised: Fundamentalist Leaders of the Middle East*, edited by R. Scott Appleby, pp. 83–181. Chicago: University of Chicago Press, 1997.

Sankari, Jamal. *Faḍlallāh: The Making of a Radical Shiʿite Leader*. London: SAQI, 2005.

OLIVIER CARRÉ
Translated from the French by ELIZABETH KELLER
Updated by JOSEPH A. KÉCHICHIAN

FAMILY. The basic social unit of Islamic society, as in many other societies, is the family. If Islam can be described as the soul of Islamic society, then the family might be seen metaphorically as its body. For centuries, the family has been the principal focus of people's emotional, economic, and political identity. Social changes in the nineteenth and particularly the twentieth centuries placed great strains on the unit, and especially on the patriarchal, extended family unit. Yet the family, together with the Islamic faith, retains a central place in the lives of people in every social class, in both rural and urban contexts, and in every Muslim-majority country.

"Family" means different things in different societies and contexts. In the Western world of the twenty-first century, "family" now includes the traditional "nuclear" family, the blended or stepfamily resulting from remarriage, the single-parent family, and the same-sex family unit. The Arabic word for family, *ahl* or *ʿaīla*, is a more comprehensive term and may include grandparents, uncles, aunts, and cousins, both paternal and maternal. In its broadest sense, the family might be perceived as an even larger unit, equal to the *ummah*, or the community of believers in Islam. Nevertheless, the family unit in many parts of the Islamic world has experienced nuclearization, the result of modernization, urbanization, and women's educational attainment.

Pre-Islamic Family. As early as 3000 BCE, in ancient Sumer, in present-day Iraq, there is evidence of a social unit similar to the contemporary Islamic family. This early manifestation, recorded in tablets and on monumental steles, was also a precursor to the family structure of Judaism and Christianity, the other two great monotheistic religions of the Middle East. Christians and Jews are known in Islam as "people of the book (*ahl al-kitāb*)," or *dhimmī*—those related to Islam through holy scripture and of whom a Muslim must be tolerant.

This early form of the family was patrilineal, a kind of social organization found in perhaps 80 to 90 percent of all human societies. In a patrilineal society, the name of the child and the inheritance are passed through the male line; children therefore are known by the names of their fathers. Although not all patrilineal families are equally patriarchal, the primacy attached to the male line reflects male dominance, both legal and informal, in the family and society. The use of the term "patriarch" to refer to the prophets of Judaism and Christianity is an indication of this tendency.

Family. The advent of Islam, in the seventh century CE, brought changes to the structure of the Arabian family. Although the basic outline of patrilineality was retained, some modifications came about with respect to women, girls, and orphans.

The Qur'ān prohibited infanticide, a practice that seems to have reached scandalous proportions in pre-Islamic Arabia, particularly in the case of infant girls. In Islam, orphans were to be treated with kindness. The Qur'ān also recognized women as having legal status as persons with rights and responsibilities. Women have the same religious duties as men, though they may be excused from fasting during Ramaḍān, for example, if they are pregnant or nursing. (Such latitude is meant to protect not only the health of the individual woman but also that of the child, either unborn or newly born, and by extension the health of the family unit itself.) The Qur'ān also gives women the right to accept or reject a marriage partner and the right to divorce in certain cases (the desertion, impotence, or insanity of the husband are most often cited). However, only men can divorce without cause. They also have the right to have up to four wives at any one time, and sons inherit twice as much as daughters.

Traditional Function of the Family. In the past, and to a great extent today, the family provided economic and emotional support to its members. An individual, as Halim Barakat points out, "inherited" his or her religious, class, and cultural identity, which was reinforced by the customs and mores of the group. In exchange for the allegiance of its members, the family group served as an employment bureau, insurance agency, child- and family-counseling service, old people's home, bank, teacher, home for the handicapped (including the mentally ill), and hostel in time of economic need. Men and women both remained members of their birth families for all of their lives, even after marriage. A divorced woman returned to her birth family, which was responsible for her support until remarriage. A divorced man returned to his birth family, and his parents cared for his children. In exchange for these services, the individual members were expected to place the group's survival above their personal desires, especially at the time of marriage, and to uphold the reputation of the family by behaving properly and "maintaining the family honor."

This, of course, was the ideal. In everyday life, ideals are not always realized. Some members have always rebelled and refused to marry the person chosen for them by their family. Some groups did not take in divorced members, sometimes because of poverty, sometimes out of spite. Vengeful fathers did not always pass on to their sons, at the time of maturity, authority over land or shops. Maintaining the family honor sometimes resulted in tragedy. The care of handicapped and elderly members often put an undue stress upon the younger members of the family. And not all women welcomed a co-wife or a divorce. Yet the institution of the Islamic family unit persisted because it met the real needs of people, especially in the absence of other institutions for social support.

Western Influence. In the West, socioeconomic and political changes led to a transformation of the family from extended to nuclear, from patriarchal to egalitarian, and from the male breadwinner/female homemaker model to a dual-income-earning model. Such a shift may be observed in the Muslim world, though not to the same extent.

The family unit in the Islamic world came under new pressures with the beginning of Western colonial rule in the late eighteenth and early nineteenth centuries. From Egypt to India, Morocco to Indonesia, European immigrants, soldiers, and administrators assumed political control. The family unit became first a religious, cultural, and social refuge from colonial domination, and eventually the site of political resistance. This action was strengthened by Western colonial policy, which in most areas left local control intact only in religious affairs and, by inference, Islamic family law, including inheritance. This was crucial for the continuation and support of the family, which, in response to the presence of strangers, turned in upon itself. Men found in their families a sanctuary, a representation of Islamic religious values wherein they were honored. Protection of Muslim women from strangers became more important as well. For example, the all-enveloping *jallābah,* with hood and face veil, found in Morocco today, dates only from about 1912, when the French conquered Morocco. Before that time, women as well as men in Morocco wore the *ḥāʾik,* a length of cloth wrapped about the body in various ways. The Qurʾānic school increased in importance as a source of religious instruction (though largely for boys) even as colonial governments were attempting to limit its influence and elites were attending the secular schools of Christian missionaries.

As organized anticolonial resistance became more serious and militant, the family became the focus of such resistance. Such resistance was often framed in terms of the protection of Islam and the family in the face of a common enemy—Western political and economic power, with its perceived secularist and anti-Islamic aims. At the same time, emergent notions of nationhood were accompanied by constructions of masculinity, femininity, and the family whereby women married and dutifully raised the next generation. A consequence was that women came to be "locked into" a patriarchal family unit, and a large proportion denied access to schooling or even a presence in public spaces, which were deemed male domains.

After independence from colonial rule in the 1950s and 1960s, few women were available for paid work in the growing modern economic sector. Muslim family laws reflected and reinforced women's family attachment and their subordination to male guardianship. During the oil-boom era in the Middle East and North Africa, state expansion and public education created a population of educated women willing to enter the workforce. The family unit also changed as male migration to locations of the oil economies increased. Although in most cases male kin tended to oversee the moral and financial well-being of the women and children, in some cases men migrating to the Gulf or to Europe effectively abandoned their families or started new ones. In the post-oil-boom era, unemployment, inflation, and poverty broke down extended family units, and forced increasing numbers of women to take up jobs outside their homes. Conflict in Israel, Palestine, Lebanon, Afghanistan, Iraq, and Sudan, as well as the effects of revolution and repression in Iran, also led to family disruption through violent deaths and forced migration. The movement in almost all Muslim-majority countries from rural to urban predominance has further challenged the customary ties of family life. It has become increasingly difficult for the traditional patriarchal family model—father as provider, mother as childbearer and rearer of children in the home—to be maintained. The dual-adult-worker pattern has not yet established itself as the norm, but there are signs that this change may be occurring in varying degrees across the Muslim world. What is more, the traditionally very high fertility rates of Muslim-majority countries have been declining. In Iran, Lebanon, Turkey, and Tunisia, the number of children per woman has fallen from six to two in just a few decades. Among the urban middle class in particular, family size is smaller, and the age at first marriage has risen to the mid- to late twenties.

Recent Changes and Challenges. The current debate throughout the Islamic world on *Sharīʿah*-based family law is a crucial one, for it not only involves the suggestion that family responsibilities be passed from the family unit to the state, but it also has implications for the definition of basic individual rights of women, men, and children. The status of women is not an isolated issue but lies at the core of the whole debate, for the woman has always been seen as the center of the family unit.

Discussions of Muslim family law reflect these concerns, as Qurʾānic family law defines relations between men and women through legislation on marriage, divorce, child custody, inheritance, and polygyny. Islamic family law currently operates in most Islamic countries, with the exception of Turkey and Tunisia. In the 1980s a number of countries moved to stiffen the application of *Sharīʿah* family law, including Saudi Arabia, Pakistan, Iran, Egypt, Algeria, and Nigeria. In the 1990s this occurred in Afghanistan and Malaysia. In both periods it reflected the growing political and cultural influence of Islamist movements, which see the family as the rock on which indigenous religious socialization and culture stand. They argue for greater family cohesion in what is perceived as a rapidly changing, unpredictable, and hostile world. At some level, the family is defined as society, and this formulation, although not stated, leads logically to the family as *ummah,* the community of believers in Islam.

After the 1979 Islamic Revolution in Iran, the family became the platform for the enunciation of the Islamic state's goals and ideals, and the subject of government legislation by the Shīʿī *ʿulamāʾ* in many areas of life other than family law—education, leisure activities, literature, politics. Since the mid-1980s, women's groups have emerged in the Muslim world to call for changes in the status of women in the family and society and for reform of family laws that place women in a subordinate position vis-à-vis husbands or male kin. They call for greater rights in marriage, divorce, child custody, and inheritance; an end to male guardianship and control over women's mobility; the right of mothers to pass on their nationality to their children (if the children are born of foreign fathers); the criminalization of "honor killings"; and greater economic and political participation. The 2003–2004 reform of the very patriarchal Mudawana, Morocco's family law, is an example of a successful campaign that was framed in terms of national development imperatives, children's well-being, women's rights, and an alternative vision of the family. Other groups and campaigns for equality and rights are Iran's One Million Signatures Campaign, Malaysia's Sisters in Islam, and Nigeria's BAOBAB for Women's Human Rights.

Modern Role of the Family. Increasing nuclearization, the changing status of women, the high cost of marriage (especially in Egypt), and the high rate of divorce (especially in Iran) have resulted in public debates, some protests, and many disappointed individuals. To some observers, such developments suggest the disintegration of the Muslim family and of Islamic culture. To others, the Muslim family is adjusting or reorganizing in response to contemporary needs. Yet others feel that the problems require appropriate public policies. Modern states have taken over some functions of the family, through programs and policies of social provisioning. Public schooling, health care, child care, government employment, family allowances, pensions, bank loans, and unemployment insurance are among the social services and social policies available to citizens. Nonetheless, especially in parts of the Muslim world devoid of a welfare or development state, the family is an essential focus of solidarity and support for its members, and affective ties remain strong.

In places where the family unit itself has been dispersed because of war, natural disaster, or economic need, the values and the functions of the family are resurfacing in different forms. Workers abroad group together on the basis of old family ties; young men entering the workforce find jobs in the same factories or businesses as their sisters, cousins, or uncles. For men of elite political groups, family ties continue to be important as political party bases shift. Newcomers to the city make connections through family members. Men on their own in a new place may turn to Islamic religious "brotherhoods," groups where, as they themselves say, they "feel like one of the family." Women whose husbands are working abroad often form kin-like ties with neighbors. Women in the workforce continue to rely on family ties for support. Through its adaptations and evolution, the family unit in the Muslim world has proven to be an interdependent and flexible social institution. For many, it remains the best way to provide for individual needs as well as group survival.

The British historian Lawrence Stone found the English family of past centuries to be a searching, acting, moving institution. The Muslim family, from its sixth-century foundations to its modern expression, might be viewed in the same way, as a structure flexible enough to deal with new pressures and strong enough in its religious and social manifestations to respond to and become part of changing conditions.

BIBLIOGRAPHY

Barakat, Halim. "The Arab Family and the Challenge of Social Transformation." In *Women and the Family in the Middle East: New Voices of Change*, edited by Elizabeth Warnock Fernea, pp. 27–48. Austin: University of Texas Press, 1985.

Charrad, Mounira M. *States and Women's Rights: The Making of Postcolonial Tunisia, Algeria, and Morocco*. Berkeley: University of California Press, 2001.

Esposito, John, and Natana DeLong-Bas. *Women in Muslim Family Law*. 2d ed. Syracuse, N.Y.: Syracuse University Press, 2001.

Fernea, Elizabeth Warnock, ed. *Women and the Family in the Middle East: New Voices of Change*. Austin: University of Texas Press, 1985.

Haeri, Shahla. *Law of Desire: Temporary Marriage in Shīʿī Iran*. Syracuse, N.Y.: Syracuse University Press, 1989.

Kholoussy, Hanan. *For Better, For Worse: The Marriage Crisis That Made Modern Egypt*. Stanford, Calif.: Stanford University Press, 2010.

Kian-Thiébaut, Azadeh. "From Motherhood to Equal Rights Advocates: The Weakening of Patriarchal Order." *Iranian Studies* 38, no. 1 (2005): 45–66.

Levy, Reuben. *The Social Structure of Islam*. Cambridge, U.K.: Cambridge University Press, 1957.

Maudūdī, Sayyid Abul Aʿlā. *Purdah and the Status of Woman in Islam*. Translated and edited by al-Ashʿarī. Lahore, Pakistan: Islamic Publications, 1972.

Minault, Gail, ed. *The Extended Family: Women and Political Participation in India and Pakistan*. Columbia, Mo.: South Asia Books, 1981.

Moghadam, Valentine M. *Modernizing Women: Gender and Social Change in the Middle East*. 2d ed. Boulder, Colo.: Lynne Rienner, 2003.

Moghadam, Valentine, and Tabitha Decker. "Social Change in the Middle East." In *The Middle East*, 12th ed., edited by Ellen Lust, pp. 65–98. Washington, D.C.: CQ Press, 2011.

Rugh, Andrea B. *Family in Contemporary Egypt*. Syracuse, N.Y.: Syracuse University Press, 1984.

Stone, Lawrence. *The Family, Sex, and Marriage in England, 1500–1800*. London: Weidenfeld & Nicolson, 1977.

Yount, Kathryn M., and Hoda Rashad, eds. *Family in the Middle East: Ideational Change in Egypt, Iran, and Tunisia*. London: Routledge, 2008.

ELIZABETH WARNOCK FERNEA
Updated by VALENTINE M. MOGHADAM

FĀRĀBĪ, ABŪ NAṢR AL-. Abū Naṣr Muḥammad ibn Muḥammad ibn Ṭarkhān ibn Awzalagh al-Fārābī (c. 873–950) was a Muslim neo-Platonist philosopher who was active mostly in ʿAbbāsid Baghdad and Ḥamdānid Damascus. He continued Abū Yaʿqūb al-Kindī's (d. 873) efforts to promote philosophy and sciences within a Muslim environment dominated by religious thought and philology. His contributions to the philosophy of language, logic, music, and politics are of singular importance. Al-Fārābī turned philosophy from its defensive position into a force of influence on Arabo-Islamic culture. He was particularly attentive to traditional Islamic disciplines (law, theology, grammar) and endeavored to upgrade their methodology, arguments, and presentation. He made logic more accessible in Arabic to those not versed in philosophy through books such as *Kitāb al-Ḥurūf* and *Kitāb al-Alfāẓ al-mustaʿmalah fī l-manṭiq*, while at the same time providing philosophers and students of philosophy with a clear and coherent philosophical corpus in Arabic. His interest in Arabic grammar facilitated contact between Arabic philologists and Aristotelian logic. As a commentator of Aristotle, his commentaries were written in an instructive and comprehensive style. Al-Fārābī's outstanding scientific and didactic abilities earned him among Muslim philosophers the title of "the second teacher" (*al-muʿallim al-thānī*)—Aristotle being the first. His authoritative neo-Platonist writings made a considerable impact on later Ismāʿīlīs as well as on Muslim philosophers such as Ibn Sīnā (Avicenna, d. 1037).

In political philosophy, al-Fārābī endorsed the ideas of Plato as found in his *Republic* and *Laws*. He made a major effort to articulate his understanding of the Platonic Perfect State into Arabic. With this in mind he attempted to reconcile the Platonic theory of state and prophecy. His own theory of civil governance, *siyāsah madanīya*, aims at achieving a happiness (*saʿāda*) that brings the perfect good to cities and nations. He avoided confrontation with the jurists who considered the Islamic *Sharīʿah* as the ultimate good for the community.

Al-Fārābī's virtuous city is modeled on Plato's *Republic*. The topics of justice, soul, non-virtuous cities, qualities of the head of the virtuous city, crafts, and happiness are all Platonic elements, essential to al-Fārābī's political teachings. However, al-Fārābī was more interested in a virtuous order than a political organization of the city. Accordingly, his political thought can be seen as ethics rather than political philosophy. Al-Fārābī does not show the same administrative and political knowledge Plato displays in the *Republic* nor is his writing as forceful. His style is expository, while Plato's approach is dialogical and highlights the deliberative and dramatic character of politics.

In al-Fārābī's utopia, the source of authority is virtue. It can be an inner disposition or it can be acquired by education. People are classified in the hierarchy of citizenship according to the degree of virtue they possess; everyone should know his or her place in the city. Like a pyramid, different classes represent different levels of the city, and equality should not be sought. Rather, the relationship among members of the city is based on service, *khidma*. Those who are on the bottom serve those who are on the top; those who are on the top serve no one—they are illuminated by the connection with the active intellect, that is, with the sum of wisdom, knowledge, and happiness a human being can acquire. Only philosophers and prophets can aspire to this status. As for those who are on the bottom, they are not served by anyone. They are, however, necessary for the city. The latter functions as the human body. Although the body is guided by the intellect, its chief organ, it also needs the other organs to subsist. The arrangement of the citizens should correspond to their virtues, their capacities, and their ranks to serve better the collective cooperation and the common good. The ultimate purpose of the virtuous city is happiness and the elimination of all evil in the city and the world.

The ignorant city (*jāhila*), the vicious city (*fāsiqa*), the altered city (*mubaddala*), and the aberrant city (*ḍālla*) are non-virtuous cities. Each of them offers a non-virtuous life centered on worldly desires. Al-Fārābī's Qurʾānic vocabulary here (*jahl, fisq, tabdīl, ḍalāl*) carries no Islamic significance, for, again, the excellence of a city is defined by virtue. The ignorant city never knows happiness and is unable to grasp its meaning. The vicious city knows virtues but behaves as the ignorant city does. The altered city was once a virtuous city but changed into a different one, in both its opinions and actions. Al-Fārābī does not elaborate on this civilizational change. Finally, the aberrant city, which is the opposite of the virtuous city, is based on falsehood although it claims to know virtue and aspires to attain happiness.

Al-Fārābī's city does not relate to the Muslim city in actual form or in its ideal one. The head of the city, the perfect man/the philosopher who connects with the active intellect, should be able to acquire the rational faculty through the passive intellect. Through the imaginative faculty he should be able to receive revelation. Thus, as the most virtuous person, the Prophet has a privileged place as the head of the city. Al-Fārābī's description of the first head of the city draws on Sunnī and Shīʿī accounts of the qualities of the Prophet and the imams. However, prophecy in the Muslim understanding (both Sunnī and Shīʿī) is not only a matter of virtue but also a divine gift. Muslims believe God chooses His prophets eternally and within different classes, while an imam's genealogy—from Qurayshī or ʿAlawī stock—matters for both Sunnī and Shīʿī. Furthermore, al-Fārābī's Prophet informs about the past and warns about the future, but Muḥammad is above all a messenger with a divine law, who is considered by Muslims as the universal end to a series of divine messengers. Al-Fārābī's city is a pure utopia along the lines of Plato's *Republic* and has no direct link to Muslim politics.

BIBLIOGRAPHY

Mahdi, Muhsin. *Al-Fārābī and the Foundation of Islamic Political Philosophy*. Chicago: University of Chicago Press, 2001.

Mahdi, Muhsin. "Al-Fārābī's Imperfect State." *Journal of the American Oriental Society* 110 (1990): 691–726.

Parens, Joshua. *An Islamic Philosophy of Virtuous Religions: Introducing Al-Fārābī*. Albany: State University of New York Press, 2006.

Walzer, Richard R. *Al-Fārābī on the Perfect State: Mabādiʾ ārāʾ ahl al-madīna al-fāḍila. A Revised Text with Introduction, Translation and Commentary*. Oxford: Clarendon Press, 1985.

ABDESSAMAD BELHAJ

FARAJ, MUḤAMMAD ʿABD AL-SALĀM.

Muḥammad ʿAbd al-Salām Faraj (c. 1954–1982) was a leader and ideologue of the radical Egyptian Islamist group Tanẓīm al-Jihād. Faraj was born in Dolongat, a province of al-Buhayra in Lower Egypt, and worked as an electrical engineer at the University of Cairo. The Cairo branch of Tanẓīm al-Jihād was responsible for the assassination of President Anwar el-Sadat (1970–1981) on 6 October 1981. Faraj's renowned political manifesto *al-Farīḍah al-ghāʾibah* (The Neglected Duty) provided the ideological justification for the assassination. *The Neglected Duty* represents the most comprehensive argument for the idea that militant *jihād* should be waged against internal enemies in general and unbelieving rulers in particular. It is the only available extended statement of radical Islamism from the 1970s and 1980s. Prior to the assassination, *The Neglected Duty* was unknown outside of Faraj's group. However, when Faraj and his fellow conspirators were put on trial, the text was used as part of their defense. Faraj and four others were executed on 15 April 1982.

Faraj sanctioned violence against Sadat by declaring him an unbeliever. He legitimized this position by referring to the medieval jurist Ibn Taymīyah (1263–1328) who declared the Mongols non-Muslims because they failed to enforce the *Sharīʿah*. Faraj professed that a Sunnī Muslim ceases to be one when he fails to keep the *Sharīʿah* or when he breaks any of the Islamic injunctions.

He found legitimacy for this position in the Qurʾān: "Whosoever does not rule by what God sent down, those, they are the unbelievers" (5:44). Faraj was thereby pronouncing *takfīr* (unbelief) on fellow Muslims, but he was less concerned with Egyptian citizens than he was with Sadat, the unbelieving Muslim ruler whom he referred to as Pharaoh, in order to imply that he was an apostate who deserved death.

As a direct result, 24-year-old Khālid al-Islambūlī of the Cairo branch of Tanẓīm al-Jihād assassinated Sadat at the annual October 6th victory parade in Cairo. When Sadat collapsed, al-Islambūlī shouted, "I have killed Pharaoh." While the group expected that Sadat's assassination would be followed by an armed Muslim uprising, it failed to ignite a revolt, and the radicals were quickly rounded up by the new Mubarak government.

In calling for the assassination of Sadat, Faraj was attempting to solve the problem that previous radical groups had faced, which was how to bring about the establishment of an Islamic state. While Sayyid Quṭb's concept of *al-jāhilīyah* (literally, "era of ignorance") established the notion of the internal enemy, Quṭb's advocacy of violence was more implicit than explicit. Faraj provided a solution to the question of what to do with the unbelieving ruler by sanctioning violence against him. This marked a radical departure from mainstream Islamic doctrine, which is generally critical of the killing of fellow Muslims or rebellion against rulers.

While Tanẓīm al-Jihād continued its violent activity throughout the 1980s and 1990s, Faraj's intellectual legacy, with its particular focus on combating the internal enemy, began to wane as the group developed in two divergent directions. In 2003, the group *al- Jamāʿah al-Islāmīyah,* formerly allied with Tanẓīm al-Jihād, called for a cease-fire. The group renounced violence, extremism, the denouncing of fellow Muslims as non-Muslims, and the killing of civilians. They argued that they had corrected their view of *jihād* and that such a correction was allowed in Islamic law. Tanẓīm al-Jihād followed suit: in 2004 one of the group's key members, Abbūd al-Zumar, declared his commitment to the electoral process, and in 2007 the Egyptian Sayyid ʿImām ʿAbd al-ʿAzīz al-Sharīf (also known as Dr. Faḍl), who was a leading figure in the global *jihād* movement, called for a halt to *jihād* activities against the West and against ruling regimes in Muslim countries.

While this renunciation of violence received approval from most of the organization's members, a segment, which for some time had been allied with al-Qaʿida, rejected it. This segment however, had moved away from Faraj's understanding of *jihād*. Āyman al-Ẓawāhirī, an Egyptian surgeon and former Tanẓīm al-Jihād member, became a prominent al-Qaʿida leader. Al-Ẓawāhirī recognized that the Islamist movement had failed to mobilize popular support. This caused him to shift from Faraj's emphasis upon struggle against the near enemy, the unbelieving ruler, to war against the far enemy, the United States and other Western countries, in the hope that the latter would help mobilize support within the Muslim world for an Islamic revolution.

[*See also* Egypt; *and* Quṭb, Sayyid.]

BIBLIOGRAPHY

Calvert, John. *Sayyid Quṭb and the Origins of Radical Islamism.* New York: Columbia University Press, 2010.

Gerges, Fawaz A. *The Far Enemy: Why Jihad Went Global.* Cambridge: Cambridge University Press, 2005.

Jansen, Johannes. *The Neglected Duty: The Creed of Sadat's Assassins.* New York: RVP Press, 2013. Contains a translation of *al-Farīḍah al-ghāʾibah.*

Kepel, Gilles. *The Prophet and the Pharaoh: Muslim Extremism in Egypt.* Berkeley: University of California Press, 2003.

Rashwan, Diaa. "The Renunciation of Violence by Egyptian Jihadi Organizations." In *Leaving Terrorism Behind: Individual and Collective Disengagement*, edited by Tore Bjørgo and John Horgan, pp. 113–132. London and New York: Routledge, 2009.

RACHEL M. SCOTT

FĀRŪQĪ, ISMĀʿĪL RĀJĪ AL-. Born in Jaffa, Palestine, Ismāʿīl Rājī al-Fārūqī (1921–1986), Islamic scholar and activist, received an education that made him trilingual (Arabic, French, and English) and provided him with multicultural intellectual sources that shaped his life and thought. He studied at the mosque school, attended a French Catholic school, the Collège des Frères (St. Joseph) in Palestine, and earned a bachelor of arts degree at the American University of Beirut (1941). Having become governor of Galilee in 1945, Fārūqī was forced to emigrate from Palestine after the creation of the state of Israel in 1948; he then earned master's degrees at Indiana and Harvard universities and a doctorate in philosophy from Indiana University (1952).

A poor job market and an inner drive brought Fārūqī back to the Arab world, where, from 1954 to 1958, he studied Islam at Cairo's al-Azhar University. He subsequently studied and conducted research at major centers of learning in the Muslim world and the West as visiting professor of Islamic studies at the Institute of Islamic Studies and a fellow at the faculty of divinity, McGill University (1959–1961), where he studied Christianity and Judaism; as professor of Islamic Studies at the Central Institute of Islamic Research in Karachi, Pakistan (1961–1963); and as visiting professor of history of religions at the University of Chicago (1963–1964).

Fārūqī then taught in the Department of Religion at Syracuse University (1964–1968) and became professor of Islamic studies and of history of religions at Temple University (1968–1986). During a professional life that spanned almost thirty years, he wrote, edited, or translated twenty-five books, published more than a hundred articles, was a visiting professor at more than twenty-three universities in Africa, Europe, the Middle East, and South and Southeast Asia, and served on the editorial boards of seven major journals.

For Fārūqī, Arabism and Islam were intertwined. Arab-Muslim identity was at the center of the man and the scholar. His life and writing reveal two phases or stages. In the first, epitomized in his book *On Arabism: Urubah and Religion* (1962), Arabism was the dominant theme of his discourse. In the second, Islam occupied center stage, as he increasingly assumed the role of an Islamic activist leader as well as of an academic. His later work and writing focused on a comprehensive vision of Islam and its relationship to all aspects of life and culture.

Living and working in the West, Fārūqī presented Islam in Western categories to engage his audience as well as to make Islam more comprehensible and respected. Like the founders of Islamic modernism in the late nineteenth and early twentieth centuries, he often presented Islam as the religion par excellence of reason, science, and progress with a strong emphasis on action and the work ethic.

If, during the 1950s and 1960s, Fārūqī sounded like an Arab heir to Islamic modernism and Western empiricism, by the late 1960s and early 1970s he progressively assumed the role of an Islamic scholar-activist. This shift in orientation was evident in the recasting of his framework: Islam replaced Arabism as his primary reference point. Islam had always had an important place in Fārūqī's writing, but it now became the organizing principle. Islam was presented as an all-encompassing ideology, the primary identity of a worldwide community (*ummah*) of believers and the guiding principle for society and culture. Like

Muḥammad ibn ʿAbd al-Wahhāb and Muḥammad ʿAbduh, Fārūqī grounded his interpretation of Islam in the doctrine of *tawḥīd* (the oneness of God), combining the classical affirmation of the centrality of God's oneness (monotheism) with a modernist interpretation (*ijtihād*) and application of Islam to modern life. In *Tawḥīd: Its Implications for Thought and Life*, he presented *tawḥīd* as the essence of religious experience, the quintessence of Islam, and the principle of history, knowledge, ethics, aesthetics, the *ummah* (Muslim community), the family, and the political, social, economic, and world orders.

This holistic, activist Islamic worldview was embodied in this new phase in his life and career as he continued to write extensively, to lecture and consult with Islamic movements and national governments, and to organize Muslims in America. During the 1970s he helped establish Islamic studies programs in the Arab world and Southeast Asia, recruited and trained Muslim students, organized Muslim professionals, established and chaired the Islamic Studies Steering Committee of the American Academy of Religion (1976–1982), and was an active participant in international ecumenical meetings where he was a major force in Islam's dialogue with other world religions. Fārūqī was a founder or leader of many organizations, including the Muslim Student Association and a host of associations of Muslim professionals, such as the Association of Muslim Social Scientists; he served as chairman of the board of trustees of the North American Islamic Trust; he established and was the first president of the American Islamic College in Chicago; and in 1981 he created the International Institute of Islamic Thought (IIIT) in Virginia.

At the heart of Fārūqī's vision was the Islamization of knowledge. He believed that the categories, concepts, and modes of analysis that originated in the secular West needed to be subordinated to the belief, ethics, and categories of Islam in order to bridge more effectively the gap between Islamic tradition and reform and revive Muslim society. His goal was to revive those methods of *ijtihād*, reinterpretation of Islam, and integrate scientific method within Islamic limits.

Fārūqī regarded the political, economic, and religio-cultural malaise of the Islamic community as primarily a product of the bifurcated state of education in the Muslim world with a resultant loss of identity and lack of vision. Fārūqī believed that the cure was twofold: the compulsory study of Islamic civilization and the Islamization of modern knowledge.

Ismāʿīl al-Fārūqī's life ended tragically in 1986 when he and his wife, Lois Lamyāʾ al-Fārūqī, also an Islamic scholar, were murdered by an intruder in their home.

BIBLIOGRAPHY

Works by Ismāʿīl Rājī al- Fārūqī

Christian Ethics. Montreal: McGill University Press, 1967.

Historical Atlas of the Religions of the World. New York: Macmillan, 1974.

"Islam and Christianity: Diatribe or Dialogue?" *Journal of Ecumenical Studies* 5, no. 1 (1968): 45–77.

"Islam and Christianity: Problems and Perspectives." In *The Word in the Third World*, edited by James P. Cotter, pp. 159–181. Washington, D.C.: Corpus Books, 1968.

Islam and Culture. Kuala Lumpur: Angatan Belia Islam Malaysia, 1980.

Islamization of Knowledge. Islamabad: National Hijra Centenary Committee of Pakistan, 1982.

"Islamizing the Social Sciences." *Studies in Islam* 16, no. 2 (April 1979): 108–121.

On Arabism. 4 vols. Amsterdam: Djambatan, 1962.

"The Role of Islam in Global Interreligious Dependence." In *Towards a Global Congress of the World's Religions*, edited by Warren Lewis, pp. 19–38. Barrytown, N.Y.: Unification Theological Seminary, 1980.

Tawḥīd: Its Implications for Thought and Life. 2d ed. Herndon, Va. International Institute of Islamic Thought, 1982.

Ed. *Essays in Islamic and Comparative Studies*. Washington, D.C.: International Institute of Islamic Thought, 1982. Collection of essays edited by al-Fārūqī.

Ed. *Islamic Thought and Culture*. Washington, D.C.: International Institute of Islamic Thought, 1982. Collection of essays edited by al-Fārūqī.

Ed. *Trialogue of the Abrahamic Faiths: Papers Presented to the Islamic Studies Group of the American Academy of Religion*. 2d ed. Herndon, Va.: International Institute of Islamic Thought, 1986. Collection of essays edited by al-Fārūqī.

Secondary Sources

Esposito, John L. "Ismail R. al-Faruqi: Muslim Scholar-Activist." In *The Muslims of America*, edited by Yvonne Yazbeck Haddad, pp. 65–79. New York and Oxford: Oxford University Press, 1991.

Wahhāb, Muḥammad Ibn ʿAbd al-. *Sources of Islamic Thought: Three Epistles on Tawḥīd*. Translated and edited by Ismāʿīl Rājī al-Fārūqī. Indianapolis: American Trust Publications, 1980.

Quraishi, M. Tariq. *Ismail R. al-Farūqi: An Enduring Legacy*. Plainfield, Ind.: Muslim Students Association of the U.S.A. and Canada, 1986.

JOHN L. ESPOSITO

FĀSĪ, MUḤAMMAD ʿALLĀL AL-.

Muḥammad ʿAllāl al-Fāsī (1910–1974) is a nationalist leader and central figure of the modern intellectual and political history of Morocco. He was raised in Fez (Ar., Fās, Morocco) in a bourgeois *fāsī* family with a strong tradition in Islamic scholarship, trade, state administration and Andalusian origins. His double interest in Islam and politics stemmed from his studies at al-Qarawiyyīn University in Fez where he graduated in 1930. There, he came under the influence of nationalist Salafī teachers who combined traditional religious teaching, the reformist ideas of Muḥammad ʿAbduh (d. 1905), and anticolonial attitudes. This complex heritage provided him with the necessary skills for an outstanding role in the struggle for Morocco's independence from France. He distinguished himself with his prolific writings, his refined manners, diplomacy, and charisma.

In 1930 he started his nationalist activities when he led the opposition to the "Berber Decree," an attempt by French colonial authorities to exempt Berbers from the application of Islamic law. He founded two of the earliest nationalist reform movements. First, in 1934, with other nationalists, he created the Committee for Moroccan Action. Then, in 1937, he launched the National Party for the Implementation of Reforms. The French Protectorate banned the party, and al-Fāsī was imprisoned and finally exiled to Gabon and Congo for nine years. Three years before his liberation, his companions founded the Istiqlāl Party in 1943. Once back, he became the leader (*zaʿīm*) of the movement and the symbol of the national aspiration for independence. However, clashes with the French, King Muḥammad V, and other nationalist activists persuaded him to lead the fight from outside the country. Thus, he carried on political missions in Latin America, Europe, and the Arab world to rally support for Moroccan independence. In 1953 his famous call from Cairo for military resistance to the French occupation accelerated the independence process.

In 1956, after independence, al-Fāsī was involved in government, then in opposition. He was a key architect of the Moroccan Constitution in 1962. In addition, in the years 1961–1963, he was minister of Islamic affairs and endowments. He was also elected a member of the parliament, where he served until 1965. However, his leadership of the Istiqlāl Party was contested by the young generation of nationalists, namely Mehdi Ben Barka (d. 1965) and his companions, who adopted radical and socialist views. Al-Fāsī maintained the party as a conservative, nationalist, pan-Arab one with centrist, liberal, and monarchist inclinations. From 1965 until his death in 1974, he was part of the opposition to King Ḥasan II (d. 1999). Although al-Fāsī was a constitutionalist monarchist, he rejected King Ḥasan's rising authoritarianism, nor did he accept King Ḥasan's pragmatic and gradual repossession of the Moroccan territories from Spain and Algeria.

As a reformist, al-Fāsī believed that authentic Islam was corrupted by despotism, colonialism, and ignorance. To be able to redress the situation, he promoted the reform of the Moroccan mind. He dedicated to this topic his most deeply thoughtful and original work *Self-Criticism*, which was published in 1952. In fact, al-Fāsī was rather concerned about the obstacles to independence and progress in Moroccan society, which was traditional, backward, and under colonial rule. Among the social vices that prevented it from developing, al-Fāsī addressed selfishness, laziness, gender inequality, poverty, analphabetism, and other social handicaps. In particular, he criticized errors of thought made by the protagonists of the nationalist struggle. Accordingly, he examines the intellectual premises, conditions of thought, and freedom as displayed by Moroccan nationalism. His criticism was followed by a reform program for an independent Morocco, led by the Istiqlāl Party. Al-Fāsī emphasized the necessity of facing the economic and social problems of Morocco as the major battle for sovereignty.

After independence, decolonization—especially constitutional and legal decolonization—was the main subject of al-Fāsī's thought. This stimulated his interest in the revival of *Sharīʿah*, to which he dedicated two of his major books. In his work *The Finalities of Sharīʿah and Its Merits*, published in 1963, he argues that ethics is the basis of public interest and the higher objectives of Islam. He emphasizes the virtues of justice and equity as essential to the teachings of Islamic law. At this point, he seems under the influence of ʿAbduh and Rashīd Riḍā (d. 1935). In their footsteps, he asserts that the finality of *Sharīʿah* is civilization, the preservation of order and cohabitation, the establishment of justice, reason, labor, and the management of resources. Although he admits the agreement of Islamic law and natural law, he sees superiority in the former where obligation stems from divine authority. In his second book, *An Apology for Sharīʿah*, published three years later, he states that law is part of religion. Subsequently, he harshly criticizes the adoption of European laws in Muslim societies and sees their presence as a colonial legacy to be removed. For him, a Muslim society should not be separated from *Sharīʿah* to adopt a foreign law. In an apologetic tone, he makes a case for the merits and the universality of *Sharīʿah*. His apology glorifying *Sharīʿah* is comparable to Salafī writings. After all, he was preoccupied with the usual double concern of Salafī reformists: the reform of Islam and the revival of the nation. However, his nationalist attitude is omnipresent, and the question of colonial use of law to exploit lands is a central issue in his thought.

BIBLIOGRAPHY

Works by Muḥammad ʿAllāl al-Fāsī

Al-Naqd al-dhātī. Cairo: al-Maṭbaʿah al-ʿĀlamīya, 1952.

Difāʿ ʿan al-sharīʿa. Beirut: Manshūrāt al-ʿAṣr al-Ḥadīth, 1972.

Maqāṣid al-sharīʿa al-islāmīya wa-makārimuhā. Beirut: Dār al-Gharb al-Islāmī, 1993.

Edited Collections and Articles in Edited Collections

Benaddi, Hassan. "Muḥammad ʿAllāl al-Fāsī: Le penseur et le combattant." In *Penseurs maghrébins contemporains*, edited by Hassan Benaddi et al., pp. 13–41. Tunis: Collectif CERES, 1993.

Johnston, David L. "ʿAllāl al-Fāsī: *Sharīʿah* as Blueprint for Righteous Global Citizenship?" In *Sharīʿah: Islamic Law in the Contemporary Context*, edited by Abbas Amanat and Frank Griffel, pp. 83–103. Stanford, Calif.: Stanford University Press, 2007.

Journal Articles

Balafrej, Ahmed. "'Allāl al-Fāsī, Héraut de l'indépendance marocaine." *Les Africains* 12 (1978): 41–59.

Talbi, Mohamed. "'Allāl al-Fāsī (1910–1974)." *Cahiers de Tunisie* 23 (1975): 301–304.

ABDESSAMAD BELHAJ

FĀṬIMID DYNASTY. The Fāṭimid dynasty was a major Ismāʿīlī Shīʿī dynasty that ruled over parts of North Africa and the Middle East from 909 until 1171. Comprising the following fourteen caliphs, the Fāṭimids were also acknowledged as Ismāʿīlī imams:

al-Mahdī (909–934)
al-Qāʾim (934–946)
al-Manṣūr (946–953)
al-Muʿizz (953–975)
al-ʿAzīz (975–996)
al-Ḥākim (996–1021)
al-Ẓāhir (1021–1036)
al-Mustanṣir (1036–1094)
al-Mustaʿī (1094–1101)
al-ʿĀmir (1101–1130)
al-Ḥāfiẓ (as regent, 1130–1132; as caliph, 1132–1149)
al-Ẓāfir (1149–1154)
al-Fāʾiz (1154–1160)
al-ʿĀḍid (1160–1171)

Early Fāṭimids. By the middle of the ninth century, the Ismāʿīlīs had organized a dynamic, revolutionary movement, generally designated as *al-daʿwah al-hādiyah* or the rightly guiding mission. The Ismāʿīlī imāms traced their ʿAlid ancestry to Ismāʿīl, the eponym of the Ismāʿīlīyah and the original heir designate of his father, the early Shīʿī Imam Jaʿfar al-Ṣādiq (d. 765 CE). The early Ismāʿīlī *daʿwah,* propagated by a network of *dāʿīs* or missionaries throughout the Islamic world, achieved particular success in North Africa as a result of the efforts of Abū ʿAbd Allāh al-Shīʿī, a *dāʿī,* when he met and converted members of the Kutāma Berbers, of Lesser Kabylia in present-day eastern Algeria, while on pilgrimage in Mecca. He established a base in their homeland in 893. By 903 Abū ʿAbd Allāh had commenced his conquest of Ifrīqiyah, covering today's Tunisia and eastern Algeria, at the time ruled by the Sunnī Aghlabids as vassals of the ʿAbbāsids. By 909 Abū ʿAbd Allāh entered Qayrawān, the Aghlabid capital, and ended their rule.

In 902 the Ismāʿīlī imam (who at that time acted as the head of the *daʿwah* and simply an ambassador to the real imam, Muḥammad ibn Ismāʿīl Saʿid ibn al-Husayn, later to be called ʿAbd Allāh al-Mahdī bi Allāh) left Salamīyah to avoid capture by the ʿAbbāsids. After brief stays in Palestine and Egypt, he was imprisoned in Sijilmāsa, in southern Morocco, from 905 to 909; he was rescued by his *dāʿī,* Abū ʿAbd Allāh. In Ramaḍān in 909, Abū ʿAbd Allāh set off at the head of his Kutāma army to Sijilmāsa, to hand the reins of power to the Ismāʿīlī imām. ʿAbd Allāh al-Mahdī entered Qayrawān on January 4, 910, and was immediately proclaimed caliph. The Ismāʿīlī *daʿwah* finally led to the establishment of a *dawlah,* or state, headed by the Ismāʿīlī imām. The Shīʿī caliphate of the Fāṭimids commenced in Ifrīqiyah and came to be known as the Fāṭimid dynasty or Fāṭimīyah, named for the Prophet's daughter and ʿAlī's wife Fāṭimah, to whom al-Mahdī and his successors traced their ancestry.

Consolidation and Resistance. The first four Fāṭimid caliph-imams who ruled from Ifrīqiyah encountered numerous difficulties while consolidating their power. In addition to the continued hostility of the ʿAbbāsids, the Umayyads of Spain, and the Byzantines, the early Fāṭimids devoted much energy to subduing the rebellious Khārijī Berbers belonging to the Zanāta confederation, especially the prolonged revolt of Abū Yazīd. They also confronted hostile Sunnī Arab inhabitants of

Qayrawān and other cities of Ifrīqiyah, led by their Mālikī jurists. The Fāṭimids were city builders and founded al-Mahdīyah and al-Manṣūrīyah (the precursor of Cairo); these served as their new capitals in Ifrīqiyah.

In accordance with their universal claims, the Fāṭimids continued their *da'wah* activities after they assumed power. The *da'wah* was reinvigorated from the time of al-Mu'izz, who firmly established Fāṭimid rule in North Africa and successfully pursued policies of war and diplomacy resulting in territorial expansion. Al-Mu'izz also made detailed plans for the conquest of Egypt, a perennial objective of the Fāṭimids in their eastern strategy of expansion. Through the combination of taxes, military, and religious reforms, al-Mu'izz through his commander Jawhar, a slave of Slavic extraction, was able to conquer Egypt in 969. A new residential and administrative complex was founded north of al-Fustāt and rapidly developed into a city, Qāhirah (Cairo). Al-Mu'izz arrived in his new capital city, brining the coffins of the deceased Fāṭimid imāms, in 973, marking the end of the North African phase of the Fāṭimid caliphate.

Fāṭimid Empire and Contributions. Naval and military power, the splendor of the court, Egypt's artistic productions, and burgeoning international trade helped to project the Fāṭimid regime as an equal of the Byzantine and 'Abbāsid empires. Politically and militarily, however, its efforts to advance through Syria were checked in the second half of the tenth century by a resurgence of Byzantine power and the armies of the Qarmaṭīs of Bahrain; and later by the incursions of the Turkish Seljuks. Despite these setbacks, by the end of al-'Azīz's reign, the Fāṭimid empire had attained its greatest extent, at least nominally, with Fāṭimid suzerainty recognized from the Maghrib to parts of the Fertile Crescent, specifically Syria and Palestine.

At the same time, Ismā'īlī *dā'īs* acting as secret agents of the Fāṭimid state continued their activities both within and outside the Fāṭimid dominions, with Cairo serving as the headquarters of the Ismā'īlī *da'wah*. But within the Fāṭimid state, the Ismā'īlī doctrines made little headway among the population at large. In Fāṭimid Egypt, the population remained predominantly Sunnī with an important community of Coptic Christians. Indeed, the Ismā'īlī *da'wah* had its greatest lasting success outside of Fāṭimid dominions, especially in Yemen, Iraq, Iran, and Central Asia.

The Fāṭimids established many institutions of learning in Cairo, including al-Azhar, originally a mosque and then converted to a university, and the Dār al-'Ilm, or House of Knowledge, set up in 1005 by al-Ḥākim. During al-Ḥākim's reign certain *dā'īs* preached extremist ideas that culminated in the proclamation of this controversial caliph/imām's divinity and the formation of the Druze movement, which was opposed by the Fāṭimid regime.

Decline and Dissent. Fueled by factional rivalries within the Fāṭimid armies, and economic troubles exacerbated by famines, plagues, and the lack of Nile floods, the Fāṭimid caliphate began to decline during the long reign of al-Mustanṣir, who was eventually obliged to call on the Armenian commander Badr al-Jamālī for help. In 1074 al-Jamālī arrived in Cairo with his Armenian troops and speedily restored relative peace and stability to the Fāṭimid state. Badr became the "commander of the armies" (*amīr al-juyūsh*) and the first of the "viziers of the sword," in addition to reaching the highest positions of the Fāṭimid state. Henceforth, military men, frequently appointed as viziers rather than caliphs, exercised effective power in the Fāṭimid state. Al-Jamālī (d. 1094) also ensured that his son al-Afḍal would succeed him as the real master of the Fāṭimid state.

On the death of al-Mustanṣir, in 1094, the Ismā'īlīs split into the Nizārī and al-Musta'lī factions, named after al-Mustanṣir's sons who claimed his heritage. Henceforth, these two branches of the Ismāʿīlīyah recognized different lines of imāms. The cause of Nizār (d. 1095), the designated successor of al-Mustanṣir who was ousted by al-Afḍal, was taken up in Iran by Ḥasan-i Ṣabbāḥ (d. 1124) who founded the independent Nizārī *daʿwah*. The Mustaʿlī Ismāʿīlīs of Fāṭimid Egypt and elsewhere acknowledged al-Mustaʿlī, who was installed to the Fāṭimid caliphate by al-Afḍal, also as their imām. By 1132, in the aftermath of al-Āmir's assassination and the irregular succession of his cousin al-Ḥāfiẓ, the Mustaʿlī Ismāʿīlīs themselves split into the Ḥāfiẓī and Ṭayyibī branches. Only the Ḥāfiẓīs, situated mainly in Egypt, recognized al-Ḥāfiẓ and the later Fāṭimids as their imāms.

The final decades of the Fāṭimid caliphate were extremely turbulent. Reduced to Egypt proper, the Fāṭimid state was continuously beset by political and economic crises, worsened by disorders within the Fāṭimid armies, the arrival of the Crusaders, and the invasions of the Zangids of Syria. Ṣalāḥ al-Dīn (Saladin), initially a lieutenant of the Zangids and the last of the Fāṭimid viziers, ended Fāṭimid rule in 1171 CE and had the *khuṭbah* (Friday sermon) read in Cairo in the name of the ʿAbbāsid caliph.

[*See also* ʿAbbāsid Caliphate; *and* Egypt.]

BIBLIOGRAPHY

Daftary, Farhad. *The Ismāʿīlīs: Their History and Doctrines*. 2d ed. Cambridge, U.K.: Cambridge University Press, 2007.

Halm, Heinz. *Die Kalifen von Kairo: Die Fatimiden in Ägypten 973–1074*. Munich: Beck, 2003.

Halm, Heinz. *The Empire of the Mahdi: The Rise of the Fatimids*. Translated from the German by M. Bonner. Leiden: E. J. Brill, 1996.

Maqrīzī, Taqī al-Dīn Aḥmad al-. *Ittiʿāẓ al-Ḥunafāʾ*. Edited by J. al-Shayyāl and M. Ḥ. M. Aḥmad. 3 vols. Cairo, 1967–1973.

Nuʿmān ibn Muḥammad, al-Qāḍī Abū Ḥanīfah al-. *Iftitāḥ al-daʿwah*. Edited by Wadād al-Qāḍī. Beirut, 1970. Translated as *Founding the Fatimid State: The Rise of an Early Islamic Empire* from the Arabic by H. Haji. London: I. B. Tauris, 2006.

Walker, Paul. E. *Exploring an Islamic Empire: Fatimid History and Its Sources*. London: I. B. Tauris, 2002.

FARHAD DAFTARY
and D. S. RICHARDS
Updated by KHALED M. G. KESHK

FATWA. A fatwa (Ar. *fatwā*) is a legal–theological opinion based on *Sharīʿah*, the religious law. The opinion is given by an authoritative scholar of Islam who in his particular capacity as jurisconsult is called a mufti (Ar. *muftī*). A mufti does not issue a fatwa on his own accord, but on the request of a person or institution, the *mustaftī*. The fatwa is nonbinding and is not to be applied by any person or institution except the fatwa-petitioner.

A fatwa can relate to any kind of query that is of importance to the petitioner, but it was intended originally to explain the finer details of *Sharīʿah* to those not learned in the law. A fatwa therefore commonly answers questions with regard to issues of ritual law, personal status law, and social interaction, but it has also gained importance in sociopolitical issues—modern examples include fatwas on entering into war, drinking coffee, using a printing press, listening to the radio, and residing under non-Muslim rule.

The practice of fatwa-giving (*iftāʾ*) finds its origin in the Qurʾān, where a number of verses addressed to the Prophet Muḥammad begin, "When they ask you for an opinion (*yasataftūnaka*) on . . . , then say (*qul*). . . ." (e.g., Qurʾān 4:127, 176). The *iftāʾ* was officially not part of Islamic legal scholarship, as *fiqh* and *uṣū al-fiqh*, but the authority of certain muftis was such that collections of their fatwas became part of that scholarship.

A fatwa should be distinguished from a ruling issued by a judge. A judge uses the law in order to make a decision in a conflict between two parties and to rule on the basis of evidence presented. The mufti, on the other hand, merely provides a single petitioner with information that is exclusively based on Islamic legal rules. Unlike the fatwa, the judicial ruling is binding and can be enforced by the state.

Another important distinction relates to the functionaries: in premodern times the judge was a civil servant of the state, whereas the mufti was not an appointed official. Ideally, the petitioner selected the mufti based on the scholar's knowledge and personal integrity. In practice, it is conceivable that a petitioner would select a mufti whose views matched those of the petitioner, perhaps even in disregard of the mufti's reputation.

In the past as well as the present, courts and rulers have also acted as *mustaftīs*. The judge might ask for a fatwa as support for the judge's understanding of the law or as a pronouncement of the law based on the bare facts given to the mufti. The ruler, on the other hand, frequently used a fatwa as support for an act he desired to take. Under the Ottomans, the muftis became part of the state apparatus, with the appointment of a state mufti (called *shaykh al-Islām*). This practice has been continued by most modern Muslim states, often alongside the establishment of a state-appointed body that issues fatwas (*dār al-iftāʾ*).

Fatwas in Modern Times. Since the late twentieth century, the practice of *iftāʾ* outside of state-institutionalized *iftāʾ* has undergone several remarkable changes with regard to content as well as procedure and methodology.

In terms of content, the traditional field of fatwa-queries has been expanded to encompass a wider array of issues than was previously the case. This can be explained by the increasing importance of Islam in the modern Muslim world, such that Islam not only pertains to issues of ritual and private social life, but also to a host of societal, economic, and political questions related to the globalizing and modern world. The prolific use of fatwas to support or condemn events of global implications—such as the 1991 allied response to Iraq's invasion of Kuwait, suicide bombings, or the attacks of 9/11—is an example of the highly politicized and altered use of this institution.

In terms of procedure, *iftāʾ* has developed in a variety of ways. Although until recently the fatwa-petitioner would generally only contact a local mufti, the petitioner now has access to muftis all over the world, who promptly issue fatwas by means of email. Moreover, fatwas are often filed in online archives that can be browsed at leisure. This phenomenon of "cyber-fatwas" not only serves the individual Muslim petitioner who is one click away from a mufti, but also yields an ever-growing corpus of fatwas on contemporary issues.

In addition to this development, the number of muftis has increased, including many whom the religious establishment of traditionally trained scholars (*ʿulamāʾ*) does not consider qualified. However, although Islamic doctrine does prescribe the general professional and personal qualifications of a mufti in the so-called *adāb al-muftī* literature, there is no central authority to uphold them. Recently, two measures have been employed to counter the increase in what is perceived by the religious establishment as unauthorized fatwas. First, religious and governmental authorities jointly issue statements emphasizing the qualitative conditions for issuing fatwas. An example is the Amman Message of 2004, a detailed statement from King Abdullah of Jordan defining Islam and the conditions for issuing fatwas, which in a consecutive process of conferences and Internet exchanges was endorsed by more than five hundred Muslim scholars and most Muslim state leaders.

The second measure is the cooperation among muftis to jointly issue fatwas that, due to their collective endorsement, will carry more authoritative weight than individual fatwas. The cooperation can take place within either a network or a collective. Networks of muftis are commonly employed by Internet sites that receive questions by the petitioner and then distribute these questions among their network of selected muftis. Although these muftis still operate in their traditional role as individual jurisconsults, the name and position of the Internet site guarantee a degree of conformity in the fatwas issued.

The collective is a historically new phenomenon through which scholars, often of different nationalities and of different schools of law (sometimes including both Sunnī and Shīʿite scholars), have organized to issue joint fatwas. This process of joint *iftāʾ* is also known as "collective legal interpretation" (*ijtihād jamāʿī*). Examples of the collective approach are the fatwa boards of Islamic financial institutions and international fatwa councils.

The third modern development in *iftāʾ* is related to the methodology employed in reaching a fatwa. The most remarkable trend is the return to the practice of *ijtihād*, a method of reasoning based on direct reference to the sources of the Qurʾān and Sunnah. Although *ijtihād* is formally not disallowed in *iftāʾ*, it is now practiced in innovative ways in fatwas, for example, allowing gender equality and banking interest. The most conspicuous use of this new approach is in fatwas with extreme militant content. Fatwas in support of suicide bombings, the indiscriminate killing of bystanders, and the declaration of individual Muslims or Muslim governments as unbelievers (*takfīr*) have contributed to the image of the fatwa as a death warrant.

Another approach of this new *ijtihād*, on the other hand, advocates a return to ruling on grounds of the underlying objectives of the *Sharīʿah* (*maqāṣid al-Sharīʿah*), rather than on the literal source material. This approach allows two important principles to be derived: what is in the interest of Muslims (*maṣlaḥah*) and what is impelled by "necessity" (*ḍarūrah*) to go against the rule. The main argument behind this new approach is that the *Sharīʿah* is meant to serve the interests of Muslims and to make their lives easier (*taysīr*) rather than more difficult—hence, contemporary fatwas have been issued that allow Muslims to take on a mortgage, to reside in non-Muslim countries as long as their religious freedom is guaranteed, or to allow fasting times to be adjusted for Muslims living in areas with long daylight hours. This form of *ijtihād* is found in particular in the elaboration of *fiqh al-aqallīyāt* (Islamic jurisprudence for Muslim minorities), which applies to Muslims living in Western countries. Opponents of this new form of reasoning argue that the interests of Muslims should not be shaping the outcome of the *Sharīʿah* since the *Sharīʿah* is meant to determine the interests of the Muslim.

The enormous production of fatwas since the late twentieth century testifies to the importance of Islamic authenticity to many Muslims, but it attests very little to the impact of these fatwas on Muslims. The extent to which Muslims acknowledge the authority of fatwas, or regulate their lives accordingly, is to date unknown. For that reason, fatwas cannot be equated prima facie with the conduct or opinions of Muslims. Fatwas may at best be read as a collective of opinions on what Muslims "ought to think" rather than "what Muslims find to be true."

[*See also* Dār al-Iftāʾ; Minority Fiqh; *and* Sharīʿah.]

BIBLIOGRAPHY

Bunt, Gary R. *Islam in the Digital Age: E-jihad, Online Fatwās and Cyber Islamic Environments.* London: Pluto Press, 2003. Analyzes contemporary developments.

Calder, Norman. "Al-Nawawī's Typology of *Muftīs* and Its Significance for a General Theory of Islamic Law." *Islamic Law and Society* 3, no. 2 (1996): 137–164. One of the many articles written on the status, practice, typology, and qualifications of muftis.

Gerber, Haim. *State, Society and Law in Islam: Ottoman Law in Comparative Perspective.* Albany: State University of New York Press, 1994.

Hallaq, Wael B. *A History of Islamic Legal Theories: An Introduction to Sunnī uṣūl al-figh.* Cambridge, U.K.: Cambridge University Press, 1997. Contains an extensive discussion of the theological and legal technicalities of fatwas.

Masud, Muhammad Khalid, Brinkley Messick, and David S. Powers, eds. *Islamic Legal Interpretation: Muftīs and Their Fatwās.* Cambridge, Mass.: Harvard University Press, 1996. Provides an overview of the use of fatwas through the ages, with an extensive introduction on the characteristics and functions of the fatwa.

Skovgaard-Petersen, Jakob. *Defining Islam for the Egyptian State: Muftīs and Fatwās of the Dār al-Iftā.* Leiden, The Netherlands: Brill, 1997.

Tyan, Émile. *Histoire de l'organisation judiciaire en pays d'islam.* 2d ed. Leiden, The Netherlands: Brill, 1960. pp. 219–229.

Walsh, J. R. "Fatwā." In *Encyclopaedia of Islam.* Vol. 2. New ed. Leiden, The Netherlands: Brill, 1960–2004. A basic introduction to the fatwa, mostly treating the classical period.

MAURITS S. BERGER

FEDĀʾĪYĀN-I ISLĀM. The Fedāʾīyān-i Islām (Fedayan-e Islam, Devotees of Islam) was an Iranian religious group founded in 1945 by Navvāb Ṣafavī, a low-rank cleric, which propagandized a fundamentalist version of Shīʿī Islam. The Fedayan favored the introduction of the *Sharīʿah* into national legislation as the only valid law and a political system led by clerics. It is not surprising that, in the aftermath of the Islamic revolution in 1979–1980, Navvāb Ṣafavī was recalled by the rightist and traditionalist factions as one of the historical personalities inspiring this event. Opposing all secular institutional establishments as anti-Islamic, the group chose political violence as its strategy and carried out a number of assassinations in the 1940s, 1950s, and 1960s. Because of this terrorist activity, Navvāb Ṣafavī was imprisoned in 1951 and executed in 1956 after a failed assassination attempt against Prime Minister Ḥusayn ʿAlā.

The Fedayan's terrorist activities targeted high-profile men from the military and political elite of the Pahlavi period. Navvāb Ṣafavī and his companions masterminded and implemented the assassinations of the intellectual Aḥmad Kasravī, in 1946, because of his secular beliefs and strident criticism of the Shīʿī *ʿulamāʾ*; and Prime Minister Hossein ʿAli Razmara, in 1951, who opposed the nationalization of the Anglo-Iranian Oil Company. In the 1950s, after the withdrawal of their support for Muḥammad Muṣaddiq's government, they tried to assassinate Muṣaddiq himself and Ḥusayn Fāṭimī, a key Muṣaddiq advisor, leaving the latter seriously injured. Fedayan's last assassination was in 1965, when they killed the prime minister, Ḥasan ʿAlī Manṣūr.

Despite its terrorism, the group gathered support from some other political forces. Indeed, the Fedayan became one of the protagonists of the events related to the overthrow of Muṣaddiq's government and the coup d'état organized against him in 1953. In mid-1952 Ayatollah Abol-Qāsem Kāshāni made overtures to the Fedayan in order to gain its support for his struggle against Muṣaddiq's government, which, according to the ayatollah, had enacted un-Islamic law and refused to appoint loyal Muslims to relevant positions. The bitterness between Muṣaddiq and Kāshāni was such that the cleric, along with the Fedayan, turned against the government, thus paving the way for British and American secret services to carry out the coup against Muṣaddiq.

The Fedayan was socially homogeneous. They appealed to the lowest strata of the Iranian society: low-ranked clerics and the urban proletariat. Poverty was common in Iranian cities during the 1950s, a situation that later convinced the shah of the necessity of a major reform plan, the so-called

White Revolution. The group opposed secularism and abhorred the modern, secular life that was, at that time, the trademark of Iran and Pahlavi's rule. It is not surprising that the group reappeared on the scene in 1965, during the implementation of the Shah's White Revolution, which was meant to bring modernity in Iran by complying with Western models of development.

BIBLIOGRAPHY

Abrahamian, Ervand. *A History of Modern Iran*. Cambridge, U.K.: Cambridge University Press, 2008.

Abrahamian, Ervand. *Iran Between Two Revolutions*. Princeton, N.J.: Princeton University Press, 1982.

Tahavi, Mohammad Ali. *The Flourishing of Islamic Reformism in Iran: Political Islamic Groups in Iran (1941–1961)*. London: Routledge, 2005.

PAOLA RIVETTI

FIQH. Since the ninth century the Arabic term *fiqh* (lit., "understanding") has denoted legal doctrine or jurisprudence, as well as the discipline that derives norms for human acts from the holy texts of the Qurʾān and Sunnah. It thus designates a scholarly activity, the explanation and elaboration of the religious law (*Sharīʿah*) through the interpretive activity of legal scholars, the *fuqahāʾ* (sing., *faqīh*). *Fiqh* is the only way for humankind to arrive at God's law.

The terms *Sharīʿah* and *fiqh* are sometimes used synonymously. The contemporary Egyptian judge Muḥammad Saʿīd al-ʿAshmāwī (b. 1932) argues that the word *Sharīʿah* in the Qurʾān means neither law (*qānūn*) nor legislation (*tashrīʿ*) but the *ṭarīq* ("path"), the divine way or method of Islam. Its meaning was inflated, he argues, to include, first, all of the rules pertaining to worship and to society found in the Qurʾān, then the *ḥadīth* literature relating to the Prophet, and, finally, all the opinions and judgments of the legal scholars. The last-mentioned is properly called *fiqh*, and thus the term *Sharīʿah* today is commonly and wrongfully used to mean *fiqh*. Al-ʿAshmāwī illustrates this with Article 2 of the Egyptian Constitution, which reads in part: "The principles of Islamic *Sharīʿah* are the principal source of legislation." This refers properly to the principles of legislation, that is, *fiqh*. The article thus also confuses *Sharīʿah* with *fiqh* and in consequence confuses the will of God with the opinions and actions of humans. Al-ʿAshmāwī recommends returning to the proper usage in which *Sharīʿah* includes only those values, principles, and law that can be found in the Qurʾān and the sound Sunnah, because these alone are protected from error by God. All deductions or extrapolations from these, and all commentaries upon them, represent fallible human effort, or *fiqh* (Shepard, 1996).

The use of the term *fiqh* for jurisprudence shows that Muslims came to regard knowledge of the sacred law as knowledge par excellence. Theology (*kalām*)—the branch of knowledge that provides rational proofs for religiously held truth—was never able to gain the same position in Islamic societies as *fiqh* (Johansen, "Muslim *Fiqh*," 1999; Calder, 2006).

History. After the Prophet's death in 632 the *fuqahāʾ* were seen, and saw themselves, as "heirs to the Prophet" in accordance with a Prophetic *hadīth*, "The learned are the heirs to the Prophet." They were thus considered the only legitimate persons to interpret the revealed texts and deduce legal rules from them. Their position in premodern Islamic societies was therefore a central one. The advice given to the ʿAbbāsid caliph al-Manṣūr by the secretary Ibn al-Muqaffaʿ (d. 756), who proposed that the caliph be a lawgiver and enact law, was not followed in public law. Rather, from the latter half of the eighth to the tenth centuries the caliphs enforced the law and nominated, appointed, and dismissed judges (sing., *qāḍī*, who came from the class of *fuqahāʾ*) but did not themselves deduce the law from the sources. Thus the *fuqahāʾ* and the norms they developed acquired increasing importance in the political and religious culture of the pre-modern Islamic states. The role of *faqīh* was not restricted to the production of legal rules to be applied by courts; it also dominated in the debates on ethical as well as legal obligations and gained what may perhaps be called "legislative authority." Islamic jurisprudence is thus termed a jurist's law (Schacht, 1964), created and further developed by private specialists independent of the state. Only in early modern and modern Islamic states does legislative power rest with the state.

Islamic law has also been called a sacred law, based as it is on the two revealed sources of Qurʾān and *ḥadīth*. The hermeneutical challenges of the texts (see "The Roots of Islamic Law," below) resulted in a wide range of differing interpretations. This plurality of possible and accepted legal rules was acknowledged by Muslims as difference in opinion (*ikhtilāf*) and is institutionally reflected in the existence of four main Sunnī and one major Shīʿī (Jaʿfarī or Twelver) schools of law (sing., *madhhab*). Not only is the plurality of schools accepted as valid, but within the schools of law themselves different opinions about the same legal or ethical question are also often found.

Islamic law does not claim universal validity; it is binding on Muslims to its full extent in the territory of the Islamic state and to a slightly lesser extent in a non-Muslim territory, and only partially binding on non-Muslims residing in an Islamic territory. Islamic law is conscious of its character as a religious ideal. For Muslims, all human acts and relationships, including those that have less to do with law in the more narrow sense of the word, are assessed according to five (religious) qualifications (*al-aḥkām al-khamsa*): obligatory, recommended, indifferent, reprehensible, or forbidden (*ḥarām*). Alongside these five qualifications exists a scale of legal validity. Both can apply concurrently to the same case. Islamic law is thus part of a system of religious duties, but the legal subject matter is not reduced to and expressed only in those terms. The sphere of law retained a technical character of its own, and juridical reasoning could develop along its own lines. The jurists were aware that in some judgments religious and ethical points of view could not be taken into account (Schacht, 1964; Johansen, "Die sündige, gesunde Amme," 1999).

The Origins of Islamic Jurisprudence. According to the traditional Muslim position, *fiqh* has developed continuously from the lifetime of the Prophet. The Prophet's behavior was always an example for his followers, who, from the beginning, espoused what he approved of as custom (*sunnah*) or tradition in the form of Prophetic sayings. This ultimately led to the development of legal schools in the eighth and ninth centuries. This view was challenged in the early twentieth century by Ignaz Goldziher and fleshed out by Joseph Schacht some fifty years later (Schacht, 1979). According to Schacht, early Muslim jurisprudence reflected a "living tradition" and did not grow out of Prophetic *ḥadīth*; Schacht regarded the jurist ʿAbd Allāh Muḥammad ibn Idrīs al-Shāfiʿī (d. 820) to be the first scholar to refer systematically to Prophetic *ḥadīth*. Traditional Muslim scholars on the other hand consider the *ḥadīths*, as collected by al-Bukhārī (d. 870) and Muslim ibn al-Hajjāj (d. 875), to be authentic expressions going back to the Prophet and a firm basis for the development of *fiqh*. The major part of Islamic legal scholarship has, in the last decades, examined Schacht's views, either rejecting or corroborating them or elaborating on them (Calder, 2006).

The Literature of Islamic Jurisprudence. *Fiqh* books appeared soon after the middle of the eighth century. The earliest texts are attributed to Mālik b. Anas (d. 795), al-Shāfiʿī, Muḥammad ibn al-Ḥasan al-Shaybānī (d. 805), and Abū Yūsuf

(d. 798). The latter two were pupils of Abū Ḥanīfa (d. 767) who, along with Mālik, al-Shāfiʿī, and later Aḥmad Ibn Ḥanbal (d. 855), gave his name to a Sunnī school of law. The Twelver Shīʿa, also called the Jaʿfariyya or Imāmiyya, developed an independent legal tradition and school; there were also many schools that did not survive, for example, the Ẓāhirīyah, followers of Dāʾūd al-Ẓāhirī (d. 884). Each school of law has its own tradition of *fiqh* literature.

Fiqh books are divided into two major parts: one on ritual law or acts of devotion (*ʿibādāt*), such as purity (*ṭahārah*) as a precondition for prayer, the ritual prayer (*ṣalāt*), alms tax (*zakat*), fasting (*ṣawm*), and pilgrimage (*ḥajj*), normally in this order; and the other on legal areas deriving from interactions of human beings with one another (*muʿāmalāt*), such as personal status law, the law pertaining to slavery, vows, the Qurʾānic criminal punishments (*ḥudūd*), the law of war, obligations, process, rules regarding food and the slaughter of animals, and criminal law (*jināyāt*), in slightly differing orders according to the school of law. Important or complex aspects of Islamic law, particularly the law of succession, were also treated in separate works, as were subjects that were directly relevant to the administration of law in practice, such as religious endowments (*awqāf*, sing., *waqf*), legal devices (*ḥiyal*), written documents (*shurūṭ)*, and the duties of the judge (*ādāb al-qāḍī*). The administration of justice and public law in general is discussed in such works as *al-Aḥkām al-sulṭānīya* of al-Māwardī (d. 1058). There are numerous treatises on the duties of the market inspector (*ḥisba*). An important group of works deals with the problem of distinguishing between seemingly parallel but systematically distinct cases (*furūq*), and with the systematic structure of positive law in general. Here, legal maxims or principles (*qawāʿid fiqhīyah*) can be mentioned. Special works deal with the definition of technical terms. There are comparative accounts of the doctrines of several schools (*ikhtilāf*). Finally, the works on *ṭabaqāt,* the classes or generations of lawyers, provide biographical and bibliographical information. *Fiqh* literature shows remarkable structural and conceptual uniformity from its first appearance until its gradual displacement or transformation in the nineteenth and twentieth centuries and contains three broad areas of discussion: the sources of law, the hermeneutical rules that permit extrapolation of norms from sources, and an elaboration of the theory of *ijtihād* (lit., "personal effort"; the interpretation of the legal rule from an inexplicit divine ruling).

Nineteenth-century Western scholars characterized the *fiqh* literature as reflecting a speculative system of religious thought thoroughly imbued with idealistic norms. Recent research has shown, however, that especially the *fatwa* literature (Hallaq, 1994) and the *ādāb al-qāḍī* literature, which contains procedural law and tips for the correct behavior of the judge (Schneider, 1990), as well as literature on *shurūṭ* (written documents; Wakin, 1972) are rooted in practice. The concept of *ḍarūrah,* "necessity," which allowed Muslims under certain circumstances to be excepted from observing the law, must be mentioned in this context, as well as the legal devices (*ḥiyal*), often legal fictions, that were used—particularly in commercial law—to avoid violating the *Sharīʿah.* Furthermore, it has been argued that *fiqh* literature is not abstract but focused on a special brand of discourse of legal problems (Schneider, 2007).

In recent years encyclopedias of *fiqh* have gained increasing importance, for example, the one initiated by the Egyptian president Gamal Abdel Nasser (*Mawsūʿat al-fiqh al-islāmī,* 1971) and the Kuwaiti one (*al-Mawsūʿah al-fiqhīyah,* 1993). Unlike in classical works of *fiqh,* the subjects in these modern reference works are arranged alphabetically.

The Roots of Islamic Law. *Fiqh* is divided into *uṣūl al-fiqh*, "the roots (or theoretical bases) of Islamic law," and *furūʿ al-fiqh*, "the branches of Islamic law." Both concepts stand for an academic discipline and a literary genre. *Uṣūl al-fiqh* is concerned with the sources of the law and the methodology of extrapolating rules from the Qurʾān and Sunnah. The *Risālah fī uṣūl al-fiqh* of al-Shāfiʿī is considered the earliest work of *uṣūl al-fiqh*; the temporal gap between it and the later literary tradition has led its influence to be challenged (Hallaq, 1993). A noteworthy feature of pre-modern Islamic law is the casuistic method.

Before al-Shāfiʿī delineated the sources of Sunnī *uṣūl al-fiqh*—(1) the Qurʾān, and (2) the Sunnah of the Prophet; and when neither of those are explicit, (3) consensus (*ijmāʿ*) among scholars, and (4) analogy (*qiyās*), in that order of importance—the jurist's personal opinion (*raʾy*) on the basis of his *ijtihād* played an important role in the legislative process. For the Shīʿī Jaʿfarī school, the sayings of the imams—the direct descendants of the Prophet—are accepted in addition to the Qurʾān and the Sunnah of the Prophet; it also acknowledges *ijmāʿ* but generally not *qiyās*.

In Sunnī *fiqh*, *ijmāʿ* is the third and in practice most important principle. It is the unanimous agreement of the scholars on a rule (*ḥukm*) imposed by God. An important argument in this context is the infallibility of the Muslim community (*ummah*) (cf. the Prophetic *ḥadīth*, "My community shall not agree on an error"). The exact definition of *ijmāʿ* has always remained controversial. The Mālikī school recognizes, alongside the general consensus of the scholars of a given period, the consensus of the (ancient) scholars of Medina, the Prophet's town. The fourth source for determining the law is *qiyās*, analogy. The juristic conclusion of reasoning by analogy relies on the existence of a common characteristic in the "basic case" and the "analogous case." It is used to find solutions for cases that have not previously been the object of explication. Whereas *ijmāʿ* was born out of the need to ensure coherence in the nascent doctrine of Islam, in the face of dispersion of the believers and the proliferation of sayings attributed to the Prophet, *qiyās* appears to have responded originally to a need for diversification and clarification of the divine law.

Ijtihād, or a jurist's effort to determine the correct ruling from an indeterminate revelatory source, has played an important role from the beginning—in determining the *fiqh*, in the methodology of the Jaʿfarī school of law, and in Sunnī *fiqh* in the modern period. In al-Shāfiʿī's view, *ijtihād* was restricted to analogy. There is a modern scholarly debate concerning the "closing of the door of *ijtihād*": Joseph Schacht (1964) used this term when arguing that in about the tenth century the point had been reached when the scholars of all schools felt that all essential questions had been thoroughly discussed and finally settled, and a consensus was reached on the demand for *taqlīd*, a term that came to mean the unquestioning acceptance by jurists of the doctrines of the established schools and authorities. *Taqlīd* is thus the opposite of *ijtihād*. Wael Hallaq (1984) and others have concluded, however, that the door of *ijtihād* was closed neither in theory nor in practice.

It was indeed never closed in Twelver Shīʿī *fiqh*. Since the eleventh century, the Shīʿah have developed a theory of *ijtihād* as intellectual constraint of reason (*ʿaql*) that was thought to propel the jurists during the absence of the twelfth imām to valuable results in theological as well as legal questions. This concept of *ijtihād* has been named an intellectual revolution in medieval Shiism and it gave the jurists a strong and independent position. Only scholars with special qualifications were considered able and licensed to do *ijtihād*—they were then called *mujtahids*. Laypeople had to rely on those scholars on the basis of *taqlīd*.

A doctrine was developed according to which no *mujtahid* is infallible but every *mujtahid* is right (*kullu mujtahid muṣīb*), because the truth is only known to God. With the ensuing differing, sometimes contradictory legal opinions and rulings, the Shīʿī *fuqahāʾ* developed an instrument of legal interpretation with enormous flexibility, especially since the sixteenth century in Iran. The practical results and the theoretical developments that emerged from this situation can be seen in the development of the concept of the "rule of the jurist" (*wilāyat-e faqīh*) as promulgated by Khomeini in 1979.

In Sunnī legal theory the early unfettered use of *raʾy* continued to be recognized as legitimate by the Ḥanafīs under the name of *istiḥsān* (lit. "approval, preference") in cases in which the strict application of analogy would have led to undesirable results. The Mālikī school prefers the method of *istiṣlāḥ*, "having regard for the public interest (*maṣlaḥah*)."

The Branches of the Law. *Furūʿ al-fiqh* is the substantive law, as opposed to the *usūl* (principles). Its books are divided into the two spheres of *ʿibādāt* and *muʿāmalāt*, as explained above.

Family law. In modern Islamic states the law of personal status still refers explicitly to rulings of the Qurʾān and the classical *fiqh*; only in Turkey has a secular code of family law been introduced. There have been adjustments, especially in the area of gender relations. Divorce—in particular a wife's petition for dissolution of her marriage—is the outstanding example. In Ḥanafī *fiqh*, a wife could obtain a judicial annulment of her marriage if her husband was incapable of consummating the marriage and, on the grounds of putative widowhood, if her husband was a missing person and ninety years had elapsed since the date of his birth. Other schools, in particular the Mālikīs, allowed a wife to ground a petition on her husband's cruelty, his refusal or inability to provide for her, his desertion, or his affliction with a serious ailment that made the continuance of the marriage harmful for the wife. On the basis of *takhayyur* "selection," the female's right of divorce in many modern states where Ḥanafī law prevailed was implemented. Another basis for reform was *talfīq*, by which legal rules are constructed by combining and fusing discrete juristic opinions, or elements therefrom, of diverse provenance. An example is the Egyptian law of inheritance of 1943 that allows a Jew domiciled in a non-Muslim state to inherit from his Christian relative domiciled in a Muslim state. This would be possible neither under Ḥanafī law, because of the different domiciles of the two relatives, nor under Mālikī law, where a difference of religion between non-Muslim relatives constitutes a bar to inheritance. The combination of the two views resulted in a law for which no authority exists in any of the Sunnī schools (Coulson, 1964).

Polygyny was combated by individual male and female actors and women's organizations on the basis of neo-*ijtihād*. The first attempts in family law to improve the situation of women materialized in the Syrian Law of Personal Status of 1953. Syrian reformers maintained that the Qurʾānic verse (4:3) that husbands were not to take additional wives unless they were financially capable of supporting them, which had always been construed by jurists as a moral exhortation only, should be regarded as a positive legal condition and enforced as such by the courts. In 1957 polygyny was banned altogether in Tunisia and made a crime.

Penal law. Here, the classical *fiqh* developed a partition into *ḥudūd*, that is, the Qurʾānic crimes (unlawful sexual relations, slanderous accusation of unlawful sexual relations, drinking of wine/alcohol, theft, robbery, and in some cases, apostasy), and homicide and bodily harm, which is punished by retaliation (*qiṣāṣ*) or the payment of blood-money (*diyah*). In most Muslim states Islamic criminal law has been replaced by Western law. But Islamic penal law is still being applied or was reintroduced in Iran, Saudi Arabia, Pakistan, Northern Nigeria, Libya, Yemen, and Qatar. The reintroduction of Islamic criminal law in Iran and Pakistan in the 1970s was accompanied by a powerful ideological discourse that was shaped by propagandists of Islamism but has its roots in deeply felt religious convictions and emotions. In some of these states, for example, in Iran, classical penal law has more or less been codified (Peters, 2005).

Public law. After Ibn al-Muqaffaʿ's unsuccessful push for state control over the law, orthodox Islam has refused to be drawn into too close a connection with the state. According to classical Sunnī public law, caliphs, and later governors and sultans, only had an active role in law via their ability to enforce it and appoint and dismiss judges. However, the ruler had the right to *siyāsah* ("administration, management," modern: "policy") that comprised the whole of administrative justice, in contrast with the *Sharīʿah*, the religious law, administered by the *qāḍī*. Public law dealt with the qualifications and functions of the caliph as the ruler of the community. Twelver Shīʿī jurists on the other hand, believing that the last direct successor of the Prophet with the exclusive right to rule the Muslim community disappeared in the ninth century and will only return as the Mahdī at the "end of the time," worked out the outlines of an Islamic state and discussed the relation of scholars with the political power. With the concept of the caliphate as the head of the Muslim community losing force in the political fragmentation of the eleventh century at the latest, the Sunnī jurist Ibn Taymīyah (d. 1328) developed a theory according to which Islamic law does not prescribe a caliph, but only a policy governed by *fiqh* (*siyāsah sharʿīya*).

The *Fuqahāʾ*: Education and Profession. Knowledge of *fiqh* was required of both *qāḍīs* and the *muftīs*, jurists who issued a non-binding legal opinions (*fatwas*). According to the *fiqh* books, the judge had to be male, free, and a Muslim. He was the central juridical authority, as there was no provision for appeal in pre-modern times. According to the classical law of procedure, revision of a judgment on the basis of *ijtihād* was not possible; the *qāḍī*'s judgment could theoretically be revised only by himself or, in certain circumstances, by his successor. It could not be quashed by the ruler, who, however, did have the right to depose the judge. The ruler's jurisdiction extended to the institution of *maẓālim* (lit., "injustices") to which his subjects had the right to turn and submit a complaint, for instance, about the non-implementation of judgments or the corruption of state officials.

The question as to what role women could and did play in the Islamic judiciary is crucial. From the eleventh century on, judges and other civil servants were trained in colleges to which women seem not to have had access (cf. the West, where, e.g., the first woman studied at the University of Zurich in 1840). Women studied in informal settings such as private houses. In the classical period we find several female scholars teaching Prophetic *ḥadīth*, but there were hardly any women *faqīhs* or female judges (Schneider, 1998). The topic of female judges is discussed in *fiqh*. The view of the Mālikīs, Shāfiʿīs, and Ḥanbalīs was that women were incompetent to hold the post of *qāḍī*. Al-Māwardī's argument was that jurisdiction is part of political leadership, for which a woman is not eligible, and he cites Qurʾān 4:34, "Men are in charge of women." According to Abū Ḥanīfah, however, a woman could act as a *qāḍī*, but he restricted her judgments to those cases at which a woman was allowed to testify, thus excluding her from penal law, especially in regard to *ḥudūd* and *qiṣāṣ* cases. Abū Jaʿfar Muḥammad ibn Jarīr al-Ṭabarī (d. 923), who was the eponym of a school of law that did not survive, was of the opinion that women could act as judges in all legal matters. He based his view on the analogy between issuing a judgment and issuing a *fatwa*, which women were authorized to do (Schneider, 2005).

Developments from the Nineteenth Century on. Since the nineteenth century Islamic states have felt the impact of Western law. Already in the Ottoman empire (thirteenth to twentieth centuries), in the Ṣafavid and Qājār dynasties in Iran (sixteenth to twentieth centuries), and in the Mughal empire (sixteenth to nineteenth centuries), rulers were eager to control the legislative and adjudicative processes. The Ottoman empire was the most effective in this sense. After World War I and the collapse of the Ottoman empire, the jurist's law was transformed to statutory law, a law promulgated by a national-territorial legislative body. The jurisdiction of Islamic law became fully integrated into the modern nation-state's system of legislation. This transformation had profound implications, the most important of which was the abolishing of the law-making authority of the *fuqahāʾ* and their investment in state legislation. Western scholars differ as to how to assess the codification of the *Sharīʿah* and the wide range of methods and mechanisms designed to apply the codified *Sharīʿah* since the mid-nineteenth century. Some maintain that this development is an expression of the *Sharīʿah*'s vitality and ability to renew itself, while others are of the opinion that codification reflects a process of detachment from the *Sharīʿah* and even its "secularization" by the creation of an alternative statutory version of it (Layish, 2004). Clearly, modern-day Muslim jurists still have a voice in Muslim states and strive to adapt *fiqh* to modern conditions. An example is Yūsuf al-Qaraḍāwī (b. 1926), who is active in promoting the *fiqh* of minority Muslims in the West (*fiqh al-aqalīyāt*). In Iran the civil-society group "One Million Signatures" campaigned for the repeal of the 2008 personal status law, arguing on the basis of *fiqh*—as opposed to, for example, human-rights conventions—and using its bargaining power vis-à-vis the government of the Islamic Republic of Iran (Schneider, 2010).

Practically all constitutions of modern-day Islamic states refer to the religion or the law of Islam as being the basis of the legal system. But how can the state make sure that legislation is Islamic? What exactly is Islamic legislation? With modernity new interpretations of the sacred law appeared, solutions for newly arisen problems were sought and found, and the plurality of hermeneutic deductions increased. Two questions are crucial for the implementation of *fiqh* in modern nation-states: Which person, institution, or organ has the right to interpret the sources of Islamic law? And which interpretation is regarded in a certain state as the "right" interpretation?

Confronted with the necessity to develop a modern code of Islamic law, especially upon the emergence of modern nation-states after World War I, *fiqh* was further developed to adapt to the changing circumstances in politics, legislation, society, and economic life. Plurality of interpretation had always been accepted in the classical schools of law; now new methods such as *takhayyur* ("selection" of a desired legal ruling from one school of law, or of a weak ruling from one's own school) and *talfīq* ("piecing together" a ruling from components of opinions of different schools of law or of the same school) gained in importance. These methods remained within the framework of the existing schools of law and thus can be termed *taqlīd*. On the other hand, *ijtihād*—now neo-*ijtihād*—became revitalized. As early as 1898 the great Egyptian jurist Muḥammad ʿAbdūh (d. 1905) advocated the reinterpretation of the principles embodied in the divine revelation as a basis for legal reform. Since then scholars have argued for reopening the door of *ijtihād*, meaning leaving behind the body of classical *fiqh* and taking a fresh interpretative approach to the Qurʾān as well as the Sunnah.

[*See also* Fatwa; Ḥisbah; Minority Fiqh; Qaraḍāwī, Yūsuf al-; Sharīʿah; *and* Siyāsah Sharʿīyah.]

BIBLIOGRAPHY

Calder, Norman. "Sharīʿa." In *Encyclopaedia of Islam*, 2d ed. Edited by P. J. Bearman et al. Leiden: Brill, 2006.

Coulson, Noel J. *A History of Islamic Law*. Edinburgh: Edinburgh University Press, 1964.

Hallaq, Wael B. "From *fatwās* to *furūʿ*: Growth and Change in Islamic Substantive Law." *Islamic Law and Society* 1 (1994): 29–65.

Hallaq, Wael B. "Was the Gate of Ijtihad Closed?" *International Journal of Middle East Studies* 16, no. 1 (1984): 3–41.

Hallaq, Wael B. "Was al-Shafiʿi the Master Architect of Islamic Jurisprudence?" *International Journal of Middle East Studies* 25, no. 4 (1993): 587–605.

Johansen, Baber. "Die sündige, gesunde Amme. Moral und gesetzliche Bestimmung (ḥukm) im islamischen Recht. " In *Contingency in a Sacred Law: Legal and Ethical Norms in the Muslim Fiqh*, by Baber Johansen, pp. 172–188. Leiden: Brill, 1999.

Johansen, Baber. "The Muslim *Fiqh* as a Sacred Law." In *Contingency in a Sacred Law: Legal and Ethical Norms in the Muslim Fiqh*, by Baber Johansen, pp. 1–106. Leiden: Brill, 1999.

Krämer, Gudrun. "Drawing Boundaries: Yusuf al-Qaraḍāwī on Apostasy." In *Speaking for Islam*, edited by Gudrun Krämer and Sabine Schmidtke, pp. 181–217. Leiden: Brill, 2006.

Layish, Aharon. "The Transformation of the Shariʿa from Jurists' Law to Statutory Law in the Contemporary Muslim World." *Die Welt des Islam* 44, no. 1 (2003): 85–113.

Motzki, Harald. *The Origins of Islamic Jurisprudence*. Leiden: Brill, 2002.

Peters, Rudolph. *Crime and Punishment in Islamic Law: Theory and Practice from the Sixteenth to the Twenty-First Century*. Cambridge, U.K.: Cambridge University Press, 2005.

Schacht, Joseph. *An Introduction to Islamic Law*. Oxford: Clarendon Press, 1964.

Schacht, Joseph. *The Origins of Muhammadan Jurisprudence*. Oxford: Oxford University Press, 1979.

Schacht, Joseph, and Ignaz Goldziher. "Fiḳh." In *Encyclopaedia of Islam*, 2d ed. Edited by P. J. Bearman et al. Leiden: Brill, 1983.

Schneider, Irene. "Civil Society and Legislation: Development of the Human Rights Situation in Iran 2008." In *Beiträge zum Islamischen Recht VII: Islam und Menschenrechte*, edited by Hatem Elliesie, pp. 387–414. Frankfurt: P. Lang, 2010.

Schneider, Irene. *Das Bild des Richters in der adab al-qāḍī-Literatur*. Frankfurt: P. Lang, 1990.

Schneider, Irene. "Freedom and Slavery in Early Islamic Times (1st/7th and 2nd/8th Centuries)." *Al-Qantara* 28 (2007): 253–382.

Schneider, Irene. "Gelehrte Frauen des 5./11. bis 7./13. Jh.s nach dem biographischen Werk des Ḏahabī (st. 748/1347)." In *Philosophy and Arts in the Islamic World: Proceedings of the Eighteenh Congress of the UEAI, held at the Katholieke Universiteit Leuven (September 3–September 9, 1996)*, edited by U. Vermeulen and D. De Smet, pp. 107–21. Leuven: Peeters, 1998.

Schneider, Irene. "The Position of Women in the Islamic and Afghan Judiciary." In *The Shariʿa in the Constitutions of Afghanistan, Iran and Egypt: Implications for Private Law*, edited by Nadjma Yassari, pp. 83–101. Tübingen: Max-Planck-Institut, 2005.

Shepard, William E. "Muhammad Saʿid al-ʿAshmawi and the Application of the Shariʿa in Egypt." *Journal of Middle East Study* 28 (1996): 39–58.

Wakin, Jeanette A. *The Function of Documents in Islamic Law: The Chapters on Sales from Ṭaḥāwī's Kitāb al-shurūṭ al-kabīr*. Albany: State University of New York Press, 1972.

IRENE SCHNEIDER

FITNAH. The Arabic root *f-t-n* ("burn") is used to refer to the melting (or trying) of gold or silver with fire. Hence it is both a burning and a trial, or a temptation, and by extension a seduction or a charming—an enchantment. Thus it is said in the Qurʾān that God tested Moses (20:40); the faithful are tested by being called out to war with infidels (9:126); the Zaqqūm tree that grows in Hell is a punishment for evildoers (37:62–63); the faithful pray not to be made a lure for tyrants to oppress (10:85); the goods and children of the faithful are a temptation to forsake righteousness (8:28); the oppression of idolaters is a worse fault than killing in the sacred month (2:217); and God allows Satan to cast his own verses into the revelations of the prophets as a temptation for those in whose hearts is sickness (22:53), among other examples.

The Arab lexicons give "error" or "crime" as definitions of *fitnah*. Satan is *al-fātin* or *al-fattān*, because he leads people into error. One who is *maftūn* is afflicted with madness or demonic possession. Thus, the early jurist Ibn Hurmuz of Medina (d. 765) stated as his defense, when apprehended in the ʿAlid rebellion against the ʿAbbāsids in 762, that he had been carried away by a general *fitnah,* and he was forgiven. The term is also used for the final inquisition in the grave by the angels Munkar and Nakīr, and for the trials of the dead in their graves.

Although *fitnah* (pl. *fitan*) is generally negative, it can have positive aspects. A girl today may be named Fātin, or Fitnah, in the hope that she will be not a seductress, but charming or alluring. However, some see in the name Fitnah for a beautiful woman evidence of a negative view toward women generally among Muslims. There is also a *ḥadīth* to the effect that the greatest *fitnah* for men is women, and the *ḥadīth* is sometimes explained by reference to the story of Adam and Eve.

***Fitnah* in Early Islam.** In early Islam, the term is used particularly for trials and temptations to which the Muslim community was exposed. The first *fitnah* was the division that occurred from the assassination of the third caliph ʿUthmān in 656, through the Battle of the Camel when ʿAlī defeated ʿUthmān's followers, and the subsequent schisms that led to the formation of the sectarian groups of the Khawārij and the Shīʿa and the seizure of power by Muʿāwiyah, founder of the Umayyad dynasty, in 661. Here, *fitnah* is civil strife, war, division, and those situations that tempt Muslims to depart from the straight path of unity and right action. The second major *fitnah* began with the rebellion and death of the Prophet Muḥammad's grandson Ḥusayn ibn ʿAlī in 680, and the third with the overthrow of the Umayyad dynasty by the ʿAbbāsids in 750.

The major *ḥadīth* collections, such as those by al-Bukhārī and Muslim, have sections on *fitan,* trials of the community, represented as foretold by the Prophet and leading up to the signs that will usher in the great *fitnah*: the return of Jesus, the end of the world, the resurrection, and the final judgment. The term later came to be applied to any group departure from the collective, as well as to religious uprisings such as those of the ʿAlids, when it was easy for people to be confused as to which course to follow, or the riots between the Ashʿarīs and the Ḥanbalīs in Baghdad in the tenth century. The disorders that brought the collapse of the Umayyad caliphate in Andalusia and the rise of the factional kings in the early eleventh century were also called the *fitnah* in that part of the Muslim world.

Again, *fitnah* is generally a negative term, and the *ʿulamāʾ* warn against it. The Successor and preacher al-Ḥasan al-Baṣrī (d. 728) is quoted as saying that anyone who instigates *fitnah* is an innovator in religion, who, according to the *ḥadīth,* will go to Hell. Here, apparently, civil strife and rebellion against the authorities are intended; al-Baṣrī was known to consider the actions of tyrants as a trial to be patiently endured rather than opposed by arms.

Historical Examples. The *kalām* treatises usually discuss *fitnah* in connection with the imamate or caliphate. When there is no clear imam, there will be *fitnah*; an imam is necessary to prevent schism in the community. There is discussion as to whether an imam should be appointed during a time of *fitnah*: not if it will make things worse, but certainly if it will help bring *fitnah* to an end, since nothing is worse than *fitnah*. Even tyranny is greatly preferable. Ibn Jamāʿah (d. 1333) states that if a king gains power by usurpation or force in a Muslim country, the caliph should recognize him and delegate the affairs of that place to him in order to avoid *fitnah* and to guarantee Muslim unity.

The appearance of a claim to be the Mahdī was seen as a clear invitation to *fitnah,* so rulers were instructed to punish such claimants fittingly. The Delhi Sultan Fīrūz Shāh (r. 1351–1388) proudly records that he executed a man who claimed to be the Mahdī but only imprisoned a man who claimed to be God. Ibn Khaldūn (d. 1406) regards the whole Mahdī idea as an occasion for *fitnah* and argues that it has no real basis in Islam, because all of the *ḥadīth*s upon which it rests are spurious. This helps explain why in modern times those claiming to be the Mahdī have been ruthlessly punished. In the early 1860s one Aḥmad al-Ṭayyib, who had been acclaimed as the Mahdī in Upper Egypt, was massacred with his followers by government troops, even though they had not made an uprising. This attitude has continued in modern times, even when it meant using armed force in the Holy Mosque at Mecca (on the basis of Qurʾān 2:191) in 1979. The very appearance of a Mahdī brings *fitnah,* and this may be reckoned one of the signs of the Hour.

As the Saudi mosque incident shows, the Qurʾānic saying "*Fitnah* is worse than killing" (2:191, 217) is used to justify putting down peasant revolts and urban unrest by often harsh methods. In 1605 the heterodox *shaykh* Yaḥyā ibn ʿĪsā al-Karakī was judged by the *ʿulamāʾ* of Damascus deserving of execution on the grounds that he had a following among the rural immigrants to the Maydān quarter of the city and might cause a *fitnah.*

In some of the *fiqh* books, selling weapons at a time of *fitnah* to a person known to be engaged in it is a reprovable practice because it will lead to sin. If it is not known that the person is so engaged, then there is no harm in it.

A curious example of the use of the term occurred in sixteenth-century Syria, when a Shāfiʿī *qāḍī* accused the new Ottoman regime of provoking a *fitnah* in Islam by imposing a marriage fee, a practice unknown under the previous Mamlūk regime. He seems to have meant that it was a scandalous and innovative practice.

The term could on occasion be applied to situations outside the Muslim community. The first Muslims to write about the French Revolution of 1789 identified it as a *fitnah* and clearly took a negative view of it.

Modern Politics. *Fitnah* in a social sense is thus seen almost always as highly undesirable, a temptation to Muslims to forsake the service of God, and "worse than killing." As a term of opprobrium, it can conveniently be used to characterize the actions of opponents, as it often is in modern journalism and polemical literature. The uprising of the supporters of the Muslim Brotherhood in Hamah, Syria, decisively put down by armed government forces in 1982, was called a *fitnah* by their opponents. Attacks on Christians by Islamists in Upper Egypt are called *fitnah,* and the word is occasionally used to describe the activities of Islamists in North Africa. Anything that might polarize or divide society may be called *fitnah*; on the other hand, attempts by governments to put an end to potentially destabilizing activities by Islamic religious groups may in turn be labeled *fitnah* by adherents of those groups.

In political discourse, *fitnah* is a value-laden term that can be used to discredit opponents. Frequently the division of the original community upon the occasion of the first *fitnah* is evoked as a fearful and deterrent example.

[*See also* Rebellion; *and* Tyranny.]

BIBLIOGRAPHY

al-ʿAqīqī, Anṭūn Ẓāhir. *Thawrah wa-fitnah fī Lubnān.* Translated from the Arabic by Malcolm H. Kerr as *Lebanon in the Last Years of Feudalism, 1840–1868.* Beirut: Catholic Press, 1959.

Esposito, John L., and John O. Voll. *Islam and Democracy*. New York: Oxford University Press, 1996.

Fīrūz Shāh Tughluq. *Futūḥāt-i Fīrūz Shāhī*. Aligarh, India: Aligarh Muslim University, 1954. Partial translation from the Urdu in *History of India, as Told by Its Own Historians: The Muhammadan Period*, by H. M. Elliot, edited by John Dowson, vol. 2, pp. 378–379. London: Trübner and Co., 1877; reprint, New York: AMS Press, 1966.

Gardet, Louis. "Fitna." In *Encyclopaedia of Islam*, 2d ed. Leiden: Brill, 1960–2004.

al-Jurjānī, ʿAlī ibn Muḥammad. *Sharḥ al-Mawāqif*, vol. 8, pp. 344–345. Cairo: Maṭbaʿat al-Saʿāda, 1907.

Kepel, Gilles. *Fitna: Guerre au coeur de l'Islam*. Paris: Gallimard, 2007.

al-Marghinānī, Burhān al-Dīn. *Al-Hidāyah*, vol. 4. Beirut: Dār al-Arqam, n.d. Translated by Charles Hamilton as *The Hedàya, or Guide*. 2d ed. London: W. H. Allen, 1870. See p. 90.

Mernissi, Fatima. *Beyond the Veil: Male-Female Dynamics in Modern Muslim Society*. New ed. London: Saqi Books, 2011.

Pandolfo, Stefania. *Impasse of the Angels: Scenes from a Moroccan Space of Memory*. Chicago: University of Chicago Press, 1997. For *fitnah* as it relates to women.

Williams, John Alden. "The Expected Deliverer." In *Themes of Islamic Civilization*, by John Alden Williams, chap. 4. Berkeley: University of California Press, 1971.

JOHN ALDEN WILLIAMS
Updated by PERI BEARMAN

FRANCE. Following their invasion of Spain in 711 CE, Muslim forces pushed into southern France, where they were defeated at the Battle of Tours in 732. Further attempts at Muslim penetration continued into the tenth century but were unsuccessful; nevertheless, the Muslim invaders left their mark on several regions of southern France. At the beginning of the seventeenth century, a group of Spanish Muslims deported from Spain later settled in France.

Modern Muslim Presence. The Muslim presence in France in modern times is the product of the French colonization of North Africa beginning in 1830. Algeria was made a department of France, although Muslims did not become French citizens, and at the turn of the century, the first groups of Algerian, and later Moroccan, workers arrived in metropolitan France. During World War I, more than 132,000 North Africans were brought to France to replace French workers called to active duty, and more than 15,000 others were called to arms.

Although many of these people were repatriated after the war, the influx into France of workers from North Africa continued until the depression of the 1930s, resumed after World War II, and peaked in the 1960s. In 1974 the French government interrupted the immigration of labor, and until the early 1980s, it sought to reduce the number of foreign residents, particularly Algerians. Efforts to reverse the flow of immigrants proved largely unsuccessful, and in the process, questions of immigration and national identity became increasingly politicized in France. Meanwhile, the Muslim community increased and diversified with the arrival of immigrants from Africa, Asia, and the Middle East.

Muslim Identity. French law prohibits the inclusion of questions concerning religious affiliation or race in the national census; therefore, the exact size of the Muslim population in metropolitan France is unknown. On the lower end, the Pew Research Center in a 2010 survey estimated the Muslim population to be 3,574,000, or 5.7 percent of the total population. On the higher end, a 2010 study by the National Institute of Statistics and Economic Studies (Institut National de la Statistique et des Études Économiques—INSEE) and the National Institute of Demographic Studies (Institut National d'Études Démographiques—INED) estimated there were 5 to 6 million Muslims in metropolitan France. In either case, France is the European country with the highest percentage of Muslims as well as the highest absolute number of Muslims.

Brouard and Tiberj (2005) are among the few scholars to explore the percentage of the Muslim population who are actually observant Muslims. Their survey of French of African, Maghribī, and Turkish origin, including immigrants, showed that 66 percent declared themselves to be Muslim and 16 percent without religion, the remaining persons belonging to other religions. Although the level of "practice," measured as at least monthly attendance at a "religious service," was similar to that of a non-immigrant "mirror" population (22 percent versus 19 percent), the proportion of persons considering their religion "extremely important" was comparatively high (19 percent versus 4 percent). Furthermore, 72 percent of self-declared Muslims said that their religion was "very" or "extremely important" for "guiding their conduct." Observant Muslims constitute the second largest religion in France behind Roman Catholics.

Modes of Organization and Institutions. According to conservative government estimates, the number of prayer rooms and mosques in France increased from around 255 in 1983 to about 1,600 in 2005. The geographic distribution of these facilities gives a rough idea of the distribution of Muslim life. More than four hundred are located in the Île-de-France area including Paris, 219 in the Rhône-Alpes area, 173 in the Provence–Alpes–Côte-d'Azur area, and 101 in the Nord–Pas-de-Calais region. Although French legislation does not allow for the establishment of confessional cemeteries, there are designated enclosures for Muslims in more than sixty cemeteries, as well as one exclusively Muslim cemetery created during World War I.

Since the early 1990s, a number of institutions of higher education in Islamic sciences have been set up, primarily in the Paris area. In addition to offering courses in Arabic and French, these institutes offer a stage for a growing number of French Muslim scholars and intellectuals. Several of these institutes also train imams and educators. The prospect of adding a Muslim element to the vast state-subsidized school system, which now includes several Muslim high schools, is slowly becoming more realistic. The number and variety of francophone Muslim media have also dramatically increased since 1990. This development has contributed to the growth of a national Muslim audience, as does the emerging Muslim music industry.

Muslim institutions and practices are affected by the secular legal framework of France, which establishes a comparatively strict separation between state and religion. The most important element of this framework of *laïcité* (laicism), whose central laws were adopted in the late nineteenth and early twentieth centuries, is that the state does not recognize or subsidize religions. Consequently, the overwhelming majority of mosque associations are registered as cultural as opposed to religious associations, which entitles them to public funding. Although France guarantees freedom of religion, a large number of cases exist in which unfavorable administrative or political decisions make it difficult or impossible for Muslims to practice their religion freely. The wearing of head coverings, the sacrifice of animals on the Feast of Sacrifice (ʿĪd al-Aḍḥā), the construction of mosques, the establishment of Muslim enclosures in public cemeteries, and the creation of Muslim schools have all been politically sensitive issues in recent years.

The French State and Islam. The so-called Islamic-veil affair, which in France mostly involved head scarves as opposed to veils, put Islam on the political agenda of France in 1989, and it has remained there since that time. From the question of whether Muslim girls can wear the *ḥijāb* in state schools, the debate expanded to consider the right of students to wear any conspicuous sign of religious expression in state schools, to a prohibition on face-shrouding veils (burqas) in public, to a ban on street prayer in front of overcrowded mosques. In part, these debates reflected a widespread, legitimate concern with how to reconcile Islam with the principle of *laïcité*, and in part they reflected concerns with security and the threat of Islamist terrorism. More generally at issue are unresolved questions concerning the citizenship of Muslims and the failure of integration in France.

Since 1989 the government's main focus involving the politics of Islam in France has been on the creation of a unified representative body of Muslims. This body is intended to complement existing Catholic, Protestant, and Jewish institutions of the same type. In 2003 this institution emerged as the French Council of Islamic Worship (Conseil Français du Culte Musulman—CFCM), a nonprofit organization or association as defined in the law of 1901 and intended to serve as an interlocutor to the state. According to its statutes, the CFCM aims to defend the dignity and interests of Islam in France; to promote and organize the sharing of information and services between places of worship; to encourage dialogue between religions; and to provide the state with representatives of Muslim places of worship. Members of the various national or regional branches of the council are elected by delegates from their places of worship, with the seats on the council apportioned according to the square footage of each place of worship.

In certain respects, the CFCM marks a rupture with earlier modes of state governance of Islam. For a long time, the French government has relied in its policies on the Grand Mosque of Paris (GMP) and on the network of mosques associated with it. The GMP, built by France after World War I in gratitude for the services of Muslim soldiers during the war, has been controlled since 1957 by the Algerian state. During the consultations preceding the creation of the CFCM, successive French governments became increasingly concerned with the degree to which their Muslim partners actually represented the Muslim communities and started to broaden the scope of Muslim partners acceptable to the state. Ultimately even the highly controversial Union of Islamic Organizations of France (Union des Organisations Islamiques de France—UOIF), commonly regarded as fundamentalist and linked to the Muslim Brotherhood, was included in the CFCM. However, although the government included various independent Muslim personalities during the consultations prior to the CFCM's creation, the latter's structure, based as it is on places of worship, works to strengthen the position of France's major Muslim federations. Today, the CFCM is dominated by the GMP, the National Federation of French Muslims (Fédération Nationale des Musulmans de France—FNFM), closely related to Morocco, and the independent UOIF. Moreover, contrary to the government's proclaimed aim to work via the CFCM for the establishment of an "Islam of France," the centerpiece of its policies on Islam consolidates foreign influence on French Islam and ethnic divisions inside the Muslim community. To a certain degree, it also marginalizes French-born Muslims, who are not well represented in the leadership of France's Muslim federations.

[*See also* Algeria; Citizenship; Education, Muslim; Islam and Politics in Europe; Islamophobia; Morocco; Secularism; *and* Union des Organisations Islamiques de France.]

BIBLIOGRAPHY

Arkoun, Mohammed, ed. *Histoire de l'islam et des musulmans en France du Moyen Âge à nos jours.* Paris: Albin Michel, 2006.

Bowen, John R. *Can Islam Be French? Pluralism and Pragmatism in a Secularist State.* Princeton, N.J.: Princeton University Press, 2010. An anthropological examination of how Muslims are responding to the conditions of life in France.

Brouard, Sylvain, and Vincent Tiberj. *Français comme les autres? Enquête sur les citoyens d'origine maghrébine, africaine et turque*. Paris: Presses de la Fondation nationale des sciences politiques, 2005.

Keaton, Trica Danielle. *Muslim Girls and the Other France: Race, Identity Politics, and Social Exclusion*. Bloomington: Indiana University Press, 2006. Examines the life and experience of Muslim girls growing up in the *banlieues* (suburbs) of Paris.

Laurence, Jonathan, and Justin Vaisse. *Integrating Islam: Political and Religious Challenges in Contemporary France*. Washington, D.C.: Brookings Institution Press, 2006. Explores the many challenges to be met by Muslims and non-Muslims alike to achieve a full integration of Islam into French society.

Thomas, Elaine R. *Immigration, Islam, and the Politics of Belonging in France: A Comparative Framework*. Philadelphia: University of Pennsylvania Press, 2012. Explores the interaction between policy debate and contested concepts in contemporary France.

FRANK PETER
Revised by RONALD BRUCE ST JOHN

FREEDOM. The Arabic word for freedom, *ḥurrīyah*, is a modern usage of this derivative of the Arabic root *ḥ-r-r*. The Qurʾān uses derivatives of this root only when speaking of freedom and slavery—*ḥurr* is a free man, and *taḥrīr*, the verbal noun, means setting someone free. This entry deals primarily with the modern notion of freedom, which includes religious freedom and civil liberties, as well as freedom of speech and political action. However, it will be useful to begin with a word on the issue of slavery and how it was rationalized in Islam. Islam did not abolish slavery, which continued to be practiced and tolerated until recently in parts of the Muslim world. Muslim scholars, however, have maintained that Islam sought to abolish slavery gradually by employing an attractive reward for manumitting slaves and limiting the acquisition of new slaves, creating a situation whereby fewer slaves would be introduced and more freed. And despite their limited freedom, liabilities, and rights, slaves are regarded essentially as human beings, and as such are equal to their masters in humanity. After all, both slaves and masters are God's own slaves.

This view of God's sovereignty over all people also extends to politics. Upon the death of the Prophet Muḥammad in 632 CE, the Muslim community dealt with the issue of succession: Who would succeed the Prophet, how would he be chosen, and what powers would he have? Those who would come to be called Shīʿī Muslims insisted that the Prophet designated his cousin and son-in-law, ʿAlī, as imam, the spiritual and political guide of the community to whom unconditional obedience was due. The majority Sunnīs, however, held that Muslim rulers ought to be chosen freely by the Muslim community, whose oath of allegiance (*bayʿah*) was a requirement of legitimate rule. These rulers did not have unrestricted authority, and obedience was due to them provided they obeyed God and the Prophet, a notion attributed to the Prophet's first successor, Abū Bakr. Other reports show his successor, ʿUmar ibn al-Khaṭṭāb, warning his governors against abusing their political authority and oppressing people. These and similar incidents provided the principles that governed, in theory, all issues related to the freedom of the ruled in their relation with the state. Both were subject to God's law as it was interpreted.

More often than not, however, Muslim rulers enjoyed unlimited powers, and the oath of allegiance, although still indispensible in theory, was reduced to a mere formality. Rulers typically ascended to the throne in hereditary systems or by overthrowing an incumbent potentate. People did not have channels to exercise "political freedom," and although admonishing the ruler remained a theoretical religious duty, it was seldom exercised by laypeople. *Shūrā*, a Qurʾānic term that refers to consultation among Muslims and of

Muslims by the ruler, was considered praiseworthy but not mandatory. People did not challenge this lack of political freedom not only because they did not have a modern notion of political freedom but also because many of them preferred stability and security to chaos and schism, a quietist approached that was endorsed by most religious scholars.

Since the nineteenth century, the issue of freedom has been on top of the agenda of most Muslim "reformist" scholars. Generally speaking, these scholars seek to demonstrate that there is no irreconcilable contradiction between Islam and freedom. To do this, they emphasize two points. The first is the spirit and broad principles of Islam. For example, justice is a basic concept in Islam. God is just and he requires us to be just. Justice, they maintain, entails human freedom, for one can justly be held accountable for one's deeds only if one has the freedom to think and act. Reflecting these principles, evidence from early Islam indicates that early Muslims enjoyed a great deal of political freedom. Other evidence demonstrates the active participation of Muslim women in politics and war in early Islam. Further, history has demonstrated that the lack of political freedom leads to injustice, which is antithetical to Islam.

This focus on the principles of Islam requires the historical contextualization of some of its teachings and some of the practices and views of medieval Muslim societies. For example, restrictions on women's freedom should be understood against the backdrop of the lack of security in seventh-century Arabia, where Islam arose. The traditionally prescribed capital punishment for apostasy (conversion from Islam to another religion) was probably the product of a time when conversion from Islam threatened the unity of Muslims when they were weak or outnumbered by followers of other faiths. In addition to contradicting the very notion of religious belief, which is supposed to be voluntary and sincere, this view contradicts a clearly stated Qurʾānic rule, that is, that there is no compulsion in religion (Qurʾān 2:256). This points to the necessity of distinguishing between the teachings of Islam itself and the culture of medieval Muslim societies that did not necessarily reflect the original message of Islam.

In the view of these Muslim reformist scholars, Islam can incorporate most aspects of the modern notion of freedom. However, although only a few of them would advocate a freedom that is not restricted by some understanding of religious norms, there are many critics of their methodologies and views in Muslim societies. Some conservative religious scholars question their credentials (many of these reformist scholars are not graduates of traditional religious seminaries) and motives, accusing them of subjecting Islam to foreign norms. Others criticize their apologetic discourse and selectivity of texts and reports. For example, reports indicate that Qurʾān 2:256 addressed a case where a Muslim father wanted to force his sons to convert to Islam. Thus, it prohibits forced conversion *to* Islam, but does not necessarily allow the freedom to convert *from* Islam. Nonetheless, this verse is regularly used by reformist scholars to argue that freedom of religion, including conversion from Islam, has a textual basis in Islam.

Most Muslim countries have now adopted modern constitutions that guarantee freedom of speech and of religion and protect the right of the citizens to choose their leaders and political systems. However, Muslim countries usually rank low in freedom surveys, although some recent research has suggested that there is no necessary correlation between Islam per se and authoritarianism. There definitely is a discrepancy between theory and practice in Muslim countries resulting from socioeconomic, cultural, and political factors. On one end of the spectrum, some Muslim countries, such as Saudi Arabia, restrict most forms of political expression, regarding them as a potential threat to the unity and values of the Muslim community. This attitude is always associated with limiting the freedom of women and religious minorities. On the other end, Muslim countries like Turkey (some setbacks notwithstanding) have gone a long way in allowing a degree of personal and political freedom close to that found in Western democracies. Theoretical debates and bargaining between political forces are underway in other Muslim countries, and while it can be argued that there is a general acceptance of the necessity of expanding political freedom, genuine disagreements exist on the limits of personal, religious, and social freedom.

Bibliography

Abou El Fadl, Khaled. *Islam and the Challenge of Democracy.* Edited by Joshua Cohen and Deborah Chasman. Princeton, N.J.: Princeton University Press, 2004.

Fish, M. Steven. "Islam and Authoritarianism." *World Politics* 55, no. 1 (2002): 4–37.

Freedom House. "Freedom in the World, 2011: The Authoritarian Challenge to Democracy." http://www.freedomhouse.org/

Hunter, Shireen T., ed. *Reformist Voices of Islam: Mediating Islam and Modernity.* Armonk, N.Y.: M. E. Sharpe, 2009.

Kamrava, Mehran, ed. *The New Voices of Islam: Reforming Politics and Modernity; A Reader.* London: I. B. Tauris, 2006.

Amr Osman

Freedom Movement of Iran. The Freedom Movement of Iran (*Nahẓat-i Āzādi-yi Īrān,* FMI) was established in 1961 by two University of Tehran professors, Mehdi Bazargan and Yadollah Ṣaḥābi, and a cleric, Ayatollah Sayyid Maḥmud Ṭāleqāni. The origins of the FMI date back to the period of the premiership of Muḥammad Muṣaddiq (1951–1953), the nationalization of oil, the bid for democratic reforms, and the British-American coup that brought down Muṣaddiq's nationalist government in August 1953. As supporters of Muṣaddiq, both the leadership and membership of the FMI participated in the National Front, a coalition that was established by supporters of Muṣaddiq during the period of oil nationalization. The National Front was an association of Muṣaddiq supporters from various strata of Iranian society, including secular and religious nationalists, students, and intellectuals. Following the crackdown on Muṣaddiq supporters, a group of political activists led by Bazargan, Ṭāleqāni, and Ṣaḥābi put together a new underground organization named the National Resistance Movement (*Nahẓat-i Muqāvamat-i,* NRM). The NRM campaigned for a free and fair election in 1954 and pushed for the opening of the political system. The shah's severe repression prevented a free election in 1954, and the NRM was later disbanded under the pressure of political suppression.

The Second National Front was established in 1960. The membership represented a wide spectrum of views held by opponents of the shah. Disenchanted by the conservatism of many in the National Front coalition, Bazargan, Ṭāleqāni, and Ṣaḥābi established the FMI. The goal was to resort to more politically challenging activities against the regime and to also encourage the religious sector of the population to participate in opposition against authoritarianism and the call for change. The FMI succeeded in attracting the religious-nationalist segment of the Iranian population, mostly those within the intelligentsia. They quickly established support among religious segments of the population, including seminarians and merchants. After a short period of activity, the leadership was arrested and sentenced to lengthy prison terms.

As the FMI leadership languished in prison, a group of younger members migrated to the United

States and Europe and established FMI branches there. Ibrāhīm Yazdī, Muṣṭafā Chamrān, ʿAlī Sharīʿatī, and Sadiq Ghotbzadeh were a few of these activists who established the first FMI branches abroad in the 1960s and began to mobilize Iranian students studying abroad against the shah's regime.

When Ayatollah Khomeini arrived in Paris in 1978, Yazdī, Chamrān, and Ghotbzadeh joined him there to orchestrate the revolutionary campaign. FMI members both outside and inside Iran were very active in the revolutionary process, and their role was crucial to the success of the Iranian Revolution of 1979.

After the success of the revolution, FMI members and supporters filled many positions within various institutions of the country, from the Revolutionary Council to other government positions. Khomeini appointed Bazargan prime minister of the provisional government. As an intellectual, religious nationalist, and reformer, Bazargan had fame and a good reputation in Iran after the revolution. Many intellectuals, especially those who were religiously oriented, joined the revolution because of Bazargan and his party's participation in it.

A rift quickly developed between Bazargan and his FMI organization, and Khomeini on major political issues and policies. The FMI membership became the first group to oppose Khomeini's regime and political ideology in the post-revolutionary period. Following the seizure of the American Embassy in November 1979 and the subsequent holding of its staff as hostages, Bazargan's government resigned in protest. From that point, Bazargan and his political party became vocal critics of the government. They opposed the hostage-taking, radicalism inside and outside the country, and the continuation of war with Iraq after Iraqi forces were expelled from the country in 1982. The revolutionary zeal and radicalism that characterized post-revolutionary politics made the FMI very unpopular, but Bazargan and the party continued its opposition.

When Bazargan died in 1995, Yazdī was elected to replace him as party leader. The FMI supported Muḥammad Khatami's presidency (1997–2005) and rejected the result of the presidential elections in both 2005 and 2009. Party members have been subject to repeated harassment and imprisonment. Yazdī himself was repeatedly arrested despite advanced age and ill health. In March 2011 Abdolali Bazargan, a son of Mehdi Bazargan, succeeded Yazdī as secretary-general of the FMI. As a party with religious convictions and a commitment to democratic norms, the FMI continues to challenge the Iranian regime's authoritarianism on both religious and political grounds.

BIBLIOGRAPHY

Abrahamian, Ervand. *Iran between Two Revolutions*. Princeton, N.J.: Princeton University Press, 1982.

Chehabi, H. E. *Iranian Politics and Religious Modernism: The Liberation Movement of Iran*. Ithaca, N.Y.: Cornell University Press, 1990.

Dabashi, Hamid. *Theology of Discontent*. New York: New York University Press, 1993.

MEHDI NOORBAKSH

G

Germany. With an estimated population of more than four million, Germany's Muslims constitute the second largest Muslim immigrant community in the European Union, after that of France, and constitute approximately 5 percent of the country's population. The community's immigrant status, as well as its internal differentiation along national, ethnic, linguistic, doctrinal, and political lines, shapes its internal dynamics and its interactions with the institutions and politics of the majority society, which is mostly antagonistic to expressions of Muslim identity. Over 60 percent of Muslims in Germany hail from Turkey, while one-fifth emigrated from the former Yugoslav republics of Bosnia, Kosovo, and Macedonia. Muslims from Turkey are further differentiated as Turks, Kurds, and Alevis, a heterodox religious community distinguished by a distant Shīʿī ancestry. The latter two groups are estimated at somewhere between half and one million. Other notable communities are Arabs, particularly from Iraq, Lebanon, Egypt, and the Maghrib, as well as smaller Twelver Shīʿī congregations from Iran. Not all Muslims in Germany identify primarily by creed, are organized in religious associations, or attend mosque regularly. Evidence based on Friday prayer attendance and membership in "burial funds," however, suggests that at least half of Turkish Muslims are associated with organized community life in one way or the other.

Legacies: *Orientpolitik*, Holocaust, and Immigration. Even though Islam in Germany is a phenomenon inextricably linked to the labor immigration that began in the late 1950s, the political field of Islam and Muslims has been shaped by a set of historical legacies preceding the migratory movements by more than a century. Early contacts with the Muslim world began in the eighteenth century, with the arrival of the first Ottoman envoy to the Prussian Court in 1763 and the establishment of a Muslim cemetery in Berlin in 1798. The first prolonged German encounter with Muslims took place during the period of economic, military, and political cooperation with the Ottoman Empire, starting from the second part of the nineteenth century. This cooperation culminated in the German-Ottoman coalition of World War I, with results that would impact German attitudes towards Muslims, Arabs, and Turks for decades afterwards, and probably more deeply than the romantic Orientalist tradition, which also has its roots in the same period. The participation of German officers in the

Armenian genocide and the declaration of *jihād* on British and French colonial armies by Sultan Abdülhamid II are particularly noteworthy during this period. The latter was a project advanced by the maverick German diplomat Max von Oppenheim, who convinced the German Foreign Office that a partial *jihād* declared by the Sultan would weaken the war efforts of its enemies by opening new fronts in the east. While this policy had little impact at the time, Oppenheim made a comeback in World War II when the National-Socialist government reintroduced the holy war rhetoric to exploit Arab nationalist struggles against European colonial powers. Part of this strategy was the largely inconclusive attempt to enlist the Grand Mufti of Jerusalem, al-Ḥājj Amīn al- Ḥusaynī, in the Nazi war effort, even though he did accept a part in the recruitment of Bosnian Muslims for the mostly Muslim 13th Waffen Mountain Division of the SS called Handschar. Some German commentators refer to these incidents today as signs of Arab collusion with Hitler.

Another long-term effect of the ties with the Ottoman Empire was that of immigration. When the booming postwar economy of Germany required additional labor force for the reconstruction effort of the 1950s, Turkey as well as the former Ottoman and Habsburg territories of Yugoslavia emerged as the most important sending countries. A recruitment treaty was concluded with Turkey in 1961, and with Yugoslavia in 1969. Although recruitment ceased in 1973, close to three million Muslim immigrants lived in Germany by the 1980s. The 1983 law encouraging the return of migrants was an important symbolic watershed. Around 200,000 Turkish citizens left the country, while those who stayed made the decision to settle permanently.

Another defining moment was the German unification of 1989, which, among other things, created conditions for a resurgent extreme nationalist movement. A number of racially motivated arson attacks against Turks and Muslims in the 1990s were followed by a series of murders against the owners of mostly Turkish kebab restaurants in the 2000s. The killings were carried out by the neo-fascist National-Socialist Underground (Nationalsozialstischer Untergrund), which was infiltrated by members of the intelligence services, who are believed to have refrained from intervening in the murders. While these prominent cases, and the notorious stabbing in court of Marwa El-Sherbini in 2009 by a defendant in a racism trial, evidence a mainstream public sentiment in Germany shaped by suspicion towards Islam and Muslims, the fact that some of the masterminds of the 9/11 terrorist attacks had operated from Hamburg in northern Germany stoked the overwhelmingly negative majority perception of Islam and Muslims.

Contemporary Spaces of Islam and Politics. The political Muslim sphere of Germany can be separated into three distinct domains: the politics of integration and exclusion; the domain of Muslim associational life with its politics of recognition, community building, and transnational networks; and the space of Muslim actors in German politics.

The Politics of Integration and Exclusion. Much of the political debate on Islam and Muslims in Germany focuses on immigration and the perceived threat of "non-integrated" immigrants. While prominent German politicians have emphasised repeatedly that "Islam is a part of Germany," Islamophobic rhetoric has generally overshadowed public debates. Many of these debates are initiated by protagonists of a so-called Critique of Islam (Islamkritik) and imply the irreconcilability of Islamic traditions and scripture with the German constitutional order and what is often referred to as "Judeo-Christian" Europe. Recurring themes are limitations on *ḥijāb* in the public sphere, the status of women in Islam, the effects of male circumcision, and the impact of radical Islamist movements. In such debates, whether in the media or in public forums, Muslims are often invited to speak on behalf of all Muslims, but are usually expected to accept the accusations and affirm their personal allegiance to the constitutional order by distancing themselves from "extremists" or "conservatives." Comparable anti-Muslim attitudes prevail in debates addressing requests and claims made by Islamic associations and Muslim representatives, particularly in discussions about the building of mosques, provisions for fasting and *ḥalāl* food, Islamic religious education, and gender-segregated sports classes. Such imperious attitudes in the public domain have also been reflected in the agenda-setting of discussions between state representatives and Muslim associations in the German Islam Conference (Deutsche Islamkonferenz), a corporatist body set up by then Interior Minister Wolfgang Schäuble in 2006. Although many Muslims initially welcomed it as a first step towards state recognition, the Conference eventually became a platform from which German officials presented their expectations to Muslim associations, including a "partnership for security," which effectively mandated some members of the Conference to spy on others.

Muslim Associational Life, Community, and Transnational Politics. Despite the narrow field that such an anti-Muslim sentiment in state and society leaves, Muslim immigrants have engaged in an impressively diverse, if fragmented, associational life since the 1970s. The most influential movement to emerge from these early days was the German section of Milli Görüş (National View, since 1995 Islamische Gemeinschaft Milli Görüş, Islamic Community Milli Görüş, IGMG), Turkey's mainstream Islamist political movement then led by its charismatic chairman Necmettin Erbakan. Milli Görüş created the initial infrastructure of contemporary Muslim life in Germany, mobilizing hundreds of emerging "backyard mosques" into a hierarchically structured movement providing social and religious services to the wider community. In time, these mosques would also become ports of call for Bosniaks and Albanian Muslims, who shared with Turks a Sunnī Ḥanafī tradition, the religious heritage of the Ottoman Empire, as well as the sense of limitations of the secular nation-states that succeeded it in the twentieth century. For many Bosniaks and Albanians it was easier to pray in the "Turkish mosques" beyond the control of Yugoslav authorities.

At the same time, Milli Görüş also campaigned for the establishment of an Islamic state in Turkey. Muslim activists on this political quest became increasingly radicalized after the Islamic Iranian Revolution of 1979. As the emergence of the Islamic Republic coincided with a Turkish military coup, which also targeted Erbakan's movement, Germany became a destination for leading Turkish Islamists. An offshoot of the IGMG under the preacher Cemalettin Kaplan led to the emergence of the elitist and sectarian "Union of Islamic Associations and Communities" (Verband der Islamischen Vereine und Gemeinden, Islami Cemaat ve Cemiyetler Birliği) in 1984. From its headquarters in Cologne, the Union worked towards the violent overthrow of Turkey's secular order, and it took on the epithet of the "Caliphate State" in the mid-1990s. While the Caliphate State collapsed with the incarceration and deportation of Kaplan's son and successor Metin, in 2004, Germany's IGMG gradually distanced itself from the Islamic politics of Turkey and transformed into a Muslim community committed to life in Germany, as well as to larger issues concerning the *ummah*. In a groundbreaking ethnographic study of Milli Görüş, anthropologist Werner Schiffauer described its "Post-Islamist" turn from Islamist movement to Islamic community, in terms of cadres, organizational principles, and ideological debates.

Notwithstanding this transition, the IGMG remains under the surveillance of Germany's intelligence services (Offices for the Protection of the Constitution) of the federal states (Landesverfassungschutz) and the central state (Bundesamt für Verfassungsschutz), with significant disadvantages for members and sympathizers. They may face prosecution and can be denied German citizenship. Public bodies are discouraged from dealings with this significant Muslim association in Germany, which is the second largest after the DITIB (Diyanet İşleri Türk Islam Birliği, Türkisch-Islamische Union der Anstalt für Religion, Turkish Islamic Union of the Presidency of Religious Affairs). DITIB is the German branch of Turkey's Presidency of Religious Affairs (Diyanet) and serves as the national umbrella for almost nine hundred locally constituted mosque communities. While decidedly nonpolitical, DITIB is closely tied to the religious policy of Turkish governments, with all of its religious personnel and administrative infrastructure maintained by the Diyanet. While DITIB used to stand for a "Kemalist state Islam" and hence was deeply suspicious of Milli Görüş and its political activism, this antagonistic constellation has been partly eroded during the government of the Justice and Development Party since 2002.

In addition to a range of other Turkish Muslim associations with different sectarian, political, or linguistic affiliations, Bosniaks and Albanian speakers from Kosovo and Macedonia are organized in mosque associations, which are related to their national Islamic Unions (Islamska Zajednica, Bashkësia Fetare Islame). In addition, there are many Arab Muslim organizations such as the Muslim Community of Germany (Islamische Gemeinde in Deutschland). These are rather loose associations of small numbers of mosque communities that recoil from public visibility and presence. In the case of the latter, this is also due to allegations of organizational proximity to the Egyptian Muslim Brotherhood and hence observation by the intelligence services.

Since 9/11 and the growing public scrutiny of Muslims, alongside the need for representation in the German Islam Conference, umbrella organizations have proliferated. One example is the Liberal Islamic Union (Liberal Islamischer Bund), which, despite a membership of fewer than 120, has garnered heightened media attention for its support of liberal policies such as same-sex marriage. The more prominent associations with a claim to representativeness, such as the Central Council of Muslims (Zentralrat der Muslime) and the Islam Council (Islamrat), have formed a coordination body with the leading Turkish-Muslim associations, called the Coordination Council of Muslims (Koordinationsrat der Muslime). As is evident from this unduly large number of umbrella organizations, as well as from the insistence on unity and centrality in their naming, the associational landscape of Muslim organizations is still far from representing a unified Muslim position. Surveillance of some member organizations by the intelligence services, and an antagonistic public debate keep many Muslim associations from engaging with larger societal questions, and exacerbate intra-Muslim fragmentation.

Meanwhile, the Alevi movement has taken a different route to integration and recognition, effecting a relatively successful transformation from socialist activism with roots in Turkey's revolutionary parties of the 1970s to Diasporic community building. Despite a continuing focus on "homeland politics," and specifically the campaign for Alevi rights in Turkey, the Alevi Community (Alevitische Gemeinde Deutschland, AGD) has followed an accommodationist policy towards state agencies since the 1990s. In most federal states, the AGD has been registered as a religious community with the right to teach Alevi belief in public schools: this prerogative is withheld from mainstream Muslim organizations. Intelligence services tend to treat Alevi organizations with more sympathy, and sometimes Alevis are presented as a panacea to "fundamentalist Islam." This creates political opportunities for Alevi organizations, while it pits them against Islamist or post-Islamist organizations such as Milli Görüş.

Muslims in Politics. A third domain of Muslim politics pertains to the engagement of Muslim immigrants in German political parties and in federal and state parliaments, where the number of representatives particularly of Turkish and Kurdish descent is high in European comparison. The growing presence of Muslim Members of Parliament as well as of ministers at the state level within the parties of the left has had some impact on the politics of recognition of Muslims and immigrants, even though the country's citizenship regime remained relatively restrictive despite attempts at reform. Since 1999 citizenship has been based on the principle of territorial descent (*ius solis*) rather than the lineage of blood (*ius sanguinis*), yet the law has also explicitly outlawed dual citizenship, thereby significantly limiting its appeal particularly for Turkish immigrants. Some members of the principal party on the right, the Christian Democrats, continue to hold on to a "Judeo-Christian" notion of European civilization and revert to anti-Muslim rhetoric, yet even there, a growing number of Muslims have begun to take political posts in local and federal state parliaments. In most cases, however, Muslim politicians' portfolios tend to be limited to "immigration and integration" issues, curtailing their impact on larger policy issues. With the exception of Turkey, most foreign policy areas have remained outside the reach of Muslim politicians. This is particularly true for "Muslim concerns" such as Israel, Palestinian rights, and opposition to Western intervention in the Muslim world.

Muslim Futures in Germany. Germany's transformation from its postwar ethno-nationalist orientation towards an open society based on immigration and diversity has been erratic and is far from completion. The resulting approach towards Islam and Muslims by both state and society appears to owe more to ontological insecurities rooted in German history, Orientalism, and the Holocaust than to the actions or politics of Muslims as such. It does, however, account for much of the precariousness of Muslims' presence in Germany, their politics of recognition, community-building, and transnational mobilization. Considering demographic trends, German society is progressively reshaped by immigration and cultural and religious diversity. While this could further fuel insecurity in some parts of German society, it also bears the potential to open up space for Muslims in their quest for recognition and participation in the larger body politic.

The fragmented nature of the political Muslim sphere, as well as the relevance of Turkish-speaking Muslims, will almost certainly continue, while a "common Muslim space" that would be internally diverse but able to concur on core issues, is unlikely to emerge in the near future. New, non-ethnically based Muslim organizations are likely to gain more ground. Current movements such as Wheels (Zahnräder) and the Muslim Youth of Germany (Muslimische Jugend Deutschland), where Muslims of the second and third generation with different countries of origin join in the pursuit of shaping society and exploring their identity, are a case in point. While some Muslims will become more active within a German context, transnational connections will maintain their importance, whether in terms of relations with the country of origin or with other Muslim communities. Another potentially relevant development may be the very recent emergence of Salafī groups, which have succeeded in attracting a considerable number of disaffected young Muslims in urban areas. Their future, as well as that of the Muslims of Germany more broadly, will largely depend on German state policies towards Islam in general, and towards Muslim associations that operate within the confines of the constitution in particular.

BIBLIOGRAPHY

Al Hamarneh, Ala, and Jörn Thielmann, eds. *Islam and Muslims in Germany*. Muslim Minorities, vol. 7. Leiden and Boston: Brill, 2008.

Bade, Klaus J., Pieter C. Emmer, Leo Lucassen, and Jochen Oltmer, eds. *The Encyclopedia of Migration and Minorities in Europe: From the Seventeenth Century to the Present*. Cambridge, U.K., and New York: Cambridge University Press, 2011.

Mandel, Ruth Ellen. *Cosmopolitan Anxieties: Turkish Challenges to Citizenship and Belonging in Germany*. Durham, N.C. and London: Duke University Press, 2008.

Schiffauer, Werner. *Nach dem Islamismus. Eine Ethnographie der Islamischen Gemeinschaft Milli Görüş*. Berlin: Suhrkamp Verlag, 2010.

Schneider, Thorsten Gerald, ed. *Islamfeindlichkeit. Wenn die Grenzen der Kritik verschwinden*, 2d ed. Wiesbaden: VS Verlag für Sozialwissenschaften, 2010.

Sökefeld, Martin. *Struggling for Recognition: The Alevi Movement in Germany and in Transnational Space*. New York: Berghahn Books, 2008.

Yurdakul, Gökçe. *From Guest Workers into Muslims: The Transformation of Turkish Immigrant Associations in Germany*. Newcastle, U.K.: Cambridge Scholars, 2009.

KEREM ÖKTEM

GHĀMIDĪ, JĀVED AḤMAD. Jāved Aḥmad Ghāmidī (b. 1951) is a Pakistani Islamic scholar. He is known for a number of different views on religious law that differ from many other scholars, particularly on issues concerning women.

Ghāmidī was born in a small village outside Lahore, Pakistan. He graduated from Islamiya High School, Pakpattan, in 1967, and Government College, Lahore, with a bachelor's degree in English, in 1972.

He was an early member of Pakistan's Jamāʿat-i Islāmī political party. In the 1970s, Ghāmidī's thought began to diverge from the modernist interpretations endorsed by the Jamāʿat, particularly those of its founder Abū al-Aʿlā al-Mawdūdī. He was subsequently expelled from the Jamāʿat in 1977 and began a sustained critique of Mawdūdī's thought.

In his scholarship, Ghāmidī is a traditionalist: his views on contemporary issues are informed through reference to the Qurʾān and the Sunnah (traditions of the Prophet Muḥammad). His three major books are his annotated Qurʾān *al-Bayān*, his legal philosophical treatise *Burhān*, and *Mīzān*. As Ghāmidī's major exegetical work, *Mizān* is his application of Qurʾānic law to a range of social and political issues.

Ghāmidī differs from other traditionalists on various points. He interprets the Qurʾān through a form of coherence theory. Unlike most traditionalist scholars, who interpret the Qurʾān primarily at the level of the *ayāt* (verse), he insists that the text should be interpreted primarily in terms of whole *suwar* (chapters). Ghāmidī argues that Muslims in the present day are not under obligation to wage military *jihād* to spread Islam, and only as a last resort to end oppression. He also argues the stoning punishment for apostasy was specific to the Prophet's time.

Ghāmidī is also notable for his views on women. He regards women's head covering not as mandated under Islamic law but rather as a desirable Islamic custom. He has also asserted that women's testimony in court is equal to that of men's. While he holds some exceptional views regarding women and religious law, much of his underlying perspective on gender roles follows traditionalist thought. He has written that men and women do have different capacities and, in the family specifically, God has granted men a degree of control over women.

In 2006 Ghāmidī's views on proposed women's rights legislation put him in the political spotlight in Pakistan. At the time he was the head of the Council of Islamic Ideology, advising the government on proposed reforms to the *hudūd* laws, which deal with rape and other serious crimes. Ghāmidī has long argued they are un-Islamic, and his was a prominent voice pushing for reform.

After the 2010 assassination of Punjab governor Salman Taseer during his attempts to reform Pakistan's blasphemy laws, Ghāmidī was one of a few public personalities who continued to speak out against the laws. Death threats against Ghāmidī and his family increased in 2006, and he chose to flee with his family to Malaysia, where he currently resides.

BIBLIOGRAPHY

Hassan, Riffat. "Islamic Modernist and Reformist Discourse in South Asia." In *Reformist Voices of Islam: Mediating Islam and Modernity*, edited by Shireen T. Hunter, pp. 159–186. London: M. E. Sharpe, 2009.

ABBAS JAFFER

GHANNŪSHĪ, RĀSHID AL-. Rāshid al-Ghannūshī (b. 1941) is an Islamic thinker, activist, and political leader in Tunisia. Born to a peasant family in Tunisia, Ghannūshī (often spelled Ghannoushi in Western literature) is the head of the Ḥizb al-Nahḍah (Renaissance Party; formerly called Ḥarakat al-Ittijāh al-Islāmī, or Islamic Tendency Movement) and is its chief theoretician. Ghannūshī grew up in a religious household and received his early education in the traditional Zaytūnah schools. In 1968 he received a degree in philosophy from the University of Damascus, Syria. After a year in France, Ghannūshī returned to Tunisia to become a secondary-school philosophy teacher, and to establish—along with a group of young Tunisians increasingly at odds with the secular policies of Habib Bourguiba's regime—an organized Islamic movement. In 1981 he was sentenced to eleven years' imprisonment for operating an unauthorized association; he was released in 1984. In 1987 he received a life term of forced labor but was discharged in 1988. In the early 1990s Ghannūshī lived in Europe as a political exile.

Ghannūshī's thought reflects a masterful understanding of Western and Islamic philosophies and a genuine concern for reconciling the basic tenets of Islam with modernity and progress. He maintains nontraditional views on several issues, and he evaluates the West within the philosophical dimension of East-West dialogue. Unlike the Muslim Brotherhood of Sayyid Quṭb of Egypt, he perceives the West as an ideological counterweight to Islamic doctrines: the West is considered neither superior nor inferior to Islam. Ghannūshī sees coexistence and cooperation as the basis for the relationship between the two. What sets the two worlds apart, however, is the difference in their perception of the fundamental concepts, or "effective ideas," that move their cultures: the value and place of humanity in the universe. Islam replaces the Western "man-god" formula with an Islamic one, "man the vicegerent of God on earth," and posits God as the ultimate value in the universe; it acknowledges the material and spiritual essences of humanity and attempts to reconcile them; and it directs human activities according to the divine regulations and concise values embodied in the *Sharīʿah* (law based on the Qurʾān).

Ghannūshī acknowledges that the system of democracy is a direct consequence of a particular Western experience. He perceives democracy as a method of government and as a philosophy. In his view, the Muslims' problem is not with democratic institutions themselves, but with the secular and nationalistic values behind democracy. Islamic democracy is distinguished from other systems by its moral content as derived from the *Sharīʿah*.

Ghannūshī makes an important intellectual contribution by linking Westernization with dictatorship. He believes two common characteristics dominate the political systems of the Arab and larger Muslim world—Westernization and dictatorship by ruling elites. Because of its alienation from the masses, the Westernized elite resorts to violent and repressive means to impose its foreign-inspired models and perpetuate its rule.

Ghannūshī advocates an equal role for women in society and their right to education, work, choice of home and marriage, ownership of property, and political participation. He considers wearing the veil a matter of personal choice that is not to be imposed by the state.

Because he takes a gradualist stance in advocating social and political change, Ghannūshī seeks to inspire a more vital cultural model. He relies on orthodox ideas while in fact reinterpreting them to accommodate the modern issues of his society. His ideas, though sometimes controversial, are paid much attention by Muslim activists and intellectuals. Ghannūshī's intellectual contributions and political activism have gained him prominence within the contemporary Islamic movement

Following the popular uprisings that led to the removal of Ben Ali from power, Ghannūshī returned to Tunisia on 30 January 2012. As an influential politician and influential leader of the al-Nahḍah Party, he continues to play a moderating role in Tunisia's democratic transition. In 2012 Ghannūshī received the Chatham House Prize for his positive role in the transition.

[*See also* Ḥizb al-Nahḍah.]

BIBLIOGRAPHY

Esposito, John L., and John O. Voll. *Makers of Contemporary Islam*. New York: Oxford University Press, 2001.

Ghannūshī, Rāshid al-. *Fī al-Mabādiʿ al-Asāsīyah lil-Dīmuqrāṭīyah wa-Uṣūl al-Ḥukm al-Islāmī* (The Principles of Democracy and the Fundamentals of Islamic Government). Tunis: R. al-Ghannūshī, 1990.

Ghannūshī, Rāshid al-. *Maqālāt* (Essays). Paris: Dār al-Karwān, 1984.

Ghannūshī, Rāshid al-. *Ṭarīqunā ilā al-Ḥaḍārah* (Our Path to Civilization). Tunis, n.d.

Ghannūshī, Rāshid al-. "We Don't Have a Religious Problem." Interview. *Middle East* 203 (September 1991): 19–20.

Ghannūshī, Rāshid al-, and Ḥamīdah al-Nayfar. *Mā huwa al-gharb* (What Is the West?). Tunis, n.d.

Ghannūshī, Rāshid al-, and Ḥasan al-Turābī. *Al-Ḥarakah al-islāmīyah wa-al-taḥdīth* (The Islamic Movement and Modernization). Beirut: Dar al-Jeel, 1984.

Shahin, Emad Eldin. *Political Ascent: Contemporary Islamic Movements in North Africa*. Boulder, Colo.: Westview Press, 1997.

Tamimi, Azzam S. *Rachid Ghannouchi: A Democrat within Islamism*. New York: Oxford University Press, 2001.

EMAD EL-DIN SHAHIN

GHAZĀLĪ, ABŪ ḤĀMID AL-.

(1058–1111), theologian, jurist, and philosopher.

Al-Ghazālī lived a short life during the political turmoil of the late ʿAbbāsid period, during which military leaders of varied ethnicities vied for control of a very weak ʿAbbāsid caliph in Baghdad. Al-Ghazālī, seeing politics as "of little significance" (*Iqtiṣād*, p. 234), was not so much a political theorist as a theologian. But he was also, ironically, deeply engaged in the realpolitik of his time, as Hillenbrand says (2004, p. 594). His engagement in politics, therefore, is accounted for by a more existentialist as well as a practical concern that can be detected throughout his corpus. Al-Ghazālī's works, reflecting the effects of the disturbances mentioned above, make it clear that the chief motivation and the underlying concern behind his writings was to safeguard religious doctrines under which to unite the Muslims. In the works where he dealt with issues of a political nature, he was more concerned with rectifying the conditions causing the political turmoil than with forging a comprehensive Islamic political theory that could be used to legitimize any form of governance. He dealt with practical matters with a view to finding a solution to pressing problems deemed crucial for the well-being of Muslim society. His is an idiosyncratic attitude toward politics in that he attaches the utmost practical value to it insofar as it affects the religious order of society. This explains why he offered practical, sometimes ad hoc, solutions to urgent issues, which was the very reason for his engagement in realpolitik.

The fact that al-Ghazālī's overall thought was so strongly influenced by practical concerns means that most of his theological and philosophical works can be viewed as part of a greater "project" that is political in essence. He sought to restore the unity of the Muslim community as a whole under the umbrella of the *Sharīʿah*, the law, by creating a common ground: preserving the integrity of religion based on undisputed religious tenets as he understood them. To that end, for instance in the *Tahāfut al-falāsifah*, al-Ghazālī, seeing himself as a *mujaddid*, or reviver, of religion (*al-Munqidh*, p. 75), launched a religious and philosophical assault against the metaphysical conclusions of the Muslim philosophers. His objective was to discredit the philosophers, who he thought disparaged religion by introducing new-fashioned ideas, a new-fangled understanding of religion, and also religiously unacceptable doctrines into the Islamic milieu, thereby supplying theoretical ammunition for opposing groups (e.g., the Ismāʿīlis) in their violent attacks on Sunnī orthodoxy and the political order.

Political Views. It is in this context that al-Ghazālī's political attitude gains significance: polity must have an order and a ruler to maintain the religious order, so as to fulfill the more sublime end of creating a secure setting in which religious duties may be observed and fulfilled. To this end, he first argued for the indispensability of designating an imam and then, for more circumstantial reasons, for upholding the legitimacy of the ruler in power against dissenters, even if the ruler is not the best candidate according to religious principles. For al-Ghazālī, the necessity of the imam is sanctioned by the law and founded on two premises: "The order of religious matters is certainly sought for by the law-giver prophet. And . . . the establishment of the order of religion cannot be realized except through an imām who is obeyed [*al-muṭāʿ*]" (*al-Iqtiṣād*, p. 235). For "the order of religion can only be achieved by the order of the world and the order of the world can only be achieved by virtue of an imām" and "the world and the protection of life and properties can only be realized by virtue of a ruler." Hence "the ruler is necessary for the order of the world, and the order of the world is necessary for the order of religion. The order of religion is necessary to achieve happiness in the hereafter" (*al-Iqtiṣād*, pp. 235–236; *Faḍāʾiḥ*, p. 235). The presence of a ruler is vital for the establishment and the validity of all religious and social institutions, and the ruler is needed to unite people of diverging opinions. Without a ruler, chaos and disintegration would prevail, disputes would continue, and famine and disease would spread.

Upon establishing the necessity of the existence of an imam, regarding the manner of his appointment, al-Ghazālī believed that the best way is by holding elections. However, this election would not necessarily require the consent of the majority. For instance, in perilous times, the allegiance to the caliph of even one person holding military power (*shawka*) would solve the question, since the allegiance of the power-holder means the allegiance of all under him (*al-Iqtiṣād,* p. 238; Hillenbrand, 1988, p. 84). The description of the ruler needed for the order of religion as "the one who is obeyed" is particularly significant at this point.

Al-Ghazālī believed that in order to prevent disunity, power should be vested in one single ruler, who must possess certain qualities, such as competence, knowledge, intelligence, willpower, chivalry, and visionary leadership. The ruler must also have affection for his subjects and be God-fearing, well informed about current events, and a descendant of the tribe of Quraysh (*Naṣīḥat; Faḍā'iḥḥ*). Lack of these qualities, however, may be tolerated for the sake of maintaining order. Accordingly, ousting a ruler is only allowed as long as anarchy or armed conflict is not suspected. Otherwise, even imams who lack the necessary qualities must be obeyed, in order to avoid harmful consequences (*al-Iqtiṣād,* p. 235; *Iḥyā',* "Kitāb al-ḥalāl wa al-ḥarām"). Out of the same concern, al-Ghazālī was willing to acknowledge the legitimacy of the holders of military force (*shawka*), by creating a link between the caliph and these rulers (*Iḥyā'*; Hillenbrand, 1988, p. 91; Rosenthal, 1958, p. 42). Al-Ghazālī's intention was to legitimize the de facto rulers, as a working solution, in order to maintain his constant goal of political stability.

In this situation when the rulers were not completely adequate, al-Ghazālī's approach was to advise and admonish these rulers with a view to keeping them in line with religious teachings. In such works as *Iḥyā' 'ulūm al-dīn, Letters of al-Ghazālī,* and *Naṣṣīḥat al-mulūk,* the latter composed mainly in a "Mirror for Princes" style, al-Ghazālī advises rulers to be pious and observe religious duties, to heed Islamic principles in their governance, and to take the Prophet as a role model. Rulers should also be just in dealing with their people, be aware of this world's transitory nature and the perpetuity of the next, beware of injustice and corruption, consult the *'ulamā',* avoid luxury, be humble and kind to people, show clemency and good morals, comply with the law, and uphold the rights of people, including slaves. The ultimate goal is a secure environment in which people lead a happy life in accordance with religion.

[*See also* Mirrors for Princes; *and* Offices and Titles: Religious, Social, and Political.]

BIBLIOGRAPHY

Primary Sources

Ghazālī, Abū Ḥāmid al-. *Faḍā'iḥ al-bāṭinīyah (al-mustaẓhirī).* Partially translated by R. J. McCarthy in *Al-Ghazali: Deliverance from Error; Five Key Texts Including His Spiritual Autobiography* al-Munqidh min al-dalal. Louisville, Ky.: Fons Vitae, 1999.

Ghazālī, Abū Ḥāmid al-. *Iḥyā' 'ulūm al-dīn.* Beirut: Dār al-M'rifa, 1982.

Ghazālī, Abū Ḥāmid al-. *al-Iqtiṣād fī al-i'tiqād.* Edited by I. Agah Çubukçu and Hüseyin Atay. Ankara: Ankara Üniversitesi İlahiyat Fakültesi Yayınları, 1962.

Ghazālī, Abū Ḥāmid al-. *al-Munqidh min al-ḍalāl.* Translated by W. Montgomery Watt as *The Faith and Practice of al-Ghazālī.* Chicago: Kazi Publications, 1982.

Ghazālī, Abū Ḥāmid al-. *Naṣīḥat al-mulūk.* Translated from the Persian by F. R. C. Bagley in *Al-Ghazālī's Book of Counsel for Kings.* London and New York: Oxford University Press, 1964.

Qayyum, Abdul. *Letters of al-Ghazzali.* Lahore: Islamic Publications, 1994.

Secondary Works

Binder, Leonard. "Al-Ghazālī's Theory of Islamic Government." *Muslim World* 45, no. 3 (1955): 229–241.

Hillenbrand, Carole. "Islamic Orthodoxy or Realpolitik? Al-Ghazālī's Views on Government." *Iran* 26 (1988): 81–94.

Hillenbrand, Carole. "A Little-Known Mirror for Princes by al-Ghazālī." In *Words, Texts and Concepts Cruising the Mediterranean Sea,* edited by R. Arnzen and J. Thielmann, pp. 593–601. Leuven: Peeters, 2004.

Lambton, Ann K. S. "The Theory of Kingship in the *Naṣīḥat ul-mulūk* of Ghazālī." *Islamic Quarterly* 1 (1954): 47–55.

Rosenthal, Erwin I. J. *Political Thought in Medieval Islam: An Introductory Outline*. Cambridge, U.K.: Cambridge University Press, 1958.

Sherwani, H. K. "El-Ghazzâlî on the Theory and Practice of Politics." *Islamic Culture* 9 (1935): 450–474.

FEHRULLAH TERKAN

GHAZĀLĪ, MUḤAMMAD AL-. Muḥammad al-Ghazālī (1917–1996) was an Egyptian Islamic scholar and for a time a leading member of al-Ikhwān al-Muslimūn (Muslim Brotherhood). Al-Ghazālī is arguably one of the two or three most influential Sunnī Islamic thinkers of the twentieth century. Born in Buḥayrah Province in the Nile Delta, he graduated from al-Azhar in 1941 and occupied influential positions in his own country and in other Arab states. In Egypt, he was director of the Mosques Department, director-general of Islamic Call (*daʿwah*), and undersecretary of the Ministry of Awqāf (religious foundations). He has also taught at the universities of al-Azhar (Egypt), King ʿAbd al-ʿAzīz and Umm al-Qurā (Saudi Arabia), and Qatar and was the academic director of Amīr ʿAbd al-Qādir's Islamic University in Algeria.

Al-Ghazālī was dismissed from his position in the *hayʾah taʾsīsīyah* (constituent body) of the Ikhwān in December 1953, after reportedly attempting, with two other prominent members, to unseat the organization's leader, Ḥasan al-Huḍaybī (with the approval, some Muslim Brothers suspected, of Gamal Abdel Nasser and the Free Officers). Many feel that he remained an Ikhwānī in all but name, and he consistently maintained a positive evaluation of the historic role of the Muslim Brothers. However, his bold and original interpretations over his lifetime far exceeded the often stifling limitations of Brotherhood thinking.

Al-Ghazālī's Work. Al-Ghazālī's most enduring legacy resides primarily in his role as a leading member of the Egyptian new Islamist school of creative and independent Islamic thinkers who produced an impressive body of *fiqh* (jurisprudence) on all the major issues facing the Islamic *ummah*, from progressive attitudes to the arts and education, to innovative and socially responsible thinking about the economy and society (notably the role of women and non-Muslims) and innovative elaborations of democratic ideas and resistance to external pressures. Active in publishing throughout his life, al-Ghazālī wrote approximately forty titles including such important works as *Moral Character of the Muslim*, *Islam and Economic Affairs*, *Islam and Political Despotism*, *A Constitution for Cultural Unity*, and *Prejudice and Tolerance in Christianity and Islam*. He established a reputation as a reasonable, well-balanced, and independent scholar. A rigorous interpreter, although by no means a traditionalist, his positions on various issues are taken seriously by the mainstream of the Islamist movement.

Al-Ghazālī contended that contemporary Muslims paid excessive attention to matters of cleanliness, prayers, pilgrimage, and rituals while lagging far behind the West in matters of government, the economy, and finance that he regarded as being of far greater importance to the *ummah*.

As an erudite theorist, who strongly supported an expansive concept of *shūrā* (political consultation) and was willing to build on that precept to elaborate democratic principles compatible with Islam, al-Ghazālī stood out among contemporary philosophers. He was and is still regarded as a modernist in social and political matters, condemning the austere, simplistic orientation of what he termed *al-fiqh al-badawī* (the jurisprudence of nomads—implicitly referring to Wahhābī thought), and he actively encouraged consideration of the experience of other (non-Muslim) societies as a source of inspiration for Muslims. For example, he cited both historical

Islamic and contemporary non-Islamic examples to support the case that a woman may legitimately assume any high post in society, which was entirely compatible with traditional Islamic teachings.

Al-Ghazālī's main, and rather daring, methodological contribution has been his attempt to reduce excessive reliance on the *ḥadīth* (pl. *aḥādīth*) in contemporary jurisprudence or, to put the issue another way, to insist on the priority of the Qur'ān over the *ḥadīth*. His voluminous writings admit only the *ḥadīth*s that have a Qur'ānic credibility and exclude *aḥādīth al-āḥād* (single sayings), if they appear odd or poorly reasoned. He maintained that "a little reading of the blessed Qur'ān and a lot of reading of the *aḥādīth* does not give an accurate picture of Islam." In his view, it was this lopsided methodology in approaching Islam that partly explained what he regarded as the "infantile" and "half-educated" attitude of militant Islamists; they were obsessed with power but poorly trained.

Al-Ghazālī's strict scrutiny of the *ḥadīth* thus enabled him to criticize simultaneously both the Muslim social reactionaries, who used *ḥadīth*s on the flimsiest grounds to justify such practices as beating and sodomizing wives, and the Islamist political radicals, who used similar *ḥadīth*s to justify forcing their own views and authority on society at large.

With consistently centrist positions, which inevitably exposed him to attacks from both Islamist traditionalists and violent extremists, al-Ghazālī attracted the antipathy of militant secularists as well. Because they were generally opposed to all Islamists in public life, belligerent foes did not welcome the interpretive successes of the new Islamist school to which al-Ghazālī belonged. His place in public life was marked by periodic crises when his views came under sharp, often vicious attack.

The Case of the Farag Foda Assassination. One such incident proved particularly damaging. When Islamist extremists resorted to terror and assassinated the secularist Farag Foda in 1992, al-Ghazālī and the new Islamists stood against them with an unambiguous condemnation. Still, it was not always possible to avoid being drawn into the controversies around such deplorable incidents. Al-Ghazālī, for example, was called to testify as an expert on *Sharīʿah* for the defense in the trial of Foda's murderers. He did so in a strict and unimpeachable way, but was nevertheless vilified when his testimony was distorted in tendentious ways as a justification of the assassins. Al-Ghazālī offered no such justification in his narrow but accurate clarification of the provisions of *Sharīʿah* in such cases. Naturally, he assumed some responsibility for the uproar his testimony generated, because his final response on punishment for those who take it upon themselves to chastise an apostate, though technically correct, was too brief and too insensitive to the context within which this narrow legal question was posed. Earlier in the court session, al-Ghazālī elaborated on the *fiqh* surrounding the issue of apostasy, and he indicated clearly his own opinion that *Sharīʿah* did not, as the extremists claimed, demand a death sentence. He could and should have done the same on the issue of those who usurped authority. After all, what was at stake in the trial was precisely the fate of those accused of the murder of an alleged apostate, and such an elaboration would have been even more germane than the one he offered on apostasy in general terms.

Regrettably, and because he failed to take this opportunity, al-Ghazālī made himself vulnerable to attack. He was repeatedly accused of "not [being] closely identified with the militant cause" and frequently appeared on state-run television to criticize extremists, all of which drew the ire of revolutionaries. His 1989 book *al-Sunnah al-nabawīyah bayna ahl al-fiqh wa-ahl al-ḥadīth*, severely criticized *Ahl al-ḥadīth,* which was a term thought to be a euphemism for Wahhābīs that, for complicated reasons, he could not openly identify. The controversial volume prompted both unfavorable "major conferences . . . in Egypt and Saudi Arabia" (Abou El Fadl, 2005, p. 93) and highly critical articles in the Saudi-owned newspaper *Asharq Al-Awsat.* While some questioned "his motives and competence," few could deny the scholar's credentials as well as his impressive contributions to mainstream Islamic thought.

[*See also* Egypt; *and* Muslim Brotherhood.]

BIBLIOGRAPHY

Abou El Fadl, Khaled. *The Great Theft: Wrestling Islam from the Extremists.* New York: HarperSanFrancisco, 2005.

Baker, Raymond William. *Islam Without Fear: Egypt and the New Islamists.* Cambridge, Mass.: Harvard University Press, 2003. In-depth treatment of al-Ghazālī's life work, emphasizing his role, along with Shaykh Yūsuf al-Qaraḍāwī, as a leading figure of the New Islamist School of independent and enlightened Islamic thinkers.

Ghazālī, Muḥammad al-. *Humūm dā'iyah* (Concerns of an Islamic Caller). Cairo, 1983. Useful collection illustrating al-Ghazālī's position on several religious and social issues.

Ghazālī, Muḥammad al-. *Al-sunnah al-nabawīyah bayna ahl al-fiqh wa-ahl al-ḥadīth.* Cairo: Dār al Sharuq, 1991. Tenth edition (in two years) of a book in which al-Ghazālī illustrates how his methodology of *uṣūl al-fiqh* may be applied to the analysis of various religious and social issues.

RAYMOND WILLIAM BAKER
Updated by JOSEPH A. KÉCHICHIAN

GHULĀT. *See* Rebellion.

GLOBALIZATION. Globalization, or "becoming global" (Ar., *'awlama*), refers to the dramatic increase in the flow of goods, information, and people between different parts of the world. It can be understood primarily as the phenomenon of predominance of global economic forces over local ones, with concomitant political, cultural, and social ramifications. It is a phenomenon that has challenged religion (or other comprehensive doctrines) and conventional political systems, democratic or authoritarian.

Like "modernity," "reason," and "justice," "globalization" is a term as much in vogue as it is laden with meanings and consequences. The occurrence of globalization is widely accepted (although some dismiss the term as a euphemism for imperialist hegemony of the U.S. military and the neoliberal business elite), whereas its human and moral consequences are endlessly disagreed on. In its contemporary sense, it is best understood as primarily an economic phenomenon that has enveloped the world since the last quarter of the twentieth century. If defined loosely as an increase in global relationships and transfer of goods, information, and people, its roots are as old as ancient human commerce, travel, and conquest, with significant surges in these activities during Islamic (seventh century), Mongol (thirteenth century), and then European (nineteenth century) imperial expansions. Some key theorists, such as Immanuel Wallerstein, trace the roots of the current wave of globalization with an essentially economic logic in the rise of capitalism and the attendant colonialism in early modern Europe. If defined more narrowly, it can be dated to the Euro-American policies of neoliberalization that began in the 1980s with the administrations of Ronald Reagan and Margaret Thatcher. These policies require, in theory, the flow of goods, services, and labor uninhibited by politically created barriers, and prescribe as the supreme good the health of the market and financial institutions at the cost of jobs, services, social justice, and most other desirables. These were a response primarily by the Euro-American capitalist class to the "Keynesian compromise" between state-managed and free market capitalism that had characterized the Western world in the years surrounding the two world wars. The neoliberal partisans of globalization, which include the world's economic and political elites and institutions, see the Keynesian era of social ("inward-looking") democracies as the exception to the natural globalizing arc of modernity (IMF Staff, "Globalization"). Its critics see the Anglo-American shift to neoliberalism as an immensely successful revolt of big business against the politically and democratically enacted constraints to protect democracy, the environment, and social responsibility (Harvey, 2007).

While there is little consensus on globalization, the adverse effect of globalization on the power and autonomy of the state, including democratic politics, is generally agreed upon (Osterhammel and Petersson, 2009). Its critics qualify that globalization has eroded the autonomy of the state only vis-à-vis international economic centers and corporations, whereas it has aggrandized the power and authoritarianism of the state vis-à-vis social actors, such as the civil society, environmental groups, or cultural and religious forces, within the polities. Some theorists point out that war, along with the consequent aggrandizement of the state, has indeed been the major force of globalization in history (Barkawi, 2005).

The advocates of economic globalization see the replacement of politics by economics as desirable and globalization as the culmination of modernity, holding that political systems have become irrelevant except as facilitators and protectors of business and finance. On the other hand, the advocates of democracy, social justice, environment, and local autonomy, independently and from various vantage points, decry the negative effects of globalization, which in some cases, such as the environment, appear to be irreversible and drastic. Sheldon Wolin, an influential American political theorist, sums up the judgment of most political thinkers when he dubs the rise of neoliberalism and its concomitant global corporation as "inverted totalitarianism"—that is, unlike the totalitarian states of the mid-twentieth century that co-opted their economies, today's economies have so overwhelmed the states as to render the democratic process ineffective even in the world's most powerful states.

Globalization has polarized the conventional "elites"—provoking often strong disapproval from the intellectual elite and strong endorsement by the capitalist elite, and rendering the political elite beholden to the latter rather than the former. The activists concerned with the destructive consequences of the economic globalization on the environment and the immense global disparity of wealth are divided on the alternatives, their responses ranging from a reversal of globalization to its redeployment by the sharing of information and resources it enables as essential in combating global climate degradation and other challenges (Bennholdt-Thomsen et al., 2001).

The Muslim world, with the exception of the new Muslim global capitalist class, has experienced globalization as little more than a new phase of Western colonialism. As elsewhere in the developing world, globalization has weakened postcolonial Muslim states' autonomy and provided opportunities to the unelected autocrats of various kinds for crony capitalism. However, given the limited reach of the weakly legitimated post colonial secular states and relatively weak nationalism (the strength of which is variable from one state to another and generally proportional to the depth of prior colonial penetration), the effects of globalization in societies shaped for centuries by Islamic tradition have peculiar dimensions. Globalization in the Muslim world, as elsewhere, has manifested as increasing U.S. influence. In particular against the backdrop of the end of the Cold War and the rise of the United States as the sole superpower, most Muslim states, like Sadat's Egypt or Zia's Pakistan, abandoned any socialist pretensions and embraced neoliberalism in the late 1970s and 1980s, leading to rising unemployment, economic disparity, and social dislocations. Even in authoritarian states with socialist sympathies that resisted leaning toward the United States, such as Syria, the essential dynamic has not been different (Haddad, 2012).

The response of the various Islamic movements to globalization is complex and evolving. First, there is a crisis of religious authority, which began over a century earlier with colonialism, but has been aggravated and transformed by globalization, in particular, the rise of the Internet, satellite news and other media, and the cultural values of neoliberalism (individualism, consumerism, sexual freedoms, economic inequality) that have now penetrated the Muslim world as never before. Second, as Olivier Roy has pointed out, there has been a turn in Islamic movements since the 1980s from state-centered ideologies concerned with social justice (in the manner of Ḥasan al-Bannā or Abū al-Aʿlā al-Mawdūdī) to apolitical responses through either personalist religiosity (Wahhābī-Salafism or televangelists such as Amr Khaled) or militancy (al-Qaʿida, Taliban). Third, the establishment of substantial Muslim minorities in the West has influenced both Muslim and Western countries significantly (if not always predictably or positively); Islam can no longer be dismissed as an Eastern religion by Westerners but increasingly forms an indigenous presence (or perceived threat). On the other hand, Western-educated Muslims, already dominant as secular rulers or intelligentsia in the postcolonial Muslim world, are now finding representation in the leadership of Islamist movements and the institutions of traditional learning like al-Azhar. Fourth, the most far-reaching impact of globalization on the Muslim world has manifested itself in the rise of free and credible Arab media outlets such as Al Jazeera since the late 1990s and in the powerful Arab public sphere these outlets have enabled. The spread of the Arab Spring of 2011 to virtually all Arab countries can be credited to this single influence. Finally, the oil- or neoliberal business and political Muslim elite remain the primary "native informants" of Islam to the global business (and thus, political) elite. Most of all, it is perhaps the lavish monuments in the oil-rich ports of global business and pleasure that represent the most telling symbols of the marriage of Islam to economic globalization. Another instance of a far deeper instance of the same relationship is Turkey's Islamic parties, in particular AKP, whose accommodation of and by the Turkish secularist and military class, Islam's most implacable adversary in the Muslim world, is testimony to the power of economic neoliberalism. The Turkish case is unsurprisingly held up as a model to and by the aspiring Islamists of Egypt and the Arab world generally.

The Arab Spring of 2011 was intimately yet ironically connected to globalization. On the one hand, the tremendous economic grievances that motivated the uprisings were more or less a direct consequence of the neoliberal policies of their authoritarian governments and of the global disparity of power globalization has aggravated. Yet on the other hand, the protestors' slogans of freedom, democracy, and human rights were and continue to be couched in a language and projected through the technology enabled by globalization. Finally, the neoliberal path is being presented to the fledgling democracies as the only way to progress and prosperity, yet, arguably, the failure of neoliberal dogma even in the United States, as evidenced by the economic downturns of the last decade, has given many pause. The most telling sign of the paradoxes of contemporary globalization is the way the Occupy Movement of disenfranchised Western populations against the economic elite has drawn on the symbols of the Arab Spring.

BIBLIOGRAPHY

Barkawi, Tarak. *Globalization and War*. Lanham, Md.: Rowman & Littlefield, 2005.

Bennholdt-Thomsen, Veronika et al., eds. *There Is an Alternative: Subsistence and Worldwide Resistance to Corporate Globalization*. Melbourne: Zed Books, 2001.

Haddad, Bassam. *Business Networks in Syria: The Political Economy of Authoritarian Resilience*. Stanford, Calif.: Stanford University Press, 2012.

Harvey, David. *A Brief History of Neoliberalism*. Oxford: Oxford University Press, 2007.

Hirst, Paul, Grahame Thompson, and Simon Bromley. *Globalization in Question*, 3d ed. Cambridge, U.K.: Polity Press, 2009.

IMF Staff. "Globalization: A Brief Overview." May 2008. Accessed May 09, 2012, http://www.imf.org/external/np/exr/ib/2008/053008.htm.

Osterhammel, Jürgen, and Niels P. Petersson. *Globalization: A Short History*. Princeton, N.J.: Princeton University Press, 2009.

Roy, Olivier. *Globalized Islam*. New York: Columbia University Press, 2006.

OVAMIR ANJUM

GOVERNANCE. The contemporary word for "government" in Arabic and other Islamicate languages is *ḥukūmah*. The root *ḥ-k-m* in Arabic has the original meaning "to restrain or prevent someone from acting in evil or foolish manner" or "rein in [a horse]." Since pre-Isalmic times, *ḥukm* has been used to refer to judgment, arbitration, passing sentence, decisionmaking, and, in later Islamic history, political authority or government. *Ḥukūmah*, another infinitive noun from the same root that was originally synonymous with *ḥukm*, has been used since the early modern period more specifically to mean government, whereas *ḥukm* maintains its more general meaning.

In the Qurʾān, the derivatives of the root *ḥ-k-m* that are relevant to governance and arbitration are *ḥukm*, *ḥikmah*, and *ḥukkām*. *Ḥukm* connotes the act or power of judgment, which is said, in the ultimate sense, to belong to God alone. Indeed, it is attributed only to God in the Qurʾān with a few exceptions in which *al-ḥukm* refers to the divine wisdom (or set of divine judgments) given to prophets (6:89, 19:12, 45:16). This observation may have been the cause of the Kharijite consternation against attributing *ḥukm* to anyone else. The famous verse they invoked, "The *ḥukm* is for none but God," is repeated thrice in the Qurʾān (6:57; 12:40; 12:67), and *ḥukm* appears on several other occasions with the same meaning. The wisdom given to prophets and to the righteous generally is referred to more frequently as *ḥikmah* (2:269, 38:20). The form *ḥakkama* (inf. n., *taḥkīm*; subj. n., *ḥakam* (sing.) or *ḥukkam* (pl.)) is reserved for human arbitration or authority in specific disputes (2:188, 4:65, 5:43), which must nonetheless be based on divine guidance. A *ḥakam* was an arbiter in pre-Islamic times, often a neutral outsider known for his or her wisdom, called on to judge on tribal disputes. The term *ḥukūmah,* which in the premodern period bore the same connotations as *ḥukm* (i.e., judgment on a dispute), or the dispute itself, does not appear in the Qurʾān. Lewis notes that since the Seljuk period (eleventh century), the term *ḥukūmah* denotes the office or function of governorship, usually provincial or local, and this usage continues into the Ottoman period. By the end of the eighteenth century the word seems to have acquired the more abstract sense of rule, the exercise of political authority, or the institutions of government.

Political Concepts and Vocabulary in Premodern Islam. The conceptual history of government in Islam is complex, and often the attempts to tie it to the etymology of some equivalent terms have led to the omission of crucial facts. The family of words that attended political discourse in Islamic history included terms such as *siyāsah* (politics, policy), *sulṭa* (*sulṭān*) (authority; ruler), *khilāfah* (successorship or deputyship), *mulk* (dominion, kingship), and *dawlah* (dynasty, reign), and, last but not least, *al-amr* (*ulū al-amr, amīr, imāra, imra*). This last is the most difficult to accurately translate, for *amr* as such means any matter or issue, but, as modern Egyptian scholar Muḥammad ʿImārah has persuasively argued, it, rather than any of the above, was the most frequently used term in the first century of Islam that was employed to refer to the "collective matter," "political rule," or "government."

We may capture some of the issues modern scholars have raised surrounding this history under the following questions: whether government, understood in an abstract sense, was a concept of which early Muslim thinkers were conscious; that is, whether they imagined it as an abstraction distinguished from the specific individuals in charge; whether they imagined it, as moderns do, as a set of institutions extricable from the individuals holding power; whether they took the origin of government for granted as being a necessary outgrowth of monotheism or whether they could reflect on its human origins; and finally, whether government as a rational, human endeavor (rather than God's direct rule through deputies, a Semitic idea they inherited) could be imagined.

Bernard Lewis (2012) links the modern Arabic term *ḥukūmah* (Persian *ḥukūmat*, Turkish *hükümet*) to "government," understood as a "group of men exercising the authority of the state" and observes that it was first used in the Ottoman period in the nineteenth century. He suggests that Turkish and Arabic writers made the "distinction between the state (*devlet, dawla*) and the government (*ḥukūmet, ḥukūma*) . . . following European practice" while also continuing to use the word *ḥukūmah* in the general, abstract sense of government, régime. Persian, however, has not adopted this distinction, and still uses *dawlat* for both the state and the government, while *ḥukūmat* has the more general sense of political authority. This claim is called into question by Riḍwān al-Sayyid's observation that Abū Hilāl al-ʿAskarī (d. c. 1005), an Arabic literary critic and rhetorician of Persian extraction, distinguishes between authority in the abstract (*mulk*) and the group of individuals who come to possess it: "The difference between *mulk* (dominion, authority) and *dawla* is that *mulk* means power, the ability to coerce the majority of people, whereas *dawla* connotes the transfer of fortune from one group of people to another" (R. al-Sayyid, Introduction to al-Māwardī's *Tashīl al-naẓar wa-taʿjīl al-ẓafar* (Beirut: Dār al-ʿUlūm al-ʿArabīya, 1987), p. 7, quoting Abū Hilāl's *al-Furūq al-lughawīya*). Furthermore, some medieval Muslim thinkers, such as Ibn Taymīyah (d. 1328), focused on the substance of government and criticized those who focused solely on the personal qualities of the ruler in judging legitimacy and nature of rule (Anjum, 2012).

Patricia Crone (2004) has observed that early Muslims took government for granted rather than asking, as early modern Western theorists do, where government came from. But asking philosophical questions about the nature or origin of government is by no means a self-evident human enterprise, and hardly one in which most moderns engage. Political theorists and historians observe that such inquiry often takes place in times of crisis and upheaval and is an exception rather than the rule, including in stable modern Western polities. This precisely was the case with the early Muslim community, for it did, indeed, right after the demise of its prophet, struggle with the question of whether and how to justify its authority over the rest of Arabia, and the so-called apostasy wars were precisely the response of the Medinan leadership to that question. Crone's argument for the lack of Muslim reflection on the origin of government was intended to show that "[a]s medieval Muslims saw it, government was the inseparable companion of monotheism, and since humans had originated in a monotheistic polity, the problem was not how they had come to live in states but rather why government has so often been corrupted thereafter, or disappeared altogether" (Crone, p. 14). This need not be true, for that theoretical distinction between the problem of the origin of the first human government (which occupied early modern European thinkers) and that of its reenactment after its disappearance is moot, which might explain why Muslims did indeed reflect on such issues quite early on, and found foreign literature on the subject sufficiently relevant to assimilate (Marlow, 2010). Crone's main point that Semitic monotheism led even the earliest Muslims to rely directly on God as the only ruler with no need for human government is not corroborated by the earliest sources (Anjum, 2012). The disputes surrounding the famous arbitration (*taḥkīm*) between the camps of the fourth caliph, ʿAlī, and Muʿāwiyah were couched by the objectors, the Khawārij, in the language of *ḥukm* as they invoked the Qurʾānic verse, "The *ḥukm* is for none but God." In response, the fourth caliph is reported to have said, in both Sunnī and Shīʿī sources, with slight variants: "The *ḥukm* is indeed for God, and on earth are *ḥukkām*. (What they really are refusing is *imārah*,) People cannot do without a chief (*amīr*)—be he [in his person] pious or impious—who reins in the chaos, gathers the scattered affairs, distributes the revenues, fights the enemy [*yujāhid al-ʿaduww*], taking from the strong for the weak, so that the pious may be at peace and saved from the impious" (Sayyid, 1997, p. 28; for further discussion, see Anjum, 2012, p. 60; the statement in parentheses appears in some reports).

Concerning the question of how early Muslims imagined human government, and whether they imagined it as any activity apart from applying divine judgments, we may turn to the general Qurʾānic depiction of the nature and purpose of authority in the community it spawned. According to this depiction, the Muslim community (*ummah*) inherits the prophetic mission (referred to, in its earthly, political dimension, simply as *al-amr*, as Muḥammad ʿImāra has argued), whose affairs are managed by authorities from within it (*ulū al-amr*) through consultation (*shūrā*) with the believing community, wisdom, and decrees (*ḥikmah, ḥukm*) given by God. The crucial point is that this sense of limited self-government represents a conscious break from the Israelite tradition in the sense that God's spokesmen now no longer ruled directly. This break is remarkable, for, in most ways, continuity with the Israelite tradition remained the rule. The Qurʾān referred to the Israelites frequently as an earlier community of Muslims from whose examples, both good and bad, Muslims were to learn. Yet, there is evidence in early Islam of the recognition of a categorical difference between Islamic and Israelite attitudes toward government or political power, for Islam's prophet is the last one and his successors were neither divinely chosen nor guided in a direct sense. This break is expressed in the following *ḥadīth* report: "The Israelites used to be led by prophets (*kānat Banū Isrāʾīl tasūsuhum al-anbiyāʾ*); whenever a prophet died, another followed him. But after me, there is no prophet, but there will be many deputies (*khulafāʾ*)" (reported in *Musnad Aḥmad*, al-Bukhārī, and Muslim; see Anjum, 2012). The root *s-w-s* that appears in the word *tasūsuhum* in reference to the Israelite prophets' management and leadership of their people also provides the Arabic word for politics, *siyāsah*.

All this suggests that the earliest Muslims disputed about, and hence considered alternative ways of imagining, the role of human agency in government, despite acknowledging God's ultimate authority of arbitration. It appears that the abstraction of power from those who exercised it was not quite absent. It may therefore be that premodern Muslims were unwilling, rather than unable, to think of government as institutions alone and treat individuals as interchangeable occupiers of offices in institutions, as early modern Western political thought came to do. The Qur'ānic emphasis on moral formation through worship, self-discipline, and mutual advice (as embodied in the duty of "commanding right and forbidding wrong"), and the moral authority of such exemplars as a requisite of the good governance of the community of faith, may have been seen as a requirement that could not be replaced by institutional rules, checks, and balances. We need more textured studies of this conceptual development before any judgment could be made with confidence.

Theories of Government. All Muslim sects and schools, including the Sunnī as well as the Shīʿah, consider government a religious obligation (with some reported exceptions in early Islam). The key difference between the two is that the Shīʿah consider it part of their creed, meaning that without giving one's allegiance to the proper imam one cannot be considered a proper Muslim, whereas Sunnīs consider it an obligation, which means that establishing the caliphate is an obligation on all but not doing so results in a sin rather than invalidation of one's Islam (Tabataba'i, 2000; Anjum, 2012).

Although conflicts and hence thinking about government and legitimacy were the very first questions Muslims encountered, explicit, systematic treatises on the nature and function of Islamic government in Sunnī Islam can be dated to the ninth and tenth centuries, the onset of the classical period. Three distinct bodies of literature can be identified that treated the problem of government from different vantage points. The *ʿulamāʾ* began to theorize the ideal caliphate, at about the same time, ironically, that the central caliphate was losing its power. This effort was prompted by this very circumstance, in fact, for it is in the treatises of theological polemics directed against the Shīʿī theological and political threat, in particular in Baghdad under the Būyids (932–1062), that the earliest treatments of the subject can be found. There had been two other bodies of literature growing that more closely guided the practical life of the two types of the elite of the classical period: the *fiqh*, the legal discourse of the *ʿulamāʾ*, who were the social elite par excellence, and statecraft literature or "mirrors for princes," which comprised a discourse composed for the rulers and often by the rulers or some member of their entourage.

The first of these discourses was based on Islamic sources, although, as it developed in polemical heat, it was primarily the early historical disputes around political and historical deployment of the scriptural texts, rather than the texts themselves, that supplied much of the motivation and arguments for much of the polemics on all sides. It was not until Ibn Taymīyah (d. 1328) that a thorough reliance on scriptural sources is brought to critique the Sunnī as well as Shīʿī classical theories of the imamate.

The Sunnī discourse on the caliphate, especially as it consolidated in its Ashʿarī form, concerned itself with Islamic theological and legal rulings concerning government of the Muslim community, not of a particular territorial unit. It is primarily focused on the qualifications of the leader of the community, whom it envisions as a successor (*khalīfa*) of the Prophet without being infallible or religiously supreme (for instance, Sunnī theory does not give precedence to the caliph's interpretation even on disputed points of law, and exhorts caliphs to resort to the teachings of the *salaf*; e.g., Abū Yūsuf's *K. al-Kharāj*). One, but by no means the only or even the major, authoritative Sunnī treatise on the subject in this regard is al-Māwardī's *al-Aḥkām al-sulṭānīya,* which inaugurates the practice of bringing together jurisprudential discourses of various Sunnī schools relevant to the job of the caliph and the Sunnī theological polemics that addressed its nature, functions, qualifications, and justifications. Al-Māwardī's is the first Sunnī treatise to treat the office of the caliph as a ritual necessity for the Sunnī community and also gives the caliph enormous powers in the political as well as religious realm, while reducing the role of election and consultation by the community to a mere ritual. Later jurists disagreed with him on many points, as he had disagreed with his predecessors in crucial respects.

One of the most developed Sunnī theories of government appears in the writings of Ibn Taymīyah who stands out for his emphasis on the law, *Sharīʿah,* rather than the individual ruler as the object of political thinking and programs, and reconciles the two separate strands of political thinking in Islam: on the one hand was the orthodox strand of the caliphate discourse weaved together by theologians and jurists over the centuries, which responded to the caliphate's loss of power by ritualizing the caliphal office, and on the other hand there was the actual statecraft driven by power and pragmatism, starting already in the Umayyad period but more explicitly with the Seljuks. For Ibn Taymīyah, an Islamic government was not merely a matter of ritual continuity with the past, but a direct requirement of scriptural imperative, grounded in the obligation of the Muslim community to "command right and forbid wrong." It was an obligatory institution, furthermore, whose basic parameters could be broadly determined by the scriptural texts and the practice of the rightly guided caliphs; any institutional developments after this normative period he considered relative and nonessential (Anjum, 2012, ch. 6).

Statecraft. Early Islamic statecraft was a form of Arab traditional tribal diplomacy and warfare that was shaped, as Fred Donner (1981) has shown, by significant and in some cases decisive influence of Islamic beliefs, identity, and legal institutions. The tensions created by the piety of an otherworldly and egalitarian religion on the one hand and the contingencies of governing and keeping together a rapidly expanding Islamic imperial system on the other, and the triumph of the latter consideration over the former (i.e., of unity and pragmatism over equality and piety), defined the overall Umayyad statecraft. The Abbasids inherited in the eighth century the Umayyad problems and eagerly adopted and developed the emerging Umayyad solutions, but increasingly employed the Persian-Sassanid political heritage and wisdom, which included a highly stratified social ideal, a professional army, religion as an arm of government and a divinized emperor. One major challenge for the Abbasids that had been only a fledgling concern for their predecessors was that posed by the *ʿulamāʾ*, the group of pious scholars who claimed the authority of the religious tradition, thus frustrating the Abbasid caliph al-Maʾmūn's historic attempt, known as the *miḥnah,* to accumulate Sassanid-style unified authority. The High ʿAbbāsid Caliphate started giving way in the central regions during the ninth century to a fragmented empire ruled increasingly by provincial governors, whose power in turn gave way during the tenth and eleventh centuries to a series of Central Asian nomadic invaders, starting with the Turkoman tribes such as the Seljuks in the tenth century and continuing until the Mongol onslaught in the thirteenth. The resulting statecraft was a mix of Persian-Sassanid, Central Asian tribal, and Islamic models, and is reflected in the political advice literature, in particular the mirrors for princes genre (Marlow, 2010). Central Asian nomadic tribes, whether Turkoman or Mongol, had been hierarchically organized rather than egalitarian and hence their clash with Persian statecraft had been less than with the original Arab egalitarianism, which had for all purposes been already tamed, but not eliminated, by the Persian tradition. Variants of this statecraft could also be found throughout the Muslim world.

[*See also* Imamate, Theories of the; Muslim Political History; *and* Sovereignty.]

BIBLIOGRAPHY

Anjum, Ovamir. *Politics, Law and Community in Islamic Thought: The Taymiyyan Moment*. Cambridge, U.K.: Cambridge University Press, 2012.

Crone, Patricia. *God's Rule: Six Centuries of Medieval Islamic Political Thought*. New York: Columbia University Press, 2004.

Donner, Fred. *Early Islamic Conquests*. Princeton, N.J.: Princeton University Press, 1981.

ʿImāra, Muḥammad. *Al-Islām wa-falsafat al-ḥukm*, 3d ed. Cairo: Dār al-Shurūq, 2009.

Lewis, Bernard. "Ḥukūma." *Encyclopaedia of Islam*, 2d ed. Brill Online, 2012.

Marlow, Louise. "Advice and Advice Literature." In *Encyclopaedia of Islam*, 3d ed., edited by G. Krämer, D. Matringe, J. Nawas, and E. Rowson. Leiden: Brill, 2010.

Sayyid, Riḍwān al-. *Al-Jamāʿa wa-al-mujtamaʿ wa-al-dawla*. Beirut: Dār al-Kitāb al-ʿArabī, 1997.

Tabataba'i, S. M. Hosayn. *Islamic Teachings: An Overview*, 2d ed. Translated by R. Campbell. New York: Alavi Foundation, 2000.

Ovamir Anjum

Great Britain. According to the 2001 census on the United Kingdom, there were around 1.6 million Muslims in Britain, and more recent estimates put the figure at around 2.5 million in 2010. After small-scale immigration from various parts of the British Empire during the 19th and early 20th centuries, the major change took place beginning in the 1950s when people (mostly men) from the Indian subcontinent started arriving in large numbers. Legislation limited labor immigration from 1962, with increasingly restrictive rules introduced later. For a long time, however, women and children were allowed to join their menfolk, driving a trend of family reunion and community settlement. According to the 2001 census, almost 1.1 million Muslims were of Indian subcontinent origin, two-thirds of them Pakistani. In addition there were notable numbers of Turks, Cypriots, Arabs, and sub-Saharan Africans and some tens of thousands of converts (a figure that cannot be deduced from the census). Muslims live mainly in the major cities and towns, over a third of them in London, with Birmingham, Bradford, Blackburn, and Manchester being other significant centers. They are served by some two thousand mosques of various sizes.

Organizations and Institutions. Soon after the Muslim communities began to form, they were followed by organized networks from the countries of origin. The most notable of these is rooted in the Jamāʿat-i Islāmī of Pakistan and includes the U.K. Islamic Mission, which runs a series of mosques with education and community work, and the Islamic Foundation, a center for research, training, and publishing. In the early 1990s the foundation started the Markfield Institute of Higher Education, which offers courses for professionals as well as master's and PhDs awarded by a neighboring university. It has also cooperated with government in joint projects and produced reports on aspects of the situation of Muslims in Britain.

Although successful, this network is not the largest. The Deobandī and Barelwī movements have also spread to Britain, where they often find themselves continuing the rivalry begun at home. The Deobandī network is more organized than that of the Barelwīs, with several seminaries providing a growing number of imams and teachers for Deobandī mosques. The Tablīghī Jamāʿat is also active in Britain, often in cooperation with the Deobandī networks. The Barelwī network is fragmented among various prominent pirs and their lieutenants. Overlapping with the Barelwīs are a number of Ṣūfī orders, with branches of the Naqshbandīs and Chishtīs especially prominent.

The 1990s saw a growth in Shīʿī organized activity, apart from that associated with local communities in places like Birmingham, Manchester, and parts of London. The Khoei Foundation, based in London, is mainly Arab in its constituency and springs from the Iraqi family of religious leaders of the same name. Apart from educational and social activities for the Arab Shīʿī community, the foundation has also been active in interreligious networks and cooperation with official institutions. The Islamic Cultural Centre in north London is an Iranian initiative that has established connections with some of the Shīʿī communities of South Asian origin.

There have long been attempts to form national umbrella organizations. The first was the Union of Muslim Organisations (1970), which, although it did not achieve its aim, still exists in name. Since then several other attempts have been made, some sponsored by the Saudi-based Muslim World League and one by the Libya-based Islamic Call Society. The Muslim Institute, founded in 1972 by the journalist Kalim Siddiqui, was linked with Iran for most of the 1980s. In 1991 it set up the so-called Muslim Parliament, which was greeted with skepticism by most of the British Muslim community.

In 1997 the Muslim Council of Britain (MCB) was formed as a result of consultations between the government and groups sympathetic to the Jamāʿat-i Islāmī–related networks. Although it initially had good access to government, relations soured when the MCB distanced itself from the invasion of Iraq in 2003. Usually regarded as close to the Muslim Brotherhood, the Muslim Association of Britain (MAB), also founded in 1997, achieved prominence in its active campaign against the war in Iraq. More closely related to the Barelwī movement, the British Muslim Forum (BMF) brings together about one-quarter of the mosques in Britain. In 2009 these three groups and the Khoei Foundation came together, with the active encouragement of the government, to form the Mosques and Imams National Advisory Board (MINAB).

Between Security and Accommodation. Britain was a frequent choice of exile for Islamic political activists caught up in crises in their own countries, and as early as the 1980s London became home for political refugees from a number of Muslim countries, much to the annoyance of their governments and the governments of some European countries. From the late 1990s the security authorities were paying growing attention to the political activities of Muslim exiles, and from 1998 antiterrorism legislation was taking into account possible activities from Muslim quarters. This was markedly strengthened after the 2001 attacks in the United States, the 2003 intervention in Iraq, and the 2005 attacks in London. While the government continued to seek to cultivate positive relations with the Muslim communities, the increasingly visible security agenda also strengthened the popularity of both more conservative groups—there has been a marked growth in groups and meetings that can broadly be described as Salafī—and more radical groups. Ḥizb al-Tahrīr gained ground on a number of university campuses during the 1990s. Certain individual preachers, especially in London, attracted notoriety and suspicion of involvement in militant activity and had some success in recruiting small numbers of individuals to a radical view of Islam sympathetic to activities in the style of al-Qaʿida.

As young Muslims born in Britain have grown up, they have begun to loosen their links with the countries and cultures of their parents. Since the early 1990s many, especially the better-educated, have begun to move into the management of existing Muslim organizations. Others have established their own youth organizations. In the universities, they have become the dominant force in Islamic student societies previously controlled by foreign students. The younger Muslims are much more actively concerned with events in places like Bosnia, Iraq, and Palestine than with developments in their parents' regions of origin. Although some have been attracted by radical groups, the great majority continue to develop modes of participation that include local and national activity within Britain as well as a concern for wider issues in the Muslim world community. This is reflected in the development of Islamic Relief, which was started by a group of young Muslims in the 1980s and is today one of the largest European Muslim aid and emergency relief organizations.

With this background the government had to find a balance between the momentum toward integration and the security responses to threatened acts of violence based in extremist Muslim circles. Security measures and frequent arrests of people suspected of terrorist links ran parallel to policies with the general aim of "social cohesion." A program named Prevent invested in encouraging Muslim organizations that, it was judged, could counteract extremist violence. An organization with the name the Quilliam Foundation (named after the English convert who in the late 1880s founded the first mosque in Britain, in Liverpool) was seen as especially promising, as it was run by young people who had dropped out of extremist movements such as Ḥizb al-Tahrīr. Other parts of the program included increased monitoring of groups and areas that were felt to be potentially dangerous. When a new Conservative–Liberal Democrat coalition took over the government in spring 2010, it withdrew funding from many such activities and started a thorough review of the Prevent program.

Islam Remains Contested. In Britain as elsewhere in Europe, Islam has become a focus of mistrust in the general population, while opinion polls and other surveys also indicate that Muslims are exposed to harassment, discrimination, and hate speech more frequently than others. Apart from fears of terrorism, the two main focuses of such mistrust, at least in the media, have been perceptions of Muslim women and separate Islamic family law practices. On the whole Britain has been rather more relaxed about female Islamic head covering than mainland Europe, although a few politicians have raised the possibility of banning face covering, without finding much support. The practice of Islamic family law has been much more controversial, with the existence since the 1980s of national and local *Sharīʿah* councils and, since 2007, the Muslim Arbitration Tribunal. Whereas the legal status of the former is unclear, the latter claims to work within the legal system under the Arbitration Act of 1996. A number of organizations have mobilized against such initiatives, while on a populist level others have started street actions against Muslims generally, led by the English Defence League. On the other hand, leaders of both church and law have expressed sympathy with Muslim concerns.

Although a few Muslims continue to quietly withdraw into their own enclaves, while others actively campaign against Muslims voting in elections, for example, it clearly remains the case that the majority has elected for full participation in British society and politics, often with significant support from and cooperation with other groups.

BIBLIOGRAPHY

Abbas, Tahir, ed. *Islamic Political Radicalism: A European Perspective.* Edinburgh: Edinburgh University Press, 2007. Parts 3 and 4 discuss the reasons for and effects of British Muslim radicalization.

Gilliat-Ray, Sophie. *Muslims in Britain: An Introduction.* Cambridge, U.K.: Cambridge University Press, 2010.

Lewis, Philip. *Young, British and Muslim*. London: Continuum, 2007.

McLoughlin, Seán. "From Race to Faith Relations, the Local to the National Level: The State and Muslim Organisations in Britain." In *Muslim Organisations and the State: European Perspectives*, edited by Axel Kreienbrink and Mark Bodenstein, pp. 123–149. Nuremberg, Germany: Bundesamt für Migration und Flüchtlinge, 2010.

Modood, Tariq. *Multicultural Politics: Racism, Ethnicity and Muslims in Britain*. Edinburgh: Edinburgh University Press, 2005.

Peach, Ceri. "Muslims in the 2001 Census of England and Wales: Gender and Economic Disadvantage." *Ethnic and Racial Studies* 29, no. 4 (2006), pp. 629–655.

JØRGEN S. NIELSEN

GROUPE ISLAMIQUE ARMÉ. The al-Jamāʿah al-Islāmīyah al-Musallaha, better known in Algeria by its French name, Groupe Islamique Armé (GIA, Armed Islamic Group), emerged to oppose the military dictatorship that ruled the North African state. Although its initial goal was murky—to establish just rule via elections—it resorted to extreme violence after 1992 and declared the establishment of an Islamic government in Algiers. This drew the ire of conservative forces in both the government and Paris, both of which mobilized to defeat it, although with mixed results.

After the Islamic Salvation Front—known as the FIS (Front Islamique du Salut)—gained a significant legislative electoral victory in December 1991, and after insecure military officers voided this result, a number of Islamists adopted violent tactics. Between 1992 and 1998 groups operating under the GIA umbrella conducted an exceptionally violent campaign against civilians, both domestic and foreign. An estimated 150,000 Algerians were killed during these atrocities, along with more than a hundred expatriate workers, mostly French, living in the country. Various kidnappings and assassinations were attributed to the GIA, including a particularly vicious attack, by decapitation, in May 1996 against seven monks serving in the Tibhirine monastery who, ironically, were known to have assisted GIA dissidents. The Tibhirine monks, who followed the Roman Catholic Trappist Order of Cistercians of the Strict Observance, were kidnapped, held for two months, and then found dead under mysterious circumstances. Although the GIA claimed responsibility, General Francois Buchwalter, then the French military attaché, alleged that they were accidentally killed by the Algerian army in a rescue attempt. Algierian secret services apparently, although impossible to verify, decided to use the tragedy to trap GIA leaders.

Origin and Development. A well-known "Arab Afghan," Mansouri Meliani, broke away in early 1992 from the then emerging Mouvement Islamique Armé (MIA), an organization led by the renowned Islamist leader Abdelkader Chebouti, to establish the GIA some time around July of that year. Meliani proved ineffective against the Chedli Benjedid government, which promptly arrested him in January 1993. ʿAbdelhak Layada, perhaps under the spiritual guidance of an Afghanistan-trained cleric by the name of Omar El-Eulmi, succeeded Meliani. As the second GIA leader, Layada served from 1993 to 1994, steered by El-Eulmi, who professed his opposition to political pluralism. Lax internal security resulted in a systemic infiltration by Algerian security forces at this time. Consequently several successive GIA leaders were killed in the early 1990s, including Cherif Gousmi, who was gunned down in September 1994 and Djamel Zitouni in July 1996.

After 1992 GIA principals issued death threats against several FIS and MIA members and called for the killing of anyone ostensibly collaborating with the military government in Algiers. All government employees, including teachers and civil servants, became legitimate targets. Prominent journalists and intellectuals, among others, were assassinated.

As the killings multiplied after 1993 and were generously reciprocated by government personnel, leading FIS sympathizers joined the GIA. Muḥammad Saʿid, Anwar Haddam, and Saʿid Makhloufi—ironically wanted by the GIA for egregious shortcomings—left the FIS to declare, on 26 August 1994, that a caliphate was established in Algeria under Cherif Gousmi. Muḥammad Saʿid was declared the prime minister of this short-lived Islamic government of Algeria; Haddam, then living in exile in the United States, was made foreign minister; and Makhloufi became a provisional interior minister. The latter was the first to withdraw—less than twenty-four hours after his appointment—because the GIA deviated from Islam. Makhloufi insisted that the "caliphate" was nothing more than Muḥammad Saʿid's scheme to gain control over the GIA, although informed Algerian military sources claimed several years later that the idea was, in fact, a clever counterespionage invention by the security services.

At the height of this epochal reassessment, and under Zitouni, the GIA exported its actions to France. On 24 December 1994 an Air France flight from Algiers to Paris was hijacked. French commandoes stormed the plane on 26 December, killing all the hijackers, because authorities feared they would crash the plane into the Eiffel Tower.

Bombings and killings in Algeria continued throughout the ensuing years, justified by *fatwas* issued by Abū Qatada al-Falasṭīnī and others. Angered by negotiations with Algiers, GIA constituents assassinated the FIS cofounder, Abdelbaki Sahraoui, in Paris on 11 July 1995. An internecine conflict emerged as GIA and FIS elements targeted each other throughout 1995 when new parliamentary elections were scheduled. The GIA threatened to kill anyone who participated in what it determined were illegal elections, using the slogan "one vote, one bullet," although intra-GIA disputes and murders were so frequent that few citizens were deterred by the threats. After Zitouni was murdered in July 1996, his successor, Antar Zouabri, asserted that an Algerian who refused to join the GIA was impious. He served for six years, as the GIA was slowly transformed into a *takfīrī* group. Calls to purify Algerian society became regular pronouncements as the country's military officers accepted the appointment, and eventual election, of the affable foreign minister, Abdelaziz Bouteflika, as president. After Zouabri was murdered in February 2002, the group's leadership passed to Rachid Abou Tourab, who in turn was killed in July 2004, and Boulenouar Oukil. Oukil was arrested on 29 April 2004, with his successor, Nourredine Boudiafi, also apprehended in late 2005.

The GIA's fundamental error was in engaging in repeated massacres of civilians, which drained popular support, even if security forces were also involved in some of the massacres or, perhaps, even manipulated the group. Under Bouteflika a 1999 amnesty law was passed, which was rejected by the GIA but accepted by many rank-and-file Islamist fighters who surrendered their arms and returned to civilian life. The Salafist Group for Call and Combat (GSPC), a GIA splinter faction, eclipsed the original group and was considered to be far more effective. GIA and GSPC leaderships rejected Bouteflika's amnesty though neither engaged in fresh attacks on civilians.

According to the Algerian government, the GIA was no longer a viable organization after 2006, although that was probably due to attrition among the rank-and-file Islamist community, rather than an ideological reconciliation with the military-dominated government.

[*See also* Algeria; *and* Islamic Salvation Front.]

BIBLIOGRAPHY

Aggoun, Lounis, and Jean-Baptiste Rivoire. *Françalgérie crimes et mensonges d'États: Histoire secrète, de la guerre d'indépendance à la "troisième guerre" d'Algérie*. Paris: Découverte, 2005. Alleges that after 1980 Algerian generals launched a "third war" and blamed it on Islamists to retain power with the complicity of rogue French officials.

Fisk, Robert. "Anything to Wipe Out a Devil...." In his *The Great War for Civilisation: The Conquest of the Middle East*. New York: Alfred A. Knopf, 2005. Rare insights on GIA killings in the 1990s.

Kiser, John W. *The Monks of Tibhirine: Faith, Love, and Terror in Algeria*. New York: St. Martin's, 2003. A complete assessment of the murky tragedy.

Labat, Séverine. *Les islamistes algériens: Entres les urnes et le maquis*. Paris: Seuil, 1995. A first-rate scholarly assessment.

Martinez, Luis. *The Algerian Civil War, 1990–1998*. Translated by Jonathan Derrick. New York: Columbia University Press, 2000. Contains useful information on the GIA's interaction with the Islamic Salvation Front.

Souaïda, Habib. *La sale guerre: le témoignage d'un ancien officier des forces spéciales l'armée algérienne*. Paris: Editions La Découverte, 2001. A dissident Algerian officer's account of the war describing the military's goal to "terrorize the terrorists."

Le Sueur, James D. *Algeria since 1989: Between Terror and Democracy*. London: Zed Books, 2010. An objective assessment of dramatic changes that occurred in the early 2000s.

JOSEPH A. KÉCHICHIAN

GÜLEN, FETHULLAH. Fethullah Gülen (1941–), the founder of Turkey's largest faith-oriented Islamic movement, is one of the country's most important Muslim thinkers and a prolific writer. His followers collectively constitute the Gülen movement, a branch of one of the strongest Islamic movements in Turkey, the Nurcu, founded by Said Nursî (1876–1960) in the early years of the Turkish Republic.

Gülen is from the eastern Anatolian province of Erzurum. His first impressions of Islam were influenced by Ṣūfī-oriented movements such as the Naqshbandīyah. He attended a traditional *madrasah*, later educated himself, and graduated from high school by passing outside exams; he served as an official preacher of the Turkish government's Directorate of Religious Affairs (Diyanet), for approximately thirty years; and devoted himself to writing, especially after he retired. He is deeply involved in interfaith dialogue and met with Pope John Paul II at the Vatican and with other prominent religious leaders from around the world. Although Gülen and movement members try to give the impression that they are not political and do not want to influence the political process, in practice they are extremely political and participate in the political process.

In the late 1960s Gülen was appointed as a preacher of Kestanepazari Mosque in İzmir, and soon became a formidable force through his sermons and youth-focused summer camps and activities. Because of his religious and social activities, Gülen was arrested and imprisoned for seven months in 1971. Nevertheless from a small nucleus in İzmir, Gülen created the most influential, well-organized Islamic movement in Turkey.

His movement proposes a correlation of Islam and the vocabulary of the modern discourses of human rights, science, and democracy, and also puts them into practice through his movement's educational institutions. His community has more than three hundred schools, seven universities with numerous dormitories, and it sponsors university entrance examination courses in Turkey and in other parts of the world. In addition his movement has considerable media resources, including its own television channel (Samanyolu), a newspaper (*Zaman*), and several religious and political journals, such as *Aksiyon*, *Yeni Ümit*, and *Sızıntı*. Furthermore there are several financial institutions, such as Bank Asya and Isik Sigorta, that also belong to the community.

The 1990s were the golden years of the Gülen community, when it was the most popular religious movement. Despite its nationalist and statist stand, however, the movement could not save itself from the soft coup that took place in 1997. After the state-led campaign against him, Gülen came to the United States, where he lives in Pennsylvania.

Gülen's movement has become a transnational education movement with the goal of crafting a Muslim character through education. He deals forthrightly with the questions of modernity, identity, coexistence, and democracy. Gülen explains Islamic principles and the desire for justice and the common shared good. He explains how the current understandings of Islam and the meaning of the "good life" are no longer workable and calls on contemporary Muslims to return to the authentic sources (the Qurʾān and *ḥadīth*) in order to build practical models for today's environment, rather than to try to patch old, broken models developed by medieval scholars. He addresses many facets of daily life including education, politics, and economics.

Gülen's writings offer Muslims useful analytical tools to begin this effort, but ultimately assign responsibility for concrete solutions to community leaders rather than individual Muslims, thereby taking into account circumstances unique to each situation. Thus there is communalism without individualism. Gülen is at his best when he evaluates the human quest for the "good life." He argues that modern reality reflects such a multitude of paths to the good life, not only among different people but also within a single group, that to assume a single ideal is incompatible with modern life. Thus one has to take religious ideals into account to redefine the meaning of the good life.

Gülen's conceptualization of science, nature, state, politics, and personhood makes sense only within Islamically rooted ethical values. The concepts he has developed are resources to understand and theorize about the rapidly changing everyday life of Turkish society. Gülen's conceptual world is not abstract and distanced from reality; it is an attempt to comprehend reality in religiously rooted thought. By knowing the moral language of Turkish society, Gülen argues that modern relations, which cannot be derived from interest alone, become meaningful and stable if they are framed within a traditionally religious moral view. Islamic thought, for Gülen, plays an active role in articulating its own claims to normative authority and empowering ordinary people to develop their own conceptual debate.

Gülen gives priority to illuminating the mind and soul. He believes nutrition for the brain is positive science, whereas nutrition for the soul is faith. For Gülen faith is an instrument to serve humanity and improve human dignity. This can be done only when faith is reconciled with reason, and education is the only way for this reconciliation to take place. He is a pacifist, and supports majoritarian (not liberal) democracy. As for his economic ideas, he calls on Muslims to engage with the market and if possible to control it. The Gülen movement is most popular among merchants and the new Anatolian bourgeoisie. Gülen recognizes ignorance, poverty, conflict, and dissension as sources of problems in the Muslim world, and he proposes education, economic development, cooperation, and tolerance as solutions.

Although Gülen has never been an outspoken critic of the Kemalist establishment, in influential circles, especially in the powerful military, his ideas and activities have been perceived as a national security threat. The militant secularism of the Kemalist political elite has made the state, since the outset of the new Turkish Republic in 1923, suspicious about religious leaders and movements. Relatively independent religious leaders like Gülen have always been treated as potential threats. The Kemalist elite does the most it can to intimidate, harass, and, if possible, convict independent religious leaders. This attitude is not directed only at Gülen, but it stems from the extremely antireligious nature of Kemalist secularism.

[*See also* Islam and Politics in Central Asia and the Caucasus; *and* Turkey.]

BIBLIOGRAPHY

Hunt, Robert A., and Yüksel A. Aslandoğan, eds. *Muslim Citizens of the Globalized World: Contributions of the Gulen Movement*. Somerset, N.J.: The Light, 2007.

Yavuz, M. Hakan, and John L. Esposito, eds. *Turkish Islam and the Secular State: The Gülen Movement*. Syracuse, N.Y.: Syracuse University Press, 2003.

HAKAN YAVUZ

GULF COOPERATION COUNCIL. When the six conservative Arab Gulf monarchies (Bahrain, Kuwait, Oman, Qatar, Saudi Arabia, and the United Arab Emirates [UAE]) established the Cooperation Council for the Arab States of the Gulf (CCASG)—better known as the Gulf Cooperation Council (GCC)—on 25 May 1981, they specifically identified their "common characteristics and similar systems founded on the Creed of Islam" as the defining reasons for their effort. The foreign ministers of the six member-states provided even clearer justifications for their endeavor at their first pre-summit meeting in Taif, Saudi Arabia, when, on 4 February 1981, they issued a communiqué that read, in part, that the conservative monarchies wished to unite "out of consideration of their special relations and joint characteristics stemming from their joint creed, similarity of regimes, unity of heritage, similarity of their political, social and demographic structure, and their cultural and historical affiliation." Similar statements followed but what they all purported to declare was that unity on the Arabian Peninsula was widespread and, more important, that potentially negative underlying currents—including ethnic and religious differences—were the figment of Orientalist imaginations.

Still, the reality of the GCC in 1981 was evident—that a political and economic union was necessary to shelter largely tribal societies from perceived multifaceted threats. These emanated from, among others, the February 1979 Iranian Revolution, the December 1979 Soviet invasion of Afghanistan, and the 1980–1988 Iran-Iraq War.

Entrusted to the first secretary-general, ʿAbdallah Bisharah of Kuwait (1981–1993), the GCC brought unity to the peninsula even if it was not in it. Over the years Bisharah's successors, Fahim bin Sultan Al Qasimi (UAE, 1993–1996), Jamil bin Ibrahim Al Hujaylan (Saudi Arabia, 1996–2002), and Abdul Rahman bin Hamad Al Attiyah (Qatar, 2002–2011), recorded significant achievements though, as events since 1981 in every Gulf state amply illustrated, major differences remained. The current secretary-general, ʿAbdullatif bin Rashid Al Zayani (Bahrain), confronted grave differences in several countries but especially in Bahrain, Kuwait, and Saudi Arabia, where dormant ethnic and religious divisions awakened long before the 2011 Arab uprisings that literally shook the vast majority. Amidst the 2011 Bahraini protests, for example, Saudi, Kuwaiti, and Emirati forces were sent to Manama in March, which further highlighted existing tensions.

Although the six monarchies shared many attributes: oil wealth, low populations, limited military capabilities, similar socioeconomic setups and common religion, language, and culture, various obstacles faced them in unison. Leaders were preoccupied with both Iran and Iraq, and wished to keep the two hegemonic powers at safe distances. Likewise the smaller shaykhdoms contemplated how best to dissuade Saudi Arabia from reasserting itself over them, even if plans to establish a strong intervention force failed to materialize by 2011.

Still the primary goal of the GCC was to unify military cooperation, multilaterally through the Dara'a al-Jazirah (Peninsula Shield) Force, and bilaterally between individual countries and leading Western powers. Nevertheless, and despite significant military expenditures during the past few decades, the moderate Arab Gulf monarchies fielded weak military forces when measured vis-à-vis their needs.

Among the stated objectives of the GCC were the adoption of joint economic policies, along with mutually beneficial trade, customs, tourism, and administration measures. A unified economic agreement was signed on 11 November 1981 in Abu Dhabi, which created a common market after 2008 that intended to grant nationals equal treatment wherever their toiled. The effort was meant to remove all trade barriers although it quickly confronted bilateral Free Trade Agreements signed between Bahrain, Oman, Qatar, and the United States, which in effect undercut the GCC's agreement. Naturally the steps caused friction, which hindered efforts to adopt a common currency, the khaleeji. In December 2006 Oman withdrew from the project and, following the announcement that the central bank for the monetary union would be located in Riyadh, and not in Abu Dhabi as previously envisaged, in May 2009 the UAE announced its withdrawal from the monetary union project too.

The logo of the GCC consisted of two concentric circles, with the *bismillah* written on the upper part of the larger circle, while the Council's full name in Arabic was reproduced in the lower part of that circle. The inner circle contained an embossed hexagonal shape representing the Council's six member countries, with the inside of the hexagon filled by a map encompassing the Arabian Peninsula, on which the areas of the member countries were colored brown. Interestingly no borders were depicted, even if such disputes lingered. The Republic of Yemen was the only country on the Arabian Peninsula that was not a GCC member-state, though Sanaa repeatedly made appropriate overtures for consideration. On 10 May 2011 Jordan and Morocco expressed their interests to join, even if no decisions were immediately reached.

BIBLIOGRAPHY

Ibrahim, Badr El Din A. *Economic Co-operation in the Gulf: Issues in the Economies of the Arab Gulf Co-operation Council States*. London and New York: Routledge 2007. A useful analysis of topical issues such as the long-discussed monetary union, intra-GCC national labor movements, and Islamic banking.

Peterson, Erik R. *The Gulf Cooperation Council: Search for Unity in a Dynamic Region*. Boulder, Colo.: Westview Press, 1988. One of the first detailed descriptions of the institution and a useful reference source.

The Cooperation Council for the Arab States of the Gulf maintains a web page at http://www.gcc-sg.org/eng/, which includes all the key documents issued by the organization and provides pertinent links.

JOSEPH A. KÉCHICHIAN

GULF STATES. Bahrain, Kuwait, Qatar, and the United Arab Emirates stand at the intersection of several combustible currents in Islamic politics. The Iranian revolution of 1978–1979 mobilized the Shīʿī communities of Bahrain and Kuwait, but provoked little agitation in the United Arab Emirates and had no impact on Qatar. All four countries have subsequently exhibited two sets of overlapping tensions, one between moderate Islamists pushing for marginal reforms and Islamist radicals who demand fundamental political change; and another pitting movements that champion the interests of disadvantaged Shīʿīs against Sunnī closely allied to the regimes. Sectarian conflict diminished in the late 1990s, as both Shīʿī and Sunnī Islamists advocated civil liberties and religious activists participated in local elections, but tensions revived markedly during the first decade of the twenty-first century.

Bahrain has been ruled since the late eighteenth century by shaykhs of the Khalīfah clan. The Āl Khalīfah are Sunnīs who adhere to the Mālikī school of Islamic jurisprudence, which favors strict interpretations of the Qurʾān and the traditions of the Prophet (*ḥadīth*) but tolerates flexibility in applying the law. The commercial elite consists of both Sunnīs of the Shāfiʿī school, most of whom immigrated to Bahrain from southern Iran, and rationalist (Uṣūlī) Twelver Shīʿīs linked to Iran and southern Iraq. There are also pockets of Sunnīs who follow the literalist Ḥanbalī school, and Shīʿīs of the ecstatic Akhbārīyah school, which takes a strict constructionist view of the Qurʾān and the traditions of the first twelve imams. Shīʿīs make up 70 percent of the citizenry.

Discontent within the Shīʿah precipitated riots in 1923. British agents deposed the ruler and inaugurated administrative reforms. Sunnīs responded by organizing the Bahrain National Congress to demand the restoration of the ruler and the creation of an advisory council. Shīʿīs remained largely aloof, but petitioned the ruler in 1934 to promulgate a basic law and institute proportional representation on local councils. Sunnī notables demanded a popular assembly (*majlis*) in late 1938. When students and oil workers threatened to call a general strike to back the *majlis* movement, the regime's British protectors deported leading reformers to India.

Violence between Sunnīs and Shīʿīs erupted in late 1952 over the composition of the Manama municipal council. Over the next two years workers struck to protest the oil company's policy of employing expatriates, while liberals focused discontent against the British and away from sectarian grievances. The strategy galvanized support for a Higher Executive Committee made up of four Sunnīs and four Shīʿīs and helped launch several grassroots organizations, including the Shīʿī Jaʿfarī League, which demanded fundamental political change. In late 1956 liberals, about to lose control over the movement, acquiesced to the suppression of the radicals.

Smoldering discontent among Shīʿīs resurfaced during the Iranian Revolution. Reformist associations such as the Sunnī Society for Social Reform and the Shīʿī Party of the Call to Islam steadily lost ground to radical groups like the Sunnī Islamic Action Organization and the Shīʿī Islamic Front for the Liberation of Bahrain. In December 1981 the authorities announced the discovery of a network of saboteurs affiliated with the Islamic Front.

Sectarian conflict flared in December 1994. Draconian measures imposed on Shīʿī critics of the Āl Khalīfah fragmented the reform movement along sectarian lines. A four-year uprising left Shīʿis more alienated and highly mobilized than ever. When the new ruler, Emir Ḥamad bin ʿĪsā Āl Khalīfah, set up an elected advisory council, Shīʿī activists joined Sunnī liberals in applauding. Islamist candidates won forty-two of fifty seats in the May 2002 municipal elections. Half of the victorious Islamists belonged to the Shīʿī National Pact Society; most others represented the Sunnī Muslim Brothers. State officials then reconfigured voting districts in ways that boosted pro-regime candidates in the October 2002 parliamentary elections. Government interference, along with the announcement that the appointed upper house would exercise legislative powers equivalent to those of the elected lower house, led the National Pact Society to boycott the balloting. Confronted with a National Assembly dominated by Muslim Brothers and pro-regime representatives, the National Pact Society contested the

November 2006 parliamentary elections, and came away with seventeen of forty seats. Muslim Brothers and other Sunni Islamists won twelve. The radical Shīʿī movement Truth remained outside the assembly.

Shīʿī radicals clashed with police in August 2010, after civil rights activists and a leader of Truth were forcibly detained. The National Pact Society condemned the arrests but called for calm in the run-up to parliamentary and municipal elections scheduled for October. Avowedly secularist movements, including the National Democratic Action Society and the leftist Progressive Platform, charged that the National Pact Society had fueled sectarian animosity and failed to improve the lives of the poor by working inside the National Assembly. Sunnī critics of the regime organized the National Integrity Gathering to challenge pro-regime Islamists. Escalating popular unrest culminated in large-scale demonstrations in February 2011, orchestrated by radicals outside the existing political associations. Large numbers of Sunnīs rallied behind the regime, and security forces inflicted severe punishment on Shīʿī protesters. State officials charged that Shīʿī activists in general, and the National Pact Society in particular, were tools of Iran, and Sunnī vigilantes in December 2011 started attacking Shīʿī funeral processions. Disaffected Sunnīs formed the Conqueror Youth Union to push for more effective governance. By early 2012 political life in Bahrain had splintered along sectarian lines.

Since the early eighteenth century, Kuwait has been ruled by shaykhs of the Ṣabāḥ clan. The Āl Ṣabāḥ are Sunnīs and adhere to the Mālikī school of Islamic jurisprudence. The merchant elite consists primarily of Twelver Shīʿīs from southern Iraq and Iran, along with a small number of Sunnīs following the Shāfiʿī school who migrated from southern Iran. Shīʿī tribespeople based in southern Iraq and Saudi Arabia straddle the northern and western borders, while poorer Twelver Shīʿīs arrived after World War II to work in petroleum and construction. Shīʿīs make up a quarter of the citizenry.

Religious conflict played little part in the reform movements of 1921 and 1938, although the elected council (*majlis*) that grew out of the latter accused the ruler's Shīʿī chief adviser of mobilizing coreligionists against the Sunnī-dominated *majlis*. Expatriate teachers founded a branch of the Muslim Brothers in 1951, which became the moderate Social Reform Society. Representatives to the National Assembly mandated by the 1962 constitution coalesced into two blocs: supporters of the Āl Ṣabāḥ, including settled Bedouin, prominent Shīʿīs, and moderate Sunnī Islamists, versus liberals critical of the regime. Conflict between the assembly and the cabinet prompted the prime minister to tender the government's resignation in August 1976, thereby suspending the parliament.

Disadvantaged Shīʿīs staged demonstrations during the Iranian Revolution; the authorities deported the most influential Shīʿī notable and banned posters depicting Ayatollah Ruhollah Khomeini. Protests erupted again when Sunnī militants seized the Grand Mosque in Mecca. A group of Shīʿī intellectuals then accused the government of removing Shīʿīs from command positions in the armed forces. These events prompted a backlash against the local Shīʿah: in October 1983 militant Sunnīs attacked workers building a Shīʿī mosque.

In February 1985 Islamist candidates were trounced in National Assembly elections. Moderate Sunnīs lost support due to a Saudi scholar's legal ruling (*fatwa*) against coeducation and Western music. Only one prominent Shīʿī won a seat. Disaffection within the Shīʿah prompted an attack on the ruler's motorcade in May; a month later, a café at a senior citizens' meeting house sponsored by the Āl Ṣabāḥ was bombed. These events precipitated the dissolution of the National Assembly in July 1986.

Sunnīs and Shīʿīs joined in agitating for restoration of the National Assembly. Professional associations, university students, and trade unionists petitioned the ruler in February 1990 to authorize elections, and former delegates petitioned the prime minister directly in March. These actions convinced the cabinet in April to form a National Council charged with charting parliament's future, but deliberations were interrupted by the Iraqi invasion that August. During the occupation, two Sunnī organizations, the moderate Social Reform Society and the radical Heritage Revitalization Society, coordinated the distribution of food, medicine, and fuel.

National Assembly elections took place in October 1992. Islamist candidates—both Sunnī and Shīʿī—won eighteen seats, giving critics of the regime thirty-one delegates in the fifty-member body. Sunnīs coalesced into two blocs, a reformist Islamic Constitutional Movement with ties to the Muslim Brothers and a conservative (*salafī*) Islamic Popular Alliance. Both blocs advocated amending the 1962 constitution to make *Sharīʿah* the sole basis of Kuwaiti law.

Just before the July 1999 elections, the ruler granted full political rights to all adult female citizens. Islamists expressed outrage, calling the decree unconstitutional. After a heated campaign the Islamic Constitutional Movement won six of the fifty seats, the Islamic Popular Alliance two, and the Shīʿī National Islamic Alliance two. Elections in June 2006 resulted in a virtually identical distribution of seats, with greater representation for the Heritage Revitalization Society and independent conservatives. Three years later Islamist candidates suffered a major electoral defeat.

Persistent allegations of ministerial corruption sparked popular protests in March 2011, but the young demonstrators who occupied the parliament building on 16 November exhibited no sectarian characteristics. Sunnī Islamists emerged from the February 2012 elections with twenty-three seats in the National Assembly, leaving only nine secularist liberal representatives.

Since the late nineteenth century Qatar has been ruled by shaykhs of the Thānī clan. Almost all citizens adhere to the literalist Hanbalī school of Sunnī Islam, and to the strict interpretation formulated by the eighteenth-century reformer Muhammad ibn ʿAbd al-Wahhāb. Consequently the country's religious elite exercises great influence over judicial and educational affairs. A minority of prominent merchants consists of Shīʿī immigrants from Iran, along with Sunnīs who came from southern Iran at the turn of the twentieth century. Shīʿīs make up around one-sixth of the citizenry.

Liberal nationalists have joined dissident Āl Thānī shaykhs in challenging the regime. The National Unity Front of the early 1960s included oil workers and younger members of the ruling family alike. In December 1991 fifty Qatari families, both Sunnī and Shīʿī, petitioned the ruler to authorize an elected national council. Religious issues played no role in the municipal council elections of March 1999, April 2003, April 2007, or May 2011. In February 2005 Qatar became only the second Arab Gulf state, after Bahrain, to set up a Shīʿī judiciary to deal with matters of personal law. Concerns about Islamic authenticity led the authorities to ban sales of alcoholic beverages in the expatriate-oriented Pearl district in December 2011.

The United Arab Emirates is governed by the ruling families of the federation's seven states—Abu Dhabi, Dubai, Sharjah, Ras al-Khaimah, Ajman, Umm al-Qaiwain, and Fujairah. These clans share an adherence to Sunnī Islam and the Mālikī school of legal interpretation, while the federation's commercial elite is divided along sectarian lines in a number of ways: in Dubai, the most influential merchants are Sunnīs from southern Iran, with some Twelver

Shīʿīs; in Sharjah, Shīʿīs from South Asia predominate; Abu Dhabi's smaller commercial elite consists primarily of Sunnīs, aong with a cluster of Twelver Shīʿīs. For the federation as a whole, Shīʿīs account for some 20 percent of citizens.

Sectarian conflict played no part in the 1938 reform movement in Dubai, and opposition to the ruling families during the 1950s emanated from young professionals rather than Sunnī or Shīʿī Islamists. The revolution in Iran failed to elicit political agitation from resident Shīʿīs. Only in the wake of the September 2001 attacks on the United States did any sign of radical Islamist activity appear, as connections were uncovered between local financiers and al-Qaʿida militants. Beginning in December 2011, prominent members of organizations affiliated with the Muslim Brothers, most notably Reform and the Holy Qurʾān Foundation, had their citizenship rights rescinded after they criticized the authorities for excluding Islamist candidates from elections to the federation's consultative council.

BIBLIOGRAPHY

Abdullah, Muhammad Morsy. *The United Arab Emirates: A Modern History*. London: Croom Helm, 1978. Particularly good on the 1938 reform movement in Dubai.

Brown, Nathan J. *Pushing toward Party Politics? Kuwait's Islamic Constitutional Movement*. Carnegie Papers No. 79. Washington, D.C.: Carnegie Endowment for International Peace, 2007. Sophisticated analysis of Kuwait's primary Sunnī Islamist political association.

Crystal, Jill. *Oil and Politics in the Gulf: Rulers and Merchants in Kuwait and Qatar*. Cambridge, U.K., and New York: Cambridge University Press, 1990. Conceptually and empirically rich study of elite interaction both before and after oil.

Davidson, Christopher M. *The United Arab Emirates: A Study in Survival*. Boulder, Colo.: Lynne Rienner, 2005. Comprehensive survey of politics, economics, and society.

Gause, F. Gregory. *Oil Monarchies: Domestic and Security Challenges in the Arab Gulf States*. New York: Council on Foreign Relations Press, 1994. Lucid account of political activism following the 1990–1991 Gulf War.

Khalaf, Abdul Hadi. *Unfinished Business: Contentious Politics and State-Building in Bahrain*. Lund, Sweden: University of Lund, 2000. Authoritative treatment of Bahrain's popular movements.

Lawson, Fred H. *Bahrain: The Modernization of Autocracy*. Boulder, Colo.: Westview Press, 1989. Overview of Bahrain's modern political and economic history, with an extensive bibliographic essay.

Louer, Laurence. *Transnational Shia Politics: Religious and Political Networks in the Gulf*. New York: Columbia University Press, 2008. Path-breaking survey of regional connections among Islamist movements.

Tétreault, Mary Ann. *Stories of Democracy: Politics and Society in Contemporary Kuwait*. New York: Columbia University Press, 2000. Accessible treatment of the Arab Gulf's most vibrant electoral system.

Fred H. Lawson

Ḥadd. *See* Sharīʿah.

Ḥalāl. *See* Sharīʿah.

Ḥamās. *This entry contains two subentries:*

Overview *and*
Parliamentary Reform.

Overview

The organization Ḥarakat al-Muqāwamah al-Islāmīyah (Movement of Islamic Resistance), the most important Palestinian Islamist organization in the West Bank and Gaza Strip, is known by its acronym "Ḥamās." A non-Qurʾānic word, *ḥamās* means "zeal." The organization was established in December 1987, at the very beginning of the first Palestinian uprising (*intifāḍah*), as an expression of the Muslim Brotherhood in Palestine. Therefore, participation in the anti-Israeli resistance after two decades of Islamic political quietism stood at the heart of the Ḥamās credo. Since 2006 Ḥamās has formed the majority party of the Legislative Council of the Palestinian Interim Self-Government Authority. Its armed wing is known as the ʿIzz al-Dīn al-Qassām Brigades, a reference to the *shaykh* killed by the British at the beginning of the great Palestinian revolt in 1936.

Emergence of Ḥamās. Before the emergence of Ḥamās, Islam had rarely constituted the primary justification for the contemporary liberation struggle of the Palestinians; rather Arab or Palestinian nationalisms were the ideological pillars used by various leaders. At the end of the 1970s, however, new types of Islamic activism appeared. Present in Jerusalem as a benevolent organization since the 1940s, the Muslim Brotherhood articulated, as its primary goal, the reinvigoration of an Islamic identity. As political Islam and Islamism expanded in the region in the 1970s, the Muslim Brotherhood became more active but confined its political measures to the struggle against the Palestinian Communist Party. The group's failure to confront Israel's occupation of the Palestinian territories (i.e., the West Bank and Gaza)—ongoing since 1967, in violation of UN security regulations—cost the group political legitimacy in the view of many Palestinians. But its large social-welfare network (consisting of schools, orphanages, healthcare clinics, and the like) in the Gaza Strip, established under the charismatic leadership of the handicapped schoolmaster Shaykh Aḥmad Yāsīn (killed by the Israeli army in 2004), endeared the group to others. Notably, the Brotherhood earned popular support in a majority of Gaza mosques, and came to control Gaza's Islamic University. In the West Bank, however, the group failed to establish a strong network or find a charismatic leader; its only strongholds were in the universities. At this time, Fatah, the dominant wing of the Palestinian Liberation Organization (PLO), and Jordan, still linked to the West Bank, encouraged Islamist attacks on leftist elements, and Israel encouraged the religious group to counter the militant nationalist leaders.

When some new Islamist groups adopted a strongly anti-Israeli discourse, arguing that Israel constituted the spearhead of Western aggression against Islam, the liberation of Palestine was transformed into a fundamentally religious question. Under the leadership of the physician Fatḥī Shiqāqī (1951–1995), various factions engaged in *jihād* against Israel, including initiating armed struggle, a central religious duty. In doing so activists claimed to be acting on the authority of Sayyid Quṭb, the Egyptian Muslim Brotherhood leader executed in 1966 and the inspiration of the Egyptian Islamic *Jihād* as well as the Islamic revolution in Iran. In 1986 and 1987 *Jihād* cells embarked on a series of anti-Israeli guerrilla operations, some of which were bloody affairs.

By 1987, and in the wake of military operations, the whole Palestinian population mobilized against the Israeli occupation through the *intifāḍah*. Muslim Brotherhood leaders then concluded that their survival as an associative movement dedicated to preaching largely depended on permanent political mobilization. As the "strong arm" of the Brotherhood in the Palestinian Uprising, Ḥamās was created in Gaza by the physician ʿAbd al-ʿAzīz al-Rantīsī (killed by the Israeli army in 2004); Salah Shihādah (killed by the Israeli army in 2002), chief of the security apparatus of the Brotherhood; and other young Brotherhood members with Shaykh Yāsīn's approval.

With the political, military, and social commitment of the Brotherhood, Ḥamās integrated religion and patriotism, monopolized until then by nationalist forces, and secured growing popular support. Shortly after its foundation Ḥamās opened representative bureaus outside Palestine, and entered (and won) student and professional elections.

Political Activities. Ḥamās's aims and strategies, similar to those of the Muslim Brotherhood in Egypt and Jordan, were first summarized in a covenant (*mīthāq*) published in August 1988. In it Palestine was declared an eternal religious trust, no part of which may be given up. Therefore, recognizing the legitimacy of the Israeli state—as the PLO did in 1988—was deemed unacceptable. Ḥamās leaders nevertheless declared, in the mid-1990s, that they would accept a long-term truce in return for a complete withdrawal by Israel from the West Bank (including East Jerusalem) and the Gaza Strip, as well as the establishment of a Palestinian state.

Beyond the covenant, Ḥamās boycotted Palestine's 1996 presidential and legislative elections, along with the 2005 presidential election, ostensibly because it could not condone the Israeli-Palestinian Interim Agreements. However in 2005 Ḥamās participated in Palestine's municipal elections—with the justification that its participation was in the social interest of the Palestinian people—and took control of many municipalities. In 2006 it gained the majority of seats in the Palestinian legislature, and Ismāʿīl Hanīyah (1962–), one of Ḥamās's leaders in Gaza, became prime minister of the Palestinian Authority.

To end Ḥamās rocket attacks on Israeli border towns, Egypt obtained a ceasefire in June 2008, which secured a pledge to prevent fresh assaults. The agreement was breached four months later when Israel carried out a military action ostensibly targeted to avert an abduction. After Israel discovered tunnels dug under the border security fence, it organized the assassination of seven

Ḥamās operatives that led to retaliations. A barrage of rockets led to the December 2008 Israeli raids. Starting on 27 December 2008 Israel bombarded Gaza in what it termed "Operation Cast Lead," which resulted in hundreds of casualties. A unilateral ceasefire was declared on 17 January 2009, although none of the underlying causes that led to the confrontations had been solved.

In July 2009 Khālid Mishʿal, the Ḥamās political bureau chief headquartered in Damascus, Syria, stated his willingness to cooperate with a resolution to the Arab-Israeli conflict that included a Palestinian state based on the 1967 borders. His conditions, that an undetermined number of Palestinian refugees should be given the right to return to Israel and that East Jerusalem should be recognized as the new state's capital, were rejected. In May 2011 Mishʿal decided to move to Doha, Qatar, in the aftermath of the uprisings that shook the Syrian capital. Ḥamās was once again in search of a home, even if this latest relocation increased its distance from Palestine.

The Ḥamās movement is banned by Israel and is listed as a terrorist organization by the United States and the European Union. After the 2004 killings of the Ḥamās founder Shaykh Yāsīn and his successor al-Rantīsī, the identity of Ḥamās's leader is not officially known. Many believe that Mahmud al-Zahhār, a Gaza physician who was Palestine's minister of foreign affairs in 2006, leads the group.

BIBLIOGRAPHY

The Palestinian Information Center, http://palestine-info.co.uk/en (also available in Arabic, French, Urdu, Persian, Russian, and Malay), is the unofficial website of Ḥamās. The ʿIzz al-Dīn al-Qassām Brigades Information Office has an official website, http://www.qassam.ps/, available in Arabic, English, and Turkish).

Abu-Amr, Ziad. *Islamic Fundamentalism in the West Bank and Gaza: Muslim Brotherhood and Islamic Jihad*. Bloomington: Indiana University Press, 1994.

Chehab, Zaki. *Inside Hamās: The Untold Story of the Militant Islamic Movement*. London and New York: Nation Books, 2007.

Hroub, Khaled. *Hamās: A Beginner's Guide*. 2d ed. London and New York: Pluto Press, 2010.

Hroub, Khaled. *Hamās: Political Thought and Practice*. Washington, D.C.: Institute for Palestine Studies, 2000.

Legrain, Jean-François. "Palestinian Islamisms: Patriotism as a Condition of Their Expansion." In *Accounting for Fundamentalisms: The Dynamic Character of Movements*, edited by Martin E. Marty and R. Scott Appleby. Chicago: University of Chicago Press, 1994.

Mishal, Shaul, and Avraham Sela. *The Palestinian Hamās: Vision, Violence, and Coexistence*. 2d ed. New York: Columbia University Press, 2006.

Shadid, Mohammed. "The Muslim Brotherhood Movement in the West Bank and Gaza." *Third World Quarterly* 10, no. 2 (April 1988): 658–682.

Tamimi, Azzam. *Hamas: A History from Within*. Northampton, Mass.: Olive Branch Press, 2011.

Tamimi, Azzam. *Hamās: Unwritten Chapters*. New ed. London: Hurst, 2009.

Jean-François Legrain
Updated by Joseph A. Kéchichian

Parliamentary Reform

Ḥamās won the Palestinian legislative elections of 25 January 2006. In doing so it became one of the first Islamic movements in the Arab world to assume majority control of a government following a series of internationally verified elections. Running under the parliamentary bloc name "Change and Reform," Ḥamās won 74 out of the 132 Palestinian Legislative Council (PLC) seats, gaining a 56 percent majority position with over 42 percent of the popular vote. Ḥamās's unexpected and unprecedented victory—called by some an "electoral tsunami"—ended more than four decades of political domination by Fatah, Ḥamās's most formidable electoral opponent and a secular-nationalist rival. Fatah's widespread reputation for incompetence, cronyism, and corruption was widely perceived as contributing to Ḥamās's sweeping electoral victory.

The decision to participate in the 2006 PLC elections marked a transformational moment for Ḥamās, a twenty-year-old Palestinian Islamic nationalist movement established in the early months of the first Palestinian *intifāḍah* (uprising). In 1996 the group had boycotted the Palestinian legislative elections because of their affiliation with the Oslo peace process, which Ḥamās ideologically and militantly opposed. In March 2005 Ḥamās leaders reversed this oppositional stance, justifying their decision by disassociating the 2006 elections from the Oslo peace process, which was declared obsolete. Furthermore they emphasized the exigencies and benefits for extending its diversified array of activist work within the electoral sphere, which proved to be a significant contribution. Always engaged in humanitarian, social, and educational outreach alongside more militant activities, Ḥamās, now added legislative participation to its cache of strategies, which were designed to achieve two core goals: ensuring the emergence of a sovereign Palestinian state and improving the plight of Palestinians within and outside of the occupied territories.

Despite Ḥamās's previous rejection of electoral participation at the legislative level, it had neither opposed nor boycotted such participation at the societal, local, or municipal levels; indeed, it had vigorously contributed to such elections since its founding. Ḥamās leaders repeatedly called for municipal-level elections during Yasir Arafat's tenure, calls that went unheeded until shortly after his death in 2004. Once such elections were announced, Ḥamās immediately affirmed its participation, launched a well-orchestrated campaign, and eventually achieved numerous electoral victories in both the Gaza Strip and the West Bank. Despite gaining fewer votes overall than Fatah in the 2004–2005 municipal elections, Ḥamās's successful performance signaled two new trends within Palestinian affairs: the end of Fatah's unilateral political domination and the beginning of Ḥamās's political involvement—perhaps even domination—at the highest levels of the Palestinian government.

Campaign electoral strategies and political agendas were outlined in "The 2005 Electoral Platform for Change and Reform," a twenty-page document addressing eighteen substantive topics in roughly eight thousand words. With the exception of two themes, "Our Essential Principles" (Article 1) and "Religious Guidance and Preaching" (Article 8), the eighteen other subjects addressed (i.e., domestic policy, administrative reform, legislative policy, educational policy, citizens' rights and liberties) were typical of ordinary secular political movements, both Western and non-Western. The text was notable for its minimal religious and militant content, expansive scope, substantive detail, and predominantly mundane tone, all of which stood in stark contrast to the more inflammatory rhetoric and sectarian-militant phraseology characteristic of older Ḥamās publications, especially its 1988 founding charter. Illustrating a newfound level of political sophistication and intellectual maturity, Ḥamās's Change and Reform agenda represented a new phase in the movement's ideological evolution, namely an embrace of legislative and electoral politics as additional ways to effect change and ultimately bring about an independent Palestinian state.

Still, mired in controversy since its January 2006 electoral victory, the Change and Reform government prevented Ḥamās from implementing the program outlined in its Electoral Platform. Preoccupied with the ever-present threat of civil war, the increasingly dire effects of an international economic boycott imposed by Israel and the International Quartet (the United Nations, the United States, the European Union, and Russia), the detention of many of its elected members by Israel, and intensified Israeli retaliatory incursions into the Gaza Strip and West Bank, the Ḥamās government was unable to implement substantive components of its agenda.

Instead, during its first year in power, the Ḥamās-led government focused almost exclusively on political survival, leading to numerous attempts to forge a unity government with other Palestinian political factions. After many failed attempts to do so, a national unity government was finally announced, with the assistance of Saudi mediation, in March 2007. Despite hopes that this would lead to the cessation of both the international economic boycott and domestic factional infighting, internal violence and ongoing clashes with the Israeli army escalated, the economic boycott persisted, and international criticism of Ḥamās's involvement in politics continued to mount.

By June 2007 domestic infighting led to the demise of the national unity government formed and headed by Ḥamās and resulted in an unprecedented phenomenon—a military and political split between the Gaza Strip and West Bank, with Ḥamās assuming control of the Gaza Strip and Fatah assuming control of the West Bank. In response to Ḥamās's military takeover of the Gaza Strip, the Palestinian president Mahmoud Abbas dissolved the national unity government, replaced the Ḥamās-appointed prime minister, outlawed Ḥamās's newly appointed security force (the so-called Executive Force), and declared a state of emergency. This internal disunity was exacerbated by the response of Israel and many Western nations, most notably the United States, which moved to further isolate Ḥamās, including its democratically elected politicians, while financially, politically, and militarily bolstering the Fatah-affiliated President Abbas. Consequently Ḥamās's parliamentary bloc remained not only excommunicated but outlawed from participating in the Palestinian government it legitimately and democratically gained access to in the elections of January 2006.

Lingering disputes between the two leading factions lasted into late April 2011 when an accord among eleven Palestinian groups was signed in Cairo, Egypt. Ḥamās and Fatah reached an agreement on 28 April 2011, ending what was a nearly four-year rift that spread death and destruction. Palestinian Authority President Mahmoud Abbas's Fatah party and Ḥamās Prime Minister Ismāʿīl Hanīyah, agreed to hold national elections as soon as possible. The Israeli prime minister Benjamin Netanyahu denounced the pact, positing that the agreement dealt a severe blow to the peace process. He also said that his government would withhold tax revenue collected on behalf of the Palestinians until it was certain that the funds would not end up in the hands of Ḥamās. Tensions were high among the principle protagonists, each accusing the other of bad faith. Abbas insisted, nevertheless, that Fatah would set all foreign policy matters in any unity government with Ḥamās, and that the Palestinian Authority would seek a negotiated peace agreement with Israel leading to the establishment of a Palestinian state in the West Bank, Gaza Strip, and East Jerusalem.

BIBLIOGRAPHY

Brown, Nathan J. "Aftermath of the Hamas Tsunami." Carnegie Endowment for International Peace, February 2, 2006. http://www.carnegieendowment.org/publications/index.cfm?fa=view&id=17975&prog=zgp&proj=zdrl,zme.

Fuller, Graham E. "Hamas Comes to Power: Breakthrough or Setback?" *Strategic Insights* 5, no. 2 (February 2006).

Gunning, Jeroen. *Hamas in Politics: Democracy, Religion, Violence.* New York: Columbia University Press, 2009.

Hroub, Khaled. *Hamas: A Beginner's Guide.* 2d ed. London and New York: Pluto Press, 2010.

Hroub, Khaled. *Hamas: Political Thought and Practice.* Washington, D.C.: Institute for Palestine Studies, 2000.

Hroub, Khaled. "A New Hamas Through its New Documents." *Journal of Palestine Studies* 35, no. 4 (Summer 2006): 6–27.

International Crisis Group. *After Mecca: Engaging Hamās*. Report no. 62, February 26, 2007. http://www.crisisgroup.org/en/regions/middle-east-north-africa/israel-palestine/062/after-mecca-engaging-hamas.aspx.

International Crisis Group. "Enter Hamas: The Challenges of Political Integration." Report no. 49, January 18, 2006. http://www.crisisgroup.org/en/regions/middle-east-north-africa/israel-palestine/049-enter-hamas-challenges-of-political-integration.aspx.

Malka, Haim. "Forcing Choices: Testing the Transformation of Hamas." *The Washington Quarterly* 28, no. 4 (Autumn 2005).

Milton-Edwards, Beverly. "Prepared for Power: Hamas, Governance, and Conflict." *Civil Wars* 7, no. 4 (Winter 2005): 311–329.

Mishal, Shaul, and Abraham Sela. *The Palestinian Hamas: Vision, Violence, and Coexistence*. 2d ed. New York: Columbia University Press, 2006.

Roy, Sara. "Hamas and the Transformation(s) of Political Islam in Palestine." *Current History* 101, no. 13 (January 2003): 13–20.

Tamimi, Azzam. *Hamas: Unwritten Chapters*. New and updated ed. London: Hurst and Co., 2009.

Chrystie Swiney
Updated by Joseph A. Kéchichian

Ḥarakat Mujtamaʿ al-Silm [HAMS].

See Movement for the Society of Peace.

Ḥarām.

See Sharīʿah.

Haron, Imam Abdullah. To the Muslims of South Africa and particularly those in the Cape, Imam Abdullah Haron (1923–1969) has come to be regarded as both a saint and a martyr who died for the cause of justice in what was then apartheid South Africa. He was a Muslim activist who suffered the fate of countless others, including well known anti-apartheid figures such as Steven Biko, all of whom were victims of the apartheid regime. They were apprehended by the dreaded South African Security Branch which had the power to track down, detain, and torture suspected activists and opponents of apartheid. The police then attempted to cover up their murderous acts by claiming that, for instance, the detainees had committed suicide or that they had died accidentally.

The imam lived through the turbulent late 1950s and especially the 1960s, which were a transitional period in the peaceful anti-apartheid resistance when some elements in the African National Congress (ANC), including activists such as Nelson Mandela, initiated armed struggle or what was called "Umkhonto wa Sizwe" (Spear of the Nation). The apartheid regime responded by setting up a wide network of spies/informers and the Special Branch of the police to apprehend those who were seen as opponents of the regime. This was also the period when the ANC and a splinter group from it, the Pan Africanist Congress (PAC), were banned and forced to go underground.

How did Imam Haron get involved in the anti-apartheid struggles? Before answering this question, let us first present a brief sketch of the imam's life and career up to the period when he became a person of special interest to the authorities.

Haron was born on 8 February 1923 in Newlands-Claremont, a suburb of Cape Town. The youngest of five children, he was still an infant when his mother died. As a result his father sent him to live with his childless aunt Maryam, who raised him. After completing the sixth grade at a local school he pursued Islamic studies for two years in Makkah, Saudi Arabia, under the tutelage of Shaykh al-Alawi al-Maliki, returning to South Africa (according to his son who is writing his biography) before the outbreak of World War II. He continued his studies with a number of teachers and mentors, among whom the most prominent were the al-Azhar-trained South African scholar Shaykh Ismail Ganief Edwards, who influenced his social welfare activism or working to provide services to the poor and needy, and

Shaykh Abdullah Taha Gamieldien. He was also influenced by progressive ideas circulating within South Africa through his interactions with certain individuals he met as well as from his reading of the literature of activist Muslim groups such as the Muslim Brotherhood of Egypt and their educational and social outreach programs.

In 1955 Haron was appointed imam of al-Jamiʿa Mosque in Claremont where he served until that fateful day when he was picked up by the police. One of the first things he did was to set up the Claremont Muslim Youth Association with its newsletter, *al-Islam*, as a vehicle for disseminating information on Islamic teachings and contemporary Islam and society. He also began to conduct classes for adults and children. He encouraged women to attend his mosque classes and, in addition, created a discussion forum for the exchange of ideas and helped members of his mosque community with their financial and personal problems. He also circulated the anti-apartheid pamphlet of the Call of Islam in 1961 and as well as kept up with the anti-apartheid struggles by the different groups. In his Friday sermons he offered critiques of the white minority government and attacked its racist laws as being inhumane and un-Islamic.

He refused to be paid a salary and drew an income from working at his father's grocery store. After the store closed he worked as a sales representative for a British-based candy company in another area of the town mainly inhabited by African Xhosa speakers. He had been issued a permit that allowed him to be in an area that would otherwise have been off-limits for him as a non-African (a Cape Malay). This provided him with his first significant opportunity to establish close contact with Africans from Langa, Guguletu, and Nyanga in a country where people were segregated by ethnicity, race, and class that determined where they lived, where they were educated, where they worked, and eventually where they died and were buried. This was by virtue of apartheid laws that had been enacted by the white supremacist government to exploit the labor of the non-white majority for the benefit of the economically and politically favored descendants of Europeans. Under the National Party laws such as the Immorality Act, the Mixed Marriages Act, and especially the Group Areas Act were established to keep the races "apart" (hence the racist ideology of apartheid or racial "apartness"). The Imam himself was forced to relocate to a new area and build his new home opposite the Rugby stadium as a result of the implementation of the Group Areas Act.

The warm, friendly, helpful imam and candy salesman was readily embraced by the Africans. They affectionately nicknamed him "Mfundisi" (the priest) due to his love of children and the respect and humane treatment he displayed for Africans. He did whatever he could to help them and their families, especially after he discovered that many of the African breadwinners in the Cape townships (who had aligned themselves with the PAC) had been killed or imprisoned for their sociopolitical activities against the apartheid state. This left their family dependents in dire economic needs with no source of income. He provided whatever assistance he could for these families. More significantly his interfaith dialogues and contacts began to generate funds for his relief work primarily from the International Defence League, which was strongly supported by the Christian churches internationally. As he got deeply involved in the affairs of the victims of apartheid he too ended up throwing his weight behind the PAC which, along with ANC, he now supported. Furthermore, in 1968 Haron traveled to Mecca, where, among other things, he met the Saudi Arabian minister of education as well as King Faisal. He was also in Egypt where he addressed a Muslim conference that was attended as well by PAC and ANC representatives.

Haron's activities had already drawn the attention of the Security Branch, which kept a watchful eye over him and monitored closely his clandestine activities over a period of time. In fact, some close friends, fearing for his personal safety if he returned, advised him to consider going into exile. Such a course of action, however, was not attractive given that his ailing father was not willing to emigrate.

Finally on 28 May 1969 the dreaded Security Branch apprehended him under the 180-Day Terrorism Act of 1967. He was in police custody for four months until his death on 27 September 1969 from torture by the police. The police claimed that he died of wounds suffered in an accidental fall from a staircase in prison. His autopsy revealed a totally different story. His Muslim funeral prayer at the City Park Rugby Stadium was attended by almost thirty thousand people. The Imam was survived by his wife and three children.

It would take another decade before the Imam became a symbol and icon for the Muslim struggle against apartheid. By then his role had been integrated in the community's memory by the creation of a legendary martyr status deployed to make sure his efforts and sacrifices did not fall by the wayside. As has been pointed out, the creation of the Haron myth reflects a historical transfiguration that served to maintain an image of the Muslim commitment to the struggle against apartheid. The perception of the Muslim contribution to liberation being out of proportion to their numbers (less than 2 percent of the population) is still contested.

BIBLIOGRAPHY

Davids, Achmat. "Imam Haron: Legend and Myth in the Making of History." *Boorhaanol* 31, no. 1 (February 1996): 15–20.

Desai, Barney, and Cardiff Marney. *The Killing of the Imam*. London and New York: Quartet Books, 1978.

Gunther, Ursula. "The Memory of Imam Haron in Consolidating Muslim Resistance to the Apartheid Struggle." In *Religion and the Political Imagination in a Changing South Africa*, edited by Gordon Mitchell and Eve Mullen. Münster, Germany, and New York: Waxmann, 2002.

Haron, Muhammad. "A Man of Justice: Towards a Sacred Biography. The Life and Times of Imam Abdulla Haron." *Muslim Views* (1994): 2–6.

Haron, Muhammad. "Towards a Sacred Biography. The Life and Thoughts of Imam Abdulla Haron." *Journal of Islamic Studies* 14 (1994): 63–83.

Abdin Chande

Ḥasan II of Morocco. King Ḥasan II (1929–1999), the twenty-first sovereign of the Alaouite dynasty, ruled Morocco for thirty-eight years. He displayed two distinct faces: one of a brutal and unforgiving autocrat and the other as a unifier and eloquent statesman.

Ḥasan was educated at the Imperial College in Rabat and the University of Bordeaux, where he received a law degree. In 1956 his father, King Muḥammad V, appointed him head of the armed forces and in 1960 as minister of defense and deputy prime minister. After his father's death, Ḥasan became king (in March 1961), at the age of thirty-two. Although he produced Morocco's first constitution in 1962 and created a multiparty system, Ḥasan ruled as an absolute monarch. He suspended parliament from 1965 until 1970 and assumed emergency powers. A new constitution in 1972 established the king as "Supreme Representative of the Nation" and outlawed criticism of the monarchy.

Coup attempts in 1971 and 1972, the latter led by General Mohamed Oufkir, one of the king's closest aides, ushered in a period of even greater repression. Oufkir's betrayal, along with the lingering challenge posed by leftist activists, heightened Ḥasan's sense of insecurity and led him to take harsh measures against those he deemed traitors. The mid-1960s through the late 1980s, known as *les années de plombe* (years of lead), saw the killing, imprisonment, and "disappearance" of thousands of opposition activists. While willing to use repression, Ḥasan was also successful at co-opting political parties and civil society, providing them benefits and patronage in return for their acceptance of the legitimacy of the monarchy.

Ḥasan treated his position as a divine right; his was a highly personalized form of rule. He anointed himself the "Commander of the Faithful" and regularly emphasized his religious legitimacy as a descendent of Prophet Muḥammad. This made it more difficult for Islamist groups in Morocco to gain traction. A critical point came in 1975, when he led more than 300,000 Moroccans to claim Western Sahara, precipitating Spain's withdrawal. The success and symbolism of the "Green March" added to the king's legitimacy, allowing him to consolidate his power even further.

Valued for maintaining stability, Ḥasan developed strong relationships with Western nations during and after the cold war. He was a skilled diplomat and played a key, albeit secret, role in Arab-Israeli negotiations, including Camp David in 1979. During his reign, he kept Morocco in the moderate pro-Western camp in the Arab world. He sent troops to defend Saudi Arabia during the 1990–1991 Gulf crisis. In 1994 he hosted the first Middle East and North Africa Economic Summit, which encouraged Arab-Israeli economic cooperation.

In the early 1990s the repressiveness of Ḥasan's rule was mitigated by his establishment of the Consultative Council for Human Rights. He began releasing hundreds of political prisoners, closing down the notorious desert prison at Tazmamart. After falling seriously ill in 1995 during a trip to the United Nations in New York, Ḥasan began to worry about succession to the throne. As Islamists began to gain ground, he once again revised the constitution, brought longtime opposition parties into a governing coalition, and appointed the leftist leader Abderrhamane Youssoufi as prime minister.

When he died on 23 July 1999 King Ḥasan's nearly four decades of rule left behind rising inequality, a declining education system, inadequate public services, endemic corruption, and a growing number of jobless youth who believed their only future rested beyond Morocco's borders. Even so Ḥasan's foresight to ensure the continuation of the monarchy and preserve stability has given Morocco a more peaceful history than that of many of its neighbors. His legacy, therefore, will largely depend on who is measuring it. King Ḥasan II was succeeded by his eldest son, Muḥammad VI.

[*See also* Morocco.]

BIBLIOGRAPHY

Hassan II. *The Challenge: The Memoirs of King Hassan II of Morocco*. Translated by Anthony Rhodes. London: Macmillan, 1978.

Howe, Marvine. *Morocco: The Islamist Awakening and Other Challenges*. Oxford and New York: Oxford University Press, 2005.

Hughes, Stephen O. *Morocco under King Hassan*. Reading, U.K.: Ithaca Press, 2001.

Willis, Michael, and Nizar Messari. "Analyzing Moroccan Foreign Policy and Relations with Europe." *The Review of International Affairs* 3 (Winter 2003): 152–172.

Shadi Hamid
and James Liddell
Updated by Nael Shama

Ḥawwā, Saʿīd. (1935–1989), chief ideologue of the Muslim Brothers (Muslim Brotherhood) society in Baʿthist Syria. Ḥawwā was born and raised in a poor quarter of Hama, Syria, to a father who was active in the local anti-landlord movement. Passing through the state school system, he graduated in 1961 from the *Sharīʿah* Faculty at the University of Damascus. In high school Ḥawwā was influenced by the charismatic teacher of religion Muḥammad al-Ḥamid, who was an adept in the Ṣūfī Naqshbandīyah order, as well as a founding member of the Hama branch of the Muslim Brothers society. Ḥawwā joined the Muslim Brothers at his teacher's instigation in 1953, at the same time immersing himself in Ṣūfism.

Ḥawwā rose in the ranks of the Brotherhood to membership on the Brotherhood International Guidance Council and was a member of the leadership of the Syrian Brotherhood between 1978–1962. He was imprisoned five times between 1973 and 1978. He lectured and gave speeches in many Arab, Muslim, and Western countries.

In the wake of the Hama disturbances of 1964, which followed the rise of the Baʿth to power, Ḥawwā was nominated acting head of the Muslim Brothers society in the city. Two years later he left for Saudi Arabia to reformulate the movement's doctrine. Returning to Syria after Hafez al-Assad's seizure of power, Ḥawwā was imprisoned for his role in the opposition to the 1973 constitution, which failed to mention that the president's faith must be Islam. On his release in 1978 he fled to Jordan and joined the collective leadership of the Islamic Front in the confrontation with the regime, which ended in the Hama debacle of 1982. Ḥawwā died in exile in Jordan seven years later. He was partially paralyzed in 1987, entered a coma in 1988, and died on 9 March 1989.

Ḥawwā's literary output reached almost thirty works. These range from multivolume Qurʾān and *ḥadīth*, commentaries, through extensive expositions in the spheres of theology, law, Sufism, and *daʿwah* (preaching), to a detailed autobiography and pamphlets on current issues. Ḥawwā was critical of the radical wing of the Islamic movement, the followers of the Egyptian Muslim Brotherhood ideologue Sayyid Quṭb. Although sharing the radicals' analysis of the lamentable state of the Islamic world and its inferiority to the West in the modern age, he objected to their denunciation of contemporary Muslim societies as *jāhilī* (living in ignorance, as in the pre-Islamic period). Instead, Ḥawwā maintained that Muslims might degenerate into a state of *riddah* (apostasy) if they were not guided on the right path. This entailed striking a new balance between the Salafī call to follow the example of the pious ancestors and a reformed type of a spirituality to fight present-day materialism.

In both doctrinal and organizational matters, Ḥawwā claimed to follow the original program of the Muslim Brothers society as delineated by its Egyptian founder Ḥasan al-Bannā. His ideas also reflected the positive democratic experience of the Muslim Brothers in post-independence Syria. Ḥawwā accepted the idea of an Arab national identity, as part of the larger Islamic *ummah* (community) and as an indispensable stage in the formation of the universal Islamic state. He called for the reinstitution of the caliphate, the holder of the office to be elected by *shūrā*, a permanent consultative organ consisting of *ʿulamāʾ* (religious scholars) proficient in both the religious sciences and worldly affairs. The role of the Islamic movement in Ḥawwā's scheme was to organize all Islamic forces under a unified political leadership and remold society, essentially by peaceful means, into a party of God.

In the wake of the establishment of the ʿAlawī-based authoritarian Baʿth regime, Ḥawwā offered the Syrian Muslim Brothers a new program, which he called *al-iḥyāʾīyah al-rabbānīyah* (divine revival). This was modeled on the reformist tradition he had adopted from his former teacher Muḥammad al-Ḥamid. The essence of Ḥawwā's scheme was to create a loose grassroots organization of Islamic groups around local mosque-schools. The *rabbānīyah* circles were to provide the Islamic movement with spiritual guidance and restrain the radicals who called for immediate confrontation with the regime. Unable to convince his colleagues of the need for moderation, Ḥawwā joined the 1982 Islamic uprising, which ended, as he had feared it would, in disaster.

BIBLIOGRAPHY

Abd-Allah, Umar F. *The Islamic Struggle in Syria*. Berkeley, Calif.: Mizan Press, 1983.

Hinnebusch, Raymond A. "Syria." In *The Politics of Islamic Revivalism: Diversity and Unity*, edited by Shireen T. Hunter. Bloomington: Indiana University Press, 1988.

Mayer, Thomas. "The Islamic Opposition in Syria, 1961–1982." *Orient* 4 (1983): 589–609.

Weismann, Itzchak. "The Politics of Popular Religion: Sufis, Salafis, and Muslim Brothers in Twentieth-Century Hamah." *International Journal of Middle East Studies* 37 (2005): 39–58.

Weismann, Itzchak. "Said Hawwa and Islamic Revivalism in Baathist Syria." *Studia Islamica* 85 (1997): 131–154.

Weismann, Itzchak. "Said Hawwa: The Making of a Radical Muslim Thinker in Modern Syria." *Middle Eastern Studies* 29 (1993): 601–623.

Ahmad Moussalli

ḤAWẒAH. In the Shīʿī shrine cities of Najaf and Karbala in Iraq and in Qom, Iran, *ḥawẓah* denotes a community of learning that encompasses circles of study, scholarly activities, and social bonds and offers organizational and financial assistance. Karbala emerged as the leading center of learning and religious leadership in Shiism following the 1722 fall of the Ṣafavids in Iran, with Najaf succeeding it from the 1840s. The *ḥawẓah* centered on individual *mujtahids* who gave their own classes, and sometimes supported lower-level teachers. Students were regarded as disciples of a specific *mujtahid*, and not of the *madrasah* as an institution. Najaf and Karbala were sustained primarily by donations from believers and fees for religious services provided to pilgrims, while Qom also enjoyed income from landed endowments.

Typical of traditional Muslim institutions of learning, the *ḥawẓah* lacked formal organization and hierarchy. The regularization of curriculum and the certification system was based on conventions that crystallized and persisted over time. Social hierarchy and status were based on scholarship and acumen in building networks of patronage in addition to a certain charisma. Consequently the *ḥawẓah* was open to newcomers and offered them upward social mobility.

The subjects and modes of study were influenced by Sunnī institutions of learning, as they were divided into transmitted sciences (*al-ʿulūm al-naqlīyah*) and rational sciences (*al-ʿulūm al-ʿaqlīyah*). However, great prominence was given to principles of jurisprudence (*uṣūl al-fiqh*), because of the central role of *ijtihād* in Shiism.

Ḥawẓah studies comprised three stages: preliminaries (*muqaddamāt*), which focused on acquiring a firm knowledge of Arabic grammar, logic (*manṭiq*), and rhetoric (*balāghah*). At the beginning level (*suṭūḥ*), jurisprudence (*fiqh*) and the principles of jurisprudence (*uṣūl al-fiqh*) were the two main topics. Students could attend courses in Qurʾān commentary (*tafsīr*), critical study of the *ḥadīth* (*dirāyah*), biographies of transmitters of *ḥadīth* (*rijāl*), ethics (*akhlāq*), theosophy (*ḥikmah*), and history (*tārīkh*).

Each subject had its own specific books that were read successively. Ordinarily, passage from one stage of learning to another depended upon completing the reading of the required books, but students could leave a teacher earlier. There was no fixed number of years for education, and students could continue their studies for as many years as they chose. The highest stage, the *dars al-khārij* or *baḥth al-khārij*, aimed at the attainment of *ijtihād*. These courses were given by senior *mujtahids* on topics in *uṣūl* or *fiqh* of their own choice. The teaching of this course reflected the teacher's senior rank and aspiration for religious leadership (*marji'īyah*).

The culmination of the process of learning was the attainment of *ijāzah ijtihād*, a certification that allowed the student to practice *ijtihād* and issue rulings from one or as many *mujtahids* as possible, though not all students attained it. During the 1940s Ayatollah Moḥammad Hosayn Borujerdi introduced reforms in the Qom *ḥawẓah* that centralized its finances and certification process. In the early 1960s Ayatollah Muḥammad Bāqir al-Ṣadr sought to modernize the curriculum in Najaf, but with little success, but in 1993 Ayatollah 'Alī al-Sīstānī introduced a new mode of teaching in the traditional *dars al-khārij* courses.

Karbala and Najaf served as centers for the 1920 anti-British rebellion, but, following the establishment of modern Iraq, the Sunnī-led government curtailed their status as centers of the Shī'ī community. They experienced a decline from the 1940s, parallel with the rise of Qom to prominence from 1927, and suffered severe repression under Ba'thist rule in Iraq (1968–2003). With the formation of a new Shī'ī-led state following the 2003 U.S. invasion, Najaf regained its importance as a political center in Iraq and possibly as a future center of learning for the Shī'ī world.

[*See also* Ṣadr, Muḥammad Bāqir al-.]

BIBLIOGRAPHY

Litvak, Meir. *Shī'ī Scholars of Nineteenth-Century Iraq: The 'Ulamā' of Najaf and Karbala*. Cambridge, U.K., and New York: Cambridge University Press, 1998.

Nakash, Yitzhak. *The Shī'īs of Iraq*. Princeton, N.J.: Princeton University Press, 1994.

MEIR LITVAK

ḤIRĀBAH. The Arabic term *ḥirābah*, from the root *ḥ-r-b* meaning "to wage war," is defined in the Qur'ān as "corruption in the land." Referred to as the *ḥirābah* verse, 5:33–34 clearly stipulates the possible punishments for the crime of *ḥirābah*, which can include execution, crucifixion, severance of limbs, or exile, but leaves undefined the precise elements or behaviors that constitute the crime itself. Because of this omission, the term *ḥirābah* has always been characterized by definitional ambiguity and subject to varied interpretation.

The *ḥirābah* verse has been read to include highway robbery, piracy, rebellion, sedition, and, most recently, terrorism. Indeed, in the post–September 11 era, the term has been used to distinguish terrorism from *jihād*. Advocates of this usage hope to preserve the nonviolent denotations attached to the word "*jihād*" while simultaneously preventing Islamic terrorists from coopting and misusing religious phraseology to justify their terrorist acts.

Historically Muslim scholars have disagreed over the precise definition and the intended subjects of the *ḥirābah* verse, with some jurists insisting that it could apply to polytheists and apostates who waged war on Muslims and exegetes insisting that it applied only to Muslims who committed certain egregious acts. Complicating the disagreement were the many conflicting reports (sing., *ḥadīth*, the second of the law's sources) about the verse's occasion of revelation. By the twelfth and thirteenth centuries the dominant legal position circumscribed the crime of *ḥirābah* as applying to Muslims engaged in the act of brigandage or highway robbery. By settling on a narrow definition, the Muslim jurists hoped to ensure that the particularly grievous punishments associated with *ḥirābah* were applied only to a small category of vicious criminals. Historical records suggest that certain Islamic rulers, including some Umayyad and 'Abbāsid caliphs, applied the condemnatory language and harsh penalties of the *ḥirābah* verse to their political opponents—so-called "rebels"—whose misdeeds should have been covered under the less severe laws of rebellion (*aḥkām al-bughāh*).

The jurisprudence (*fiqh*) underlying the crime of *ḥirābah*, at least as articulated by the early jurists, is complex but tends to advocate punishments commensurate with and at times identical to the particular crime committed. Accordingly most Sunnī schools of law held that if a murder was committed in the process of a highway robbery, the robber must be not only killed, but crucified; if a robber unlawfully seized property, the robber's limbs must be amputated from opposite ends; and if a criminal inflicted terror but without causing death or stealing property, the criminal must be exiled. Despite the harshness of these penalties, clemency was permitted under the laws of *ḥirābah* if the criminal repented prior to his capture. For an explanation of the different schools' approaches, see Peters 2005.

While defining *ḥirābah* in ways typical of earlier jurists, some nineteenth- and twentieth-century Muslim thinkers expanded the term's meaning to encompass an even broader variety of crimes. Muḥammad ʿAbduh (d. 1905) and Rashīd Riḍā (d. 1935), for example, viewed *ḥirābah* as not only a threat to public security, but also as a threat to the sanctity of Islamic law. Riḍā in particular emphasized that *ḥirābah* is the crime of arming oneself for the purpose of preventing the application of religious law. Similarly for the Islamist Sayyid Quṭb (d. 1966) *ḥirābah* involved opposition to legitimate Muslim authority.

After the September 11 attacks on the United States, some scholars established a linkage between *ḥirābah* and domestic terrorism. While notable differences between the two legal categories do exist, such as *ḥirābah*'s broader scope, many similarities characterize the two terms, including their mutual elements of intimidation, spreading fear, and, as the fourteenth-century Ḥanbalī jurist Taqi al-Dīn ibn Taymīyah pointed out, helplessness. Moreover *ḥirābah*, like modern-day terrorism, is defined by "publicly directed violence" and the severest of punishments (Jackson 2001). The strict evidentiary requirements for a *ḥadd* (pl., *ḥudūd*) crime, of which *ḥirābah* is one, such as Muslim male eye-witness testimony or a confession to the crimes, might be the reason for trying cases of domestic terrorism instead as crimes of "corruption in the land," as has happened in several instances in Saudi Arabia, one of the few Muslim countries that still applies Islamic law.

[*See also* Combat; *and* Rebellion.]

BIBLIOGRAPHY

El Fadl, Khaled Abou. "Rebellion." In *Encyclopaedia of the Qurʾān*, edited by Jane Dammen McAuliffe. Leiden, Netherlands: Brill, 2007.

Guirard, James. "Ḥirābah Versus Jihad: Rescuing Jihad from the al-Qaeda Blasphemy." *The American Muslim*, July 6, 2003. http://theamericanmuslim.org/tam.php/features/articles/terrorism_ḥirābah_versus_jihad_rescuing_jihad_from_the_al_qaeda_blasphemy/.

Jackson, Sherman A. "Domestic Terrorism in the Islamic Legal Tradition." *The Muslim World* 91, nos. 3–4 (2001): 293–310.

Peters, Rudolph. *Crime and Punishment in Islamic Law: Theory and Practice from the Sixteenth to the Twenty-First Century*. Cambridge, U.K., and New York: Cambridge University Press, 2005.

Vogel, Frank. "The Trial of Terrorists Under Classical Islamic Law." *Harvard International Law Journal* 43, no. 1 (2002): 53–64.

Chrystie Flournoy Swiney
Updated by Peri Bearman

Ḥisbah. The term *ḥisbah* largely refers to the jurisdiction of a legal official, the *muḥtasib*, who was appointed in Muslim societies historically (and in a very few places in the modern period) to carry out the duty to command right and forbid wrong on behalf of the appointing ruler. While *muḥtasib* is often rendered "market inspector," this is too narrow a translation, because the *muḥtasib* had jurisdiction over all public spaces: "inspector of public places" is more precise. Some scholars—notably al-Māwardī (d. 1058) in *al-Aḥkām al-sulṭānīyah* and al-Ghazālī (d. 1111) in his magnum opus *Iḥyāʾ ʿulūm al-dīn*—used the term *ḥisbah* synonymously with "commanding right and forbidding wrong," even though technically the function of *ḥisbah* refers only to appointed officials and not to Muslims who undertake the duty as individuals. As a result, modern scholarship sometimes defines *ḥisbah* as both the duty of the individual Muslim and the jurisdiction of the appointed official.

The origins of the concepts of *ḥisbah* and *muḥtasib* are uncertain. The standard account of the *muḥtasib*'s origins focuses on market regulation, beginning with the assumption that, in pre-Islamic Arabia, markets had their own regulatory and dispute-resolution mechanisms. These markets continued in the early Islamic period, and others developed that also needed regulation. The Prophet reportedly appointed people to monitor the markets in Medina—including a woman—under the title *ʿāmil al-sūq* (guardian of the market) or the virtual synonym *ʿāmil ʿalā al-sūq*. The Umayyads took the concept of the market inspector with them, and thus, in the Umayyad-era sources of the Islamic west, the position appears as *ṣāḥib al-sūq*. The standard account of origins then suggests that in an effort to "Islamize" the institutions of the Umayyads, the ʿAbbāsids gave wide-ranging powers to what had mainly been a market-inspecting position and connected it to the broader Qurʾānic notion of commanding right and forbidding wrong. Linking the term *muḥtasib* to the Qurʾānic concept was thus a later development, intended to infuse the position with a broad Islamic component. The position continued in the central and eastern Islamic lands under this name, flourishing in the Fāṭimid (909–1171), Ayyūbid (1174–1250), and Mamlūk (1250–1517) eras in particular. This account is not entirely persuasive. The term *muḥtasib* may be as early as its synonym *ṣāḥib al-sūq*, as Patricia Crone has argued. Furthermore the claim that market regulation under the *ṣāḥib al-sūq* was purely commercial and not infused with legal and ethical concerns derived from the Qurʾān, ignores the existence of juridical opinions on marketplace behavior, many of which are based on Qurʾānic verses that require fair dealings when using weights and measures.

The origins of the terminology are also uncertain. An earlier prominent view believed that *ṣāḥib al-sūq* is the Arabic translation of the Greek term *agoranomos* (market inspector), an official in cities charged with checking for fraud in the market and watching over temples that were located in the market areas. Under this theory the Arabs found this position to be a useful one and retained it, although with an Arabic name. Benjamin Foster, however, has traced carefully the use of the term *agoranomos* in pre-Islamic Egypt, Syria, and Palestine to show that its usage in the sense of market inspector had ceased around the end of the third century. The root of the terms *ḥisbah* and *muḥtasib* (and the related verb *iḥtasaba*) suggests that the act is done for God, without personal or worldly motives (see Cook, 2000, p. 448 and n. 136). Yet an appointed *muḥtasib* typically received a salary from the treasury (or compensation from the merchants) and so did receive a tangible benefit.

The most thorough theoretical treatment of the position of *muḥtasib* by a premodern author is al-Māwardī's treatise *al-Aḥkām al-sulṭānīyah*. Al-Māwardī was interested in the substance of the *muḥtasib*'s duties as well as in the larger concepts of the position's jurisdiction, and he depicted the jurisdiction of the *muḥtasib* as standing between that of a judge and the sultan (see Stilt, 2011, p. 42–47). One salient distinction is that, unlike the judge, the *muḥtasib* does not need to wait for a complainant to appear before acting; the official may act on his own initiative to command or forbid on the basis of any public event (but may not, with some exceptions, spy in order to carry out his work). The *muḥtasib* as an individual should be knowledgeable enough in matters of Islamic law so that he knows what acts are agreed upon as prohibited or required, but the *muḥtasib* does not need to be familiar with juridical differences because he should not, on his own accord, enforce matters of disagreement. Al-Māwardī's description of the *muḥtasib* also included other general understandings about the position, such as punishment power: the *muḥtasib* has broad enforcement mechanisms at his disposal, including verbal chastisement and physical punishment, but in punishing corporally, the official is limited to discretionary punishment (*taʿzīr*) and may not carry out the *ḥadd* penalties (unless instructed to do so by a competent official).

A genre of literature developed to guide *muḥtasib*s in their work. The authors of these manuals were not typically well known as jurists; rather, they seem to have had enough knowledge of Islamic law alongside a good sense of the practices in the marketplace to write these instructional manuals, which typically listed the qualifications for the person serving as *muḥtasib*, described the official's areas of duties, cautioned against specific types of fraud and how to detect them, and suggested means of punishment. (See the three Mamlūk-era manuals in the bibliography.)

The practice of the *muḥtasib* is an important yet understudied topic. Most of the research of this kind has been focused on Mamlūk Egypt due to the availability of source materials. In Mamlūk Cairo and Fustat the *muḥtasib*s took action in a wide range of substantive areas, including Muslim devotional and pious practices, serious crimes and minor offenses, the public behavior of Christians and Jews, market regulation and consumer protection, currency, taxes, and public order generally. While the office in Cairo and Fustat was filled in the early Mamlūk period by jurists and individuals with administrative experience in the sultanate, over time the position was also held by individuals whose main credentials were connections to the rulers, and then *mamlūk* soldiers and even the sultan himself held the position toward of the end of the period.

[*See also* Commanding Right and Forbidding Wrong; *and* Māwardī, Abū al-Ḥasan al-.]

BIBLIOGRAPHY

Primary Works

Ibn Bassām, Muḥammad ibn Aḥmad. *Nihāyat al-rutbah fī ṭalab al-ḥisba*. Edited by Ḥusām al-Dīn al-Sāmarrāʾī. Baghdad: Maṭbaʿat al-Maʿārif, 1968. An instructional manual for the *muḥtasib*.

Ibn al-Ukhūwah, Muḥammad ibn Muḥammad. *Maʿālim al-qurbah fī aḥkām al-ḥisba*. Edited by Muḥammad Maḥmūd Shaʿbān and Ṣiddīq Aḥmad ʿĪsā al-Muṭīʿī. Cairo: al-Hayʾa al-Miṣriyya al-ʿĀmma li-l-Kitāb, 1976. Also edited under same title with an English abstract of contents, glossary, and indices by Reuben Levy (Cambridge, U.K.: Cambridge University Press for the E. J. W. Gibb Memorial Trust, 1938). An instructional manual for the *muḥtasib*.

Shayzarī, ʿAbd al-Raḥmān ibn Naṣr al-. *Kitāb Nihāyat al-rutbah fī ṭalab al-ḥisba*. Edited by al-Sayyid al-Bāz al-ʿArīnī (Cairo: Lajnat al-Taʾlīf wa-l-Tarjama wa-l-Nashr, 1946). Translated by R. P. Buckley as *The Book of the Islamic Market Inspector = Nihāyat al-rutba fī ṭalab al-ḥisba: The Utmost Authority in the Pursuit of Ḥisba* (Oxford: Oxford University Press, 1999). An instructional manual for the *muḥtasib*.

Secondary Works

Cook, Michael. *Commanding Right and Forbidding Wrong in Islamic Thought*. Cambridge, U.K., and New York: Cambridge University Press, 2000.

Crone, Patricia. *Roman, Provincial and Islamic Law: The Origins of the Islamic Patronate*. Cambridge, U.K., and New York: Cambridge University Press, 1987.

Foster, Benjamin R. "Agoranomos and Muḥtasib." *Journal of the Economic and Social History of the Orient* 13 (1970): 128–144.

"Ḥisba." In *Encyclopaedia of Islam*, 2d ed. Edited by P. J. Bearman, et al. Leiden, Netherlands: Brill, 1960–2004.

Stilt, Kristen A. *Islamic Law in Action: Authority, Discretion, and Everyday Experiences in Mamluk Egypt*. Oxford: Oxford University Press, 2011.

Abdul Rahman I. Doi
Updated by Kristen A. Stilt

Historiography. The political history of early Islam has often informed subsequent theological and sectarian disputes. The critical evaluation of the relationship between history, historical writing, and politics investigates also claims of identity, legitimacy, authenticity, and relations of power. In this synoptic essay, I begin by examining some of the trends of classical and medieval Islamic historiography, followed by a brief discussion of modern scholarship on early Islamic history, after which I conclude with methodological remarks on historiography by turning to the relationship between Islam and politics in modern contexts.

Muslims historians produced voluminous works that should be counted among the textual sources through which cultural literacy was articulated and disseminated. In fact history was a popular topic animating scholarly conversations in premodern Islam: "Historical events and anecdotes were frequently the topic of conversations and dictation in circles of learned men" (Robinson, 2003, p. 116). In this way historical writing "was richly compensated for its theoretical inferiority by the domination it exercised over the minds of the young and the thinking of men of political influence and general culture. And the Muslim historians had the right to feel and, as a rule, did feel confident about the value of their work" (Rosenthal, 1968, p. 53). For early Muslim historians, the writing of history was "a kind of narrative practice" (Robinson, 2003, p. 6) in which they invoked the paradigm of world history.

The earliest forms of historical reports were transmitted orally, implying that attention was given to archiving those narratives and memories of the past that were immediately relevant. Because early Muslim historiography relied so heavily on oral reports, it cannot be understood as a discourse independent of the political realities prevalent in the Umayyad and the ʿAbbāsid caliphates. As Chase Robinson notes, "Whereas written history *can* be made to conform closely to the imperative of the present, oral history *always* conforms to it" (Robinson, 2003, p. 10). On the one hand, oral transmission allowed for a greater flexibility in the retrieval of memory, enabling reporters and their audiences to improvise historical narratives for specific purposes. But on the other hand, because of this flexible tendency it became easier for the ruling elite to invoke and canonize only those narratives that legitimated their sovereignty.

According to Robinson, historiography was largely a political instrument in early Islam in at least two senses. First, "The spectacular success of empire building during the seventh and eighth centuries created a market of readers hungry for historical narrative, especially several forms of chronography, which offered lessons and models to rulers, their courts and urban elite; and this market survived the breakup of the empire during the tenth and eleventh centuries, when many successor states rationalized their experience of political power by patronizing local historiography" (Robinson, 2003, p. 188). Second, many traditionists were "enthusiastic about those historiographic forms that reinforced traditionist institutions (especially the schools of law) and attitudes (especially reverence for the Prophet Muhammad, whose model they claimed to transmit)" (Robinson, 2003, p. 188).

It is important to note that the various interpretations of the Qurʾān, the Prophet Muḥammad's example, and the schools of jurisprudence originating in the eighth and ninth centuries did not always mediate exclusively the relationship between governance and religion in the history of Islam. Muslim rulers also relied on local customs, precedents from Roman or Persian legal codes, the discourses of literary and aesthetic moral education (*adab*), and translations of ancient texts on classical political philosophy, especially the texts of Plato and Aristotle. The history of political theology in Islam is marked by the seeming tensions between a state grounded in reason and a state founded on divine law. These tensions not only characterized classical and medieval Muslim political theology but they also form the conceptual nexus on which modern and contemporary versions of Muslim political theology are proposed, enforced, and contested.

Early Muslim rulers conceived of history as a source of political wisdom. Robinson calls this role of history as the "didactic function of historiography in the world of politics" wherein chronological and annalistic history encompassed "lessons to teach about everything from just rulership to administrative geography" (Robinson, 2003, p. 115). History was also used for purposes of verifying reports of legal norms coming down from the Prophet Muḥammad and the foundational generations of Muslims. For political practice this meant that a legal policy could be contested if the religious intelligentsia found fault with its chain of transmission. Thus the famous legal scholar of the ninth century, Aḥmad ibn Ḥanbal (d. 855), was skeptical of reports pertaining to the *maghāzī* (battles) because the transmissions of these reports did not meet his criteria for sound transmission. However, the objections of religious authorities did not necessarily imply that the ruling elites paid any heed to their protestations. In fact when such objections posed a threat to the legitimacy of the ruling elite, the rulers employed history to counter their opponents. As Robinson points out, "historiography offered a medium through which states could broadcast claims about the past, present or future, legitimize themselves and undermine their critics" (Robinson, 2003, p. 119).

One of the central questions that has preoccupied modern historians of Islam concerns the origin and function of the premodern political imaginary. Historians such as Ira M. Lapidus contextualize where Islam converged with and diverged from other contemporaneous Near Eastern ideological forces "The formation of the Islamic community in Arabia established in a hitherto marginal region a type of religious polity which had already been created under Jewish, Christian, and Zoroastrian auspices throughout the Middle East" (Lapidus, 1988, p. 36). The political effects of Muḥammad's preaching and his followers did not happen in an historical vacuum; rather they contributed to making the inhabitants of the Arabian peninsula claim their own form of "universal confessional religion" and "political unity" (Lapidus, 1988, p. 36). Modern historians of Islam have spilt much ink on the nature of the Islamic state. It is safe to say that during the caliphal period (632–661), Muslim society was not organized around a centralized government akin to the state.

On Patricia Crone's reading, for early Muslims "truth and power appeared at the same times in history and regulated the same aspects of life," though this conviction of theirs became untenable with "post-conquest developments" (Crone, 2004, p. 16). For Crone early Islam assumed religion, state, and society as identical collective experiences. After six centuries of Muslim rule governance and religion had diverged from each other a great deal. As Crone explains,

> The Shariʿa did cover the caliphate, holy war, taxation and other aspects of public organization, but its rules on these subjects were commonly ignored, and there was in any case a good deal more than that to politics. Government now formed an almost completely detached

> circle of its own, devoted to the upkeep of Islam but not generated by it. But as far as society (or at least urban society) was concerned, the overlap remained almost total. Insofar as one can tell, society continued to be based largely on the Shariʿʿa in respect of marriage, divorce, succession, and commercial transactions, an admixture of customary law notwithstanding; and it continued to display its loyalty in visible ritual law. (Crone, 2004, p. 396)

Giving an alternative account, Muhammad Qasim Zaman examines closely the relationship between religion and the ʿAbbāsid state to suggest that the caliphs themselves took part in the construction of "proto-Sunni trends." Zaman argues that official state patronage and self-alignment with the religious authorities "crystallized in the reign of Harūn al-Rashīd" (Zaman, 1997, p. 11). At about the same time in ʿAbbāsid society, there emerged the beginnings of what Zaman calls a "pattern of collaboration between the caliphs and the *ʿulamāʾ*" (Zaman, 1997, p. 12). Religious authorities expected the caliphs to be involved in religious matters, as is exemplified in al-Maʾmūn's *Miḥna*. This trend of collaboration makes it hard to accept Crone's thesis that gradually religion and state went their separate ways. Zaman's more recent work has shown how in contemporary times the *ʿulamāʾ* continue to exercise considerable political authority in Muslim states and have become "custodians of change" (see Zaman, 2002).

Let us now consider two examples of contemporary historiographical methods in the study of Islamic history. Our first example shows that the task before historians of Islam and politics requires of them to think about the macrohistorical framework that comes as a given with Islam and the microhistorical context in which substantial and useful analyses find their historical data. A rigorous thinking of the universals and particulars of history can only happen when we turn our attention to situated histories of specific contexts. For example, in the case of the Sudan the work of scholars such as Abdullahi A. Gallab, Abdel Salam Sidahmed, Gabriel Warburg, and Kim Searcy has taught us the importance of examining current political phenomena and practices in wider historical, socioeconomic, and political frameworks that pay attention to historical relations of power, especially colonialism. When we examine Islamism in the Sudan we find that concepts such as fundamentalism lack the rigor required to paint a comprehensive portrait of the political landscape of that country. We have to pay attention to civil wars, droughts, the implementation of religious economic reforms (Islamic banking), regime changes, the question of minority rights (given Sudan's significant Christian population), and the historical struggles against colonialism that took their inspiration from Ṣūfī fellowships rather than Salafī texts (Sudan's Mahdist revival in the late nineteenth century).

Our second example will illustrate that before, during, and after the age of colonialism, Muslims have not always had the privilege of embodying religious observance under Muslim states. Therefore we should incorporate within the purview of the historiography of Islam and politics those cases in which Muslims negotiated their religious identity outside Islamdom. To take but one example, let us travel to Tsarist Russia and the work of scholars such as Adeeb Khalid and Robert D. Crews. Around the year 1900 there were approximately 20 million Muslims in the Russian Empire, making up "the largest non-Orthodox group" (Crews, 2006, p. 1). The complex history of Russia's Muslim populations from 1613–1917 (the years of the Romanov dynasty) precludes simple conclusions regarding the relationship between the tsarist state and its Muslim subjects. There were instances in which the Romanovs saw their Muslims subjects as an internal threat and forced harsh policies or outright expulsion upon such subjects. But as Crews argues, expulsion was not the modus operandi of the tsarist state in dealing with its Muslim minorities. Rather the Romanovs grounded their own authority in religion. The relationship between the tsarist regime and Muslims became dialectical, one in which imperial authority and local religious authority collaborated to secure social and political order. Thus the history of Muslims in non-Muslim lands shows that the antagonistic relationship between Muslim minorities and non-Muslim states was often transcended by collaborative negotiations. In the case of Tsarist Russia Muslims looked toward the state to secure the sanctity of Islamic law in everyday life. As Crews notes, "Petitions, denunciations, court records, police reports, and numerous Muslim sources reveal how, within the broader framework of tsarist toleration, Muslim men and women came to imagine the imperial state as a potential instrument of God's will" (Crews, 2006, p. 20). The specific ways in which Muslims inhabited everyday life in the multinational Romanov empire shows that "Islam and Muslim culture. . . are far from immutable characteristics; rather, they change and evolve and do so through debate and the struggle of different groups in Muslim society" (Khalid, 1998, p. xiii).

My two modern examples emphasize distinct points that underscore the value of a hermeneutic of difference when it comes to the demands of historiography. Chase Robinson's illuminating words emphasize how historical writing is always more than the mere notation of data: "History writing is a potent source of legitimacy and criticism not simply because it can deliver particular versions or reconstructions of the past. It can also reflect (or impose) ways of thinking about time, about change, about how the individual relates to the state, and the state to the world" (Robinson, 2003, p. 121).

BIBLIOGRAPHY

Black, Antony. *History of Islamic Political Thought: From the Prophet to the Present*. Edinburgh: Edinburgh University Press, 2001.

Crews, Robert D. *For Prophet and Tsar: Islam and Empire in Russia and Central Asia*. Cambridge, Mass.: Harvard University Press, 2006.

Crone, Patricia. *God's Rule: Government, and Islam Thought*. New York: Columbia University Press, 2004.

El-Hibri, Tayeb. *Parable and Politics in Early Islamic History: The Rashidun Caliphs*. New York: Columbia University Press, 2010.

Gallab, Abdullahi A. *The First Islamist Republic: Development and Disintegration of Islamism in the Sudan*. Burlington, Vt.: Ashgate, 2008.

Khalid, Adeeb. *The Politics of Muslim Cultural Reform: Jadidism in Central Asia*. Berkeley: University of California Press, 1998.

Khalidi, Tarif. *Arabic Historical Thought in the Classical Period*. Cambridge, U.K., and New York: Cambridge University Press, 1994.

Khalidi, Tarif. *Islamic Historiography: The Histories of Masʿūdī*. Albany: State University of New York Press, 1975.

Lapidus, Ira M. *A History of Islamic Societies*. Cambridge, U.K., and New York: Cambridge University Press, 1988.

Masʿūdī, Abū al-Ḥasan ʿAlī al-. *Murūj al-dhahab wa-maʿādin al-jawhar*. 4 vols. Edited by Mufīd Muḥammad Qumayḥah. Beirut: Dār al-Kutub al-ʿArabiyyah, 1990.

Noth, Albrecht, and Lawrence I. Conrad. *The Early Arabic Historical Tradition: A Source-Critical Study*. Translated by Michael Bonner. 2d ed. Princeton, N.J.: Darwin Press, 1994.

Robinson, Chase F. *Islamic Historiography*. Cambridge, U.K., and New York: Cambridge University Press, 2003.

Rosenthal, Franz. *A History of Muslim Historiography*. 2d ed. rev. Leiden: E. J. Brill, 1968.

Searcy, Kim. *The Formation of the Sudanese Mahdist State: Ceremony and Symbols of Authority: 1882–1898*. Leiden, Netherlands, and New York: E. J. Brill, 2011.

Sidahmed, Abdel Salam. *Politics and Islam in Contemporary Sudan*. New York: St. Martin's Press, 1997.

Warburg, Gabriel. *Islam, Sectarianism, and Politics in Sudan since the Mahdiyya*. London: Hurst, 2003.

Wellhausen, Julius. *The Arab Kingdom and its Fall*. Translated by Margaret Graham Weir. Calcutta: The University of Calcutta, 1927; reprinted New York: Routledge, 2000.

Zaman, Muhammad Qasim. *Religion and Politics under the Early ʿAbbāsids: The Emergence of the Proto-Sunnī Elite*. Leiden, Netherlands, and New York: E. J. Brill, 1997.

Zaman, Muhammad Qasim. *The Ulama in Contemporary Islam: Custodians of Change*. Princeton, N.J.: Princeton University Press, 2002.

ALI ALTAF MIAN

ḤIZB AL-ʿADĀLAH WA-AL-TANMIYAH.

See Justice and Development Party.

ḤIZB AL-DAʿWAH AL-ISLĀMĪYAH.

Daʿwah for short, Ḥizb al-Daʿwah al-Islāmīyah is the party of Iraq's first two elected prime ministers after the fall of Saddam Hussein in 2003, namely Ibrāhīm Jaʿfarī and Nouri al-Maliki. The first predominantly Shīʿī Islamist party in Iraq, Daʿwah was organized in Najaf in October 1957 by a small group of junior religious scholars and pious laymen. Ideologically progressive and inclusive, the party has advocated the concept of *wilāyat al-ummah* (governance of the people), as outlined by its spiritual leader, Muḥammad Bāqir al-Ṣadr (1935–1980). This concept is at odds with the notion of *wilāyat al-faqih* (governance of the jurist) championed by Ruhollah Khomeini and enshrined in the constitution of the Islamic Republic of Iran. Daʿwah membership has consisted primarily of an intellectual elite.

Worried by increasing secularism and the popularity of Western ideas among Iraqi society, Daʿwah set out to "call" the people to Islam through education in preparation for the ultimate aim of forming an Islamic state. The party successfully won over many young intellectuals through the promotion of Islamic social justice as a counter to the appeal of communism in Baghdad's huge al-Thawra slum (later renamed Saddam City, then Sadr City). By the late 1960s Daʿwah had spread to other parts of the Middle East, notably Lebanon and the Persian Gulf monarchies. From this network of affiliated groups evolved several other Shīʿī parties.

In Iraq the Baʿthist government that took power in 1968 cracked down on religious institutions. Daʿwah became the target of persecution, with the execution of ʿAbd al-Ṣāḥib Dakhail in 1971 and five senior members in 1974, including the group's operational leader Shaykh ʿĀrif al-Baṣrī. Confrontation intensified during the so-called Safar uprising of 1977, when Daʿwah used its mobilizing power to rally about thirty thousand worshipers in defiance of a government ban on a march to commemorate the anniversary of the martyrdom of Imam Ḥusayn. Several marchers were killed and hundreds arrested. In June 1979 the detention under house arrest of Muḥammad Bāqir al-Ṣadr triggered large demonstrations, and in April 1980 the ayatollah and his sister Bint al-Hudā were executed.

State oppression, as well as the revolution in neighboring Iran in 1979, emboldened Daʿwah to adopt more militant tactics against the Iraqi regime. While under house arrest Ayatollah Bāqir al-Ṣadr had issued calls for armed struggle, along with a *fatwa* prohibiting Iraqi Shīʿī from joining the Baʿth Party. The government's harsh crackdown on Daʿwah forced most of the party into exile. Branches were established in Tehran, Damascus, and in the late 1980s, London, but clandestine cells remained in Iraq. Activists carried out attacks against government targets in Iraq, including the assassination attempts against Foreign Minister Tariq Aziz in April 1980, Saddam Hussein in 1982, and his son Uday in 1996. The interests of pro-Iraqi governments abroad, mainly in Kuwait, were also targeted. After the Iran–Iraq War (1980–1988) Daʿwah stopped all armed activities outside Iraq.

The Gulf War (1990–1991) and its aftermath opened possibilities for dialogue and cooperation between various Iraqi opposition groups, as well as with Western governments and their Arab allies such as Saudi Arabia. Daʿwah participated in conferences in Beirut in December 1990 and March 1991, and in Ṣalāḥ al-Dīn in October 1992, but by the mid-1990s it had withdrawn from the Iraqi National Congress.

Several splits marked the history of Daʿwah in exile, due mainly to the Islamic Republic of Iran and its model of government, and the balance of power between clerics and laymen in the party. When the Supreme Council for the Islamic Revolution in Iraq (SCIRI) was formed in 1982, as an umbrella for Iraqi opposition groups under Ayatollah Khomeini's patronage, some Daʿwah members joined the new organization, including the splinter group al-Daʿwah al-Islāmīyah led by ʿAbd al-Zahra ʿUthmān (best known as ʿIzz al-Dīn Salīm). Other activists advocated independence and created the Tehran branch. A number also left for Damascus, London, and elsewhere. The erosion of the power of senior (pro-Iran) *ʿulamāʾ* in Daʿwah started in 1984, with the abolition of the party's Majlis al-Fuqahā (Council of Jurists). In 1987 a dispute over the powers of Sayyid Kāẓim al-Hāʾirī, then spiritual adviser of Daʿwah, led him and some followers to leave the party.

After Iraq's Baʿthist government was ousted, Daʿwah opened dozens of offices. With its large splinter group the Daʿwah Party–Iraq Organization, it took part in post-sovereignty governments, advocating a democratic, federal, and unified Iraq with the provinces to be determined geographically, rather than ethnically. It has supported a government run by the laity in accordance with the tenets of Islam, as recommended by Ayatollah ʿAlī al-Sīstānī and Muḥammad Bāqir al-Ṣadr before him. Former exiles Ibrāhīm Jaʿfarī and Nouri al-Maliki have served successively as Iraq's prime minister from 2005, the former deciding to form his own party after a Daʿwah conference held in April 2007 elected al-Maliki as the party's secretary general.

Like other Islamic groups, Ḥizb al-Daʿwah al-Islāmīyah has proved its capacity to adapt to, and take advantage of, the political changes it has faced throughout its existence. Its striving for independence, sustained by a strong commitment to Iraq, has contributed to its identity as an Islamist-nationalist party.

BIBLIOGRAPHY

Dai, Yamao. "Transformation of the Islamic Daʿwa Party in Iraq: From the Revolutionary Period to the Diaspora Era." *Asian and African Area Studies* 7, no. 2 (2008): 238–267.

Islamic Dawa Party official website. http://www.islamicdawaparty.com/.

Shanahan, Rodger. "Shiʿa Political Development in Iraq: The Case of the Islamic Daʿwa Party." *Third World Quarterly* 25, no. 5 (2004): 943–954.

Wiley, Joyce N. *The Islamic Movement of Iraqi Shiʿas.* Boulder, Colo.: Lynne Rienner, 1992.

Amatzia Baram
Updated by Joyce N. Baram
and Elvire Corboz

Ḥizb al-Nahḍah. Formerly called al-Ittijāh al-Islāmī (Mouvement de la Tendance Islamique [MTI]), the political movement that adopted the name Ḥarakat al-Nahḍah (Renaissance Movement) in 1988 was the banned representative group of Islamist thought and political expression in contemporary Tunisia. The movement's relations with the government of President Zine el Abidine Ben Ali was contentious, but survived successive waves of repression. It was thought to have the diffuse support of as much as one-third of the Tunisian population. In the aftermath of the Jasmine Revolution that toppled the Ben Ali regime, the interim government in Tunis granted the group permission to reconstitute a legal political party, Ḥizb al-Nahḍah, on 1 March 2011.

The contemporary Islamist movement traced its roots to the Qurʾānic Preservation Society

(QPS), a cultural association founded in 1970 in reaction to modernist reforms promulgated in the 1960s, and to the Pakistan-based Daʿwah (The Call), which spread across the Maghrib in the early 1970s, "calling" Muslims to return to the faith. Out of this group emerged a nexus of activists who were satisfied with neither the cultural critique of the QPS nor the more personal approach of the Daʿwah, but who focused rather on the role of Islam in society and openly preached reform (*tajdīd*). As these sentiments sorted themselves out in the 1970s, young men with beards and women in the chador-like *ḥijāb* (veil) became a common sight in Tunis and other cities. By 1979 one group identifying itself as "progressive Islamists" and concentrating on the renewal of Islamic thought (*ijtihād*) had split off to pursue essentially intellectual matters. The energies of those who sought political action coalesced around Rāshid al-Ghannūshī (Rashid Ghannoushi) and Abdelfatah Mourou. Al-Ghannūshī, who studied in Damascus between 1964 and 1968, returned to Tunis in 1970 after a year in France. Along with Sadiq Shourou, a jurist who was a fellow student at the Zaytūnah University in Tunis, al-Ghannūshī announced the formation of the MTI at a press conference in April 1981, where they called for the reconstruction of economic life on a more equitable basis, the end of single-party politics, and a return to the "fundamental principles of Islam" through a purging of what was viewed as well-entrenched "social decadence." Furthermore, MTI representatives announced that they were seeking recognition as a political party according to guidelines established by the government in the preceding autumn. That request was denied, and less than two months later most of the MTI's leaders were imprisoned. Al-Ghannūshī and several of his followers were sentenced to eleven years in prison in Bizerte.

Despite this repression—or perhaps because of it—the MTI survived and even gained strength in the early 1980s. It found allies in other Tunisian opposition forces, including the Movement of Democratic Socialists and the new Tunisian League of Human Rights, and its discourse took on egalitarian and republican overtones. Under pressure the Tunisian government released MTI leaders in 1984, but its basic stance remained unchanged. The MTI's second bid for legal recognition was rejected in 1985, and, in a symbolic gesture, the government outlawed the *ḥijāb* in state-run institutions. As the MTI's condemnatory rhetoric once again gathered steam, Tunis intensified its efforts in the spring of 1987 to eradicate the movement, arresting more than three thousand of its alleged supporters. The party's leaders were tried en masse before the State Security Court in August for ill-defined capital crimes, and several were sentenced to death in absentia. Al-Ghannūshī was sentenced to a life term, but was released a year later.

The specter of politically motivated executions and uncontrollable social responses created a backdrop for the coup instigated by Prime Minister Zine el Abidine Ben Ali a few months later. Islamists were the primary beneficiaries of the liberalizing policies introduced by the new regime. As prisons were emptied, a multiparty system embraced, and the franchise restored to those who had previously been imprisoned, an atmosphere of détente raised hopes among Islamists that they would be allowed to participate in the political system. To comply with new rules prohibiting parties from capitalizing on religious sentiments, the MTI changed its name.

The renamed Ḥarakat al-Nahḍah reached a turning point in relations with the new regime in April 1989. Without legal recognition Islamists were prevented from participating openly in Tunisia's first contested legislative elections, but the independent slates they fielded nevertheless garnered 14 percent of the popular vote (30 percent in certain Tunis suburbs) and sent shock waves through the government. Al-Nahḍah's pending request for recognition was denied, educational reforms aimed at curtailing Islamist influence were implemented, and the movement's remaining leaders in Tunisia were taken in for questioning. Tensions were exacerbated by the war for Kuwait, which aggravated anti-Western sentiments, and the growing influence of the Islamists in neighboring Algeria. The death of one Islamist student, shot by government militia during a demonstration, sparked protests that inspired a new wave of arrests and further restrictions. Al-Ghannūshī went into self-exile in London. An assault allegedly by Islamists on an office of the ruling Democratic Constitutional Rally (RCD) in February 1991, which killed one guard and injured another, heightened the political confrontation. Al-Nahḍah's formal responsibility for that attack was never made clear, but together with the discovery in subsequent months of two alleged plots to overthrow the government, the event fueled a campaign of repression that resulted in more than eight thousand arrests. In 1992, 279 al-Nahḍah members were tried before military tribunals; leaders in the government's custody were sentenced to life in prison.

It is unclear how much al-Nahḍah was affected by the far-reaching efforts to stifle it under Ben Ali. To be sure, its leadership changed, and while Rāshid al-Ghannūshī was still formally recognized as the head of al-Nahḍah in 1993 Shourou formally dissociated himself from the unauthorized party in 1991 following the attack on the RCD office. A new cadre of leaders emerged, and the government claimed to have uncovered a covert military wing. Meanwhile *al-Fajr*, the al-Nahḍah publication that was to have illuminated its thought, was silenced.

Concerted pressures in the early 1990s made al-Nahḍah less visible; in particular many young women ceased to wear the symbolic *ḥijāb*. There has been evidence all the same that the Islamist movement continues to enjoy popular support—perhaps more than ever in the wake of disappointment with the Ben Ali government. A membership once described as young and chiefly comprised of students has now aged, without obvious attrition. Students, particularly those in religious and technical institutes, continued to supply recruits, but the Islamist message of social and political resistance and reform resonated in the humanities and social sciences as well. The movement held particular appeal for sectors of society that felt relatively disenfranchised by the modernist regime, and economic pressures in recent years only increased those sentiments. Parents and others of an older generation were now commonly identified as sympathizers, and the movement was largely supported from abroad by a broad network of Tunisian students. It remained the most significant opposition group in contemporary Tunisia until early 2011.

After Ben Ali was ousted al-Ghannūshī returned to Tunisia on 30 January 2011. Rapidly unfolding political developments in the North African country meant that the party was coerced by die-hard supporters to "quickly carve out a place" in the Tunisian political scene by "taking part in demonstrations and meeting with the prime minister." Still progress was slow because al-Ghannūshī's network was no longer credible and, equally important, because Tunisians were no longer willing to simply follow. Many were impatient with promises made by both opposition and official representatives. Others, especially women, were not ready to surrender significant social gains made during the Ben Ali years. Although al-Nahḍah was legalized on 1 March 2011, and ranked first in polls conducted at that time, its overall popularity stood at less than 30 percent, with the Progressive Democratic Party at 12.3 percent.

[*See also* Ghannūshī, Rāshid al-.]

BIBLIOGRAPHY

Centre National de la Recherche Scientifique. *Annuaire de l'Afrique du Nord, 1979*. Paris: Centre National de la Recherche Scientifique, 1981. Yearbook devoted to the special topic of Islam in the Maghrib, containing several articles on Tunisia.

Esposito, John L., and John O. Voll. *Makers of Contemporary Islam*. Oxford and New York: Oxford University Press, 2001.

King, Stephen J. *Liberalization against Democracy: The Local Politics of Economic Reform in Tunisia*. Bloomington: Indiana University Press, 2003.

Perkins, Kenneth J. *A History of Modern Tunisia*. Cambridge, U.K., and New York: Cambridge University Press, 2004.

Tamimi, Azzam S. *Rachid Ghannouchi: A Democrat Within Islamism*. Oxford and New York: Oxford University Press, 2001.

Waltz, Susan. "Islamist Appeal in Tunisia." *Middle East Journal* 40 (Autumn 1986): 651–670.

Zartman, I. William, ed. *Tunisia: The Political Economy of Reform*. Boulder, Colo.: L. Rienner, 1991. Contains several insightful articles on Islam in Tunisia.

SUSAN WALTZ
Updated by JOSEPH A. KÉCHICHIAN

ḤIZB AL-TAḤRĪR AL-ISLĀMĪ. Known as the Islamic Liberation Party, it is a transnational Islamist political movement and party. It aims to establish a caliphate through coup and seizure of the reins of any Muslim state. Despite its radical discourse, its nonviolent methods and active denunciation of violence has given it relative freedom to operate in the West—though it remains repressed in much of the Arab world and only minimally tolerated in most Muslim states.

Origins and History. Ḥizb al-Taḥrīr al-Islāmī was established in 1953 in Jerusalem by Taqī al-Dīn al-Nabhānī (1909–1977), a graduate of al-Azhar University in Cairo, a secondary school teacher, and a *qāḍī* (judge). Born in Ijzim, in northern Palestine, Nabhānī established the party along with others who had left or were disenchanted with the Cairo-based Muslim Brotherhood. Ḥizb al-Taḥrīr al-Islāmī gained some political traction early in its life, particularly in the West Bank and Jordan, where some of its sympathizers were elected to the Jordanian parliament as independents. While never legal, Ḥizb al-Taḥrīr was tolerated until 1957, when all political parties not loyal to the U.S.- and U.K.-backed monarchy were suppressed and emergency martial law announced. Ḥizb al-Taḥrīr continued to work clandestinely, holding underground meetings, preaching in mosques and prayer circles, and disseminating information through the regular issuance of leaflets and books. By the mid-1950s, Ḥizb al-Taḥrīr had extended its reach beyond the West Bank and Jordan, with branches appearing in surrounding countries, particularly Syria, Lebanon, Kuwait, and Iraq, but it remained relatively small and marginal yet substantial in its output and broader public awareness of its politics. Pan-Arabism, particularly Nasserism, remained dominant throughout the mid-1950s to mid-1960s, but Ḥizb al-Taḥrīr remained effective in building a base and moved beyond dissemination of its ideas when in 1968 and 1969 it attempted two coups against King Hussein of Jordan. Ḥizb al-Taḥrīr attempted coups in other capitals as well, including Baghdad in 1972, Cairo in 1974, and Damascus in 1976.

It remained marginalized in the 1980s, despite the rise of Islamist political movements. In Palestine and Jordan, Ḥizb al-Taḥrīr was unable to capitalize on the rise of Islamic forces, with Ḥamās and the Islamic *Jihād* in the ascendant in Palestine and the Islamic Action Front in Jordan gaining widespread support. However, since the early 1990s Ḥizb al-Taḥrīr has exhibited a significant revitalization, with branches emerging once again across the Arab world. Moreover it has expanded significantly in the broader Muslim world, where, given its nonviolent politics, it has garnered relative tolerance by state security. It organizes activities in Turkey, India, Bangladesh, Indonesia, and Malaysia publicly and with little state intervention, but in Central Asia, where is has attained significant prominence since the late 1990s, it is often met with repressive state response, particularly in Uzbekistan, Tajikistan, and Kazakhstan. Further abroad there are small but active chapters of the party within Muslim communities in the United States, Australia, and most visibly in Western Europe—particularly the United Kingdom, where despite its controversial public image it is nonetheless permitted to conduct its activities openly.

Ideology and Structure. Ḥizb al-Taḥrīr believes that the most important aim of an Islamist movement is to establish an Islamic state. In this way a new caliphate (*khilāfah*) would replace the colonial and postcolonial states that had veered away from Islam, uniting Muslims under one banner (*raya*). This distinction from other Islamist movements is made in its main political slogan, "*Khilāfah* is the solution," consciously contrasting itself to the Muslim Brotherhood slogan, "Islam is the solution."

In seeking this *khilāfah*, Ḥizb al-Taḥrīr is modeled on an idealized notion of a caliphate system and its conceptualization of the nature of leadership and authority. The executive of the party is called the *amīr*, to whom fealty is required, with a council of advisers (*shūrā*) offering nonbinding guidance. More structurally, the party is often compared to a vanguardist formation, with a clear and centralized line of authority and a demand for ideological conformity and discipline through every level of the party.

Ḥizb al-Taḥrīr is unique in its ideological consistency and comprehensive political program. Emerging from the cold war, Ḥizb al-Taḥrīr consciously articulates Islam as an ideological alternative to capitalism and communism. Nabhānī's books, disseminated widely and required reading for all members, outline Islam as a rational doctrine that must be at the center of Muslim thought and the backbone of any state. To that end, it adopted a constitution detailing the political, economic, and social systems of the new caliphate. In this constitution executive and legislative powers are vested in an elected caliph. Party plurality is encouraged as a mechanism by which citizens can contest caliph policies, although democracy is regarded as non-Islamic, with sovereignty in the hands of God, and his viceroy, the caliph.

Given this ambition Ḥizb al-Taḥrīr's primary objective is to gain the reins of power through a coup d'état, focusing primarily on the security elements of the state and the army. Concerned therefore with the politics of the state, the party expressly rejects social base-building or reform. Much of its output is concerned with bringing about public political consciousness of the continued incipient role of colonialism in the Muslim world and the need for a new Islamic order.

Impact on Political Dynamics and Future Prospects. When ʿAbd al-Qadim Zallum, an early member, succeeded Nabhānī in 1977, he focused on the outward expansion of the group across the Muslim world and in Muslim communities elsewhere. Zallum's successor in 2003, ʿAṭāʾ Abū al-Rushtah (b. 1943) has focused mostly on the expansion of Ḥizb al-Taḥrīr's public image. In particular Ḥizb al-Taḥrīr began to organize even larger mass *khilāfah* rallies throughout the world, especially in London, garnering significant media attention. Its primary distinction, particularly after 11 September 2001, as a nonviolent movement that nonetheless advocates for an Islamic state, has given it a maneuverability not achieved by other political parties with similar pan-Islamic aspirations. Indeed, despite its small political impact across the Arab and Muslim world, it is this maneuverability that as given it a larger-than-life image.

BIBLIOGRAPHY

Hizb-ut-Tahrir official website. http://www.hizb-ut-tahrir.org.

International Crisis Group. "Radical Islam in Central Asia: Responding to Hizb ut-Tahrir." International Crisis Group Report 58, June 30, 2002. http://www.crisisgroup.org/en/regions/asia/central-asia/058-radical-islam-in-central-asia-responding-to-hizb-ut-tahrir.aspx.

Taji-Farouki, Suha *A Fundamental Quest: Hizb al-Tahrir and the Search for the Islamic Caliphate*. London: Grey Seal Books, 1996.

SUHA TAJI-FAROUKI
Updated by MEZNA M. QATO

ḤIZB-I ISLĀMĪ AFGHĀNISTĀN. An Islamist political party that has, for more than three decades, promoted the idea of establishing an Islamic state in Afghanistan. Its principal leader is Gulbuddin Hekmatyar, and while other figures have broken away from the party on occasion, his position as its leader has never been seriously challenged from within.

The Ḥizb emerged from the earlier Muslim Youth Organization of Afghanistan, which in turn had drawn on Islamist networks that took shape at Kabul University in the late 1960s. These networks included Professor Ghulam Muhammad Niazi, Professor Burhanuddin Rabbani, and the young Hekmatyar, at that time an engineering student. Hostile to the monarchical regime of Muḥammad Zāhir Shāh—and after the July 1973 coup, to the republican regime of Zāhir Shāh's cousin Muḥammad Dāʾūd—the activists began to mobilize against the state. In August 1975, however, a planned uprising against the government failed badly, and Hekmatyar, already enjoying sanctuary in the Pakistani city of Peshawar, was joined by the survivors of the uprising. In 1976 a growing rift between Hekmatyar and Rabbani, both aspiring leaders of the exiled movement, led to the establishment on 11 May of the Ḥizb-i Islāmī under the compromise leadership of Qazi Amin Waqad. The truce was short-lived: in late 1977 Rabbani broke away to form his own party. Shortly thereafter Hekmatyar secured the leadership of the Ḥizb, which he has held ever since.

For much of the 1980s, confusion persisted because of the decision by another Afghan religious figure, Mawlawī Yūnus Khāliṣ, to establish a party of the same name. Khāliṣ, of an earlier generation than Hekmatyar, was a well-known pamphleteer, but his base of support was regional and tribal. Originally a Khogiani Pushtun from Nangahar, his strength always lay in eastern Afghanistan, where he enjoyed close relations with the prominent Arsala family and support from the resistance commander Jalāluddīn Ḥaqqanī. After the collapse of the Afghan communist regime in April 1992, Khāliṣ's Ḥizb remained focused on the east and in effect faded away, in the face of the expansion of the Taliban movement from 1994. Khāliṣ died in his late eighties in July 2006.

The significance of Hekmatyar's personality and leadership style cannot be underestimated in explaining the durability of the Ḥizb-i Islāmī. The party was made up mainly of ethnic Pushtuns, and Hekmaytar himself was a Khorati Ghilzai Pushtun from the Kunduz area. Nonetheless, tribal identity was not the basis of its strength. In contrast to most other leaders of Afghan émigré parties in the 1980s, Hekmatyar was genuinely charismatic, although he was also a secretive figure who concentrated on inspiring a network of extremely loyal supporters rather than building a mass following. More importantly, he set out to control the Ḥizb with an iron hand. This led one observer to describe it as an "Islamo-Leninist" force, recalling Lenin's advocacy of a vanguard party of professional revolutionaries in his 1902 essay "What Is To Be Done?" Hekmatyar's party was highly centralized and authoritarian and deployed *madrasah*-trained religious officers to monitor the performance of its military commanders. One result of the lack of intra-party democracy was that defections from the Ḥizb were common, starting with Qazi Amin Waqad's resignation in 1985. The underlying cause was often Hekmatyar's willingness to make breathtaking tactical shifts, such as his willingness in March 1990 to support the communist defense minister, Shahnawaz Tanai, in an attempt to displace the communist leader Najibullah. Hekmaytar was also an adherent of the doctrine of *takfīr*, which in effect allowed him to deny the claims of others to be Muslim if they happened to differ from him politically.

Until the Soviet invasion of Afghanistan in December 1979 the Ḥizb-i Islāmī was a minor player in Afghan politics. This position was transformed by the invasion, as Pakistan-based *mujāhidīn* (resistance) parties became conduits in a Cold War context for the delivery of aid to field commanders attacking Soviet forces. The Ḥizb rapidly developed a well-oiled propaganda machine. Hekmatyar spoke competent English, but kept some distance from Western figures; the main liaison role was played by his spokesman Nawab Saleem, who had studied in the United States. As a military force, however, the Ḥizb was much less significant than groups such as Aḥmad Shāh Masʿūd's Shūrā-i Nazar (Supervisory Council) or Jalāluddīn Ḥaqqanī's combatants in Paktia. Indeed, in the eyes of many other resistance groups, the Ḥizb was a sinister force, implicated in the killing of Western aid workers and of other resistance commanders—most notoriously in July 1989, when a Ḥizb commander murdered thirty Shūrā-i Nazar commanders on their way from a planning meeting with Masʿūd. In hindsight, it is clear that a great deal of the weaponry supplied to the Ḥizb during the 1980s was not used against the Soviet military but stockpiled for future use against moderate resistance actors.

The Ḥizb was able to do this because of its special relationship with the Inter-Services Intelligence Directorate of the Pakistan Armed Forces (ISI). The ISI had been in contact with Hekmatyar since before the April 1978 communist coup in Afghanistan, and the ISI saw the Ḥizb as unlikely to threaten Pakistan's interests. In addition, in an era in which "Islamization" was being promoted by the Pakistani regime of General Muhammad Zia ul-Haq, the ideological position of the Ḥizb went down well with the ISI leadership. As a result the Ḥizb received the bulk of U.S.-funded weaponry channelled through ISI, even though Hekmatyar was by far the most militantly anti-Western figure to lead a resistance party. When the Afghan communist regime collapsed in 1992, the ISI was very keen to see Hekmaytar emerge as leader of Afghanistan. This was to set the scene for two decades of hostility between Pakistan and those Afghans who did not support the Ḥizb.

The problem faced by the Ḥizb in 1992 was that it lacked significant support in Afghanistan on either territorial or tribal bases. It had become a "rentier party"—heavily dependent on aid from Pakistan and on income from narcotics, with a September 1989 news report identifying it as the likely owner of the world's largest heroin factory. An attempt by Hekmatyar's supporters to take Kabul in April 1992 failed; instead, it fell under the control of Masʿūd and other moderate parties. Hekmatyar adopted a "spoiler" strategy of rocketing the capital, causing enormous civilian losses, and prompting Rabbani, by this time president of Afghanistan, to label him a "dangerous terrorist." Pakistan's support switched from the Ḥizb to its new client, the Taliban movement. In early 1995 Hekmatyar's forces were finally driven from their vantage point just south of Kabul, but in a clumsy move at reconciliation, Rabbani agreed in May 1996 to appoint Hekmatyar as prime minister, a post he assumed on 26 June. His tenure was short-lived, lasting only until the Taliban seized Kabul on 26 September; the decrees he issued at this time differed little from those that the Taliban subsequently promulgated.

The Taliban occupation of Kabul from 1996 removed Hekmatyar from any claim to exercise state power and weakened the position of the Ḥizb considerably. Masʿūd, who had always been deeply skeptical of Rabbani's efforts to reconcile with Hekmatyar, pursued his own campaign against the Taliban until he was assassinated by al-Qaʿida agents on 9 September 2001. Hekmatyar, by contrast, left Afghanistan and received sanctuary from Iran. He did not, however, detach himself entirely from Pakistan, and his son-in-law Ghairat Baheer continued to represent the Ḥizb in Pakistan until after the September 2001 attacks. These attacks left the Ḥizb extremely exposed. Hekmatyar was forced to leave Iran in February 2002, and Baheer was detained in Pakistan, handed over to U.S. forces, and held at Bagram until May 2008. Nonetheless, as U.S. attention to Afghanistan drifted following the March 2003 invasion of Iraq, the Ḥizb resumed its activities, both politically through the issuing of statements by Hekmatyar, and militarily with attacks on troops in Afghanistan deployed as part of the International Security Assistance Force under NATO command. On their own, these attacks were not large enough to pose a real threat to the ISAF mission, but they succeeded in winning some access for the Ḥizb: after his release from US custody, Baheer was able to meet with President Hamid Karzai, a privilege denied most Afghans.

At one level the Ḥizb might appear a spent force. Among the armed opponents of the Karzai government, it is typically viewed as less militarily significant than either the Taliban under the direction of the so-called Quetta Shura or the Ḥaqqanī network of militants inspired by former Mujāhidīn commander Jalāluddīn Ḥaqqanī. Hekmatyar and his associates are aging, and there is little evidence that their militant brand of Islamism enjoys much support in Afghanistan. Nonetheless, in President Karzai's immediate circle and in the lower house (Wolesi Jirga) of the Afghan parliament, there are several key figures with ties to the Ḥizb. This may point to a "Trojan Horse" strategy for promoting the Ḥizb's wider objectives.

BIBLIOGRAPHY

Ahmad, Ishtiaq. *Gulbuddin Hekmatyar: An Afghan Trail from Jihad to Terrorism*. Islamabad: Society for Tolerance and Education, 2004.

Edwards, David B. *Before Taliban: Genealogies of the Afghan Jihad*. Berkeley: University of California Press, 2002.

Hekmatyar, Gulbuddin. *Secret Plans Open Faces: From the Withdrawal of Russians to the Fall of the Coalition Government*. Translated by Sher Zaman Taizi, edited by S. Fida Yunas. Peshawar: Area Study Centre, University of Peshawar, 2004.

Hussain, Rizwan. *Pakistan and the Emergence of Islamic Militancy in Afghanistan*. Aldershot, U.K., and Burlington, Vt.: Ashgate, 2005.

Roy, Olivier. *Islam and Resistance in Afghanistan*. 2d ed. Cambridge, U.K., and New York: Cambridge University Press, 1990.

Sinno, Abdulkader H. *Organizations at War in Afghanistan and Beyond*. Ithaca, N.Y.: Cornell University Press, 2008.

William Maley

ḤIZBULLĀH. There are several organizations, some permanent and others ephemeral, who bear the name Ḥizbullāh (party of God) in the Middle East and the broader Muslim world. The term is derived from the Qurʾānic term *ḥizb Allāh* (occurring in *suwar* [chapters] 5 and 58) and refers to the body of Muslim believers who are promised triumph over *ḥizb al-Shayṭān* (the Devil's party). This article will focus on three *ḥizbullāh* movements in the Middle East: the Ḥizbullāh in Iran and Lebanon, and the Kurdish Ḥizbullāh in Turkey.

Ḥizbullāh in Iran. Ḥizbullāh entered the Iranian political scene during the 1978–1979 revolutionary upheaval. Recruited mainly from the ranks of the urban poor, the *bāzārīs* (small businessmen), and the lumpenproletariat, the Ḥizbullāhīs played an important role in organizing demonstrations and strikes that led to the downfall of the Pahlavi regime. Following the victory of the revolution they served as the unofficial watchdogs and storm troopers of the clerically dominated Islamic Republican Party (established in 1979 and dissolved in 1987).

Often led by the firebrand Ḥujjāt al-Islām Hādī Ghaffārī, the Ḥizbullāhīs used clubs, chains, knives, and guns to disrupt the rallies of opposition parties, beat their members, and ransack their offices. The Ḥizbullāhī ruffians—nicknamed *chumāqdār*s (those with clubs) by the opposition—were instrumental in the undoing of President Abol-Hasan Bani Sadr, the closing of the universities, the enforcement of veiling, the suppression of the press, and the browbeating of people into silence. In addition the Ḥizbullāh provided an inexhaustible pool of faithful warriors who enlisted for the war with Iraq. The recruitment of many of these veterans by such organizations as the Basīj youth volunteers, Jihād-i Sāzandigī (Reconstruction Crusade), and Pasdaran has so far prevented the establishment of a formal party called Ḥizbullāh. On the contrary, some Ḥizbullāhī squads have now been transformed into the private militias of powerful clerics and have even set on each other's benefactors.

The Iranian Ḥizbullāh is reported to have transnational links with like-minded groups in the region, in particular with its namesake in Lebanon. The Lebanese Ḥizbullāh was organized, trained, and financed by the Iranian Pasdarans who were dispatched to Lebanon in 1982. The two groups share certain characteristics, such as a militant interpretation of Shīʿī doctrines, adoration for Ayatollah Khomeini, anti-Zionism, and suspicion of Western governments. Furthermore some of the leading personalities of these two groups are linked through family ties or can boast of having studied with the same mentors at theological seminaries in Najaf and Qom. However, while the Ḥizbullāh of Lebanon operates as a formal political party, the Iranian Ḥizbullāhīs for the most part continue to operate as vigilante bands.

In Iran Ayatollah Mohammad Baqir Kharrazi serves as the secretary-general of the World Organization of Ḥizbullāh. The Iranian Ḥizbullāh has gone through seven periods of transformation. In the first stage of its development in the years immediately preceding the victory of the 1979 revolution, the Ḥizbullāh was simply a loose association of a group of young religious activists in Qom who were engaged in learning urban warfare against the shah's forces. In the second stage the organization focused its activities on disseminating religious and political tracts against the monarchy and leading a number of attacks against military and economic targets in Iran. The Ḥizbullāh's third stage was augured by the victory of the revolution, and its focus shifted to what it called political and cultural activities while attacking presumed internal enemies of and dissidents in the Islamic Republic. During the Iran–Iraq War (1980–1988), the Ḥizbullāh ceased its anti-dissident activities inside the country and sent its forces to fight in this war. During this (fourth) phase of its evolution the Ḥizbullāh lost many of its committed members in the Iran-Iraq War.

After the end of this war the Ḥizbullāh initiated its fifth phase of development by resurrecting its domestic organizational structure and targeting its attacks on what it viewed as cultural threats to Iran. In the sixth stage of its development the Ḥizbullāh undertook a major expansion of its membership base and infrastructure as it perceived its very existence being threatened by the maturation of the governmental structure in

Iran and the initiation of the reform movement in the country. Finally, in the last (current) stage of its transformation, the Ḥizbullāh has continued to focus on solidifying its base by expanding its sociocultural activities.

Ḥizbullāh in Lebanon. The foundations of Ḥizbullāh were laid years before the 1979 Iranian Revolution in the ties that bound the Shīʿī *ʿulamāʾ* (religious scholars) of Iran and Lebanon. Many of these men attended Shīʿī theological seminaries in Iraq, especially in the shrine city of Najaf. During the late 1950s and the 1960s these academies formulated an Islamic response to nationalism and secularism. Prominent *ʿulamāʾ* lectured and wrote on Islamic government, Islamic economics, and the ideal Islamic state. In Najaf the Iraqi ayatollah Muḥammad Bāqir al-Ṣadr and the exiled Iranian ayatollah Ruhollah al-Musavi Khomeini both subjected the existing political order to an Islamic critique. Lebanese *ʿulamāʾ* and theological students joined in these debates.

Sayyid Muḥammad Ḥusayn Faḍlallāh, the future spiritual leader of Ḥizbullāh, was an exemplary product of Najaf's mix of scholasticism and radicalism. Faḍlallāh was born and schooled in Najaf, where his father, a scholar from south Lebanon, had come to study. He imbibed the ideas then current in Najaf and went to Lebanon in 1966, where he made his Beirut *ḥusaynīyah* (a Shīʿī congregation house) into a center of Islamic activism. Although Sayyid Mūsā al-Ṣadr was the dominant Shīʿī voice and by far the more influential religious authority (*marjaʿ*) in Lebanon, he nevertheless welcomed Faḍlallāh, with whom he shared several common goals. After al-Ṣadr disappeared on a visit to Libya in 1978, and with the onset of Iraqi expulsions of more than a hundred Lebanese theology students from Najaf, Faḍlallāh gathered these mobilized voices around him. These men formed the core of an emerging Ḥizbullāh, even though the guerrilla movement would not become active until 1982. By the time of Faḍlallāh's death in July 2010 Ḥizbullāh had established a formidable presence in the Lebanese political landscape.

The formal and sustained partnership between Lebanese Shīʿī and Iran was greatly strengthened in 1982, following the Israeli invasion of Lebanon and the deployment of American, French, and Italian peacekeeping forces in Beirut. When Iran offered to assist in mobilizing Lebanese Shīʿī, who became the target of Israeli onslaught, Syria approved, allowing Iran to send about a thousand Revolutionary Guards to the Bekáa (al-Biqāʿ) Valley in eastern Lebanon. There they seized a Lebanese army barracks and turned it into their operational base.

Emboldened by the arrival of the Iranians Faḍlallāh and a number of young *ʿulamāʾ* declared *jihād* against the Israeli presence in Lebanon while pledging their allegiance to Khomeini. Similarly, a faction of the Amal militia led by a former schoolteacher, Ḥusayn al-Mūsawī, went over to the Revolutionary Guards, disappointed that the Amal movement had failed to resist Israel's invasion. Iran's ambassador to Damascus after 1981, ʿAlī Akbar Muḥtashimī, established a council to govern the new movement, which brought together Lebanese *ʿulamāʾ* and security strongmen responsible for secret militia operations. Later the council created the post of secretary-general, held successively by Shaykh Ṣubḥī al-Ṭufaylī, Sayyid ʿAbbās al-Mūsawī, and Sayyid Ḥasan Naṣrallạh. Faḍlallāh declined all formal office, but his rhetorical genius and seniority assured his moral prestige in the movement.

The movement drew its support from various components of the Shīʿī society, especially from the larger Shīʿī clans of the Bekáa Valley. The message of Ḥizbullāh also appealed to Shīʿī refugees who were forced by war into the dismal slums of southern Beirut known as the Dahīyah. They included Shīʿī driven from their homes in the Phalangist assault on Palestinians in the eastern

Beirut neighborhoods of Nabaʿ and Burj Hammud in 1976. Many more fled the south following the Israeli invasions of 1978 and 1982, further swelling Beirut's less-privileged suburbs.

From the outset Ḥizbullāh conducted its struggle on three discrete levels—open, semi-clandestine, and clandestine. Faḍlallāh and the *ʿulamāʾ* openly preached the message of resistance to Islam's enemies and fealty to Khomeini in mosques and *ḥusaynīyah*s, which became the focal points for public rallies. The Revolutionary Guards trained the semi-clandestine Islamic Resistance, a militia-like formation that successfully attacked and drained Israeli forces in south Lebanon.

As Ḥizbullāh's military attacks on Western forces in Lebanon intensified, its stature among the Lebanese increased. Throughout the 1980s assassinations of individual foreigners escalated into massive bombings, some of them conducted by "martyrs," which destroyed the U.S. embassy and its annex in two separate attacks in 1983 and 1984; the Beirut barracks of American and French peacekeeping troops in two attacks on the same morning in 1983; and command facilities of Israeli forces in the south in 1982 and 1983. Hundreds of foreigners died in these bombings, the most successful of which killed 241 U.S. Marines in their barracks. As a result the United States and France withdrew their forces from Lebanon; Israel, whose troops also came under attack by the Islamic Resistance, retreated to a narrow "security zone" in the south.

For its part Ḥizbullāh also lost several of its leaders when they became the targets of assassination and abduction. Faḍlallāh narrowly missed death in a massive car bombing in 1985 that killed eighty and injured more than four hundred; Israel abducted a local Ḥizbullāh cleric, Shaykh ʿAbd al-Karim ʿUbayd, in 1988; and Israeli helicopter gunships killed Ḥizbullāh's secretary-general, Sayyid ʿAbbās al-Mūsawī, and his family in an attack on his motorcade in 1992. Upon Mūsawī's assassination Shaykh Ḥasan Naṣrallāh became the secretary-general of Ḥizbullāh.

As Ḥizbullāh gained momentum, it sought unimpeded access to the south so it could promote the struggle against Israel. As Israeli deaths in Lebanon increased—Ḥizbullāh took credit for the estimated sixteen hundred killed between 1982 and 2000, even though its own casualties were probably much higher—the party gained added legitimacy. Among Shīʿī Lebanese casualties was Ḥasan Naṣrallāh's eldest son, Muhammad Hadi, who was killed by Israeli forces in the Jabal al-Rafiʿ in 1997. In fact Ḥizbullāh's military campaigns were probably a major factor in the Israeli decision to withdraw from southern Lebanon in 2000. Ḥasan Naṣrallāh played an important role in the prisoner exchange with Israel in 2004, when four hundred Palestinians and thirty Ḥizbullāh detainees were freed—and the remains of fifty-nine deceased Lebanese men were returned to their families—in exchange for Israeli businessman (and former colonel) Elchanan Tenenbaum, as well as the remains of three Israeli soldiers. Remarkably this accord catapulted Ḥizbullāh to new heights in Arab political circles.

Ḥizbullāh also cooperated with Iranian aid agencies to fund a wide range of social and economic projects. These include hospitals and pharmacies in Beirut, small textile factories and sheltered workshops to employ families of members and "martyrs," book allowances and scholarships for students, street paving in Beirut, and the digging of wells and reservoirs in rural areas. Ḥizbullāh sponsored a scout movement, summer camps, and a soccer league. The movement published a weekly newspaper and operated an independent radio station, as well as the widely popular al-Manār television network. These activities broadened the base of the movement and enhanced its ability to field fighters.

Although Ḥizbullāh still considers itself the flagship of Lebanese resistance movements against Israeli threats and occupation, it has now been fully integrated into the mosaic of Lebanon's political structure. Ḥizbullāh now regularly participates in all Lebanese elections and has representatives at all levels of Lebanese sociopolitical structures, including the Parliament. In fact, since 2000 Ḥizbullāh has acted both as a political force and a crucial power broker in Lebanon's fractured political system.

On 12 July 2006 Ḥizbullāh troops kidnapped two Israeli soldiers and killed three others in order to force Israel to release hundreds of Lebanese Shīʿī prisoners. This episode resulted in a massive Israeli retaliation and the Ḥizbullāh counteroffensive. The war lasted until 14 August. More than 2,500 Lebanese and 165 Israelis were killed. On 11 August 2006 the United Nations Security Council unanimously approved Resolution 1701, ushering in a ceasefire with the deployment of a strengthened UN peacekeeping force to police the border.

With undeniable military capabilities—lobbing thousands of short- and long-range rockets into Israel—Ḥizbullāh demonstrated rare fighting abilities that earned it Lebanese and Arab praise. Sunnī and Christian Arabs believed that Ḥizbullāh restored their dignity, because its fighters did what mighty Arab armies failed to do. However Ḥizbullāh's reputation has been somewhat damaged after the Special Tribunal for Lebanon, which had been set up to investigate the death of former prime minister Rafiq Hariri, issued arrest warrants on 30 June 2011 for senior Ḥizbullāh members. Ḥasan Naṣrallāh rejected the charges as a plot against his organization. Ḥizbullāh's support for the Syrian regime of Bashar al-Assad has also diminished its luster among some Arabs.

The Kurdish Hizbullah in Turkey. Hizbullah is the largest militant Islamic group currently active in Turkey. It is often referred to as "Kurdish Hizbullah" (KH), to distinguish it from the Lebanese group using the same name.

In the 1970s a group of Turkish and Kurdish Islamists, including KH's founders, believed that an Islamic state could be established through democratic processes and to this end joined the National Turkish Student Association (Milli Türk Talebe Birliği, MTTB), the youth organization of the National Salvation Party (Millî Selamet Partisi, MSP). After the 1980 military coup, however, Hizbullah's founders concluded that Turkey's powerful military was determined to maintain secularism as the basis of the Turkish state and abandoned all hope for success through the ballot box.

Thus a group of Kurdish Islamists including Hüseyin Velioğlu and Fidan Güngör left MTTB in 1980 and formed the Union Movement (Vahdet Hareketi). The movement opened bookstores for recruitment and training purposes. Two bookstores, Menzil (Destination) in Diyarbakır, owned by Fidan Güngör, and İlim (Science) in Batman, owned by Huseyin Velioğlu, were competing centers of Islamic activity, which led to a division among Islamists and the formation of new militant Islamic movements, Hizbullah/Menzil and Hizbullah/İlim.

Between 1990 and 1993 Hizbullah/Menzil led by Fidan Güngör and Hizbullah/İlim led by Huseyin Velioğlu, had competed to prevail in Islamic activities. In 1993, by killing many members of the Menzil group, Hizbullah/İlim prevailed in the Kurdish region and adopted a new name, "Hizbullah."

In order to maintain its dominant position among Kurdish communities, KH had also confronted the Marxist Kurdish terror organization, the Kurdistan Workers' Party (PKK). In this period of confrontation KH conducted numerous murderous operations against the PKK. Between 1992 and 1995, in the southeastern cities of Diyarbakır and Batman, KH killed roughly five hundred members of the PKK, suffering two hundred deaths themselves. These clashes took place without interference from Turkish security forces which were also in hot pursuit of the PKK. For this reason much of the general public had come to regard KH as a quasi-official terrorist, or counterterrorist, organization. However the truth behind these violent clashes is that the PKK claimed to be the only true spokesman of Kurdish nationalism in Turkey, and KH viewed this claim as a threat to its own identity that had to be crushed.

Velioğlu foresaw Hizbullah developing through three distinct stages:

1. Propaganda (*tebliğ*): an educational period of raising religiopolitical consciousness. KH members in this period were expected to strive to persuade the people to adopt Islamic religious practices.
2. Community (*cemaat*): communities are restructured in accordance with Islamic rules and practices.
3. *Jihād* (*cihat*): armed struggle to safeguard the Islamic way of life.

Under the new leadership of İsa Altsoy, a Turkish Kurd living in Germany, the organization has given up violence in order to reestablish grassroots support. (In doctrinal terms, this represents a retreat to the *tebliğ*, or propaganda, stage.) KH is conducting publicity, fund-raising, and recruitment operations throughout the Kurdish diaspora in Europe as well as in Turkey. It is printing books and publishing magazines in Turkey and Europe and has opened new bookstores in eastern Turkey. The following magazines are believed to be publications of KH: *Gönülden Gönüle Damlalar*, *İnzar*, and *Müjde*. The Association for Human Rights and solidarity with the Oppressed (Insan Hakları ve Mustazaflarla Dayanişma Derneği) was established to advocate for the rights of imprisoned KH members.

KH wants all organizations that originated in or are based in Kurdistan to consider the Kurdish question in an Islamic framework. If Islamic societies are liberated, it contends, the Kurdish problem will automatically be solved. To this end Bagaşi argues, "Hizbullah as an Islamic movement is dedicated to defend the Muslim Kurds' Islamic and Human Rights, and to find solutions to historic, social, political, economic, and cultural problems through an Islamic approach. Hizbullah's duty is to struggle against oppression, tyranny, and injustice to make Kurds free."

BIBLIOGRAPHY

Fuller, Graham E. "The Hizballah–Iran Connection: Model for Sunni Resistance." *The Washington Quarterly* 30, no. 1 (Winter 2006–2007): 139–150.

Hamzeh, Ahmad Nizar. *In the Path of Hizbullah*. Syracuse, N.Y.: Syracuse University Press, 2004.

Noe, Nicholas, ed. *Voice of Hezbollah: The Statements of Sayed Hassan Nasrallah*. Translated by Ellen Khouri. London and New York: Verso, 2007.

Norton, Augustus Richard. *Hezbollah: A Short History*. Princeton, N.J.: Princeton University Press, 2007.

Ranstorp, Magnus. *Hizb'allah in Lebanon: The Politics of the Western Hostage Crisis*. New York: Palgrave Macmillan, 2003.

Saad-Ghorayeb, Amal. *Hizbullah: Politics and Religion*. London: Pluto Press, 2002.

Sankari, Jamal. *Fadlallah: The Making of a Radical Shiʿite Leader*. London: Saqi Books, 2005.

Uslu, Emrullah. "From Local Hizbullah to Global Terror: Militant Islam in Turkey." *Middle East Policy* 14, no. 1 (Spring 2007): 124–141.

Mehrzad Boroujerdi, Martin Kramer, Emrullah Uslu, *and* Nader Entessar

Ḥojjatīyeh Society. A Shīʿī lay organization that was formed in the period between 1953 and 1979 by Sheikh Maḥmūd Ḥalabī. Although the association never had more than a thousand active members, and despite the fact that its explicit objective was restricted to providing a response to the theological challenge and missionary activities of the Bahāʾī faith, it had an indirect and unintended impact on the elites of the Islamic revolution of 1979, more than ten thousand of whom had passed through the teaching and training courses of the association and had been imbued with a sense of mission, discipline, and activism. The curriculum of the association included vignettes of both Islamic and Bahā'ī texts, as well as debating techniques, public speaking instruction, and intelligence-gathering skills concerning the Bahā'ī proselytization plans. In the late 1960s the association became more bureaucratic and expanded to most Iranian cities as well as a few neighboring countries.

The Ḥojjatīyeh Society was a manifestation of traditional Islam's struggle to accommodate modernity. Members of the society, unlike their traditional brethren in seminaries, were groomed for success in the modern world. The association's pledge to stay away from political activities helped maintain it in the public sphere in an otherwise restrictive political milieu, but it opened the association after the Revolution of 1979 to charges of complicity with the shah's regime.

The 1970s witnessed more bureaucratic reforms in the association, indicative of an increasing division of labor and a demand for compartmentalization and efficiency. The result was a structure in which graduates of the basic (*payeh*) and middle-level (*vijeh*) training were absorbed into newly differentiated specialist teams dubbed debaters, public speakers, instructors, and intelligence researchers. Two governing formations known as board of directors and implementers emerged as the top decision-making bodies. The graduate level of instruction was accessible only to a small group of elites through written entrance examinations.

Bahā'īs generally reacted to the Ḥojjatīyeh challenge by avoiding open debates with the members of the association, convincing the Ḥojjatīyeh of the effectiveness of its strategy. Among politicized religious rivals of the Ḥojjatīyeh, discontent grew on the grounds that the association had grown beyond the perceived threat of Bahā'ī proselytization and was threatening to deplete the finite pool of talented young Muslim volunteers.

The Islamic revolution caught Ḥojjatīyeh by surprise. Its initial noncommittal stance caused widespread defections within its ranks. With the success of the revolution, Ḥojjatīyeh attempted to placate the revolutionary leadership but was bluntly rebuffed. Ayatollah Khomeini, despite his earlier approval of the association, allowed open criticism of its erstwhile apolitical nature and its conservative "bias." Finally two years after the Islamic revolution, Khomeini publically threatened to annihilate the association. The founder, Sheikh Maḥmūd Ḥalabī, responded by terminating all of the activities of the Ḥojjatīyeh in a brief notice published in the daily newspaper *Keyhan*.

In the years that followed, Ḥojjatīyeh was publicly vilified and its members barred from education and employment. Ironically the Islamic republic's treatment of Bahā'īs and the Ḥojjatīyeh members is similar. Conspiracy theories about its clandestine "mission" and its mafia-like powers abound as well. However the original members, due to their penchant for secrecy, their apolitical frame of reference, and their fear of reprisals have hitherto declined to respond. In what little remains of the former Ḥojjatīyeh, instruction and debate sessions focus on a rather pietistic version of Shī'ī mysticism that has, in recent years, been described as "the school of distinction" (*maktab-i tafkīk*).

BIBLIOGRAPHY

Hakimi, Mohammad Reza. "Maktab e Tafkik." *Keyhan Farhangi*, February 1980.

Ḥalabī, Maḥmūd. *Bayāniya-ye tawaq-qof-e faāliyathā-ye Ḥojjatiya* [statement of cessation of Ḥojjatiya activities]. *Keyhān*, 25 March 1984, p. 1.

Ḳalḳāli, Ṣādeq. *Khāṭirāt-i Shaykh Ṣādiq Khalkhāli*. Tehran, 2001.

Rafsanjānī, ʿAlī Akbar Hāshimī. *ʿObur az boḥrān.* Tehran, 1999.

Sadri, Mahmoud. "Anjoman Hojjatieh va Bahaian." *Payam e Bahaʾi* (April 2012).

Sadri, Mahmoud. "Halabi." In *Encyclopedia Iranica*, edited by Ehsan Yarshater, vol. 11. London and Boston: Routledge, 1982–.

Sadri, Mahmoud. "Hojjatieh." In *Encyclopedia Iranica*, edited by Ehsan Yarshater, vol. 12. London and Boston, Routledge, 1982–.

Soroush, ʿAbdolkarim. *Reason Freedom and Democracy in Islam: Essential Writings of ʿAbdolkarim Soroush.* Translated by Mahmoud Sadri and Ahmad Sadri, pp. 5–6. New York: Oxford University Press, 2000.

Mahmoud Sadri

Horn of Africa. The region known as the Horn of Africa stretches over much of the area between the Red Sea and the Nile Valley, that is, over today's states of Somalia, Djibouti, Ethiopia, and Eritrea. Historically, it often also included the Sudan. Though lying quite close to those parts of Arabia where Islam was born, and though the two shores of the Red Sea were partially integrated in the century prior to the days of the Prophet, Islam, as an empire and as a political system, hardly included the Horn. Islam's political and military energies were diverted from Arabia in other directions, and the region's dominant state remained Ethiopia, which adopted Christianity in 333–334. Moreover, in the early centuries of Islam, the Christian Nubians prevented the penetration of Islamic armies that came from the direction of Egypt. Yet Islam, from its very inception, did spread in the Horn. Its local history dates back to the "first Hegira," the hasty emigration of the Ṣaḥābah in 615–616 from their pagan persecutors in Mecca to seek asylum with Ethiopia's Christian king. This formative episode left Muslims with a dual message regarding Ethiopia, of acceptance of the Christian kingdom as a good neighbor, as well as of delegitimization of Christian Ethiopia after her king, who saved the Ṣaḥābah, had allegedly converted to Islam and was consequently betrayed by his people.

Islam continued to spread in the Horn, influenced by scholars, traders, and immigrants from both Arabia and Egypt. However, lacking the direct backing of an Islamic Middle Eastern imperial order, Islam was adopted in the Horn mainly by diverse local populations and groups that resisted the local hegemony of Ethiopia. They generally remained loyal to their different languages, cultures, and tribal or clannish structures, and developed their Islam in mostly popular modes. More orthodox Islam and the use of Arabic were better established in some urban centers along the Red Sea and the Indian Ocean, and in the inland walled town of Harar, considered as of the twelfth century to be the capital of Islam in the Horn. Between the ninth and the mid-sixteenth centuries, various local Islamic sultanates of Sidama, Somali, Adari, as well as other linguistic groups, notably the Shoa, Ifat, and Adal, existed on the coast and in the southern Ethiopian plateau, but as they failed to unite, they were often dominated by Christian Ethiopia, especially in Ethiopia's prime, under the Solomonian dynasty, 1270–1529.

The major event in the premodern history of Islam in the Horn was a Harar-centered moment of religious politicization combined with Islamic momentum in the Middle East and Arabia. Inspired and aided by the rising Ottomans and by Arabian scholars, the local Harari *amīr*, Aḥmad ibn Ibrāhīm, nicknamed Gran (in Amharic *grañ̃*, left-handed), united local Islamic power. Accompanied by Somalis, Sidamas, Afars, Hararis, and others—all also motivated by the desire to control the fertile highlands—Aḥmad ibn Ibrāhīm led his armies of Islamic holy warriors into Ethiopia in 1529. Emperor Lebna Dengel (who reigned from 1508) died in isolation in a mountain fortress in 1540, and, with the exception of the Lake

Tana islands, the entire Christian kingdom fell to the Muslims. According to Ethiopian records, nine out of ten Christians were forced to convert to Islam and all churches were looted and destroyed. The traumatic memory of the Gran conquest remains alive among Christians to this day.

Although Aḥmad ibn Ibrāhīm enjoyed the support of Islamic scholars from Arabia, and benefited from military aid sent by the Ottomans, he failed to consolidate his occupation of the country. Old ethnic rivalries and quarrels over booty undermined his unifying revolution. In 1540 the Portuguese sent troops to help the Ethiopians, and, on 21 February 1543, Aḥmad ibn Ibrāhīm was killed. After his death the entire Islamic enterprise in Ethiopia collapsed, and the remnants of his army returned to Harar. At the same time the Ottomans, for their part, having lost their struggle with the Portuguese over control of the sea route to India, established a foothold on what is the coastal zone of Eritrea today. But this "Province of Ethiopia" (Habesh Eyalet, Turk., Eyalet-ı Habeş) enterprise was defeated by the Ethiopians in 1578. Following that, Islam in the Horn of Africa would not regain political momentum until the modern era. Ethiopia's Christianity was also eroded politically and for some three centuries, the state lost its centralized order. The Christian's longstanding fear of Islam grew when some of the Oromo tribes of the south took advantage of the chaos in the sixteenth century, penetrated the core Christian highlands, and, in the seventeenth century, adopted Islam to further solidify their local independence in the Ethiopian heartland.

From the mid-nineteenth century and well into the twentieth century, both Islam and Christianity were revived as political religions in the Horn of Africa. Ethiopia's Emperor Tewodros II, a self-conceived crusader (1855–1868), restored central authority, and Emperor Yohannes IV (1872–1889) initiated the massive Christianization of Oromo Muslims. Emperor Menelik II (1889–1913) conquered vast Muslim-inhabited territories in the south (Harar was occupied in 1887), shaped the boundaries of today's Ethiopia, and put Somali, Afar, Sidama, Oromo, and other groups, mostly Muslims, under his Christian government.

Islamic communities that did not fall to the Ethiopians at that time came under other foreigners. First the modern, Westernizing, state of Egypt under Khedive Ismāʿīl (1863–1879) occupied the Red Sea and Indian coasts of the Horn (as of 1870), and in 1866 reestablished effective Egyptian control of the Sudan (which had been occupied by Egypt in 1821). Then, following the collapse of the Egyptian imperial enterprise in 1884–1885, the same regions were occupied and divided among the Ethiopians, the British, the French, and the Italians. Resistance to all these occupiers stimulated a new period of Islamic politicization throughout the Horn.

The Mahdīyah in the Sudan was arguably one of the most successful Islamic political revival movements of that time, and directly impacted affairs in the Horn. The Mahdists established an independent state (1884–1898), which radiated militant Islam to Ethiopia itself and mainly to the area that would (in 1890) become the Italian colony of Eritrea. In this part of the Horn the Mahdists' radical Islam competed with the more flexible Sufism of the Mīrghānīyah movement, which had been introduced and supported by the Egyptians. In March 1889 the Mahdīyah army was defeated by the Ethiopians, and the Mahdist state was finally destroyed by an Anglo-Egyptian army in 1898.

Political Islam in the Horn was soon revived from another direction. Between 1899 and 1920 a Somali movement of resistance to the British, Italian, and Ethiopian occupiers was led by "the Sayyid," Muḥammad ibn ʿAbd Allāh Ḥasan (better known by his British nickname, "the Mad Mullah").

The "Sayyid" mixed Islamic orthodoxy—he had been trained in Mecca—with local Ṣūfī traditions to create and lead a liberation movement under the banner of Islamic religious war. Though he failed to unite the Somalis, his long struggle is still considered by many to be the formative experience of modern Somali nationalism. Among other efforts he tried to build an alliance, during World War I and with Ottoman inspiration, with the Ethiopian successor to Menelik II, Lij Iyasu. Iyasu, grandson of Menelik and the son of a Muslim Oromo chief who had converted to Christianity, was said in 1916 to have returned to Islam, gambling on Ottoman victory and the eventual creation of a comprehensive Islamic empire in the Horn. He was consequently deposed that year by Ethiopia's Christian elite, led by future emperor Haile Selassie, supported by the British, the French, and the Italians.

After the death of the Somali "Sayyid" in 1920, political Islam in the Horn was not significantly revived prior to our time. The colonized Somalis, Eritreans, and Sudanese developed various forms of modern national ideologies which would motivate their liberation movements and politics until the late 1980s. Islam, as interpreted by the Somalis, was hardly helpful in bridging the various clannish rivalries and after an experiment with liberal parliamentarianism, the Republic of Somalia (independent as of 1960) came under the military Marxist regime of Mohamed Siyad Barre (1969–1991). The Muslims of Eritrea initiated a revolt (in 1961) against the annexation of the former Italian colony to Ethiopia, but they did so under the banner of modern, revolutionary Arabism, not Islam. By the mid-1980s, however, the leadership of the Eritrean struggle was captured by a Marxist movement (EPLF) dominated mostly by local Christians, who would lead the country—independent since 1991—into the twenty-first century. Sudanese nationalism and the Sudanese republic's various regimes after independence in 1956 were also mainly oriented toward modern revolutionary Arabism rather than Islam.

Ethiopia's Muslims generally remained politically passive and disunited under Haile Selassie (1930–1974). The Marxist military dictator Mangistu Haile Mariam (1974–1991) officially abolished Christian hegemony, but the country's Muslims suffered even more, because his centralized economy undermined their traditional role as urban entrepreneurs and traders.

Islam as a political religion was revived in the Horn as of the late 1980s, and has remained central to local developments. In Sudan President Jaʿfar Nimeiri (al-Numayrī, 1969–1985) reoriented his policy on Islam and the *Sharīʿāh* as of late 1983. In 1989, four years after Nimeiri's removal, General ʿUmar al-Bashīr took power and joined with the Islamicist scholar and leader Ḥasan al-Turābī. Their policy in Sudan had direct implications on the Horn. Al-Turābī hosted Osama Bin Laden in Khartoum between 1992 and 1996, and together they worked to radicalize Islam in the Horn as well, extending help to movements in Somalia, Eritrea, and Ethiopia, especially among the Oromos of the southern regions. In 1999 al-Bashīr broke with al-Turābī and Sudan mended fences with Ethiopia, but Sudan continued to radiate political Islam to the Horn.

In Somalia Siyad Barre was ousted in 1991, and the country has been unstable since. Various clannish militias engaged in internal fighting and efforts to restore coalition governments have mostly failed. Many Somalis, despairing of clannish rivalries, turned to Islam to provide cohesiveness and restore order. Of the various Islamic movements in Somalia, the Islamic Courts Union (ICU) proved the more effective. It itself was torn between radicalism, inspired by foreign movements like al-Qaʿida, and the more moderate wing, inspired by the flexibility of traditional local Somali Sufism. Moreover the radical faction strove to forcefully reclaim the Somali-inhabited territories of Ethiopia, and worked to promote Islamic militancy there. In June 2006 the ICU, led by its more radical wing, managed to capture the capital of Mogadishu. Proclaiming a regime of rigid Islamic law, it banned music and inflicted severe punishment on those who practiced Ṣūfī customs as well as on women whose behavior was less than fully strict. The ICU also called for a holy war on Ethiopia. In December of that year an Ethiopian army invaded Somalia, occupied its capital, and crushed the ICU government. Following this trauma the ICU split and its more pragmatic wing reestablished a government indirectly supported by Ethiopia. The radical wing integrated with the militant movement of al-Shabāb, which controlled parts of the land and continued to struggle, with the help of outsiders, to gain victory for their kind of Islam in Somalia and the entire region.

The regime which in 1991 replaced Mangistu's dictatorship in Ethiopia reorganized the country along decentralized, federal lines. Based mainly on ethnic criteria, it also enabled considerable religious pluralism. Since the 1990s Ethiopia's various Islamic communities have made revolutionary progress in terms of active participation in all dimensions of Ethiopian life. Religious freedom and economic openness—all still in need of further progress—enabled the emergence of thousands of mosques and the institutionalization of Islamic culture, including the rapid spread of the Arabic language among the young. In general the Muslims of Ethiopia, arguably representing half the population, are said to be divided between a majority that identifies with this kind of new Ethiopianism, and a minority, substantial enough to be significant, that strives for the victory of Islam in the entire Horn of Africa. The initial dichotomy stemming from the dual messages of the "first hegira," between good neighborliness and religious victory, continues to inspire the region's political developments.

BIBLIOGRAPHY

Ahmed, Hussein. "Coexistence and/or Confrontation? Towards a Reappraisal of Christian-Muslim Encounter in Contemporary Ethiopia." *The Journal of Religion in Africa* 36, no. 1 (2006): 4–22.

Carmichael, Tim. "Contemporary Ethiopian Discourse on Islamic History: The Politics of Historical Representation." *Islam et Sociétés au Sud du Sahara* 10 (1996): 169–187.

De Waal, Alex, ed. *Islamism and Its Enemies in the Horn of Africa*. London: Hurst, 2004.

Erlich, Haggai. *Islam and Christianity in the Horn of Africa: Somalia, Ethiopia, Sudan*. Boulder, Colo.: Lynne Rienner, 2010.

Erlich, Haggai. *Saudi Arabia and Ethiopia: Islam, Christianity, and Politics Entwined*. Boulder, Colo.: Lynne Rienner, 2007.

Jhazbhay, Iqbal. "Islam and Stability in Somaliland and the Geo-Politics of the War on Terror." *Journal of Muslim Minority Affairs* 28, no. 2 (August 2008): 173–205.

Miran, Jonathan. "A Historical Overview of Islam in Eritrea." *Die Welt des Islams* 2 (2005): 177–215.

Pirio, Gregory Alonso. "Radical Islam in the Greater Horn of Africa." http://www.ephrem.org/dehai_news_archive/2005/feb05/0038.html.

Shank, Michael. "Understanding Political Islam in Somalia." *Contemporary Islam* 1, no. 1 (June 2007): 89–103.

Shinn, David. "Al-Qaeda in East Africa and the Horn." *The Journal of Conflict Studies* 27 (Summer 2007): 47–75.

Shinn, David. "Ethiopia and Sudan: Conflict and Cooperation in the Nile Valley." In *Narrating the Nile: Politics, Cultures, Identities*, edited by Israel Gershoni and Meir Hatina, pp. 203–226. Boulder, Colo.: Lynne Rienner, 2008.

Terdman, Moshe. "Somalia at War: Between Radical Islam and Tribal Politics." Tel Aviv University, The Faniel Abraham Center, Research Paper 2, 2008. http://www.xtome.org/docs/countries/somalia/somalia_-_Mar08.pdf.

Uhlig, Siegbert, ed. *Encyclopaedia Aethiopica*. 4 vols. Hamburg: Universität Hamburg, 2003–2010.

Haggai Erlich

HUMANISM. Humanism has been defined in diverse and sometimes contradictory ways. In the seventeenth century, humanism appeared as both a critique of religion and as "Christian humanism"; in the nineteenth century, one humanism was hostile toward science, while another was devoted to it; Marxism, existentialism, and personalism have all been termed humanisms; some Stalinists called themselves humanists; and some people "supported the humanistic values of the National Socialists" (Foucault, 1984). Given these disparate claims, combined with contested, multiple understandings of Islam, a brief review of humanism and Islam will necessarily be selective and partial. As a starting point I assume that "humanism" refers to discourses in the "modern West," traceable to the Enlightenment, which revolve around celebrating "radical freedom, creativity, and the autonomy of humanity" (Schweiker, 2003, p. 541).

The difference between Islamic humanism and nonreligious humanism may be in what authorities and claims are invoked. If one presumes that humanism describes a religious system with no reference to God, then by definition there is little scope for Islamic humanism other than in the historical/civilizational sense. It is not clear, however, that Islam is necessarily less centered on humanity simply because it proclaims "God." Following William Schweiker (2003), if humanism is to rightly value and properly esteem human beings, and if to be human is to have some orienting "good," the ethical and theological question that follows is what good can and ought to be trusted. Religious humanism can thus be imagined as religious actors who promote the human good as they perceive it, while engaging with their tradition on their own terms (Flood, 2006, p. 153).

Diverse figures from premodern Islamic history have been invoked as expressions of humanism. In identifying an "Islamic humanism" Lenn Goodman points to philosophical tracts, literary works, commentaries on ethics, and historiographic shifts toward a universal history. According to Joel Kraemer, Muḥyī al-Dīn ibn ʿArabī, al-Ḥusayn ibn Manṣūr al-Ḥallāj, ʿAbd al-Karīm al-Jīlī, and Shihāb al-Dīn Suhrawardī are well-known premodern authorities that placed man at the center of being and thus constitute an expression of humanism. Another figure, Abū Bakr Muḥammad ibn Zakarīyā al-Rāzī "advocated autonomy of reason in a manner reminiscent of the European Enlightenment" and also articulated the idea of scientific progress, further expressions of humanism (Kraemer, 1984, p. 145). Mohammad Arkoun labeled Abū Hayyān al-Tawḥīdī a "tortured" humanist and Abū ʿAlī ibn Miskawayh a "serene" humanist, arguing that an "Islamic humanism" can be discerned insofar as thinkers "confided to human reason alone the task of confirming by logic the profound truths disclosed by revelation" (Kraemer, 1984, p. 146). As evidence supporting his claims about humanism in Islam, Emad Shahin cites texts by al-Fārābī, al-Kindī, Miskawayh, and Abū Ḥāmid al-Ghazālī.

Humanistic tendencies reached a high point in the tenth century, during the ʿAbbāsid period, which Mohammad Arkoun, Joel Kraemer, and George Makdisi have labeled an Islamic "Renaissance" (Shahin, 2010). The period's "urbane, humanistic culture" became more universalistic in its humanism as its *adab* began including non-Arabic literature. Muʿtazilī approaches emphasize independent human reason as capable of producing knowledge, and appear particularly humanistic in the Enlightenment sense suggested by Kraemer.

In the modern period Muḥammad ʿAbduh, Mohammad Iqbal, and Syed Ameer Ali have been labeled humanists; ʿAbduh advocated "a liberal and humanistic Islam, free of rigid traditional formulations and invigorated by rational and historical methods of criticism" (Vatikiotis, 1957, p. 18). More recently, Abdulaziz Sachedina has argued that the Qurʾān offers a "vision of a universal humanity." This essential message of human unity can promote harmony and cooperation, and it affirms diversity as valuable (49:14; "so that you may know one another") rather than inevitably producing tension. Emad Shahin suggests that five discernible features form humanistic tendencies in Islam. First "the value of human beings as the center of the universe"; second "cosmopolitanism and the unity of humanity (*wihdat al-khalq*)"; third "attainment of happiness (taḥṣīl *al-saʿāda*)"; fourth "knowledge and reason as the driving force for the attainment of happiness and progress"; and fifth "universal cooperation to achieve global happiness (*al-taʿāwun fī al-insanīya*)" (Shahin, 2010, p. 6).

An Islamic humanism, or significant elements thereof, can be found in Khaled Abou El Fadl's assertion that a Muslim must be committed to the well-being of other humans. Vindicating the rights of human beings is "our prime moral responsibility on earth"; "commitment in favor of human rights is a commitment in favor of God's creation and ultimately a commitment in favor of God" (Abou El Fadl, 2003). The Qurʾān does not differentiate the sanctity of a Muslim and a non-Muslim, and repeatedly asserts that humans cannot limit or regulate divine mercy. Thinkers of the twentieth and twenty-first centuries continue to wrestle with the question of whether Islam can make human dignity the sole criterion for social and political entitlement in an Islamic political context.

One question is how religious humanism in the Islamic context fares in competition with other visions. The Khārijites of early Islamic history represent an exemplary antihumanist posture. Their slogans, which have parallels in some recent Islamist groups, included "Dominion belongs to God" and "the Qurʾān is the Judge." They alleged that ʿAlī ibn Abī Ṭālib had forsaken the dominion of God and instead accepted the judgment and dominion of human beings. In Abou El Fadl's critique, the Khārijite position rested on the fiction that some humans can entirely set aside their own proclivities and perfectly access and execute God's will, and some Muslim puritans in the modern period assume a neo-Khārijī position.

Contemporary religious identity-based conflict groups, some espousing the widespread "clash of civilizations" narrative, also contradict universalistic religious humanism. Against this tendency, a significant recent effort is the Common Word document, which has notable signatories from different schools of thought and claims to offer an authoritative interpretation of a Qurʾānic verse. The Common Word to which it appeals is the greatest commandment, to love God, and the second great commandment, to love thy neighbor. While this is narrower than "all humanity" because it is explicitly addressed to Christians, the second commandment that it affirms is not restricted to any faith group. It is a religious version of the Golden Rule, which is found in other ethical systems. To the extent that humanist doctrine is centered on the shared responsibility implied by "want for your neighbor what you want for yourself," the Common Word initiative forms a potential supporting plank for an Islamic religious humanism.

Nonreligious humanist claims about social needs are by definition not couched in theological terms. In this regard nonreligious humanism overlaps with a political prescription for a secular state in a religious Islamic context by Abdullahi An-Naʿim (2008). An-Naʿim proposes that a modern Muslim polity should not allow *Sharīʿah* to be publicly invoked as the reason for favoring (or opposing) a particular policy because it quickly shuts down the deliberative process by implicitly challenging the piety of those with counterproposals. This can be detrimental to policy-making, and to achieving the public good, which, ironically, is usually considered to be a goal of *Sharīʿah*. In place of invoking claims about *Sharīʿah*, An-Naʿim advocates the use of "public reason," akin to "civic reason" described by Habermas. In terms of invoked authorities in public deliberations on policy matters, An-Naʿim's prescription differs little from what might be expected in a nonreligious humanist polity.

BIBLIOGRAPHY

Abou El Fadl, Khaled. "Islam and the Challenge of Democracy: Can Individual Rights and Popular Sovereignty Take Root in Faith?" *Boston Review*, April/May 2003). http://bostonreview.net/BR28.2/abou.html.

An-Naʿim, Abdullahi. *Islam and the Secular State: Negotiating the Future of Shariʿa*. Cambridge, Mass.: Harvard University Press, 2008.

Common Word Signatories. "A Common Word Between Us." http://www.acommonword.com.

Flood, Gavin. "Response to William Schweiker." *Journal of the American Academy of Religion* 74, no. 1 (March 2006): 152–154.

Foucault, Michel. "What is Enlightenment?" ["Qu'est-ce que les lumières?"]. In *The Foucault Reader*, edited by Paul Rabinow, pp. 32–50. New York: Pantheon Books, 1984. http://foucault.info/documents/whatIsEnlightenment/foucault.whatIsEnlightenment.en.html.

Goodman, Lenn E. *Islamic Humanism*. Oxford: Oxford University Press, 2003.

Kraemer, Joel L. "Humanism in the Renaissance of Islam: A Preliminary Study." *Journal of the American Oriental Society* 104, no. 1 (January–March 1984): 135–164.

Sachedina, Abdulaziz. *The Islamic Roots of Democratic Pluralism*. Oxford and New York: Oxford University Press, 2001.

Schweiker, William. "Theological Ethics and the Question of Humanism." *The Journal of Religion* 83, no. 4 (October 2003): 539–561.

Shahin, Emad El-Din. "Toleration in a Modern Islamic Polity: Contemporary Islamist Views." In *Toleration on Trial*, edited by Ingrid Creppell, Russell Hardin, and Stephen Macedo. Lanham, Md.: Lexington Books, 2008.

Vatikiotis, P. J. "Muḥammad ʿAbduh and the Quest for a Muslim Humanism." *Arabica* 4, no. 1 (January 1957): 55–72.

ANAS MALIK

HUMAN RIGHTS. The term "human rights," or *huqūq al-insān* in Arabic, has only recently come into common use, as have the analogous terms *huqūq-i insān* in Persian, *insan haklari* in Turkish, and *hak asasi anusia* in Bahasa Indonesia (Indonesian).

Early Formulations and Influences. Concepts analogous to human rights have certain precursors in Islamic philosophy and theology, but human rights lack precise equivalents in medieval *fiqh* (jurisprudence). In *fiqh* the category *ḥaqq al-ʿabd*, the right of the individual Muslim, was used to distinguish cases in which legal actions against a wrongdoer were left to the discretion of the injured party or parties from other cases belonging to the category of the right of God, *ḥaqq Allāh*, in which prosecution was mandatory and to be undertaken by the government. One settled *fiqh* principle corresponding to a modern right was the right of the owners of property to seek legal relief against interference with their property.

Rather than constructing doctrines or proposing institutions designed to curb the powers of the ruler or to protect the individual from the ruler's oppression, Islamic legal thought long concentrated on defining the theoretical duties of believers, including rulers, vis-à-vis God. According to the prevailing perspective, rulers had the obligation to rule according to *Sharīʿah* law; their subjects were to obey them unless the order constituted a sin. The development of institutions that could place real curbs on rulers' despotism or make them accountable to those they ruled was neglected; rebellion was commonly proposed as the remedy for tyranny.

To deal with the practical problems of protecting rights and freedoms, Muslim intellectuals and statesmen began to adopt the principles of European constitutionalism in the nineteenth century. In the latter half of the twentieth century, after the common acceptance of the principles of constitutionalism, the related question of the compatibility of international human rights principles with Islamic doctrine was raised. This debate was, however, highly politicized because of the legacy of colonialism and imperialism. During the latter half of the twentieth century Western support for Israel, despite its ongoing violation of UN Security Council resolutions, and for many authoritarian Arab/Muslim regimes brought charges of double standards and hypocrisy to the human rights debate.

The strongest influences on Muslims' ideas came from French concepts and legal principles developed during the Enlightenment and the French Revolution. These included the first great statement of modern human rights, the 1789 Declaration des Droits de l'Homme et du Citoyen, and the 1791 French constitution, as well as concepts of public liberties. In the areas of the Muslim world ruled by Britain, which lacked a written constitution expressly guaranteeing specified rights, the models were democratic freedoms as developed in the common-law tradition and Britain's system of parliamentary government.

Many nineteenth-century officials, diplomats, and writers from Muslim countries played roles in disseminating European ideas of constitutionalism and public liberties. They included the Egyptian *shaykh* Rifāʿah Rāfiʿ al-Ṭahṭāwī (1801–1871), an al-Azhar scholar who studied French legal and political institutions in Paris from 1826 to 1831. He prepared a report on concepts of political rights, the rule of law, liberty, equality, and the ideas of the Enlightenment, and translated the French constitution into Arabic; in 1839 his report was translated into Turkish. The Persian diplomat Mīrzā Malkom Khān (1833–1908), who was educated in Paris, had lived in Turkey, and later became the Persian ambassador to Great Britain, wrote extensively on European concepts of government, the rule of law, and liberty, claiming that these could be reconciled with Islam. In the Ottoman realm the literary figure Namık Kemal (1840–1888) was prominent in disseminating ideas of rights and freedoms and the notion of their compatibility with Islam.

Nonetheless, it needs to be emphasized that the European colonial powers in the aftermath of the Age of Enlightenment routinely and systematically violated the rights of the colonized. Thus human rights were introduced mainly in the breech with loss of life, systematic torture in the case of France in Algeria, and the denial of liberty and freedom of speech when imperial rule was threatened. The subjugated did however use the ideas and rhetoric of rights to morally disarm their colonizer and propel their cause. It is estimated that in Algeria alone, upward of a million people died in the protracted and bitter struggle against French colonialism.

Constitutionalism and Rights. In the nineteenth century early debates developed over differences between inherited Islamic doctrines and modern norms regarding rights, particularly concerning the equality of Muslims and non-Muslims before the law, as European powers pressed for the elimination of the disabilities traditionally imposed on non-Muslims.

The most important early reforms in the direction of realizing rights were undertaken in the Ottoman Empire, which had many non-Muslim subjects and which, because of its military and economic vulnerability, was also exposed to pressures from European powers. The *hatt-ı şerif* (noble edict) of 1839, reinforced by the *hatt-ı hümayun* (imperial edict) of 1856, was part of a series of modernizing reforms in the Tanzimat period intended to establish the security of life, honor, and property, fair and public trials, and equality before the law for all Ottoman subjects irrespective of religion. The principle of nondiscrimination based on language and race was added by the *hatt-ı hümayun*. In 1840 the new penal code affirmed the equality of all Ottoman subjects before the law.

By mid-century reformist pressures prompted the adoption of the 1876 Ottoman constitution, which contained a section on the *hukuk-i umumiye* (public liberties) of Ottoman subjects, providing for equality regardless of religion, free exercise of religions other than Islam, and freedom of worship, inviolability of personal freedom, and guarantees against arbitrary intrusions, extortion, arrest, or other unlawful violations of person, residence, or property. There were also provisions for freedom of the press, association, and education. This constitution was suspended in practice and not revived until after the Young Turk Revolution in 1908, a central goal of which was to revive the constitution and establish the equality of all Ottoman citizens. The Young Turks' reforms expanded constitutional rights protections, prohibited arrests and searches except by established legal procedures, abolished special or extraordinary courts, and guaranteed press freedom. Turkey's second republic saw in 1961 the promulgation of a constitution that undertook in its preamble to ensure and guarantee "human rights and liberties" and made men and women equal (Article 12).

In the area of free exercise of religion, conditions were imposed to safeguard the policy of secularism adopted by Mustafa Kemal Atatürk (1881–1938), the first president of the Turkish Republic. Article 2 of the 1982 Turkish constitution proclaimed Turkey to be a law-state that respects human rights. In Republican Turkey the energetic pursuit of Kemalist secularism, beginning in 1925, led to the repression of various Islamic groups, especially Ṣūfī orders.

Popular agitation against the despotism of the Qājār shahs culminated in Persia's first constitution in 1906–1907. Persia's Shīʿī clerics were divided about the religious legitimacy of constitutionalism and its attendant rights provisions. One group of proconstitutionalist clerics, whose most articulate champion was Ayatollah Muḥammad Ḥusayn Nāʾīni (1860–1936), argued that a democratic constitution was compatible with the core values of Islam and should be supported because it placed limits on monarchial tyranny. Another group led by Ayatollah Fażlullāh Nūrī (1842–1909) opposed the constitution, citing opposition to the equality in law between Muslims and non-Muslims, freedom of the press and speech and the supremacy of human-made law over divine law.

After the 1979 Islamic Revolution in Iran official spokesmen invoked Islam as the reason for the clerical regime's hostility to international human rights, which they often dismissed as products of an alien, Western cultural tradition; however Iran did not repudiate its ratification of the International Covenant on Civil and Political Rights. The 1979 Iranian constitution in Article 20 states that all citizens shall be protected by the law and enjoy "human, political, economic, social, and cultural rights" but then qualifies them by stating they must be "in conformity with Islamic criteria." Other articles in the constitution (Articles 21–42) that refer to basic rights and freedoms are similarly qualified by reference to religion and in case there is any doubt, Article 4 states that Islamic principles shall prevail over the entire constitution and that Islamic jurists of the non-elected Guardian Council are the interpreters of what constitutes Islamic criteria. The limitations placed on human rights correlated with the policies of Iran's clerical leadership after 1979.

The principle of equality and equal protection for women and religious minorities was breached in many ways. In the name of implementing Islamic criminal justice, the regime ignored principles of criminal procedure designed to protect the rights of the accused both before and during trial, as well as prohibitions of cruel and inhuman punishment. Religious minorities and individuals and groups opposed to clerical rule or the regime's religious ideology were excluded from the political process and were often subjected to harsh persecution. During the Reformist presidency of Mohamed Khatami (1997–2005) the human rights situation improved, especially during his first term. This was attributed in part to his own commitment to defend the rights of the people and to strengthen civil society. The proliferation of independent newspapers and the reformist-dominated sixth parliament (2000–2004) helped expose human rights abuses. Most of these gains, however, were rolled back during Khatami's second term in office in a conservative backlash against the reform movement. Since the election of the ultraconservative President Mahmoud Ahmadinejad in 2005, the human-rights situation has continued to deteriorate.

In the Arab world a fundamental pact announced in Tunisia in 1857 under European pressure guaranteed equality for all before the law and in taxation as well as complete security for all inhabitants irrespective of religion, nationality, or race. Tunisia was the first Muslim country to promulgate a constitution, doing so in 1861 and affirming the rights established in the pact; however the constitution was suspended by the French Protectorate (1881–1956). In Tunisia as in many other Muslim countries, the independence struggle against European domination heightened people's consciousness of the importance of rights and democratic freedoms. After independence the 1956 Tunisian constitution stated that the republican form of government was the best guarantee of "human rights."

By the end of the twentieth century all Muslim countries had adopted constitutions containing some or all of the rights principles set forth in international human rights law. The 1989 Algerian constitution was noteworthy for its guarantee of equality before the law regardless of gender (Article 28), fundamental liberties and human rights (Article 31), and human rights advocacy (Article 32). Like most Muslim countries, however, Algeria retained Islamic personal-status rules and constitutional provisions according Islam a privileged status, perpetuating the ambiguous relationship between religious and constitutional norms.

Traditional interpretations of Islamic law survived longest as the official law of the land in Saudi Arabia, but changes inaugurated in 1992 suggested that the country might be moving gradually toward a governmental system that would accord at least limited recognition to rights and constitutionalism, albeit subject to Islamic criteria. The principle that Islam entails limits on human rights was adopted in the Basic Law of Government promulgated by the Saudi Arabian regime in 1992; Article 26 provided that "the state protects human rights in accordance with the Islamic *sharīʿah*." What the *Sharīʿah* limits on rights would entail was not defined. The basic law provided for many citizen entitlements in the area of social welfare, but only a few rights in the political or civil area were recognized. These included the provision that no one should be arrested, imprisoned, or have his actions restricted except as provided by law (Article 36); that homes should not be entered or searched save in cases specified by statutes (Article 37); that communications should not be confiscated, delayed, read, or listened to except in cases defined by statute (Article 40); and that private property must be protected and could only be taken for the public interest and with fair compensation (Article 17).

Women's Rights. One of the areas where the clash between traditional interpretations of Islamic principles and international human rights norms remains most acute is that of women's rights. Although conservatives propounded the notion that full equality for women violated Islamic precepts, feminists argued that it was patriarchal attitudes and inadequate study of the Islamic sources that led to the notion that Islam required keeping women in a subordinate position.

In the late nineteenth century, liberal writers such as the Egyptian Qāsim Amīn (1865–1908) had already propounded the thesis that certain problems facing Middle Eastern societies—despotism, moral degeneration, and the degraded status of women—were not intrinsic to Islam but were the products of corrupting influences and social customs. While not advocating full equality for women, Amīn demanded that women's rights should be enhanced. He also linked the cause of women's freedom to the realization of freedom and rights for citizens in general. Feminists such as the Egyptian Hudā Shaʿrāwī (1882–1947) became prominent advocates of women's rights and emancipation. One of the boldest attempts to reconcile Islam with full equality for women was offered by al-Ṭāhir al-Ḥaddād, an Islamic reformer, who in 1930 published *Imraʾatunā fī al-sharīʿah wa-al-mujtamaʿ* (Our Women in the *Sharīʿah* and Society), which propounded the idea that Islam had envisaged a progressive emancipation of women; he advocated the reform of Islamic laws to eliminate obstacles to male-female equality in the domestic as well as the public sphere. For the boldness of its thesis the book was condemned with particular vehemence by conservatives and its author denounced as a heretic.

Women's equality was also a common theme among Indian Muslim modernist reformers. Mumtāz ʿAlī (1860–1935) wrote manifestos arguing for women's equality. A conservative Muslim cleric, he broke with his traditionalist brethren to articulate an Islamic exegetical basis for women's equality and founded, along with his wife, a journal on women's rights.

Unequivocal support for full equality for women came from Kemal Atatürk, who, in the wake of the Turkish war of independence, proclaimed that women had the right to equality; he subsequently took measures to remove the disabilities imposed by Turkish custom and Islamic law—without attempting to reconcile his reforms with Islamic precepts. In the Arab world the most dramatic reform was embodied in the Tunisian Law of Personal Status of 1956, promulgated by President Habib Bourguiba. Presented as an Islamic law, the code undertook bold reforms improving women's status, such as abolishing polygamy and establishing equal rights for men and women in divorce.

Into the late twentieth century many Muslim countries preserved laws that discriminated against women and denied them full civil and political rights, often in the face of constitutional provisions mandating the equality of all citizens. In general laws afforded women considerable equality outside the family; it was in the area of personal status that discriminatory features taken from traditional interpretations were retained. Saudi Arabia was notable for its reliance on its own narrow and rigidly sectarian interpretation of traditional Islam to justify its refusal to grant women rights and freedoms widely enjoyed elsewhere in the Muslim world. Saudi Arabia has also been accused by international human rights organizations of systematically discriminating against Shīʿī Muslims and religious minorities.

Few Muslim countries ratified the 1979 Convention on the Elimination of All Forms of Discrimination Against Women, and those that chose to ratify did so subject to reservations regarding various central provisions. The reservations made by Bangladesh, Egypt, Libya, and Tunisia were specifically justified by their need to adhere to Islamic law.

Human Rights Movements. Independent nongovernmental organizations founded for the defense of human rights have spearheaded campaigns to improve respect for human rights in Muslim countries. One of the earliest Muslim human rights organizations was established by Moroccans in December 1933 in the Spanish-controlled enclave of Tetouan as an affiliate of a Spanish human-rights organization. A human rights group with Islamic affiliations, the Iranian Committee for the Defense of Freedom and Human Rights, was formed with the participation of several religious figures; it aimed primarily at achieving democratization and the elimination of torture and of political trials in camera. A central participant was Mehdi Bazargan (1907–1995), a proponent of Islamic liberalism who went on to become Iran's first prime minister after the Islamic Revolution. He and his associates later broke with the leader of the 1979 Islamic Revolution, Ayatollah Khomeini, over the question of human rights abuses and democracy following the seizure of the U.S. embassy in Tehran. Human rights organizations in which educated professionals were prominent proliferated throughout the Muslim world in the 1980s in the face of daunting obstacles and dangers. One of the most important was the Arab Organization for Human Rights, which, like the overwhelming majority of independent human rights organizations, espoused the human rights standards set forth in international law. These organizations collaborated with international human rights organizations.

Muslim States and International Human Rights Law. It was in the immediate aftermath of World War II that the modern international formulations of human rights were produced, setting standards that came to be incorporated in public international law. Muslim countries were among the founding members of the United Nations, whose 1945 Charter called for respect for human rights and fundamental freedoms; all Muslim countries eventually joined the UN.

Recent scholarship has shown that Muslim countries and their representatives actively participated in the formulation and negotiation of the Universal Declaration of Human Rights (UDHR) and two legally binding covenants (the International Covenant on Civil and Political Rights [ICCPR] and the International Covenant on Social, Economic, and Cultural Rights/ [ICESCR]. Some were supportive and others were not. Charles Malik representing Lebanon and Omar Loutfi representing Egypt participated in the discussions on the UDHR, Malik from its very inception.

There was no voice of Muslim unanimity but instead a diversity of opinions reflecting national and individual interests. Pakistan's foreign minister, Sir Muhammad Zafaru'llah Khan, an Aḥmadī Muslim, argued strongly for freedom of religion. Saudi Arabia wished to omit the phrase dealing with the freedom to change religion from Article 18. Both the Indian delegate Mohammed Habib and the Pakistani delegate Zafrullah Khan opposed the Saudi motion.

The Iraqi female delegate Bedia Afnan insisted on wording that recognized gender equality, resulting in Article 3 within the ICCPR and ICESCR. Another strong proponent for women's rights was the Pakistani female delegate Shaista Ikramullah.

Aspects of the Universal Declaration of Human Rights passed by the General Assembly in 1948 provoked criticism from representatives of Muslim countries, although in the end only Saudi Arabia opposed its passage. Muslim nations differed greatly in their willingness to ratify the human rights conventions subsequently drafted under UN auspices. Muslims sometimes charged that international rights norms had a Western or Judeo-Christian bias that prevented their acceptance in Muslim milieus. In terms of the compatibility of international rights norms and Islamic law, the alleged conflicts centered on civil and political rights; issues of the compatibility of Islam with economic, social, and cultural rights were rarely raised. The principles of freedom of religion—notably the right to convert from Islam to another faith—and the full equality of persons regardless of sex or religion seemed to pose particular problems.

The charter of the Organization of the Islamic Conference (OIC), an international organization founded in 1969 to which all Muslim countries belong, stated in its preamble that the members were "reaffirming their commitment to the UN Charter and fundamental human rights." (The organization changed its name in 2011 to the Organization of Islamic Cooperation.) The OIC charter came into force in 1973. In 1990, however, the OIC issued the Cairo Declaration on Human Rights in Islam, which diverged significantly from international human rights standards; it was not made clear how this declaration was to be reconciled with the conflicting obligations undertaken by OIC members in ratifying international human rights covenants or in their individual constitutional rights provisions, which in many cases corresponded to the international norms.

The OIC declaration extensively borrowed terms and concepts from the International Bill of Human Rights, presenting a mixture of elements taken from traditional Islamic and international law. The OIC Declaration asserted that "fundamental rights and universal freedoms in Islam are an integral part of the Islamic religion," but then proceeded to insert qualifications and conditions on the rights and freedoms guaranteed under international law—in conflict with international human rights theory, which does not permit religious criteria to override rights. Representative provisions included the rule in Article 24 that all the rights and freedoms stipulated in the declaration were subject to the *Sharīʿah*, without defining what limits this would entail.

There was no provision for equal rights for all persons regardless of sex or religion. Instead Article 1 stated that "all human beings are equal in terms of basic human dignity and basic obligations and responsibilities (not "rights"), without any discrimination on the grounds of race, color, language, sex, religious belief, political affiliation, social status or other considerations." Article 6 further provided that "woman is equal to man in human dignity" (not "rights"), but it imposed on the husband the responsibility for the support and welfare of the family. In contrast Article 13 provided that men and women were entitled to fair wages "without discrimination." Article 5 provided that on the right to marry there should be "no restrictions stemming from race, color, or nationality," but did not prohibit restrictions based on religion.

The provisions regarding religion did not aim at neutrality: Article 10 stated that Islam was the religion of unspoiled nature and prohibited "any form of compulsion on man or to exploit his poverty or ignorance in order to convert him to another religion or to atheism." Article 9 called for the state to ensure the means to acquire education "so as to enable man to be acquainted with the religion of Islam." The favored treatment of Islam carried over to freedom of speech, with Article 22(a) stating that expressing opinion freely was allowed "in such manner as would not be contrary to the principles of the *sharīʿah*." Article 22(c) barred the exploitation or misuse of information "in such a way as may violate sanctities and the dignity of Prophets, undermine moral and ethical values or disintegrate, corrupt or harm society or weaken its faith." Article 18 stipulated a right to privacy in the conduct of private affairs, in the home, in the family, and regarding property and relationships. Article 15 set forth "rights of ownership" to "property acquired in a legitimate way, barring expropriation except for the public interest and upon payment of immediate and fair compensation."

Notable for their absence were provisions calling for the observance of democratic principles in political systems and guarantees of freedom of religion, freedom of association, freedom of the press, and equality and equal protection of the law. Although torture was prohibited in Article 20, there were no provisions explicitly endorsing international rights norms in the area of criminal procedure—only the vague assurance in Article 19 that the defendant would be entitled to "a fair trial in which he shall be given all the guarantees of defense." Since Article 25 stated that the *Sharīʿah* "is the only source of reference or the explanation or clarification of any of the articles of this Declaration," the possibility was left open that a trial would be deemed "fair" as long as it was conducted in conformity with *Sharīʿah* norms, which were historically underdeveloped in the area of criminal procedure. There was no principle of legality per se; the provision in Article 19 that there should be no crime or punishment except as provided for in the *Sharīʿah* seemed to open the door to the application of *taʿzīr* ([discretionary] penalties), as well as rules regarding the fixed punishments for *ḥadd* crimes, such as amputation of the hand for theft. Article 2 prohibited taking away life except for a reason prescribed by the *Sharīʿah*. Reflecting the third-world setting in which Muslim nations elaborate their positions on rights, Article 11 prohibited colonialism and stated that "peoples suffering from colonialism have the full right to freedom and self-determination." In sum the OIC Declaration suggested that the official approach of Muslim countries to civil and political rights was distinguishable from that of non-Muslim countries by reason of their reliance on *Sharīʿah* rules.

Today "secular" discourses in the Muslim world are widely discredited and viewed as inauthentic. Thus contemporary Muslim human rights scholars have attempted to anchor human rights discourses within an Islamic paradigm; that is, the universal is particularized within the dominant idiom of Muslim societies. Among the more visible proponents include: the human rights activist Shirin Ebadi who won the 2003 Nobel Peace Prize and the Yemeni activist Tawakkol Karman who was a co-recipient of the 2011 Nobel Peace Prize.

Shirin Ebadi won her peace prize on behalf of her struggle for the rights of children and women in her native Iran. Tawakkol Karman is a prominent human rights activist who rose to prominence for her pro-democracy struggles during the Arab Spring. Other intellectual voices include Khaled Abou El Fadl and ʿAbd Allāh al-Naʿīm. Khaled Abou El Fadl has offered critiques of modern day fundamentalists and articulated a reading that emphasizes a rights-based discourse that is premised on Islamic values and the legal debates of Islamic jurists from the medieval era. Al-Naʿīm has argued that Islamic law—and understandings of *Sharīʿah*—must be contested and not treated as unsusceptible to reinterpretation; that is, *Sharīʿah* is not divine writ itself, but rather is based on human interpretation that is inherently fallible and subject to change. He also believes that the state should not enforce *Sharīʿah* on society.

Muslim feminists in recent years have argued that Muslim men have arrogated to themselves alone the role of interpreters of religious law, and they now contest vigorously patriarchal interpretations of Islam. Among the most prominent proponents of an indigenous feminist reading are Zainah Anwar, Hatoon Al-Fassi, and Ziba Mir-Hosseini.

In a post–September 11th world, the ubiquitous authoritarian state remains the most significant human rights abuser in the Muslim world where torture, illegal detention, and the absence of judicial process are common. And human rights abuses at Abū Ghurayb prison in Iraq and the Guantanamo Bay detention camp and drone attacks have severely tarnished the reputation and made hollow the claim of the West as the standard-bearer of universal human rights. In Europe Muslim minorities find themselves increasingly besieged and their religious freedoms impinged. Governments, organizations, and individuals throughout the Muslim world continue to take a variety of opposing positions on human rights.

The Arab Spring witnessed the emergence of Islamic political parties that have participated in the Egyptian and Tunisian elections. They hold a variety of positions on human rights ranging from quietist and reluctant support on the part of the Muslim Brothers to Salafīs who wish to further restrict the rights of women and non-Muslim minorities. The conflicts in Iraq and Syria have also intensified and solidified the sectarian divide and conflict between the Sunni and Shīʿah. In Egypt, four Shīʿah were lynched and murdered in Greater Cairo on 23 June 2013, by a Salafī mob. In Pakistan, the Pakistani Taliban have combined ever-increasing levels of misogyny and lethal violence directed against women and girls, even going so far as to forbid girls' education and attacking those girls who resist their strictures—most famously, Malala Yousafzai, the Pakistani teenage activist. The various terror activities against female education have no justification in Islamic legal thought and contemporary tribal practice. Pakistan's Islamist political parties remain reluctant to criticize or even accept the culpability of the Pakistani Taliban for these actions. Throughout the Islamic world, apostasy and blasphemy laws are used to target liberal Muslim thinkers, heterodox Muslims, and non-Muslim minorities. Non-state actors (jihadist groups) use these laws to legimitate extra-judicial killings of those tried, but not found guilty, particularly non-Muslim minorities in Pakistan.

There is a divide between those using "Islamic" discourses to legitimate human rights and those that interpret sacred text to obtain the opposite meaning. It remains unclear which forces are ascendant, though polling consistently reveals that a plurality of Muslims do admire and support human rights and democracy. An ever-growing number of Muslim scholars and activists are continuing the slow and deliberative process of interpreting Islamic legal principles in a way that is consonant with human rights.

[*See also* International Law; Organization of Islamic Cooperation; Taliban; *and* Tanzimat.]

Bibliography

Abou El Fadl, Khaled. "Cultivating Human Rights: Islamic Law and the Humanist Imperative." In *Law and Tradition in Classical Islamic Thought: Studies in Honor of Professor Hossein Modarressi*, edited by Michael Cook et al. New York: Palgrave Macmillan, 2012.

Abou El Fadl, Khalid. *The Great Theft: Wresting Islam from the Extremists*. New York: HarperSanFrancisco, 2005.

Abou El Fadl, Khaled. *Islam and the Challenge of Democracy*. Edited by Joshua Cohen and Deborah Chasman. Princeton, N.J.: Princeton University Press, 2004.

Abou El Fadl, Khaled. "The Human Rights Commitment in Modern Islam." In *Human Rights and Responsibilities in the World Religions*, edited by Joseph Runzo, Nancy M. Martin, and Arvind Sharma. Oxford: Oneworld Publications, 2003.

Abou El Fadl, Khaled. "Islamic Law, Human Rights and Neo-Colonialism." In *Oxford Amnesty Lectures 2006: The "War on Terror,"* edited by Chris Miller. Manchester, U.K.: Manchester University Press, 2009.

Abou El Fadl, Khaled. *Speaking in God's Name: Islamic Law, Authority and Women*. Oxford: Oneworld Publications, 2001.

Ahmad, Eqbal, and Stuart Schaar. "Tahar Haddad: A Tunisian Activist Intellectual." *Maghreb Review* 21, nos. 3–4 (1996): 240–255.

Ali, Kecia. *Sexual Ethics and Islam: Feminist Reflections on Qur'an, Hadith, and Jurisprudence*. Oxford: Oneworld, 2006.

An-Na'im, Abdulahi. *Islam and Human Rights: Selected Essays of Abdullahi An-Na'im*. Edited by Mashood A. Baderin. Aldershot, U.K.: Ashgate, 2010.

An-Na'im, Abdullahi. *Islam and the Secular State: Negotiating the Future of Shari'a*. Cambridge, Mass.: Harvard University Press, 2008.

An-Na'im, Abdullahi. "Islam, Sharia and Democratic Transformation in the Arab World." *Die Friedens-Warte* [Journal of International Peace and Organization] 87 (2012): 27–41.

An-Na'im, Abdullahi Ahmed. *Toward an Islamic Reformation: Civil Liberties, Human Rights, and International Law*. Syracuse, N.Y.: Syracuse University Press, 1990.

An-Na'im, Abdullahi. "Transcending Imperialism: Human Values and Global Citizenship." In *The Tanner Lectures on Human Values*, edited by Suzan Young, vol. 30, pp. 71–144. Salt Lake City: University of Utah Press, 2012.

An-Na'im, Abdullahi. "Why Should Muslims Abandon Jihad? Human Rights and the Future of International Law." *Third World Quarterly* 27, no. 5 (2006): 785–797.

Anwar, Zainah. "Negotiating Gender Rights under Religious Law in Malaysia." In *New Directions in Islamic Thought: Exploring Reform and Muslim Tradition*, edited by Kari Vogt, Lena Larsen, and Christian Moe. London: I. B. Tauris, 2009.

Baderin, Mashood A. *International Human Rights and Islamic Law*. Oxford: Oxford University Press, 2003.

Badran, Margot. *Feminism Beyond East and West: New Gender Talk and Practice in Global Islam*. New Delhi: Global Media Publications, 2007.

Bano, Masooda, and Hilary Kalmbach, eds. *Women, Leadership and Mosques: Changes in Contemporary Islamic Authority*. Leiden, Netherlands: E. J. Brill, 2012.

Barlas, Asma. "Believing Women." In *Islam: Unreading Patriarchal Interpretations of the Qur'ān*. Austin: University of Texas Press, 2002.

Blaustein, A. P., and G. H. Flanz, eds. *Constitutions of the Countries of the World*. Dobbs Ferry, N.Y.: Oceana Publications, 1971–.

Coulson, Noel J. "The State and the Individual in Islamic Law." *International and Comparative Law Quarterly* 6 (1957): 49–60.

Ebadi, Shirin, and Azadeh Moaveni. *Iran Awakening: A Memoir of Revolution and Hope*. New York: Random House, 2006.

Hairi, Abdul-Hadi. *Shi'ism and Constitutionalism in Iran: A Study of the Role Played by Persian Residents of Iraq in Iranian Politics*. Leiden, Netherlands: E. J. Brill, 1977.

Hammer, Juliane. *American Muslim Women, Religious Authority, and Activism: More than a Prayer*. Austin: University of Texas Press, 2012.

Hourani, Albert. *Arabic Thought in the Liberal Age, 1798–1939*. London and New York: Oxford University Press, 1962.

Johansen, Baber. "The Relationship Between the Constitution, the Sharī'a and the Fiqh: The Jurisprudence of Egypt's Supreme Constitutional Court." *Zeitschrift für ausländisches öffentliches Recht und Völkerrecht* [Heidelberg Journal of International Law] 64, no. 4 (2004): 881–896.

Keddie, Nikki R. *Women in the Middle East: Past and Present*. Princeton, N.J.: Princeton University Press, 2006.

Kurzman, Charles, ed. *Liberal Islam: A Source Book*. Oxford and New York: Oxford University Press, 1998.

Lewis, Bernard, et al. "Dustūr." In *Encyclopaedia of Islam*, new ed., vol. 2, pp. 638–677. Leiden, Netherlands: E. J. Brill, 1960–.

Lewis, Bernard. *The Emergence of Modern Turkey*. 3d ed. New York: Oxford University Press, 2002.

Mayer, Ann. *Islam and Human Rights: Tradition and Politics*. 5th ed. Boulder, Colo.: Westview Press, 2013.

Mernissi, Fatima. *The Veil and the Male Elite: A Feminist Interpretation of Women's Rights in Islam*. Translated by Mary Jo Lakeland. Reading, Mass.: Addison-Wesley, 1991.

Mir-Hosseini, Ziba. "Classical Fiqh, Contemporary Ethics and Gender Justice." In *New Directions in Islamic Thought: Exploring Reform and Muslim Tradition*, edited by Kari Vogt, Lena Larsen, and Christian Moe. London: I. B. Tauris, 2009.

Moosa, Ebrahim. "The Dilemma of Islamic Rights Schemes." *Journal of Law and Religion* 15, nos. 1–2 (2000–2001): 185–215.

Rosenthal, Franz. *The Muslim Concept of Freedom Prior to the Nineteenth Century*. Leiden, Netherlands: E. J. Brill, 1960.

Saeed, Abdullah, and Hassan Saeed. *Freedom of Religion, Apostasy, and Islam*. Aldershot, U.K., and Burlington, Vt.: Ashgate, 2004.

Şentürk, Recep. "Sociology of Rights: 'I Am, Therefore I Have Rights': Human Rights in Islam between

Universalistic and Communalistic Perspectives." *Muslim World Journal of Human Rights* 2, no. 1 (2005). http://www.bepress.com/mwjhr/vol2/iss1/art11.

Wadud, Amina. *Qur'ān and Woman: Rereading the Sacred Text from a Woman's Perspective*. 2d ed. New York: Oxford University Press, 1999.

Waltz. Susan. "Universal Human Rights: The Contribution of Muslim States." *Human Rights Quarterly* 26, no. 4 (2004): 799–844.

NADER HASHEMI
and EMRAN QURESHI

ḤUSAYN IBN ʿALĪ. Ḥusayn ibn ʿAlī (626–680) was the third Shīʿī imam, son of ʿAlī ibn Abī Ṭālib and grandson of the Prophet Muḥammad. As Muḥammad had no male heirs, Ḥusayn and his elder brother Ḥasan are believed to have continued the Prophet's line through his daughter Fāṭimah and his cousin ʿAlī. Hagiographical tradition abounds with tales of love and affection of the Prophet for his two grandsons.

ʿAlī was assassinated in 661 after a short and turbulent caliphate and was succeeded by his elder son, Ḥasan. But Ḥasan soon abdicated as he realized the disunity and fickleness of his followers and the superiority of Muʿāwiyah's well-organized forces.

Ḥusayn reluctantly accepted his brother's compromise and refused to pay allegiance to Muʿāwiyah. However, during Muʿāwiyah's long reign (661–680), Ḥusayn honored his brother's agreement with the Umayyad caliph. Among the stipulations of this agreement was that, after Muʿāwiyah's death, his successor would either be chosen through *shūrā* (consultation) or, according to Shīʿī reports, the caliphate would revert to one of the two sons of ʿAlī.

Ḥasan died in 671, and Muʿāwiyah appointed his own son Yazīd as his successor. Yazīd is reputed to have been a lewd character given to drinking and other illicit pleasures. Many, particularly in the Hejaz and Iraq, opposed Yazīd's appointment, and a small number of notables, including Ḥusayn, withheld their allegiance. Wishing to assert his authority and quell opposition at any cost, Yazīd in 680 ordered his governor in Medina to take everyone's oath of allegiance and execute anyone who refused.

Ḥusayn left Medina (Madīnah) secretly and sought protection in the sanctuary of Mecca (Makkah). There he received numerous letters from the Shīʿah of Kufa inviting him to lead them in an insurrection against Yazīd. Ḥusayn sent his cousin Muslim ibn ʿAqīl to Kufa to investigate the situation. Muslim sent word that support for Ḥusayn was strong and that he should hasten to Kufa without delay.

Apprised of these developments Yazīd dismissed the governor of Kufa and extended the authority of ʿUbayd Allāh ibn Ziyād, the governor of Basra, to include Kufa. Ibn Ziyād was a shrewd and ruthless politician. By means of threats and bribes he quickly contained the uprising and sent a small detachment to prevent Ḥusayn from reaching Kufa. He captured Muslim and had him executed with some of his close supporters.

Ḥusayn now set out for Iraq with his women and children and a small band of followers. Learning of Muslim's fate along the way, he released his relatives and followers from all obligations and advised them to go. Many did, and he was left with a small group of loyal supporters and family members. He was intercepted by a small detachment and diverted away from Kufa to a place called Karbala on the banks of the Euphrates.

An army of about four thousand men was then assembled to confront Ḥusayn and his band of seventy-odd followers. The army was headed by ʿUmar ibn Saʿd ibn Abī Waqqāṣ, the son of a respected companion of the Prophet. Ibn Ziyād also made sure that some of Ḥusayn's Kufic supporters were conscripted.

Ḥusayn arrived at Karbala on the second of the month of Muḥarram. After a week of fruitless negotiations between Ḥusayn and ʿUmar ibn Saʿd, Ibn Ziyād sent an alternative leader, Shamir ibn Dhī al-Jawshan, with instructions to execute the reluctant ʿUmar ibn Saʿd should he refuse to carry out his orders. Ḥusayn, Ibn Ziyād ordered, should either surrender and be brought to him as a war captive or be killed in battle. For some days Ḥusayn and his followers were denied water from the Euphrates in order to force them to surrender.

On the morning of 10 Muḥarram AH 61/10 October 680, the battle began. Greatly outnumbered, Ḥusayn and his followers were annihilated by the early afternoon. Ḥusayn witnessed his own children and other relatives fall, one by one. Even an infant whom he held in his arms was slain. Finally, after a brave fight, Ḥusayn himself fell. On orders from Ibn Ziyād, Ḥusayn's corpse was trampled by horses and his head and those of his followers were paraded in Kufa as a warning to others.

Few personalities in Muslim history have exerted as great and enduring an influence on Islamic thought and piety as Imam Ḥusayn. For Sunnī, and particularly Ṣūfī, piety, Ḥusayn is the revered grandson of the Prophet and member of his household (*ahl al-bayt*). Ḥusayn's shrine-mosque in Cairo is a living symbol of Sunnī devotion to the martyred imam.

Ḥusayn's revolt against Umayyad rule inspired not only religious Muslims, but also secular socialists. A powerful portrayal of Ḥusayn the revolutionary was made by the socialist Egyptian writer ʿAbd al-Raḥmān al-Sharqāwī in his two-part play *Ḥusayn the Revolutionary* and *Ḥusayn the Martyr*.

Although these ideas are also shared by many educated Shīʿīs, Ḥusayn occupies a central place in Twelver Shīʿī faith and piety. Pilgrimage (*ziyārah*), actual or ritualistic, to his tomb is second in importance to the *ḥajj* pilgrimage. Moreover, the ʿĀshūrāʾ and other *taʿzīyah* (passion play) celebrations have given the Shīʿī community an ethos of suffering and martyrdom that distinguish it sharply from the rest of the Muslim community.

The meaning and significance of the revolution, struggle, and martyrdom of Imam Ḥusayn continues to grow with changing times and political circumstances of Muslim society. He has become a symbol of political resistance for many Muslims, regardless of their ideological persuasion or walk of life. For Shīʿī Muslims Ḥusayn is also a symbol of eschatological hope, as the expected Mahdī (messiah) will finally avenge his blood and vindicate him and all those who have suffered wrong at the hands of tyrannical rulers.

Since the Middle Ages special mosque annexes appropriately called *ḥusaynīyah* have served as centers for the memorial observances of the sufferings and martyrdom of Ḥusayn and his family and the social and political lessons that can be learned from this tragedy. It was in such centers in Beirut and south Lebanon that the first Shīʿī resistance movements were born. It was also in the Ḥusaynīyah-i Irshād that the ideas of ʿAlī Sharīʿatī kindled the final spark of the Iran's Islamic Revolution. Indications are that the example of Ḥusayn will continue to inspire Muslim resistance and religious fervor for a long time to come.

[*See also* Taʿzīyah.]

BIBLIOGRAPHY

Alsarat. *The Imam Ḥusayn*. Vol. 12. Edited by the Muhammadi Trust of Great Britain and Northern Ireland. London, 1986. Collection of papers presented at the Imam Ḥusayn Conference from a variety of Shīʿī and Sunnī scholars representing both traditional and modern views of Ḥusayn's personality and martyrdom.

Ayoub, Mahmoud M. *Redemptive Suffering in Islām: A Study of the Devotional Aspects of ʿĀshūrāʾ in Twelver Shīʿism*. The Hague: Mouton, 1978. Offers a useful discussion of the development of the ʿĀshūrāʾ celebrations and their place in Shīʿī popular piety and culture.

Bukhārī, Muḥammad ibn Ismāʿīl. *Sahīh al-Bukhārī: The Translation of the Meanings of Sahih al-Bukhari.* With the Arabic Text. Translated by Muhammad Muhsin Khān. Riyadh, Saudi Arabia: Darussalam, 1997.

Gordon, Matthew. *The Rise of Islam.* Westport, Conn.: Greenwood Press, 2005.

Mufīd, Muḥammad ibn Muḥammad. *The Book of Guidance into the Lives of the Twelve Imams = Kitāb al-irshād.* Translated by I. K. A. Howard. Elmhurst, N.Y.: Tahrike Tarsile Qurʾan, 1981. Classic work presenting a generally balanced account of Ḥusayn's life and martyrdom, by a respected tenth-century Shīʿī scholar. See part 2, chapter 2, "Imām al-Ḥusayn ibn ʿAlī," pp. 296–379.

Ṭabarī, Muḥammad ibn Jarīr al-. *The Caliphate of Yazīd b. Muʿāwiyah.* Translated by I. K. A. Howard. Vol. 19 of *The History of al-Ṭabarī.* Albany: State University of New York Press, 1990. The earliest account by an authoritative classical historian, based on the oldest sources.

MAHMOUD M. AYOUB

HYPOCRITES. Hypocrites (*munāfiqūn*) typically refers to people who outwardly profess to be Muslims while harboring disbelief or failing to fulfill the manifest duties of a Muslim. The Arabic terms for hypocrite (*munāfiq*) and hypocrisy (*nifāq*) derive from the root *n-f-q*. The form I noun *nafaq*, which appears in Qurʾānic verse 6:35, means "tunnel," and classical Arabic dictionaries frequently offer as an example the tunnel of the jerboa (*yarbūʿ*, *Jaculus orientalis*), a small desert rodent found in Central Arabia and North Africa. The jerboa hides in elaborate dens with many entrance and exit holes that confuse its predators. That the term *munāfiq* derives from this root suggests that hypocrites similarly use obfuscation and deceit to mask their true positions. While the term *nifāq* was used in pre-Islamic Arabic (as the plural of *nafaqah*, meaning "expenditures"), the specialized meaning of "hypocrisy" and its association with the term *munāfiq-ūn*, first appears in the mid-seventh century in the context of opposition to the rise and spread of Islam in Central Arabia (Ibn Manẓūr, *Lisān al-ʿarab*), thus emerging as a distinctly human characteristic and an important Islamic ethico-religious concept.

The Qurʾān describes hypocrites in terms of their moral, cognitive, and behavioral traits; assesses them according to how far their beliefs and actions deviate from normative Islamic values and practices; and situates them as a liminal class between believers and disbelievers. Hypocrites are the subject of an entire chapter of the Qurʾān (*sūrah* 63, "The Hypocrites"), which opens with a concise description of their dubious status: "They take their oaths as a screen [to conceal their misdeeds]. . . . That is because they believed and then disbelieved" (63:2–3). Hypocrites also appear in several other, mainly Medinan, chapters (e.g., 3, 4, and 9). The Qurʾān describes hypocrites in a parabolic fashion, associating them broadly with doubt (8:49 and 9:64), polytheism (4:61, 140), deceit (63:1), arrogance and showmanship (4:142 and 9:101), and disobedience during times of great struggle, such as during the battles of Uḥud and the Trench (3:167 and 59:11). According to the Qurʾān, hypocrites do the opposite of believers when they "enjoin what is evil and forbid what is just" (9:67), and are therefore subject to communal reproach and divine punishment (9:101). Frequently hypocrites/hypocrisy are mentioned alongside disbelievers/disbelief (*kāfirūn/kufr*) (e.g., 9:97 and 33:1), and it is unclear whether the two are synonymous or whether hypocrites/hypocrisy comprise an entirely separate class or a discrete subclass of disbelievers/disbelief. The Prophet is twice exhorted to "strive hard against the disbelievers and the hypocrites" (9:73 and 66:9), and while the Qurʾān frequently warns hypocrites of their impending judgment and punishment at the hands of God (4:145 and

9:68—again alongside the disbelievers), it stops short of actually stipulating the terms of their punishment at the hands of the Prophet and ordinary Muslims. The ambiguous social status of hypocrites makes the label "hypocrite" an especially malleable and provocative tool in Islamic political polemic.

The *ḥadīth* and exegetical literature (*tafsīr*) elaborate on the Qurʾānic paradigm of the hypocrite outlined above, and the political contexts and specific examples offered in these works provide models for later medieval, modern, and contemporary applications of the term in political discourses. Among the more frequent historical examples are the hostile activities of certain tribes (e.g., Aws and Khazraj) and tribal leaders (e.g., ʿAbd Allāh b. ʿUbayy b. Salūl and al-Jadd b. Qays) during critical moments in the history of the fledgling community, such as the battles of Uḥud the Trench, and the expedition to Tabuk. These reports echo the Qurʾān's depictions of hypocrites as deceitful, lazy, selfish, and arrogant, and reflect Muslims' attempts to carry out the Qurʾānic exhortations to "strive hard" against them. Many of these examples suggest that a hypocrite is not equivalent to a disbeliever but rather aligns—albeit perfidiously—with believers, yet fails to uphold the duties of full membership in the believers' community. A few references suggest more of a synonymous relationship between hypocrisy and disbelief, such as when the exegete Abū al-Ḥasan al-Wāḥidī (d. 1076) indicates that the disbelievers mentioned in Qurʾān 3:28 refer to the hypocrites ʿAbd Allāh b. ʿUbayy and his cohorts.

After the Prophet's death, allegations of hypocrisy emerge in the debates over succession to political and/or spiritual leadership of the believers' community. Various Muslim politicians, religious leaders, and historians apply the epithet "hypocrite" to the Muslim whose erroneous political alignment (and concomitant moral deviance) poses an imminent danger to the solidarity and prosperity of the Muslim polity, and therefore must be corrected or eliminated. Thus we find the Khārijites and the *qurrāʾ* (Qurʾān reciters) refusing to obey ʿAlī on account of his allegedly hypocritical statements to them during the Ṣiffīn conflict; the Sunnī historian and exegete al-Ṭabarī (d. 923) describing the Sabaʾīyah (an early pro-ʿAlid sect) as a party of hypocrites who used deceit to cloak their political opposition to Abū Bakr in pious garb; the proto-Shīʿah explaining ʿAlī's failure to secure succession at the Saqīfah, and later during the *shūrā*, on the basis of a conspiracy of selfish hypocrites to deny the Banū Hāshim their rightful place as leaders of the *ummah*; the Ilkhanid sultan Ghazan (r. 1294–1304) and the Mamluk sultan al-Nāṣir Muḥammad (r. 1293–1294 and 1299–1341) exchanging rival accusations of hypocrisy; and contemporary Salafists like Yūsuf al-Qaraḍāwī (b. 1926) and Āyman al-Ẓawāhirī (b. 1951) calling for *jihād* against non-Muslim disbelievers and hypocrites alike. Given the dubious status of the alleged hypocrite, one's objective in dealing with them may range from reform and normalization to ostracization and combat. The former objective typically involves an emphasis on the tentative and malleable character of the hypocrite, while the latter typically involves a thorough and irrevocable conflation of hypocrisy and disbelief.

BIBLIOGRAPHY

Primary Sources

Ibn Manẓūr. *Lisān al-ʿarab*. Al-Baheth al-Arabi. Available online at http://www.baheth.info/. This website provides a searchable edition of Ibn Manẓūr's widely cited late-thirteenth-century Arabic lexicon.

Qaraḍāwī, Yūsuf al-. *The Lawful and Prohibited in Islam*. Translated by K. al-Hilbawi, M. Siddiqi, and S. Shukri. 2d ed. Cairo: Al-Falah Foundation, 2001. Al-Qaradāwī is an influential Egyptian Sunnī scholar and theologian whose views are widely disseminated through Arabic television networks (e.g., Al Jazeera's program *Shariah and Life*), the Internet (e.g., http:/ www.islamonline.com/ and http://www.qaradawi.net/), and in several printed works (e.g., *Islamic Awakening between Rejection and Extremism*).

Quranic Arabic Corpus. http://corpus.quran.com/. This website provides several of the major English interpretations of the Qur'ān (e.g., Arberry, Pickthall, Sahih International, and Yusuf Ali) and shows the Arabic grammar, syntax, and morphology for each word in the Qur'ān.

Zawahiri, Ayman al-. *Loyalty and Separation: Changing and Article of Faith and Losing Sight of Reality*. Excerpted in *Al Qaeda in Its Own Words*. Edited by Gilles Kepel and Jean-Pierre Milelli, pp. 206–234. Translated by Pascale Ghazaleh. Cambridge, Mass.: Belknap, 2008. Considered by many to be Osama Bin Laden's replacement as head of al-Qa'ida, al-Ẓawāhirī represents the militant and highly conservative branch of Salafīyah, which tends to view Muslim states that conduct diplomatic relations with non-Muslim states as illegitimate hypocrites against whom Muslims are required to fight.

Secondary Sources

Ayoub, Mahmoud. *The Qur'an and Its Interpreters*. Vol. 2. Albany: State University of New York Press, 1992. Provides the English reader with a comprehensive sample of Sunnī and Shī'ī exegeses of *sūrah*, al-'Imrān (The House of 'Imrān), which includes multiple references to hypocrites.

Broadbridge, Anne F. *Kingship and Ideology in the Islamic and Mongol Worlds*. Cambridge, U.K.: Cambridge University Press, 2008. Uses mainly the diplomatic correspondences (epistles, proclamations, treaties, etc.) exchanged between the Mamlūk Sultanate and several rival Mongol dynasties in the east (e.g., the Ilkhanids and Timurids). Both claimed to be the rightful Commanders of the Believers, and both used the term "hypocrite" to denigrate their Muslim political opponents.

Crone, Patricia. *God's Rule: Government and Islam*. New York: Columbia University Press, 2004. Shows how Muslim religio-political groups made use of ethico-religious concepts such as hypocrisy and disbelief in discourses on legitimate leadership.

Donner, Fred. "The Historical Context." In *The Cambridge Companion to the Qur'ān*. Ed. Jane Dammen McAuliffe, pp. 23–39. Cambridge, U.K.: Cambridge University Press, 2006. Provides a concise presentation of the major events that occurred during the prophetic career of the Prophet Muḥammad (c. 610–611/632) that, according to both Islamic and Western scholars, played a role in shaping the revelation and the community to which it is addressed.

El-Hibri, Tayeb. *Parable and Politics in Early Islamic History: The Rashidun Caliphs*. New York: Columbia University Press, 2010. Argues that accounts of the Prophet's life and career, early community, and debates over succession during the era of the "rightly guided" caliphs consciously followed a narrative and thematic trajectory that can be traced back to biblical roots.

Kohlberg, Etan. "Some Zaydī Views on the Companions of the Prophet." *Bulletin of the School of Oriental and African Studies* 39, no. 1 (1976): 91–98. Provides a concise discussion of the principle differences in Zaydī and Imāmī (or Twelver) Shī'ī attitudes toward the Companions of the Prophet during the era of the "rightly-guided" caliphs.

Watt, W. Montgomery. *Islamic Political Thought*. Edinburgh: Edinburgh University Press, 1998. Argues that initially the Islamic concept of the caliph (*khalīfah*) closely resembled pre-Islamic notions of inherited authority. Under the Umayyad and 'Abbāsid Caliphates *khalīfah* was transformed into a merit-based institution, where the degree of merit was determined according to the candidate's religious virtues (e.g., early conversion and meritorious service), and political and historical narratives began to employ Islamic terminology, such as "hypocrites," to distinguish qualified Islamic leaders from pretenders.

Adrian De Gifis

I

ʻIBĀDĀT. *See* Sharīʿah.

IBN BĀJJAH, ABŪ BAKR. Abū Bakr ibn Bājjah (d. 1138), known in Latin as Avempace, was born in Saragossa in Muslim Spain, lived for some time in Seville and Granada, and died an untimely death in Fez. His work marks the beginning of original philosophical thought in the Muslim West and sets the stage for the later accomplishments of Ibn Ṭufayl (d. 1185) and Ibn Rushd (Averroës, d. 1198). He was a Neoplatonist in the vein of earlier eastern Muslim philosophers such as al-Fārābī (d. 950), in addition to being well informed concerning the philosophical, theological, and Ṣūfī ideas formulated by al-Ghazālī (d. 1111). He was also active in politics and served as vizier for the Almoravids (r. 1062–1147), which gave him a unique perspective on the relationship between the individual, society, and the state in light of the paradigm of human nature and purpose that emerges in that intellectual current. Secondhand accounts of his life by contemporaries, including Ibn Ṭufayl, describe him as a brilliant thinker hampered in his philosophical writing by financial and political preoccupations. Thus his life was itself an example of the tension between the transcendent calling of the philosopher, understood in Neoplatonic terms, and the obstructions posed to that by the corporeal dimension of human nature. His insights in this regard are found mainly in two works: *Ittiṣāl al-ʿaql bi-al-insān* (The Contact of the Intellect with Man) and *Tabdīr al-mutawaḥḥid* (The Conduct of the Solitary).

Following the Neoplatonist paradigm of his Muslim predecessors, Ibn Bājjah understands philosophy as the pursuit of knowledge for the sake of happiness. Happiness is the fulfillment of the objective purpose of the human being, understood as *ittiṣāl*, or contact, of the individual soul with the active intellect, the transcendent source from which emanates the intelligibility, and thus the very being, of the universe. This is the state that some Ṣūfīs described as "union" with God; and though Ibn Bājjah followed the Neoplatonists in insisting that the precise description is not union, but contact, it is clear that he conceives the philosophers and the Ṣūfīs as having a similar aim. In "The Contact of the Intellect with Man," he proposed a solution to the problem of explaining how the individual soul both maintains its individual existence and also is one with all created intellects in the state of contact with God.

Ibn Bājjah inherits the Neoplatonic schema of the human psyche propounded by the Muslim philosophers of the East. It is essentially immaterial but related to matter to various degrees, corresponding to its various faculties, ranging from the external senses, directly connected to matter; to the imagination, standing midway between matter and spirit; to pure intellect, which cognizes the intelligible forms completely independent of matter. The human essence is completely immaterial, and contact with the active intellect can be achieved only through a process of liberation from one's material entanglements. One's relation to matter, then, is only of concern insofar as it contributes to this liberation. The arrangement of these relations in such a way as to facilitate this liberation is, following Plato and al-Fārābī, the definition and proper function of the just state, understood as the Platonic Republic.

What, then, of the individual who lives not in the just state but in one of the degenerate states that nearly always prevail in the world? This raises a problem in light of the Aristotelian insight that man is a political animal. If the right kind of social life is vital to the actualization of human potential, then how, if at all, is it possible for the individual to attain contact with the active intellect in an unjust society, or under the rule of an unjust regime? This problem is the focus of Ibn Bājjah in "The Conduct of the Solitary." One solution, of course, is for the philosopher to emigrate to a just society. Such a state, however, is very rare. Perhaps no such state has ever existed since the rule of the philosopher king in the person of the Prophet Muḥammad in Medina.

Thus, Ibn Bājjah argues, while it is true that man is a social animal and that therefore life in a just society is vital to human development, a dysfunctional state can only be harmful and obstructive to the aims of the philosophical individual. In such circumstances it would be the lesser of two evils to withdraw as far as possible from social and political engagement in favor of a life of solitude in order to pursue liberation from the entanglements of the material world and contact with the divine, either individually or in the private company of others of like mind. Ibn Bājjah's pessimistic view of politics in relation to the high aspirations of the philosopher, and the quietist elitism that follows from it, would find its echo both in Ibn Ṭufayl's *Ḥayy ibn Yaqẓān*, and Ibn Rushd's strict definition of the boundary between philosophical and religious discourse.

BIBLIOGRAPHY

Al-Maʿsumi, Muhammad Saghir Hasan. "Ibn Bājjah." In *A History of Muslim Philosophy, with Short Accounts of Other Disciplines and Modern Renaissance in Muslim Lands*, edited by M. M. Sharif. 2 vols., vol. 1, pp. 506–525. Wiesbaden: Harrosowitz, 1963–1966.

Fakhry, Majid. *A History of Islamic Philosophy*. New York: Columbia University Press, 1970.

Goodman, Lenn E. "Ibn Bājjah." In *History of Islamic Philosophy*, edited by Seyyed Hossein Nasr and Oliver Leaman, pp. 294–312. London and New York: Routledge, 1996.

EDWARD MOAD

IBN AL-FARRĀʾ, ABŪ YAʿLĀ. Based in Baghdad during the eleventh century, Abū Yaʿlā b. al-Farrāʾ (d. AH 458/1066 CE) is most famous for his work, *al-Aḥkām al-sulṭāniyya*, a political treatise in which he expands on his ideas concerning the imamate that he had previously addressed in his larger work, *Kitāb al-Muʿtamad fī uṣūl al-dīn*. Although Abū al-Ḥasan al-Māwardī's (d. AH 450/1058 CE) similarly titled work on the imamate has eclipsed that of Abū Yaʿlā in the medieval and modern study of the development of the classical theory of the caliphate, Abū Yaʿlā's approach to the topic and his conclusions make him an essential voice in the discourse on medieval political culture. A staunch Ḥanbalī by character and practice, Abū Yaʿlā eschewed official association with the ruling powers (e.g., ʿAbbāsids and Saljūqs) during his lifetime, but in his discussion of the imamate he displays a keen insight into the reality of the contemporary political arena and, more specifically, the essential and integral nature of the Sunnī caliphate for the larger Muslim polity (*ummah*).

In his treatise, Abū Yaʿlā approaches his topic in a traditional and systematic fashion. After stating unequivocally in his introductory remarks that the necessity of the imamate is understood through revelation—not reason—Abū Yaʿlā then turns to the process by which the ruler (*imām*) is selected. Relying almost exclusively on examples from the Prophet, the Companions and first generation after the Prophet (*salaf*), and Aḥmad b. Ḥanbal transmitted *ḥadīth*, Abū Yaʿlā states that the ruler may be selected either by "those who loose and bind" (i.e., *ahl al-ḥall wa-al-ʿaqd*) or by the previous ruler. Support for this claim comes from the precedents set during the era of the first four caliphs (*Rāshidūn*) and addresses the requirements for both the electors (*ahl al-ikhtiyār*) and the candidates. Whereas the electors must embody justice, knowledge, and wisdom, the potential ruler's qualifications are more rigorous. Unlike al-Māwardī, who lists seven requirements for rulers, Abū Yaʿlā provides four: of Qurashī descent; fulfillment of the requirements to be a judge (*qāḍī*); ability to wage *jihād* and apply prescribed penalties; and be the most meritorious (*afḍal*) in terms of knowledge and piety. It is with this last qualification that Abū Yaʿlā—much like al-Māwardī—shows a realpolitik approach. Using an interlocutory method in his discussion, Abū Yaʿlā provides a hypothetical case in which there are two viable candidates for the imamate; in this case, the candidate who fits the current needs of the community is selected.

This realistic approach carries over to his discussion of the duties and delegating authority of the ruler. The central theme embodied in Abū Yaʿlā's discussion of the rights and obligations of the ruler is that the role of the ruler is to establish a society that allows for the preservation of the correct religion (*ḥifẓ al-dīn*) and the avoidance of discord (i.e., *fitnah*). Following this line of thought, Abū Yaʿlā spends the majority of his work outlining the appointment of civilian and military officials (e.g., viziers and amirs, respectively) and discussing the criteria that must be met before a ruler can and should be replaced. Simply put, the authority of all governmental officials is only licit if it is delegated through the ruler. The contemporary and practical nature of this discussion is best exemplified in Abū Yaʿlā's discussion of the "amir of seizure [of territory]" (*amīr al-istīlāʾ*). Abū Yaʿlā supports the legitimacy of the amir of seizure as long as he is duly appointed by the ruler and upholds the laws of Allah. In justifying these amirs and their role in regional affairs, Abū Yaʿlā was recognizing the reality of the role that the Būyid amirs and Seljuk sultans played with regard to their control over administrative and military matters. In light of the ʿAbbāsid caliphate's loss of temporal power in 946 CE, Abū Yaʿlā and his contemporaries were emphasizing the central importance of the authority of the imamate and thus were legitimating a fait accompli with regard to the contemporary political arena. Supporting this argument is the fact that whereas Abū Yaʿlā meticulously supported his discussion of the nature and selection process of the imamate with historical precedents and scripture, his discussions in the later section of his work are less well supported and more matter of fact in tone.

To summarize, Abū Yaʿlā's work should be viewed as part of the classical theory of the caliphate, albeit overshadowed by al-Māwardī's work. Modern scholars (Little 1974, Hanne 2004, and Melchert 2010) have addressed the identical nature of al-Māwardī's and Abū Yaʿlā's works, noting the differences in methodology in addition to addressing the issue of which work preceded the other; Melchert's recent work provides strong evidence for Abū Yaʿlā's precedence in this case.

[*See also* Ahl al-Ḥall wa-al-ʿAqd; Fitnah; *and* Caliphate, Theories of.]

BIBLIOGRAPHY

Crone, Patricia. *God's Rule: Government and Islam.* New York: Columbia University Press, 2004.

Hanne, Eric. "Abbasid Politics and the Classical Theory of the Caliphate." In *Writers and Rulers: Perspectives on Their Relationship from Abbasid to Safavid Times*, edited by Louise Marlow and Beatrice Gruendler, pp. 49–71. Wiesbaden, Germany: Reichert Verlag, 2004.

Ibn al-Farrāʾ, AbūYaʿlā Muḥammad. *al-Aḥkām al-sulṭāniyya* [Statutes of Government]. Cairo, 1966.

Little, Donald. "A New Look at *al-Aḥkām al-Sulṭāniyya.*" *Muslim World* 64 (1974): 1–15.

Melchert, Christopher. "Māwardī, Abū Yaʿlá, and the Sunni Revival." In *Prosperity and Stagnation: Some Cultural and Social Aspects of the Abbasid Period (750-1258)*, edited by Krzystof Kościelniak, pp. 37–61. Kraków, Poland: UNUM, 2010.

Mikhail, Hanna. *Politics and Revelation: Mawardi and After.* Edinburgh: Edinburgh University Press, 1995.

ERIC J. HANNE

IBN ḤANBAL. *See* Schools of Jurisprudence, *subentry* Sunni Schools of Jurisprudence.

IBN ḤAZM, ʿALĪ IBN AḤMAD. Alī Ibn Aḥmad Ibn Ḥazm (994–1064), was an Andalusī theologian, jurist, man of letters, and principal exponent of the doctrine of the Ẓāhirī legal school. The son of a vizier, Ibn Ḥazm grew up in Córdoba. With the fall of the ʿĀmirids in 1009, the family suffered loss of position and wealth, and Ibn Ḥazm began a wandering life, at first as an active supporter of Umayyad claimants to the Andalusī caliphal throne. These failed and, following a period of imprisonment, he retired from politics. It was a little before this time, in 1022, that he began work on his semiautobiographical work entitled *Ṭawq al-hamāmah.* Living in several of the small *tāʾifah* kingdoms of eleventh-century al-Andalus, he became a scholar and a prolific writer with a strong polemical bent. One of his sons claimed that he produced some four hundred works; fewer than forty, many very short, survive today. There is some evidence that Ibn Ḥazm may have been a Shāfiʿī before becoming a great proponent of the Ẓāhirī school, after denying the viability of *qiyās*. He definitely had issues with the Mālikīs, the dominant *madhhab* in al-Andalus, whom he felt were proponents of the anti-Umayyad groups who were responsible for his and family's political demise. It was a combination of the lack of followers and his intellectual exile by the authorities that stifled the Ẓāhirī school, which never grew into as prominent a *madhhab* as the other four, and his works on religion and law were little read. In the modern era, however, there has been a concerted effort by American Muslims to revive this *madhhab*.

Ibn Ḥazm is best known today for several works. *Fiṣal* (or *Faṣl*) *fī al-milal wa-al-ahwāʾ wa-al-niḥal* is an encyclopedic guide to Islamic sects and reveals extensive knowledge of Jewish and Christian scriptures. It has frequently been regarded as an early work of comparative religion, though its main aim is to demonstrate the correctness of the Ẓāhirī *madhhab* over against the others. *Al-Muḥallā* and *Kitāb al-iḥkām fī uṣūl al-aḥkām* are concerned with *fiqh* and the bases of legal reasoning.

In the field of history, Ibn Ḥazm produced the *Jamharat ansāb al-ʿarab*, a huge genealogical work whose aim was to preserve knowledge of the ancestries of those who could claim Arab descent. Its composition perhaps demonstrated that, by his time, real knowledge of such genealogies, as also the significance attached to them, had largely faded. Ibn Ḥazm's other principal work in this field is *Naqṭ al-ʿarūs*, a lightweight collection of historical anecdotes written for entertainment rather than as a contribution to scholarship.

Ibn Ḥazm also wrote many shorter works, on such subjects as education (*Marātib al-ʿal-t*) and logic (*Kitāb al-taqrīb li-ḥadd al-manṭiq*), and minor essays on a wide variety of topics, including the virtues of al-Andalus as compared with other Islamic territories, the permissibility of listening to music, and, the best-known of them today, his attack on the Jewish vizier of Zīrid Granada, Samuel ha-Nagid. Based mainly on material in the *Fiṣal*, this is a political pamphlet, attacking Jewish participation in *ta'ifah* politics, dressed up as a religious polemic.

His political ideal was that of the Umayyads and their proximity to the Arab "ideal." Although he recognized that Islam, and thus piety, was that which God will measure people, his family experience and many of his works specify the importance of genealogy. He maintains that a caliph has to be from Quraysh and that, even though the East held sway in terms of caliphal families, he believed in the independence and uniqueness of Spain.

Cultured and learned in the manner of many in al-Andalus, Ibn Ḥazm stands out in his time and place for both the fierce independence and the failure of his political and religious views.

[*See also* Andalusia.]

BIBLIOGRAPHY

Works of Ibn Ḥazm

Abenházam de Córdoba y su Historia crítica de las ideas religiosas. Translated with a commentary by Miguel Asín Palacios. 5 vols. Madrid: Tip. de la "Revista de archivos," 1927–1932. Translation of and commentary on *Fiṣal fī al-milal wa-al-ahwāʾ wa-al-niḥal*.

The Ring of the Dove: A Treatise on the Art and Practice of Arab Love. Translated by A. J. Arberry. London: Luzac, 1953. Translation of *Tawq al-Hamāmah*.

Secondary Works

Arnaldez, Roger. *Grammaire et théologie chez Ibn Hazm de Cordoue: Essai sur la structure et les conditions de la pensée musulmane*. Paris: J. Vrin, 1956.

Turkī, ʿAbd al-Majīd. *Théologiens et juristes de l'Espagne musulmane: Aspects polémiques*. Paris: G.-P. Maisonneuve et Larose, 1982.

David J. Wasserstein
Updated by Khaled M. G. Keshk

Ibn Jamāʿah, Badr al-Dīn. Badr al-Dīn ibn Jamaʿah (1241–1333) was a Mamlūk-period Shāfiʿī jurist, chief judge, and author of a well-known treatise on government. He was born in the Syrian city of Ḥama and died in Cairo. His family traced its lineage to the north Arabian tribe of Kināna. His father, Ibrāhīm ibn Saʿd Allāh, was a teacher of jurisprudence and tradition, and a Ṣūfī in Ḥama who finally settled and died in Jerusalem. With his modest ancestry Ibn Jamāʿah attained, with his learning and skill, the highest office available to a free-born Arab in the Mamlūk reign, the chief *qāḍī* of Egypt. His family, the Banū Jamāʿah, benefitted from his distinguished career and continued to enjoy prominence as scholars, teachers, and judges after him for generations. Ibn Jamāʿah distinguished himself as a scholar and was appointed to the position of the teacher (*mudarris*) at al-Ṣalāḥiyya in Damascus and then to that of the Friday sermon giver (*khaṭīb*) of al-Masjid al-Aqṣā, the third most sacred shrine in Islam; this position remained in his family for two centuries. He was then appointed chief judge of Egypt and a *shaykh al-shuyūkh* (head of Ṣūfī fraternities) by the Mamlūk sultan al-Ashrāf Khalīl in 1291. He was dismissed in 1294 upon the murder of the sultan but was appointed to the same office, chief judge and head of Ṣūfī orders, in Damascus. As was typical for the *ʿulamāʾ* of his time, his appointments followed political winds, and he was dismissed and reappointed to this position between Egypt and Damascus several times. Dismissed by the sultan al-Nāṣir in 1310, he was reappointed in 1311 in Egypt and retained his position until his final retirement in 1327.

He is known for his treatise on jurisprudence concerning government, *Taḥrīr al-aḥkām fī tadbīr ahl al-Islām* (Compendium of Rulings Concerning the Governance of the People of Islam). The treatise is written in a genre inaugurated by another and much more accomplished Shāfiʿī jurist three centuries earlier, Abūal-Ḥasan al-Māwardī (d. 1058). That genre had brought together issues concerning governance that had been debated before al-Māwardī in disparate discourses, such as theological polemics and jurisprudential rulings concerning *jihād*, taxation, and treatment of rebels. Ibn Jamāʿah's treatise is thematically organized, more or less like al-Māwardī's *al-Aḥkām al-sulṭānīyah*, beginning with a summary of the typical Shāfiʿī-Ashʿarī positions on the imamate, with slight adjustment or reinterpretation, followed by jurisprudential issues. The content, however, is quite different: rather than detailed discussion of the jurisprudential opinions of the three major schools that al-Māwardī included, Ibn Jamāʿah's treatise consists of simple Qurʾānic verses and traditions from the Prophet and the early Muslims, as if written for nonexperts and for exhortatory purposes. Furthermore, due perhaps to the persistent threat of Mongol attacks, the obligation of the government to keep an army for defense is a key concern. In fact, as is evident from the list of chapter titles reproduced below, modern scholars have misinterpreted this treatise as being a political treatise; its sole purpose seems to be exhortation to the Mamlūk rulers to defend their lands against the Mongols. The treatise is divided into nineteen chapters, listed (in slightly paraphrased translation) here:

1. On the obligation of imamate;
2. The rights and responsibilities of the imam and sultan [understood to be the same person];
3. The traditions and functions of viziers;
4. The [necessity of the military] leaders' preparation to combat the enemy;
5. The protection of the conditions and functions of the Sharīʿah, it being the terminus ad quem of the Prophet Muḥammad's mission;
6. Creating and maintaining an army for establishing the obligation of *jihād*;
7. The sultan's grants [to his *amīrs*] and types of land-grants (*iqṭāʿāt*);
8. Proper distribution of army stipends and the deserts of those who perform *jihād*;
9. Preparation of horses, arms, and a skilled army for the obligatory *jihād*;
10. Maintaining the *dīwān* (chancellery or registry for the army and officials);
11. On the merits of *jihād* and who is qualified to carry it out;
12. The conditions of fighting the battle and patience in the face of a tough enemy;
13. The spoils of war, the types of spoils, and their detailed rulings;
14. The ruling concerning the conquered land;
15. Distributing the spoils;
16. On truce, protection, and conditions of peace and protection;
17. Fighting Muslim rebels;
18. Rulings concerning the contract of protection (*ʿaqd al-dhimmah*);
19. What constitutes the *dhimmī*'s breaking of contract.

Modern scholars have singled out Ibn Jamāʿah's treatise, in particular the following passage, as an example of the crisis of political legitimacy in medieval Islam to the point that jurists seemed willing to acknowledge any coercive usurpation as legitimate. Ibn Jamāʿah wrote in the *Taḥrīr*:

> When there is no imam and an unqualified person seeks the leadership and compels the people by force and by his armies, without any *bayʿah* [oath of allegiance] or succession, then his *bayʿah* is validly contracted, and obedience to him is obligatory, so as to maintain the unity of the Muslims and preserve agreement among them. This is still true, even if he is barbarous or vicious, according to the best opinion. When the leadership is thus contracted by force and violence to one [person], and then another arises who overcomes the first by his power and his armies, then the first is deposed and the second becomes imam, for the welfare of the Muslims and the preservation of their unity, as we have stated. (pp. 55–56)

The list of chapter themes above suggests that the political legitimacy of the Mamlūk sultans may not have been important to Ibn Jamāʿah. Instead, his object was only to urge these sultans, "barbarous or vicious" as they may have been, and their subjects to prepare for *jihād* to defend the borders of (Sunnī) Islam against the Mongol invaders.

[*See also* Imamate, Theories of the; *and* Sovereignty.]

BIBLIOGRAPHY

Rosenthal, E. I. J. *Political Thought in Medieval Islam: An Introductory Outline*. Cambridge, U.K.: Cambridge University Press, 1958.

Ibn Jamāʿah, Badr al-Dīn. *Taḥrīr al-aḥkām fī tadbīr ahl al-Islām*. 3d ed. Edited by Fuʾād ʿAbd al-Munʿim Aḥmad. Doha, Qatar: Dār al-Thaqāfa, Riʾāsah al-Maḥākim al-Sharʿīyah, 1988.

Lambton, Ann K. S. *State and Government in Medieval Islam: An Introduction to the Study of Islamic Political Theory*. Oxford: Oxford University Press, 1981.

Salibi, Kamal. "Banū Jamāʿa: A Dynasty of Shāfiʿī Jurists in the Mamluk Period." *Studia Islamica* 9 (1958): 97–109.

OVAMIR ANJUM

IBN KHALDŪN, ʿABD AL-RAḤMĀN. Ibn Khaldūn (1332–1406), a renowned Muslim sociologist and historian, began his career as a courtier, statesman, and thoughtful observer in various cities, empires, and deserts in North Africa and elsewhere in the Arab world. Based on his observations, supplemented with a more systematic collection of historiographic material from these regions, he wrote the works that made his name as a philosopher of history and politics, and, some scholars would say, a premodern progenitor of social science who anticipated the development of the modern disciplines of political science and sociology. In addition to works on theology and an autobiography, his major works were his universal history, the *Kitāb al-ʿibar* (Book of Admonitions), which is devoted mainly to Arab and Berber history, and its *Muqaddimah* (Introduction, or Prolegomena), which can stand on its own.

Ibn Khaldūn's Personal Experience of Disordered Polities. Ibn Khaldūn was the scion of a prestigious Arab family in his place of birth, Tunis. He received an Islamic education based on the Qurʾān, traditions (*ḥadīth*), jurisprudence, and literature; he studied philosophy, mathematics, and the natural sciences under Abū ʿAbd Allāh al-Ābilī. In 1352 Ibn Khaldūn moved to Fez, putting his scholarly skills at the disposal of the energetic Sultan Abū ʿInān; however, charged with conspiracy, he was imprisoned for over a year. Following the sultan's death in 1359, Ibn Khaldūn pledged allegiance to the new sultan, Abū Sālim. He served in the *maẓālim* (tribunal of iniquities). The hostility of other courtiers, however, induced him in 1363 to leave for Granada, Spain, which was ruled at the time by the Nasrids—the last Muslim dynasty in Spain. There Ibn Khaldūn was appointed ambassador to the court of Peter the Cruel, the king of Castile. His unusually swift advancement led to envy and, notwithstanding the support of his friend and notable figure Ibn al-Khatīb, he was again forced to leave, this time for Bougie (in present-day Algeria), to the court of the *amīr* Abū ʿAbd Allāh Muḥammad, who appointed him to the high position of chamberlain. In Bougie Ibn Khaldūn undertook another profession, that of jurist and teacher of Malikī jurisprudence. When Abū ʿAbd Allāh Muḥammad was killed by his rival, the *amīr* of Constantine, Ibn Khaldūn defected and entered the service of the victor, only to leave it abruptly and escape to Biskra, Algeria.

Ibn Khaldūn spent many years weaving together political coalitions in confused and complex situations in which there was no lasting dominant power. He seems to have hoped to raise a powerful Maghribi force in order to unify the land and reconstruct a centralized authority similar to that which had existed under the Almohad dynasty (c. 1130–1269). His autobiography reveals his repeated experience of failed attempts to overcome the challenges of administration, government, and politics. He returned to Fez in 1372 (where he was again imprisoned), then to Tlemcen, Algeria, where he witnessed the murder of his friend Ibn al-Khatīb. Persuaded of the necessity to leave the dangerous life of politics, Ibn Khaldūn and his family took refuge with the Awlād ʿArīf Berber tribe, under their protection in the seclusion of the Qalʿah (fortress) Ibn Salāmah.

The need to secure historiographic materials led Ibn Khaldūn to Tunis where, under the protection of the Ḥafṣid sultan Abūal-ʿAbbās, he taught jurisprudence and continued writing. As had happened in turbulent times before, hostility toward his intellectual pursuits compelled him to leave again, this time for Egypt. Purporting to make the pilgrimage to Mecca, Ibn Khaldūn stopped in Alexandria for a month in 1382, before settling in Cairo where he took up judicial and academic office. His last major adventure transpired in October 1400 when he accompanied the Mamlūk sultan al-Nāṣir Faraj to meet Tamerlane, who was besieging Damascus. The Tatar ruler appreciated his knowledge and shrewdness, and though Ibn Khaldūn was unable to prevent the sacking of the city, he may have succeeded in persuading Tamerlane not to invade Egypt. Ibn Khaldūn lived the remainder of his life in Cairo.

Ibn Khaldūn's Core Insights. Ibn Khaldūn's wide, checkered experience of political order and disorder in the Middle East and North Africa help to illuminate his interventions and reforms in historical analysis and writing, which some scholars consider an early attempt at a sociological style of research. His purpose in writing both the *Kitāb al-ʿibar* and its introduction, the *Muqaddimah*, was to analyze and explain his epoch, in order ultimately to help improve life in these regions. He excoriated the inaccuracies, falsehoods, and distortions that he found in existing historical writing and sought to set and maintain a standard of reliability and consistency with the factual and documentary record. Ibn Khaldūn was highly original in both of these major works, but the *Muqaddimah* features his most striking innovations. In it, he returns to a concept common to Greek philosophy (originating with Plato and Aristotle) and Islamic political philosophy (most fully articulated by al-Fārābī): that man is a political animal. In this aspect Ibn Khaldūn's historical methods are rooted in philosophy (*ḥikmah*), the fruits of which may be regarded as comparable to those of other premodern philosophers. Ibn Khaldūn writes that social organization is a necessity; humanity cannot do without that pinnacle of human collective life, the *madīnah* (city).

According to the *Muqaddimah* there are two types of human organization: *badawī* (rural, bedouin) and *ḥaḍarī* (urban).The bedouin are physically strong and courageous; they are of fitter mettle and moral fiber. Conversely the people accustomed to urban, sedentary civilization become physically weaker, and along with their martial prowess their character and moral rectitude degrades. Even as city living makes people soft and corrupt, it also bestows upon them wealth, culture, learning, and prosperity—all of which reach their apex in the cities.

Whether in rural or urban settings social organization and cooperation is necessary to facilitate the satisfaction of human needs such as food and security. However, when people live together they also have greater scope to enact their natural tendency toward aggression. Humans' hostile, selfish impulses necessitate the institution of an authority over the community. Ibn Khaldūn's assumptions concerning the formation and development of political society are similar to those of the English political philosopher Thomas Hobbes (1588–1679): humankind lives in a natural state of violence and mutual opposition; a restraining authority is needed, and the individual or group that exercises that restraint becomes the head of the state.

ʿAṣabīyah (group feeling or solidarity) is the chief dynamic element in Ibn Khaldūn's analysis of history, and it is the engine that both creates and destroys sovereign authority. *ʿAṣabīyah* is especially strong in *badawī* society, and weaker in the *ḥaḍarī*. *ʿAṣabīyah* may be grounded on the ties of blood (*ṣilat al-raḥīm*) that are the hub of rural, nomadic communities. It is this close connection (*iltiḥām*) that moves humans instinctively to support their associates by defending them and by avenging any offenses that they suffer. *ʿAṣabīyah* may also be created through sworn alliance (*ḥilf*) and clientelism (*walāʾ*). The possibility of alliances and patron-client relations reinforces the internal ties of cooperation in tribal societies. The culmination of *ʿaṣabīyah* is the institution of a ruling authority, termed "royal authority" (*mulk*). Ibn Khaldūn believed that religion, while not a prerequisite to order and civilization, could help make a people more susceptible of governance. In his analysis of early Islamic history, Ibn Khaldūn surmises that the Prophet Muḥammad succeeded in propagating and expanding the appeal and reach of Islam by means of the strong group feeling of the Meccan emigrants (*muhājirūn*) and the Medinan helpers (*anṣār*).

In a tripartite typology Ibn Khaldūn enumerated the following versions of royal authority: natural sovereignty (*mulk ṭabīʿī*), which is autocratic; political or rational sovereignty (*mulk siyāsī*), corresponding to the secular state, ruled in accordance with rational principles; and the caliphate (*khilāfah*), which is tantamount to a rational and political *mulk* but the legislation of which is of divine and revealed origin. Ibn Khaldūn held that justice is a necessary element for each type. The ruler should avoid perpetrating injustice (*ẓulm*): uncompensated confiscations of property or other assets, forced labor, or otherwise unfair treatment of subjects or iniquitous behavior of sovereigns each diminish the authority's legitimacy. According to a retrospective utopianism in Ibn Khaldūn's history, the epoch of the first Muslim community in Medina and the first caliphate were the most nearly just and perfect human societies.

A chief reason Ibn Khaldūn's method foreshadows the modern social sciences is his attempt (notwithstanding his concern with justice), to bracket normative values and to find patterns or law-like, nomothetic propositions that describe complex, varied historical phenomena. Reasons and empirical factors and regularities, rather than aspirations or sentiment, comprise the moving parts of the *Muqaddimah*. In political-scientific terms Ibn Khaldūn is a realist; modern readers may find not so much a realistic as a pessimistic outlook in his works, but, then, the time in which he lived was marked by political instability and (frequently violent) turmoil.

Two Moroccan scholars who have studied Ibn Khaldūn's thought from a theoretical perspective are Abdallah Laroui and Muḥammad ʿAbed al-Jābrī. On Laroui's reading there is common ground between Ibn Khaldūn and the Italian political philosopher Niccolò Machiavelli (1469–1527), because each overcame the dichotomy between ideal analysis and factual description. Laroui contends that today Ibn Khaldūn's ideas can assist in solidifying the foundations of secularism in the Arab states. Al-Jābrī maintains that Ibn Khaldūn shares the rationalism of the Andalusian-Maghribi philosophical tradition, as exemplified by the philosophy of Ibn Rushd (Averroës), and that in the contemporary world Ibn Khaldūn may provide Arabs guidance leading them toward greater civilizational achievements and modernity.

In Ibn Khaldūn's philosophy of history, the state—like humans and their bodies—naturally declines and inevitably dies. States decline because of the diminution of *ʿaṣabīyah* over time, and because rulers inexorably degenerate into tyrants, losing their commitment to and observance of the demands of justice. Ibn Khaldūn specifies the time it takes a community to degenerate: five generations. Luxury and civilization destroy the purity of *badawī* customs, while urban society loses its vigor and succumbs to inactivity and unrestrained expenditure and waste. Rulers appropriate the state and its revenue and interfere in productive enterprises by transforming the market economy into a private estate. All the admirable qualities of any state, over time, vanish. The cyclical character of history consists in the cyclic transition from rural (*badawī*) to urban (*ḥaḍarī*) civilization, and back again. In a slightly more auspicious respect, the process is not wholly negative and repetitive, as the civilizational gains of past *ḥaḍarī* phases are not completely lost between one cycle and the next, implying that history demonstrates—however unevenly and uncertainly—an evolutionary tendency.

Transmission and Summing Up. Scholars suggest Ibn Khaldūn contributed to a revival of historical writing in the fifteenth century in Egypt. Several Ottoman historians in the sixteenth and seventeenth centuries took an interest in the *Muqaddimah* and translated portions into Ottoman Turkish. With the first translations of his works into French in the nineteenth century, his insights became available to a Western audience. At present Ibn Khaldūn's intellectual legacy can be seen in the esteem his thought enjoys in Arab scholarly discourse. Not only did he understand the dynamics of social and political evolution in the Arab world and suggest a new methodology for the analysis of history, he also provided the tools for shaping and predicting the future development of Arab societies.

Between his birth in Tunis and his death in Cairo, Ibn Khaldūn's own diplomatic, juristic, and political career shaped his empirically based historiography of North Africa and the Middle East. While some scholars may overstate comparisons between the positivistic methods and findings of Ibn Khaldūn and contemporary social science, there is no doubt that his major works remain a substantial advance in the study of Arab societies and history and continue as a resource that scholars mine for theoretical insights about the complex dynamics of sociopolitical change and how to investigate and represent that change.

BIBLIOGRAPHY

Works of Ibn Khaldūn

The Muqaddimah: An Introduction to History. Translated by Franz Rosenthal. Princeton, N.J.: Princeton University Press, 1967.

Discours sur l'histoire universelle (Discourse on Universal History). 2d ed. rev. Translated by Vincent Monteil. Paris: Sindbad, 1978. Translation of *Kitab al-ʿibar*.

Le livre des exemples. Translated, edited, and annotated by Abdesselem Cheddadi. Paris: Gallimard, 2002.

Secondary Works

Ahmad, Zaid. *The Epistemology of Ibn Khaldūn*. London: Routledge Curzon, 2003; repr. London: Taylor and Francis, 2010.

Chabane, Djamel. *La pensée de l'urbanisation chez Ibn Khaldûn (1332–1406)*. Pairs: L'Harmattan, 1998.

Jābrī, Muḥammad ʿAbed al-. *Introduction à la critique de la raison arabe*. Translated by Ahmed Mahfoud and Marc Geoffroy. Paris: Découverte, 1994.

Lacoste, Yves. *Ibn Khaldūn: The Birth of History and the Past of the Third World*. Translated by David Macey. London: Verso, 1984.

Laroui, Abdallah, *Islam et modernité*. Paris: Découverte 1986.

Scott Morrison

Ibn al-Muqaffaʿ, ʿAbd Allāh. One of the earliest contributors to the genre of "mirrors for princes" literature, ʿAbd Allāh Ibn al-Muqaffaʿ (720–757) was a Persian convert to Islam who became a prominent writer and an influential chancery secretary (*kātib*). This brilliant guide to the uncle of the caliph al-Manṣūr was a pioneering figure who shaped the emergence of classical Arabic literature through his translations from Persian, such as the Indo-Persian epic *Kalīlah wa-Dimnah*, as well as his authorship of several *Fürstenspiegels* (a series of writings that advise young princes on how to conduct themselves, adopt ethical norms, and discharge government responsibilities). Of special significance are his *al-Adab al-kabīr* (Great Learning), *al-Adab al-ṣaghīr* (Small Learning), and *Risālah fī al-ṣaḥābah* (Letters in Friendship), which are replete with political advice to the caliph and his courtiers, derived from the *khudāy-nāmah* chronicles of Persian kings as well as his own experiences and involvements in the affairs of state, which, tragically, led to his early death at the hands of his enemies.

Ibn al-Muqaffaʿ was born in Gor, the present Fīrūzābād in Iran, around 720 CE, into a noble Persian family. He was the son of an Umayyad tax collector named Daduya (Mubārak) who earned the nickname "the Shriveled Hand" (al-Muqaffaʿ) because he was allegedly tortured for embezzling some of the money entrusted to him (Sourdel, 1954, p. 308). Converted to Islam from (Zoroastrianism) by 743, the young man became an Umayyad *kātib* in Shāpūr, Fars, which led to various clashes. He was embroiled in hostilities between his master, the governor Masīḥ ibn al-Ḥawārī, and the man sent to replace him, Sufyān ibn Muʿāwiyah al-Muhallabī. To avoid conflicts, Ibn al-Muqaffaʿ moved to Kermān and, after the fall of the Umayyads, cultivated ties with the Banū ʿAlī officials. As the paternal uncles of the first two ʿAbbāsid caliphs, the Banū ʿAlī appreciated the *kātib*'s refined manners and deep respect for Persian traditions, while meticulously observing Arab ways. Because of his impeccable mastery of both Persian and Arabic, ʿĪsā ibn ʿAlī offered him a permanent post in his court, where Ibn al-Muqaffaʿ outshone members of the Arab ruling class. A witty person, he was nevertheless an intellectual who did not suffer fools, whom he could belittle and ridicule. One of the victims of his derision was Sufyān ibn Muʿāwiyah, who took his revenge when Ibn al-Muqaffaʿ offended the caliph al-Manṣūr, allegedly for encouraging the Banū ʿAlī, and especially his uncle ʿAbd Allāh ibn ʿAlī, to rise against the ruler. Ibn al-Muqaffaʿ was murdered in Basra around 756 on the order of the second ʿAbbāsid caliph, AbūJaʿfar al-Manṣūr, reportedly for heresy, in particular for attempting to import Zoroastrian ideas into Islam, although this was a pretext, because Zoroastrianism was not seen as as much of a threat as it became later, especially under the reign of al-Mahdī (775–785).

Epic Translation. Ibn al-Muqaffaʿs translation of the fables *Kalīlah wa-Dimnah* from Middle Persian is considered one of the first masterpieces of Arabic literary prose. This rendition of animal fables, mostly of Indian origin, involving two jackals, Kalīlah and Dimnah, was introduced with an original prologue and, perhaps, with four added stories that were not in the original. Over the years, many versions of the fables emerged, although his endured on account of the clarity of expression and plain syntax.

Original Works. Ibn al-Muqaffaʿ produced an Arabic adaptation of the late Sassanian *Khwadāy-nāmag*, a chronicle of pre-Islamic Persian kings, princes, and warriors. A mixture of legend, myth, and fact, the *Khwadāy-nāmag* served as a quasi-national history that was inspired by a vision of kingship as a well-ordered autocracy whose sacred duty it was to rule and to regulate the conduct of subjects within a carefully arranged system of government. Interestingly, the narrative offered practical advice on civil and military matters, focusing on tactics, customs, court manners, and other matters that were typical of various works on Sassanian institutions.

Remarkably, Ibn al-Muqaffaʿs most important work was the *Adab al-kabīr*, which was divided into four parts, the first of which offered a brief rhetorical overview on the excellence of the Sassanian legacy of spiritual and temporal knowledge. This is followed by a miniature "mirror for princes" epistle, whose audience, apparently the caliph's son, is counseled in the rules of conduct (*adab*). A future leader is thus guided to learn his priorities by mastering the fundamentals of power and how to apply his authority to avoid pitfalls, especially seduction by flattery. In the traditions of Islam, Ibn al-Muqaffaʿ urges the prince to cultivate men of religion as potential aides and intimates and to stay faithful to his moral goals. He encourages the future leader to listen to advice, even when it is unpalatable, from qualified counselors. Naturally, the recommendations aim to protect the monarch from friends and foes alike, to transform apprehension into prudence, and nurture both justice and the appearance of impartiality. In the third part of the *Adab al-kabīr*, Ibn al-Muqaffaʿ provides a pragmatic survival guide for a ruler's intimates. He offers advice in a high moral vein, without insisting on epochal philosophical, ethico-religious, or spiritual bases like several of his successors, including al-Jāḥiẓ (776–868), Ibn Qutaybah (828–889), al-Māwardī (974–1058), Niẓām al-Mulk (1018–1092), al-Ghazālī (1958–1111), al-Ṭurṭūshī (1059–1126), or Ibn Ẓafar al-Ṣiqillī (1104–1170). The fourth and longest part of the *Adab* treats relations with colleagues and acquaintances in order to forge friendship and avoid enmities. Remarkably, Ibn al-Muqaffaʿ stresses the need for fidelity, loyalty, and devotion as critical means of protection against all caustic elements. For him, friendships must always be formed with those who may be superior to one's station, precisely to prevent envy from coloring enduring ties.

Legacy. Ibn al-Muqaffaʿ was a pioneer in the introduction of literary prose narrative to Arabic literature and paved the way for later innovators, such as al-Hamadānī and al-Saraqusṭī. He also established a powerful precedent in the "mirror for princes" genre. His most significant contribution was to transform the absolutist model of Persian kingship into a more humanistic practice of rulership constrained by the Islamic faith, with its laws, obligations, and equality of all believers before God.

Bibliography

Arjomand, Said Amir. "ʿAbd Allah Ibn al-Muqaffaʿ and the ʿAbbasid Revolution." *Iranian Studies* 27 (1994): 9–36.

Gabrieli, F. "Ibn al-Muḳaffaʿ." *Encyclopaedia of Islam, Second Edition*. Edited by: P. Bearman, Th. Bianquis, C. E. Bosworth, E. van Donzel, W. P. Heinrichs. Brill Online, 2013. http://referenceworks.brillonline.com/entries/encyclopaedia-of-islam-2/ibn-al-mukaffa-SIM_3304.

Latham, J. Derek. "Ebn Al-Moqaffaʿ, Abū Moḥammad ʿAbd-Allāh Rōzbeh." In *Encyclopædia Iranica*, edited by Ehsan Yarshater, vol. 8, fasc. 1, pp. 39–43. London: Routledge, 1997. http://www.iranica.com/articles/ebn-al-moqaffa.

Rosenthal, Erwin I. J. *Political Thought in Medieval Islam: An Introductory Outline*. Westport, Conn.: Greenwood, 1985. See esp. pp. 68–73.

Sourdel, Dominique. "La biographie d'Ibn al-Muqaffaʿ d'après les sources anciennes." *Arabica* 1 (1954): 307–323.

Joseph A. Kéchichian

Ibn Qayyim al-Jawzīyah. Shams al-Dīn Muḥammad ibn Abī Bakr ibn Qayyim al-Jawzīyah (1292–1350) was a leading Ḥanbalī jurist and scholar of *ḥadīth*, *tafsīr* (Qurʾānic exegesis), *uṣūl al-fiqh* (legal theory), and *furūʿ al-fiqh* (substantive law). He did for the thought and work of his teacher Taqī al-Dīn Aḥmad Ibn Taymīyah (d. 1328), what Abū Yūsuf did for Abū Ḥanīfah: popularize and spread his thoughts and ideas. Born in Damascus, Ibn Qayyim began his early religious studies under his father, who was an attendant (*qayyim*) at the local al-Jawzīyah *madrasah*. His zeal for knowledge while still in his early youth led him to sit with several great masters, studying with them several sciences, including *uṣūl al-dīn* (fundamentals of faith), *ḥadīth*, and *fiqh* (jurisprudence).

Ibn Taymīyah had the greatest influence on Ibn Qayyim, who attended the former's study circles at the age of twenty-one and eventually became, along with Ibn Kathīr (d. 1373), one of his foremost students and disciples. Ibn Qayyim's dedication to Ibn Taymīyah was without exception, and together they would be persecuted and imprisoned in the citadel of Damascus for their views on certain matters pertaining to theology and law. It was not until Ibn Taymīyah's death, while they were in prison, that Ibn Qayyim was released. Ibn Qayyim's political output is to be found in his book *al-Ṭuruq al-ḥukmiya* (Ways of Government), which is based largely on Ibn Taymīyah's *Kitāb al-siyāsah al-sharʾiyah* (Religio-politics). Thereafter, he continued to defend Ibn Taymīyah's positions and propagate his teachings until the end of his life. He is buried in Damascus, in the cemetery of Bāb al-Saghīr.

While he was tremendously influenced by Ibn Taymīyah, Ibn Qayyim was far less polemical. His contemporaries, including his most famous disciple, Ibn Rajab (d. 1393), and Ibn Kathīr, have described him as being, inter alia, deeply pious and magnanimous, with a keen insight and a profound wisdom. As a preacher (*wāʿiẓ*), he was captivating and inspiring, possessing extraordinary oratorical skills. Not only was he gifted in speech, but he was also a highly talented and eloquent writer. Among his more famous works is *Zād al-maʿād* (Provisions for the Hereafter), from which is extracted the popular book *al-Ṭibb al-nabawī* (The Medicine of the Prophet). While he authored several books, many of which deal with *tafsīr*, *ḥadīth*, and *fiqh*, most of his writings are compilations and editions of the works of Ibn Taymīyah. Several manuscripts in his own handwriting have been preserved and are today in the Central Library in Damascus.

Much of Ibn al-Qayyim's thought reflects, with good reason, the teachings of Ibn Taymīyah. His conservatism is typical of Ḥanbalī scholars, strictly opposing any authority other than that of the Qurʾān and prophetic traditions and referring to the *salaf* (early Muslims) only in matters in which the former are silent. Though Ibn Qayyim has been highly revered throughout the Sunnī tradition for his scholarly achievements, he has drawn criticism from within Sunnī circles for certain theological views he espoused (in following Ibn Taymīyah), particularly concerning his seemingly anthropomorphic interpretation of the attributes of God. His lengthy poem on the tenets of faith, titled *al-Qasīda al-nūnīyah* (Ode Rhyming in the

Letter *Nūn*), is filled with corporeal renderings of the attributes of God and continues to be taught in schools into the twenty-first century (especially in Saudi Arabia). Such renderings have been rejected outright and deemed erroneous by the majority of Sunnī scholars throughout Islamic history (who hold true to Qurʾān 42:11, which explicitly states that there is nothing like God). Among those who have vehemently denied these renderings are the Ashʿarīs, whom Ibn Qayyim castigates in their denial, comparing them to the most deviating of Muʿtazilī factions.

Ibn Qayyim continues to be widely respected throughout the Sunnī community, and many of his works (dealing with both legal and spiritual matters) appeal to different Sunnī trends, including Ṣūfī and Salafī. He is especially popular in conservative Sunnī circles, and his influence is most pronounced among the Wahhābī and modern-day Salafī movements, who claim him to be among the older authorities representing the practice of the *salaf*. These movements have generally adopted some of Ibn Qayyim's thought and views. They accept his interpretation of the attributes of God and his opposition to individual Muslims resorting to *taqlīd* (imitation) of the four Sunnī *madhāhib* (schools of law). This view maintains that individual Muslims should interpret the Qurʾān and *sunnah* independently, with no need for an intermediary. They also adopt his generally harsh rhetoric towards *ahl al-dhimmah* (people of the covenant, that is, Jews and Christians); this rhetoric has also influenced Sayyid Quṭb, as reflected in some of his writing. In fairness to Ibn Qayyim, his stance toward non-Muslims should, arguably, be understood in light of his time, taking into account the mistrust that Muslims generally had for non-Muslims, as a result of the Crusades and Mongol invasions.

[*See also* Fiqh; Ibn Taymīyah, Taqī al-Dīn Aḥmad; *and* Quṭb, Sayyid.]

BIBLIOGRAPHY

ʿAbd al-Mawjūd, Salāh al-Dīn Alī. *Biography of Imam Ibn al-Qayyim*. Translated by Abdul-Rafī Adewale Imām. Riyadh, Saudi Arabia: Darussalam, 2006.

Ibn Qayyim al-Jawzīyah, Muḥammad ibn Abī Bakr. *Provisions for the Hereafter*. Abridged by Muḥammad ibn ʿAbd al-Wahhāb. Riyadh, Saudi Arabia: Darussalam, 2003.

Misrī, Aḥmad ibn Naqīb al-. *Reliance of the Traveller: The Classic Manual of Islamic Sacred Law ʿUmdat al-sālik*. Edited and translated by Nuh Ha Mim Keller. Rev. ed. Beltsville, Md.: Amana, 1999.

Mohammad A. Abderrazzaq
Updated by Khaled M. G. Keshk

Ibn Qutaybah, ʿAbd Allāh. Abū-Muḥammad ʿAbd Allāh b. Muslim al-Dīnawarī Ibn Qutaybah (828–889) was a chief Sunnī philologist, theologian, and man of letters who flourished in early ʿAbbāsid Iraq. He was described by the Ḥanbalī jurist and theologian Ibn Taymīyah (d. 1328) as the preacher of *ahl al-sunnah*. He associated himself with different, often overlapping, intellectual circles. As a traditionalist theologian, he followed prominent authorities of Sunnī traditionalism, such as Isḥāq b. Rāhawayh (d. 853) and Aḥmad b. Ḥanbal (d. 855). In this regard, he played an active role in the Sunnī rebuttal of the Muʿtazilah, adhering to the Sunnī policy of the caliph al-Mutawakkil (r. 847-861). In his theological writings, he supports the Ḥanbalī creed, affirming divine attributes and rejecting allegorical interpretation. He benefitted from the ʿAbbāsid patronage and became a judge and a justice officer. Above all, he built a solid scholarly reputation on his literary and historical skills as an *adab* compiler. Much of the materials he collected were available to him through the circle of Baghdadi littérateurs. His treatises are predominantly philological, on lexicography, grammar, and morphology. This left a lasting effect on his style, as can be seen in his theological and literary writings.

Through his *Taʾwīl mushkil al-Qurʾān* and *Taʾwīl mukhtalif al-ḥadīth*, Ibn Qutaybah made a major contribution to Islamic hermeneutics. In the first work, a Sunnī traditionalist approach of Qurʾānic interpretation is offered as an alternative to Muʿtazilī Qurʾānic hermeneutics. The second book defends the Sunnī doctrines on divine attributes and acts. In addition, he employs allegoric interpretation to resolve what he perceived as ambiguity in the Qurʾān. Ibn Qutaybah accuses his opponents of a lack of philological understanding of the Arabic language. Beyond Muʿtazilīs, Ibn Qutaybah also refutes anti-Qurʾān heretics who claim the Qurʾān is contradictory. The Ḥanbalī-Muʿtazilī dispute on the createdness of the Qurʾān largely frames his discussions. In addition, his views should be read as a reaction to the challenge of Muslim heretics and the *shuʿūbīyah* (anti-Arab) followers. Qurʾān criticisms were also endorsed by atheists and freethinkers. Using his philological skills, mainly with respect to Arabic dialects, Ibn Qutaybah dismisses any criticism of variations in Qurʾānic recitation. He also defends the Qurʾānic style and grammatical mistakes (*laḥn*). He considers all inconsistencies as rhetorical devices of the Qurʾānic style that demonstrate its inimitability, eloquence, and richness. Thus, the book reads as both a philological source and a work of apologetics. For every variation, inconsistency, or ambiguity, he provides a justification either from literature (narrations, poetry) or linguistic sciences (lexicography, grammar, morphology). In Ibn Qutaybah's Qurʾānic hermeneutics, interpretation is a tool of coherence and orthodoxy.

In the same vein, Ibn Qutaybah's *ḥadīth* hermeneutics is an attempt to resolve contradictions between the prophetic traditions. He uses his considerable philological arsenal to conciliate between opposing meanings of specific *ḥadīths*. In addition, the coherence of the *ḥadīth* is proved by theological deliberations. Ibn Qutaybah enlarges the list of his adversaries to include the Khārijīs, the Murjiʾah, and the Shīʿī Twelvers, whose political use of prophetic reports to support their claims he contests. He objects to their justifications by denying any political message in the traditions under consideration. He defends the reliability of Muḥammad's companions against the deprecations of the Muʿtazilī al-Naẓẓām (d. 846). Further, Ibn Qutaybah rebuts accusations of anthropomorphism, an argument frequently used against traditionalists. Besides rational theology, Ibn Qutaybah criticizes the Ḥanafī jurists who rely on opinion (*raʾy*), analogy (*qiyās*), and equity (*istiḥsān*). Closer links between Iraqi Ḥanafīs and Muʿtazilīs might have been the reason he added rational jurists to his rebuttal of rational theologians. *Taʾwīl mukhtalif al-ḥadīth*, although a classical treatise of *ḥadīth* hermeneutics, could be seen as a defense of the traditionalists of *ahl al-ḥadīth* in both theology and jurisprudence.

Ibn Qutaybah's theological writings show a Ḥanbalī tendency. He locates the Sunnī orthodoxy between *jahmīyah* (Muʿtazilah) and *mushabbihah* (anthropomorphism). That is, while he affirms divine attributes, he rejects anthropomorphist voices within the *ahl al-ḥadīth*. He refutes the negation of attributes as well as allegoric interpretation. He vehemently rejects the Muʿtazilī doctrine of the createdness of the Qurʾān. Ibn Qutaybah devotes long discussions to disproving the interpretation of the divine throne, divine sitting, or divine fingers. Thus, he adheres to the *bilā kayf* doctrine, which makes his contribution acceptable within early Ḥanbalīsm and Ashʿarism. Likewise, on the issue of divine acts, Ibn Qutaybah refutes the deniers of *qadar* (Muʿtazilim) but also the Jabrīyah (determinists). While often disparaging some excess in traditionalist circles, his theology restates the Sunnī belief as was understood by the *ahl al-ḥadīth*.

With reference to the *imāmah* issue, he refutes both the *nawāṣib* and the Rawāfiḍ—the anti-ʿAlī party and the Twelvers. Calling for a moderate appreciation of ʿAlī, the fourth caliph (d. 661), he sticks to the standard position of the *ahl al-ḥadīth* on the matter. Rather than criticizing Shīʿī Twelvers, Ibn Qutaybah seems to be more alarmed about anti-ʿAlī sentiment among the traditionalists.

Ibn Qutaybah's most well-known intellectual achievement by far is his *Adab al-kātib*, a philological compendium written for ʿAbbāsid scribes. He claims to have been motivated by the philological shortcomings of philosophers, littérateurs, and scribes. He depicts them as superficial, badly informed, and theoretical. Further, Ibn Qutaybah blames philosophers for objecting to Islamic traditions. His reprimand of the philosophers and scribes could be seen as part of the conflicts among the elite. It also reflects the transition of the ʿAbbāsids towards Sunnīzation. Principally, for Ibn Qutaybah, a good scribe should improve his philological knowledge, speech, and handwriting. In addition, he is required to master the Arabic names of animals, professions, tools, and plants. To be able to speak and write correctly, Ibn Qutaybah advises mastering orthography, grammar, and morphology. Ibn Qutaybah's *Adab al-kātib* is a philological encyclopedia that hides a social criticism of the rival secular intellectual elite in Baghdad. In sum, Ibn Qutaybah uses philology as an instrument of social and political criticism. Put in their sectarian and religious contexts of the ʿAbbāsid ninth century, his philological works make him an outstanding philologist and ideologue of the *ahl al-ḥadīth*.

Bibliography

Ḥusaynī, Isḥāq Mūsā. *The Life and Works of Ibn Qutayba*. Beirut: American Press, 1950.

Ibn Qutaybah, ʿAbd Allāh b. Muslim. *Le traité des divergences du ḥadīṯ d'Ibn Qutayba (mort en 276/889): Traduction annotée du Kitāb taʾwīl muḥtalif al-ḥadīṯ*. Translated by Gérard Lecomte. Damascus: Institut Français de Damas, 1962.

Lecomte, Gérard. *Ibn Qutayba (mort en 276/889): L'homme, son oeuvre et ses idées*. Damascus: Institut Français de Damas, 1965.

Schmidtke, Sabine. "The Muslim Reception of Biblical Materials: Ibn Qutayba and his *Aʿlām al-nubuwwa*." *Islam and Christian-Muslim Relations* 22 (2011): 249–274.

Abdessamad Belhaj

Ibn Rushd, Abū al-Walīd Muḥammad Aḥmad.

Abū al-Walīd Muḥammad ibn Aḥmad Ibn Rushd (1126–1198 CE) was often regarded as the outstanding Aristotelian in the Islamic world. Known as Averroës in Latin, he came to revolutionize philosophy in medieval Europe where Christian and Jewish theologians and philosophers benefited from his insights, which helped create and shape the movement that led to the European Renaissance. He was a polymath who mastered Aristotelian and Islamic philosophy, theology, Mālikī law and jurisprudence, logic, psychology, politics, Arabic music theory, and the sciences of medicine, astronomy, geography, mathematics, physics, and celestial mechanics, and worked as a physician, lawyer, and theologian. Ibn Rushd became a significant political and legal figure in his native Córdoba (in modern-day Spain) during the period of Islamic rule under the Almohad regime, something that made his life difficult at times when political conditions changed. He was sometimes exiled, and indeed ended his life in Marrakesh, Morocco, though precisely why he was banished is unknown.

His main influence is undoubtedly his contribution to the understanding of Aristotle, whose works were introduced to him by Ibn Ṭufayl (1105–1185), a renowned Andalusian physician/philosopher. Ibn Rushd wrote a variety of commentaries, explaining and clarifying a difficult and technical thinker like Aristotle in such a way that others could more readily engage with his ideas and develop them. He wrote three different kinds of commentary on most of Aristotle's texts—a long *tafsīr* for scholars, and medium-length *talkhis* and shorter *jamis* for a wider public. Frequently in these briefer commentaries Ibn Rushd expressed his own opinions quite directly on a range of philosophical and theological issues, but in the long commentaries he tried, on the whole successfully, to preserve a dispassionate academic tone. In addition to his commentaries on Aristotle's works and his commentary on *The Republic* by Plato, Ibn Rush wrote at least sixty-seven original works, including twenty-eight works on philosophy, twenty on medicine, eight on law, five on theology, and four on grammar.

He was also a trenchant defender of his kind of philosophy, often labeled peripatetic (*mashshā'ī*), which had been recently attacked by al-Ghazālī and had also come under suspicion by the religious authorities of al-Andalus for its apparent heterodoxy. Al-Ghazali and others feared that teachings based on Aristotelian philosophy would undermine the teachings of Islam, which was an egregious position from a philosophical perspective, but an eminently logical one to espouse from a political perspective. Never one to avoid a challenge, Ibn Rushd argued in his *Decisive Treatise* that not only is it acceptable to study philosophy, Muslims are in fact obliged to do so, and they must also seek philosophical solutions to theological problems, since the theologians are incapable themselves of resolving such dilemmas as how to interpret the Qur'ān. It is hardly surprising that this sort of defiant response did not endear him to the enemies of philosophy. In fact, after his death his works fell very much out of favor in the Islamic world, even in the West, and he was largely ignored in the Arab world until he was rediscovered in the nineteenth century and viewed as one of the original inspirations of the Arab Renaissance (*nahḍah*).

Ibn Rushd's arguments showed how to reconcile religion with reason, thus bringing religion together with modernity and science, one of the pressing ideological issues of the Middle East in the premodern and modern periods. Whether the radical directions in which his work was taken actually represented his own views seems unlikely. He did, however, develop the thesis that religion and reason are different routes to the same truth, and within a cultural context where religion is regarded as the major route to the truth, as in medieval Europe and the modern Islamic world, Ibn Rushd seems subversive. Ibn Rushd believed that truth was of two kinds: a knowledge of truth in religion that, because it was based in faith, could neither be tested nor required any training to understand, and a philosophical truth reserved for learned individuals with the intellectual capacity to undertake its study. This was entirely understandable from a trained mind, a scholar that devoted his life to the study of logic and order.

Ibn Rushd's works had a strong influence on the Jewish and Christian communities of his time. He was regarded as the commentator par excellence, particularly on Aristotle, the most popular and highly regarded thinker of the time. Although Ibn Rushd did not write a commentary on Aristotle's *Politics*, to which he did not have access, his translations and ideas were assimilated by Siger of Brabant and Thomas Aquinas, and others, within the Christian scholastic tradition, which valued Aristotelian logic. Aquinas considered him to be so significant that he referred to him as "the Commentator" while calling Aristotle "the Philosopher." Under his Latin name, Averroës, he continued for many centuries to be read in Latin as the main authority on Aristotle. A movement grew in Christian Europe called "radical Averroism," which based itself on some of his arguments and argued for a radical split between religion and reason. This provided the grounds for those who argued that he led the way to the tendency of the European Renaissance itself and the later Enlightenment to depose traditional religion and elevate reason. Often linked with Maimonides, Ibn Rushd was a significant figure in Jewish philosophy for a very long time, although his *Decisive Treatise* stressed the importance of analytical thinking as a key prerequisite to interpreting the Qurʾān.

[*See also* Ghazālī, Abū Ḥāmid al-.]

BIBLIOGRAPHY

Averroës. *The Book of the Decisive Treatise Determining the Connection between Law and Wisdom, and Epistle Dedicatory*. Translated by Charles E. Butterworth. Provo, Utah: Brigham Young University Press, 2001.

Averroës. *Averroës on the Harmony of Religion and Philosophy*. Translated by George Hourani. London: Luzac, 1961.

Leaman, Oliver. *Averroës and His Philosophy*. Oxford: Clarendon, 1988.

Wohlman, Avital. *Al-Ghazali, Averroës, and the Interpretation of the Qurʾan: Common Sense and Philosophy in Islam*. Translated by David Burrell. London: Routledge, 2010.

Oliver Leaman
Revised by Joseph A. Kéchichian

Ibn Sīnā, Abū ʿAlī.

Abū ʿAlī al-Ḥusayn ibn ʿAbd Allāh Ibn Sīnā (b. c. 980, d. 1037), commonly known as Ibn Sīnā or by his Latinized name, Avicenna, was one of the foremost Persian thinkers in the tradition of Medieval Hellenism. His philosophy was based on the concept of reality and reasoning, which allowed Ibn Sīnā to understand progress that finally led him to God, the ultimate truth. A polymath who delved in the sciences, Ibn Sīnā stressed the importance of knowledge based on four specific activities: developing one's sense of perception, strengthening the aptitude for retention, expanding imagination, and honing judgment skills. He concluded that imagination was the intellect's principal role, as it allowed an individual to compare. For Ibn Sīnā, the ultimate object of knowledge was God, both essence and existence, although he distinguished between essence itself and existence for man. In fact, he believed that essence simply considered the nature of things, and was independent of mental as well as physical realizations. A soul, he assumed, was spiritual and therefore immune to destruction. In a remarkable assertion, he held that the soul was an agent that helped choose between good and evil, which in turn led to rewards or punishment as the case warranted. Such insights enriched Ibn Sīnā's voluminous writings, which were studied at leading European universities for centuries, and which influenced many Christian philosophers, including Thomas Aquinas.

Ibn Sīnā's father, ʿAbd Allāh, was a respected Ismāʿīlī scholar from Balkh, in present-day Afghanistan, while his mother, Setareh Khanum, hailed from Bukhara, in present-day Uzbekistan. Empowered to govern a village in one of the royal estates, ʿAbd Allāh focused on the education of his precocious son, who displayed exceptional intellectual capabilities. A child prodigy who memorized the Qurʾān by the age of ten, he memorized Persian poetry too and learned Indian arithmetic, studied *fiqh* under the Ḥanafī scholar Ismāʿīl al-Zahid, and started reading various works of philosophy. Aristotle's *Metaphysics* troubled him as he struggled to understand what he was reading. Only al-Fārābī's magisterial commentary on the *Metaphysics* soothed Ibn Sīnā's troubled mind, though he struggled with philosophy for the rest of his life. Still, philosophical inquiries strengthened his faith, as he frequently interrupted his studies with prayers. At sixteen,

Ibn Sīnā opted to study medicine under a physician named Kūshyār, which allowed the young apprentice to treat patients using new methods. By the age of eighteen, he was a tested doctor, and his fame spread quickly. This expertise brought him to the attention of the ailing sultan of Bukhara, Nuh ibn Mansur, whom he treated successfully. Consequently, Ibn Sīnā received permission to use the sultan's library and its rare manuscripts, which greatly helped his research efforts.

When the sultan died, the heir to the throne, ʿAlī ibn Shams al-Dawlah, asked Ibn Sīnā to continue as vizier, but the philosopher sided with another son of the late king, ʿAlāʾ al-Dawlah. Caught in an intradynastic struggle, the philosopher-physician went into hiding near Rey, in the vicinity of modern Tehran. It was at this time that Ibn Sīnā composed his major philosophical treatise, *Kitāb al-shifāʾ* (Book of Healing), a comprehensive account of learning that ranged from logic and mathematics to metaphysics and the afterlife. Regrettably, Ibn Sīnā was arrested and imprisoned, but managed to escape to Isfahan disguised as a Ṣūfī, to rejoin ʿAlāʾ al-Dawlah. His best works were written in Isfahan, including the *Kitāb al-najāt* (Book of Salvation), *al-Mantiq*, translated as *The Propositional Logic of Ibn Sina*, and *al-Ishārāt wa-al-tanbīhāt* (Remarks and Admonitions). His fourteen-volume *al-Qānūn fī al-ṭibb* (Canons on Medicine), became a standard medical text throughout the Islamic world and in much of Europe until the eighteenth century. The remaining years of his life were spent in the service of ʿAlāʾ al-Dawlah, whom he accompanied as physician and general literary and scientific adviser, even on his numerous campaigns. He died in June 1037, in his fifty-eighth year, and was buried in Hamadān, Iran.

A devout Muslim, Ibn Sīnā understood the very existence of God within the logic of the nexus of causes and effects, and since such a link needed to have a first cause, for him God's existence was assured. At a time when theologians hotly debated major doctrinal questions, Ibn Sīnā's reasoning was heavily criticized, including by al-Ghazālī, the great Persian mystic from Khorāsān. Al-Ghazālī rejected the logic that God only governed the universe, as he posited that God governed individual human actions too. Moreover, al-Ghazālī asserted that God could give bodies to resurrected souls in the afterlife, something Ibn Sīnā rejected, arguing that since God was the only Necessary Being, a physical feature for human souls was not required. Such debates were not the only controversies that surrounded Ibn Sīnā. The Shīʿī *faqīh* Nurullah Shushtari and historian Seyyed Hossein Nasr maintained that Ibn Sīnā was most likely a Twelver Shīʿī, although the philosopher was tutored in the Ḥanafī *madhhab* under Ismāʿīl al-Zahid. Dimitri Gutas held that Ibn Sīnā was a Sunnī Ḥanafī, while the theologian Henry Corbin considered that Ibn Sīnā, just like his father, was a good Ismāʿīlī. The philosopher, one surmised, was far more preoccupied with the human soul. His focus was on knowledge and metaphysics in the quest for the ultimate truth.

BIBLIOGRAPHY

Davidson, Herbert A. *Alfarabi, Avicenna and Averroes on Intellect: Their Cosmologies, Theories of the Active Intellect, and Theories of the Human Intellect*. New York: Oxford University Press, 1992. A thorough consideration of Ibn Sīnā's theory of the intellect in relation to Hellenistic and Arabic philosophy.

Goodman, Lenn E. *Avicenna: Arabic Thought and Culture*. London: Routledge, 2002.

McGinnis, Jon. *Avicenna*. New York: Oxford University Press, 2010.

Ibn Sīnā, Abū ʿAlī al-Ḥusayn ibn ʿAbd Allāh. *The Life of Ibn Sina: A Critical Edition and Annotated Translation*. Edited and translated by William E. Gohlman. Albany: State University of New York Press, 1974. The only critical edition of Ibn Sīnā's autobiography, supplemented with material from a biography by his student Abū ʿUbayd al-Jūzjānī. A more recent translation of the autobiography appears in Dimitri Gutas, *Avicenna and the Aristotelian Tradition: Introduction to Reading Avicenna's Philosophical Works* (Leiden, Netherlands: E. J. Brill, 1988). See also Ibn Sīnā's *al-Qānūn fī al-ṭibb* (Canons on Medicine), http://ddc.aub.edu.lb/projects/saab/avicenna/index.html.

JOSEPH A. KÉCHICHIAN

IBN TAYMĪYAH, TAQĪ AL-DĪN AḤMAD.

(1263–1328), Taqī al-Dīn Aḥmad Ibn Taymīyah was a prominent, influential, and sometimes controversial thinker and political figure, was born in Harran, a city located in modern-day Turkey, to a family of Ḥanbalī scholars (including his paternal grandfather, uncle, and father). Although Ibn Taymīyah was himself a Ḥanbalī scholar in many juridical and theological matters, he espoused Salafī views on a wider plane, which translated into strong influences on conservative Sunnī circles, especially in modern times.

Ibn Taymīyah's life was a mix of intellectual activity, preaching, politics, and periodic persecutions and imprisonments. This was in the context of the great disruptions caused by the Mongol invasions of the Urartian plateau in contemporary Turkey. In 1268, when the future *ʿalim* was five years old, he was taken with his family to Damascus, in flight from the Mongol threat. He was educated there in the traditional religious sciences, took over for his father as head of the Sukkarīyah mosque, and became a professor of Ḥanbalī law in about 1282. Ibn Taymīyah taught and preached elsewhere in Damascus and in other cities, though he incurred the wrath of some Shāfiʿī and other *ʿulamāʾ* (religious scholars) and theologians for some of his teachings on theology and law. He was persecuted and imprisoned in both Syria and Egypt, for his *tashbīh* (anthropomorphism), while several of his rulings—which were derived through *ijtihād* (independent reason)—along with his idiosyncratic legal judgments (e.g., on *ṭalāq* [divorce]), shocked many. Ibn Taymīyah was active in anti-Mongol propaganda, and his legal and theological definitions used in determining whether the Mongols (particularly Mongol rulers) were Muslims or *kuffār* (nonbelievers) proved influential. *Jihād* against the Mongols, he affirmed, was not only permissible but obligatory because the latter ruled not according to Sharīʿah but through their traditional, and therefore manmade, Yassa code. This essentially meant that Mongols were living in a state of *jāhilīyah*. Both Ibn Qayyim al-Jawzīyah and Ibn Kathīr, two of Ibn Taymīyah's most renowned disciples, confirmed the *ʿalim*'s pronouncements on the matter.

Ibn Taymīyah wrote numerous works (estimated between 350 and 500 books and/or pamphlets), most of which were published and translated, that described in some detail his doctrine, which was, in Ḥanbalī fashion, based on the supremacy of the Qurʾān and *sunnah* (received custom), as well as the *salaf* (early Muslim models) as ultimate authorities. He applied an austere exegetical literalism to the sacred sources and condemned the popular practice of saint veneration and pilgrimages to the *ziyārat al-qubūr* (tombs of saints) as *bidʿah* (innovation). All of these were tantamount to worshiping something other than God. Moreover, and in sharp contrast to scholars who practiced evolving but accepted practices, he rejected as alien the methods and content of *ʿilm al-kalām* (discursive theology), *falsafah* (peripatetic philosophy), and metaphysical Sufism (though he did encourage pietistic Sufism). Consequently, his conservatism evolved into the basis of Ibn Taymīyah's argument against blind obedience to *taqlīd* (established legal judgments), which was revolutionary, to say the least. In his view, the *salaf* needed to balance the sacred sources with their own *ijtihād* to better understand and live according to God's laws, and the same was required of modern generations. Ibn Taymīyah thus employed an *ijtihād* that relied more on *qiyās* (analogical reasoning) than jurists before him. For Ibn Taymīyah, *īmān* (a deep pietistic belief) was the source and power of all religion, as well as its epistemological foundation. Without it, he thought, doctrine could have no meaning or force and in his own life as a pietistic Ṣūfī, he exemplified such beliefs. His treatise on *īmān* (*Kitāb al-īmān*) was one of the most profound and subtle treatments of the subject produced in medieval Islam.

Several of Ibn Taymīyah's ideas were relevant to society and politics, including his notion of the closeness between religion and state; his defining of the Mongols as *kuffār*, in spite of their public Islamic discourse; and his general antipathy toward the *ahl al-kitāb* (people of the book). Indeed Ibn Taymīyah's significance for modern Islamic thought and culture gained momentum in conservative and Islamist circles precisely because of his avowed antipathies that, allegedly, preserved the integrity of the faith. Still, some liberal thinkers invoked his doctrines too, especially his notion of *ijtihād* and his antipathy to *taqlīd*. Insofar as modern Islam was profoundly preoccupied with issues of religion, state, and society, Ibn Taymīyah's influence was present, whether implicitly or explicitly, particularly in the Arab world.

For example, the Unitarian (Wahhābī) movement and the Saudi state that emerged from it were deeply affected by several of Ibn Taymīyah's ideas. The Wahhābī emphasis on Qur'ān and *sunnah*; a literalistic exegesis; a distaste for speculative strains of theology, the four schools of Sunnī legal thought, and mysticism; a rejection of the visitation of tombs; and a conception of the early *ummah* (community) in Medina as the model for a modern Islamic state all reflected Ibn Taymīyah's outlook.

Many later Islamist thinkers drew heavily on Ibn Taymīyah's principles for their general worldview, especially in their conception of Islam and the *ummah* and the close connection between politics and religion. This was clear in the thoughts of Ḥasan al-Bannā in Egypt, whose insistence on Islam as a synthesis of religion and state (*dīn wa-dawlah*), and his practical religious tendencies owed much to the earlier thinker.

With the Egyptian Sayyid Quṭb (1906–1966), this tendency became pronounced, as the leading member of the Muslim Brotherhood developed his notion of *jāhilīyah* (ignorance). For Quṭb the non-Islamic modern culture of moral and intellectual relativism, along with the absolute conflict between God's law and that culture, exemplified Ibn Taymīyah's sharp distinction between basic concepts within Islam and their absence in other religions. For example Quṭb's persistent attack on Muslim rulers, regimes, and so-called members of the intelligentsia for allegedly ruling and teaching according to secular principles, rather than Islamic teachings, were firmly based on Ibn Taymīyah's far-reaching pronouncements concerning the status of the Mongols within Islam. In this view leaders of modern nation-states were akin to those Mongols who publicly espoused Islam but acted against its principles. They thereby confused Muslim subjects whose faith was already weak, which meant that—based on Ibn Taymīyah's assertion—it was permissible to question such modern rulers as to the veracity of their Muslim identities. Some militant fundamentalist groups, particularly in the Arab world (and Iran), argued explicitly for *takfīr* (excommunication), branding such rulers as *kuffār*.

There is a prominent example of the principle of *takfīr* in the widely disseminated tractate *al-Farīḍah al-ghā'ibah* (The Absent Precept), by Muḥammad ʿAbd al-Salām Faraj. Faraj, the intellectual voice of the group that engineered Anwar el-Sadat's assassination, quoted Ibn Taymīyah's *fatwa* (ruling) on the Mongols as a legal precedent in his *takfīr* of contemporary rulers and religious authorities. Since then, the Egyptian religious establishment has concluded that the book was offensive, doctrinally wrong, and dangerous. Three decades after Sadat's murder, the *Majallat al-Azhar* (Journal of al-Azhar) published a special 112-page booklet in July 1993, criticizing Faraj's tractate point by point. Concerning Ibn Taymīyah's *takfīr* of the Mongols as a universal precedent, the al-Azhar booklet argued that Ibn Taymīyah's *fatwa* was time-bound, relevant only to that particular case and not to twentieth-century Egypt. It asserted:

> Can there be any comparison between these people [the Mongols] who did to Muslims [the things] carried within the history books and [modern] Egypt, its rulers and its people? Can one really compare those with these?...These explanations...[which we have given] of the reasons for [Ibn Taymīyah's] *fatwā* show that Ibn Taymīyah took his position [solely] with regard to the contemporary situation of the Tartars. [Thus in his view] they were, non-Muslims [*kuffār*], even though they spoke the language of Islam in an attempt to lead Muslims astray...(The Absent Precept, *Journal of al-Azhar*, July, 1993)

With the polarization of modern Islamic political thought on these issues in the latter half of the twentieth century, Ibn Taymīyah's influence, through Sayyid Quṭb, the Islamic movements, and others, dominates the discourse on one side of the political debate, which has perpetuated the *ʿalim*'s influence up to the present.

[*See also* Salafī Movements; *and* Sufism.]

BIBLIOGRAPHY

Works of Ibn Taymīyah

The Goodly Word. Abridged and translated by Ezzedin Ibrahim and Denys Johnson-Davis. Cambridge, U.K.: Islamic Texts Society, 2003. A translation of *Kalim al-Tayyib.*

Un Dieu hesitant? Translated and annotated by Yahya Michot. Paris: Éditions Albouraq, 2005. A French translation of *Fatāwā.*

Mardin: Hégire, fuite du péché et "demeure de l'Islam." Translated by Yahya Michot. Paris: Éditions Albouraq, 2005. A French translation of more *fatāwā.*

Mécréance et pardon: Ecrits spirituals d'Ibn Taymiyya. Michot, Yahya, trans. Paris: Éditions Albouraq, 2005. A French translation of various writings.

Kitab al-Iman [Book of Faith]. Bloomington, Ind.: Iman Publishing House, 2010.

Secondary Works

DeLong-Bas, Natana J. *Wahhabi Islam: From Revival and Reform to Global Jihad.* Oxford and New York: Oxford University Press, 2004.

Ibn Qayyim al-Jawzīyah, Muḥammad ibn Abī Bakr. *Asmāʾ muʿallafāt Ibn Taymīyah* Damascus, 1953. Catalogue of Ibn Taymīyah's main works, written by a great disciple.

Laoust, Henri. *Essai sur les doctrines sociales et politiques de Takī-d-Dīn b. Taimīya.* Cairo: l'Institute Français d'Archéologie Orientale, 1939. Standard book on Ibn Taymīyah's social and political thought.

Laoust, Henri. *La biographie d'Ibn Taimīya d'après ibn Katīr.* Damascus, 1943. The best biography of Ibn Taymīyah.

Makari, Victor E. *Ibn Taymiyyah's Ethics: The Social Factor.* Chico, Calif.: Scholars Press, 1983. Interesting and valuable discussion of Ibn Taymīyah's theory of social ethics.

Memon, Muhammad Umar. *Ibn Taymīya's Struggle against Popular Religion.* The Hague: Mouton, 1976. Excellent account of Ibn Taymīyah's ideas on popular religious practices. The book also includes a valuable discussion of Ibn Taymīyah's refutation of Ibn ʿArabī's metaphysical Sufism.

Rapoport, Yossef, and Shahab Ahmed. *Ibn Taymiyya and His Times.* New York: Oxford University Press, 2010.

RONALD L. NETTLER
Updated by JOSEPH A. KÉCHICHIAN

IBN ṬUFAYL, ABŪ BAKR. Abū Bakr ibn Ṭufayl was born at the beginning of the twelfth century in a small village northeast of Granada. He taught and practiced medicine, and served as minister to the governor of Granada and other members of the Almohad dynasty before becoming minister and chief physician to Sultan Abū Yaʿqub Yūsuf. The sultan, who was an avid patron of the sciences, and Ibn Ṭufayl introduced and recommended scholars from around the world to the court, including Ibn Rushd (Averroës), who eventually became Ibn Ṭufayl's successor as court physician.

Ibn Ṭufayl is best known for his allegorical *Ḥayy ibn Yaqẓān* (Alive, Son of Awake). As the story goes Ḥayy grows up from infancy on an uninhabited island, raised by a fawn in complete isolation from human society. The story recounts his intellectual development as he progresses through successive stages of a Neoplatonic Ṣūfī epistemic hierarchy toward Truth. In childhood Ḥayy imitates the animals he is raised with, and develops feelings of attraction and aversion to things in his environment. Then practical reason develops as he begins to use leaves and skins to protect his body and fashions weapons to protect himself against animals. When his fawn-mother dies, and he tries to find a way to revive her, it leads to him to conceive the notion of an animating principle the return of which would bring her back to life—the soul. This leads to a phase of empirical research in which Ḥayy studies things in his environment, dissecting animal bodies and experimenting with fire, in search of this animating principle. This leads to a metaphysical stage of thinking in which Ḥayy is led, by a consideration of unity and multiplicity, to a Platonic formalism; and through a consideration of change, to deduce the existence of God.

When he considers the question whether or not the world is infinite and eternal, he arrives through the resulting antinomy to the limits of reason. This culminates in a direct experience of contact with the Divine, in which Ḥayy is stripped of his awareness of anything other than God. Thereafter he turns his focus away from the material world and toward the Divine, leading life of even barer simplicity and spiritual contemplation. All of this occurs, importantly, without the use of language or human society, the implication being that neither is a necessary condition of full self-actualization, as envisioned in the tale.

On a neighboring island, in a society whose laws are based on the teachings of an ancient prophet (i.e., a Muslim society ruled by Sharīʿah law), there live two religious scholars. Absāl, the esoterically inclined of the two, retreats to the uninhabited island for a life of solitude; Salāmān, the exoterically inclined, remains and becomes the leader of his society, enforcing outward compliance with its religious law. Absāl encounters Ḥayy on the island, where they both eventually realize that Ḥayy's spiritual state is in fact the ultimate purpose and meaning of the political state established by the religion of Absāl's society. Revealed and natural wisdom, individual reflection and social coercion converge in one truth.

Both men return to Absāl's island to explain this to the inhabitants, encouraging them to go above and beyond the minimal requirements of their religious law and aspire to the higher levels of spiritual awareness that are its aim. But they find them and their leader Salāmān resistant to this message. Realizing that most of the people are incapable of receiving it, Ḥayy apologizes for his misguided attempt to instruct the masses in the esoteric dimension of their religion, and enjoins them to continue strictly following its outward injunctions. He and Absāl then return to their island to continue their spiritual quest in solitude.

The political import of this is to define and manage relations between the social classes (the intellectual-spiritual elite and the masses) by advocating both an ultimate harmony and a strict discursive segregation between them. It also asserts the intellectual and moral independence of certain elite individuals from society at large.

It reflects the needs of a state that seeks to avail itself of the benefits of autonomy and the patronization of an international cadre of intellectuals, but whose political legitimacy and ability to control society depend largely on a more provincial application of public religion.

BIBLIOGRAPHY

Work by Ibn Ṭufayl

Ibn Ṭufayl's Ḥayy Ibn Yaqẓān: A Philosophical Tale. Translated by Lenn Evan Goodman. Updated ed. Chicago: University of Chicago Press, 2009.

Secondary Works

Conrad, Lawrence I., ed. *The World of Ibn Ṭufayl: Interdisciplinary Perspectives on Ḥayy Ibn Yacẓān.* Leiden, Netherlands, and New York: E. J. Brill, 1996.

Fakhry, Majid. *A History of Islamic Philosophy.* New York: Columbia University Press, 1970.

Siddiqi, Bakhtyar Husain. "Ibn Ṭufayl." In *A History of Muslim Philosophy, with Short Accounts of Other Disciplines and the Modern Renaissance in Muslim Lands.* Edited by M. M. Sharif. 2 vols., pp. 526–539. Wiesbaden: Harrosowitz, 1963–1966.

EDWARD MOAD

IMAMATE, THEORIES OF THE.

In Arabic, *imām* signifies a leader. In Islamic usage, its designations vary, ranging from one who simply leads the Muslim ritual prayer (*ṣalāh*) to the supreme religious or religio-political leader of a group; only context determines what is intended. To the Sunnīs, it may mean a great leader, the highest master of a science, or the political head of the Muslim community. In its last sense, the term *imām* is interchangeable with *khalīfah* (literally, "deputy"). To the Shīʿī, the imam is the supreme religious and political leader, and it is on the infallible guidance of a series of such early imams, from the lineage of the Prophet, that Shīʿī religious doctrine is based. This article treats only the political theories of imamate in the sense of the supreme political or religio-political leader.

Imamate is the cardinal doctrine that separates Shiism from Sunnism. According to Shiism, revelation has an exoteric (*ẓāhir*) and an esoteric (*bāṭin*) aspect, both possessed in their fullness by the Prophet, who is at once *nabī* (prophet) and *walī* (saint), the *nubūwah* being connected with his exoteric function of bringing a divine law and the *walāyah* with his esoteric function of revealing the inner meaning of religion. With the death of the Prophet the "cycle of prophecy" (*dāʾirat al-nubūwah*) came to an end, but the "cycle of initiation" (*dāʾ irat al-wilāyah*) continues in the person of the imam.

Twelver Shiism. According to the Ithnā ʿAsharīyah (Twelver) Shīʿī, the imams are: (1) ʿAlī ibn Abī Ṭālib (d. 661), (2) al-Ḥasan ibn ʿAlī (d. 669), (3) al-Ḥusayn ibn ʿAlī (d. 680), (4) ʿAlī ibn al-Ḥusayn (Zayn al-ʿĀbidīn) (d. 714), (5) Muḥammad al-Bāqir (d. 733), (6) Jaʿfar al-Ṣādiq (d. 765), (7) Mūsā al-Kāẓim (d. 799), (8) ʿAlī al-Riḍā (d. 818); (9) Muḥammad Jawād al-Taqī (d. 835); (10) ʿAlī al-Naqī (d. 868); (11) al-Ḥasan al-ʿAskarī (d. 874), and (12) Muḥammad al-Mahdī (called al-Qāʾim and al-Ḥujjah), who entered major occultation in 940.

The imams are said to have instructed their followers during their lifetime directly, leaving behind disciples and sayings that became the basis of later Shīʿī intellectual life. In Shiism the *ḥadīth* literature includes the sayings of the imams in addition to those of the Prophet. Imamate is one of the five "principles of religion" (*uṣūl al-dīn*) in Twelver Shiism, the others being unity (*tawḥīd*), justice (*ʿadl*), prophecy (*nubūwah*), and resurrection (*maʿād*). The imam has three functions: to rule over the Islamic community, to explain the religious sciences and the law, and to be a spiritual guide to lead men to an understanding of the inner meaning of things. Because of this triple function, he cannot possibly be elected. A spiritual guide can receive his authority only from on high. Therefore, each imam is appointed through the designation (*naṣṣ*) of the previous imam by Divine command. Moreover, the imam must be inerrant (*maʿṣūm*) in order to be able to guarantee the survival and purity of the religious tradition. His function is at once human and cosmic. The twelfth imam (the Mahdī) is hidden; he is alive yet not seen by the majority of men, but will appear to the outside world toward the end of time. He is the guarantee of the preservation and continuation of the Sharīʿah and the supreme spiritual guide (*quṭb*). Without the imam, men would cease to understand the inner levels of meaning of the revelation, and without him all temporal rule is marked by imperfection; only his reappearance can establish that ideal state based on divine justice which Islam envisages in its teachings (Nasr).

Other Shīʿī branches are the five-imāmī school of the Zaydīyah and the seven-imāmī school, known as Ismāʿīliyah. Many other Shīʿī sects that emerged in the early period are now mostly extinct.

Ismāʿīlī (or Seveners). The Ismāʿīlīyah, branching off after the death of Imām Jaʿfar, believe in the permanent need for a sinless and infallible imam as the sole legitimate political and religious leader of humankind; in addition, under Neoplatonic influences, they added a cyclical view of history. In each prophetic era, seven imams followed the speaker-prophet (*nāṭiq*) and his *waṣī* (executor) or *asās* (base). The seventh imam in this heptade would rise to the position of speaker-prophet of the next era. In the sixth era, which was inaugurated by the Prophet as the speaker-prophet and ʿAlī as the executor, the seventh imam was Muḥammad ibn Ismāʿīl ibn Jaʿfar. In pre-Fāṭimid Ismāʿīlism, he was expected to return after his disappearance as the seventh speaker-prophet, who was identified with the Mahdī, opening the eschatological seventh era. This belief was modified in Fāṭimid doctrine by the recognition of the Fāṭimids as imams of the sixth era, removing the eschatological expectations further and further into the future. The irregularities of the succession led to constant readjustment of the doctrine and the creation of more and more elaborate back-projections. The imam represents a grade (*ḥadd*) in the religious hierarchy below the speaker-prophet and the executor and above the *ḥujjah* (proof), and assumes the function of the speaker-prophet in expounding and preserving the exoteric (*ẓāhir*) meaning of the revealed law, while his proof reveals its esoteric interpretation (*tāʾwīl*).

Zaydīyah. The Zaydīyah, supporters of the revolt of Zayd ibn ʿAlī in 740, unlike the Imāmiyah (Twelvers and Seveners) did not recognize a hereditary line of imams but were prepared to support any member of the *ahl al-bayt* who claimed the imamate by "rising" (*khurūj*) against the illegitimate rulers. While some Zaydīs as late as the tenth century considered all descendants of ʿAlī's father Abū Tālib as eligible for the imamate, the prevalent doctrine restricted it to the descendants of al-Ḥasan and al-Ḥusayn. During the eighth century, Zaydism was divided doctrinally into two major groups, the Baṭrīyah and the Jārūdīyah. The Baṭrīyah, following the traditions of the moderate wing of the Kufan Shīʿī, upheld the imamate of Abū Bakr and ʿUmar and of ʿUthmān during the first six years of his rule, on the basis that ʿAlī had pledged allegiance to them. They repudiated ʿUthmān during the last six years of his rule, just as they repudiated all opponents of ʿAlī. Considering ʿAlī the most excellent of men after the Prophet, they permitted the imamate of the less excellent. The Jārūdīyah, adopting the more radical views of the Imāmiyah, rejected the imamate of the first three caliphs and held that the Prophet had invested ʿAlī as his executor (*waṣī*) by designation (*naṣṣ*). Holding that the great majority of the companions of the Prophet had gone astray by following Abū Bakr and ʿUmar, they, unlike the Batriyah, rejected the tradition of the law handed down by them and relied for religious knowledge on the descendants of al-Ḥasan and al-Ḥusayn as a whole, not merely those recognized as imams. From the ninth century onward, the tendencies of the Jārūdīyah came to prevail in Zaydīsm. The major points of Zaydī doctrine, as it was fully developed during the tenth century in discussions with representatives of Muʿtazilī and Imāmī doctrine, included the following elements. The establishment of an imam is obligatory on the community, according to the common view, because of his functions under the revealed law, not on rational grounds. The first three imams—ʿAlī, al-Ḥasan, and al-Ḥusayn—were invested by the Prophet through designation (*naṣṣ*). This designation was obscure (*khafī*, *ghayr jalī*), so that its intended meaning could be discovered only by investigation. Through this doctrine the Zaydīyah, in contrast to the Imāmiyah, tended to alleviate the sin of the early community in disobeying the order of the Prophet. After al-Ḥusayn, the imamate belongs to any qualified descendant of al-Ḥasan or al-Ḥusayn who calls to his allegiance and rises against the illegitimate rulers. The imamate becomes legally valid through the formal "call" to allegiance (*daʿwah*) and "rising" (*khurūj*), not through election (*ikhtiyār*) and contract (*ʿaqd*), as Sunnīs believed. The qualifications of the imam were, aside from his descent, essentially the same as in Sunnī and Muʿtazilī doctrine. The imamate is forfeited by the lack of any of the qualifications, in particular by moral offenses. Whether an existing imam must be replaced by a more excellent claimant is disputed. The existence of two separate Zaydī communities, in the southern coastal areas of the Caspian Sea and in Yemen, led in some cases to a later recognition of two contemporary claimants as imams.

Sunnī Discourse on Imamate/Caliphate. All Sunnīs, including the Ashʿarīs, Māturīdīs, and traditionalists (Atharīs, or Ahl al-Ḥadīth), consider the imamate/caliphate an obligation. Yet, it has been claimed by almost every major scholar writing on the subject since Henri Laoust that Ibn Taymīyah denied the obligation of the Sunnī caliphate; this is entirely incorrect, as has been demonstrated in some new studies (Hassan; Anjum). The formulation of the Sunnī caliphate discourse was the work almost exclusively of the Sunnī theologians of Baghdad of the tenth and eleventh centuries. After the confrontation between the rising religious leaders of the community, the Sunnī *ʿulamāʾ*, and the caliphate, during the Miḥnah of the "createdness of the Qurʾān," the relationship became one of mutual dependency. As the ʿAbbāsids' fortunes and prestige fell precipitously and they lost effective power to a series of Shīʿī military adventurers, the Sunnīs became the caliphs' supporters. At this point there existed various attitudes among the Sunnīs toward the caliphate, and political quietism was not the only Sunnī option. Sunnī political thought began to consolidate as Sunnī *kalām* took off in the tenth century when al-Ashʿarī and his followers took up the banner of defending the traditionalist orthodoxy represented by Ibn Ḥanbal and vindicated by his triumph in the Miḥnah. The rise of Shīʿī dynasties that ruled over a Sunnī majority and their open support for Shīʿī political theology spurred Sunnī *kalām* scholars to consolidate and defend Sunnī orthodoxy and provide a theoretical basis for the Sunnī caliphate. The challenge for Sunnī theologians now was to theorize the existing caliphate while attempting to defend the historical legitimacy of the early caliphate against attacks by the Shīʿa and the Khārijīs. Equally significant foes were the Muʿtazilīs, who had backed and fueled the Miḥnah, whose rationalist theology was both the main target as well as the source of the intellectual tool set of Sunnī *kalām*.

The key Ashʿarī theologians in this discourse are: the Mālikī al-Bāqillānī (d. 1013), ʿAbd al-Qāhir

Ṭāhir al-Baghdādī (d. 1037), Abūal-Ḥasan al-Māwardī (d. 1058), Abūal-Ma'ālī al-Juwaynī (d. 1085), and Abū Ḥāmid al-Ghazālī (d. 1111). The traditionalist or Atharī scholars, in particular Abū Ya'lā (d. 1066) and Ibn Taymīyah (d. 1328), generally stayed true to the early model of the caliphate and were less swayed by Shī'ī polemics. The development of the caliphate doctrine on major issues is presented in the following.

The necessity of the imamate. With the exception of some of the Khārijīs and the Baghdādī Mu'tazilīs, all sects agreed on the necessity of installing an imam. For the Baghdādī Mu'tazilīs, the imamate was only a rational necessity, while the Basran Mu'tazilīs, with the exception of al-Jāḥiẓ, seem to have considered reason as well as revelation the provenance of the obligation; Ibn Taymīyah supported this view. All Ash'arīs insist that the imamate is an obligation by revelation, not reason.

The circumstance of appointment. This point is designed to counter the Shī'ī claim of having an invisible imam—the Sunnīs, Baghdādī maintains, require an imam who is visible.

The number of imams at any given time. Al-Bāqillānī stipulated that there be only one imam of the *ummah* at any given time, while al-Ash'arī, al-Baghdādī and others held that more than one imam is possible if separated by a sea—an obvious concession to the Spanish Umayyads. Al-Māwardī, al-Juwaynī, and al-Ghazālī rejected the possibility of coexistence of more than one imam. Clearly, when they wrote, they had in mind the threat of the Fāṭimid counter-caliphate.

The race and tribe of the imam. All Sunnīs agree on the requirement of Qurayshī descent, although al-Bāqillānī and al-Juwaynī express some doubts, and Ibn Khaldūn provided a sociological, rather than religious, explanation for this choice.

The qualifications for the imam. The requirements for the imam for all of the Sunnīs were, with some variations: (1) Qurayshī descent; (2) the qualifications of a *mujtahid* in knowledge—al-Bāqillānī required the qualifications only of a *qāḍī*, a rank lower than *mujtahid*; (3) the probity (*'adālah*) of an acceptable witness before a judge; (4) judgment and capacity to command in peace and war. Al-Māwardī famously accepts the imamate of one overpowered and confined (*ḥajr*) by someone who is not openly rebellious and disobedient—an unveiled concession to the Būyid control of Baghdad but also a veiled warning to the Būyids, and possibly the oncoming Saljūqs, to watch their limits. Al-Juwaynī adds to al-Baghdādī's list physical fitness (as does al-Māwardī), but more important, independent power and self-sufficiency (*istiqlāl* and *kifāyah*), which is more than the capacity required by most—al-Juwaynī here means actual power, in conscious contrast to al-Māwardī's potentially overpowered caliph. Al-Ghazālī transfers the requirement of actual power to the ruling sultan and reduces the caliph to a ritual position that is absolutely necessary to safeguard and hence cannot be deterred by unfeasible requirements. Ibn Taymīyah considers a powerless caliph irrelevant and focuses instead on a substantively Islamic government, ruled by Sharī'ah and justice, as more important than the formal requirements for the caliph. He upholds the obligation of the caliphate and deems kingship or sultanate sinful, but tolerable if nothing else is possible.

Impeccability. Sunnīs reject the Shī'ī requirement of infallibility (*'iṣma*).

The means whereby the imam is established in office. Most agreed that the imamate is established by: (1) election (*ikhtiyār*) by one or more electors (commonly termed *ahl al-ḥall wa-al-'aqd*, those who untie and tie), followed by a contract (*bay'ah*); (2) testamentary designation by the previous imam (*'ahd*); (3) brute force (*ghalbah*). This last appears, especially starting with al-Juwaynī, as another independent way of (self-)appointment of the imam.

In the early phase of the caliphate discourse, there existed significant disagreement about whether testamentary designation is an independent means of appointing an imam. The

Muʿtazilīs consider it invalid altogether. The Mālikī al-Bāqillānī, the Ḥanbalī Abū Yaʿlā, and others consider it valid only if followed by *bayʿah* by the electors, thus effectively reducing its value to mere nomination. Al-Baghdādī considered designation legitimate but without explicitly specifying whether the confirmation by the electors is necessary. He does state, however, that if the designated person is fit for the imamate, it is an obligation upon the *ummah* to accept it—as in the case of Abū Bakr's designation of ʿUmar—which would mean that the electors' confirmation is unnecessary if the designated imam is suited for the office (he does not tell us who makes that decision). Al-Māwardī was the first to not only claim a consensus on the issue but also to consider designation a method of appointment independent of confirmation by the electors. Others suggested that the caliphate could be contracted, using the analogy of a marriage, by a single guardian of legal probity, yet others required at least two electors; in case of multiple simultaneous elections, some suggested drawing lots or redoing.

***The appointment of imam after the death of the Prophet and inheritance and testament in regard to the imamate* (naṣṣ).** The appointment of Abū Bakr after the Prophet and the election of the three subsequent caliphs are the critical historical points around which most controversies regarding the imamate revolved. The Sunnī political theology rejected the Shīʿī doctrine on two main points, a normative one, that is, the obligation upon God of appointing an infallible imam, and a corresponding historical one, the historical claim of the Prophetic testament (*naṣṣ*) to appoint ʿAlī as the next imam.

BIBLIOGRAPHY

Anjum, Ovamir. *Politics, Law and Community in Islamic Thought: The Taymiyyan Moment.* Cambridge, U.K.: Cambridge University Press, 2012.

Dumayjī, ʿAbd Allāh ibn ʿUmar ibn Sulaymān al-. *Al-Imāmah al-ʿuẓmā ʿind ahl al-sunnah wa-al-jamāʿah.* Riyadh: Dār Ṭība, 1987.

Hassan, Mona. "Modern Interpretations and Misinterpretations of a Medieval Scholar: Apprehending the Political Thought of Ibn Taymiyyah." In *Ibn Taymiyya and His Times*, edited by Y. Rapoport and S. Ahmed. Karachi, pp. 338–366. Oxford University Press, 2010.

Hillenbrand, C. "Islamic Orthodoxy or Realpolitik? Al-Ghazālī's Views on Government." *IRAN* 26 (1988): 90.

Lambton, Ann K. S. *State and Government in Medieval Islam: An Introduction to the Study of Islamic Political Theory: The Jurists.* New York: Oxford University Press, 1981.

Laoust, Henri. *Essai sur les doctrines sociales et politique de Taki-D-Din Ahmad b. Taymiya.* Cairo: L'institute français d'archéologie Oriental, 1939.

Madelung, W. "Imāma." *Encyclopaedia of Islam*, 2d ed. Brill Online, 2012.

Nasr, S. H. "Ithnā ʿAshariyya." *Encyclopaedia of Islam*, 2d ed. Brill Online, 2012.

Sayyid, Riḍwān al-. *Al-Jamāʿa wa-al-mujtamaʿ wa-al-dawla.* Beirut: Dār al-Kitāb al-ʿArabī, 1997.

OVAMIR ANJUM

IMĀRAH. In the Prophetic traditions, *imārah* connotes commandership. It derives from the Arabic root *a-m-r*, which means "to command," and belongs to the pattern of *fiʿalah*, which makes *imārah*, literally, "the profession of commanding." Without distinguishing between military commandership and political leadership, it is understood by early reports as the responsibility of ruling a community. As such, the political authority of the *imārah*, or emirate, is comparable to that of the caliphate, the imamate, or the leadership (*wilāyah*). Nevertheless, even in the earliest traditions, the emirate did not have a religious status, as did the caliphate or the imamate. Rather, the emirate covers executive, administrative, and military commanderships, albeit at the highest level. It is more concerned with the worldly order than with the community's religious life. The Prophet warns his followers from accepting the position of emirate, for it is a risky duty that could lead one to a terrible fate in the hereafter. The overall negative image of the emirate in the traditions reflects mistrust in the Muslim political leaders. However, a few *ḥadīths* praise the emirate if undertaken in accordance with justice and piety. In some early narrations, the reigns of the first two caliphs, Abū Bakr al-Ṣiddīq (d. 634) and ʿUmar ibn ʿAbd al-Khaṭṭāb (d. 644), were described as *imārah* as well. In particular, ʿUmar assumed the title of commander of the faithful, *amīr al-muʾminīn.* In his case, the emirate is a supreme religious and political leadership, similar to the caliphate. This means that the emirate is one of the earliest forms of Muslim political organization.

Increasingly, with the centralization and expansion of the Muslim empires, *imārah* came to convey a more restricted meaning: commanding an army, a military campaign, or ruling an area. For instance, Khālid ibn al-Walīd (d. 642), a general of the conquering Muslim armies, was in charge of the leadership of the army, *imarat al-jaysh.* Several traditions attributed to companions and successors who lived in the caliphate period indicate that the emirate is a secondary position compared to the supreme leadership of the caliphate. In the Umayyad era, ʿUmar ibn ʿAbd al-ʿAzīz (d. 720) was reported to have said he always wanted the emirate, meaning governorship, and once he had it, he aspired to the caliphate. He became first an Umayyad governor in Medina and then caliph in Damascus.

In the eleventh century, administrative and military commanderships were separated in public law. This can be seen in Abūal-Ḥasan al-Māwardī's (d. 1058) *al-Aḥkām al-sulṭānīyah wa-al-wilāyāt al-dīnīyah.* The author calls the administrative commandership *al-imāra ʿalā al-bilād,* which is a governorate appointed by the caliph over an area or a city. It can be general or specific. The general contract clearly defines the territory and the tasks of the appointed emir. His responsibilities would include commanding the army and *jihād,* supervising finances, the judiciary, and the pilgrimage, preserving religion, applying criminal punishments, and leading collective prayers. It may be considered a mini-caliphate reporting to the central caliph. This general emirate is of two sorts: contracted either by commission, *imārat istikfāʾ*, or by force, *imārat istīlāʾ*. The first takes place when a caliph, by his will, appoints an emir to rule an area for him. As for the emirate by force, it occurs when a commander holds power in a country or a city against the central authority. Left with no choice, the caliph appoints him, de jure, as a governor. Although this emir is in fact a despot who monopolizes governance, al-Māwardī asserts, the caliph provides him, through his permission, an authority to rule in the name of Islam. Thus, his contract is validated. With reference to the Sunnī political tradition based on choice, al-Māwardī admits that this type of emirate is an anomaly. Nonetheless, he approves it since it preserves the Muslim public order, which should not be run into chaos and corruption. Like most of the Muslim jurists, al-Māwardī is a realist. He justifies a situation in which the caliph should legitimize the emirate by force by its exceptionality. Under an order brought by force and obligation, certain things are allowed that normally should not be permitted in the appointment of governors by choice. The difference lies in the conditions of capacity (emirate by commission) and incapacity (emirate by force). Under conditions of a powerful caliph, no emir should be accorded exceptions. Al-Māwardī, who lived under a weak ʿAbbāsid caliphate, saw the caliphs legalizing the rule of the Būyids (934–1055) and the Seljuks (1037–1194). As for the specific emirate, it defines the domain of a commander or a governor whose responsibilities are to supervise the army, to govern the community, and to assure security. He should not intervene in the issues of law or taxes. As such, the specific emirate is regional executive governance.

Beside the emir of governance, the caliph appoints an emir of war, *al-imārah ʿalā al-jihād.* The latter is secondary to the former in order of importance, and his major task is to wage war. An emirate of war is also of two sorts: general and specific. In case of the general one, the emir leads the army into battle, disposes of the war booty, and contracts peace. It is comparable to the general emirate of governance. The specific emir of war leads only the army during war, making his responsibilities more restricted and equivalent to the specific emir in the administrative emirate. Warlords were a real threat to the political stability of the caliphate and frequently aspired to autonomy or independence. In later periods of Islamic political history, as the caliphate weakened, emirates acquired greater sovereignty. Some emirs recognized the caliph's suzerainty formally, but generally the emir possessed both military and administrative powers, supported by his clan, tribe, or an alliance of tribes.

In the twentieth century, the emirate was a political system adopted in the Middle East by small Arab states on the margins of the Ottoman Empire or as a consequence of its collapse. Similarly to the medieval emir, the modern emir leads the state and governs with the help of his clan or tribe. His functions are those of an absolute king or sultan. For example, Moroccan kings still hold the religious title *amīr al-muʾminīn* (commander of the faithful) as the symbol of their religious authority over their subjects.

In the current Arabic political vocabulary, another modern usage of *imārah* can be seen in the Islamist literature. So far, the most elaborated Islamist political reflection on *imārah* was produced by the Syrian Saʿīd Ḥawwā (d. 1989), who was the ideologue and spiritual leader of the Syrian Muslim Brotherhood. In his *Fuṣūl fī al-imrah wa-al-amīr,* he deliberately uses the term *imrah* rather than *imārah*, claiming the former to be more inclusive, as it encloses all positions of responsibility, which range from the patriarchal family to the caliphate. Ḥawwā sees three sorts of political *imrah*: first, the *imrah* of the commander of the faithful, who should be the general commander of the whole Muslim community; second, the *imrah* of the commanders of provinces, who enjoy the executive authority; finally, there is the *imrah* of the commanders of Islamic movements. The tasks of the first two is the establishment of Islamic governance, based on Sharīʿah and human experience. As for the third, it strives for the achievement of Islamic objectives, namely, the establishment of an Islamic state. Although his book is embedded with Islamist political ethics, it is modeled on the genre of *al-Aḥkam al-sulṭānīyah.* The latter provides justification for an Islamist emirate. Ḥawwā validates every institution and policy through Islamic traditions and juristic principles borrowed from this genre. Alienated from a reality in which emirate, in its medieval sense, is anecdotal, his work is a normative treatise on what an ideal emir should be like. The result is an Islamist emirate, midway between a modern state and a caliphate; it disposes of the centralization of the modern nation-state, and the ruler has the ethics of justice, compassion, and benevolence of an idealized caliph. Still, a tension exists between the structures of a modern state and Ḥawwā's emirate. For instance, he requires the emir to know everything about the issues of his subjects. Thus, in his political imagination, he recalls the idealized caliphs of the past who, in several narratives of the Islamic "golden era" were attentive to the everyday affairs of people. Conversely, the modern state is an abstract form of public interest. No supreme leader is able, or required, to know everything about his citizens, even with the most powerful intelligence service.

In the twenty-first century, several Islamist emirates are established in grey zones throughout the Muslim world. The most notable is the emirate of the Taliban in Afghanistan. Other similar although minor emirates, based on a *jihād* mode of life and economy, subsist in the Caucasus, Azawad, and Somalia. These are armed Islamist movements, practicing guerrilla insurgency against central governments, which they perceive as un-Islamic and corrupt, and foreign powers, who are fought for supporting the governments and invading Muslim territories. The emir is appointed by the members of his movement through the process of allegiance (*bay'ah*). He enjoys religious, political, and military authority until his death.

BIBLIOGRAPHY

Al-Māwardī, Abū al-Ḥasan. *The Ordinances of Government*. Translation by Wafaa Hassan Wahba of *al-Aḥkām al-sulṭānīyahwa-al-wilāyāt al-dīniyya*. Reading, Pa.: Garnet, 2000.

Ḥawwā, Sa'īd. *Fuṣūl fī al-imrah wa-al-amīr*. Cairo: Dar al-Salam, 1950.

Lewis, Bernard, *The Political Language of Islam*. Chicago: University of Chicago Press, 1988.

Muslim, Ibn al-Ḥajjāj al-Qushayrī, *Ṣaḥīḥ Muslim*. Edited by Abū 'Abd Allāh Muḥammad Ubbī et al. Beirut: Dār al-Kutub al-'Ilmīyah, 2008.

ABDESSAMAD BELHAJ

INDIA. At approximately 160 million people, the Muslim population of the Republic of India, some 14 percent of the whole, constitutes one of the largest Muslim populations in the world. Muslims form a majority only in the contested state of Kashmir. In the populous states of Uttar Pradesh and Bihar, the Muslim population stands at about 15 to 20 percent; in Malabar and West Bengal, one-quarter of the whole; and in Assam, about one-third. Muslims vary by such regional and linguistic affiliations as Bengali, Deccani, Gujarati, Hindustani, Mappila, Tamil, Oriyya, and Punjabi. They are characterized by multiple sectarian or denominational affiliations. Most are Sunnī, with Ḥanafī law predominating and some Shāfi'ī in the south. About 10 percent are Shī'ī, mostly Ithnā 'Asharī. A small but significant Shī'ī community is the Ismā'īlī under the leadership of the Aga Khan; the core Ismā'īlī population are traders based in western India. Most Muslims in the subcontinent have participated in the institutions of the Ṣūfī orders.

Modern cultural, religious, and political movements account for further intellectual and even sectarian differences. Among figures influential beyond the subcontinent are Sayyid Aḥmad Khān (1817–1898), whose Aligarh Muslim University (1875) gave Islamic modernism in India its name; the Islamist Abū al-A'lā Mawdūdī (1903–1979), founder of the Jamā'at-i Islāmī (1941); Muhammad Iqbal (c. 1877–1938), regarded as the poet of Pakistan; Mawlānā Muḥammad Ilyās (1885–1944), the inspiration to the Tablīghī Jamā'at; and Abū al-Ḥasan 'Alī al-Nadvī (1914–1999), long associated with the Nadwat al-'Ulamā' (1908), an academy meant to produce reformed religious leaders fluent in Arabic, and a scholar and public intellectual within India and in international organizations such as the Muslim World League.

The Nineteenth Century and Establishment of British Institutions. Following the suppression of the so-called Indian Mutiny of 1857, Britain abolished the East India Company, and India came under direct British government rule. Reprisals against Muslims were particularly severe because they were regarded as the displaced rulers. The British also, however, identified people whom they considered conservative "natural leaders," among them large landlords and princes whose polities included about a quarter of the population. Aristocrats like the Muslim rulers of Rampur, Bhopal, and Hyderabad were patrons of Islamic learning, music, and Greco-Arabic medicine. British administrative policy imagined an India divided into "religious communities" (like "Hindu" and "Muslim") in keeping with what was taken to be India's backward stage of civilization. Sayyid Aḥmad Khān responded to the opportunity to argue that the "Muslim" minority was well suited to cooperate in governing because of their former experience as rulers and shared monotheism with the British. Leaders of the *ʿulamāʾ* in these years established themselves as a popularly supported class oriented toward grassroots education and guidance. The *ḥadīth*-oriented Deobandi *ʿulamāʾ* pioneered a Dār al-ʿUlūm (1867) with its formal organization based on colonial schools. Other orientations that crystallized in this period include the Ahl-i Ḥadīth, which favored direct use of sacred texts, and the Barelwīs (who called themselves the Ahl-i Sunnat va Jamāʿat), who were Ḥanafī but more supportive of customary devotional practices. The Ahmadis were followers of Mīrzā Ghulām Aḥmad (1839–1908), excoriated to the present on the grounds of compromising the finality of Muḥammad's prophethood. They are a Ṣūfī-like, highly educated community committed to missionary work. All utilized the new technology of inexpensive publications and engaged in both intra-Muslim debate and debates with Hindus and Christians.

Although Sayyid Aḥmad Khān opposed the program of the Indian National Congress (1885) out of fear that minority interests would suffer in councils where their numbers would be small, other Muslims participated, and Muslim issues became part of public discussion, especially their numbers in governing councils, in schools, in public employment, and so on.

Twentieth Century to Partition. Three early-twentieth-century issues shaped a Muslim political agenda: first, the 1905 division of the Bengal presidency on ostensibly administrative grounds into two new provinces (the eastern half emerging as a Muslim-majority area), rescinded in 1911 in the face of protests by Bengali nationalists; second, the first of three pre-independence Council Reform Acts, stimulating the organization of the Muslim League (ML) of landed and aristocratic leaders and resulting in the provisions of the Morley-Minto Reforms of 1909 for reserved seats for Muslims as well as separate electorates in which only Muslims could vote for Muslim representatives; and third, a surge in "Pan-Islamic" concerns, focused on what were seen as European efforts to undermine the Ottoman Empire in the Balkans and in the Hijaz. This last produced social service organizations and medical missions under the leadership of *ʿulamāʾ* and the secularly educated. Abū al-Kalām Azād (1888–1958), who would become a prominent Congress member and India's first minister of education, rose to prominence over Ottoman issues.

British policy after World War I dashed heightened expectations for self-rule. Wartime emergency legislation continued, and the Montagu Chelmsford Reforms (1919) offered only limited constitutional reform. Postwar dismemberment of the Ottoman Empire was taken as evidence of colonial perfidy. The Khilāfat movement, which sought to defend the position of the Ottoman sultan and his symbolic role as the caliph of all Muslims, allied with the Gandhian non-cooperation movement.

In Punjab and Bengal, landlord parties in the interwar years reflected a powerful class rather than religious interest. There, too, however, there was Muslim-Hindu friction at the popular level and competition that often manifested itself in communal riots. Three significant movements led by religious leaders emerged. The Jamiʿat ʿUlamāʾ-i Hind (JUH; 1919) was organized to support the *khilāfat* and Indian nationalism as anti-colonial causes. JUH, which included many

Deobandis, was committed to an independent India in which Muslims would control their own educational and jurisprudential lives; they strongly opposed Partition in 1947. The Tablīghī Jamāʿat emerged in the face of Hindu "reconversion" movements of the 1920s; it has remained one of the most influential Muslim movements worldwide. Apolitical and non-confrontational, without overarching institutionalization, it calls on every Muslim to provide nonjudgmental guidance to other Muslims in homes, mosques, and tours. The Jamāʿat-i Islāmī, formed shortly before Partition, turned to the secularly educated to create the "vanguard" of a new "order"—in the spirit of other twentieth-century "isms"—based on a purified Islam, understood as a "system" and "a complete way of life" in contrast to the decadent, materialist West. The writings of the founder, Mawlana Mawdūdī, have been significant in Pakistan and abroad, influencing figures like the Egyptian Sayyid Quṭb (d. 1966) whose writings have inspired contemporary militants, but in their political form are of marginal importance within India.

After little success against the Congress in the provincial elections following the Government of India Act of 1935, Mohammad Ali Jinnah (1876–1948), a Bombay lawyer who had been active in the Congress, determined to make the Muslim League into a mass party and himself the sole spokesman for Muslims. In 1940, the ML passed the Lahore Resolution in favor of a separate Muslim state, arguably a "bargaining chip" to gain guaranteed weight in councils where Muslims were a minority and there was weak central authority over the provinces, five of which had Muslim majorities. The League gained ground during World War II, when much of the Congress leadership was imprisoned for opposition to a war they had not entered independently. With the failure of a negotiated settlement, a divided India became independent on 15 August 1947. Partition was the fruit of decades of religio-political movements that had drawn ever-sharper boundaries around communities, and it was a *pis aller* for Congress leaders who saw decentralized federalism as an obstacle to a strong, "developmentalist" center. The early date set for independence and the failure to prepare for the aftermath reflected an exhausted Britain eager to end its responsibilities. Gandhi opposed Partition to the end. Many hoped that Partition would end communal violence.

The Republic of India. In the horrific course of the Partition of British India, as many as 12 to 18 million people may have migrated; perhaps a million others died. The rulers of the various princely states, abandoned by Britain, were forced to make a choice of India or Pakistan. The Hindu rulers of Kashmir, adjoining both India and Pakistan, had notoriously discriminated against their Muslim majority population. While the maharaja vacillated, Pakistani irregular troops invaded in the hope of forcing Kashmir's accession to their new state. The maharaja's subsequent decision to opt for India defied the logic of Partition, but for India it confirmed India's claim to be a secular rather than a Hindu state. At the end of the conflict in 1948, Pakistan secured some regions of the state, but India held the rich Srinagar valley. A "line of control" has persisted through two subsequent wars, United Nations resolutions, and various negotiations until today. In the late 1980s, Indian Kashmir was overtaken by a separatist movement that has endured into the early twenty-first century.

Mutual animosity has been a theme in the nationalism of both new states and a particular burden for India's Muslim population. The horrors of Partition, as well as revulsion at Hindu extremism after the 1948 murder of Mahatma Gandhi by a Hindu extremist, contributed to a period of quiescence. Gandhi's assassination, ostensibly motivated by his intervention in adjudicating

Pakistan's share of undivided India's cash assets, revealed a deep Hindu nationalism, or "Hindutva," that identified India's Christians and Muslims as "foreigners." This would resurface in the 1970s during a period of emergency rule and again during the social dislocations of economic change from the 1980s. All evidence to the contrary, Muslim Indians have borne the burden of suspicion as Pakistani loyalists have been unfairly tainted by outrages like the terrorist attacks launched from Pakistan on Mumbai in 2008.

India's constitution (1950) laid the framework for a secular liberal democracy; it rejected both separate electorates and reservation of seats on religious grounds. Two provisions were meant as temporary accommodations: the continuation of religiously defined family law (Hindu, Muslim, and Christian) until the minorities gained sufficient confidence to accept a Universal Civil Code; and reservations for Dalits, the "untouchables" whose status was now made illegal, and who needed, as it was seen, the temporary "helping hand" of affirmative action. Both provisions continue to the present. Muslim Personal Law has persisted as a key symbol of Muslim cultural autonomy, particularly important as anti-Muslim sentiment grew by the end of the twentieth century. Muslims, like other Indians, long supported the Congress party, which espoused secularism and wooed Muslim votes. By the turn of the century, Muslims were voting primarily for regional parties deemed likely to support their interests. Three of those filling the largely ceremonial role of India's president have been of Muslim background.

Beginning in 1984, Hindu activists made a Mughal mosque, the so-called Babri Masjid in Ayodhya, the symbol of anti-Muslim antagonism. Historical evidence to the contrary, they insisted that the mosque was built on the ruins of a temple built to honor the birthplace of the god Rama. Led by the Vishva Hindu Parishad (World Hindu Organization, or VHP) and often supported by the political party Bharata Janata Parishad (BJP), pressure grew to replace the mosque with a temple. VHP-led mass actions, like processions transporting bricks to rebuild the temple, led to far-reaching anti-Muslim violence. On 6 December 1992, activists tore down the entire stone mosque. In the violence that followed, nearly 2,000 died, the vast majority Muslim, particularly in Bombay where the complicity of officials led commentators to speak of the action as a "pogrom." In the following year, bomb blasts rocked Bombay, leading to perhaps 200 deaths. In 2007, court judgments were handed down against perpetrators of this latter terrorism, instigated by gangsters of Muslim background, but virtually no action was taken against those responsible for the earlier shocking attacks on Muslims.

Anti-Muslim sentiment, like the suspicion of minorities generally, is useful to modern nationalism and helped bring the BJP to power as head of a ruling coalition in the central government from 1998 to 2004. Indian Muslims became a surrogate for opposition to what was seen as an immoral and increasingly intrusive state structure. Muslims were imagined as a vested interest with special privileges who were disloyal to the Indian state and who had connections to "foreign" interests in Pakistan, the Gulf, and elsewhere—a community unassimilable to the values of Hindu morality. With the dislocations brought about by economic liberalization and the increased political activism of previously suppressed social classes, class tension was displaced onto religion. In case after case, demands for affirmative action for lower strata of society evolved into anti-Muslim violence, with Muslims a foil for creating majoritarian unity.

In the Gujarati town of Godhra in 2002, a railway fire, in which several dozen Hindu activists returning from Ayodhya were killed, sparked a weeks-long anti-Muslim pogrom. Hindu nationalist activists, using official computer printouts, identified Muslim shops and residences and killed, raped, and mutilated with impunity until the army was deployed. At the very least, 1,000 Muslims were killed and 150,000 driven to relief camps. The BJP state government was subsequently reelected; trials against perpetrators were frustrated; and rehabilitation of those impacted was marginal.

In 2004 a Congress ministry, headed by the distinguished economist Manmohan Singh, took office, reelected to a second five-year term in 2009, with a commitment to sustain economic growth and redirect attention to the soaring disparities that placed huge populations outside the mainstream. Despite individual success stories, Muslims continue to number among the poorest citizens in India, as definitively confirmed in the 2006 "Sachar Report." Muslims are dramatically underrepresented in the armed forces, the police, and the public sector generally; for the most part, have not benefited from the economic boom; and are woefully behind in literacy and education. They have faced evident discrimination, limited job prospects, and systematic underinvestment in education and other services in Muslim localities; most lack access to credit and are self-employed or employed in small undertakings or the informal sector. The report described Muslims as divided into three strata, roughly analogous to other Indians: (a very small) "upper caste", "other backward castes", and "scheduled castes", the former "untouchables." This distinction had ongoing relevance to the controversial question of whether at least some Muslims should be eligible, as has been increasingly demanded in recent years, for official affirmative action, from which they have been largely excluded. That demand, as well as the fact that they are among the most outspoken defenders of secularism and the rule of law, makes clear the extent to which Muslim Indians are active participants in India's democratic political culture.

[*See also* Aḥmad Khān, Sayyid; Aḥmadīyah; All-India Muslim League; Barelwīs; Chirāgh ʿAlī; Deobandīs; Iqbal, Muhammad; Jamāʿat-i Islāmī; Jamʿīyatul ʿUlamāʾ-i Hind; Jinnah, Mohammad Ali; Khilāfat Movement; Mawdūdī, Sayyid Abū al-Aʿlā; Qadarites; *and* Tablīghī Jamāʿat.]

BIBLIOGRAPHY

Ahmed Irfan. *Islamism and Democracy in India: The Transformation of Jamaat-e-Islami*. Princeton, N.J.: Princeton University Press, 2009.

Ahmed, Rafiuddin. *The Bengal Muslims, 1871–1906*. Delhi and New York: Oxford University Press, 1981.

Bayly, Susan. *Saints, Goddesses, and Kings: Muslims and Christians in South Indian Society, 1700–1900*. Cambridge, U.K.: Cambridge University Press, 1989.

Chatterjee, Joya. *Bengal Divided: Hindu Communalism and Partition, 1932–1947*. Cambridge, U.K.: Cambridge University Press, 1994.

Freitag, Sandria B. *Collective Action and Community: Public Arenas and the Emergence of Communalism in North India*. Berkeley: University of California Press, 1989.

Gilmartin, David. *Empire and Islam: Punjab and the Making of Pakistan*. Berkeley: University of California Press, 1988.

Hardy, Peter. *The Muslims of British India*. Cambridge, U.K.: Cambridge University Press, 1972.

Hasan, Mushirul. *Nationalism and Communal Politics in India, 1885–1930*. Delhi: Manohar, 1979.

Jalal, Ayesha. *The Sole Spokesman: Jinnah, the Muslim League and the Demand for Pakistan*. Cambridge, U.K.: Cambridge University Press, 1985.

Lelyveld, David. *Aligarh's First Generation: Muslim Solidarity in British India*. Princeton, N.J.: Princeton University Press, 1977.

Metcalf, Barbara D. *Islamic Revival in British India: Deoband, 1860–1900*. 2d ed. New Delhi and New York: Oxford University Press, 2002.

Metcalf, Barbara Daly, ed. *Islam in South Asia in Practice*. Princeton, N.J.: Princeton University Press, 2009.

Metcalf, Barbara D. "Traditionalist Islamic Activism." http://blogs.ssrc.org/tif/2011/09/07/traditionalist-islamic-activism/.

Metcalf, Barbara D., and Thomas R. Metcalf. *A Concise History of Modern India*, 3d ed. Cambridge, U.K.: Cambridge University Press, 2012.

Minault, Gail. *The Khilafat Movement: Religious Symbolism and Political Mobilization in India*. New York: Columbia University Press, 1982.

Mujeeb, Mohammad. *The Indian Muslims*. London: Allen and Unwin, 1967.

Rai, Mridu. *Hindu Rulers, Muslim Subjects: Islam, Rights and the History of Kashmir*. Princeton, N.J.: Princeton University Press, 2004.

Ramaswamy, Sumati, ed. *Barefoot across the Nation: Maqbool Fida Husain and the Idea of India*. New York: Routledge, 2011.

Shani, Ornit. *Communalism, Caste and Hindu Nationalism: The Violence in Gujarat*. Cambridge, U.K.: Cambridge University Press, 2007.

Zaman, Muhammad Qasim. *The Ulama in Contemporary Islam: Custodians of Change*. Princeton, N.J.: Princeton University Press, 2007.

BARBARA D. METCALF

INDIVIDUALISM. A discussion of individualism requires the choice of a definitional starting point, although the term's historical "baggage" is problematic. Three visibly contested areas—property rights, the role of women, and interpretative authority—illustrate the possibility for individualism among diverse and often polarized claims about Islam.

"Individualism" carries historically contingent meanings that are loaded with contemporary norms, complicating the discussion. The term is entangled with modern liberal theories that are embedded in modern Enlightenment-based subjectivism, which conceives of the "self" as "an agent disengaged from any context of relations, whether these relations are attributed to the world, human language, existence, or the Divine" (Kalin, 2010, p. 48). The acontextual, autonomous subject presumed in the conception of the modern individual influences claims about individualism in Islam, yet this influence sometimes goes uninterrogated, making genuine dialogue more difficult. From a spectrum of possible understandings, this essay presumes that "individualism" asserts individual agency and emphasizes protections for individual choice, particularly when those choices diverge from collective preferences. Claims about the Islamic understanding of these two areas thus speak to the topic of individualism and Islam.

Recognition of the capacity for individual choice rests in part on claims about human agency. The question of human agency has arisen in theological positions taken by the Muʿtazilī and Ashʿarī, a binary presumed by Sachedina (2001, pp. 20–21). The Muʿtazilī view describes humans as free agents responsible before a just God; good and evil are rational categories that can be discerned through reason, which is a source of spiritual and ethical knowledge. The Ashʿarī position is that God directly creates all actions, sometimes making the individual a voluntary, responsible agent, and the divine will is known through revealed guidance. In Sachedina's view, the Muʿtazilī thesis has prevailed over traditional and Ashʿarī approaches in Sunnī exegesis, particularly with respect to the individual freedom of conscience and the opportunity to negotiate his or her own spiritual destiny. In Abou El Fadl's view, Muslims' belief in God's sovereignty does not provide an escape from human agency (Abou El Fadl, 2003).

Another claim suggesting the human capacity to choose is based on *fiṭrah*, a Qurʾānic term. According to Sachedina, *fiṭrah* is a primordial nature given to all humans at birth, and imparts "the necessary cognition and volition to fulfill the goals of humanity and to recognize and serve God," suggesting that it is every individual's responsibility "to discern what it means to be a witness to God and to serve humanity" (Sachedina, 2001, p. 26). Claims recognizing individual capacity and volition fit with individualism.

Individualism can be counterposed to collectivism. In individualism, the rights of the individual are paramount over social needs, while in collectivism, the rights of the group (society, community, or nation) are paramount. In individualism, there is more personal freedom of choice, while in collectivism, the group is more empowered to pursue collective goals. Some assert a collectivist essence to Islam (Tibi, 1994, p. 289; Brohi, 1982), while others see this as a mistaken impression (Abou El Fadl, 2003; Shahin, 2010). According to Abou El Fadl, "the notion of individual rights is actually easier to justify in Islam than a collectivist orientation. God created human beings as individuals, and their liability in the Hereafter is individually determined as well" (2003). Numerous juristic positions condemning torture and coerced confessions, and affirming the presumption of innocence, appear oriented to the protection of individual rights. Abou El Fadl further asserts that while the five values of *Sharīʿah* with regard to human necessities (religion, life, intellect, honor/lineage, and property) have often been reduced to technical objectives, they "could serve as a foundation for a systematic theory of individual rights in the modern age" (2003).

Lexically, Islam has been translated as "submission," and to the extent that the act of submission is predicated on individual choice, a theological claim about individualism in Islam can be made. Qurʾān 2:256 ("Let there be no compulsion in religion...") can be interpreted as a divinely ordained right for each person to make religious choices without coercion (Sachedina, 2001, p. 25). Whether this extends to Muslims who commit apostasy remains debated. One view is that apostasy is not in itself a crime punishable by *Sharīʿah,* but a sin for which punishment is promised in the hereafter; apostasy may be punishable if it amounts to treason (a more imaginable possibility in the medieval era, when citizenship was based on religious rather than territorial ties; Intisar Rabb interview, Merica, 2011).

Whether and how polity design can recognize individual choice while also recognizing collective groupings remains a key area for debate (Mahmood, 2004; Kymlicka, 1991; Kukathas, 2003; Malik, 2008). One consonance within the Islamicate context is the Ottoman millet system, which recognized groups and offered some autonomy. To the extent that millet recognition reinforced hierarchies within communities, empowering religious leaders, the system more closely resembles collectivism over individualism. Yet there were protections for individual rights extended to Muslims and non-Muslims, based on claims about Islamic law (Aral, 2004). Ottoman arrangements provide one example of how the central state's purview was circumscribed in a way that promoted choice.

The liberal discourse within which individual rights are often discussed contains assumptions about the "public" and "private" realms. These distinctions were not used in the pre-modern period. A key institutional space in Islamicate societies, the *waqf* (endowment), is neither public nor private (Asad, 2003, p. 683). This matters because it suggests room for engagement between the individual and community in ways that may escape the public/private dichotomy that shapes liberal polity discussions. With the rise of states, *awqāf* may be in decline as autonomous spaces.

Property rights are foundational to individualistic notions of freedom found in the ideology of such economic liberals as Milton Friedman. The right to property was discernible in the right of compensation, according to Muslim jurists (Abou El Fadl, 2003). Imad ad Din Ahmad (1991) sees grounds for private property rights in Qurʾānic injunctions on contracts and on honesty in measures, and points to Muslim historical exemplars who zealously applied private property rights regimes. This contrasts with views that advocate nationalizing some resources, or views that promote redistribution of wealth.

A prominent issue in the human rights nongovernmental organization (NGO) community is the ostensible clash between women's choices and Islamic legal positions as codified in personal status laws (Modirzadeh, 2006). These are entangled with individualism, because they touch on contested claims about the protections for choice. Claims about protections for women's choices can be found in well-established *fiqh* schools, particularly with reference to independent property rights, inheritances, the ability to stipulate terms in a marriage contract, and the consent required for contractual arrangements in general. Other claims are drawn from self-consciously non-patriarchal interpretations of religious text (e.g., Wadud, 1999).

In general, the interpretative freedom of conscience that individuals exercise might be understood as an individualistic element in Islamic normative practice. After the Prophetic period, "the absence of the only authoritative interpreter of the message, namely the Prophet himself, precludes any claim to a definitive understanding of the Koran on the part of the community" (Sachedina, 2001, 16). In contrast to the Roman Catholic Church, in which an organized hierarchy claims the exclusive right to offer final, authoritative guidance on what the correct religious teaching is, the Islamic (especially the Sunnī) tradition has remained open in principle to individual religious interpretation. In practice, there is a high bar to the interpretation in Islamic tradition, leaving religious legal interpretation largely in the hands of specialists—*ʿulamāʾ*—who have the requisite knowledge. One possible trend is the erosion of traditional qualifications and the increasing voice of non-*ʿulamāʾ* in making theological claims, amid such shifts as new technologies of dissemination and the rise of the *salafīyah*.

BIBLIOGRAPHY

Abou El Fadl, Khaled. "Islam and the Challenge of Democracy." *Boston Review* (April/May 2003). http://bostonreview.net/BR28.2/abou.html.

Ahmed, Imad ad Din. "An Islamic Perspective on the Wealth of Nations." Paper presented at the conference on the Comprehensive Development of Muslim Countries (August 1–3, 1994) in Subang Jaya, Malaysia. http://www.minaret.org/malaysia.htm.

Aral, Berdol. "The Idea of Human Rights as Perceived in the Ottoman Empire." *Human Rights Quarterly* 26 (2004): 454–482.

Asad, Talal. "Boundaries and Rights in Islamic Law: An Introduction." *Social Research* 70, no. 3 (Fall 2003): 683–686.

Brohi, A. K. "The Nature of Islamic Law and the Concept of Human Rights." In International Commission of Jurists, Kuwait University, and Union of Arab Lawyers, *Human Rights in Islam: Report of a Seminar Held in Kuwait, December 1980*, pp. 43, 48.

Kalin, Ibrahim. "Islam, Christianity, the Enlightenment: 'A Common Word' and Muslim-Christian Relations." In *Muslim and Christian Understanding: Theory and Application of "A Common Word,"* edited by Waleed El-Ansary and David K. Linnan. New York: Palgrave Macmillan, 2010.

Kukathas, Chandran. *The Liberal Archipelago: A Theory of Diversity and Freedom*. New York: Oxford University Press, 2003.

Kymlicka, Will. *Liberalism, Community, and Culture*. New York: Oxford University Press, 1991.

Mahmoud, Saba. "Is Liberalism Islam's Only Answer?" In *Islam and the Challenge of Democracy*, edited by Khaled Abou El Fadl. Princeton, N.J.: Princeton University Press, 2004.

Malik, Anas. "Challenging Dominance: Symbols, Institutions, and Vulnerabilities in Minarchist Political Islam." *The Muslim World* 98 (October 2008): 501–518.

Merica, Dan. "Pastor's Possible Execution Reveals Nuances of Islamic Law." 2011. http://religion.blogs.cnn.com/2011/10/07/pastors-possible-execution-reveals-nuances-of-islamic-law/?hpt=hp_t2.

Modirzadeh, Naz. "Taking Islamic Law Seriously: INGOs and the Battle for Muslim Hearts and Minds." *Harvard Human Rights Journal* 19 (Spring 2006). http://www.law.harvard.edu/students/orgs/hrj/iss19/modirzadeh.shtml.

Sachedina, Abdulaziz. *The Islamic Roots of Democratic Pluralism*. New York: Oxford University Press, 2001.

Shahin, Emad. "Islam and Politics: Toward a Humanistic Approach." Henry R. Luce Inaugural Lecture, March 25, 2010, University of Notre Dame.

Tibi, Bassam. "Islamic Law/Shariʿa, Human Rights, Universal Morality and International Relations." *Human Rights Quarterly* 16, no. 2 (May 1994): 277–299.

Wadud, Amina. *Qurʾan and Woman: Rereading the Sacred Text from a Woman's Perspective*. New York: Oxford University Press, 1999.

ANAS MALIK

INDONESIA. Approximately 85 to 90 percent of Indonesia's more than 245 million people are followers of Islam, the largest population of Muslims of any country in the world today. They are almost all Sunnīs and followers of the Shāfiʿī school. The remainder of the population are Christian, Hindu, animist, or adherents of various Confucian and Buddhist sects.

Historical Development. There is some dispute as to when Islam arrived in the East Indies. There were Arabs in the archipelago before the Hijrah, and Muslim merchants resided in East and Southeast Asia in the succeeding centuries. Islam became established in the local population of the East Indies in the thirteenth century and expanded markedly in the fifteenth and sixteenth centuries. By the eighteenth century, the vast majority of the populations of Java and Sumatra had become Muslim. Islam appears to have been transported by Muslims from several countries. The initial sources of Islamic missionary activity apparently were Gujarat and Malabar in western India, followed by Arabia, especially the Ḥaḍramawt, in the south of the peninsula. The people of the East Indies were generally converted to Islam through peaceful means. It was first transmitted through traders who brought with them religious scholars, and its spread was furthered by the conversion of the elite and by political alliances. From the beginning, state and popular Islam were imbued with a Hindu culture, reframed within the local traditions that had previously dominated the country. Rather than being obliterated by the new religion, Hindu and other non-Muslim elements became embedded in traditional rule, poetry, dance, and music, and influenced the way in which many converts, particularly on Java, approached Islamic thought and practice.

Early Islam was also greatly influenced by Ṣūfī views, and by the sixteenth century many of the archipelago's best-known Muslim scholars were from the Ṣūfī orders. In the years that followed, Ṣūfī orders such as the Qādirīyah and Naqshbandīyah attracted many Indonesians into their ranks, and branches were formed in many parts of the islands. Ṣūfī mysticism, with its tolerance of local traditions, further abetted the growth of Islam in the islands. It also helped to frame the syncretic and eclectic nature of Indonesian Islam through the centuries. By the eighteenth century, more orthodox Arab scholars from the Hadhramaut began to make their views on Islam felt, and external influences on Indonesian Islam began to shift from its former center on the Indian subcontinent to the Middle East. In spite of this, mysticism has remained an important characteristic of Indonesian Islam.

Until the nineteenth century, contact with the rest of the Muslim world was intermittent compared with the burgeoning interaction that was to follow. Muslim scholars from the Middle East and the Indian subcontinent continued to be the transmission channels for Islamic ideas, and a small but important group of Indonesians traveled to centers of Muslim learning in the Arab world. Arabs and Turks also acted as political and religious advisers in local sultanates, but the number of Indonesians making the arduous journey of the *ḥajj* remained small.

The nineteenth and early twentieth centuries saw a significant increase in Indonesia's involvement with the rest of the Islamic world. The number of pilgrims to Mecca grew to the point where they were termed the "rice of the Hejaz," reaching 123,052 in 1926–1927. There was also a significant rise in the number of Indonesian scholars going to the Middle East for religious studies. During the mid-1920s there were about two hundred Southeast Asian students (mostly Indonesian) studying in Cairo, and despite a decline in pilgrims during the Great Depression, there were reportedly more than two thousand residents of Saudi Arabia claiming East Indies citizenship during World War II. Some of these individuals, the Jawa—as Southeast Asians were called by Arabs—became well-respected scholars in Mecca. Those who returned from Middle Eastern training became the backbone of religious education in the East Indies, along with immigrants from Arab states who taught religion and Arabic in the *pesantren* (Islamic boarding schools) and *madrasah* (Islamic schools).

This was also a period in which new religious ideas, particularly modernism, made strong inroads into religious thinking in the East Indies. These reformers were particularly critical of the syncretic, "non-Islamic" elements of Islam as it had developed in the archipelago and sought to eliminate these "un-Islamic" accretions. They also argued in support of *ijtihād* (independent judgment) and rejected *taqlīd* (adherence to tradition). Initially spread among Arab residents in Jakarta, modernism found a strong base in West Sumatra. It was in Yogyakarta in East Java that the most important modernist organization, the Muhammadiyah, was founded in 1911. Its founder, Kiyai Hadji Ahmad Dahlan and other key members were trained in Cairo by followers of Muḥammad ʿAbduh. The Muhammadiyah became heavily involved in education and social change, although its focus varied according to area: in Sumatra it was more involved in purifying the faith, while on Java it was more inclined to confront Western challenges.

The postwar era was a time of great ferment in Indonesian Islamic circles. Independence, an increasingly educated population, funds for religious development from the Middle East, and the ability to communicate ideas more easily across the Islamic world brought Indonesia even more firmly into the intellectual and political core of Islam. The number of Indonesian students in the Middle East grew markedly from the hiatus of the Depression, World War II, and the struggle for independence. In 1987 there were 722 students in Cairo (585 of them in al-Azhar University), and 904 in Saudi Arabia. Religious students from these institutions tended to assume lower-level religious educational and technical posts upon their return to Indonesia. Of considerable importance in influencing Islamic thinking in postwar Indonesia were those who did graduate work in North American, British, and Commonwealth universities. Many of these individuals became the religious conduits of contemporary revivalist thinking into the archipelago. Arab teachers have also remained important, particularly in language and literature.

Religious thought in postwar Indonesia was characterized by a burgeoning indigenous literature on Islam and by the large-scale importation and translation of works by Islamic writers from abroad. More traditional Indonesian religious writers, such as Hamka, as well as those considered more current (e.g., Nurcholish Madjid and Abdurrahman Wahid), are now well-recognized interpreters of Islamic thought in the islands. There has also been an increase in the number of periodicals emphasizing Islamic issues, including *Panji Massyarakat*, *Dahwah*, *Kiblat*, and *Pesantren*. The most widely published foreign Muslim writers in Indonesian have been ʿAlī Sharīʿatī, Sayyid Quṭb, Abū al-Aʿlā Mawdūdī, al-Ghazālī,

Ḥasan al-Bannā, and Muhammad Iqbal. There has also been some penetration of Shīʿī ideas. Part of this has been the result of romanticism among youth regarding the Iranian Islamic Revolution, but there has also been an intellectual interest in the more speculative and abstract elements of Shīʿī thought. A number of Shīʿī books and tracts have been translated into Indonesian and published in the islands.

Character of Contemporary Indonesian Islam. While contemporary Indonesian Islam has been unified by its almost unanimous acceptance of its Sunnī roots, it has also been pluralistic in terms of belief and practice. At one level, Indonesian Muslims have been divided into those "nominal" Muslims who have been more deeply influenced by non-Muslim traditions and the more "orthodox" who follow a more universalistic pattern of belief and practice. The former, usually referred to as *abangan*, have been described as imbued with Hindu and animist elements reinforced by Sufism to create forms of rituals and mysticism peculiar to Indonesia and especially to Java. Within this culture, ritual feasts (*slametan*), spirit beliefs, traditional medical practices, and Hindu art and ceremonial forms intertwine with Muslim precepts. The latter group, termed *santri*, have perceived themselves as followers of a "purer" faith, adhering more rigidly to rituals such as prayer and fasting and less contaminated by animistic and mystical beliefs.

This dichotomy is weakened, however, both by the extent to which individuals in both groups oscillate in belief and practice, and by the development in the postwar era of a more universalistic Islam. As late as 1960, the Ministry of Religion argued that only a small minority of Muslims in Indonesia practiced their faith by prayer, *zakāt* (alms), and fasting. In some areas of Java, Hindu beliefs dominated the religious ways of nominal Muslims, and elements of belief in spirits infused the faith of individuals in all religions throughout Indonesia. Greater contact with the rest of the Muslim world, however, and the teaching of Islam to Indonesia's growing school population have provided a stronger foundation for a more universalistic interpretation of the religion. The teaching of religion in the schools is now compulsory, and though often superficial, it does project a less parochial interpretation of Islam. Recent decades have seen major growth in the number of people attending Friday prayer and adhering more closely to other rituals, such as observing Ramadan. There has also been a greater interest in the *ḥajj*, more wearing of Islamic dress by women, and concern over *ḥalāl* (ritually lawful) products. This closer observance of Islamic practice has been particularly noticeable among educated youth, but it is also to be found in the villages. Part of this change is the result of missionary activities (*dakwah*; Ar., *daʿwah*) by organizations seeking to "make Muslims better Muslims" or to "Islamize Muslims." The postwar era has seen a proliferation of Muslim organizations, tracts, magazines, study groups, and lectures seeking to bring Indonesians a better understanding of Islam.

It would be an oversimplification to divide Indonesian Islam sharply between modernists and traditionalists. There is general agreement that the principle of Sharīʿah is the foundation for all Muslims and that Islam should regulate personal and state actions. A core issue that has divided the adherents of these two views has been partially resolved by a gradual closing of the gap on the question of *ijtihād*. While there has not been any significant official change in interpretation of the problem by traditional organizations such as Nahdatul Ulama, individual leaders have displayed greater flexibility. Even with this growing consensus among Indonesian Muslims, however, there still exist significant variations in belief and practice throughout the archipelago, not only in terms of adherence to the core of universal Islamic patterns, but also in the manner in which local cultural influences frame perception and maintenance of the religion.

Islam and Politics. Islam played an important role in twentieth-century Indonesian politics. The first mass nationalist organization was Sarekat Islam, formed in 1912 and the dominant political organization of the colony for more than a decade. Given the great ethnic and linguistic diversity across the archipelago, Islam provided the one common thread for the vast majority of the population. It differentiated the Indonesians from their Christian masters and gave them a sense of identity with a universal cause. This seeking to be part of the wider community (*ummah*) was reflected in the large number of Indonesians making the *ḥajj* and the interest of many Indonesian nationalists in such international Islamic issues as the Caliphate and the Pan-Islamic movement. Sarekat Islam also had an economic agenda that reinforced its religious platform. From the beginning it criticized Chinese and Dutch economic power in the islands. For its part, the Dutch colonial administration tended to see Islam as a danger to domestic peace and order and expressed suspicion of returning pilgrims and students who had studied in foreign Muslim educational institutions. It was especially disturbed by what administrators saw as loyalties to authority outside the colony.

In the decades preceding World War II and during the Japanese occupation, Islam's role in domestic politics was weakened, first by the challenge of more secular nationalism and Dutch repression and later by Japanese suspicions of Muslim political loyalty to Japan's goals. In the first instance, Sarekat Islam began to break up in the 1920s because of poor internal administration and competition from radical (especially communist) elements; it was ultimately overshadowed by more secular nationalist parties. Through these years Islamic political power was further fractured by religious differences among Muslims who formed competing organizations. In 1926 Nahdatul Ulama was founded as a traditionalist counter to the reformist aspects of Sarekat Islam and to what its founders saw as an undermining of the power of the *'ulamā* (those who have had special training in Islamic religion and law). This vacuum gave rise to an increased role for nonpolitical groups like the modernist-oriented Muhammadiyah organization.

When Japan occupied the East Indies during World War II, it assumed a somewhat ambivalent position regarding Islam. It sought to foster public support by championing Islam against the Christian Dutch, but once in control, Japan attempted to direct Indonesian loyalties away from the Middle East and toward an East Asian community. The concept of the unity of Muslims did not fit the Japanese effort to emphasize the Greater East Asian Co-Prosperity Sphere. Leadership of the wartime nationalist movement tended to fall to secular forces, and Islam did not enter the independence years as a united political force.

Two major political parties sought to dominate the Muslim majority in the new republic; both groups reflected the historic division among Muslims. Nahdatul Ulama supported more traditional nonmodernist views, and Masjumi was formed as a modernist Islamic socialist party. They vied to lead Indonesians who were interested in a government based on Muslim values and expressed strong opposition to secular and particularly communist influences. Although it was believed that the majority of Indonesians supported the Muslim cause, in the country's first election in 1955, the Masjumi (a modernist Islamic socialist party) and Nahdatul Ulama each received approximately 20 percent of the national vote, and other Muslim parties obtained only a small percentage; the remainder went to primarily secular parties. The combined vote for all

Muslim parties was 43.5 percent. The Masjumi became increasingly frustrated with its inability to influence the growing secularism of Indonesian politics, and in 1960 the party was outlawed for supporting dissidents who were fighting the central government. This left the more traditional Nahdatul Ulama and small splinter parties to act as the legal voices of Islam at the national level.

During this period, Muslim political leaders were particularly concerned with establishing Islam firmly within the Indonesian constitutional framework. An original agreement among nationalist factions in 1945 would have obliged Muslims to practice Sharīʿah law and would have required that the head of state be a Muslim, but a compromise altered the charter to reflect a more secular and pluralist view of the role of religion in the state. A new national ideology, the Pancasila (Sanskrit, "five principles"), proclaimed as one of its tenets "belief in God" but did not define this in Muslim terms, allowing Indonesians freely to choose their own religion. President Sukarno originally explained the concept as pluralist in nature:

> The principle of Belief in God! Not only should the Indonesian people believe in God, but every Indonesian should believe in his own God. The Christian should worship God according to the teachings of Jesus Christ, Moslems according to the teachings of the Prophet Mohammad, Buddhists should perform their religious ceremonies in accordance with the books they have. But let us all believe in God. The Indonesian State shall be a state where every person can worship his god as he likes. The whole of the people should worship God in a cultured way, that is, without religious egoism.

The 1945 constitution and provisional constitutions in 1949 and 1950 did not change this interpretation, and when President Sukarno reestablished the 1945 constitution in 1959 he gave strong support to the pluralist definition of the Pancasila. This issue of the place of Islam within the national ideology remained a core source of Muslim dissatisfaction in the postwar era.

The third thread of Islam in the early years was the activities of radical Muslim military units such as Dar ul Islam, a Muslim militant group formed in West Java in 1948. In part, Dar ul Islam rationalized its war against the Indonesian Republic on the grounds that secularist forces had rejected Islam as the basis of the state. Through much of the 1950s, the Dar ul Islam forces caused considerable destruction in West Java, and the government appeared incapable of controlling its activities as Dar ul Islam spread its influence into East Indonesia. During this period other Muslim groups in Sumatra and Sulawesi also prepared to employ force to defend Islam against what they saw as a secular regime in Jakarta. Negotiations largely brought an end to this period of conflict in 1959, but the leader of Dar ul Islam was not captured and executed until 1962, and the Sulawesi rebellion did not collapse until 1965. The influence of Dar ul Islam could be seen within some radical Islamic groups in the early twenty-first century.

Following an attempted coup in 1965, in which the Indonesian Communist Party was involved, some Muslim youth groups, along with the military, killed large numbers of communists, perhaps 300,000 or more. Communists were considered enemies of Islam because of their perceived atheistic views and, to a lesser degree, because many landowners were members of religiously powerful families. These events led to the fall of the Sukarno regime; the military-dominated government of General, later President, Suharto held power in Indonesia until he was forced to resign in 1998. It was initially hoped that the military would work closely with Muslim political organizations, and there was even a strong faction in the armed forces that sought to make Islam the unifying spiritual cement within the military. In the ensuing years, however, important cleavages developed between elements of the Muslim community and the Suharto regime. While the factors responsible for these differences were complex, they centered on three core issues: government efforts to establish secular bases for centrally important areas of interest to Muslims, such as education and marriage; attempts to emasculate Muslim political power; and the reimplementation of the Pancasila as the national ideology.

In the first instance, elements of the Muslim community were antagonized by such government efforts as the formulation of regulations that divorced the school calendar from Ramadan and discouraged Islamic dress for girls in public schools. The most incendiary issue was the marriage bill of 1973, by which the Suharto regime attempted to give precedence to civil authority in cases of marriage and divorce. This policy was promulgated without consultation with Muslim leaders or organizations. Muslims were particularly affronted by requirements in the bill for civil permission for marriage, divorce, and polygamous marriage, and by the provision that religious differences were not to be an obstacle to marriage. This bill was considered by many Muslims to be a direct attack on Muslim law and religious authority, and the depth of opposition led the government to withdraw the bill. Islamic codes remain the foundation for family law in the country.

The second point of contention was Suharto's efforts to limit the political power of Islam. After the 1965 coup, the outlawed Masjumi party was not allowed to reform its structure, and in 1973 all Muslim parties were forced to unite in a single organization, the United Development Party (Partai Persatuan Pembangunan, or PPP). In the 1970s the Muslim parties became the preeminent legal opposition to the government's party, Golkar. The majority of Golkar's membership reflected *abangan* religious views, but there were elements in the party that were critical of specific government policies, such as the opening of schools during Ramadan. Although both the PPP and Golkar employed Islam as campaign tools—for example by having candidates participate publicly in Muslim rituals—further attempts were made in the ensuing years to emasculate the political power of Islam. Faced with the effective containment policies of the government, Muslim organizations were unable to launch successful political challenges to the central authorities in the 1970s and 1980s. The Jakarta government sought to ensure that religion did not become the source of political ideology in contemporary Indonesia, a policy similar to that of the Dutch colonial regime.

During the later 1970s and the 1980s, small radical elements in the Muslim community turned to violence to express their opposition to what they perceived to be an un-Islamic government; they demanded the formation of an Islamic state and the elimination of "yellow culture." One organization, Kommando Jihad, was accused of conspiring to overthrow the government; another, the Islamic Youth Movement, allegedly attacked shopping centers in the name of Islam; and the Indonesian Islamic Revolution Board was charged with seeking Iranian support to eliminate Suharto's regime. There were isolated acts of airplane hijacking, arson, and store bombings, and the placing of bombs on the Borobudur, the famous Buddhist monument in Java. There were largely unproven charges that seditious organizations were being aided by certain Middle Eastern governments, particularly Iran and Libya. Islamic religious spokesmen also released cassette recordings criticizing what they perceived as the corrupt and anti-Islamic activities of the Suharto administration. The government forcefully repressed these activities and used the incidents as further proof of the need to remove religion from politics.

This move to de-emphasize Islam in politics reached its zenith with the demand by the Suharto government that all mass organizations affirm that the Pancasila was their only ideology. The government had previously emphasized the need proclaimed by Sukarno for all Indonesians to believe in God: to do otherwise would arouse suspicion of communist tendencies. Initially, Muslim groups were strongly opposed to the state policy on ideology on the grounds that the principle of "Belief in God" proclaimed in the Pancasila was at best agnosticism. They believed that the acceptance of that ideology as their sole foundation refuted their own religious bases and feared that it would become the official national religion. After strong criticism from the Muhammadiyah, President Sukarno personally guaranteed that it would not become a religion. Under the Suharto regime, those expressing public opposition to the Pancasila, as well as some Muslim religious leaders who attacked the government in the name of Islam, found themselves faced with long prison sentences. However, Nahdatul Ulama and other organs of the PPP ultimately capitulated and accepted the Pancasila as their only ideology. Toward the end of his regime, Suharto sought to co-opt the Islamic agenda, publicly proclaiming himself a devout Muslim and sponsoring the ICMI (Ikatan Cendekiawan Muslim Indonesia, or Association of Muslim Intellectuals), which some criticized as a tool of the state.

The return to democracy in Indonesia at the end of the twentieth century meant both change and continuity. Islamic parties did not gain a majority in parliament (the Dewan Perwakilan Rayat, or People's Representative Council) in the 1999, 2004, and 2009 national elections. Legislation sponsored by Islamic parties, however, often received support from more secular parties that recognized the religious attitudes of their constituents. In this period several high officials were drawn from Islamic organizations, including a president, vice president, leader of the lower house of parliament, and justice minister.

Outside the institutions of the state, Islamic interests played significant roles in the new democracy. The two largest organizations in the Republic were Islamic: the Muhammadiyah, claiming 30 million members, and Nahadatul Ulama claiming 40 million. Members of both have held major government posts. Militant radical Islamic groups, however, have received the greatest international attention.

Anti-Christian rhetoric and actions have a long history in the archipelago and grew during the last years of the Suharto regime. An anti-Christian and anti-Western bias is prevalent in these radical Islamic groups, and the influence of conservative Salafī tenets has been common in several organizations. These beliefs, heavily influenced from Saudi Arabia, have tended to be politically anti-pluralist and religiously intolerant. Leaders of nonmilitant Muslim organizations such the Muhammadiyah have also been suspicious of Christians. In the post-Suharto years the largest Islamic militant group was the now defunct Laskar Jihad, which was charged with the death of thousands of Christians, particularly in East Indonesia. The Laskar Jihad leadership articulated Salafī beliefs and had close ties with elements of the Indonesian military. Other radical Islamic groups included the Islamic Defenders Front, a violent wing of the Majelis Mujahidin Indonesia, the Hizbullah Front, Laskar Jundullah and, most noteworthy, the multinational Jemaah Islamiyah (JI). The JI was held responsible for bombings throughout the islands and reportedly is tied to al-Qaʿida. None has been successful at the parliamentary level, and all have suffered from government pressure causing fragmentation and weakening of their organizations.

Islam and Foreign Policy. Islam was not a major factor in Indonesian foreign policy in the Sukarno and Suharto eras, but it did play a positive role during Indonesia's postwar effort to seek allies in its fight for independence from the Dutch. At that time it made major efforts to gain the support of Arab leaders, and the Arab League recommended that all its members recognize the new republic. It was in this period that Indonesia initiated diplomatic relations with Arab states.

In the succeeding years the Indonesian government tended to downplay Islam as a primary basis for foreign policy decisions, reflecting partly the more secular viewpoint of the country's leadership and partly the government's wish not to reinforce religious loyalties at home. Thus, although Indonesia criticized Israel's actions against the Palestinians and its Arab neighbors and the Soviet invasion of Afghanistan, it did so more in the name of Third World solidarity than in that of Islam. Jakarta was also cautious about becoming involved in disputes among other Muslim countries, calling for peaceful solutions but not actively engaging in efforts to end these conflicts.

Although President Sukarno did support the Africa-Asia Islamic Conference in 1964—in part to gain support for his confrontation with Malaysia—Indonesia did not formally participate in the Rabat and Jiddah meetings that formed the Organization of the Islamic Conference (OIC). Although a member of the OIC since its inception in 1969, it did not attend the meeting that promulgated the OIC charter in 1972 and initially did not sign the charter. It was argued that by joining the organization Indonesia would have to accept the OIC's Islamic principles and declare itself an Islamic state. Since that time, Indonesia has worked more closely with the OIC and has become involved in a number of economically oriented Islamic international organizations. Indonesians in their private capacities have also been very active in many nongovernmental Islamic groups, such as the World Islamic League and the World Assembly of Muslim Youth.

In the new democratic era, Islam has played an even greater role in Indonesian foreign policy, and the government has become more involved in Islamic world issues. Public rhetoric in the twenty-first century reflects a more Islamic tenor than that of earlier periods. Several political leaders and government spokespeople have expressed opposition to U.S. policies in the Middle East and to Israeli actions in Palestine and Lebanon. Polls consistently show public support for these positions. While the government has cooperated with the United States in the "war on terror," polls show that the majority of respondents view it instead as a war on Islam.

Islam and the Courts. During most of the period of Dutch rule from the end of the nineteenth century, the colonial government held the view that *ʿādāt* (native customary law) was the legal framework within which the indigenous population was to be ruled, and that Islamic law was only to be enforced to the degree that it was accepted by *ʿādāt*. From 1882 to 1937, the so-called Priestraad (Religious Court, later called Penghulu Court) on Java and Madura had general jurisdiction over marriage, divorce, alms, and inheritance. In 1937, inheritance was officially taken from the religious courts, although they continued to rule on such issues.

During the Japanese occupation, a Department of Religion (Syumubu) was established, and in 1946 the new Indonesian Republic formed a Ministry of Religion to govern all the nation's faiths. This ministry was not always considered a friend of Islam by Muslim leaders and organizations, particularly after 1971 when it came under the control of less traditional ministers. While the ministry has directorates for other faiths, its main focus is on Islam. It supervises religious education in both Muslim and state schools, the organization of the pilgrimage, Muslim foundations, Islamic marriage laws, and religious courts, and it supports Muslim places of worship.

After independence, the government initially maintained the former Dutch system of courts, but in 1957, Penadilan Agama (Courts of Religious Justice) were formed for most districts. The courts of first instance and of appeals cover marriage, divorce, child support, charity, and religious foundations. Inheritance is not included, and in certain regions ʿ*ādāt* law takes precedence. It is the general view of Muslim legal scholars that the "reception theory"—that Sharīʿah laws apply only if they have become part of ʿ*ādāt* law—is no longer valid and that Islamic law has equal standing with ʿ*ādāt* and Western law. For the most part, however, the religious courts in Indonesia have a quite restricted role.

Aceh, the home of decades of rebellion, was given the right to implement partial Sharīʿah law in the province in 2002 as part of peace agreements. Aslo, numerous regencies (subprovincial governments) and municipalities have established local regulations based upon the Sharīʿah.

Many Indonesian Muslims would like to see a greater infusion of Islamic principles into the juridical system, but there is no agreement on how Sharīʿah should be implemented. Groups and individuals disagree as to whether to accept only the Shāfiʿī school of law, as well as on the role of *ijtihād*, the rights of non-Muslims, the place of ʿ*ādāt*, and the meaning of the term "Islamic state."

[*See also* Darul Islam Movement; Daʿwah; Islam and Politics in Southeast Asia; Masyumi Party; Muhammadiyah; Nahdatul Ulama; Partai Persatuan Pembangunan; *and* Sarekat Islam.]

Bibliography

Alfian. *Muhammadiyah: The Political Behavior of a Muslim Modernist Organization under Dutch Colonialism.* Yogyakarta: Gadjah Mada University Press, 1989.

Barton, Greg. *Indonesia's Struggle: Jemaah Islamiyah and the Soul of Islam.* Singapore: University of Singapore Press, 2004.

Boland, B. J. *The Struggle of Islam in Modern Indonesia.* Translated by C. A. Franken. The Hague: Martinus Nijhoff, 1971.

Geertz, Clifford. *The Religion of Java.* Glencoe, Ill.: Free Press, 1960.

Hefner, Robert W. *Civil Islam: Muslims and Democratization in Indonesia.* Princeton, N.J.: Princeton University Press, 2000.

Hefner, Robert W. *The Politics of Multiculturalism: Pluralism and Citizenship in Malaysia, Singapore, and Indonesia.* Honolulu: University of Hawaii Press, 2001.

Hilmy, Masdar. *Islam and Democracy in Indonesia: Piety and Pragmatism.* Singapore: Institute of Southeast Asia Studies, 2010.

Hooker, M. B., ed. *Islam in South-East Asia.* Leiden: E. J. Brill, 1988.

Kipp, Rita Smith, and Susan Rodgers, eds. *Indonesian Religion in Transition.* Tucson: University of Arizona Press, 1987.

Noer, Deliar. *The Modernist Muslim Movement in Indonesia, 1900–1942.* Singapore and London: Oxford University Press, 1973.

Ramage, Douglas E. *Politics in Indonesia: Democracy, Islam and the Ideology of Tolerance.* London: Routledge, 1995.

Pringle, Robert. *Islam in Indonesia: Politics and Diversity.* Honolulu: University of Hawaii Press, 2010.

von der Mehden, Fred R. *Religion and Nationalism in Southeast Asia: Burma, Indonesia, the Philippines.* Madison: University of Wisconsin Press, 1963.

Woodward, Mark R. *Islam in Java.* Tucson: University of Arizona Press, 1989.

Fred R. von der Mehden

Indonesian Mujahidin Council. The Indonesian Mujahidin Council (Majelis Mujahidin Indonesia, MMI) is one of the leading hardline Islamist organizations in a post–New Order Indonesia. It was established in Yogyakarta in 2000 as a pro-Sharīʿah (Islamic law) advocacy organization, with the stated goal of creating an Islamic state in the country. Indonesia's best-known radical cleric, Abu Bakar Bashir, was the supreme leader (*amīr*) of the organization until he and his close allies split from the MMI to form another jihadist organization, *Jamāʿah Ansharut Tauhid* (JAT) in 2008.

The prime goal of the MMI is the implementation of Sharīʿah, including the creation of a state based on their narrow, dogmatic interpretation of Islamic laws. The MMI formally supports the implementation of *ḥudūd* and *qiṣāṣ*, draconian Islamic punishments. It is an aboveground organization primarily focused on *daʿwah* (missionary) education as well as sermons and lectures by Bashir.

Many suspect its linkage with the Jemaah Islamiyah (JI), a notorious militant jihadist network which is responsible for many terrorist attacks and clandestine activities across the archipelago, including the deadly attacks in Bali. A number of famous terrorists were members of both organizations, most prominently Bashir, the spiritual leader of JI. Other prominent examples include: the MMI's board members Abu Jibril and Agus Dwikarna who headed JI's two paramilitary arms and were both members of the JI *syuro* (executive council); Fikri Sugundo, an MMI *amīr* beneath Bashir, who was the JI secretary and a principal of an elementary school of Al-Mukmin, an Islamist boarding school (*pesantren*) run by Bashir.

Despite its alleged association with JI and other illegal activities, the MMI itself does not officially promote or use violence as its primary strategy to achieve its ideological and political goals. Leaders of the organization typically run and use their *pesantrens* to propagate Islamist ideology and doctrines and to recruit young men into the MMI. In its heyday the MMI had branches in nearly thirty cities throughout Indonesia, although its official membership is unknown. Its major asset and source of popularity was without doubt its charismatic leader, Bashir, and his celebrity status within the jihadist community in Southeast Asia.

A rift emerged between Bashir and fellow members of the MMI after his release from prison in 2006, which ultimately led to the declining prominence of the MMI. Bashir was allegedly discontented with the nature of the leadership structure, arguing that the MMI gave its leader only a symbolic role and that the real authority lay in a body called the Ahl al-Ḥall wa-al-ʿAqd (AHWA), where decisions were made collectively. For him, such structure was un-Islamic because an Islamic organization should be led by an *amīr* with full authority, although the *amīr* could consult with others in an executive council (*majelis syuro*). He criticized MMI leaders and members for using a secular structure to undermine his authority as the supreme leader, while his opponents accused him of behaving like an autocrat.

The deepest cause of the internal rift seems to have been Bashir's lack of accountability, both politically and financially. One of the MMI leaders, for example, accused Bashir of claiming leadership for life and infallibility without any need to answer to the broader community. Some were also increasingly frustrated by the influence of Bashir's family, especially his son Abdul Rohim in decision-making and management of the organization. On the other hand Bashir's family believed that the MMI was exploiting Bashir's popularity for its own purposes.

Moreover Bashir and his loyalists disagreed with other leaders over the organization's strategy, whether the MMI should adopt a strategy that some hardliners consider "un-Islamic," such as lobbying the government on issues such as an anti-pornography law. The hardcore jihadists believed that the MMI should avoid all contact with a secular government and not even try to influence it, because a secular government was *thaghut* (anti-Islamic). In contrast, other members accused the hardliners in the organization, such as Halawi Makmum, head of MMI's Islamic law department, of being too radical because they were too quick to declare Muslims who did not apply Islamic law as apostates.

After Bashir resigned as the MMI's leader to form JAT in July 2008, some MMI branches went over to JAT wholesale, as in Samarinda, in East Kalimantan, which led to the collapse of the MMI there. Much of West Java, traditionally an Islamist stronghold, also went over to JAT. As a result, MMI has lost much of the prominence and efficacy it once enjoyed within the jihadist community in the country.

BIBLIOGRAPHY

Abuza, Zachary. *Militant Islam in Southeast Asia: A Crucible of Terror*. Boulder, Colo.: Lynne Rienner Publishers, 2003.

International Crisis Group. "How Indonesian Extremists Regroup." *Asia Report* no. 228, 16 July 2012. http://www.crisisgroup.org/en/regions/asia/south-east-asia/indonesia/228-how-indonesian-extremists-regroup.aspx.

International Crisis Group. "Indonesia: The Dark Side of Jama'ah Ansharut Tauhid (JAT)." *Asia Briefing* no. 107, 6 July 2010. http://www.crisisgroup.org/en/regions/asia/south-east-asia/indonesia/B107-indonesia-the-dark-side-of-jamaah-ansharut-tauhid-jat.aspx.

KIKUE HAMAYOTSU

INTERNATIONAL INSTITUTE OF ISLAMIC THOUGHT. Founded in 1981 by Ismā'īl Rājī al-Fārūqī, a Palestinian-American professor of Islam and comparative religion, the institute focuses on issues of Islamic thought. Al-Fārūqī's research emphasis and interests varied over the years, beginning with his position as a Pan-Arab Muslim and changing over the years to a focus on Pan-Islamism, a development that led to his creation of the International Institute of Islamic Thought (IIIT). Al-Fārūqī and his wife were murdered in their home in 1986, ending his short tenure as the head of IIIT.

Dr. Taha Jabir al-Alwani assumed the leadership of IIIT after the death of his friend. Like al-Fārūqī, he was a product of Al-Azhar University, but he was preoccupied with epistemology and how that influences research and its agenda. Al-Alwani was more focused on Pan-Islamism and how the Muslim minority in North America might adjust and be beneficial to U.S. and Canadian society. Al-Alwani saw North America as a place for Islamic rebirth and progress. He created the Islamic Jurisprudential Council (the Fiqh Council of North America) in 1986, and he founded Cordoba University in 1993, signifying his belief that North America is where Islam will advance in lieu of Muslim Spain, in an era that is marked by scientific, medical, and theoretical advances in Muslim history.

Since its founding, IIIT's mission has focused on revitalizing and reclaiming Islamic thought. IIIT has acted as a beacon of knowledge that was and still is involved in recovering and reforming Islam in light of contemporary changes in society. The pursuit of dynamism in Islamic thought is an affirmation of the institute's stress on cultural and civilizational identity.

IIIT also hosts academic conferences that confirm its commitment to creating a bridge for Western and Islamic cultural and educational exchange. Among IIIT's achievements is its progressive approach to modernity in the fields of sciences as well as the social sciences, that is, its engagement in the public discourse on issues that deal with contemporary developments in all fields. The institute is also very active in teaching and training people from different professions about Islam, publishing books, and supporting scholars who study the subject matter.

IIIT therefore may be described as an Islamic think tank that strives to educate and foster the growth of an understanding of Islam and Muslims.

The institute's impact is felt in educating others about Islam in the United States and various areas of the Muslim world. Its role is not limited to affecting and reforming the faith and its followers in North America; it plays an international role through its conferences and publications.

IIIT became a supporter of moderate Muslims to confer and publish. It was a magnet to international and North American Muslim scholars who were interested in Islam as a faith and culture. Contributors to IIIT have ranged from Rāshid al-Ghannūshī (leader of Tunisia's Islamic party, Renaissance) and Yūsuf al-Qaraḍāwī (ideologue of the Egyptian Muslim Brotherhood) to Emad Shahin and Suhail Hashimi (both editors of this work).

The academic activities in which IIIT engaged were markedly changed following the events of 11 September 2001, in the United States. After 9/11, Muslim organizations in the United States were viewed with suspicion and were placed under tight scrutiny. Dr. al-Alwani left his position at IIIT, and the institute was left to struggle after losing both its academic momentum and its financial resources in the face of legal allegations of involvement with "terrorism." As a result, IIIT is slowly recovering, like other Islamic organizations, and is struggling to restore its academic and scholarly vigor.

BIBLIOGRAPHY

"Center for the Study of Islam and Democracy." https://www.csidonline.org/about-csid/board-of-directors/past-directors/24.

"History Commons." March 20, 2002. www.history-commons.org.

"Islamic Epistemology." http://i-epistemology.net/tahar-jabir-al-alwani.html.

"International Institute of Islamic Thought." www.iiit.org.

"Ismail Faruqi." www.ismailfaruqi.com/.

McCarthy, Andrew. "International Institute of Islamic Thought and the Muslim Brotherhood." *National Review*, July 24, 2010. www.nationalreview.com.

Deina Abdelkader

International Islamic Organizations. Transnational pan-Muslim organizations and institutions, including the Rābiṭat al-ʿĀlam al-Islāmī (World Muslim League), the Organization of Islamic Cooperation (OIC, formerly known as the Organization of the Islamic Conference), and Islamic Relief Worldwide, seek to bring together representatives from different Muslim majority states and significant Muslim minority communities. Many of these organizations engage in political and social activism as well as humanitarian aid work, seeking to represent Muslim communities and Islamic causes on the world stage.

Rābiṭat al- ʿĀlam al-Islāmī (Muslim World League). The Muslim World League, which is one of the largest operating international Islamic organizations, was founded on 18 May 1962, during a meeting of Muslim religious leaders from over twenty countries in the city of Mecca, Saudi Arabia. The organization's charter defines its mission as providing education on the religion of Islam and its principles and tenets, while also defending it from "false allegations." According to the charter, the organization sees its activism as part of its members' "obligation towards God," the most important of which is proclaiming Islam worldwide as well as unifying all of the world's Muslims. At its core, the Muslim World League was founded as a missionary education (*daʿwah*) organization seeking to educate Muslims about the "correct" interpretation and practice of Islam. It holds observer status in the United Nations General Assembly as well as the Organization of Islamic Cooperation, and it is a member of the United Nations Children's Fund (UNICEF) and the Islamic Educational, Scientific and Cultural Organization (ISESCO).

The Muslim World League was founded in the midst of a bitter political conflict between the Saudi monarchy, which represented the more conservative Arab Gulf states and the Zaydī imamate in North Yemen, and the wave of pan-Arab nationalism ushered in by the charismatic president of Egypt, Gamal Abdel Nasser. The organization received significant financial and political backing from Fayṣal ibn ʿAbd al-ʿAzīz Āl Saʿūd, who reigned as the Saudi king from 1964 until his assassination in 1975 by a disgruntled relative, and served in part as a tool to combat secular pan-Arabism. The political competition between the Saudis and Nasser, which lasted roughly between 1958 and 1970, included a proxy military conflict in North Yemen, with the Saudis backing that country's Zaydī monarchy and the Egyptians backing rebels seeking to replace the monarchy with a republican government. This political conflict was famously dubbed the "Arab Cold War" by Malcolm Kerr, a scholar of Middle East politics and president of the American University of Beirut, who was murdered by unknown gunmen in 1984.

The founding principle of the Muslim World League is abiding by Islamic law (Sharīʿah). Its chief goals include coordinating Islamic political and social activism across nation-state borders, further *daʿwah* and other educational programs with the goal of deepening Muslims' understanding of their religion through seminars, conferences, and classes, as well as spreading Islam globally; bringing together Muslim religious scholars (*ʿulamāʾ*), jurists (*fuqahāʾ*), and other leaders and intellectuals, particularly during the annual *ḥajj* pilgrimage to Mecca; establishing offices designed to further its activism; supporting the maintenance and upkeep of mosques; and promoting the Arabic language.

The organization is led by an executive wing, the General Secretariat, which is based in Mecca and tasked with supervising day-to-day activities and implementing the resolutions and policies adopted by its governing Constituent Council. The Muslim World League's current secretary-general is ʿAbd Allah ibn ʿAbd al-Muḥsin al-Turkī. The organization hosts regular meetings, termed "general Islamic conferences," during which its members meet to discuss issues deemed pressing to Muslim communities and countries around the world. Resolutions and other measures are discussed and adopted at these meetings. Its members take the opportunity provided by these meetings to adopt resolutions on prominent ongoing political issues such as Palestinian statehood.

The Constituent Council serves as the organization's governing body and is composed, usually, of around sixty Muslim scholars representing both majority Muslim countries and significant Muslim minority communities. New members are selected by sitting members. A requirement for membership is active participation in *daʿwah*. The council must approve resolutions proposed by either the General Secretariat or three members of the council itself. Members are unsalaried.

One of the Muslim World League's most important offices is the World Supreme Council for Mosques (WSCM), whose declared mission is to promote the centrality of the mosque to Muslims' social and religious lives. Founded in 1975, its mission is based on the belief of the centrality of the mosque as a communal center during the lifetime of the Prophet Muḥammad and his successors in the first decades of Islam. The WSCM is also dedicated to protecting the sanctity of Islamic trusts (*awqāf*) and the rights of minority Muslim communities in non-Muslim majority states. It is made up of forty unsalaried volunteer members selected from both Muslim majority countries and Muslim minority communities.

The WSCM develops plans to revive the role of the mosque in Muslim communities as an educational, religious, and social services center. In order to promote its work, it publishes a magazine, *Message of the Mosque*, as well as numerous books and pamphlets. The council also sponsors *da'wah* trips by Muslim religious scholars and preachers to mosques around the world and organizes courses designed to enhance the skills and efficiency of prayer leaders and preachers.

The Muslim World League maintains country and regional offices around the world. They distribute free literature, often in pamphlet form, via the Internet and in paper copies designed to counter negative impressions of Islam and Muslims. Topics covered include Islam and terrorism, the Qur'ān and its interpretations, the life and traditions of the Prophet Muḥammad, defending minority Muslim communities, manuals on how to perform the obligatory daily prayers (*ṣalāt*), the nature of God and His absolute unity (*tawḥīd*), and ritual practices such as funerals, relations with family, and marriage. These offices also sponsor their own activities, such as seminars and competitions, including Qur'ān recitation and memorization. Muslim youth are a focal point of the organization's educational programs, which seek to train them to be the next generation of Muslim leaders as well as to ward off "extremism."

Organization of Islamic Cooperation. The Organization of Islamic Cooperation (OIC), formerly the Organization of the Islamic Conference, is the second-largest intergovernmental organization after the United Nations. Founded in 1969 after an international meeting in Rabat, Morocco, the OIC is composed of fifty-seven member states, up from the original twenty-five founding member states. In addition to Muslim-majority countries, a number of other states with significant Muslim populations and Islamic and international organizations hold observer status in the OIC. These include Bosnia and Herzegovina, Russia, Turkish Cyprus, Thailand, the Central African Republic, United Nations, the Non-Aligned Movement, the Arab League, the African Union, the Economic Cooperation Organization, and the Moro National Liberation Front in the Philippines. The OIC's inaugural meeting was held in 1970 in the Saudi coastal city of Jiddah, which is also the host city for the organization's general secretariat. The current secretary-general is Ekmeleddin İhsanoğlu, a Turkish academic and former diplomat, who assumed office in January 2005, after he was elected by the organization's Council of Foreign Ministers. In April 2011, the United Nations General Assembly adopted a resolution welcoming cooperation with the OIC.

The OIC revised its founding charter in March 2008 at its eleventh Islamic Summit, which was held in Dakar, Senegal. The organization's mission is to represent the international Muslim community (*ummah*) and increase its voice by bringing together the world's Muslim-majority states and minority Muslim communities on the world stage. The OIC also seeks to assist member states in resolving armed conflict and other disputes, in accord with the charter's goal to "enhance and consolidate the bonds of fraternity and solidarity among the Member States." The political, economic, and social cooperation of member states is a top priority for the organization, which seeks to establish an international "Islamic common market" and to support efforts to achieve sustainable and comprehensive human development through economics, science, and technology. The charter also encourages inter-civilizational and inter-religious dialogue between Muslims and non-Muslims as well as between Islam's different sub-groups.

Member states are required to make a commitment to the United Nations Charter as well as to settling their disputes through peaceful means rather than the use of threat of force. Each member state must also respect the national sovereignty and territorial integrity of the others and refrain from interfering in their internal affairs. They must dedicate themselves to the principles of good governance, human rights, and the rule of law.

The OIC is divided into three main bodies, the Islamic Summit, the Council of Foreign Ministers, and the General Secretariat. The Islamic Summit consists of the heads of state of member states, who collectively serve as the organization's highest authority. They meet once every three years in order to discuss pressing issues and vote on policy decisions of concern to both member states and the *ummah*. The Council of Foreign Ministers is composed of the foreign ministers of each member state and meets once annually in order to discuss and adopt resolutions for the organization to implement and review the implementation of previously adopted decisions and resolutions. The General Secretariat is the executive organ of the OIC and is tasked with the implementation of resolutions and decisions made by the Islamic Summit and the Council of Foreign Ministers. Since its founding, there have been eleven Islamic Summit conferences and thirty-eight meetings of the Council of Foreign Ministers.

The organization includes a number of committees, nearly all of which are at the ministerial level, though some are chaired by heads of member states, which are dedicated to particular issues. These include the Al-Quds Committee, which is dedicated to protecting the sanctity of the contested city of Jerusalem, the Standing Committee for Information and Cultural Affairs, the Standing Committee for Economic and Trade Cooperation, and the Standing Committee for Scientific and Technological Cooperation. These committees work toward implementing the OIC's goals of improving economic, scientific, cultural, legal, technological, and educational well-being.

In December 2005, at the Third Extraordinary Conference in Mecca, Saudi Arabia the member states of the OIC adopted the Ten-Year Program of Action. The conference was convened by Saudi Arabia's king, ʿAbd Allāh ibn ʿAbd al-ʿAzīz Āl Saʿūd, who offered to serve as host. The program seeks to coordinate the actions of member states to promote solidarity of member states, tolerance and moderation among Muslims, combat Islamophobia, and implement substantial reforms in all fields with the goal of promoting advances in science and technology, the economies of member states, education, good governance and human rights, family values, and enhancing free trade. The attendees also rejected the usefulness of unilateral sanctions, continued to support the rights of minority Muslim communities as well as the Palestinians, and dedicated themselves to combating the spread of extremism among Muslims. The conference also agreed that a renewed focus was needed on Africa in order to address the continent's severe problems of poverty, disease, illiteracy, famine, and debt.

As part of its promotion of cooperation and solidarity among member states, the OIC's Ten-Year Program addressed the need for Muslims to understand and accept the "multiplicity of Islamic jurisprudence." This requires the strengthening of dialogue among Islam's different jurisprudential schools, recognition of the Muslim identity of their adherents and the rejection of "excommunication" (*takfīr*) of Muslims with differing views, and the protection of the inviolability of every Muslim's person and property. The program also rejected the "audacity of those who are not qualified in issuing religious juridical rulings (*fatāwā*, sing., *fatwā*), thereby flouting the tenets and pillars of the religion and the well-established schools of jurisprudence." Muslim jurists must agree to abide by the "relevant provisions" regarding the issuing of *fatāwā* adopted at the International Islamic Conference held in July

2005 in Amman, Jordan, as well as the recommendations made by the Forum of Muslim Scholars and Intellectuals at its summit in Mecca in September 2005. As part of its program of regulating the issuing of *fatāwā*, the program called for the International Islamic Fiqh Academy (IIFA) to coordinate juridical rulings with existing religious authorities in the Muslim world and to combat those rulings that contravene the teachings of Islam. The IIFA is a subsidiary of the OIC, founded in 1988 with the objectives of unifying the *ummah* and developing cooperation and respect among the different schools of thought in Islam.

The combating of illegitimate *fatāwā* issued by unqualified individuals was part of the OIC's initiative to combat terrorism and extremism among Muslims. The Ten-Year Program emphasized the organization's "condemnation of terrorism in all its forms and [rejection] of any justification or rationalization for it." Terrorism must be seen as "a global phenomenon that is not connected with any religion, race, color, or country" and it must be distinguished from "the legitimate resistance to foreign occupation, which does not sanction the killing of innocent civilians." The OIC reiterated its dedication to "criminalize all terrorist practices as well as all practices to support, finance, or instigate terrorism," which would include cooperating with international counterterrorism efforts.

The program emphasized the danger of spreading Islamophobia and called for the OIC to work together with the international community through the United Nations to combat it. The program called for all nations to "enact laws to counter it, including deterrent punishments." The main way to combat Islamophobia, the program said, was to engage in "structured and sustained dialogue in order to project the true values of Islam and empower Muslim countries to help in the war against extremism and terrorism."

To promote its programs, initiatives, and other activities, the OIC publishes a newsletter and the *OIC Journal* and maintains an extensive official website in English, French, and Arabic. The organization also publishes annual reports on Islamophobia.

BIBLIOGRAPHY

Al-Mashet, Abdel Monem. *The Organization of the Islamic Conference in a Changing World*. Cairo: Friedrich-Ebert-Stiftung, 1994.

Kerr, Malcolm H. *The Arab Cold War, 1958–1967: A Study of Ideology in Politics*. New York: Oxford University Press, 1967.

Khan, Saad S. *Reasserting International Islam: A Focus on the Organization of the Islamic Conference and Other Islamic Institutions*. Karachi: Oxford University Press, 2001.

"Muslim World League." http://www.themwl.org/.

"Muslim World League, Canada Office." http://www.mwlcanada.org/.

"Muslim World League, London Office." http://www.mwllo.org.uk/.

"Organization of Islamic Cooperation." http://www.oic-oci.org/.

"Organization of Islamic Cooperation, Charter." http://www.oic-oci.org/page_detail.asp?p_id=53.

"Organization of Islamic Cooperation, Ten-Year Programme of Action." http://www.oic-oci.org/page_detail.asp?p_id=228.

CHRISTOPHER ANZALONE

INTERNATIONAL LAW. International law may be understood through three legalistic stances that Muslims take toward international society: (1) a doctrinal one, in terms of the Islamic legal tradition, which sets forth the conduct of international relations within the framework of Islamic law (Sharīʿah); (2) a practical one, in terms of state participation in the legal institutions and practices of the international, and largely non-Muslim, order; or (3) a normative one, in terms of how Muslims (whether or not organized as states) should comport themselves on the global stage at the present time.

Doctrines of Islamic international law. *Siyar* (Islamic international law) came to mean the conduct of the Prophet in his wars, and has come to mean the (correct) conduct of Muslim rulers in international affairs (Hamidullah, 1977). The *siyar* was most influentially set forth as a loose body of law, dealing with a set of interrelated questions, by the Ḥanafī legal scholar Muḥammad ibn al-Ḥasan al-Shaybānī (d. 805), who is widely credited with originating the field of Islamic international law.

Because the *siyar* is part of the law and the will of God, al-Shaybānī, and Islamic scholars since his time, made use of the traditionally authoritative sources of legal knowledge—Qurʾān, *sunnah*, consensus, and analogy—to extrapolate the rules. What emerged is a very pragmatic, even problem-oriented, approach to what anachronistically might be called international relations. The *siyar* instructs Muslims what to do in various situations in which they are likely to find themselves engaged with unbelievers.

The most fundamental distinction drawn by the *siyar* is between two contexts: either one is within the *ummah*, the community of believers, where God's law is obeyed, or one is outside the *ummah*, among the unbelievers. The territory controlled by Muslims is called *dār al-Islām*, 'the abode of Islam', or, by implication, the abode of peace, since Muslims are not to make war upon one another. Territory controlled by unbelievers is *dār al-ḥarb*, usually translated as "the abode of war."

Although these two "abodes" are conceived in terms of a diametrical opposition, the actuality is more complicated. The following questions arise: Under what circumstances, if any, may Muslim rulers fight other Muslim rulers? Under what conditions, if any, may Muslim rulers ally themselves with non-Muslim rulers? Under what circumstances, if any, may Muslims regard themselves as neutral? May Muslims sign peace treaties with non-Muslims, and if so, what is the legal effect of such treaties?

The fact that actual relations—and thus the *siyar*—may be complicated should not obscure the fact that, in theory at least, the relationship between *dār al-Islām* and *dār al-ḥarb* is essentially antagonistic. While war may be postponed, the *siyar* presumes struggle (*jihād*) between the two abodes and thus, either explicitly or by implication, war. The *siyar* presumes that over time, *dār al-Islām* will seek to incorporate *dār al-ḥarb*, by force if necessary.

Given the *siyar*'s preoccupation with *jihād*, it is perhaps unsurprising that much of the law treats what may be done by Muslim forces in the course of prosecuting a war; for instance, under what circumstances may Muslims retreat? What is to be done with spoils? How are Muslims to treat prisoners of war? More generally, how are Muslims to treat the inhabitants of conquered lands?

A second important classification of situations—and hence a host of practical rules—addresses different kinds of non-believers. Islamic law does not treat all those who do not subscribe to Islam in the same way. Distinctions are drawn between a *dhimmī* (a taxpaying non-Muslim living in Muslim lands); a person of the *hudnah* ("truce"; a non-Muslim who is protected by agreement); and a *mustāmin* (a protected enemy alien, such as a messenger, merchant, or student).

The *siyar* tends to be expressed in personal terms, as rules that not only constrain but also guide actions taken by Muslims. Obedience to the law is an act of faith. The law, therefore, is more of a "how" than a "what." It thus stands in some contrast with Western notions of law's promulgation as an internally consistent and somewhat self-referential corpus, which, once established, governs as the law of a place, a jurisdiction.

Muslim Criticism of the Siyar. The *siyar* has been subjected to three kinds of criticism. The first is that the *siyar* is too enmeshed in historical circumstances that no longer exist. Many of its rules are based upon scholarly recording or interpretation of events of long ago, and the historical figures at the center of these events, in contemporary circumstances, might have acted or reacted differently.

A second criticism is that the *siyar*'s substantive scope is too narrow, and many issues that are of great concern to Muslims are simply not addressed. The *siyar* says much more about war than it does about peace, although most international relations happen in peacetime. Here it should be recalled that public international law—in the sense of the tradition guarded by the International Court of Justice—articulates only a tiny fraction of the legal relations on the global stage, and questions of trade or human rights, for example, may be addressed by a part of Islamic law not traditionally considered within the more military purview of the *siyar*.

Third, and combining these concerns, the fundamental bifurcation between the two abodes has been contested doctrinally, as not compelled by either the Qurʾān or the Prophetic tradition. The *siyar*, in this view, should be understood historically as a Ḥanafī response to the needs of the ʿAbbāsid caliphate and not as binding on contemporary Muslims.

The Practice of Muslim States. An individual might also look for "the law" not in abstract doctrine, but in state practice: what is the Islamic legal significance of an act by a Muslim state? This question should be considered in two broad historical contexts. First, from at least colonial times to the present, the ability of states to bind themselves has been understood to provide the grammar of interstate legal relations both inside and outside the Muslim world, but the legitimacy and even autonomy of many states has been open to question. Second, one should also ask after the traditional practice of Muslim rulers in the centuries after al-Shaybānī and before the adoption (coerced or not) of Westphalian understandings of international law.

Contemporary Practice. At first glance, it might seem that the question of "Islamic" views of contemporary international law is inapposite. Muslim states sign treaties with other Muslim states and with non-Muslim states. Muslim states conduct diplomatic and trade relations, and participate in the United Nations and other international institutions. Muslim states go to war, not only with non-Muslim states, but with other Muslim states. In short, international law governs Muslim and non-Muslim states alike. From this perspective, Islam seems irrelevant to international law, at least as currently practiced by Muslim states, if not as doctrinally articulated by the *siyar*.

While there is truth to this view, at least two qualifications should be made. First, Islamic law, including Islamic international law, is the law of God. Law's authority is God's authority. Consequently, the law cannot be understood apart from belief. Thus, to state baldly that international law does not require faith, that the Westphalian project transcends religion—yet still claims to be legal—may be fundamentally objectionable or simply implausible. (Public international law refers to its ability to have law without shared belief by allusion to Westphalia, where treaties ended the religiously articulated Thirty Years War in Europe without solving the religious controversies.) Such doubts are hardly unique to Muslims.

Second, although Muslim states do in fact participate in international law in all sorts of ways, the legitimacy of many such states has not been beyond question. Most of the boundaries of the Middle East, and many of the regimes, are direct results of twentieth-century decolonization, and many Muslim states today cannot draw particular legitimacy from representing peoples specific to that state, or from a long history as a state. Nor can such states draw much legitimacy from the Islamic legal tradition, because Islamic law is concerned with rulers, the *ummah*, and nonbelievers, but has no real discourse of the state. Moreover, although "Muslim" and "Arab" are not synonymous, it should be kept in mind that throughout the twentieth century there have been calls for pan-Arab unity, and even for a single Arab state, implicitly calling into question the legitimacy of current, less than pan-Arab, entities. Thus the legitimacy of Muslim, especially Arab, states that participate in international affairs may not be presumed, and has in fact been challenged. By extension, the legitimacy of international commitments entered into by such states may also be questioned. This potential is more likely to be realized in areas of substantive conflict with other legal systems, for example, the status of women, democracy, or other human rights.

Traditional Practice. Throughout the Muslim world, and for centuries after al-Shaybānī, Muslim rulers had to deal with one another and with non-Muslim rulers. These rulers' practices might indicate Islamic international law after the fashion of custom in most legal systems, including public international law. Understanding Islamic international law in this way offers at least two important advantages. First, what transpired was not the product of decisions by non-Muslim colonial powers; and second, those practices covered the usual range of foreign relations.

However, the territorial expanse of *dār al-Islām* and the area ruled by the caliph, the caliphate, are traditionally thought to be one and the same. Although effective administration often required the devolution of power to regional and local authorities, all such authorities traditionally derived their authority from, and owed their allegiance to, the caliph. Indeed, the relations among Islamic "states" within the caliphate tend to be discussed under the rubric of what does and does not constitute rebellion. Thus if the caliphate is perceived to be a single legal entity—the institutional aspect of the *ummah*—then the actions of regional administrators do not reflect, much less create, law, but instead reflect the practical exigencies of rule.

International law thus instantiates an issue found elsewhere in Islamic law, which is whether state policy (*siyāsah*) of Muslim rulers is essentially mere politics and thus outside the law—traditionally the province of religious scholars (*ʿulamāʾ*)—or a part of the law, in which case "administrative" decisions made in all parts of the caliphate can be examined for their legal sense, akin to what, in the public international-law tradition, is called *opinio juris*. If *siyāsah* were not part of Sharīʿah, then the current and indeed historical practice of Muslim governments would be rather untethered in the Islamic legal tradition.

At present, however, there exists no analysis of the external relations of Muslim governments over the last millennium with anything like the reach and authority of al-Shaybānī's treatment of *siyar*. Thus, even if an Islamic international law theoretically might be founded on practice, it must be said that the bulk of such work remains to be done.

Islamic Law in Global Society. The question that organizes the *siyar*—how are Muslims to comport themselves vis-à-vis non-Muslims—may be asked slightly differently: How are Muslims to conduct themselves vis-à-vis a global modernity largely comprised of non-Muslims? With regard to a number of issues—democracy; human rights; international norms of dress (the veil controversy) and publication (the Danish cartoon controversy); Israel's status; *jihād*; recognition of new governments, for example, in Kosovo or Libya; terrorism; the treatment of Muslims in non-Muslim majority states—discourses have emerged that are simultaneously legal, international in extension, and avowedly Islamic.

In general, these are not issues that are organized in the first instance, or in some cases at all, by the dealings among states. They are more reliant on what Islam (and so Islamic law) requires, but the context of that requirement is both larger than a given nation-state and, in an important sense, separate from the discourses of states. To call such issues matters of trans- or even supranational law only reinscribes the identification of law with the state. But the requirements of Islamic law reflect independence from the state, often in social spaces that public international law—due to its own conceptual structure—denominates "international."

[*See also* Combat; Jihād; Minorities in Muslim States; Rebellion; Sharīʿah; Siyāsah Sharīʿah; *and* Treaties.]

BIBLIOGRAPHY

Abū Sulaymān, ʿAbdul Ḥamīd A. *Towards an Islamic Theory of International Relations: New Directions for Islamic Methodology and Thought.* 2d rev. ed. Herndon, Va.: International Institute of Islamic Thought, 1993.

Al-Shaybānī, Muḥammad. *The Islamic Law of Nations: Shaybānī's Siyar*, translated by Majid Khadduri. Baltimore: The Johns Hopkins University Press, 1966.

Bedjaoui, Mohammed. "The Gulf War of 1980–1988 and the Islamic Conception of International Law." In *The Gulf War of 1980–1988: The Iran–Iraq War in International Legal Perspective*, edited by Ige F. Dekker and Harry H. G. Post. Dordrecht, The Netherlands: Kluwer Academic, 1992.

Bouzenita, Anke I. "The Principle of Neutrality and 'Islamic International Law' (Siyar)." *Global Jurist* 11 (2011). http://www.bepress.com/gj/vol11/iss1/art4.

Hamidullah, Muhammad. *Muslim Conduct of State: Being a Treatise on Siyar.* 7th ed. Lahore: Sh. Muhammad Ashraf, 1977.

Moinuddin, Hasan. *The Charter of the Islamic Conference and Legal Framework of Economic Co-Operation among Its Member States.* New York: Oxford University Press, 1987.

Roy, Olivier. *Globalized Islam: The Search for a New Ummah.* New York: Columbia University Press, 2006.

Roy, Olivier. *The Failure of Political Islam.* Cambridge, Mass.: Harvard University Press, 1998.

Westbrook, David A. "Islamic International Law and Public International Law: Separate Expressions of World Order." *Virginia Journal of International Law* 33 (1993): 819–897.

DAVID A. WESTBROOK

INTERNATIONAL RELATIONS AND DIPLOMACY. When referring to the historical documents and scripts of Muslim authors, analogous concepts of international relations can be found in the early stage of Islamic history; thus one can easily conclude that international and diplomatic realms are incorporated within Islam. During this period, diplomacy was used as a tool to spread information on the divine principles. After the treaty of al-Ḥudaybīyah (the Prophet's agreement with the Meccans in 628) had been concluded and peace with the Quraysh (pagans) had been in place for at least ten years, the Prophet Muḥammad was highly satisfied with the victory, despite some objections raised on that ground. After this victory, the Prophet Muḥammad sent messages to the neighboring countries, aiming at spreading the messages of Islam. These messages, sent to Jews and Christians of the Arabian Peninsula, including Abyssinia, Byzantium, Egypt, and Persia, Rome, Ethiopia, Syria, and others, were considered clear examples of an early Islamic diplomatic practice. Despite the assumption that *jihād* against infidels is an unremitting obligation, the treaty of al-Ḥudaybīyah has become the prototype of a truce (though not lasting peace) between combatants. Following this precedent, the fifth Umayyad caliph, ʿAbd al-Malik (r. 685–705), concluded a truce with the Byzantine ruler.

During the reign of Caliph Hārūn al-Rashīd (r. 786–809), Islamic civilization flourished; the period was often referred to as the "golden age" of Islamic civilization. Later, the ʿAbbāsids furthered international relations as such. They routinely concluded different treaties with foreigners, using a particular approach to treaties that were related to prisoners of war. Moreover, they also regularly and lavishly received foreign envoys in Baghdad under the capacity of representatives of fellow sovereigns. Around the year 800, for example, Caliph Hārūn received an ambassador from Charlemagne and sent an ambassador in return. Even during the Crusades, there were several formal treaties with Christian princes, such as the agreement in 1192 between Saladin (Ṣalāḥ al-Dīn, r. 1186–1193) and the English king Richard I, which facilitated Christian pilgrimage to the Holy Land.

The Politics of Conflict and Competition. In the Qurʾān, the means of negotiation and diplomacy are explicitly stated, referring to "inviting people to God's mean with proper advice, and negotiate with them in a peaceful way, and have discussions with them in the best manner" (16:125). However, despite the logic of solving disputes in a peaceful way, as expressed in the Qurʾān and as demonstrated in the early history of Islam and international relations, the polemicists often disregard these facts by concluding that Islam is preeminently concerned with the creation of a universal Muslim community and is intolerant of those who are not Muslims. These arguments are supported by the fact that the Qurān and the traditions of the Prophet have many references to the need and desirability of fighting the unbelievers, often to the bitter end. This is one dimension of *jihād* that is especially emphasized in the case of polytheists: the Qurʾān urges the believers to fight them "wherever you find them" until they repent or are defeated (9:5), and a *ḥadīth* records the Prophet as saying, "I am ordered to fight until they [the polytheists] say 'there is no God but Allah.'" Ahl al-Kitāb (People of the Book), other monotheists such as Jews or Christians, are also to be fought until they pay a special tax and are "subdued" or "humbled" (9:29). Generally, the *ḥadīth* tell us that "whoever fights to make Allāh's Word superior fights in God's cause," and that even a single journey for this purpose is "better than the world and all that is in it."

This expansionist zeal accounts for the ʿAbbāsid elaboration of a bifurcated and conflict-ridden world—*dār al-islām* (the Islamic realm of peace) and *dār al-ḥarb* (the non-Islamic realm of war). Moreover, within the realm of Islam, the Islamic state's non-Muslims citizens who pay *jizyah* (tax) as a sign of subjection to the Islamic state's laws receive in return protection as well as certain rights, such as the permission to practice their faith, to be protected from the outside aggression, and so on. Nevertheless, the Islamic state's non-Muslims citizens who pay *jizyah* suffer certain disadvantages compared to Muslim citizens. The former are not allowed to display their religious symbols openly or to carry arms. The former condition applied to non-Muslim Western military forces stationed in Saudi Arabia during the Persian Gulf crisis of 1990–1991.

Though Islamic political theory is far more complex than described above, it is sometimes seen as a twofold theory. On one hand, Islam is associated with the phenomenon of *jihād* as an instrument of Islamic militancy and religion expansionism; on the other hand, the alternative view describes a tolerant, nonviolent Islam that calmly accommodates itself to the reality of political pluralism and non-Muslim centers of power. The legitimacy of the first approach derives from the Muslim motivation to commit one's wealth and one's life (61:11) to "strive" ceaselessly against falsehood. The second approach is supported by the obligation to avoid combat at all if possible. The latter approach goes on to claim that fighting is enjoined for self-defense only. According to the

Qurʾān, one should "fight in the cause of God those who fight you, but one should not be aggressive, for God does not love aggressors" (2:190). This approach is widely used to perceive the Muslim world as similar to the international actors. As a clear example, Muslims may even in certain circumstances conclude a treaty with the enemy that would take precedence over any obligations to their fellow Muslims: "If they [Muslims] ask for help in the matter of religion, it is your duty to help them, except against a people with whom you have a treaty" (8:72).

The history of conflict and competition between the Muslim and non-Muslim world is replete with historical facts of conflict resolution by legal means as well as through armed conflict. Yet, it is worth mentioning that although Muslims did not concede that Western states were equal to them, Muslim states regularly entered into territorial agreements and concluded peace, such as the Ottoman treaty with Russia in 1739. Concerning the early debate that was widely discussed among jurists in the sixteenth century, related to the length of truce between Muslims and non-Muslims, an answer was given by Muslim practice. Invoking the treaty of al-Ḥudaybīyah, jurists of at least two legal schools argued that such agreements could not last more than ten years. But the treaty of 1535 between the Ottoman ruler Süleyman the Magnificent (r. 1520–1566) and Francis I of France endorsed the idea of "valid and sure peace" between them for their lifetimes; thus this historical experience redefined the theoretical approach.

Compatibility of Islam and Nationalism. Islamic theory reserves a significant role for the idea of inclusiveness of the worldwide community. According to the Qurʾān, there is no distinction among believers except in piety (49:13) and the fraternity of the faith will inevitably extend to incorporate all peoples. Other bonds of loyalty, such as to tribe or race, must be replaced by common submission to the one God, and as the influential Indian/Pakistani writer Abūal-Aʿlā Mawdūdī (1903–1979) states, the Islamic community (*ummah*) can only be "universal and all-embracing, its sphere of activity...coextensive with the whole human life" (*Political Theory of Islam*, Lahore, 1960, p. 26). Yet one can also point to ideological, political, and territorial divisions that Islam recognizes. The Qurʾān seems to sanction such divisions. It claims that God divided men into nations and tribes for a purpose—to come to "know each other" (49:13)—and the divisions of language and color "are signs for those who know" (30:22). At another point, the Qurʾān says, "If God had so willed, He would have made them one community" (42:8).

A large literature has developed which argues that Islamic law enshrines territorial divisions to which the law must bend, while Muslim medieval intellectuals sought to prove that there was pluralism within the Islamic realm, as well as between the latter and the non-Islamic realm. Among the best-known advocates of the idea of pluralism in Islam is al-Ghazālī (1058–1111), who argued that caliphs owed their position to decisive, non-caliphal centers of power. Ibn Taymīyah (1263–1328) went further, stressing that, because of Islam's essential religious unity, it does not need to have only one political regime. Ibn Khaldūn (1333–1406) endorsed the idea of pluralism by arguing that the rise and decline of political units are natural and in accord with the divine plan.

In parallel to this intellectual thought stands the flexibility that Muslim statesmen have demonstrated. In addition to maintaining regular diplomatic relations with non-Muslims, Muslims have come to accept the reality of separate sources of power within the Islamic *ummah* itself. An early example is the dispute between ʿAlī (c. 600–661), the Prophet's son-in-law and the fourth caliph, and Muʿāwiyah (c. 602–680), the governor of Syria and later the first Umayyad caliph, over legitimate succession to the caliphate. The text of the arbitration between them is remarkable for the way it rendered the two caliphs equal as territorially based sovereigns.

In the twentieth century, Muslim-Western relations and inter-Muslim relations came indisputably to be measured by the yardstick of territorial and national sovereignty. From the end of the eighteenth century onward, European colonialism had implanted itself, fostering in turn the growth of indigenous nationalisms. Local elites realized that they needed to rid themselves of imperial control, while simultaneously protecting their own prestige and power against rival claimants to postcolonial leadership. They recognized that, to achieve both goals, they had to play by the rules of the international game. In order for international rules to be put in place, they first needed to ensure recognition from the great powers, then enhance the sense of national uniqueness in the greater society of nation-states. As a consequence of this approach, "the Arab region, traditionally a medieval system of overlapping authorities, was subdivided as modern territorial state units with national boundaries" (Bacik, 2008, p.1)

As far as inter-Muslim relations are concerned, starting from 1930 and continuing into the twenty-first century, the paramount norm has been the acknowledgment of strengthening the spiritual and cultural unity of the faith while insisting on the preservation of territorial divisions and sovereignty. When scrutinizing the bilateral and multilateral agreements, one can distinguish that the majority of them explicitly express the individual sovereignties of the contracting parties, making it clear that the form of association agreed upon must not be seen as a derogation of the individual sovereignties of the contracting parties. The Arab League Pact (1945), for example, although "the willingness of strengthening the close relations and numerous ties which link the Arab states" (Preamble), is committed to preserving the independence and sovereignty of its members (Article 2) and requires that "each member state shall respect the systems of government established in the other member states and regard them as the exclusive concerns of those states" (Article 8). Another similar example is the Charter of the Organization of the Islamic Conference (OIC, 1972) which unambiguously affirms that the organization is based on the "abstention from the threat or use of force against the territorial integrity, national unity or political independence of any member State" (Preamble) and on the principles of "respect of the sovereignty, independence and territorial integrity of each member State" (Article 2b).

Many Muslims, however, such as Mawdūdī, have rejected the institution of the nation-state as alien and destructive of pan-Islamic union. The most notable recent exponent of this view was Ayatollah Ruhollah Khomeini (1902–1989), who, as the supreme leader of Iran, committed the government to promoting Islamic unity. Yet for all his wider aspirations, Khomeini implicitly accepted the legitimacy of the territorial state of Iran when it was under attack by the Iraqis during the Iran–Iraq War (1980–1988). In effect, Iran was validated as the vanguard of the Islamic Revolution. The demands of political and economic intercourse, the development of an intellectual and pragmatic consensus, even if unenthusiastically so, and the pervasive influence of modern, nationalized educational systems have combined to make nationalism and the nation-state a powerful presence on the modern Muslim landscape. Indeed, for all their criticisms of the status quo, most Islamists have been less concerned about supplanting the nation-state system than with making the state more "Islamic."

Transnationalism of Islam. Political Islam is clearly an international phenomenon, but as international politics has become more complex and is now more accurately described by the concept of world politics, Islam is therefore more than simply international. This is demonstrated by the activities of the Muslim Brotherhood (al-Ikhwān al-Muslimūn), which, although rooted in individual countries, operates simultaneously in Egypt, Sudan, Syria, Jordan, Palestine, and even South Asia, among other locations, and exhibits some degree of linkage among them. The Muslim Brotherhood is a pan-Islamic nonstate actor that was founded as a religious and social organization and then expanded its target to state-level issues, exercising an impact on the state system.

Nonstate actors are an increasingly prominent aspect of modern Islamic life, particularly in the field of *daʿwah* (the "call" to Islam). Such organizations as the Egyptian Muslim Brotherhood and the Palestinian Ḥamās (Ḥarakat al-Muqāwamah al-Islāmīyah, the Islamic Resistance Movement) are involved in providing a range of social welfare activities through such institutions as health clinics, schools, and housing cooperatives, which by their very efficiency and popularity provide a powerful challenge to the legitimacy of state institutions. Although their bases are securely located in their own national territories, there is no doubt that assistance in the training of activists, significant funding, and intellectual stimulation are derived from external sources.

Governments often seek to channel popular Muslim sentiments by sponsoring their own *daʿwah* organizations. The Islamic Propagation Office in Iran is concerned with various dimensions of the export of the Iranian revolutionary message, but like its counterpart in Libya, the Islamic Call Society (Jamʿīyat al-Daʿwah al-Islāmīyah), the degree of success can be overstated. The Saudi government, with its sponsorship of the Muslim World League (Rābiṭat al-ʿĀlam al-Islāmī), has been more successful in facilitating the spread of a non-revolutionary but nonetheless assertive strain of Islamic activism. Through such journals as *Al-Rābiṭah* (The League; English edition: *Journal of the Muslim World League*) and *Al-Nahḍah* (The Renaissance, the journal of the allied Regional Islamic Daʿwah Council of Southeast Asia and the Pacific), transnational *daʿwah* groups provide a potent communications and information network. Such a network encourages the mobilization of Muslim opinion on broader, pan-Islamic issues, such as the *jihād* against the Soviet authorities in Afghanistan in the 1980s, the plight of Muslim minorities in places like the Philippines and Thailand, and the future of Muslim Chechnya or Kosovo Muslims.

The Islamic transnational network was also an instrument in generating and sustaining the negative reaction to the publication in 1988 of Salman Rushdie's novel *The Satanic Verses*, which was widely regarded as blasphemous of the prophet Muḥammad, and to the award of a knighthood to Rushdie in 2007. Britain and Iran broke off diplomatic relations over the original affair and the European Community and the Organization of the Islamic Conference (OIC) put it near the top of their agendas. But in addition to these foreign policy results, the Rushdie affair generated more complicated politics.

One of the distinctive features of the Rushdie affair was the replication of both Saudi–Iranian rivalry and the fragmented Islamic politics of South Asia on British soil. Partly because of the lack of full assimilation into British economic, social, and political life, linguistic pluralism, and ethnic differences, there was a built-in competitiveness in British Muslim communities, reflected in identifiably sectarian mosques and schools and a susceptibility to outside influences. These latter included Barelwī or Deobandī *ʿulamāʾ*, the Tablīghī Jamāʿat, and Jamāʿat-i Islāmī from the Indian subcontinent. Correspondingly, the reactions of Muslim groups in Britain and their support for Ayatollah Khomeini's *fatwa* against the novel in February 1989 had an impact on the factionalized politics of Iran.

Paradigmatic Challenges. Even before the unsettling events of 11 September 2001, commentators had questioned the relevance of conventional ways of conceptualizing international relations, among Muslim societies and beyond. This questioning has taken four dimensions.

First, Samuel Huntington argued that cultures and civilizations are diverging in the post–Cold War order and are likely to be the main source of conflict. The advent of al-Qaʿida and global terrorism in the name of Islam appeared to confirm this assumption, first put forward eight years before the attacks on Washington and New York. But critics have argued that his depiction of the "centuries-old military interaction between the West and Islam" ("The Clash of Civilizations?" *Foreign Affairs* [Summer 1993]: 31–32) simplifies history, overlooks the heterogeneity of Muslim societies, and understates the possibilities of cross-cultural cooperation. Whereas Huntington refers to Islam's "bloody borders" and others have explicitly spoken of the "Islamic threat," critics of these views argue that, owing in great part to the potency of global communications, ideas and norms easily move across supposed cultural barriers, and cross-cutting alliances become possible when interests dictate.

Second, a set of challenges that can be summarized as globalization has also arisen. Although Muslims have long developed a self-conscious sense of the cosmopolitanism of Islam, notions of territory, time, and authority may be in the process of rapid redefinition because of the greater intensity of economic interdependence, cultural exchange, and political interaction. Some Muslim intellectuals, broadly in common with leftist, liberal, and secular critics, have objected to the polarizing, marginalizing, and homogenizing effects of globalization. Others see it as an ally in efforts to reduce poverty or as a way to disseminate Islamic ideas. Muslim political leaders have found that globalization may enhance as well as reduce the regulatory powers of the state and produce "reforms" that redound to the advantage of entrenched elites. This ambivalence points to the persistence of the old rules of the game, even as challenges to them are formulated.

Third, Muslim radicals have advanced a powerful criticism of contemporary order that calls into question the past acquiescence of Muslim elites in the prevailing international order. In this view, the great powers, particularly the United States, and international institutions such as the United Nations and the World Trade Organization manipulate and exploit Muslims. Local regimes of the Muslim world, preeminently the Saudi monarchy, have allied themselves with such oppressive forces. Muslims aspire to "recapture" the unity of the *ummah* and, especially in the program of Ḥizb al-Tahrīr al-Islamī (the Islamic Liberation Party), to restore the caliphate. Individual Muslims function as heroic *mujāhidīn* against the "Crusaders" (*al-sālibīyīn*), "Jews," and "infidels" (*kuffār*) of the age. For some, terrorism becomes an integral part of what is presented as a "defensive" *jihād*, and in the view of Osama bin Laden, even civilians can become legitimate targets. World politics is thus conceived as targeting peoples rather than states and territory, and within a religiously charged framework rather than a geopolitical one, such as balance of power. But implicit notions of territorial and political differentiation are also found in lively debates over where the lines between *dār al-Islām* and *dār al-ḥarb* lie today.

Fourth, a preoccupation with "Islamic" or domestic matters has suggested to some that the internal, rather than the external, realm is the main site of political activity today. This inward turning comes from two sources. Just as the secular Arab nationalists a generation earlier had concluded that they would never prevail over Israel as long as their own governments were corrupt, the vast majority of Islamists have put at the heart of their program an overturning of secular, impious government and a vaguely defined Islamization of society. In addition, others—women, human rights, and other special interest groups—are also increasingly making their views heard and are enhancing the pluralism, perhaps even contributing to the democratization of Muslim societies.

The combined effect has not been to displace the state or interstate politics; the tacit acceptance of this framework so long as it appears to have some Islamic legitimacy continues to be a major, if not the predominant, trend. But the shifting of focus to the *ummah* for many, on the one hand, and to society and governance, on the other hand, suggests a more complex politics of identity than the one that had prevailed in the past.

[*See also* Bin Laden, Osama; Daʿwah; Human Rights; International Law; Nation; Organization of Islamic Cooperation; Pan-Islam; *and* Ummah.]

BIBLIOGRAPHY

Abu-Rabiʿ, Ibrahim M. "Globalization: A Contemporary Response." *The American Journal of Islamic Social Sciences* 15, no. 3 (Fall 1998): 15–45.

Abū Sulaymān, ʿAbdulḥamīd A. *The Islamic Theory of International Relations: New Directions for Islamic Methodology and Thought*. Herndon, Va.: International Institute of Islamic Thought, 1987.

Abū Zahrah, Muḥammad. *Al-ʿalāqāt al-duwalīyah fī al-Islām* (International Relations in Islam). Cairo: al-Dār al-Qawmīyah, 1964.

Ahsan, Abdullah, al-. *Ummah or Nation? Identity Crisis in Contemporary Muslim Society*. Leicester, U.K.: Islamic Foundation, 1992.

Bacik, Gokhan. *Hybrid Sovereignty in the Arab Middle East: The Cases of Kuwait, Jordan, and Iraq*. New York: Palgrave Macmillan, 2008.

Dawisha, Adeed, ed. *Islam in Foreign Policy*. Cambridge, U.K.: Cambridge University Press, 1983.

Djalili, Mohammad-Reza. *Diplomatie islamique: Stratégie internationale du khomeynisme*. Paris: Presses Universitaire de France, 1989.

Hamidullah, Muhammad. *Muslim Conduct of State*. 4th rev. ed. Lahore: Sh. Muhammad Ashraf, 1961.

Hurewitz, J. C., ed. *The Middle East and North Africa in World Politics: A Documentary Record*. 2 vols. 2d ed. New Haven, Conn.: Yale University Press, 1975.

Iqbal, Afzal. *Diplomacy in Islam*. Lahore: Institute of Islamic Culture, 1977.

Khadduri, Majid. *War and Peace in the Law of Islam*. Baltimore: The Johns Hopkins University Press, 1955.

Khan, Saad A. *Reasserting International Islam: A Focus on the Organization of the Islamic Conference and Other Islamic Institutions*. Karachi: Oxford University Press, 2001.

Landau, Jacob. *The Politics of Pan-Islam: Ideology and Organization*. Oxford and New York: Oxford University Press, 1990.

Moinuddin, Hasan. *The Charter of the Islamic Conference: The Legal and Economic Framework*. Oxford: Oxford University Press, 1987.

Proctor, J. Harris, ed. *Islam and International Relations*. New York: Praeger, 1965.

Rajaee, Farhang. *Islamic Values and World View: Khomeyni on Man, the State and International Politics*. Lanham, Md.: University Press of America, 1983.

Saleem, Musa. *The Muslims and the New World Order*. London: ISDS Books, 1993.

Schulze, Reinhard. *Islamischer Internationalismus im 20. Jahrundert: Untersuchungen zur Geschichte der Islamischen Weltliga*. Leiden: Brill, 1990.

Siddiqui, Kalim. *Beyond the Muslim Nation-State*. London: Open Press, 1980.

JAMES PISCATORI
Updated by KETRINA ÇABIRI
and KLODIANA KAPLLANI (NÉE ÇABIRI)

INTIFĀḌAH. Arabic term meaning literally "a shaking off," used to describe the popular Palestinian uprising of 1987. It has since entered the global lexicon, and lent its name to the Palestinian uprising of September 2000, the "al-Aqsā Intifāḍah."

The 1987 *intifāḍah* was a turning point in the history of the Israeli-Palestinian conflict. It was one of a long succession of protests resisting the dispossession of land that began well before the establishment of Israel in 1948, on three-quarters of what used to be British Mandate Palestine. But it was the first to mobilize all sectors of society, crossing class, gender, and rural-urban barriers, and, as such, was a defining moment for the Palestinian national consciousness. The *intifāḍah* began in December 1987 in the Gaza Strip as a response to an Israeli truck killing four Palestinian workers and ended with the signing of the Oslo Accords in 1993. During this period, more than 1,100 (some say 1,300) Palestinians were killed by Israelis, more than a quarter of whom were under sixteen years of age, over 100,000 were wounded, and some 2,000 homes were demolished. An additional 1,000 Palestinians were killed by other Palestinians on suspicion of collaboration. By contrast, 160 Israelis were killed by Palestinians during this period, sixty of whom were soldiers. Only five were under the age of seventeen.

The *intifāḍah*'s most enduring image is that of rock-throwing youths, wrapped in checkered kaffiyehs (head scarves), confronting Israeli tanks. But protest methods ranged from bombing, shooting, and kidnapping to shopkeepers' strikes, boycotts of Israeli goods, and tax rebellion. The initial weeks saw spontaneous mass protests sweeping the Gaza Strip and the West Bank (the two geographically separate parts of the Palestinian territories occupied by Israel in 1967). But local grassroots leaders soon began to direct the *intifāḍah* in coordination with the leaders of the Palestine Liberation Organization (PLO) in exile. The United Leadership of the Uprising, a coalition of nationalist and leftist factions (though not the Islamists), coordinated everything from protests to providing medical, schooling, and welfare services, and kept the general population informed through a sophisticated underground distribution system of leaflets.

The *intifāḍah* began spontaneously, but both its beginnings and its longevity had their roots in factors that had been years in the making. At one level, it was a response to twenty years of occupation, increasingly harsh and repressive military tactics, and the gradual loss of land to Israeli settlements. By 1987, more than half of the West Bank and almost half of the Gaza Strip had been expropriated to make way for settlements and military installations. The rise of the Likud Party in Israel and its more explicitly expansionist claims on the occupied territories convinced the Palestinians that theirs was an existential struggle for survival.

At another level, the *intifāḍah* was a response to the dire economic conditions within the territories. Israeli-imposed restrictions on land use, external trade, and industrial development, Israel's refusal to maintain, let alone develop, the territories' basic infrastructure, and the subordination of the Palestinian economy to the Israeli economy combined with the regional recession of the 1980s to create unprecedented levels of economic hardship. By the mid-1980s, only about a fifth of school leavers and university graduates could find employment.

But the *intifāḍah* was also the culmination of a series of far-reaching structural changes. Inside the occupied territories, socioeconomic changes, triggered by the integration of the Palestinian territories into the Israeli economy, the 1970s rise in oil prices, the concomitant expansion of tertiary education, and the expropriation of land, had led to the weakening of the traditional landowning elite and the emergence of a counter-elite, drawn predominantly from the lower and lower-middle classes. This counter-elite was the driving force behind the expansion of the civil society organizations that would form the backbone of the *intifāḍah*.

By the late 1980s, economic growth had been superseded by recession. Expanding population growth and the out-migration of those seeking employment elsewhere had resulted in an increasingly youthful population, producing the volatile combination of a predominance of youths (in 1987, around half the population was under fourteen years old), economic hardship, and thwarted expectations—particularly among the newly graduated, who went on to play a leading role in the *intifāḍah*.

Israel's suspension of Palestinian municipal elections in 1980 and its attempts at decapitating the emerging nationalist leadership inside the territories had served both to remove the more temperate leadership and to discredit traditional politics. By 1987, Palestinians inside the occupied territories had moreover come to realize that no external actor would come to their rescue. Despite fiery rhetoric and repeated attempts, the surrounding Arab states had failed to deliver a Palestinian state. The national Palestinian leadership in exile had similarly failed. In 1982, it had been driven out of Lebanon by the Israeli army and forced to retreat to Tunisia, where it had then been weakened by internal divisions.

Into this vacuum stepped the grassroots activists of the counter-elite, politicized by their participation in the newly created student unions and civil society organizations, and radicalized by their encounters with the Israeli army and years spent in Israeli prisons. Predominantly young and with a lesser stake in the status quo, they were more willing to embrace radical methods. Israel's adoption of "iron fist" tactics in the early 1980s only served to exacerbate this process. The *intifāḍah* had a profound effect on the Arab-Israeli conflict. It led Jordan to renounce its claims to the West Bank, paving the way for a two-state solution based on an independent Palestinian state, as opposed to a Palestinian-Jordanian federation. It revived the PLO, enhancing its international leverage, but also increased the pressure to accept a two-state solution, leading to the PLO's historic recognition of Israel in November 1988. It forced Israel to reconsider its policy of creeping annexation and triggered a process of economic and political separation that strengthened the argument for a two-state solution. And it affected public opinion across the world, inverting Israel's image as a Jewish David against an Arab Goliath and (temporarily) supplanting the 1970s image of the "Palestinian terrorist" with that of the stone-throwing Palestinian youth.

The *intifāḍah*'s legacy, though, was double-edged. It laid the foundations for a participatory democracy through its incredible success in mobilizing society. But it simultaneously sowed the seeds for civil society's demise by exhausting it, spawning armed militias that marginalized civil society organizations and triggering a peace process that was designed, in part, to enable the PLO leadership to reassert itself and subjugate civil society. It paved the way for the reintegration of the internal and exiled leaderships, but it also helped to consolidate divisions between a resurgent internal leadership and the exiled leaders, which played a role in Fatah's electoral defeat in the 2006 legislative elections. It empowered women's organizations, yet served to reinforce conservative gender hierarchies. It forced the PLO and Israel to explore diplomatic avenues, yet laid the foundation for the more radical violence of the 1990s.

Perhaps the *intifāḍah*'s greatest paradox was that it both propelled the PLO back into the spotlight and triggered the establishment of the Islamic resistance movement Ḥamās. Like the *intifāḍah*, Ḥamās creation had been long in the making. However, the *intifāḍah* provided the impetus for the Muslim Brotherhood to establish Ḥamās as a resistance wing and helped to create the conditions that enabled it to become the main opposition party. Other factors played a part, such as the demise of the Soviet Union and its effect on the Palestinian Left, or the outbreak of the Gulf War and Arafat's decision to side with Saddam Hussein, which almost bankrupted the

PLO. But the *intifāḍah* both provided opportunities for Ḥamās to take center stage and helped create an ideological climate within which its rejectionist and conservative message gained rapidly in popularity.

[*See also* Arab-Israeli Conflict; Ḥamās; *and* Palestine Liberation Organization.]

BIBLIOGRAPHY

Freedman, Robert, ed. *The Intifāḍah: Its Impact on Israel, the Arab World, and the Superpowers.* Miami: University Press of Florida, 1991. Assesses the *intifāḍah* in the context of regional and global politics.

Mishal, Shaul, and Reuben Aharoni. *Speaking Stones: Communiqués from the Intifāḍah Underground.* Syracuse, N.Y.: Syracuse University Press, 1994. Collection of leaflets distributed during the *intifāḍah.*

Nassar, Jamal R., and Roger Heacock, eds. *Intifada: Palestine at the Crossroads.* New York: Praeger Publishers, 1990. Provides a balanced account of the relevant events.

Robinson, Glenn E. *Building a Palestinian State: The Incomplete Revolution.* Bloomington: Indiana University Press, 1997. Places the *intifāḍah* in its wider historical context.

JEROEN GUNNING

IQBAL, MUHAMMAD. (1877–1938), poet and philosopher of the Indian subcontinent and one of the principal intellectuals of Muslim modernism in the twentieth century. He was one of the main proponents of the two-nations theory propounded by the Muslim League, which led in 1947 to the partition of India and the creation of Pakistan.

Iqbal's early education was in Sialkot, a town in the northern Punjab, where he finished high school and then joined the Scotch Mission College, subsequently named Murray College. After studying for two years there, he went on to the Government College in Lahore, fifty miles to the south. Iqbal graduated cum laude from Government College and was also awarded a scholarship for further study toward a master's degree in philosophy. By far the most pervasive influence during his years at Government College was that of Sir Thomas Arnold, an accomplished British scholar of Islam and modern philosophy. In Arnold, Iqbal found a loving teacher who combined a profound knowledge of Western philosophy and a deep understanding of Islamic culture and Arabic literature. Arnold helped to instill this blending of East and West in Iqbal and inspired him to pursue further graduate studies in Europe.

In 1905 Iqbal traveled to Europe, where he studied in both Britain and Germany. In London he studied at Lincoln's Inn in order to qualify for the bar and at Trinity College of Cambridge University, where he enrolled as a student of philosophy while simultaneously preparing to submit a doctoral dissertation in philosophy at Munich University. The German university exempted him from a mandatory stay of two terms on the campus before submitting his dissertation, "The Development of Metaphysics in Persia." After his successful defense of the dissertation, Iqbal was awarded a doctorate in philosophy on 4 November 1907.

At Cambridge, Iqbal came under the influence of the neo-Hegelians John McTaggart and James Ward. Two outstanding Orientalists at Cambridge, E. G. Browne and Reynold A. Nicholson, also became his mentors. The latter translated Iqbal's Persian masterpiece *Asrār-i khūdī* (The Secrets of Self) when it was first published at Lahore in 1915.

Iqbal was never at home in politics, but he was invariably drawn into it. In May 1908 he joined the British Committee of the All-India Muslim League. With one brief interruption, Iqbal maintained his relationship with the All-India Muslim League throughout his life.

When Iqbal came back from Europe in 1908 after earning three degrees in Britain and Germany, he embarked simultaneously on three professional careers—as an attorney, college professor, and poet. At length, however, the poet and philosopher won out at the expense of the professor and attorney, although he continued to be active to some degree as a political leader.

Iqbal was elected a member of the Punjab Legislative Assembly for a period of four years from 1926 to 1930 and soon emerged as the political thinker among the unionist politicians led by Sir Fazal-i Hussain. In the period 1930–1934, Iqbal provided the ideological leadership for the All-India Muslim League, articulating the Muslims' demand for a separate Muslim state. His presidential address at the 1930 Muslim League conference is a landmark in the Muslim national movement for the creation of Pakistan. Delivered in Allahabad, the address formulated the two-nations theory, which subsequently would be championed by Mohammad Ali Jinnah. Even though Iqbal was by no means a skillful or committed politician, he nevertheless must be seen as a political mentor of Jinnah in regard to the creation of Pakistan.

The opportunity for another journey to the West was provided by the second (1931) and third (1932) London Round Table Conferences, called by the British government to consult with Indian leaders on the problems of constitutional reforms for India. In February 1933 Iqbal was back in Lahore. Seven months later, Muḥammad Nādir Shāh, the king of Afghanistan, invited him to visit Kabul along with Sayyid Sulaymān Nadvī and Sir Sayyid Ross Masood. The Afghan king wanted Iqbal to advise his government on the establishment of a new university and the reorganization of higher education, utilizing the best of modern Western and traditional Islamic values; however, not much is known about the educational recommendations made by Iqbal and his associates.

After his return from Afghanistan, Iqbal's health steadily deteriorated. His intellect remained sharp, however, and during this time he conceived many new projects, including proposed studies on Islamic jurisprudence and the study of the Qur'ān. During this period Iqbal also invited a younger Muslim scholar, Sayyid Abū al-Aʿlā Mawdūdī, to the Punjab, where he began to publish his well-known journal, *Tarjumān al-Qur'ān*. Iqbal had hoped that Mawdūdī would become a modernist scholar who would update Islamic ideas. After 1947 Mawdūdī moved to Lahore and involved himself in the struggle for power in Pakistan.

By 1938 Iqbal's health had sharply declined, and he died on 20 April of that year. He was buried to the left of the steps leading to the Badshahi Mosque in Lahore; construction of the present mausoleum was started in 1946, the marble being provided by the government of Afghanistan.

Religious and Political Thought. Iqbal's life was spent exclusively under British colonial rule, during which Muslims in the Indian subcontinent were profoundly influenced by the religious thought of Shāh Walī Allāh (1703–1762) and Sir Sayyid Aḥmad Khān (1817–1898). Iqbal's philosophical and political prose works are very few. Most notable among them are three works, including his published dissertation, *The Development of Metaphysics in Persia* (Cambridge, 1908). *The Reconstruction of Religious Thought in Islam* (Lahore, 1930) was a collection of seven lectures delivered in December 1928 in Madras. Iqbal took three years to compose these lectures and considered them reflective of his mature philosophical and rational approach to Islam. In the sixth lecture, Iqbal deals most directly with political concerns. He begins by dwelling on the importance of *ijtihād,* which he broadens from its technical meaning in Islamic jurisprudence to a core concept in the Islamic ethos. For Iqbal, *ijtihād* is nothing short of the "principle of movement in the structure of Islam." He expected the younger generations to follow him in a responsible *ijtihād*, the interpretation of the Qurʾān and the *sunnah* and the formation of an entirely new approach to Islamic law that would address the malaise of Muslim societies through analytical deduction. Iqbal hoped to lay the groundwork for religion and science to discover mutual harmonies that would enable Muslims to learn modern sciences and to use technology to improve their material existence. In the political realm, he championed a republican form of government of the sort then being implemented in Turkey not only as consistent with Islamic principles but as a necessity given the conditions of the modern era. The ancient juridical principle of *ijmāʿ*, Iqbal argued, must be understood in the modern age as parliamentary democracy, in which the people's representatives have the right to legislate anew according to the needs of their society.

Finally, his *Presidential Address to the Annual Meeting of the All-India Muslim League*, 1930, is a very extensive review of the interaction among the British, the All-India National Congress, and the All-India Muslim League, from the perspective of a Muslim thinker who was anxious about the political and cultural future of Muslims in the Indian subcontinent. Iqbal here expounded the concept of two nations in India. Subsequently this address came to be known as the conceptual basis for the state of Pakistan, although Iqbal did not use the name "Pakistan." On the contrary, Muslim nationalism is emphasized, giving shape and content to the national liberation movement of Muslims in India. Iqbal stressed the necessity of self-determination for the Muslims: "I'd like to see the Punjab, North-west Frontier Province (NWFP), Sindh and Baluchistan, amalgamated into a single state. Self government within the British empire or without the British empire, and the formation of a consolidated Northwest Muslim Indian State appears to have to be the final destiny of the Muslims, at least of Northwest India."

Intellectually, however, Iqbal was not an enthusiastic supporter of nationalism, and especially nationalism among Muslims. He attempted to resolve this dilemma by positing Muslim nationalism not as an end but a means to the end of broader Muslim unity and fraternity. As he wrote in *The Reconstruction of Religious Thought in Islam*: "It seems to me that God is slowly bringing home to us the truth that Islam is neither Nationalism nor Imperialism but a League of Nations which recognizes artificial boundaries and racial distinctions for facility of reference only, and not for restricting the social horizons of its members."

And in a letter to Jawaharlal Nehru, his younger contemporary, he explained:

> Nationalism in the sense of love of one's country and even readiness to die for its honor is a part of the Muslim faith; it comes into conflict with Islam only when it begins to play the role of a political concept and claims...that Islam should recede to the background of a mere private opinion and cease to be a living factor in the national life. Nationalism was an independent problem for Muslims only in those countries where they were in the minority. In countries with a Muslim majority, nationalism and Islam are practically identical, but in countries where Muslims are in the minority, their demands for self-determination as cultural unification is [*sic*] completely justified. ("Reply to Questions Raised by Pandit Jawaharlal Nehru," in S. A. Vahid, ed., *Thoughts and Reflections of Iqbal*, Lahore, 1964)

Iqbal composed his poetry in both Persian and Urdu. His six Persian works are *Asrār-i khūdī va Rumūz-i bīkhūdī* (Secrets of the Self and Mysteries of Selflessness, 1915), *Payām-i Mashriq* (Message of the East, 1923), *Zabūr-i ʿAjam* (Scripture of the East, 1927), *Javīd-nāmah* (Book of Eternity, 1932), *Pas chih bāyad kard, ay aqvām-i sharq* (What Should Be Done, O Nations of the East, 1926), and *Armaghān-i Ḥijāz* (A Gift of the Hijaz, 1938). His Urdu works, which are primarily responsible for his popularity in Pakistan as well as in India, are *Bang-i darā* (The Call of the Caravan Bell, 1924), *Bāl-i Jibrīl* (Gabriel's Wing, 1935), and *Ẓarb-i Kalīm* (The Rod of Moses, 1936). Poetry, like visual art, is susceptible to varied interpretations; consequently, his admirers, relying primarily on his poetry, have variously attempted to prove him a Pakistani nationalist, a Muslim nationalist, a Muslim socialist, and even a secularist.

Before Iqbal, Indian Muslim political thought was primarily concerned with the fate of India's large Muslim minority. For instance, Sayyid Ahmad Khan characterized love as a pyramid; at the top was the noblest form of love—love for the universe. This kind of love, however, "was unattainable." In the middle was love for those who "share human qualities with us." For Sayyid Ahmad, this was far too elusive a quality to be comprehended. He reasoned that at the bottom of the pyramid is placed the love of nation, "which I understand and I am capable of." Iqbal's intellectual evolution was the reverse of Sayyid Ahmad's. In his early works, Iqbal was absorbed in himself, agonizing over his personal disappointments. His emotional horizons then expanded to include India, particularly the Indian Muslims and the larger world of Islam. Then his love enveloped mankind, and at a still later stage it changed into a passionate involvement with the universe. Despite his commitment to the concept of a separate Muslim state, he remained a philosophical humanist, and humanism was truly his message.

Iqbal's thought influenced a diverse range of Muslim intellectuals and activists during the twentieth century. Abū al-Aʿlā Mawdūdī claimed to be his intellectual heir, but Mawdūdī's opponents, particularly the modernist scholar Fazlur Rahman, vehemently rejected such assertions. Similarly, two very different ideologues and activists, Sayyid Quṭb in Egypt and ʿAlī Sharīʿatī in Iran, seem to have borrowed elements of Iqbal's critique of secular modernity and his call for an enlightened Islamic reform that combines faith and reason.

BIBLIOGRAPHY

Aziz, Ahmad. *Studies in Islamic Culture in the Indian Environment*. Oxford and New York: Oxford University Press, 1964.

Beg, Abdulla Anwar. *The Poet of the East: The Life and Work of Dr. Sir Muhammad Iqbal*. Lahore: Qaumi Kutub Khana, 1939.

Iqbal, Muhammad. *The Reconstruction of Religious Thought in Islam* (1930). Lahore: Iqbal Academy Pakistan 1989.

Malik, Hafeez. *Iqbal: Poet-Philosopher of Pakistan*. New York: Columbia University Press, 1971.

Mir, Mustansir. *Iqbal: Makers of Islamic Civilization*. London: I. B. Tauris, 2007.

Mir, Mustansir. *Tulip in the Desert: A Selection of the Poetry of Muhammad Iqbal*. Montreal and Kingston: McGill-Queen's University Press, 2000.

Saiyidain, Khwaja Ghulam. *Iqbal's Educational Philosophy*. Lahore: Sh. Muhammad Ashraf, 1945.

Schimmel, Annemarie. *Gabriel's Wing*. Leiden, Netherlands: E. J. Brill, 1963.

Vahid, S. A., ed. *Thoughts and Reflections of Iqbal*. Lahore: Sh. Muhammad Ashraf, 1964.

HAFEEZ MALIK
Updated by SOHAIL HASHMI

IRAN, ISLAMIC REPUBLIC OF. The Islamic Republic of Iran came into existence following the 1979 revolution. The politics, perspective, and personality of Ayatollah Khomeini—Khomeinism—became the dominant discourse of post-revolutionary Iran. However, Khomeinism was one among many sociopolitical forces of the revolution. Pre-revolutionary Iran never experienced a homogeneous Islamist political culture. Diverse ideological discourses within the alliance led to the 1979 revolution. The first three Islamic discourses were Khomeinism, ʿAlī Sharīʿatī's Islamic-left ideology, and Mehdi Bazargan's liberal-democratic Islam. The fourth discourse was that of the socialist guerrilla groups, with Islamic *mujāhidīn* and Marxist *fidāʾī* variants; the fifth was that of secular constitutionalism, with the pro-Mossadegh nationalist and the Marxist Tudeh varieties. Nonetheless, Khomeinism has dominated post-revolutionary Iran.

One Regime and Fifth Republics. After the Iranian Revolution of 1979, Ayatollah Khomeini established a new regime called the Islamic Republic of Iran, which transformed Iran from a monarchy into a republic, but the regime he founded was a complex mixture of Islamic clericalism and secular republicanism. He created a hybrid regime that has undergone five consecutive phases—five republics—that simultaneously combined elements of totalitarian, authoritarian, and democratic politics (Chehabi, 2000, pp. 48–70). Each republic presented a different face of Khomeinism.

The First Republic (1979–1989). In the aftermath of the revolution, a division among the Islamists, nationalists of secular thinking, and various groups on the secular Left became visible. Each group held different opinions on the future of post-revolutionary politics. For Khomeini, the leader of the revolution, Iran's government could only be an Islamic republic, but the nature of this republic remained undefined. Khomeini moved to implement his theory of *vilāyat-i faqīh* (guardianship of the jurist), merging clericalism and republicanism. Hence, both concepts were redefined.

Khomeini's theory of *vilāyat-i faqīh*, which was developed through a series of lectures in Najaf in the early 1970s, challenged the conventional Shīʿī doctrine of the imamate, which states that the legitimate leadership of the Muslim community belongs to the Prophet and his twelve successors, the Shīʿī imams. He redefined the role of clergy, suggesting that in Islam there is no distinction between temporal and religious power. He rejected the prevalent notion that the jurists' task should be limited to understanding and interpreting the Sharīʿah, but rather stipulated that their duty is to implement the law. The role of the imam, he suggested, "should be represented by a *faqīh*, as the sole holder of legitimate authority" (Khomeini, 1978, pp. 28–40, 77–79, quoted in Bashiriyeh, 1983, pp. 62–63). Khomeini's definition of politics was an individual's conformity to the Sharīʿah. For Khomeini, the structure of authority was divine, and the state was instrumental in the implementation of the Sharīʿah. He proposed the novel idea that "our duty to preserve Islam" by establishing an Islamic government "is one of the most important obligations incumbent upon us; it is more necessary even than prayer and fasting" (Algar, 1981, p. 75). He suggested the task of creating an Islamic government justified on the basis of the "secondary ordinances" (*aḥkām-i sānaviyeh*), where the "primary ordinances," that is, *Sharīʿah* law, are silent or nonexplicit (ibid., p. 124). The *Sharīʿah* law cannot be fully implemented without an Islamic state; Islamic government is the only legitimate tool to put the Islamic rules into practice. The just *vali-ye faqīh* is the only qualified ruler to undertake this task after the Prophet and imams.

Khomeini also redefined the concept of republicanism in accordance with clerical rule. The people's participation in politics, or republicanism, resembled for Khomeini the traditional Islamic concept of *bayʿah*, meaning the vote of allegiance to authority. According to one view, for Khomeini, the *vali-ye faqīh* derives his popularity from the people, but his legitimacy is divine. Another interpretation suggests that both popularity and legitimacy of the *vali-ye faqīh* derive from the people. Khomeini combined his theory of *vilāyat-i faqīh* with the republican institutions inherited from the Iranian Constitution of 1906. The republican institutions are subordinated to the rule of the *vali-ye faqīh*. The Majlis (parliament) in the Iranian state must share legislative authority with the Guardian Council, whose jurist members are appointed by the *vali-ye faqīh*. Constitutionally, in the absence of the Guardian Council, the Majlis is devoid of authority. The Majlis must also share its legislative authority with the Expediency Council, whose chair and most members are appointed by the *vali-ye faqīh*. Similarly, the president in the Islamic republic is ranked next to the *vali-ye faqīh*. Furthermore, the *vali-ye faqīh* holds many institutional "extended arms," ranging from the powerful Revolutionary Foundations to the parallel institutions accountable not to the republican institutions but to the *vali-ye faqīh*.

Incorporating the theory of the *vilāyat-i faqīh* into state institutions required time and experience. Khomeini appointed Mehdi Bazargan, a moderate Muslim technocrat, to head the interim government. Bazargan reluctantly accepted Khomeini's offer, hoping "he would be able to influence the new regime from within" (Chehabi, 1995, p. 135). In Paris, Khomeini said "the *ʿulamāʾ* themselves will not hold power in the government," but instead "exercise supervision over those who govern and give them guidance" (Schirazi, 1997, p. 24). But by the end of 1979, Iran had a quasi-theocratic constitution, and by the summer of 1981, Khomeini's theory was in practice. After the fall of Bazargan's government in November 1979 and the dismissal of President Bani Sadr in June 1981, the regime shut down all political parties and arrested, executed, or jailed the opposition. There were 600 opposition figures executed by 1 September, 700 by October, and 2,500 by December 1981 (Abrahamian, 1989, p. 220). The first clerical president and the Islamic republic's third president was ʿAlī Khameneʾi, then secretary general of the Islamic Republican Party and the future successor of Ayatollah Khomeini as *vali-ye faqīh*.

The Islamic republic turned into a "clerical oligarchy," a polity with the repressive apparatus of ideological, military, and economic control. The state not only kept the shah's military and police structures but created new revolutionary institutions to expand its control: the Islamic Revolutionary Guard Corps with some 100,000 members, the Basīji with over 300,000 armed men, a number of Islamic Associations in public administrations, universities, and workplaces, and formal and informal organized gangs called Hizbollahi groups (Rahnema and Moghissi. 2001, p. 2).

The state under Ayatollah Khomeini's leadership was a mishmash of totalitarianism, authoritarianism, and semi-democracy. Khomeini's religious and revolutionary charisma, the revolutionary fever, the boost in global oil price (to $50 per barrel), and the Iraq-Iran war (1980–1988) were all instrumental in mobilizing the masses and consolidating a revolutionary, populist, and semi-totalitarian polity in the first republic. Yet the results were far from what Ayatollah Khomeini had intended. The decentralization of Islamic faith and relative diversity of opinion, together with pragmatism and the elite factional politics, contributed to the development of limited pluralism in the Iranian state and overruled the success of totalitarian tendencies (Chehabi, 2000, pp. 56–59).

By 1981, the state succeeded in eliminating and dismantling most of the opposition, including Muslim and secular-leftist groups such as the People's Mujāhidīn Organization (MKO), the Organization of Iranian People's Fidāʾī Guerrillas (Minority), the Worker's Path Organization (Rāh-i Kārgar), and a number of pro–ʿAlī Sharīʿatī groups, such as the Ideals of Dispossessed (Armān-i Mostazʿafin) and the Irshad Association.

In less than six months, thousands of opponents were executed, imprisoned, or had fled. In 1983, the Islamic republic eliminated the Tudeh Party and other non-militant Marxists such as the Organization of Iranian People's Fidā'ī (Majority), who had supported the regime's reign of terror against the liberals, progressive Muslims, and the militant leftists. The regime's anti-imperialist rhetoric, the hostage crisis involving American embassy personnel, the Iran–Iraq War, and the legacy of Third Worldism contributed to the confusion of some of the opposition about the nature of the state.

Sectarianism severely weakened the institutional power of the opposition, because of "confusions and disagreements over the issue of the nature of the regime—whether to support or confront it" (Rahnema, 2004, pp. 253–254). The People's Mujāhidīn Organization, the Fidā'ī (Minority), Rāh-i Kārgar, Peykār, and the Kurdish parties took a radical path against the state and were marginalized. Others such as the Tudeh Party, the Fidā'ī (Majority), and the Militant Muslims Movement (Jonbesh-i Musalmānān-i Mubāriz) sided with the clerics and fought the liberals.

The legacy of the Iran–Iraq War was contradictory. The war provided Khomeini with a historic opportunity to consolidate his vision of the revolution and eliminate or neutralize the state's rivals and enemies, and yet the war changed relations between the state and society as it simultaneously created a mass society with unfulfilled demands. By 1987, it became "too clear that the regime's emphasis on Islam, war, revolutionary discourse, and the persona of Khomeini were insufficient for governing Iran" (Moslem, 2002, p. 72). The crisis in the economy, the frustration and alienation in society, and the systematic deadlock and ideological factionalism in politics alarmed the regime, pushing the state to take some initiatives for change. The change was aimed at the institutionalization of the *vilāyat-i faqīh* and made Khomeini into an absolute (*mutlaqeh*) *vali-ye faqīh*. Three issues exemplified this transformation:

The Absolute Rule of the State over Religion. The nature of the Islamic state brought to the fore divisions within the Khomeinist camp. The conservative or traditional Right, backed by the *bāzārī* merchants and the orthodox clergy, held a conservative position on the nature of the Islamic state and "wanted strict implementation of Sharī'ah in the sociocultural spheres." The Society of Combatant Clergy (Jāme'eh Rūhānīyat-i Mubāriz) and the Allied Islamic Society (Jam'īyāt-i Mo'talefeh-i Islami) supported the conservative Khomeinists. The revolutionary elites, by contrast, "supported state-sponsored redistributive and egalitarian policies." The Mujāhidīn of the Islamic Revolution Organization (Sāzmān-i Mujāhidīn-i Enghilāb-i Islami) and the Society of Combatant Clerics (Majma'-i Rūhāniyūn-i Mubāriz) supported the revolutionary Khomeinists. The central committee of the Islamic Republican Party, until its dissolution in 1986, was more inclined to the revolutionary Khomeinists and less to the conservatives. They believed that primary Islamic ordinances (*aḥkām-i awaliyeh*), derived from the two Islamic sources of the Qur'ān and the Tradition of the Prophet (the *sunnah*) were insufficient and therefore Muslims living in modern times needed to issue secondary ordinances (*aḥkām-i sānaviyeh*) (Moslem, 2002, pp. 47–49). Ayatollah Khomeini trusted both factions, but by 1987, his policy of "dual containment" was no longer effective, given the ever-increasing disagreements over economic, sociocultural, and military policies between the two factions (Moslem, 2002. p. 65). From December 1987 until his death in June 1989, Khomeini issued various decrees to clarify his sociopolitical positions and sided with the revolutionary camp. Khomeini also created the Expediency

Council (Majmaʿ-i Tashkhīs-i Maṣliḥat-i Niẓām), an institutional mediator between the two Khomeinist camps in the Majlis and the Guardian Council, paving the way for further institutionalization of the *vilāyat-i faqīh*. In January 1988, he made clear that "the state that is a part of the absolute vice-regency of the Prophet of God is one of the primary injunctions of Islam and has priority over all other secondary injunctions, even prayers, fasting and *hajj*.... The government is empowered to unilaterally revoke any *sharia* agreement" (Ettelaʾat, 1988, quoted in Moslem, 2002, p. 74). Khomeini provided the state "with the authority not only to intervene in the economy but the right to use its discretion to suspend even the pillars of Islam" (Moslem, 2002, p. 74).

The "Poisoned Chalice" of Peace. Ayatollah Khomeini accepted the ceasefire in the Iran–Iraq War in the summer of 1988. He subsequently expressed his "absolute" authority in three specific events. First, following the end of the war, the People's Mujāhidīn Organization, the opposition group based in Iraq, launched a military attack against Iran. The regime's response was harsh: the Mujāhidīn's forces were massacred on the battlefronts and several thousand jailed political opponents were executed in the prisons (Abrahamian, 1999). Second, Khomeini's *fatwa* against Salman Rushdie's novel *Satanic Verses* created tension between Iran and the West. Third, after a decision made by the Assembly of Experts in 1985, Khomeini's loyal student, Ayatollah Ḥusayn-ʿAlī Muntazirī, was expected to succeed him. Muntazirī was the only high-ranking cleric who supported Khomeini's theory of *vilāyat-i faqīh* and contributed to its institutionalization. However, Muntazirī frequently criticized the violation of human rights by the regime. He challenged the regime's new reign of terror in the summer and autumn of 1988. Consequently, Khomeini asked him to resign and ordered the Assembly of Experts to meet and make a decision on the future leadership of the republic. The purge of the only ayatollah loyal to the doctrine of the *vilāyat-i faqīh* set the stage for the revision and the redefinition of this core institution.

The Succession. The 1979 constitution was explicit on the theological qualifications of the *vali-ye faqīh*, indicating that only one among the grand ayatollahs, as the prominent *marjʿa-e taqlīd*, or "source of imitation," could hold the office. None among the grand ayatollahs was sympathetic to Khomeini's theory of *vilāyat-i faqīh*. Moreover, the leading grand ayatollahs lacked the personal charisma or political qualifications required for the office. However, a number of middle-ranking clerics accepted Khomeini's theory and held the necessary political requirements. The pragmatic solution was to revise the constitution to save the state.

The 1989 constitution expanded the power of the *faqīh* by transferring the president's task of coordinating the three branches of government to the office of the *vilāyat-i faqīh*. It made explicit that the *vali-ye faqīh* holds an "absolute" power by adding the phrase *mutlaqeh* to Articles 107–110, defining his absolute authority. Article 109 of the amended constitution separated the position of the *marjʿa* from that of the *faqīh*, setting the stage for the selection of a new *vali-ye faqīh* who could be a middle-ranking cleric. The *vali-ye faqīh* no longer needed to hold the religious qualification of the *marjʿa-e taqlīd*. Khomeini's priority for the interests of the state led him to revise his own theory of *vilāyat-i faqīh*. Khomeini died on 3 June 1989, and the Assembly of Experts appointed ʿAlī Khameneʾi as the new leader of the Islamic republic.

The Second Republic (1989–1997). His lack of personal charisma and clerical credentials caused Sayyed ʿAlī Khameneʾi to be perceived at most as one among equals. Unlike Khomeini, who depended on his own charismatic authority,

Khameneʾi depended on his conservative peers. Having been concerned about the leader's lack of charismatic authority, the clerical oligarchy emphasized an absolutist version of the *vilāyat-i faqīh*, suggesting a complete and full obedience to the *faqīh*, or "melting into the *vilāyat*" (*zob-e dar vilāyat*).

As president of the second republic, ʿAlī Akbar Hāshimī Rafsanjānī initiated a neo-liberal policy of reconstruction *(sāzandegi)* to resolve the state's sociopolitical crisis. However, the politics of *sāzandegi* weakened the social base of the regime, escalated elite factionalism, and forced the regime to open up public space and allow a limited degree of sociopolitical liberalization. The politics of *sāzandegi*, "neo-liberal Khomeinism," prioritized economic development over political development. The policy was far from a success because Iran in the mid-1990s was experiencing a growing socio-ideological disenchantment. The youth in particular were politically disappointed and economically dissatisfied. By the 1990s, Iran was grappling with the consequences of demographic changes of a population, 70 percent of which was under thirty. Rapid urbanization, the expansion of higher education, and the need for employment of women were among the structural factors pushing for change. Moreover, civil society managed to challenge the repressive intentions of the state by resisting the clerical cultural codes. Youth and women brought the public sphere into their private lives by watching forbidden shows and openly discussing sociopolitical taboos. The state, in sum, had failed to create the individual or the society that the revolution had promised. The unintended consequences of the Khomeinist state was to empower and enlighten the public and undermine the intellectual foundations of the state.

Independent intellectuals managed to publish some journals such as *Iran-e Farda*, *Goftego*, and *Kiyan*. Religious and secular intellectuals posed serious challenges to the ideological foundations of Khomeinism. Abdolkarim Soroush challenged authoritarian religious thinking: Clerics, like other "professional groups," hold a corporate identity, "a collective identity and shared interest," and thus possess no divine authority (Soroush, 1995, quoted in Brumberg, 2001, p. 205). The rule of the *vali-ye faqīh*, Mojtahed Shabestari argued, is not divine and thus has to be subjected to democratic procedures. Ayatollah Muntazirī came up with a more accountable interpretation. The *vali-ye faqīh* "envisaged in the constitution has his duties and responsibilities clearly defined. His main responsibility is to *supervise*" (Muntazirī, 1997, quoted in Brumberg, 2001, p. 238). The devastating eight-year Iran–Iraq war with no clear victory, the decline of the global oil price ($10 or less per barrel), the end of the revolutionary fever, the rise of a new generation, and the failure of the state to meet their demands all contributed to the crisis of legitimacy in the second republic. By the late 1990s, the division among the elites was a fact, providing much opportunity for the unexpected victory of the reformist presidential candidate Muḥammad Khātamī.

The Third Republic (1997–2005). If Ayatollah Khomeini's death and the end of the Iraq–Iran War terminated the first republic, the explosive demands for greater pluralism and freedom put an end to the second. The unexpected presidential election of Muḥammad Khātamī, a moderate, reformist cleric, on 23 May 1997, marked the beginning of the third republic. Khātamī became the candidate for change and received the people's protest vote, making him a "Cinderella candidate" (Milani, 2001, p. 29) and eventually an "accidental president" of the Islamic republic (Bakhash, 2003, p. 119).

The reformist republic stood on three intellectual pillars: Islamic constitutionalism, the promotion of civil society, and Islamic democracy.

All three were bound to the legacy of Khomeinism, which created a limited and inchoate subjectivity never independent of the *vali-yefaqīh*.

The reform movement under Khātamī suffered largely from an ineffective presidency. Khātamī was neither an extension of the will of the political establishment nor an opposition to the establishment. He belonged to the establishment and yet was determined to reform it without harming it. As a result, he remained in a difficult and paradoxical position, making him marginal for both the state and the reform movement. Moreover, the reformists lacked the strong, grassroots, and inclusive organizations required for a successful public mobilization. In addition to the domestic factors, international politics proved detrimental to the success of the reformists. Khātamī's idea of "dialogue between civilizations" gained recognition by the United Nations, which declared the year 2001 the official year of dialogue between civilizations. Khātamī's UN speech "raised hopes for a détente" with the United States, but President Bush's "axis of evil" speech in 2002 increased speculation that the United States was bent on regime change in both Iraq and Iran. Bush's speech shocked the reformists, provided a pretext to Iran's hard-liners to raise the flag of national security, and persuaded some reformers "to put their hopes on the back burner waiting for better days" (Abrahamian, 2004, pp. 93–94).

The electorate cast their vote for Khātamī's democratic reform twice, in the 1997 and 2001 presidential elections. They also voted overwhelmingly for the reformers in the municipal elections of 1999 and the parliamentary elections of 2000. Incapable of meeting the public demands and unable to deal with the counter-reform forces, reformists in power began to lose public support in three major elections: the February 2003 second municipal elections, the February 2004 seventh parliamentary elections, and eventually the June 2005 ninth presidential elections. The reformist republic gave birth to a republic of hard-liner conservatives, the fourth republic of post-revolutionary Iran.

The Fourth Republic (2005–2013). The 2005 presidential election marked a new era in the Khomeinist state: neoconservative Khomeinism. The president of Iran's fourth republic (2005–2013), Mahmoud Ahmadinejad, was a product of the state-security apparatus, the office of the *vilāyat-i faqīh*, and Iran's neoconservatives. Sadeq Mahsouli, former minister of welfare under Ahmadinejad, and Mohammad-reza Rahimi, Ahmadinejad's vice president, among others, were members of the new oligarchy. The former was a billionaire real estate broker and the latter was another billionaire benefiting from exclusive political rents. The populist slogans in the fourth republic were instrumental in serving their pragmatist purpose, that is, to replace the old oligarchy with a new one and to establish a populist, centralized state backed by the lower classes and sponsored by petro-dollars.

With the rise of Iran's neoconservatives to power, the Islamic republic's social base may have shifted from the coalition of the *mullah*-merchant to that of the revolutionary security and military forces. The conservatives, in spite of their internal conflicts, gained complete control of the state, and the absolute rule of the *vali-ye faqīh* Khamene'i seemed at hand. However, for the first time in the Islamic republic, the public and the reformist elites openly challenged the authority and legitimacy of the *vali-ye faqīh* in the popular democratic Green Movement in 2009.

The Fifth Republic (2013). In the presidential elections on 14 June 2013, Hassan Rouhāni was elected as the seventh president of the Islamic Republic of Iran. His four-year term, which started on 3 August 2013, brought to an end Iran's fourth republic (Ahmadinejad's presidency) and began Iran's fifth republic.

Rouhāni is not a reformist. He is close to *vali-ye faqīh* Khamene'i and the traditional conservatives. However, he is also close to Hāshimī Rafsanjānī, the pragmatist president of the second republic. In his presidential campaign, Rouhāni openly challenged domestic and foreign policies of Ahmadinejd. He promised to pull Iran back from the brink of the negative economic growth, political repression, and international sanctions. Muḥammad Khātamī, the reformist president of the third republic, supported Rouhāni's plan for change. The electorate cast their vote for his campaign slogans of "moderation" (*e'tedāl*), "hope" (*omid*), and "wisdom" (*tadbīr*). It remains to be seen whether he is competent to normalize Iran's relations with its neighbors and the West, resolve the nuclear issue, push back the rising power of the state-security apparatus in the economy and politics, fix the economy, ease the political repression, and release the political prisoners, including the public figures of the Green Movement.

The Green Movement. The Green Movement formed in the wake of the disputed June 2009 presidential election. The incumbent president Mahmoud Ahmadinejad claimed victory in the election, and the *vali-ye faqīh* Khamene'i endorsed these results. However, the reformist candidates Mir-Hossein Mousavi, a former prime minister, and Mehdi Karroubi, former speaker of the Majlis, challenged them. Grand Ayatollah Muntazirī gave his blessing to the movement. Millions of people from religious and secular backgrounds demonstrated in the streets. They chanted *Ra'ye man kojāst?* (Where is my vote?), waving green banners, the color Mousavi used for his campaign. Pro-government forces attacked the peaceful demonstrations and killed, jailed, and tortured many demonstrators.

The Green Movement is the latest chapter in the Iranian people's long quest for freedom and social justice. It marks a turn in the country's politics to a still-emerging post-Islamist phase.

Post-Islamism. Similar to Islamism, post-Islamism accepts public religion. Contrary to Islamism, it rejects the concept of Islamic state. While religion might play a constructive role in civil society, the state should be a secular entity, no matter who the statesman is. The Islamic state in theory is an oxymoron; in practice, it is no less than a clerical oligarchy, a leviathan that protects the interests of the ruling class. Hence, the concept of the Islamic state marks a distinction between post-Islamism and Islamism, including moderate Islamism.

Today's Iran is on the brink of a post-Islamist turn, as the first post-Islamist civil society in the Middle East is in the making. Post-Islamism in Iran maybe divided into three main intellectual trends: semi-post-Islamism represented by reformists such as Mir-Hossein Mousavi, Mehdi Karroubi, Muḥammad Khātamī, and Ayatollah Muntazirī; liberal post-Islamism represented by Abdolkarim Soroush, Mohammad Mojtahed-Shabestari, and Mostafa Malekian, among others; and neo-Sharī'atī discourse represented by 'Alī Sharī'atī's family, Reza Alijani and Taqi Rahmani (Mahdavi, 2011). The scope and intensity of the discursive changes toward post-Islamism are evident in the statements of public figures of the Green Movement. Although Mousavi still believes in the doctrine of *vilāyat-i faqīh*, he has gradually moved toward greater recognition of pluralism in the nation, claiming that his position is one among many other secular and Islamic voices in the Green Movement (Mousavi, 2010). In his statement known as a working draft of the "Covenant of the Green Movement," Mousavi advocates the separation of "religious institutions and clergymen from the state," although he acknowledges the "presence" of religion in the future of Iran. He "opposes the use of religion as an instrument and coercing people into an ideology." People want nothing short of "popular sovereignty." Similarly, Mehdi Karroubi questions the authority of the *vali-ye faqīh* Khameneʾi. In his last public speech in support of the Green Movement, Ayatollah Muntazirī boldly argued that this regime is neither Islamic nor a republic; it is a mere dictatorship (Montazeri, 2010). The Green Movement, in sum, signifies a radical epistemic shift in Iran's political culture toward celebrating pluralism, coexistence of religious and secular agents, and embracing nonviolence.

Many of the reformist Khomeinists, those who accompanied Khomeini on his return to Iran from France, are now in open revolt. Khameneʾi and his cronies, they believe, have betrayed Khomeni's legacy. The reformist Khomeinists seek a peaceful transformation within the Khomeinist system. On the other hand, the political spectrum of the Green Movement is both broader and more radical than the reformist discourse. In addition to the quest for free elections and civil rights, it seems that Khomeini's legacy of the absolute *vilāyat-i faqīh* is no longer acceptable to the public. Iran seems to be inching toward the post-Khomeinism era.

BIBLIOGRAPHY

Abrahamian, Ervand. "Empire Strikes Back: Iran in U.S. Sights." In *Inventing the Axis of Evil*, edited by Bruce Cumings, Ervand Abrahamian, and Moshe Ma'oz. New York: The New Press, 2004.

Abrahamian, Ervand. *Radical Islam: The Iranian Mojahedin*. London: I. B. Tauris, 1989.

Abrahamian, Ervand. *Tortured Confessions: Prisons and Public Recantations in Modern Iran*. Berkeley: University of California Press, 1999.

Algar, Hamid. *Islam and Revolution: Writings and Declarations of Imam Khomeini*. Berkeley: Mizan Press, 1981.

Amir Arjomand, Said. "Authority in Shiism and Constitutional Development in the Islamic Republic of Iran." In *The Twelver Shia in the Modern Times: Religious Culture and Political History*, edited by Rainer Brunner and Werner Ende. Leiden: Brill, 2001.

Ansari, Ali M. *Modern Iran since 1921: The Pahlavis and After*. London: Pearson Education, 2003.

Bakhash, Shaul. "Iran's Remarkable Election." In *Islam and Democracy in the Middle East*, edited by Larry Diamond, Marc F. Plattner, and D. Brumberg. Baltimore: The Johns Hopkins University Press, 2003.

Bashiriyeh, Hossein. *The State and Revolution in Iran, 1962–1982*. New York: St. Martin's Press, 1984.

Brumberg, Daniel. *Reinventing Khomeini: The Struggle for Reform in Iran*. Chicago: University of Chicago Press, 2001.

Chehabi, H. E. "The Political Regime of the Islamic Republic of Iran in Comparative Perspective." *Government and Opposition* 36, no.1 (2000): 48–70.

Chehabi, H.E. "The Provisional Government and the Transition from Monarchy to Islamic Republic in Iran." In *Between States: Interim Governments and Democratic Transitions*, edited by Yossi Shain and J. Linz. New York: Cambridge University Press, 1995.

Khomeini, R. *Velayat-e Faqih, Hokomat-e Islami* [The Rule of the Jurisprudent, Islamic Government]. Tehran: Amir Kabir, 1978.

Mahdavi, Mojtaba."Post-Islamist Trends in Postrevolutionary Iran." *Comparative Studies of South Asia, Africa and the Middle East* 31, no. 1 (2011): 94–109.

Milani, Mohsen M. "Reform and Resistance in the Islamic Republic of Iran." In *Iran at the Crossroads*, edited by John L. Esposito and R. K. Ramazani. New York: Palgrave, 2001.

"Montazeri's Last Public Statement." *Jaras* (Rahesabz online), February 2010, www.rahesabz.net/story/8775/.

Moslem, Mehdi. *Factional Politics in Post-Khomeini Iran*. Syracuse, N.Y.: Syracuse University Press, 2002.

Mousavi, Mir-Hossein. *The 18th Statement*. http://khordaad88.com/?cat=1.

Rahnema, Saeed. "The Left and the Struggle for Democracy in Iran." In *Reformers and Revolutionaries in Modern Iran: New Perspectives on the Iranian Left*, edited by Stephanie Cronin. London and New York: Routledge Curzon, 2004.

Rahnema, Saeed, and Haideh Moghissi. "Clerical Oligarchy and the Question of Democracy in Iran." *Monthly Review* 52, no. 10 (2001).

Schirazi, Asghar. *The Constitution of Iran: Politics and the State in the Islamic Republic*, translated by John O'Kane. London and New York: I. B. Tauris, 1997.

MOJTABA MAHDAVI

Iranian Revolution of 1979. The Iranian Revolution of 1979 was many years in the making. In simple terms, the regime of Muhammad Reza Shah Pahlavi was overthrown by a coalition of opposition forces dominated by Shīʿī Muslim fundamentalists. The acknowledged leader of the revolution was Ayatollah Ruhollah al-Musavi Khomeini (1902–1989). Although the specific events leading up to the ouster of the shah took place over a period of approximately one year before his departure from Iran on 16 January 1979, the social conditions underlying the revolution spanned several centuries.

Early Religious-Secular Conflict. The Ithnā ʿAsharī (Twelver) branch of Shīʿī Islam had been the official state religion in Iran since the founding of the Ṣafavid dynasty in the sixteenth century. Almost from the beginning of Ṣafavid rule, religious officials criticized the court for laxity in observance of Islam, establishing an opposition between religious and secular leadership that continued into the twentieth century.

The impoverished shahs of the nineteenth-century Qājār dynasty found themselves in military and economic conflict with European powers. They faced growing criticism by the clergy over territorial losses, foreign economic penetration, and incompetent government. The Qājārs began to sell agricultural and commercial concessions to foreigners to raise money. Religious leaders, inspired by the efforts of the reformer Jamāl al-Dīn al-Afghānī (d. 1897), became alarmed at the marketing of the Iranian patrimony and launched a series of public protests. This culminated in the Constitutional Revolution of 1905–1911, in which the Qājār monarch was forced to accept a constitution and a parliament. About twenty years later the dynasty collapsed.

The rivalry between the successor Pahlavi dynasty (1925–1979) and Khomeini had a long history. In 1921, Reza Khan, an army officer, emerged as a national leader. Ruhollah Khomeini was then entering theological studies in the shrine city of Qom south of Tehran. In 1926 Reza Khan formally crowned himself Reza Shah and established the Pahlavi dynasty. Khomeini was qualified as a *mullah* that same year.

Reza Shah ignored the new constitution and ruled by decree, initiating a series of drastic reforms in Iranian life designed to modernize the nation, many of which were directed at the religious establishment. Religious institutions were placed under the control of the state, thus depriving the clergy of a major source of power and income. Public protests, supported by the clergy against these reforms, were ruthlessly suppressed.

In September 1941 Reza Shah was forced by the Allied powers to abdicate for his pro-German sentiments. He was succeeded by his young son, Muhammad Reza. Ayatollah Ruhollah Khomeini then began a long career of attacking the Pahlavi regime. He started in 1941 in an essay, "Kashf al-Asrār" (Unveiling of the Mysteries), in which he suggested that decisions from the throne should first involve consultation with the clergy. His frustration with the shah's rule increased from year to year, culminating in December 1969 and January 1970 in a series of lectures in which he espoused the controversial view that the *mullah* should not just teach and advise; they should play the central role in governing the country. This doctrine decrees that the legitimate rule of the twelfth imam of Twelver Shiism, Muḥammad al-Mahdī, who disappeared into "occultation" in the ninth century, should be carried out under the doctrine of *wilāyat al-faqīh* (regency of the chief religious jurisprudent), who would govern until the Mahdī's return to earth.

In 1964 Khomeini, now acclaimed as an Ayatollah, was exiled by the shah. His religious status prevented his outright execution. After seven months in Turkey, he settled in the Shīʿī holy city of Najaf, Iraq, where he continued to issue pronouncements against the Pahlavi regime.

The National Front. Secular oppositionists with claims to leadership also arose in the years following World War II. Chief among these was a coalition of parties known as the National Front, established in 1949 and led by Mohammad Mossadegh. Mossadegh had opposed Reza Shah's ascent to the throne in 1926. The National Front espoused many of the revolutionary ideals of the Islamic reformers, such as limiting the powers of the shah and ending foreign domination, but it did not advocate Islamic dominance of government.

The popularity of the National Front brought Mossadegh to power as prime minister in 1951. He came into conflict both with religious leaders and with the shah, who tried unsuccessfully to oust him from office. The shah was forced to flee in 1953, but the United States and Great Britain promptly restored the shah to power. This act established the United States as the chief foreign interventionist in Iranian affairs.

Another important opposition group was the Mujāhidīn-i Khalq (People's Warriors), established in 1965 from other similar opposition groups. Their doctrine combined Islamic religious commitment with socialist doctrine.

Prelude to Revolution. The United States continued active support of the shah. It anointed him as a protector of Western interests in the Persian Gulf and sold Iran advanced weaponry to support a powerful military. Under U.S. pressure, the shah launched a massive economic and social reform program in 1963 known as the White Revolution. Economic growth was furthered through foreign investment in partnership with the throne and other economic elites.

In 1971 Britain withdrew its military from the Persian Gulf, and the United States began to arm Iran even more heavily. Then, in 1973 Iran and Saudi Arabia led the Organization of Petroleum Exporting Countries (OPEC) in a massive price increase in crude oil, providing the shah with even more funds for military and economic development.

Growth of the gross national product (GNP) continued, but the national income was derived almost exclusively from petroleum sales, and profits were limited largely to the top echelons of society. The shah thus achieved financial independence from the Iranian people and enjoyed seemingly unlimited control in the exercise of power.

Consequently, the shah and his largely technocratic ministries turned the nation into a private economic and social laboratory based largely on Western modernist thinking. Life became uncomfortable, as the traditional population was shocked by the sudden appearance of public behavior that they deemed indecent. One noted social critic, ʿAlī Sharīʿatī (1933–1977), accused the regime of "Westoxication" or "Occidentosis" (*gharbzadagī*, literally "West-struckness") in the pursuit of Euro-American modernity at any social price. By 1975, despite GNP growth, inflation had begun to make itself felt at a rate exceeding 60 percent. Agricultural production went into a steep decline. Iran became a net importer of meat and grains for the first time. Housing costs rose precipitously. Ordinary Iranians, particularly those on fixed incomes, or on rigidly limited government salaries, began to suffer. The government of Jamshīd Amūzgār (August 1977) cut off subsidies to the clergy and religious institutions that had been instituted by the former prime minister, Amīr ʿAbbās Huvaydah. The shah later identified this act as the mistake that caused his downfall. Large sections of the traditional population became alienated. This gave the religious establishment its opening, and the revolutionary exhortations of Ayatollah Khomeini began to take effect throughout the population.

The Revolution. On 9 January 1978, theology students in the city of Qom began a protest against a pseudonymous article published in the newspaper *Itt'ilā'āt* accusing Ayatollah Khomeini of licentious behavior and crimes against the state. The author was widely thought to have been Minister of Information Daryūsh Humāyūn (Daryoush Homayoun). The demonstration met with violent confrontation by the police. Several students died, touching off a cycle of mourning ceremonies, which turned into increasingly violent public demonstrations.

Protests increased throughout the spring and summer. On 7 September 1978, the shah declared martial law and banned all demonstrations. Unfortunately, word of this decree had not spread. A demonstration in Jaleh Square in Tehran was confronted by the military, and a large number of defenseless people were shot. Protests then spread to every part of the nation.

The shah seemed to have no strategy for dealing with the crisis. Though it was not generally known at the time, he was sick with lymphatic cancer, which contributed to his irresolute behavior. He tried a number of tactics to defuse the revolution, changing prime ministers and ordering arrests. Finally, he coerced Iraqi officials into expelling Khomeini, who eventually settled in Neauphle-le-Château, a suburb of Paris. Ironically, he was better able to communicate with internal revolutionary forces from Paris by way of long-distance telephone than from Iraq. Khomeini's powerful central message was the same one that religious oppositionists had been preaching for a hundred years: the shah had conspired with foreign powers—primarily the United States—to exploit the Iranian people and undermine Islam.

Eventually, it became clear to the shah that he must leave Iran if stability were to be preserved. He attempted to appoint several different men to serve as prime minister in a caretaker role, but all refused. Finally, Shahpour Bakhtiar (Shāpūr Bakhtiyār), a venerable National Front politician, accepted the job in order to allow the shah to leave. On 16 January 1979, the shah left Iran. The United States dispatched General Robert Huyser to Tehran to ensure the support of the Iranian military for the Bakhtiar government. Bakhtiar was, however, doomed from the start, as Khomeini appointed his own Provisional Revolutionary Government headed by another National Front politician, Mehdi Bāzargān. The real power during January and February of 1979 resided in roving *komitehs* (committees) of revolutionaries organized in mosques. They joined veteran guerrilla fighters, such as the Mujāhidīn-i Khalq, to rule the streets of the large cities.

Khomeini returned to Iran on 1 February 1979, with great public enthusiasm. Units of the military began to defect. Tension between military groups reached a climax on 9 February 1979, in the victory of air force cadets and technicians who had declared their loyalty to Khomeini over the shah's Imperial Guards at the air force base at Doshan Tappeh on the outskirts of Tehran. This touched off a series of armed confrontations throughout the capital. On 11 February, the Supreme Military Council announced that the military would no longer participate in the political crisis. Bakhtiar fled to Paris and the Khomeini-led government officially assumed power. The anniversary of the Revolution is now designated as 11 February.

The Aftermath of the Revolution. February to November 1979 was a transitional period in which the religious leaders fully established themselves in power in Iran. The Provisional Revolutionary Government established by Khomeini consisted largely of nonclerical National Front leaders. These leaders favored a secular democracy based on European models. Hard-line religionists, however, had a different vision, favoring an outright Islamic theocracy. On 30–31 March, the Provisional Revolutionary Government held a national referendum asking whether Iran should become an Islamic republic. Official tallies put the "yes" vote at 98 percent.

The nation next decided on a constitution for the new government. After several drafts, the proposed constitution invested ultimate power in a *faqīh* (chief jurisprudent), along with a five-person religious Council of Guardians. The secular National Front leaders led extensive public opposition, fearing, as Bāzargān asserted, a new "dictatorship of the clergy." Fate intervened in the constitutional ratification process. The former shah, now deathly ill, appealed to the United States for medical treatment. Despite dire warnings from the U.S. embassy in Tehran, the Carter administration allowed him to fly to New York on 22 October 1979.

The reaction in Tehran was immediate. On November 4 a group of students took over the U.S. embassy and took all its personnel hostage. The Americans remained captive for 444 days, touching off huge anti-American protests. Officials of the Provisional Revolutionary Government, notably Bāzargān, were blamed for the decision to seek refuge for the shah in the United States and subsequently resigned. On 2–3 December 1979, the nation accepted the new constitution with a 99 percent "yes" vote, establishing a theocracy with Khomeini at its head.

In the ten years from the onset of the revolution until Khomeini's death on 3 June 1989, the new government groped its way toward stability. Despite continued infighting between political factions, internal political transitions were generally peaceful. A debilitating war with Iraq, begun in September 1980, was fought to a standstill in July 1988. The continued power of the *komitehs* and their successors, the Sipāh-i Pāsdārān-i Inqilāb-i Islāmī (Revolutionary Guard), caused alarm. These groups continued to enforce a rough-and-ready Islamic morality, in addition to keeping the peace. The new government continued to be hostile toward the United States but improved its relations with most other nations. Ayatollah Khomeini was replaced by Ayatollah ʿAlī Khameneʾi,one of his followers, who had also served a term as president.

Although opposition to the monarchy had long existed in Iran, no one could have predicted with certainty that the final outcome of the revolution would be a theocratic government. For Muslims eager for reform and escape from Western domination, in Iran and in other nations, the revolution was a deeply inspirational event. For secular nationalists and for most of the Western world, the Revolution continues to be seen as a threat.

[*See also* Afghānī, Jamāl al-Dīn al-; Iran, Islamic Republic of; Khomeini, Ruhollah al-Musavi; Sharīʿatī, ʿAlī; *and* Wilāyat al-Faqīh.]

BIBLIOGRAPHY

Akhavi, Shahrough. *Religion and Politics in Contemporary Iran: Clergy-State Relations in the Pahlavi Period*. Albany, N.Y.: State University of New York Press, 1980. Important work laying out the background leading to systematic clerical opposition to Pahlavi rule in Iran.

Arjomand, Said Amir. *The Turban for the Crown: The Islamic Revolution in Iran*. New York and Oxford: Oxford University Press, 1988. One of the most complete accounts of the events of the revolution from an acknowledged expert on Iranian contemporary history and politics.

Bakhash, Shaul. *The Reign of the Ayatollahs: Iran and the Islamic Revolution*. Rev. ed. New York: Basic Books, 1990. Account of the revolution by a seasoned journalist and historian, highly critical of the religious regime.

Beeman, William O. *The "Great Satan vs. the Mad Mullahs": How the United States and Iran Demonize Each Other*. Westport, Conn.: Praeger, 2005. Extensive treatment of the estrangement of the United States and Iran as a result of the Revolution.

Bill, James A. *The Eagle and the Lion: The Tragedy of American-Iranian Relations*. New Haven, Conn.: Yale University Press, 1988. Account of relations between the United States and Iran during the Pahlavi era showing how the Iranian government systematically hid its internal political actions from U.S. officials.

Ebadi, Shirin, and Azadeh Moaveni. *Iran Awakening: A Memoir of Revolution and Hope*. New York: Random House, 2006. Nobel Peace Prize winner Ebadi teams with *Time* correspondent and author Moaveni to present a personal memoir of an intrepid reformer in the post-Revolutionary period.

Fischer, Michael M. J. *Iran: From Religious Dispute to Revolution*. Cambridge, Mass.: Harvard University Press, 1984. Classic anthropological work showing how the revolution was constructed in Shīʿī religious symbolic terms by the militant clergy.

Huyser, Robert E. *Mission to Tehran*. New York: Harper and Row, 1986. The final word by the American general thought to have engineered the Iranian military's capitulation to the Kohmeini-led revolutionary government.

Keddie, Nikki R. *Roots of Revolution: An Interpretive History of Modern Iran*. New Haven, Conn.: Yale University Press, 1981.

Keddie, Nikki R., ed. *Religion and Politics in Iran: Shiʿism from Quietism to Revolution*. New Haven, Conn.: Yale University Press, 1983. Two important works by a premier historian of Iran detailing centuries of confrontation between religious and secular officials.

Khomeini, Ruhollah. *Islam and Revolution: Writings and Declarations of Imam Khomeini*. Translated and annotated by Hamid Algar. Berkeley, Calif.: Mizan Press, 1981. Ayatollah Khomeini's philosophy of revolution and government in his own words.

Kurzman, Charles. *The Unthinkable Revolution in Iran*. Cambridge, Mass.: Harvard University Press, 2004. Sociologist Kurzman examines five sets of analytic accounts of the Iranian revolution—political, organizational, cultural, economic, and military—and finds each valid but problematic.

Ramazani, Ruhollah K. *Revolutionary Iran: Challenge and Response in the Middle East*. Baltimore: The Johns Hopkins University Press, 1986. Excellent account of government and international relations in postrevolutionary Iran.

Rubin, Barry. *Paved with Good Intentions: The American Experience and Iran*. New York: Oxford University Press, 1980. Masterful review of U.S. military and development efforts in the period leading up to the revolution.

Sick, Gary. *All Fall Down: America's Tragic Encounter with Iran*. New York: Random House, 1985. The Iranian Revolution from the standpoint of a U.S. military analyst who saw it all.

Wright, Robin. *In the Name of God: The Khomeini Decade*. New York: Simon and Schuster, 1989. A journalist's account of Khomeini's leadership in Iran, replete with facts and dates.

Wright, Robin. *The Last Great Revolution: Turmoil and Transformation in Iran*. New York: Alfred A. Knopf, 2000. Journalist Robin Wright provides many insightful interviews and direct observations of ordinary Iranians highlighting the effects of the Revolution.

Zonis, Marvin. *Majestic Failure: The Fall of the Shah*. Chicago: University of Chicago Press, 1991. The author's account of the shah's failure to respond to the revolutionary challenge to his regime is based on his theory that the shah was unable to cope psychologically with a series of personal tragedies in the last years of his regime.

WILLIAM O. BEEMAN

IRAQ. Since its inception, Iraq has been perilously divided among three key constituent communities—the Shīʿī, the Sunnī Arabs, and the Kurds. Sunnī Arabs have historically dominated the state, and are the primary force that led to the creation, development, and bureaucratization of the modern Iraqi state. However, since 2003 there has been a significant change in fortunes. The Kurdish population has managed to attain, as a formal, legal matter, the broad self-rule it had long sought for itself, and the Shīʿī dominate Iraqi politics from Baghdad. It is now the Sunnī Arabs who feel marginalized and alienated. Irrespective of who is in control, however, the same core problem remains for Iraq that existed at the time of its creation; namely, the difficulty of finding a way for three distinct identitarian communities with vastly different conceptions of ideal state structure and organization to coexist in the same political state as a single nation.

Historical Background: 1921–2003. Iraq was created by a League of Nations mandate awarded to the British in 1920. In many ways, its existing severe political divisions date back to its turbulent formation. The British chose Faisal ibn Hussein ibn ʿAli, who had led the Arab revolt against the Ottomans during the World War I, to lead the Iraqi government as its reigning monarch. The Iraqi notables who gathered around Faisal to form the backbone of the Iraqi government were those loyal to him from the days of the Arab revolt.

Sunnī Arabs dominated the Iraqi political scene from its inception until the fall of the Saddam Hussein regime in 2003. The political movements they led, which in turn led the state, were generally pan-Arab in outlook, from the monarchy to the nationalists who led the 1958 revolution to the even more pan-Arab Baʿath, who eventually took complete control of the state apparatus in 1968 and remained in control until 2003.

The Kurds and the Shīʿīs, by contrast, largely populated other parties. For the Kurds, the dominant political movement was the Kurdish Democratic Party, or KDP, formed by younger Kurdish notables, chief among them Muṣṭafā al-Barzānī, during the 1930s. A second party, known as the Patriotic Union of Kurdistan, or PUK, eventually emerged as well, led by Jalal Talabani and Ibrāhīm Aḥmad, the latter of whom broke off from the KDP after differences with Barzānī. The two parties were often in conflict with one another, though both purported to be established on the principle of demanding greater self-rule for the Kurds. Indeed, their negotiations with Baghdad were generally framed around this central demand.

The other major, national party with significant Kurdish following in Iraq's early years was the Iraq Communist Party, or ICP. This was equally true of the Shīʿī, making the ICP perhaps the only large party that extended broadly across ethnic and sectarian lines. The appeal of communism to these two politically marginalized and economically disadvantaged communities, who together constituted nearly three-quarters of Iraq's population, caused no small amount of consternation among Iraq's traditional ruling elites. Though some Iraqi leaders, among them ʿAbd al-Karīm Qāsim and even the Baʿath, sought to negotiate with the communists at various times throughout Iraqi history, no lasting means of integrating them into Iraq's ruling framework was found. In the end, the communists were ruthlessly suppressed by the Baʿath throughout the 1970s and disappeared from the political scene after that.

A second political movement developed among the Shīʿīs after communism, largely in the 1970s, and it has come to dominate Shīʿī politics in the contemporary era. This is political Islam, defined in its early days in Iraq in the personality of the Najaf-trained cleric Muḥammad Bāqir al-Ṣadr. Through the political party he helped found—Daʿwah, or the Islamic Call—al-Ṣadr sought to reinvigorate Islam as a social and political force and enhance the role of the Shīʿī clergy at the center of this revival. Though al-Ṣadr made efforts at ecumenism, particularly in his early work, Daʿwah was unmistakably Shīʿī, with little or no Sunnī or Kurdish representation. Ultimately, al-Ṣadr espoused a theory of juristic rule in politics that resembled Khomeini's famed Guardianship of the Jurist, and he paid for his political activism with his life in 1980.

Severe repression of Shīʿī Islamist movements followed al-Ṣadr's execution, and their presence in Iraq came to an end. The views of the quietist Grand Ayatollah Abul Qasim al-Khuʾi, who disdained any role for the jurists in politics, came to dominate Najaf. The Islamists were killed by the Ba'ath, or they fled. Two of the sons of the long deceased but still highly respected Grand Ayatollah Muḥsin al-Ḥakīm, Muḥammad Bāqir al-Ḥakīm and ʿAbdul ʿAzīz al-Ḥakīm, left for Iran and founded a group known as the Supreme Council for the Islamic Revolution in Iraq

(SCIRI). Other Daʿwah leaders fled to Syria or the West. With the forceful suppression of Daʿwah throughout the 1980s, the existence of all political associations and organizations other than the Baʿath came to an end. Baʿath domination of Iraqi politics became total.

Iraq: 2003–2005. With the fall of the Saddam Hussein regime in 2003, exile parties were the first to fill the vacuum that had been created by the sudden removal of a totalitarian party. As was the case throughout Iraq's history, the parties were largely organized around ethnicity and sect. Chief among the Shīʿī parties were SCIRI, still led by the Ḥakīm brothers, and a remnant of Daʿwah, initially led by Ibrāhīm Jaʿfarī. These parties had largely moderated their Islamist message, no longer seeking juristic control of the state, though they did seek to project religious authority prominently in some areas and to assert constitutional controls over the enactment of legislation deemed contrary to core Islamic sensibilities. Most telling, in the early years, was their effort to repeal Iraq's Personal Status Code and to replace it with no more than uncodified Sharīʿah, with each person bound by the rules of his own sect. If such a repeal is ever put in place—and it is contemplated under Article 41 of Iraq's current constitution—it would be a dramatic realignment of rule-making authority in the area of personal status, away from the state and in favor of the Najaf clergy.

Within a year of Saddam's fall, one other lasting Shīʿī political movement arose, also Islamist, the Sadrist Trend. Led by Muqtadā al-Ṣadr, the core support of the Sadrist Trend lay among the substantial numbers of neglected Shīʿī poor who found Muqtadā a compelling figure, a scion of a clerical family who had remained in Iraq throughout the entirety of Baʿath rule. In the early years, the Sadrist Trend, while engaged politically, often found itself at odds with the state. It fought a series of battles with the United States, and later the Iraqi army, and sought to project authority and control unilaterally in various parts of Iraq.

Among the Kurds, the KDP and the PUK had largely unified insofar as national politics were concerned, and they came to dominate the Kurdish political scene. Their main aim has been the preservation and extension of the autonomy that the Kurds have enjoyed since 1991 by virtue of a no-fly zone imposed over their region by the United Nations Security Council after the First Gulf War.

As for the Sunnīs—who had long dominated the state and whose domination was coming to an end after a foreign intervention to which they had not consented—they were initially broadly alienated and isolated from the state. Little was done to encourage their participation by either the United States or the historically persecuted Shīʿīs or Kurds, all of whom seemed more intent on exacting revenge, most often by removing (often Sunnī) Baʿathists from their positions in the government, than finding a means of reintegrating Sunnīs. The immediate result of this marginalization and consequent disaffection was the rise of a Sunnī insurgency and the dangerous proliferation of a terrorist organization dubbing itself al-Qaʿida in Iraq.

Finally, beyond the political parties and their constituencies, it would be a mistake to disregard Najaf's clerics themselves, and chiefly the leader of Najaf since the fall of Saddam Hussein, Grand Ayatollah ʿAlī al-Sīstānī. Sīstānī was the main domestic political force behind accelerated elections and the subsequent drafting of an Iraqi constitution. Sīstānī hardly desired political authority himself in the manner that Khomeini and Ṣadr had once espoused, but he did seek to marginalize American influence and solidify Shīʿī control of the state apparatus at the earliest available opportunity. He insisted as early as June 2003 that the body that would write the constitution of Iraq would have to be elected by the Iraqi people. He also used the maximum leverage available to him as Iraq's supreme jurisprudent to create a unified Shīʿī list to run in that first election, held in January 2005. The Kurds proved amenable to this timetable and ran a combined list of the KDP and the PUK, thereby resulting in a healthy proportion of the body responsible for preparing a constitution for referendum. The problem lay in the fact that the Sunnīs remained as disaffected as ever and boycotted the election. Thus, an election demanded by the Shīʿī clerical elite had exposed the raw fault lines of ethnicity and sect that ran the course of Iraq's history, in a manner that proved existentially dangerous.

The United States belatedly recognized the problem and used maximum influence to successfully force Sunnī inclusion into constitutional negotiations, over Shīʿī and Kurdish objections. Ultimately, however, the drafting process ended in acrimony. The appointed Sunnī leaders, Arab nationalists in the historic Sunnī tradition, regarded with anathema the possibility that autonomous regions other than Kurdistan (the latter of which was a fait accompli since 1991) could be created in Iraq. SCIRI and the Kurds were equally insistent that the option be retained. The constitution contemplated the possibility, SCIRI threatened to exercise it, and the Sunnīs abandoned the negotiations and voted against the constitution in large numbers in a subsequent referendum. Their opposition, however, was not sufficient to prevent the constitution's ratification. Sunnī disaffection continued, the security situation continued to deteriorate, and Iraq entered into a horrific phase of sectarian bloodletting after the bombing of a Shīʿī holy shrine, the al-Askari Mosque, in 2006.

Iraq since 2006. Much has transpired since that sectarian conflict, much of it salutary. Having long abandoned what turned out to be a disastrous electoral boycott, Iraq's Sunnī population now regularly elects its leaders. The first party to enjoy broad Sunnī support was the coalition known as Tawāfuq, moderately Islamist in orientation and led by Aʿyād al-Samarraʾī, who served as speaker of Iraq's legislature. The elections of 2010 were devastating to Tawāfuq, which retained only one seat. The primary party enjoying Sunnī support currently is, entirely in keeping with historical tradition, a nationalist one, known as Iraqīya, more secular than Tawāfuq and more strident in its criticisms of Iraq's current government. It purports to be nonsectarian, and, indeed, one of its primary leaders, ʿAyād ʿAllāwī, is Shīʿī, but whatever Shīʿī support it enjoys is limited to a small sliver of Baghdad's urban intelligentsia. In almost every Shīʿī-dominated province, Iraqīya does remarkably poorly.

While the same principal Islamist protagonists continue to dominate Shīʿī politics, there has been a sea change respecting their relative influence. SCIRI's influence has waned, and Daʿwah has surged, having emerged under the unchallenged leadership of the current prime minister, Nūrī al-Mālikī, under the new banner "The Coalition for the State of Law." The Sadrist Trend also enjoyed something of a political renaissance. After a series of devastating military and electoral setbacks that came about after they sought to project authority through their militia, the Sadrists began to deemphasize their earlier reliance on violence and to engage more seriously in Iraqi politics. Since then, their political base has remained loyal and stable. They are a potent force in the Iraqi legislature. They are also staunchly Islamist and unreservedly anti-American.

In addition, both they and Daʿwah, under Mālikī, are centralists, resembling the traditional Sunnī parties in their calls to Iraqi nationalism and their objections to the fragmentation of the state through the deployment of strong forms of federalism. This has gone some way toward mollifying Sunnī nationalists, at least in their concerns over the creation of Shīʿī autonomous regions. Sunnī leaders have as a result largely reassessed their earlier criticisms of the constitution, now going so far as to invoke its provisions when they feel that Mālikī has transgressed them.

Ironically, and more ominously, disaffected Sunnīs in various provinces have begun to invoke the same federalist demands that had led to the initial Sunnī abandonment of constitutional negotiations in 2004, with some provinces going so far as to call for a referendum to enable them to become autonomous regions. Such moves have seemed isolated and lacking in political momentum, having failed to gather even the support of Iraqīya's strong nationalist leaders in Baghdad. They are nonetheless telling of the extent of continued Sunnī disaffection with the state, which could prove extremely destabilizing over the medium to long term. Such disaffection has led to mass demonstrations in Sunnī parts of the country that began late in 2012 and has continued into 2013. Whether such demonstrations will lead to the outbreak of another eruption of sectarian violence, or whether the Iraqi government will be able to mollify the protestors through concessions, remains an open question.

The least change has been among the Kurds, where the PUK and the KDP continue to dominate the political landscape. Since late 2008, an opposition party, known as Goran or Kurdish for "change," has emerged. It has castigated the major parties for mismanagement and corruption and has considerable support among the Kurdish urban youth disaffected by the sclerotic bureaucracy and rampant corruption evident throughout the region. However, as for now, Goran remains a distinctly minority party, both in the regional legislature of Kurdistan and in Iraq's parliament in Baghdad.

Iraqi politics therefore remains as perilously divided as it has always been. Its parties are built upon strong historical edifices that are largely defined by ethnicity and sect. However, levels of violence are dramatically reduced from where they were only a few years ago, and severe political disputes, at least for now, are resolved in legislature and meeting hall, pursuant to a constitution that all parties purport to regard as legitimate and sovereign. While the situation is hardly ideal, such a divided society could easily be in a worse political condition than this.

BIBLIOGRAPHY

Allawi, Ali A. *The Occupation of Iraq: Winning the War, Losing the Peace.* New Haven, Conn.: Yale University Press, 2007.

Farouk-Sluglett, Marion, and Sluglett, Peter. *Iraq since 1958: From Revolution to Dictatorship.* Rev. ed. London: I. B. Tauris, 2003.

Hamoudi, Haider Ala. "Identitarian Violence and Identitarian Politics: Elections and Governance in Iraq," *Harvard International Law Journal (Online)* 51 (2010): 82–95.

Istrabadi, Feisal. "A Constitution Without Constitutionalism: Reflections on Iraq's Failed Constitutional Process," *Texas Law Review* 52 (2009):1627–1655.

Mallat, Chibli. *The Renewal of Islamic Law: Muhammad Baqer as-Sdr, Najaf, and the Shi'i International.* Cambridge, U.K.: Cambridge University Press, 1993.

Marr, Phebe. *The Modern History of Iraq.* 2d ed. Boulder, Colo.: Westview Press, 2004.

Packer, George. *The Assassins' Gate: America in Iraq.* New York: Farrar, Straus, and Giroux, 2005.

Shadid, Anthony. *Night Draws Near: Iraq's People in the Shadow of America's War.* New York: Henry Holt, Picador, 2006.

Visser, Reidar. "The Kurdish Issue in Iraq: A View from Baghdad at the Close of the Maliki Premiership." *Fletcher Forum for World Affairs* 34 (2010): 77–94.

BARAK A. SALMONI
Updated by HAIDER ALA HAMOUDI

ISLAM AND ECONOMICS. The last two centuries have seen the emergence of modern government in the Islamic world. An important part of this process has involved the creation of institutions for macroeconomics management. The role of the state in the economy has been formalized, with the introduction of ministries of finance, planning, industry, agriculture, and commerce. At the same time, central banks have been created, and a large number of organizations that play some role in the regulation of economic activity, from chambers of commerce to syndicates of workers and trade unions, have emerged. Some of these are mere agents of government, but others enjoy considerable autonomy.

Western economics often purports to be universally applicable, reflecting the assumed value-free and culturally independent nature of its methodology. At the policy level, however, experience from many parts of the world indicates that such assumptions are simplistic, if not completely misleading. Yet the universality of economic epistemology is seldom questioned in the West, though it is in the Islamic world, where the subject has its own axioms. The school of Western thought known as institutional economics has perhaps a more relevant approach for dealing with Islamic societies. Its leading advocates, Thorstein Veblen, Wesley Mitchell, and Gunnar Myrdal, did not concern themselves with Islamic societies, though Myrdal, in his classic study, *Asian Drama: An Inquiry into the Poverty of Nations* (London: Allen Lane, 1968), demonstrated an awareness of the issues.

Institutionalists believe that the political and social structures of a country influence how its economy works and that other disciplines, including law, sociology, and anthropology, are relevant to economic problems. A neoclassical approach, which tries to isolate demand and supply from the market environment in which they operate, is not very instructive in Islamic societies. Indeed, excessive abstraction may not be very fruitful in any social context. The institutions involved in economic policy formation, or its execution, are staffed by individuals with beliefs and values. Simplistic economic models that assume so-called rational maximizing behavior fail to explain much of what is actually taking place in particular economies, where, after all, it is social beings who are the economic agents, not impersonal mechanistic forces.

Islamic Financial Administration. There have, of course, been institutions concerned with the collection of taxation and the disbursement of the proceeds since the time of the Prophet. The Bayt al-Māl is the institution with traditional responsibility for the administration of taxes. Its role and responsibilities with respect to the Muslim community are broadly defined, and there is no exact equivalence in modern societies. One function was that of Bayt al-Māl al-Khāṣṣ, literally, the royal treasury or privy purse. This was concerned with the management of the finances of the caliph (*khalīfah*), or ruler, including the disbursement of funds to cover his personal expenses. The Bayt al-Māl al-Khāṣṣ was also responsible for the upkeep of palaces, the salaries of the royal guards, gifts to foreign rulers, and the maintenance of the *ḥarīm* (harem, the royal ladies-in-waiting).

The finances of the Muslim community were administered separately from those of the royal household through the Bayt al-Māl al-Muslim, which was often administered from buildings adjacent to the chief national or provincial mosque, and the work was supervised by the religious authorities. Responsibilities were wide-ranging, from public works such as the construction and maintenance of roads and bridges to social expenditures that were designed to help the poor and needy. The latter were financed with revenue from *zakāt*, the Islamic taxation on wealth, from which the ruler could not profit as the proceeds were earmarked for socially worthwhile purposes.

The Bayt al-Māl performed some of the functions of a modern central bank, as it acted as government financier, but it was not concerned with the management of financial intermediation or currency issue. It could undertake most of the essential public financing required in societies where exchange was based either on barter or the use of precious metals, such as silver and gold, as mediums of exchange. The Bayt al-Māl, however, was not involved in deficit financing, which would have been questionable under Sharīʿah, as it usually involves the issue of bills bearing *ribā* (interest), which is unacceptable under Islamic law. Such limitations were not a constraint in preindustrial economies, but clearly meant that the ruler and his subjects had fewer economic options than in Western societies. Modern Islamic economists argue that the constraints imposed by the Bayt al-Māl practices and procedures were both desirable and justified. The institutional framework was appropriate for an Islamic society, and its workings reflected Muslim values and aspirations.

Management of Shared Productive Resources. Islam recognizes the private ownership of property; indeed, there are well-defined laws governing the inheritance of property, which are clearly set out in the Qurʾān itself. However, there has always been provision for the voluntary transfer of land and other privately owned assets to a *waqf* (charitable trust), and such transfers have been actively encouraged throughout Islamic history. The assets transferred are administered by the *waqf* on behalf of the Muslim community as a whole residing in a particular area or state.

Typically the land transferred was used for the construction of mosques, schools, health facilities, or other buildings that served the local community. *Waqf* land could also be rented out and the income used for the payment of teachers and religious scholars. Rental income could be used directly for socially beneficial purposes, including helping the poor and needy. Sharecropping arrangements sometimes stipulated that a proportion of the crop would accrue to the tenant and his family, but the rest might go to support sick and disabled Muslims who were unable to work. Hence there was basic social security provision for the Islamic faithful, independent of family and kinship connections.

In Islam, land and other resources represent the bounty of Allāh. They are to be used and not squandered. The emphasis is on the productive use of what God has provided. Those concerned with the administration of a *waqf* have a duty to see that *waqf* property is put to good use, and tenants on the property are expected to work effectively. In many contemporary Islamic states, responsibility for *waqf* property has been taken over by a government ministry. In Saudi Arabia, for example, there is a Ministry of Pilgrimage and Endowments, which has a deputy minister responsible for *waqf*. In some states, this responsibility resides with the Ministry of Religious Affairs, and in others with the Ministry of Justice, where there are specialists in Sharīʿah. Occasionally, as in Iran under the shah, responsibility for the management of *waqf* lands and property remained with the religious authorities in control of the mosques. This gave religious leaders considerable economic power, which they resisted giving up even when the Islamic republic was established.

Secular Economic Influences. During the nineteenth century, the influence of Western ideas steadily increased throughout the Islamic world, and commercial laws modeled for the most part on the British, French, and Dutch equivalents were introduced in many countries. Government ministries were modernized and restructured, but usually this was associated with an increasing role for the state, as it took on new economic functions. The changes in the organization of government were not challenged by the local Muslim populations on religious grounds, but were seen as part of the modernization process rather than as secularist trends with new commercial codes drawn up to coexist in parallel with Sharīʿah. Often the new laws applied to trade with foreigners as the economies were opened up, and frequently even local business was conducted by foreigners. As far as the mass of the Muslim population was concerned, the new laws were irrelevant; they governed the dealings of the infidel, not their own lives.

The organization of government economic ministries became more formalized as contacts with industrial powers increased, and many Muslim states became European colonies. State expenditures increased substantially in the nineteenth century, usually outstripping tax revenues and, as a consequence, debt financing became a major preoccupation of treasury officials. The Ottoman government in particular incurred substantial debt, not just to European governments but also to private foreign financiers. In some respects, its situation was similar to that of contemporary Third World debtor nations, with Ottoman bonds and bills trading far below their face values in international financial markets. This, of course, raised questions with implications for Islam, as borrowing by issuing interest-bearing bills and bonds means in practice dealing in *ribā*, and profiting from bond-price movements may amount to speculation or even gambling. Under Islamic law, *gharar* (speculation) is *ḥarām* (forbidden). This government borrowing problem has been solved today by the development of sovereign *ṣukūk* securities, which serve the same purpose as bonds but pay non-interest returns based on rents or profit sharing and are asset-backed.

Ottoman authorities were under severe pressures from their European creditors and as a consequence were driven to compromise on matters of principle. Under a law passed in 1887, interest was permitted, as long as it did not exceed the principal of the loan. This was a highly dubious interpretation of *sūrah* 3:130 of the Qurʾān, which states, "O ye who believe, devour not usury doubled and multiplied." This verse makes no mention of the principal. Some jurists have interpreted it to mean that compound rather than simple interest is *ḥarām*, but both were permitted in the Ottoman Empire by the nineteenth century, although under the 1887 act domestic interest was subject to a ceiling of 9 percent. It is not clear how this figure was arrived at. Modern *fuqahāʾ* (Islamic jurists) generally regard all interest as *ribā*.

The extent of Western secular influence was most strongly manifest in Egypt, where there were separate courts established for non-Muslim foreigners resident in the country. These courts dealt with both civil and criminal cases and were called to make judgments in commercial cases involving payments, defaults, and false disclosures by parties involved in trade. The Sharīʿah law is very clear on such matters, but Islamic *fiqh* (jurisprudence) was ignored when foreigners were involved. With the 1952 revolution, these separate courts were finally abolished as an unacceptable inheritance from the Ottoman "capitulations" that permitted European officials to protect and impose legal sanctions on their own nationals. Egyptian president Gamal Abdel Nasser saw this as an infringement of national sovereignty. Modern Muslims view such practices as a violation of the sovereignty of Islam.

Institutional Development. The expanding role of the state in Islamic economies necessitated the enlargement of government ministries of finance and agriculture and led to the creation of new ministries dealing with planning, industry, petroleum, tourism, and other economically important activities. Modern economies are quite different in their scope and nature from the type of agricultural and trading activity that prevailed at the time of the Prophet more than fourteen hundred years ago. It is only in the past fifty years that Islamic economists have sought to discover how the principles of Sharīʿah could be applied in such fields as macroeconomic policy, project appraisal, accounting, and national planning.

The introduction of *fiqh* into these new areas has raised many questions, as the ongoing debate clearly illustrates, while many issues remain to be resolved. *Shūrā* (consultation) between government and Muslim populations is needed to determine how policy should evolve, and the *ʿulamāʾ* and increasingly educated Muslim professionals are involved in this process in most Islamic states. Determining exactly what is *ḥarām* and what is *ḥalāl* (permitted) in modern economies with increasingly sophisticated financial and commercial systems is often far from straightforward.

Macroeconomic policies have Islamic implications, for example, as excessive demand can result in inflationary conditions that can destroy a financial system based on *murābaḥah* (funded trade) and *muḍārabah* (equity participation). It also raises the issue of interest to compensate for inflation that most *fuqahāʾ* would still regard as *ribā*. Nevertheless, excessive constraints on demand can result in an underutilization of capacity, a waste of resources, and unemployment. This can result in *ẓulm*, a term that refers to inequity, injustice, exploitation, oppression, and wrongdoing. In a recession induced by government in the interests of the control of inflation, it is usually the weak and marginal employees who are the first to be dismissed. If the Islamic community or *ummah* suffer from such policies, this is intolerable.

Economic planning is much less in vogue since the collapse of the centrally planned economies of Eastern Europe, but in most Muslim countries there are planning ministries, and national plans are produced to cover each five-year period. In many Muslim countries, the plans are a legacy of the nationalistic, and in some cases socialistic, post-independence period. The *ʿulamāʾ* have often been unhappy with the plans, as there has been little *shūrā* outside government circles. Infrastructure and industrial projects have frequently involved the employment of large numbers of infidels from outside the Islamic world, and there has been unease concerning the social and cultural impact of these employees.

The new industries have often been a threat to the traditional craft and trading activities which are highly regarded in Islamic societies. The Qurʾān itself has much to say on fair-trading practice. Dealing in commodities, as opposed to mere monetary transactions, is regarded as a productive activity, according to *sūrah* 2:275: "God hath permitted trade and forbidden usury." The bazaar and souk trading economies have been undermined by the growth of employment in the modern sector, which has benefited from government subsidies, protectionism, and artificial pricing policies. Finance has been made available on generous terms to the modern sector, while the traditional sectors have been starved of funds. This has raised the price of bazaar finance, opening up the whole issue of usury. In such circumstances, it is hardly surprising that the bazaar merchants in Iran were among the most fervent supporters of the Islamic revolution. Some Islamic economists are critical of free trade, however, because of the unfair practices often used, and would like to see the institution of the *ḥisbah* (consideration) revived, an institution that traditionally regulated markets to ensure transactions complied with Sharīʿah.

International Islamic Institutions. The Organization of the Islamic Conference is the major intergovernmental institution in which all Muslim states are represented. The institution became increasingly active in the late 1960s, and it was responsible for the founding of the Islamic Development Bank in 1974. International humanitarian issues affecting Muslims are discussed, and representatives from the Red Crescent, the Islamic equivalent of the Red Cross, have attended some of the meetings. There is a solidarity fund, which disburses grants rather than advancing funds through *murābaḥah* and *muḍārabah*, as is the practice of the Islamic Development Bank. The poorest Muslim countries, such as Bangladesh, Afghanistan, and Somalia, have all been beneficiaries of these grants.

At the meetings of the Islamic Conference international issues are discussed at heads-of-state level, but it is the sessions involving finance ministers that are primarily concerned with economic matters. The conference has a distinctive contribution to make on questions, such as Third World debt, which have deeply worried many Muslim states. The cause of the payment difficulties is seen as the *ribā*-based nature of the international financial system, which imposes unfair interest burdens on many developing countries. Swapping debt for equity appears at first sight to be an acceptable solution, as *muḍārabah* funding can replace *ribā* finance. There is some caution over this, however, if it means the transfer of ownership of assets in Muslim debtor nations to the control of infidels.

[*See also* Organization of Islamic Cooperation; *and* Waqf.]

BIBLIOGRAPHY

Al-Sadr, Mohammad Baqir. *Our Economics*. London, 2000.

Chapra, Mohammad Umer. *The Future of Economics: An Islamic Perspective*. Leicester, U.K.: Islamic Foundation, 2000.

El-Ashker, Ahmed, and Rodney Wilson. *Islamic Economics: A Short History*. Leiden, Netherlands: E. J. Brill, 2006.

Iqbal, Munawar. *Distributive Justice and Need Fulfilment in an Islamic Economy*. Leicester, U.K.: Islamic Foundation, 1988.

Khan, M. Fahim. *Essays in Islamic Economics*. Leicester, U.K.: Islamic Foundation, 1995.

Kuran, Timur. *Islam and Mammon: The Economic Predicaments of Islamism*. Princeton, N.J.: Princeton University Press, 2004.

Naqvi, Syed Mawab Haider. *Perspectives on Morality and Human Well-Being: A Contribution to Islamic Economics*. Leicester, U.K.: Islamic Foundation, 2003.

Nomani, Farhad, and Ali Rahnema. *Islamic Economic Systems*. London: Zed Books, 1994.

Pramanik, Ataul Huq. *Poverty, Inequality, and the Role of Some Islamic Economic Institutions*. Islamabad, 1981.

Rahman, Afzalur. *Banking and Insurance*. London: Muslim Schools Trust, 1979.

Rodinson, Maxime. *Islam and Capitalism*. New York: Pantheon, 1974.

Saleh, Nabil. *Unlawful Gain and Legitimate Profit in Islamic Law*. Cambridge, U.K.: Cambridge University Press, 1986.

Siddiqi, Muhammed Nejatullah. *Role of the State in the Economy*. Leicester, U.K.: Islamic Foundation, 1996.

Warde, Ibrahim. *Islamic Finance in the Global Economy*. Edinburgh: Edinburgh University Press, 2000.

Wilson, Rodney. *Economics, Ethics, and Religion: Jewish, Christian, and Islamic Economic Thought*. New York: New York University Press, 1997.

Wilson, Rodney. "The Development of Islamic Economics: Theory and Practice." In *Islamic Thought in the Twentieth Century*, edited by Suha Taji-Farouki and Basheer Nafi. London: I. B. Tauris, 2004.

RODNEY WILSON

ISLAM AND POLITICS IN AFRICA.

Islamic expansion in North Africa was centered on the religion's commercial and at times military attributes, whereas in West and East Africa its diffusion manifested commercial characteristics associated with its dissemination in other parts of the world. In North Africa, as in the Near East, Islam was intricately connected to the process of Arabization, or the creation of new Arabs, even when significant numbers of people in the region identified—and still continue to identify—as Berbers. A similar pattern did not develop in sub-Saharan Africa, where people maintained their separate identities as non-Arabs but who, as Muslims, joined or became part of the universal Muslim *ummah*, or community of believers, over space and time. In this expanded *ummah*, Islam provided new influences and impacted local cultures and languages, without, however, displacing them or the local practices associated with them. This may be described as a unity in diversity.

The impact of cross-cultural trade in the regions of Africa connected to trans-Saharan, Red Sea, and Indian Ocean trading networks reinforced cultural self-identity and allowed, in the later centuries, a growth in commitment to Islam. It also fostered a pluralistic structure in which commerce, Islam, and the indigenous African system supported the urban network (with which Islam has been associated). Thus a balance was established between local ritual precepts and the universal norms of Islam. This strengthened allegiance to Islam's religious system and fostered at the same time commitment that ranged from parochial ethnic self-identity on one hand to Islamic all-embracing community self-identity, universal and trans-ethnic in scope, on the other. Islamic diffusion in the rural areas, slow and gradual, came later.

This peaceful phase of Islamic expansion in some parts of Africa was later interrupted for a time by the more assertive or revivalist phase of Islamic consolidation in what was the frontier, the ecological transition zone (the Sahel) between the Sahara Desert and the forest region. These reformist efforts, with millenarian and Mahdist overtones, represented for the most part an increasing commitment to scriptural Islam by Islamic scholars, especially among the Fulani, to establish Islam as a state religion in such West African regions as Senegambia, Mali, and Guinea, on the basis of the model that had existed earlier, for instance, during the period of the Askiya dynasty in fifteenth- and sixteenth-century Songhay. These Islamic scholars reacted to what they saw as widespread corruption, arbitrary taxation and seizure of property, oppression of the poor and slave trading that was indiscriminately claiming even fellow Muslims as victims. Nevertheless, these militant state-building experiments, which reached a peak in the nineteenth century (the era also of the Sudanese Mahdi, the archetypal figure with apocalyptic associations) were brought to an end with the rise of European powers competing to carve out states in Africa following the European scramble for territories. From that time, Muslims faced a dual challenge in the colonial subjugation: the arrival of triumphant Atlantic states, armed with superior technology and accompanied by a political agenda in the service of an imperial project; and the emergence of European missionary Christianity as a cultural rival to Islam with its own schools, clinics, and so on, as vehicles for evangelization. Muslims found themselves forced to choose between accommodation (as, for instance, the Murid Ṣūfī brotherhood did in Senegal) and resistance to a racist settler-based colonial system (as the Algerians did against the French both in the nineteenth century and again in the 1950s) in their response to these new political realities.

Islam: Prospects and Challenges of Colonial Rule and Modernity. The relationship between colonialism and Islam was a very complex one. First, while colonialism arrested the spread of Islam in, for instance, Uganda, in other areas of Africa—as far apart as Tanzania (Tanganyika) in East Africa and in Senegal and, indeed, in much of West Africa—it facilitated the growth of Islam through the activities of Muslim brotherhoods (Ṣūfī orders), traders, and others. Newly established communications and transportation infrastructure allowed Muslims, despite their loss of political power to Europeans, to expand the scope of their activities and to increase exchange between different Muslim communities across a wide region. As a result, Muslim communities made significant inroads in much of West Africa and in the interior of Tanganyika. Second, colonialism and colonial policies in some parts of Africa had the unintended result of making some African groups turn to Islam. This, for instance, happened with Amadu Bamba M'Backe's Murid (Ṣūfī) brotherhood in Senegal, which converted thousands of uprooted Africans whose earthly kingdoms had been shattered by colonialism. Third, colonial policies also inadvertently aided the growth of Islam in some parts of Africa by preserving the powers of the previous Muslim elites (for instance, the descendants of the militant, reform-minded Shaykh Usuman dan Fodio, who had established the Sokoto caliphate in northern Nigeria) in return for their cooperation with European colonial rule. This provided Muslim rulers with legitimacy and a platform from which to expand and build their influence among non-Muslims in their areas. Moreover, Europeans restricted the activities of Christian missionaries in those areas where such cooperative arrangements or cordial relationships with Muslim elites existed.

Nevertheless, colonialism also facilitated the work of Christian missionaries by entrenching their domination of the colonial educational system, which later had disastrous consequences for Muslims. For instance, in both East Africa (Uganda, Kenya, and Tanzania) and West Africa (Nigeria, Ghana, Sierra Leone, and others), Muslims found themselves unable to compete with the relatively better educated African Christians. In fact, Muslim political and social activism, both during and after the colonial era, has its basis in Muslim dissatisfaction with their socioeconomic status, especially in those countries where Muslims do not constitute an absolute majority, that is, are between 10 and 55 percent of the total population. It is not a coincidence, therefore, that in both Tanzania (though only some) and Nigeria, for instance, Muslims attempted to lobby the British colonial government to postpone granting independence until Muslims had gained educational parity with Christians.

Islam, Politics, and the Multiethnic State: Case Studies. It is important to note first that the existence of peaceful relations between Muslim and non-Muslim communities in some parts of Africa and, more important, the prevalence of ethnic, regional and, in some cases, religious tensions between them in other parts of the continent have much to do with the policies and politics of colonial territorial engineering. Colonial powers had a vested interest in creating artificial, ethnically fragmented countries in which ethnic, linguistic, or religious groups were thrown together or separated in different states. This sowed the seeds for later ethnic, religious, and regional conflict in these countries. More specifically, when two regions with varying cultural and historical trajectories, such as northern and southern Nigeria, northern and southern Sudan (which recently became independent), northern and southern Chad, and northern and southern Ivory Coast, were amalgamated, European powers exacerbated relations between them through implementation of the policy of "divide and rule." Thus the construction of ethnic, linguistic, regional, and religious differences and divisions dictated the course of national identity politics. As a result, power sharing in such countries was and continues to be elusive, with open hostilities sometimes erupting into violence or civil wars that have claimed thousands of lives.

Since gaining independence in the 1950s, Sudan has been plagued by religious and other divisions that have periodically erupted into violence between the Muslim north and the non-Muslim south and factionalism within the north between the Anṣār Mahdī, Khatmīyah, the Muslim Brotherhood, Arab nationalists, and others. The Muslim Brotherhood, for instance, seeks to reorient Sudanese society to more familiar patterns of existence embracing the utopian image that seeks to reintegrate all levels of Islam's personal, communal, and political life. The growing tension between the north and south expressed in an intractable civil war that raged on and off for the last half century (1955–1972 and 1983–2005) left Sudan with no option but to grant independence to the much economically neglected southern region of Sudan, despite the challenges of border disputes, displaced populations, and a sustainable oil revenue–sharing mechanism that lie ahead. In both northern Sudan and northern Nigeria, where Islam was more entrenched, the post-independent Sharīʿah controversy, for instance, that has pitted supporters of Western/secular legal institutions in the south against some of their northern compatriots who seek a reinstatement of pre-colonial legal system, should be viewed within the context of pre-independent historical developments. In other words, the prior existence of the Sharīʿah in pre-colonial times is often the justification for calling for its reintroduction as the level of politicization of Islam deepens. It is important to point out, though, that in Sudan it was not the followers of Ansar Mahdi or their leader al-Ṣādiq al-Mahdī (a descendant of the Mahdī) who have been behind such calls but the Bashir military government, supported previously by the Muslim Brotherhood, whose members are committed to the establishment of an Islamic government even if under the sponsorship of a military dictator as is currently the case in Sudan.

The increasing politicization of both Islam (hence the specter of Islamic revivalism in northern Nigeria, stimulated by Islamic currents from both within and without) and Christianity ("born again" versions of it that have become equally assertive) has provided the idiom of political struggles between Christians calling for a secular state and Muslims advocating the establishment of an Islamic state. Yet the persistence of many problematic issues—the failure of the modern secular state in Nigeria to deliver on its economic promises, the endemic corruption that exists especially at the federal level and has made Nigeria one of the countries at the top of the global corruption chart, the mismanagement of the economy that many Nigerians complain about, and the widespread prevalence of crime—has led Muslim groups in northern Nigeria to call for a Sharīʿah-based judicial system, which they claim will reform the economic and moral system in the country. In fact, the divisive Sharīʿah debate has become part of the public discourse in Nigeria that has pitted secular nationalists, particularly those in the south, against Islamic-oriented groups. Nevertheless, Nigerians have been and will be able to work out compromises for themselves between the two systems (even with the establishment of the controversial Sharīʿah Court of Appeal) if politicians refrain from using the Sharīʿah debate simply as a vehicle for gaining political power.

Complicating matters in Nigeria are ongoing concerns on the part of northern Nigerian Muslims about politics at the federal level and especially the ruling Peoples Democratic Party's (PDP) internal arrangement of power rotation, which had confirmed a southerner, not a northerner, as the PDP's presidential candidate for the 2011 elections. The outcome of this election confirmed the fact that since 1999, with the return of civilian rule, Nigeria has effectively known two Christian presidents, both from the south (first Olusegun Obasanjo, 1999–2007, and then Goodluck Jonathan, who will be in office until 2015). Similarly, the southerners had their own concerns, among which was the previous northern monopoly of power by successive Muslim-headed military governments in the period before 1999. Clearly, therefore, power sharing has to be negotiated across ethnic, regional, and religious lines.

In contrast to the Nigerian situation of ethnic, regional, and religious divisions, in Senegal, which has a different ethnic and historical/cultural mix, Muslims, Christians, and followers of African traditional religions live and have lived rather amicably with one another (just as they do in the Yoruba region of southwestern Nigeria, the key as to whether Nigeria will survive or self-destruct as a state) in an environment of religious pluralism. In Senegal, considered a model of a stable democracy with a Muslim population that constitutes over 90 percent of the national total, Muslims and especially Murid (Ṣūfī) leaders cooperated with and voted for President Léopold Senghor, a Catholic, who ruled the country for two decades (1960–1980). This cooperation has its roots in the colonial period when the French government relied on the Murid for export production of peanuts. The relationship of partnership between politicians and Muslim leaders involves the government using the Muslim leaders (marabouts) to mobilize support for its programs while in turn allowing them to have a voice or exercise influence on the shaping of society and polity, even though they do not participate in making policy.

Ethiopia, unlike Senegal, presents a totally different model in which historically the state has been identified with the Coptic Church or Orthodox Christianity, reputed to be the establishment religion of the country. The political and social marginalization of Muslims in Ethiopia as such makes the likelihood of a Muslim becoming the president of Ethiopia any time soon rather slim. This is despite the fact that Muslims make up nearly half the total population of the country and Islam has been in the country since the inception of the religion in Arabia. Moreover, from the end of the monarchical period (Emperor Haile Selassie was removed from power in 1974) to the present, successive Ethiopian governments, including the current ethnic-based Tigrean-dominated regime, have played the "Arab/Islamic threat" card to court the support of Western countries, the United States in particular, especially in the war against global terrorism. Ethiopia's involvement in the affairs of neighboring Somalia, for instance, has much to do with its own internal issues (the threat from Ogaden Somalis and, more seriously, from the Oromo, who make up almost 40 percent of the total population of the country). Therefore, any Western alignments with Ethiopia have the potential of reviving old antagonisms and stirring up ethnic and religious nationalisms in the Horn of Africa that go as far back as the late nineteenth and early twentieth centuries. That was when militant, reformist Islam was deployed against both the expansionist Ethiopian state under Menelik II and Western/Christian colonial powers vying for control of territories in the area. The Muslim Youth, or al-Shabāb, an offshoot of the Islamic Courts Union and champions of radical political Islam (the U.S. government labels them as a terrorist organization) see themselves as defenders of "pure" Islam against the corrupt, ineffective successive transitional Somali governments supported by Ethiopia and the United States. These ideologically committed Muslim youths (who operate in the same atmosphere of chaos and ethnic/factional fighting as the Taliban did in Afghanistan and are also known for their quick and tough justice against thieves and other offenders) seek to play the same role in a politically fragmented drought-stricken country, or what has been called a "failed state," as the man whom the British characterized as the "mad Mullah" (Abdille Hassan) of Somalia did in the early 1900s. He conducted a guerrilla warfare to resist the territorial ambitions of the British, the Italians, and the Ethiopians.

Interaction between the State and Religion: East Africa. Turning to Tanzania, which has a different political culture, there is relatively far more peaceful coexistence between different ethnic and religious groups in (mainland) Tanzania than in any other part of East Africa. At the same time, however, some Muslim groups have expressed concern about the distribution of economic opportunities (specifically, underrepresentation in civil service and other sectors of the economy) over the different religious groups and constituencies. As far back as 1959, the All Muslim National of Union of Tanganyika (AMNUT) urged the British government to delay independence until Muslims had acquired sufficient education to be able to compete with the educated African Christians. The majority of Muslim leaders, however, rallied behind the nationalist party, Tanganyika African Union (TANU) and opposed AMNUT. When individuals within TANU advanced what were labeled as "Muslim demands," the party took action by creating an Elders Section within TANU. It was dominated by coastal Muslim elements in Dar es Salaam and Tanga. Furthermore, in 1958, President Julius Nyerere expelled one of these elders, Shaykh Taqdir, from the party for complaining that there were not enough Muslims on the TANU election slate. In other words, Taqdiri was accused of mixing religion with politics when he drew attention to TANU's putting forward more Christian than Muslim candidates. Perhaps he thought that TANU was attempting to replace the Muslim trader-politician with the more educated Christian.

In the post-independence period, Nyerere's one-party rule continued its efforts to co-opt every group in the country to its Ujamaa socialism as a vehicle to change conditions that promoted inequality in the country. Yet, by the time Nyerere stepped down as president of Tanzania in the mid-1980s, Ujamaa socialism had not delivered on its economic promises to equalize opportunities between regions and between religious communities. Moreover, with the restoration of multiparty politics in the early 1990s Muslims became increasingly assertive. Under these circumstances, the ruling party, Chama Cha Mpinduzi (CCM), seems to have informally opted for a system of presidency that alternates between Muslim and Christian candidates as one way to deal with this issue.

In newly independent African states (with their secular constitutions) the repeated calls by top government officials for the separation of religion and politics are contradicted at the same time by the state's attempts to monopolize legitimate authority and to exercise it without tolerating competitors or challengers from any quarters. For instance, the political leadership in East Africa as well as in other parts of Africa has discouraged criticism or any open discussion of public policy on the part of religious figures or organizations, even as it has attempted to co-opt them to the state's political agendas, especially during the period of the one-party or military dictatorships where these have existed. As far as these organizations were concerned, however, who else, if not representatives of civil society, was going to speak for their disadvantaged communities in countries where there were growing social inequalities, falling standards of living, and increasing arbitrariness of the state which in some cases has worsened conditions of ethnic tensions and interethnic and communal violence?

More specifically, the efforts to bureaucratize Muslim communities in East Africa as well as elsewhere in Africa, through the establishment of national associations such as SUPKEM (Supreme Council of Kenyan Muslims), BAKWATA (Baraza Kuu La Waislamu wa Tanzania), and the Uganda Muslim Supreme Council (UMSC) should be viewed as attempts on the part of politicians and Muslim leaders to mobilize Muslims, supposedly to protect and to advance their interests in a single centralized body. This was necessitated by the absence of institutions or a hierarchical organization similar to that of, for instance, the Catholic Church, through which the ruling elite might contact a leading religious figure who speaks on behalf of the whole community. The outcome has been that not just politicians, but Muslims themselves, have sought to establish a centralized Muslim council to channel their energies and efforts in the realization of their goals.

The creation of a corporate identity (for instance, SUPKEM in Kenya in 1973) to assist in channeling social influence, campaigning for legalization of Islamic law, promoting Muslim educational facilities, and so on, has not, however, been without its challenges. While the attempted bureaucratization of Muslim communities has provided an opportunity for political leaders to exercise control over the Muslim leadership, it has also fostered the growth of oppositional groups that compete against and function independent of the officially recognized national Muslim organization. Some Muslim groups have expressed their dissatisfaction with the central Muslim leadership for not representing their interests or for not standing up to the politicians by forming their own independent organizations. In each of the three East African countries, Muslim groups have viewed their national Muslim council as an instrument to manage the state's domination of the Muslim community. This demonstrates quite clearly that monolithic control has not been possible due to the nature of diffused religious authority, particularly in Sunnī Islam, in contrast to Christianity with its hierarchical church organization.

Muslim-state relations in Kenya under President Daniel arap Moi (in office 1978–2002) have been characterized by suspicion and dissatisfaction with the distribution of positions of power, economic opportunities, and privileges that favored up-country Africans, especially Moi's kinsmen. Unlike the previous president, Jomo Kenyatta, whose economic policies benefited mainly his fellow Kikuyus, Moi worsened the situation by subsequently privileging both ethnicity (the Kalenjin people) and religion (Christianity). Moi's increasingly autocratic government continued to politically marginalize Muslims during the period of worsening political and economic situation in the country. In a political system plagued by patronage and ethnic lobbying, Muslim politicians (labeled Moi loyalists) accomplished little in terms of promoting the interests of Muslim masses. This situation led some Muslims, especially young preachers, to become active on behalf of their community by relating their sermons to the issues of the day. A noted feature of this era was a rising Muslim political consciousness, which in the coastal region found expression in, for instance, the formation of a Muslim advocacy group, the Islamic Party of Kenya (IPK), headed by Shaykh Khalid Balala, a graduate of the Islamic University of Medina, in Saudi Arabia.

The process of Muslim activism in the case of Kenya was further facilitated by the growth of the number of Muslim graduates of secular education at the country's four local universities. Like other Kenyans, these Muslim youths have become a bit disillusioned by the performance of their postcolonial national state. The worldwide impact of and heightened awareness created, at least initially, by the success of the Islamic revolution in Iran generated far more assertiveness and a sense of political awareness than was the case before.

Islamic Reform in East Africa. Several factors contributed to this rise in Muslim activism from the mid-1970s into the early twenty-first century. These include the growth of global Muslim networks, which have expanded as well as promoted opportunities for higher Islamic education in the Muslim world. This has led to the rise (in East Africa as in West Africa) of a new group of *'ulamā'* (religious scholars), locally or foreign trained, with a more pan-Islamic or global outlook. They include Muslim "puritans" or idealists, otherwise known as Salafi in different parts of Africa, whose rise to prominence reflects deepening local Muslim contacts with centers and sources of global resurgent Islam in the Islamic heartlands. This is part of a worldwide phenomenon that has been noted in far flung Muslim communities in different regions of the world. The agents of this renewal and reform are young Muslim preachers who seek to reform the practice of Islam in different local contexts, as well as to deepen Muslim involvement in the affairs of their communities, even as they call on scripture and invoke memories of an Islamic past in support of their efforts.

In the case of Uganda in the 1990s the influential Muslim reformers (many products of the Islamic University of Medina) fragmented into two: the larger and more moderate wing of the Salafī movement was led by Shaykh Kakeeto, whereas the fringe or more radical and political Islamist wing was headed by Shaykh Mukulu. Critical of the Uganda Muslim Supreme Council (UMSC) for its ineffectual leadership, the Mukulu faction became radicalized over leadership issues in the Muslim community and began at the same time to defy central authority as being unjust. By 1995, Shaykh Mukulu had fled the country (further weakening his movement) even as the Uganda Muslim Liberation Army (UMLA) arose to champion Muslim rights. The Museveni government accused these young Muslims (who do not have the backing of the Muslim community) as being misguided and supported by the Hassan al-Turabi faction in Sudan. Shaykh Kakeeto and other Muslim leaders have distanced themselves from these radical young Muslims.

While Shaykh Kakeeto and his followers, as well as the majority of Muslims of Uganda, do not support armed resistance against the government, they do, however, challenge or question the inherited colonial and Christian missionary construction and the "mapping" of Islam and Muslims as being the "other" in Uganda. When Idi Amin seized power in the early 1970s, Muslims hoped that he would be able to correct this situation. Unfortunately, Amin's tyrannical military government, while empowering Muslims (especially his own narrowly defined "Nubi" or Kakwa ethnic group and other northwestern Ugandans), alienated many people and contributed to economic mismanagement of the country.

Yet the legacy of Amin's rule is that Uganda has an Islamic university and Islamic institutes (built mainly with funds from oil-rich Saudi Arabia) that have prepared a new generation of Muslim scholars with a reformist orientation. Moreover, Uganda during the rule of Amin was among the African states whose leaders (including Omar Bongo of Gabon, who converted to Islam) were wooed politically and in other ways by the ideologically eclectic President Muʿammar al-Qadhdhāfī. Later, Qadhdhāfī provided funds for the construction of a mosque in Uganda, considered to be one of the largest in Africa. Some scholarships were also given to Ugandans to study in Libya. Uganda also became a member of the Organization of Islamic Conference (OIC, which changed its name to the Organization of Islamic Cooperation in 2011). The consequence of these developments was that Muslim activism in Uganda as well as elsewhere in Africa began to receive an enormous boost from Arab petrodollars, thus leveling the missionary playing field for both Muslims and Christians (who received funding from the West).

It is important to note here the consequences of the tragic episode of the embassy bombings in Kenya and Tanzania in August 1997, as well as the 9/11 terrorist attacks in the United States in 2001, all of which negatively impacted the Muslims of Uganda, Kenya and Tanzania. The tragic events in East Africa complicated matters for Muslims, particularly those of the coastal region of Kenya, who complained of Muslim profiling and harassment by law enforcement agents. Even prior to these events, coastal Muslims had complained for years about being treated as strangers, as there was a tendency in Kenya of associating Muslims with Arabs on the coast.

In Uganda, too, there were indiscriminate arrests of Muslims for investigation following the 1997 bombings. This was also the period in which there were reports of human rights abuses, as well as disappearances of Muslims, as the Museveni regime attempted to come to terms with rebel groups belonging to the Allied Democratic Front (ADF), which had some Muslim fighters.

Nevertheless, relations between Muslims and the Museveni government have improved. Some of the Muslims who had been arrested before were released, and some of those who had fled the country were allowed to return. Nevertheless, Shaykh Mukulu has not returned and it is not clear what would happen if he did.

BIBLIOGRAPHY

Brenner, Louis, ed. *Muslim Identity and Social Change in sub-Saharan Africa*. Bloomington: Indiana University Press, 1993.

Chabal, Patrick, and Jean-Pascal Daloz. *Africa Works: Disorder as Political Instrument*. Oxford: James Currey, 1999.

Chande, Abdin. "Muslim-State Relations in East Africa under Conditions of Military and Civilian or One-Party Dictatorships." *Historia Actual Online* 17 (October–November 2008): 97–111.

Chande, Abdin. "Radicalism and Reform in East Africa." In *History of Islam in Africa*, edited by Randall Pouwels and Nehemiah Levtzion, pp. 349–372, Columbus: Ohio University Press, 2000.

De Waal, Alex, ed., *Islamism and Its Enemies in the Horn of Africa*. London: Hurst, 2004.

Dickson, David. *Political Islam in Sub-Saharan Africa: The Need for a New Research and Diplomatic Agenda*. United States Institute of Peace Special Report no. 140. Washington, D.C.: U.S. Institute of Peace, 2005.

Eickelman, Dale, and James Piscatori. *Muslim Politics*. Princeton, N.J.: Princeton University Press, 1996.

Haynes, Jeffrey. *Religion and Politics in Africa*. London: Zed Books, 1996.

Kabe, Lansine. *The Wahhabiyya: Islamic Reform and Politics in French West Africa*. Evanston, Ill.: Northwestern University Press, 1974.

Kane, Ousmane. *Muslim Modernity in a Post-Colonial Nigeria: A Study of the Society for the Removal of Innovation and Reinstatement of Tradition*. Leiden: E. J. Brill, 2003.

Kasozi, Abdu B. K. "The Uganda Muslim Supreme Council: An Experiment in Muslim Administrative Centralization and Institutionalization, 1972–82." *Journal Institute of Muslim Minority Affairs* 6 (1985): 34–52.

Kokole, Omari. "Idi Amin, 'the Nubi' and Islam in Ugandan Politics." In *Religion and Politics in East Africa*, edited by Holger Hansen and Michael Twaddle. London: James Currey, 1995.

Mamdani, Mahmood. *Good Muslim, Bad Muslim: America, the Cold War, and the Roots of Terror*. New York: Pantheon, 2004.

Mazrui, Ali. "Shariacracy and Federal Models in the Era of Globalization: Nigeria in a Comparative Perspective." *American Journal of Islamic Social Sciences* 26, no. 3 (Summer 2009): 24–40.

Miles, William. "Islamism in West Africa: Conclusions." *African Studies Review* 47, no. 2 (2004): 109–117.

Quinn, Charlotte, and Frederick Quinn. *Pride, Faith, and Fears: Islam in Sub-Saharan Africa*. New York: Oxford University Press, 2003.

Seesmann, Rudiger, and Roman Loimeier, eds. *The Global World of the Swahili*. Berlin: LIT, 2006.

Soares, Benjamin, and Rene Otayek, eds. *Islam and Muslim Politics in Africa*. New York: Palgrave MacMillan, 2007.

Soares, Benjamin, and Rene Otayek, eds. *Muslim Christian Encounters in Africa*. Leiden: E. J. Brill, 2006.

Villalón, Leonardo A. *Islamic Society and State in Senegal: Disciple and Citizens in Fatick*. Cambridge: Cambridge University Press, 1995.

Westerlund, David, and E. E. Rosander, eds. *African Islam and Islam in Africa: Encounter between Sufism and Islamists*. Athens: Ohio University Press, 1997.

Abdin Chande

Islam and Politics in Central Asia and the Caucasus.

Central Asia and the Caucasus are tremendously diverse. They contain Central Asian oases that were some of the most important centers of Islam worldwide; vast steppes and deserts, home to pastoral nomads; and remote mountain areas. Historically, Ḥanafī law of Sunnī Islam predominated, and Sufism played a role in most of this region. Later, Russian imperialism and Soviet communism unified the region. Today, the legacy of Soviet rule continues to shape Islam and politics. While the post-Soviet successor states have grown increasingly different, they all pursue policies toward Islam that reflect a deep anxiety that it could become a powerful force opposing Soviet-style secularism and undermining existing regimes. These policies include constitutional declarations of secularism, laws that restrict religion and limit outside Islamic influences, state bodies that enforce religious laws, and state-controlled muftiates. Simultaneously, they exploit local Islam (a synthesis of scriptural, pre-Islamic, and customary practices) for political purposes.

Political and Ethnic Subdivisions. Each subregion displays considerable internal diversity. The South Caucasus comprises Armenia, Georgia, and Azerbaijan, as well as Iranian Azerbaijan in northwestern Iran and adjacent parts of Turkey. In this region the Sunnī- Shīʿī divide is accentuated. Jaʿfarī Shīʿīs constitute 85 percent of Muslims in the Republic of Azerbaijan and the overwhelming majority in Iranian Azerbaijan. In other parts, however, such as the autonomous regions of Adjaria, Abkhazia, and Ossetia in Georgia, Sunnī Muslims constitute a significant minority among a predominantly Christian population.

The North Caucasus includes "autonomous republics" within the Russian Federation—Adygea, Karachay-Cherkessia, Kabardino-Balkaria, North Ossetia-Alania, Ingushetia, Chechnya, and Dagestan—all of which have some Muslim population. The eastern part of the North Caucasus, especially in Dagestan and Chechnya, is the only part of the former Russian Empire where Shāfiʿī law of Sunnī Islam predominated. Today, Ṣūfī Islam of the Naqshbandīyah and Qādirīyah orders plays an important role in the societies of those republics.

In the steppe region, from the Crimean Peninsula to the Volga basin, and the Kazakh Steppe, from the Ural Mountains north of the Caspian Sea eastward into Siberia, a population of predominantly Turkic pastoral nomads adopted Islam under the Golden Horde in the early fourteenth century, when its leader, Öz Beg Khan, made it the religion of state. As with pastoral nomads elsewhere, Ṣūfī orders were instrumental in the spread of Islam. Tatars from Kazan and the steppe region played a key role as translators and cultural mediators in the Muslim territories of Russian expansion, particularly in the Kazakh Steppe and southern Central Asia. They also led Muslim reformist movements which spread across the Russian Empire in the late nineteenth century, and they provided leadership for the Muslim political movements that emerged after Russia's 1905 liberal reforms.

Finally, the largest Muslim populations of the former Soviet domain inhabit Central Asia. This region includes the lands between the Caspian Sea and the Pamir–Tian Shan mountain system (Turkmenistan, Uzbekistan, Tajikistan, Kyrgyzstan, and Kazakhstan), as well as adjacent areas in western China and northern Afghanistan. The Umayyad Caliphate incorporated the southwestern part of this region, in today's Turkmenistan and Afghanistan, in the mid-seventh century, and Muslims controlled most of the populated oases of Mawarannahr (the lands between the Amu Darya and the Sir Darya) by the mid-eighth century. By the end of the ninth century, the cities of Bukhara and Samarkand began to acquire the status of major cultural centers in the Islamic world. The Central Asian oases retained their stature as important centers of Islamic learning and culture, as market centers on the Silk Road, and as the core of major world and regional powers from the Sāmānids to the Chagatayids, Timurids, and Shibānids. The Naqshbandīyah Ṣūfī order, founded in Bukhara in the fourteenth century, became one of the most influential Ṣūfī orders across the Muslim world, and Bukhara remained a spiritual center of regional importance even after the Russian conquest, as Bukharan *madrasahs* continued to attract students and scholars from many parts of the eastern Islamic world.

Russian and Soviet Domination. Islam in Central Asia and the Caucasus suffered severely from Russian conquests and Soviet anti-religious policies. Czarist policy toward Islam varied from highly suspicious, considering that fanatical Islam caused uprisings against czarist authorities, to tolerant and broadly supportive, reflecting the idea that Islam could be a civilizing factor, especially among nomads.

Soviet policy toward Islam also varied, but after a period of relatively limited interventions in the decade following the Revolution, the Soviet regime unleashed a very severe campaign to suppress Islam. It attempted to transform or liquidate those aspects of society in Central Asia and the Caucasus that it perceived as blocking the "building of socialism," and it classified Islamic leaders as the "class enemy." Under the campaigns against Islam, it closed virtually all mosques, as well as all *maktabs* and *madrasahs*; eventually it reopened just two Islamic schools during periods of relatively liberal policy toward Islam. It also targeted violently and coercively many other "patriarchal-feudal" practices associated with Islam, including women wearing veils, visitation of shrines, and customs associated with marriage, circumcision, and burial. In the late 1930s and at other times, the severe suppression of Islam included exiling people to Siberian gulags and eliminating religious elites.

Meanwhile, the Soviet regime also sought accommodation with Muslim societies. During World War II, for example, to secure Muslim support in the war effort, it greatly relaxed the assault on Islam. Since much of the communist leadership consisted of people from the Muslim community, local officials often served to mediate central policies to the community. Although periodic campaigns continued through the Soviet period, their impact was limited. Many communist officials remained aligned with Islam and often became more devout after retirement. While never officially accepted, Muslims maintained practices such as Islamic education conducted in homes, gathering at unofficial mosques, visitation of officially closed shrines, and the traditional life-cycle rituals.

The Study of Islam and Politics in Central Asia and the Caucasus. Due to limited access to the region under Soviet rule and Soviet efforts to weaken religion, Islam and politics in Central Asia and the Caucasus is understudied. During the Cold War, most Western scholarship on contemporary Islam in this region focused on whether Islam survived the impact of Soviet repression sufficiently that it could serve as a basis for political mobilization to help bring down the Soviet regime. Alexandre Bennigsen argued that, although the Soviet regime severely repressed religion, Muslim identity and underground Islamic organizations—especially Ṣūfī organizations—remained strong and would probably destabilize the Soviet Union.

Following the demise of the Soviet Union, scholarship that is no longer guided by the political agenda of the Cold War era, which has vastly improved access to field and archival sources, has grown. Little of the Cold War–era analysis of Islam in the Soviet Union has borne up under empirical investigation. It has become clear that the interactions between the Soviet system and Islamic practices were much more complicated than the unrelenting repression and control posited by the Bennigsen school, and that, in many areas, the practice of Islam was indeed sustained, though little of this activity had the orientation of opposition to the Soviet regime, as Bennigsen had argued. In the post-Soviet era, some intellectual voices sustain the narrow focus of Cold War–era scholarship on the supposed threat that Islam posed for the regime, in that they still devote attention to the question of whether Islamic opposition forces pose a challenge to existing regimes. The difference is mainly that the "Islamic threat" was formerly seen as an antidote to Soviet ascendancy, while some now view it as a danger for stability and a potential vector for international terrorism.

Additionally, there is important new research that takes advantage of improved archival access to examine the complex relationship between Islam and the Soviet state—which was by no means exclusively repressive—as well as the religious positions and social agendas of Muslim leaders, both in official institutions that the Soviet regime supported and in the "underground." Scholars also give much attention to the developments that were taking place in Islam in the Russian Empire on the eve of the Bolshevik Revolution, notably the movements to reform Muslim society chiefly through education (Jadīdism), and the way that these developments fed into the revolution and its aftermath, as some Jadīd leaders were recruited for national leadership in the communist government and then were mostly repressed in the purges of the late 1930s.

Assessments of the Character of Islam and Politics in the Region. One of the persistent questions in scholarship on Islam and politics in Central Asia and the Caucasus is whether Muslims in this region have a "strong" enough Muslim orientation to lead them to rise up against secular rulers. Researchers often trace answers to this question back to the original method of conversion of a given people to Islam. They imagine that conversion either by coercion under conquest or by a leader on behalf of the entire group yields only a superficial or "weak" adoption of Islam that does not give rise to Islamism. Conversions, however, occurred hundreds of years ago, and the extent of early coercive conversion in the region is undoubtedly exaggerated. Scholars in both Soviet and Western traditions also theorize that Islam is incompatible with a nomadic lifestyle because of the lack of fixed structures for mosques and schools, as well as low levels of literacy, which supposedly hinder the maintenance of the strong textual tradition presumed to be essential for strong devotion to Islam. There is no consistent relationship, however, between high levels of literacy and devotion to Islam, as the faith found strong adherents among Arab nomads.

Scholars also argue that local traditions with pre-Islamic origins practiced by Muslims in the region displace and dilute true Islamic devotion, supposedly creating a safe buffer between Muslims of this region and more radically oriented Muslims of the Middle East. Such arguments were common among Soviet ideologists and academics who wished to demonstrate that Muslims under Soviet rule are not really so Muslim and thus might more easily abandon Islam in favor of secular values. Such arguments are often advanced today as well by the secularly oriented post-Soviet regimes, as well as by many observers, who hope that "weak" Islam will help to avoid the prospect of Islamic revival or opposition. These assessments, of course, replicate the views, common both in Western scholarship on Islam and among many Muslims with a "radical fundamentalist" orientation, that "true" Islam is strictly based on the textual tradition of the Qur'ān and *ḥadīth,* and that all other practices and beliefs represent deviations from the faith. However, only a small percentage of Muslims in Central Asia and the Caucasus practice Islam in this way.

References to "shamanistic elements," Ṣūfī traditions, and the shallow character of nomadic Islam combine to create an image of the Eurasian nomads as no more than superficially Muslim. Political and intellectual elites of post-Soviet states embrace this idea, but it does not square with the importance of Islam that is evident in these cultures. Further doubt is cast on the depth of devotion of Muslims in Central Asia and the Caucasus based on the notion that the period of Soviet rule was so transformative, and so disruptive of Islamic practices and institutions, that it reduced the population's orientation toward the faith to nothing more than an attribute of their national identity. This claim is also embraced by the political leaders of post-Soviet states, who maintain the Soviet modernist antipathy for religion and would like to see Islam play only a symbolic role in their countries.

To ensure that Islam stays out of politics, recent legislation in Central Asia and the Caucasus tightens long-standing controls on religion, including Islam. In 2011, for example, Kazakhstan (while recognizing the historical role of Ḥanafī Islam) and Azerbaijan followed other regional states as they revised their religious laws to make it harder for "non-traditional" Muslim groups to proselytize, distribute literature, and form associations. On the other hand, some political leaders in Kyrgyzstan foster Islamic financing, and the president of Chechnya promotes morality regulations like dress codes for women in public places.

Sufism. Central Asia is one of the key regions from which Sufism spread widely in the Islamic world. Sufism is a multidimensional phenomenon, which makes it very difficult to conceptualize or analyze. During Soviet times, Western scholars examining the role of Islam and politics in Central Asia and the Caucasus often believed that Sufism represented an oppositional force to the Soviet regime that could operate easily in the underground and could rely on the devoted, even fanatical support of its followers. Thus, the strength of opposition to Russian conquest and Soviet rule observed in the North Caucasus was attributed to Sufism. Paradoxically, Sufism is also often characterized as a deeply spiritual and internal orientation and as open and syncretistic, and thus politically moderate. Scholars often characterize the Naqshbandīyah order, the most widely practiced form of Sufism in this region, as "sober," practicing silent *dhikr* (ritual invocation), in contrast to other Ṣūfī groups categorized as "ecstatic." They often counterpose Sufism to "orthodox" Islam, but in this region there is no broad opposition—political or religious—between an "orthodox" tradition and Sufism.

Sufism had a tremendous impact on both Sunnī and Shīʿī traditions in the region. From the Timurid dynasty onward, some Ṣūfī figures were very closely associated with ruling regimes in the region, and this has also been true in Soviet and post-Soviet times. Sufism and politics, for example, remain connected today in eastern parts of the North Caucasus. It is also true that Ṣūfī figures led some of the major revolts against rulers, including the resistance to Russian occupation of the North Caucasus led by Imam Shāmil (1797–1871) and the Andijan Uprising of 1898. The multidimensional reality of Sufism has not kept scholars and secular political leaders from assessing Sufism in simplistic, contradictory terms.

In the post-Soviet period, there has been growing contention over practices related to Sufism and shrines. They are often called "un-Islamic innovations" (*bidʿah*) by those who now aspire to bring Islam in the region back to its "true" roots in the tradition of Middle Eastern fundamentalist movements.

Muslim Reform. As elsewhere in the Islamic world, efforts to reform Muslim society have been a recurrent theme since the earliest days of Islam in this region. Over the past century or so, these efforts have had two main, interrelated orientations, which may be termed "revivalist," calling for a return to the uncorrupted form of Islam of the time of the Prophet and the early caliphs, and "modernist," calling for an end to the conservatism of Muslim societies that prevents them from acquiring the benefits of modernization.

The Jadīd movement of the late nineteenth and early twentieth centuries criticized the corruption of traditional Muslim rulers and religious leaders in the region and sought to transform their Muslim societies through modern education, which would lead to improvements in health, economic well-being, and spiritual enlightenment. The Soviet regime and the Islamic institutions that it established in the 1940s to represent and direct Islam officially adopted some of the threads of Jadīdist reformism. These included efforts to eradicate practices associated with Islam that it viewed as being at odds with successful modernization, such as restrictions on women's roles, payment of bride-price in arranged marriages, and expensive celebrations associated with circumcision, marriage, and other community events.

Those imams who led prayer in the limited number of mosques that were allowed to function during Soviet times, and those who taught in the two educational institutions that opened during and after World War II, as well as those who worked in the four regional "spiritual directorates" (*muftiates*), were in an ambiguous position as representatives both of the policies of an aggressively atheist regime and of the *ummah*. It is not clear to what extent *fatwa*s issued by official *muftī*s aimed at supporting Soviet modernization, for example, were viewed as the authoritative positions of an authentic Islamic leadership. Yet, it is striking to note the extent to which those who occupied official positions of authority during Soviet times have maintained leadership roles for the post-Soviet Muslim communities throughout the region. That the "Soviet Muslim clergy" was not simply an extension of the Soviet ideological apparatus or the KGB is evident in the diverse positions that these figures are now known to have taken in traditionalist versus reformist debates in Soviet times, and the more open debates on these issues that are taking place in the post-Soviet period.

Reformist agendas took many new directions following the liberalization of Soviet religious policy under Gorbachev's programs of *glasnost* and *perestroika* and especially following independence. There has been a broad social consensus among most Muslims that the effects of Soviet suppression of Islam must be reversed. This has even been embraced by the one-time communist leaders who still dominate the political elite all across the region and who promote historical figures and cultural practices associated with Islam as part of their revival of national culture more broadly. In most cases, however, the political elite views Islam as potentially threatening to the established secular order, and after an initial period of relatively liberal policies (c. 1990–1993), they sought to bring Islam back under state control through direct control over mosques, Islamic schools, and so on, and to exclude Islam from the political arena entirely except as a form of cultural symbolism. Meanwhile, popular views have generally moved in the opposite direction, in part under the influence of greater exposure to the practice of Islam in other countries such as Turkey, Egypt, and Pakistan. This at times creates competing visions of the role of Islam in the state.

The governments of the region apply the terms "Wahhābī" and "fundamentalist" to virtually any Islamic orientation that they deem politically unacceptable, and they treat these terms as synonymous with "Islamic terrorist." Anti-"Wahhābī" laws in the Russian republics of Dagestan and Ingushetia, for example, allow government leaders beholden to Moscow to conduct campaigns against those they label extremists. Violent extremists, however, are still in the minority. They are relatively marginal groups with radical positions determined more by their conflict and confrontation with Russian authorities—especially in the context of the brutal suppression of the Chechen struggle for independence—than by outside influences. One such group is the secessionist/Islamist Caucasus Emirate. While these minority militants primarily attack the police, they have increased attacks on official Islamic clergy.

Meanwhile, there are widespread debates across the region today that echo those in reformist movements throughout the Islamic world. For example, there is much debate about the proper role for women, with some calling for a reversal of key aspects of the "emancipation" that the Soviet regime achieved, such as women's participation in politics and the workforce, education for girls, modern dress standards, and the integration of women and men in public. Much of the focus of reformist debates is on practices associated with Sufism, such as shrine visitation rituals and spiritual healing, as well as aspects of local burial practices, wedding celebrations, and so on, which are seen as reflecting the influences of pre-Islamic religions or Soviet-style secularization. Debates touch on all aspects of society and politics: whether polygamy should be made legal, how prayer should be conducted, whether it is acceptable to use non-Islamic religious symbols in national symbolism, and whether Islamic law should form the basis of state law.

Assessments of Islam and Politics in the Soviet and Post-Soviet Periods. During the Soviet period, the prevailing assessments of Islam and politics in Central Asia and the Caucasus represented two diametrically opposed positions. Some viewed Soviet policies as having been so thoroughly repressive and effective that Islam had been utterly transformed and retained little of the social or political importance that it had in pre-Soviet times. Others saw Islam, for better or worse, as having such an indomitable vitality that it was able to resist all Soviet assaults on it. These opposing views reverberate in the post-Soviet period in the widespread expectations that Islam would serve as a powerful radicalizing force, once the "lid was taken off" Soviet totalitarianism, as well as the claims that Islam would have no political role—barring nefarious outside intervention in the region—because it had been reduced to merely an aspect of national cultural identity. Neither of these assessments captures the complexity of the Soviet or post-Soviet situations. The region is growing more diverse as Soviet unity recedes into the past, as states develop divergent policies, and as social and political developments take their different courses, ranging from violent upheaval in Tajikistan and the North Caucasus, to sharply repressive policies on religion in Uzbekistan and Azerbaijan, to growing social stratification in the relatively prosperous economies of Kazakhstan and Tatarstan.

Yet there are important commonalities that characterize the region as a whole. Everywhere, the legacy of Soviet-style governance is strong, and the political leadership is working to ensure that there will be no development of movements with an Islamic orientation that could challenge their position or the secular character of their regimes. And everywhere, there is a strong impulse within the societies to assign a new importance to Islam as a guiding principle for changes in the social, political, and moral order, in ways that will present challenges for both the traditional practice of Islam and the secular character of societies.

[*See also* Azerbaijan; Chechnya; Kazakhstan; Russia; Sufism; *and* Uzbekistan.]

BIBLIOGRAPHY

Balci, Bayram. "Between Sunnism and Shiism: Islam in Post-Soviet Azerbaijan." *Central Asian Survey* 23, no. 2 (2004): 205–217.

Bennigsen, Alexandre, and Marie Bennigsen Broxup. *The Islamic Threat to the Soviet State*. New York: St. Martin's Press, 1983.

Bregel, Yuri. *An Historical Atlas of Central Asia*. Leiden, Netherlands: Brill, 2003.

DeWeese, Devin. "Islam and the Legacy of Sovietology: A Review Essay on Yaacov Ro'i's Islam in the Soviet Union." *Journal of Islamic Studies* 13, no. 3 (2002): 298–330.

DeWeese, Devin. *Islamization and Native Religion in the Golden Horde: Baba Tükles and Conversion to Islam in Historical and Epic Tradition*. University Park: Pennsylvania State University Press, 1994.

Dudoignon, Stéphane A., ed. *Devout Societies vs. Impious States? Transmitting Islamic Learning in Russia, Central Asia, and China, Through the Twentieth Century*. Berlin: Schwarz, 2004.

Exnerova, Vera. "Caught Between the Muslim Community and the State: The Role of the Local Uzbek Authorities in Ferghana Valley, 1950s–1980s." *Journal of Muslim Minority Affairs* 26, no. 1 (2006): 101–112.

Frank, Allen J. *Muslim Religious Institutions in Imperial Russia: The Islamic World of Novouzensk District and the Kazakh Inner Horde, 1780–1910*. Leiden, Netherlands: Brill, 2001.

Frank, Allen J., and Jahangir Mamatov. *Uzbek Islamic Debates: Texts, Translations, and Commentary*. Springfield, Va.: Dunwoody Press, 2006.

"Islam in Central Asia." Special issue. *Central Asian Survey* 25, no. 3 (2006).

Knysh, Alexander. "Sufism As an Explanatory Paradigm: The Issue of the Motivations of Sufi Resistance Movements in Western and Russian Scholarship." *Die Welt des Islams* 42, no. 2 (2002): 139–173.

Louw, Maria. *Everyday Islam in Post-Soviet Central Asia*. London: Routledge, 2007.

Olcott, Martha Brill. "The Roots of Radical Islam in Central Asia." Carnegie Papers, no. 77. Washington, D.C., 2007.

Privratsky, Bruce G. *Muslim Turkistan: Kazak Religion and Collective Memory*. London: Curzon Press, 2001.

Ro'i, Yaacov. *Islam in the Soviet Union: From the Second World War to Gorbachev*. New York: Columbia University Press, 2000.

Turam, Berna. "The Politics of Engagement between Islam and the Secular State: Ambivalences of 'Civil Society.'" *British Journal of Sociology* 55, no. 2 (2004): 259–281.

Yemelianova, Galina M. *Radical Islam in the Former Soviet Union*. London: Routledge, 2010.

JOHN SCHOEBERLEIN
Updated by DAVID E. MERRELL

ISLAM AND POLITICS IN EUROPE.

There has been a significant Muslim presence in Europe for centuries, particularly in the eastern portion of the continent. In Western Europe, Muslim communities are a more recent phenomenon arising primarily out of post-1945 immigration. Across the continent there has been a growing focus on these communities and the issues they raise in local and national politics. At the same time, the Muslin communities have become increasingly active in national and international politics.

European Muslim Domestic Politics and Transnational Networks. In recent years, much focus has been directed at changing and often conflicted developments in relationships between European governments and their domestic Muslim communities. One of the consequences of communist rule in Eastern Europe in some countries, following a period of fascist dictatorship between the two world wars, was the tight state control of religion, which essentially marginalized it. Many religious edifices were closed, especially churches and mosques, as a form of official Islam was established (except in Albania, where all religion was outlawed), with a central office led by a senior official or mufti, who was known as the *ra'īs al-'ulamā'* in Yugoslavia. This person was in effect nominated and appointed by the state, often with the close involvement of internal security services. After the collapse of the Soviet system in 1989–1991, there was a process of often radical change, which formally entailed a break between the state and the official Muslim structures, as religious freedom and more equality among various communities were introduced. However, in most countries, new constitutions tended to maintain a distinction between the traditional religions of the country, often including Islam, and new ones. In these circumstances, traditional Islamic institutions found that they no longer enjoyed a monopoly of public representation, as rival organizations appeared, especially among the growing number of new immigrants from the Muslim world. In the successor states to the former Yugoslavia, there was the added complication of the role of the former central Islamic administration based in Sarajevo, now in Bosnia-Herzegovina. While most of the Islamic administrations in the new countries accepted some form of primacy, if not direct governance, of Sarajevo, the Serbian Islamic administration was split between those who insisted on complete independence and those who wanted to retain a relationship. In many cases, governments continued to interfere in the internal affairs of Muslim organizations, in some cases in the face of judgments from the European Court of Human Rights in Strasbourg, as was the case in Bulgaria.

While the relationship between the state and the Muslim community in the countries of Eastern Europe is based on a deep-rooted history, the situation in Western Europe has been different. Although there has been history of immigration going back many generations, the situation has been determined mainly by the arrival of people from various parts of the Muslim world since the 1950s, some as immigrant workers and their families and some as refugees. As they started to organize for religious purposes, they increasingly had to navigate within existing organizational forms and legislation. In some countries, such as the United Kingdom and Denmark, groups can form associations without having to register, a requirement that becomes necessary only when tax exemption and other advantages are involved. In other countries, like France and Germany, legislation requires the registration of voluntary organizations, which must meet certain requirements as far as their internal governance is concerned.

Once the processes of organization reached the national level, they ran into the historical patterns of church-state relations. In France there was an official separation between religion and state in 1905, but there has traditionally been a formal liaison forum with the main religions. In the early 1990s, the first attempt was made to establish something similar for Islam. The third attempt took place with the founding in 2002 of the Conseil Français du Culte Musulman (CFCM). This entity continues to function, even though there are regular tensions between various constituent groups. A number of countries have a form of official recognition: Belgium, Germany, and Austria (going back to legislation from 1912; revived in 1979). In these countries, recognition entails state support for confessional religious education, although in Germany only a few federal states have yet recognized Islam for purposes of religious education. In Spain, Denmark, and Britain, a form of recognition is available that gives civil recognition to marriages conducted by an Islamic authority. Variations on these formats can be found elsewhere.

One of the functions of the various forms of state recognition is to manage the place of religion, including Islam, in the public sphere. This fits into a general historical European pattern in which religion is considered a potential threat to the state—understandable given European states' conflicted history with religion. However, in recent years this tension between religion and the public sphere has especially focused on Islam. Since Muslims in Western Europe began organizing in the 1970s, the relationships with local and national authorities have tended to be pragmatic. Local problems have been sorted out locally, and at the national level there has tended to be a low-profile process of steady negotiation. This started changing, as Islam became a factor in international politics after the 1979 Iranian Revolution. The level of domestic attention rose markedly in 1989, when Muslim protests against Salman Rushdie's book *The Satanic Verses* had international repercussions. Later in the year, the expulsion of three students in a Paris suburb for refusing to remove their head scarves opened a simmering debate in France about the nature of the secularity of the state. Both cases provoked major debates across Western Europe.

During the 1990s, international events became an even stronger factor influencing public attitudes towards Muslims. The discourse of "Islam as the new enemy" was reinforced by responses to Samuel Huntington's "The Clash of Civilizations," first published in 1993. But this period also saw the coming of age of the children of immigrant parents. As they began to take an interest in both domestic and international politics, a growing number of people began to take part in politics with Islam at least as part of their profile, initially in local politics and then in national affairs. By the beginning of the twenty-first century, most European parliaments had Muslim members, usually representing parties of the Left (e.g., Labour and Social Democrats), but also occasionally of the Right.

The position of Muslims and attitudes toward Islam were also mobilized for electoral political purposes, often to the advantage of Far Right nationalist parties. The Danish "cartoons affair" in 2005–2006 drew international responses after what appeared to be anti-Islamic cartoons garnered scorn, while in the Netherlands the Far Right politician Geerd Wilders built up a new political party, the Party for Freedom (PVV), with strong Islam-critical campaigns. The perceived threats to national cohesion and identity attributed to Muslims were a marked dimension of the two most recent French presidential elections as well.

The issue of head scarves especially has become a symbol of national political debate across Europe. A growing number of nationalist parties have used the head scarf as well as full face-covering dress (burqa or *niqāb*) in campaigns against what some have alleged is a threatening Islamic takeover. Bans on the public wearing of face covering have been instituted in France and the Netherlands, and silhouettes of burqa-clad women have been prominent symbols in campaigns against expressions of Islam in the public space, including in a Swiss referendum held in November 2009, leading to a ban on the building of minarets on mosques. Following a French example in 2004, a ban on girls wearing head scarves in secondary school was discussed elsewhere, including in 2010 in Kosovo. A German court had some years earlier paved the way for a ban on schoolteachers wearing head scarves.

An underlying theme in the public debates on Islam has been demographic: the immigrant population of Europe, overwhelmingly Muslim, was believed to be growing exponentially with continuing immigration and high rates of fertility. Some versions predicted that half of Europe's population would be Muslim by the end of the century or earlier. Official statistics, in fact, indicate that birthrates among communities of Muslim background are falling fast to approximate the general levels of the countries of residence. The fear of a Muslim "takeover" (planned or not) became part of a more general uncertainty about national identities in an ever more complex world, which has its roots in Europe in the 1980s.

This was one reason that the 1989 French head scarves affair attracted so much attention: it was the year that France celebrated the bicentenary of the French Revolution. Debates across the region have with increasing regularity focused on national values—whether Muslims accept them and can integrate into them, and whether national identities are being threatened.

Muslim Transnational Networks. The first generation of immigrants from Muslim countries maintained links with their countries and districts of origin, and in their new locations organized in ethnic patterns and often in mosques and organizations with reference to their districts of origin. These links were kept alive by regular travel back and forth, especially among Turks and North Africans, where distances were short enough to allow annual visits home.

These networks could be mobilized for a variety of purposes. Centrally, of course, it meant that extended families could stay in touch, in particular by arranging cross-border marriages, and by the substantial financial remittances that were a significant part of the international economy of the countries of origin, at least in the early phases. These were often the networks through which immigrant Muslim communities acquired their first imams and religious teachers, as they began to organize as religious communities. This often meant that the community had an individual in a position of religious authority who was not well trained, which put them at a disadvantage when attempts were made to establish links with other religious communities, especially churches, in their immediate neighborhoods.

All the countries of origin experienced various forms of Islamic revival over the nineteenth and twentieth centuries, out of which arose a variety of movements of different character and with different programs and activities. Many of these very quickly followed immigration into Europe.

The import of workers from Turkey into Germany was arranged at an official central government level. As families were established, the arrangements included the emigration of Turkish schoolteachers to Germany to teach Turkish children their native language and culture. (These teachers tended to be secularists in the Kemalist tradition who therefore ignored religion.) During the 1980s, emigration to Germany provided the opportunity for Turkish Islamic movements—which were often banned in Turkey, including the Süleymancıs, Milli Görüş, and Nursis—to set up mosques and other facilities. The official Turkish religious authority, the Diyanet İşleri Başkanlığı (commonly called the Diyanet), a department of the prime minister's office, also established itself with a German branch, known as DITIB, with a head office in Cologne. As Turkey drifted toward civil war during the late 1980s, most of the parties to the conflict received substantial support among the Turks in Germany. When the army took over in Ankara in September 1980, it immediately set about strengthening the role of the Diyanet, both internally and among the expatriate communities, including those in the Netherlands, Belgium, and France, as well as in Germany. The number of DITIB-related mosques in Germany grew markedly, while some of the other organizations declined. The Milli Görüş, especially, came under surveillance by the German security services due to suspicions about its political character. Since the beginning of the twenty-first century, tensions among various Islamic movements in Turkey eased, especially since the Adalet ve Kalkınma Partisi (Justice and Development Party, or AKP) came to power in 2002. At the same time, the neo-Nursi movement of Fethullah Gülen expanded. These changes were apparent in Germany, where previous rivalries eased and were replaced by sometimes quite close cooperation at the local level. In 2006, the federal ministry of the interior set up a consultative project, the German Islam Conference, and in response the major Muslim umbrella organizations came together very loosely in the Coordination Council of Muslims in Germany.

In France, men from the North African colonies of Morocco, Algeria, and Tunisia served in the French army in both world wars, and together with immigrant workers made for a substantial number of North Africans in France by the 1950s. The Algerian war of independence created major tensions among these people, which meant that the independence movement enjoyed extensive support in France, and many thousands of Algerians were imprisoned as a direct consequence of their activities. When the war ended in 1962, large numbers of Algerians who had supported the French were forced to leave Algeria and were settled in camps. The Islamic Centre and Grand Mosque of Paris, built by the French state in the 1920s in recognition of North Africans' contribution during World War I, now gradually became the representation of official Islam in Algeria. Opposed to it were a number of Muslim organizations, loosely associated with the Muslim Brotherhood, today represented in the Union des Organisations Islamiques de France. In a similar manner, the Fédération Nationale des Musulmans de France brings together mainly Moroccan Muslims. The establishment in 2002 of the CFCM was the culmination of a long process of French pressure for Muslims to present a single voice with which the government could negotiate. Internal tensions among the member organizations regularly resurface, especially when political tensions in the country of origin transfer to France.

As late as the 1990s, Moroccan authorities sought to keep their émigrés under control from afar, going so far as to decree that they should not participate in local elections when rules were amended to allow foreign residents to do so. This particularly affected local elections in the Netherlands in the 1990s. There, as also in Belgium and France, Moroccan authorities attempted to keep Moroccan mosques under control in an official federation, though a number of smaller mosques managed to stay independent.

In Britain, it is primarily organizations of South Asian origin that have attracted attention. The two main movements that were established in response to full British rule after the Indian uprisings of 1857, the Deobandīs and the Barelwīs, very quickly began to function among Muslim immigrants in Britain in the 1960s and early 1970s. People from the much smaller political movement, the Jamāʿat-i Islāmī, founded by Abūal-Aʿlā Mawdūdī (1903–1979), were active from the early 1970s. While the Barelwīs have remained a loose network of mosques focused around individual spiritual leaders, the Deobandīs have concentrated on a growing network of colleges, Dār al-ʿUlūm, where teenage boys receive education and Islamic training. A growing number of them have become imams after following higher education at Islamic universities in the Middle East. Both these networks have maintained close links to their colleagues in the Indian subcontinent, especially in Pakistan.

The Jamāʿat-i Islāmī–related institutions, on the other hand, have been established to meet particular needs among Muslims in British society, especially concerning the Islamic instruction of young people. The Islamic Foundation outside the city of Leicester has been active mostly in research, higher education, and the training of community leaders. It cooperates closely with British local and central government in the provision of advice and consultancy and in providing courses for public officials.

While some of these organizations work with British authorities, others keep varying degrees of distance, although none appears actively to be engaged in activities opposed to the authorities. However, they have all in one way or another become active in public campaigns against specific government policies, especially foreign policy in the Middle East.

Since the late 1980s, transnational Islamic networks have grown. Especially among Sunnī Muslims, networks have developed that have bases in the countries of the Arabian Peninsula, especially Saudi Arabia. Saudi embassies and certain central government agencies have made a variety of efforts to spread their impact among the Muslim communities of various ethnic and national origins. First, there is the organization of the annual *ḥajj*, for which the issuing of visas and travel arrangements are an important dimension. Each year *ḥajj* authorities also invite prominent Muslim personalities as official guests. Since the communist collapse, Saudi authorities have also sponsored large numbers of pilgrims from Eastern European countries. Through the 1980s, the Saudi office of *daʿwah* sponsored the appointment of imams to a variety of mosques around Europe, at one time more than twenty in the United Kingdom alone. Various government agencies also have contributed substantial sums to the construction of new mosques, although not nearly as many as the media suggested. In this Saudi Arabia was not alone, with most Muslim states at one time or another doing so, not to mention donations from a number of wealthy private individuals. It is, however, difficult to assess how much financial support also influenced the political stances of the groups being supported. Various sources suggest that at the time of the Iraqi invasion of Kuwait in 1990, the Saudi authorities found it difficult to translate their financial investment into support for Saudi Arabia's political stance in the military alliance against Iraq.

Most prominent among such sponsorship agencies was the Muslim World League (Rābiṭat al-ʿĀlam al-Islāmī). Headquartered and significantly funded by Saudi Arabia, the League is an international nongovernmental organization concerned with supporting Islamic educational and other charitable purposes and spreading awareness of Islam. The League has been a major mover in sponsoring the building of mosques, especially in areas of war and civil strife, including regions of former Yugoslavia. In some areas this has led to accusations of the imposition of Saudi concepts of Islam, even of supporting salafism, although the evidence of the latter is weak.

From the late 1970s, Libya also sought to present its interests through support for Muslim activities. At a time when the countries of communist Eastern Europe were beginning to allow a few native Muslims to receive Islamic studies training in the Muslim world, they preferred to allow them to go to countries that could be politically approved. Libya was included on this list, particularly in the form of the World Islamic Call Society. A number of Islamic leaders in Eastern Europe were thus trained at the Society's college outside Tripoli. After the collapse of communism, it became easier to find training elsewhere, especially in Egypt, Saudi Arabia, and Malaysia.

European Foreign Policy and Islam. During the first phases of immigration and settlement in Western Europe, the political activists among Muslims were primarily interested in issues that directly affected themselves. Internationally, this meant issues to do with the countries of origin. As already mentioned, this meant an active interest among Algerians in France in the struggle for independence in the years up to 1962 and then, in the 1990s, in the civil war in Algeria. Before the military coup in September 1980, Turks in Germany were likewise frequently engaged in events "back home." In fact, it was often difficult to distinguish between transnational religious, family, and political links. Pakistani politics have regularly divided communities of Pakistani origin in Britain in complex manners, although the local expressions of such divisions have tended to be quieter than in the subcontinent itself, even when events there have been violent, especially in 1971, when East Pakistan broke away by war to become Bangladesh, and in 1979, when Pakistan's military government executed Zulfikar Ali Bhutto, the leader of the Pakistan People's Party, which had a large popular following in Britain. One issue on which virtually all British-Pakistanis could agree was the injustice of India's role in Kashmir, a sensitive territorial as well as religious conflict.

Once the children of immigrants became politically active, their interests broadened. As many of them became more consciously Muslim, they developed interests in a wider range of "Muslim causes," in addition to those that concerned their parents. The 1990s offered a number of such causes for young Muslims to identify with. Initially mobilized by the Rushdie and head scarf affairs in Britain and France, many young Muslims proceeded to throw their energies into such issues. The affairs of 1989 were followed in 1990–1991 by the First Gulf war following Iraq's invasion of Kuwait, and questions were raised about Muslims as a potential security issue when they took a high profile in protests against the war. Soon after, Yugoslavia broke down and the war in Bosnia became a theme, which brought many young Muslims together across national and ethnic boundaries. The Algerian civil war during the 1990s occasionally spilled over into violent incidents in France with growing talk of Islamic terrorism. At the same time, events in Chechnya and, around the turn of the century, in Kosovo offered other causes for concern. The plight of Palestine was a continuing sore. Terrorist attacks on New York and Washington, D.C., on 11 September 2001 (9/11), followed by attacks in Madrid in March 2003 and in London in July 2005, strongly encouraged security-led policy responses in a number of European countries as well as fears of "home-grown terrorists." Anti-terrorism legislation was tightened, as were border controls; numerous projects and programs to counter "radicalization" of young Muslims were introduced; and Muslims generally were made to feel that they were the target of public suspicion.

It became increasingly common to see Muslims demonstrating in connection with these events in various European capitals. Muslim organizations, as well as the small but growing number of politicians of Muslim background, began to lobby their governments on foreign policy questions other than those of their countries of origin. Some voices in the British Foreign Office had already made informal contacts with selected Muslim organizations as early as the early 1990s, with the argument that in a democracy they needed to listen also to interested minority voices. This coincided with the development of a policy line of "engaging with Islam." During the war in Bosnia in 1992–1995, there was a good deal of frustration among Muslims around Europe at their governments' lack of willingness to engage substantially with events. When, toward the end of the decade, European governments took a more active stance toward developments in Kosovo, this was widely welcomed. In London, the Muslim Council of Britain held a reception to thank Prime Minister Tony Blair and the foreign secretary for their role in curbing Serbian attacks.

When the second Iraq War started in March 2003, Muslim activists across Europe became prominent in an alliance with a variety of other groups against the war. In the biggest demonstration anywhere in the world, the antiwar demonstration in mid-February 2003 in London had a collective leadership in which Muslims worked together with political parties, trade unions, Christian and other religious organizations, women's and youth groups, and so on.

Assessment. The relationship between Muslims and Islam in Europe and the broader societies and states in Europe is complex. The experiences of Muslims living in Europe range from the centuries-old communities in Eastern and parts of central Europe to the recent arrivals of labor migrants and refugees. Their national, ethnic, and cultural backgrounds differ widely, as do their experiences and conceptions of Islam and their degrees of attachment to their religion, from completely secularized to deeply pious. They are variously impacted by the European contexts in which they live in terms of social and economic environment, work, and educational experience.

When it comes to politics, there is probably more common ground among various Muslim groups than on most other issues, at least when the matter is one of foreign policy. Both the European political environment and the international Islamic networks have imagined Europe's Muslims as being a rather more uniform community than it really is. This has contributed to encouraging innate tendencies toward a unified Muslim response to many of the foreign policy issues that have appeared in the headlines in the last quarter of a century.

Such common policy stances have, however, remained absent in the politics of Muslim groups on the domestic scene, where the variety referred to earlier often takes precedent. It seems reasonable to expect such domestic variety to continue to be a factor, although with the passage of time those dimensions, which are linked to the country of origin, will weaken in influence compared to those related more directly to the lived situation.

BIBLIOGRAPHY

Al-Azmeh, Aziz, and Effie Fokas, eds. *Islam in Europe: Diversity, Identity and Influence*. Cambridge, U.K.: Cambridge University Press, 2007.

Bougarel, Xavier, and Nathalie Clayer, eds. *Le nouvel Islam balkanique: Les musulmans, acteurs du post-communisme 1990-2000*. Paris: Maisonneuve et Larose, 2001.

Bowen, John R. *Can Islam be French? Pluralism and Pragmatism in a Secular State*. Princeton, N.J.: Princeton University Press, 2010.

Cesari, Jocelyne. *When Islam and Democracy Meet: Muslims in Europe and the United States*. 2d ed. New York: Palgrave Macmillan, 2006.

Fetzer, Joel S., and J. Christopher Soper. *Muslims and the State in Britain, France and Germany*. Cambridge, U.K.: Cambridge University Press, 2005.

Klausen, Jytte. *The Islamic Challenge: Politics and Religion in Western Europe*. Oxford: Oxford University Press, 2005.

Marechal, Brigitte, Felice Dassetto, Stefano Allievi, and Jørgen S. Nielsen. *Muslims in the Enlarged Europe*. Leiden, Netherlands: E. J. Brill, 2003.

Nielsen, Jørgen S. *Muslims in Western Europe*. 3d ed. Edinburgh: Edinburgh University Press, 2004.

Nielsen, Jørgen S., et al., eds. *Yearbook of Muslims in Europe*. Leiden, Netherlands: E. J. Brill, 2009–.

Sinno, Abdulkader, ed. *Muslims in Western Politics*. Bloomington: Indiana University Press, 2009.

JØRGEN S. NIELSEN

ISLAM AND POLITICS IN NORTH AMERICA. The subject of Islam and politics in North America can be discussed according to two interrelated issues: the first issue addresses how Islam, embodied by the practice of its adherents, is accommodated in North America, according to the distribution of privileges afforded to constituents of North American societies. The second is the issue of how Muslims, as adherents of Islam, inform the distribution of privileges in said societies through political action, such as forming voting blocs, action committees, alliances, civil rights organizations, and activism.

Islam as a Feature of American Universalism. Muslims have been present in North America and, more particularly, the United States throughout the formative period of the latter, mostly as a result of the trans-Atlantic slave trade. It is difficult to ascertain what percentage of slaves may have been Muslim; there is little doubt that many were, however. Notwithstanding the long presence of Muslims in North America, this entry is concerned with the politics of such a presence—and less with its history. In the United States, privileges associated with citizenship or other political affiliations were extended to Muslims by the so-called founding fathers.

George Washington, John Adams, Thomas Jefferson, and James Madison all in one way or another solidified the unique form of American secularism by insisting on religious freedom for Muslims (as well as others). The expressed concern with religious freedom for Muslims reflects two overarching qualities regarding the founders: first, they insisted on religious freedom for Muslims at a time when hostilities between the nascent United States and Muslim countries flared, therefore denoting American principles of secularism as a fundamental feature of both the polity and its countenance toward the international community. For example, during the late eighteenth century, the United States found itself at war with the North African, predominately Muslim, principalities. At the conclusion of the conflict, the United States entered into a peace treaty. Below is an excerpt from the Treaty of Tripoli (1797):

> As the Government of the United States of America is not, in any sense, founded on the Christian religion, as it has in itself no character of enmity against the laws, religion, or tranquility, of Mussulmen [Muslims], and as the said States never entered into any war or act of hostility against any Mahometan [Muslim] nation, it is declared by the parties that no pretext arising from religious opinions shall ever produce an interruption of the harmony existing between the two countries. (Treaty of Peace and Friendship)

The above excerpt suggests that the United States was "not, in any sense, founded on the Christian religion," thus militating against any notion that the United States was a denominational state. This principle could be said to be a basic building block of American secularism. The second overarching quality, which stems from the first, is the universal nature of American secularism. "Virtue," as a recall of Hellenic referents, is a philosophical underpinning of American society as conceived by the early authors of American doctrine. According to John Adams:

> All sober inquirers after truth, ancient and modern, pagan and Christian, have declared that the happiness of man, as well as his dignity consists in virtue. Confucius, Zoroaster, Socrates and Mohamet (Muhammad), not to mention authorities really sacred, have agreed to this. (Adams, p. 3)

The above passage asserts, quite emphatically, not only the open nature of "American political thought," if such a denotation is possible at the time, but the ecumenical assumptions underlying it. The impetus of the pursuit of virtue is not the rejection of various religious, spiritual, or philosophical traditions—quite the opposite. Virtue is postulated as a universal value and all of the great "sober inquirers of truth" are credited for consecrating virtue's centrality. In terms of this principle, the explicit way in which many of the founders advocated for religious freedom for Jews and Muslims, beyond merely various Christian denominations, is more readily understood. The founders valued the presence of spiritual and religious diversity as indispensable to the manifestation of virtue's universality and, by extension, America's unique capacity to accommodate it.

In this regard, one can begin to examine ways in which this principle has been lived out according to the distribution and protection of privileges associated with being an American.

Muslims in America. It is quite common to begin any discussion about Muslims in America by drawing attention to the trans-Atlantic slave trade. Since it is difficult to know just how many slaves were Muslim and how many, though doubtless thousands, were forcibly converted to Christianity, it is not possible to shed much light on the politics of Muslims in America through this example. Slaves were deprived of any and all privileges and thus could be said to have been denied a political status altogether. Furthermore, since countless slaves, if not the majority, were certainly not Muslim, the denominational background of African slaves is incidental to the political climate affected by the slave trade. Rather, it will be necessary to draw attention to specific issues—legislation, discrimination, accommodation, and the like—to discuss Islam and politics.

Since the establishment of the United States and Canada, mosques have been constructed, census figures accumulated, and immigrants accommodated. Notwithstanding isolated incidents and figures, little can be said about the political nature of Islam in America from the eighteenth century through the twentieth. There are instances of individual Muslims who ascended to the national stage and affected the political discourse—for example, Malcolm X (d. 1965) and Muhammad Ali (b. 1942)—but these men inform our thoughts on the civil rights movement in America, especially as it pertains to the plight of African Americans. In addition, although "the Islam," if you will, of both men certainly drew the ire of white conservatives, "their Islam" was not responded to by an effective national discourse that sought to curb the privileges of American Muslims on the basis of their being practitioners of Islam exclusively.

Such a discourse emerges in both the United States, and to a lesser extent in Canada, after the attacks of 11 September 2001, which were carried out by militant Muslims against high profile U.S. targets. Subsequent to those attacks, a sharp increase in federal hate crimes, as well as lesser forms of discrimination, has been well-documented. The nature in which such crimes are enabled through popular discourse is an aspect of the politics of Islam in America. Since perhaps 1979 and certainly 2001, an ever growing organization of pundits, self-proclaimed scholars, activists, and even Christian and Jewish leaders have formed a loose federation of alliances intent on three things: (1) insisting that Islam is uniquely inimical to Western values, and (2) arguing that Muslims are, therefore, not a natural part of the Western social fabric, which forms the premise for (3) taking legal action to prevent Muslims from practicing their faith in the United States and other Western states. This discourse can be summarized as "Islamophobia."

Islamophobia, or the intentionally engendered irrational fear of Muslims, can be seen playing itself out in the contest over the distribution of privileges. In addition, Islamophobia has lent itself to foreign policy debates, nudging certain political circles into believing that a protracted war with the Muslim world is both necessary and inevitable. The 2003 invasion of Iraq, largely seen as illegal throughout much of the world, and the unconditional support for Israel are two key foreign policy positions that distinguish the Islamophobic network.

The Politics of Islamophobia: General Features. Islamophobia involves not only the irrational fear of Muslims, but actions, resulting in policy, to be taken predicated on such fears; thus Islamophobia is overtly political. For example, since November 2010, over twenty states in the United States have passed or proposed bills to ban Sharīʿah (guidelines for living an Islamic life). Several important political implications may be noted here: first, the sharp contrast between attempts to ban Sharīʿah, which amounts to essentially banning Islam, and the ethos of the founders. Whereas the founders sought to extend the privilege of religious freedom to Muslims to strengthen the American polity, this new movement seeks to restrict Muslim freedoms in an effort to re-align the polity according to unprecedented configurations. Individuals who restrict Muslim freedom often argue that Islam is incompatible with American values because America is a Christian nation. As noted above, some of the founders argued that it is not.

Second, by attempting to ban Sharīʿah and effectively ban the practice of Islam, this movement revolves around the principle that some constituents should be denied privileges, while others should not. The inequitable distribution of privileges (whether material or emancipatory) facilitates competition, which in turn is embodied in partisan politics, thus substantiating a system of variegated political parties, platforms, and agendas. Individuals and groups then associate themselves with such parties accordingly or due to a prioritization of the privileges they seek to advocate on behalf of themselves or society as a whole.

The last political implication is that many of the campaigns to ban Sharīʿah coincide with elections. They thus displace more traditional political issues, like the distribution of resources, to make space for the politicization of non-material cultural privileges. In other words, emphases on wealth distribution, education, and health care at a state or federal level are reduced and concerns over the freedom of Muslims to practice their faith on the state or federal level are elevated. Needless to say, the skewing of popular emphasis shifts the entire political landscape.

The Trajectory of Islamophobic Politics: Neoconservatism. Two events converge to form the dynamics that characterize the American Muslim context: the First Gulf War and the attacks of 11 September 2001. Many American Muslims did not support American efforts against Iraq; as a result, the Gulf states withdrew their support for many Islamic organizations in America. These Islamic organizations underwent a period of "re-assessment" (Haddad, 2000, p. 31). These organizations could no longer consider themselves as extensions of the "home" countries or as largely overlooked minorities whose civil rights were not perceived as under threat. The First Gulf War, coinciding with the collapse of the Soviet Union, fomented an environment for the creation of a "new enemy" with global reach. "Islam" emerged as an abstract, yet simultaneously identifiable, enemy.

Between the 1967 Arab–Israeli War and the Iranian hostage crisis of 1979, Muslims remained a dormant yet consistent fear in the American public imagination. This fear was due in part to concrete events that took place overseas and in part due to a narrative perpetuated by the various institutions that deal with the Muslim world. This narrative, as mentioned earlier, insisted that conflict between the West and Islam was perennial. This type of narrative can only be substantiated by generalizing upon acts carried out by Muslims, or by misattributing such acts to Islam, or by reducing complex developments to an identification with Islam. And though these methods can be found among any and all peoples involved in the generation of stereotypes, they resonate as a political logic in only one place—the neoconservative movement. Islam occupies a central place on the neoconservative political platform.

Economic theory underlies traditional conservatism. It is believed that the economy is both self-regulating and the basis of human interaction. Government action can only interfere with this natural process, thus resulting in economic and, by extension, social decline; thus traditional conservatives argue for a laissez-faire economy. Social conservatism is a natural concomitant to economic conservatism since the insistence on economic liberty necessitates limitations on political institutions. Political institutions are responsible for the mandated redistribution of resources, among other things, such as providing security and arbitrating disputes. The power of such institutions is limited in a conservative society and, due to the absence of governing bodies, culture enjoys a de facto autonomy to replicate itself, sustaining its consistent nature. Economic conservatism facilitates a de facto cultural conservatism. Neoconservatives reverse this dynamic: they insist on privileging culture in their political rhetoric. Evasive concepts such as "the West" or "the Judeo-Christian tradition" operate as political platforms; when enacted as a political project, the emphasis on sustaining a "cultural heritage" liberates political institutions from the conventional task of redistributing wealth. Thus a project to "conserve culture" facilitates a de facto free economy.

Such a political ideology requires *cultural* enemies, both domestic and foreign. Domestically, homosexuals, immigrants, Muslims, progressives, atheists, and others are depicted as "threatening" the American way of life. Since this discussion is concerned with Islam and politics, it will be informative to look at some specific examples. Whatever conflicts arise out of the Muslim world and are translated into American political discourse, for whatever reason, are often processed in a unique manner, according to general stereotyping methods.

For example, the attacks of 11 September 2001, were often attributed to the Islamic doctrine of *jihād*, in which it was supposed that Islam "commands *jihād*" against non-believers. Since the attacks of 2001 involved the kamikaze-like act of militant suicide, comparisons were immediately drawn between these events and attacks against Israelis carried out by Palestinian fighters, which throughout the same time period displayed similar characteristics. It was argued by many that militant suicide (i.e., the willingness to terminate oneself in an effort to carry out militant attacks) was encouraged by Islamic doctrines that offered "virgins" in Islamic "paradise." It is never explained, however, why the vast majority of Muslims do not opt out of life through militant suicide to enjoy the supposedly generous sexual activity it affords. It has been well documented that neoconservatives were enthusiastic activists for the 2003 U.S.-led invasion of Iraq. Whether or not such thinkers truly believed in a "clash of civilizations" is irrelevant; these analysts, as part of their political logic, invest heavily in notions of culture and distinguish themselves from traditional conservatives in this regard.

What makes America uniquely American for neoconservatives is its culture, not its constitutional principles. For the neoconservatives, being a Christian or a Jew, or a supporter of Israel, or a heterosexual, or "tough" on immigration has inherent political value. Naturally, in order for this platform to be operative, it must be juxtaposed to the non–Judeo-Christian, the homosexual, and the immigrant. The civilizational reach of Islam, along with the fact that Israel occupies largely (though not exclusively) Muslim lands, makes Islam a suitable anti-hero or antagonist. Neoconservatives have been just as responsible for the politicization of Islam as Muslims themselves. And a distinct correlation exists between Islamophobia and the politics of the Right.

Muslims as Political Actors. Just as much of the twenty-first-century neoconservative movement was forged by the First Gulf War and the 11 September 2001, attacks, Muslim political life has been as well. Between the specific ascendancy of the neoconservatives during the Bush era and the more general politics of Islamophobia, in which Americans are called upon to ban Sharīʿah, Muslim have come to see their civil rights under threat. Notwithstanding the context of the Patriot Act, which is largely seen as targeting Muslims, it is the more specific efforts to target Islamic modes of life that concern Muslims. Just as states have attempted to ban Sharīʿah, local councils have held up the construction of new mosques and Islamic cultural centers. The most well-known example is the Park51 Cultural Center, near

"Ground Zero." Data suggested that 70 percent of Americans opposed the center, citing various but related reasons. Most of these reasons pertained to the perceived pain that building the center would supposedly cause. Mayor Rudy Guiliani of New York argued that building the center amounted to a "desecration; Nobody would allow something like that at Pearl Harbor.... Let's have some respect for who died there and why they died there" (Haberman, 2010).

The notion that building a religious affiliated center in the United States could be a desecration obviously informs discussions over the equal distribution of rights. Muslims have made an increasing presence on the political landscape, gravitating toward organizations in ever increasing numbers. Organizations like CAIR (the Council on American Islamic Relations) are especially devoted to Muslim civil rights. The effectiveness of these organizations remains to be seen.

Lastly, the emergence of a new breed of American Muslim intellectuals and activists is changing the political landscape. Historically, Muslims have had to either assimilate to the dominant culture or segregate themselves. For the former, events like those of 11 September 2001, and its consequences have made smooth assimilation more difficult. For the latter, such events have turned them into suspects. Since the politics of the Muslim world and its vast resources affect political discourse in the United States, American Muslim intellectuals are now beginning to actively pursue reform in the Muslim world while defending Muslim civil rights in the United States, thus adopting an openly cosmopolitan identity.

This cosmopolitanism distinguishes such Muslims from their forebearers insofar as they (1) do not rely on notions of civil rights but increasingly notions of human rights; and (2) openly challenge the status quo in Muslim-majority countries as Muslims who do not subscribe to dominant American policies, political platforms, or affiliations. In other words, such intellectuals possess "street credit" inside Muslim countries and are known in these countries, thanks to advanced forms of communication, yet they also pose a deep confidence in political values such as freedom and democracy, due to their American experiences. The politics motivating such Muslims, in no particular order, are (1) genuine humanitarian concerns over social justice in the West and the Muslim world; (2) an awareness of the correlation between Islamic politics and the situation facing American Muslims; and (3) strictly Muslim intellectual concerns over the content of Islam. The Arab Spring has brought these intellectuals, who have far from everything in common, in sharp relief. Ahmed Rehab, Mona Eltahawy, M. Yaser Tabbara, and Reza Aslan are a few examples of such American Muslims.

BIBLIOGRAPHY

Asad, Talal. *Formations of the Secular: Christianity, Islam, Modernity.* Stanford, Calif.: Stanford University Press, 2003.

Bowen, John R. *Blaming Islam.* Cambridge, Mass.: MIT Press.

CNN/Opinion Research Poll, 11 September 2010.

Center of American Progress. "Fear, Inc: The Roots of the Islamophobia Network in America." http://www.americanprogress.org/wp-content/uploads/issues/2011/08/pdf/islamophobia.pdf.

Curtis, Edward E. *Muslims in America: A Short History.* Oxford: Oxford University Press, 2009.

Federal Bureau of Investigation. http://www.fbi.gov/about-us/investigate/civilrights/hate_crimes.

Haberman, Maggie. "GZ Mosque Is a 'Desecration,' "Decent Muslims' Won't Be Offended." http://www.politico.com/blogs/maggiehaberman/0810/Rudy_Mosque_is_a_desecration_.html.

Haddad, Yvonne Yazbeck. "The Dynamics of Islamic Identity in North America." In *Muslim on the Americanization Path?,* edited by Y. Y. Haddad and J. Esposito, p. 31. Oxford: Oxford University Press, 2000.

Hutson, James. "The Founding Fathers and Islam." *Library of Congress Information Bulletin* 61/65 (May 2002).

"Jihad Watch." http://www.jihadwatch.org/2012/07/raymond-ibrahim-in-who-is-telling-the-truth-about-islam.html.

Pipes, Daniel. "Moderate Islam May Be Key to Winning War on Terror." *New York Sun*, 5 December 2006.

Southern Poverty Law Center. http://www.splcenter.org/get-informed/hate-map.

Treaty of Peace and Friendship. Article 11. The Avalon Project. New Haven, Conn.: Yale Law School.

Laith Saud

Islam and Politics in South Asia.

Islam initially spread in South Asia as a result of the region's trade links with the Arab world, but it was not until the Arab invasion of 711 that the first of many small Muslim states were established in the region.

The Sultanate of Delhi. The weakening of the ʿAbbāsid caliphate in Baghdad allowed South Asia to become more independent and gave powerful military dynasties opportunities to gain control over large parts of the area. Among the first to do so were the Ghaznavids, Turkish slaves of the Seljuks, who invaded India in the tenth century. Maḥmūd of Ghaznā (d. 1030), in particular, was presented by local historians such as Bārānī (d. 1357) as an ideal Muslim ruler who fought both rebellious Hindus and heretical rebels and brought honor to Muslims. However, Maḥmūd's destruction of Hindu temples in Somnath and elsewhere has also been cited by Hindu nationalists as proof of Islam's intolerance.

The Ghūrīds displaced the Ghaznavids and Shamsuddin Iltutmish (d. 1236), a former slave of the Ghūrīd ruler Quṭb al-Dīn Aybak (d. 1210), established the Delhi Sultanate, which was subsequently presided over by the Khaljīs (1290–1320), the Tughluqs (1320–1414), the Sayyids (1414–1451), and the Lodhīs (1451–1526). Like Maḥmūd, the sultans of Delhi justified their rule, at least in part, based on their defense of Sunnism, defending their realm as *dār al-Islām* and Delhi as its fortress (*qubbah*), striking coins with Islamic inscriptions, imposing *jizyah* on non-Muslim *dhimmī* (although not consistently) and obtaining recognition of their status as *amīr*s from the caliph. The sultans also set up a system of *qāḍī* courts, which applied Sharīʿah law. Ibn Baṭṭūṭah, the renowned traveler, served as a *qāḍī* not only in Delhi under Muḥammad Shah Tughluq (r. 1325–1351) but also in the Maldives, where he acted as a *qāḍī* for the Mālikī population. Most of the sultans also engaged in *jihād* against Hindus and heretics such as the Ismāʿīlīs but also against rival Muslims. Some dynasties also accommodated the adoption of Hindu culture and intermarriages with Hindus, prompting a warning from figures such as Bārānī who saw in such marriages an upsetting of the social order.

The sultans were also divided over their policy toward Sufism, which has played a major role in consolidating Muslim identity in South Asia and has represented, at different times, both Sharīʿah-minded orthodoxy and an escape from the latter. While many of the sultans patronized Ṣūfī saints and burial sites, some, such as Ghiyāth al-Dīn Tughluq (r. 1320–1325), his successor Muḥammad al-Dīn (d. 1351) (who reportedly received Ibn Taymīyah's students in his court), Bahlūl (r. 1451–1489), and Sikander Shah Lōdhī (r. 1489–1517) were opposed to Ṣūfī practices, which they regarded as undermining the Sharīʿah. However, many Ṣūfīs, such as al-Hujwīrī (d. 1077) and Nizām al-Dīn Awliyāʾ (d. 1325) used juristic arguments in support of their controversial practices such as *samāʿ*, as seen in Hujwīrī's *Kashf al-maḥjūb*. In some cases, Ṣūfīs such as ʿAbd al-Quddūs Gangōhī (d. 1538) acted as a check to the despotism of the sultans, reminding them of their duty to uphold the Sharīʿah. Because the mass popularity of Ṣūfīs often transcended confessional boundaries—as seen in the example of Farīd al-Dīn Ganj Shakkar (d. 1265), whose teachings have been incorporated in the Sikh Guru Granth—most earned popularity and respect.

The Moghuls. Unlike the Delhi sultans, who traced their ancestry to the Turks, Mughals took pride in their descent from the Mongol Tīmūr (d. 1405). Bābur (d. 1530), the ruler of Kabul and Ghaznī, founded the dynasty by invading India and conquering Delhi in 1526, justifying his assaults on local Hindus as a *jihād*. His successor, Humāyūn, who was forced into exile in Ṣafavid Iran, embraced Shiism and, upon his restoration, recognized the Ṣafavid ruler as the Imām, ordering coins to be minted in the latter's name and for prayers to be sent on him during *khuṭbahs* (Friday sermons).

Akbar (d. 1605), who acceded to the throne at the age of thirteen, promoted a state-enforced syncretism named the Divine Faith (Dīn-i Ilāhī), which merged Islam, Hinduism, and Christianity (the first Jesuit missionaries having arrived in Agra in 1580). Presiding over this faith was the emperor himself, whose quasi-divine authority was justified with reference to illuminationist doctrines and the discourse of the Shīʿī philosopher Naṣīr al-Dīn al-Ṭūsī, (d. 1274). However, Akbar also patronized Ṣūfī orders, particularly the Chishtī, which had been brought to India by Muʿīnuddīn Chishtī (d. 1236) in 1193. Inasmuch as Chishtī and his closest disciples had generally shunned association with the rulers, some of the strongest opposition to Akbar's policies thus came from the Chishtī jurist and historian Badaʾūnī (d. 1615) and Aḥmad Sirhindī (d. 1624), who hailed from a Chishtī family and later became a *khalīfah* of the Naqshbandī Bāqī Billah (d. 1603).

Hailed as the "revivalist of the second millennium," Sirhindī criticized not just Akbar's Dīn-i Ilāhī but also Ibn al-ʿArabī's unity of being (*waḥdat al-wujūd*), which was used by some Ṣūfīs, such as the Chishtī Shaykh Muḥibb Allāh (d. 1648), to argue for an inclusivist theology which could find a place for Hindu deities within Islam's *tawḥīd*. In its place, Sirhindī championed the concept of *waḥdat al-shuhūd*. Sirhindi's influence was also felt in Ottoman Turkey through the Kurdish Shaykh Khalid al-Baghdādī (d. 1826). Opposition to Akbar's policies also came from the Qadirī Ṣūfī ʿAbd al-Ḥaqq Dihlawī (d. 1642), who championed *ḥadīth* studies and wrote important works in the field.

The death of Shāh Jahān in 1666 brought the tradition of liberal inclusivism—represented by his eldest son, Dārā Shukūh (d. 1659), who had advocated the use of Hindu scriptures to interpret the Qurʾān—which brought his supporters, such as Muḥibb Allāh, into open conflict with Shāh Jahān's third son, Awrangzīb ʿĀlamgīr, and the circle of Sirhindī, which inclined toward Sunnī orthodoxy. Awrangzīb's victory over his rivals allowed him to patronize orthodox Sunnism, for instance by sponsoring the production of the *Fatāwā Alamgīrīyah* (also known as the *Fatāwā Hindīyah*), a collection of authoritative Ḥanafī legal responses compiled by state-employed *muftīs* under the supervision of Shaykh Niẓam Burhānpūrī (d. 1679). Unlike previous attempts by local rulers to compile *fatāwā*, such as the *Fatāwā Tatar khānīyah* compiled by Fīrūz Shāh Tughluq (r. 1351–1388), the *Alamgīrīyah* tended to record the most relied-upon opinions in Ḥanafī *fiqh* and also represented a record of the ongoing process of living *ijtihād* within the school. Its composition also marks a unique model of interaction between the scholarly class and a modernizing, bureaucratic state. The almost immediate translation of the work into Persian also shows the tremendous impact it had on *qāḍīs* and *muftīs* in the period.

In 1670 Awrangzīb also reintroduced the office of the *muḥtasib*, officials whose office empowered them to ensure compliance with the Sharīʿah in the public realm. Another major development in the period was the bestowal of hereditary land grants to religious scholars, which in effect created a landed Muslim gentry, often associated with hereditary shrines. One such grant of land and buildings in the foreign quarter (Farangī Maḥall) was made to Quṭb al-Dīn Sihalwī (d. 1692), the author of a book on the rules of war commissioned by Awrangzīb. The former's grandson, Mullā Nizām al-Dīn (d. 1784), was to found the educational system for religious scholars known as the *dars-i nizāmī,* which would be adopted throughout South Asia.

Awrangzīb also abolished non-Islamic taxes such as transit dues and forbade the construction of Hindu temples and the public commemoration of Muḥarram. He also set a personal example of great asceticism and piety (forbidding imperial portraits and biographies and choosing to be buried in a simple grave next to a Chistī saint), which made him an exemplar of Islamic piety among later Muslim historians.

The British. As European piracy had already caused Awrangzīb to order the seizure of all European trading missions in 1702, the arrival of the colonial powers also produced a revival of interest in *jihād* among South Asian Muslims. The *Tuḥfat al-mujāhidīn* of Aḥmad Zayn al-Dīn al-Maʿbarī, written in Arabic around 1584, was a response to Portugese intervention in South Asia. Similarly, Tipu Sultan of Mysore (d. 1799), who became a fierce opponent of the English in South Asia, ordered the compilation of *fatāwā* related to *jihād* entitled *Fatāwā-yi Muḥammadī.*

With the 1803 British annexation of Delhi, Muslim power in South Asia came to an end. British historians depicted Muslims as external invaders like themselves, and it has been argued that the British created and enforced strict and distinct religious identities in order to legitimize their own rule, presenting themselves as the ones most qualified to preserve peace between India's indigenous religious communities. In the disciplines of law and education (particularly the new discipline of Oriental studies), the English promoted a view of Islam (and Hinduism) as fixed and unchanging. For instance, English judges regarded the *Hidāyah* (translated by Charles Hamilton, as *The Hedaya, or Guide*, London, 1791) of al-Marghinānī (d. 1197) as the authoritative version of the Ḥanafī school, disregarding the *Fatāwā Alamgīrīyah,* which represented a living tradition of Islamic legal discourse.

Modern Movements. Starting in the eighteenth century, a renewed interest in revivalist ideas was recorded, often expressed in a desire for educational reform and *jihād.* Both trends are associated with the circle of Shāh Walī Allāh (d. 1762), who wrote important works on *ḥadīth,* law, and mysticism, bringing his ideas together in his *Ḥujjat Allāh al-Bālighah* (God's Manifest Argument). Walī Allāh also supported the reform of the Dārs-i Niẓāmī to privilege the study of *ḥadīth* over the study of philosophy and *kalām.* Walī Allāh's sons produced the first Urdu translation of the Qurʾān. His grandson, Shāh Ismāʿīl (d. 1831) and Sayyid Ahmed of Rāē Barēlī (d. 1831) (a disciple of Walī Allāh's son Shāh ʿAbd al-ʿAzīz) also became leaders of a revivalist movement, the Tarīqah-yi Muḥammadiyyah (the Prophetic Path) that swept through India, warning against the prevalence of shirk and Sufi doctrines such as *waḥdat al-wujūd* and the intercession of saints and waging a *jihād* against the Sikhs. These ideas lead to the movement being labeled "Wahhābī" by its opponents. Although the Tarīqah-i Muḥammadiyyah suffered a military defeat, its ideas nourished subsequent revolts, such as the Faraizi movement in Bengal and the rebellion of 1857, which was prompted by several *ʿulamāʾ* endorsing a *fatwa* holding that *jihād* would become individually obligatory if the British attacked Delhi.

A second great wave of revivalist thought occurred in the aftermath of the 1857 rebellion, which was defeated, emphasizing the importance of *jihād*. It also sought to achieve an internal revival of Islamic society. This revivalist thought eventually crystallized into three main movements. The Ahl-i Ḥadīth, influenced by the thought of Ibn Taymīyah (d. 1328), Shāh Walī Allāh, and more immediately by their contacts with the Yemeni revivalist Shawkānī (d. 1834), rejected *taqlīd* of the established Sunnī schools of law in favor of a direct reliance on the Qurʾān and *ḥadīth*. They produced some prominent scholars in the latter discipline such as ʿAbd al-Raḥmān Mubārakpūrī (d. 1935). The movement was generally supported by rich, educated elites, such as the consort of the Begum of Bhopal, Ṣiddīq Ḥasan Khān Qannawjī (d. 1890). The Deobandī movement, which began in 1867, also focused on the study of *ḥadīth* as a means of bringing about an internal reform within Islamic society, although it advocated *taqlīd* of the Ḥanafī school (wherein lay their difference with the Ahl-i Ḥadīth) and adhered to the relatively sober Naqshbandī Sufi order, rather than the exuberant Qādirī order favored by their fellow Ṣūfī Ḥanafīs. Under its initial leaders, such as Muḥammad Qāsim Nānōtwī (d. 1877) and ʿAbd al-Rashīd Gangōhī (d. 1905), the Deobandī *madrasah* followed a traditional curriculum while adopting modern trends in pedagogy. The third and numerically most significant group was the Ahl al-Sunnat wa-al-Jamāʿat, also called the Barelwīs, after their leader, Aḥmad Raza Khan of Bareily (d. 1922). While adhering to the Ḥanafī school in matters of ritual worship, this school advocated relying on the dead as intercessors with God and asserted that the Prophet was both omnipresent and omniscient, leading their opponents to label them polytheists.

The greatest threat to traditional revivalism came from modernists such as Sayyid Aḥmad Khān (d. 1898), who advocated the adoption of British education and manners by Muslims, setting up institutes for the purpose in 1870. However, Sir Sayyid's loyalty to the British made him a target even for modernists such as Jamāl al-Dīn al-Afghānī (d. 1897), who visited India in the 1850s. Sir Sayyid was often accused of unbelief, as was Mirzā Ghulām Aḥmad (d. 1908), who also advocated loyalty to the British and adopted a pacifist reinterpretation of *jihād*, going so far as to label himself the promised Messiah. His followers, the Qādiyānīyah, who regard him as a prophet, are officially regarded as non-Muslims in Pakistan. A different sort of threat came from the Ahl-i Qurʾān, such as ʿAbd Allāh Chakrālvī (d. 1930) and Ghulām Aḥmad Parvīz (d. 1986), who rejected the authority of *ḥadīth* material altogether and thus challenged Sunnī orthodoxy.

Another major influence on South Asian Islam was the poet and philosopher Muhammad Iqbal (d. 1938). His poems "Shikwā" (1911) and "Jawāb-i Shikwā" (1912) are a lament on the state of contemporary Islam and an attempt to develop an Islamic theodicy in the twentieth century, while "Iblīs kī Majlis-e Shūrā" (the Parliament of Satan) represents an Islamic critique of non-Muslim political and economic philosophy. In his religious writings, Iqbal also advocates a new form of *ijtihād* and *kalām*, one that is based on a strong sense of heroic individualism. Iqbal was also influential in articulating the idea of a separate Islamic state in the subcontinent and in persuading figures such as the Austrian man of letters Muhammad Asad (born Leopold Weiss) to contribute to the cause.

One of the most influential movements to emerge from South Asia has been the Tablīghī Jamāʿat, founded by Muḥammad Ilyās Kandhālwi (d. 1944), near Delhi. The group shuns politics and favors a program of individual spiritual reforms, which highlight the importance of ritual obligations such as prayer and charity. Its annual gathering in Raiwind, Pakistan, is the second largest worldwide gathering of Muslims, after the *ḥajj* in Saudi Arabia. Curiously, the other most popular ideological export of the region has been the highly politically charged doctrine of Abū al-Aʿlā Mawdūdī (d. 1979), who founded the Jamāʿat-i Islāmī, a small but influential actor in Pakistani, Indian, and Bangladeshi politics. Mawdūdī's ideas on *jāhilīyah* and *ḥākimīyah* also influenced the Egyptian radical Sayyid Quṭb, although Mawdūdī himself never adopted Quṭb's radical stance and participated in Pakistan's democratic elections till the end of his life.

Partition and Beyond. The marginalization of Muslims after 1857 produced a growing sense of exclusion, particularly among middle-class Muslims, who felt that the British discriminated against Muslims, who were tainted with the mark of sedition, in favor of Hindus. However, Muslims and Hindus could occasionally come together through organizations such as the Indian National Congress to collectively agitate for greater rights for Indians and to complain about the problems of colonial rule. Nevertheless, the All India Muslim League was formed to agitate specifically for the rights of (upper and middle class) Muslims and to advocate for middle-class Muslim demands such as separate electorates. After World War I, a prominent demand among most Muslim circles was the protection of the Ottoman Caliphate, a demand that was supported by the prominent Congress leader Mohandas K. Gandhi (d. 1948) and that soon became a mobilization call for the expression of anti-British and anti-colonial sentiment.

In 1930, Iqbal presented his views on the concept of two nations in India to the Muslim League Annual Meeting, arguing that Islam could only survive as an ethical ideal if it was not divorced from its laws and institutions. Muslims in the provinces of Punjab, Sindh, Baluchistan, and the Northwest Frontier Province should, Iqbal suggested, come together to form a consolidated Muslim state, later given the name of Pakistan ("land of the pure") by some of his supporters. However, the League's lack of popular support among ordinary Muslims, who continued to share the traditional scholar's distrust of the League's Western-educated and reformist elites, meant that despite its adoption of Iqbal's resolution, the League could not present itself as the voice of the Muslims on the subcontinent. By 1940, Mohammad Ali Jinnah, a British-educated Muslim lawyer who had been trying to bolster the League's popularity among Muslims, publicly called for a separate Muslim state in the famous Lahore Resolution. The League also began an active program of Islamic campaigning, seeking popular support through the use of religious edicts supporting their policies and electoral candidates and employing slogans such as *Pakistan ka maṭlab kyā? Lā ilāha illa Allāh* ("What does Pakistan mean? There is no God but Allāh"). The effect of such slogans in mobilizing the support of a largely illiterate Muslim electorate cannot be overemphasized. However, the explicitly Islamic vision of the state sold to the people was quite different from the vision privately harbored by feudal landowners and members of the bourgeoisie who led the League.

As a result, when India was partitioned in August 1947, there were significant differences among Muslim citizens of the newly created country of Pakistan about the role of Islam in the state. These differences have continued to influence the political trajectory of Pakistan. On the one hand, the country's Constitution (especially after 1985, when the Objectives Resolution became an operative part of the Charter) explicitly calls for the state to be based on the recognition of the fact that sovereignty belongs not to it but to God. The Constitution also calls for any non-Islamic law to be struck down and establishes a Federal Shariat Court to supervise the application of Islamic law in the country. However, the radical tenor of these provisions has been tamed by the interpretations of the largely Western-trained judges of the High Courts and Supreme Court, who, like their British forebears, have incorporated what they see as Islamic principles and legal reasonings into their interpretations but have so far not been sympathetic to any challenges to the order that called for its complete overhaul on the basis of its incompatibility with Islam. Parliament, too, has proceeded slowly in bringing about an Islamization of the country's legal code, and the country's Islamic political parties, while retaining enormous influence on the public, have failed to translate that influence into electoral success.

Of course, a significant number of Muslims had decided not to migrate to Pakistan upon partition and, officially, some 13 percent of the population of India is Muslim. The princely state of Hyderabad, a center of Muslim culture and learning, had initially decided to remain independent, but its forced annexation to India in 1948 was, for Indian Muslims, a reminder of the new realities that now governed their lives as a minority religious community. Their political efforts would henceforth be directed at protection of the Islamic legal code, particularly in the area of personal law, from the reach of the state. However, increasing levels of violence against Muslim communities, as in Gujrat in 2002, have also played a role in defining Islam in India. The growth of international jihādism, which has found a base in some parts of South Asia, looks set to change the nature of Islam in the region once again.

BIBLIOGRAPHY

ʿAbd, al-Ḥaqq S.-D. D, and Salmān -H. Nadwī. *Muqaddamah fī uṣūl al-ḥadīth*. Lucknow: Kullīyat al-Sharīʿah, Dār al-ʿUlūm li-Nadwat al-ʿUlamā', 1984.

Anooshahr, Ali. "Mughal Historians and the Memory of the Islamic Conquest of India." *The Indian Economic and Social History Review* 43, no. 3 (2006): 275.

ʿAzīz Aḥmad, Muḥammad. *Political History & Institutions of the Early Turkish Empire of Delhi (1206–1290 A.D.)*. Lahore: M. Ashraf, 1949.

ʿAzīz Aḥmad, Muḥammad. *Islamic Modernism in India and Pakistan, 1857–1964*. London: Oxford University Press, 1967.

Eaton, Richard M. *Sufis of Bijapur, 1300–1700: Social Roles of Sufis in Medieval India*. Princeton, N.J.: Princeton University Press, 1978.

Elliot, Henry M., and John Dowson. *The History of India, As Told by Its Own Historians*. London: Trübner, 1877.

Hardy, Peter. *The Muslims of British India*. Cambridge, U.K.: Cambridge University Press, 1972.

Hujvīrī, ʿAlī ibn ʿUthmān. *The Kashf al-mahjúb: The Oldest Persian Treatise on Sufiism*. Trans. Reynold A. Nicholson. London: Luzac, 1976.

Hunter, William W. *The Indian Musulmans*. Delhi: Indological Book House, 1969.

Ismāʿīl, Muḥammad. *Taqwiyat-ul-imān: Strengthening of the Faith*. Riyadh, Saudi Arabia: Dar-us-Salam Publications, 1995.

Iqbal, Muhammad. *The Reconstruction of Religious Thought in Islam*. Oxford: Oxford University Press, 1934.

Malik, Jamal. *Islam in South Asia: A Short History*. Leiden: E. J. Brill, 2008.

Mubārakfūrī, Muḥammad ʿAbd al-Raḥmān ibn ʿAbd al-Raḥīm, ʿAbd al-Wahāb ʿAbd al-Laṭīf, ʿAbd al-Raḥmān Muḥammad ʿUthmān, and Muḥammad ibn ʿĪsā Tirmidhī. *Tuḥfat al-aḥwadhī bi-sharḥ Jāmiʿ al-Tirmidhī*. Medina: al-Maktabah al-Salafīyah, 1963.

Niẓām, al-Shaykh, and Samīr M. Rabāb. *Al-fatāwā al-Hindīyah fī madhhab al-Imām al-Aʿẓam Abī Ḥanīfah al-Nuʿmān*. Beirutt: Dār Iḥyā' al-Turāth al-ʿArabī, 2002.

Nizami, Khaliq A. *Religion and Politics in India During the Thirteenth Century*. New Delhi: Oxford University Press, 2002.

Metcalf, Barbara D. *Islamic Revival in British India: Deoband, 1860–1900*. Princeton, N.J.: Princeton University Press, 1982.

Mill, James, and William Thomas. *The History of British India*. Chicago: University of Chicago Press, 1975.

Minhāj, Sirāj J, and H. G. Raverty. *Ṭabakāt-i-nāṣirī: A General History of the Muhammadan Dynasties of Asia, Including Hindustan from A.H. 194 (810 A.D.) to A.H. 658 (1260 A.D.) and the Irruption of the Infidel Mughals into Islam*. Kolkata: The Asiatic Society, 2010.

Riexinger, Martin. *Sanā'ullāh Amritsarī (1868–1948) und die Ahl-i-Ḥadīs im Punjab unter britischer Herrschaft*. Würzburg: Ergon, 2004.

Roy, Asim. *Islam in History and Politics: Perspectives from South Asia*. New Delhi: Oxford University Press, 2006.

Sanyal, Usha. *Devotional Islam and Politics in British India: Ahmad Riza Khan Barelwi and His Movement, 1870–1920*. Delhi: Oxford University Press, 1996.

Taylor, David. *Islam in South Asia*. London: Routledge, 2010.

Ulughkhānī, ʿAbd Allāh Muḥammad ibn ʿUmar, and E. Denison Ross. *An Arabic History of Gujarat: Ẓafar ul-wálih bi-Muẓaffar wa ālih*. 3 vols. London: J. Murray, 1910–1928.

Walī Allāh al-Dihlawī, and Marcia K. Hermansen. *The Conclusive Argument from God: Shāh Walī Allāh of Delhi's Hujjat Allāh al-bāligha*. Islamabad, Pakistan: Islamic Research Institute, 2003.

Ziyā al-Dīn Baranī, W. Nassau Lees, and Kabir al-Din Ahmad.*The Táríkh-i Feroz-sháhí of Ziaa al-Din Barni*. Calcutta, 1862.

Abdul Rahman Mustafa

Islam and Politics in Southeast Asia. More than 250 million Muslims live in Southeast Asia, primarily in three Muslim-majority states—Indonesia (the world's most populous Islamic country), Malaysia, and the small oil-rich sultanate of Brunei Darussalam—though significant Muslim minorities reside in Myanmar (formerly known as Burma), Thailand, the Philippines, and Singapore. Only in Singapore does a Muslim minority account for more than 6 percent of the total population. Contemporary Islam and politics interact in this region primarily in four ways: (1) as the basis of political parties; (2) with regard to issues defining the role of Islam and the state; (3) as one the key factors fostering demands for separatism and autonomy among Muslim minorities; and (4) in defining the character of Islamic militancy.

Islamic Oriented Political Parties. Political parties with an expressly Islamic platform have played a significant role only in Indonesia and Malaysia. Brunei's political system has only small parties with very limited power. There were Muslims in important ministerial posts in Burma before the military took power in 1962, and Muslims in cabinet-level positions in the Philippines, but they were not representatives of Islamic parties. Muslims from Thailand organized themselves into the Wadah faction, a quasi-party that has held several cabinet posts.

Indonesia. In the Dutch East Indies, divisions arose between Muslims supporting a modernist Islamic approach and those fostering a more traditional perspective; these divisions continued to impact Islamic political parties after Indonesia was formed. Sarekat Islam (Islamic Union) reflected more modernist views. Founded in 1914 as a commercial organization, it became the largest pre-war nationalist movement in the years after World War I. Although it initially supported the Dutch administration and had membership in the colonial legislature when it opened in 1917, by 1920 it was espousing a strongly anti-colonial and anti-capitalist agenda. It was loosely organized and vulnerable to differences in political and religious approaches; these divisions, combined with colonial repression, ultimately led to its decline by the 1930s. The Islamic traditionalist elements in the Dutch East Indies sought to counter Sarekat Islam and other secular trends by forming the orthodox Nahdatul Ulama (Awakening of the Ulama, or NU) in 1926. It began largely as a religious social and educational organization and expanded significantly in the next two decades.

The post–World War II years saw this division replicated by the contest between the Masjumi Party and Nahdatul Ulama. Founded in 1945, the Masjumi (Partai Majelis Syuro Muslimin Indonesia, or Council of Indonesian Muslim Associations) initially included both modernist members and the Nahdatul Ulama. Its religious platform espoused an Islamic state and promotion of the Sharīʿah. After the NU left the party in 1952, the Masjumi continued to uphold these religious ideals, but also reflected the modernist and social democratic views of its leadership. Its political base was in the islands outside Java. During the liberal democratic era of 1950–1957, it was a member of five of the six coalitions that dominated the national legislature. It held a series of cabinet posts, and there were three Masjumi prime ministers. Representing the traditional Muslim community, Nahdatul Ulama had increased its membership markedly. Its electoral base was primarily in Java. NU members held several cabinet posts in the democratic era, but did not retain their leadership at the national level, as did the Masjumi.

In the first national elections in 1955, the Masjumi received 20.9 percent of the vote and Nahdatul Ulama 18.4 percent. However, liberal democracy gave way to "Guided Democracy" in 1957 when then President Sukarno began a series of measures that ended parliamentary democracy. Reactions to Sukarno's policies led to rebellions outside Java in which the Masjumi was implicated, and the party was banned in 1960. The NU was less critical of Sukarno's policies and continued as a political party, albeit with little power.

Islamic-based parties in the democratic era of 1950–1957 were not able to implement their religious agenda, and efforts to foster national acceptance of Sharīʿah came to naught. Instead, they were faced with a Sukarno-inspired ideology, the Pancasila (Five Principles), one of which called for the recognition of all religions. This was seen by many Muslims as agnostic and un-Islamic. The lack of success of the Masjumi and the NU can be explained by the fractured nature of the Indonesian national legislature. The 1955 elections produced four major parties, the Masjumi, the NU, the secular Nationalist Party, and the Communist Party, along with a large number of minor parties. Islamic party representatives were split between the Masjumi, the NU, and other minor Islamic parties, including a remnant of Sarekat Islam, the Partai Sarekat Islam Indonesia. They also had to deal with a charismatic president, backed by secular political parties, who was not sympathetic to their goals.

Islamic political parties were not to play a significant role in Indonesian national politics until the end of the twentieth century. Following the ouster of Sukarno by the military in 1967, the "New Order" was established, with power in the hands of the armed forces and its chosen parties. Ultimately, all Islamic parties were forced to join into one coalition, the PPP (Partai Persatuan Pembangunan, or United Development Party). During this period the PPP was banned from using Islam in its platform and displaying the Kaʿbah as its party symbol. In 1983 it was forced to accept the Pancasila as its only ideology, which led Nahdatul Ulama to leave party politics.

The year 1999 saw the end of the New Order and the return to competitive party politics. During the following dozen years, Indonesia held three national elections for its House of Representatives, the Dewan Perwakilan Rakyat, and three presidential elections, the last by direct vote. In this environment, Islamic political power was fragmented between several political parties that were a minority in a more secular legislature. Votes for Islamic political parties have actually declined since the return to democracy. Their combined total dropped from 38 percent in the first elections in 1999 to 32 percent in 2004 to 24 percent in 2009. These parties differed over ideological and political issues. Among the ten Islamic-oriented parties, the major ones include a reformulated PPP that has pressed a conservative Islamic agenda and requires all members to be Muslims; the Partai Kebangkitan Bangsa (National Awakening Party, or PKB, initially led by democratic pluralist leader from a major *ʿulamāʾ* family who refused to put Islam in the party's name and pursued the idea of an inclusive

Islam; the Partai Keadilan Sejahtera (Prosperous Justice Party, or PKS), which has ties to the Muslim Brotherhood and supports conservative religious teachings but not the mandatory implementation of the Sharīʿah; and the Partai Amanat Nasional (National Mandate Party), which has its roots in the Muhammadiyah, a modernist organization.

While these Islamic-oriented parties have been able to influence individual pieces of legislation, they have not been able to implement a major Islamic agenda. This difficulty arises from a variety of causes. There is a fragmentation among and within these organizations. They are divided between purists and pluralists with regard to their religious identity. Representatives at the cabinet level generally have not been highly regarded. There have been numerous charges of corruption, although the PKS was initially less vulnerable to these accusations. Finally, party leaders do not appear to be capable of addressing the social and economic needs of the electorate and appear to be more interested in personal self-aggrandizement. However, in Indonesia's multiparty legislature, Islamic party votes are often necessary to achieve a ruling coalition, giving them a continued role in national governance. They have used their power to influence legislation on religion and morality.

Malaysia. Malaysia has been governed by a multi-ethnic coalition (initially called the Alliance and the Barisan Nasional since 1973), with its dominant member the United Malays National Organization (UMNO). Founded in 1946, it was the most prominent party in the colony until independence in 1957. Since 1957 members of UMNO have held the core cabinet posts of prime minister, deputy prime minister, home minister, and in recent decades finance minister. The party has presented itself as the representative of both Malay and Muslim interests in a society in which there is a co-identity between Malay ethnicity and being Muslim.

In its first decades UMNO leadership did not emphasize Islam, although it did hold itself as a protector of Muslim interests and supported projects such as the construction of mosques. UMNO prime ministers until 1981 directed their attention to economic and social development programs. The inauguration of the National Development Plan (NEP) in 1971 brought special emphasis to raising the economic and educational levels of Malays. It was during the long tenure (1981–2003) of Mahathir Mohamed that Malaysia launched a series of steps fostering Islamic goals. While these were accomplished under a multi-ethnic and religious coalition, it was UMNO's leadership that directed this process, not always to the liking of its non-Muslim partners.

Some of these programs were institution building such as the establishment of the International Islamic University, Islamic banking, the Pusat Islam (Islamic Center) to implement greater Islamization and the Institut Kefahaman Islam Malaysia (Malaysian Institute of Islamic Understanding, or IKIM). Founded in 1992 IKIM was developed as the intellectual vehicle to support Mahathir's religious and social policies. It has its own radio station and has an active publishing agenda. There were also a series of policies that aided the development of Islamic schools, the sending of students to the Middle East, and increasing Islamic study in public schools.

An important element of Mahathir's program was to ensure the growth of UMNO's views of a moderate Islam and to control "deviant Islam." A central actor in this process has been the Jabatan Kemajuan Islam Malaysia (Department of Islamic Development in Malaysia, or JAKIM). One of its roles is to assess organizations and publications for practices or statements that it defines as "deviant Islam." It monitors those seen as outside generally accepted Malaysian Islam, such as Wahhābī-Salafī and Shīʿī beliefs. One of its tasks is to coordinate *dakwah* (Islamic missionary) groups. Another is to aid the government in developing family law and morality issues. While JAKIM does not have the power to implement its recommendations, other avenues have been available to the government. For example, it has used the Internal Security Act against Islamic militants and the Printing Press and Publicity Act and Societies Act to control "deviant" or "seditious" public statements or organizations. The University and University Colleges Act does much the same to restrain campus activities and statements. The federal government of Malaysia under Mahathir also attempted to expand its control over religious education. This effort had its antecedents in earlier policies to control the Islamic curricula in public schools and to make Islam one of the required fields for the Malaysian High School Certificate. In reaction to possible teaching of radical Islam in private schools, after 9/11 the government turned to controlling their activities.

The culmination of this program of Islamization came in 2001. Mahathir announced that, given what had been accomplished in implementing Islam in Malaysia, it was already an Islamic state and a model Islamic state. This assertion was not positively received by UMNO's non-Muslim partners or its Islamic political opposition.

UNNO's Islamic political party opposition has come from the Parti Se-Malaysia (Islamic Party of Malaysia, or PAS). Initially registered in 1955 as the Parti Islam Se-tanah Melayu, or PMIP, PAS presented a more conservative Islamic agenda that opposed the idea of allying with non-Muslim parties. It espoused an Islamic state based upon the Qurʾān and *sunnah*, although it was not until 2001 that it defined the parameters of that state. However, it provided little serious opposition to UMNO in its first decades. It received only one seat in the 1955 elections and was part of the UMNO-led coalition from 1974 to 1977. It was more successful at the state level of Malaysia's federal system, capturing Kelantan (1955–1977 and 1999 to the present) and Terengganu (1959–1961). It showed far more success in the 1999 and 2008 national elections, when it expanded its parliamentary membership, gained control over Kedah, and was part of the coalition governing Selangor. PAS has experienced internal disputes between purists who want to maintain the party's Islamic identity without cooperation with non-Muslim groups and those who have seen electoral alliances outside the Muslim community as a means of gaining greater political leverage. The 1999 and 2008 elections could be seen as the outcome of the rise of the accommodationists.

PAS criticisms of UMNO have included attacks on its cooperation with non-Muslims, accusations that UMNO seeks to install only parts of the Sharīʿah rather than its entirety, charges that UMNO was not truly Islamic and that the declaration by Mahathir about Malaysia being an Islamic state was false, and characterizations of UMNO leadership as corrupt and materialistic. On its part, UMNO has called PAS an opponent of the government's efforts to develop a moderate and modern Islam. It has accused PAS of ties with extremism and has had PAS members arrested for alleged seditious behavior. Members of both parties have accused the other of being infidels.

Thus, the role of Islamic-oriented political parties has varied markedly between Indonesia and Malaysia. The latter has a history of divisiveness within the Muslim political community within an environment that has allowed the development of secular political parties composed of Muslims. They have not been able to successfully implement a national Islamic agenda. In Malaysia it has only been in recent years that Malay Muslims have supported non-Islamic oriented parties, and UMNO's dominance of the national coalition has allowed it to promulgate a series of programs to foster Islam at both the state and federal level.

Religious Issues. The two interlocking religious issues that have dominated political considerations of the role of Islam have been the implementation of an Islamic state and the adoption of the Sharīʿah. Debates concerning an Islamic state have centered upon whether it should be established and, if so, how such a state is to be defined. Brunei is officially an Islamic state. The promulgation of an Islamic state is supported by both major Islamic-oriented parties in Malaysia, although it was initially rejected by UMNO and Mahathir. Mahathir announced that Malaysia was already an Islamic state, but stated that there was no need to change the constitution and that the rights of non-Muslims would be maintained. In Indonesia an Islamic state has been espoused by the United Development Party and some smaller Islamic-oriented groups and parties, but historically the leaders of both the National Awakening Party and the National Mandate Party have opposed the idea. While the Prosperous Justice Party has ties to the Muslim Brotherhood and has members who call for an Islamic state, there have been divisions within the party, and it does not support its implementation. The formation of an Islamic state has been the central principle of militant groups throughout the region.

A core issue regarding the idea of an Islamic state has been how it is to be defined. One fault line has been the rights of non-Muslims. Anti-pluralist groups such as most militant groups have demanded that non-Muslims should be excluded and some have called for their expulsion. Political parties in Malaysia and Indonesia espousing an Islamic state have defined it being only mandatory for Muslims. PAS has stated that it would be an option for Muslims to be governed by Islamic penal codes (*ḥudūd* laws).

The second core issue has been the role of the Sharīʿah and the extent to which it should be implemented. Public opinion polls in both Malaysia and Indonesia have shown popular support for an increased role for the Sharīʿah. PAS has declared that the Sharīʿah should be the law of the land, including *ḥudūd* laws. It has criticized UMNO for accepting a piecemeal approach and has declared that Mahathir's statement that Malaysia was already an Islamic state was false, since such a state needed to accept the Sharīʿah as a whole. The Indonesian national legislature has not proposed the imposition of the Sharīʿah for the nation. However, it did agree to the establishment of Sharīʿah courts and laws in Aceh in an effort to ameliorate a long-standing conflict with that religiously conservative province. Aceh has adopted a series of laws involving such issues as personal behavior, gambling, and elements of Islamic penal laws. Human rights groups have criticized some of these actions and what they see as the overzealous actions of Sharīʿah police. In addition, many local governments throughout the archipelago have attempted to implement the Sharīʿah.

Muslim Separatists. Muslims have sought independence or various levels of autonomy in Myanmar, Thailand, and the Philippines. These goals have been driven only in part by religious considerations. Other significant factors have been ethnicity, economic grievances, and perceptions of repression by the majority-led government. In each of these three cases, there has been a co-identity between religion and ethnicity, both of which have set them apart from the rest of the nation. The Arakanese of southwestern Myanmar are the descendants of Bengalis who began moving to Burma when it was still attached to colonial India. The Myanmar government does not recognize them as Myanmar nationals but considers them *kalas* (foreigners). As such, they have not received support for education and development, and the government has imposed limitations on their activities. In southern Thailand, the

Muslims not only differ from the Buddhist majority on religious grounds, but they are Malay, with a history of being part of old Malaya until the early twentieth century. They have rejected past efforts at assimilation and have sought to maintain their own ethnic identity. The Muslims in the southern Philippines are historically not of one ethnic unit, but have come to see themselves as a Moro community seeking to stave off Christian incursions into their homeland.

In addition, these groups have not achieved the economic and educational levels of the majority community, and there has been a history of government neglect. The regions inhabited by these minorities have been geographically isolated and did not receive the level of government development support given the majority areas. Efforts have been made to improve conditions in recent years in Thailand and the Philippines. There has also been the incursion of majority groups into lands previously held by these minorities, leading to further dissatisfaction.

This discontent has led both to demands for greater autonomy and armed rebellion. In Thailand there have been a number of militant groups that have fought Thai forces, but they have differed on tactics and interpretations of Islam. Earlier active organizations, such as the Patani United Liberation Organization (PULO) and the New PULO, have been decimated, but major violence continues. In the southern Philippines, the two largest separatists organizations, the Moro National Liberation Front (MNLF) and the Moro Islamic Liberation Front (MILF), a more Islamic-oriented militant group, have shown a willingness to negotiate with the government. The one very violent actor is the relatively smaller Abu Sayyaf Group. Expressing radical Islamic views influenced by Wahhābī-Salafī interpretations of Islam, it has been responsible for killings, bombings, and kidnappings. Some consider it to be a criminal organization. Violent actions by separatists have brought government reprisals that many in minority communities have seen as persecution.

Militant Islam. Militant Islam is defined as the espousal or use of violence as a means of achieving Islamic goals. This pattern has involved regional organizations as well as domestic groups, most particularly in Indonesia and Malaysia. The dominant regional actor has been Jeemah Islamiyah (Islamic Organization, or JI). Much of the history and organization of the JI has been murky, with its early leadership coming from Indonesians in exile in Malaysia. It has its roots in Darul Islam (Abode of Islam), an Indonesian group that sought to establish an Islamic state in the 1940s and 1950s. The JI also seeks to foster an Islamic state throughout the region. Initially decrying violence, it shifted to a more aggressive stance in the late 1990s. There are accusations of links to al-Qaʿida, and it is believed to have had cells in Indonesia, Thailand, Malaysia, the Philippines, and Cambodia. It is considered to have been responsible for a series of violent acts, including the Bali bombings, attacks on the Australian embassy and the Marriott hotel in Jakarta, Indonesia, bombings in Manila, and attacks on Christian churches. Efforts by governments in Southeast Asia, aided by states outside the region, have led to the arrest of key leaders and divisions within the organization. The result has been a serious weakening of the JI.

Aside from actions involving separatist movements, domestic Islamic militancy has been most apparent in Malaysia and Indonesia. In Malaysia the government has emphasized the dangers of radical Islam, although the levels of violence have been low, with a small number of casualties compared to Indonesia. In 1980 exiled Muslim Chams attacked a police station and eight Chams were killed. In 1985 in the "Memali Incident," government forces fought villagers over a controversial charge of the teaching of "deviant Islam" by a PAS member. Reports indicated that eighteen police and villagers were killed. In the mid-1990s authorities supposedly faced an organization called the Kampulan Militan Malaysia (Malaysian Militant Group, or KMM), although there was little evidence of its activities. UMNO has regularly charged PAS with being in league with radical and extremist groups.

Indonesia has faced violent Islamic groups since 1948 when Darul Islam fought against the Dutch and then the Republic until the late 1960s. Its major announced goal was the formation of an Islamic state. Elements of the organization later turned to criminal activities, leading to a loss of popular support. Nevertheless, its Islamic ideals have continued to resonate in Indonesia. Its influence can be seen in militant organizations such as Kommando Jihad (Holy War Command), Jeemah Islamiyah, Laskar Jihad (Holy Warriors), and the Majelis Mujahidin Indonesia (Indonesian Mujahidin Council, or MMI). The Kommando Jihad was a shadowy group active in the 1970s and the early 1980s that espoused an Islamic state. It was held responsible for a dramatic plane hijacking in 1981. There have been questions as to Suharto government involvement in its initial formation. Laskar Jihad was active from 2000 to 2002, when it disbanded. It had up to 20,000 members at its height. Salafī interpretations of Islam were a significant foundation of its beliefs. It was primarily involved in the clash between Christians and Muslims in East Indonesia. The conflict, which had its roots in communal tensions going back to the colonial era, caused heavy casualties and involved attacks on schools, banks, markets, homes, and holy places. The MMI has included leaders tied to extremist groups such as Jeemah Islamiyah. A group defining itself as a protector of Islamic interests, but often described as "thugs" or opportunists, is the Front Pembela Islam (Islamic Defense Front). It is widely known for its public attacks on places that it considers immoral, such as bars and massage parlors. Targets have also included Westerners and members of Christian, Aḥmadīyah, and Shīʿī communities.

The Indonesian government was slow to act when militant Islam began to erupt into violence in the late 1990s; in part this was due to fears of possible repercussions from Islamic-oriented parties and organizations. There were also signs of aid to Laskar Jihad from elements of the Indonesian armed forces and public sympathy for the plight of Muslims in East Indonesia. The United States was also reluctant to act because of Indonesia's domestic issues and did not term Jeemah Islamiyah a "terrorist" group until after the Bali bombing and has not put Laskar Jihad on its "terrorist" list. However, there has been a serious decline in militant activity in recent years as governments have developed more sophisticated means of control and the populace has shown little support for the militants. It should be noted that all Islamic-oriented parties in the Indonesian national legislature espouse democracy, and no representative of a militant group has been elected to that body.

These Southeast Asian militant groups have in common an agenda that calls for the establishment of an Islamic state and with it the promulgation of the Sharīʿah. They also oppose religious and political pluralism.

Bibliography

Feith, H. *The Decline of Constitutional Democracy in Indonesia*. Singapore and Jakarta: Equinox Press, 2007.

Kahin, George. *Nationalism and Revolution in Indonesia*. Ithaca, N.Y.: Cornell University Press, 1952.

Liow, Joseph. *Piety and Politics: Islamism in Contemporary Malaysia*. New York: Oxford University Press, 2009.

Means, Gorden. *Political Islam in Southeast Asia*. Boulder, Colo.: Lynne Riener, 2009.

Nasr, Sayyed Vali Reza. *Islamic Leviathan: Islam and the Making of State Power.* New York: Oxford University Press, 2001.

Sidel, John. *Riots, Pogroms, Jihad: Religious Violence in Indonesia*. Ithaca, N.Y.: Cornell University Press, 2002.

Yegar, Moshe. *Between Integration and Secession: The Muslim Communities in Southern Thailand, Southern Philippines and Western Burma/Myanmar*. Lanham, Md.: Lexington Books, 2002.

FRED R. VON DER MEHDEN

ISLAM AND POLITICS IN SUB-SAHARAN AFRICA. Islam has had a presence in Africa since the earliest days of its history. Biāl, one of the first converts to Islam and the first muezzin of the Muslim community of Medina, was a former black slave, probably from Abyssinia. This same region was the destination of the first *hijrah* (emigration) of a small group of Muslims around the year 615, about seven years before the well-known *hijrah* from Mecca to Medina. Muslims established a permanent presence in Egypt following the military conquests led by ʿAmr ibn al-ʿĀṣ in 641. Centuries later the Nile valley would become one of the avenues for the spread of Islam into sub-Saharan Africa. According to the Arab geographer and traveler Abū ʿAbd Allāh al-Bakrī, who visited the Soninke rulers of the great medieval empire of Ghana, in West Africa, in 1067, there was a Muslim neighborhood in the capital, and the ruler had Muslim ministers and advisers. With the rise of the Almoravids (from Arabic *al-Murābiṭūn*), a puritanical Berber Islamic movement that emerged in the second half of the eleventh century in the Western Sahara, Islamic influences soon prevailed in Ghana and reached the Senegal valley, where the ruler of the Takrur State embraced Islam and introduced Sharīʿah law even before the advent of the Almoravids. In Hausaland (modern northern Nigeria), Usuman Dan Fodio established the Sokoto Caliphate in 1809, one of the most important seats of power in modern West Africa.

The Nilotic Sudan, the Horn, and East Africa. In spite of its proximity to Egypt and the Arabian Peninsula, the upper Nile valley was Islamized late. The gradual saturation of the Christian kingdoms in the Nubian region to the south by Arab traders led to a decisive shift in the religious situation only during the fifteenth and sixteenth centuries, although the Mamlūks of Egypt had led repeated incursions into Nubian territory in the late thirteenth and early fourteenth centuries. Arab immigrants settled along the Somali coast as early as the ninth century and established trading posts in the hinterland, which was populated by Somali-speaking nomads.

The Colonial Period. The late nineteenth and the earliest twentieth centuries saw large-scale conversion of Africans to Islam. Though colonial governments tried to apply various strategies to prevent Islam from spreading into new territories, they also established working relationships with important Muslim local rulers and religious leaders to better control their Muslim subjects. The best-known examples of such Muslim notables are the so-called marabouts in the French colonies, originally a generic term for Muslim teachers and healers that came to describe the leaders of the Ṣūfī orders, most notably the Tijānīyah, the Qādirīyah, and the Murīdīyah. The French elevated Seydou Nourou Tal (c. 1880–1980), the grandson of the nineteenth-century *jihād* leader al-Ḥājj ʿUmar Tal based in Dakar, to the rank of Grand Marabout de l'A.O.F. (Afrique Occidentale Française) and sponsored his frequent travels throughout the French colonies from the 1920s onward. In the period after World War II French fears of organized Muslim resistance were rekindled by a new wave of Islamic reforms. As most proponents of the new trend had been inspired by visits to Saudi Arabia, French administrators referred to them as Wahhabis. They were more critical of colonial rule than the old Muslim establishment had been and were very outspoken in their attacks on the Ṣūfī orders and the marabouts.

In East Africa the encounter between Muslims and European rule yielded similar results, albeit under different local conditions. After the two most notable anticolonial struggles, the *jihād* of Muḥammad ʿAbd Allāh Ḥasan in northern Somalia (1898–1920) and the Maji Maji Rebellion in Tanganyika (present-day Tanzania, 1904–1907), had faded, Muslims became resigned to European rule. The Sultanate of Oman—based in Zanzibar and until the late nineteenth century in control of the coastal strip from Mogadishu in the north to the Portuguese dominions of Mozambique in the south—was gradually forced to relinquish control to Germany and Britain.

The Postcolonial Period. With few exceptions (Ethiopia and the special case of South Africa under apartheid rule), all sub-Saharan nation states started off with secular constitutions, even though there are cases in which the head of state was expected to be a Christian (as in Ethiopia) or a Muslim (as in Sudan). In Nigeria, the most populous country of the continent, where the Christian and Muslim populations are nearly equal, the Muslim elites in the north were forced to accept the fact that there was no return to the precolonial political and legal system. The long search for a compromise or a power-sharing formula has left a strong imprint on the postcolonial history of Nigeria and occasionally erupted into violent confrontations; it took a heavy toll during the Biafran War (1967–1970).

The latest chapter of this history is the enactment of Sharīʿah laws in most of the northern federal states of Nigeria from 2001 onward, which continues to pose a challenge to national unity. New Islamic associations draw their financial resources form a variety of sources. In the 1970s Saudi Arabia emerged as one of the major players in the Islamic field in sub-Saharan Africa. Philanthropists, many of them based in the rich Gulf states, continue to provide African Muslims with significant funds.

Countries such as Ghana, Kenya, and Ethiopia, whose governments have long appeared to ignore the existence of their sizable Muslim populations, have now turned to repressive policies that do nothing to ease the religious tensions. On the other hand Muslims in minority contexts have also contributed to the strains in their relations with Christians by campaigning for the reapplication of Islamic law. These struggles, which highlight tensions between nation-states that trace their history to the colonial period, conceptions of religious freedom, and the role played by local and international politics in the manifestation of these tensions, continue today.

Bibliography

Bang, Anne K. *Sufis and Scholars of the Sea: Family Networks in East Africa, 1860–1925*. London and New York: RoutledgeCurzon, 2003.

Batran, Aziz A. *The Qadiriyya Brotherhood in West Africa and the Western Sahara: The Life and Times of Shaykh al-Mukhtar al-Kunti (1729–1811)*. Rabat, Morocco, 2001.

Brenner, Louis. *Controlling Knowledge: Religion, Power, and Schooling in a West African Muslim Society*. Bloomington: Indiana University Press, 2001.

Cruise O'Brien, Donal B. *The Mourides of Senegal: The Political and Economic Organization of an Islamic Brotherhood*. Oxford: Clarendon Press, 1971.

Kaba, Lansiné. *The Wahhabiyya: Islamic Reform and Politics in French West Africa*. Evanston, Ill.: Northwestern University Press, 1974.

Kane, Ousmane. *Muslim Modernity in Postcolonial Nigeria: A Study of the Society for the Removal of Innovation and Reinstatement of Tradition*. Leiden and Boston: Brill, 2003.

Loimeier, Roman. *Islamic Reform and Political Change in Northern Nigeria*. Evanston, Ill.: Northwestern University Press, 1997.

Loimeier, Roman, and Rüdiger Seesemann, eds. *The Global Worlds of the Swahili: Interfaces of Islam, Identity, and Space in 19th and 20th-Century East Africa*. Berlin: Lit, 2006.

Levtzion, Nehemia, and Randall L. Pouwels, eds. *The History of Islam in Africa*. Athens: Ohio University Press, 2000.

Maghīlī, Muḥammad ibn ʿAbd al-Karīm. *Sharia in Songhay: The Replies of al-Maghīlī to the Questions of Askia al-Ḥājj Muḥammad.* Translated, with a commentary by John O. Hunwick. Oxford and New York: Oxford University Press, 1985.

Pouwels, Randall L. *Horn and Crescent: Cultural Change and Traditional Islam on the East African Coast, 800–1900.* Cambridge, U.K., and New York: Cambridge University Press, 1987.

Robinson, David. *The Holy War of Umar Tal: The Western Sudan in the Mid-Nineteenth Century.* Oxford and New York: Oxford University Press, 1985.

Robinson, David. *Paths of Accommodation: Muslim Societies and French Colonial Authorities in Senegal and Mauritania, 1880–1920.* Athens: Ohio University Press, and Oxford: James Currey, 2000.

Rosander, Eva Evers, and David Westerlund, eds. *African Islam and Islam in Africa: Encounters between Sufis and Islamists.* Athens: Ohio University Press, 1997.

Soares, Benjamin. *Islam and the Prayer Economy: History and Authority in a Malian Town.* Edinburgh: Edinburgh University Press, 2005.

Soares, Benjamin, ed. *Muslim-Christian Encounters in Africa.* Leiden and Boston: Brill, 2006.

Soares, Benjamin F., and René Otayek, eds. *Islam and Muslim Politics in Africa.* New York: Palgrave Macmillan, 2007.

Triaud, Jean-Louis, and David Robinson, eds. *La Tijâniyya: Une confrérie musulmane à la conquête de l'Afrique.* Paris: Karthala, 2000.

Trimingham, John Spencer. *The Influence of Islam upon Africa.* 2d ed. London and New York: Longman, 1980.

Umar, Muhammad Sani. *Islam and Colonialism: Intellectual Responses of Muslims of Northern Nigeria to British Colonial Rule.* Leiden and Boston: Brill, 2006.

Rüdiger Seesemann
Updated by Sarah Eltantawi

Islam and Politics in the Middle East and North Africa. Many Muslims in the modern Middle East and North Africa lived between "memory and desire"—the powerful memory of a glorious pre-modern past and the desire for the benefits of modernity reconciled with Islamic tradition. After independence from European powers from the 1920s to the 1960s, the Arab world seemed to be locked in an inescapable crisis of economic stagnation, authoritarianism, and absolutist state control of resources and governance. This stagnant disquiet exploded into a tsunami of protest in the revolts of 2011—the so-called Arab Spring. Indeed, the breaking point came as an increasingly youthful population took to the streets in waves of protest, given that most were no longer disconnected from the rest of the world. Al-Jazeera, the Internet, and other media outlets opened the floodgates, overwhelming countless ministries of information and propagandists.

Yet, technology was only a means, not a source, of revolution. While a technologically literate and Western-leaning, educated youth confronted fresh dilemmas—the face of demonstrations in Cairo's Tahrir Square, the main boulevards in Tunis, and so many other scenes of utter chaos throughout the region—protestors found success only by gaining the support of two often-opposed camps: the military and the long-standing community of Muslim activists. Indeed, as sources of unity and resistance to the state, religious parties had provided a place for religiously veiled civic discourses for most of the post-independence period. Islam often stood virtually alone against the domination of dictators. While the state, through "official Islam," controlled many aspects of religious experience through the vetting of Friday sermons and the appointing of religious scholars, it could not completely suppress the inherently egalitarian aspects of the Islamic *ummah* that struggled to find a balance between religiosity and secularizing trends.

Although they often overlap, Islamic and Arab identities are not the same. Arab nationalism, which became a favorite mantra in the 1950s and 1960s, referred to a pan-Arab identification that focused on language and ethnic identity. The League of Arab States, which came into existence at the height of World War II, represented the modern, institutional expression of this form of identity. In contrast, Islamic identity was much broader in scope and included Muslims the world over; as such, it was accurate to state that Islamic identity was a large tent that included ethnic divisions, among Arab as well as other ethnic groups. Moreover, Islamic reassertions gained momentum, after pan-Arab popular ideals lost most of their followings after the 1960s. One of the most important reasons for the appeal of Islam to all of these groups was the unifying impetus of pan-Islamic identity.

Historical Overview of Major Developments. Leading observers have claimed that Islam and modernity were inherently in conflict. Proponents of modernization theory, led by the influential sociologist Max Weber (d. 1940), argued that Islam was antithetical to capitalism and, thus, to modernization. In fact, Weber identified Islam as the polar opposite of Puritanism, and it was safe to state that many of his ideas influenced scholars who sought to explain the relative economic disparities between the Islamic world and the West—disparities that could be even higher without the critical role that oil played since the mid-twentieth century in global economic affairs. Another observer, Samuel Huntington, famously suggested a religious basis for fundamental differences and clashes in world politics after the Cold War, even if his *Clash of Civilizations and the Remaking of the World Order* was perceived as an anti-Muslim political treatise.

Inasmuch as modernization theory assumed that Islam had not changed in any significant way since the times of the Prophet, and because of the legacy of foreign occupations that had lasted six centuries, Arab political developments acquired complex features. In fact, the relationship between Islam and modernity was interpreted in radically different ways, depending on the country or society; thus anthropological studies scored far better in providing useful analyses. Ernest Gellner, for example, discussed how Islam as a religious institution fostered almost all of the same work-oriented, industrial tendencies in most Arab countries as Protestantism did throughout Europe. Egalitarianism, a concept made sacred in Islamic thought, was similarly conducive to modernity, even if colonial pressures had prevented felicitous outcomes. Consequently, it was important to note that clashes between Western and Muslim civilizations, which often make the news because of their dramatic qualities, did not represent majority views. In fact, extremists who learned how to manipulate media outlets did not represent the majority of Muslims who, it is worth repeating, aspired for the same democratic values as those of people living in Western societies.

Rise and Influence of Islamic Movements. While most *madāris* (religious schools, sing., *madrasah*) and mosques in the Muslim world were under the control of governments, state authorities could never entirely manage the populist strains of Islamic activism. Behind a tailor's shop, one might find an impromptu mosque and a room for teaching the young outside a state's strict regulations. It was often mentioned how sudden and unexpected the Arab Spring was to veteran observers of the region, though the rise and influence of Islamic movements was neither sudden nor unanticipated. Rather, the effective, civil, non-state nature of the opposition to the state, both religious and liberal, accounted for this lack of predictability. Most opposition activities happened far from the view of the state apparatus. Even in those instances when states were able to intervene, they often attempted to co-opt religious movements, instead of simply suppressing them. For despite some very public executions or expedient statements of religiosity, so-called secular strongmen by and large failed to fully repress or mollify religious opposition.

Although it enjoyed universal appeal, Islam was a highly diverse religion, and regardless of specific manifestation of belief—mystical Ṣūfī, traditional Salafī, or militant jihādist—unofficial Islam has often been an alternative to the monopoly of power claimed by the modern nation-state. Over decades, Muslim groups formed to provide charities, social networks, community foundations, and a means of organizing beyond the reach of state control. As much as they allowed Muslims to fulfill spiritual yearnings, leaders of secular states understood that the strict application of Sharīʿah law did not always provide immediate, practical solutions. Iran, in particular, exemplified some of the limits of a theocratic system and adopted secular inspired institutions, such as a constitution, republic, and parliament. Moreover, it was the 1979 Islamic revolution that awakened largely dormant opposition groups, as several emulated Tehran's mullahs under the guise of revolts against authoritarianism and stagnation. As Islamic political organizations—Sunnī or Shīʿī, Ṣūfī or Salafī—were tested, many became keenly aware of the need to reconcile political Islam with aspects of modernity.

Clash between These Movements and Secular Nation-builders. Because the ideal relationship between state and religion in majority-Islamic societies was different from that in the West, with the Qurʾān, *ḥadīth* (sayings of the Prophet), and the *sunnah* in Islam forming the original corpus of all legal sources, inevitable clashes emerged between Muslim movements and secular nation-builders. The Qurʾān included specific legal provisions governing some matters of personal status, such as marriage, divorce, and inheritance, as well as certain forms of social transactions and legal stipulations. The *ḥadīth* formed another essential basis for Islamic law. In contrast, and through most of Islamic history, legitimate rulers, called caliphs, or successors of the Prophet, claimed to follow the Prophet Muḥammad's example as closely as possible. Indeed, a caliph with symbolic leadership, if not outright power over a large number of Muslims, existed throughout most of Islamic history before the fall of the last Ottoman sultan-caliph, Abdülmecid II, in 1924. What occurred in the twentieth century, however, was the gradual imposition of the secularized nation-state system that emphasized the role of central authority and the need for positive laws.

In the post-independence period, after the fall of the British and French empires in the 1960s, leaders such as Sayyid Quṭb of the Muslim Brotherhood contrasted the "golden age" of Islam—the first decade of rule under the Prophet and his immediate successor, the Rightly Guided Caliphs—with the rule of irreligious, secular, and populist strong men. Quṭb's magnum opus, *Fī ẓilāl al-Qurʾān* (In the Shade of the Qurʾān) focused on the period when the Holy Scriptures were revealed to Muḥammad and drew an ideological framework that sought to delegitimize the post-independent secular state and to question its fundamental basis. Unlike Quṭb, however, contemporary reformist Muslim thinkers such as Abdulaziz Sachedina and Fatima Mernissi have seen in the golden age examples of Islamic forms of democracy. Tariq Ramadan, for his part, called for a renaissance of ideas in the Middle East and a reconciliation of Islam with the principles of democracy and human rights. In fact, Ramadan emphasized that the life of the Prophet was the basic model, the historical, exemplary ideal, which was universal and, therefore, completely compatible with modern life.

Still, the challenge of implementing religious promise simply according to scriptural or founding ideals was daunting since those emerged in a particular historical context. A separation between the original ideals and Muslim practices emerged a few decades after the death of the Prophet Muḥammad. Caliphs, turning into monarchs, fell short of fulfilling the promise of revelation. Another difficulty with Islamic law, especially law strictly interpreted, was the growing inability of Muslim jurists to adapt it to current social and political circumstances. Generally, the exercise of *ijtihād* (independent reasoning) became limited, and the body of Muslim jurisprudence suffered from imitation and stagnation. While some regimes claimed secular, or pan-Arab nationalist visions and ideologies, they were also the first to be challenged. Indeed, there appeared to be a resurgence of Islamic politics and religious values tied to the Prophet's original Islamic state. Monarchs who survived the recent uprisings largely through their appeal to a more localized religious legitimacy or through the support of Western powers and oil revenues, donned similar cloaks.

Although Islam and monarchy did not mix easily, Arab rulers were influenced by Persian and Byzantine style of rule and established effective dynasties. Of course, Islamic thinkers like Ḥasan al-Bannā (d. 1949), the founder of the Muslim Brotherhood in Egypt, rejected these "dynasties." They represented, he asserted, decadence, even if contemporary Arab rulers were consensus-driven. Modern scholarship avowed some of al-Bannā's conclusions; Lisa Anderson underscored the astonishment of Western scholars at the continued viability of kings, emirs, and sultans in various Middle Eastern states. While many predicted the downfall of such systems in the post-colonial period as monarchs faced the king's dilemma—the expansion of economy and society leads to pressures to expand the area of participation and thus loss of control and power—it was clear that the existential risks of the king's dilemma were avoided, or at least minimized, precisely because of the emphasis on consensus and the use of the state's resources to secure the support of the population. Others argued that the longevity was merely coincidental, since the survival of Arab monarchies, emirates, and sultanates in Jordan, Morocco, Oman, Saudi Arabia, and the Gulf—despite persistent and significant calls for revolution and reform during the Arab Spring—incorporated narrower political factors.

Among the many reasons that Arab monarchs survived were innate mechanisms to withstand the enormous pressures of change that overthrew entrenched secular dictatorships in Tunisia and Egypt. In his *Commander of the Faithful* (1982), John Waterbury described the fundamentally religious role appropriated by the king of Morocco, who served not merely as a political leader but as a religious symbol tied by blood to the family of the Prophet through Sharīfī heritage, as a good illustration of legitimacy. The dynasty of Muḥammad VI, as one of the oldest in history, was the focus of the independence movement under the French protectorate and somehow associated its fate with that of the nascent state. Likewise, in Jordan, the king claimed an illustrious background as a member of the Hashemite dynasty, whose historical roots overcame colonial boundaries. In both cases, the rulers resorted to their religious roles in society.

Even if the emirates of the Gulf were different, since none claimed to be a descendant of the Prophet, their legitimacies were nevertheless historically tied to direct interaction with a small citizenry. Only recently have monarchical assertions been implemented that secured the power of succession with advisory councils and traditional systems of consensus replaced by newer *shūrā* (consultative) traditions. Rulers of the region, including the *shayhk*s of Qatar, found a renewed role through assuming a regional influence. Bahrain was an interesting example of the creativity in which monarchies engaged, as the ruler simply changed his title from emir to king in 2002. In most instances, current rulers became significant only under the auspices of British colonial rule, which recognized them in the nineteenth century.

Still, contemporary monarchies maintained their powers by forging close ties with religious authorities. The first founder of what is now Saudi Arabia, Muḥammad ibn Saʿūd famously signed a pact with the founder of the Wahhābī movement Muḥammad ibn ʿAbd al-Wahhāb, agreeing to support the implementation of strict Islamic law as long as Wahhābī clerics supported the Saudi dynasty. That pact, although often tenuous with the constant threat of revolt and Islamist uprising, survived. Western support, in the form of oil revenues and security guarantees, further shore up this and other Arabian Peninsula dynasties.

Iranian Revolution and Impact in the Region. Unlike conservative Arab Gulf monarchies, the most important and influential models of a functioning, democratic, and successful republics in the present-day Islamic world are Turkey and Iran, though they are at opposite ends of the spectrum.

Although it remained an outlier, Turkey's growing influence could not be underestimated, as the ruling, moderate Justice and Development Party (Adalet ve Kalkınma Partisi, or AKP) was a model for many Islamist groups. Prime Minister Recep Tayyip Erdoğan wrested power from the secular generals who saw it as their duty to uphold the state and ideals of Turkey's secular founder Mustafa Kemal (d. 1938), known as Atatürk (father of the Turks). Atatürk instituted top-down radical secularization in the wake of the disastrous Ottoman breakup after World War I. The Turkish republic was ruled by the military for much of its modern history, though Erdogan gradually re-introduced Islam into the public sphere and has shown the possibility of harmony between democratization and Islamic politics. Simultaneously, Erdogan's politics were often more moderate and dependent on secular institutions than the Muslim Brotherhood in Egypt or Ḥizb al-Nahḍah in Tunisia, which partially explained its successes.

The situation in Iran was different, as the clergy claimed an increasingly large sphere of influence after the 1979 revolution. The supreme leader, Ayatollah ʿAlī Khamaneʾi succeeded Ayatollah Ruhollah Khomeini, while an elected president, Mahmoud Ahmadinejad, managed the country's day-to-day affairs. A twelve-member guardian council was appointed by the supreme leader and the judiciary, tasked to ensure that laws conformed to the constitution of the Islamic Republic. The president and the assembly were elected, but candidates required a thorough vetting by clerics. Moreover, the supreme leader delineates the general policies of the republic, which meant that this system was a hybrid clerical-democratic rule at best—a "guardianship of the Islamic jurists." Although some Sunnī Islamists might suggest theocratic ideas, the idea of a *vilāyat-i faqīh* (rule of the jurist) in Sunnī-majority Arab Middle Eastern countries was probably untenable. For the most part, there was no such thing as an established, clerical hierarchy in Sunnī Islam, and Islamists who criticized the "luxury" of monarchies and called for uprisings gathered little support. Even the Muslim Brotherhood in Egypt or the Ḥizb al-Nahḍah in Tunisia have, for the most part, maintained a much less hierarchical system than that found in Iran, as Mohammed Morsi surrendered his membership in the Brotherhood upon his election as president of Egypt to project a more egalitarian authority.

Islam in the Arab Spring. The glory days of secularist strongmen in the Middle East have ended. Tunisia, Egypt, Libya, and Syria, among others, which appeared to be stable with sophisticated security systems, ushered in dramatic transformations. The overthrow of Saddam Hussein, as much a consequence of internal divisions and American intervention, seemed to herald the possible end of an era. Founded in Syria following World War II, the Baʿthist movement combined socialism, pan-Arabism, nationalism and anti-imperialism. It involved many prominent Christian Arabs as well as majority, Sunnī Arabs who attempted to harmonize political and national unity across borders. Even Nasserism, a movement largely focused on the personality of Gamal Abdel Nasser (d. 1970), who was leader of the 1952 Egyptian revolution and who called for pan-Arab unity and national ideals, gave way to less ideologically driven governments. In fact, the promise of Baʿthist and Nasserist ideologies—nationalist as well as pseudo-socialist systems that were never fully implemented and that heavily relied on Cold War dynamics and Soviet support to justify themselves—faded into insignificance. Nasserist revolutions and calls for pan-Arabism and political unity in the 1960s were frustrated by the differing demands of the nation-states. A short-lived union between Syria and Egypt in 1958, for example, fizzled three years later. The 1967 pan-Arab war with Israel called *al-Naksa* (setback), ended in an ignominious defeat, further eroding the appeal of the Nasserists and Baʿthists. Yet, even as their ideologies faltered, the regimes held on for decades, substituting the promise of national ideology with brute force and suppression by police states.

With the Arab Spring, most secular dictators disappeared, as the Bashar al-Assad regime in Syria fought tooth and nail to survive. In Algeria, which remained somewhat of an outlier in this respect, the military successfully appropriated control and tempered dissent. Although it is too soon to know for certain, the downfall of the Yemeni strongman, ʿAlī ʿAbd Allāh Ṣalīh, seems to have led to the rise of an equally security-oriented strongman, ʿAbd al-Rabbah Manṣūr al-Hadī. It is in the scattered ruins of these regimes that the failure of Baʿthism and Nasserism, at least as they were manifested in the form of highly corrupt police states, finally became apparent.

Theoretical Disputes between Islamists and Secularists. The future of Islam and politics in the region could be described as being cautiously optimistic. Contrary to the predictions of Western experts and Middle Eastern regimes, revolutionaries and Islamic parties have proven their ability to outlast and overcome secular dictatorships. Their promise of Islamic democracy, although not fully articulated, could undoubtedly lead to a far greater promise of equality and representation. Religious parties in the West, such as the Christian Democrats, and religious states, such as Anglican England, can exist within a strong democratic framework. It will be largely up to the newly liberated populations, with careful stewardship by their leaders, to maintain a balance between religious values and the maintenance of pluralistic, democratic institutions.

After the first democratic legislative election in Algeria in 1991, the initial victory of the Islamic Front (FIS) led to the invalidation of the election by the military, which rejected any "Islamist" democracy. In the aftermath of more recent upheavals, this sort of secular military coup was no longer possible, as Islamist parties were forced to moderate their positions in the face of political realities. Even as the West was partially responsible for the ills of the past, Islamists re-established ties with the most powerful economies of a globalized world, precisely to withstand new expectations. There was always the risk that these new regimes would simply turn Islamic politics into ideological screens for corruption and effective dictatorship that, in fact, many Arabs and Muslims were no longer willing to tolerate. Once thought to be dormant, these masses asserted their power to change by pouring into the streets, though vigilance will be required to maintain pressure on new systems of government, so that demands for transparency and representative governance may thrive.

BIBLIOGRAPHY

Arkoun, Mohammed. "Present-Day Islam Between Its Tradition and Globalization." In *Intellectual Traditions in Islam*, edited by Farhad Daftary, pp. 179–222. London: I. B. Tauris, 2000.

Black, Antony. *The History of Islamic Political Thought: From the Prophet to the Present*. New York: Routledge, 2001.

Entelis, John, ed. *Islam, Democracy and the State in North Africa*. Bloomington: Indiana University Press, 1997.

Esposito, John. *Islam and Politics*. 4th ed. Syracuse, N.Y.: Syracuse University Press, 1998.

Gause, Gregory. "Can Democracy Stop Terrorism?" *Foreign Affairs* 84, no. 5 (Sept-Oct. 2005): 62–76.

Heck, Paul. *Sufism and Politics: The Power of Spirituality*. Princeton, N.J.: Markus Weiner, 2007.

Humphreys, R. Stephen. *Between Memory and Desire: The Middle East in a Troubled Age*. Berkeley: University of California Press, 1999.

Kamrava, Mehran, ed. *The New Voices of Islam: Rethinking Politics and Modernity: A Reader*. Berkeley: University of California Press, 2006.

Lindholm, Charles. *The Islamic Middle East: Tradition and Change*. Oxford: Blackwell, 2002.

Milton-Edwards, Beverly. *Islam and Politics in the Contemporary World*. Princeton, N.J.: Polity Press, 2004.

Mernissi, Fatima, and Mary Jo Lakeland. *The Veil and the Male Elite*. New York: Basic Books, 1992.

Quṭb, Sayyid. *Fī ẓilāl al-Qur'ān (In the Shade of the Qur'an)*. Translated by M. A. Salahi and A. A. Shamis. Wamy, 1995.

Quṭb, Sayyid. *Milestones*, New York: Islamic Book Service, 2006.

Roy, Oliver. *Global Islam: The Search for a New Ummah*. New York: Columbia University Press, 2004.

Ramadan, Tariq. *In the Footsteps of the Prophet: Lessons from the Life of Muhammad*. New York: Oxford University Press, 2009.

Ramadan, Tariq. *Islam and the Arab Awakening*. New York: Oxford University Press, 2012.

Shehata, Samer, ed. *Islamist Politics in the Middle East: Movements and Change*. New York: Routledge, 2012.

Sachedina, Abdulaziz. *The Islamic Roots of Democratic Pluralism*. New York: Oxford University Press, 2007.

Waterbury, John. *Commander of the Faithful*. New York: Columbia University Press, 1982.

ALLEN FROMHERZ

ISLAMIC ACTION FRONT. The Islamic Action Front (Jabhat al-ʿAmal al-Islāmī, IAF), Jordan's most influential political opposition movement, was formed by members of the Jordanian Muslim Brotherhood, an Islamic reform movement, in 1992, following the legalization of political parties by Jordan's King Hussein. The Jordanian branch of the Muslim Brotherhood emerged in 1945 and was initially dedicated to the maintenance of a unified, Arab-majority Palestine and against the formation of the state of Israel. Although it maintains relations with the original Muslim Brotherhood movement in Egypt, Jordan's branch is in practice autonomous, and its members pursue their own political programs. During the 1950s–1970s, the Jordanian Muslim Brotherhood was permitted to expand its base of support, particularly among the Palestinian refugees to Jordan following the formation of Israel in 1948–1949 and following the occupation of the West Bank by the Israelis in June 1967.

Unlike its Egyptian counterpart, the Jordanian Muslim Brotherhood maintained good ties with the Jordanian monarchy and in return was permitted to operate without the repression that befell the country's secular communist and socialist opposition parties. The pro-monarchy faction of the Muslim Brotherhood prevailed in the early 1970s and supported the government's crackdown on Palestinian paramilitary groups connected to the Palestine Liberation Organization following a failed coup attempt, popularly known as "Black September," which began in September 1970 and continued into the summer of 1971. Significant numbers of prominent Muslim Brotherhood leaders served in successive Jordanian governments since the movement's formation. Its goal was to reform, not overthrow, the government by Islamicizing it and moving it toward a political path that, in the eyes of the IAF and Muslim Brotherhood leaderships, would be more in line with religious principles.

The Jordanian monarchy's relationship with the Muslim Brotherhood has been one of mutual convenience. King ʿAbdullāh I and King Hussein drew upon the Brotherhood's support in times of political or social need, and the Brotherhood was permitted to operate relatively freely as long as it did not challenge the sovereign authority of the monarchy. Despite this understanding, the Brotherhood and its political party, the IAF, have undergone periods of harassment for being too critical of the monarchy, particularly about its foreign policy, such as its continued close ties to the United States and Great Britain and the 1994 peace treaty signed by King Hussein and Israeli prime minister Yitzhak Rabin. The pattern has continued under King ʿAbdullāh II. In one highly publicized incident in June 2006, Jordanian authorities arrested four IAF members of parliament—the senior leader and prominent preacher Shaykh Muḥammad Abū Fāris, Jaʿfar al-Hūrānī, ʿAlī Abū Sukkar, and Ibrahīm al-Mashwakhī—for attending the wake of Jordanian militant leader Abū Muṣʿab al-Zarqawī following his death in a U.S. air strike in Iraq.

The IAF and the Jordanian Muslim Brotherhood have relied primarily on social service organizations such as schools, health clinics, religious education programs, and charitable institutions to build a following. The Brotherhood's central social services organization is the Islamic Center Charity Society. Its schools teach the nationally mandated curriculum as well as a program of religious education aimed at creating new generations of religiously observant Jordanian youth to form a support base for the IAF and the Muslim Brotherhood. In addition to its educational and health care facilities, the Muslim Brotherhood has also founded organizations such as the Society for the Preservation of the Qurʾān, which seeks to protect Jordan's "religious heritage," furthering the movement's goal of leading the country's citizens back toward Islamic principles. The main bases of electoral support for the IAF and Muslim Brotherhood are located in Islamist political strongholds such as al-Zarqāʾ, an industrial city northwest of the capital city, Amman, and include members from across Jordan's socioeconomic classes. The IAF is particularly popular among Palestinian Jordanians because of its strong support of the Palestinian national cause and its criticisms of Israel and its backers.

The IAF is characterized by its on-and-off decisions to participate in or boycott parliamentary elections. In July 2003, for example, IAF candidates secured 20 out of 84 seats. The 64 remaining seats were won by non-partisan deputies, while the prominent National Democratic Block failed to win a single post. By August 2007, however, the 25 IAF candidates up for election in municipal elections were withdrawn, allegedly because Amman (the Jordanian Government) manipulated the ballot boxes. In the event, voter turnout was low, though four IAF supporters, including two mayors, assumed elected positions. A few months later, the IAF fielded 22 candidates for the Jordanian national elections. Six won, resulting in the lowest showing to date of the Islamist party, further illustrating the IAF's waning influence. IAF leaders accused Amman of vote buying and ballot-box stuffing.

In the aftermath of dramatic political uprisings in Tunisia and Egypt starting in February 2011, street protests in major Jordanian cities mobilized the IAF as well as the Jordanian monarchy. King ʿAbdullah II replaced Prime Minister Samir Rifai with Maʿrouf Bakhit, a former prime minister, and asked him to "launch a genuine political reform process." IAF leaders called on the monarch to address sorely needed economic reforms. IAF secretary-general Hamzah Mansour insisted that genuine reforms must focus on "the manner in which the government is formed, the way lawmakers are elected and the issue of taxes." Unlike opposition forces elsewhere in the region, the

IAF, still the largest resistance group in Jordan, did not call for regime change.

[*See also* Arab-Israeli Conflict; Islamism; Jordan; Muslim Brotherhood; *and* Palestine.]

Bibliography

"Islamic Action Front Party: Jabhat al-ʿAmal al-Islāmī." http://www.jabha.net/. Official website of the Islamic Action Front.

Harmsen, Egbert. Islam, *Civil Society and Social Work: Muslim Voluntary Welfare Associations in Jordan between Patronage and Empowerment*. Amsterdam: Amsterdam University Press, 2008.

Schwedler, Jillian. *Faith in Moderation: Islamist Parties in Jordan and Yemen*. Cambridge, U.K., and New York: Cambridge University Press, 2006.

Wiktorowicz, Quintan. "Islamists, the State, and Cooperation in Jordan." *Arab Studies Quarterly* 21, no. 4 (Fall 1999): 1–17.

Wiktorowicz, Quintan. *The Management of Islamic Activism: Salafis, the Muslim Brotherhood, and State Power in Jordan*. Albany, N.Y.: State University of New York Press, 2001.

Christopher Anzalone
Updated by Joseph A. Kéchichian

Islamic Banking.

See Islamic Finance.

Islamic Constitutional Movement.

The Ḥarakāt al-Dusturiyah al-Islāmīyah, known as Ḥadas in Arabic, is the Islamic Constitutional Movement (ICM), one of Kuwait's leading Sunnī Islamist organizations and political associations. It was formed in 1991 following the War for Kuwait (the first Gulf War). Created and led by affiliates of the Kuwaiti Muslim Brotherhood, with which ICM remains closely linked, Ḥadas is a politically and socially conservative movement intent on eliminating corruption, promoting electoral reform, and instilling traditional Islamic values. The individual most responsible for the creation of the ICM is Jasim al-Muhalhil, who spearheaded participation in successive Kuwaiti parliamentary elections, starting in 1992, and encouraged representation in the Majlis.

Although political-party status is prohibited under Kuwaiti law, ICM is often referred to as an informal political party and is considered one of Kuwait's leading political actors. Its candidates have won seats in every post–Gulf War parliamentary election, and its ranking members have accepted executive-level cabinet appointments, including the Ministers of Trade and Islamic Endowments.

At the time of ICM's emergence, the Kuwaiti parliament was inoperative, having been dissolved in 1986. Following the revival of parliamentary elections in 1992, however, ICM won four of the fifty available seats in Kuwait's unicameral National Assembly. Since then, ICM has achieved recurring electoral successes, earning between four and six seats in many subsequent elections. In 2003, only two ICM deputies were elected, although three managed to win in 2008, when Jamaan al-Harbash, Abdulaziz al-Shayji, and Nasser al-Sane were elected. In 2009, Kuwait held its third election in less than three years—and the third in which women were allowed to vote and stand for parliament. It was the three ICM parliamentarians who set the 2009 elections in motion when, in March of that year, they filed requests for the prime minister, Shaykh Nasser Mohammad al-Ahmed al-Jaber al-Sabah, a nephew of the emir, to face questioning over policy decisions and alleged financial irregularities at his office. The move backfired, as only al-Harbash was reelected in 2009, although another deputy, Falah al-Azmi, considered himself to be affiliated with the Muslim Brotherhood.

ICM generally adopts a gradualist, nonconfrontational, and often pragmatic approach in its political endeavors. It supports both the liberalization and the Islamization of Kuwaiti politics, and it has proven willing and able to coordinate with its traditional rivals to press for change. As its name implies, ICM views itself as a rigorously constitutional yet fundamentally Islamic movement, dedicated to constructively opposing the government when its actions violate either the constitution or traditional Islamic values. Because of its dual commitments to Islam and the constitution, ICM's political identity is founded on political liberalization and cultural conservatism, which may sound contradictory but is eminently logical for its members.

ICM's Islamic agenda has, broadly speaking, focused on promoting traditional values and eliminating so-called moral corruption, such as lurid broadcasts, religiously offensive publications, and mixed-gender classrooms. In an ultimately unsuccessful effort to advance its Islamic agenda, ICM lobbied strenuously for Islamic law to constitutionally represent the sole source of legislation, as opposed to one of many sources. Following the Kuwaiti emir's veto of the proposed amendment, ICM narrowed its constitutional reform efforts to focus on the enforcement of particular aspects of Islamic law, such as the payment of *zakāt*.

ICM's political liberalization agenda has generally emphasized the elimination of political corruption, ensuring governmental accountability, expanding citizens' rights, and promoting electoral reform. Some of the reform initiatives it has supported include the passage of a political parties law, the enlargement of parliament, the adoption of financial disclosure laws, and the creation of a constitutional monarchy. With respect to women's rights, the movement has taken a position of compromise, calling for women's suffrage but not the full panoply of political rights. In May 2005, the National Assembly approved legislation granting women full political rights. Subsequently, the prime minister appointed Kuwait's first female minister, Dr. Massouma al-Mubarak, as planning minister and minister of state for administrative development affairs, and the government appointed two women to Kuwait's Municipal Council. Following the resignation of the cabinet in March 2007, Dr. al-Mubarak was joined by a second woman, Nouriya Subih, in the cabinet. In 2009, the ICM welcomed four female deputies, Aseel al-Awadi, Rola Dashti, Salwa al-Jassar, and Massouma al-Mubarak (who had served as planning minister and minister of state for administrative development affairs since 2005), and did not object when Moudhi al-Humoud was appointed minister of education in May 2009. She became the sole female cabinet member in 2011. Regarding economic matters, the ICM supports free market liberalization measures consistent with Islamic law; on foreign policy, it supports, among others, the Palestinian Ḥamās and Kuwait's traditional security relationship with the United States.

ICM comprises a general assembly, secretary general, secretariat, technical office, and eight-member political bureau. Membership is based on recruitment and achieved following a period of probation. While membership recruitment occurs primarily in the mosques, leadership recruitment occurs primarily on university campuses. Consequently, ICM leadership tends to include educated, middle-class professionals, while the membership tends to include a broad cross-section of Kuwaiti society.

BIBLIOGRAPHY

Brown, Nathan. *Pushing Towards Party Politics? Kuwait's Islamic Constitutional Movement.* Carnegie Paper No. 79. Washington, D.C.: Carnegie Endowment for International Peace, February 2007. See the comments made by Mohammed Hussein al-Dallal, political relations official and member of the ICM political bureau in Kuwait, on this paper at http://www.carnegieendowment.org/publications/index.cfm?fa=view&id=19168&prog=zgp&proj=zdrl,zme.

Country Profile: Kuwait. London: The Economist Intelligence Unit, 2006–2011.

Hamid, Shadi, and Amanda Kadlec. *Strategies for Engaging Political Islam*, Washington, D.C.: Friedrich-Ebert-Stiftung [Foundation] and Project on Middle East Democracy, November 2009.

"Islamic Constitutional Movement." http://www.icmkw.org/. In Arabic.

"Muslim Brotherhood." http://www.ikhwanweb.com/tagBView.php?id=Islamic%20Constitutional%20Movement. The Muslim Brotherhood's official English web page provides detailed reportage on the ICM in Kuwait.

Valenti, Peter C. "The New Shape of Kuwait's Elections." *Washington Report on Middle East Affairs* 25, no. 6 (August 2006): 40–41.

CHRYSTIE SWINEY
Updated by JOSEPH A. KÉCHICHIAN

ISLAMIC DEVELOPMENT BANK. *See* Islamic Finance.

ISLAMIC FINANCE. Islamic finance—shorthand for "banking transactions in compliance with Islamic principles"—is a form of modern banking that has evolved in the context of modern-day global financial markets. Claiming to abide by the prescriptions of Islamic law, Islamic finance is arguably the most important area where Muslim economic doctrines are put into practice. In 2007, an aggregate of USD 500 billion were reported to be under management according to Islamic principles and, with annual growth rates of 15 to 20 percent, Islamic finance is generally hailed as a success story. Whether Islamic finance also is faithful to its overarching goals, namely, to establish an alternative financial system that is compliant with Muslim business ethics, and whether such a system is superior to the conventional financial system, continue to be subject to debate.

Islamic Finance and Islamic Law. The rich and diverse tradition of Islamic jurisprudence did not regulate banking transactions in any detail, nor did it develop a general theory of obligations. This means that the legal principles underpinning Islamic financial transactions are essentially a product of contemporary Islamic scholarship, formulated and legitimized in accordance with the canonical texts of Islamic law. Although many details continue to be disputed, certain core principles have emerged: (1) interest on loans is prohibited. This prohibition is derived from the Qurʾanic ban of *ribā*, that is, "illicit gains" in commercial transactions (2:275). The prohibition of *ribā* is held to proscribe any excess or gain in consideration for the deferral of a debt; (2) speculation is unlawful. This principle is derived from the prohibition of *gharar*, that is, (excessive) uncertainty in bilateral transactions. In principle, the object of a contract must be determined and ready for delivery when the contract is concluded; and (3) profit is only permissible if it is based on an (entrepreneurial) risk. This means that all financing parties should participate in the fate of the financed venture or asset. This renders a fixed return on a certain investment impermissible.

The Emergence of the Islamic Finance Industry. The first Islamic financial institution was set up in 1963 in the town of Mit Ghamr, in the Egyptian Nile Delta. It was structured as a credit cooperative and its founder, Dr. Aḥmad al-Najjār, who was influenced by the German concept of savings banks (*Sparkassen*), promoted compliance with Islamic principles as a prerequisite in order to reach the conservative rural population.

The Iraqi scholar Muḥammad Bāqir al-Ṣadr (d. 1980), one of the foremost (Shīʿī) jurists of the twentieth century, is credited with masterminding the concept of the Islamic bank based on the application of Islamic legal principles and a reinterpretation of traditional contractual structures of Islamic law. In his seminal book "The Interest-Free Bank in Islam" (*al-Bank al-lā ribāwī fi l-Islām*, 1969), he proposed that an Islamic financial system be based on Sharīʿah principles and that the most important principle was the ban of interest on loans.

Since the Village Bank in Mit Ghamr, the Islamic finance industry has changed considerably, due to a combination of the doctrine of Islamic economics and the oil wealth of the Arab Gulf countries. The first commercially oriented Islamic bank was the Dubai Islamic Bank, established in 1975, and by the end of the decade there were many others throughout the Middle East. In 1981 a major transnational company, the Dār al-Māl al-Islāmī, was set up, based in Geneva. These institutions engaged in corporate finance and retail transactions targeting wealthy Muslim investors, pursuing a commercial agenda with a business model that was predicated, however, on the claim to abide by religious prescriptions. With their promotion of "interest-free" banking, the prohibition of interest became the key concept of Islamic banking.

In 1974 the Organization of the Islamic Conference (OIC) summit in Lahore created the Islamic Development Bank (IDB). In addition to acting as a development bank for the Muslim world, this intergovernmental organization was entrusted with providing training and advice to Islamic financial institutions. Although the IDB did gain a certain role in development finance in the Muslim world, its influence on the Islamic finance industry at large remained limited.

Since the 1990s, Islamic finance has witnessed a considerable internationalization. The rapid growth of the economies in the Arab Gulf and Southeast Asia, along with the emergence of new financial hubs in Bahrain, Qatar, and Dubai, have globalized Islamic financial practices. In 2011, most international banks are active in Islamic finance—some through a wholly Islamic subsidiary (such as CIIB, the Islamic Bank of Citi Group), others as part of their normal product range (e.g., Deutsche Bank)—and Islamic banking has matured into one aspect of global finance.

Islamic Financial Transactions. Islamic banks have developed contractual structures that cover the full range of (conventional) banking services.

Islamic loans. The most important Islamic financing transaction is the *murābaha* ("mark-up") loan. Under a *murābaha*, a bank acquires an asset and sells it on deferred terms with a mark-up. Thus, instead of extending a loan, the bank engages in the purchase (and sale) of an asset, and instead of charging interest, the bank achieves a trading profit. Most contractual structures envisage that the risk of loss in transit is exclusively borne by the customer, who also waives any and all rights with regard to defects of the asset. As a result, the risk structure of a standard *murābaha* loan is similar to a conventional loan. This is even more obvious with a *tawarruq* ("commodity *murābaha*"), by way of which the bank sells certain traded commodities to the customer (which the customer, in turn, can convert into cash through the commodity exchange). This structure, in particular, has been criticized by more conservative Islamic scholars for merely mimicking a conventional credit transaction.

Asset Finance. Leasing transactions (*ijāra*) are widely used in Islamic finance. Since Islamic principles require the lender to participate in the ownership risk, Islamic banks assume the risk of the commodity and pass it on to a third party on the basis of a maintenance agreement. Another structure, also used in project financing transactions, is the contract of manufacture (*istisnā'*). As with a *murābaha*, the bank undertakes the construction of a certain project on behalf of the customer (and sells it to the latter on deferred terms). Again, instead of lending money, the bank engages in "real" economic activity.

Capital Market Instruments. Islamic banks have developed a number of capital market instruments, most importantly the *sukūk* (Islamic bond). Under a *sukūk* transaction, the issuer sells and transfers a certain asset (e.g., a real-estate portfolio) to a special purpose vehicle (SPV) and rents it back for a specific time period. The SPV funds the acquisition by issuing *sukūk* certificates to investors, which provide for their participation in the rental income of the underlying transaction (equivalent to a coupon in a conventional transaction). At the end of the contractual term, the issuer repurchases the asset, which allows the SPV to redeem the *sukūk* certificates (economically speaking, to repay the bond). It is a source of debate among Islamic scholars whether it is permissible to determine the redemption price in advance (with the effect that the *sukūk* effectively is turned into a fixed-income instrument).

Fund Structures and Private Equity. There are various Islamic structures under which the lender participates as silent partner (*mudāraba*) or in the equity (*mushāraka*) of a business. These profit- and loss-sharing structures implement the Islamic principle of "no profit without risk sharing" most faithfully. In practice, however, they only play a marginal role, as they are cumbersome to manage and raise regulatory issues (no guarantee of the deposits). On the investment side, banks have set up Islamic investment funds (investing normally in real estate or equities) that are based on these structures. All permissible investments must comply with an Islamic screening. As far as equities are concerned, certain industries are excluded (such as alcohol, pork, and pornography), as are target companies that have a high debt ratio or receive considerable income from interest payments.

Islamic Insurance Schemes. Commercial insurance, whereby the insurer undertakes against a premium to indemnify the insured (or to pay a certain sum of money) in case a certain event occurs, is not permissible from an Islamic perspective, as it is deemed unlawful speculation. Islamic insurance schemes (*takāful*) thus are based on the concept of cooperative insurance, whereby all participants exposed to the same risk contribute to an indemnity fund. Often a commercial insurance company will serve as the *takāful* fund's manager and the conditions are comparable to those offered by commercial insurers.

Scholars, *Fatwas,* and Sharīʿah Boards. Normally, Islamic financing transactions are reviewed and certified by a board of Islamic scholars (the Sharīʿah board), which renders an opinion (*fatwa*) as to their compliance with Islamic principles. The scrutiny and approval of complex financial transactions is a challenging task, however, which requires a thorough knowledge of Islamic jurisprudence and a sound understanding of modern banking practices; although some Islamic scholars have begun to specialize in it, the circle of internationally recognized scholars remains small (estimates range from twenty to fifty), so that Islamic legitimacy is a scarce resource. There are conflicts of interest, due to the combined advisory and auditing function of many scholars, and the certification process itself has often been criticized for being slow and nontransparent. Also at odds with the requirement of standardization in the global banking industry are the discursive tradition of Islamic jurisprudence and the plurality of opinion. In response, industry organizations such as the Accounting and Auditing Organization for Islamic Financial Institutions (AAOIFI, Bahrain) and the Islamic Financial Services Board (IFSB, Kuala Lumpur) were established to, inter alia, define Sharīʿah standards for the Islamic finance industry, which will replace the ad hoc certification by individual scholars, at least to the extent financial innovations are concerned.

Islamic Finance and the State. Islamic finance developed independently from the state. The driving force behind it was an alliance of petro-dollar banking and Muslim revivalism. Only very few states—among which are Iran, Pakistan, and Sudan—have made attempts to "Islamize" the banking sector by banning interest-bearing loans, and none has been particularly successful in establishing an alternative, Islamic financial system. It appears that Islamic finance hubs fare better in jurisdictions where the official law does not enforce Islamic prescriptions relating to interest and speculation. Nevertheless, the contractual practices of Islamic finance do intersect with state law in certain areas, among them banking regulation and litigation. Here, the relationship between Islamic finance and the state has not always been easy.

Terrorism Finance? In the aftermath of 9/11, Islamic banks were suspected of providing a financial platform for Muslim terrorism. Although some may have been used to fund terrorist activities, there is no hard evidence that their Islamic orientation in any way promoted this. Moreover, the informal money transfer (*ḥawāla*), which is an attractive way of transferring illicit funds as it works on a basis of personal trust without leaving a paper trail, takes place outside the formal banking system and is not practiced by Islamic financial institutions. The issues with *ḥawāla* banking lie mainly in the lack of proper regulation (which, for example, has caused the UAE Central Bank to take action against *ḥawāla* operators recently), not the mechanism as such.

Banking Regulations. Another issue for states is the extent to which they should adopt special rules tailored to Islamic banks and their needs. Some countries, such as Malaysia, Kuwait, Bahrain, and Dubai, have enacted a separate regulatory regime for Islamic financial institutions; others, such as the United Kingdom, have exempted Islamic financial institutions from certain regulatory rules that are in conflict with Islamic financing structures. More recently, it seems as if financial regulators have entered into a competition for the best regulatory environment for Islamic banks, with the international financial centers London, Luxembourg, and Geneva (in addition to the new financial centers in the Arab Gulf) vying for the prize. One of the central issues discussed in European jurisdictions is the exemption from the "double stamp duty" that is triggered when title to an asset first transfers to the bank before it is transferred to the customer.

Islamic Finance Litigation. Litigation arising out of Islamic financing agreements can be a particular challenge for state courts. Normally, Islamic financing agreements are governed by the law of a specific legal order (e.g., English law, which is a preferred choice of law in financing transactions). However, at times parties to the litigation also invoke principles of Islamic law, arguing that they have transacted with an Islamic bank. In view of the interpretative pluralism of Islamic law, this can be a considerable challenge for commercial courts. In a series of cases, English courts have judged that an Islamic financing agreement is governed by the agreement of the parties and cannot be challenged on the basis of Islamic principles. According to this approach, adjudication on the Islamic permissibility of the transaction is left to the Sharīʿah board and cannot be raised in court. This approach must be seen in the context of English commercial law, which provides the parties with wide discretion to determine the content of transactions. It remains to be seen whether courts in a Middle Eastern jurisdiction, which to a certain extent claim to validate provisions of Islamic law, will take the same approach.

Form vs. Substance: The Discussion of Muslim Business Ethics. From an economic perspective it is often difficult to see the difference between an Islamic and a conventional transaction, in particular with regard to Islamic loan and bond structures; as both transactions are asset-based, one can argue that the transaction is linked to the real economy (the bank trades in precious metals and engages in a sale and lease-back transaction, respectively). This link to the real economy, however, is artificial, and critics of Islamic finance point out that the risk profile of these transactions is very similar to conventional deals. In their view, Islamic finance has failed to establish a true alternative to the conventional financial system and the Islamic scholars have designed complicated and opaque legal devices with the sole aim of circumventing the prescriptions of Islam.

For this reason, critics such as the U.S.-based economist Mahmoud El-Gamal have attacked the formalism of Islamic banking and argued in favor of a renewal of Islamic banking based on an Islamic value system. According to this line of thinking, only a value orientation of Islamic finance, substituting substance for form, would justify its existence. This calls for a debate on how to design an Islamic financial system that is substantially different from conventional finance and how to determine the guiding ethical principles of such a venture. However that may be, the question of whether Islamic finance is a viable alternative to the existing financial system gained greater interest when, during the financial crisis of 2007, mainstream economists noted that Islamic banks were not affected, and their interest in Islamic finance was piqued.

[*See also* Islam and Economics]

BIBLIOGRAPHY

Bälz, Kilian. "Insurance: Islamic Law." In *The Oxford Encyclopedia of Legal History*, edited by Stanley N. Katz, vol. 3, pp. 254–257. New York: Oxford University Press, 2009. An introduction to Islamic insurance, with further references.

Bälz, Kilian. "Islamic Financing Transactions in European Courts." In *Islamic Finance: Current Legal and Regulatory Issues*, edited by Nazim Ali, pp. 61–75. Cambridge, Mass.: The Islamic Finance Project, Harvard Law School, 2005. An overview of Islamic finance litigation with reference to court cases.

Bälz, Kilian. *Sharia Risk? How Islamic Finance Has Transformed Islamic Contract Law*. ILSP Occasional Publication, 9. Cambridge, Mass.: Islamic Legal Studies Program, Harvard Law School, 2008. Discusses the transformation of Islamic contract law as applied by Islamic banks.

El-Gamal, Mahmoud A. *Islamic Finance: Law, Economics, and Practice*. Cambridge: Cambridge University Press, 2006. Probably the most influential critical work on Islamic finance.

Hamoudi, Haider Ala. "The Muezzin's Call and the Dow Jones Bell: On the Necessity of Realism in the Study of Islamic Law." *American Journal of Comparative Law* 56 (2008): 423–70. An excellent discussion of Islamic finance from a critical legal perspective.

Henry, Clement M., and Rodney Wilson, eds. *The Politics of Islamic Finance*. Edinburgh: Edinburgh University Press, 2004. An overview of Islamic financial institutions and their relationship to Middle Eastern politics.

Iqbal, Zamir, and Abbas Mirakhor. *An Introduction to Islamic Finance: Theory and Practice*. Singapore: John Wiley & Sons, 2007. A good overview of the instruments used by Islamic banks.

Saeed, Abdullah. *Islamic Banking and Interest: A Study of the Prohibition of Riba and Its Contemporary Interpretation*. 2d ed. Leiden: Brill, 1999. A good discussion of the prohibition of interest and its application in present-day Islamic finance.

Saleh, Nabil A. *Unlawful Gain and Legitimate Profit in Islamic Law: Riba, Gharar, and Islamic Banking*. 2d ed. London and Boston: Graham and Trotman, 1992. The authoritative work in the English language on the prohibition of interest and speculation in Islamic law.

Vogel, Frank E., and Samuel L. Hayes III. *Islamic Law and Finance: Religion, Risk, and Return*. The Hague and Boston: Kluwer Law International, 1998. The authoritative work in the English language on Islamic finance from a legal perspective.

Warde, Ibrahim. *Islamic Finance in the Global Economy*. Edinburgh: Edinburgh University Press, 2000. The authoritative work on Islamic finance from a political economy perspective.

AAOIFI [http://www.aaoifi.com].

IFSB [http://www.ifsb.org].

KILIAN BÄLZ

Islamic Reform. Intellectual reform (*iṣlāḥ*) is related to the shock that was transmitted by the first mission that Muḥammad ʿAlī Pasha (r. 1805–1848) sent to France, as is clear in Rifāʿah Rāfiʿ al-Ṭahṭāwī's book *Takhlis al-Ibriz fi Talkhis Bariz*, published in 1834. In this book, al-Ṭahṭāwī (1801–1873) creates the foundation of combining (*tawlif*) the principles of the French Revolution (liberty, justice, and fraternity), in addition to the doctrine of *waṭan* (homeland), with Islam and its traditions. Al-Ṭahṭāwī began an intellectual trend that has offered the Arab world the basis of a liberal reform, or "modernism" (*al- ḥadātha*). Al-Ṭahṭāwī was followed by leaders and thinkers such as Adīb Isḥāq (1856–1885), Faraḥ Anṭūn (1874–1922), Shiblī Shumayyil, ʿAbd al-Raḥman al-Kawākibī, ʿAbd Allāh al-Nadīm, Muṣṭafā Kāmil, and Salāmah Mūsā. Other Muslim reformers, including Jamāl al-Dīn al-Afghānī (1837–1897) and Muḥammad ʿAbduh (1849–1905), were influenced by his thinking and the ideals of the French Revolution. Followers of ʿAbduh, such as Aḥmad Luṭfī al-Sayyid, Qāsim Amīn, Ahmd Fathi Zaghlūl, and Saʿd Zaghlūl, formed a liberal wing in the Arab world. The same applies to the grand shaykh of Al-Azhar, Muṣṭafā ʿAbd al-Rāziq, and his brother, ʿAlī ʿAbd al-Rāziq, as well as Aḥmad Amīn and Khālid Muḥammad Khālid.

Pan-Islamism (reformism, *iṣlāḥīyah*) promoted both Islamic unity and national unity. Jamāl al-Dīn al-Afghānī called for not differentiating between people on the basis of national identity—Arab or non-Arab—because religion is based on belief, not on tribalism or nationalism. However, the feudal system of the Ottoman Empire was based on feudal exploitation, which disabled nationalist aspirations. The coming to power of Muḥammad ʿAlī in Egypt and Syria challenged the basis of the feudal system and the development of other productive systems. Thus his attempt at unifying Egypt and Syria was aborted by the Ottoman Empire with the help of European powers.

In the eighteenth century, the Ottoman Empire experienced a real threat to its existence from external factors, such as the scientific revolution that turned Europe into an economic and political force. Muslim intellectuals then believed in the need to imitate European models in state building. However, in the middle of the nineteenth century, when Arab sensibilities were provoked, nationalism was born. Sulayman Mūsā tells us that the first Arab attempt, either by the Egyptians under the leadership of Ibrāhīm Pasha or by the Wahhābīs, failed to establish an Arab state or unite Arab land. Included in this period were thinkers like ʿAbd al-Raḥman al-Kawākibī and Najīb ʿAzūrī.

The history of the Arab world between the two world wars is the history of the Arab nationalist movement. While aiming at independence, this movement saw the solution through religious and political reform, developed along European notions of change. Most representative of this movement are Ṭāhā Ḥusayn, Mansur Fahmī, and ʿAlī ʿAbd al-Rāziq, in addition to Shiblī Shumayyil, Salāmah Mūsā, and Faraḥ Anṭūn. However, most Muslim thinkers believed that the causes for the rise of civilization in the West were derived from progress in science. Science should be a value in itself, but the nationalist movement opted for ideology, or the ideologization of science, as it did with religion and other disciplines.

Other thinkers describe various defining moments and elements of reform: (1) the French invasion of Egypt (1798–1801), which brought modern Western civilization and its political doctrines and administrative systems; (2) the scientific mission to Egypt that Muḥammad ʿAlī Pasha initiated, as well as the influx of French experts and technicians, beginning in 1820; (3) the great waves of missionary schools in the nineteenth century, such as ʿAyntūrah in 1834, al-Jamiʿīyah al-Surīyah in 1847, the Protestant Syrian College in 1866, and the Jesuits in 1874, which led to the active spread of translations and the modernization of Arabic—an act that influenced the idea of an Arab Renaissance; (4) printing, which led to propagating historic great books and the translation of European books; and (5) the press, which carried the political campaign for Arab unity. In addition, in Syria there was a great campaign for translation, which was restricted mostly to religious books. However, Muḥammad ʿAlī wanted the translation of European books to serve as an instrument of modernization of the state. European literary and scientific associations were introduced as well, such as Jamiʿīyat al-Adab wa-al-ʿUlūm (in 1847), with the help of American missionaries, and al-Jamiʿīyah al-ʿIlamīyah al-Surīyah (1852) and Jamiʿīyat Shams al-Biʾr (1869), which was a branch of the American YMCA. However, in Egypt, the literary and scientific associations, such as al-Maʿhad al-Maṣrī (1859) and al-Jamiʿīyah al-Jughrafīyah al-Khiduawīyah (1875), were set up by the French. Thus, one finds two trends that galvanized the Arab intellectuals—the admiration of Western civilization and the acceptance of Arab backwardness—which in turn explain the focus of the Arab Renaissance on reviving the Arab spirit and imitating the advanced European peoples.

However, Jamāl al-Dīn al-Afghānī and Muḥammad ʿAbduh deemed it necessary to study the components and elements of Western civilization that Muslims should adopt and those Islamic religious components and elements that they should maintain. Therefore, they tried to distinguish between Islam as a religion and Islam as a civilization and determined that it is politics, not Islam as such, that played a major role in Muslims' backwardness.

While al-Afghānī paved the way for an intellectual Muslim modernist and reformist trend, this trend did not develop. It was cut short by the rise of a nationalist trend inspired generally by Western liberal secular thinking and particularly by the doctrines of the French Revolution. Al-Afghānī and ʿAbduh educated an entire generation of intellectuals, including Aḥmad Luṭfī al-Sayyid, Muḥammad Ḥusayn Haykal, Ṭāhā Ḥusayn, and Aḥmad Amīn. However, this generation opted for association with Western thought and disconnection from Islamic thought. Thus the Arab reform remained superficial and did not penetrate basic social fabrics. The Arab reform blindly and unconditionally adopted Western thought and generalized its suitability to the Arab world. This view of Western thought paralyzed the possibility of developing Islamic civilization from within and linked liberation movements of that time to the very doctrines used to exercise and justify Western domination. Therefore, Western domination and powers were replaced by their distorted images, that is, authoritarian Arab domination and powers that raised, like Western powers, the slogans of freedom, development, science, and secularism.

The writings of Amir Shakīb Arslān, who experienced firsthand the failures, victories, and weakness of the Ottoman Empire as well as the Arab Renaissance, represent the trend of rising nationalism and rationalism to confront challenges from the West. He devoted his writing to proving Islam's capacity to strike a revival and Arabism's ability to confront political invasions. The challenge of Islam/Arabism versus the West was the central characteristic of the Arab Renaissance: conflict with the West and the rise of nationalism, both of which developed with regional and social fragmentation. Thus, Islamic reformism evolved into a movement that linked political bankruptcy to religious bankruptcy, that is, lack of justice and freedom. Arslān launched an anti-Western campaign revolving around the West's claims of civility and progress. His famous book *Limādhā taʾakhkhara al-Muslimūn, wa-limādhā taqaddama ghairuhum* is an example of such a revolt against both the Islamic world and the West, which provoked the French to confiscate his writings.

Arslān finds that the central cause for Arab backwardness is the Muslims' deficiency in developing science, and in this Arslān is in agreement with al-Afghānī, al-Ṭahṭāwī, and Khayr al-Dīn al-Tūnīsī. Islam is civil in nature, and its call for deep belief in a divine creed as a source for unity among humankind to fight ignorance and injustice was the cause for the rise and expansion of the first state of Arabs and Muslims. However, the backwardness and deterioration of Muslims are the result of the loss of such a belief and thus the loss of knowledge and power.

It is therefore obvious that the reformist reading of past Islamic heritage (*turāth*) is an attempt to adjust to the modern age and the employment of an Arab revival. However, this reading has led to the acknowledgment of the supremacy of Western thought by requiring the West to reform understanding of Islamic cultural heritage. Thus, the discourses of Arab enlightenment and Islamic reform turned into attempts to forge (*talfīq*) doctrines such as nationalism, democracy, and socialism into selective components of Islamic heritage.

The discourses of reformism or modernism took roots in societies that were fragmented after the collapse of the Ottoman Empire, and these discourses turned into radical discourses of struggle and independence. Thus, these discourses were the consequence of the intersection between Western culture and Islamic culture at the moment of the collapse of the universal Islamic Empire. Therefore, the relationship between the West and the Islamic world turned into a question of the factors that led to that collapse. The birth of the culture of the reform took place during the weakness of the Islamic nation; therefore, both questions and answers over failure and success were distorted to a large extent.

The Muslim reformers thought that they could reread and reinterpret Islamic heritage from a liberal perspective, which could constitute a prelude to a democratic national revolution under the umbrella of Islam. Thus, Islam was turned into conceptual justifications for democracy, social justice, and modernization. Muḥammad ʿAbduh tells us that real modernization is identical to Islam. Under the pretext of absorbing the dominant concepts of the West, Muslim reformers fell under spell of Western epistemological and political domination during a period of imperialist and capitalist expansion.

BIBLIOGRAPHY

Adams, Charles. *Islam and Modernism in Egypt*. New York: Russell and Russell, 1986.

Binder, Leonard. *Islamic Liberalism: A Critique of Development Ideologies*. Chicago and London: University of Chicago Press, 1988.

Hefner, Robert. "Multiple Modernities: Christianity, Islam, Hinduism in a Globalizing Age." *Annual Review of Anthropology* 27 (1998): 83–104.

Hourani, Albert. *Arabic Thought in the Liberal Age, 1798–1939*. Cambridge, U.K.: Cambridge University Press, 1983 [1962].

Landau, Jacob M. *The Politics of Pan-Islam: Ideology and Organization*. Oxford: Clarendon Press, 1990.

Mohammadi, Ali, ed. *Islam Encountering Globalization*. London: RoutledgeCurzon, 2002.

Moussalli, Ahmad. *Moderate and Radical Islamic Fundamentalism: The Quest for Modernity, Legitimacy and the Islamic State*. Gainesville: University Press of Florida, 1999.

Moussalli, Ahmad. *The Quest for Democracy, Pluralism and Human Rights*. Gainesville: University Press of Florida, 2001.

Moussalli, Ahmad. "Two Tendencies in Modern Islamic Political Thought: Modernism and Fundamentalism." *Hamdard Islamicus* 16, no. 2 (Summer 1993).

Najjar, Fauzi. "The Arabs, Islam and Globalization." *Middle East Policy* 12, no. 3 (Fall 2005): 91–106.

Zebiri, Kate. *Mahmud Shaltut and Islamic Modernism*. Oxford: Oxford University Press, 1995.

AHMAD MOUSSALLI

ISLAMIC REPUBLICAN PARTY. Founded in February 1979, shortly after the fall of the Iranian monarchy, the Islamic Republican Party (IRP) had the approval of Ayatollah Ruhollah Khomeini (1902–1989), and its key founding members were among his top clerical loyalists. Foremost among them were Muḥammad Bihishtī, ʿAbd al-Karīm Mūsavī Ardabīlī, ʿAlī Khameneʾi, ʿAlī Akbar Hāshimī Rafsanjānī, and Muḥammad Javād Bāhunar. All were also members of the Revolutionary Council. Bihishtī was the secretary general of the IRP and the Revolutionary Council concurrently. The close connection between the two bodies was acknowledged by Rafsanjānī during the first party congress in 1983. The Revolutionary Council, however, had been disbanded in July 1980.

The IRP was not a regular political party. It neither institutionalized a party structure nor encouraged increased membership. Formal membership was never emphasized and did not seem important. From the start, the party served as a mobilizer of some of the traditional and reactionary forces of Iranian society. It formed a united front through a loose coalition of various Islamic groups and organizations, clerics, and nonclerical elements that endorsed Khomeini's version of an Islamic government. A multitude of persons and groups whose interests ran counter to the religious moderates, secularists, liberals, and leftists were utilized by the IRP to undermine these voices. The divided character of the non-IRP groups, their ideological, organizational, and personal conflicts, as well as their inexperience in the intricacies of governance, helped contribute to the IRP success.

Under the shrewd leadership of Bihishtī, the IRP moved swiftly toward monopolizing state power. It became a focal point for unleashing Islamic forces on grassroots organizations and independent groups, and it organized Islamic associations inside the workplace to counter the independent workers' councils. On university and college campuses, Islamic student groups were encouraged to take matters into their own hands. The IRP organized rallies and demonstrations against other groups, advocated purges of government institutions and the overhaul of the state bureaucracy, pushed for the execution of the officials of the previous regime, and ordered the confiscation of their properties and the takeover of some sectors of the Iranian economy. The IRP also played an important role in the takeover of the American Embassy in Tehran in November 1979.

These activities did not always occur under the rubric of the IRP or the person of Ayatollah Khomeini. The presence of autonomous and semiautonomous groups and individuals in the party facilitated a chain of action with the sole purpose of eliminating those perceived as the enemies of the revolution and guaranteeing governance for the Khomeini loyalists. For example, although Sipāh-i Pasdarān-i Inqilāb-i Islāmā (the Revolutionary Guards) and the Ḥizbullāh (the Party of God) adherents were not part of the IRP, they served as its agents. Also, not all pro-Khomeini clerics and groups were supportive of the IRP or of Bihishtī. The most prominent among these nonsupporters were members of the religiously conservative Jamʿīyah-yi Mudarrisīn-i Qom (Theological Teachers' Association of Qom). The teachers' group was sharply critical of the idea of a political party, but since such groups could not dominate the political scene or single-handedly eliminate the liberal or leftist factions, it sided with the IRP. Other groups, such as the Jamʿīyah-yi Rūḥānīyat-i Mubāriz (Association of the Combatant Clerics), never directly joined the IRP but formed a temporary coalition in order to gain a foothold in the 1980 parliamentary elections.

A majority of the elected candidates to the Majlis-i Khabarīgān (Assembly of Experts), a crucial body charged with drafting a new constitution, came from the IRP coalition. Ayatollah Bihishtī became vice chair of the Assembly of Experts and ran most of its public and private meetings. The Revolutionary Council and the IRP campaigned vigorously for the approval of the constitution in the December 1979 referendum.

Abol-Hasan Bani Sadr's election in January 1980 as the first president of postrevolutionary Iran was a significant setback for the IRP. The party had pressed for the postponement of the presidential elections until the last day. Bani Sadr's close connection to Khomeini, his popularity among the anti-IRP groups, and the top clerics' general ambivalence about the IRP's capability to govern joined to bring about the IRP defeat in January 1980. Yet in February, Bihishtī, maintaining all his previous positions, became the head of the Supreme Court.

Thereafter, the IRP put all of its efforts into gaining a majority in the first parliamentary elections after the revolution, to be held in March 1980. Several developments are of political significance. In mid-February 1980, the Revolutionary Council decided to change the election law. An absolute majority was required in order to win the first round of balloting, failing which the top two candidates had to participate in a runoff election. With the exception of the IRP, most groups and organizations opposed the two rounds of balloting, arguing that it worked to the disadvantage of small parties. The IRP then moved to form a grand coalition of diverse Islamic groups. It also used its connections and clout to change the boundaries of various constituencies to the IRP's advantage. Obstruction of the campaigns of other political parties was systematic. Many small-party candidates were disqualified and demonstrations were disallowed; Friday prayer sermons and religious broadcasts on television and radio were used as campaign forums. On the day of the elections, fraud and irregularities were rampant. The result was an impressive success for the IRP and the independent Islamic elements. About half of those elected in the first round in March and more than half in the second round of elections in May were part of the IRP coalition. Rafsanjānī was elected speaker of the Majlis (parliament) on 20 July 1980.

IRP control of the parliament presented an added challenge to Bani Sadr. The IRP and the president clashed over many issues, including the choice of a prime minister and cabinet heads. Muḥammad ʿAlī Rajāʾī, a Majlis deputy from Tehran and an IRP member, was imposed as prime minister on the president, touching off a constitutional crisis and immobilizing state functions. Ignoring the chain of command, Rajāʾī regularly opposed Bani Sadr. These confrontations came to symbolize anticlerical versus clerical rule. Petitions were signed and demonstrations were held asking for the dissolution of the IRP. Grand Ayatollahs ʿAbd Allāh Shīrāzī and Ḥasan Ṭabāṭabāʾī Qummī declared their support for the president. Ayatollah Khomeini interceded, asking all sides to cease their quarrels, but to no avail. The IRP's propaganda and mobilization of street mobs and parliamentary deputies eventually resulted in Bani Sadr's removal by Khomeini on 22 June 1981, and a major crackdown against all anticlerical groups. The Temporary Council of the Presidency was established to oversee the change. Its three members were Bihishtī, Rajāʾī, and Rafsanjānī.

On 28 June 1981, the IRP headquarters in Tehran was destroyed in a major bomb blast. Seventy-four people were killed, including Bihishtī, Majlis deputies, high-ranking government officials, and other party members. Although the government blamed the organization known as the Mujāhidīn-i Khalq, no one claimed responsibility for the blast. This fueled rumors that interclerical rivalry and anti-Bihishtī sentiments were responsible for the bombing.

Muḥammad Javād Bāhunar, the minister of education, became secretary-general of the party; in July elections Rajāʾī was elected president (confirmed by Khomeini on 2 August 1981), and he chose Bāhunar as his prime minister. Mūsavī Ardabīlī replaced Bihishtī as the head of the Supreme Court. On 30 August 1981, both Bāhunar and Rajāʾī were killed in another bomb blast in the premier's office. Again, with impressive speed, the regime moved to fill the gap. Khameneʾi became secretary-general of the IRP and, in October, was elected the third president of the Islamic Republic of Iran. He held both positions concurrently until the dissolution of the IRP in 1987.

The goals of the IRP were not spelled out until its first (and last) party congress in May 1983. Many observers believe that the congress was convened in order to regroup the party and save it from internal fracture. Prior to this date, the IRP had not issued any document on its general ideological outlook. The congress revealed that the goal of the party was to bring together and coordinate dispersed Islamic forces in order to prevent them from neutralizing each other. Difficulties and sharp ideological divisions in the party were acknowledged, yet party members were urged to cooperate with nonparty persons and groups, because they were a valuable asset to the Islamic regime. No statements were made on possible plans to increase membership. Reports indicated that around a thousand members and several nonparty political dignitaries were invited as guests and observers. For the first time, a general plan of action was approved and members were voted on for two councils: the Central Council of the party and the Council of Jurisdiction. The latter's task was to mitigate infighting and to remove factional disputes. Its five members were Khameneʾi, Rafsanjānī, Muḥammad-Mahdī Rabbānī Amlishī, ʿAbbās-Vaʿẓ Ṭabarsī, and Muḥammad ʿAlī Muvaḥḥidī Kirmānī.

The precise ideological orientation of the IRP is more difficult to describe. It was a goal-oriented party whose task, the institutionalization of an Islamic state, had already been accomplished. It is clear, however, that the fall of Bani Sadr and the death of Bihishtī prompted a resurfacing of personal and ideological conflicts among Islamic forces. Bihishtī's death, in particular, marked the beginning of the end for the IRP. His sagacious and farsighted managerial skill and his ability to bring together diverse and hostile forces under the party umbrella were lost forever. The nature of the intra-elite conflict remains obscure owing to its fluid nature, secrecy, and personalism. Personal rivalries were often disguised as ideological disagreements, and individuals shifted their positions and allegiances from one group or issue to another. Adding to the confusion is that certain groups and individual clergy already independent from the IRP still worked with the party on issues of mutual interest. This was acceptable to the party, which did not attempt to coerce any entity into joining the organization; there was no particular reward or punishment for membership. These independent centers of power were a source of both attraction and emulation by inner circles of the party.

Observers of elite factionalism have identified various tendencies within the IRP. Although a concise categorization is an impossible task, some conflicting ideological tendencies are identifiable. In 1983, on the eve of the formation of the Assembly of Experts to decide on a successor to Khomeini, a number of ideological clashes resurfaced. The naming of Husein Ali Montazeri (Ḥusayn ʿAlī Muntazirī) as the successor to Khomeini prompted a public display of political and personal rifts. Two prominent camps were referred to as the Maktabī and the Ḥujjatīyah groups. Each embraced several minigroups with clerical adherents from the IRP. The two groups seem to have differed on the type of leadership that they wanted in the post-Khomeini era (individual cleric versus collective leadership), the nature of social and economic reform (strong centralized government versus less government monopoly), the extent of clerical involvement in politics (more active versus a less-visible role), and several other issues. In the summer of 1983, the Ḥujjatīyah group was attacked in the media and accused of being antirevolutionary and in doubt of Khomeini's leadership. Then, public references to the Ḥujjatīyah suddenly ceased, prompting rumors that the group had suspended its activities. Rarely was there any mention of even the Maktabīs after this incident. Public displays seemed to have turned private again.

It is not certain which clerical elite belonged to which faction. Both Khameneʾi and Rafsanjānī were rumored to belong to either group. Bihishtī, Bāhunar, and Muḥammad Riḍā Mahdavī-Kānī were identified with the Ḥujjatīyah. Prime Minister Mīr Ḥusayn Mūsavī, Mūsavī Ardabīlī, Muḥammad Mūsavī, Khūʿīnīha (the leader of the Students of the Imam's Line—the group that took over the American embassy in November 1979), and ʿAlī Mashkīnī (chair of the Assembly of Experts) were rumored to be Maktabīs.

Throughout 1984, 1985, and 1986, elite factionalism in the party's top leadership intensified. Khameneʾi and Rafsanjānī were rumored to be heading opposing factions of the party. In public, however, they acknowledged the presence of factionalism but exhibited camaraderie toward each other. Some observers believe that the nature of the conflict was in terms of Left versus Right; the leftists were understood to be more militant on foreign policy and favored a state monopoly of principal economic assets, and the rightists were believed to be dominated by the rich *bāzārīs* and to favor less central control and the toning down of anti-imperialist rhetoric. The two factions were unable to reach an agreement or to compromise.

Another dimension of this conflict is the dubious role played by small associations, individual cliques, and sympathizers. The followers of one faction who worked in semiautonomous institutions and government offices and ministries could easily undermine any coherent action by the opposite side. Smaller groups were splitting into several subfactions.

In an environment of much less diversity and of clerical domination, war with Iraq, popular discontent, and elite factionalism, the second parliamentary elections were held in 1984. Voters were told that they had options other than the Islamic Republican Party and the clerics. The IRP list of candidates appeared along with other groups and associations' lists. Almost two-thirds of the candidates appeared on most lists, yet beneath the surface, there was fierce competition between the two dominant party factions. The election resulted in the IRP being the only political party and holding a little less than half of the parliamentary seats.

In October 1985, Khameneʾi became president for a second term. Factionalism remained and rivalries were exposed in the presidential campaign, as well as in the nomination of Prime Minister Mūsavī. A significant feature of this presidential election was the way in which groups and individuals were trying to disassociate themselves from the party. For instance, Sayyid Maḥmūd Kāshānī, who was an IRP member, ran against Khameneʾi, claiming that he was not a member of the party. Meanwhile, both Khomeini and Montazeri made repeated appeals to various factions to stop their infighting.

Public exposure of the secret negotiations with the United States and the Reagan administration in the Iran-Contra affair further worsened the inner-party struggle. A major meeting of the party elite failed to bring about a peaceful resolution. The Central Council of the IRP discussed the viability of different options, including maintaining the party, dissolving it, or dividing it into several parties. Arguments raised at the inception of the IRP were raised again with more vigor. Ḥizbullāh, for example, unhappy with the title of "party" for anyone but the Party of God, now raised its objections again to the idea of continuing the IRP. Worsening conflict penetrated provincial and city levels, hindering party activity. In many parts of the country, party headquarters were either closed or operated part-time.

It is unclear which faction originally recommended the end of the IRP. It was rumored that the right wing favored the continuation of the party. Officially, however, Khamene'i and Rafsanjānī, in a letter to Khomeini, explained that under the circumstances there was no need for a political party and that the two opposing camps might hurt national unity. By order of Ayatollah Khomeini, on 2 June 1987, the Islamic Republican Party was officially dissolved.

[*See also* Ḥizbullāh; Iran, Islamic Republic of; Iranian Revolution of 1979; *and* Khomeini, Ruhollah al-Musavi.]

BIBLIOGRAPHY

Scholarship devoted exclusively to the Islamic Republican Party is scarce. Information was obtained from primary sources and the following works.

Akhavi, Shahrough. "Elite Factionalism in the Islamic Republic of Iran." *Middle East Journal* 41 (Spring 1987): 181–201. Outstanding analysis of the nature of intra-elite conflict and its impact on public policy.

Bakhash, Shaul. *The Reign of the Ayatollahs*. New York: Basic Books, 1984. Insightful account of developments leading to the clerical takeover of the state apparatus.

Bayat, Assef. "Labor and Democracy in Post-Revolutionary Iran." In *Post-Revolutionary Iran*, edited by Hooshang Amirahmadi and Manoucher Parvin, pp. 41–55. Boulder, Colo., and London: Westview Press, 1988. Excellent analysis of the relationship between the independent workers' councils and Islamic forces, including the Islamic Republican Party.

Hiro, Dilip. *The Iranian Labyrinth: Journeys through Theocratic Iran and Its Furies*. New York: Nation Books, 2005.

Martin, Vanessa. *Creating an Islamic State: Khomeini and the Making of a New Iran*. London: I. B. Tauris, 2003.

Menashri, David. *Iran: A Decade of War and Revolution*. New York and London: Holmes and Meier, 1990. Interpretive survey of developments in Iran based on more than a dozen newspapers and periodicals and an array of reports from news agencies, radio stations, and monitoring services.

Schahgaldian, Nikola B. *The Clerical Establishment in Iran*. Santa Monica, Calif.: Rand, 1989. Useful analysis of the evolution of Shīʿī clerical rule, including various Islamic associations and groups.

Takeyh, Ray. *Hidden Iran: Paradox and Power in the Islamic Republic*. New York: Holt Paperbacks, 2007.

ELIZ SANASARIAN

ISLAMIC SALVATION FRONT. The Islamic Salvation Front (Front Islamique du Salut, FIS; in Arabic, Jabhat al-Islāmīya li-al-Inqādh) emerged in Algeria in the aftermath of the riots in October 1988, which eventually led to the introduction of political pluralism by President Chadli Benjedid. The FIS was formally founded on 18 February 1989, and was legalized in September 1989. It soon developed strong capabilities for mass mobilization, as became evident by its organization of massive relief after the Tipasa earthquake on 29 October 1989, when the state remained inactive. In June 1990, the FIS scored a surprising victory in local and regional elections by winning 54 percent of the vote and controlling 856 of 1,541 communal assemblies and 31 of 48 provincial assemblies. In a conflict over the electoral laws and after challenging the presidency and the army, the FIS leadership was arrested in June 1991. Nevertheless, the FIS could run for national elections and continued its success in the first round on 26 December 1991, when it secured, with a quarter of the total registered electorate,

188 seats of 386, thereby heading toward a possible 75 percent majority in the final vote. After the suspension of the second electoral round by a military coup on 11 January 1992, President Benjedid was forced to resign, and a High State Committee (Haut Comité d'État, HCE) was established as a transitional executive body. The FIS was declared illegal in March 1992 and remains forbidden in the early twenty-first century. Thousands of its activists were arrested.

Algerian Islamism goes back to the reform movement of the 1920s, organized since 1931 by the Association of Algerian Muslim Ulema (Association des Oulémas Musulmans Algériens) of Shaykh ʿAbd al-Hamid Ben Badis (1889–1940), which joined the Front de Libération Nationale (FLN) and dominated "official Islam" until the 1980s. Then, a new trend emerged, inspired by preachers and thinkers from Egypt and Saudi Arabia, which was politically far more radical. The FIS competed with other, still active Islamic parties.

All elements of the previous Algerian Islamist discourse fed into the ideology of the FIS: the call for cultural authenticity and for a reform of the educational system; a religious and conservative vision for the role of women and the demand for the segregation of the sexes in public; a puritanical censorship of morals (*hisbah*, e.g., forbidding alcohol or immodest dresses); the condemnation of corruption and arbitrariness in government; and the call for justice and good government based on the Sharīʿah (Islamic law) and *shūrā* (mutual counseling). The FIS, however, added some new elements: liberalism in economic policy; a call for the immediate establishment of an Islamic republic; the central themes of Algerian nationalism (like the anti-French policy and an anti-imperialist and pan-Arabist stance), uncommon for other Algerian Islamist groups with their pan-Islamic and *ummah*-oriented views; and a particular discourse on the FLN. The FIS presented itself as the heir of the good historic FLN (prior to independence in 1962), as opposed to the bad and corrupt FLN (since 1962). Islamism, populism (e.g., criticizing the living conditions or the violence of the armed forces), and Algerian nationalism allowed for the mobilization of the popular masses (the poor and urban youth).

The FIS was led by a council, Majlis al-Shūrā, of thirty to forty members, and had several thematic committees. It was similarly structured top-down on every level, including the quarters where the basis of the FIS remained in the "free mosques" that operated outside state control.

In 1999, ʿAbbāsī Madanī (b. 1931), a professor of education science at the University of Algiers and former president of the FIS who was imprisoned from June 1991 until July 2003, supported the ceasefire by the Islamic Salvation Army (AIS, Armée Islamique du Salut; the armed branch of the FIS that had been fighting the state and its security agencies since the dissolution of the FIS in March 1992), which had been unilaterally declared in 1997. In January 2000, the approximately 7,000-member AIS dissolved after a general amnesty by President Abdelaziz Bouteflika.

Madanī could claim revolutionary credentials, as he was one of the men who began of the war for independence in November 1954. His vice president, Ali Belhadj (b. 1956), the imam of El Sunna mosque in the popular quarter Bab El Oued in Algiers, represented the Salafīyah trend of Algerian Islamism. Both were arrested on 30 June 1991, when the electoral process was stopped, and were sentenced by a military court on 15 July 1992, to twelve years in prison. Released in July 2003, Madani went into exile in Qatar. Belhadj returned to Algiers and has been arrested several times since then. Both men—as well as the "FIS Executive Committee abroad"—still comment on Algerian politics through interviews and declarations.

BIBLIOGRAPHY

International Crisis Group. *Islamism, Violence and Reform in Algeria: Turning the Page*. ICG Middle East Report No. 29. Cairo and Brussels, July 30, 2004. www.icg.org.

Roberts, Hugh. "From Radical Mission to Equivocal Ambition: The Expansion and Manipulation of Algerian Islamism, 1979–1992." In *Accounting for Fundamentalisms: The Dynamic Character of Movements*, edited by Martin E. Marty and R. Scott Appleby, pp. 428–429. Chicago: University of Chicago Press, 1994.

Rouadjia, Ahmed. *Les frères et la mosquée: Enquête sur le movement islamiste en Algérie*. Paris: Karthala, 1990.

Jörn Thielmann

Islamic Society of North America.

Based in Plainfield, Indiana, the Islamic Society of North America (ISNA) is one of the largest and oldest Islamic organizations in North America. It provides a variety of social, educational, and religious services to Muslims in the United States and Canada. It also is actively engaged in reaching out to non-Muslims, seeking to educate the larger community about Islam, and running several interfaith programs to eliminate prejudices between Muslims and the adherents of other faiths. ISNA's annual convention, which is usually held on the Labor Day weekend in early September, is the largest gathering of Muslims in North America, with approximately 50,000 attendees.

ISNA has its roots in the Muslim Students Association (MSA), which was established in 1963 at the University of Illinois, Urbana-Champaign. The MSA was founded to help coordinate the activities of existing Muslim student associations at various universities across North America. After its inception, the association, on the one hand, worked toward the preservation of Islamic identity and lifestyle among Muslim students, and on the other, promoted Islam to non-Muslims. The publication and distribution of Islamic books and magazines served both purposes.

In time, the MSA gained popularity, which allowed it to extend beyond university campuses into larger Muslim communities. This growth necessitated departmentalization and, eventually, a change in its institutional structure. The founding of separate institutions and, subsequently, of ISNA as an umbrella organization over them was the result of this process.

As of 2012, there are eight constituent organizations in the United States and Canada that operate in a variety of fields, ranging from education to finance, under the umbrella of ISNA: Muslim Students Association of the United States and Canada, North American Islamic Trust, Islamic Medical Association of North America, Association of Muslim Scientists and Engineers, Canadian Islamic Trust Fund, Muslim Youth of North America, Council of Islamic Schools of North America, and Islamic Media Foundation. Some of these organizations are autonomous; others receive directions from ISNA.

In addition to these constituent organizations, ISNA is affiliated with various Islamic centers and organizations in North America. Both individuals and institutions can become paying members of ISNA. Paid membership comes with the eligibility to vote in elections for the president, vice presidents, and board of directors (Majlis al-Shūrā) of ISNA.

It should be noted, however, that membership in ISNA is limited to practicing Muslims. The official website of ISNA states that "[a]ny Muslim, 18 years of age or more living in North America who endeavors to practice Islam as a total way of life may become a member of ISNA." This strong emphasis on the practice of Islam and its prioritization as a lifestyle constitute the common ground that brings a diverse body of members together; in the context of ISNA, the ethnic or denominational identities of members are secondary at best, if at all relevant. Accordingly, the activities of ISNA primarily revolve around issues that are of interest to all practicing Muslims in North America. This inclusionary orientation helps ISNA remain a mainstream organization and increases its ability to represent Muslims in North America.

BIBLIOGRAPHY

"Islamic Society of North America." http://www.isna.net/.

Serdar Kaya

Islamic Supreme Council of Iraq. An association of groups committed to establishing Islamic government in Iraq, the Islamic Supreme Council of Iraq (ISCI) (al-Majlis al-Aʿlā al-Islāmīyah al-ʿIrāqīyah) was organized in November 1982 as the Supreme Council for the Islamic Revolution in Iraq (SCIRI) when Iraqi opposition groups in Iran banded together at the behest of the Iranian government. The group's name was changed in May 2007 to reflect the fact that revolution was no longer a goal, given that Iraq's new political system provides for the peaceful transfer of political power through public elections.

The groups that formed SCIRI were Ḥizb al-Daʿwah al-Islāmīyah (Party of the Call to Islam); Harakāt al-Mujāhidīn (Movement of Fighters in a Holy Cause); Munazzama al-ʿAmal al-Islāmīyah (Islamic Task Organization); Harakāt al-Mujāhidīn fī al-ʿIrāq (Movement of Iraqi Fighters in a Holy Cause) led by Jalāl al-Dīn al-Saghir; Harakāt al-Mujāhidīn fī al-ʿIrāq (Movement of Iraqi Fighters in a Holy Cause) led by ʿAbd al-ʿHakīm; Jund al-Imām (Soldiers of the Imam); al-Daʿwah al-Islāmīyah (Call to Islam); and al-Harakāt al-Islāmīyah fī al-Kurd (the Kurdish Islamic Movement, or KIM). All were Arab Shīʿī groups except the latter, which consisted of Sunnī Kurds. SCIRI was committed to an Iraq united within the framework of Islamic brotherhood and to self-rule for the Kurds. Its governing body was a central committee elected by a general assembly representing the constituent Islamic movements. Funding came from the Iranian government and from the *marjiʿīyah*, the Shīʿī religious establishment.

The leader of SCIRI was Muḥammad Bāqir al-Ḥakīm (b. 1939–d. 2003), the charismatic son of the deceased Grand Ayatollah Muḥsin al-Ḥakīm, Iraq's chief religious authority in the 1960s. Among the other leaders were Ḥizb al-Daʿwah's Sayyid Ibrāhīm al-Jaʿfarī, who became prime minister of Iraq in 2005, and Shaykh Kāzim al-Ḥāʾiīr, who became a prominent ayatollah in Iran. SCIRI acknowledged the Islamic Republic of Iran as the foundation of the world Islamic revolution and aimed to establish a representative Islamic government in Iraq by pursuing two paths: militarily resisting the tyrannical regime of Saddam Hussein and uniting Iraqi opposition groups. To those ends SCIRI formed an alliance with the Kurdish National Union led by the Barzānīs, Iraq's most powerful Kurdish family. Later the group also allied with the Patriotic Union of Kurdistan, Iraq's other major Kurdish party. The constituent groups met annually and opened offices in Iraqi Kurdistan, Damascus, London, and elsewhere.

SCIRI oversaw prisoner-of-war camps for Iran during the Iran–Iraq War (1980–1988) and organized conferences to call attention to the plight of the Iraqi people. SCIRI's military arm was the Badr Brigade (*faylaq badr*) set up in cooperation with Iran's Revolutionary Guards and trained by them near the Iranian city of Dezfūl. Members of the Badr Brigade were predominantly ex-Iraqi army personnel, tribesmen, and former Iraqi policemen who were captured by Iran or fled to Iran during the war. The Badr Brigade carried out guerrilla operations inside Iraq and secured the Iraqi village of Ḥaj ʿUmrān near Sulaymānīyah in 1983. SCIRI's executive director, Abū Thaʿir al-Ḥasan, was killed in Ḥaj ʿUmrān by an Iraqi government chemical attack in November 1987.

Prior to relocating to Iran, Ḥizb al-Daʿwah, a major component of SCIRI, rejected the principle of *wilāyat al-faqīh* (the guardianship of the jurist) as a principle of Islamic governance. In Iran, pressure on SCIRI members to accept that Islamic government had to be controlled by the *ʿulamāʾ* (clergy) resulted in most of Hizb al-Daʿwah leaving SCIRI by 1984. Muḥammad Bāqir al-Ḥakīm, who had been a prominent Ḥizb al-Daʿwah leader, accepted the guardianship of Imam Khomeini and the leadership of SCIRI.

During the first Gulf War of 1990–1991, SCIRI worked with other Iraqi opposition groups to set up a plan for governing Iraq in the event Saddam Hussein's government was toppled. The plan called for elections and Kurdish autonomy. From 1991 to 2003, SCIRI carried out guerrilla actions in southern Iraq and the mountains of northern Iraq. In August 2002 SCIRI was one of six Iraqi groups invited to the United States prior to U.S. military action against Iraq in March 2003.

In connection with the 2003 U.S. invasion, SCIRI returned to Iraq from its exile in Iran. The Badr Brigade, led by Hadī al-Amīrī from the mid-1990s, fought in Diyala Province against the defenders of the Baʿthist regime. When law and order in Iraq collapsed after the fall of the Iraqi government, the ten-thousand-man Badr Brigade provided security in such places as Baʿqūba and Majar al-Kabir and distributed food and other supplies trucked in from Iran. In response to U.S. demands, most of the Badr Brigade disarmed in September 2003 and the name was changed to Badr Organization.

In August 2003, Ayatollah Muḥammad Bāqir al-Ḥakīm was killed in a terrorist bombing in Najaf. His brother Sayyid ʿAbdul ʿAzīz al-Ḥakīm (1950–2009), SCIRI's executive director and military leader, became the SCIRI leader. As a member of the Iraqi Governing Council set up by U.S. occupation authorities, Sayyid al-Ḥakīm in December 2003 pushed through a replacement of Iraq's 1959 personal status law with a law returning jurisdiction over family matters to religious courts, a prospect that led thousands of Iraqi women to protest in the streets. Women lobbied courageously and got some political parties on their side. After ten weeks, L. Paul Bremer, head of the Coalition Provisional Authority, opted not to sign the decree.

As insurgent attacks on the Shīʿī community mounted in the absence of government-provided security, many Shīʿī areas were protected by the Badr militia. The Badr Organization competed with other Shīʿī groups for control of southern Iraqi cities, such as Basra. On occasion, the Badr militia joined *peshmerga* (Kurdish guerrilla) units to supplement American troops in Sunnī areas.

SCIRI was a leader of the United Iraqi Alliance (UIA) of Shīʿī groups, which won both of Iraq's elections in 2005. In the January provincial elections, SCIRI won six of the eight Shīʿī-majority provinces, emerging as the dominant political power outside Kurdistan. SCIRI supported the October 2005 constitution outlining a loose federal state with a weak central government, a position opposed by Sunnī Arab groups as likely to fragment Iraq into several mini-states. Having won the most seats in parliament in 2005, SCIRI led four ministries, including the powerful Interior Ministry, and SCIRI member ʿAdil ʿAbdul Mahdi became vice president.

During the civil war of 2006–2007, militant Sunnīs attacked Shīʿites who ultimately cleansed much of Baghdad of Sunnīs. When men in Interior Ministry uniforms began kidnapping and killing young men from Sunnī neighborhoods, many blamed the Badr militia. As security deteriorated from its already low level, Sayyid al-Ḥakīm announced support for an Iraqi federal system consisting of three large provinces: a Kurdish state in the north, a Shīʿī confederation in the south, and a Sunnī Arab state in the center. This position met SCIRI's longtime commitment to the Kurds but was inimical to Baghdad's Shīʿī majority, who would be in the Sunnī province, and to Arab Sunnīs who anticipated that the central province would have difficulty getting oil revenues, given that the oil is in the south and the north. As the governing party in most of the South, SCIRI was blamed by many there for the lack of security and the ubiquitous poor living conditions in the region.

At the time of the organization's 2007 name change to ISCI, its constituent groups were the Badr Organization, Iraqi Ḥizbullāh, the Shahīd al-Mahrab Foundation, and the Sayyid al-Shuhadāʾ Movement. Lebanon's Grand Ayatollah Muḥammad Ḥusayn Faḍlallāh (1935–2010) was clerical guide for most of the group, meaning they no longer supported *wilāyat al-faqīh*. ISCI's general assembly consisted of 163 members and its central committee of 15 members. Its official newspaper remained *al-Istiqāmah* (Straightness).

In the 2008 fighting in the south, ISCI joined U.S. troops and Iraqi government troops against Fadhila (Islamic Virtue Party) and Muqtadā al-Ṣadr's Mahdī Army, groups purporting to represent Iraq's poor Shīʿī. Given ISCI's association with Iraq's traditional clerical establishment and Prime Minister al-Maliki's Ḥizb al-Daʿwah party's beginning as an organization of educated Shīʿī laymen, the fighting bared class divisions within the Shīʿī community.

In the 2009 provincial elections, ISCI ran candidates under the name al-Mahrab Martyr List, referring to the martyred Ayatollah Muḥammad Bāqir al-Ḥakīm, and received only 6.6 percent of the vote and control of one province, Muthanna. In August of 2009 Sayyid ʿAbdul ʿAzīz al-Ḥakīm died and his son ʿAmmar took over leadership of ISCI. In the run-up to the March 2010 elections, ISCI joined the Iraqi National Alliance with the Sadrists. ISCI won only twenty seats in the 325-seat parliament. In the nine months before a unity government was formed, ISCI supported its own candidate, Vice President Adil Abd Al-Mahdi, for prime minister. Eventually, the Badr Organization came out for Prime Minister al-Maliki, followed finally by the rest of ISCI. In the government proposed by Prime Minister al-Maliki and endorsed by Iraq's parliament in December 2010, Vice President Mahdi retains his position, Hadī al-Amīrī, head of the Badr Organization, is Minister of Transportation and Ḥasan al-Raḍi of ISCI is Minister of State without portfolio. ISCI's governing body remains its General Assembly, with day-to-day decisions made by a seven-member Consultative Committee headed by President ʿAmmar al-Ḥakīm.

[*See also* Ḥizb al-Daʿwah al-Islāmīyah; *and* Iraq.]

Bibliography

Ali, Nadje al-, and Nicola Pratt. *What Kind of Liberation? Women and the Occupation of Iraq*. Berkeley, Calif., and London: University of California Press, 2009. Account of the effect military occupation and conservative Islamic groups had on Iraqi women after the ouster of Saddam Hussein's government in 2003.

Herring, Eric, and Glen Rangwala. *Iraq in Fragments: The Occupation and Its Legacy*. London: Hurst, 2006. A good account of the events of 2003–2006 in Iraq and SCIRI's part in them.

Musawi, Karim al-. "Brief History of the Supreme Council for the Islamic Revolution in Iraq (SCIRI)." Washington, D.C., 2007. Eight-page history written by the SCIRI representative in the United States.

Official Site of the Islamic Supreme Council of Iraq. http://www.isci-iraq.com (English); http://www.almejlis.org (Arabic).

Wiley, Joyce N. *The Islamic Movement of Iraqi Shi'as*. Boulder, Colo.: Lynne Rienner Publishers, 1992. Account of the contemporary movement to establish Islamic government in Iraq.

Joyce N. Wiley

Islamic Youth Movement of Malaysia. Also known as Angkatan Belia Islam Malaysia, or ABIM, the Islamic Youth Movement of Malaysia is one of the leading religious-based social movements in Malaysian society and politics. The movement was founded in 1971 by a group of Muslim youth activists, the most famous of whom was Anwar Ibrahim. In their formative years, the movement was primarily committed to religious duties and social-welfare programs as a *da'wah* (Malaysian *dakwah*, religious missionary) movement. It gained prominence since it not only voiced concerns about social injustice, such as poverty and inequality in Malaysian society, but also did not hesitate to take political action against the authorities. It grew rapidly on the major university campuses and around cities such as Kuala Lumpur, recruiting urban, educated Muslim youth who grew more pious in their beliefs and outlook while also becoming more conscious about the plight of Muslim communities both at home and abroad. Due to their critical attitudes and the radical actions they sometimes took against the authorities, ABIM was often seen as antigovernment and was branded as radical and even militant. The organization also aspired to build a religious society based on Islamic principles and demanded preferential policies for Muslim Malays, raising anxieties and fears among non-Muslim communities against the backdrop of rising influence of political Islam globally.

The political and ideological orientation of ABIM and its relations with the government began changing after its charismatic leader, Anwar Ibrahim, and some other prominent members of the movement were inducted into the ruling party, the United Malays National Organization (UMNO), after Mahathir Mohamad came to power in 1981. It is believed that the rising influence of ABIM in the Muslim community and its allegedly close relations with the major Muslim-based opposition party, the Islamic Party of Malaysia (PAS), posed a threat to the political dominance of UMNO in the Malaysian polity. This perception resulted in UMNO's preemptive move to co-opt ABIM and its leadership into the UMNO fold.

The presence of Anwar and his extensive grassroots networks was expected to contribute immensely to the government's Islamization campaigns under Mahathir by giving the latter a more authentically Islamic outlook. Further, it was expected to help outperform PAS's conservative Islamic vision and programs. Soon after joining the government, Anwar was elevated to the position of deputy minister in the prime minister's department in charge of Islamic affairs, and he began playing a central role in piloting the Mahathir administration's Islamization enterprise. He helped to formulate new Islamic policies that put the administration into competition with PAS and other *da'wah* movements in civil society.

Due to the movement's heavy reliance on Anwar and its close association with the ruling party and regime, however, ABIM somewhat lost its credentials as a social movement, with the fate of the movement largely conditioned by the political rise and fall of Anwar and his close allies in government. This was not surprising since some former ABIM leaders apparently had joined UMNO to gain access to powerful positions and lucrative business deals. ABIM's survival was suddenly put in danger when Anwar was ousted from the ruling party and government in 1999 as a result of his falling-out with Mahathir; he subsequently was arrested for corruption and sodomy charges. Probably based on such extraordinary experiences and the bitter lessons learned from them, ABIM, under new leadership, has been trying to regain its reputation and credentials as an independent social movement committed to *daʿwah* and social justice. However, some observers are concerned about the movement's increasingly conservative, dogmatic, and discriminatory outlook and orientation in recent years.

Bibliography

"BBC News Asia." http://www.bbc.co.uk/news/world/asia/.

Jomo, Kwame Sundaram, and Ahmed Shabery Cheek. "The Politics of Malaysia's Islamic Resurgence." *Third World Quarterly* 10, no. 2 (1988): 843–868.

Zainah, Anwar. 1987. *Islamic Revivalism in Malaysia: Dakwah among the Students*. Petaling Jaya, Malaysia: Pelanduk.

Kikue Hamayotsu

Islamism. Islamism is one of many sociopolitical concepts continuously contested in scholarly literature. It is a neologism debated in both Muslim and non-Muslim public and academic contexts. The term "Islamism" at the very least represents a form of social and political activism, grounded in an idea that public and political life should be guided by a set of Islamic principles. In other words, Islamists are those who believe that Islam has an important role to play in organizing a Muslim-majority society and who seek to implement this belief. As such, Islamist activism is a public manifestation of religiously informed political will, often expressed as resistance to various types of competing ideas, policies, and even lifestyles. The ideological dimension of Islamism has developed primarily during the second half of the twentieth century.

The primary method of diffusion of activists' ideas has always been through the persuasion of the Muslim masses—*daʿwah* or *tarbīyah*. This form of awareness-raising campaigns has been used by virtually all Islamist groups, be they violent (radical) or nonviolent (moderate). Increasingly, many Islamist groups have adjusted their claims to sociopolitical realities in various political contexts, translating these claims through liberal and human rights discourse. Many of the organizations have toned down their previous emphasis on the past, resulting in increased popular support and gradual Islamization of the political discourse centering on democratization of their societies. Most notably, Islamists have become increasingly aware of the sociopolitical and economic "needs" of the populations they addressed. They have responded by organizing social welfare and education programs, as well as political parties and lobby associations. Such organizations are frequently labeled as moderate Islamists.

Other organizations are reactionary in their approach to social change. Many of these groups tend to employ violence to achieve their goals. Their ideas for the transformation of contemporary Muslim majority societies into ideal Islamic polities are frequently linked with some form of coercion. Some of the contemporary reactionary organizations are located in places that have experienced protracted periods of violence before the emergence of Islamist ideas. Such groups are often labeled as radical Islamists because they demonstrate little interest in adjusting their ideological claims to the political realities of their respective locations. An explicit trait of intransigent groups in this category is the ideology of *takfīr*, excommunicating or pronouncing their Muslim opponents as unbelievers.

Early Islamic Revivalist Movements. Islamism's political dimension is complex and is largely attached to its supporters' identity politics.

Nevertheless, Islamist ideas are to a great extent a part of Muslim modernism, which can be traced back for more than a century. Islamism has its roots in the late nineteenth century, when a number of Muslim intellectual movements were formed. These were essentially the intellectual elites' response to the political decline of the Ottoman Empire and the subsequent strengthening of colonial control of Muslim societies by European imperial powers. One of the main early intellectuals to formulate the idea of Islamic revival was Jamāl al-Dīn al-Afghānī (d. 1897). He promoted the idea of the restoration of Muslim-majority societies' scientific and cultural vitality. His activism was directed primarily toward developing an Islamic response to European secularism and materialism. As a methodological tool for revival, al-Afghānī proposed *ijtihād*, a process of deductive reasoning derived from the Islamic legal tradition. *Ijtihād* was necessary, al-Afghānī argued, to recapture the dynamism of early Islamic intellectual life. This principle became a rallying cry of modernists across the Muslim world.

One of al-Afghani's most prominent students was Muḥammad ʿAbduh (d. 1905), an Egyptian jurist and a graduate of al-Azhar University. He was an outspoken critic of British colonial authorities, earning him exile first from Cairo (1879) and briefly from Egypt (1882). Gradually, ʿAbduh developed his own ideas of revival and distanced himself from al-Afghānī. He focused on developing a methodology of *ijtihād* by analyzing the legislative reasoning of the early Muslims, the so-called pious predecessors, or *al-salaf al-ṣāliḥ*. They had, argued ʿAbduh, been remarkably innovative in solving complex sociopolitical issues encountered through Islamic expansion, creating a new, syncretistic civilization. They were creative enough to interpret the Qurʾān in a way that was beneficial for the populations at the time. This principle, called *maṣlaḥah*, was central in ʿAbduh's reformist methodology and resonated well with the Egyptian conservative intelligentsia.

After his falling out with al-Afghānī, ʿAbduh was allowed to return to Cairo, where he promptly rose through the administration of the prestigious al-Azhar University, becoming an influential member of its ruling body. Soon thereafter he was installed as Egypt's highest ranking Islamic jurist (*muftī*). During his brief tenure ʿAbduh was able to promote his ideas of revival far and wide. In the process he started cooperating with another Islamic scholar, Muḥammad Rashīd Riḍā (d. 1935). The principal outcome of their collaboration had been establishment of the influential journal *Al-Manār*. ʿAbduh used the journal as a platform for furthering his revivalist agenda. ʿAbduh and Riḍā attempted to develop a non-literalist reading of Islamic sources as a way of more effective reconciliation of the Islamic tradition with the Western scientific progress. They hoped to stimulate cultural reform (*iṣlāḥ*) and religious moderation (*iʿtidāl*) in Muslim societies, which, according to them were pillars of the success of the early Islamic civilization. After Abduh's death and under the continued European colonialism of the Middle East, Riḍā gravitated towards religious conservatism as a method for cultural revival and resistance to foreign domination.

During the same period there was a parallel intellectual awakening in India. Its central figures were Sayyid Ahmad Khan (d. 1898) and Muhammad Iqbal (d. 1938). These two thinkers were concerned with largely the same issues as al-Afghānī and ʿAbduh: the sociopolitical stagnation of Muslim societies. Iqbal's primary contribution to Islamic revivalist thought is his conception of a dynamic and purposeful interpretation of the religious sources. His constant referral to the early generation of Muslims, their interpretive approach to the Qurʾān, and their cultural success matches the ideas of ʿAbduh point by point.

However, Sayyid Ahmad Khan and Muhammad Iqbal faced a political challenge at home that was peculiar to the Indian subcontinent. The large Muslim population of British India constituted a relatively small percentage of the total Indian population. Both men thought that Muslims in India would need to separate from the majority Hindu population. Iqbal strongly urged that the northwestern provinces (today's Pakistan) should be ruled by an autonomous Muslim authority in order to facilitate a viable sociocultural revival.

Muhammad Ali Jinnah (d. 1948) was the inheritor of Khan's and Iqbal's ideas and the driving force behind the formation of Pakistan. Initially, Jinnah favored Muslim-Hindu political unity, but with the tilt of the Indian independence movement toward Hindu motifs and appeals under the leadership of Mahatma Gandhi, Jinnah came to fear that Muslim identity and privileges would not be safeguarded in a united India and thereafter adopted Iqbal's separatist agenda. Jinnah was also wary of religious zealotry in any form. It is possible that his wariness came from the fact that he belonged to the Shīʿī Muslim minority, making him a part of a minority within the overwhelming Sunnī majority, which in turn was a small minority among a large Hindu majority.

Islamist Trajectories. In Egypt, the early modernist discourse of ʿAbduh and Riḍā was adopted and applied by a schoolteacher named Ḥasan al-Bannā (d. 1949). In 1928 he and a group of his close associates organized a society of Muslim Brothers, one of the first Islamist social movements and, later, political organizations. Al-Bannā and the first generation of Muslim Brothers rendered their world meaningful through a process of reinterpretation of sociopolitical conditions. This was primarily done by a process of reconceptualizing modern notions of science, politics, the state, and so on, in an Islamic idiom, most prominently by linking them to the classical Islamic juridical and ethical tradition. This effort was essentially rooted in the ideas of ʿAbduh and Riḍā; however, the Brothers took those ideas a step further, organizing an educational program that they applied by forming small neighborhood groups all across Egypt. The organization quickly attracted large numbers of followers. They represented a new perspective on Islamic teachings in contrast to the traditional elite of Azharī *ʿulamāʾ*. Even though ʿAbduh and Riḍā were educated as traditional Islamic scholars, the overwhelming number of subsequent Islamist thinkers, such as al-Bannā, were not.

The Muslim Brotherhood's popularity depended greatly on al-Bannā's charisma and his straightforward analysis of the sociopolitical conditions of the Egyptian state. The Brotherhood's Islamist vision has traditionally been presented through a religious discourse relating contemporary problems with analogous difficulties from the Islamic past. Al-Bannā proposed solutions to many of the social problems of the time in a language that people could understand and relate to. Many different groups of people, from peasants and workers to middle-class professionals, could relate to the Islamists' core message that social ills can be remedied through improved personal piety and effective social mobilization. The core of the Islamist message has always been an appeal to the notion of authenticity: their vision and their agenda is the true Islamic worldview as it is based in the divine sources of Islam.

Al-Bannā's articulation of the Brotherhood's overall purpose and the organization's mobilization strategies inspired many Egyptians at the time. Al-Bannā explained that the Brotherhood was guided by and organized through "a *salafīyah* message, a Sunnī way, a Ṣūfī truth, a political organization, an athletic group, a scientific and cultural union, an economic enterprise, and a social idea" (Mitchell, 1969, p. 14). A "*salafīyah* message" implies that Muslims in general and the

Muslim Brotherhood specifically have a responsibility to strive for authenticity in their doctrinal beliefs and religious practices in what relates to their socio-political convictions. This had not been directly related to the reactionary *salafiyah* movement of the time. Authenticity alludes to conformity with the message of the Qurʾān and the practice (*sunnah*) of the Prophet and his pious companions (the *salaf*). Adherence to the *sunnah* is the way to revive moral values and thereby rejuvenate Islamic civilization. The emphasis on revival was important for al-Bannā, as it diminishes the need to rely on "imported" ethical values (e.g., European cultural influences, such as arts, fashion, and political traditions). Al-Bannā was here much closer to the late Riḍā's attitude towards foreign influences than ʿAbduh's reconciliatory ideas. These ideas are akin to the "Ṣūfī truth" focused on a purity of faith, introverted religious practice, and individual spiritual development; indeed, Sufism's influence on al-Bannā is evident not only in the ideology of the Muslim Brotherhood but also in its organizational structure.

In the decades to come, the Brotherhood branched out to virtually every country in the region, establishing local cells of committed members loosely attached to national leaderships. Shortly after al-Bannā founded the Muslim Brotherhood in Egypt, Abūal-Aʿlā Mawdūdī (d. 1979) began building the most important Islamist organization in South Asia, the Jamāʿat-i Islāmī. As a young contemporary of Jinnah, Mawdūdī was attracted to his use of Islamic symbols and rhetoric to mobilize the Indian Muslim masses. Mawdūdī shared Jinnah's vision of Muslim unity and cultural independence for the millions of Indian Muslims, but he viewed Jinnah as a rival and doctrinal deviant primarily because of Jinnah's scant religious credentials and openly secularist vision. Mawdūdī saw himself—not Jinnah—as the true heir to Muhammad Iqbal's legacy.

Like ʿAbduh, Mawdūdī believed that power came from the written word. He expressed his ideas for Muslim revival in the newspaper *Tarjumān al-Qurʾān*. His goal was to encourage a Muslim minority among the Hindu majority to create a separate polity based on the Islamic principles derived from the divine sources, the Qurʾān and the *sunnah*. Initially, he was supported by Iqbal, who assisted him in establishing an activist base in Punjab. Mawdūdī focused much of his attention initially on the negative impacts of colonial occupation of India. Subsequently he gave more consideration to issues of internal reform within the Muslim community as a way to establish a stabile Islamic polity.

His organization, Jamāʿat-i Islāmī, was the primary tool to reform what he considered detrimental parts of the Muslim Indian culture. These included the general public's reverence of traditional Muslim religious and landed notables. Most important, however, Mawdūdī intended to purify the Indian Muslims' religious practices from any not found in the religious sources. A Muslim, Mawdūdī argued, is a person who is obedient to God in practice, not one who merely accepts the validity of Islamic teachings. He therefore saw the institutional process of creating a Muslim-majority state as a way of implementing his doctrinal framework. Politics was a set of practical tools for instituting the Sharīʿah-based polity. He also maintained that the separation of administrative and judicial functions of government is necessary to secure the supremacy of the Islamic legal system.

What is common among the modernist Islamist organizations has been their nonviolent, reformist, and gradualist approach to establishing the Sharīʿah-based society. Both the Muslim Brotherhood and Jamāʿat-i Islāmī consider politics as an inseparable part of the Islamic tradition; however, a framework within which politics is practiced should be delineated by religious principles. In order for such framework to function well, these groups argue, the reform process starts with education of an individual Muslim, then families, followed by social institutions and lastly political authority. The organization's strategy and structure was copied throughout the Muslim communities in the Southeast Asian region.

Similar movements exist in almost every Muslim majority country. In North African states, a variety of Islamist organizations can be found. Some, such as Morocco's Justice and Development Party, which has its roots in a small political group founded in the late 1960s, have accepted participation in parliamentary elections, much the same as the Muslim Brotherhood and Jamāʿat-i Islāmī. In Algeria, the Islamist experience has been far more volatile.

The Islamic Salvation Front, one of the major Islamist organizations, was formed in 1989 to promote the establishment of a Sharīʿah-based Algerian state. Their political discourse, similar to that of the Brothers, combined Islamic terminology with political solutions to social problems. As a result of their grassroots activism, good communication skills, and a widespread network of supporters, they swept the polls in the local elections in 1990. Their rhetoric, based on the reestablishment of Islamic-Arab identity, resonated well with the disenfranchised urban masses, especially young university graduates. The regime quickly reacted and arrested the movement's leadership before going ahead with the first round of parliamentary elections.

The Islamic Salvation Front won more votes than any other political party, including the ruling National Liberation Front. The results were quickly canceled by the regime and the Islamist party was effectively banned. The brutal civil war that followed was initially not endorsed by the organization; however, a year later (1993), a part of its leadership called for armed resistance. Soon after, several small factions of armed Islamist guerrilla groups disassociated themselves from the Islamic Salvation Front's ideology, denouncing democratic politics and the majority of the Algerian population as Muslim heretics. The most notable of these violent Islamist groups is the Armed Islamic Group. The organization can be considered a radical Islamist organization holding explicit *takfīr*-based ideology.

Takfīr, excommunication of a Muslim from the realm of Islam, can be found at an extreme end of the Islamist ideological spectrum. In Egypt, the Society of Muslims (later dubbed *al-Takfīr wa-al-Hijrat*) was formed in the early 1970s and represented an intensely reactionary view of Islamist politics. For instance, the *takfīrīs*' main premise regarding the ruling regimes in Muslim-majority countries is that they are apostates because of their "un-Islamic" beliefs and political practices. This intransigent custom is not new. Ideas of *takfīr* can be traced to the first Muslim sectarian group, the Khawārij. The group formed about 657 CE in the midst of inter-Muslim fighting between followers of Muʿāwiyah I and ʿAlī. Their name, which means "those who secede," was given to them by their detractors because they left ʿAlī after he agreed to arbitration with Muʿāwiyah. They understood that God decides who is right and who is wrong by giving victory and political dominance to the righteous. Because of their stringent notions of piety they declared any Muslim who committed a major sin (e.g., adultery, consumption of alcohol, rape, murder, etc.) as an apostate (*kāfir*), and thus subject to killing. The Khawārij, as a *takfīrī* sect, did not last; those who were more tolerant, such as the Ibāḍīyah and Ṣufrīyah, accepted other Muslims as *muʿāhadūn* (monotheists) but not *muʾminūn* (true believers).

In the early twenty-first century, there are very few Islamist groups who adopt the concept of *takfīr* in their activism. Nevertheless, these are the groups that are readily labeled as radical and reactionary, primarily due to their readiness to engage in violence against other Muslims in order to bring about sociopolitical change. Some al-Qaʿida affiliated groups certainly fall into this category, as well as the above mentioned organizations.

Another type of Islamist organization includes those who passively support other Islamists' violence at the same time distancing themselves from violent tactics. Ḥizb al-Taḥrir (Liberation Party) is one such organization that is considered to be an Islamic party working toward the establishment of a pan-Islamic state (*khilāfah*). The party is, at least in part, an ideological spin-off of the Muslim Brotherhood. Its founder, Taqī al-Dīn al-Nabāhni, was a Palestinian cleric who was initially a member of the Muslim Brotherhood. The party had primarily been a response to the Muslim Brotherhood's loss of political influence in Egypt after Gamal Abdel Nasser's 1954 coup d'état. The party had based all its organizational and strategic decisions on its own interpretation of Islam, strictly staying away from liberal political jargon (e.g., human rights and democracy).

The party rejects political participation of any kind, except in an Islamic system where the Caliph would be responsible for the socio-political and economic affairs of Muslims. The organization works for the establishment of a confederate system of Muslim states, held together by the office of a *khilāfah* (i.e. the Prophet's, or God's, representative, depending on the interpretation). Such a confederation would essentially be governed through a Sharīʿah-rooted judiciary—thus implementing Islamic version of the rule of law. On the other hand, individual states would be free to organize their particular political systems, as long as such processes do not contradict the principles of Sharīʿah. Ḥizb al-Taḥrir could therefore be considered ideologically radical but strategically moderate. Its primary bases of popular support are in the Central Asian republics and Indonesia.

Shīʿī Islamism is likewise diverse and multifaceted, albeit more geographically constrained. It includes a variety of groups and interpretations of the divine sources. Nevertheless, what is most noticeable about this version of Islamism is that one of its strands actually gained political control of a state—Iran. The chief ideologue of Shīʿī Islamism has been Ayatollah Khomeini, who succeeded in taking control of the state in the wake of the popular revolution in 1979. The main principle around which the political authority was organized has been *vilāyat-i faqīh* (guardianship of the jurisprudent). The concept of supreme authority of a scholar, or group of scholars, is seemingly a new concept in the classical body of Shīʿī (Jaʿfarī) jurisprudence. Although some political freedoms are allowed in Iran, the religious clerics are ultimately setting the pace and limits of the political process. Other competing Islamist groups are either marginalized or banned.

Iran Freedom Movement is one such opposition group that has opposed the concept of *vilāyat-i faqīh*, arguing that it contradicts Sharīʿah principles developed in the traditional Shīʿī teachings. The organization had been formed in 1961 with no real Islamist agenda, but rather with liberal ideas, similar to the political understanding of former Iranian prime minister Mohammed Mossadegh. The group was formed by Mehdi Bazargan. After the revolutionary events of 1979, the organization was marginalized and later banned from politics by Khomeini himself.

Khomeini's writings have also had a great influence on Shīʿī communities in Iraq and Lebanon. Shīʿī Islamism has not developed significantly among significant non-Arab Shīʿī population centers (e.g. Azerbaijan, Afghanistan, Pakistan). Ḥizbullāh (Party of God) is one the most notable Shīʿī Islamist organizations. It was formed in 1982 by two Lebanese students of Khomeini, ʿAbbās al-Musawī and Subḥī al-Tufaylī. The organization received the full support and endorsement of the

Iranian regime, which viewed it as a useful tool for exporting the Islamic revolution. Ḥizbullāh's primary initial task was to organize armed resistance against the Israeli occupation of southern Lebanon. The party has since branched out its activities, endorsing party politics and regularly participating in parliamentary elections, and it is today a part of the Lebanese government. The organization views itself as a part of an Islamist resistance to Israeli occupation. In reality, however, the party functions as a political representative of the Shīʿī in the Beirut suburbs and southern Lebanon, its primary popular strongholds. Ḥizbullāh could be described as an armed Islamist organization and a pragmatic political party with a highly sophisticated administrative structure.

Dynamics of Islamism. As Islamist social movement organizations operate in many different sociopolitical contexts, they have also learned to adjust their claims and adapt their strategies, all in accordance with the character of their relationship with various domestic ruling regimes. During this process of discursive and strategic calibration, many Islamist organizations have progressively incorporated much of what was thought to be "foreign" political terminology into their reform programs. One reason behind such adjustment might have been these organizations' ideological pragmatism. This is primarily connected to the positive resonance of their modification process and their nuanced messages with large segments of the marginalized public in many Muslim-majority countries.

These various forms of Islamist activism are products of institutional and sociocultural contexts of Muslim-majority countries. The ideological components of religiously inspired groups are important, as they provide a general framework of meaning to their supporters. This includes specific normative guiding principles for the organization. On the other hand, external and structural factors have had a highly significant impact on the size, shape, and mobilization strategies of Islamist groups.

For instance, the violent conflict between Hosni Mubarak's security forces and Jamāʿat al-Islāmīyah, the Islamic Group, in 1992–1997 forced the Islamist organization to reconsider its strategies. The leadership denounced violence as an activist strategy, hence refocusing their mobilization toward the grassroots. Such decisions allowed them to renew popular support, most notably among the most disadvantaged inhabitants of rural Upper Egypt and the poor urban areas of Cairo and other cities. Their efforts were focused mostly on proselytizing a version of a nonviolent *salafī* movement. Due to its strategic evaluation and denunciation of violent tactics in 1997, a group of the organization broke off, consisting mainly of activists outside Egypt, who rejected the change of course. These activists readily adopted the *takfīrī* ideas, joining other groups that shared a similar understanding.

Those in the organization who denounced violence refocused their activism on the poorest regions (e.g., the Cairo suburb of Imbābā), engaging in social work and solving the practical problems of the inhabitants. The organization established soup kitchens for the poorest, literacy courses for the illiterate, and health services, and provided help with small-scale entrepreneurship. Often during the Islamic holidays, they organized celebrations and additional assistance to the poor. Its activists were most frequently energetic and religiously zealous young men in their early and late twenties who were largely responsible for rapidly organizing and deploying these social services.

In the early 2000s, the Islamic Group, although a shadow of its former organizational presence, has been transformed into a *salafīt* piety movement, attracting a massive following among a new generation of Egyptians. The wide reach of satellite TV stations and the emergence of independent *salafī* televangelists had broadened support for this type of Islamism. Consequently, *salafī* activism has promoted high standards of individual piety and generally an apolitical stance in relation to the regime. In the face of state repression and restricted political participation, many young people found *salafī* mobilization an alternative to the more pro-active and pragmatic Muslim Brotherhood.

In 2006, another, much smaller, *salafī*-oriented Islamist organization in Egypt, Islamic Jihād (Jihād al-Islāmī) followed the example of the Islamic Group, revising its ideological justification for violent government overthrow. One of its founding members and an early associate of Āyman al-Zawāhirī, Sayyid Imam al-Sharīf, a well-known reactionary ideologue, renounced violence as a legitimate Islamist mobilization tactic. He proclaimed in a series of texts that his previously held stance was essentially breaching the rules of Sharīʿah, the very thing he wanted to uphold. In his revisionist texts, al-Sharīf argues that the priority of Muslims' basic rights is far greater than the obligation to change rapidly (i.e., violently) the sociopolitical system. Sociopolitical reform, in other words, can be legitimate only if it does not break the basic principles given by God, such as causing insecurity in society, harming and killing individuals, and destroying property).

In the post-revolutionary Egyptian context, *salafī*-oriented Islamist groups have formed several political parties. All have won a substantial number of seats in the lower house of the Egyptian parliament. Previously violent and reactionary Islamist groups have shifted their mobilization tactics, substantially demonstrating the power of sociopolitical context on Islamist activism. In contrast, the Egyptian Muslim Brotherhood's slow-grinding reformist strategy has given the organization enough popular support to outperform all other political forces after the fall of the Mubarak regime. The Brotherhood's efforts to win over critical elements within the general public (e.g., middle-class professionals, university students, and merchants) have resonated strongly with the Egyptian masses.

Contemporary Islamism. Contemporary Islamism has as much to do with identity politics as with party politics. On the organizational level, Islamist political parties propagate for a general Sharīʿah-informed political system—differing widely on its format and contents. On the personal level, Islamism guides individual political actions delineating between insiders and outsiders, conformists and non-conformists, and so on. Therefore an understanding of such ideological precept is not fixed, including its contents. What is certain, however, is that Islamism is concerned with identity creation, and focuses on the particular and local, incorporating partly the uniform and abstract. Islamic movements in general have set about reforming Muslim political identity and encouraging Muslims to become active participants in a collective whole—be they moderate or radical. Islamist organizations often refer to their interpretation of Islam as a comprehensive (including social, political, economic issues) and authentically pious lifestyle, which should be appealing to insightful Muslims. In general, Islamists have developed a local culture of resistance to the ruling elites, authoritarian or otherwise. This does not necessarily include resistance to modernity and consumerism, but more readily to perceived socioeconomic and political decadence. It is because of this perception of being engaged in collective resistance that many Islamists have developed a deep sense of solidarity, comradeship, and a set of affirmative attitudes. This makes many of them deeply committed to their respective organizations. Islamists re-adjust contemporary meanings by referring to traditional Islamic authenticity, thus creating friction with other competing understandings of, among other things, globalization, modernity, and most notably politics. Islamist claims have evolved and thus have been adjusted to the present institutional order far beyond the Middle East.

Islamism, therefore, is the religiously informed ideological framework of a broad social movement and should not be treated as sui generis, distant and separate from socioeconomic and political realities and moral dilemmas. Islamism and its proponents are interlinked with larger sociopolitical contexts, and as such, ultimately are subjected to a continuous process of organizational change and even ideological and strategic modifications. Due to increasing secularization and volatile political fragmentation in a number of Middle Eastern and North African states after the Arab Revolutions in 2011 there is heightened risk of open confrontation between Islamists and their political opponents, including the powerful remnants of the old regimes. Regardless of a short-term outcome of these political tensions, Islamists seem to remain, if not the principal part, a pivotal part in the evolving political landscapes in the region.

BIBLIOGRAPHY

Abu-Rabiʿ, I. *Contemporary Arab Thought: Studies in Post-1967 Arab Intellectual History*. London: Pluto Press, 2004.

Al-Hudaibi, M. *The Principles of Politics in Islam*. Cairo: Islamic Publishing, 2000.

Al-Nafisi, A., ed. *Al-Ḥarakah al-islāmīyah: Ru'yah mustaqbalīyah* (The Islamist Movement: Prospective Outlook). Cairo: Maktabat Madbūlī, 1989.

Al-Qaradawi, Y. *State in Islam*. 3d ed. Cairo: Al-Falah Foundation, 2004.

Ashour, O. *The De-Radicalization of Jihadists: Transforming Armed Islamist Movements*. New York: Routledge, 2009.

Ayoob, M. *The Many Faces of Political Islam*. Ann Arbor: University of Michigan Press, 2008.

Ayubi, N. *Political Islam: Religion and Politics in the Arab World*. London: Routledge, 1991.

Barker, R. W. *Islam Without Fear: Egypt and the New Islamists*. Cambridge, Mass.: Harvard University Press, 2003.

Crone, P. *God's Rule: Government and Islam*, New York: Columbia University Press, 2004.

Dabashi, H. *Theology of Discontent: The Ideological Foundations of the Islamic Revolution in Iran*. New York University Press, 1993.

Esposito, J. *The Future of Islam*. Oxford: Oxford University Press, 2010.

Esposito, J., and J. Voll. *Islam and Democracy*. Oxford: Oxford University Press, 1996.

Feldman, N. *The Fall and Rise of the Islamic State*. Princeton, N.J.: Princeton University Press, 2008.

Hafez, M. *Why Muslims Rebel: Repression and Resistance in the Islamic World*. Boulder, Colo.: Lynne Rienner Publishers, 2003.

Ismail, S. *Rethinking Islamist Politics: Culture, the State and Islamism*. London: I. B. Tauris, 2006.

Karam, A. *Transnational Political Islam: Religion, Ideology, and Power*. London: Pluto Books, 2004.

Kepel, G. *Jihad: The Trail of Political Islam*. London: I. B. Tauris, 2006.

Martin, B., and A. Barzegar, eds. *Islamism: Contested Perspectives on Political Islam*. Stanford, Calif.: Stanford University Press, 2010.

Mitchell, R., *The Society of the Muslim Brothers*, London: Oxford University Press, 1969.

Meijer, R., ed. *Global Salafism: Islam's New Religious Movement*. New York, Columbia University Press, 2009.

Wiktorowicz, Q., ed. *Islamic Activism: A Social Movement Theory Approach*, Bloomington: Indiana University Press, 2004.

EMIN POLJAREVIC

ISLAMIZATION OF KNOWLEDGE AND SOCIETY.

The expression "Islamization of knowledge" (IOK) first appeared in a book by the Malaysian scholar Syed Muhammad Naquib al-Attas published in 1978 under that title *Islām and Secularism*. The idea was later picked by a group of scholars who turned the idea into a worldwide project devoted to the mission of Islamizing knowledge. The group founded the International

Institute of Islamic Thought in 1983, which became the impetus for the efforts to bring a new interpretation of culture and society as part of the "Islamization of Knowledge" project.

The project emerged in response to cultural and educational division in postcolonial Muslim societies that split educational institutions into Sharīʿah-based and secular-based, creating educational and cultural dualism in Muslim societies. The objectives and general plan of the project were set forth in a monograph authored by Ismāʿīl R. al-Fārūqī, a leading figure in the IOK movement, and was first published by the International Institute of Islamic Thought (IIIT) in 1982 under the title *Islamization of Knowledge: General Principles and Work Plan*. In this monograph, al-Fārūqī singled out two factors as being responsible for the perpetuation of the adverse conditions of the Muslim community (*ummah*)—conditions he termed the malaise of the *ummah*, namely, the current secular-religious duality of the educational system in Muslim societies and the lack of clear vision to guide and direct Muslim action. The rejuvenation of the *ummah*, he argued, is contingent on the integration of Islamic and secular sciences—in a word, on ending educational duality:

> The task confronting the ummah in the fifteenth century Hijrah is that of solving the problem of education. There can be no hope of a genuine revival of the ummah unless the educational system is revamped and its faults corrected. Indeed, what is needed is for the system to be formed anew. The present dualism in Muslim education, its bifurcation into an Islamic and secular system, must be removed and abolished once and for all. The two systems must be united and integrated. (Fārūqī, 1987, p. 9)

According to al-Fārūqī, the desired integration of Muslim education is the task of academicians who are well versed in both modern disciplines and Islamic legacy. This integration of knowledge, whose concrete manifestation is the production of university-level textbooks containing "Islamized knowledge," is the essence of what al-Fārūqī called "Islamization of knowledge." "Islamizing knowledge," he wrote, "[is] in concrete terms, to Islamize the disciplines, or better, to produce university level textbooks recasting some twenty disciplines in accordance with the Islamic vision (Fārūqī, 1987, p. 9).

The philosophical underpinnings of the IOK project were rooted in the Qurʾānic concept of *tawḥīd* (unity of God). Al-Fārūqī identifies five principles of Islamic methodology, expressed in terms of five unities: the unity of Allah, of creation, of truth, of life, and of humanity. These principles of unity belong to the theory of being (ontology), and hence constitute the ontological presuppositions of an Islamic theory of knowledge (Fārūqī, 1987, p. 14).

Transcending Traditional Knowledge. Scholars engaged in "Islamizing" knowledge are in many ways forward-looking ones who do not advocate a return to traditional Islamic knowledge but rather a synthesis between Islamic values and modern approaches. The IOK project insists that classical Islamic sciences are themselves inadequate for guiding modern scientific activities. This inadequacy has been highlighted by a number of scholars. Al Fārūqī, for instance, argued that the inadequacy of traditional methods reveals itself in two diametrically opposed tendencies. The first tendency is to restrict the field of *ijtihād* to legalistic reasoning, that is, subsuming modern problems under legal categories, thereby reducing the *mujtahid* to a *faqīh* (jurist), and reducing science to legal science. The other tendency is to eliminate all rational criteria and standards by adopting "a purely intuitive and esoteric methodology." This sought-after methodology should avoid the excesses of these two approaches. That is to say, it should avoid restricting reasoning to the extent that modern problems confronting Muslim scholarship are placed outside the realm of scientific research, and should not, at the same time, allow the admission of fiction and superstition into the realm of true knowledge (Fārūqī, 1987, p. 19).

The same concern is echoed by Abdul Hamid Abu Sulayman, who links the crisis of modern Muslim intellectualism to the methodological inadequacy besetting contemporary Muslim thought, manifesting itself in the employment of exclusively linguistic and legalistic patterns of thinking. According to Abu Sulayman, the dilemma of contemporary Muslim intellectualism is that while the *faqīh* as jurist is trained to handle legal/moral problems, he continues to be perceived as an all-round, universal intellectual, capable of resolving all problems of modern society. As he puts it:

> The crisis [of Islamic thought] also lies in the nature of our Islamic methods of research, which are confined to textual studies of language, traditions and orthodox jurisprudence. These two attitudes are manifested in our tendency to regard the *faqih* (jurist) in the historical sense as one who is capable of resolving the crisis of thought, culture, and knowledge. (Abu Sulayman, pp. 268–269)

Another aspect of the inadequacy of classical methods is highlighted by Mona Abul-Fadl. The reason classical methods are inadequate, she points out, is that while the study of social phenomena requires a holistic approach whereby social relations are systemized according to universal rules, classical methods are atomistic, relying primarily on analogical reasoning. Taha Jabir Al-Alwani, an Azhar University graduate, has also made concerted effort to open up the *uṣūl al-fiqh* tradition to modern influences.

Objections to IOK. The drive toward developing an Islamic methodology elicited two types of responses. The first response, represented here by Muḥammad Saʿīd al-Būṭī, denies the need for the development of a new Islamic methodology. However, al-Būṭī claims that an Islamic methodology has already been "discovered" by classical Muslim scholars. In a paper presented at the Fourth International Conference on Islamic Methodology and Behavioral and Education Sciences held in Khartoum, Sudan, in 1987, and later published by IIIT, al-Būṭī contended that the scientific method is a fact (*ḥaqīqah*) that belongs to the "objective world." Like all "material things" it has a fixed nature, completely independent in both its structure and existence from human thought and reasoning. According to al-Būṭī, the objectivity and permanence of the scientific method (*manhaj al-maʿrifah*) is necessitated by its function. Since the scientific method is an instrument, a scale (*mīzān*) for ensuring the correctness and soundness of thinking, its validity has to be independent of the thinking process itself. Hence, al-Būṭī concludes, the scientific method cannot be modified or altered by reason; otherwise, one would have to seek another method for its modification, leading to infinite regress. He therefore argues that since the scientific method is fixed and permanent, it is not susceptible to development and innovation. This means that the role of human intellect (in this case Muslim intellect) is limited to identifying or discovering the "sound method" (Būṭī, 1990, p. 59).

Further, contemporary Muslims need not bother discovering the "sound method" of knowledge, he contends, for this discovery has already been accomplished by early Muslims in the "golden age of Islam" (Būṭī, 1990, p. 59) As to the question of the role of contemporary Islamic scholarship in relation to scientific methodology, al-Būṭī proposes a twofold program, whereby contemporary Muslim scholars work, firstly, to reorganize the already-discovered method so as to make it more responsive to existing needs and, secondly, to recast it in contemporary language so that it can once again guide Muslim discourse.

Al-Būṭī's argument is problematic for at least two reasons. First, it confuses the methods of scientific research with the fundamental principles of reason. For while one may argue that the principles of reason (the principle of consistency or of noncontradiction) are intrinsic to human reasoning, and hence unalterable, one can hardly say the same about the techniques and procedures used in *uṣūl al-fiqh* (e.g., *istiḥsān*). But beyond that, al-Būṭī fails, secondly, to recognize that the methods of *uṣūl al-fiqh* were not "discovered" but were rather developed over several centuries. Indeed, al-Būṭī's suggestion that classical methods need to be recast in contemporary language points to the inadequacy of classical methods for modern research. For if the use of language is a matter of function and not of fashion, why should anyone call for recasting the perpetual scientific method in a new language, unless there are some intrinsic conceptual or procedural differences between the old and the new?

The other, and more sympathetic, response came from Fazlur Rahman, who advanced an argument reminiscent of Ibn Rushd's contention that methods are basically tools independent of any religious orientation. Fazlur Rahman, like al-Būṭī, disagreed with the project of Islamization of knowledge, but for completely different reasons. In an article appearing in the *American Journal of Islamic Social Sciences* (*AJISS*) shortly after his death, Fazlur Rahman, while agreeing that much of contemporary knowledge reflects a Western ethos, strongly contended that one cannot devise a methodology or detail a strategy for achieving Islamic knowledge. The only hope Muslims have for bringing about Islamic knowledge, he argued, is to nurture the Muslim mind, as he put it:

> So far as the problem under consideration—Islamization of knowledge—is concerned, I, therefore, conclude that we must not get enamored over making maps and charts of how to go about creating Islamic knowledge. Let us invest our time, energy and money in the creation, not of propositions, but minds. (Rahman, 1988, p. 10)

While anyone who has given the question of revitalization of Muslim scholarship some thought can hardly disagree with Fazlur Rahman that a state of Islamized knowledge can never materialize unless it is produced by scholars who are both highly competent in their fields and strongly committed to the ideals of Islam, one has to reject an outright denial of the value of methods. Indeed, Fazlur Rahman himself could not maintain his claim till the end of his article. In the early parts of the article, he contended that one cannot develop a method for guiding human reason, for "human thought," he proclaimed, "has its own mode of operation. We still do not know what the nature of the human thought process is" (Rahman, 1988, p. 11). Aristotle tried, he contended, to discover the structure of human thinking. His efforts culminated in the theory of syllogism. But Aristotle failed because, Rahman added, "absolutely nothing of this sort happens in actual reality. Human thought does not behave syllogistically" (Rahman, 1988, p. 10).

Yet one paragraph later, the article takes a surprising turn when Rahman outlines in the conclusion of his article a twofold strategy in which he calls upon Muslim scholars to examine, first, Muslim tradition and, second, Western tradition. To undertake this examination, he adds, Muslim scholars have to establish "certain criteria" that "must obviously come initially from the Qurʾān." The establishment of this set of criteria is what IOK scholars have focused on in their writings and literature.

Fazlur Rahman's concluding paragraph seems to contradict his earlier argument against methods, or at least reveals a certain inconsistency and ambiguity in the author's attitude toward methodology. For if one is to concede that there is a need for "certain criteria" to guide the examination of Muslim and Western intellectual traditions, one has to concede as well the need for rules to guide the derivation and application of these criteria—that is, a methodology.

Islamization of Society. The Islamization of knowledge project seems to have reached a plateau by the turn of the twenty-first century. The work of the 1980s and 1990s has led to a consensus that Muslim scholarship need to engage both modern sciences and traditional sciences in a critical way. While IIIT continues advancing the tradition of Islamization of knowledge, the intensity of the workshops, seminars, conferences, and publications, including more than four hundred books published in English and Arabic, has subsided. Yet it can be argued that IOK played a pivotal role in bridging the cultural and scholarly divide between traditional and modern knowledge in Arab and Muslim societies. There is today a greater harmony between the modern and traditional, as well as the religious and the secular, in the Arab and Muslim worlds. The spread of interest-free Islamic banking is only one aspect of the impact the Islamization of knowledge movement has made since the 1980s.

BIBLIOGRAPHY

Abul-Fadl, Mona. *Naḥwa manhajīyah lil-taʿāmul maʿa maṣādir al-tanẓīr al-Islāmī*. Cairo: Al-Maʿhad al-ʿĀlamī lil-Fikr al-Islāmī, 1996. See esp. pp. 206–207.

Abu Sulayman, Abdul Hamid. "Islamization of Knowledge." pp. 268–269.

Attas, Naquib al-. *Islām and Secularism*. Kuala Lumpur, Malaysia: International Institute of Islamic Thoughts and Civilization, 1978.

Būṭī, Muḥammad Saʿīd al-. "Azmat al-maʿrifah wattlajuha fi hayatina al-Islamryah ul-mu'fisirah" (The Crisis of Knowledge and Its Treatment in Our Contemporary Intellectual Life). In *Al-Manhajīyah al-Islāmīyah wa-al-ʿulūm al-sulūkīyah wa-al-tarbawīyah: Buḥūth wa-munāqashāt al-Muʾtamar al-ʿĀlamī al-Rābiʿ lil-Fikr al-Islāmī*, pp. 55–85. Herndon, VA: International Institute of Islamic Thought, 1990.

Fārūqī, Ismail R. al-. *Islamization of Knowledge: General Principles and Work Plan*. Herndon, VA: International Institute of Islamic Thought, 1987.

Rahman, Fazlur. "Islamization of Knowledge: A Response." *American Journal of Islamic Social Sciences* 5, no. 1 (1988): 3–11.

LOUAY M. SAFI

ISLAMOPHOBIA. Islamophobia is the "shorthand way of referring to the dread or hatred of Islam and, therefore, to fear or dislike all or most Muslims" based upon an "unfounded hostility towards Islam." This is the definition set out in the influential report *Islamophobia: A Challenge for Us All* (Runnymede Trust, 1997, p. 1), also known as the Runnymede report, and is the definition that has shaped and influenced most of the understandings of the term, although the term remains contested and is sometimes used interchangeably with neo-Orientalism, anti-Muslimism, anti-Muslim racism, or "new" or cultural racism. Much debate has surrounded the use of the term, questioning its adequacy as an appropriate and meaningful descriptor. However, since Islamophobia has broadly entered the social and political lexicon, arguments about the appropriateness of the term now seem outdated.

Since 1990 Islamophobia has gained a greater discursive prevalence, emanating primarily from Europe but more recently finding resonance in the United States, the Middle East, the Indian Subcontinent, and Australia. First used by Etienne Dinet and Slima Ben Ibrahim in 1925, this term only began to be used to describe an ideological "unfounded hostility" toward Muslims in the late twentieth century. It is important to note that while many have suggested that today's Islamophobia is merely a contemporary manifestation of a centuries-old hatred of Islam (Sardar,

1995), Islamophobia in the contemporary setting is recognized as a new word for a new reality. Contemporary Islamophobia has been primarily shaped by the British context. Shortly after its adoption at the grassroots level, the term made its appearance in print in the American journal *Insight* and in a book review by Tariq Modood in the *Independent* newspaper. In both instances the term was used without explanation, as it was in the 1993 Runnymede Commission on Antisemitism's report *A Very Light Sleeper*. It was this report that led to the Commission on British Muslims and Islamophobia being established three years later.

With the Runnymede report published, the term Islamophobia received wider public and political recognition in Britain. Setting out a typology of "closed" and "open" views through which Islamophobia could be identified, the report has been criticized for oversimplifying a complex issue by scholars, including Fred Halliday (Halliday, 2003), and Kenan Malik (Malik, 2005). Outside Britain, however, the term "Islamophobia" remained less operative. This is highlighted by a European Monitoring Centre for Racism and Xenophobia project in 2001 that sought to establish operable EU-wide definitions for racism, anti-Semitism, and Islamophobia (Clayton, 2002). It found that in seven of the fifteen European Union member states, there was no clear or known operational definition of Islamophobia. Of the rest, two noted that the term was nonoperational but were able to provide definitions; three referenced the Runnymede report, while the others offered quite different and incomplete definitions.

It could therefore be argued that 9/11 was the main catalyst for propelling Islamophobia into the much wider European and global setting. As the largest monitoring project undertaken into Islamophobia, Allen and Jørgen Nielsen's summary report on Islamophobia in the European Union following the 11 September 2001 attacks (Allen and Nielsen, 2002) identified a strong EU-wide backlash against Muslims. While the project failed to offer a concrete definition of what Islamophobia was, it observed that Islamophobia was in evidence. One of the possible reasons for the relative ambiguity of the report's observations is that, despite Islamophobia's growing prevalence, it remained highly protean, grouping together different forms of discourse, speech, and acts that emanate from an irrational fear—hence "phobia"—of Islam (Maussen, 2006).

A sense of disagreement about what Islamophobia is and where it comes from thus drastically impacts upon ensuing debates and arguments. Nevertheless, specific incidents of indiscriminate attacks against Muslims following events such as the bombings of the London underground and Madrid trains, the murder of Theo van Gogh and the assassination of Pim Fortuyn in the Netherlands, the social unrest in the Paris suburbs, or the publication of the cartoons of the Prophet Muḥammad in the Danish *Jyllands-Posten* newspaper that have received attention from scholars in books and reports. The Organization of the Islamic Conference (OIC) established an observatory to monitor and report incidences of Islamophobia.

Concerned scholars, policy makers, and civil organizations have suggested strategies to combat Islamophobia in the West by rooting out its political, economic, social, and cultural causes. The OIC and other organizations are placing great emphasis on intercivilizational and interfaith dialogues to help promote respect for all faiths and all colors.

BIBLIOGRAPHY

Allen, Christopher, and Jørgen S. Nielsen. *Summary Report on Islamophobia in the EU after 11 September 2001*. Vienna: European Monitoring Centre on Racism and Xenophobia, 2002.

Clayton, Dimitria. "Data Comparability, Definitions and the Challenges for Data Collection on the Phenomenon of Racism, Xenophobia, anti-Semitism and Islamophobia in the European Union," in *European Monitoring Centre on Racism and Xenophobia Colloque*, June 25, 2002. Vienna: EUMC.

Esposito, John L. and Ibrahim Kalin, eds. *Islamophobia: The Challenge of Pluralism in the 21st Century.* New York: Oxford University Press, 2011.

Gottschalk, Peter, and Gabriel Greenberg. *Islamophobia: Making Muslims the Enemy.* Lanham, Md.: Rowman & Littlefield, 2008.

Halliday, Fred. *Islam and the Myth of Confrontation: Religion and Politics in the Middle East.* Rev. ed. London: I. B. Tauris, 2003.

Malik, Kenan. "The Islamophobia Myth." http://www.kenanmalik.com/essays/prospect_islamophobia.html.

Cesari, Jocelyn, ed. *Securitization and Religious Divides in Europe, Muslims in Western Europe after 9/11: Why the Term Islamophobia is More a Predicament Than an Explanation.* Paris: Challenge, 2006.

Organization of the Islamic Conference. *Fourth OIC Observatory Report on Islamophobia (Intolerance and Discrimination against Muslims) May 2010 to April 2011.* Jiddah, Saudi Arabia: Organization of the Islamic Conference, 2011.

Runnymede Trust. *Islamophobia: A Challenge for Us All.* London: Runnymede Trust, 1997.

Sardar, Ziauddin. "Racism, Identity, and Muslims in the West." In *Muslim Minorities in the West*, edited by Syed Z. Abedin and Ziauddin Sardar, pp. 1–17. London: Grey Seal, 1995.

CHRIS ALLEN
Updated by ABDUL RASHID MOTEN

ISRAEL. In September 2012, the Arab and Druze minority in Israel numbered approximately 1,636,000, constituting 20.6 percent of the total Israeli population (Arab residents of East Jerusalem are estimated to number 285,000). Eighty-four percent of the Arab minority was Arab Muslim, whereas the rest were Arab Christian (7.9) and Druze (8.1 percent). Muslims in Israel are mostly Sunnī. The annual growth rate of Muslims in Israel was 2.5% in 2010.

The Post-1948 Period. The 1948 Arab-Israeli War created a structural vacuum in the life of the Israeli Muslim community. Organized Islam virtually disappeared. Muslims in the newly established state of Israel were left without religious court judges, prayer leaders, and other functionaries necessary to sustain the religious life of the community. The Supreme Muslim Council ceased to exist, having been superseded by the Jordanian religious authorities.

Israel was faced with the challenging task of reestablishing the Muslim religious apparatus and applying the Sharīʿah in the new Jewish state. Muslim religious affairs, including the administration of *awqāf* (religious endowments), devolved to Israeli authorities, primarily the Muslim Department of the Ministry of Religious Affairs.

The Sharīʿah court system was gradually reconstructed over years, because few people were qualified to assume religious appointments. By necessity, underqualified men were occasionally engaged. In May 1961 the Knesset (parliament) ratified the Qādīs Law, which stipulated that the *qādīs* (judges) be selected by a committee with a Muslim majority, appointed by the president of Israel, and dispense justice in accordance with Israeli laws.

Muslim religious courts in Israel were granted exclusive and extensive jurisdiction in matters of personal status and *awqāf* (charitable religious foundations). The Knesset, however, restricted the jurisdiction of the Sharīʿah courts in certain areas with the intention of thoroughly reforming the legal status of women.

As Aharon Layish has shown (Layish, 1965, pp. 50–79), Israeli legislation in matters of personal status proceeded along two different lines. With regard to marriage and divorce, the Knesset imposed several restrictions: it prohibited the marriage of girls under seventeen, outlawed polygamy, and forbade divorcing a woman against her will. The secular legislation did not supersede religious law in these matters, but it was enforced by penal sanctions. The other entailed the supersession of Muslim religious law; for example, the Knesset's legislation that only natural guardianship of the mother was binding. With the 1965 Succession Law, the exclusive jurisdiction of the Sharīʿah courts in matters of succession and wills was abolished, and the power to deal with these matters was transferred to the state district courts. In 2011, eight Sharīʿah courts operated in Israel: in Acre, Nazareth, Haifa, Bāqa al-Gharbīya, Taiba, Jaffa, Jerusalem (also the site of the Supreme Sharʿī Court of Appeal), and Beersheba.

After 1948, Muslim *waqf* properties whose administrators or beneficiaries were absentees were entrusted to a special custodian. Consecrated Muslim sites and their secular appurtenances were administered by the Muslim Department of the Ministry of Religious Affairs, which served as an agent of the Custodian of Absentees' Property. The law was amended in 1965 to allow the release of *waqf khayrī* property (established for a particular public good) to several Muslim trustee committees.

Islamic Revival. Since the late 1970s, the Muslim community in Israel has been undergoing a process of Islamic revival. Renewed contacts with the Palestinians of the West Bank and Gaza after the 1967 war strengthened the religious component of Israeli Muslims' collective identity. The resurgence of Islam must be seen against the background of the Arab sector's socioeconomic crisis. Since the early 1970s, the Arab sector in Israel has become increasingly aware of and distressed by its socioeconomic situation relative to that of the Jews. The sizable gap between the Arab and Jewish populations in such fields as education, health services, housing, and industrialization has become increasingly acute. The gaps developed partly through governmental neglect and partly through the government's inability to meet the growing needs caused by the Arabs' rapid population growth. The ultimate outcome was a deepening sense of Arab bitterness, frustration, alienation, and dissent.

As the discrepancies between Jews and Arabs widened, the Arab community became increasingly eager for external forces to remedy the imbalance. Ayatollah Ruhollah Khomeini's rise to power in Iran led to the formation of the first clandestine group of Islamic militants in Israel. Set up within a year of the Iranian revolution, it called itself Usrat al-Jihād (the Jihād Family) and was organized as a paramilitary unit. The group's objective was to wage *jihād* against Israel, undermine the basis of Jewish-Zionist existence, and cause the state to collapse from within. Usrat al-Jihād carried out a number of acts of sabotage, including arson; it also took action against secular or liberalizing trends among Israeli Muslims. However, soon after their first sabotage operations in 1981, all seventy members of the organization were arrested and sentenced to prison terms ranging from one to fifteen years. The arrest and trial dampened Muslim militancy in Israel.

In the mid-1980s the Islamic activist Shaykh ʿAbd Allāh Nimr Darwīsh moved to center stage. A resident of Kufr Qasim, Darwīsh was a graduate of the Nablus Sharīʿah College. In 1979 he joined Usrat al-Jihād; he was arrested and convicted in1981 and released in 1983. When Darwīsh resumed his politico-religious career, he gave Islamic activism in Israel a new nonmilitant direction. Darwīsh focused on the community, trying to win the hearts of the local Muslims by means of religious education and community work. Islamic associations were soon founded in a number of Arab localities. The Islamic Movement, as it came to be known, succeeded in changing the face of Arab village society. Mosque attendance increased; the number of mosques in Israel grew from sixty in 1967 to eighty in 1988, 240 in 1993, and 363 in 2003. According to some estimates, 40 percent of the 363 mosques throughout Israel are headed by imams affiliated with the Islamic Movement (figures from 2003). The Islamic Movement found solutions to many of the daily hardships that resulted from the authorities' failure to meet the Arab sector's needs.

In line with the Muslim Brotherhood's doctrine advocating a gradualist approach in performing the necessary socioreligious transformation, the Movement deployed an efficient network of organizations, institutions, and officially registered volunteer associations, whose operations covered numerous spheres of life, grounded in the concept of Islam as a social religion with a moral message. The Movement was particularly active in the fields of education, infrastructure projects, healthcare, charity and welfare, culture and the arts, and recreation.

This approach proved to be a prescription for success. In the 1998 municipal elections, the Islamic Movement won representation in thirteen localities, including the mayorship of five towns and villages: Umm al-Faḥm, Kafr Qāsim, Rāhaṭ, Jaljūlīya, and Ṭamra. In the 2003 municipal elections, it won representation in only nine localities, but it still maintained its power, especially in Umm al-Faḥm, the second largest Arab town in Israel, where the Movement's candidate for mayor, Shaykh Hāshim ʿAbd al-Raḥmān, won 75 percent of the ballots, defeating a rival candidate representing a secular coalition. He thus preserved the Movement's dominance in the city since 1989. The Islamic Movement also kept its strong grip in Nazareth, the largest Arab town in Israel which was traditionally dominated by the Christian-Communist party, where the Movement's candidates secured eight out of seventeen seats in the city's council, of the same number as the Christian-Communist-list candidates.

During the 1990s, the Al-Aqṣā Association for the Preservation of the *Waqf* and the Islamic Holy Sites, established by the Islamic Movement in 1991, mounted a campaign to restore the *waqf* properties to their lawful owners in the Muslim community. In March 2001, the Islamic Movement established a Supreme Muslim Council, intended in part to serve as the elected Islamic body to which the *waqf* properties would be reinstated.

The success of the Islamic Movement was not only the result of the religious appeal. For many, it was a vote of confidence in a movement that successfully dedicated itself to the social, economic, and cultural advancement of the Arab sector.

The religious views of the Islamic Movement appear to have been influenced by various forces. One is the traditional orthodox Sunnī approach taught in Arab schools and Islamic colleges in the West Bank. A second is the ideas of nineteenth- and twentieth-century Islamic reformists and modernists. The third, and perhaps most important, is the doctrine of the Muslim Brotherhood.

From its inception, the local Islamic Movement has been torn between three competing foci of loyalty or solidarity—Islam, Israel, and Palestine. The Islamic Movement's program genuinely reflected the problematic interrelationship among Islamic revivalism, the declared secular character of Palestinian nationalism, and the need to act within the boundaries of Israeli law. This gave rise to confusion and often ambiguous language on sensitive issues, such as the components of identity, the Palestine Liberation Organization, the solution of the Palestinian problem, the idea of a Palestinian Islamic state, the Islamic movements in the territories (Ḥamās, Islamic Jihād), the *intifāḍah*, and the Palestinian/Islamic armed struggle.

The complexities facing the revivalists can best be exemplified by their treatment of the issue of national identity. The four orbits of identity often mentioned by the Islamic Movement in Israel are Islam, Arabism, humanism, and Palestinian nationalism. Some local Islamic leaders refrain from mentioning Israel at all; others, wary of provoking a harsh reaction on the part of the Israeli authorities for implicitly denying Israel's existence, mention the state, but only with reference to the technicality of citizenship. Leaders of the Movement have been put under house arrest, and the Movement's press has been temporarily closed in reaction to the publication of what was described as inflammatory material.

Similarly complex is the question of a Palestinian Islamic state. Unlike their counterparts in the territories—who do not hesitate to call for a state from "the River to the Sea," that is, from the Jordan to the Mediterranean—the Israeli Islamists are reserved. Some, like Shaykh Darwīsh, make a clear distinction between their support of the idea that genuine Islamic states should be established in the region and their rejection of the idea that an Islamic state should replace Israel. Others fully endorse the views of Ḥamās that the land of Palestine is an Islamic endowment (*waqf*), which Sharīʿah requires Muslims to liberate. They do not, of course, expound pursuing this goal, for this would compel the Israeli authorities to take action against them.

The question of whether or not to participate in the Knesset elections aroused an internal controversy within the Islamic Movement's ranks. One of the most important developments before the 1996 elections was the Movement's reversal of its long-held position of staying out of Israeli parliamentary elections. In March 1996 the Movement's General Congress endorsed its participation in the Knesset elections within the framework of a unified Arab party headed by an Islamic Movement candidate.

The initiative to reverse the previous decision made in 1995 came from the group of Islamic leaders associated with Shaykh Darwīsh. The motivation for this effort was the desire to unite the fragmented Arab vote and prevent a situation in which, as a result of increased factionalism, Arab representation in the Knesset would be weakened or even eliminated.

This new decision caused an immediate crisis within the Movement ranks. Two of the more radical leaders, Shaykh Kamāl Khaṭīb and Shaykh Rāʾid Ṣalāḥ, mayor of Umm al-Faḥm at the time, announced that they did not view themselves bound by the Movement's resolution to participate in the Knesset elections, a move that eventually caused a split within the Movement's ranks into two factions: The first, headed by Shaykh Darwīsh, adopted a more pragmatic view toward integration into the Israeli society, including participation in Knesset elections. The second, headed by Shaykh Rāʾid Ṣalāḥ, maintained a more dogmatic one.

Representatives of the latter faction argued that the Islamic Movement cannot integrate into the Israeli system, because it is based on a set of Jewish-Israeli laws that stood in complete contradiction to the very essence of Islamic law. Hence, this faction endorsed the idea of taking independent institutions for the Arab population in Israel a step further. As part of its social worldview, especially in light of events in October 2000, when twelve Israeli Arab citizens were killed during bloody clashes with Israeli security forces near Arab localities in the Galilee and in the Triangle area (in central Israel), the dogmatic faction considered establishing an alternative social infrastructure for a community that was capable of relying on itself (*al-mujtamaʿ al-ʿiṣāmī*, "self-help society") by means of independent industrial, commercial, and financial institutions, and by its own health, security, and education services. However, no significant practical steps have been taken to realize these ideas.

The more moderate faction of the Islamic Movement, also known by its geographic dimension as the southern faction, has been represented in the Knesset since 1996. Shaykh Ibrahim Sarsur, leader of the faction, was elected to the Seventeenth Knesset in 2006, running as head of the United Arab List, which included the Islamic

Movement, the Arab Democratic Party, and the Arab Movement for Change. Sarsur replaced the lawyer ʿAbd al-Mālik Dehamshe (Dahāmsha), who had served as the faction's representative in the Knesset since 1996. Two members represented the Islamic Movement in the Eighteenth Knesset (elected in 2009): Ibrahim Sarsur and Masʿūd Ghanāyyim.

In May 2003, some central figures of the dogmatic faction, including the leader of the faction, Shaykh Ṣalāḥ himself, had been arrested for money laundering and transfer of money to Islamic activists in the West Bank. The faction's press was temporarily closed due to what was described as publication of inflammatory material. Some of the detainees were released in January 2005 and the rest, including Shaykh Ṣalāḥ, were released four months later. Since his release, Shaykh Ṣalāḥ has been active in organizing protests against Israel's excavations on the Temple Mount, under the slogan "Al-Aqṣā Is in Danger." In April 2009, some 150 Islamist activists affiliated with Shaykh Ṣalāḥ's northern faction demonstrated near the Old City of Jerusalem to protest Jewish groups' intention to hold prayers and allegedly gain control of the Temple Mount. In January 2010, the Jerusalem Magistrate's Court sentenced Shaykh Ṣalāḥ to nine months in jail for attacking and spitting on a policeman during a demonstration in the Old City that took place in February 2007.

The Islamic Movement's continued success in Israel depends on the skill of its balancing act: its relentless promotion of the Islamization of Israeli Muslims in their personal conduct and community life, on the one hand, and, on the other, its keeping political action and propaganda compatible with the anomaly of a Muslim-Arab minority living in a Jewish state.

[*See also* Arab-Israeli Conflict; Ḥamās: *subentry* Overview; *and* Palestine Liberation Organization.]

BIBLIOGRAPHY

Ali, Nohad. "Political Islam in an Ethnic Jewish State: Historical Evolution, Contemporary Challenges, and Future Prospects." *Holy Land Studies* 3, no. 1 (May 2004): 69–92.

Israeli, Raphael. *Muslim Fundamentalism in Israel.* London: Brassey's, 1993.

Layish, Aharon. "Muslim Religious Jurisdiction in Israel." *Asian and African Studies* 1 (1965): 49–79.

Layish, Aharon. "The Muslim Waqf in Israel." *Asian and African Studies* 2 (1966): 41–47.

Layish, Aharon. *Women and Islamic Law in a Non-Muslim State: A Study Based on Decisions of the Sharīʿa Courts in Israel.* New York: John Wiley, 1975.

Mayer, Thomas. *Hitʿorerut ha-Muslemim be-Yisraʿel.* Givʿat Ḥavivah, Israel: Ha-Makhon le-Limudim ʿArviyim, 1988.

Peled, Alisa Rubin. "Towards Autonomy? The Islamist Movement's Quest for Control of Islamic Institutions in Israel." *Middle East Journal* 55, no. 3 (Summer 2001): 378–398.

Rekhess, Elie. "The Islamic Movement following the Municipal Elections: Rising Political Power?" In *Ha-beḥirot ha-munitsipaliyot ba-yishuv ha-ʿAravi veha-Druzi (2003): Ḥamulatiyut, ʿadatiyut, u-miflagtiyut,* edited by Elie Rekhess and Sarah Ozacky-Lazar, pp. 33–41. Tel Aviv: Tel Aviv University, 2005.

Rekhess, Elie. "Resurgent Islam in Israel." *Asian and African Studies* 27 (1993): 189–206.

Rekhess, Elie, and Arik Rudnitzky. "Israel: Arab Population." *Encyclopaedia Judaica*, 2d ed., edited by Fred Skolnik, vol. 10, pp. 728–733. Detroit: Macmillan Reference USA, 2007.

ELIE REKHESS

IZETBEGOVIĆ, ALIJA. Alija Izetbegović (1925–2003), was the first president (1992–1996) and later co-president (1996–1998, 1999–2000) of independent Bosnia and Herzegovina during the tumultuous last decade of the twentieth century, during which the country and surrounding region suffered from wars of independence, near-genocide, and strained efforts at reconstruction and reconciliation. He was seen and portrayed as the father of the modern Federation of Bosnia and Herzegovina. A key European Muslim thinker of the twentieth century, Izetbegović authored a number of books that reflected his experience with religion and politics, Islam in Europe, and the identity and future of the Balkans.

Izetbegović graduated with a degree in law from the University of Sarajevo in 1956 and spent the rest of his life as a lawyer, activist, and politician. He was an outspoken critic of communism, particularly its role in the repression of religious sentiment, and it was for this reason that he was first imprisoned, after World War II. He was imprisoned again from 1983 to 1988 for allegedly inciting Muslims to establish an Islamic political state in communist Yugoslavia through the publication and propagation of his works *The Islamic Declaration* and *Islam between East and West.*

Izetbegović cofounded the Party of Democratic Action in 1990, one of the first after the ban on the multiparty system enacted by communist Yugoslavia in 1945. Although Izetbegović's name would become synonymous with the independence of Bosnia and Herzegovina, he was, at first, in favor of the political reconstruction of Yugoslavia rather than provincial sovereignty. Although Bosnians and Croats voted overwhelmingly for sovereignty, the Serbian constituency did not.

The move for independence threw Bosnia and Herzegovina into war. Throughout the war, Izetbegović remained in favor of a unified but multiethnic Bosnia with central governance. He spent his presidency besieged in Sarajevo by Serbian factions. He represented the Bosnian government during the negotiations that came to be called the Dayton Peace Accord (21 November 1995; signed in Paris on 14 December 1995) and was thus instrumental in bringing about a conclusion to the war, though he himself was unconvinced of the fairness of the terms of that peace.

Izetbegović was widely heralded as an intellectual, moderate, and democratic political leader who skillfully led a multiethnic and multinational country to independence. Still, he was a controversial figure. He was criticized for accepting foreign Muslim soldiers during the war, and was accused of transforming it into a religious conflict and exacerbating ethnic tensions in the region. At the time of his death, Izetbegović was being investigated by the International Criminal Tribunal for the former Yugoslavia for involvement in war crimes, but the inquiry was unsubstantial and closed upon his death.

Izetbegović was awarded numerous international honors, including the 1996 International Democracy Award presented by the Centre for Democracy at the United Nations. He is remembered as a political philosopher who encouraged Muslims to learn from the strengths of Western democracy and culture. His advocacy of Islamic renaissance sought to revitalize the practice of Islam among Muslims while embracing their European heritage. He died of heart failure in Sarajevo on 19 October 2003, at the age of seventy-eight.

[*See also* Bosnia and Herzegovina.]

BIBLIOGRAPHY

Izetbegović, Alija. *Inescapable Questions: Autobiographical Notes.* Translated by Saba Rissaluddin and Jasmina Izetbegović. Leicester, U.K.: Islamic Foundation, 2002.

Izetbegović, Alija. *Islam between East and West.* 2d ed. Indianapolis, Ind.: American Trust, 1989.

Nada Unus

J

JAMĀʿAT-I ISLĀMĪ. Jamāʿat-i Islāmī (Islamic Party) was founded in 1941 by Sayyid Abū al-Aʿlā Mawdūdī (d. 1979), an Islamist thinker and activist. Mawdūdī's call for the creation of an organization that would better address the predicament facing Muslims was supported by a number of young *ʿulamāʾ* who joined him in this cause. Mawdūdī was elected as the Jamāʿat's first *amīr* (president). Between 1941 and 1947, the Jamāʿat spread its message across British India through widely distributed literature and public sessions (*Ijtamaa*). However, in the independence movement, Jamāʿat-i Islāmī opposed both the Indian National Congress and Muslim League.

History and Politics. Following the partition of India, Mawdūdī migrated to Pakistan, where national politics proved receptive to Jamāʿat, and the party soon found a niche in the political arena. Jamāʿat organized a network of activists who propagated Mawdūdī's views and enabled the party to wield power. However, due to its radical Islamic base, the party soon became a main rival of more liberal state machinery. Pakistani authorities accused the Jamāʿat of pro-Indian sympathies and anti-Pakistan activities. Several Jamāʿat leaders, including Mawdūdī, were incarcerated, and the party was declared a seditious entity. Following Mawdūdī's release from prison in 1950, the Jamāʿat became directly active in politics by taking part in the Punjab elections. It was, however, the anti-Aḥmadīyah agitations in 1953–1954 that catapulted the Jamāʿat to the forefront of Pakistani politics. The government again arrested Mawdūdī, convicting him of sedition and sentencing him to death. That sentence was later reversed by Supreme Court.

In 1957, despite opposition within the party, Mawdūdī directed the Jamāʿat to participate in the national elections. The constitutional victory was, however, short-lived, as General Muhammad Ayub Khan took power in 1958 and declared martial law. As a result the Jamāʿat's offices were closed down and its activities were restricted. Mawdūdī himself was imprisoned twice during Ayub Khan's rule. Consequently, the Jamāʿat joined the opposition alliance that advocated an end to Ayub Khan's hegemony and supported the candidacy of Fatimah Jinnah in the presidential elections of 1965. In 1970 Jamāʿat participated in national elections but won only four seats in the National Assembly. In the 1971 civil war Jamāʿat mobilized its resources with the help of the

Pakistani army; its paramilitary organizations, al-Shams and al-Badr, played a key role in fighting alongside the Pakistani army to crush Bengali separatism. The secession of East Pakistan and the rise of Zulfiqar ʿAli Bhutto to power in 1971 intensified the Jamāʿat's political activism, notably during the movement against recognition of Bangladesh in 1972–1974 and the anti-Aḥmadīyah disturbances of 1974. The Jamāʿat's religio-political program was instrumental in shaping the anti-Bhutto opposition alliance Tehreek Nizam-e-Mustafa. In the 1977 elections, widely believed to have been rigged, the Jamāʿat won nine of the thirty-six seats won by opposition. However, when in the midst of antigovernment protests, General Zia ul-Haq proclaimed martial law and dismissed Bhutto, the party's popularity soared further. Zia's eleven-year rule from 1977 to 1988 was a period of unprecedented political influence for party. Jamāʿat leaders occupied important government offices, including cabinet posts, and the party's views were reflected in government programs. Though later Jamāʿat developed some differences with Zia, his generally close ties with the party leadership was facilitated by Jamāʿat's direct role in Zia's Islamization of the country and then in the Afghan *jihād*.

Nevertheless, the rise in the fortunes of the Jamāʿat turned out to be a pyrrhic victory, as, despite its influence at the top, the party failed to expand its social base. As a result Jamāʿat performed badly in the national elections of 1985 and won only ten seats in the National Assembly. Its performance grew worse in subsequent elections, after the restoration of democracy, in 1988, 1990, and 1993, when despite forming alliances with major parties it won only eight, eight, and three seats, respectively. The Jamāʿat boycotted the 1997 polls. For the 2002 elections, Jamāʿat allied with other religious parties, including Mutahiddah Majlis-i-Amal (MMA). This alliance was able to cash in on anti-American sentiment within Pakistan (especially its Pashtun-majority areas) in the post-9/11 scenario and following the ouster of the Taliban regime in Afghanistan, and thus made unprecedented electoral gains, winning sixty seats in the National Assembly and also forming provincial governments in two Pakistani provinces bordering Afghanistan. However in a dramatic move, the MMA in 2003 supported Pervez Musharraf, a staunch American ally, in his bid to gain a vote of confidence from parliament and on the proposed seventeenth amendment. This step eventually worsened the image of Jamāʿat and MMA. In 2007, Jamāʿat along with other major opposition parties announced it would boycott the elections. Nevertheless, after the assassination of Benazir Bhutto in December 2007, the main opposition leader, Nawaz Sharif, reversed the decision and announced participation in these elections. Nevertheless Jamāʿat failed to evaluate the rising unpopularity of military rule and stuck with the decision to boycott. This decision ultimately proved fatal and as a result Jamāʿat was out of the national and provincial assemblies.

Party Structure. The party consists of members (*arkān*, sing., *rukn*) and a coterie of sympathizers (*muttafiqs* and *hamdards*) who form a cadre of workers (*kārkun*), but only members may hold office in the party. In 1947 the Jamāʿat had 385 members; in 1989 this figure stood at 5,723, when the party also boasted 305,792 official affiliates. The Jamāʿat is guided by the *amīr* in consultation with the Shūrā (consultative assembly). The administrative affairs are supervised by the *qayyim* (secretary-general). The party has also a women's wing, a student wing (Islāmī Jamʿīyat-i Ṭulabā, Islamic Students Association), and some semiautonomous organizations such as publication houses and unions. The Jamāʿat has been led by four *amīrs*; Sayyid Abu al-Aʿlā Mawdūdī (1941–1972), Miyān Ṭufayl Muḥammad (1972–1987), Qāzī Ḥusayn Aḥmad (1987–2008), and Munawer Hasan (2008–).

The party has compensated for its restricted social base by developing ties with students, bureaucrats, and intellectuals. It is its success with students that best explains the Jamāʿat's growing influence in the bureaucracy. This strategy also manifests Mawdūdī's doctrine of Islamizing the state by the conversion of society.

[*See also* Aḥmadīyah; Mawdūdī, Sayyid Abū al-Aʿlā; *and* Pakistan.]

BIBLIOGRAPHY

Adams, Charles J. "Mawdudi and the Islamic State." In *Voices of Resurgent Islam*, edited by John L. Esposito, pp. 99–133. New York: Oxford University Press, 1983.

Binder, Leonard. *Religion and Politics in Pakistan*. Berkeley: University of California Press, 1961.

Haqqani, Husain. *Pakistan: Between Mosque and Military*. Washington, D.C.: Carnegie Endowment for International Peace, 2005.

Hasan, Masudul. *Sayyid Abul Aʿala Maududi and His Thought*. 2 vols. Lahore: Islamic Publications, 1984–1986.

Nasr, Seyyed Vali Reza. "Islamic Opposition to the Islamic State: The Jamāʿat-i Islāmī, 1977–88." *International Journal of Middle East Studies* 25, no. 2 (May 1993): 261–283.

Nasr, Seyyed Vali Reza. *Mawdudi and the Making of Islamic Revivalism*. New York: Oxford University Press, 1996.

Nasr, Seyyed Vali Reza. *The Vanguard of the Islamic Revolution: The Jamaʿat-i Islami of Pakistan*. Berkeley: University of California Press, 1994.

KAMRAN BOKHARI
Updated by MUHAMMAD ATIF KHAN

JAMĀʿAT AL-ISLĀMĪYAH, AL-. Several Islamic organizations in Egypt use the name al-Jamāʿat (al-Gamāʿah or al-Jamāʿah) al-Islāmīyah (Islamic Groups). The largest, and most significant, of these groups is al-Jamāʿat al-Islāmīyah (the Islamic Group). Up until the late 1990s, and along with the Egyptian Islamic *Jihād* group, the Jamāʿah aimed to overthrow the government of former Egyptian president Hosni Mubarak, which it perceived as corrupt and repressive, and replace it with an Islamist state. Most Egyptian congregations operate primarily through independent mosques and student unions on university campuses and appeal primarily to Egyptian youths. There appears to be no unifying leadership; instead, the groups reflect the general trend in Egyptian society toward Islamic resurgence. However, because violent clashes occurred between government forces and more politically militant groups acting under the banner of al-Jamāʿah al-Islāmīyah between the mid-1980s and 1999, Cairo remains vigilant. The spiritual leader of al-Jamāʿah al-Islāmīyah is Sheikh Omar Abdel Rahman (ʿUmar ʿAbd al-Raḥmān), a blind preacher from El Faiyûm who lived in exile in the United States in the early 1990s and is serving a life sentence in jail for his involvement in the 1993 attack on the World Trade Center in New York.

Origins and Support. The use of the name "al-Jamāʿat al-Islāmīyah" originated in the early 1970s under the government of President Anwar Sadat. Sadat officially permitted new Islamic organizations to form on university campuses under the umbrella of al-Jamāʿah al-Islāmīyah. This move to reconstruct the conservative religious sectors of society was an early sign of a shift in Egypt's political course. Throughout the 1970s, as Sadat developed his plans to restructure the state's political structure, socioeconomic outlook, and foreign policy alliances, various Islamic groups served as an important counterbalance to the old Nasserist constituency and others further to the left. While the regime reduced government programs and encouraged general privatization, the number of private (*ahlī*) mosques in the country doubled in one decade from twenty thousand to forty thousand.

Ahlī mosques and the many Islamic organizations associated with them played critical roles in large urban areas, including Cairo, Alexandria, Port Said, and Suez in Lower Egypt, and Asyūṭ, El Faiyûm, and El Minya in Upper Egypt. Continued rural migration to these cities, combined with the government's restructuring policy, exacerbated social and economic tensions and led to a growing sense of urban alienation. While Cairo reduced its social welfare programs, al-Jamāʿah al-Islāmīyah provided a sorely needed safety net through private mosques, with centers for the distribution of food and clothing as well as for the study of the Qurʾān.

Sadat faced growing opposition after signing the Camp David agreement with Israel in 1978. In response, several independent religious leaders associated with al-Jamāʿah al-Islāmīyah gained popularity by criticizing the regime. Prominent among these were Shaykh Aḥmad al-Maḥallawī at Qaʿīd Ibrāhīm Mosque in Alexandria and Shaykh Ḥāfiẓ Salāmah of al-Shuhādāʾ Mosque in Suez and al-Nūr Mosque in Cairo. Just before his assassination in 1981, Sadat publicly chastised both Shaykh Maḥallawī and Shaykh Salāmah. For his part, Shaykh Omar Abdel Rahman was also critical of the regime, and was later charged with having links to the group that carried out Sadat's assassination. His trial ended with a not-guilty verdict. In the crackdown on public opposition that followed the assassination, these religious leaders all suffered state censorship and imprisonment; Karam Zuhdī eventually expressed regret for conspiring with Islamic *Jihād*. Zuhdī was among nine hundred militants who were released in April 2006 as the Mubarak government introduced new controls.

Methods and Aims. It is difficult to generalize about the ideology, practices, and aims of the various groups that operate under the umbrella of al-Jamāʿah al-Islāmīyah. They tend to advocate stronger Islamic rule and oppose non-Islamic practices in Egyptian society. They call for the adoption of *Sharīʿah*, the Islamic legal code, as the official law of the state, and oppose attempts by the government to control and supervise—through the *shaykh* of al-Azhar and the Ministry of Awqāf (religious endowments)—the work of mosques and religious groups.

The main difference between the activities of al-Jamāʿat al-Islāmīyah and those of *Jihād* was the former's use of methods openly designed to mobilize popular resistance through public preaching and conferences, whereas *Jihād* activities were secret and aimed at overthrowing the regime through a military coup. In addition, the *Jihād* group rejected the leadership of Shaykh Omar Abdel Raḥmān because of his blindness, as they believed this deficiency hindered him from leading the group efficiently. On the theological level, the two groups differed over their understanding of the concept of *al-ʿudhr bi-al-jahl* (the excuse of ignorance). While the leaders of al-Jamāʿat al-Islāmīyah believed that the violation of Islamic rules is excused from punishment if the violating party is uninformed about these rules, leaders of *Jihād* maintained that punishment would still be valid as long as the violating party did not exert the required effort to thoroughly study these Islamic rules.

Confrontation with the State. The level of conflict between al-Jamāʿah al-Islāmīyah followers and Cairo increased in the early 1990s, with military troops, armored vehicles, and helicopters deployed to several cities. The nature of the confrontation also assumed three new forms. First, the political assassinations of People's Assembly speaker Rifʿat al-Maḥjūb in October 1990 and of liberal author Faraj Fawdah in June 1992 were blamed on al-Jamāʿah al-Islāmīyah members. Attacks on prominent officials continued, such as the attempted assassination of Prime Minister ʿĀṭif Ṣidqī, in November 1993, and that of President Mubarak on several occasions. Second, in 1991 violent clashes between Muslims and Christians erupted in key cities of Upper Egypt, notably Dayrut; the government claimed these were instigated by members of al-Jamāʿah al-Islāmīyah, although dormant rivalries probably contributed to the malaise. Third, by late 1992, extremist elements in al-Jamāʿah al-Islāmīyah claimed responsibility for at least two attacks on foreign tourists visiting pharaonic monuments in Upper Egypt. The government claimed al-Jamāʿah al-Islāmīyah was pursuing a new strategy to disrupt the tourist trade to damage and weaken the national economy. Attacks on foreign tourists continued throughout the 1990s.

In part to address such assaults on Western visitors, Cairo pushed through its subservient parliament a strict new antiterrorism law. It required that all mosques and prayer leaders follow vetted guidance from state-sanctioned authorities. One of the most spectacular operations carried out by al-Jamāʿah al-Islāmīyah militants was the attack at the Temple of Hatshepsut in Luxor on 17 November 1997, in which six men machine-gunned and hacked to death fifty-eight foreign tourists and four Egyptians. The attack stunned Egyptian society, severely curtailed the booming tourist industry, and shattered popular support for violent Islamism among devout Muslims.

Deradicalization and After. In 1997, the jailed leaders of al-Jamāʿat al-Islāmīyah declared a unilateral cease-fire with the Egyptian regime. This step was followed by wide doctrinal revisions that thoroughly changed the ideological outlook of the group. Decades of state repression and the decline of popular support may have prompted the pursuit of reconciliation with state and society. According to the spiritual leaders' new understanding of Islam, *jihād* (holy war) is to be used only against outside enemies in the event of war. Accordingly, the use of violence against both Muslims and non-Muslims is prohibited. Furthermore, Muslims rulers were no longer perceived as apostates even if they declined to apply the Sharīʿah. Thousands of al-Jamāʿat al-Islāmīyah followers have repented following this extensive deradicalization process and were released from prisons.

The opening up of Egypt's political system after the 2011 revolution encouraged many former militant Islamists to form political parties and join electoral politics. Al-Binnaʾ wa-al-Tanmiyah (Building and Development) Party, established by former members of al-Jamāʿat al-Islāmīyah, was recognized by court order in October 2011 after the Committee of Political Parties Affairs had rejected it the on the grounds that its program was founded on a religious basis. The party's participation in the 2011 parliamentary elections further integrated al-Jamāʿat al-Islāmīyah members in Egypt's postrevolution politics. The party won thirteen seats in these elections, most of them in Upper Egypt governorates.

[*See also* Egypt; Muslim Brotherhood; *and* Rahman, Omar Abdel.]

BIBLIOGRAPHY

Ashour, Omar. "Lions Tamed? An Inquiry into the Causes of De-Radicalization of Armed Islamist Movements: The Case of the Egyptian Islamic Group." *Middle East Journal* 61 (2007): 596–625.

Baker, Raymond William. *Islam without Fear: Egypt and the New Islamists*. Cambridge, Mass.: Harvard University Press, 2003.

Blaydes, Lisa, and Lawrence Rubin. "Ideological Reorientation and Counterterrorism: Confronting Militant Islam in Egypt." *Terrorism and Political Violence* 20 (2008): 461–479.

Gunaratna, Rohan, and Mohamed Bin Ali. "De-Radicalization Initiatives in Egypt: A Preliminary Insight." *Studies in Conflict and Terrorism* 32 (2009): 277–291.

Kenney, Jeffrey T. *Muslim Rebels: Kharijites and the Politics of Extremism in Egypt*. Oxford: Oxford University Press, 2006.

Rubin, Barry. *Islamic Fundamentalism in Egyptian Politics*. Rev. ed. New York: Palgrave Macmillan, 2002.

Zakariyya, Fouad. *Myth and Reality in the Contemporary Islamist Movement*. Translated by Ibrahim M. Abu-Rabiʿ. London: Pluto, 2005.

Ibrahim Ibrahim
Updated by Joseph A. Kéchichian
and Nael Shama

Jamāʿat Izālat al-Bidʿa wa Iqāmat al-Sunna. A Nigerian Muslim reformist movement founded in 1978 by Malam Ismaila Idris and others in Jos (central Nigeria) and most active in the northern, Hausa-speaking part of Nigeria. Its spiritual leader was Alhaji Abubakar (Arabic, al-Ḥājj Abū Bakr) Gumi (1922–1992). The movement is popularly known in Hausa as *Izala*—the name used henceforth in this entry to refer to it—and its members are called *'Yan Izala* but often prefer to use the Arabic name *ahl al-sunna* (people of the Prophet's tradition) in reference to themselves. Because of the strong personal and ideological links of the movement with Wahhabism, its detractors in Nigeria, especially members of the Ṣūfī brotherhoods, sometimes refer to it derogatorily as *Wahabiyawa* (Wahhābīs). However, despite the obvious Saudi influence, the tradition of reform represented by the Izala has deep roots in the local culture of northern Nigeria.

Izala is a typical representative of the religious reform movements widespread in the modern Muslim world, and, like these, it phrases its reform program in terms of a "return" to "original" Islamic norms and a wholesale eradication of reprehensible innovations (sing. *bidʿa*). This reform tradition in Nigeria gained particular momentum during the *jihād* of Usuman Dan Fodio (d. 1817), a historical antecedent routinely invoked by contemporary Nigerian Muslim reformers, including Gumi himself.

Contemporary Nigeria has a wide variety of Islamic movements and associations. These have differing views, goals, and methods and draw their inspiration from different sources. Some Islamic movements concentrate on providing education and social welfare in a dysfunctional and corrupt state, others stress *daʿwa* (missionary activity), yet others have a strongly political and revolutionary agenda. Izala is not a militant or revolutionary group comparable to, say, the Islamic Movement (or Muslim Brothers) of Ibrahim El-Zakzaky, strongly influenced by Iran and thus known in Hausa as *'Yan Shia* (Shīʿī). It tends to mix criticism of corrupt government with occasional cooperation with the state. Indeed Abubakar Gumi himself held the official position of grand *qāḍī* of northern Nigeria in the 1960s and was on good terms with a number of prominent (mainly Muslim) politicians.

The name of the movement clearly states its agenda. At the core of its teachings is the eradication of all *bidʿa*. The main target of Gumi's work *al-ʿAqīda al-ṣaḥīḥa fī muwāfaqat al-sharīʿa* (The Right Faith According to the Shariʿa, 1972) was Sufism, specifically the two locally dominant brotherhoods, the Qādiriyya and the Tījāniyya. Indeed Izala encourages its followers to oppose all forms of traditional authority, including Ṣūfī leaders as well as parents who do not subscribe to reformist teachings. This element of rebellion against authority makes Izala especially attractive to the younger generations of poor Muslims, as does its opposition to high brideprice and expensive traditional social ceremonies. Folk customs are also regular targets of Izala, who brand all these phenomena *bidʿa*.

Izala is not opposed to modernity as such. It has always used modern means of communication and actively encouraged the use of vernacular languages, instead of Arabic, to disseminate the message of Islam. Education, including women's education, is another important area of its activity.

Following its foundation in 1978 Izala quickly spread to all major cities of northern Nigeria and came to prominence in local and national politics and culture during the 1980s. In its first decade its anti-Ṣūfī stance caused serious strife in many communities between its followers and Ṣūfīs, and conflict over the control of local mosques often led to the establishment of separate mosques for the Izala. In the late 1980s, however, Izala began to curb its aggressive and divisive tactics. Gumi and other Izala ideologues gradually came to realize that internal disagreements within the Islamic community only served the interest of Christian pressure groups and severely jeopardized the proportional representation of Muslims in Nigerian politics by splitting the Muslim vote. This realization brought about a sort of reconciliation between Ṣūfī leaders and Izala in 1988. After the death of Gumi in 1992 disagreement over the acceptable degree of cooperation with the state led to the emergence of two factions within Izala (led by Ismaila Idris and Musa Mai Gandu, respectively), and more recently various splinter groups were formed, some of which now focus on development projects and the provision of social welfare to poor Muslims. Today Izala has over 2 million followers in Nigeria, and it is also present to some extent in adjoining Hausa-speaking parts of Niger.

BIBLIOGRAPHY

Gumi, Abubakar, and Ismaila A. Tsiga. *Where I Stand*. Ibadan, Nigeria: Spectrum Books, 1992.

Gwarzo, Tahir Haliru. "Activities of Islamic Civic Associations in the Northwest of Nigeria: With Particular Reference to Kano State." *Afrika Spectrum* 38, no. 3 (2003): 289–318.

Kane, Ousmane. *Muslim Modernity in Postcolonial Nigeria: A Study of the Society for the Removal of Innovation and Reinstatement of Tradition*. Leiden and Boston: Brill, 2003.

Loimeier, Roman. *Islamic Reform and Political Change in Northern Nigeria*. Evanston, Ill.: Northwestern University Press, 1997.

ZOLTAN SZOMBATHY

JAMʿĪYAT AL-SHUBBĀN AL-MUSLIMĪN.

A Pan-Islamic Egyptian political association founded in 1927 in Cairo, the Jamʿīyat al-Shubbān al-Muslimīn was apparently modeled in part on the YMCA and is often referred to as the Young Men's Muslim Association (YMMA). It was created in the midst of the social and political turmoil in Egypt following the 1919 nationalist revolution and was one of many societies and associations, of a variety of political stripes, formed in Egypt in that period. No doubt the most important of these groups was the Muslim Brotherhood (al-Ikhwān al-Muslimūn) under the leadership of Ḥasan al-Bannā. Al-Bannā played an active role in the creation of the YMMA and is said to have related the group's founding to an increasing dissatisfaction among younger Egyptian activists seeking a central role for Islamic ideals in political and social life in the face of a perceived unwillingness of the al-Azhar religious hierarchy to address contemporary issues. Despite his support for the YMMA, al-Bannā never devoted his full attention to the group, and, ironically, his assassination in 1949 took place outside the organization's headquarters.

Among those involved in the creation of the YMMA and in the formulation of its initial policies and activities were ʿAbd al-Ḥamīd Bey Saʿīd, at the time a leading nationalist and member of the Egyptian parliament; Muḥībb al-Dīn al-Khaṭīb, a bookseller and editor of *Majallat al-fatḥ*, a weekly publication promoting Islamic views that is often associated with the Salafīyah movement; and Yaḥyā Aḥmad al-Dardīrī, who served as the editor of the official publication of the YMMA, to which he was a frequent contributor. Al-Dardīrī also published a history of the organization titled *al-Ṭarīq* (The Way). Like the Muslim Brotherhood, the YMMA set out quickly to establish branches in other areas of the Middle East, chiefly in Palestine, Syria, and Iraq. Branches were established in Jerusalem, Acre, Haifa, and Jaffa by the end of 1928 and in Baghdad and Basra by 1929.

The group was established initially as a social, cultural, and religious organization seeking to appeal directly to Egypt's youth. Its headquarters was the center of literary and educational gatherings, and its members were encouraged to set a moral example for their peers. Perhaps inevitably the leaders of the YMMA joined in the many political debates of their day. In writings and lectures, al-Dardīrī, along with other spokesmen for the group, addressed grievances related to the presence of a large non-Muslim population in Egypt and its influence on Islamic life; they attacked Jewish immigration to Palestine and the activities of Zionist organizations; and they criticized the French colonization of Algeria and Morocco.

A YMMA branch was founded in 1985 in the Israeli-occupied city of Hebron to become a major charity providing various services. Catering to fifteen hundred students in four schools, the YMMA looked after orphans who paid no tuition or fees, as the organization managed to raise funds locally. Palestinian leaders, whether part of Fatah or Ḥamās, acknowledged the association's contributions to culture, education, and youth and sports activities, all in accordance with Islamic traditions. In fact, the Hebron YMMA continued earlier Egyptian practices by assisting with a full kitchen in its four schools, where local women were employed to prepare home-cooked food for students and staff. The group increased its activities during the first decade of the twenty-first century, providing sorely needed services to thousands who, in the absence of such assistance, would be deprived of basic aid. Importantly, and in addition to the financial assistance disbursed by Palestinian supporters, the group received modest aid from the European Union too.

[*See also* Bannā, Ḥasan al-; *and* Muslim Brotherhood.]

BIBLIOGRAPHY

Coury, Ralph M. *The Making of an Egyptian Arab Nationalist: The Early Years of Azzam Pasha, 1893–1936.* Reading, U.K.: Ithaca, 1998.

Høigilt, Jacob. *Raising Extremists? Islamism and Education in the Palestinian Territories.* Oslo: Fafo, 2010.

Husaini, Ishak Musa. *The Moslem Brethren: The Greatest of Modern Islamic Movements.* Translated by John F. Brown and John Racy. Beirut: Khayat's College Book Cooperative, 1956.

Mitchell, Richard P. *The Society of the Muslim Brothers.* New York: Oxford University Press, 1993.

MATTHEW S. GORDON
Updated by JOSEPH A. KÉCHICHIAN

JAMʿĪYATUL ʿULAMĀʾ-I HIND. An organization of Sunni Muslim religious scholars (*ʿulamāʾ*) of India, the Jamʿīyatul ʿUlamāʾ-i Hind (Association of the ʿUlamāʾ of India) was founded in November 1919, when numerous *ʿulamāʾ* from throughout India participated in the anti-British Khilāfat Movement. Many of the members of the Jamʿīyatul ʿUlamāʾ-i Hind were associated with the Dār al-ʿUlūm (House of Knowledge) of Deoband, in what was then the United Provinces of India (present-day Uttar Pradesh).

The leadership of the Jamʿīyatul ʿUlamāʾ-i Hind had established themselves as part of the political process in the crystallizing Indian nationalist movement of the early twentieth century, though serving more as guides than as politicians. At this time, Indians of all religious affiliations united in the anti-British Khilāfat struggle, including Mohandas Gandhi. Later, Jamʿīyatul ʿUlamāʾ-i Hind participated in the noncooperation movement with Gandhi's party, the Indian National Congress. It maintained an overall pro-Congress attitude throughout much of the struggle for India's independence, leading those South Asian Muslims who supported a united India. Jamʿīyat had opposed the movement for the creation of Pakistan as a separate state for India's Muslim minority. However, some leading members of Jamʿīyatul ʿUlamāʾ-i Hind, under the leadership of Mawlānā Shabbīr Aḥmad ʿUs̱mānī (d. 1949), seceded in 1945–1946 and established the Jamʿīyatul ʿUlamāʾ-i Islām, which supported the establishment of Pakistan. Such individuals questioned the Jamʿīyatul ʿUlamāʾ-i Hind's emphasis on a united India under the rule of a Hindu majority.

Alternate Theories of Nationalism. The main contribution of the Jamʿīyatul ʿUlamāʾ-i Hind to Indo-Muslim political thought in the twentieth century was the theory of "united nationalism" (*muttaḥidah qawmīyah*). This theory—which was elaborated in speeches and writings of the Jamʿīyat's leadership and particularly in the works of its longtime president, the Dār al-ʿUlūm Deoband graduate Ḥusayn Aḥmad Madanī (1879–1957)—served as an alternative to the "two nations theory" of the Muslim League, which formed the ideological basis of the Pakistan movement. The League argued that both a Hindu and a Muslim nation had been living in British India and that two separate homelands should emerge at the end of foreign rule owing to cultural and religious differences between the two groups. However, the Jamʿīyat's "united nationalism" theory proposed that nations can be composed of groups that differ in such areas as religion, race, language, and color, much as individuals differ from one another in appearance and character yet share a common humanity: Muslim Indians differed religiously from other Indians and belonged to a distinctly Muslim *qawm*, yet shared the same homeland and belonged to the same nation as other Indians. To prove its nationalist credentials, the Jamʿīyatul ʿUlamāʾ-i Hind backed the Indian National Congress's call to the British to "quit India" in 1942.

The Jamʿīyatul ʿUlamāʾ-i Hind accepted the idea of territorial nationalism. This was novel in Islamic thought, and the *ʿulamāʾ* devoted considerable intellectual effort to legitimizing it. The Jamʿīyat's leaders repeatedly cited the Charter of Medina (*ʿahd al-ummah*), the document that the Prophet Muḥammad purportedly issued to regulate the relationship between the Emigrants (Muhājirūn), the Helpers (Anṣār), and the Jews in Medina after the Hijrah. One of its sections states that "the Jews of [Banū] ʿAwf are one community with the believers; the Jews have their religion and the Muslims theirs." The *ʿulamāʾ* concluded from this passage that the Prophet included Muslims and non-Muslims in the same nation. The Jamʿīyat also drew on an idealized view of Muslim-dominated Mughal India to exemplify and justify the composite nationalism theory. According to them, the Mughal period knew no communalism; their rulers treated all Indians equally. Despite the foreign roots of the Muslims who established the Mughal Empire, they became an inextricable part of Indian nationhood once they settled in South Asia. Echoing the allegations of other Indian nationalists, the Jamʿīyat argued that the interreligious violence that would culminate in the horrors of partition resulted from British policies. The withdrawal of the British should thus give rise to reunification, not physical division. The Jamʿīyat's nationalism, however, always presumed separate religious and juridical administrations for Muslims and other religious communities.

In the independent and united India that the *ʿulamāʾ* envisaged and sought to create, Muslims would have significant influence, their family law and religious institutions would be maintained, and governments with a Muslim majority would be established in several provinces. On the basis of these expectations, they appealed to Muslims not to join the Muslim League, even declaring membership in it a sin. The Jamʿīyat's *ʿulamāʾ* maintained that the establishment of Pakistan would not solve the communal problem because millions of Muslims would remain in the Indian part of the subcontinent and live in an atmosphere of hate generated by partition. On the other hand, the establishment of a strong and united India, in which the Muslims would be an influential and significant minority, would benefit Muslims throughout the world.

Independence and Partition. The views of the Jamʿīyat did not prevail during the struggle for independence, and in 1947 the subcontinent was partitioned between India and Pakistan. In independent India the Jamʿīyat acquired greater political importance. In contrast with the Muslim League and other organizations that supported Pakistan's creation, the Jamʿīyat possessed impeccable credentials of opposition to partition and was a natural candidate to represent Indian Muslims. Shortly after independence, the *ʿulamāʾ* called upon Indian Muslims to declare loyalty to India and to embrace the idea of a secular state, which they conceived as neutral in matters of religion, not interfering in the affairs of the *qawm*, judicially or otherwise.

Since independence, the Jamʿīyat has supported the Indian government's policies even on some issues that were sensitive for Muslims. These included the accession of Kashmir (a Muslim-majority state included in the Indian Union following a military intervention) and Hyderabad (present-day Andhra Pradesh, a Muslim-ruled but Hindu-majority state annexed in a "police action") to the Indian Union. However, they have acted defiantly on some issues. In 1961–1962, for example, the Jamʿīyat opposed even the investigation of possible changes to Muslim personal law by the government. Consistent with their understanding of a composite nation, they would not tolerate the weakening of the Muslim autonomy that allowed them to live under a separate civil-law system. Cases such as the controversial 1986 Shah Bano divorce were judged according to Sharīʿah, not a nationally uniform civil code. The violent destruction by Hindu nationalists of the Bābarī Masjid in Ayodhya, India, in 1992 and the resulting communal riots and preponderance of Muslim victims propelled the Jamʿīyat in two different directions: some members sought to hold the central government responsible and have the mosque rebuilt, but most counseled restraint.

The Jamʿīyat's membership still remains largely restricted to the Hindi-speaking areas of northern India, principally the states of Bihar, Madhya Pradesh, and Uttar Pradesh. The organization continues to hold its annual conferences, in which the *ʿulamāʾ* a have taken stances on the central issues of the day. The Jamʿīyat had criticized the Indian government's often harsh measures to curb the mainly Islamist-oriented secessionist movement in Jammu and Kashmir. Even so, in its 2010 Kashmir Conference the general secretary of the Jamʿīyat, Maulānā Maḥmūd Madanī stated that his organization will "never allow further division of the country and community" (Madani, 2010).

The Jamʿīyatul ʿUlamāʾ-i Hind continues to struggle for the rights of Indian Muslims as its leadership perceives that India's sizeable Muslim minority lags behind the Hindu majority in terms of economic, social, and political advancement within Indian society. Nonetheless, its commitment to promote its vision of Islam based upon composite Indian nationalism appears to be undiminished.

[*See also* All-India Muslim League; India; *and* Pakistan.]

BIBLIOGRAPHY

Friedmann, Yohanan. "The Attitude of the Jamʿiyyat al-ʿUlamāʾ-i Hind to the Indian National Movement and to the Establishment of Pakistan." *Asian and African Studies* 7 (1971): 157–180.

Friedmann, Yohanan. "The Jamʿiyyat al-ʿUlamāʾ-i Hind in the Wake of Partition." *Asian and African Studies* 11 (1976): 181–211.

Hardy, Peter. *Partners in Freedom and True Muslims: The Political Thought of Some Muslim Scholars in British India, 1912–1947.* Lund, Sweden: Studentlitteratur, 1971.

Hasan, Mushirul. *Legacy of a Divided Nation: India's Muslims since Independence.* Boulder, Colo.: Westview, 1997.

Madani, Mahmud. "Jamiyat Kashmir Conference" (31 October 2010). http://www.Jamiatulama.org/kashmir_conference_delhi/press_release_delhi.html

Minault, Gail. *The Khilafat Movement: Religious Symbolism and Political Mobilization in India.* New York: Columbia University Press, 1982.

Pirbhai, M. Reza. *Reconsidering Islam in a South Asian Context.* Leiden, Netherlands: Brill, 2009.

PETER GOTTSCHALK
Updated by RIZWAN HUSSAIN

JAMʿĪYATUL ʿULAMĀʾ-I PĀKISTĀN. The Jamʿīyatul ʿUlamāʾ-i Pākistān (JUP) was formed in Karachi in 1948 at the behest of Mawlānā ʿAbdulḥamīd Badāʾunī, Sayyid Muḥammad Aḥmad Qādirī, and ʿAllāmah Aḥmad Saʿīd Kāẓimī. After the Jamʿīyatul ʿUlamāʾ-i Islām, it has been the largest *ʿulamāʾ*-led party of Pakistan. The Jamʿīyat follows the Barelwī school of Islamic thought.

The Barelwī *ʿulamāʾ* formed the Jamʿīyatul ʿUlamāʾ-i Pākistān in 1948 in opposition to the Jamʿīyatul ʿUlamāʾ-i Islām. Between 1947 and 1958, the Jamʿīyat participated in political debates over the nature of the state of Pakistan and the necessity of an Islamic constitution. It did not envisage a role for itself in national politics.

By the late 1960s, the Jamʿīyat had become embroiled in politics because of the increasing prominence of the Jamʿīyatul ʿUlamāʾ-i Islām and other Islamic parties such as the Jamāʿat-i Islāmī. The Jamʿīyat challenged the Jamāʿat-i Islāmī in the national elections of 1970, defeating their opponents in several contests and dividing the religious vote in others to the advantage of secular parties.

The Jamʿīyat was not immune to the attraction of political power; moreover, it did not wish to leave the growing religious vote to revivalist parties or to the Jamʿīyatul ʿUlamāʾ-i Islām or the Jamāʿat-i Islāmī. The decision to participate in the national elections of 1970, the first for the Jamʿīyat, was made after the Jamāʿat-i Islāmī flaunted the electoral potential of Islamic symbolism by introducing its campaign with the Yawm-i Shawkat-i Islām (Day of Islam's Glory), which was held throughout Pakistan in May 1970.

The Jamʿīyat became involved in politics in response to the challenge of the secular regime (1958–1969) of Field Marshal Muhammad Ayub Khan. The Jamʿīyat opposed Ayub's modernist agenda but was especially perturbed by the government's appropriation of religious endowments and takeover of the management of religious shrines and mosques. By the mid-1960s, under the leadership of Mawlānā Shāh Aḥmad Nūrānī, the Jamʿīyat became a vociferous actor in the political arena; it now included lay members and leaders and addressed issues of national concern. Mawlānā Shāh Aḥmad Nūrānī was elected to the National Assembly in 1970.

Following the secession of Bangladesh in 1971—which the Jamʿīyat opposed—and the rise of the populist Zulfiqar ʿAli Bhutto to power, the Jamʿīyat became more involved in politics. It coordinated its activities with other parties in the antigovernment Niẓām-i Muṣṭafā (Order of the Prophet) movement. The Jamʿīyat agitated to have the 1973 Constitution based more on the principles of Islam. It joined the Pakistan National Alliance in opposition to Zulfiqar ʿAli Bhutto in 1977.

The Jamʿīyat was the first Islamic party to distance itself from the Zia ul-Haq regime, and Zia held its leader, Mawlānā Shāh Aḥmad Nūrānī, under house arrest for a long time. The party was not, however, able to escape the increasingly strict orthodoxy that swept Pakistan in the 1980s. By then, elements within the Jamʿīyat had moved close to the doctrinal positions of Jamʿīyatul ʿUlamāʾ-i Islām and the Jamāʿat-i Islāmī. Clashes over policy decisions divided the Jamʿīyat into factions in its preparations to contest the 1988 elections, the first democratic elections since Zia's coup. One faction, led by Nūrānī, avoided joining the Islāmī Jumhūrī Ittiḥād (IJI, Islamic Democratic Alliance) and allied itself with an offshoot of the Jamʿīyatul ʿUlamāʾ-i Islām to form the Islamic Democratic Front. The other faction, under the leadership of the late Mawlānā ʿAbdussattār Niyāzī, decided to remain with the IJI.

Since the early 1990s, the Jamʿīyat has lost much of its support in Karachi, following the meteoric rise of the ethnic party Muttahida Qaumi Mahaz (MQM) in the urban centers of Sindh. In the 1970 elections the JUP had received 8.2 percent of the popular vote and won seven seats in the National Assembly. By 1990, its share had fallen to 1.47 percent and only four seats.

The rise of militant Deobandī parties in Pakistan and the Pakistani military's involvement in the emergence of the Taliban movement in Afghanistan in the mid-1990s resulted in marginalizing the Jamʿīyat in mainstream Pakistani politics. However, the Nūrānī faction continued to play a mediating role in Pakistani Islamic politics by emphasizing the commonalities among Pakistan's diverse Muslim sects. Despite continuing differences among the Deobandī parties, the Jamʿīyatul ʿUlamāʾ-i Pākistān developed a shared platform with the Deobandīs and other orthodox Sunnī groups in response to the post-9/11 Muslim world. The Jamʿīyat opposed the U.S.-led intervention in Afghanistan in October 2001 and condemned the Anglo-American invasion of Iraq in March 2003. Within Pakistan the Jamʿīyat factions remained opposed to the pro-U.S. policies of the military-dominated regime of General Pervez Musharraf. It was a key player in the creation of the Muttahida Majlis-i Amal (MMA, United Action Forum), a coalition of six Islamic political parties, and Nūrānī was elected the coalition's chief and president. The MMA succeeded in winning the 2003 provincial election in the Northwest Frontier Province (now Khyber Pakhtunkhwa) and formed the government there, and shared power in Baluchistan. These electoral victories brought a great deal of attention to Nūrānī, as coalition chief, and to his Jamʿīyat faction.

However, Nūrānī died soon thereafter, in December 2003, and was succeeded by his son, Shah Anas Noorani, who resigned as the Jamʿīyat's president in 2008. The Jamʿīyat fragmented further, with one faction being led by Mawlānā Shāh Faridul Haq and another by K. M. Azhar. The Jamʿīyat remains a skeleton organization, with no written position on matters of foreign, economic, or domestic policy, limiting its political involvement to occasional statements on religious issues. The Jamʿīyat failed to win seats in the Pakistani legislatures in the February 2008 elections, though some of its members were elected who had been nominated by other Islamic political parties. What was now called the JUP-F had often publicly declared its opposition to religious extremism as espoused by its Deobandi rivals in the Jamʿīyatul ʿUlamāʾ-i Islām. In 2009, it opposed the military-devised peace deal with the pro-Taliban Tehrike-Nifaz-e-Shariat-e-Mohammadi (TNSM) that had resulted in the imposition of the Islamic Nizam-e-Adl (System of Justice) act in Khyber Pakhtunkhwa province's Malakand region. In May 2009, it joined together with seven other Barelwī political parties to form the Sunni Ittehad Council (SIC) to fight against the growing Talibanization of Pakistan.

In recent years, major Barelwī groups in Pakistan have tried to reinvolve themselves in the country's politics, which have been increasingly Deobandī-influenced. Various JUP factions attempted in 2012 to reorient their focus to forge a multiparty, all-Pakistan Barelwī alliance. Sahibzada Abul Khair Zubair and Haji Muhammad Fazal Karim represented the two more influential factions of the JUP. Fazal Karim, the leader of JUP-F faction, served a second consecutive term as a National Assembly member, although on a Pakistan Muslim League N (PML-N) ticket.

[*See also* Barelwīs; Deobandīs; Jamāʿat-i Islāmī; *and* Pakistan.]

BIBLIOGRAPHY

Ahmad, Mumtaz. "Islam and the State: The Case of Pakistan." In *The Religious Challenge to the State*, edited by Matthew C. Moen and Lowell S. Gustafson, pp. 239–267. Philadelphia: Temple University Press, 1992.

Ahmad, Mumtaz, Dietrich Reetz, and Thomas H. Johnson. *Who Speaks for Islam: Muslim Grassroots Leaders and Popular Preachers in South Asia*. NBR Report 22. Seattle: National Bureau of Asian Research, 2010.

Binder, Leonard. *Religion and Politics in Pakistan*. Berkeley: University of California Press, 1961.

Ewing, Katherine. "The Politics of Sufism: Redefining the Saints of Pakistan." *Journal of Asian Studies* 42, no. 2 (1983): 251–268.

Metcalf, Barbara Daly. *Islamic Revival in British India: Deoband, 1860–1900*. Princeton, N.J.: Princeton University Press, 1982.

Nasr, S. V. R. "Islam, the State, and the Rise of Sectarian Militancy in Pakistan." In *Pakistan: Nationalism without a Nation?*, edited by Christophe Jaffrelot, pp. 85–114. London: Zed, 2002.

Nawab bin Mohamed Osman, Mohamed. "The *Ulama* in Pakistani Politics." *Journal of South Asian Studies*, n.s., 32, no. 2 (August 2009): 230–247.

Pirzada, Sayyid A. S. *The Politics of the Jamiat Ulema-i-Islam Pakistan, 1971–77*. Karachi: Oxford University Press, 2000.

Shafqat, Saeed. "From Official Islam to Islamism: The Rise of Dawat-ul-Irshad and Lashkar-e-Taiba." In *Pakistan: Nationalism without a Nation?*, edited by Christophe Jaffrelot, pp. 131–147. London: Zed, 2002.

KAMRAN BOKHARI
Updated by RIZWAN HUSSAIN

JERUSALEM. One of Islam's three holiest cities, Jerusalem is most widely believed to have originated as an old Canaanite settlement where David, king of Israel, built his capital and David's son Solomon built the Temple. Considering the importance of Jerusalem to millions of Muslims, Jews, and Christians, it is extraordinary that the city is not particularly ancient when compared to the venerable cities of Damascus and Jericho. The archaeologist Kathleen Kenyon discovered some of the earliest evidence of settlement on the Ophel, a hill near the Gihon Spring, dating to 1800 BCE, many millennia after the beginning of human settlement in the Levant. Jerusalem, the English rendition of this pre-Hebraic Canaanite word of possible Jebusite origin, is not mentioned by name in the Qurʾān. Generally called simply "the Holy" (al-Quds) by Muslims, the Islamic tradition unanimously sees a reference to it in the allusion in *sūrah* 17:1 in which the Prophet Muḥammad was borne by night from Mecca to "the Distant Shrine" (al-Masjid al-Aqṣā). The Prophet moved the *qiblah*, or direction of prayer, from Jerusalem to Mecca in 623 CE. Al-Quds also figures prominently in the *ḥadīth* literature, in which it is also referred to by the terms "the Sacred House" (Bayt al-Maqdis) and "the Holy Land" (al-Arḍ al-Muqaddasah). Muslim armies took Jerusalem without resistance in 635 CE and immediately set to refurbishing its chief holy place, the neglected Temple Mount of the "noble sanctuary" (al-Ḥaram al-Sharīf). They first built at its southern end their congregational mosque (al-Aqṣā) and, by 692, had completed at its center the splendid shrine called the Dome of the Rock, revered as both the terminus of the Night Journey and the biblical site of Abraham's sacrifice and Solomon's Temple. Jerusalem and surrounding areas would remain in Muslim hands almost continuously until its loss by the Ottomans during World War I.

Excavations of extensive buildings south of the Ḥaram suggest that the Umayyad Muslim rulers may have had ambitious political plans to make Jerusalem their political center, which they apparently aborted when Damascus became their new capital. It was the Umayyad caliph ʿAbd al-Malik who constructed the Dome of the Rock. During the Crusades Christians and Jews (Jerusalem was filled with Christians and Christian holy places, and the Jews had been permitted by the Muslims to return to the city for the first time since their ban by the Romans in 135 CE) may have outnumbered Muslims. The Egyptian ruler al-Ḥakīm bi-Amr Allāh had the Christians' Church of the Holy Sepulchre burned down in 1009, one of the events that provoked the Europeans' invasion of Palestine and their occupation of Jerusalem in 1099. According to their own chronicles, the Crusaders killed a large proportion of Jerusalem's Jewish, Christian, and Muslim population, famously wading in blood up to their knees after their successful siege. The Latin Christian interregnum in Jerusalem lasted a scant century before Ṣalāḥ al-Dīn (Saladin) drove them out in 1187, long enough, however, for the Crusaders to convert the Dome of the Rock into a church and al-Aqṣā into the headquarters of the Knights Templar.

Under Ṣalāḥ al-Dīn, the Muslim holy places were restored to their original use, and it was he, aided by popular preachers, who raised Muslim appreciation of what was, after Mecca and Medina, the third holiest city in Islam. The Frankish Crusade appears to have taken the Muslims by surprise, but thereafter they were well aware of European intentions toward Jerusalem. In the centuries after the Crusades, the level of hostility between the Muslims and the indigenous Christian population, and particularly the European pilgrims who continued to visit the city (and whose accounts graphically document life there), rose appreciably. Ṣalāḥ al-Dīn also wished to make Jerusalem a safely Sunnī city; the Shīʿah were regarded as far more subversive enemies than the Christians. His goal was realized under the Mamlūks, his family's successors in Egypt and Palestine. From their accession in 1250 they invested heavily in Jerusalem; many of the Sunnī colleges (*madrasahs*) and Ṣūfī lodges (*khānqāhs*) they constructed around the northern and western margins of the Ḥaram still retain some of their expensive elegance, although they are now empty of the students and Ṣūfīs who used to inhabit them.

The Ottomans, who inherited the city in 1517 from the Mamlūks, continued their predecessors' generous support of the holy city. The walls that still set off the "Old City" today were built by the Ottomans, uselessly, perhaps, because the greatest threat to the city came from abroad, not in the form of armed warriors. The might of the Ottomans was tested and broken in the Balkans during the seventeenth to nineteenth centuries; consequently, their control of their own affairs in their own dominions was progressively eroded. Even before the Crusades, the Christians of Jerusalem, the Latins, Greeks, and Armenians, had learned the benefit of invoking the protection of the more powerful of their coreligionists; somewhat later, the European powers learned what benefits might accrue to them from manipulating those invocations.

The disintegration of Ottoman sovereignty was nowhere more evident than in Palestine and Jerusalem in the nineteenth century. The city began to fill up with European consulates, European missionaries, and, finally, European archaeological missions, many of them instruments of national policy and all of them far beyond the reach of the Ottoman authorities in what was by then an exceedingly poor city. Even the Jews, always the least considerable and most hapless of Jerusalem's medieval population, discovered that they, too, had powerful friends and benefactors in Europe. With the aid of those benefactors, the Montefiores and Rothschilds chief among them, their numbers began to spiral upward. By 1900, there were 35,000 Jews out of a total population of 55,000 (Muslims and Christians numbering 10,000 each).

Ottoman Turkey joined Germany in its unsuccessful war against the Allies in 1914; in December 1917 Jerusalem fell, without damage, to General Edmund Allenby and a British Expeditionary Army. It rested under the uneasy control of British governors during the entire Mandate period (1922–1948). When the British withdrew in 1948, the Jordanians hastened to occupy the Old City, while members of the United Nations recommended internationalization. It remained a part of Jordan until the 1967 war, when the Israelis took it after fierce fighting. The whole city has since been integrated into the State of Israel and proclaimed its capital, though this has been declared in violation of international law by UN Resolution 478. There is a stark political, religious, and cultural division between East Jerusalem, which is mainly Palestinian, and West Jerusalem, the primarily Jewish city. Palestinians still claim East Jerusalem, the area of the city under Jordanian control until 1967, as their capital. In June 1967, the Israeli minister of defense, Moshe Dayan, acknowledged the entire al-Ḥaram al-Sharīf to be the possession of the Muslims. The policy has been repeatedly rendered meaningless. In September 2000, Israeli prime minister Ariel Sharon visited the Temple Mount with a sizable police escort and reportedly asserted it and the Islamic holy sites thereafter and permanently to be in Israeli control, sparking the Second Intifada. The building of the Israeli West Bank barrier wall since 2002 has also complicated questions of Palestinian rights to Jerusalem.

The status of Jerusalem and the Temple Mount and questions regarding who should exercise sovereignty over portions of each continue to be contested issues between Israeli and Palestinian authorities. Indeed, as the firestorm surrounding the publication of Nadia Abu El-Haj's *Facts on the Ground* attests, this dispute can be seen especially in the fields of archaeology and historical research as both groups claim historic rights to specific parts of the city. It is repeatedly invoked as one of the main issues on which the acceptability of a peace agreement hinges, and has figured prominently in peace talks including the Middle East Peace Summit at Camp David of July 2000 and the Taba Summit in January 2001. Various suggestions were proposed but not adopted, including a proposition that the city serve as capital to two states and Arab and Israeli neighborhoods be given to the jurisdiction of their respective communal authorities.

[*See also* Arab-Israeli Conflict; *and* Israel.]

BIBLIOGRAPHY

Abu El Haj, Nadia. *Facts on the Ground: Archaeological Practice and Territorial Self-Fashioning in Israeli Society*. Chicago: University of Chicago Press, 2001.

Armstrong, Karen. *Jerusalem: One City, Three Faiths*. New York: A. A. Knopf, 1996.

Busse, Heribert. "The Sanctity of Jerusalem in Islam." *Judaism* 17 (1968): 441–468.

Goitein, S. D. "Al-Ḳuds, Part A: History." In *Encyclopaedia of Islam*, new ed., vol. 5. Edited by H. A. R. Gibb, pp. 322–339. Leiden, Netherlands: E. J. Brill, 1986.

Grabar, Oleg. *The Dome of the Rock*. Cambridge, Mass.: Belknap Press of Harvard University Press, 2006.

Grabar, Oleg. "Al-Ḳuds, Part B: The Monuments." In *Encyclopaedia of Islam*, new ed., vol. 5. Edited by H. A. R. Gibb, pp. 339–344. Leiden, Netherlands: E. J. Brill, 1986.

Johns, Jeremy, ed. *Bayt al Maqdis*. Part 2, *Jerusalem and Early Islam*. Oxford: Oxford University Press, 1999.

Peters, F. E. *The Distant Shrine: The Islamic Centuries in Jerusalem*. New York: AMS, 1993.

Silberman, Neil Asher. *Digging for God and Country: Exploration, Archeology, and the Secret Struggle for the Holy Land, 1799–1917*. New York: A. A. Knopf, 1982.

F. E. Peters
Updated by Nada Unus
and Allen Fromherz

JIHĀD. Connoting an endeavor toward a praiseworthy aim, the Arabic word *jihād* bears many shades of meaning in the Islamic context. It may express a struggle against one's evil inclinations or an exertion for the sake of Islam and the *ummah* (Islamic community), for example, in trying to convert unbelievers or working for the moral betterment of Islamic society ("*jihād* of the tongue" and "*jihād* of the pen"). In books on Islamic law and commonly in the Qurʾān, the word means an armed struggle against the unbelievers. Sometimes the "*jihād* of the sword" is called "the lesser *jihād*," in opposition to the peaceful forms named "the greater *jihād*." Often used today without religious connotation, its meaning is roughly equivalent to the English word "crusade" (e.g., "a crusade against drugs"). Either "Islamic" or "holy" is currently added to the word when it is used in a religious context (e.g., *al-jihād al-Islāmī* or *al-jihād al-muqaddas*).

Origin. The concept of *jihād* goes back to the wars fought by the Prophet Muḥammad and their written reflection in the Qurʾān. The concept was influenced by the ideas on war prevailing among the pre-Islamic tribes of northern Arabia, among whom war was the normal state, unless a truce had been concluded. War between tribes was regarded as lawful, especially if the war was a response to aggression. Ideas of chivalry forbade warriors from killing noncombatants, especially children, women, and old people. These rules were incorporated into the doctrine of *jihād* in the eighth and ninth centuries.

The Qurʾān frequently mentions *jihād* and fighting (*qitāl*) against unbelievers. *Sūrah* 22:40 ("Leave is given to those who fight because they were wronged—surely God is able to help them—who were expelled from their habitations without right, except that they say 'Our Lord is God'"), revealed not long after the *hijrah*, is traditionally considered to be the first verse dealing with the fighting of unbelievers. Many verses exhort the believers to take part in the fighting "with their goods and lives" (*bi-amwālihim wa-anfusihim*), promise reward to those who are killed in *jihād* (3:157–158, 169–172), and threaten with severe punishments in the hereafter those who do not fight (9:81–82, 48:16). Other verses deal with practical matters such as exemption from military service (9:91, 48:17), fighting during the holy months (2:217) and in the holy territory of Mecca (2:191), the fate of prisoners of war (47:4), safe conduct (9:6), and truce (8:61).

It is not clear whether the Qurʾān allows Muslims to fight unbelievers only as a defense against aggression or under all circumstances. In support of the first view, a number of verses can be quoted that expressly justify fighting on the strength of aggression or perfidy on the part of the unbelievers: "Fight in the way of God with those who fight you, but aggress not: God loves not the aggressors" (2:190), and "If they break their oaths after their covenant and thrust at your religion, then fight the leaders of unbelief" (9:13). Other verses seem to order the Muslims to fight the unbelievers unconditionally: "Then, when the sacred months are drawn away, slay the idolaters wherever you find them, and take them, and confine them, and lie in wait for them at every place of ambush" (9:5), and "Fight those who believe not in God and the Last Day and do not forbid what God and His Messenger have forbidden—such men as practice not the religion of truth, being of those who have been given the Book—until they pay the tribute out of hand and have been humbled" (9:29). Even in the case of these verses, however, the context could be used to infer that they also refer to cases of self-defense. Classical interpretation of the Qurʾān, however, did not go in this direction. It regarded the "sword verses," with the unconditional command to fight the unbelievers, as having abrogated all previous verses concerning intercourse with non-Muslims. This idea is connected with the pre-Islamic concept that war between tribes was allowed unless there existed a truce between them, the Islamic *ummah* being considered to have taken the place of a tribe.

The first comprehensive treatise on the law of *jihād* was written by ʿAbd al-Raḥmān al-Awzāʿī (d. 774) and Muḥammad ibn al-Ḥasan al-Shaybānī (d. 804). The legal doctrine of *jihād* grew out of debates and discussions that had continued since the Prophet's death. This period in which the doctrine of *jihād* was formulated coincided with the period of the great Muslim conquests, in which the conquerors were exposed to the cultures of the conquered, and the doctrine of *jihād* may have been influenced by Byzantine thought, in which the idea of religious war and related notions were very much alive. It is, however, difficult to identify these influences; if there are similarities, they may result from parallel developments rather than from borrowing.

Classical Doctrine. The doctrine of *jihād* as expounded in the works on Islamic law developed from Qurʾānic prescriptions and the example of the Prophet and the first caliphs, as laid down in the *ḥadīth* (traditions). The crux of the doctrine is the existence of a unified Islamic state, ruling the entire *ummah*. It is the duty of the *ummah* to expand the territory of this state in order to bring as many people as possible under its rule. The ultimate aim is to bring the whole earth under the sway of Islam and to extirpate unbelief: "Fight them until there is no persecution [or "seduction"] and the religion is God's entirely" (2:192 and 8:39). Expansionist *jihād* is a collective duty (*farḍ al-kifāyah*), which is fulfilled if a sufficient number of people take part in it. If this is not the case, the whole *ummah* is sinning. Expansionist *jihād* presupposes the presence of a legitimate caliph to organize the struggle. After the conquests had ended, the legal specialists ruled that the caliph must raid enemy territory at least once a year in order to keep alive the idea of *jihād*.

Sometimes *jihād* becomes an individual duty (*farḍ al-ʿayn*), as when the caliph appoints certain persons to participate in a raiding expedition (*ghazāh*) or when someone takes an oath to fight the unbelievers. Moreover, *jihād* becomes obligatory for all free men capable of fighting in a certain region if this region is attacked by the enemy; in this case, *jihād* is defensive.

Sunnī and Shīʿī theories of *jihād* are similar in all respects but one crucial one: Twelver Shīʿah hold that *jihād* can only be waged under the leadership of the rightful imam. After the occultation of the last (twelfth) imam in 873 CE, theoretically no lawful expansionist *jihād* could be fought, but because defense remains obligatory and the *ʿulamāʾ* (religious scholars) are often regarded as the representatives of the Hidden Imām, several wars between Iran and Russia in the nineteenth century have been called *jihād*.

War against unbelievers may not be mounted without summoning them to Islam or submission before the attack. A *ḥadīth* lays down the precise contents of the summons:

> Whenever the Prophet appointed a commander to an army or an expedition, he would say: "When you meet your heathen enemies, summon them to three things. Accept whatsoever they agree to and refrain then from fighting them. Summon them to become Muslims. If they agree, accept their conversion. In that case summon them to move from their territory to the Abode of the Emigrants [i.e., Medina]. If they refuse that, let them know that then they are like the Muslim Bedouins and that they share only in the booty, when they fight together with the other Muslims. If they refuse conversion, then ask them to pay poll tax. If they agree, accept their submission. But if they refuse, then ask God for assistance and fight them." (*Ṣaḥīḥ Muslim*)

This *ḥadīth* also neatly sums up the aims of fighting unbelievers: conversion or submission. In the latter case, the enemies are entitled to keep their religion and practice it, against payment of a poll tax (*jizyah*); see *sūrah* 9:29, quoted above. Although the Qurʾān limits this option to the People of the Book, that is, Christians and Jews, it was in practice extended to other religions, such as the Zoroastrians (Majūs) and even eventually to adherents to nonmonotheistic faiths such as Hinduism.

Whenever the caliph deems it in the interest of the *ummah*, he may conclude a truce with the enemy, as the Prophet did with the Meccans at al-Ḥudaybīyah. According to some schools of law, a truce must be concluded for a specified period of time, no longer than ten years. Others hold that this is not necessary if the caliph stipulates that he may resume war whenever he wishes. The underlying idea is that the notion of *jihād* must not fall into oblivion.

Function. The most important function of the doctrine of *jihād* is to motivate Muslims to take part in wars against unbelievers in fulfillment of their religious duty. This motivation is strengthened by the idea that martyrs (*shāhids*) who die in battle will go directly to Paradise. When wars were fought against unbelievers, religious texts circulated replete with Qurʾānic verses and *ḥadīths* extolling the merits of *jihād* and vividly describing the reward waiting in the hereafter for the slain.

Another function was to enhance the legitimation of a ruler or movement. After 750 CE, the political unity of the *ummah* was lost and has never been restored. One way to acquire greater legitimacy was to wage *jihād* against unbelievers, one of the main tasks of the lawful caliph. A related function was to validate the struggle against others who were ostensibly Muslims. When two Muslim states were at war with one another, muftis on one side would usually find cause to label those on the other as rebels or heretics. Moreover, throughout Islamic history, but especially in the eighteenth and nineteenth centuries, radical movements striving for the establishment of a purely Islamic society proclaimed *jihād* against their opponents, both Muslims and non-Muslims. To justify the struggle against their Muslim adversaries, they branded them as unbelievers for their failure to follow and enforce the strict rules of Islam.

A final function of the *jihād* doctrine was to provide a set of rules governing warfare, including the initiation, conduct, and termination of war and the treatment of combatants, noncombatants, and prisoners of war during and after conflict.

Jihād in History. Although the legal doctrine had not yet been fixed in all its details, the notion of *jihād* played a crucial role as a motivating force during the wars of conquest in the first century of Islam. It provided a unifying ideology that transcended tribal factionalism. After the initial conquests, the idea of *jihād* was kept alive by raiding enemy territory, but this did not result in substantial territorial gains. The main purpose of *jihād* was the defense of Muslim lands. This became especially important during the Crusades (eleventh to thirteenth centuries CE), when many works were written exhorting the Muslims to take up *jihād* against the "Franks" and extolling the sacredness of Jerusalem. From the fourteenth century the Ottoman sultans expanded their territory in northwestern Anatolia at the expense of the Byzantine Empire, which lost its capital, Constantinople, in 1453. Some Western historians have argued that the Ottoman state owed its existence to the struggle against the unbelievers. Although this is now disputed, the importance of *jihād* in Ottoman history is beyond doubt. Ottoman sultans meticulously observed the rules of *jihād* in their foreign policies. The last instance was the call for *jihād* issued by the Ottoman government when it entered World War I in 1914.

Jihāds were prominent in the growth of other regions of the Muslim world, most especially in

India under Awrangzīb (1658–1707) and in western Africa under Shehu Usuman Dan Fodio (1804–1812). Most of the anticolonialist movements of the nineteenth and early twentieth century in Africa, India, and the Caucasus employed the language of *jihād* against the encroaching infidel. It should be noted, however, that a number of these *jihād*s were equally of a purificationist bent (such as that of Dan Fodio in northern Nigeria) and did not attack non-Muslims at all. Some scholars note the role of these *jihād*s as protonationalist movements, such as that of Muḥammad ʿAbd Allāh Ḥasan in Sudan (the "Mad Mullah," 1899–1920).

Changing Modern Interpretations. The colonial experience affected the outlook of some Muslim intellectuals on *jihād*. Some argued that in view of the military superiority of the colonizer, *jihād*, on the strength of *sūrah* 2:195—"and cast not yourselves by your own hands into destruction"—was no longer obligatory. Others, however, elaborated new interpretations of the doctrine of *jihād*.

The first to do so was the Indian Muslim thinker Sayyid Aḥmad Khān (1817–1898). After the Mutiny of 1857 the British began favoring the Hindus in the army and in government service. Sayyid Aḥmad Khān wanted to show that Islam did not forbid cooperation with the British colonial government; in this he was motivated by his desire to safeguard employment for the young Muslims from the middle and upper classes. On the basis of a new reading of the Qurʾān, he asserted that *jihād* was obligatory for Muslims only in the case of "positive oppression or obstruction in the exercise of their faith . . . impair[ing] the foundation of some of the pillars of Islam" (Ahmad Khan, 1872, pp. xviii–xix). Because the British did not, in his opinion, interfere with the practice of Islam, *jihād* against them was prohibited.

Middle Eastern Muslim reformers like Muḥammad ʿAbduh (1849–1905) and Muḥammad Rashīd Riḍā (1865–1935) did not go as far as Sayyid Aḥmad Khān. On the strength of those Qurʾānic verses that make fighting against unbelievers conditional upon their aggression or perfidy, they argued that peaceful coexistence is the normal state between Islamic and non-Islamic lands and that only defensive *jihād* is permitted. This view, however, left open the possibility of *jihād* against colonial oppression, as the colonial enterprise was clearly an attack on the territory of Islam. Following this reasoning, *jihād* has recently been presented as a form of Muslim international law, and *jihād* has been equated with just war. Those who have elaborated this theory point out that Muḥammad al-Shaybānī had formulated a doctrine of international law long before Hugo Grotius (d. 1645).

Twenty-first-century thinking about *jihād*, however, offers a wider spectrum of views. Apart from the conservatives, who adhere to the classical Islamic legal interpretation, the ideologues of the radical Islamic opposition call for *jihād* as a means to spread their brand of Islam. Some of these radical groups call for the use of violence to defeat the established governments. They are faced, however, with a serious doctrinal problem as they preach an armed revolution against Muslim rulers: Islamic law permits revolt only in rare circumstances. One of these is when a ruler abandons his belief; as the apostate deserves capital punishment, fighting against him is permitted. Throughout Islamic history, governments and opposition movements have declared their Muslim adversaries to be heretics or unbelievers (*takfīr*, declaring someone to be a *kāfir*, unbeliever) in order to justify their struggle against them. This line of reasoning is used by modern radical Islamic groups to legitimate their use of arms against rulers who are to all appearances Muslims. In modern times these views were first propagated by fundamentalists like Sayyid Quṭb (d. 1966) and Abū al-Aʿlā Mawdūdī (d. 1979).

The most eloquent and elaborate statement of this view can be found in a pamphlet published by the *Jihād* Organization, whose members assassinated President Anwar el-Sadat of Egypt in 1981. The pamphlet is called *al-Farīḍah al-ghā'ibah* (The Absent Duty), referring to the duty to wage *jihād*, which, according to the author, Muḥammad ʿAbd al-Salām Faraj, is no longer fulfilled. The author, borrowing his arguments from two *fatwas* issued by the jurist Ibn Taymīyah (1263–1328), argues that because the Egyptian government fails to implement Sharīʿah and is therefore apostate, it is an individual duty of Muslims to attack the government in order to liberate the country from the regime of "unbelievers."

The Globalization of Jihād. When the Soviet Union occupied Afghanistan, resistance was offered not only by local militants but also by volunteers from elsewhere in the Muslim world, who were motivated by *jihād*. When the Soviet Union was defeated in 1989 and withdrew its troops, many of the international *mujāhidūn* (*jihād* fighters) remained. One of their organizations was al-Qaʿida, led by the Saudi national Osama Bin Laden. After the Gulf War of 1991 and the stationing of American troops on Saudi territory, Bin Laden became convinced that the United States was the main enemy of Muslims. In 1996 he issued a twenty-three-page declaration of war against the United States in which he exhorted all Muslims to support the Muslims struggling in Palestine and Saudi Arabia and help them defeat the enemies who occupy Islamic holy places. This was followed in 1998 by a *fatwa* signed by him and four other radical Muslim leaders. Its conclusions were more specific: "Killing the Americans and their allies—civilians and military—is an individual duty for every Muslim who is capable of it and in every country in which it is possible to do so. This will continue until al-Aqṣā Mosque and the Holy Mosque in Mecca have been liberated from their grip, and their armies have moved out of all the lands of Islam, being defeated and unable to threaten any Muslim." This *fatwa* heralded the bombings of the American embassies in Dar es Salaam and Nairobi in August 1998 and the attacks on the World Trade Center and the Pentagon on 11 September 2001.

Thus *jihād* became globalized: it was no longer conceived as a local struggle against an enemy occupying Muslim lands, but as a global struggle conducted by *mujāhidūn* without a well-defined regional basis and hitting the enemy wherever possible, attacking civilians and soldiers alike. Many Muslims protested the 9/11 attacks, especially because these were aimed at civilians, but staunch defenders of Bin Laden issued *fatwas* declaring the attacks lawful under Sharīʿah. They made two arguments; the first was that the Prophet Muḥammad during his lifetime had attacked towns at night or with catapults. Because it would be impossible to distinguish between combatants and noncombatants during such attacks, the Prophet must have condoned incidental harm to noncombatants. And second, that there are no innocent Americans, because the United States is a democracy and the people of the United States are liable for the acts of the government they have chosen. These arguments, however, were not widely accepted by Muslims.

In the early twenty-first century the most popular methodology of *jihād* of those most vocally claiming to be waging it is akin to traditional guerrilla methods, and involves pitting a Muslim underdog population under occupation (or perceived to be under occupation) against a superior foe utilizing traditional *jihād* slogans and employing the example of the Prophet Muḥammad's battles. This model has been adopted by al-Qaʿida, the Taliban, and their supporters in Afghanistan and Iraq (against the United States); both Ḥamās and Ḥizbullāh (against Israel); Filipino radicals (in the southern Philippines); and Kashmiri radicals (against India).

In its ideal form it involves not only the creation of a fighting force but an entire countersociety, complete with social welfare programs, in which the core doctrines of radical Islam are spread through the educational system rather than through outright coercive methods. It was owing to the creation of this infrastructure that both Ḥamās and Ḥizbullāh were able to achieve political power. Radicals who have been unable to create this infrastructure are open to the accusation that they are promoting nihilistic violence and ultimately alienate the Muslim populations upon which they depend.

[*See also* ʿAbduh, Muḥammad; Aḥmad Khān, Sayyid; Bin Laden, Osama; Mawdūdī, Sayyid Abū al-Aʿlā; Quṭb, Sayyid; *and* Rashīd Riḍā, Muḥammad.]

BIBLIOGRAPHY

Ahmad Khan, Syed. *Review of Dr. Hunter's "Indian Musalmans: Are They Bound in Conscience to Rebel against the Queen?"* Benares, India: Medical Hall Press, 1872.

Bonner, Michael. *Jihad in Islamic History: Doctrines and Practices*. Princeton, N.J.: Princeton University Press, 2006.

Bonney, Richard. *Jihad: From Qu'ran to Bin Laden*. Basingstoke, U.K.: Palgrave Macmillan, 2004.

Cook, David. *Martyrdom in Islam*. Cambridge, U.K.: Cambridge University Press, 2007.

Firestone, Reuven. *Jihad: The Origin of Holy War in Islam*. New York: Oxford University Press, 1999.

Gerges, Fawaz A. *The Far Enemy: Why Jihad Went Global*. Cambridge, U.K.: Cambridge University Press, 2005.

Ghunaimi, Mohammad Talaat al-. *The Muslim Conception of International Law and the Western Approach*. The Hague: Martinus Nijhoff, 1968.

Hamidullah, Muhammad. *Muslim Conduct of State*. 6th ed. Lahore, Pakistan: Muhammad Ashraf, 1973.

Kelsay, John, and James Turner Johnson, eds. *Just War and Jihad: Historical and Theoretical Perspectives on War and Peace in Western and Islamic Traditions*. New York: Greenwood, 1991.

Kepel, Gilles. *Jihad: The Trail of Political Islam*. Translated by Anthony F. Roberts. 4th ed. London: I. B. Tauris, 2006. A detailed discussion of late twentieth and early twenty-first-century *jihād* movements.

Khadduri, Majid. *War and Peace in the Law of Islam*. Baltimore: Johns Hopkins University Press, 1955. Reliable survey of the classical doctrine of *jihād*.

Kohlberg, Etan, "The Development of the Imami Shiʿi Doctrine of Jihâd." *Zeitschrift der Deutschen Morgenländischen Gesellschaft* 126 (1976): 64–86.

Peters, Rudolph. *Islam and Colonialism: The Doctrine of Jihad in Modern History*. The Hague: Mouton, 1979.

Peters, Rudolph. *Jihad in Classical and Modern Islam: A Reader*. 2d ed. Princeton, N.J.: Markus Wiener, 2005.

Shaybānī, Muḥammad ibn al-Ḥasan. *The Islamic Law of Nations: Shaybānī's "Siyar."* Translated by Majid Khadduri. Baltimore: Johns Hopkins University Press, 1966. Translation of one of the earliest works on *jihād*.

RUDOLPH PETERS
and DAVID COOK

JIHĀD GROUPS.

During the 1990s and particularly after the 11 September 2001 attacks in the United States, *jihād* organizations gained notoriety as fundamental actors in contemporary world affairs as major agents of disruption, threat, and instability at the local as well as global levels. Driven by sensationalism, most of these groups drew attention from the media, decision makers, and academics alike. In the perception of many Westerners, several became the ultimate, new post–Cold War enemies that jeopardized the livelihoods and values of many—whether in Europe and North America or in the Muslim world. The complexity of these groups as well as their diversities were not sufficiently acknowledged, and one group, al-Qaʿida, received disproportionate attention.

Jihād organizations can be defined in a broad way as representative of Islamist groups that consider violence a necessary means of political action. One should keep in mind that such violence is not always targeted at civilians and cannot always be seen as random, indiscriminate, or blind, because such acts often have a specific agenda that cannot be ignored. Thus, automatically equating *jihād* with terrorism, which is by definition indiscriminate violence, or even with a kind of nihilism, is largely incorrect. Indeed, however similar their names might be, *jihād* organizations are diverse; they have different objectives, multiple strategies, and various targets, some of which can be considered legitimate ways of resisting oppression. Furthermore, in certain cases, the war they wage should not be considered necessarily unjust simply because it is legitimized through a religious vocabulary. The growing role and number of such organizations does not say as much about Islam, as is often assumed, as it does about attempts to exploit Islam politically and to fill an ideological vacuum.

Discourse. Upon their emergence in the 1970s as new actors, prominent *jihād* organizations legitimized themselves and their actions through Islamic discourses, mainly because the Islamic treatise became an alternative to the founding myths of the postindependence nationalist governments that were present in many parts of the developing world. Such discourse proved effective in mobilizing segments of the population and, from its main (although not exclusive) cradle in the Arab world and particularly Egypt around Sayyid Quṭb (executed in 1966) and his book *Maʿālim fī al-ṭarīq* (Milestones), as well as a reinterpretation of Ibn Taymīyah's fourteenth-century teachings on *jihād*, spread and adapted itself elsewhere. More specifically, the repression of the Muslim Brotherhood by various governments in Egypt, Syria, Iraq, and several other countries meant that Islamists were not able to confront them efficiently through peaceful means. Moreover, and in the aftermath of the humiliating 1967 Arab defeat by Israel, certain cells became progressively more radical.

The word *jihād* is often translated in the West as "holy war," although the original Islamic concept does not have an exclusively military connotation. *Jihād* in Arabic simply means "struggle" or "effort," and it is a religious duty imposed on Muslims, to spread Islam by waging war four different ways: by the heart, the tongue, the hand, and the sword. In Islamic history and classical jurisprudence, the struggle (including within oneself) on behalf of the cause of Islam, and imposes war with other nations only as a defensive measure when the faith is in direct danger. Nevertheless, in classical and modern times, Islamic governments, or more accurately governments that base their legitimacy on Islamic rationalization, repeatedly used the word to describe all combat efforts of their armies. This restrictive and partial representation of *jihād* as holy war became dominant.

Global versus National Organizations. In the turbulent politics of contemporary affairs throughout the Muslim World in the early twenty-first century, radical opposition groups fought with the same weapons that have been used against them by their own governments. Over the years, *jihād* organizations emerged with two types of ideals: national and global. The first, exemplified by groups or parties such as the Palestinian Ḥamās, engaged in national level struggles against foreign occupation or local rulers considered to be illegitimate. The other, among which al-Qaʿida was the most significant incarnation, fought at a global level against the "far enemies," whether the Americans, Russians, French, Israelis, or British, accused of being responsible for modern-day oppression and corruption. Just as the governments of Muslim countries exploited Islam for purely political purposes, radical opposition groups espoused Islam as an ideology to attribute their violent deeds to Islamic requirements, claiming that resorting to violence and defending oneself was a religious obligation. While many groups in the Middle East regularly used the phrase "Islamic Jihād" as the name for various organizations, it was important to note that those organizations were not necessarily in cooperation with one another. The same was true within al-Qaʿida, which emerged as a label that largely autonomous groups adopted without necessarily taking their orders from its leaders.

Local social and political dynamics appeared to be the main determinants of the means and ends of the diverse *jihād* organizations and of their levels of social and political inclusion, and the level of repression (whether local or international) also shaped operational strategies. Torture, deprivation, imprisonment, domination, and humiliation were likely to increase the violence of these groups, while participation and inclusion had opposite effects.

Among the "national" *jihād* organizations, the most notorious were probably the Palestinian Ḥamās, the Lebanese Ḥizbullāh, and the Algerian Groupe Islamique Armée (GIA). Others, such as the Kashmiri Lashkar-i-Tayyiba, the Libyan Islamic Fighting Group, or the Islamic Movement of Uzbekistan, drew less media attention but were nevertheless active.

Jihād Organizations in the Middle East. Throughout the 1950s and up until the 1980s, Arab leftist and nationalist groups were the most prominent and active in using the term *jihād*. In the Middle East, the term *jihād* later reemerged within groups such as the Organization of the Islamic Jihād, or the Detachment of the Islamic Jihād. This organization was believed to be tied to the faction within Fatah that was under the control of the late Palestine Liberation Organization leader Khalīl Ibrāhīm al-Wazīr whose nom de guerre was Abū Jihād. The Ḥarakāt al-Jihād al-Islāmī fī Filasṭīn (Palestinian Islamic Jihād Movement), simply known as the Palestinian Islamic Jihad (PIJ), emerged in 1979 after Fatḥī Shiqāqī and ʿAbd al-Azīz ʿAwdah, affiliated with the Egyptian Muslim Brotherhood conducted various operations against Israel.

Created in 1987 by Aḥmad Yāsīn, Ḥamās was the Palestinian branch of the Muslim Brotherhood, although the organization gained autonomy since 2000. Owing to its numerous activities in the social field, it quickly emerged as a popular grassroots movement that claimed responsibility for many attacks against soldiers as well as Israeli civilians, particularly during the mid-1990s, when it violently opposed the 1993 Oslo Accords between Israel and Fatah. Following the assassination of Aḥmad Yāsīn in March 2004 by an Israeli missile, Ḥamās changed its strategy, participated in various elections, and tried to emerge as a respectable movement. It won the January 2006 general elections, when Ismail Haniyeh (b. 1963) was named prime minister of Palestine. Tensions with Fatah leaders inevitably led to a severe internal crisis, though Ḥamās accepted a cease-fire in June 2008. Still, when Israel killed seven Ḥamās soldiers near a tunnel dug under the so-called border security fence on the Egyptian-Palestinian frontier, the conflict restarted. A barrage of Ḥamās rockets on Israeli towns led to a late December 2008 retaliation, when Israel opened a month-long campaign on the Gaza Strip.

The Lebanese Shīʿī Ḥizbullāh, despite its strong institutional links to the Islamic Republic of Iran, was also a "nationalist" *jihād* organization. It was created in 1982 to confront the Israeli occupation of southern Lebanon. During the Lebanese civil war, it participated in different attacks and took foreign hostages. Like Ḥamās, Ḥizbullāh was active in charity organizations and, building on its various political successes, tried to normalize its position as a prominent political party in Lebanon, actively participating in elections and seeking to become a legitimate international actor.

From the end of the 1970s onward, the internal doctrinal evolutions inside the various Egyptian *jihād* organizations influenced many of the contemporary violent Islamist groups, characterized by their global outreach as well as their refusals to compromise. The assassination of Egyptian president Anwar el-Sadat in October 1981 by Khālid al-Islambūlī, who had known links to the organization al-Jihād headed by Muḥammad ʿAbd al-Salām Faraj, was indeed a radical way of protesting against the government, highlighting its incapacity to implement and respect Islamic law. In that sense, this assassination appeared to be an example of the "national" type of *jihād* fighting against a "corrupt" ruler.

Emergence of Transnational Jihād Organizations. At times, foreign interventions created misunderstandings and tension between groups because local combatants did not always share the same objectives as the transnational *jihādīs*. Consequently, certain organizations such as Ḥamās rejected the trend, preferring to fight on narrower terms. In the early 1990s, Muqbil al-Wādiʿī's Salafī groups in Yemen refused Osama Bin Laden's proposal to help them wage war against the socialists of the former South Yemen and criticized many of the outcomes of the *jihād* in Afghanistan. The idea of a globalized *jihād* was not as appealing to everyone.

In the 1990s, al-Qaʿida managed to merge various groups, including the Egyptian Islamic Jihād headed by Āyman al-Ẓawāhirī (b. 1951), and in 1998 Bin Laden and al-Ẓawāhirī published a militant text, *Jihad against Jews and Crusaders*, in which they declared the killing of Americans and their allies to be a legitimate duty to liberate Palestine and the holy lands of Mecca and Medina from foreign occupation. Settling in Afghanistan after 1996, the two al-Qaʿida leaders then planned the 11 September 2001 attacks on the World Trade Center and the Pentagon in the United States. For partisans as well as enemies, al-Qaʿida represented the paragon of transnational *jihād* organizations and therefore immediately became the main target of the "global war on terror" waged by Washington and its allies.

In March 2003, the American-led war against Iraq and the subsequent occupation of the country created yet another battlefield for different *jihād* organizations. In that context, new techniques of violent warfare were implemented, and the Internet became a fundamental tool of communication for *jihādīs*: videos of attacks and assassinations were broadcast around the world, giving a sense of chaos and of purely indiscriminate violence. While a large number of national *jihād* organizations emerged, such as the Shīʿī Mahdī Army or the Sunnī Association of Muslim Scholars, transnational groups (most of which were Sunnī) also became prominent and, more explicitly than before, contributed to the violent stigmatization of the Shīʿah. Western media attention focused on the role of foreign fighters, especially on the figure of Abū Muṣʿab al-Zarqāwī, a Jordanian who claimed to head al-Qaʿida in the "Land of the Two Rivers" (Iraq), but probably overestimated their importance in the insurgency that followed. Zarqāwī was killed on 7 June 2006, in Baʿqūbah, when two 500-pound (230 kg) guided bombs on were dropped on his safe house. Osama bin Laden was shot and killed inside a private residential compound in Abbottabad, Pakistan on 2 May 2011 in a covert operation by U.S. Navy SEALs and CIA operatives.

This brief account highlights the many different trends and debates within the broad spectrum of *jihād* organizations in the contemporary Islamic world. These groups, whether structured as formal parties or as underground cells, emerged as major disruptors of world politics, even if they were often misunderstood because their actions became overideologized and linked to a specific aspect of Islam. Indeed, *jihād* organizations, despite their apparently rigid doctrines, adapted to their changing environments. Their violence, however despicable, only became intelligible when it was confronted with other forms of violence.

BIBLIOGRAPHY

Abou Zahab, Mariam, and Olivier Roy. *Islamist Networks: The Afghan-Pakistan Connection*. Translated by John King. London: Hurst, 2004.

Kepel, Gilles. *Muslim Extremism in Egypt: The Prophet and the Pharaoh*. Translated by Jon Rothschild. Rev. ed. Berkeley: University of California Press, 2003.

Lia, Brynjar. *Architect of Global Jihad: The Life of Al-Qaida Strategist Abu Mus'ab al-Suri*. New York: Columbia University Press, 2008.

Moghadam, Assaf, and Brian Fishman, eds. *Fault Lines in Global Jihad: Organizational, Strategic, and Ideological Fissures*. Milton Park, U.K.: Routledge, 2011.

AS'AD ABU KHALIL
Updated by LAURENT BONNEFOY
and JOSEPH A. KÉCHICHIAN

JINNAH, MOHAMMAD ALI. Mohammad Ali Jinnah (1876–1948) was the *quaid-i azam* (*qā'īd-i a'ẓam*, great leader) and first governor-general of Pakistan. Born in Karachi, the eldest child of well-to-do Khojas, young Jinnah was sent to London in 1893 and apprenticed to a British managing agency. He was bored by business, however, and turned to the study of law at Lincoln's Inn and also aspired to acting. Jinnah helped the "grand old man" of India's National Congress, Parsi Dadabhai Naoroji, win a seat in the House of Commons, and with Dadabhai's support joined the Indian National Congress in 1906. By then a successful Bombay barrister, Jinnah also joined the Muslim League in 1913 and was instrumental in drafting the jointly adopted Congress-League Lucknow Pact of 1916. As the brightest ambassador of Hindu-Muslim unity, Jinnah seemed destined to lead a united Indian dominion after World War I, but Mohandas K. Gandhi returned from South Africa to revolutionize the Congress Party and become its postwar leader. Jinnah tried his best to dissuade Congress from following Gandhi's "dangerous" and "radical" lead, but he failed in 1919 and withdrew.

Jinnah then focused on his legal practice and served as an independent Muslim member, elected from Bombay, on the viceroy's legislative council in Calcutta and New Delhi. In 1930 he sailed back to London to attend the first Round Table Conference on Indian Constitutional Reforms, just when Muhammad Iqbal (1877–1938) was presiding over the Muslim League in Allahabad. The latter called for "a consolidated North-West Indian Muslim state" for the first time from any League platform, a decade prior to the Lahore "Pakistan Resolution." Jinnah and Sir Shah Nawaz Bhutto managed in London to win separate provincial status for their home province of Sind, which in 1935 became the only Muslim-majority province of British India (Eastern Bengal and Assam having been reunited with West Bengal in 1910). Liaquat Ali Khan (1896–1951) lured Jinnah back from London to become permanent president of the Muslim League. But Congress won most of the provincial contests in 1937 and refused to admit any League leaders to its provincial cabinets. Outraged by Congress arrogance, Jinnah now appealed to India's Muslim masses, transforming himself at his League's Lucknow session of 1937 into their *quaid-i azam*. By March 1940, when the League met in Lahore, Jinnah insisted that British India's Muslims were no longer a "minority" but a "nation." The Lahore Resolution's demand for a separate, single Pakistan became his sole platform and a goal to which he devoted the rest of his life and fast-failing energies. He survived long enough to preside over his new nation's birth in mid-August 1947, but died of lung cancer before he could bring to fruition his fondest dream of firmly establishing in Pakistan a secular and democratic polity free of corruption and internal conflicts.

[*See also* All-India Muslim League; Iqbal, Muhammad; *and* Pakistan.]

BIBLIOGRAPHY

Ahmed, Akbar S. *Jinnah, Pakistan, and Islamic Identity: The Search for Saladin*. London: Routledge, 1997.

Javed, Ajeet. *Secular and Nationalist Jinnah*. New Delhi: Kitab, 1997.

Jinnah, Mohammad Ali. *The Collected Works of Quaid-e-Azam Mohammad Ali Jinnah*. Vol. 1. Compiled by Syed Sharifuddin Pirzada. Karachi: East & West, 1984.

Wolpert, Stanley A. *Jinnah of Pakistan*. 3d ed. New York: Oxford University Press, 1996. Standard biography of Jinnah.

STANLEY WOLPERT

JORDAN. The modern state of Jordan first emerged in 1921 as the Emirate of Transjordan. Until the end of World War I, this area had been part of Greater Syria under Ottoman rule. After the defeat of the Ottoman Empire in 1918, the Allied powers split the Middle East into spheres of influence, with Transjordan and Palestine under British mandate and trusteeship. In 1946 Transjordan achieved independence to become the Hashemite Kingdom of Jordan, with its emir, Abdullah ibn al-Hussein, becoming its first monarch (as emir, r. 1921–1946; as king, r. 1946–1951). The Hashemite family originated in Saudi Arabia and claims legitimacy to rule based in part on its descent from the Prophet Muḥammad.

After Abdullah's assassination in 1951, succession passed quickly from his son, King Talal ibn Abdullah, who abdicated after less than a year due to mental illness, to his grandson, King Hussein ibn Talal, who ruled until his death, from cancer, in 1999. Upon his death, his son, King Abdullah II, assumed the throne and has ruled since then.

In 1921 Jordan's population was estimated to be between 200,000 and 400,000 (a rough estimate because of the mobility of the Bedouin segment). Two significant waves of Palestinian refugees dramatically increased Jordan's population: a first wave (750,000) after the partition of Palestine in 1948 and a second (400,000) following the 1967 Israeli occupation of the West Bank. A third influx occurred with the return from Kuwait and Saudi Arabia of more than 300,000 Palestinians and Jordanians during the 1990–1991 Gulf War. Since the 2003 U.S.-led Iraq War, as many as a million Iraqi refugees have entered Jordan, significantly increasing the total population and altering the ethnic composition of the country. In 2011, Jordan's population was estimated at approximately 6.5 million people.

Jordan occupies nearly 57,354 square miles, more than two-thirds of it semiarid. Over 92 percent of the land under cultivation depends on annual rainfall, and less than 10 percent of all the land receives more than the approximately 20 centimeters (7.8 inches) required annually for cultivation. The regime has supplemented its water needs by tapping nonrenewable aquifers, resulting in serious environmental degradation. Because agriculture's contribution to the national economy fluctuates with rainfall, Jordan relies on food imports to meet its basic needs. Jordan's only natural resources are potash and phosphates, and therefore the nation also depends on imports to meets its energy needs, although it is currently exploring opportunities to develop more renewable and indigenous energy sources.

Since 1999, macroeconomic stability has allowed Jordan to develop its emerging knowledge economy, with tourism, banking, real estate, and information communication technology sectors becoming increasingly competitive. Jordan also attracts significant foreign investment and growing foreign trade thanks to the regime's focus on maintaining strong relations with the United States, the Arab Gulf states, and, until 2011, Syria. These diplomatic efforts also contribute to high levels of foreign aid (grants and soft loans) extended to Jordan by the United States in return for continuing peaceful relations with its neighbor Israel. However, rising food prices, high inflation, and poor living conditions are major challenges Jordan has yet to overcome.

Islam is the dominant religion in Jordan, and 92 percent of the population is Sunnī Muslim. Another 2 percent consists of Druze and Bahā'īs; Christians comprise the remaining 6 percent. Before the twentieth century, most residents of Jordan were farmers and small merchants residing in villages and towns. Since then, migrants from the Balkan states, the Caucasus, Syria, Lebanon, Palestine, Egypt, Iraq, and the Arabian Peninsula have arrived, transforming Jordan.

Politics, Reform, and Islamic Movements. In 1948 the United Nations partitioned Palestine, and the Arab-Israeli war began. At the end of the war, Jordan annexed the West Bank of the Jordan River and restructured its parliament to provide equal representation for West and East Bank populations. This structure continued until 1967, when Israeli forces occupied the West Bank and Gaza Strip during the 1967 War. As a result, the Jordanian king suspended parliament and declared martial law. In 1970, the regime fought militant Palestinians based in the East Bank. In a confrontation known as "Black September," the regime defeated the militants and banished the Palestinian organizations from the country.

Parliament was reconvened in 1984, and by 1990 Jordan had severed its legal and administrative ties with the West Bank, held parliamentary elections involving only residents of the East Bank, and lifted martial law. Although Jordan continues to hold fairly regular parliamentary elections, political freedoms have been steadily curtailed in the name of stability and economic reform. The king retains the power to approve legislation and dissolve parliament, which he has done multiple times since 2009.

The most influential social and political groups in Jordan are Islamic in orientation. All seek full implementation of Islamic law in all fields of social, economic, and political life, but their varying priorities and activities render some more explicitly political—in the sense of active engagement in domestic political processes—than others. In the nonpolitical realm, the most prominent is the Muslim Brotherhood, established as a socioreligious philanthropic organization in 1946 with the blessing of King Abdullah I. Other groups that focus exclusively on religious issues include various Ṣūfī orders, as well as the Jamā'at al-Tablīgh, and the Jamā'ah al-Salafīyah. Two Islamic political parties function legally: the Islamic Action Front (Jabhat al-'Amal al-Islāmī), licensed in 1993, and the Islamic Center Party (Ḥizb al-Wasaṭ al-Islāmī), licensed in 2004. Other explicitly political groups have no legal status at all, including the Islamic Liberation Party (Ḥizb al-Taḥrīr al-Islāmī), the Islamic Holy War Party (Jamā'at al-Jihād al-Islāmī), Ḥamās, Muḥammad's Army (Jaysh Muḥammad), and the Muslim Youth Movement (Ḥarakat Shabāb Nafīr al-Islāmī). These latter groups, with the exception of Ḥamās, have called for the overthrow of ruling Arab regimes and their replacement by Islamic governments.

The Jordanian branch of the Muslim Brotherhood has had a fluctuating relationship with the government. Following its inception, it quickly become popular for its support of Palestinians and active participation in the Arab-Israeli War. Kings Abdullah I and then Hussein actively supported the group, in part for its advocacy of conservative religious values, but also for its loyalty and political conservatism as Jordan increasingly faced internal and external political pressures. Particularly as leftist and pan-Arab nationalist movements gained popularity in the 1950s and 1960s, the Muslim Brotherhood proved a staunch ally of the regime. The Muslim Brotherhood in Jordan focuses on building organizations and institutions that provide services to the public, including private Islamic schools, Qurʾānic teaching centers, mosques, hospitals, and health care clinics, transmitting its religio-political message through them. Popular support for the Brotherhood came particularly from Palestinian segments of the population, and the movement's focus on Israel and Palestinian issues reflects their support base. Although they oppose violence against civilians in Jordan or elsewhere, their support of attacks against Israeli soldiers in the Palestinian territories and U.S. soldiers in Iraq has generated friction with the Jordanian regime, which desires good relations with these countries.

The positive dynamic between the Muslim Brotherhood and the Jordanian regime changed in the 1980s when it became critical of the regime. Alarmed and under political pressure from riots over food prices, King Hussein attempted to moderate the movement by allowing the organization to participate in parliamentary elections in 1989. Since then, and especially after the creation of their political wing, the Islamic Action Front, in 1993, relations have deteriorated as both Hussein and Abdullah II attempted to limit the political power of the movement even as they allowed it to compete in elections. Of particular contention is the "one man, one vote" system implemented in 1993, which disadvantages Islamic parties, as they tend to have higher support in densely populated, majority-Palestinian areas.

The Islamic Liberation Party has not been legalized. Its founder, Shaykh Taqī al-Dīn Nabhānī, was born in Palestine in 1910. After the partition of Palestine in 1948, al-Nabhānī submitted an official request to the Jordanian government to allow the party to operate legally within the political system, but this was denied. Continual pressure by the government, harsh treatment, and imprisonment forced many party leaders to leave Jordan. Al-Nabhānī fled to Syria in 1953 and then to Lebanon, where he lived until his death in 1974. Ideologically, the Islamic Liberation Party maintains that Islam is not only a religion, but that it defines and includes every other aspect of life. With this view, the party urges Muslims to replace current governments with an Islamic caliphate, by force if necessary. Because the leadership thought that its ideology would appeal to the masses and be accepted rapidly, it sought to expedite its objectives by wresting authority from the hands of corrupt regimes. This led to an unsuccessful attempt to take over the Jordanian government in 1969.

Ḥamās, another secretly organized Islamic religio-political movement, developed in the occupied West Bank and Gaza Strip. This organization played an important role in the *intifāḍah* that began in 1988. It has publicly declared no other political interest than the liberation of Palestine from the Israelis.

Other nonlegal religio-political Islamic groups, less popular than the Islamic Liberation Party, include the Islamic Holy War Party, Muḥammad's Army, and the Islamic Youth Organization. Over the last two decades, these groups were involved, according to the Jordanian government, in more than one attempt to overthrow the regime in Jordan, and many of their members have been arrested.

The organized Islamic groups that have no political agenda include the Ṣūfī orders and the groups Jamāʿat al-Tablīgh and Jamāʿah al-Salafīyah. The orders, which spread into Jordan from various neighboring countries since the mid-twentieth century, emphasize individual spiritual and religious conduct and relationship to God. All Ṣūfī orders disregard materialistic values, which they believe corrupt people. Ṣūfī orders that practice in Jordan include the Shādhilīyah al-Yashruṭīyah, Kilānīyah, Qādirīyah, Rifāʿīyah, Naqshbandīyah, Taymīyah, and Tijānīyyah. Members gather on a regular basis to recite religious songs and versus from the Qurʾān; a major effect of their activities is heightened awareness of Islam.

The Jamāʿat al-Tablīgh, which began in India, emphasizes spreading God's word and Islam. Members are required to devote an hour a day or one full day a month to preaching God's word. The Jamāʿah al-Salafīyah calls for a return to the Qurʾān and *sunnah* as well as the practices of the early centuries of Islam.

The Arab Spring and Regime Responses. The "Arab Spring" has not so far seriously challenged the Jordanian regime, with most protesters at first demonstrating against corruption, poverty, and the peace treaty with Israel rather than demanding the overthrow of the regime. Protests began in Jordan on 14 January 2011 and have generally been peaceful relative to those in other Arab countries, the most violent exception being on 25 March 2011, when protestors clashed with progovernment forces, culminating in one death and a slew of injuries.

However, as pressure continues, increasing numbers have expressed doubts over whether the regime's reform efforts are genuine, and the king, once beyond public criticism, has increasingly come under direct attack. Islamic groups have been intimately involved in unrest since 2011, spearheading anticorruption and poverty demonstrations and challenging the political system that they say restricts their representation. Salafī movements have been particularly energetic, although the Muslim Brotherhood has generally made clearer public demands. Responding to a 2012 electoral law that they argued further disadvantaged them, the Muslim Brotherhood, its political wing, the Islamic Action Front, and several other opposition parties, boycotted the January 2013 elections. This was the second election in a row that Islamists have boycotted, a worrying trend for those seeking to improve the integrity and legitimacy of elections in the eyes of the public.

The regime has generally followed a strategy of attempting to appear tolerant (relative to the responses in other countries) yet using force against demonstrators when it decides the protesters have gone too far. Facing regional and domestic unrest, King Abdullah II has responded by repeatedly replacing the cabinet and prime minister and promising further economic and political reforms. Between February 2011 and December 2012, Jordan had five different prime ministers.

More broadly, the regime has responded strongly to violent Islamic movements, while allowing limited political space for more moderate groups. After the bombing of three Amman hotels in 2006 by Iraqi militants and other threats of violence, King Abdullah II put increasing pressure on the mainstream Islamists to keep hard-line elements in check. The regime has also targeted Islamic movements they deem a threat to the state, imprisoning both their leaders and sympathizers. Simultaneously, as Islamic groups increase in influence and power as a result of the Arab Spring, the Jordanian regime also reached out to groups such as Ḥamās in early 2012, seeking to placate their bases of popular support and ensure Jordan's stability.

BIBLIOGRAPHY

Boulby, Marion. *The Muslim Brotherhood and the Kings of Jordan, 1945–1993*. Atlanta: Scholar's Press, 1999.

Brown, Nathan J. *Jordan and Its Islamic Movement: The Limits of Inclusion?* Carnegie Papers 74. Washington, D.C.: Carnegie Endowment for International Peace, 2006.

Clark, Janine A. *Islam, Charity, and Activism: Middle-Class Networks and Social Welfare in Egypt, Jordan, and Yemen*. Bloomington: Indiana University Press, 2004.

Dalacoura, Katerina. *Islamist Terrorism and Democracy in the Middle East*. New York: Cambridge University Press, 2011.

Schwedler, Jillian. *Faith in Moderation: Islamist Parties in Jordan and Yemen*. New York: Cambridge University Press, 2006.

Tobin, Sarah A. "Jordan's Arab Spring: The Middle Class and Anti-Revolution." *Middle East Policy* 19, no. 1 (Spring 2012): 96–109.

Wiktoriwicz, Quintan. "The Salafi Movement in Jordan." *International Journal of Middle East Studies* 32, no. 2 (May 2000): 219–240.

JESSIE MORITZ

JURISPRUDENTIAL COUNCIL OF NORTH AMERICA. The Islamic Jurisprudential Council of North America (ISNA) started out in the 1960s as the Religious Affairs Committee of the Muslim Students Association of the United States and Canada. The council was created to respond to many personal status questions that concern Muslims in the United States and Canada such as divorce, marriage, dietary habits, child custody, and the like. After the creation of the Islamic Society of North America (ISNA) in 1981, the committee came under its auspices. Finally, in 1986, the committee was transformed into an independent body of scholars. By 2003 the council faced financial difficulties and therefore it returned to ISNA's leadership as the head organization.

The Islamic Jurisprudential Council is currently composed of seventeen members, headed by an executive council that was initially appointed to handle managerial issues but instead became the central decision-making body.

The council's independence in 1986 helped foster a more academic community that was less involved with the ISNA as a quasi-political organization. The leader of the council's transformation in 1986 was Dr. Taha Jaber al-Alwani, a religious scholar, who was also the head of the International Institute of Islamic Thought.

The council is an association of Muslims who interpret Islamic law within the United States and Canada. The seventeen members of the council are Muslims who issue religious rulings, resolve disputes, and answer questions relating to the Islamic faith. As outlined in its bylaws, the council's primary objective is: "To consider all transactions from a Shari'ah perspective and offer advice on specific undertakings, transactions, contracts, projects, or proposals, guaranteeing thereby that the dealings of American Muslims fall within the parameters of what is permitted by the Shari'ah."

The religious opinions/edicts (*fatwas*) that the council issues are not binding, as is typical of a Sunnī institution. Therefore, the people might follow the edicts depending on how convincing the argument made by the jurisconsult(s) is. Islamic law is decentralized and therefore the council is composed of scholars who are trained in Islamic legal institutions in their home countries, like al-Azhar. This makes it nearly impossible for the council to enforce any of its edicts, but as jurisprudential scholars, the members reflect on and analyze the law. The council also utilizes the principle of "consensus" (*ijmāʿ*) and analogical reasoning (*qiyās*) to issue those edicts. Thus living in a majority non-Muslim country requires the academic rigor that the council applies so that the Muslim community can adjust to life in its new homeland.

Some examples of the council's edicts that have been accepted by a majority of American Muslims have dealt with the issues of the determination of Ramadan and the condemnation of terrorism.

Although the legal opinions of the council are not binding or enforceable, the council's opinions serve as academic opinions built on Islamic legal thought and epistemology.

BIBLIOGRAPHY

Barsky, Yehudit. "The Fiqh Council's Fatwa: Actions, Not Words, Needed." *Global Jewish Advocacy*, 2 August 2005, http://www.ajc.org/site/apps/nl/content3.asp?c=ijITI2PHKoG&b=846739&ct=1256033.

Fiqh Council of North America Web site: http://www.fiqhcouncil.org/.

Investigative Project on Terrorism. "Backgrounder on the Fiqh Council of North America and the Council on American-Islamic Relations." http://www.investigativeproject.org/FCNA-CAIR.html.

DEINA ABDELKADER

JUSTICE. The most common referent for "justice" in Arabic, with a semantic field covering the concepts of "balance," "mean," "straightness," "fairness," "equal" and "equity," are words derived from the root *ʿ-d-l*, usually *ʿadl*, but also *ʿadāla*, particularly in modern usage. *Inṣāf*, often glossed as justice, equity, or fairness, is semantically related to "half," "middle," or "medium." *Qisṭ*, more often used along the lines of "equity" in distribution, is related to the concepts of "share," "part," "allotment," or "measure." Finally, *ḥaqq* covers a semantic field that includes concepts of "right," "truth," and "correctness."

Justice in the Qurʾān. The Qurʾān mostly makes use of words derived from *ʿ-d-l* and *q-s-ṭ*—twenty-eight and twenty-five times, respectively. Most references to a morally substantive value of "justice" use these roots. The well-known verse (4:3) that establishes the permissibility of polygamy, for example, uses them as near synonyms:

> And if you have reason to fear that you might not act equitably (*tuqsiṭū*) towards orphans, then marry from among [other] women such as are lawful to you—[even] two, or three, or four: but if you have reason to fear that you might not be able to treat them with equal fairness (*taʿdilū*), then [only] one—or [from among] those whom you rightfully possess. This will make it more likely that you will not deviate from the right course.

By and large, as in the above verse, the Qurʾān refers to "justice" in ways that presume knowledge of the substantive obligations of justice, directing believers instead to the obligatoriness and importance of acting in accordance with them: "Whenever you judge between people, judge with justice (*bi-l-ʿadl*)" (4:58); "Be ever steadfast in your devotion to God, bearing witness to the truth in all equity (*bi-l-qisṭ*); and never let hatred of anyone lead you into the sin of deviating from justice (*a-lā taʿdilū*)" (5:8); "Behold, God enjoins justice (*ʿadl*), and the doing of good, and generosity towards [one's] fellow-men" (16:90); "Verily, God loves those who act equitably (*al-muqsiṭīn*)!" (49:9).

The justice that humans are enjoined to uphold in the Qurʾān is characterized in both intuitive and revealed terms. Morality and justice are often referred to as "that which is known" (*maʿrūf*) and immorality as "that which is denied" (*munkar*). One need not accept a rationalist or naturalist interpretation of Islamic ethics to accept the idea that the Qurʾān expects certain basic understandings of justice and morality to be widely known and valued. "Justice" is first about acting and judging impartially with no morally irrelevant characteristics such as kinship or wealth serving as the basis for advantage. As in all universalist conceptions of justice which reject the idea of justice as "helping friends and harming enemies," the obligations of justice are both distinct from and have priority over one's personal affective attachments and obligations to particular persons. As seen above, the Qurʾān warns against letting "your hatred of a people cause you to act unjustly" and counsels "when you voice an opinion, be just (*fa-ʿdilū*), even though it be [against] one near of kin" (6:152).

Here one can discern a fundamental connection to the idea of "equality (of value)" or "equal measure" in the concept of *ʿadl*. Unbelievers are thrice blamed for "making equivalence" (*yaʿdilūna*) between God and others (6:1, 6:150, 27:60); and the idea of *ʿadl* as one's "ransom" on the Day of Judgment for one's earthly sins (2:48, 2:123, 6:70) suggests the idea of an equal or equivalent exchange (of which, of course, there is none). For example, the Qurʾān exhorts, "kill no game while you are in the state of pilgrimage. And whoever of you kills it intentionally, [shall make] amends in cattle equivalent to what he has killed... or else he may atone for his sin by feeding the needy, or by the equivalent thereof in fasting (*ʿadlu dhālika ṣiyāman*)" (5:95). At the same time, an intriguing Qurʾānic passage refers to God's creation of man's nature "in just proportions (*fa-ʿadalaka*)" (82:8).

But if humans are expected to have some intuitive conception of justice as equity, fairness, balance, and impartiality, justice in the Qurʾān is ultimately about enacting God's revealed and commanded positive rules. Another verse, which also elides the difference between *q-s-ṭ* and *ʿ-d-l*, exemplifies this:

> O you who have attained to faith! Be ever steadfast in upholding equity (*qisṭ*), bearing witness to the truth for the sake of God, even though it be against your own selves or your parents and kinsfolk. Whether the person concerned be rich or poor, God takes precedence over [the claims of] either of them. Do not, then, follow your own desires, lest you swerve from justice (*taʿdilū*): for if you distort [the truth], behold, God is indeed aware of all that you do! (4:135)

Thus what it means to apply justice in defiance of personal ties or preference for the powerful is to uphold "God's precedence," meaning the rules God has laid down and the claims he has made for himself.

Justice is also known by its negation. The opposite of justice in the Qurʾān is expressed primarily as *ẓulm* or *jawr*. There are hundreds of Qurʾānic references to words derived from the root *ẓ-l-m*. Many of them are used in connection with God, and it is thus to the question of God's justice that we now turn.

Divine Justice. One of the earliest and most enduring theological and dogmatic controversies in Islam related to God's justice. A significant number of Qurʾānic verses make reference to God not acting unjustly towards his creatures (e.g., 4:40, 18:49.) However, a perennial theological question plagues the idea of God's justice, namely, is it an expression of his wisdom and perfection, or rather his unconstrained will and power?

The Muʿtazilite school of theology pointed to the above verses to support their rational arguments in defense of the former view. Along with his oneness (*tawḥīd*), the idea of God's justice was the core principle of Muʿtazilite theology—thus their moniker for themselves, "the people of divine unity and justice" (*ahl al-tawḥīd wa-l-ʿadl*). For the Muʿtazilites, justice is a quality that corresponds to the perfection of God. God must be just and equitable in his judgments, may not be unjust or arbitrary, and must always do what is optimal (*aṣlaḥ*) for his creation. More controversially, his acts cannot be incompatible with universal criteria accessible to reason for distinguishing good from evil. What makes determinations of good and evil accessible to reason is that certain actions are in themselves good or evil; good and evil are essences that inhere in certain acts. For example, on this view it is irrational to deny that lying is bad (*qabīḥ*) by essence and that justice is good (*ḥasan*) by essence, and not merely by convention, command, or consequence.

The Muʿtazilite view thus required an affirmation of the freedom of the human will or *ikhtiyār* ("choice"). For if God is just, and does not wrong his servants, then his punishments and rewards on the Day of Judgment must be in response to actions for which humans are themselves responsible. To punish humans for disbelief or acts of sin that God himself has caused and constrained humans to perform is tantamount to injustice and tyranny, traits that are *a priori* reasoned to be excluded from God's essence. Man is thus the creator, author, and agent of his actions, and all evil and injustice in the world must be attributable to humans, not to God.

However, these views were found by early Muslim theologians to be in tension with certain Qur'ānic statements that God has created everything on earth and all motions in the universe. They also introduce the possibility that rational and revelatory accounts of justice might be in conflict, thus raising the question of which is to be accorded priority and authority. Despite the frequent assertion that any apparent contradictions between reason and revelation were only that—apparent and not real—the troubling nature of the mere possibility of these tensions led many theologians to accord a primacy not to God's everlasting wisdom and reason, but to his will and power.

In response, the Ashʿarite school of theology tended to assert the following points of doctrine: God is radically free to create and command moral values; the content of justice is determined by what he has set out as the law in revelation; human destiny is predetermined by God; and human acts are caused by God. As to the ontology of justice, the important point is that acts (lying, killing, praying) do not have essences in which their justness or badness inheres, but are given a moral value only by God's sovereign determination. In the words of al-Juwaynī (d. 478/1085): "The intellect does not ascertain the goodness of a thing or its badness. Something being good or bad falls solely within the disposition of the law.... What is meant by 'obligatory' refers merely to the act which, because the law commands it, is obligatory." On the question of whether God can be regarded as the author of evil and injustice, which the Muʿtazilites found ludicrous, al-Ashʿarī (d. 324/935) insisted that God was indeed the author of human injustice in the world, but he distinguished between his willing injustice on his own part, unmediated, and willing injustice men do to one another.

While this solved the problem of how to consistently uphold God's power, it raised other awkward questions about just deserts and human agency. Sunnīs writing within the Ashʿarite and Māturidī traditions thus articulated the doctrine of acquisition (*kasb*). This doctrine held that while God does in fact create all human actions in an ultimate sense, there is space for humans to "acquire" a certain measure of authorship and agency over their deeds. This was a way of theorizing both divine power over the world and human moral responsibility for those acts that God has already created.

Muʿtazilite views about God's justice and human free will survived in both the Twelver and Zaydī Shīʿī traditions. The tenth-century Twelver creed of Ibn Bābawayh asserted that God is just ("He requites a good act with a good act and an evil act with an evil act") but also "treats us with something better, namely, grace (*tafaḍḍul*)." He also recorded the doctrine that "human actions are created in the sense that God possesses foreknowledge and not in the sense that God compels man to act in a particular manner." The attractiveness of these Muʿtazilite doctrines for the Twelvers and the Zaydīs may have had sociopolitical origins as much as intellectual or spiritual ones. With Ashʿarism ascendant under ʿAbbāsid rule by the late ninth century, there may have been an elective affinity between disaffected Muʿtazilites and oppositional sects. Muʿtazilite doctrines of justice, responsibility, and free will also hold a clear appeal for parties in opposition as they deny that might reflects right and discourage the oppressed from accepting existing realities on fatalist grounds.

The argument for God's justice reached an intellectual apex in the works of *falsafa*, particular those of Ibn Rushd (d. 595/1198). In *al-Kashf ʿan manāhij al-adilla fī ʿaqāʾid al-milla* (Exposition of the Methods of Argumentation in Religious Doctrines) he writes that the Ashʿarite position that justice is only that which is commanded by the law and there is nothing just or unjust in itself, "is not only not the one proposed by revelation, but opposed to it" and "of the utmost absurdity." Intriguingly and more than a little provocatively, he historicizes and relativizes the Ashʿarite doctrine by conjecturing that Ashʿarites needed to assert their doctrine that God created both good and evil in the world since "they needed to explain that God is described as just and the creator of all things, both good and evil, because in the past many nations believed erroneously that there are two gods, one creating good and the other creating evil. Accordingly, they asserted that God is the creator of both."

Ibn Rushd's own treatment of God's justice focuses on the knotty question of why God willed that there be unbelievers in the world, since "if God had so willed, He surely would have gathered them all under his guidance" (6:35). As will be recalled, this was the basis for one of the arguments advanced by the Muʿtazilites for human free will: since God is just, it is unthinkable that he has damned certain people to eternal torment through no fault of their own; therefore, humans must have free will to believe or disbelieve, and act justly or act sinfully, thus meriting their recompense in the hereafter.

Ibn Rushd concedes that God has "allowed for the existence of some misguided people among the different kinds of existing entities, people who are predisposed to error by their very natures and driven to it by what surrounds them of misleading causes, whether internal or external." His response, however, is to emphasize less the problem of God's justice qua judge as his wisdom qua creator. God's choice was either not to create humanity at all, or to create humanity with the stipulation that among humanity will be some who are wicked and who disbelieve. Thus the just action was to advance the greater good (the creation of humanity) rather than abstain from this creation in order to avoid a small amount of evil.

For all of the appeal of the ideas that God's judgments are somehow substantively and objectively just and that humans deserve their treatment in the hereafter as a result of their freely chosen actions in this world, it was the view of God as defined by power and will first that prevailed in Muslim theological and juridical circles. Even those (Muʿtazilites or Muʿtazilite-sympathizers) who were inclined on principle to believe that certain actions are inherently good or evil and that God's revelation merely reflects this did not necessarily deny that human behavior in this world should be judged according to the standards of the law as revealed by God. Thus it was primarily through the discourse of discovering the law that the substantive requirements of justice were articulated.

Legal Justice. In his famous *Risāla*, al-Shāfiʿī (d. 204/820) defined justice simply as "acting in obedience to God." Thus the primary approach to the study of punitive, contractual, and distributive justice in Islam is simply to study the rules of Islamic *fiqh* in these areas. Short of outlining the specific rules of justice in individual areas of the law—translations into English exist of a number of canonical legal manuals—it is possible to note a few general aspects of Islamic legal thought that indicate assumptions about the content of legal justice.

The publicity of the law's justification and articulation is such an aspect. Ideally, all claims to moral and legal knowledge are justified publically to a community of equals through agreed-upon methods of proof and argumentation. This alone represents a commitment to justice between moral equals not present in moral theories where political and moral obligations can be worked out in an insular fashion by elites or experts with no obligation to publically present and justify those obligations in the same terms as they were arrived at by the insular community.

The core features of Islam's publicity are the claim that (a) humans may justify impositions and obligations on one another as religious obligations only on the basis of proof from texts shown to be authentically from God; (b) the meaning of these texts is linguistically accessible to humans and their legislative force can in principle be apprehended through the application of certain interpretive methods; and (c) it is understood and publicly acknowledged that scholars do not have conclusive knowledge of the divine legislative ruling (*ḥukm*) on specific acts, and thus the scholarly community may not arbitrarily censor opinions arrived at through interpretive methods or close off scholarly inquiry. Indeed, Sunnī Islam's commitments to universal public justification go even deeper than this, to the idea that rational proofs of both God's existence and the veracity of Muḥammad's prophecy must be provided to those subject to its ordinances.

A further commitment is to the universality of the law. In principle, there is one law for all believers. Rulers, scholars, and notables are all subject to it. "Law" is not a "noble lie" for the masses with opt-out clauses for statesmen, philosophers, gentlemen, or, importantly, mystics. However, while the scholars were able to monopolize (more or less) religious epistemic authority, they were not (until Khomeini's doctrine of *wilāyat al-faqīh*) in charge of the state. They were thus often in the position of justifying certain departures from the ideal. Some of these efforts are noteworthy for their egalitarian and justificatory commitments.

For example, is it permissible to apply discretionary punishment (*taʿzīr*) differentially to social notables as opposed to the masses (the jurists held that there were no exceptions in the application of the mandatory *ḥudūd* punishments)? The idea seems deeply un-Islamic. Wealth, power, and social standing are not marks of virtue and do not privilege their possessors morally. In reality the elite always have special access to the halls of justice. Consider the eleventh-century jurist al-Māwardī's exposition of this problem: "The censure due to people of dignity and honor is milder than that given to the contemptible or the impudent." The justification for gradations of discretionary punishment (viz., ignoring, reprimand, vituperation, detainment, beating) is that the same goals can be achieved ("reform and rebuke") with different people through different means. People of honor are deterred by public shunning or reprimand, while the base require detainment or beating. There are elements of social stratification creeping into the law (not to mention culture), but even here the jurists feel the burden of public justification.

Raising the subject of substantive inequalities within a law that proclaims equality and universality immediately invokes the three main classes of persons excluded from social equality: women, slaves, and non-Muslims. Non-Muslims are obviously expressly excluded from the justificatory community, although this does not preclude moral and legal obligations to them as prescribed by the law. Slavery and the social inequality of women are institutions that appear in the revealed texts. For Muslim jurists, treating slaves and women according to different rules is not in itself a violation of Islamic justificatory commitments as the theologians and jurists understood them, for these were not social customs or arbitrary preferences but textually redeemable practices. More than women, slaves—like non-Muslims—were excluded from the justificatory community, although slaves could convert and acquire their freedom, thus erasing any legally and religiously justifiable social distinction. Women, on the other hand, as Muslims were from the beginning part of the justificatory community; fidelity to divine sovereignty would require of them no less than of men that they accept the results of the investigation into the revealed texts.

Legal values of procedural fairness and impartiality are often expressed as requirements of judges. Legal manuals (as, e.g., Ibn Naqīb's *ʿUmdat al-sālik*) command judges to treat both litigants with equal impartiality (*yusāwī baynahumā*), seating them in places of equal honor and attending to them equally. Judges are "to be stern without harshness, and flexible without weakness" and not to decide cases when their temperament or mood might affect the decision. They are to sit with "tranquility and gravity" and consult both credible witnesses and learned scholars. Judges may not accept gifts or decide cases involving relatives or business partners. Further requirements of procedure, evidence, and testimony are outlined in the manuals in order to advance fairness and impartiality.

Within the context of legal justice, it must also be noted that "justice" is also a personal quality of persons. The Qurʾān (5:95, 5:106, 65:2) speaks of the need for witnesses or scribes present during important transactions to be possessed of *ʿadl*. This quality, which the juridical tradition would eventually include as a necessary legal condition for those who discharge the obligations of witnesses, judges, market inspectors, and rulers, refers to an individual's moral probity in a wide, but not impossibly demanding, sense.

In principle it is the jurists' task to develop the particular rulings of the law so as to anticipate as many possible areas of its application and to ensure that it is thus both predictable and depersonalized; in this way the legal scholars also summarized basic legal principles to make maxims of law (*qawāʿid fiqhiyya*) to assist in the adjudication and application of the law. These maxims are often procedural or coordinative, but just as often contain substantive (if rather generic) statements about the requirements of justice. Some of the best known and important for the study of justice are: "A matter is determined according to intention"; "Injury cannot exist from time immemorial"; "Latitude should be afforded in the case of difficulty"; "An injury cannot be removed by the commission of a similar injury"; and "Necessity does not invalidate the right of another."

Political Justice. The question of political justice raises a number of distinct questions. Most important among them are what the characteristics of a just ruler are, what claims of justice the subjects of political power have, and whether there are any limits to obeying an unjust ruler or regime.

Rulers are exhorted to be just in all genres of Islamic theological, legal, and political writing. In the earliest period of Islam, the ruler's justice was to a large extent the function of his legitimacy. A just ruler was one who came to power through the approved procedure, whether by appointment by a predecessor, by "election" on the part of the "people who loose and bind," or through inheritance via a designated line of descent. The first two conditions were variations on the conception of legitimacy that came to constitute Sunnism, whereas the last is the defining characteristic of Twelver Shiism.

Once in office, what makes a legitimate ruler just or unjust? The simplest answer is that a just ruler is one who applies God's law, either directly or by appointing and then getting out of the way of judges. As noted in the previous section, the substantive content of justice to be executed by rulers and scholars is elaborated in the manuals and compendia of *fiqh*. However, treatises on the rules of governance (*al-aḥkām al-sulṭāniyya*) cover the most important duties made obligatory on the ruler within the *Sharīʿah* (his *sharʿī* duties), namely, the public legal validation of the Muslim community (*umma*), the validation of public worship, the execution of *ḥudūd* punishments, the waging of both defensive and expansionary *jihād*, the commanding of right and forbidding of wrong, the preservation of religion, and the collection of *Sharīʿah*-prescribed taxes.

But Islamic legal and political writing anticipates a space for the ruler to act at his own discretion, what might today be referred to as public policy, and here his justice is a measure of his own qualities and deeds. Rulers were expected to uphold and advance the welfare of their subjects, not to tax them beyond reasonable limits, to apply the law impartially, to listen to grievances (*maẓālim*), and to engage in consultation (*shūrā*) with important representatives of one's community. Jurists sometimes also speak about the ruler's duties beyond those prescribed by the *Sharīʿah* (his non-*sharʿī* duties): to use public power to protect internal security, improve infrastructure (roads, bridges, inns, walls, mosques, etc.), promote charity and social welfare, provide public medical services, and sponsor religious education. Many of these were provided by non-ruling notables and others in addition to the "state."

Interestingly, and in this latter vein, justice is not always assumed to be coterminous with Islam. Naturally, the purest and most comprehensive standard of justice is that set out within the *Sharīʿah*. But for some scholars it is consistent to describe a ruler or a regime as believing-and-unjust or as unbelieving-yet-just. The *locus classicus* for this sentiment is found in Ibn Taymiyya's (d. 728/1328) work on the *ḥisba*, the purview of the market inspector-cum-morals police, wherein he elaborated much of his political theory. In this treatise, the great Ḥanbalī theologian and jurist writes, "God preserves the just state even if it is unbelieving and does not preserve the oppressive state even if it is Muslim. It is said that the world persists with justice and unbelief and does not persist with oppression and Islam. . . . This is because justice is the order of all things. Thus if the affairs of the world are arranged with justice, then they are upheld even if the one responsible has no share of the hereafter." While Ibn Taymiyya does not elaborate in any detail what conditions an unbelieving state must fulfill to be regarded as just, such a statement can only be read to comprise a certain kind of universal understanding of political justice that involves the rule of law, limitations on arbitrary power, and public coercion allowed only in the service of public goods and interests rather than the private interests of those in power.

If the subjects of political power have a right to expect the performance of these duties, do they have a right to demand them? The standard response within Sunnī thought is that while the ruler has an obligation to be just and is exhorted to fear God while exercising power, obedience to an unjust ruler is an absolute requirement of the ruled. Sunnism, after all, emerged out of the desire to maintain communal unity and prevent both the wanton bloodshed and religious schism that arose out of rebellion to political rulers in the early years of Islam. *Fitna*—sedition, chaos, civil strife—became the supreme political evil within Sunnism. An oft-invoked expression proclaims that a terrifyingly long period of time (thirty years, one hundred years) under an unjust ruler is preferable to a single day of *fitna*.

This stern conception of political obligation did not rise to the level of that demanded by the "divine right of kings" doctrine of medieval and early modern Europe or by Hobbesian social contract theory. Indeed, a contrary principle proclaims that "there is no obedience to a creature in disobedience to the Creator." But this did not authorize the anarchy of a private right of veto on the part of any individual Muslim against any act of public power deemed impious. Furthermore, treatises on the rules of governance (*al-aḥkām al-sulṭāniyya*), later often styled as treatments of "religiously legitimate governance" (*al-siyāsa al-sharʿiyya*), anticipate and authorize the ruler acting according to his own judgment, both beyond the letter of *Sharīʿah* and also at times in opposition to it.

The right to disobey tended to be limited to egregious cases of a ruler's interference in purely religious matters (of creed or worship) or, in the extreme case, if he abandoned Islam and sought to undermine it within his area of rule. It is this idea that has been seized upon in the modern period to justify rebellion against nominally Muslim rulers. It has been argued, most famously by ʿAbd al-Salām Farāj in his treatise justifying armed revolt against the Egyptian government of Anwar Sadat, *The Neglected Duty* (*al-Farīḍa al-Ghāʾiba*), that imposing foreign, secular, non-Islamic laws on Muslims constitutes nothing less than apostasy from Islam, since God has proclaimed in the Qurʾān that "those who do not rule [judge] by what God has revealed, those are the unbelievers" (5:44). As unbelievers, such rulers may be killed as apostates or rebelled against as traitors. Thus the classical principle of obedience to any ruler who provides security and stability (reaffirmed, if awkwardly, by the clerics of al-Azhar during the anti-Mubarak uprising of January and February 2011) collapses into a tautology reminiscent of the early Khārijite doctrine: Muslims are commanded to obey their rulers; rulers are commanded to enforce the *Sharīʿah*; departure from the *Sharīʿah* negates the obligation to obey; those subject to power will judge what constitutes departure from the *Sharīʿah*. This is the precise logic of replacing the will and judgment of the ruler with one's own understanding of God's will, which horrified Sunnī scholars in the eighth century (as well as Thomas Hobbes in the seventeenth century).

While few Muslims embrace the utopianism and *Sharīʿah*-formalism of Farāj and his heirs in the radical Islamist movement, many no longer accept the near-absolute duty of obedience often asserted in the Sunnī tradition. The Green Movement in Iran and the events of the Arab Spring seem to have consigned the "better thirty years of injustice than a day of *fitna*" doctrine to the proverbial dustbin of history. Events now have caught up with a century of thinking, some of it tentative or formulaic, about how to institutionalize traditional Islamic commitments to political justice, the rule of law, and the duty to consult within modern constitutional and democratic forms.

Social Justice. Another modern contribution to the Islamic tradition of thinking about justice is the discourse on "social justice." In response to both the eruption of what is sometimes called "the social question" in Muslim societies (mass poverty or inequality combined with the emergence of mass politics) and the challenge of avowedly secular socialist or communist ideologies and movements, many twentieth-century Muslim thinkers rediscovered a commitment to "social justice" within Islamic ethics. Thinkers such as Sayyid Quṭb recast Islam as a religion not only of charity and care, but of social solidarity (*takāful*), or, as in the case of ʿAlī Sharīʿatī in Iran, a religion of revolutionary socialism.

One of the most common themes of modern Islamic political thought across the ideological spectrum is that Islam is superior to other religions like Christianity and other ideological rivals like socialism because it is the only doctrine or ideology that takes all of man's innate needs equally seriously. A common Muslim reading of Christianity is that it is merely a religion of the spirit and thus either impossibly demanding ("love thy enemy"; "turn the other cheek"; "harder to get a rich man into heaven than a camel through the eye of a needle") or unacceptably antinomian and libertine (since all that matters is faith and works are in vain). Similarly, a common reading of socialist ideologies is that they are merely materialist, only concerned with man's body. Islam, so goes the refrain from Muḥammad ʿAbduh and Rashīd Riḍa through Sayyid Quṭb, al-Mawdūdī, and Ayatollah Khomeini to ʿAlī Sharīʿatī, is the "natural religion" (*dīn al-fiṭra*), which on this modern reading comes to mean the religion that responds to all of man's psychological, emotional, material, and spiritual inclinations. Thus Muslims can have all of the care and solidarity of a socialist safety net while sacrificing neither their spiritual yearnings nor, crucially, their natural and understandable desire to be rewarded for their efforts and pass on their wealth to their children.

In Sayyid Quṭb's case, the problem of social justice is given a politico-moral twist reminiscent of Rousseau. Made of both clay and God's spirit (38:71–72), both good and evil, man naturally inclines toward the morality called for by God, according to Quṭb. However, in order to remain true to this morality, he needs not only personal commitment and a cultivated moral disposition, but the security that comes only from the faith that all of his fellows in society are equally so committed and from emancipation from domination by other humans—a political regime that not only enforces the letter of Islamic morality, but also exemplifies the principle of human subjugation only to God. In addition to domination or oppression, the innate inclination to morality can be undone by the fear, need, and servility that come from poverty. Whatever nobility the grateful, pious pauper may have in Quṭb's eyes, the average man will be morally disfigured by the experience, unable to experience the security and dignity needed for the development of moral personality. Thus the need for an economic regime that not only enforces the letter of Islamic rules regarding charity, but also exemplifies the belief that all property belongs ultimately only to God. Social justice is therefore not only an obligation incumbent on Muslims, but the secret to the realism and feasibility of Islam's utopian vision. The Muslim who experiences social justice will not only have no further grievances, but will experience no atavistic desires or motives contrary to the demands of religious morality.

[*See also* Ashʿarīs; Muʿtazilah; Quṭb, Sayyid; *and* Religious Beliefs.]

BIBLIOGRAPHY

Abou El Fadl, Khaled. *Rebellion and Violence in Islamic Law*. Cambridge, U.K.: Cambridge University Press, 2001.

Al-Azmeh, Aziz. *Muslim Kingship: Power and the Sacred in Muslim, Christian and Pagan Polities*. London: Tauris, 1997.

Crone, Patricia. *God's Rule: Government and Islam*. New York: Columbia University Press, 2004.

Holland, Muhtar, trans. *Public Duties in Islam: The Institution of the Ḥisba, by al-Shaykh al-Imām Ibn Taymīya*. Leicester, U.K.: The Islamic Foundation, 1982.

Kamali, Mohammad Hashim. *Freedom, Equality and Justice in Islam*. Cambridge, U.K.: Islamic Texts Society, 2002.

Kassem, Hammond. "The Idea of Justice in Islamic Philosophy." *Diogenes* 20 (1972): 81–108.

Keller, Nu Ha Mim, trans. *Reliance of the Traveller: The Classic Manual of Islamic Sacred Law ʿUmdat al-salik*. Beltsville, Md.: Amana Publications, 1999.

Khadduri, Majid. *The Islamic Conception of Justice*. Baltimore: Johns Hopkins University Press, 1984.

Khadduri, Majid, trans. *al-Imām Muḥammad Ibn Idris al-Shāfiʿī's al-Risāla fī uṣūl al-fiqh: Treatise on the Foundations of Islamic Jurisprudence*. Cambridge, U.K.: Islamic Texts Society, 1997.

Kuran, Timur. "On the Notion of Economic Justice in Contemporary Justice Thought." *International Journal of Middle East Studies* 21 (1989): 171–191.

McCarthy, Richard J., trans. *The Theology of al-Ashʿarī: The Arabic Texts of al-Ashʿarī's Kitāb al-Lumaʿ and*

Risālat istiḥsān al-khawḍ fī ʿilm al-kalām. Beirut: Imprimerie Catholique, 1953.

Najjar, Ibrahim Y., trans. *Faith and Reason in Islam: Averroes' Exposition of Religious Arguments*. Oxford: Oneworld, 2001.

al-Māwardī, Abū l-Ḥasan. *The Ordinances of Government: al-Aḥkām al-Sulṭāniyya w'al-Wilāyat al-Dīniyya*. Translated by Wafaa H. Wahba. Reading, U.K.: Garnet, 1996.

Otto, Jan Michiel, ed. *Sharia Incorporated: A Comparative Overview of the Legal Systems of Twelve Muslim Countries in Past and Present*. Leiden: Leiden University Press, 2010.

Sharīʿatī, ʿAlī. *On the Sociology of Islam: Lectures*. Translated by Hamid Algar. Berkeley: Mizan, 1979.

Shepard, William E. *Sayyid Qutb and Islamic Activism: A Translation and Critical Analysis of* Social Justice in Islam. Leiden: Brill, 1996.

Vasalou, Sophia. *Moral Agents and Their Deserts: The Character of Muʿtazilite Ethics*. Princeton, N.J.: Princeton University Press, 2008.

Walker, Paul E., trans. *A Guide to Conclusive Proofs for the Principles of Belief: Kitāb al-irshād ilā qawāṭiʿ al-adilla fī uṣūl al-iʿtiqād [by] Imām al-Ḥaramayn al-Juwaynī*. Reading, U.K.: Garnet, 2000.

Walzer, Richard, trans. *Al-Farabi on the Perfect State: Abū Naṣr al-Fārābī's Mabādiʾ ārāʾ ahl al-madīna al-fāḍila*. Oxford: Clarendon Press, 1985.

Watt, William M. *Islamic Creeds: A Selection*. Edinburgh: Edinburgh University Press, 1994.

Andrew F. March

Justice and Benevolence Party.

The Justice and Benevolence Party (ʿAdl wa-al-Iḥṣān) is the largest Islamic organization in Morocco. Shaykh Abdessalam Yassine (ʿAbd al-Salām Yāsīn) officially founded the organization in 1987, although it had existed under other names before that date. The Justice and Benevolence Party is opposed to the institution of the Moroccan monarchy, which was a point of view first expressed in a letter written by Shaykh Yassine to King Ḥasan II titled "Islam or the Deluge." In that letter Shaykh Yassine remonstrated with King Ḥasan, urging him to "repent" as an impious ruler. In response to his criticism King Ḥasan interned Shaykh Yassine in a psychiatric hospital until 1978. From 1978 until 2000 he was either in jail or under house arrest. King Muḥammed VI finally released him from custody in May 2000.

The Justice and Benevolence Party is not a political party that participates in elections. It refuses to participate in the electoral system because it does not recognize the legitimacy of the Moroccan monarchy. The organization formally objects to the provision in the Moroccan constitution that designates the king of Morocco as the *amīr al-muʾminīn*, or "commander of the faithful," and it objects to the constitutional provision that the king's person and reputation is inviolable. Because of its position regarding these two issues, the organization believes it cannot recognize the monarchy. The party, however, is tolerated by the regime, and it organizes demonstrations and engages in charitable and educational endeavors.

The Justice and Benevolence Party has emphasized spiritual and social development for its members, which springs from Shaykh Yassine's experiences as a Ṣūfī practitioner. Before founding the Justice and DevelopmentParty, Shaykh Yassine was a member and leader within the Būtshīshīyah Ṣūfī order, which had been led by Ḥājj ʿAbbās al-Qādirī. After the death of Shaykh ʿAbbās in 1972, Yassine left the Būtshīshīyah order. He then established the Justice and Benevolence Party in 1987. The party's orientation, organization, and leadership have emphasized moral and spiritual development, which reflect its Ṣūfī origins. Besides focusing on spiritual and moral development, Shaykh Yassine's critique of the Moroccan monarchy is part of a longer tradition of Moroccan religious leaders who were also influenced by Sufism, including Hassan Lyousi (b. 1631) and Muḥammad ibn ʿAbd al-Kabīr al-Kattānī (1873–1909).

The organization does not participate in formal electoral politics in the traditional sense. It remains the largest Islamist organization in Morocco, however, and as such remains influential in politics because it can either counsel or direct its followers to vote for candidates or parties that are standing for political office. Because of its capability to mobilize its members to vote, it remains a politically potent despite much criticism leveled at it by Salafist organizations and parties that do not endorse its Ṣūfī inspired principles. Despite this Salafist critique of its Ṣūfī orientation, this branch of Ṣūfī mysticism has deep roots and continues to have influence in Morocco. Both the party's Ṣūfī orientation and its advocacy for the amelioration for the conditions of the poor and for political reform have attracted wide following in Morocco.

The organization has a pyramidal structure; the basic unit of the organization is the *usrah*, or family, which consists of two to ten persons. The members of the *usrah* try to meet three times a week to pray, study, and provide mutual assistance within a family setting. The various *usrah* are overseen by a general council and a supreme guide. Besides providing a supportive environment through the *usrah*, the organization provides formal medical, social, recreational, and financial services.

The liberalization of the Moroccan regime that began in the mid-1990s has somewhat weakened the Justice and Benevolence Party's influence, but it remains the largest Islamist organization in Morocco. As it has weakened, the influence of its former rival the Justice and Development Party has grown. Despite the relative growth of the Justice and Development Party, the Justice and Benevolence Party remains important within the fragmented opposition to the Moroccan monarchy. It remains an important agent for social and political mobilization.

BIBLIOGRAPHY

Lauzière, Henri. "Post-Islamism and Religious Discourse of ʿAbd al-Salam Yasin" *International Journal of Middle East Studies* 37 (May 2005): 241–261.

Munson, Henry, Jr. *Religion and Power in Morocco*. New Haven, Conn.: Yale University Press, 1993.

Shahin, Emad Eldin. *Political Ascent: Contemporary Islamic Movements in North Africa*. Boulder, Colo.: Westview, 1997.

Yāsīn, ʿAbd al-Salām. *Rijāl al-qawmah wa-al-iṣlāḥ*. [Rabat, Morocco]: Manshūrāt al-Ṣafāʾ lil-Intāj, 2001.

Ricardo Laremont

Justice and Development Party.

Although the Justice and Development Party (ʿAdālah wa-al-Tanmiyah; Le Parti de la Justice et du Développement [PJD]) of Morocco was officially founded in 1998, its origins can be found in a predecessor party, the Ḥizb al-Ḥarakah al-Shaʿbīyah al-Dustūrīyah al-Dīmuqrāṭīyah or Mouvement Populaire Démocratique et Constitutionnel (MPDC; Popular Constitutional and Democratic Party) that was founded by ʿAbd al-Karīm al-Khaṭīb in 1967. Al-Khaṭīb was a well-respected senior politician who was favorably viewed by the Moroccan monarchy. The activists who eventually founded the PJD had belonged to a clandestine organization known as al-Shabībah al-Islāmīyah, which, because of its more radical views regarding the use of violence for political change and their questioning of the legitimacy of the monarchy, had not met with palace approval. Beginning in the 1990s core activists within al-Shabībah al-Islāmīyah began moderating their views and created a politically strategic link with al-Khaṭīb that enabled them to join his party and stand for office in the parliamentary elections of November 1997. In that election the MPDC won nine seats in the parliament. In 1998, with the MPDC now controlled by al-Shabībah al-Islāmīyah members, the organization changed its name to the Justice and Development Party.

The PJD is an Islamist-oriented party whose stated objective is the improvement of the socio-economic conditions of the Moroccan people. It does not oppose the institution of the Moroccan monarchy, and because of this policy position the monarchy has approved its operation as a party. The PJD has tried to position itself as a moderate Islamist party, even consciously modeling itself upon Turkey's Justice and Development Party (AKP). There is not, however, a formal connection between these two parties. The PJD's economic program has focused upon the objective of obtaining GDP growth rates of 7 percent per annum in Morocco, which, under most circumstances, is difficult to attain. It remains an Islamist party, yet its foreign policy it has placed great emphasis on maintaining favorable relations with the West and especially with the European Union. The European Union constitutes Morocco's principal export market and attracts a considerable number of Moroccan migrant workers.

In the next set of parliamentary elections, which were held on 27 September 2002, the party advanced its political position and became the leading opposition party in Morocco by winning 42 of 325 seats in the national legislature. Five years later, when the September 2007 parliamentary elections were held, it increased its representation in the national legislature to forty-six members. During the November 2011 parliamentary elections it won 107 of 395 seats to become the leading vote-getting party. After winning the plurality of the vote in that election it proceeded to form a coalition government with three other parties: the socialist Parti du Progrès et du Socialisme (PPS), the nationalist Istiqlāl party, and the royalist Mouvement Populaire (MP). On 29 November 2011, Abdelillah Benkirane, the leader of the PJD, was appointed prime minister of Morocco by King Muḥammed VI.

The PJD recognizes the legitimacy of the monarchy within the framework of the Moroccan state. The party's position stands in contrast with the Justice and Benevolence Party (a key rival in the Moroccan political system), which does not accept either that the Moroccan monarch as the leader of the faithful (*amīr al-muʾminīn*) or that the monarch's person is inviolable Because the PJD has accepted the monarchy's legitimacy, the monarchy has accepted it as a viable political player within the Moroccan political system. Also, the PJD has distanced itself apart from other Salafist parties because it does not advocate a state that would be ruled exclusively by Sharīʿah, or Islamic law. It has developed into a conservative party that is keen on upholding traditional moral values, working with the monarchy, and continuing to oppose the more negative aspects of western culture. It pragmatically works to maintain positive economic and diplomatic relations with the West. By staking moderate positions on social and political matters, the PJD has notably expanded its electoral success while still maintaining a core of political support from its constituents, who are attracted to its Islamist-informed rhetoric and frames of political reference.

With its victory in the November 2011 parliamentary elections the PJD moved from being the principal opposition party to being the leader within a coalition government. In terms of political practice it has not sought to dominate the political arena but rather has worked with other parties that do not share its Islamist views. For the most part the PJD's political positions have not been rigid or unpredictable. Although the PJD has consistently called for the prohibition of the consumption and distribution of alcoholic beverages, and while it has challenged the media when it believes that Islam has been insulted, in 2005 it supported the adoption of a new, more liberal version of the country's code regulating marriage and family life, known as the Mudawwana. The PJD's support for the revision of the Mudawwana provoked considerable criticism from Morocco's more conservative Islamist groups in Morocco. Despite these conservative criticisms, its support of the revision of the Mudawwana arguably advanced the social status of women in Morocco. Its pursuit of moderate positions and support of the monarchy have enhanced the party's success with the electorate and has distanced it from the positions taken by the more conservative Islamists.

Bibliography

Hamzawy, Amr. *Party of Justice and Development in Morocco: Participation and its Discontents*. Carnegie Papers 93. Washington, D.C.: Carnegie Endowment for International Peace, Middle East Program, 2008.

Tozy, Mohamed. *Monarchie et Islam politique au Maroc*. Paris: Presses de la Fondation Nationale des Sciences Politiques, 1999.

Wegner, Eva, and Miguel Pellicer. "Islamist Moderation without Democratization: The Coming of Age of the Moroccan Party of Justice and Development?" *Democratization* 16, no. 1 (2009): 157–175.

Ricardo Laremont

Just War. As a term of art, the phrase "just war" translates the Latin *bellum iustum*. It is thus of Roman provenance and is characteristically associated with developments in those areas where Latin continued as the language of learned people for the centuries following the collapse of the Western empire in the fifth century CE In this sense, the terminology would seem to have little relevance to Muslim ideas concerning war. However, the continuation of the eastern portions of the Roman Empire ensured that something of the old models in politics and war remained in place, not least in a number of the areas that came under Muslim rule following the conquests of the seventh century. While one ought not overestimate the impact of Roman (or Byzantine) notions related to the justification and conduct of war on the development of Islam—which in fact drew on a number of religious and cultural sources—it nevertheless remains the case that the earliest works in which Muslim jurists pronounce on the rights and wrongs of armed force reflect the basic structure of *bellum iustum*. It is difficult to avoid the conclusion that this Roman (and Christian) notion influenced developments in Muslim discourse.

At least since the time of Cicero (106–43 BCE), discussions of just war pointed to three requirements: right authority, just cause, and right intention, with the last indicated by right conduct. Right authority pointed to war as a public affair. Fighting between individuals or between two or more parties within the state might occur; it did not constitute war, however. In just war discourse, that formal designation was reserved for fighting authorized by recognized officials. This restriction in fact rendered a number of types of fighting suspect. Rebellion, for example, did not carry a positive valence, and could often be seen as a criminal activity. *Bellum iustum* was in fact conceived as a way of countering the more anarchic forms of fighting associated with war or violence more generally.

Just cause again reflects the reservation of the right of war to public authority. That is, for war to be just the cause must reflect legitimate political interests: recovery of territory wrongly taken by an enemy, the need to secure boundaries or to protect the good represented by the order of the state, and more generally the protection of justice are typical examples.

Finally, right intention points to norms related to the conduct of war. *Bellum iustum* required that those considering the use of armed force seek to resolve differences with an enemy by offering terms of peace. In Cicero's formulation, the religious officials known as *fetiales* served as emissaries, delivering an "official demand for satisfaction," joined with a warning that a refusal would lead to war. In the context of fighting, those claiming the mantle of just war were bound to observe any agreements with or promises made to enemy forces. They should also avoid direct harm to noncombatants and eschew the use of poisons or other unjust means. As such, *bellum iustum* provided a vocabulary by which one might distinguish rightful uses of armed force from those that are wrong.

With this background, it is a relatively simple matter to track just war concerns in Muslim discourse. Al-Shaybānī's *Kitāb al-siyar* contains opinions characteristic of the Ḥanafī school of jurisprudence in the early ʿAbbāsid period (c. 750–805). One of the basic texts on which these opinions are based relates the orders given to fighters by the Prophet Muḥammad. They are to fight "in the path of God." They are to fight "only those who disbelieve" and who display this by refusing to accept terms of peace with the Muslims. And they are not to "cheat or commit treachery," to "mutilate anyone or to kill children." Reading through the al-Shaybānī's text, it is clear that the collected opinions suppose that approved fighting involves a command from publicly established authorities, for causes consistent with the establishment and maintenance of a territory in which the freedom to practice Islam is secure, and conducted in ways that suggest an honorable intent. With respect to the last, in particular, the prohibition of killing children already mentioned is expanded to include women, the old, the lame, the blind, monks, and others who do not participate in fighting; as well, restrictions on the use of certain tactics and weapons follow. The analogy with *bellum iustum* seems very clear. Indeed, the procedures outlined in the report of the Prophet's orders appear to track Cicero's description of the traditions of the *fetiales* so closely that one wonders whether some experience of the Roman way of war may in fact be a source for this tradition.

The various terms associated with fighting are also of interest in connection with notions of just war. Both *ḥarb* (usually translated "war") and *qitāl* ("killing," "slaughter") suggest activities that may be approved in some contexts and disapproved in others. Qurʾān 47:4, for example, refers to enemy fighters captured during battle. These may be used to bargain with the enemy "until the war [*al-ḥarb*]" is over. By contrast, 5:33 condemns those who "wage war [*yuhāribūna*] against God and His Messenger." At 2:190, believers are commanded to "fight [*qātilū*] in God's way against those who fight you [*yuqātilūnakum*]" though they are to avoid violating certain limits. Both activities obtain justice in connection with *jihād*, that is, the struggle to bring oneself and one's world into conformity with divine guidance.

By contrast with these, terms like *fitnah* ("strife," "dissension") and *fasād* ("corruption") seem always to carry negative valence. Used in connection with fighting, they indicate an activity that is unjust. Thus, Qurʾān 2:191 indicates that *fitnah* is worse than killing, while 5:33 extends the negative judgment on those who make war against God and God's Messenger by adding that they spread *fasād* in the land.

In connection with the attempt to distinguish just from unjust fighting, one of the more interesting features of juridical discourse has to do with the set of judgments related to *al-bughāt* and *al-khawārij*. The basic meanings of these terms seems to be negative. The former suggests "tyrants," in the sense of a group of people who seek to impose their will upon others, while the latter indicates "secessionists" and was historically associated with a group or groups unwilling to adhere to a settlement negotiated between parties in the fighting (*fitnah*) between ʿAlī and

Muʿāwiyah. In the works of jurists, however, the terms come to stand for "rebels," and much attention is given to directing the forces of the established regime to limit their response so that reconciliation remains possible. In this regard, jurists developed a number of criteria by which rebels might be distinguished from others who might become the target of legitimate force (for example, apostates, brigands, and highwaymen). Parties of a certain size, whose complaint against an existing regime had an Islamic basis, and who provide the government with real provocation (that is, something beyond critical speech), should be treated differently from others. In this sense, historic Muslim reasoning created a limited space for something like just rebellion.

Since the eighteenth century, many of the best known cases of Muslims engaged in fighting have involved resistance—to European imperial or colonial forces, as well as to Muslim regimes considered inadequate or corrupt. In this sense, the political and military conditions in which Muslims speak about just and unjust wars are importantly distinct from those in which scholars like al-Shaybānī promulgated their opinions. While some of the old terms are still utilized, albeit controversially (*jihād*, to take the most obvious case), others seem to have fallen into disuse (*bughāt*, for example). Instead, contemporary Muslims make use of a number of other terms, for example, *thawrah* (revolution), *inqilāb* (overturning), and *intifāḍah* (awakening). Distinguishing the just from the unjust in connection with these terms is an ongoing task, with much import for the future of Muslim discourse about war.

As to as the conduct of war, most mainstream Muslim scholars embrace the international law of armed conflict, codified in such international agreements as the Geneva Conventions, as entirely compatible with Islamic law and ethics. Many of these scholars have been outspoken critics of terrorism and terrorist groups such as al-Qaʿida. Evident in much of the Muslim discourse on *jihād* today is a conscious effort to align Islamic theory with Western notions of just war.

Bibliography

Hashmi, Sohail H., ed. *Just Wars, Holy Wars, and Jihads: Christian, Jewish, and Muslim Encounters and Exchanges*. New York: Oxford University Press, 2012.

Johnson, James Turner. *The Holy War Idea in Western and Islamic Traditions*. University Park: Pennsylvania State University Press, 1997.

Johnson, James Turner, and John Kelsay. *Cross, Crescent, and Sword: The Justification and Limitation of War in Western and Islamic Tradition*. New York: Greenwood, 1990.

Kelsay, John. *Arguing the Just War in Islam*. Cambridge, Mass.: Harvard University Press, 2007.

Kelsay, John. *Islam and War: A Study in Comparative Ethics*. Louisville, Ky.: Westminster John Knox, 1993.

Kelsay, John, and James Turner Johnson, eds. *Just War and Jihad: Historical and Theoretical Perspectives on War and Peace in Western and Islamic Traditions*. New York: Greenwood, 1991.

Zawati, Hilmi M. *Is Jihad a Just War?: War, Peace, and Human Rights Under Islamic and Public International Law*. Lewiston, N.Y.: Edwin Mellen, 2001.

John Kelsay

Juwaynī, ʿAbd al-Mālik al-. Al-Juwaynī (d. 1085) was a distinguished jurist of the Shāfiʿī school, a key figure in Ashʿarī theology (*kalām*), and one of the pioneers of theoretical jurisprudence (*uṣūl al-fiqh*). He was born near Nishapur, the chief city of Khorāsān, to a respected Shāfiʿī jurist, Abū Muḥammad al-Juwaynī (d. 1047), who was also his first teacher. Among his other teachers was the redoubtable Abū al-Qāsim al-Isfarāyīnī (d. 1060). After he was banned from the pulpits by the Ḥanafī vizier of the Seljuk sultan Tughril Beg (r. 1055–1063), reportedly because he advocated Ashʿarī theology, al-Juwaynī lived in exile for four years in Mecca and Medina, where he served as an imam—hence his honorific "Imām al-Ḥaramayn" (the prayer leader of the two sacred mosques). With the succession of Alp Arslan in 1063 or possibly earlier, the Seljuk vizier Niẓām al-Mulk (r. 1063–1092), an ardent Shāfiʿī, appointed al-Juwaynī, barely thirty years of age, as the head of the grand *madrasah* of Baghdad, al-Niẓāmīyah.

Al-Juwaynī made his name primarily as a jurist and theologian. His treatise on legal theory, *al-Burhān fī uṣūl al-fiqh,* is regarded as both pioneering and brilliant, while his *al-Irshād ilā qawāṭiʿ al-adillah fī uṣūl al-iʿtiqād* is considered a definitive reference work in Ashʿarī theology (and, according to Ibn Khaldūn, the last great work in *kalām* before al-Ghazālī, al-Juwaynī's illustrious student, mixed it with *falsafah*). As an Ashʿarī, his chief intellectual adversary was the Muʿtazilī school, which had also been adopted by the Shīʿah. A crucial backdrop for al-Juwaynī's political ideas was the rout of the Shīʿī Būyids by his Sunnī patrons—the uncouth but orthodox Seljuks—in various battles ending in 1060.

Al-Juwaynī's major work on governance is *Ghiyāth al-umam fī iltiyāth al-ẓulam* ("Aid to Nations Enshrouded in Darkness"; also called *al-Ghiyāthī,* after the vizier Ghiyāth al-Dīn Niẓām al-Mulk), a treatise on the leadership of the (Sunnī) Muslim community, which stands out in the Ashʿarī tradition for its realist streak. It is divided into three parts. The first part, which occupies a little over half of the treatise, corresponds to the conventional Sunnī caliphate discourse. This discourse, pioneered by the Ashʿarīs al-Bāqillānī (d. 1013) and al-Baghdādī (d. 1037), had its classical statement in the treatise *al-Aḥkām al-sulṭānīyah* of al-Māwardī (d. 1058). The second part addresses the emergency scenario in which the Muslim community lacks an imam (i.e., a caliph); the third contemplates the extinction of "the carriers of the Sharīʿah"—namely, the *ʿulamāʾ*. Given the significance of the continuance of the caliphate for Sunnīs and the fact that Sunnīs like al-Māwardī had not effectively dealt with the reduction of the caliphal office to a mere symbol, al-Juwaynī's bold contemplation of the extinction of the caliphate and even of scholars must have been startling for its originality, realism, and pessimism.

Al-Juwaynī follows the main contours of the caliphate discourse on the whole, adding a conspicuous emphasis on power as a key element of caliphal legitimacy. To install a caliph, al-Juwaynī holds, is an obligation, if it is possible. He is willing to compromise on some of the qualifications Sunnīs required of the caliph—that he be righteous, learned, capable, and Qurashī in lineage. But, in conscious contrast with al-Māwardī, who was willing to legitimize an "overpowered" caliphate—the ʿAbbāsid caliphs had been essentially under house arrest under the Būyids—al-Juwaynī requires of the caliph independent power and self-sufficiency (*istiqlāl* and *kifāyah*). In his discussion of methods of appointment, al-Juwaynī is the first to add brute force (*ghalbah*); scholars before him had tolerated the self-appointment of a ruler only if ratified by the community or at least the influential electors (*ahl al-ḥall wa-al-ʿaqd*).

With his daring proposal that, at least in an emergency, a non-Qurashī, such as Niẓām al-Mulk or another capable Seljuk sultan, could legitimately hold the imamate, al-Juwaynī clashed with al-Māwardī; he also took al-Māwardī to task for not mentioning disagreements about issues surrounding the caliphate and for neither being attentive to the nature of the evidence proffered for them nor differentiating between conclusions based on definitive proofs (*qaṭʿī*) and opinions based on speculative evidence (*ẓannī*, or *maẓnūn*). Al-Juwaynī agreed with al-Māwardī on the necessity of reconciling with the military patronage state (sultanate) but criticized him for not going far enough in supporting it and instead suggesting excessive measures to protect an ineffectual symbol of the caliphate. To al-Juwaynī reverence had been granted to the ʿAbbāsid caliphate for two reasons beyond its lineage and the inherited Sunnī consensus: protection of the unity of the Muslim community and society (prevention of civil war and other internal strife) and fighting the enemy (defense of the house of Islam). The new power sultans also fulfilled both of these requirements. Al-Juwaynī thus allowed for the legitimization of an imamate by force, or, more accurately, the transfer of the title of Imam to the military commanders, the Seljuks. While far from the ideal candidates for the caliphate and however unruly they were as people, these new defenders of Sunnī Islam could still put power in service of religion, he opined. They were acceptable as long as they consulted the *ʿulamāʾ* and applied the divine law.

Although it has been suggested that, in contrast with al-Māwardī, who emphasized the "sacrosanctity of the imam," al-Juwaynī "detached the imamate altogether from the domain of prophecy and sacred objects," thus demoting the imam "to a temporal functionary, though still responsible for the well-being of the religion" (Hallaq 1984, p. 30), it is more accurate to say that al-Juwaynī rejected the excessive sanctification of the caliphate that had been al-Māwardī's innovation. The functions al-Juwaynī assigned to the imam comprised religious ones, including the support of all Sunnī schools in law but in theology only Ashʿarism, *jihād* against the enemy, administration, appointment of judges, and, most importantly, application of the Sharīʿah. Like al-Māwardī, al-Juwaynī dispenses with the *ahl al-ḥall wa-al-ʿaqd* (those who loose and bind) and considers the imam's choice of his heir apparent (testamentary designation, *ʿahd*) irrevocable, even, like al-Māwardī but unlike al-Bāqillānī, allowing the imam to choose a succession of heirs, thus theoretically strengthening the assumption that the imam is the owner of the office rather than a representative of the community. Also, in al-Juwaynī's theory the role of the *ʿulamāʾ* increased notably, for he mentioned them in an advisory capacity, whereas al-Māwardī did not.

[*See also* Ahl al-Ḥall wa-al-ʿAqd; Māwardī, Abū al-Ḥasan al-; Niẓām al-Mulk; Seljuk Dynasty; *and* Tyranny.]

BIBLIOGRAPHY

Anjum, Ovamir. *Politics, Law, and Community in Islamic Thought: The Taymiyyan Moment*. Cambridge, U.K.: Cambridge University Press, 2012.

Hallaq, Wael B. "Caliphs, Jurists, and the Saljūqs in the Political Thought of Juwaynī." *Muslim World* 74, no. 1 (1984): 26–41.

Juwaynī, Abū al-Maʿālī al-. *Ghiyāth al-umam fī iltiyāth al-ẓulam*. Edited by Haytham Khalīfah al-Ṭuʿaymī. Beirut: al-Maktabah al-ʿAṣrīyah, 2006.

Juwaynī, Abū al-Maʿālī al-. *A Guide to Conclusive Proofs for the Principles of Belief*. Translated by Paul E. Walker. Reading, U.K.: Garnett, 2000.

OVAMIR ANJUM

K

KĀNŪN. The Ottoman system of justice operated within a diverse legal environment. The officially recognized religious minorities (until the mid-nineteenth century the Greek Orthodox, Armenian, and Jewish communities), and some other groups, notably tribal entities, enjoyed limited legal autonomy in the realm of personal status law as well as in most civil and criminal actions exclusively involving members of their respective communities. Certain geographical regions, depending on the circumstances of their conquest, continued to be administered under local customary laws, some dating back to previous Islamic or Christian regimes. Official recognition of these various usages, however, arose from the allowances of *kānūn*, or state legislation, and Sharīʿah, Islamic law, the two pillars of the entire imperial legal system.

Sharīʿah law was scripturally based, deriving primarily from the Qurʾān and the recorded practice of the Prophet Muḥammad. Kānūn (T., < Ar. *qānūn*) can be understood as state law, deriving from the principle of *ʿurf* (T. *örf*), the sultan's executive right and initiative as sovereign ruler. The term *kānūn* can refer to a specific piece of legislation, whether an individual law or a set of regulations pertaining to a particular subject. It also refers in a more general sense to any non-Sharīʿah legislation of the ruler's making. Decrees, statutes, orders, and regulations, in the Ottoman case bearing such names as *kānūn*, *hükm*, *kanunname*, *hatt-ı hümayun*, *hatt-ı şerif*, *nizam*, *emr*, *buyuruldu*, *yasak*, *berat*, and *ferman*, were all varieties of such legislation, that is, they constituted state law promulgated by the sultan or, on his authority, by his officials. The sultan's right to legislate was regarded as sanctioned by the sharīʿah, and his laws and ordinances were generally accepted as consonant with sharīʿah tenets and principles. Rulers were eager to stress these affinities in order to underscore both the rectitude of their official decrees and their own legitimacy as Islamic sovereigns.

In general, *kānūn* legislation was supplementary to the Sharīʿah in that it applied to areas of law that the Sharīʿah either did not address or did not fully elaborate. The province of *kānūn* typically included land tenure, taxation apart from taxes imposed by Sharīʿah, administrative practice, military governance, and public order, as well as the specification of crimes and penalties relating to transgressions in any of these. In theory, an incumbent sultan's issuances were valid only for the duration of his reign. State decrees therefore had to be renewed by successors. In practice, reaffirmation seems to have occurred almost by default, unless and until a successor explicitly revoked or replaced a predecessor's rulings. The conception of state law as finite, not binding on successors, increased new rulers' independence. Perhaps more importantly, it reflected the *ulema*'s reluctance to admit of any law save divine law, Sharīʿah, as binding for all time.

Although *kānūn* and Sharīʿah had quite different provenances, the two were conjoined in the person of the sultan, who ultimately presided over both. In practice, the purview of each legal realm overlapped with the other in several ways. For one thing, the sultans often linked the two rhetorically, invoking the religious licitness of state legislation by inserting Qurʾānic phrases into the *kānūn* text, or including an explicit statement pronouncing the legislation to be in accord with Sharīʿah. The interpenetration of *kānūn* and Sharīʿah also occurred substantively in the case of Sharīʿah-defined offenses that did not stipulate precise penalties. For example, Sharīʿah law identifies malicious wounding (Ar. *jurḥ*; T. *cerh*) as a punishable offense, but it does not assign penalties beyond saying that such offenses are subject to the discretionary judgment (Ar. *taʿzīr*) of the Islamic court judge (Ar. *qāḍī*; T. *kadi*). Sharīʿah also does not put forward preventive public order measures, like curfews or citizen watch patrols, that might guard against criminal assault. Rulers or their designees thus could themselves determine whether punishments should be corporal or monetary, and how much of either type should be exacted. The sultan might simply endorse customary usage in such matters, or he or a successor might decide that previous punishments, regardless of longstanding custom, were too lenient. The openness of the Sharīʿah formulation enabled sultans to establish the parameters of punishments. It also increased the likelihood that the severity of discretionary punishments would vary over time and space, as indeed occurred in Ottoman jurisprudence. The silence of the Sharīʿah regarding preventative measures against these sorts of criminal acts gave the ruler further scope for tying his own public order enactments to a Sharīʿah preoccupation and thereby to religious sanction.

Ottoman Law in Practice. The functions of Ottoman Sharīʿah court judges give additional evidence of the often porous boundary between the two kinds of law. *Kadi*s were appointed to judgeships on the strength of their expertise in Islamic law. However, they were responsible for helping to implement the requirements both of *kānūn* legislation and of the Sharīʿah law for which they had expressly trained. For most of the history of the Ottoman Empire, although especially after the mid-sixteenth century, when the major components of the religious educational system and legal apparatus were fully in place, Sharīʿah court judges were assigned to virtually every corner of the empire, administering justice in regular or circuit courts and also serving as administrative adjuncts—central government watchdogs—in the provinces. The Sharīʿah court system, with its hundreds of *kadi*s and judicial adjuncts, was the backbone of the legal system as a whole until the mid-nineteenth century and the reforms of the Tanzimat era. It was also a—arguably the—principal conveyor of Ottoman Islamic norms and values throughout the vast empire.

With respect to the implementation of *kānūn* and the locus of senior authority in the adjudication of *kānūn*, the councils of provincial governors (T. *beylerbeyi*, *vali*) and district heads (T. *sancak beyi*), as well as the imperial divan itself, functioned as courts at the highest levels. It was these courts that handled cases involving officialdom. Such cases included complaints, petitions, and appeals—emanating either from official quarters or from the ordinary populace—regarding the action or lack of action of imperial appointees.

The history of state legislation in the Ottoman empire dates back to the earliest sultans. However, it was only in the reign of the seventh, Mehmed II (r. 1451–1481), the Conqueror of Constantinople, that *kānūn* laws covering vast regulatory areas were issued in codified form. In fact, the *kanunname*, code of laws or book of laws, attributed to Mehmed II contains material from earlier and later periods, thus casting doubt on its mid-fifteenth-century origin and on the dating of all its rules and strictures to Mehmed's reign. Indeed, specific clauses appear to relate to the late sixteenth and early seventeenth centuries, suggesting that later legislators either saw advantage in invoking the Conqueror's foundational reign or, more likely, that Mehmed's legislation had been added to and revised. *Kanunname*s were by their nature revisionary and accretional, with some older measures dropped and others carried forward into new times and forms. *Kānūn* law, then, was essentially dynamic. Nonetheless, like many features of Ottoman rule, the sultan's enactments were usually cloaked in the comforting language of time-honored precedent and Sharīʿah sanction.

The *kanunname* of Mehmed II is one of several surviving examples of empire-wide, comprehensive codes that were promulgated or emerged in revised form in the fifteenth through the seventeenth centuries. These covered most aspects of imperial governance and the socioeconomic order. Mehmed's *kanunname* opened with sections on crimes and punishments. It went on to spell out tax rates, payers, exemptees, and collectors; the organization and responsibilities of institutions from military fiefs (T. *timar*), government bureaus, and the imperial mints to the education and ranking of *kadi*s and other *ulema*; protocol regarding the person of the sultan and palace ceremonial; and the fratricidal law of succession, which Mehmed II thereby regularized. More common were law codes drawn up for specific regions or for designated areas of law. An example of the former, among any number of codes issued over the centuries for individual provincial areas (T. *sancak*, *liva*), is that produced for the Hungarian region of Buda around the time of its conquest in 1540. An example of the latter includes codes dealing specifically with market regulations and standards, such as the *Kanunname-i ihtisab* issued by Bayezid II (r. 1481–1512), son and successor of Mehmed II, for each of the municipalities of Bursa, Edirne, and Istanbul.

Mehmed's great-grandson, Süleyman I (r. 1520–1566), "the Magnificent," is most closely associated with ensuring the legacy of Ottoman *kānūn*. Süleyman was memorialized among the Ottomans themselves as *Kanuni*, "Lawgiver," for his achievements in producing numerous exemplary codes for the many regions and pursuits of his vastly expanded realm, and for doing so without compromising the notion of the compatibility of *kānūn* with Sharīʿah law. His efforts were aided by the *şeyhülislam* (< Ar. *shaykh al-islām*) or Grand Mufti of the time, Mehmed Ebüssuʾûd (d. 1574), who has come to be regarded as the most important of Ottoman jurists. Codes and individual decrees credited to Süleyman and understood to have been vetted by Ebüssuʾûd became the basis of Ottoman governance for centuries to come.

Modern scholarship has discarded the old view of *kānūn* and Sharīʿah as completely separate legal spheres. However, the connections and accord between the two should not be overstated. Not all *ulema* accepted the principle of a legislative authority other than God, or legislation other than divinely ordained law. Even *ulema* who were comfortable with the concepts of *ʿurf* and the public good (Ar. *maṣlaḥa*) objected to particular laws when they regarded them as impinging on Sharīʿah. For their part, various sultans were keen to expand the scope of their sovereignty irrespective of Sharīʿah limitations or the claims of *ulema* more conventional in their orthodoxy than Ebüssuʾûd. The legal history of the empire in fact reflects struggles between exponents of one or the other position. The focus of these struggles, especially in the first three Ottoman centuries, the fourteenth through the sixteenth, was the legislation of individual sultans. In the later centuries the conflict over how best to manage the uniquely diverse and increasingly more beset empire tended to arise from the differences in perspective and interest between *kānūn*-minded officials, who were concentrated in the central bureaucracy, and the Sharīʿah-minded, led by members of the *ulema*.

Halil İnalcık has argued (1969, p. 136) that from the early seventeenth century until the nineteenth-century reforms, state legislation was increasingly subject to Sharīʿah curbs and considerations. In the nineteenth century, although especially as of the latter half of the reign of Mahmud II (r. 1808–1839), *kānūn* legislation as a vehicle for reasons of state regained ascendancy. The rise of the bureaucracy as the chief architect of secularizing Ottoman reform policies in the nineteenth century was one of the signal features of the institutionalized domination of state law over Sharīʿah. At the same time, the issuance of laws promising religious egalitarianism and of entire legal codes independent of the Sharīʿah marked the important, though still partial, displacement of Sharīʿah from major segments of Ottoman law.

[*See also* Ottoman Empire; *and* Siyāsah Sharʿīya.]

BIBLIOGRAPHY

Heyd, Uriel. *Studies in Old Ottoman Criminal Law.* Edited by V. L. Ménage. Oxford: Clarendon Press, 1973.

Imber, Colin. *Ebu's-su'ud: The Islamic Legal Tradition.* Stanford, Calif.: Stanford University Press, 1997.

İnalcık, Halil. "Ḳānūnnāme." In *The Encyclopaedia of Islam*, 2d ed., edited by P. J. Bearman et al. Leiden: Brill, 1960–2004.

İnalcık, Halil. "Suleiman the Lawgiver and Ottoman Law." *Archivum Ottomanicum* 1 (1969): 105–138.

Lowry, Heath. "The Ottoman *Liva Kanunnames* Contained in the *Defter-i Hakani*." *Journal of Ottoman Studies* 2 (1981): 43–74.

Peirce, Leslie. *Morality Tales: Law and Gender in the Ottoman Court of Aintab.* Berkeley: University of California Press, 2003.

Peters, Rudolph. *Crime and Punishment in Islamic Law.* Cambridge: Cambridge University Press, 2005.

MADELINE C. ZILFI

KARAKĪ, ʿALĪ AL-. Abū al-Ḥasan ʿAlī ibn al-Ḥusayn ibn ʿAbd al-ʿĀlī al-ʿĀmilī al-Karakī (1466–1534), known by the honorific al-Muḥaqqiq al-Thānī ("the Second Verifier/Investigator"), was an Arab Ithnā ʿAsharī ("Twelver") Shīʿī jurist, born into a family of Shīʿī *ʿulamāʾ* from the scholarly community of Karak Nūḥ in the Bekáa Valley. A distinguished figure in the evolution of Ithnā ʿAsharī substantive law (*fiqh*) and legal theory (*uṣūl al-fiqh*), al-Karakī is most remarkable as a major player in the religio-juridical-political landscape of early Ṣafavid Persia. His importance stems from his circumvention of a long-held Ithnā ʿAsharī doctrine of disassociation from temporal governments, his subsequent legal and administrative contributions to the sovereignty of the Ṣafavid polity, his active promulgation of scholastic-juridical Shiism in Ṣafavid domains, and his development (and implementation) of key theories bearing upon the administrative powers of qualified Shīʿī jurists.

Legal Scholarship and Political Influence. Al-Karakī's career developed at a time when the Shīʿī rulers of Ṣafavid Persia endeavored to legitimize and bolster their sovereignty (in the eyes of both their heterodox subjects and Ottoman foes) by promulgating the scholastic-juridical Shiism developed by the independent, highly respected *madrasahs* of the Jabal ʿĀmil and Bekáa (whose scholars were collectively referred to as ʿĀmilīs). Ṣafavid shahs invited prominent ʿĀmilīs to promote and administer a standardized, systematic Shiism in their domains; ʿĀmilī émigrés—through legal formulation, disputation, and administrative enactment—proved instrumental in placing Ṣafavid sovereignty on a strong foundation and converting the new empire's subjects.

Al-Karakī was first among prominent ʿĀmilī émigrés. After establishing himself as an exceptional jurist and teacher in Najaf, he soon accepted an invitation to the Ṣafavid court of Shāh Ismāʿīl I (r. 1501–1524), later returning to Najaf with a significant annual stipend. During the subsequent reign of Shah Ismāʿīl's son Ṭahmāsp (r. 1524–1576), al-Karakī came to exert a powerful influence at court; providing a measure of legitimacy through his rulings and actively engaging in the persuasion of heterodox subjects, he was rewarded with new powers and titles. Ṭahmāsp bestowed unprecedented honors on al-Karakī, designating him *Murawwij al-Madhhab* ("Propagator of the [Shīʿī] Doctrinal School") and—by *farmān* (official decree)—*Khātam al-Mujtahidīn* ("Seal of the *Mujtahids*"), *Mujtahid al-Zamān* ("*Mujtahid* of the Age"), and *Nā ʾib al-Imām* ("Deputy of the *Imām* [during the Occultation]"). Exceptional powers of appointment and dismissal were granted him, along with extensive, perpetual land endowments; officials and notables alike were enjoined to pay al-Karakī obedience and to model themselves after his example.

Such titles and powers were won through scholarly exactitude and disputational skill, and through these al-Karakī exerted an unparalleled legal-administrative influence. Via scholarly networks and manuals he instructed government officials directly—especially with regard to the administration of the land tax (*kharāj*). His reinstitution of the Friday prayer (a prerogative of the *imām* or his appointed deputy [*nāʾib*], long held to be in abeyance), his delegation of prayer leaders, his revival of the public cursing of the first two caliphs (a markedly anti-Sunnī ritual), and his permissive ruling that scholars might receive gifts from temporal rulers, were all controversial enactments pregnant with political implications.

Author-Jurist and Master Dialectician. Al-Karakī was a prolific and meticulous author-jurist; his rational and well-argued scholarship is preserved in numerous works, several of which have served as standard juridical manuals. Notably, he authored a prodigious number of treatises (*ras ā ʾil*) on the difficult legal controversies (*mas ā ʾil*, sing. *masʾalah*) of his day; of special import are his solutions to new problems attending the unprecedented executive powers bequeathed by an officially Shīʿī polity. On the whole, his work is marked by scrupulous analysis and rational inference in an instructional-dialectical style: extended question-and-answer sequences outline all the premises and responses that might arise in disputation over a particular *masʾalah*.

Al-Karakī's scholarship and administrative career, in fact, is everywhere marked by disputation (of particular note are his encounters with Ghiyāth al-Dīn al-Dashtakī and Ibrāhīm ibn Sulaymān al-Qaṭīfī). Nor was this a purely scholastic function; dialectical disputation certainly spurred the evolution of Ithnā ʿAsharī legal theory and substantive law, but the outcomes of formal disputations often had direct political consequences (e.g., the bolstering of a particular policy, or the dismissal of an opposing official) and proved a powerful dynamic in the dissemination of scholastic-juridical Shiism (persuading the heterodox population and combating Sunnī Ottoman propaganda).

Al-Karakī and the Powers of the Mujtahid. A thorny *masʾalah* throughout the evolution of Ithnā ʿAsharī Shiism (and bearing enormous political consequences in modern times) has been whether and to what extent a fully qualified legal scholar (*mujtahid*) may act as deputy (*nā ʾib*) for the Hidden Imām—that is, as an authoritative executive agent during the *imām*'s occultation. Key aspects of al-Karakī's career are his review and development of foundational arguments for the *mujtahid* as *nā ʾib al-imām*, his self-designation—and later investiture—as *nā ʾib al-imām*, and whatever role all this may have played in the doctrinal progression leading eventually to formulations of *wilāyat al-faqīh* (the jurist's assumption of total legislative and executive authority). However, notwithstanding certain claims that a protoformula may be extracted from his writings, al-Karakī's theorizing (and practice) never approached the comprehensive scope of *wilāyat al-faqīh*; he is best understood as an accommodationist *mujtahid*, interweaving his *ijtihād* with the executive authority of a temporal (though ostensibly Shīʿī) polity.

BIBLIOGRAPHY

Abisaab, Rula Jurdi. *Converting Persia: Religion and Power in the Safavid Empire*. London: I. B. Taurus, 2004.

Arjomand, Said Amir, ed. and trans. "Two Decrees of Shāh Ṭahmāsp Concerning Statecraft and the Authority of Shaykh ʿAlī al-Karakī." In *Authority and Political Culture in Shiʿism*, edited by Said Amir Arjomand, pp. 250–262. Albany: State University of New York Press, 1988.

Karakī, ʿAlī ibn al-Ḥusayn, al-. *Jāmiʿ al-maqāṣid fī Sharḥ al-qawāʿid*. Edited by Muʾassasat Āl al-Bayt li-Iḥyāʾ al-Turāth. 13 vols. Qom, Iran: Muʾassasat Āl al-Bayt li-Iḥyāʾ al-Turāth, 1987.

Karakī, ʿAlī ibn al-Ḥusayn al-, and Muḥammad al-Ḥassūn, ed. *Ḥayāt al-muḥaqqiq al-Karakī wa-Āthāruhu*. 12 vols. Tehran: Manshūrāt al-Iḥtijāj, 2002.

WALTER EDWARD YOUNG

KĀSHĀNI, ABOL-QĀSEM. Ayatollah Abol-Qāsem Kāshāni (1882–1962) was an Iranian religious and political leader during the national movement in the 1950s. Born in Tehran, Kāshāni made a pilgrimage to Mecca at the age of fifteen and settled in Najaf, Iraq, to pursue his education. His political activity began against British rule in Iraq when his father was killed in an uprising in April 1916. Sentenced to death in absentia, he escaped to Iran around February 1921.

Between 1921 and 1941, Kāshāni initially enjoyed the support of Reza Shah Pahlavi and was elected to the Constituent Assembly, which approved the establishment of the Pahlavi dynasty in 1925. However, he soon lost the shah's favor, withdrew from politics, and confined himself to teaching.

Toward the end of Reza Shah's reign, Kāshāni became involved in pro-German activities. In January 1942, following the British and Soviet invasion and occupation of Iran, Kāshāni, General Fazlullah Zahedi, and several army officers and politicians founded the Nahzat-i Millīyūn-i Īrān (Movement of Iranian Nationalists). The group was soon discovered, its members arrested, and Kāshāni sent into exile.

Returning to Iran at the end of World War II, Kāshāni expanded his power and popularity enormously during the movement to nationalize the Iranian oil industry. In the Majlis and outside, his followers began to mobilize support for the National Front under Mohammad Mossadegh's leadership. On 30 April 1951, Mossadegh was appointed prime minister.

Kāshāni's relations with the secular Mossadegh were marked by tension and suspicion from the beginning. By October 1952, relations between the two men had broken down, and Kāshāni finally abandoned Mossadegh and turned to General Zahedi and the Pahlavi court, leaving Mossadegh isolated when he was deposed in a CIA-financed coup d'état on 19 August 1953. The main reasons for the break were Kāshāni's expectation of more power and control over the cabinet, Mossadegh's desire to keep the clergy out of the governmental process, Mossadegh's inability to settle the Anglo-Iranian oil dispute and the crippling boycott of Iranian oil that resulted, and the clergy's fear of the growth of communism.

Mossadegh's downfall also ended Kāshāni's political career. General Zahedi, the new prime minister, offered Kāshāni a seat in the senate. Kāshāni rejected the offer and pressured Zahedi to implement the oil nationalization law. Zahedi ignored the ayatollah, who then declared Zahedi a dictator. Kāshāni's continued activities against Zahedi's government resulted in his arrest and imprisonment in July 1956 on charges of cooperation with the Fidāīyān-i Islām in the assassination of Prime Minister Razmara in 1951. However, Kāshāni's old age and the intervention of Ayatollahs Mohammad Hosayn Borujerdi and Abū al-Fazl Zanjānī saved his life. In 1958 Kāshāni's son Mustafā was mysteriously poisoned. This tragic event and disillusionment with politics caused Kāshāni to withdraw from public life. He died on 14 March 1962.

Kāshāni advocated the unity of the spiritual and temporal spheres, seeing the separation of religion and politics as a colonial plot. However, he never sought direct rule by the clergy. His major contribution to the status of the Iranian *ʿulamāʾ* was his revival of their traditional leadership role as spokesmen of popular discontent. The clerical opposition toward the government after 1963 and the developments that led to the 1979 revolution were considerably influenced by Kāshāni's ideas and activities. Although his views differed greatly from his clerical successors regarding Iranian nationalism, the place of Sharīʿah in society, and attitudes toward the West, many of his ideas were borrowed and developed by Ayatollah Khomeini and formed the foundations of his government. The role of the *ʿulamāʾ* as heirs to the Shīʿī imams that Kāshāni so often emphasized was expanded by Khomeini and formulated in the doctrine of *vilāyat-i faqīh*. Finally, Kāshāni's most important legacy was his dream of a nonaligned political bloc of all Muslim states, which found resonance in Khomeini's "neither East nor West" foreign policy.

BIBLIOGRAPHY

Abrahamian, Ervand. *Khomeinism: Essays on the Islamic Republic*. Berkeley: University of California Press, 1993.

Akhavi, Shahrough. "The Role of the Clergy in Iranian Politics, 1949–1954." In *Musaddiq, Iranian Nationalism, and Oil*, edited by James A. Bill and Roger Louis, pp. 97–117. London: I. B. Tauris, 1988.

Faghfoory, Mohammad H. "The Role of the Ulama in Twentieth-Century Iran with Particular Reference to Ayatullah Haj Sayyid Abul-Qasim Kashani." Ph.D. diss., University of Wisconsin–Madison, 1978.

Richard, Yann. "Ayatollah Kashani: Precursor of the Islamic Republic?" In *Religion and Politics in Iran: Shiʿism from Quietism to Revolution*, edited by Nikki R. Keddie, pp. 101–124. New Haven, Conn.: Yale University Press, 1983.

MOHAMMAD H. FAGHFOORY

KASHMIR.

See India; Pakistan.

KAWĀKIBĪ, ʿABD AL-RAḤMĀN AL-.

ʿAbd al-Raḥmān ibn Aḥmad al-Kawākibī (1854–1902) was an Islamic revivalist and advocate of an Arab caliphate. Al-Kawākibī was born to a prominent family known for its dedication to scholarship in Aleppo, Syria, and was educated thoroughly in religion, Ottoman administrative law, Arabic, Turkish, and Farsi. He began his career in journalism and the law and from 1879 to 1896 held several senior public posts. After suffering from the intrigues of Ottoman officials, in 1898 al-Kawākibī fled to Egypt, where he remained until his death in 1902.

Al-Kawākibī is best known for his two books, *Umm al-qurā* (The Mother of the Villages, one of the names of Mecca), and *Ṭabāʾi ʿ al-istibdād* (The Attributes of Tyranny). He published them in Cairo under the pen names al-Sayyid al-Furātī and Raḥḥālah "Kāf" (Traveler K), respectively, to avoid harassment by the Ottoman authorities. Published in 1899, *Umm al-qurā* is an account of the proceedings of a fictitious secret congress (the Congress of Islamic Revival) in Mecca attended by twenty-two Muslim delegates from various Muslim countries. The participants' purpose was to discuss the causes of the decline of the Muslim peoples and design a reform program for their recovery.

Al-Kawākibī attributed this decline to religious, political, and moral factors. Influenced by the reform ideas of Jamāl al-Dīn al-Afghānī and Muḥammad ʿAbduh, he advocated a return to the original purity of Islam, which had been distorted by alien concepts and currents such as mysticism, fatalism, sectarian divisions, and the passive and uncritical imitation of previous scholars. These distortions had led to ignorance among the Muslims and their submission to stagnant theologians and despotic rulers who suppressed freedoms, promoted false religion, and corrupted the moral, social, educational, and financial systems of the Muslim nation.

Al-Kawākibī proposed the formation of a society, with branches throughout the Muslim world, to educate Muslims and promote among them the aspiration for progress. Holding non-Arabs, specifically the Turks, accountable for the degeneration of Islam, he called for an Arab caliphate, which would exercise religious and cultural leadership, not temporal authority, and become the basis for the revival of Islam and an Islamic federation. He stipulated that the caliph be from the tribe of Quraysh, have limited powers, and be subject to election every three years and accountable to an elected council. He viewed the true Islamic state as one based on political freedoms and government accountability.

Alluding to the autocratic rule of the Ottomans, *Ṭabāʾi ʿal-istibdād* is an outright attack on tyranny and the misrule of the Ottoman sultan Abdülhamid II. Al-Kawākibī discussed the nature of despotism and its devastating effects on society as a whole. A despotic state controls the affairs of its citizens without fear of accountability or punishment, suppresses their rights, and prevents their education and enlightenment. Its purpose is to keep the people acquiescent and inactive; consequently, it destroys their moral, religious, and national bonds. Al-Kawākibī advocated education and gradualism as the means to uproot tyranny.

Sylvia Haim developed the thesis that al-Kawākibī's two books were heavily influenced by nineteenth-century Western writings. She argued that *Umm al-qurā* echoed the ideas expressed by W. S. Blunt in *The Future of Islam* (1882), and that *Ṭabāʾi ʿal-istibdād* was largely derived from the Italian writer Vittorio Alfieri's *Della tirannide* (1800), but this thesis was rejected by many scholars, most notably Khaldun Husry (Husry, 1966).

Al-Kawākibī contributed greatly to the evolution of Arab nationalist thought. Unlike the proponents of Pan-Islamism at the time, he drew a clear distinction between Arab and non-Arab Muslims, exalting the former on the basis of their language, descent, and moral attributes, and explicitly called for an Arab state. His fictional congress in *Umm al-qurā* inspired many reformers who later adopted the idea and put it into practice. Thus, he gave an organizational form and a political content to the cause of reform and to the Arabs' aspiration for independence from the Ottomans. Al-Kawākibī was far from being a secularist; in his endorsement of an Arab spiritual leadership and a restricted caliphate, however, he separated the temporal and spiritual, a division that represented a break from classical Islamic thought.

[*See also* Arab Nationalism; *and* Caliphate, Theories of the.]

BIBLIOGRAPHY

Amīn, Aḥmad. *Zuʿamāʾ al-iṣlāḥ fī al-ʿaṣr al-ḥadīth.* Cairo: Maktabat al-Nahḍah al-Miṣrīyah, 1979. Chapter on al-Kawākibī is a thorough study of his two books.

ʿAqqād, ʿAbbās Maḥmūd al-. *ʿAbd al-Raḥmān al-Kawākibī: Al-raḥḥālah "Kāf."* Beirut: Dār al-Kitāb al-ʿArabī, 1969. Excellent analysis of al-Kawākibī's background, thought, and contributions.

Husry, Khaldun S. al-. *Three Reformers: A Study in Modern Arab Political Thought.* Beirut: Khayats, 1966. Chapter on al-Kawākibī is a thorough and insightful study of his life and thought. Husry attempts to refute Haim's thesis.

Kawākibī, ʿAbd al-Raḥmān al-. *Al-aʿmāl al-kāmilah li-ʿAbd al-Raḥmān al-Kawākibī.* Edited by Muḥammad ʿImārah. Cairo: al-Hayʾah al-Miṣrīyah al-ʿĀmmah li-al-Taʾlīf wa-al-Nashr, 1970. Al-Kawākibī's works are prefaced by a detailed study of his life and thought.

Rahme, Joseph G. "ʿAbd al-Raḥmān al-Kawākibī's Reformist Ideology, Arab Pan-Islamism, and the Internal Other." *Journal of Islamic Studies* 10 (1999): 159–177.

EMAD EL-DIN SHAHIN
Updated by NAEL SHAMA

KAZAKHSTAN. Islam was introduced to the territory of what is now southern Kazakhstan during the late eighth and early ninth centuries. The conversion of nomads inhabiting the vast steppes to the north proved to be a gradual and protracted process. The peripatetic Ṣūfī order established by Aḥmad ibn Ibrāhīm al-Yasavī (1106–1166 CE) played a particularly important role in the Islamization of Turkic tribes. The Yasavī tradition successfully blended Islamic religious practice with local traditions steeped in animism, shamanism, and the cult of ancestors. The final affirmation of Sunnī Islam of the Ḥanafī school across the territory of present-day Kazakhstan toward the end of the eighteenth century was the result of proselytizing efforts from the Emirate of Bukhara, the Khanate of Khoqand, and the Russian Empire. The tsarist authorities used Muslim Tatar subjects to pacify the pastoral nomads with whom the expanding Russian state came into increasing conflict. By the middle of the nineteenth century, Islam was making inroads among the Kazakh aristocracy, and by the 1860s there were Qurʾānic schools in some Kazakh cities.

Traditional Kazakh society was shattered from the time of the widespread Central Asian Rebellion of 1916 to the end of the civil war in 1922, and then again during the Soviet collectivization drive of 1929–1934. In those decades, over 3 million Kazakhs died and over 1 million were driven into exile, reducing the population to about one-third of what it had been in 1916. Prominent among the victims were the mullahs, who were imprisoned or killed during the aggressive antireligious campaigns of the Soviets from the late 1920s until World War II. Anti-Islamic campaigns also closed *madrasahs*, *mekteps* (Kazakh adaptation of Arabic *maktab*), and mosques throughout Central Asia. Furthermore, the Soviet authorities banned the Arabic script and introduced the Latin script, later replaced by the Cyrillic alphabet (1940).

In 1943 the antireligious pressure eased somewhat as part of Stalin's effort to ensure that the Soviet people would fight the Nazis. An official Spiritual Directorate of Muslims of Central Asia and Kazakhstan (SADUM) was established in Tashkent (Uzbekistan) to give the appearance of religious independence for Muslims, whose practice in fact remained severely restricted.

In 1961, the Kazakh Soviet Socialist Republic had only twenty-five registered mosques with approximately forty thousand regular attendants (compare to 2,500 mosques in the early twenty-first century). While Soviet antireligious pressure all but eliminated doctrinal Islam, it had little impact on traditional practices in Kazakhstan or elsewhere, which remained a mixture of Islamic and pre-Islamic cultural rituals. Since the perestroika and glasnost of the Gorbachev era and following the independence of Kazakhstan in 1991, the authorities relaxed their opposition to religion, a significant part of Kazakhs identified themselves as Muslim believers, and many more retained vestiges of Islamic practice within families or communities. There has been a remarkable resurgence of religious activity; many mosques and religious schools have opened and new building has begun, financed in part by Saudis, Turks, Egyptians, and others, as well as by contributions from local Muslims. The largest mosque in Central Asia, built in the new capital, Astana, and named after Aḥmad Yasavī, Hazrat Sultan, was opened by President Nursultan Nazarbayev in 2012.

Since the early 1990s, the proportion of Kazakhs identifying themselves as Muslims has doubled, surpassing 80 percent; piety and observance have increased dramatically, especially at the individual level. Most Muslims in Kazakhstan practice Islamic funeral, wedding, and circumcision rites, while some of them fast and pray regularly. The Islamic fervor appears to be higher in the southern regions. Hundreds of young Kazakhstanis received religious training abroad, mostly in Turkey, Egypt, Saudi Arabia, and Pakistan, and numerous Islamic missionaries visited the country.

Independent Kazakhstan is a secular republic in which no religion has official status. The government of President Nursultan Nazarbayev has declared a policy of confessional and ethnic tolerance in a country where ethnic Kazakhs account for only half of the population. According to the official sources, the Republic of Kazakhstan is a model of peaceful coexistence of over forty confessions and denominations and 130 ethnic groups. Many Russians and Ukrainians are members of the Russian Orthodox Church. Members of other religious denominations, including Catholics, Protestants, Jews, and Buddhists are represented as well in the multicultural country. In addition, some Kazakhs and other people of Islamic background converted to Protestantism and other nontraditional religions. The republic's constitution specifically guarantees freedom of religious worship and makes no mention of an Islamic dimension to the nation's past or identity. Despite these declarations, the authorities continue to restrict freedom of religion, tightening state control over various religious organizations and increasing penalties for participation in "illegal" religious activities across the country. President Nazarbayev has been careful to cater to the Islamic sensibilities of the Kazakhs without compromising the secular foundations of the state. He performed *ḥajj* in 1994, and, like other Central Asian heads of state, he has endorsed making Muslim holy days official holidays. Unlike neighboring Uzbekistan, Kazakhstan under the rule of Nazarbayev developed a legal framework for Islamic banking services, becoming the first post-Soviet country to welcome and facilitate Islamic banking and finance. Nursultan Nazarbayev has positioned himself as an ecumenical leader and a champion of the dialogue of civilizations. Pope John Paul II visited Kazakhstan at his personal invitation in 2001, and three congresses of the Leaders of World and Traditional Religions took place in Astana (2003, 2006, and 2009).

The Islamic establishment is led by the Muslim Spiritual Administration of Kazakhstan (DUMK), headed by a chief *muftī*. The Muslim Spiritual Administration of Kazakhstan separated from the Tashkent-based SADUM in 1990, while Kazakhstan was still part of the Soviet Union.

While the DUMK remains officially independent of the state, it is loyal to the Nazarbayev government, cooperates with authorities in the fight against extremism, and eagerly supports domestic and foreign policy initiatives of the president. In general, there is no tension between the Nazarbayev administration and the state-sanctioned Muftiat. The republic is less repressive than other Central Asian countries (Uzbekistan, Turkmenistan, and Tajikistan) in dealing with Islamic activism.

Until the late 1990s government officials did not strive for intrusive control of the *muftī*'s jurisdiction and Muslim communities at large. Increasing concerns about Islamic extremism and the government's perception of growing radicalism prompted the National Security Council, chaired by President Nazarbayev, to launch a policy review over the following decades. As a result of the radicalization of some Muslim groups, the new laws adopted to combat extremist activity give security services a broad mandate to monitor and close down offending groups. The Agency for Religious Affairs of the Republic of Kazakhstan requires all religious organizations to be officially registered with the central and local governments, imposing new restrictions on unregistered religious groups.

[*See also* Islam and Politics in Central Asia and the Caucasus.]

BIBLIOGRAPHY

Cummings, Sally N. *Kazakhstan: Power and the Elite.* London: I. B. Tauris, 2005.

Gleason, Gregory. *The Central Asian States: Discovering Independence.* Boulder, Colo.: Westview, 1997.

Maggs, Peter. "Islamic Banking in Kazakhstan Law." *Review of Central and East European Law* 36, no. 1 (April 2011): 1–32.

Olcott, Martha Brill. *Kazakhstan: Unfulfilled Promise.* Washington, D.C.: Carnegie Endowment for International Peace, 2002.

Soucek, Svat. *A History of Inner Asia.* Cambridge, U.K.: Cambridge University Press, 2000.

MARTHA BRILL OLCOTT
Updated by KIRILL NOURZHANOV
and ANARA TABYSHALIEVA

KHALED, AMR. (1967–), born in Alexandria, Egypt, and currently residing in London, a Muslim preacher and televangelist. Selected by *Time* as one of the top one hundred most influential people who shape our world, Khaled is one of the key figures of the contemporary Islamic revivalist movement that spans the Arab world. The *New York Times* described him as "the world's most famous and influential Muslim televangelist" (Shapiro, 2006). His official website (www.amrkhaled.net) is accessible in eighteen languages, including English, French, Dutch, and Hebrew, it is the third most popular Arabic Web site in the world, behind Al Jazeera and an e-mail portal. His message of self-empowerment based on a spiritual, values-driven interpretation of Islam has resonated with youth across the Muslim world. In scores of interviews conducted with Arab youth in Qatar, Syria, and Jordan, Amr Khaled was the only individual selected as the "top contemporary role model" by the majority of the youth interviewed (Ahmed, 2007). His "rock star" popularity is not confined to the Arab world, as evidenced by the flock of fans that surrounded him during appearances in the United States (Wright, 2007).

His website and forum best illustrate the source of Khaled's popularity. On his site, he shares experiences and thoughts of his everyday spiritual journey through videos, sermons, articles, and comments. His videos reflect a personable, soft-spoken, spiritually inclined person who integrates religious advice into personal stories or reflections on prophetic history. His forum motivates members to move beyond discussion into action. One of his most recent forum topics, after the fall of the Mubarak regime in Egypt, is "Plan for Egypt." In this forum topic, Khaled asks Egyptian youth, whom he refers to as "the youth of the Renaissance" (*shabāb al-nahḍah*) and *sunaʿ al-ḥayāh* (life-makers), to formulate concrete projects ideas in the fields of health, education, technology, international relations, and academic research for the development of Egyptian society. The team with the best project idea will receive twenty thousand Egyptian pounds and present their idea on the satellite TV show *Bukrah Aḥlā* (Tomorrow Will Be More Beautiful).

Unlike traditional religious scholars, Khaled received a secular education. He graduated from Cairo University in 1988 with a degree in accounting. In 2001 he received a diploma from the Islamic Studies Institute. In 2010, he received his Ph.D. in Islamic Studies from Wales University. Amr Khaled is clean-shaven, wears a suit (no robes), and speaks in colloquial Arabic, which has attracted millions of youth throughout the Arab world, making him an unlikely superstar. Amr Khaled targets Muslim Arabs aged fifteen through thirty-five who come from the upper-middle class, because he believes they are the ones capable of changing the Islamic world. Young people can often relate to him because of his friendly and humorous style and his practical message, which focuses on issues of everyday life, such as diet, prayer, small acts of kindness, and small changes that can lead to dramatic progress. For example, a young Palestinian woman in the West Bank tells David Hardaker from the *Independent* how she has heeded Amr Khaled's call for Muslims to get fit and therefore has begun to jog two thousand laps across the hallway in her home each day. Another young woman in Cairo has planted a small tomato vine on top of her ten-floor apartment building. She says that Khaled encourages his listeners to plant vegetation, which could possibly become a small source of revenue in a city where money in short supply. The forum on his website is replete with hundreds of personal stories from members, who share how Khaled's message has transformed their lives.

He encourages youth to focus not on the things they cannot change but on those they can, such as their attitude, behavior, and character. Amr Khaled's message is one of hope. He argues that Muslim youth can change the conditions of their societies and countries by first changing their own conditions. He writes, "Our problem is that we have got used to taking without ever giving. In other words, we are living as parasites on the rest of the world."

Unlike traditional religious clerics and preachers, his message avoids the typical religious admonitions one might hear at a mosque or TV show. Instead of focusing on the "dos and don'ts" of Islam, Khaled is more interested in illustrating a path of spirituality that encourages, not shuns, worldly achievement and inner happiness. One section of his web site is a radio show titled *Life Has Taught Me*, which encourages listeners to overcome self-destructive habits and take concrete steps toward becoming better spouses, better parents, and more fulfilled individuals. Although his message is imbued with religious advice from the Qurʾān, prophetic tradition (*sunnah*) and prophetic history (*sīrah*), his focus is primarily on self-empowerment and self-development. For example, one section of his website, on self-education, teaches important life skills such as time management, leadership skills, and the important inner qualities for being a great person.

Scholars such as Reza Aslan believe that Khaled represents an "Islamic Reformation," as billions of Muslims are able to bypass the authority of traditional clerics and instead seek advice from the televised programs of Amr Khaled, who is not a cleric and has not been traditionally trained in Islamic law. Nevertheless, through his website and weekly television programs, millions of viewers and Internet users have chosen to model their opinions on his. According to Aslan, the decentralization of religious authority through satellite TV and the Internet is playing a role in the Islamic Reformation because it allows Muslims to "draw upon the opinions of not only their own clerical leaders, but also of a host of Muslim activists and academics who are propounding fresh and innovative interpretations of Islam" (Aslan, 2006).

After moving to Birmingham, England, in 2004, Khaled began to focus his attention on the second-generation Muslims of Europe. In lectures to Muslim audiences in the West, he implores them to reflect the best of Islam and to remove barriers of fear and intimidation. In an interview with Robin Wright of the *Washington Post* in 2007, he said, "My message is, Please be rightful representatives for your religion. Please show people here your good manners, your attitude of hard work, how you can succeed in this society, what you can add, your positive integration while maintaining pride in Islam—so people know how really great this religion is" (Wright, 2007.)

One of his goals is to create a bridge between the East and West. When the Danish cartoon crisis erupted, Khaled convened an interfaith conference in Copenhagen (9–10 March 2006) called Know the Prophet. Although the conference was endorsed by forty-two prominent preachers and Islamic scholars, Khaled received much criticism for his move to initiate a dialogue with the Danes at that time. In response to the criticism he received, Khaled is quoted as saying, "We have to ask ourselves what we want: co-existence or conflict? What is in Muslims' best interest? Can we have a renaissance in the presence of continued, non-stop, conflicts?" ("Now Danes Respect Muslims," 2007). Khaled believes that an Islamic renaissance is more likely to take place with the world at peace, rather than in conflict.

BIBLIOGRAPHY

Ahmed, Akbar. *Journey into Islam: The Crisis of Globalization*. Washington, D.C.: Brookings Institution Press, 2007.

Amr Khaled website. http://www.amrkhaled.net

"Now Danes Respect Muslims." *Al-Ahram Weekly*, March 23–29, 2006. http://weekly.ahram.org.eg/2006/787/eg11.htm.

Shapiro, Samantha M.. "Ministering to the Upwardly Mobile Muslim." *New York Times Magazine*, April 30, 2006. http://www.nytimes.com/2006/04/30/magazine/30televangelist.html?pagewanted=1&ei=5090&en=4c56a0ffa67fa4ca&ex=1304049600&partner=rssuserland&emc=rss.

Wright, Robin. "Islam's Up-to-Date Televangelist: Amr Khaled Has Bridged the Religious and Secular with His Feel-Good Message." *Washington Post*, September 11, 2007.

HADIA MUBARAK

KHĀLID, KHĀLID MUḤAMMAD.

Khālid Muḥammad Khālid (1920–1996) was an Egyptian writer and essayist known for his popular writings related to religion and society. Born in Sharqīyah Governorate, he graduated from al-Azhar University (in Cairo) in 1947 with an *ʿālimīyah* degree from the Faculty of Sharīʿah (qualifying him as one of the *ʿulamāʾ*) and then earned a teaching certificate, also from al-Azhar. He worked as an Arabic-language teacher in Cairo and then in the Cultural Bureau (Idārat al-Thaqāfah) of the Ministry of Education and with the Writers' Committee (Hayʾat al-Kuttāb) connected to the Ministry of Culture. He later became a supervisor in the Department for the Publication of the Heritage (al-Ishrāf ʿalā Idārat Taḥqīq al-Turāth). He wrote more than thirty books, as well as articles in newspapers and magazines, such as *al-Sharq al-awsaṭ* (London), *al-Muslimūn*, *al-Muṣawwar*, *al-Ahrām*, and *al-Wafd*.

His first and most controversial book was produced in 1949 under the title *Bilād man?* (Whose Country?) but was banned by censor, in part because of objections from al-Azhar. It was then republished in 1950 under the title *Min hunā nabdaʿ* (From Here We Begin), after a change of government, and finally released by order of the Cairo district court. In this book he mounted a passionate attack on "priesthood" (in all times and places, but clearly having the Muslim *ʿulamāʾ* as a class in view). In particular he claimed that it has used religion to justify social inequality, tyranny, and ignorance. He likewise attacked "religious government" and called for separation of religion and state, using arguments reminiscent of those made in the 1920s by ʿAlī ʿAbd al-Rāziq. He also called for a moderate and democratic socialism, effective birth control, and furtherance of the rights of women, going into some detail on these issues. The book was notably criticized by Muḥammad al-Ghazālī (1917–1996), then a member of the Muslim Brotherhood and later one of the leading Islamists of his time, in his book *Our Beginning in Wisdom* (*Min hunā naʿlam*) in 1951.

Khālid expressed similar views in other passionately written books in the 1950s and early 1960s, such as *Muwāṭinūn... la raʿāyā* (Citizens... Not Subjects, c. 1951), also banned under the monarchy but released after the 1952 revolution; *Maʿan ʿalā al-ṭarīq... Muḥammad wa-al-Masīḥ* (Together on the Road: Muḥammad and Christ, 1958), in which he presented both prophets as standing for the same values of humanity, life, love, and peace; *Al-dīmuqrāṭīyah abadan* (Democracy Forever, 1953); and many others. Some of the ideas in these books influenced the laws enacted by the post-1952 government, although he did not favor Nasser's one-party system.

Beginning in the early 1960s, Khālid turned his attention to specifically Islamic topics, writing several books on the Qurʾān and on Muḥammad and other early Islamic heroes, presented as models of faith and moral inspiration for society. Among these were *Kamā taḥaddatha al-Qurʾān* (As the Qurʾān Speaks, 1962), *Kamā taḥaddatha al-Rasūl* (As the Messenger Speaks, 1963), *Rijāl ḥawl al-Rasūl* (*Men around the Messenger*, 1964), and *Muʿjizat al-Islām: ʿUmar ibn ʿAbd al-ʿAzīz* (The Miracle of Islam: ʿUmar ibn ʿAbd al-ʿAzīz, 1969). This move is reminiscent of an earlier generation of secularists, such as Ṭāhā Ḥusayn, Muḥammad Ḥusayn Haykal, and especially ʿAbbās Maḥmūd al-ʿAqqād, who began to write on Islamic figures in the 1930s and 1940s. This involved an effort to recapture the Muslim heritage (*turāth*) but not a rejection of secularism. The same seems to be the case with Khālid at this stage.

He did reject secularism, however, in his 1981 book *Al-dawlah fī al-Islām* (The State in Islam), which was a best seller that year. He described the call for separation of religion and government in his first book as "exaggerated." It was, he said, the result two errors that no longer influenced him: ascribing to deviant Muslim rulers the extreme characteristics of some Christian governments, and treating the violent actions of some of the Muslim Brothers as an indication of what a government in the name of Islam would be like. Islam has nothing to do with "religious government" as represented by these, but it does have a civil as well as a religious mission and does call for the state to apply Islamic principles. An Islamic state aims at liberty and opposes despotism. It is characterized by *shūrā* (consultation) and *bayʿah* (oath of allegiance to the ruler by the people), which today take the form of parliamentary democracy, including parliament, elections, recognized opposition, freedom of speech and press, and separation of executive, legislative, and judicial powers. The Qurʾān is its constitution; but while this is given by God, it is the people who accept it. The linkage of these modern forms to traditional concepts is more often asserted than argued in detail, although he does argue in some detail that the ruler is obligated to follow the advice he receives from *shūrā*, a view that backs up the power of parliament in modern times. It appears that his actual prescriptions for society are not so different from those of his first book, but they are now given Islamic form and justification. Here, though, there is little detailed discussion of these prescriptions, and little on economic justice and the position of women, such as are found in the first book. The stress is rather on the moral value of Islamic prescriptions and of the Islamic heritage. The book includes as a lengthy appendix a chapter from his book on ʿUmar ibn ʿAbd al-ʿAzīz, presented as an ideal ruler. The ideological position of this book is best labeled "Islamic reformist" or "Islamic modernist," standing in the tradition of people such as Muḥammad ʿAbduh.

The development of Khālid Muḥammad Khālid's thinking reflects the shift of much Egyptian and Muslim thinking from the 1950s to the 1980s and later, from a strong emphasis on social justice and reform, or even revolution, to a greater concern for Islamic authenticity. Like the majority, he did not move on to the extreme forms of Islamism that have received so much attention in recent years.

BIBLIOGRAPHY

Branca, P. "Riformismo e identità islamica nel pensiero di Khalid Muhammad Khalid." *Islàm: Storia e Civiltà* 5 (1986): 97–107.

Eccel, A. Chris. *Egypt, Islam and Social Change: Al-Azhar in Conflict and Accommodation*. Berlin: Klaus Schwarz, 1984.

Ghazzālī, Muhammad al-. *Our Beginning in Wisdom*. Translated by Isma'il R. al Faruqi. Washington, D.C.: American Council of Learned Societies, 1953.

Khālid, Khālid Muḥammad. *From Here We Start*. Translated by Isma'il R. el Faruqui. Washington, D.C.: American Council of Learned Societies, 1953.

Khālid, Khālid Muḥammad, *Men around the Messenger*. Translated by Muhammad Mustafa Gemeiah. Rev. ed. Kuala Lumpur: Islamic Book Trust, 2005.

William E. Shepard

Khamene'i, ʿAlī. ʿAlī Khamene'i was born in 1939 in Mashhad, Iran. His father, Sayyid Javad, was a low-ranking cleric. Khamene'i attended local elementary and intermediate Qur'ānic schools in Mashhad. He began to study with various scholars in Najaf in 1957, including Muḥsin al-Ḥakīm (d. 1970) and Mahmud Shahrudi (d. 1974), but he returned to Iran after about only a year and attended courses at the seminary in Qom from 1958 to 1964. It is said that among his teachers were Moḥammad Ḥosayn Borujerdi (d. 1962), as well as Ruhollah al-Musavi Khomeini (d. 1989), the eventual founder of the Islamic Republic of Iran (IRI). He returned to Mashhad and likely pursued further study with Ayatollah Hadi Milani (d. 1975). Although his official biography states that by that time he had become a *mujtahid* (one qualified to practice *ijtihād*, or independent judgment in search of a legal rule), this is not certain. He apparently did not obtain the highest level of education and did not write a *risālah* (dissertation). Nonetheless, it has been suggested that he received, through political pressure, a diploma (*ijāzah*) of *ijtihād* from Ayatollah Muḥammad Taqī Bahjāt, a relatively obscure clergyman—though when this occurred, if it did, is unknown.

Khamene'i has stated that among those who influenced him politically was Navvāb Ṣafavī (d. 1955), the founder in 1945 of the Fidāʾīyān-i Islām, who gave a rousing speech at Khamene'i's seminary in 1952. When Khomeini attacked the regime in 1962 for permitting women to vote and allowing non-Muslims to run for office, Khamene'i joined this effort and thereafter remained politically active in the opposition to the monarchy. He is said to have been arrested six times between 1964 and 1978.

In late 1978, he became a member of the then-clandestine Revolutionary Council. After the revolution, Ayatollah Khomeini appointed Khamene'i to be his representative in the Pasdaran (Revolutionary Guard Corps) and the Supreme Defense Council. Khamene'i was also one of the leaders of the Islamic Republican Party when it was formed in 1979. Khomeini also appointed him to be the Friday Mosque Prayer Leader of Tehran when Ayatollah Ḥusayn ʿAlī Muntaẓirī stepped down in 1980. In 1980, Khameneʾi was elected to parliament. On 27 June 1981, he was the target of an assassination attempt and lost the use of his right hand. Then on 30 August, the president of Iran, Muḥammad ʿAlī Rajāʾī, was assassinated, whereupon Khameneʾi succeeded him. He served two terms, from 1981 to 1989. In 1988, Ayatollah Khomeini publicly rebuked Khameneʾi for arguing that the actions of the supreme jurist were bound by the constitution. Khomeini proclaimed that the IRI could even suspend prayer or the *ḥajj* if doing so were necessary to defend its interests, on the grounds that it was a genuine embodiment of the Islamic state, whose interests must not be undermined.

When Ayatollah Khomeini died, in June 1989, the Council of Experts elected Khameneʾi to succeed him in the office of leader. Because of Khameneʾi's lower qualifications, constitutional amendments were passed deleting the requirement that the leader had to possess the highest clerical title (*marjaʿ al-taqlīd*). Efforts to confer upon him the title of ayatollah eventually succeeded, but several campaigns to endow him with the sobriquet of *marjaʿ al-taqlīd* failed. In 1995, he publicly stated that he did not seek to be *marjaʿ* for Iranians but would accept that status for Shīʿah outside Iran. He is routinely referred to in government sources as *āyatullāh ʿuẓmā* (grand ayatollah), but most of the top clergy have refused to acknowledge him in that capacity. In 1997, Ayatollah Ḥusayn ʿAlī Muntaẓirī, at one time considered Khomeini's successor, openly stated that Khameneʾi lacked the qualifications to use these titles.

Nevertheless, Khameneʾi has made use of his control of the state financial and administrative apparatus to bureaucratize the process by which the *marjiʿīyah* is conferred. There can be no doubt that he is the most powerful individual in the Islamic Republic, although whether most of the politically aware population accepts the legitimacy of his rule is a contentious matter.

Popular erosion of Khameneʾi's authority, however, has not stopped him from asserting his power on many occasions. Among his autocratic interventions one must include his order to violently suppress protests by opposition groups who claimed that the regime had rigged the presidential elections of 2009 in favor of Mahmoud Ahmadinejad, then running for his second term as president. In addition, one must note Khameneʾi's command that the latter be exempt from parliamentary interpellation or impeachment, despite the constitutional vesting of such rights in the parliament.

Khameneʾi has also been at the center of the crisis between Iran and the United Nations (particularly the Western powers) over the issue of the country's determination to enrich uranium, which he and his supporters justify on grounds of civilian energy use but which his adversaries fear is for the purposes of building nuclear weapons. He has, on more than one occasion, declared that he regards nuclear weapons to be prohibited by the tenets of Islam. However, the fact that the Iranian government failed to disclose the country's nuclear research program until 2003, when it was publicly exposed, a failure that was in violation of the Nuclear Non-Proliferation Treaty, to which Iran is a signatory, has given the Iranian government's critics ample reason to distrust his proclamations on nuclear weapons.

Ironically, despite his interventions on behalf of Ahmadinejad, Khameneʾi found himself locked in a bitter internal dispute with him over the role of the clergy in leadership positions and a host of public policy issues as the president's second term of office drew to a close in 2013. No doubt Khameneʾi is the more powerful figure, but he has sometimes retreated in the face of Ahmadinejad's obdurate opposition to some of his positions and policies. What may explain Khamene'i's reluctance to force the issue with the president is the latter's vague threats to reveal certain secrets that would prove more than embarrassing to the power elite in Iran.

The four rounds of UN sanctions against Iran as a result of the country's continuing nuclear program have weakened Iran's economy and caused severe inflation and currency devaluation. The key to Khamene'i's holding on to power since 1989 seems to be his ability to satisfy enough of his ardent supporters among the Revolutionary Guard and the Youth Rally (known as the Basīj), as well as elements of petite bourgeoisie and urban poor, especially through subsidy programs.

BIBLIOGRAPHY

Buchta, Wilfried. *Who Rules Iran: The Structure of Power in the Islamic Republic*. Washington, D.C.: Washington Institute for Near East Policy, 2000.

Khalaji, Mehdi. *The Last Marja': Sīstānī and the End of Traditional Religious Authority in Shiism*. Washington, D.C.: Washington Institute for Near East Policy, 2006.

Khamene'i, 'Alī. *Ajwibat al-istiftā'āt*. Kuwait: Dar al-Naba' li-al-Nashrwa al-Tawzi', 1995.

Walbridge, Linda S. "The Counterreformation: Becoming a Marja' in the Modern World." In *The Most Learned of the Shi'a: The Institution of the Marja' Taqlid*, pp. 230–245. New York: Oxford University Press, 2001.

SHAHROUGH AKHAVI

KHAN, MAULANA WAHIDUDDIN.

Maulana Wahiduddin Khan was born on 1 January 1925 in Azamgarh, a town well known for its *madrasahs* (Islamic seminaries), in Uttar Pradesh, India. He received a traditional Islamic education and was part of the Jamā'at-i Islāmī movement in India and was briefly associated with the Islamic Da'wah movement Tablīghī Jamā'at. Since 1976, he has run his own Islamic Center in New Delhi, which publishes his journal *al-Risālah* and his numerous books and essays. The author of nearly two hundred books and booklets in addition to numerous journal articles, he lectures worldwide and is now an active user of social and Internet media to disseminate his ideas.

In spite of controversy surrounding his thought and politics, Maulana Wahiduddin has for decades enjoyed a reputation as a thoughtful, independent, and critical Muslim thinker in India. Since the death of Abulḥasan 'Alī al-Nadvī in 1999, Maulana Wahiduddin, though not enjoying the widespread respect that 'Alī Nadvī commanded, has been the most prominent scholarly voice on Islam and Muslim Affairs in India. Both mainstream and Muslim media follow his activity and he has shaped the debate on key issues, including the Bābarī Masjid conflict, the Salman Rushdie *fatwa*, the plight of Muslim minorities in India, and Hindu-Muslim relations, as well as the current global issues concerning blasphemy against the Prophet of Islam.

Maulana Wahiduddin's thought has two main characteristics: his undiluted commitment to nonviolence and his firm belief in the principle of *ijtihād*. Over the decades, he advanced the thesis that Islam teaches nonviolence. The *mawlānā* relies on the direct textual meaning of several verses of the Qur'ān that express God's displeasure with those who cause trouble on earth, such as 2:205: "And when he goes away, he strives throughout the land to cause corruption therein and destroy crops and animals. And Allah does not like corruption." By focusing on the last part of this *sūrah*, "Allah does not like *fasād*" (corruption), Maulana Wahiduddin Khan builds his case for pacifism. With the justification that Islam is a religion of peace, and in order to advance his pacifist ideas, the *mawlānā* essentially ignores the *sunnah* (prophetic tradition), the history of Islam, and even the traditional understanding of Qur'ānic teachings. By identifying specific verses in the Qur'ān with literal meanings in support of pacifism, especially when they are taken out of their historical and textual context, he builds his thesis around them.

The second constituent of Maulana Wahiduddin Khan's work is his emphasis on *ijtihād*. The meaning of *ijtihād* varies widely, because a conservative jurist uses analogical reasoning when sacred texts (Qur'ān, *ḥadīth*, and the record of the opinions of early Muslims) do not directly speak to an issue, while a modernist like Maulana Wahiduddin relies on *ijtihād* as a license to think and exercise one's reason even on subjects that sacred texts have spoken on to reinterpret them in the light of new existential realities. Advancing, defending, and putting into practice this understanding of *ijtihād* is a contribution to Islamic thought, but Maulana Wahiduddin Khan's methodology of reinterpretation is often simplistic and relies primarily on selective reading of the Qur'ān.

Still, this *ijtihād* has made several reinterpretive contributions, including advocacy for science and gender equality. Not only has Wahiduddin Khan argued that Islam and science were compatible, but he posited that the Qur'ānic message itself was scientific and encouraged Muslims to reflect on the scientific basis of nature and creation. He insisted that science only authenticated the basic message of Islam, though it was imperative that Muslims rethink their understanding of Islam in the light of science. Thus in his worldview, science becomes a pathway rather than a hindrance to faith. In a similar vein he insists that Islam always intended gender equality. Maulana Wahiduddin Khan argues that Islamic sources, the Qur'ān and authentic *aḥādīth*, clearly intended gender equality, but Muslim legal traditions and culture have obscured the principle and introduced patriarchy.

One limitation of the *mawlānā*'s work is his style. He presents his thoughts based solely on selective reading of sources and without a systematic and rigorous critique of the traditional viewpoint that too often uses the same sources to advance interpretations of Islam contrary to his viewpoint. This has allowed traditional thought to thrive in India in spite of all his efforts.

A subject of several controversies, Maulana Wahiduddin Khan was once associated with the Bharatiya Janata Party, viewed by many Muslims as anti-Muslim and determined to undermine Muslim welfare in India. Equally controversial were his theological debates that did not always advance the cause of Islamic revivalism or of reform but merely served to undermine his own influence within the Muslim community while raising his profile outside of it. His suggestions that perhaps the Christian model of prophecy was better for Muslims than the prophetic model of Muḥammad attracted criticism from Muslim orthodoxy and alienated many young believers who otherwise would have found in Maulana Wahiduddin Khan a spiritual model and guide. His position on the Bābarī Mosque controversy, which appeased the Hindu communalists, generated anger among Indian Muslims. His assertion that in some areas of life Jesus was a better role model than Muhammad also resulted in outrage. Controversial positions like these have made him popular with Hindu groups in India and perhaps Christian groups in the West, though they also jeopardized his reform agenda.

BIBLIOGRAPHY

"A Conversation With: Maulana Wahiduddin Khan." *India Ink* (blog), *New York Times*, January 27, 2012, http://india.blogs.nytimes.com/2012/01/27/a-conversation-with-maulana-w-khan/.

Wahiduddin's Web: Living from the Heart. http://wahiduddin.net/.

M. A. MUQTEDAR KHAN

KHĀRIJITES. The term Khārijites (lit., "those who went out") is a term that has been used to describe a range of groups within Islam that have theological differences with both the Sunnīs and the Shīʿī. They emerged as a distinct group after a schism that took place during the Battle of Ṣiffīn, in 657 CE, and they are represented now by the Ibāḍī in Oman and Zanzibar, and also some isolated areas of North Africa.

Soon after ʿAlī became caliph he was challenged by people who felt that his conduct was suspect with regard to the assassination of ʿUthmān ibn ʿAffān, the third caliph. With some of the early companions, specifically Ṭalḥah and al-Zubayr, ʿĀʾishah went to Basra, where she fought ʿAlī at the battle of the Camel, in 656. Ṭalḥah and al-Zubayr were killed and ʿĀʾishah was sent back to Medina. At the Battle of Ṣiffīn, a year later, ʿAlī with his Iraqi supporters faced Muʿāwiyah and his Syrian supporters. The two armies fought for a long time with no decisive outcome. On 26 July, ʿAlī's supporters quickly gained an advantage over their opponents and looked as though they would carry the day. It was at this point that Muʿāwiyah had his soldiers attach copies of the Qurʾān to their lances. This act caused widespread disquiet in ʿAlī's army, and both leaders accepted the calls for arbitration that the raising of the Qurʾān had indicated. Each side decided to appoint a representative: The Syrians selected ʿAmr ibn al-ʿĀṣ and the Iraqis chose Abū Mūsā al-Ashʿarī.

While the negotiations were under way, a schism was being created by the dissenters from ʿAlī's forces. Most of this dissenting minority were from the Banū Ḥanīfah and the Banū Tamīm, both Arabian tribes. The dissenters were angered by ʿAlī's acceptance of arbitration, which they felt should not have occurred, because the outcome of battles should be left to God. ʿAlī and his cousin ʿAbd Allāh ibn ʿAbbās went to the camp of the seceders, who had gathered at Ḥarūrāʾ, on the Nahrwan Canal, and hence they were originally called Ḥarūrī. ʿAlī tried to explain that the negotiations at the Battle of Ṣiffīn were fully in keeping with the teachings of the Qurʾān and they had misunderstood his actions. However he wanted the Khārijites to accept his leadership. Their representatives said that they knew they had committed some wrongs, and were prepared to repent, but ʿAlī himself should do the same. This was never going to be acceptable to ʿAlī, who felt that he was not at fault for the schism.

The basic difference was that the rebels believed that the negotiations lacked legitimacy. This was because they felt that ʿAlī should have obeyed the Qurʾān (8:39–40): "Fight them until there is no *fitnah* [temptation], and religion is wholly unto God." This was in contrast to the Qurʾān (49:9): "If two parties of the faithful fight each other, then conciliate them." The rebels had wanted ʿAlī to destroy his opponents, and when this did not happen, they decided to reject ʿAlī as their leader.

It was not long before the Ḥarūrī became known as the Khārijites. ʿAlī and ʿAbd Allāh ibn ʿAbbās managed to get some of the Khārijites to return to follow ʿAlī's leadership. However, most of them clearly were not going to do so. The result was the Battle of Nahrwan, in 658, with ʿAlī's loyalists defeating the Khārijites, who were then dispersed.

Although the Khārijites had been defeated militarily, their core members kept to their beliefs, which began to be influential in certain sectors in Mesopotamia. They continued to intrigue and three years after their military defeat, ʿAbd al-Raḥmān ibn Muljam, a member of the Khārijites, entered the Great Mosque of Kufa with a dagger coated in poison. He struck ʿAlī on his forehead with the dagger, and ʿAlī died two days later. The assassin stated that he had sought retribution for the "slain of Nahrwan."

It was during the second civil war (680–692) when the full force of the movement was felt in the nascent Islamic state. At first, the movement was able to support and give aid to ʿAbd Allāh ibn al-Zubayr, but it was soon plagued by internal dissention over the piety or lack thereof of their leaders. The most powerful group, and one that remained a threat to the Umayyads until 699, was the Azāriqah, led by Nāfiʿ ibn al-Araq.

The ideas of the Khārijites spread steadily. They soon gained a reputation for their dislike of compromise on religious disputes. They argued that a Muslim who commits a *kabīrah* (major sin) is to be regarded as an apostate from Islam and no longer protected by Islamic laws, but they always argued that all Muslims should be treated equally, regardless of their race or tribe. Indeed, they were the first to elect a non-Qurashī to be caliph. They felt that any Muslim, regardless of tribal or ethnic background, can be the leader of the Muslim community—the caliph. This resulted in their numbers growing and traders taking their ideas far and wide across the Islamic world. Although their intellectual center was Basra, the teaching of the Khārijites soon began to influence parts of North Africa and won the support of several Amazigh (Berber) tribes. There were soon small but strong Kharijite communities in several centers of learning, such as Sijilmāsa in southern Morocco, Mzāb in the Sahara, in modern-day Algeria, Jerba in modern-day Tunisia, and Jabal Nafūsa and Zuwāghah in Libya. In all these places, it was travelers who brought the ideas of the Khārijites. Their view on equality also won them support from some slaves, including some of those in the Zanj Rebellion, which took place in Basra (869–883).

In spite of the spread of Khārijī ideas in the eighth century, the Ibāḍīyah are now the only surviving Khārijī sect. Their survival was based on two doctrines in which they differed from the rest of the Khārijites: The most important is their acceptance of, and intermarriage with, non-Khārijī Muslims. The second is their quietism, which also made it unnecessary to have an *imām*. They also reject supplications while standing during prayer.

The Ibāḍīs still dominate Oman, and the ruling family in the Sultanate of Oman is Ibāḍī. They also make up most of the Muslim communities in the ports along the East African coast, especially on the island of Zanzibar. There are fewer than a million, and the Ibāḍīs in Oman do not regard themselves as Khārijites. Instead, they emphasize their own connections with other Muslims, and many prefer to be regarded as Sunnīs, in spite of some religious and doctrinal differences.

BIBLIOGRAPHY

Crone, Patricia. "A Statement by the Najdiyya Khārijites on the Dispensability of the Imamate." *Studia Islamica* 88 (1998): 55–76.

Hitti, Philip K. *History of Syria, Including Lebanon and Palestine*. 2d ed. London: Macmillan, 1957.

Levi della Vida, G. "Kharidjites." In *The Encyclopaedia of Islam*, rev. ed., vol. 4, edited by E. van Donzel, B. Lewis, and Ch. Pellat, pp. 1074–1077. Leiden: Brill, 1978.

Salem, Elie Adib. *Political Theory and Institutions of the Khawārij*. Baltimore: Johns Hopkins University Press, 1956.

Veccia Vaglieri, Laura. *An Interpretation of Islam*. Translated by Aldo Caselli. Zurich: Islamic Foundation, 1980.

Williams, John Alden. "Khawarij." In *The Oxford Encyclopedia of the Modern Islamic World*, edited by John L. Esposito, pp. 419–421. New York: Oxford University Press, 1995.

JUSTIN J. CORFIELD

KHATAMI, MOHAMED. (1943–), an Iranian scholar and politician, is a leading Shīʿī religious figure whose lineage goes back to the Prophet Muḥammad's family. Khatami was born into a religious family in Ardakān, Yazd Province, Iran. His father was a well-known member of the religious establishment with special privileges.

He is married to Zohreh Sadeghi and has two daughters and a son.

His early education followed the traditional pattern common among clerical families in Iran, and he graduated with a high school diploma in 1961. He spent the next four years in Qom studying religious sciences. The 1960s in Iran were a politically tumultuous period when the shah consolidated his program of modernization through Westernization and marginalization of the religious establishment and their seminaries. Under these circumstances Khatami pursued a university degree in Isfahan in 1965. He graduated with a bachelor's degree in 1969, having studied philosophy, among other subjects. In 1970 he entered the University of Tehran for a graduate degree, and, after obtaining his master's degree, he returned to Qom to continue his philosophical studies.

His public career can be traced back to the 1970s, another watershed in modern Iranian history, when leading such as like Murtażā Muṭahharī, Sayyid Muḥammad Ḥusayn Bihishtī, and ʿAlī Sharīʿatī challenged the domestic religious status quo. In 1964 Ayatollah Khomeini had openly defied the autocratic rule of the shah, which in turn emboldened the younger clerics, including Khatami, to call for internal reform of the religious institutions to make them compatible with modernity. In 1978 Khatami headed the Islamic Center in Hamburg, Germany, which provided him with a rare opportunity to learn about the West directly and apply his Islamic learning to guide the Iranian Shīʿī living abroad during the critical unfolding of the Islamic Revolution. After the shah's fall in 1979, he returned to Iran and was elected to the national assembly, becoming minister of culture and Islamic guidance (1982–1992). His stay abroad and his earlier inclination toward philosophical studies made Khatami one of the few moderate religious leaders among the revolutionary supporters of Khomeini. Under his tenure, the Ministry of Islamic Guidance adopted a moderate stance on major controversies connected with publications, films, art, and music, but he was ultimately forced to resign after being charged with liberalism. Khatami subsequently served as director of the National Library (1992–1997) and a presidential adviser.

In 1997, the outgoing president, Hāshimī Rafsanjānī, supported Khatami in his bid for the presidency. With strong support from political moderates, intellectuals, students, and women he won 70 percent of the vote. His victory paved the way for the creation of a broad coalition of reformist parties known as Dovum-e Khordad (the second of the month of Khordad, the date of Khatami's election). This coalition won an overwhelming majority of seats in the 2000 parliamentary elections. As president, he appointed a relatively liberal cabinet and called for democratization and the advancement of women. He also advocated rapprochement between Iran and Arab states as well as improving relations with the West, including the United States. However, hardline conservatives in the clergy, judiciary, and military opposed many of his reforms, and his first administration was unable to produce significant economic improvements. He reluctantly ran for a second term and was reelected with more than three-quarters of the vote in 2001. But this term was little different from the first, as he was unable to take a firm stance against the hardliners. This was a weakness of his position as a "robed" politician in a culture in which direct confrontation with the religious establishment after the revolution was avoided at any cost. After eight years in office, he left the presidency in August 2005. Although highly respected abroad for his moderate stance on many issues connected with democratic governance and protection of basic freedoms in Iran, Khatami's domestic support has dwindled under the impact of the upsurge in the conservative politics of his successor, Mahmoud Ahmadinejad. His project on the "dialogue among civilizations" (in response to Samuel Huntington's study of the clash of civilizations), which was supported by the UN in 2001, remains dormant, with little or no support within Iran and almost no constructive engagement internationally. Khatami is the author of *Bīm-i mawj* (Fear of the Wave; 1993), an essay collection, and *Az dunyā-yi shahr ta shahr-i dunyā* (From the World of the City to the City of the World; 1994), a study of Western philosophical and political thought.

[*See also* Iran, Islamic Republic of.]

BIBLIOGRAPHY

Ansari, Ali M. *Iran, Islam, and Democracy: The Politics of Managing Change*. 2d ed. London: Royal Institute of International Affairs, 2006. Lucid account of Khatami's election and presidency.

Ehteshami, Anoushiravan, and Mahjoob Zweiri, eds. *Iran's Foreign Policy: From Khatami to Ahmadinejad*. Reading, U.K.: Ithaca, 2008.

Khatami, Mohammad. *Hope and Challenge: The Iranian President Speaks*. Binghamton, N.Y.: Institute of Global Cultural Studies, Binghamton University, 1997.

Khatami, Mohammad. *Islam, Dialogue, and Civil Society*. Canberra: Centre for Arab and Islamic Studies (The Middle East & Central Asia), Australian National University, 2000.

Tazmini, Ghoncheh. *Khatami's Iran: The Islamic Republic and the Turbulent Path to Reform*. London: Tauris Academic Studies, 2009.

ABDULAZIZ SACHEDINA
Updated by NAEL SHAMA

KHILĀFAT MOVEMENT. An agitation on the part of some Indian Muslims, allied with the Indian nationalist movement, during the years 1919 to 1924, the Khilāfat movement sought to influence the British government to preserve the spiritual and temporal authority of the Ottoman sultan as the caliph of Islam. Integral with this was the Muslims' desire to influence the treaty-making process following World War I in such a way as to restore the prewar boundaries of the Ottoman Empire. The British government treated the Indian Khilāfat delegation of 1920, headed by Muhammad Ali Jauhar, as quixotic Pan-Islamists, and did not change its policy toward Turkey. The Indian Muslims' attempt to influence the provisions of the Treaty of Sèvres failed; the European powers went ahead with their territorial adjustments, including the institution of mandates over formerly Ottoman Arab territories.

The significance of the Khilāfat movement, however, lies less in its supposed Pan-Islamism and its attempt to influence British imperial policy in the Middle East than in its impact on the Indian nationalist movement. The leaders of the Khilāfat movement forged the first political alliance among Western-educated Indian Muslims and *ʿulamāʾ* over the issue of the *khilāfah* (caliphate). This leadership included the brothers Muhammad Ali Jauhar and Shawkat ʿAlī, who were products of Aligarh College; their Sunnī spiritual guide Mawlānā ʿAbdulbari of Firangi Mahal in Lucknow; the Calcutta journalist and Islamic scholar Abū al-Kalām Āzād; and the leading Deobandī *ʿālim* (scholar), Mawlānā Maḥmūdulḥasan. These publicist-politicians and *ʿulamāʾ* viewed the European attack on the authority of the caliph as an attack on Islam and thus as a threat to the religious freedom of Muslims under British rule.

The Khilāfat issue crystallized anti-British sentiment among Indian Muslims that had been increasing since the Tripolitan and Balkan wars of 1911–1912, followed in 1914 by the British declaration of war against the Ottomans. Further, the violence that had followed the British demolition of a portion of a mosque in the Indian city of Kanpur in 1913, and the subsequent agitation that resulted in its restoration, had demonstrated the effectiveness of religious issues in political mobilization. The Khilāfat leaders, most of whom had been imprisoned during the war, were already nationalists. Upon their release in 1919, the religious issue of the Khilāfat provided a means to achieve pan-Indian Muslim political solidarity in the anti-British cause, as well as a vehicle of communication between the leaders and their potential mass following.

The Khilāfat movement also benefited from Hindu-Muslim cooperation in the nationalist cause that had grown during the war, beginning with the Lucknow Pact of 1916, when the Indian National Congress and the Muslim League agreed on proposals for postwar governmental reforms, and culminating in the protest against the Rowlatt antisedition bills in 1919. The Congress, now led by Mohandas K. Gandhi, had called for peaceful demonstrations against the Rowlatt bills, but violence broke out in several places. In the Punjab on 13 April 1919, soldiers fired on a peaceful meeting in Amritsar, killing 379 and injuring many more. The Amritsar massacre, together with the Khilāfat issue, provided the stimulus for the Muslim-Congress alliance in the Noncooperation movement of 1919–1922. Gandhi espoused the Khilāfat cause, seeing in it an opportunity to rally Muslim support for the Congress. The ʿAlī brothers and their allies in turn provided the Noncooperation movement with some of its most enthusiastic troops.

The combined Khilāfat-Noncooperation movement was the first India-wide agitation against British rule. It saw an unprecedented degree of Hindu-Muslim cooperation, and it established Gandhi and his technique of nonviolent protest (*satyāgraha*) at the center of the Indian nationalist movement. Students boycotted schools, lawyers boycotted the courts, voters boycotted elections, and Indians began to spin, weave, and wear homespun cloth as a protest against British economic domination. Mass mobilization using religious symbols was remarkably successful, and the British Indian government was shaken.

In late 1921 the government moved to suppress the movement. The ʿAlī brothers were arrested for incitement to violence, tried in Karachi, and imprisoned. The Noncooperation movement was suspended by Gandhi early in 1922 following a riot in the village of Chauri Chaura, in Uttar Pradesh, in which the local police force was incinerated inside their station by a mob. Gandhi was arrested, tried, and imprisoned soon thereafter. The Turks dealt the final blow by abolishing the Ottoman sultanate in 1922 and the caliphate in 1924.

The aftermath of the Khilāfat movement saw a rise in interreligious violence. The Mappila rebellion of 1921, in which the Muslim peasantry of Malabar rose against their Hindu landlords, increased Hindu-Muslim suspicions, even though the Khilāfat leadership denounced the Mappilas for resorting to violence. During the period 1922–1924, Hindu-Muslim relations deteriorated further, with riots often fomented by communal organizations. Among these organizations were the Hindu Mahāsabha, an exclusively Hindu political party, and Shuddhī and Sangathan, groups dedicated to "purification" and "solidarity" among Hindus. Tanẓīm and Tablīgh, groups devoted to solidarity among Muslims and the propagation of the faith, responded aggressively. Thus the Khilāfat movement, launched amid Hindu-Muslim amity and cooperation, ironically resulted in an aggravation of communal differences. Muslims, aroused to anti-British political activity by the use of religious symbols, found that religious issues separated them from their fellow Indians. The Indian National Congress under Gandhi's leadership found that many of their national symbols were alienating to Muslims. It was a dilemma that ultimately had no solution.

[*See also* Āzād, Abū al-Kalām.]

BIBLIOGRAPHY

Bamford, P. C. *Histories of the Non-co-operation and Khilafat Movements*. Delhi: Deep, 1974. Government intelligence report issued shortly after the collapse of the movement. First published 1925.

Brown, Judith M. *Gandhi's Rise to Power: Indian Politics, 1919–1922*. Cambridge, U.K.: Cambridge University Press, 1972. Perceptive study of Gandhi's early career in India.

Hardy, P. *The Muslims of British India*. Cambridge, U.K.: Cambridge University Press, 1972. The best short intellectual history of Muslims in nineteenth- and twentieth-century India.

Hasan, Mushirul, ed. *Communal and Pan-Islamic Trends in Colonial India*. Rev. ed. New Delhi: Manohar, 1985. Useful collection of articles.

Hasan, Mushirul. *Nationalism and Communal Politics in India, 1885–1930*. New Delhi: Manohar, 1991. Balanced study of the relationship between Muslims and the Congress in the period 1916–1929.

Hasan, Mushirul, and Margrit Pernau, eds. *Regionalizing Pan-Islamism: Documents on the Khilafat Movement*. New Delhi: Manohar, 2005.

Minault, Gail. *The Khilafat Movement: Religious Symbolism and Political Mobilization in India*. New ed. New York: Oxford University Press, 1999. Standard work on the Khilāfat movement.

Nanda, B. R. *Gandhi: Pan-Islamism, Imperialism, and Nationalism in India*. Bombay: Oxford University Press, 1989. Study of the Khilāfat movement from the point of view of Congress.

Qureshi, M. Naeem. *Pan-Islam in British Indian Politics: A Study of the Khilafat Movement, 1918–1924*. Leiden, Netherlands: Brill, 1999.

Robinson, Francis. *Separatism among Indian Muslims: The Politics of the United Provinces' Muslims, 1860–1923*. London: Cambridge University Press, 1974. Important study of the early development of Muslim politics in India through the Khilāfat movement, with emphasis on British sources and viewpoints.

GAIL MINAULT

KHOʾI, ABOL-QĀSEM AL-. (Abū al-Qāsim Khūʾī; 1899–1992) was one of the most influential and widely followed Shīʿī *ʿulamāʾ* in the second half of the twentieth century. He was born into a *sayyid* family (and thus descended from the Prophet Muḥammad) in the city of Khoʾi in the province of West Azerbaijan, Iran. Following an early education in his birthplace, he entered formal religious training in the *ḥawẓah* (center of religious learning) of Najaf, Iraq. He later studied at the highest level of the religious curriculum with Shaykh Fatḥ Allāh (al-Sharīʿah) al-Iṣfahānī and the theoretician of constitutionalism Shaykh Muḥammad Ḥusayn Nāʾīnī, among others. Khoʾi remained in Najaf, becoming a renowned teacher of jurisprudence and theology, writer, and spiritual leader of millions of Shīʿī Muslims in Iraq, Iran, Lebanon, Pakistan, India, and elsewhere.

With the death of Ayatollah Muḥsin al-Ḥakīm in 1970, Khoʾi became the most widely followed Shīʿī *marja ʿ al-taqlīd* (supreme juridical authority). He maintained contact with believers through a well-organized network of local representatives, using the abundant religious tithes (*khums*) given to him to help the poor, provide stipends to seminary students, and establish religious, educational, and social projects worldwide. He also distributed humanitarian relief aid to the victims of the many conflicts and natural disasters that hit Middle Eastern and South Asian countries during his time as a *marjaʿ*. He remained politically neutral during the Iran-Iraq War of 1980–1988, trying to provide equal assistance to civilians on both sides and prevent Tehran and Baghdad from politicizing his humanitarian work. In 1989, the Al-Khoei Benevolent Foundation was set up in London in his name to centralize the administration of his religious funds and charitable services, an initiative that had no precedent in the history of the *marjiʿīyah*.

Khoʾi's scholarly legacy lies in great part in his role as a teacher. His direct and indirect students numbered in the thousands and included *mujtahid*s (interpreters of law) who rose to prominence after him, such as Sayyid ʿAlī al-Sīstānī and Shaykh Muḥammad Isḥāq al-Fayyāḍ in Iraq and Sayyid Muḥammad Ḥusayn Faḍl Allāh (d. 2010) in Lebanon, as well as several clerics with political profiles such as the Iraqi Sayyid Muḥammad Bāqir al-Ṣadr (d. 1980); Sayyid Mūsā al-Ṣadr (d. 1978) and Sayyid Mahdī Shams al-Dīn (d. 2001), successive heads of Lebanon's Higher Islamic Shīʿī Council; and Sayyid ʿAbd al-Karīm Mūsavī Ardabīlī, former chief justice of Iran. Among Khoʾi's ninety books and manuscripts are *al-Bayān fī tafsīr al-Qurʾān* (Exegesis in Qurʾānic Commentary), *al-Masāʾil al-muntakhabah* (Selected [Religious] Questions), and *Minhāj al-ṣāliḥīn* (The Path of the Righteous), a two-volume work on religious practices and law. The scholar also specialized in the field of *ʿilm al-rij ā l* (the science of the biographies of those who transmit tradition).

In his theology, Khoʾi was traditional and scholarly, in his personal life, austere. In the political sphere, he advocated clerical aloofness from state affairs, yet he occasionally interfered in politics in defense of Islam. In the early 1960s, he joined Ayatollah Muḥsin al-Ḥakīm, the most widely followed *mujtahid* of the time, in his condemnation of communism in Iraq. In the same period, Khoʾi denounced the un-Islamic reforms of Iran's White Revolution and what he perceived as Bahāʾī and Zionist domination of society and government in the country. He also actively mediated the release of Khomeini and other Iranian clerics following the attack of March 1963 by the Imperial Guard on the Fayẓīyah School in Qom, Iran, and the crushing of the 15 Khordād demonstrations in June of that year. Khoʾi generally privileged a diplomatic approach to the Iranian monarchy in order to advise it, not foment popular opposition against it. As such, he failed to provide unconditional support to the Iranian revolution of 1978–1979. If he initially displayed signs of solidarity with the protesters by canceling his class in Najaf, he made the unforgivable move, in the eyes of revolutionaries, of receiving Queen Farah Diba of Iran in November 1978.

For this, Khoʾi was subjected to severe criticism from Khomeini's followers. Moreover, he disapproved of Khomeini's interpretation of an all-encompassing *vilāyat-i faqīh* (guardianship of the jurist). Methodologically, the doctrine was problematic to him, in that it referred to traditions with a weak chain of transmission. The jurists could only exercise limited authority in the affairs of the community—the control of the observance of Islamic principles, the authority to issue legal decrees, and the capacity to act as guardian for the orphans, minors, and the insane—not assume leadership in political matters. After the establishment of the Islamic Republic in Iran, Khoʾi called into question Khomeini's claim to *vilāyat-i faqīh*—which was theoretically the prerogative of a *marjaʿ*—by addressing him in a telegram with the low-rank title of *ḥujjat al-Islām*. Afterwards, relations between Khoʾi and the Iranian leadership remained cool, without, however, turning into open animosity on either side.

Khoʾi's relationship with the Iraqi Baʿth regime was also tense. In the early 1980s, his funds were confiscated, and his students and relatives were arrested, tortured, or killed. In spite of this, Khoʾi held to his refusal to give Baghdad its much-wanted endorsement of the Iraqi war effort against Iran. In 1990, he implicitly condemned Iraq's invasion of Kuwait with his *fatwa* forbidding Shīʿīs to purchase goods brought from Kuwait, on the grounds that the goods were stolen. As another affront to the regime, Khoʾi issued two religious edicts during the March 1991 Shīʿī uprising, the latter providing for the creation of a committee of clerics to supervise public, religious, and social affairs in Najaf. In retaliation, the regime forced Khoʾi to appear on state television with President Saddam Hussein, before putting him under house arrest for the rest of his life.

Khoʾi is justly remembered more for his legacy as a religious scholar and philanthropist than for his role in state affairs, but his political record illustrates that the traditional categorization of quietism cannot be understood in a restrictive sense: political aloofness and activism are not two definitive positions Shīʿī clerics choose to endorse, but rather options to be used according to circumstance.

[*See also* Al-Khoei Benevolent Foundation.]

BIBLIOGRAPHY

Khoʾi, Yousif al-. "Grand Ayatollah Abu al-Qassim al-Khoʾi: Political Thought and Positions." In *Ayatollahs, Sufis and Ideologies: State, Religion, and Social Movements in Iraq*, edited by Faleh Abdul-Jabar, pp. 223–230. London: Saqi, 2002.

Sachedina, Abdulaziz A. "Translator's Introduction: Al-Khūʾi and the Twelver Shīʿites." In *The Prolegomena to the Qurʾan*, by Abū al-Qāsim ibn ʿAlī Akbar Khūʾī, translated by Abdulaziz A. Sachedina, pp. 3–22. New York: Oxford University Press, 1998.

Walbridge, Linda S. *The Most Learned of the Shiʿa: The Institution of the Marjaʿ Taqlid*. New York: Oxford University Press, 2001.

JOYCE N. WILEY
Updated by ELVIRE CORBOZ

KHOMEINI, RUHOLLAH AL-MUSAVI.

Born on 24 September 1902 in Khomein, west-central Iran, Ayatollah Ruhollah Khomeini was a leading Shīʿī Muslim jurist and a revolutionary figure who led the 1979 Islamic Revolution in the overthrow of the Pahlavi monarchy and the establishment of the first Shīʿī theocracy in the modern era. As a theologian, political figure, mystical philosopher, and poet, Khomeini is best known for reconstructing Shīʿī Islam into a revolutionary movement and institutionalizing a theocratic political order led by jurists.

Early Life and Education (1902–1934). Ruhollah was brought up in a clerical family of Musavi *sayyids* who claimed descent from the Prophet Muḥammad. His father, Mostafa Hindi (1861–1902), a landed provincial cleric, was murdered on his way to the town of Arak just months after the birth of Ruhollah. The young Ruhollah was raised by his mother and his aunt Sahebeh, a woman with considerable strength and political influence in Khomein. Ruhollah's early education was in the local *maktab* (mosque school), and by his teens he had acquired an education in advanced Arabic and theology under private clerical tutorship. He was also versed in classical poetry and wrote poetry. Toward the end of his teen years, after the death of his mother and aunt in 1918, Ruhollah began his studies at the seminary of Arak under Ayatollah ʿAbdol Karīm Ḥāʾirī Yazdi (1859–1937), a leading Shīʿī cleric known for his scholarship and aloofness from politics. In 1921, he married Batul, the daughter of a Tehran-based cleric. In 1922, along with his mentor, Ayatollah Ḥāʾirī, Ruhollah moved to the Fayḍīyah seminary of Qom, where he would continue his studies to become a major scholar.

Rise to Mujtahid (1934–1962). At Qom, Khomeini underwent the traditional cycle of seminary school as a *ṭalabah*, or student, with the task of studying the Sharīʿah (religious law) and juristic practices of ruling and interpretation of religious principles, together with logic and philosophy. In the mid-1920s, he completed the study of *fiqh* (jurisprudence). In 1934 or 1935, with the ability to issue rulings for everyday problems based on the Qurʾān and the *ḥadīth*, he attained *ijazah*, or "permission" to practice *ijtihād*, or independent judgment based on Islamic law at the age of thirty-two or thirty-three. Now as a *mujtahid* (learned jurist), carrying the title of *hujjat al-Islām* (proof of Islam), Khomeini began his scholarly career with the publication of a number of important books. Written in Arabic, books such as *Ādāb al-salāt* (Prayer Literature) and *Miṣbāḥ al-hidāya* (Book of Guidance) were mostly religious tracts on worship and prayers, with some mystical overtones. He also wrote Persian mystical poetry and taught medieval mystical philosophy, originally taught to him by a number of mystical theologians such as Sayyid Abū al-Ḥasan Qazvīnī (d. 1976) and, more importantly, Mīrzā Muḥammad ʿAlī Shāhābādī (d. 1950), a leading clerical figure.

With the death of Ḥāʾirī in 1937, Khomeini followed the *marjiʿīyah*, or religious leadership, of Ayatollah Moḥammad Ḥosayn Borujerdi (1875–1961), also known for his quietism. However, by the 1940s Khomeini had begun to create his own network of seminary students who admired him and visited his house on a regular basis. His 1943 *Kashf al-asrār* (Unveiling of Secrets) provided his students with an important political work on how governance based on Islamic values and supervised by the *ʿulamāʾ* is possible. *Kashf al-asrār* also attacked secular intellectuals and liberal clerics who had become increasingly vocal in the Iranian public sphere under the reign of Reza Shah Pahlavi (1925–1941), whose secular-nationalist modernization project had deprived the clerics of much institutional authority in Iranian society. However, under Reza Shah's reign and even up to the 1953 coup, when Prime Minister Mohammad Mossadegh's government was overthrown by covert British and American intervention, Khomeini kept out of politics, largely in obedience to Ayatollah Borujerdi, who, in deference to the monarchy, prohibited clerics from participating in politics.

Beginnings of Political Activism (1961–1965). With the death of Ayatollah Borujerdi in 1961, Khomeini's activities became increasingly political. In 1963, he entered the political arena, not as a revolutionary figure but as a critical cleric who disapproved of the White Revolution, the modernization and reform policies of Mohammad Reza Shah Pahlavi (r. 1941–1979). The White Revolution promised to change the structure of Iranian society, focusing mainly on land reform, industrial development, and such social problems as illiteracy and women's status. The enfranchisement of women in particular was problematic to Khomeini and his socially conservative followers, who saw such social reforms as a Westernizing project, reminding many of Reza Shah's mandatory unveiling policy. On 22 January 1963, Khomeini publicly denounced the government's new polices, which were put to a referendum on 26 January. Other *ayatollahs*, including many known to be conservative and quietist, also condemned the referendum. The shah, on an official visit to Qom, responded by attacking the clerics as a "stupid" reactionary class. Confrontations between antireferendum activists and the regime security forces followed in Qom, where many seminarians called for the boycott of the referendum. When the shah's policies were approved by an overwhelming majority in the referendum, Khomeini called for more resistance and raised new issues to challenge the monarchy.

While he did not, during this period, have a definite vision of Islamic polity, Khomeini saw the shah as a transgressor, a ruler who had failed to live up to the guidelines of the constitution, which had guaranteed that state policies would never contradict Islamic law. On the religious day of ʿĀshūrāʾ, 3 June 1963, Khomeini's aggressive speech denouncing the shah as a "wretched, miserable man" while advising him to steer away from Israel and learn from the mistakes of his father (who had been dethroned by foreign powers), angered the monarchy. When Khomeini was arrested on 5 June, his followers, organized demonstrations and attacked major government institutions around the country. With the support of other leading clerics, Khomeini was released from prison. However, he increased his antigovernment activities after the October 1964 capitulations (Status of Forces Agreement), by which the monarchy granted diplomatic immunity to American military personnel based in Iran. When Khomeini condemned the agreement for undermining Iranian sovereignty, he was arrested again and this time exiled to Turkey in 1965.

Birth of a Revolutionary Cleric in Exile (1965–1979). The arrest and subsequent exile of Khomeini solidified his rise to leadership in the years to come. He was now recognized not only as a *marjaʿ al-taqlīd* (source of imitation) for thousands of Shīʿī Muslims but also as a political figure who had stood up bravely to the powerful regime of the shah. While in exile in Turkey, Khomeini wrote his second most important political work, *Taḥrīr al-wasīlah* (A Clarification of Questions), in which he sharpened his conception of Islamic government by assigning greater authority to the clerics as public figures responsible for looking after the welfare of the community.

In October 1965, the *ayatollah* moved to the city of Najaf, Iraq, where he began his new activities as a scholar and a revolutionary thinker. The Najaf years (1965–1978) marked a critical period in the intellectual and political life of Khomeini and his followers. His movement, known as the Nahẓat, had begun to grow in numbers and organizational strength. Students, merchants, pilgrims, and admirers would visit him in Najaf, while carrying back his speeches and sermons to Iran. Khomeini's works were translated and published in Lebanon and later transported to various countries, especially Iran, by followers.

In 1969–1970 Khomeini gave the most important series of lectures on the Islamic state, namely, *Hukūmat-i Islāmī: Vilāyat-i faqīh* (Islamic Government: Guardianship of the Jurist), which argued that the supreme authority in the state, based on Islamic principles, should rest with the clerics. Until the return of the Twelfth Imam, whose reappearance at the end of time would establish a truly just government, the clerics have the responsibility to defend Islamic values, prevent corruption, and resist foreign domination by taking over the affairs of the state.

Khomeini challenged not only the Iranian monarchy but also hundreds of years of traditional Shīʿī Twelver jurisprudence on the imamate, or leadership of the community, which primarily viewed the authority of clerics during the occultation of the Twelfth Imam as limited to the custodianship over seminary students and the poor and needy, such as orphans, widows, and the insane. It is important to note that during this period Khomeini still did not commonly use the term *inqilab*, or "revolution," though it does appear once in his *Hukūmat-i Islāmī*, most likely inserted by his students. What was revolutionary at this stage, however, was the growing organizational clout of his Nahẓat, whose leading figures, such as Murtaẑā Muṭahharī (1920–1979), ʿAlī Khameneʾi, and Moḥammad Beheshtī (1928–1981) were increasingly incorporating Marxist conceptions of revolutionary action and network strategies into the movement. While his recorded political statements attracted many young activists in Iran, leading Najaf-based quietist clerics such as Ayatollah Abū al-Qāsīm al-Khūʾī (1899–1992), who had a huge following in the Shīʿī world, maintained their opposition to Khomeini.

The Founder of a Theocratic Republic and a Statesman (1979–1989). Pressured by the shah, the Saddam Hussein government forced Khomeini to leave Iraq for Kuwait, but he was refused entry at the border. On 12 October 1978, Khomeini arrived in France, where he resided in the suburbs of Paris, delivering anti-shah speeches and cultivating the image of a spiritual figure of revolutionary fervor. Khomeini was cautious, however, as he avoided assertions about the incumbency of clerical rule, which could have alienated secular-Marxist and liberal democratic forces. He emphasized the image of an ascetic cleric denouncing the corruption of the shah and the imperialism of the United States, a populist image that appealed to many, especially the younger generation from both lower- and middle-class backgrounds who were influenced by the works of ʿAlī Sharīʿatī (1933–1977), a Paris-educated sociologist of Third Worldism popular for fusing socialism with Islam. With the initial sparks of the revolution in 1978, Khomeini had become the leading figure of the mass street protests.

By late 1978 the wave of revolutionary mobilization had peaked, and the shah was forced to appoint a liberal-democratic politician, Shahpour Bakhtiar (1914–1991), as his prime minister. On 16 January 1979, the shah fled the country for Egypt. On February 1, Khomeini returned to Iran to a jubilant crowd of millions. With the appointment of liberal Muslim Mehdi Bazargan (1907–1995) as head of an interim government and the declaration of the army's neutrality on 11 February, Bakhtiar's government collapsed and, along with it, the monarchy. After the overwhelming passage of the March 1979 national referendum on creating an Islamic Republic, Khomeini called for a new constitution.

The new constitution, adopted by referendum on 24 October 1979, played a critical role in solidifying Khomeini and his allies' power in the Islamic republic. The Revolutionary Council, consisting of Khomeini loyalists, drafted a constitution that established Khomeini's vision of *vilāyat-i faqīh*. The constitution also institutionalized the Guardian Council, appointed by the leading jurist in power, as the watchdog group with a veto power over the legislative branch. The Assembly of Experts, made up of clerics, would be in charge of appointing the supreme leader and ensuring that authority would remain in the hands of the clerics. But the new constitution also ensured "free" elections for the presidency and the Majlis, the national parliament. The result was a political order that mixed elected and unelected institutions, with the clerics dominating the latter and subordinating the elected elements.

Khomeini emerged as a revolutionary statesman. As head of the state, he served as the supreme guardian of the revolution and the Islamic Republic with complete veto power over various branches of government. He also became the leader of a populist revolutionary state that sought transnational influence over all Muslims and "oppressed" people around the world. On 4 November 1979 pro-Khomeini students seized the U.S. embassy and took American personnel hostage for 444 days. Khomeini supported the seizure for many reasons, but the most significant was to neutralize the influence of the Marxist and leftist Islamist groups and marginalize liberal forces, who saw the seizure as an illegal act. He also used the crisis to help the Iranian revolution gain international recognition as an anti-imperialist movement, partly to build transnational support in case of a possible U.S.-led coup.

The Iraqi invasion of Iran on 22 September 1980 was also a watershed in Khomeini's early career as a statesman. The war allowed Khomeini and his allies to further consolidate their power and to prolong the revolutionary fervor, now directed against Saddam Hussein.

Yet, within the country, the new Islamic Republic faced enormous challenges. With militant Marxist groups and Islamist leftists (especially the Mujāhidīn-i Khalq Organization, or MKO) challenging the new political system, Khomeini and his supporters, now mostly members of the newly formed Islamic Republican Party (IRP), used the outbreak of the war to stifle dissent, control the press, and crack down on the opposition. Following the ouster of the newly elected liberal president, Abol-Hasan Bani Sadr (r. 4 February 1980–21 June 1981), the Islamic

Republic had come under the full control of Khomeinists.

The postrevolutionary period was marked by a number of failed military coups, assassination plots, an expanding economic crisis—the result of sanctions and war—and, most importantly, a long-lasting conflict with Iraq, which was very costly in terms of lives and treasure. During this period, Khomeini, now living in northern Tehran, proved an authoritarian ruler, as he oversaw the consolidation of his theocracy and the suppression of dissidents, including quietist clerics such as Ayatollah Sharīʿatmadārī (1905–1986), who viewed *vilāyat-i faqīh* as heretical to the Shīʿī religion. In early 1989, when Ayatollah Ḥusayn ʿAlī Muntaẓirī (1922–2009), his designated successor, criticized him for infringement on citizens' freedoms and allowing the execution of numerous prisoners, Khomeini demoted and stripped him of his title as a senior cleric.

But Khomeini was also a pragmatist. In terms of domestic politics, he maintained the role of a mediator between various factions with competing visions of governance. In terms of foreign policy, he remained openly defiant against the United States even as he approved secret arms purchases from the Reagan administration that would become public in the Iran-Contra affair. In terms of social issues, Khomeini also proved to be far more liberal than his fellow traditional clerics in Qom or Najaf. Despite his support for Islamization policies such as banning alcohol and enforcing Islamic dress for women, he approved artificial insemination and sex change, along with the public display of art, music, and film, as long as it was deemed to be "Islamic" by the Ministry of Culture and Islamic Guidance. However, when in February 1989 he issued a *fatwa* for the death of Salman Rushdie for his novel *The Satanic Verses*, Khomeini's image as an intolerant zealot was solidified, especially in the West.

On 3 June 1989, Khomeini died from cancer and other complications. Before his death, he designated President ʿAlī Khameneʾi, one of the leading figures of Khomeini's pre-revolutionary Nahẓat and a major politician in the early revolutionary period, as his successor. During his funeral, millions of his grief-stricken devotees flocked to see their leader buried near a cemetery outside of Tehran. The date of his death is commemorated annually by the Iranian government.

BIBLIOGRAPHY

Abrahamian, Ervand. *Khomeinism: Essays on the Islamic Republic*. London: I. B. Tauris, 1993.

Arjomand, Said Amir. *The Turban for the Crown: The Islamic Revolution in Iran*. New York: Oxford University Press, 1988.

Brumberg, Daniel. *Reinventing Khomeini: The Struggle for Reform in Iran*. Chicago: University of Chicago Press, 2001.

Enayat, Hamid. "Iran: Khumayni's Concept of the 'Guardianship of the Juristconsult.'" In *Islam in the Political Process*, edited by James P. Piscatori, pp. 160–180. New York: Cambridge University Press, 1983.

Enayat, Hamid. *Modern Islamic Political Thought*. London: Macmillan, 1982.

Khomeini, Ruhollah. *Imam Khomeini's Last Will and Testament*. Washington, D.C.: Embassy of the Democratic and Popular Republic of Algeria, Interest Section of the Islamic Republic of Iran, 1989.

Khomeini, Ruhollah. *Islam and Revolution: Writings and Declarations of Imam Khomeini*. Translated by Hamid Algar. Berkeley, Calif.: Mizan, 1981.

Martin, Vanessa. *Creating an Islamic State: Khomeini and the Making of a New Iran*. London: I. B. Tauris, 2000.

Mottahedeh, Roy. *The Mantle of the Prophet: Religion and Politics in Iran*. New York: Simon & Schuster, 1985.

Moin, Baqer. *Khomeini: Life of the Ayatollah*. London: I. B. Tauris, 1999.

Nakash, Yitzhak. *Reaching for Power: The Shiʿa in the Modern Arab World*. Princeton, N.J.: Princeton University Press, 2006.

Nasr, Vali. *The Shia Revival: How Conflicts within Islam Will Shape the Future*. New York: W. W. Norton, 2006.

BABAK RAHIMI

KHURŪJ. *See* Rebellion.

KHUṬBAH. An address called a *khuṭbah* is delivered by a *khaṭīb* (orator) as part of a religious service. As a sacred ritual with fixed rulings, the *khuṭbah* fulfills a holy mandate associated with specific occasions such as the weekly congregational Friday service, the two ʿĪd holidays, and the Day of ʿArafāt (the ninth of the month of Dhū al-Ḥijjah) during *ḥajj*. The *khuṭbah* is also delivered on other occasions, such as a marriage-contract ceremony or during an eclipse or excessive drought. In the Friday service, the *khuṭbah* precedes the prayer, whereas the prayer precedes the *khuṭbah* during the two ʿĪd sacraments.

Before the Prophet migrated to Medina, the Muslim community did not hold Friday services in Mecca. The institution of the Friday (*jumʿah*) ceremony developed later on in Medina, as a result of the revelation of the Qurʾānic *sūrat al-jumʿah*.

The Prophet, and eventually his political successors—the caliphs and provincial governors—became imams, or leaders of the collective worship, which took place in the chief mosque of the city. Because some sort of address was made at the gathering, which was identified as a political community, a tradition emerged concerning the role of the sovereign. The significance of the mosque gathering was embodied in the *minbar* (pulpit), an elevated structure from which the *khuṭbah* is delivered, following the precedent of Muḥammad. The *minbar* gradually became a kind of throne or, more accurately, the chair of state of the sovereign, who used it on official occasions. In his inauguration ceremony, for example, the caliph would ascend the *minbar*, receiving the homage of the community, and deliver a *khuṭbah*. In the provinces, governors stood in the same relation to the central mosque as did the caliph in the capital, as they too made their formal entry into office by ascending the *minbar* and delivering a *khuṭbah*.

There also developed a political custom that enemies of the ruler and his party could be condemned from the *minbar*. Along with this tradition emerged the practice of bestowing a blessing on the ruler in whose name the Friday *khuṭbah* was delivered. The *khuṭbah* was also used for defending policies, stirring public emotion, and disseminating propaganda, and thus it became an ideal vehicle to announce the deposition of a ruler, an accession, nomination of an heir, a declaration of war, or a notification of its termination.

During the ʿAbbāsid period (750–1258 CE) the expansion of the Islamic domain and the preoccupation of the caliphs with ceremonials and traditions of the Persian monarchy prevented officials from delivering the *khuṭbah* personally. Instead, a man learned in religious matters was appointed to the position of *khaṭīb*. After the Prophet Muḥammad's death, religious scholars developed several schools of legal thought.

With the expansion of Islam, the appearance of imperial caliphal administration, the emergence of popular preachers, and the development of independent religious authorities, the mosque became less an instrument of polity and more a place for religious practices. The *khuṭbah*, which in earlier days was pronounced by the sovereign himself or his delegates and principally dealt with political, military, and other state affairs, became tangential.

Nonetheless, the political character of the mosque never entirely disappeared. Utterance of prayers for the ruler during the *khuṭbah* remained one of the recognized tokens of sovereignty under Muslim rule; its omission was a signal of revolt. The political character of the mosque had also been retained in another sense. The religious scholars endorsed the validity of praying for the leader of the Islamic state, as long as the leader was not praised for things that were untrue. In the case of a major crisis or community dissatisfaction, members flocked to the mosque to discuss the problem or seek remedy, which strengthened the institution in the eyes of believers. Throughout the history of Islam the mosque witnessed numerous uprisings, revolts, and social movements, often led from the *minbar*. In this respect, the role of the *minbar* in the nineteenth and twentieth centuries was especially notable during periods of unrest precipitated by Western incursion into Islamic territory.

Colonization of Muslim lands and the increasing political and commercial influence of the Christian West shocked Muslim leaders. The experience of colonialism motivated widespread use of the *minbar* in anticolonial movements. Shāh ʿAbd al-ʿAzīz (1746–1824), a well-known religious leader, issued a *fatwa* declaring all land under British occupation to be *dār al-ḥarb*, or the territory of the enemies of Islam. Through his preaching from the *minbars* of two chief mosques in Delhi, he maintained contact with the masses and disseminated his anticolonial views.

After abolishing the monarchy in 1952, and despite secularist tendencies, the new regime in Egypt recognized that Islam remained the widest and most effective basis for consensus both within Egypt and among Arabs more generally. Cairo manipulated religious sentiments as necessary and, in 1968, proclaimed that the mosque, state, and community would be closely associated under government guidance. In practice this meant not only that opposition parties such as the Muslim Brotherhood were barred from the mosque, but also that the content of the Friday *khuṭbah* was under strict control. Henceforth, Egyptian preachers were directed by the state to amalgamate socialism, nationalism, and industrial development with the tenets of Islam, all of which required gargantuan—and even contradictory—efforts. Remarkably, the new regime revived the symbolic fusion of state and religion in Islam and, during the invasion of Egypt by England, France, and Israel in 1956, Gamal Abdel Nasser, as president of the republic, performed the Friday prayer of the assembly in al-Azhar Mosque in Cairo on 2 and 9 November; he then ascended the *minbar* and delivered orations similar to his other fiery speeches.

King Muḥammad V of Morocco and President Nasser of Egypt used the *khuṭbah* to promote modernist policies in the garb of "true Islamic traditions"; by contrast, Abdur Rauf, a Pakistani social scientist, has openly recommended the Friday *khuṭbah* as an instrument for social change and for transforming traditional lifestyles. Rauf has suggested that a mass movement for the development of rural life in Pakistan could be extensively and effectively implemented through the Friday *khuṭbah*. He argued that the problems of apathy, ignorance, ill health, and low productivity could be effectively solved with the help of communication via the *minbar*, backed by such measures as a well-planned training program for mosque leaders and promotion of the attendance of women and children at Friday prayers.

The *khuṭbah* expanded beyond its function as a religious ritual and became a forum for the expression of political concerns. In the case of Iran, because of the split between the state and religious leaders, the *minbar* evolved into a rallying point of opposition to the government after the turn of the twentieth century. In Morocco and Egypt, with the revival of the fusion of state and religion, both governments consistently used the *khuṭbah* to their own advantages. For instance, in Egypt the mosque was transformed into an arm of the government and was often used as an instrument for the legitimization of its programs.

BIBLIOGRAPHY

Alkhairo, Wael. *Speaking for Change: A Guide to Making Effective Friday Sermons (Khutbahs)*. Beltsville, Md.: Amana, 1998.

Fathi, Asghar. "The Islamic Pulpit as a Medium of Political Communication." *Journal for the Scientific Study of Religion* 20, no. 2 (1981): 163–172.

Ibn al-Jawzī, Abū al-Faraj ʿAbd al-Raḥmān ibn ʿAlī. *Ibn al-Jawzī's Kitāb al-Quṣṣās wa'l-Mudhakkirīn*. Translated and edited by Merlin L. Swartz. Beirut: Dar El-Mechreq, 1971.

Jumʿah, ʿAlī. *Al-bayān li-mā yashghalu al-adhhān*. 2 vols. Cairo: al-Muqaṭṭam li-al-Nashr wa-al-Tawzīʿ, 2005–2009.

Mubarak, Ali. "The Khuṭba: A Symbol of Royalty in Islam." *Sind University Research Journal, Arts Series, Humanities and Social Sciences* (1979): 89–96.

Pedersen, Johannes. "Khaṭīb." In *Encyclopaedia of Islam*, 2d ed., edited by P. J. Bearman, Th. Bianquis, C. E. Bosworth, et al., vol. 4, pp. 1109–1111. Leiden, Netherlands: E. J. Brill, 1978.

Sakr, Ahmad H. *Khutab from Mihrab*. Lombard, Ill.: Foundation for Islamic Knowledge, 1998.

Samb, A. "Masdjid." In *Encyclopaedia of Islam*, 2d ed., edited by P. J. Bearman, Th. Bianquis, C. E. Bosworth, et al., vol. 6, pp. 644–707. Leiden, Netherlands: E. J. Brill, 1991.

HADIA MUBARAK
Updated by JOSEPH A. KÉCHICHIAN

KINDĪ, ABŪ YŪSUF YAʿQŪB IBN ISḤAQ AL-. The first thinker of the Islamic tradition to engage explicitly with the Greek tradition, al-Kindī (d. after 870) was a polymath who wrote on nearly all areas of philosophy. His output on political philosophy is unfortunately lost. We know from the *Fihrist* ("List") of the tenth-century bookseller Ibn al-Nadīm that this output consisted mostly of a single work. Although twelve titles are listed under al-Kindī's "books on politics" (*kutubuhu al-siyāsīyāt*), the titles show that all but one were actually about ethics (several of these are still extant and are discussed below). The exception is the "Great Epistle on Governance" (*siyāsah*), which, unfortunately, is not known to be extant.

Yet al-Kindī is of some significance in the history of Islamic political thought. This is, firstly, because of his own relation to the politics of his day. He was born into an influential line of the tribe of Kindah, and could trace his ancestry to a Companion of the Prophet. Closer to al-Kindī's own day, his grandfather was a governor under the ʿAbbāsids. Exploiting this background, al-Kindī attached himself to several ʿAbbāsid caliphs. He is said to have had dealings with al-Maʾmūn (r. 813–833), but the height of his success seems to have been under the caliph al-Muʿtaṣim (r. 833–842), whose son Aḥmad al-Kindī tutored. Both caliph and son are addressees of works by al-Kindī. In part because of these connections, it is speculated that al-Kindī had an intellectual affinity with the Muʿtazilah, the theologians whose stance on the createdness of the Qurʾān was championed in the infamous *miḥnah*, a "test" or "inquisition" in which several ʿAbbāsid caliphs required adherence to this Muʿtazilī doctrine. This could explain, for instance, al-Kindī's stress on the createdness of the world: he was attempting to safeguard the claim that eternity is unique to God alone.

As for political ideas, these must be inferred from al-Kindī's works on other topics. Like al-Fārābī after him, al-Kindī seems to see a parallel between God as providential ruler of the world and a just political order. Thus, for instance, in a work explaining why the stars are said in Qurʾān 55:6 to "prostrate themselves" before God, al-Kindī says that this means the heavens are obedient to God's command. They carry out the divine command in such a way as to bring about the workings of providence, since their motions have an effect on the world below the heavenly spheres, where we live. It is not far-fetched to assume that al-Kindī expects us to draw a parallel between the well-ordered political regime and the constant and regular phenomena in the natural world (he mentions the cycle of the seasons, for instance). Elsewhere, he compares the rational faculty in the soul to a king. This, too, suggests that for al-Kindī the proper political arrangement consists in rule by a rational king, which is greeted by unquestioning obedience.

For insight into the proper behavior of such a rational king, we can turn to al-Kindī's extant ethical writings. In a work entitled "On Dispelling Sorrows," he first sets out the basic ethical principle that one should disdain the goods of the physical world and turn towards the "world of the intellect." He then gives a series of anecdotes, sayings, and bits of advice intended to help us achieve this. Several of these feature historical rulers—Alexander the Great comes out well; Nero does not. The anecdotes convey the message that a good king is wise enough to expect death and loss, and does not value wealth over virtue. Furthermore, al-Kindī compares the attitude we should take toward pleasure to the manner of "exalted kings" who greet visitors calmly and without eagerness. Al-Kindī saw Socrates as an exemplar for this kind of virtue. In another work collecting sayings and anecdotes about Socrates, he is portrayed in dialogue with kings, giving them lessons on humility and even the correct attitude toward God.

This brings us to a final point: if God is akin to the perfect ruler and the cosmos to the perfectly ruled state, then the prophet is, of course, God's representative. However, al-Kindī resists the idea that a prophet has access to truths or knowledge inaccessible to the rest of us. In the incongruous setting of a treatise on Aristotle's works, he explains that the advantage of prophecy lies in the effortless and immediate way the prophet can have knowledge, as contrasted to the philosopher who gets the same truths only by great effort. In this way, al-Kindī anticipates the notorious view found in al-Fārābī and Averroës (Ibn Rushd) that a prophet is someone who brings truths also discovered through rational means by the philosopher.

Bibliography

Adamson, Peter. *Al-Kindī*. New York: Oxford University Press, 2007.

Adamson, Peter, and Peter E. Pormann. *The Philosophical Works of al-Kindī*. Karachi: Oxford University Press, 2012.

Druart, Thérèse-Anne. "Al-Kindi's Ethics." *Review of Metaphysics* 47 (1993): 329–357.

Kindī, Abū Yaʿqūb al-. *Le moyen de chasser les tristesses, et autres textes éthiques*. Translated by Soumaya Mestiri and Guillaume Dye. Paris: Fayard, 2004.

Kindī, Abū Yaʿqūb al-. *Rasāʾil al-Kindī al-falsafīyah*. Edited by Muḥammad ʿAbd al-Hādī Abū Rīda. 2 vols. Cairo: Dār al-Fikr al-ʿArabī, 1950–1953.

Peter Adamson

Kishk, ʿAbd al-Ḥamīd. (1933–1996), more fully, Shaykh ʿAbd al-Ḥamīd ʿAbd al-ʿAzīz Muḥammad Kishk, was an immensely popular Egyptian preacher, known to many of his followers as Shaykh ʿAbd al-Ḥamīd. Born in Shubrākhīt, a village not far from Damanhūr, near Alexandria, Kishk went to school in the city and became blind at the age of twelve, following an illness. Graduating from the *uṣūl al-dīn* (dogmatics) faculty of al-Azhar, he worked for some time in the service of the Egyptian ministry of *awqāf* (religious endowments) as a mosque preacher and imam. From 5 May 1964 until 28 August 1981, he was an independent preacher in the ʿAyn al-Ḥayāh Mosque on Miṣr wa-al-Sudān Street in the Cairo quarter known as Ḥadāʾiq al-Qubbah. This mosque is also known as the Masjid al-Malik. It was from here that his fame and popularity spread.

Under the regime of President Gamal Abdel Nasser (r. 1952–1970), Kishk came into conflict with the authorities over several questions. Among his more controversial positions was his staunch refusal to issue a *fatwa* that approved of the death sentence imposed by the regime on Sayyid Quṭb in 1966, followed by an equally contentious rejection of Arab socialism's compatibility with Islam. By such attitudes he identified himself as a dissident and as a result spent time in prison. His first incarceration, which began in 1965, lasted two and a half years.

Under the regime of Anwar el-Sadat (r. 1970–1981), Kishk's sermons became immensely popular, with crowds of ten thousand or more gathering to hear his humorous renditions. In these, he continued to criticize sharply any behavior that he regarded as a deviation from the norms of Islam. However, the regime was a little more tolerant of such criticisms, since it needed the support of the Islamic movement in the struggle against "communism and atheism." Nevertheless, Shaykh Kishk, unlike Islamists such as Shaykh al-Shaʿrāwī, did not appear on state-run television or publish in the official printed media.

In spite of the official media boycott, Kishk's sermons were widely distributed on cassette tapes, as in the same period were those by the Iranian leader Ayatollah Khomeini, who came to power in 1979. Hence, the Western media have sometimes called Kishk an Egyptian Khomeini. It became more obvious than it was in the 1980s that the resemblance between the two men was superficial at best. Whereas Khomeini founded a revolutionary movement that came to power in Iran and survived the death of its founder by years, Kishk's political views (as far as they could be found in his books) resembled a form of anarchism. He wrote, for instance, with great nostalgia about the days when there were no policemen to stop people and ask for their driver's licenses, or frontier guards to ask for passports and entry or exit visas: those were the days when the Muslims conquered the world, as Kishk wanted his audiences to remember.

Anarchism, obviously, was too strong and too Western a word to describe the traditional dislike for rulers and government officials in the Middle East and elsewhere. This common attitude was perhaps best put into words by Saʿd Zaghlūl (1857–1927; prime minister of Egypt from January to November 1924), who once remarked that Egypt's citizens tended to look at their rulers in the same way birds gazed at hunters.

The emphasis in Kishk's preaching fell on personal and private piety, not on something as transitory as worldly power. The *shaykh* was occupied with the end of the world, the miracles of the Ṣūfī saints, the metaphysics of the soul, eschatology, and death. Nevertheless, in a politically tense atmosphere the statements he made about this world were often understood as veiled demands for the introduction of a theocracy, especially by those who were in favor (or in fear) of an Islamic theocracy. There can, however, be little doubt that many in the *shaykh*'s audiences, in the traditions of the Islamic quietist Ṣūfī movements, were only superficially interested in political (Islamic) utopias, if at all.

"The believer's creed must be compressed into: loving God," Kishk once wrote (*Maktabat* 13, p. 159). It was not plausible, although admittedly possible, that such an emphasis on love, also known from Islamic mysticism, accompanied political ambitions, revolutionary schemes, and participation in the struggle for worldly power. Yet Kishk's social criticisms were thought to imply political consequences. In a sermon on 12 December 1980, he attacked Jews, Christians, lax Muslims, and a former rector of al-Azhar University, as well as a soccer captain and a businessman who was reported to have presented his wife with an expensive coat. Since the *shaykh* was repeatedly sent to jail, one had to assume that those in power were concerned about the force of such sweeping criticisms.

In the first days of September 1981, on the eve of the assassination of Sadat, which took place on 6 October, Kishk was again thrown into prison. He shared this fate with 1,526 others of all political persuasions who were put under "precautionary arrest." In anticipation of the publication of a complete official list of detainees, the first page of *al-Ahrām* on 4 September noted the imprisonment of Kishk along with a small number of prominent Egyptians. In spite of controls on the media, the *shaykh*'s fame had clearly spread.

On 24–25 January 1982, Kishk was released from detention on orders from President Hosni Mubarak (r. 1981–2011), under the strict condition that the *shaykh* end his career as a public activist. In February 1982, the Egyptian semiofficial weekly devoted to religious affairs, *al-Liwāʾ al-Islāmī*, contained minor contributions by Kishk, an indication that a compromise with the regime of Hosni Mubarak had been reached. Popular with many listeners, his cassette tapes continued to be widely available, with Gilles Kepel documenting service-taxi drivers in Cairo, Casablanca, and the North African district of Marseilles, among others places, tuning in (Kepel, 2003). With Kishk's life as a public preacher over, the ʿAyn al-Ḥayāh Mosque in Cairo was converted into a public-health center. He died in Cairo on 6 December 1996.

Kishk's uniqueness was closely tied to the way in which he chanted his sermons. His voice expressed nostalgia for the kingdom of heaven in a way that moved many members of his audiences, and, despite his political views, Kishk harbored a spiritual approach that emphasized private piety.

[*See also* Egypt.]

BIBLIOGRAPHY

Ajami, Fouad. *The Arab Predicament: Arab Political Thought and Practice since 1967*. Rev. ed. New York: Cambridge University Press, 1992. See esp. pp. 60–73.

Jansen, Johannes J. G. *The Neglected Duty: The Creed of Sadat's Assassins and Islamic Resurgence in the Middle East*. New York: Macmillan, 1986.

Jansen, Johannes J. G. "The Voice of Sheikh Kishk." In *The Challenge of the Middle East: Middle Eastern Studies at the University of Amsterdam*, edited by Ibrahim A. El-Sheikh, C. Aart van de Koppel, and Rudolph Peters, pp. 57–67. Amsterdam: Institute for Modern Near Eastern Studies, University of Amsterdam, 1982.

Kepel, Gilles. *Muslim Extremism in Egypt: The Prophet and Pharaoh*. Translated by Jon Rothschild. Rev. ed. Berkeley: University of California Press, 2003.

Kishk, ʿAbd al-Ḥamīd. *Fatāwā al-Shaykh Kishk: Humūm al-Muslim al-yawmīyah*. Cairo: al-Mukhtār al-Islāmī, n.d. [1988].

Kishk, ʿAbd al-Ḥamīd. *Al-khuṭab al-minbarīyah*. Cairo: Maktabat al-Ṣaḥāfah, 1987.

Kishk, ʿAbd al-Ḥamīd. *Maktabat al-Shaykh Kishk*. Cairo: al-Maktab al-Miṣrī al-Ḥadīth, 1979–.

Kishk, ʿAbd al-Ḥamīd. *Qissat ayyāmī: Mudhakkirāt al-Shaykh Kishk*. Cairo: al-Mukhtār al-Islāmī, n.d. [1986]. Autobiography.

JOHANNES J. G. JANSEN
Updated by JOSEPH A. KÉCHICHIAN

KISHK, MUḤAMMAD JALĀL. An Islamist intellectual and renowned journalist, Muḥammad Jalāl Kishk was born in 1929, in the city of Asyūṭ, in Upper Egypt. His father was a Sharīʿah judge, and he graduated from the faculty of commerce, Fuad University (now Cairo University), in 1952. Kishk led a rich activist and intellectual life. His politics were very much shaped by the Egyptian milieu of the 1940s that yearned for independence, unity, and social justice. He joined the Communist Party at the age of seventeen as a platform to fight both the British and the king. Before the Egyptian Revolution of 1952, he advocated the establishment of a republican system and called for the formation of a popular party for the *falaḥīn* (Egyptian peasants) and for the nationalization of the Suez Canal and the cancellation of any foreign concessions. Kishk left the Communist Party soon afterward because of differences regarding the party's position towards the Wafd Party, which spearheaded the nationalist movement. He never joined another political party or political movement, except for a brief period when he joined the Wafd.

Kishk wrote more than forty books and hundreds of articles. His first two books, which were banned, were entitled *Miṣrīyūn—lā ṭawā'if* (Egyptians, Not Factions) and *al-Jabhah al-sha'bīyah* (The Popular Front); in these he criticizes the Muslim Brotherhood and the Wafd, respectively. He was jailed twice; the first time was during the reign of King Farouk for an article that questioned the legitimacy of the king and for calling for his removal by the people. The second time, 1954–1956, was under Nasser's regime, ironically for the book *al-Jabhah al-sha'bīyah*, which was construed as evidence of his conspiring to create an actual "popular front" against Nasser's regime. After his release he worked for several (by that time) government-run newspapers and magazines such as *al-Jumhūrīyah*, *Akhbār al-Yawm*, and *Rūz al-Yūsuf*.

Kishk was critical of Marxism at the peak of Nasser's socialist experiment and wrote *al-Mārksīyah wa-al-ghazw al-fikrī* (Marxism and Cultural Invasion) in 1965. Seeking a freer environment for his ideas, he left Egypt for Beirut, Lebanon, in 1969, where he worked for the weekly magazine *al-Ḥawādith* until the start of the 1975 civil war. During this time he published several books that focused on explaining the reasons behind the June 1967 Arab defeat by Israel, the need to restore Arab and Muslim vitality and shun alien models and imported intellectual frameworks. He addressed these issues in his books *al-Qawmīyah wa-al-ghazw al-fikrī* (Nationalism and Cultural Invasion), *al-Naksah wa-al-ghazw al-fikrī* (The Setback and Cultural Invasion), and *al-Tarīq ilā mujtama' 'aṣrī* (The Road to a Modern Society), among others. Kishk continued to work for *al-Ḥawādith* from 1975 until 1979, as its owner, Salīm al-Lawzī, had moved the newspaper to London. After Lawzī was assassinated by Syrian Intelligence in Beirut, Kishk left the newspaper and became devoted to his books and freelance journalism until his death in 1993.

Kishk's books focus on the issue of "cultural invasion" and the need to devise an indigenous model of modernization. He believed that Western-inspired ideas, whether secular, progressive, or leftist, as well as Westernized intellectuals, paved the way for a continued hegemony and control by the West over the Arab nation. Kishk insisted on highlighting the distinction between Westernization and modernization. Westernization in all its forms marks an internal defeat and lack of confidence in one's own values, whereas modernization is the belief that one's values are capable of achieving vitality and progress.

His writings reflect an understanding of Islam as a civilizational movement and cultural framework that has as its roots in the religion itself. He saw in Islam a system encompassing all the necessary tools to establish a just and viable framework for believers and nonbelievers alike. His criticism of capitalism, communism, and Arab nationalism is built upon that system. While viewing capitalism and communism as ideologically bankrupt and exploitative, he believed that Arab nationalism did not provide an ideological answer to the problems of the Arabs. It was divisive and raised unnecessary tension between the Arabs and other ethnic minorities such as the Kurds and the Berbers/Amazigh. For him Islam has always provided a bond that cemented these ethnic groups together. He entered many intellectual battles against the advocates of Nasserism and Westernization and critics of Islam. Kishk was staunchly against violence as a means for change and believed in the power of ideas as the instrument of change.

BIBLIOGRAPHY

Kishk, Muḥammad Jalāl. *al-Ghazw al-fikrī*. Cairo: Al-Dār al-Qawmīyah li-al-Ṭabaʿah wa-al-Nashr, 1966.

Kishk, Muḥammad Jalāl. *Wa-dakhalat al-khayl al-azhar*. 3d ed. Cairo: Dār al-Zahrah, 1990.

EMAD EL-DIN SHAHIN
and KHALED M. G. KESHK

KNOWLEDGE (ʿILM). *See* Education, Muslim.

KURDS. Arab-Muslim interactions with Kurds have long been recorded in Arabic literature and chronicles, beginning with the Arab-Muslim conquests. But there is evidence in Greek, Armenian, and Aramaic sources that Kurds played significant roles in the region prior to the coming of Islam. Kurdish was recognized as an official language in Iraq alongside Arabic and gained the status of a regional language in Iran and that of a minority language in Armenia.

The push of the Arab-Muslim armies to the north of Iraq after 630 CE brought them into contact with Kurds, some of whom joined Arab-Muslim armies and participated in the rise of the Umayyad Empire (661 to 750). Their cooperation with the Umayyads allowed the Kurds to retain considerable autonomy. During the ʿAbbāsid Empire (759–1258), much of the fighting between Arab armies and Kurds occurred in the vicinity of Mosul (Mawṣil), demarcating a frontier between the two ethnic groups that still exists. The Kurds managed to maintain governmental sovereignty over the majority of their lands until the establishment of the Seljuk Empire in 1055.

The fragmentation of the ʿAbbāsid Empire in the tenth century allowed Kurds to assert themselves more forcefully as they began to establish a series of feudal principalities stretching from Azerbaijan to southern Iran. What resulted was a relative stability, which some historians referred to as the "Kurdish interlude"—a time of stability between the disintegration of the ʿAbbāsid Empire and the coming invasions of the Seljuk Turks.

The relative stability during the Kurdish interlude did not last long. The invasion of the Turkmens, which led to the creation of the Seljuk Empire (1055–1258), diminished the role of Kurdish principalities. Ironically, it was during this period that the word "Kurdistan" (land of the Kurds) first appeared, though this seems to have been an administrative term with no political significance. Kurds, however, continued to play important roles during the Seljuk period, especially as warriors against Christian Crusaders, who invaded the eastern Mediterranean littoral from 1091 to 1204. One of the most celebrated events in Muslim history was the reconquest of Jerusalem in 1189 by Ṣalāḥ al-Dīn al-Ayyūbī, known in the West as "Saladin," a Kurd from Tikrīt in northern Iraq and the founder of the famous Ayyūbid Dynasty that ruled Egypt and Syria from 1169 to 1260.

Another celebrated event in Kurdish history, the Battle of Chaldiran (northeast of Lake Van in modern Turkey), occurred in 1514 when the Ottoman Empire's armies defeated Shah Ismāʿīl, founder of the Ṣafavid dynasty. While Shah Ismāʿīl was a Turk, the founder of the Ṣūfī order that produced the Ṣafavid Empire was a Kurd named Shaykh Ṣafī al-Dīn. The battle of Chaldiran was momentous in that it was not merely a clash between two empires but between powers that used different theological discourses to justify their respective legitimacies; the Ottomans adopted Sunnism while the Ṣafavids adhered to Shiism. Consequently, Kurds were called upon to choose between the two empires, and this decision was made by Idris-i Bitlisi, a Kurdish adviser to the Ottoman sultan (Yavuz) Selim (1512–1520), who sided with the Sunnī Ottomans. This meant that for the next four hundred years, the majority of Kurds would remain Sunnī, affiliating with the Ottoman Empire.

The destruction of Kurdish principalities and traditional leadership through the centralization polices of the Ottoman government from 1830 until the coming of Abdülhamid II caused a significant change among Kurds of the Ottoman Empire. The leadership of Kurdish communities was taken over by *shaykh*s belonging mostly to Ṣūfī orders; it was the end of leadership by traditional princes (*mir*s; *derebey*s; *hukmdar*s). Henceforward, the main leadership cadres would come from the *shaykh*s, lay intellectuals, and military officers.

Kurds suffered over half a million deaths in World War I, though they were pawns of the Young Turk government, as it deported Armenians en masse. From 1915 to 1918, and again between 1921 and 1923, under Mustafa Kemal Atatürk, Kurdish support for the Young Turk government and for the Republic of Turkey after 1923 confirmed the active participation of Kurds in the Armenian Genocide. While Kurdish leaders seized the opportunity to confiscate abandoned Armenian lands and property, and although they remained loyal to the new Republic of Turkey with the explicit understanding that the Kurds would suppress or destroy any Kurdish nationalist groups or movements that might rise, past allegiances were not reciprocated. Neither Constantinople nor the cooperative Kurdish leadership was entirely successful in forging a semi-independent place in the nascent Republic of Turkey that emphasized Turkish nationalism. In 1925 and 1930 and from 1937 to 1938, Kurds staged large-scale rebellions against the government, but they were all brutally suppressed.

From 1920 to 1958, there was Kurdish opposition to the British-backed Iraqi government. The Iraqi Arab government was compelled by the British government to recognize certain Kurdish linguistic, cultural, and political rights. Despite this benign policy, Kurdish nationalist movements continued to gain strength, especially under the leadership of Mullā Muṣṭafā Barzānī (1903–1979), the *shaykh* of a Naqshbandī order. After many skirmishes with the British and Baghdad, Barzānī was able to establish the Kurdish Democratic Party (KDP), Iraq's first Kurdish-led political party, in 1945. However, when Mullā Muṣṭafā fled to the Soviet Union in 1947, after the collapse of the Kurdish Republic of Mahabad in Iran in December 1946, the party languished.

In 1976, Jalal Talabani, the descendent of Qādirī *shaykh*s, created another political party—the Patriotic Union of Kurdistan (PUK)—in opposition to the KDP. Despite the establishment by the United States and Britain of a "safe haven" for the Kurds in northern Iraq after the 1991 Gulf War for Kuwait, conflicts between Barzānī, Talabani, and their respective constituencies continued, hindering political cooperation among Iraqi Kurds right up to the U.S. invasion and occupation of Iraq in March 2003. The Kurds cooperated militarily with the United States, which allowed them more autonomy in the three provinces that they governed—Dohuk, Arbīl, and Suleymānīyah. The subsequent war and disintegration of Arab Iraq compelled the two parties to cooperate, and in 2006 they agreed to integrate their parties into a joint KDP and PUK government. By then, the Kurds of Iraq were poised to declare an independent state, although foreign powers prevented this. Instead, Washington persuaded Kurds to remain active in the nascent post–Saddam Hussein Iraq, as the country's political makeup was transformed. Representatives of Iraq's largest Shīʿī political parties were granted the prime ministership by parliament, while the presidency of the republic went to Jalal Talabani in 2006, which underscored a prominent political spot for Iraqi Kurds.

Developments in Iran. It was in Iran that Kurds experienced their most dramatic achievement of the twentieth century: the establishment of an independent state called the Kurdish Republic of Mahabad, which lasted for one year (December 1945 to December 1946).

After the destruction of the Kurdish Republic of Mahabad, Kurdish nationalism in Iran adopted a leftist hue, resulting in the creation of the Committee for the Revival of Kurdistan (Komala-e Jiyanawi Kurdistan; KJK) in 1942. It was the Kurdish Democratic Party-Iran (KDP-I), however, that came to dominate Kurdish politics in Iran. The KDP-I was an offshoot of the KDP of Iraq that separated from the KDP in 1957, and was more tribally based than the KJK. The KDP-I strengthened under the leadership of Abdul Rahman Qasimlu, who was secretary-general of the party from 1971 until his 1989 assassination in Vienna by operatives of the new Islamic Republic of Iran (IRI). Qasimlu's assassination indicated how threatened IRI leaders felt by Kurdish nationalism. In 1992, four more KDP-I leaders were assassinated in Berlin by IRI agents.

The savagery of the war after 2003 in the Arab part of Iraq, as well as Kurdish collaboration with the American occupying forces, allowed Iraqi Kurds to come closer than ever to an independent state, one more long-lasting than the Kurdish Republic of Mahabad. In 2004, Iraqi Kurds secured their political autonomy with the issuance of the Transitional Administrative Law (TAL), whose political assurances were embedded in the constitution of Iraq that was ratified in October 2005 and accepted as legitimate by the international community.

[*See also* Iran, Islamic Republic of; Iraq; *and* Turkey.]

BIBLIOGRAPHY

Bidlīsī, Sharaf al-Dīn. *The Sharafnâma, or History of the Kurdish Nation, 1597*. Translated by Mehrdad R. Izady. Costa Mesa, Calif.: Mazda, 2005.

Jwaideh, Wadie. *The Kurdish National Movement: Its Origins and Development*. Contemporary Issues in the Middle East. Syracuse, N.Y.: Syracuse University Press, 2006.

Koohi-Kamali, Farideh. *The Political Development of the Kurds in Iran: Pastoral Nationalism*. London: Palgrave Macmillan, 2003.

Marcus, Aliza. *Blood and Belief: The PKK and the Kurdish Fight for Independence*. New York: New York University Press, 2007.

McDowall, David. *A Modern History of the Kurds*. 3d ed. London: I. B. Tauris, 2004.

Natali, Denise. *The Kurds and the State: Evolving National Identity in Iraq, Turkey, and Iran*. Syracuse, N.Y.: Syracuse University Press, 2005.

ROBERT OLSON
Updated by JOSEPH A. KÉCHICHIAN

KUTTĀB. *See* Education, Muslim.